D1231828

Contemporary Authors®

NEW REVISION SERIES

ISSN 0275-7176

Contemporary Authors®

A Bio-Bibliographical Guide to Current Writers in Fiction, General Nonfiction, Poetry, Journalism, Drama, Motion Pictures, Television, and Other Fields

HAL MAY
JAMES G. LESNIAK
Editors

NEW REVISION SERIES volume 29

Gale Research Inc. • DETROIT • NEW YORK • FORT LAUDERDALE • LONDON

STAFF

Hal May and James G. Lesniak, *Editors, New Revision Series*

Marilyn K. Basel, Sharon Malinowski, Michael E. Mueller, Bryan Ryan, Kenneth R. Shepherd, Diane Telgen, and Thomas Wiloch, *Associate Editors*

Marian Gonsior, Cheryl Gottler, Kevin S. Hile, Margaret Mazurkiewicz, Jani Prescott, and Michaela Swart Wilson, *Assistant Editors*

Jean W. Ross, *Interviewer*

Melissa J. Gaiownik, Anne Janette Johnson, M. Gilbert Porter, and Susan Salter, *Contributing Editors*

Hal May, *Senior Editor, Contemporary Authors*

Mary Rose Bonk, *Research Supervisor*

Jane Cousins-Clegg, Alysa I. Hunton, Andrew Guy Malonis, and Norma Sawaya, *Editorial Associates*

Reginald A. Carlton, Christine Ferran, Shirley Gates, Elizabeth Parker Henry, Pamela Atsoff Jarvi, Clare Kinsman, Sharon McGilvray, and Tracey Head Turbett, *Editorial Assistants*

Gale Research Inc.
835 Penobscot Bldg.
Detroit, MI 48226-4094

Library of Congress Catalog Card Number 81-640179
ISBN 0-8103-1983-7
ISSN 0275-7176

Contents

Indexing note: All *Contemporary Authors New Revision Series* entries are indexed in the *Contemporary Authors* cumulative index, which is published separately and distributed with even-numbered *Contemporary Authors* original volumes.

Authors and Media People Featured in This Volume

Cleveland Amory (American journalist and animal-rights activist)—Appreciated for his caustic wit, Amory began his career with satires of Boston's high society but has more recently devoted his attention and talents to environmental and wildlife concerns. In his bestselling *The Cat Who Came for Christmas,* he shares the humorous and moving story of how he acquired his longtime feline companion. (Entry contains interview.)

Louis Auchincloss (American novelist, short story writer, lawyer, and literary critic)—Though a prolific author of short fiction, Auchincloss is best known for his well-crafted novels of manners, such as *The Rector of Justin* and *Honourable Men.* His chronicles of the upper class in early twentieth-century New York City have earned him frequent comparisons with F. Scott Fitzgerald, Henry James, and Edith Wharton. (Entry contains interview.)

Saul Bellow (American novelist and short story writer)—An internationally acclaimed literary artist, Bellow is the recipient of three National Book Awards, a Pulitzer and Nobel Prize, and the National Medal of Arts. Anchoring his work, which includes *The Adventures of Augie March, Herzog,* and *Mr. Sammler's Planet,* is the conviction that art is more important than science in understanding the twentieth-century experience.

Kay Boyle (American novelist, short story writer, poet, and essayist)—A member of the Paris literary set during the twenties and thirties, Boyle has steadily created an oeuvre of fiction that measures the central issues of our time. Especially recognized for her stylistic inventiveness, she has earned several awards for lifetime achievement in literature.

Simon Brett (British mystery writer)—Brett's series of mystery novels about Charles Paris, an actor and amateur detective, enjoy popularity on both sides of the Atlantic. Witty, ironic, and entertaining, the books reveal a behind-the-scenes look at British show business.

Jeremy Campbell (British-born science writer)—Although Campbell works from highly technical sources, he employs metaphors and analogies that illuminate scientific concepts for the general reader. His *Grammatical Man* surveys the developing field of information theory, and *Winston Churchill's Afternoon Nap* examines chronobiology, the study of how biological clocks and mental perceptions of time may influence human nature. (Entry contains interview.)

Nicholas Delbanco (British-born novelist and short story writer)—Well-regarded in literary circles for his poetic and stylistically experimental novels, Delbanco is best known for *Possession, Sherbrookes,* and *Stillness,* the books that comprise his Sherbrookes trilogy.

Walter Farley (American author of young adult fiction who died in 1989)—Farley bequeathed to generations of young readers the memorable stories of his "Black Stallion" series. Unflaggingly popular since their publication in the 1940s, his books have sold over twelve million copies in the United States, and most remain in print.

Erich Fromm (German-born American psychoanalyst and philosopher who died in 1980)—Advocating the importance of economic and social factors upon the human psyche, Fromm authored such popular works as *Escape from Freedom, To Have or To Be, The Sane Society,* and *The Art of Loving,* which profoundly influenced postwar thought.

William Goldman (American novelist and screenwriter)—Goldman regards himself as a "novelist who writes screenplays" but is successful in both genres. The creator of such box-office hits as "Butch Cassidy and the Sundance Kid" and "Marathon Man," based on his novel of the same title, Goldman is widely considered to have defined a standard for movies as entertainment.

Ruth Prawer Jhabvala (German-born British-American author of fiction and screenplays)—Drawing upon her experience of growing up in colonial India, Jhabvala examines cultural conflicts between East and West in her Booker Prize-winning novel *Heat and Dust,* which she also adapted for the screen. She has excelled in adapting classic novels to film, earning a Writers Guild of America Award and an Academy Award for her work on "A Room with a View." (Entry contains interview.)

Jonathan Kellerman (American mystery writer)—A psychologist by training, Kellerman earned an Edgar Allan Poe Award for best first novel in 1986 for *When the Bough Breaks* and is well known for his series of mysteries featuring psychologist Alexander Delaware. (Entry contains interview.)

Denise Levertov (British-born American poet and essayist)—Levertov's verse is in the tradition of William Carlos Williams and the Black Mountain poets, in that it portrays the mundane in a most extraordinary light. Having published poetry since the 1940s, she has increasingly charged her verse with a keen political consciousness. (Entry contains interview.)

Penelope Lively (British novelist and children's writer)—Evoking a strong sense of the past, Lively's fiction is noted for its imaginative blend of personal history and fantasy. Recipient of several literary awards, Lively received the Booker Prize in 1987 for *Moon Tiger.*

Olivia Manning (British novelist who died in 1980)—Manning was best known for the novels in her "Balkan" and "Levant" trilogies, which were especially recognized for their authentic rendering of the events surrounding World War II.

Richard Marius (American biographer and historian)—A distinguished Renaissance scholar, Marius has written highly acclaimed biographies of the religious leaders Thomas More and Martin Luther. He has also edited the Yale University Press editions of the complete works of More.

John McGahern (Irish novelist)—Often compared with James Joyce, McGahern depicts characters struggling to free themselves from a repressive and dour environment. His novel *The Barracks* won the A. E. Memorial Award and a Macauley fellowship.

James R. Mellow (American biographer and art critic)—A biographer of such literary figures as Gertrude Stein, Nathaniel

Hawthorne, and F. Scott Fitzgerald, Mellow has received a National Book Award nomination and an American Book Award for his efforts.

Eve Merriam (American poet and playwright)—Winner of the Yale Younger Poets Award for her book *Family Circle,* Merriam is best known for her children's poetry. Her play "The Club" earned an Obie Award in 1976.

Christopher Middleton (British-born poet)—A poet concerned with creating new verse structures, Middleton has been called "easily the most intelligent and serious of our innovators" by Alan Brownjohn of *New Statesman.* His works include *Torse 3: Poems, 1949-1961, The Lonely Suppers of W. V. Balloon,* and *111 Poems.*

Robin Morgan (American feminist poet)—Morgan is an outspoken feminist whose poetry collections, including *Monster* and *Lady of the Beasts,* present her social and political views. She has also edited the anthologies *Sisterhood Is Powerful* and *Sisterhood Is Global.*

Robert Nye (British poet and novelist)—Specializing in ribald and fantastic retellings of old legends and myths, Nye's poems and novels have earned the Eric Gregory Award and the Hawthornden Prize. Among his books are *Doubtfire, Darker Ends, Falstaff, Merlin,* and *Faust.*

Norman Vincent Peale (American self-help author)—Peale's best-selling *The Power of Positive Thinking* stresses the importance of a positive attitude in overcoming life's problems. He has won a Medal of Freedom and been named Clergyman of the Year.

Tom Robbins (American novelist)—A part of the "West Coast" literary movement, Robbins writes about personal freedom and Eastern religions in such novels as *Another Roadside Attraction, Even Cowgirls Get the Blues, Still Life with Woodpecker,* and *Jitterbug Perfume.*

James Tate (American poet)—Tate writes an energetic and playful poetry that probes the limits of linguistic expression. The youngest poet to ever win the prestigious Yale Younger Poets Award, Tate has produced more than two dozen works, including *The Lost Pilot* and *Constant Defender.*

Colin Thubron (British novelist and travel writer)—Thubron combines history, description, and personal observation in such award-winning travel books as *Among the Russians (or) Where Nights Are Longest* and *Behind the Wall: A Journey through China.*

Margaret Truman (American mystery novelist and biographer)—Truman has written best-selling biographies of her father, President Harry S. Truman, and mother, Bess, but equally renowned are her popular murder mysteries set in Washington's halls of power.

Richard Wilbur (American poet and translator)—Acclaimed for his great technical skill as a poet, Wilbur has won the Pulitzer Prize, the National Book Award, and the Bollingen Prize, and has been named Poet Laureate of the United States. His books include *Things of This World, Tartuffe,* and *Walking to Sleep.* (Entry contains interview.)

Geoffrey Wolff (American critic, biographer, and novelist)—Although Wolff has garnered praise for such biographies as *Black Sun: The Brief Transit and Violent Eclipse of Harry Crosby* and *The Duke of Deception: Memories of My Father,* he is also the creator of distinguished narratives. His crime novel *Providence* contains "some of the tightest, meanest dialogue this side of Elmore Leonard," according to a *Time* critic.

Jane Yolen (American fantasist and children's writer)—Drawing from ancient myths and legends, and from the oral storytelling tradition, Yolen writes tales in a beautiful, poetic language. Among her works are *The Emperor and the Kite, The Girl Who Cried Flowers, and Other Tales,* and *Owl Moon.* (Entry contains interview.)

Preface

The *Contemporary Authors New Revision Series* provides completely updated information on authors listed in earlier volumes of *Contemporary Authors (CA).* Entries for active individual authors from *any* volume of *CA* may be included in a volume of the *New Revision Series.* The sketches appearing in *New Revision Series* Volume 29, for example, were selected from more than twenty previously published *CA* volumes.

As always, the most recent *Contemporary Authors* cumulative index continues to be the user's guide to the location of an individual author's listing.

Compilation Methods

The editors make every effort to secure information directly from the authors. Copies of all sketches in selected *CA* volumes published several years ago are routinely sent to the listees at their last-known addresses. Authors mark material to be deleted or changed and insert any new personal data, new affiliations, new writings, new work in progress, new sidelights, and new biographical/critical sources. All returns are assessed, more comprehensive research is done, if necessary, and those sketches requiring significant change are completely updated and published in the *New Revision Series.*

If, however, authors fail to reply or are now deceased, biographical dictionaries are checked for new information (a task made easier through the use of Gale's *Biography and Genealogy Master Index* and other Gale biographical indexes), as are bibliographical sources such as *Cumulative Book Index* and *The National Union Catalog.* Using data from such sources, revision editors select and revise nonrespondents' entries that need substantial updating. Sketches not personally reviewed by the biographees are marked with an asterisk (*) to indicate that these listings have been revised from secondary sources believed to be reliable, but they have not been personally reviewed for this edition by the authors sketched.

In addition, reviews and articles in major periodicals, lists of prestigious awards, and, particularly, requests from *CA* users are monitored so that writers on whom new information is in demand can be identified and revised listings prepared promptly.

Format

CA entries provide biographical and bibliographical information in an easy-to-use format. For example, individual paragraphs featuring such rubrics as "Addresses," "Career," and "Awards, Honors" ensure that a reader seeking specific information can quickly focus on the pertinent portion of an entry. In sketch sections headed "Writings," the title of each book, play, and other published or unpublished work appears on a separate line, clearly distinguishing one title from another. This same convenient bibliographical presentation is also featured in the "Biographical/Critical Sources" sections of sketches where individual book and periodical titles are listed on separate lines. *CA* readers can therefore quickly scan these often-lengthy bibliographies to find the titles they need.

Comprehensive Revision

All listings in this volume have been revised and/or augmented in various ways, though the amount and type of change vary with the author. In many instances, sketches are totally rewritten, and the resulting *New Revision Series* entries are often considerably longer than the authors' previous listings. Revised entries include additions of or changes in such information as degrees, mailing addresses, literary agents, career items, career-related and civic activities, memberships, awards, work in progress, and biographical/critical sources. They may also include extensive bibliographical additions and informative new sidelights.

Writers of Special Interest

CA's editors make every effort to include in each *New Revision Series* volume a substantial number of revised entries on active authors and media people of special interest to *CA*'s readers. Since the *New Revision Series* also includes sketches on noteworthy deceased writers, a significant amount of work on the part of *CA*'s editors goes into the revision of entries on important deceased authors. Some of the prominent writers, both living and deceased, whose sketches are contained in this volume are noted in the list on pages vii-viii headed Authors and Media People Featured in This Volume.

Exclusive Interviews

CA provides exclusive, primary information on certain authors in the form of interviews. Prepared specifically for *CA,* the never-before-published conversations presented in the section of the sketch headed "*CA* Interview" give users the opportunity to learn the authors' thoughts, in depth, about their craft. Subjects chosen for interviews are, the editors feel, authors who hold special interest for *CA*'s readers.

Authors and journalists in this volume whose sketches contain exclusive interviews are Cleveland Amory, Louis Auchincloss, Jeremy Campbell, Ruth Prawer Jhabvala, Jonathan Kellerman, Denise Levertov, Belva Plain, Amy Schwartz, Richard Wilbur, and Jane Yolen.

Contemporary Authors Autobiography Series

Designed to complement the information in *CA* original and revision volumes, the *Contemporary Authors Autobiography Series* provides autobiographical essays written by important current authors. Each volume contains from twenty to thirty specially commissioned autobiographies and is illustrated with numerous personal photographs supplied by the authors. Common topics of discussion for these authors include their motivations for writing, the people and experiences that shaped their careers, the rewards they derive from their work, and their impressions of the current literary scene.

Autobiographies included in the series can be located through both the *CA* cumulative index and the *Contemporary Authors Autobiography Series* cumulative index, which lists not only personal names but also titles of works, geographical names, subjects, and schools of writing.

Contemporary Authors Bibliographical Series

The *Contemporary Authors Bibliographical Series* is a comprehensive survey of writings by and about the most important authors since World War II in the United States and abroad. Each volume concentrates on a specific genre and nationality and features approximately ten major writers. Series entries, which complement the information in other *CA* volumes, consist of three parts: a primary bibliography that lists works written by the author, a secondary bibliography that lists works about the author, and a bibliographical essay that thoroughly analyzes the merits and deficiencies of major critical and scholarly works.

These bibliographies can be located through both the *CA* cumulative index and the *Contemporary Authors Bibliographical Series* cumulative author index. A cumulative critic index, citing critics discussed in the bibliographical essays, also appears in each *Bibliographical Series* volume.

CA Numbering System

Occasionally questions arise about the *CA* numbering system. Despite numbers like "97-100" and "128," the entire *CA* series consists of only 97 physical volumes with the publication of *CA New Revision Series* Volume 29. The following information notes changes in the numbering system, as well as in cover design, to help users better understand the organization of the entire *CA* series.

CA First Revisions

- 1-4R through 41-44R (11 books)
  Cover: Brown with black and gold trim.
  There will be no further *First Revisions* because revised entries are now being handled exclusively through the more efficient *New Revision Series* mentioned below.

CA Original Volumes

- 45-48 through 97-100 (14 books)
  Cover: Brown with black and gold trim.
- 101 through 128 (28 books)
  Cover: Blue and black with orange bands.
  The same as previous *CA* original volumes but with a new, simplified numbering system and new cover design.

CA New Revision Series

- *CANR*-1 through *CANR*-29 (29 books)
  Cover: Blue and black with green bands.
  Includes only sketches requiring extensive change; **sketches are taken from any previously published *CA* volume.**

***CA* Permanent Series**

- *CAP*-1 and *CAP*-2 (2 books)
  Cover: Brown with red and gold trim.
  There will be no further *Permanent Series* volumes because revised entries are now being handled exclusively through the more efficient *New Revision Series* mentioned above.

***CA* Autobiography Series**

- *CAAS*-1 through *CAAS*-10 (10 books)
  Cover: Blue and black with pink and purple bands.
  Presents specially commissioned autobiographies by leading contemporary writers to complement the information in *CA* original and revision volumes.

***CA* Bibliographical Series**

- *CABS*-1 through *CABS*-3 (3 books)
  Cover: Blue and black with blue bands.
  Provides comprehensive bibliographical information on published works by and about major modern authors.

Retaining *CA* Volumes

As new volumes in the series are published, users often ask which *CA* volumes, if any, can be discarded. The Volume Update Chart on page xiii is designed to assist users in keeping their collections as complete as possible. All volumes in the left column of the chart should be retained to have the most complete, up-to-date coverage possible; volumes in the right column can be discarded if the appropriate replacements are held.

Cumulative Index Should Always Be Consulted

The key to locating an individual author's listing is the *CA* cumulative index, which is published separately and distributed with even-numbered original volumes. Since the *CA* cumulative index provides access to *all* entries in the *CA* series, the latest cumulative index should always be consulted to find the specific volume containing a listee's original or most recently revised sketch.

Those authors whose entries appear in the *New Revision Series* are listed in the *CA* cumulative index with the designation **CANR-** in front of the specific volume number. For the convenience of those who do not have *New Revision Series* volumes, the cumulative index also notes the specific earlier volumes of *CA* in which the sketch appeared. Below is a sample index citation for an author whose revised entry appears in a *New Revision Series* volume.

Clavell, James (duMaresq) 1925- CANR-26
Earlier sketch in CA 25-28R
See also CLC 6, 25

For the most recent *CA* information on Clavell, users should refer to Volume 26 of the *New Revision Series,* as designated by "CANR-26"; if that volume is unavailable, refer to *CA* 25-28 First Revision, as indicated by "Earlier sketch in CA 25-28R," for his 1977 listing. (And if *CA* 25-28 First Revision is unavailable, refer to *CA* 25-28, published in 1971, for Clavell's original listing.)

Sketches not eligible for inclusion in a *New Revision Series* volume because the biographee or a revision editor has verified that no significant change is required will, of course, be available in previously published *CA* volumes. Users should always consult the most recent *CA* cumulative index to determine the location of these authors' entries.

For the convenience of *CA* users, the *CA* cumulative index also includes references to all entries in these related Gale literary series: *Authors and Artists for Young Adults, Authors in the News, Bestsellers, Black Writers, Children's Literature Review, Concise Dictionary of American Literary Biography, Contemporary Literary Criticism, Dictionary of Literary Biography, Short Story Criticism, Something About the Author, Something About the Author Autobiography Series, Twentieth-Century Literary Criticism,* and *Yesterday's Authors of Books For Children.*

Acknowledgments

The editors wish to thank Judith S. Baughman for her assistance with copyediting.

Suggestions Are Welcome

The editors welcome comments and suggestions from users on any aspect of the *CA* series. If readers would like to suggest authors whose *CA* entries should appear in future volumes of the *New Revision Series,* they are cordially invited to write: The Editors, *Contemporary Authors New Revision Series,* 835 Penobscot Bldg., Detroit, MI 48226-4094; or, call toll-free at 1-800-347-GALE.

Volume Update Chart

IF YOU HAVE:	YOU MAY DISCARD:
1-4 First Revision (1967)	1 (1962) 2 (1963) 3 (1963) 4 (1963)
5-8 First Revision (1969)	5-6 (1963) 7-8 (1963)
Both 9-12 First Revision (1974) AND *Contemporary Authors Permanent Series,* Volume 1 (1975)	9-10 (1964) 11-12 (1965)
Both 13-16 First Revision (1975) AND *Contemporary Authors Permanent Series,* Volumes 1 and 2 (1975, 1978)	13-14 (1965) 15-16 (1966)
Both 17-20 First Revision (1976) AND *Contemporary Authors Permanent Series,* Volumes 1 and 2 (1975, 1978)	17-18 (1967) 19-20 (1968)
Both 21-24 First Revision (1977) AND *Contemporary Authors Permanent Series,* Volumes 1 and 2 (1975, 1978)	21-22 (1969) 23-24 (1970)
Both 25-28 First Revision (1977) AND *Contemporary Authors Permanent Series,* Volume 2 (1978)	25-28 (1971)
Both 29-32 First Revision (1978) AND *Contemporary Authors Permanent Series,* Volume 2 (1978)	29-32 (1972)
Both 33-36 First Revision (1978) AND *Contemporary Authors Permanent Series,* Volume 2 (1978)	33-36 (1973)
37-40 First Revision (1979)	37-40 (1973)
41-44 First Revision (1979)	41-44 (1974)
45-48 (1974) 49-52 (1975) ↓ ↓ 128 (1990)	NONE: These volumes will not be superseded by corresponding revised volumes. Individual entries from these and all other volumes appearing in the left column of this chart will be revised and included in the *New Revision Series.*
Volumes in the *Contemporary Authors New Revision Series*	NONE: The *New Revision Series* does not replace any single volume of *CA.* All volumes appearing in the left column of this chart must be retained to have information on all authors in the series.

Contemporary Authors

NEW REVISION SERIES

** Indicates that a listing has been revised from secondary sources believed to be reliable but has not been personally reviewed for this edition by the author sketched.*

ACZEL, Tamas 1921-

PERSONAL: Born December 16, 1921, in Budapest, Hungary; son of Joseph and Cornelia (Fabian) Aczel; married Eva Kadar, 1947 (divorced, 1956); married Olga Gyarmati, 1959; children: (first marriage) Julia (Mrs. Lorant Szucs); (second marriage) Thomas George. *Education:* University of Budapest, B.A., 1948; Eotvos Lorant University, M.A., 1950.

ADDRESSES: Home—34 Amity Pl., Amherst, Mass. 01002. *Office*—Department of English, University of Massachusetts, Amherst, Mass. 01003.

CAREER: Spark Publishing House, Budapest, Hungary, editor in chief, 1948-50; Eotvos Lorant University, Budapest, lecturer in modern literature, 1950-53; *Star* (Csillag) literary monthly, Budapest, editor in chief, 1950-53; Hungarian Academy of Dramatic Art, Budapest, professor of history of drama, 1953-55; *Hungarian Literary Gazette,* London, England, editor, 1957-62; University of Massachusetts, Amherst, professor of English, 1966—.

MEMBER: Modern Language Association of America, American Association of University Professors, American Association for the Advancement of Slavic Studies, PEN Club in Exile (vice-president), Hungarian Writers Association (secretary, 1953-55).

AWARDS, HONORS: Kossuth Prize for Poetry, 1949, for *Eberseg, huseg;* Stalin Prize for Literature, 1952, for *A szabadsag arnyekaban.*

WRITINGS:

Enek a hajon (poetry; title means "A Song on the Ship"), Officina (Budapest), 1942.

A szabadsag arnyekaban (fiction; title means "In the Shadow of Liberty"), Szikra (Budapest), 1947, 2nd edition, Athenaeum (Budapest), 1949.

Eberseg, huseg (poetry; title means "Vigilance and Faith"), Hungaria (Budapest), 1949.

Vihar es napsutes (novel; title means "Storm and Sunshine"), Szepirodalmi (Budapest), 1950.

Jelentes helyett (poetry; title means "In Lieu of a Report"), Szepirodalmi, 1951.

Lang es parazs (novel; title means "Flames and Ashes"), Szepirodalmi, 1953.

A foldrenges nyomaban (essays; title means "In the Wake of the Tremor"), Szepirodalmi, 1955.

(With Tibor Meray) *The Revolt of the Mind: A Case History of Intellectual Resistance behind the Iron Curtain,* Praeger, 1960, reprinted, Greenwood Press, 1975.

The Ice Age (novel), translation by John Simon and others, Simon & Schuster, 1965.

(Editor and contributor) *Ten Years After: A Commemoration of the Tenth Anniversary of the Hungarian Revolution,* Macgibbon & Kee, 1966, published as *Ten Years After: The Hungarian Revolution in the Perspective of History,* Holt, 1967.

(Translator with Laszlo Tikos) *Szabadsag a ho alatt* (poetry; title means "Freedom under the Snow: An Anthology of Russian Underground Poetry"), Aurora Koenyvek (Munich), 1968.

(Translator and editor with Joseph Langland and Tikos) *Poetry from the Russian Underground: A Bilingual Anthology,* Harper, 1973.

(Editor and author of introduction) *The Literature of Eastern Europe,* Cliff, 1980.

Illuminations (novel), Pantheon, 1981.

The Hunt (novel), Faber, 1989.

Also author of filmscript, "Two in an Apartment," 1956. Contributor to *Life, Figaro Literaire, Massachusetts Review, Forum, Saturday Review,* and other periodicals in the United States and Europe.

WORK IN PROGRESS: The Dragon Chronicles, a satirical novel; *Fugitive Years,* a collection of poems in Hungarian, 1956-89.

SIDELIGHTS: "Like Solzhenitsyn's *One Day in the Life of Ivan Denisovich,* Tamas Aczel's novel [*The Ice Age*] takes its theme from the Stalinist 'ice age' of European Communism," describes Joseph Hitrec in *Saturday Review.* Set in Aczel's native Hungary in the early fifties, *The Ice Age* focuses not on "the barbaric fringe of Stalinism," according to Hitrec, but instead "examines the subtler corruption of the human spirit under totalitarian pressure. . . . In [this] story darkness and terror prevail, and the outlook for the non-robot is bleak." The plot is relatively simple: a high party official dies after an operation, and the chief physician of the hospital comes under suspicion due to his reserved acceptance of party doctrine. When the doctor comes to trial, his sister, a clerk in a canning operation, is also denounced by her co-workers and friends, who fear their association with her will be used against them. "Before the author brings his tortured novel to a close," observes *New York Times Book Review* contributor William M. Kunstler, "all of those who have felt themselves threatened by the convulsions of the Hungarian police state have done their best to shore up their positions."

In outlining the castigation of the doctor and his sister, "[Aczel's] purpose is to dramatize the extent to which a totalitarian society can destroy every instinct in its members except that of survival," comments Kunstler. The critic adds that the author's "intent goes far beyond a caustic look backward. He condemns, as vehemently as he can, thought control and personality destruction by those who see political uniformity as the price to be exacted for a classless society." In targeting the fearful "zombies" of the regime, Aczel "writes about them with distaste and high style," asserts A. Alvarez in the *New York Review of Books.* "The book is based almost entirely on contempt, contempt working through a native Hungarian flair for elaborate, malicious gossip, and subtly qualified by his shrewd insights into the power game as it is played." As V. R. Yanitelli remarks in *Best Sellers,* "one must close on a note of praise for the insights, the contradictory perceptions, the existential reflections expressed so keenly by the author."

In his first novel written in English, *Illuminations,* Aczel "evokes the world of multilingual cosmopolites with unmistakable flair; the ambience is European, but the style is cleverly, hilariously American," states Ivan Sanders in *World Literature Today.* The critic adds that "at the same time *Illuminations* is much more than an adroit and tantalizing piece of fiction. Its many bravura passages and set pieces are anchored in significant moments of lived reality, much of it autobiographical." The protagonist of the novel is George Feldheimer, a Hungarian immigrant living happily and easily enough in London of the 1950s until he is robbed of his sight in an automobile accident. In following Feldheimer's attempts to regain his vision, *Illuminations* uses a symbolism "so heavily applied that the book runs the risk of becoming a parody of the symbolist novel," writes D. M. Thomas in the *New York Times Book Review.* "Perhaps, however, that is the author's intention," concedes the critic. "Bizarre and symbolic events punctuate Feldheimer's serious quest from the start." Melbourne *Times* contributor Graham Burns proposes that these symbols and "murky allegories" in *Illuminations* "build up an entropic vision of the end of ideologies. But they also suggest," continues the critic, "that Aczel is an ironist whose illuminations as often as not question our deepest impulse to seek order in disorder by forcing the reader to recognise the ways in which memory—and fictions—constructs narrative shapes from the otherwise incomprehensible flux of historical events."

Times Literary Supplement contributor George Goemoeri believes, however, that these allegorical asides detract from the plot's coherence; in addition, he faults the author's style as "a curious mixture of Central European cultural cliche and a far too idiosyncratic English vocabulary." On the contrary, Sanders believes that "what is most impressive about *Illuminations* . . . is its language. Aczel is liberated by his adopted English; he revels in it; he celebrates it." The critic elaborates: "[The author's] brash Americanisms mock his linguistic nostalgias, yet he devises tricks and wordplays that no native speaker would think of." "A novel of large proportions and considerable virtuosity," remarks Thomas, *Illuminations* "has to be read with the concentration one gives to poetry." While the critic adds that Aczel's language is sometimes overblown, he concludes that the novel, "though seriously flawed, [is] daring and often rewarding." Anticipating this type of criticism, Sanders asserts that "Aczel's new opus will no doubt perplex and exasperate many readers. . . . Yet, ultimately, *Illuminations* proves that the novel *can* carry this much baggage—that it's still the only form that can so exuberantly and with such high moral seriousness delve into riddle posed ceaselessly by human intelligence." "[*Illuminations* is] a virtuoso comic novel in the European modernist tradition of dark expressionist humor overlaying serious meanings, and of ironies honed to paradox," comments Burns. The critic concludes that *Illuminations* "lacks the vitality and moments of genius of [James Joyce's] 'Ulysses,' " to which some critics have compared it; nevertheless, he admits that "it is a considerable book for all that, and should find a place in the broader modern canon."

BIOGRAPHICAL/CRITICAL SOURCES:

PERIODICALS

Best Sellers, July 15, 1965.

Los Angeles Times Book Review, January 31, 1982.

New York Review of Books, November 11, 1965, December 3, 1981.

New York Times Book Review, June 13, 1965, November 15, 1981.

Saturday Review, July 31, 1965, November, 1981.

Times (Melbourne), February 3, 1983.

Times Literary Supplement, January 12, 1967, March 12, 1982.

World Literature Today, summer, 1982.

—Sketch by Diane Telgen

*   *   *

AFRICANO, Lillian 1935-
(Nora Ashby, Lila Cook, Jessica March)

PERSONAL: Born June 7, 1935, in Paterson, N.J.; daughter of John and Nadwa (Gorab) Tabeek; married Arthur Africano (a physician), June 28, 1958 (divorced); children: David, Nina, Arthur. *Education:* Barnard College, B.A., 1957; Columbia University, graduate study, 1957-58.

ADDRESSES: Home and office—45 West 10th St., New York, N.Y. 10011. *Agent*—Elaine Markson Literary Agency, Inc., 44 Greenwich Ave., N.Y. 10011.

CAREER: Teacher in Union City, N.J., 1957-59; *Villager,* New York City, theatre critic and entertainment editor, 1970-75; theatre critic for *Asbury Park Press,* 1973-80; *Acupuncture News Digest,* New York City, editor, 1975. Travel writer for *Ranch & Coast;* author of syndicated column "Theatre U.S.A.," 1975, and author of weekly column in *Woman's World* and of monthly news column in *Forum.*

MEMBER: Outer Critic's Circle, Drama Desk (vice-president, 1974-75, secretary, 1975-77), American Society of Journalists and Authors.

WRITINGS:

The Businessman's Guide to the Middle East, Harper, 1977.

(Co-author) *The Doctor's Walking Book,* Ballantine, 1980.

(Ghost writer) *Faces in a Mirror,* Prentice-Hall, 1980.

Something Old, Something New, Jove, 1983.

Passions, Jove, 1985.

(Under pseudonym Nora Ashby) *From Breely Hill,* Berkley, 1985.

(Under pseudonym Jessica March) *Illusions,* Warner, 1988.

(Under pseudonym Lila Cook) *Consenting Adults,* Charter, 1988.

Temptations, Warner, 1989.

Contributor to syndicated column, "One Woman's Voice"; contributor of articles to popular magazines and newspapers, including *National Review, Penthouse, Nation, Harper's Bazaar, Woman's Day, Reader's Digest, New York Times,* and *Christian Science Monitor.*

AVOCATIONAL INTERESTS: Travel.

* * *

AGAR, Brian
See BALLARD, (Willis) Todhunter

* * *

AGOR, Weston H(arris) 1939-

PERSONAL: Born December 30, 1939, in Salamanca, N.Y.; son of Randall Walter and Ruth (Barrett) Agor; married Eliana Bauer, August 20, 1963 (divorced, 1979); children: Lawrence B., William B. *Education:* St. Lawrence University, B.A., 1961; University of Michigan, M.P.A., 1963; University of Wisconsin, Ph.D., 1969. *Politics:* Republican. *Religion:* Protestant.

ADDRESSES: Office—ENFP Enterprises, The Pointe, 5525 North Stanton St., No. 18-D, El Paso, Tex. 79912.

CAREER: Procter & Gamble, Cincinnati, Ohio, and Toronto, Ontario, assistant brand man, marketing, 1963-65; University of Florida, Gainesville, assistant professor of political science and Latin American studies, 1971-73; Michigan State Senate, Lansing, executive assistant to majority leader, 1973-75, special assistant to governor, 1976-78; University of Miami, Coral Gables, Fla., professor of politics and public affairs and chairman of department, 1978-81; University of Texas at El Paso, professor and director of public administration program, 1982—; ENFP Enterprises, El Paso, president, 1982—. Visiting professor, Center for Public Policy Adminstration, California State University, Long Beach, 1981-82. Management consultant to several states and Latin American countries.

MEMBER: American Political Science Association, American Society of Public Administration, Texas Association of Schools of Public Affairs and Administration (treasurer, 1983-84), Beta Theta Pi, Pi Sigma Alpha, Psi Chi, Omicron Delta Kappa.

AWARDS, HONORS: Fulbright scholar in Chile, 1962-63; Danforth Foundation associate for instructional excellence, 1980-86; Alden B. Dow Creativity Center resident, 1984.

WRITINGS:

Chilean Senate: Internal Distribution of Influence, University of Texas Press, 1971.

Latin American Legislatures: Their Role and Influence, Praeger, 1971.

Intuitive Management: Integrating Left and Right Brain Management Skills, Prentice-Hall, 1984.

The Logic of Intuitive Decision Making: A Research-Based Approach for Top Management, Quorum Books, 1986.

Intuition in Organizations: Leading and Managing Productively, Sage Publications, 1989.

Contributor to journals and periodicals.

WORK IN PROGRESS: Use of hypnosis for creative management.

AVOCATIONAL INTERESTS: Tennis, music, sailing.

AKINJOGBIN, I(saac) A(deagbo) 1930-

PERSONAL: Born January 12, 1930, in Ipetumodu (Ife), Nigeria; son of Joel Esudoyin (a farmer) and Bernice (Falowo) Akinjogbin; married Josephine Adebisi Odeloye, May 6, 1959; children: Adeolu, Olufemi, Yewande, Baderinwa, Olugbenga. *Education:* Attended Fourah Bay College, University of Sierra Leone; University of Durham, B.A. (with honors in history), 1957; School of Oriental and African Studies, Ph.D., 1963. *Religion:* Christian.

ADDRESSES: Home—Isale-Apata, Ipetumodu (Ife), Nigeria. *Office*—Department of History, University of Ife, Ife, Nigeria.

CAREER: Yoruba Historical Research Scheme, Ibadan, Nigeria, junior research fellow, 1957-60; University of Ife, Ife, Nigeria, senior lecturer, beginning 1963, professor of history, 1968—, dean of faculty of arts, 1971-73, deputy vice-chancellor, 1974-76. Buel Gallagher Distinguished Professor, City College of the City University of New York, 1973-74.

MEMBER: International African Institute (London), Historical Association (Great Britain; honorary member), Historical Society of Nigeria (member of council; honorary general secretary, 1968-74).

AWARDS, HONORS: Commonwealth scholar at University of London, 1960-63; Carnegie Traveling fellow, 1970.

WRITINGS:

(Contributor) I. Espie and J.F. Ade Ajayi, editors, *A Thousand Years of West African History,* Thomas Nelson, 1966.

Dahomey and Its Neighbours, 1708-1818, Cambridge University Press, 1967.

(Editor) *The Story of Ketu,* 2nd edition, University of Ibadan Press, 1967.

(Editor) *Ewi Iwoyi* (modern Yoruba poetry), Collins, 1968.

(Contributor) Ajayi and M. Crowder, editors, *History of West Africa,* Volume I, Longman, 1971.

Topics on Nigerian Economic and Social History, University of Ife Press, 1980.

(Contributor) O. Ikime, editor, *Groundwork of Nigerian History,* Heinemann Educational Books, 1980.

(Editor and contributor) *A History of Ife from the Earliest Times to 1980,* Heinemann Educational Books, in press.

(Editor and contributor) *War and Peace in Yorubaland 1793-1893,* Heinemann Educational Books, in press.

(Co-author) *A History of Nigeria up to 1800,* Nelson-Pittman Nigeria, in press.

Nigeria in the Nineteenth and Twentieth Centuries, Nelson-Pittman Nigeria, in press.

SIDELIGHTS: I.A. Akinjogbin told *CA:* "There are two strands to my writing—the academic research-oriented studies in history and the emotional (or rational) outcries in poems. Both are rooted in the same conviction (or illusion?) that life can be understood, improved, and enjoyed if critically watched and intelligently explained, and that human experiences of the Africans are part of the storehouse of human treasure and should be treated as such by all."

* * *

ALBANY, James
See RAE, Hugh C(rauford)

ALDCROFT, Derek H. 1936-

PERSONAL: Born October 25, 1936, in Abergele, North Wales; son of Leslie Howard and Freda (Wallen) Aldcroft. *Education:* University of Manchester, B.A., 1958, Ph.D., 1962. *Politics:* Conservative.

ADDRESSES: Home—10 Linden Dr., Leicester, Leicestershire LE1 7RH, England. *Office*—Department of Economic History, University of Leicester, Leicester, Leicestershire LE1 7RH, England.

CAREER: University of Glasgow, Glasgow, Scotland, assistant lecturer in economic history, 1960-62; University of Leicester, Leicester, England, assistant lecturer, 1962-63; University of Glasgow, lecturer in economic history, 1964-67; University of Leicester, senior lecturer, 1967-70, reader, 1970-73; University of Sydney, Sydney, New South Wales, Australia, professor of economic history and head of department, 1973-76; University of Leicester, professor of economic history and head of department, 1976—. Member of advisory board of Investment Research Services.

MEMBER: Economic History Society (member of council).

WRITINGS:

(Editor) *The Development of British Industry and Foreign Competition, 1875-1914,* Allen & Unwin, 1968.

(With Harry Ward Richardson) *Building in the British Economy between the Wars,* Allen & Unwin, 1968.

British Railways in Transition: The Economic Problems of Britain's Railways since 1914, Macmillan, 1968, St. Martin's, 1969.

(With Harold James Dyos) *British Transport: An Economic Survey from the Seventeenth Century to the Twentieth,* Leicester University Press, 1969.

(With Richardson) *The British Economy, 1870-1939,* Macmillan, 1969.

(Editor with Peter Fearon) *Economic Growth in Twentieth-Century Britain,* Macmillan, 1969, Humanities, 1970.

The Inter-War Economy: Britain, 1919-1939, Columbia University Press, 1970.

(Editor with Fearon) *British Economic Fluctuations, 1790-1970,* Macmillan, 1972.

Studies in British Transport History, 1870-1970, David & Charles, 1974.

British Transport since 1914, David & Charles, 1975.

From Versailles to Wall Street, 1919-1929, University of California Press, 1977.

The European Economy, 1914-1970, Croom Helm, 1977, St. Martin's, 1978, revised and enlarged edition published as *The European Economy, 1914-1980,* Croom Helm, 1980.

(Editor with Neil K. Burton) *British Industry between the Wars: Instability and Industrial Development, 1919-1939,* Scolar Press, 1979.

The East Midlands Economy, Pointon York, 1979.

Rail Transport (bound with *Sea Transport* by Derrick Mort), Pergamon Press, 1981.

(Editor with P.L. Cottrell) *Shipping, Trade and Commerce,* Leicester University Press, 1981.

(Editor with Anthony Slaven) *Business, Banking and Urban History,* John Donald Publishers, 1982.

The British Economy between the Wars, Philip Allan, 1983.

(Editor with Michael J. Freeman) *Transport in the Industrial Revolution,* Manchester University Press, 1983.

Full Employment: The Elusive Goal, Harvester Press, 1984.

(Editor with Richard Rodger) *Bibliography of European Economic and Social History,* Manchester University Press, 1984.

(With Freeman) *The Atlas of British Railway History,* Croom Helm, 1985.

The British Economy, Volume I: *The Years of Turmoil, 1920-1951,* Wheatsheaf Books, 1986.

(Editor with Freeman) *Transport in Victorian Britain,* Manchester University Press, 1988.

Member of advisory panel of *Economic Review.*

WORK IN PROGRESS: Research on British economic growth in the twentieth century and on the stock market.

SIDELIGHTS: In a review of Derek H. Aldcroft's *British Industry between the Wars: Instability and Industrial Development, 1919-1939,* T.C. Barker writes in the *Times Literary Supplement:* "In [this] volume ten economic historians attempt [to look] at the performance of particular industries during the inter-war period. . . . This book is a courageous and commendable first shot at what is at present an impossible task, for the basic research has not yet been undertaken. [However,] this book provides new and significant insights into manufacturing problems between the wars. Above all, it brings about the need for much more research in this area."

AVOCATIONAL INTERESTS: Tennis, swimming, gardening, the stock market.

BIOGRAPHICAL/CRITICAL SOURCES:

PERIODICALS

Times Literary Supplement, April 18, 1980.

* * *

ALDERMAN, Geoffrey 1944-

PERSONAL: Born February 10, 1944, in Hampton Court, England; son of Samuel (a manufacturer's agent) and Lily (Landau) Alderman; married Marion Joan Freed (a graphic designer), September 9, 1973; children: Naomi Alicia, Eliot Daniel. *Education:* Lincoln College, Oxford, B.A. (with honors), 1965, M.A. and D.Phil., both 1969. *Religion:* Jewish.

ADDRESSES: Home—172 Colindeep Lane, London NW9 6EA, England. *Office*—Department of History, Royal Holloway and Bedford New College, University of London, Egham Hill, Egham, Surrey TW20 0EX, England.

CAREER: University of London, University College, London, England, research assistant in history, 1968-69; University of Wales, University College of Swansea, Swansea, temporary lecturer in politics, 1969-70; University of Reading, Reading, England, research fellow, 1970-72; University of London, Royal Holloway College (later Royal Holloway and Bedford New College), Egham, England, lecturer, 1972-84, reader in politics, 1985-88, professor of politics and contemporary history, 1988—. Election analyst, Independent Television, 1979; broadcaster in England, the Netherlands, Canada, and Israel.

MEMBER: Jewish Historical Society of England, British Association for Jewish Studies, Board of Deputies of British Jews (member of research committee, 1976-80, 1988—), Royal Historical Society (fellow), Political Studies Association of the United Kingdom, Society for the Study of Labour History, Historical Association, Association of University Teachers.

AWARDS, HONORS: Grant from British Academy, 1978-79; grants from British Academy, Wolfson Foundation, Leverhulme

Trust, and Economic and Social Research Council, 1985-88; grants from Leverhulme Trust and Nuffield Foundation, 1989-92.

WRITINGS:

The History of Hackney Downs School, Formerly the Grocers' Company's School, Clove Club, 1972.

The Railway Interest, Leicester University Press, 1973.

(Contributor) A. Newman, editor, *Provincial Jewry in Victorian Britain,* Jewish Historical Society of England, 1975.

The History of the Hendon Synagogue, 1928-1978, [London], 1978.

British Elections: Myth and Reality, Batsford, 1978.

The Jewish Community in British Politics, Oxford University Press, 1983.

Pressure Groups and Government in Great Britain, Longman, 1984.

Modern Britain, 1700-1983: A Domestic History, Croom Helm, 1986.

The Foundation of Synagogues, 1887-1987, Federation of Synagogues, 1987.

London Jewry and London Politics, 1889-1986, Routledge & Kegan Paul, 1989.

WORK IN PROGRESS: A study of British politics in the Thatcher era; a history of British Jewry since c. 1850.

SIDELIGHTS: In *The Jewish Community in British Politics,* British political analyst Geoffrey Alderman makes his case, writes William J. Fishman in the *Times Literary Supplement,* that "Jewish voters have always been capable of independent political behaviour, and at times, in response to the interests of the community as a whole, of using their votes as a political weapon." *London Review of Books* contributor David Katz, pointing out that "the influence exerted by Anglo-Jewry in business and at the polls has been a particularly sensitive issue," calls Alderman's work "a very sound and very courageous book." Alderman is also the author of *Modern Britain, 1700-1983: A Domestic History,* of which Martin Fagg comments in the *Times Educational Supplement:* "The panorama Dr. Alderman depicts is a broad one . . . [yet] he has trimmed his canvas to manageable proportions, and fills every part of it with an impressively bold and fluent treatment of material which, collectively and connectively, projects an astute and coherent portrait of the development of modern Britain."

Alderman commented to *CA* on his political studies: "My current interests revolve around the development of the British political system in the late nineteenth and twentieth centuries and, in particular, the processes of political socialization and integration. I am also much interested in the phenomenon of class, religion, and ethnicity in modern British society, and the factors which bear upon their salience in British political life." Alderman also remarked on what he hopes to communicate: "I want to illuminate the dark corners of recent British history and politics, and overturn widely held misconceptions. Too many political scientists simply write for their fellow academics. I believe I have a message for the general public, and if those with a vested interest in the perpetuation of false assumptions don't like what I write in my books, or say on radio and television, then I know I'm doing a good job."

BIOGRAPHICAL/CRITICAL SOURCES:

PERIODICALS

London Review of Books, October 6, 1983.

Times Educational Supplement, November 28, 1986.

Times Literary Supplement, May 4, 1973, June 17, 1983.

* * *

ALDRIDGE, Sarah
See MARCHANT, Anyda

* * *

ALDYNE, Nathan
See McDOWELL, Michael

* * *

ALEKSIN, Anatolii Georgievich 1924-

PERSONAL: Born August 3, 1924, in Moscow, U.S.S.R. *Education:* Graduated from Moscow Institute for Oriental Languages, 1950.

ADDRESSES: Office—c/o U.S.S.R. Union of Writers, Ulitsa Vorovskogo, 52, Moscow, U.S.S.R. *Agent*—Leah Siegel, 225 West 34th St., New York, N.Y. 10122.

CAREER: Author, playwright. Speaker on "Litsa druzei" (title means "The Faces of Friends"), monthly television show on children's education; editorial board member of *Yunost'* (magazine).

MEMBER: "Peace for Children of Our Planet" (president), Union of Writers of the Russian Soviet Federated Socialist Republic (secretary).

AWARDS, HONORS: Mildred Batchelder Award nomination, 1973, for *A Late-Born Child;* numerous awards in Soviet Union include the Lenin Komsomol prize from the Young Communist League, State Prize of the U.S.S.R., RSFSR Government N. K. Krupskaya Medal and prize, Order of Lenin, and two orders of the Labor Red Banner.

WRITINGS:

JUVENILES; IN ENGLISH TRANSLATION

Moi brat igraet na klarnete (also see below), 1968, translation by Fainna Glagoleva published as *My Brother Plays the Clarinet,* Progress Publishers (Moscow), 1972, published as *My Brother Plays the Clarinet: Two Stories,* illustrations by Judith Gwyn Brown, Walck, 1975.

Ochen' strashnaia istoriia, 1969, translation by Bonnie Carey published as *Alik the Detective,* Morrow, 1977.

Pozdnii rebenok, translation by Maria Polushkin published as *A Late-Born Child,* illustrations by Charles Robinson, World, 1971.

Razdel imushchestvo (juvenile; title means "Dividing the Property"), [Moscow], 1979.

Dhevnik zenikcha (juvenile; title means "A Diary of the Bride-Groom"), [Moscow], 1981.

Zdorovye i bolnye (juvenile; title means "The Healthy and the Sick"), [Moscow], 1982.

"Molodaia gvardiia" (play; based on the novel by Alexander Fadeev; title means "Young Guard"), first produced at the Central Children's Theatre in Moscow, spring, 1974, published, 1975.

Also author of *Bezumnaya Evdokiya* (title means "Crazy Yevdikiya"), *I Didn't Tell Anything,* and *The Mystery of the Old House.*

OTHER

Sasha i Shura (juvenile; title means "Sasha and Shura"), Detgiz, 1956.

Neobychainye pokhozhdeniia Sevy Kotlova (juvenile; title means "The Unusual Adventures of Seva Kotlov"), Molodaia gvardiia, 1958.
Pis'ma i telegrammy: rasskazy (title means "Letter and Telegram"), Pravda, 1966.
Pozavchera i poslezavtra (title means "The Day Before Yesterday and the Day After Tomorrow"), Pravda, 1974.
Sobranie sochinenii (selected works), Detlit, 1979-81.

Also author of *Tridtstat'odin den'* (title means "Thirty-One Days"), 1950, *Bud' dostoinym synom rodiny,* 1955, *Zapiski El'viry* (title means "Elvira's Notes"), 1956, *Dva pocherka,* 1957, *O druzhbe serdets* (title means "On the Friendship of Hearts"), 1958, *Pogovorim o sovesti* (title means "Let Us Speak about Conscience"), 1961, *V strane vechnykh kanikul* (juvenile; title means "In the Land of Holidays"), 1967, "Ty menia slyshish'?" (title means "Do You Hear Me?"), 1968, *Povesti,* 1969, *Uznaete? Alik Detkin* (collection), 1970, *Veselye povesti,* 1971, *Vstretimsia zavtra,* 1971, *Povesti i rasskazy,* 1973, *Zvonite i priezzhaite* (title means "Call and Visit Us"), 1974, *Deistvuiushchie litsa i ispolniteli* (juvenile; title means "Characters and Their Performers"), 1975, *Tretii v piatom riadu* (title means "Third Seat in the Fifth Row"), 1977, *Kolya pishet Ole, Olya pishet Kole* (title means "Kolya Writes to Olya, Olya Writes to Kolya"), *Govorit sed'moi etazh* (title means "This Is the Seventh Floor Speaking"), *Pro nashu sem'yu* (title means "About Our Family"), *A tem vremenem gde-to. . .* (title means "At the Same Time Somewhere . . . "), and "Every Fate Is Your Own." Also author of plays, including "Obratnyi adres" (title means "Return Address"), "Zvonite i priezzhaite!" (title means "Call and Visit Us!"), "Moi brat igraet na klarnete" (title means "My Brother Plays the Clarinet"), and "Desyatiklassniki" (title means "High School Seniors").

SIDELIGHTS: Anatolii Georgievich Aleksin has written over two hundred books, and his works have been translated into forty-four languages. A spokesman for the writer once told *CA:* "Anatolii Aleksin addresses his stories to children and young people, as well as to those that are responsible for educating them. The main theme of his work is the problem of training and educating a young person. Aleksin appears every month on television in his very popular program 'Litsa druzei,' which is devoted to the problems of educating the upcoming generation of children. In his works, Anatolii Aleksin primarily talks about how a young person enters the adult world. His works affirm that being an adult is not a concept of age. Rather, it is a moral concept. Adulthood is not determined by the date of birth indicated in a passport, but by a person's actions and deeds. The children and teenagers in his stories reveal their spiritual maturity and high concepts of duty through noble deeds that are imbued with true humanism."

* * *

ALLWOOD, Martin (Samuel) 1916-

PERSONAL: Born April 13, 1916, in Joenkoeping, Sweden; son of Charles S. (a radio teacher) and Aina (Akerhielm) Allwood; married Enelia Paz Gomez, December 20, 1977; children: Jens, Kristin, Carl-Martin, Maria, Peggy. *Education:* Cambridge University, B.A., 1938; Columbia University, M.A., 1949; University of Darmstadt, Dr.rer.pol., 1953. *Religion:* Christian.

ADDRESSES: Home—Marston Hill, Havstenshultliden 12, 560 41 Mullsjoe, Sweden. *Office*—Anglo-American Center, 565 00 Mullsjoe, Sweden.

CAREER: Santiniketan College, Bengal, India, lecturer in English, 1939; University of Goeteborg, Goeteborg, Sweden, lecturer in English, 1942-45; Columbia University, New York, N.Y., lecturer in English, 1947-49; Anglo-American Center, Mullsjoe, Sweden, director, 1950—. Co-director, Darmstadt Community Survey, 1950-53; speaker, Swedish Lecturing Association, 1953-59. Assistant professor, San Jose State College (now University), 1960-62; professor, Iowa Wesleyan College, 1963-68; lecturer, Nordic College of Journalism, Mullsjoe, 1983—.

MEMBER: Swedish Society of Authors, Swedish Society of Immigrant Authors (founder), Goeteborg Society of Authors (founder), Plesse Academy (Goettingen; life member).

AWARDS, HONORS: Lifetime grant from Sveriges Foerfattarfond.

WRITINGS:

IN SWEDISH; POETRY

(Editor and contributor) *Det unga Goeteborg 1944* (title means "Young Gothenberg 1944"), [Goeteborg, Sweden], 1944.
Katedralernas kyrkogaard (title means "The Cemetery of the Cathedrals"), Federativs (Stockholm), 1945.
Splittring och enhet (title means "Chaos and Unity"), Federativs, 1947.
Stationssamhaellet (title means "The Railroad Village"), Federativs, 1948.
Laeroverket (title means "The College"), Federativs, 1948.
Odelbar vaerld (title means "Invisible World"), Federativs, 1951.
Kaerlek maaste tala/Love Must Speak, Marston Hill (Mullsjoe, Sweden), 1959.
Resan till Unserland, Marston Hill, 1963.
Augustimoenster (title means "August Patterns"), Marston Hill, 1972.
Lillans dagbok (title means "The Diary of a Little Girl"), illustrations by daughter, Peggy Allwood, Marston Hill, 1972.
(Contributor) *I den svenska provinsen Smaaland* (poetry anthology), [Goeteborg], 1973.
Bildande konst, illustrations by the author, his wife, Enelia Paz Gomez, Adja Yunkers, and Igor Janczuk, Marston Hill, 1975.
(Contributor) Gottfried Pratschke, editor, *Das rechte Mass* (poetry anthology), [Vienna], 1977.
(Contributor) Ase-Marie Ness, editor, *Du mitt menneske* (poetry anthology), [Oslo], 1978.
(Contributor) *Lyrik paa Liseberg* (poetry anthology), Goeteborg Foerfattarsaellskap, 1978.
Valda svenska dikter: 1940-1965 (title means "Selected Swedish Poems: 1940-1965"), preface by Helmer Laang, illustrations by Janczuk, Persona Press (Mullsjoe), 1982.
Valda svenska dikter: 1966-1987 (title means "Selected Swedish Poems: 1967-1987"), [Mullsjoe], 1987.

IN ENGLISH; POETRY

Marginal Man, Free Press, 1947.
Collected English Poems: 1940-1965, Anglo-American Center (Mullsjoe), 1965.
Poems '66, drawings by author, Anglo-American Center, 1966.
Poems in March and Other Months, Anglo-American Center, 1971.
Way out of My Mind: Five Fits, Marston Hill, 1973.
The Truth of the Wind: Caribbean Poems, illustrations by Janczuk, Exposition, 1977.
(Contributor) M. Grassin, editor, *Sequences* (poetry anthology), [Paris], 1979.

New English Poems: 1966-1981, preface by G. Singh, [New York], 1980.

It's a Good Land: A Tribute to Haiti, Fardin (Port-au-Prince, Haiti), 1982.

Also contributor of poetry to *Lyrical Iowa.*

IN SWEDISH; LANGUAGE AND LITERATURE TEXTS

(With Arthur Wald) *Svenska som lever* (title means "Living Swedish"), Augustana Book Concern, 1947.

(With G. Eiding) *Andra aarets engelska* (title means "Second-Year English"), Hugo Gebers (Stockholm), 1947.

(Editor) *Amerika-Svensk lyrik genom 100 aar* (title means "American-Swedish Poetry through One Hundred Years"), Bonniers, 1949.

Albert Engstroem i Mullsjoe, 1888-1889, introduction by Laang, Institutet foer Samhaellsforskning (Mullsjoe), 1963.

Engelska vokabler och idiom (title means "Everyday English Words and Idioms"), Liber (Stockholm), 1964.

IN ENGLISH; LANGUAGE AND LITERATURE TEXTS

(With Keth Laycock) *An English Anthology: A Survey of English Literature from Chaucer to the Present Day,* Natur & Kultur (Stockholm), 1942.

A Little Book of Good Things: An Anthology of Anglo-Saxon Culture, Hugo Gebers, 1945.

(With Laycock) *Idiomatic English Sentences with Swedish Equivalents,* Almqvist & Wiksell (Stockholm), 1946, 4th edition, 1959.

(With Inga Wilhemsen) *Basic Swedish Word List: With English Equivalents, Frequency Grading, and a Statistical Analysis,* Augustana Book Concern, 1947.

(With Charles M. Q. McEaddy) *The English-Speaking Press: A Reader in Newspaper English,* Hugo Gebers, 1948.

Great Fun: A Reader, Natur & Kultur, 1954.

(With Martin Tegen) *English and American Songs,* Anglo-American Center, 1954.

A New English Anthology, Natur & Kultur, 1955.

(With Michael Taylor) *The Swan of Avon: Scenes from Shakespeare, His Life, and the Elizabethan Stage,* translated by C. A. Hagberg, Natur & Kultur, 1957.

About a Motor Car, [Mullsjoe], 1961.

American and British: A Handbook of Language Differences, New Prairie, 1964.

British-American Communication: A Quantitative Experiment in Mutual Verbal Comprehension, Anglo-American Center, 1968.

Oh, My!: The Best of Anglo-Saxon Culture and Humor, Anglo-American Center, 1977.

IN SWEDISH; NONFICTION

Laesare bedoemer litteratur (title means "Readers Judge Literature"), Natur & Kultur, 1942.

(With Laycock, Janos Lotz, and others) *Levande spraakundervisning* (title means "Living Language Teaching"), Natur & Kultur, 1942.

Indien (title means "India"), Europa Verlag, 1942.

(With Inga-Britt Ranemark) *Medelby,* Bonniers, 1943.

(With Folke Leander, Ebba Dalin, Hwang Tsu-Yue, Kaete Hamburger, and others) *Universiteten i en ny vaerld* (title means "The Universities in a New World"), Kooperativa Foerbundets Bokfoerlag (Stockholm), 1944.

(With Charles Allwood, Erik Wahlgren, and Laycock) *Experiment i Mullsjoe,* Hugo Gebers, 1948.

Masskommunikationsforskning i USA (title means "Mass Communication Research in the U.S.A."), Affaersekonomi (Stockholm), 1952.

Bombad stad, Europa (title means "Bombed City, Europe"), foreword by Conrad Arensberg, Affaersekonomi, 1954.

(With William Schreiber) *Ungdomen och massmedierna i Joenkoeping* (title means "Youth and the Mass Media in Joenkoeping, Sweden"), [Joenkoeping], 1962.

Bakgrund till Mexiko (title means "Background to Mexico"), Institutet foer Samhaellsforskning, 1968.

Herman och Ove Ekelund beraetter om Torestorp och John Bauer i Mullsjoe (title means "Herman and Ove Ekelund Tell the Story of Torestorp and John Bauer in Mullsjoe"), Institutet foer Samhaellsforskning, 1975.

(Editor) *Jag minns det vackra Mullsjoe* (title means "I Remember Beautiful Mullsjoe"), Institutet foer Samhaellsforskning, 1975.

(With Sture Rimbaeck and Lars Pettersson) *Motiv fraan gamla Mullsjoe* (title means "Views of Old Mullsjoe"), [Mullsjoe], 1976.

Jag bar doeden i min Kropp: En rapport fraan samtida svensk sjukvaard, Institutet foer Samhaellsforskning, 1976.

(With Arne Samuelsson) *Ryfors: En kavalkad om ett bruk och dess oede* (title means "Ryfors: A Cavalcade about a Manor and Its Fate"), Nykyrke Hembygds-foerening (Mullsjoe), 1979.

Den dansande jaetten (travelogue on Brazil; title means "The Dancing Giant"), illustrations by Janczuk, Institutet foer Samhaellsforskning, 1981.

Ryska Kulturmoenster (title means "Russian Cultural Patterns"), [Mullsjoe], 1984.

IN ENGLISH; NONFICTION

(With Knud Morgensen, Wilhelmsen, and Carl Nesjar) *The Norwegian-American Press and Nordisk Tidende: A Quantitative Content Analysis,* [New York], 1949.

(Editor) *Hobart Mass Communication Studies: 1949-1950,* Hobart College Press, 1950.

(With Pierre Bessaignet, Lindsay Lafford, and Robert Sommer) *Studies in Mass Communication: 1950-1951,* Hobart College Press, 1951.

The Changing Role of the Handwerk in Germany's Middletown: The Structure and Social Role of the Trades and Crafts in Darmstadt, Institute of Social Research (Mullsjoe), 1955.

What Is Psychoanalysis?: A Critical Introduction, [Mullsjoe], 1955.

(With Wilhelmsen and Sture Loennerstrand) *Kalle Anka, Staalmannen och vi* (title means "Donald Duck, Superman, and Ourselves"), Institutet foer Samhaellsforskning, 1955, published in summary form as *The Impact of Comics on a European Country,* Institute of Social Research, 1955.

Eilert Sundt: A Pioneer in Sociology and Social Anthropology, Olaf Norlies (Oslo), 1957.

(Editor) *The Anglo-American Center: 1924-1963,* Anglo-American Center, 1963.

The New Generation, Iowa Wesleyan College, 1964.

Toward a New Sociology, foreword by Arensberg, Iowa Wesleyan College, 1964.

(Editor) *Communication Today: In the Family, Community, and Nation,* Iowa Wesleyan College, 1965.

A Sociological Solution to the Russian Enigma, [Mount Pleasant, Iowa], 1965.

Snapshots, Costa-Amic English Library (Mexico City, Mexico), 1985.

More Snapshots, Costa-Amic English Library, 1988.

Light and Joy: Nanna Wiberg—Textile Artist, [Mullsjoe], 1988.
Essays on Contemporary Civilization, Costa-Amic English Library, 1988.

TRANSLATOR INTO ENGLISH

(With Wahlgren, Lars Forssell, Laycock, and others) *Modern Swedish Poems,* Augustana Book Concern, 1948.
(With Wilhemsen) *Modern Norwegian Poems,* [Mullsjoe], 1949.
Twentieth-Century Scandinavian Poetry: English Translations of the Poetry of Iceland, Denmark, Norway, Sweden, and Finland, 1900-1950, Kooperativa Foerbundets Bokfoerlag, 1950.
(And editor) *Swedish Songs and Ballads,* music and preface by Prince William of Sweden, [Mullsjoe], 1950, 4th edition, Anglo-American Center, 1957.
(Contributor) Creekmore, editor, *A Little Treasury of World Poetry* (poetry anthology), [New York], 1952.
(With Forssell, Laycock, Helen Asbury, Thord Fredenholm, and others) *Scandinavian Songs and Ballads,* music and preface by Prince William of Sweden, Anglo-American Center, 1953.
(With Mogensen) *Modern Danish Poems,* [Copenhagen], 1960.
(Contributor) George Steiner, editor, *Penguin Book of Modern Verse Translation* (poetry anthology), Penguin (Harmondsworth), 1966.
Karl Erik Johansson i Backe, *Just Old Pearl* (play), [Mount Pleasant, Iowa], 1967.
Tage Aurell, *Rose of Jericho* (short story collection), University of Wisconsin Press, 1968.
Ingeborg Lagerblad, *Who Lives in the Light?* (poems), [Soelvesborg], 1978.
Thomas Warburton, *Long Live the Revisionisms!* (poems), Proza Press (Rotterdam), 1978.
(Contributor) Samkaleen Prakashan, editor, *Art and Poetry Today* (poetry anthology), [New Delhi], 1978.
(With Cate Ewing and Robert Lyng) *The Collected Poems of Edith Soedergran,* introduction by Laang, Anglo-American Center, 1980.
(With others) *Modern Scandinavian Poetry: The Poetry of Greenland, Iceland, the Faroe Islands, Denmark, Norway, Sweden, and Finland, 1900-1975,* New Directions, 1982, 2nd edition, 1987.
(With Fredenholm) Nils Ferlin, *With Plenty of Colored Lanterns,* Eagleye Books International, 1986.
(With Fredenholm) Lennart Dahl, *The House of Darkness,* Eagleye Books International, 1987.

Also contributor of English translations to *American-Scandinavian Review* (now called *Scandinavian Review*) and *Norseman.*

"CONTEMPORARY SWEDISH POETRY IN ENGLISH" SERIES; TRANSLATOR WITH CHARLES RICHARDS, LAYCOCK, LYNG, AND OTHERS

Hans Evert Rene, *Poems,* Anglo-American Center, 1971.
Margareta Lind, *Lotus Lona,* Anglo-American Center, 1971.
Helge Jedenberg, *Poems,* Anglo-American Center, 1971.
Sten Hagliden, *Carvings,* Anglo-American Center, 1971.
Helmer V. Nyberg, *Dialogue with the Unseen,* Anglo-American Center, 1971.
Ulla Olin, *Meeting Ground,* Anglo-American Center, 1971.
Maj Larsson, *Water Colors,* Anglo-American Center, 1971.
Dahl, *Unexpected Image,* Anglo-American Center, 1971.
Ranemark, *The Gateway of the Senses,* Anglo-American Center, 1971.
Kerstin Thorvall, *Bad Words Feel So Good,* Anglo-American Center, 1972.
Alf Henrikssen, *Between the Lines,* illustrations by Bjoern Berg, Anglo-American Center, 1973.
Karl Bolay, *The Square Moon,* illustrations by Kjell Ivan Andersson, 1973.
Charlotte Christoff, *The Alsbach Poems,* Anglo-American Center, 1985.

TRANSLATOR INTO SWEDISH

Akiko Yosano and others, *Three Japanese Women Poets,* [Stockholm], 1946.
Clive Staples Lewis, *Maenniskans avskaffande* (title means "The Abolition of Man"), [Stockholm], 1957.
(And editor) *Vi kaempade foer Ungern* (title means "We Fought for Hungary"), Institutet foer Samhaellsforskning, 1957.
G. Singh, *Skuggor paa en rockaerm* (title means "Shadows on a Sleeve"), Eremit Press, 1978.
Enelia Paz Gomez, *Svart i Colombia* (title means "Black in Colombia"), [Mullsjoe], 1979.
Verona Bratesch, *Sten efter sten* (title means "Stone after Stone"), [Mullsjoe], 1985.
Octavio Paz, *Indiska dikter,* [Mullsjoe], 1987.

IN SWEDISH; CONTRIBUTOR OF SHORT STORIES

Barndom i Smaaland, [Vaxjoe, Sweden], 1967.
Smaalaendska skolminnen, [Goeteberg], 1971.
Automaten bloeder (title means "Blood Drips from the Slot Machine"), Marston Hill, 1976.
Ivandrarrapport, Immigrant-Institutet, 1978.

OTHER

(Contributor) *Horisont,* Bonniers, 1942.
Spraek och Fred, Stiftelsen Fredshoegskolan (Stockholm), 1945.
(Contributor) Arne Haeggquist, editor, *Litteraturtolkning i England* (title means "The Interpretation of Literature in England"), [Stockholm], 1948.
One Hundred Years of Swedish Poetry in America, [Rock Island, Ill.], 1949.
(Editor) Stanley Houghton, *The Dear Departed* (one-act play), [Stockholm], 1950.
(Contributor of English translation) *Adventures in Appreciation,* [New York], 1952.
(Contributor of Swedish translation) *Ziel en Gedachte,* [Leiden], 1954.
(Contributor of English translation) *Pen Prints,* [Indianapolis], 1959.
Den nya fegheten (title means "The New Cowardice"), edited by Melker Johnsson, [Stockholm], 1971.
(Contributor of translated poetry) *Invandrartidningen,* [Boraas, Sweden], 1974.
Det svenska brottet, Institutet foer Samhaellsforskning, 1976.
(Editor) Martin Ivandare, *Obehagliga sanningar* (title means "Unpleasant Truths"), [Mullsjoe], 1980.
Sleep Well in Medellin: An Improvisation Play, Persona Press, 1984.
The Fullness of Time, Costa-Amic English Library, 1987.

Also contributor of criticism to *Bonniers litteraera magasin.*

WORK IN PROGRESS: Collection of aphorisms; "I am turning my interest more and more to the protest of youth in the Soviet Union, Europe, and America."

SIDELIGHTS: As the director of the Anglo-American Center in Mullsjoe, Sweden, since 1950, Martin Allwood promotes Scandinavian literature in English-speaking countries throughout the world. His work as translator of the "Contemporary Swedish Poetry in English" series earned the praise of the *Times Literary Supplement* in 1971, which attributed the translation's appeal to the fact that Allwood is himself a poet. Much of Allwood's poetry is autobiographical and, yet, the *Times Literary Supplement* reviewer observes that it "depict[s], with a firm and perceptive realism, the physical world around [Allwood]."

Allwood told *CA:* "I have long been interested in the true causes of poverty—material and spiritual. To study these I have traveled in sixty-two countries and learned eight languages. The cause of poverty is not that the rich have stolen from the poor by possessing the means of production (as Marxism would have it), but that utterly irresponsible childbearing has caused overpopulation in many parts of the world. Redistributive politico-economic systems can postpone disaster, but they cannot avert it. We need entirely new and realistic thinking, not nineteenth-century ideological intoxication."

MEDIA ADAPTATIONS: Some of Allwood's poetry has been set to music, including "Svinsaang" (title means "Swine Song"), "Liten loppa" (title means "Little Flea"), "Laarken har tystnat" (title means "The Lark Is Silent"), "Mullsjoevisan" (title means "The Mullsjoe Song"), "Varen aer haer" (title means "The Spring Is Here"), and "Rodd-Anders" (title means "Row-Anders").

BIOGRAPHICAL/CRITICAL SOURCES:

BOOKS

Arensberg, Conrad, *Death Was in My Body,* [New York], 1980.
Martin Allwood: A Comprehensive Bibliography, 1941-1981, [Mullsjoe], 1981.
Valda svenska dikter: 1940-1965 (title means "Selected Swedish Poems: 1940-1965"), Persona Press, 1982.
Singh, G., *The English Poetry of Martin Allwood,* [Mullsjoe], 1976.

PERIODICALS

American Sociological Review, October, 1959.
Burlington Hawkeye, November 16, 1964.
Iowa Wesleyan Tiger, fall, 1964.
Times Literary Supplement, November 12, 1971.

* * *

ALPEROVITZ, Gar 1936-

PERSONAL: Born May 5, 1936, in Racine, Wis.; son of Julius and Emily (Bensman) Alperovitz; married Guillemette Caron, November 6, 1966 (divorced); married Sharon Sosnick, August 29, 1976; children: (first marriage) Kari Fai, David Joseph. *Education:* University of Wisconsin, B.S. (with high honors), 1958; University of California, Berkeley, M.A., 1960; Cambridge University, Ph.D., 1963.

ADDRESSES: Home—2317 Ashmead Pl. N.W., Washington, D.C. 20009. *Office*—1718 Connecticut Ave. N.W., Suite 310, Washington, D.C. 20009.

CAREER: Legislative director to U.S. Senator Gaylord Nelson, 1964-65; special assistant to assistant secretary of state for international organization affairs, Washington, D.C., 1965-66; fellow, King's College, Cambridge, England, 1964-68, Harvard University, Cambridge, Mass., 1965-68, and Institute for Policy Studies, Washington, D.C., 1968-69; Cambridge Institute, Cambridge, Mass., co-director, 1968-71; Exploratory Project for Economic Alternatives, Washington, D.C., director, 1973—. Guest professor, University of Notre Dame, 1982-83; guest scholar, Brookings Institution.

MEMBER: National Center for Economic Alternatives (president, 1978—), Phi Beta Kappa.

WRITINGS:

Atomic Diplomacy: Hiroshima and Potsdam, Simon & Schuster, 1965, revised edition, Penguin, 1985.
Cold War Essays, Doubleday, 1970.
(With Staughton Lynd) *Strategy and Program: Two Essays toward a New American Socialism,* Beacon Press, 1973.
(With Jeff Faux) *Rebuilding America: A Blueprint for the New Economy,* Pantheon, 1984.
(Editor) Roger Skurski, *American Economic Policy: Problems and Prospects,* University of Notre Dame Press, 1984.

BIOGRAPHICAL/CRITICAL SOURCES:

PERIODICALS

New York Times Book Review, May 20, 1984, August 18, 1985.

* * *

ALTON, Thomas
See BRYANT, T(homas) Alton

* * *

AMORY, Cleveland 1917-

PERSONAL: Born September 2, 1917, in Nahant, Mass.; son of Robert and Leonore (Cobb) Amory; married Cora Fields Craddock, 1941 (divorced, 1947); married Martha Hodge, 1953 (deceased); children: Gaea McCormick. *Education:* Harvard University, A.B., 1939.

ADDRESSES: Office—200 West 57th St., New York, N.Y. 10019.

CAREER: Worked as newspaper reporter for *Nashua Telegraph,* Nashua, N.H., and *Arizona Star,* Tucson, Ariz.; managing editor of *Prescott Evening Courier,* Prescott, Ariz.; *Saturday Evening Post,* Philadelphia, Pa., associate editor, 1939-41; free-lance writer, lecturer, and television commentator, 1943—. Host of syndicated radio program, "Curmudgeon at Large." Founding president, Fund for Animals, 1967—; president, New England Anti-Vivisection Society, 1987—.

MEMBER: Harvard Club, Dutch Treat Club, Coffee House.

AWARDS, HONORS: L.H.D. from New England College and Mercy College.

WRITINGS:

The Proper Bostonians, Dutton, 1947.
Home Town (novel), Harper, 1950.
The Last Resorts, Harper, 1952.
(Editor with Earl Blackwell) *Celebrity Register* (U.S. edition of *International Celebrity Register*), Harper, 1959.
(Editor with Frederic Bradlee) *Vanity Fair: Selections from America's Most Memorable Magazine; A Cavalcade of the 1920s and 1930s,* Viking, 1960.
Who Killed Society?, Harper, 1960.
The Proper Bostonians Revisited, Dutton, 1972.
Man Kind?: Our Incredible War on Wildlife, Harper, 1974.
Cleveland Amory's Animail, Windmill Books, 1976.
The Trouble with Nowadays: A Curmudgeon Strikes Back (novel), Arbor House, 1979.
The Cat Who Came for Christmas, Little, Brown, 1987.

Columnist, *Saturday Review,* 1952-72; critic, *TV Guide,* 1960-74; contributing editor, *Parade,* 1983—. Author of syndicated newspaper column, "Animail."

WORK IN PROGRESS: A sequel to *The Cat Who Came for Christmas.*

SIDELIGHTS: Self-proclaimed curmudgeon Cleveland Amory began his career as a journalist in the early 1930s. For more than two decades thereafter, the Harvard-educated writer cast his eye and caustic wit upon society, especially the more diaphanous aspects of "high society." In the 1960s, however, Amory directed his attention and talent toward environmental issues and the welfare of wildlife. In 1967, he founded the Fund for Animals which, as Amory explains to Jean W. Ross in a *CA* interview, is committed to "litigation, legislation, education, and confrontation." Struggling to ensure that the entitlement of animals is both recognized and respected, this activist group has ameliorated many dreadful conditions. Amory's involvement with the welfare of animals, though, has rewarded him in other ways as well; it has provided him with his longtime companion, Polar Bear—a curmudgeonly and increasingly famous feline, the rescue of whom he recounts in the affectionately humorous and popular *The Cat Who Came for Christmas.*

Whatever his subject, Amory approaches it sardonically. His first novel, *Home Town,* satirizes the publishing business in a tale about an Arizona journalist who travels to New York City to promote his new book. Calling the novel a "somewhat oversimplified lampoon of the ruses and devices and skepticism of book publishers, their aides and allies and outriders," Richard Manley suggests in the *New York Times* that "Amory has written his expose tersely, humorously and with muffled malice." In his second novel, *The Trouble with Nowadays: A Curmudgeon Strikes Back,* Amory targets contemporary manners by expounding upon the ills of modern society through the voice of "an opinionated, righteous, archconservative who is a sort of an erudite Archie Bunker," remarks a *Publishers Weekly* contributor, adding that the character's "outrageous suggestions make for sophisticated satire of a high order." Describing Amory in *Best Sellers* as "a lovable lunatic . . . chronicling our shenanigans with a breadth of vision," Tim Murray deems him "a ludicrous, and lucid, guide—and complainer."

Noted especially for his satirical nonfiction, Amory's early work concerns the affluent and their lavish lifestyles, poking gentle fun at society's pretentiousness. His first book, *The Proper Bostonians,* scrutinizes the more monied and familied of Boston's residents, while *Last Resorts,* his second book of nonfiction, surveys their playgrounds. Like most reviewers who judged the former well-researched and richly anecdotal, Edward Weeks declares in an *Atlantic* review that it is "written with enough impudence, accuracy, affection, and respect to make the First Families anxious lest there be a second volume." Suggesting in a *Commonweal* review that perhaps "Boston may take this deliberately outrageous book quite calmly," Mason Wade points out that "Mr. Amory is a proper Bostonian himself." In a *New York Times* review of *Last Resorts,* however, John McNulty expresses his feeling that while "Amory has the great gift of being able to enjoy the daffinesses and the grotesqueries of this class of Americans," he does so "without manifesting any socially conscious anger." Yet according to Fanny Butcher in the *Chicago Sunday Tribune,* "Amory has a quick eye for the bizarre, a quick ear for the apt riposte to the nasty thrust, and a pen as sharp as a stiletto," adding, moreover, that "he writes with stinging wit about many people and places that local legend oftener pats with tender hands."

In *Who Killed Society?,* Amory examines the origins and rise of "high society" in America, as well as the reasons for its decline. In the *Saturday Review of Literature,* C. O. Skinner finds that the book contains "moments of admirable scholarship, flashes of gleeful wit, and a number of startling instances of downright sensationalism." Finding the work "almost consistently entertaining," Charles Rolo writes in the *Atlantic* that "Amory combines a huge zest for his subject with an astringently ironic perspective." However, in the *Christian Science Monitor,* Rod Nordell exhibits a mixed reaction. While he believes that "when Amory is at his keen-eyed and keen-eared best, he records social history with zest, and human foibles with a deceptively ingratiating air," Nordell also feels that "this prodigal son of the society he chronicles seems to be wasting his substances on aspects of his world that are worth nobody's time, including his own."

With *Man Kind?: Our Incredible War on Wildlife,* though, Amory's mordant wit draws a bead on society's capacity for cruelty and outright indifference to the suffering it inflicts, especially upon animals. Calling the book "hard-hitting," Emil P. Dolensek suggests in the *New York Times Book Review* that it represents "an effective follow-up to Mr. Amory's frequent appearances on television and radio and to his newspaper and magazine columns where he has become an outspoken critic of man's inhumanity to animals." Focusing particularly on the hunting faction in society, Amory is "obviously most enraged by those who kill for the fun of killing," says Dolensek, adding that much of the book is devoted particularly to "the killing or exploitation of animals for their economic value—as a source of fur, meat and other products, and as a threat to agricultural programs." According to John Wanamaker in the *Christian Science Monitor:* "The reader will not like what he reads; he may shake with pity, anger, yes even with wrath. Yet assuredly, he will read on, so absorbing are the incidents Cleveland Amory describes in a straight-forward though often rightly angry, impatient vein."

While the general intent of Amory's prose might be to rankle readers out of complacency, his popular *The Cat Who Came for Christmas,* of which there are more than a million copies in print, employs a different approach. A personal story about the battered and ravenous cat that he rescues from a New York City alley on Christmas Eve, Amory's humorous and affectionate tale relates the companionship that develops, a companionship secured by mutual toleration as well as devotion. Although the horrors experienced by the animal world are softened by this account of one man's memorable relationship with his cat, according to Mary Daniels in the *Chicago Tribune,* the reader is "unavoidably made aware of these facts as they are sandwiched between layers of humorous prose about his own cat as well as a fresh view on the history and mystery of the cat." Although a *Publishers Weekly* contributor labeled the book "mainly for ailurophiles," Amory's purpose in writing it, however, is not simply to share a story with others who may have had similar experiences, as he makes clear in the book's conclusion: "I hope even more that those of you who have never had an animal will hie yourselves to the nearest shelter and adopt one. If you do, you will surely find that the animal will give you, every day of his or her life, not only joy and companionship but also that very special kind of love which can be understood, as I said at the beginning, only by those fortunate enough ever to have been owned by one."

CA INTERVIEW

CA interviewed Cleveland Amory by telephone on September 15, 1988, at his home in New York, New York.

CA: You've said that witnessing a bullfight in Mexico was the event that got you started on your work for animals. How did you go from that point to founding the Fund for Animals?

AMORY: Before I started the Fund, I joined just about every animal society I could find. I even got as far as being honorary vice-president of the National Catholic Society for Animal Welfare, which is surely as far as a Boston Episcopalian can go. I was jeopardizing my own future; I know lately there is some question about the gender of the Almighty, but I've never heard his or her Episcopalianism questioned. Early in my animal career I remember having an argument with a Catholic priest about the once prevalent teaching of that church that animals have no souls. I told the good father that if he and I were going in the future to some wonderful Elysian Field and the animals were not going to go anywhere, that was all the more reason to give them a little better shake in the one life they did have.

The Fund was formed in 1967, and at that time I said we needed to put cleats on the little old ladies in tennis shoes, which is what the animal workers had been called. I didn't mean any put-down on their gender or their size or their footwear; I meant that the struggles ahead would demand, as the Fund now puts it, "litigation, legislation, education, and confrontation." And looking back on those days, I don't think I could imagine then the kinds of confrontation we would later have.

One of the things the Fund is best known for is the painting of baby seals off the floes of the Magdalene Islands in Canada, which involved buying a British trawler, the *Sea Shepherd,* and filling the bow full of concrete to make an icebreaker out of it. The Canadians used huge icebreakers to cut the ice for the commercial sealers that came in from Norway and Halifax, and they boasted that we would never even find the seals. We had to bang our way through the ice for five days and five nights to get to them, but we did it, and we painted them with a red organic dye which is harmless to the seals but makes their coats worthless for what the sealers wanted to beat them to death for.

Then we used that same ship to go after a pirate whaling ship which flew a flag of convenience and was massacring whales everywhere. It was called, ironically, the *Sierra.* In those days the Russians and Japanese dominated the International Whaling Commission. Even they had ruled for certain sanctuaries, but this ship would go into them and clobber big whales, baby whales, mother whales, everything. We knew that we literally must confront this, so we took our trawler and located the *Sierra* off Portugal. The *Sierra,* incidentally, was armed, and they had said that if we came after her they would shoot the people on our deck. Our people had no arms at all. Our captain was under firm instructions to confront the whaler near the shore, in case she didn't have enough life preservers.

The first ramming took off the harpoon and all the bow paraphernalia for killing whales. Then we made a 180-degree turn and rammed her right square in the middle. Both the *Sierra* and our ship were towed back into Oporto, Portugal, and the *Sierra* was later sunk. They would have probably commandeered the *Sea Shepherd,* and they might have made a whaling ship out of it, so we sank our own ship. As a result of our action, the companies which insured those pirate whaling ships became convinced that, with people like us after them, it wasn't affordable to insure them. So we succeeded in getting rid of all five pirate whaling ships instead of just one.

The next thing we did was the thing for which the Fund is probably best known. It was the rescue of the burros in the Grand Canyon. These are not the donkeys that people go down to the bottom of the canyon on. This herd was started a long time ago when the Gold Rush people deserted some of their burros. The Park Service was determined to shoot them under the theory that they were not indigenous to the Canyon; the officials wanted to go back to some pristine time that they couldn't define. I said that if they really wanted to do that, they should get the hell out and let the Indians take over again. Shooting burros is a very difficult thing. There are only two places where they can be immediately killed, the brain and the heart. Also, the burro is very smart; he knows when there's trouble and he's good at hiding. The kind of event the Park Service had in mind would have been a ghastly mess. No previous effort to get the burros out of there had ever succeeded. We were given a quota we had to get in a certain number of days or they wouldn't let us do it anymore, and the time they gave us was the middle of the summer, when it was 120 degrees at the bottom of the canyon in midday. Even if we had found a burro, we couldn't have rescued it in that heat, because there wasn't enough lift to get the helicopter up out of there. But the operation was successful because we decided to work very early in the morning and very late in the afternoon, almost until dark, when it was cool enough to get the lift we needed.

We had put together a terrific crew of people, including a world-champion cowboy roper. The cowboys and even the pilots made a lot of fun of us when we were starting; they called us Bambi-lovers. But one day I noticed that they were arguing about something, and I went over to see what it was. It turned out they had rescued a mother and a baby, and they were arguing about which one to take up first. "If you take the baby first," one of them said, "at least the mother will know it's going somewhere, and when we come for her, she'll think she must be going to the same place." The other one said, "No, it's better to take the mother first, because the baby doesn't know anything." Then the man who had scoffed at me the most about being a Bambi-lover figured out that since they had taken a male that weighed 650 pounds, they could carry the weight of the mother and baby combined, and he said, "Let's build two slings and take them together." It's the first rescue I know of where a mother and baby were taken together. We rescued 577 burros, and from that time on, our rescues have probably been the best-known things about the Fund for Animals.

We've adopted out over seven thousand burros to homes. We made a pet out of the burro, which before had not been thought of as a pet. They are wonderful animals. I don't mean to put down ponies, but burros have a better disposition for kids. We've never had a case of a burro kicking a kid or anything like that.

We went on from the Grand Canyon operation to rescue goats on San Clemente Island, where the U.S. Navy was going to shoot them. Again we had to go to court to stop them. Finally we had to get Defense Secretary Weinberger to go against the Navy big shots and decide to give our rescue a chance. This time we used the helicopter system that was developed in New Zealand, and we got New Zealand net gunners to come over for it. They fire a net from a four-barrel gun, and it billows out like a sheet over the animal, but it's got heavy weights so that it drops down and covers him. Then the rescuers jump out of the helicopter and tie his feet together, put him in a sling, and take him back to the corral. The day we started, there must have been a hundred other helicopters from networks and movie people from all over the world. It was an awful job for our pilot to work with all those helicopters flying around, but in most cases he got a goat within three or four minutes and got it back in the corral. We worked with the best helicopter pilot in the world. He ran the 'copter always on the flat or heading up so that the goats would not go in the rocky canyons—San Clemente is a terribly difficult terrain to work. Our accomplishment has led in turn to our own government's doing a lot of that kind of rescue, actually using the same crew we used. It's very expensive helicopter time; it's not practical for a private society to have to do it on a huge scale.

We take these animals to Black Beauty Ranch, which we bought about the time we started the Grand Canyon rescue. It's now six hundred acres and has abused and injured equines. We call it the Black Beauty Ranch because the last line of the book *Black Beauty* is: "My troubles are over, and I have found a home." That's on a sign at the gate. We have all kinds of animals there: carriage horses from New York, mounted-police horses, broken down horses from the race track, cruelty cases. We have the last diving horses from Atlantic City, who used to be made to do that stupid trick of diving sixty feet into something like a swimming pool. We've got a small herd of burros I kept from the Grand Canyon; we have wild pigs from San Clemente, as well as the goats. We have Nim, the greatest of the sign-language-talking chimps, who came from a laboratory after seventeen researchers had made their careers by writing their theses on him—then they were going to let him go for experimentation. He has a pal at the ranch, Sally, who was a circus chimp. Last week we got a whole roadside petting zoo full of animals, including deer and coyotes and sheep. They were being starved in the zoo. They had been nine days without food and water when the Humane officer made the deal that he wouldn't prosecute if the owner would let us have the animals at the Ranch. Without our facility, he told us, he would not have been able to ask the judge for custody.

The Black Beauty Ranch has been a very valuable asset for the Fund, though we have still stuck to those basic things I mentioned at the beginning: litigation, legislation, education, and confrontation. The success of my book *The Cat Who Came for Christmas* has helped. Somebody told me today that it's going to be the best-selling animal book of this century. I don't know if that's true, but it got up to number two on the *New York Times* best-seller list, and there will be more than a million copies in print by this Christmas.

CA: In Man Kind?: Our Incredible War on Wildlife *you made some surprising revelations about some of the large, well-known wildlife groups. Since that book was published in 1974, have any of these groups taken a harder line on hunting?*

AMORY: No, they really haven't. One of the sadnesses of dealing with wildlife is that the whole machinery of the woods, as I call it, is run by departments of environmental conservation and other conservation boards like the Michigan Department of Natural Resources, which I call the Department of Nuts with Rifles. They're all controlled by the hunting and trapping fraternity, and this affects everybody who has land they want to post or anything like that. And yet hunters and trappers represent less than ten percent of the citizenry of this country, and their numbers are falling steadily because more and more people, I think, realize that the killing is so unjust and so horrible. Take for example the killing of fifty million mourning doves, a harmless, inoffensive bird that's actually useful to farmers.

I'd like to think that we're making progress in reaching people. Now organizations which are pro-hunting, like the National Wildlife Federation, deny that they're pro-hunting if you write in and criticize them. They try to have it both ways. But I think most people know by now that on every side of every issue, they always come down for the hunter and trapper. With the Audubon Society, the chapters can form their own policies, which may differ from the national policy. I think the average person who belongs to Audubon was shocked by the revelations in my book about the Audubon Society and its pro-hunting stance underneath the idea of helping. And I would include in the same category even the National Geographic Society, which sells so many magazines with its beautiful animal pictures. The fact that they're not even coming out against shooting mourning doves is really frightening.

It's too bad that such organizations are the very richest ones, the ones with the potential power to do something about this incredible hold the hunters and trappers have on the departments of environmental conservation. And I think people felt after my revelations that they would change their loyalties. You must remember that the numbers of the so-called animal advocates, or animals' rightists, as we're also called sometimes, are growing too. I think there are potentially two million people out there who now consider themselves on our end of the spectrum. The numbers are far larger than they ever were before, and greatly larger than they were when I started my work. Certainly the Fund for Animals has played an important part in this. We were the first ones to put on our buttons and bumper stickers "Animals have *rights,* too." I was nervous about that. At that time the word *rights* was very much associated with blacks, and I thought it would seem a sort of anti-black slogan, which I certainly didn't want, both because I hate prejudice and also because the blacks control so many of the animals in Africa and elsewhere. But it was not taken that way, fortunately. It's difficult for us in certain fights. If we're fighting, for example, for the bears in Oregon against the timber companies, the timber people visualize the bears marching on the state capitol or something like that because of the word *rights.* But animals have the right to a decent death, if nothing else, which is not one by poisoning or by bow hunting or all the other grisly methods that are used to massacre them. I think that, if it's true, as is sometimes quoted to us from the Bible, that "into our hands they are delivered," then they're God's creatures and it's more or less a God-given trust to us to treat them decently. If we continue as we are doing, I think we have failed that trust and, come judgment day, even the most merciful God isn't going to look very kindly on what we've done.

CA: There are many groups trying to raise money for animals. How can the potential donor make a wise decision about which group or groups to help?

AMORY: I will give information on the telephone to people who call and ask about ours. But I don't want to be quoted on other societies, because I find some good in all of them, even the ones that get much more money than they need. I think a person who gives regularly to a society, even a small amount—which may represent a larger amount for him or her than for somebody who is very well off—should get to know to whom they are giving, and should, at least once in a while, ask for an annual report to see how they spend their money, see if they're just building up endowments and giving huge salaries or whether they've really got dedicated people. I take no salary for animal work and never have. My chief assistant, Marian Probst, takes no salary, and none of the board members is paid. The highest salary the fund pays is $1200 a month, and that's to somebody who hasn't been off the Black Beauty Ranch in five years except to go for a physical checkup or something like that. When we have that kind of dedication, we don't need salaries. There are others who say that charity work should be paid just like business work, but I disagree. Whether we can find people to run the Fund after I've gone who will agree with my philosophy, I don't know. The usual history is that the people who start such an organization take very little money and build it up, and in the end it becomes quite managerial, with high salaries and so forth. I hope that doesn't happen to the Fund.

CA: You've chronicled the doings of society folks in The Proper Bostonians, The Last Resorts, Who Killed Society, *and other writing. How did the social scene attract your interest sufficiently to get you launched on such a body of work?*

AMORY: I think being born in the Boston resort of Nahant and growing up in the so-called society of Boston led to the first book, *The Proper Bostonians,* which was about where the Bostonians came from and how a very small number of families had imprinted themselves on the city to give it its character and its reputation. I did that, I hope, amusingly, and yet with some understanding from being one of them myself. The second book was about the famous resorts of the country. Then, since those books were generally filed in libraries under cities or resorts or travel, I wanted one book about society itself, where the word came from and what it meant or didn't mean, and that was *Who Killed Society?*

I've written two satiric novels. One is *Home Town,* and it's about what happens to an author when he's fortunate enough to have a successful book. The second is *The Trouble with Nowadays.* All the bores I've known in clubs throughout my life were more funny to me than boring, and I wrote a book about what they think of modern times. That may be the runt of the litter, but it's one of my favorites. I had breakfast in the New York Athletic Club this morning and there was a fellow there who was just like that. He was going on about the terrors of the prospect that the Democrats might get in again, which to him was a fate worse than death.

CA: The first-person complainer of The Trouble with Nowadays *does his writing in longhand, with a real fountain pen, every day. Is your way of writing anything like his, by chance?*

AMORY: Yes. I don't even use my old faithful typewriter anymore. I've put it over in the corner, and I do everything in longhand. As everybody gets more technical and more adept at word processing, I go back farther and farther. I think finally I'll be writing like the cave men on the side of a wall.

CA: You've written some clever and wise lines. What do you think will stick?

AMORY: I suppose I'll be remembered for some sayings that seem to appear in quote books a lot. One is from my social books: "A good family is one that used to be better." Another is "The mark of a civilized person is how he treats what's underneath him"; and, finally, "Man has an infinite capacity to rationalize his own cruelty." I think those are my best-known quotes, and I'd stand with them. I wouldn't mind any of them on my tombstone.

CA: Is there another book in the works?

AMORY: I'm doing a sequel to *The Cat Who Came for Christmas.* Polar Bear was a young cat in the first book, and this is about him as an old cat. I don't think he wants another book; I talked to him last night about it. He doesn't like all the fanfare. When a reporter comes to the house, he goes under the bed and doesn't want to come out. I have now Polar Star, whom I got at a shelter a couple of weekends ago in Massachusetts. He looked exactly like Polar Bear looked before I rescued him—the same coat that turned out to be white—but he has blue eyes instead of Polar Bear's green eyes. He adores attention and fuss, and he would be very good on programs and in other publicity situations that Polar Bear would hate. Polar Bear is very Republican; he doesn't like anything to happen which hasn't happened before.

I've had so far close to five thousand letters about *The Cat Who Came for Christmas,* and I've tried to answer them all. I think the one that meant the most to me was the one in which the writer felt that people who read the book would at least consider getting a cat out of a shelter. Cats have a rough time in shelters; they don't get adopted very much. If there are going to be a million books in print by Christmas 1988, if I were responsible for a lot of cats coming out of shelters—just in this country, let alone after the book is published abroad—I would feel that that was the best thing I had done.

BIOGRAPHICAL/CRITICAL SOURCES:

BOOKS

Amory, Cleveland, *The Cat Who Came for Christmas,* Little, Brown, 1987.

PERIODICALS

Atlantic, November, 1947, February, 1961.
Best Sellers, October, 1979.
Book Week, January 5, 1964.
Chicago Sunday Tribune, January 29, 1950, December 18, 1960.
Christian Science Monitor, October 10, 1947, January 2, 1964, December 10, 1974.
Commonweal, October 31, 1947.
Library Journal, February 1, 1964, October 15, 1979.
Nation, December 6, 1947.
National Review, March 28, 1975.
New Republic, November 10, 1947.
New York, December 21, 1987.
New York Herald Tribune Book Review, October 12, 1947, January 15, 1950, November 9, 1952.
New York Herald Tribune Lively Arts, December 18, 1960.
New York Times, October 19, 1947, November 9, 1952, January 18, 1988.
New York Times Book Review, December 25, 1960, October 27, 1974, July 12, 1981.
People, August 22, 1983.
Publishers Weekly, August 26, 1974, August 4, 1975, October 18, 1976, July 30, 1979, August 28, 1987, September 9, 1988.
Saturday Review, January 7, 1961.
Saturday Review of Literature, November 29, 1947, January 7, 1950.
Saturday Review/World, November 2, 1974.
Time, October 20, 1947, November 17, 1952, December 19, 1960.

—Sketch by Sharon Malinowski

—Interview by Jean W. Ross

* * *

ANDERSON, T(heodore) W(ilbur) 1918-

PERSONAL: Born June 5, 1918, in Minneapolis, Minn.; son of Theodore Wilbur (a clergyman) and Evelynn (Johnson) Anderson; married Dorothy Fisher (a clinical social worker), July 8, 1950; children: Robert Lewis, Janet Lynn, Jeanne Elizabeth. *Education:* North Park College, A.A., 1937; Northwestern University, B.S. (with highest distinction), 1939; Princeton University, M.A., 1942, Ph.D., 1945.

ADDRESSES: Home—746 Santa Ynez St., Stanford, Calif. 94305. *Office*—Department of Statistics, Stanford University, Stanford, Calif. 94305.

CAREER: Princeton University, Princeton, N.J., instructor in mathematics, 1941-43, research associate for national defense research committee, 1943-45; University of Chicago, Chicago, Ill., research associate for Cowles Commission for Research in Economics, 1945-46; Columbia University, New York, N.Y., instructor, 1946-47, assistant professor, 1947-50, associate professor, 1950-56, professor of mathematical statistics, 1956-67, acting chairman of department, 1950-51, 1963, chairman, 1956-60, 1964-65; Stanford University, Stanford, Calif., professor of statistics and economics, 1967—. Visiting associate professor at Stanford University, 1954; visiting professor at Imperial College of Science and Technology (London), University of Moscow, and University of Paris, 1967-68; academic visitor, London School of Economics and Political Science, 1974-75; research visitor, Tokyo Institute of Technology, 1977; Sherman Fairchild Distinguished Scholar, California Institute of Technology, 1980. Center for Advanced Study in the Behavioral Sciences, fellow, 1957-58, visiting scholar, 1972-73, 1980. Director of project for Office of Naval Research, 1968-82; principle investigator for National Science Foundation project, 1969, and for Army Research Office project, 1982—; scientific director of North Atlantic Treaty Organization (NATO) Advanced Study Institute on Discriminant Analysis and Its Applications, 1972. Chairman of committee on statistics, National Research Council, 1961-63. Member of National Academy of Sciences and National Research Council committees. Consultant to RAND Corp., 1949-66, and Cowles Foundation for Research in Economics.

MEMBER: International Statistical Institute, American Academy of Arts and Sciences (fellow), National Academy of Sciences, American Mathematical Society, American Statistical Association (fellow; vice-president, 1971-73), Institute of Mathematical Statistics (fellow; president, 1963; member of council), Bernouilli Society for Mathematics, Statistics, and Probability, Econometric Society (fellow), American Association for the Advancement of Science (fellow), Biometric Society, Psychometric Society (member of council of directors), American Association of University Professors, Royal Statistical Society (fellow), Indian Statistical Institute, Phi Beta Kappa, Sigma Xi.

AWARDS, HONORS: Guggenheim fellowship at University of Stockholm and Cambridge University, 1947-48; R. A. Fisher Award, Committee of President of Statistical Societies, 1985; Distinguished Alumnus Award, North Park College and Theological Seminary, 1987; D.Lit., North Park College and Theological Seminary, 1988; Samuel S. Wilks Memorial Medal, American Statistical Association, 1988.

WRITINGS:

(Contributor) Tjalling C. Koopmans, editor, *Statistical Inference in Dynamic Economic Models,* Wiley, 1950.

(Contributor) Jerzy Neyman, editor, *Proceedings of the Second Berkeley Symposium on Mathematical Statistics and Probability,* University of California Press, 1951.

(Contributor) Paul F. Lazarsfeld, editor, *Mathematical Thinking in the Social Sciences,* Free Press, 1954.

(Contributor) Dwight C. Miner, editor, *History of the Faculty of Political Science,* Columbia University Press, 1955.

(Editor) Abraham Wald, *Selected Papers in Statistics and Probability,* McGraw, 1955.

(Contributor) Neyman, editor, *Proceedings of the Third Berkeley Symposium on Mathematical Statistics and Probability,* Volume V, University of California Press, 1956.

An Introduction to Multivariate Statistical Analysis, Wiley, 1958, 2nd edition, 1984.

(Contributor) Ulf Grenander, editor, *Probability and Statistics: The Harald Cramer Volume,* Almqvist & Wiksell, 1959.

(Contributor) Ingram Olkin, S. G. Ghurye, and others, editors, *Contributions to Probability and Statistics: Essays in Honor of Harold Hotelling,* Stanford University Press, 1960.

(Contributor) Kenneth J. Arrow, Samuel Karlin, and Patrick Suppes, editors, *Mathematical Methods in the Social Sciences,* Stanford University Press, 1960.

(Contributor) R. Duncan Luce, Robert R. Bush, and Eugene Galanter, editors, *Readings in Mathematical Psychology,* Volume I, Wiley, 1963.

(Contributor) Murray Rosenblatt, editor, *Proceedings of the Symposium on Time Series Analysis,* Wiley, 1963.

(Contributor) *Proceedings of the IBM Scientific Computing Symposium in Statistics,* Data Precessing Division, International Business Machines, 1965.

(Contributor) P. R. Krishnaiah, editor, *Multivariate Analysis,* Academic Press, Volume I, 1966, Volume II, 1969, North-Holland Publishing, Volume V, 1980, Volume VI, 1985.

(Editor and contributor) S. S. Wilks, *Collected Papers: Contributions to Mathematical Statistics,* Wiley, 1967.

(Contributor) Lucien LeCam and Neyman, editors, *Proceedings of the Fifth Berkeley Symposium in Mathematical Statistics and Probability,* Volume I, University of California Press, 1967.

(Contributor) Lazarsfeld and Neil Henry, editors, *Latent Structure Analysis,* Houghton, 1968.

(Contributor) J. Malcolm Dowling and Fred Glahe, editors, *Readings in Econometric Theory,* Colorado Associated University Press, 1970.

(Contributor) R. C. Bose, I. M. Chakravarti, and others, editors, *Essays in Probability and Statistics,* University of North Carolina Press, 1970.

The Statistical Analysis of Time Series, Wiley, 1971.

(With S. Das Gupta and G. P. H. Styan) *A Bibliography of Multivariate Statistical Analysis,* Halsted Press, 1972.

(Contributor) LeCam, Neyman, and Elizabeth Scott, editors, *Proceedings of the Sixth Berkeley Symposium in Mathematical Statistics and Probability,* Volume I, University of California Press, 1972.

(Contributor) Theophilus Cacoullos, editor, *Discriminant Analysis and Applications,* Academic Press, 1973.

(With S. L. Sclove) *Introductory Statistical Analysis,* with solutions manual, Houghton, 1974.

(With Sclove) *An Introduction to the Statistical Analysis of Data,* with solutions manual, Houghton, 1978.

(Contributor) J. S. Coleman, R. K. Merton, and Peter H. Rossi, editors, *Qualitative and Quantitative Social Research,* Free Press, 1979.

(Contributor) D. R. Brillinger and G. C. Tiao, editors, *Directions in Time Series,* Institute of Mathematical Statistics, 1980.

(Contributor) *Proceedings of the Conference on Recent Developments in Statistical Methods and Applications,* Directorate—General of Budget, Accounting and Statistics (Taipei, Taiwan), 1980.

(Contributor) O. D. Anderson, editor, *Time Series Analysis: Theory and Practice 1,* North-Holland Publishing, 1982.

(Contributor) G. Kallianpur, Krishnaiah, and J. K. Ghosh, editors, *Statistics and Probability: Essays in Honor of C. R. Rao,* North-Holland Publishing, 1982.

(Contributor) Bo Ranneby, editor, *Statistics in Theory and Practice: Essays in Honour of Bertil Matern,* Swedish University of Agricultural Sciences, 1982.

(Contributor) Werner Hildenbrand, editor, *Advances in Econometrics,* Cambridge University Press, 1982.

(Contributor) Peter J. Bickel, Jkell A. Doksum, and J. L. Hodges, Jr., editors, *A Festschrift for Erick L. Lehmann,* Wadsworth, 1983.

(Contributor) F. Gerard Adams and Bert G. Hickman, editors, *Global Econometrics: Essays in Honor of Lawrence R. Klein,* MIT Press, 1983.

(With Barrett Eynon) *Minitab Guide to the Statistical Analysis of Data,* Scientific Press, 1986.

(With Sclove) *The Statistical Analysis of Data,* Scientific Press, 1986.

(Contributor) Tarmo Pukkila and Simo Puntanen, editors, *Proceedings of the Second International Tampere Conference in Statistics,* [Tampere], 1987.

Also contributor to *Linear Algebra and Its Applications,* 1979. Contributor to *International Encyclopedia of the Social Sciences.* Contributor of about seventy articles to scientific journals, including *Journal of the American Statistical Association, Econometrica, Annals of Statistics, Biometrika, Bulletin of the International Statistical Institute,* and *Australian Journal of Statistics.* Editor of *Annals of Mathematical Statistics,* 1950-52; member of editorial board of *Psychometrica,* 1954-72; associate editor, *Journal of Time Series Analysis,* 1980—; member of advisory board, *Econometric Theory,* 1985—, and *Journal of Multivariate Analysis,* 1988—.

* * *

ANDERSSON, Theodore 1903-

PERSONAL: Surname originally Levine; name legally changed in 1931; born February 18, 1903, in New Haven, Conn.; son of Seth Samuel and Anna Erika (Johnson) Levine; married Harriet Josephine Murdock, April 8, 1930; children: Theodore Murdock, Margit (Mrs. Timothy R. Clifford). *Education:* Yale University, B.A., 1925, M.A., 1926, Ph.D., 1931.

ADDRESSES: Home—1006 Lund St., Austin, Tex. 78704. *Office*—Foreign Language Education Center, University of Texas, Austin, Tex. 78712.

CAREER: Yale University, New Haven, Conn., instructor, 1927-37, associate professor of French, 1946-55, director of undergraduate instruction in French, 1946-51, director of Master of Arts in Teaching program, 1951-54, associate director, 1954-55; American University, Washington, D.C., professor of Romance languages and head of department, 1937-41; Wells College, Aurora, N.Y., associate professor, 1941-43, professor of Romance languages and head of department, 1943-45; U.S. Department of State, International Exchange, Division of Cultural Cooperation and Educational Advisors, chief of Western European Section, 1945-46; Modern Language Association of America, New York, N.Y., associate secretary and associate director, 1955-56, director of foreign language program, 1956-57; University of Texas, Austin, professor of Romance languages, 1957-68, professor of Spanish and education, 1968-80, professor emeritus, 1980—, head of department, 1959-68. Visiting professor at State University of New York at Albany, summer, 1937, Harvard University, summer, 1948, Middlebury College, summer, 1954, University of Wisconsin, summer, 1954 and 1955, Stanford University, summer, 1955, University of Washington, summer, 1958, and University of Hawaii, spring, 1959. Director of UNESCO Seminar for the Teaching of Modern Languages for World Understanding, Nuwara Eliya, Ceylon, 1953; U.S. delegate to UNESCO Institute for Education, Hamburg, Germany, 1959 and 1962; Ford Foundation program specialist for modern languages, Santiago, Chile, 1964-65; Southwest Educational Development Laboratory, U.S. Office of Education, Austin, Tex., director of bilingual design project, 1968-69, director of bilingual section, 1969-70, resources specialist, 1970-71. Organizer and chairman, Conference on Children's Language, 1971.

MEMBER: International Association of Applied Linguistics, International Institute of Ibero-American Literature (president, 1961-63), American Council on the Teaching of Foreign Languages, Modern Language Association of America, American Association of Teachers of Spanish and Portuguese (vice-president, 1972; president, 1973), International and Comparative Education Society, Teachers of English to Speakers of Other Languages, Phi Beta Kappa.

AWARDS, HONORS: Decorated Chevalier for French Legion of Honor, 1954, for contributions to Franco-American educational and cultural relations; Diploma di Benemerenza, Societa Dante Alighieri, Rome, 1974; decorated Caballero de la Order del Merito Civil, Spain, 1975; received award from Northeast Conference on the Teaching of Foreign Languages, 1975; awarded plaque for contributions to bilingual, bicultural education by National Association of Bilingual Education, 1978; awarded diploma by American Association of Teachers of Spanish and Portuguese, 1978, for services rendered.

WRITINGS:

Carlos Maria Ocantos: Argentine Novelist, Yale University Press, 1934.

(Editor with Thomas G. Borgin) *French Plays,* American Book Co., 1941.

The Teaching of Foreign Languages in the Elementary School, Heath, 1953.

The Teaching of Literature, Northeast Conference on the Teaching of Foreign Languages, 1954.

(With Felix Walter) *The Teaching of Modern Languages,* UNESCO, 1955.

(With others) *The Education of the Secondary School Teacher,* Wesleyan University Press, 1962.

(Contributor) *A Handbook for Teachers of Spanish and Portuguese,* Heath, 1968.

Foreign Languages in the Elementary School: A Struggle against Mediocrity, University of Texas Press, 1969.

(With Mildred Boyer) *Bilingual Schooling in the United States,* Southwest Educational Development Laboratory (Austin, Tex.), 1970, 2nd edition, National Educational Laboratory Publishers, 1978.

(Contributor) Merrill Swain, editor, *Bilingual Schooling: Some Experiences in Canada and the United States,* Ontario Institute for Studies in Education, 1972.

(Editor with William F. Mackey) *Bilingualism in Early Childhood,* Newbury House Publishers, 1977.

Resource Guide to Bilingual Education: A Selective Bibliography of Recent Publications, National Educational Publishers, 1978.

A Guide to Family Reading in Two Languages: The Preschool Years, Evaluation, Dissemination and Assessment Center, California State University (Los Angeles), 1981.

Contributor to *International Review of Education, Modern Language Journal, Hispania,* and other professional journals.

WORK IN PROGRESS: Research on learning of languages in early childhood, learning of reading from ages two to five, and the critical age for language learning.

SIDELIGHTS: Theodore Andersson writes: "The book I am now beginning to work on, a projected anthology of successful cases of preschool reading in one, two, or more languages, will, I hope, bring full circle an experience I had in Sweden at the age of four and five. When my father lost his job in the depression of 1907, my mother took me, an only child, to live on her parents' farm in central Sweden. Having heard some Swedish in New Haven, [Connecticut], I needed only three weeks to absorb the speech of that tiny rural community [in Sweden]. What my mother did not realize was that in the two years I spent in Sweden I could have learned to read—and write—the language almost as easily as I learned to understand and speak it. An aunt used to tell me stories at bedtime and thus transport me into the world of literature. But, though she was a primary school teacher, she did not read to me—or with me.

"To this day most educators, including reading specialists, do not realize that many children between the ages of two and five want to, can, and do learn to read, sometimes by themselves. Many others need only the example of parents who read or parents' gentle, unpressured encouragement to begin reading. Already I have collected for my anthology at least a dozen cases of successful early reading often resulting in a favorable impact on later education. As more and more parents come to realize their young children's learning potential and more children enter school already reading one or two languages, the schools will have to raise their standards to match children's out-of-school learning."

* * *

ANDRZEJEWSKI, Jerzy 1909-1983
(George Andrzeyevski)

PERSONAL: Born August 19, 1909, in Poland; died of a heart attack, April 20, 1983, in Warsaw, Poland; son of Jan (a tradesman) and Eugenia (Glinojecka) Andrzejewski; married Maria Abgarowicz (a musicologist), January 31, 1946; children: Marcin, Agnieszka. *Education:* Studied Polish philological sciences at University of Warsaw, four years.

ADDRESSES: *Home*—Swierczewskiego 53m.4, 03-402 Warsaw, Poland. *Agent*—Ernst Geisenheyner, Gymnasiumstrasse, 31 B, Stuttgart 1, West Germany.

CAREER: Full-time professional writer. Active in Polish underground movement during German occupation in World War II. Member of Polish Parliament, 1952-56.

MEMBER: Polish Writers Union (president of Krakow section, 1946-48; president of Szczecin section, 1948-52; president of Warsaw section, 1957-59), Polish Authors Organization (ZAIVS). Co-founder of Workers' Defense Committee (KOR, which later dissolved into Solidarity Union), 1976.

AWARDS, HONORS: Polish Academy of Literature Young Writers Prize, 1936, for *Lad serca;* Krakow Prize, 1946, for *Noc;* Odrodzenie Award, 1948, for *Popiol i diament;* Order of Banner of Labor (1st class), 1949; Polish Readers Prizes, 1959, 1964, 1965; Zloty Klos Award, 1965.

WRITINGS:

Lad serca (novel; title means "Order of the Heart"), ROJ, 1938.

Noc (stories; title means "The Night"), Czytelnik (Warsaw), 1946, published with a preface by Helena Teigova, Maj (Prague), 1948.

(Author of text) *Warszawa, 1939-45* (album), [Warsaw], 1946.

Popiol i diament (novel; also see below), Czytelnik, 1948, translation by D. F. Welsh published as *Ashes and Diamonds,* Weidenfeld & Nicolson, 1962, reprinted with an introduction by Heinrich Boell, Penguin, 1980.

Aby pokoj swyciezyl!, [Warsaw], 1950.

O Czlowieku radzieckim, Ksaizku i Wiedza (Warsaw), 1951.

Ludzie i dzarzenia 1952, [Warsaw], 1953.

Ksiazka dla Marcina (reminiscences; title means "The Book for Martin"), Panstwowy Instytut Wydawniczy (Warsaw), 1954.

Zloty lis (stories; title means "The Golden Fox"), Panstwowy Instytut Wydawniczy, 1955.

(With J. Zagorski) *Swieto Winkelrida* (play), Panstwowy Instytut Wydawniczy, 1957.

Ciemnosci kryja ziemie (novel), Panstwowy Instytut Wydawniczy, 1957, translation by Konrad Syrop published as *The Inquisitors,* Knopf, 1960, reprinted, Greenwood Press, 1976 (published in England as *Darkness Covers the Earth,* Weidenfeld & Nicolson, 1960).

Bramy raju (novel), Panstwowy Instytut Wydawniczy, 1958, translation by James Kirkup published as *The Gates of Paradise,* Weidenfeld & Nicolson, 1962.

Niby gaj: Opowiadania, 1933-58 (collection of stories), Panstwowy Instytut Wydawniczy, 1959.

Idzie, skaczac po gorach (novel), Panstwowy Instytut Wydawniczy, 1963, translation by Celina Wieniewska published as *A Sitter for a Satyr,* Dutton, 1964 (published in England as *He Cometh Leaping upon the Mountains,* Weidenfeld & Nicolson, 1965).

Warschauer karwoche (novel), Aufbau (Berlin), 1966.

(With others) *Cuatro dramaturgas polacos,* with an introduction by Sergio Pitol, UNAM, 1968.

Apelacja (novel), Instytut Literacki (Paris), 1968, translation by Wieniewska published as *The Appeal,* Bobbs-Merrill, 1971.

(Translator) *Shaare Gan-Eden,* Sifriyat Poalim (Tel Aviv), 1971.

(Adaptor with Andrzej Wajda) "Popiol i diament" (screenplay; based on novel of the same title), translation by Boleslaw Sulik published as *Ashes and Diamonds,* Lorrimer, 1973.

Prometeusz; Widowisko, Czytelnik, 1973.

Trzy opowiesci, Panstwowy Instytut Wydawniczy, 1973.

Teraz na ciebie zaglada, Czytelnik, 1975.

(With Kazimierz Kornilowicz) *Pomoc spoleczno—kulturalna dia mlodziezy pracujace; i doroslych,* Ossolinskich, 1976.

Juz prawie nic, Czytelnik, 1979.

Miazga, Polonia Book Fund, 1982.

OTHER

Also author of story collections *Dragi nieuniknione,* 1937, and *Three Tales,* 1973, and of a play, "Prometheus," 1971. Editor-in-chief, *Przeglad Kulturalny* (title means "Cultural Review"), 1952-54.

SIDELIGHTS: Jerzy Andrzejewski's concern for and interest in humanity were reflected both in his political activity and in his writing. In early September of 1968 he wrote to Eduard Goldstueker, the president of the Czechoslovak Writers Union, what was believed to be the first signed protest by a Polish intellectual of Poland's participation in the Russian occupation of Czechoslovakia. His letter read, in part: "The feeling of hopelessness in the face of violence and power is, of all human abasement, the most painful defeat. This defeat becomes a particularly hard burden when the best traditions of one's own nation are insulted, freedom of speech extinguished and truth trampled."

Andrzejewski, who resigned from the Communist Party in 1957, was one of thirty-four intellectuals who signed a letter in 1964 addressed to Polish Premier Jozef Cyrankiewicz which pleaded for liberalized censorship and criticized the Communist regime's rigid cultural policies. In the years after he left the party he used his novels to express his ideas. The author's method was satire, often skillfully couched in terms acceptable to the Polish political authorities. Andrzejewski's novel *The Inquisitors,* wrote Ronald Bryden in a *Spectator* article, "seems to have been greeted with the same covert delight as those classical and historical plays the French produced in Paris, in which all sorts of subversive implications could be read below a cryptically innocent surface." "His style," observed R. R. Rea in *Library Journal,* "is simple, beautifully polished even in translation, and his novel is a veritable gem."

As a result of his political activism, Andrzejewski, whose best-known work was the novel *Ashes and Diamonds,* was not permitted to publish in his own country; the original manuscript of another work, *The Appeal,* was smuggled to Paris for its first publication in 1968. Oswell Blakeston, writing in *Books and Bookmen,* called it "a baffling story. One begins reading it with the knowledge that it was banned in Poland, and so one expects another indictment of totalitarianism; but, with all the twists and turns of [the main character's] behavior, one senses that here is something more subtle than straight or satirical accusation. The proof that the book has quality lies in the fact that one does not work to try to reach the hidden message." A *Times Literary Supplement* reviewer found that the work "has great initial interest for its political testimony about the effect on the individual of living in a police state but it should also win acclaim as a novel which movingly and truthfully charts the workings of a sick mind."

The author "was bitterly criticized" in his lifetime, "not the least for the moralizing tone which purveys all his actions," according to a London *Times* obituary. "But he was an exceptionally gifted writer, with a keen insight into what was going on around him." A *New York Times* article reported that Andrzejewski's funeral in 1983 was attended by many of Poland's "leading writers and dissident intellectuals."

MEDIA ADAPTATIONS: Andrzej Wajda directed the film "Popiol i diament," with a screenplay by Hanna Okraskowa, for Centralna Poradnia Amatorskiego Ruchu Artystycznego, 1958. Andrzejewski collaborated with the Modern Polish Cinema on a film entitled "Niewinni Czarodzieje" (title means "The Innocent Sorcerers"), also directed by Wajda, 1959.

BIOGRAPHICAL/CRITICAL SOURCES:

BOOKS

Sasowski, Waclaw, *Andrzejewski,* Agencja Autorska (Warsaw), 1973.

PERIODICALS

Books and Bookmen, February, 1971.
Guardian, June 3, 1960.
Library Journal, July, 1960.
New York Herald Tribune Book Review, October 9, 1960.
New York Times Book Review, December 11, 1960.
Saturday Review, November 5, 1960, July 3, 1965.
Spectator, June 3, 1960.
Times Literary Supplement, January 29, 1971.

OBITUARIES:

PERIODICALS

Chicago Tribune, April 22, 1983.
New York Times, April 21, 1983, April 27, 1983.
Times (London), April 21, 1983.
Washington Post, April 21, 1983.*

* * *

ANDRZEYEVSKI, George
See ANDRZEJEWSKI, Jerzy

* * *

ANHALT, Edward 1914-
(Andrew Holt, a joint pseudonym)

PERSONAL: Born March 28, 1914, in New York, N.Y.; married wife, Edna (a writer), 1935 (divorced, 1956). *Education:* Attended Columbia University, 1930-32; studied filmmaking with Willard Van Dyke and Ralph Steiner, 1936-38.

ADDRESSES: Home—500 Amalfi Dr., Pacific Palisades, Calif. 90272; and 225 Central Park West, New York, N.Y. 10024. *Agent*—Paul Kohner Agency, 9169 Sunset Blvd., Los Angeles, Calif. 90069.

CAREER: Writer. Cameraman and film editor for Willard Van Dyke, 1937-38; Columbia Broadcasting System (CBS-TV), chief television cameraman, 1938-40. Writer for Columbia Pictures, 1947-50, and Twentieth-Century Fox, 1950-52. Former faculty member, Loyola-Marymount University.

MEMBER: Screen Actors Guild, Directors Guild of America, Writers Guild of America West.

AWARDS, HONORS: Rockefeller Foundation fellow, 1936-38; co-winner of Academy Award for best motion picture story, Academy of Motion Picture Arts and Sciences, and Writer's Guild nomination, both 1950, both for "Panic in the Streets"; co-nominee for Academy Award for best motion picture story, 1952, for "The Sniper"; Academy Award for best screenplay based on material from another medium, and Writer's Guild award, both 1964, both for "Becket"; Edgar Allan Poe award, Mystery Writers of America, 1968, for "The Boston Strangler," and 1978, for "Contract on Cherry Street"; Writers Guild Laurel Award, 1977.

WRITINGS:

SCREENPLAYS

"Problem Child" (documentary), Independent, 1935.
"Thunder of the Sea" (documentary), Lutheran Radio Pictures, 1936.
(With Edna Anhalt, under joint pseudonym Andrew Holt) "Strange Voyage" (based on their screen story), Monogram, 1946.
(With E. Anhalt, as Andrew Holt) "Avalanche" (based on their screen story), Producers Releasing Corp., 1946.
(With E. Anhalt) "Bulldog Drummond Strikes Back" (adapted from the novel by H. C. McNeil), Columbia, 1947.
"The Gentleman from Nowhere" (based on his screen story), Columbia, 1948.
(With E. Anhalt, John Lucas Meredyth, George F. Slavin, and George W. George), "Red Mountain," Paramount, 1952.
(With E. Anhalt) "The Member of the Wedding" (adapted from the book and play by Carson McCullers), Columbia, 1952.
(And producer, with E. Anhalt) "My Six Convicts," Columbia, 1952.

Management: Competencies and Incompetencies, Addison-Wesley, 1981.

Managing Incompetence, AMACOM, 1981.

Managing Your Boss, AMACOM, 1983.

Practical Strategic Planning: A Guide and Manual for Line Managers, Quorum Books, 1985.

(With E. N. Maddox and W. J. Wheatley) *Envisionary Management: A Guide for Human Resources Professionals in Management,* Quorum Books, 1988.

WORK IN PROGRESS: Strategic Human Resource Management.

SIDELIGHTS: William P. Anthony commented to *CA:* "Every manager is a human resource manager regardless of his organizational level or type of organization. Managers, from supervisors to corporate presidents, from bishops to government agency heads must deal with one key resource—people."

* * *

APPLEMAN, Philip (Dean) 1926-

PERSONAL: Born February 8, 1926, in Kendallville, Ind.; son of William Russell and Gertrude Collins (Keller) Appleman; married Marjorie Ann Haberkorn (a playwright and professor), August 19, 1950. *Education:* Northwestern University, B.S., 1950, Ph.D., 1955; University of Michigan, A.M., 1951.

ADDRESSES: P.O. Box 39, Sagaponack, N.Y. 11962.

CAREER: Indiana University at Bloomington, instructor, 1955-58, assistant professor, 1958-63, associate professor, 1963-67, professor, 1967-84, distinguished professor of English, 1984-86, distinguished professor emeritus, 1986—. Fulbright scholar, University of Lyon, 1951-52; International School of America, instructor in world literature and philosophy, 1960-61, instructor and field director, 1962-63, currently member of academic advisory committee; visiting professor, State University of New York College at Purchase, 1973, and Columbia University, 1974. Has given poetry readings at numerous colleges, universities, and forums. *Military service:* U.S. Army Air Forces, 1944-45. U.S. Merchant Marine, 1946, 1948-49.

MEMBER: Modern Language Association of America (chairman of English Section II, 1966), National Council of Teachers of English, College English Association, American Assocation of University Professors (member of national council, 1969-72), PEN, Academy of American Poets, Poetry Society of America (member of national governing board, 1981-85), Friends of Poets and Writers (member of advisory committee, 1985—), Poets House (Poets Advisory Council, 1986—), Phi Beta Kappa.

AWARDS, HONORS: Robert F. Ferguson Memorial Award, Friends of Literature, 1969, for *Summer Love and Surf;* poetry fellowship, National Endowment for the Arts, 1975; Castagnola Award, Poetry Society of America, 1975, for *Open Doorways;* Christopher Morley Award, Poetry Society of America; Midland Poetry Award, Society of Midland Authors.

WRITINGS:

NONFICTION

(Editor with Willam A. Madden and Michael Wolff, and contributor) *1859: Entering an Age of Crisis,* Indiana University Press, 1959.

The Silent Explosion, foreword by Sir Julian Huxley, Beacon Press, 1965, 2nd edition, 1966.

(Editor and contributor) *Darwin* (critical anthology), Norton, 1970, 2nd edition, 1979.

(Editor) Charles Darwin, *The Origin of Species,* Norton, 1975.

(Editor) *Malthus: An Essay on the Principle of Population* (critical anthology), Norton, 1976.

POETRY

Kites on a Windy Day, Byron Press, 1967.

Summer Love and Surf, Vanderbilt University Press, 1968.

Open Doorways, Norton, 1976.

Darwin's Ark (illustrated by Rudy Pozzatti), Indiana University Press, 1984.

Darwin's Bestiary, Echo Press, 1986.

Also contributor to *The Brand-X Anthology of Poetry: A Parody Anthology.*

NOVELS

In the Twelfth Year of the War, Putnam, 1970.

Shame the Devil, Crown, 1981.

Apes and Angels, Putnam, 1989.

OTHER

Contributor of poetry to numerous periodicals, including *Antioch Review, Harper's, Massachusetts Review, Nation, New Republic, New York Times, Partisan Review, Poetry, Sewanee Review,* and *Yale Review.* Contributor of articles and reviews to scholarly periodicals. *Victorian Studies,* founder, 1956, co-editor, 1956-64.

WORK IN PROGRESS: A new volume of poems; a novel.

SIDELIGHTS: Throughout his novels, poetry, and nonfiction, Philip Appleman shows concern over a wide range of social issues. His first novel, *In the Twelfth Year of the War,* combines an "overwhelming and at times devastating plea against war with an equally biting social commentary," writes David F. Sharpe in *Best Sellers,* adding that "Appleman expertly and poetically uses biting satire, black humor, and pathos to tell an excellent story." Art Seidenbaum in the *Los Angeles Times* similarly finds Appleman's second novel, *Shame the Devil,* entertaining and provocative: "Most of our modern manners are [satirized]. . . . Sex, politics and religion . . . are all examined in Appleman's loony laboratory and found in dubious health. . . . Appleman wants to amuse and drop morals without moralizing; he's smart enough to do it swiftly, knowing the warp of satire soon wears thin." And according to T. K. Burch in *Harper's,* Appleman's book of nonfiction, *The Silent Explosion,* brings "the intangibles of human problems, including moral values" into the biological and social sciences. A reviewer for the *New Yorker* comments that *The Silent Explosion* is a "lucid, moving, and convincing discussion. . . . Appleman discusses with great power the absolute need to change . . . attitudes if we are to survive on our meagre planet."

While a number of reviewers note Appleman's ability to effectively address many social issues, some have also pointed out instances in which he is not as successful. Reviewing *Open Doorways* for the *American Poetry Review,* Stanley Plumly writes that "when the considering voice in his poems is surrounded by circumstance and reporting directly from the evidence, Appleman's results are impressive. . . . But when the voice begins to lose sight of itself and its individual circumstance, when it begins to sound glibly generalized or socially self-conscious, when subject matter begins to replace the attention paid to specific objects, the poems take on a public, easing-into-profundity stance." Regarding the same book, Jay Parini notes in *Poetry* that "while there is no mistaking the technical competence of this poet, who has a marvelous ear, the language itself never measures up to the sound it makes." Parini adds, as one of Appleman's poems about Vietnam demonstrates, that "poets rarely make good poems from such inflated subject matter because the emotional overcharge already present before the poet goes to work has to be defused." Regarding *Shame the Devil,* Joseph McLellan in the *Washington Post* questions the varied subject matter: "The mind that one senses behind the story is a keen one, constantly darting off in a dozen directions at once. . . . [However,] it is when the mind comes wandering back from those dozen directions, bearing all kinds of miscellaneous loot that is poured into the story, that one begins to wonder: Has the author brought the elements of his novel toegether because they belong together or because they happened to interest and amuse him?"

Appleman has been particularly recognized for his work on the nineteenth-century naturalist Charles Darwin, including the critical anthology *Darwin* and a book of poems, *Darwin's Ark.* Critics have singled out both Appleman's grasp of Darwin's provocative theories and his ability to elucidate their social implications. Bette Chambers in *Humanist* comments on the second edition of *Darwin:* "Laypersons and scientists alike will treasure this new edition as an essential reference work. Appleman's own lucid style emerges in 'Darwin Among the Moralists' and 'Darwin: On Changing the Mind.' The scientists and informed laypersons who are today increasingly engaged in the public debate surrounding creationist efforts to legislate the teaching of creationist views in public school science courses . . . , will want to obtain both the first and second editions of Appleman's *Darwin.*" Regarding the poems of *Darwin's Ark,* Stephen Jay Gould in *Parnassus: Poetry in Review* praises Appleman for having "captured the elusive themes of Darwin's worldview and translat[ing] them into items of beauty that also provoke thought." Gould adds that Appleman "deftly captures the meaning of Darwin's revolution," citing the "central theme of continuity between man and nature." "Several times throughout *Darwin's Ark,* Appleman sets Darwin's famous prose metaphors as lines of poetry," Gould continues,". . . and in their fit (both to the form itself and to the purposes of this excellent book) we find our finest example of unity among all the styles of human thought."

BIOGRAPHICAL/CRITICAL SOURCES:

BOOKS

Contemporary Literary Criticism, Volume 51, Gale, 1989.

PERIODICALS

American Poetry Review, July/August, 1977.
Best Sellers, January 15, 1971.
Christian Science Monitor, April 29, 1965.
Contact II, fall, 1987.
Harper's, August, 1965.
Home Planet News, spring/summer, 1987.
Hudson Review, spring, 1971.
Humanist, July/August, 1980.
Los Angeles Times, April 22, 1981.
New Yorker, June 26, 1965.
New York Times Book Review, August 9, 1981.
Parnassus: Poetry in Review, Volume 14, number 1, 1987.
Poetry, August, 1977.
Prairie Schooner, fall, 1969.
Virginia Quarterly Review, summer, 1969.
Washington Post, May 15, 1981.

ARCINIEGAS, German 1900-

PERSONAL: Born December 6, 1900, in Bogota, Colombia; son of Rafael (a farmer) and Aurora (Angueyra) Arciniegas; married Gabriela Vieira, November 19, 1926; children: Aurora, Gabriela Mercedes. *Education:* Universidad Nacional, Bogota, Colombia, LL.D., 1924. *Politics:* Liberal. *Religion:* Roman Catholic.

ADDRESSES: *Home*—Calle 92 10-21, Bogota, Colombia. *Office*—Facultad de Filosofia y Letras, Universidad de los Andes, Cra. 1E-18A-10, Bogota, Colombia. *Agent*—ALA Agencia Latinoamericana, P.O. Box 343790, Coral Gables, Fla. 33134.

CAREER: Universidad Nacional, Bogota, Colombia, professor of sociology, 1925-28; *El Tiempo,* Bogota, editor, 1928-30, London correspondent, 1930-33, editor-in-chief, 1933-39, director, 1939; Government of Colombia, vice-consul in London, 1930, charge d'affaires in Buenos Aires, 1939-41, Minister of Education, 1941-42, 1945-46, ambassador to Italy, 1959-62, to Israel, 1960-62, to Venezuela, 1967-70, and to Vatican City, 1976-78; Universidad de los Andes, Faculty of Philosophy and Letters, Bogota, dean, 1979—. Member of Colombian Parliament, 1933-34, 1939-40, 1957-58. Visiting professor, Columbia University, 1943, 1948-57, University of Chicago, 1944, Mills College, 1945, and University of California, Berkeley, 1945. Director, *Cuadernos,* Paris, 1963-65; founder, Museo de Arte Colonial, Bogota; director, Ediciones Colombia; codirector, *Revista de America.*

MEMBER: Colombian Academy of Letters (Academia Colombiana de la Lengua), Colombian Academy of History (Academia Colombiana de Historia; president, 1980—), National Institute for Arts and Letters (honorary associate), corresponding member of academy of letters of Spain, Cuba, Mexico, and Venezuela, American Committee for Cultural Freedom (former vice-president).

AWARDS, HONORS: Dag Hammarsjkold Prize, 1967; honorary doctorate, Mills College.

WRITINGS:

WORKS IN ENGLISH TRANSLATION

Jimenez de Queseda, Editorial ABC (Bogota), 1939, translation by Mildred Adams published as *The Knight of the El Dorado: The Tale of Don Gonzalo Jimenez de Queseda and His Conquest of New Granada, Now Called Colombia,* Viking, 1942, reprinted, Greenwood Press, 1968, new Spanish edition published as *El Caballero de El Dorado,* Primer Festival del Libro Colombiano, 1958.

Los alemanes en la conquista de Americana, Editorial Losada (Buenos Aires), 1941, translation by Angel Flores published as *Germans in the Conquest of America,* Macmillan, 1943, reprinted, Hafner, 1971.

(Editor) *The Green Continent: A Comprehensive View of Latin America by Its Leading Writers,* translation by Harriet de Onis and others, Knopf, 1944, reprinted, 1963.

Biografia del Caribe, Editorial Sudamericana (Buenos Aires), 1945, 10th edition, 1973, translation by de Onis published as *Caribbean, Sea of the New World,* Knopf, 1946.

The State of Latin America, translation by de Onis, Knopf, 1952.

Amerigo y el Nuevo Mundo, Editorial Hermes (Mexico), 1955, 2nd edition, 1956, translation by de Onis published as *Amerigo and the New World: The Life and Times of Amerigo Vespucci,* Knopf, 1955, reprinted, Octagon, 1978.

El continente de siete colores: Hostoria de la cultura en la america latina, Editorial Sudamericana, 1965, 2nd edition, 1970, translation by Joan MacLean published as *Latin America:*

A Cultural History, Knopf, 1967, condensation of Spanish edition published as *Latinoamerica: El continente de siete colores,* edited by Cecil D. McVicker and Osvaldo N. Soto, Harcourt, 1967.

(Contributor) Cole Blasier, editor, *Constructive Change in Latin America,* University of Pittsburg Press, 1968.

(With John S. Knight) *The Twilight of the Tyrants,* Center for Latin American Studies, Arizona State University, 1973.

America en Europa, Editorial Sudamericana, 1975, translation by wife, Gabriela Arciniegas and Victoria Arana published as *America in Europe: A History of the New World in Reverse,* Harcourt, 1986.

Fernando Botero, translation by Gabriela Arciniegas, Abrams, 1977.

WORKS IN SPANISH

El estudiante de la mesa redonda, J. Pueyo (Madrid), 1932, 4th edition, Ediciones Ercilla (Santiago), 1937, reprinted, Plaza & Janes Editores-Colombia, 1982.

La universidad colombiana, Imprenta Nacional (Bogota), 1932.

Memorias de un congresista, Editorial Cromos (Bogota), 1933.

Diario de un peaton, Imprenta Nacional, 1936.

America, tierra firme, Ediciones Ercilla, 1937, 3rd edition, Editorial Sudamericana, 1966.

Los comuneros, Editorial ABC, 1938, 2nd edition, Zig-Zag (Santiago), 1967.

Que haremos con la historia?, Imprente Lehmann (Costa Rica), 1940.

En el pais del rascacielos y las zanahorias, Libreria Suramerica (Bogota), 1945.

Este pueblo de America, Fondo de Cultura Economica (Mexico), 1945.

(Editor) *El pensamiento vivo de Andres Bello,* Editorial Losada, 1946, reprinted, Plaza & Janes Editores-Colombia, 1981.

En medio del camino de la vida, Editorial Sudamericana, 1949, 3rd edition, 1964.

Entre la libertad y el miedo, Ediciones Cuadernos Americanos (Mexico), 1952, 10th revised edition, Editorial Sudamericana, 1958.

Italia, guia para vagabundos, Editorial Sudamericana, 1957, 5th edition, 1965.

America magica: Los hombres y los meses, Editorial Sudamericana, 1959, 2nd edition, 1961.

America magica II: Las mujeres y las horas, Editorial Sudamericana, 1961.

(Editor) Ricardo Arenales, *El Terremoto de San Salvador,* 2nd edition, Ministry of Education (San Salvador), 1961.

(Contributor) *Tres ensayos sobre nuestra America,* Biblioteca Cuadernos (Paris), c. 1962.

Colombia, Union Panamericana (Washington), 1962.

El mundo de la bella Simonetta, Editorial Sudamericana, 1962.

Cosas del pueblo: Cronica de la historia vulgar, Editorial Hermes, 1962, published as *Este pueblo de America,* Secretaria de Educacion Publica, Direccion General Divulgation (Mexico), 1974.

Entre el Mar Rojo y el Mar Muerto: Guia de Israel, E.D.H.A.S.A. (Barcelona), 1964.

Temas de Arciniegas: Invitacion a conversar, leer y escribir, edited by McVicker and Soto, Harcourt, 1967.

(Contributor) Marco Aurelio Alamazan, *Claroscuro,* Ultramar (Mexico), 1967.

Genio y figura de Jorge Isaacs, Editorial Universitaria de Buenos Aires, 1967, 2nd edition, 1970.

(Compiler) *Colombia: Itinerario y espiritu de la independencia, segun los documentos principales de las revolucion,* Editorial Norma (Cali), 1969.

Medio mundo entre un zapato: De Lumumba en el Congo a las brujas en Suecia, Editorial Sudamericana, 1969, 2nd edition, 1971.

Nuevo diario de Noe, Monte Avila (Caracas), 1969.

Nuevo imagen del Caribe, Editorial Sudamericana, 1970, 2nd edition, 1972.

Roma secretissima, Anaya (Salamanca), 1972.

Copernico, un hijo de America, Editorial de el Colegio Nacional (Mexico), 1973.

Estancia en Rumania, Pentru Turism (Bucharest), 1974.

Paginas escogidas (1932-1973), Gredos (Madrid), 1975.

(Editor) *El Zancudo,* Editora Arco, 1975.

(Editor) *Antologia de Leon de Greiff,* Instituto Colombiana de Cultura, Subdireccion de Communicaciones Culturales, Division de Publicaciones, 1976.

Galileo mira a America, Instituto Espanol de Cultura (Rome), 1977.

(Editor) Fernando Lorenzana, *Recuerdos de vida: diario de su viaje a Bogota en 1832 y su correspondencia con el primer representante de Colombia en Roma,* Instituto Caro y Cuervo (Bogota), 1978.

El reves de la historia, Plaza & Janes Editores-Colombia, 1980.

Bolivar, de Cartegena a Santa Marta, Banco Tequendama (Bogota), 1980.

20,000 comuneros hacia Santa Fe, Editorial Pluma (Bogota), 1981.

Los pinos nuevos, Editorial Boliviana Internacional, 1982.

Bolivar, el hombre de la gloria, Ediciones Tercer Mundo (Colombia), 1983.

Bolivar y la revolucion, Planeta (Bogota), 1984.

De Pio XII a Juan Pablo II: Cinco Papas que han conmovido al mundo, Planeta, 1986.

OTHER

Contributor to newspapers and magazines, including *La Prensa, La Nacion,* and *Cuadernos Americanos.* Editor of *Amerique Latine,* 1974—, *La Revista de la Indias,* and *Correo de los Andes.*

SIDELIGHTS: In *America in Europe: A History of the New World in Reverse,* Colombian historian, journalist, and diplomat German Arciniegas "argues that the influence of the New World on the Old has been neglected by historians" and sets out to promote another perspective, summarizes John Gross in the *New York Times.* Drawing examples ranging from the era of Columbus to more recent times, Arciniegas presents "comparisons [that] are rarely invidious and usually serve to correct the common historical underestimation of Americans' achievements," describes *New Yorker* contributor Naomi Bliven. "For example, he reminds us that [South American revolutionary general Simon] Bolivar commanded victorious armies over areas as vast as those Napoleon commanded." Because the scope of his subject is so broad, the author "has set himself a daunting task," comments Gross. "To measure its full extent would indeed be to calculate the incalculable. But Mr. Arciniegas, a veteran Colombian man of letters, is too shrewd to let himself get drawn into attempting an exhaustive survey. Instead, he concentrates on a few major themes and episodes." And while *Atlantic* contributor Phoebe-Lou Adams comments that the author's evidence "depends on mass and variety rather than upon strict demonstration of cause and effect," she admits that "it is impressively presented and impossible to ignore."

Although he praises the author's overall approach, Gross also comments that Arciniegas "tends to be unduly lyrical about romantic nationalism and revolutions in general, where a little analysis might have been in order." In addition, "his chapter on romanticism itself occasionally threatens to take off into the clouds." But Bliven thinks that the book "abounds in mental openings," especially in his chapter on the Romantic movement, which "rethinks a whole library." *America in Europe* is "intellectual history at its most entertaining," continues the critic. The book is "so saturated with the cultural heritage of the west that it seems effortless, even playful." And while Gross remarks that "every so often you feel the author's rhetoric has got the better of him," the critic admits that "for the most part it is rhetoric animated by ideas, and backed up by substantial learning." Concludes the critic: "The result is an unusually stimulating book, its novelty enhanced—for North American readers—by a Latin American viewpoint."

BIOGRAPHICAL/CRITICAL SOURCES:

BOOKS

Arciniegas, German, *Memorias de un congresista,* Editorial Cromos, 1933.

Cobo Borda, Juan Gustavo, *Arciniegas de cuerpo entero,* Planeta, 1987.

Cordova, Federico, *Vida y obra de German Arciniegas,* [Havana], 1950.

PERIODICALS

Atlantic, March, 1986.

New Statesman, October 24, 1969.

New Yorker, May 5, 1986.

New York Times, March 7, 1986.

New York Times Book Review, October 17, 1943, May 18, 1952.

Spectator, October 18, 1969.

Times Literary Supplement, December 4, 1969, March 25, 1977.

* * *

ARNDT, H(einz) W(olfgang) 1915-

PERSONAL: Born February 26, 1915, in Breslau, Germany; son of Fritz Georg and Julia (Heimann) Arndt; married Ruth Strohsahl, July 12, 1941; children: Christopher, Nicholas, Bettina. *Education:* Lincoln College, Oxford, B.A., 1936, B.Litt., 1938, M.A., 1940.

ADDRESSES: Home—14 Hopetoun Circuit, Deakin, Canberra, Australian Capital Territory 2600, Australia. *Office*—Research School of Pacific Studies, Australian National University, Canberra, Australian Capital Territory 2600, Australia.

CAREER: University of London, London School of Economics and Political Science, London, England, Leverhulme research fellow, 1938-41; Royal Institute of International Affairs, London, research assistant, 1941-43; University of Manchester, Manchester, England, assistant lecturer in economics, 1943-46; University of Sydney, Sydney, Australia, senior lecturer in economics, 1946-50; Australian National University, Canberra, professor of economics, School of General Studies, 1951-63, professor of economics and head of department, Research School of Pacific Studies, 1963-80, professor emeritus, 1981—, dean of faculty of economics, 1959-60, deputy chairman, Institute of Advanced Studies, 1976-80, visiting fellow, Development Studies Centre, 1981—.

Visiting professor, University of South Carolina, 1954, Indian Statistical Institute, and Indian Planning Committee, 1958-59; external examiner in economics, University of Malaya, 1968-70, and University of Singapore, 1968-70, 1976-80. United Nations, member of Research Division, Economic Commission for Europe, 1960-61, consultant, Conference on Trade and Development, 1966-67, member of governing council, Asian Institute for Economic Development and Planning, 1969-75, member of expert group on Economic Development Planning, Economic and Social Commission for Asia and the Pacific, 1975, 1977. Deputy director, Country Studies Division, Organization for Economic Cooperation and Development, 1972; member of expert group on World Employment Conference, International Labour Office, 1975; chairman of expert group on structural change and economic growth, Commonwealth Secretariat, 1980. Australian National University, member of research committee, Australia-Japan Research Centre, 1972—, chairman of Australian Steering Committee, Association of Southeast Asian Nations (ASEAN)-Australia Economic Relations research project, 1980—. Member of advisory council, Australian Capital Territory, 1959-63. Field work in Indonesia, 1964-83.

MEMBER: Social Science Research Council of Australia (secretary, 1957-59), Economic Society of Australia and New Zealand (president, 1957-59), Australian Association for Cultural Freedom (president, 1982-87), Academy of Social Sciences in Australia (fellow).

WRITINGS:

The Economic Lessons of the Nineteen-Thirties, Oxford University Press, 1944, reprinted, Cass & Co., 1963.

The Australian Trading Banks, F. W. Cheshire, 1957, 5th edition (with W. J. Blackert), Melbourne University Press, 1977.

(Editor with W. M. Corden) *The Australian Economy: A Volume of Readings,* F. W. Cheshire, 1963, 2nd edition published as *The Australian Economy: A First Volume of Readings,* 1972.

(With R. I. Downing and others) *Taxation in Australia: Agenda for Reform,* Melbourne University Press, 1964.

(Co-author) *Economic Survey of Europe in 1961,* Part 2: *Some Factors in Economic Growth in Europe during the 1950s,* United Nations, 1964.

(With J. Panglaykim) *The Indonesian Economy: Facing a New Era?,* Rotterdam University Press, 1966.

(Co-author) *Shipping and the World Economy,* United Nations, 1966.

A Small Rich Industrial Country: Studies in Australian Development, Aid and Trade, F. W. Cheshire, 1968.

Australia and Asia: Economic Essays, Australian National University Press, 1972.

(Editor with A. H. Boxer) *The Australian Economy: A Second Volume of Readings,* F. W. Cheshire, 1972.

Perbankan di Indonesia (title means "Banking in Indonesia"), Obor (Djakarta), 1972.

The Rise and Fall of Economic Growth: A Study in Contemporary Thought, Longman Cheshire, 1978.

(Co-author) *The World Economic Crisis: A Commonwealth Perspective,* Commonwealth Secretariat (London), 1980.

(Co-author) *Developing Asia: The Importance of Domestic Policies,* Asian Development Bank (Manila), 1982.

(Editor and co-author) *Development and Equality in Indonesia,* Macmillan, 1982.

(Editor and co-author) *Pembangunan dan Pemerataan: Indonesia di Masa Orde Baru,* [Djakarta], 1983.

The Indonesian Economy: Collected Papers, Chopmen (Singapore), 1984.

Prospects for Industrial Development and for Capital Goods Industry in Indonesia, three volumes, United Nations Industrial Development Organization (Vienna), 1984.

(Co-author) *Malaysia, the Philippines, Thailand,* United Nations Industrial Development Organization, 1985.

(Co-author) *A Course through Life: Memoirs of an Australian Economist,* National Centre for Development Studies, Australian National University (Canberra), 1985.

Economic Development: The History of an Idea, Chicago University Press, 1987.

Asian Diaries, Chopmen, 1987.

CONTRIBUTOR

The Impact of Immigration (monograph), Commonwealth Bank of Australia, 1950.

A. Davies and G. Derle, editors, *Policies for Progress,* F. W. Cheshire, 1954.

Economic Survey of Europe in 1960, United Nations, 1961.

J. Wilkes, editor, *Economic Growth in Australia,* Angus & Robertson, for Australian Institute of Political Science, 1962.

Canberra: The Next Decade, Federal Capital Press, 1963.

Australian Foreign Aid Policy, University of Adelaide, 1964.

Economic Survey of Europe in 1962, United Nations, 1964.

SEANZA Lectures, Volume 1, State Bank of Pakistan, 1964.

Anatomy of Australia, Sun Books, 1968.

J. D. B. Miller, editor, *India, Japan, Australia: Partners in Asia?,* Australian National University Press, 1968.

The Australian Role in Joint Ventures and Investment in Developing Countries of Asia and the Pacific: A Seminar Report, Australian Council for Overseas Aid, 1969.

B. Glassburner, editor, *The Economy of Indonesia: Selected Readings,* Cornell University Press, 1971.

J. A. A. Stockwin, editor, *Japan and Australia in the Seventies,* Angus & Robertson, 1972.

N. Bhagwati and R. S. Eckaus, editors, *Development and Planning: Essays in Honor of Paul Rosenstein-Rodan,* Allen & Unwin, 1972.

G. Greenwood and N. Harper, editors, *Australia in World Affairs, 1966-1970,* F. W. Cheshire, 1974.

H. Bull, editor, *Asia and the Western Pacific: Towards a New International Order,* Nelson, 1975.

B. D. Beddie, editor, *Advance Australia—Where?,* Oxford University Press, 1975.

K. Kojima and M. S. Wionczek, editors, *Technology Transfer in Pacific Economic Development,* Japan Economic Research Center, 1975.

Narongchai Akrasanee and others, editors, *Trade and Employment in Asia and the Pacific,* University Press of Hawaii, 1977.

J. P. Nieuwenhuysen and P. J. Drake, editors, *Australian Economic Policy,* Melbourne University Press, 1977.

R. T. Shand and H. V. Richter, editors, *International Aid: Some Political, Administrative and Technical Realities* (monograph), Australian National University, 1979.

International Encyclopedia of the Social Sciences, Macmillan, 1979.

W. Prest and R. L. Mathews, editors, *The Development of Australian Fiscal Federalism: Selected Readings,* Australian National University Press, 1980.

Indonesia: Australian Perspectives, Australian National University Press, 1980, Volume 2: *Indonesia: Dualism, Growth and Poverty,* edited by R. Garnaut and P. McCawley, Volume 3: *Indonesia: The Making of a Nation,* edited by J. A. C. Mackie.

J. A. Lozoya and A. K. Bhattacharya, editors, *Asia and the New International Economic Order,* Pergamon, 1981.

Yoo Se-Hee, editor, *Political Leadership and Economic Development: Korea and China,* Hanyang University (Seoul), 1983.

Conference on Experience and Lessons of Economic Development in Taiwan, Institute of Economics, Academia Sinica (Taipei, Taiwan), 1983.

K. Jackson, editor, *ASEAN Security and Economic Development,* University of California Press, 1984.

Between Two Nations: The Indonesia-PNG Border and West Papuan Nationalism, R. Brown (Bathurst, Australia), 1986.

L. T. Evans and J. D. B. Miller, editors, *Policy and Practice: Essays in Honour of Sir John Crawford,* Australian National University Press (Syndey), 1987.

Industry and Development, United Nations Industrial Development Organization, 1987.

OTHER

Author of official papers for the United Nations, India, and Australia. Contributor of more than one hundred articles to economic, banking, and other journals, including *Asian Development Review, Southeast Asian Affairs,* and *World Development.* Member of editorial board, *Economic Record,* 1956-74; editor, *Bulletin of Indonesian Economic Studies;* co-editor, *Quadrant,* 1981-83; editor, *Asian Pacific Economic Literature,* 1987—.

WORK IN PROGRESS: Research on developments in the Indonesian economy; ASEAN-Australian economic relations; the history of the development objective; international monetary economics.

* * *

ASCHER, Carol 1941-
(Carol Lopate)

PERSONAL: Born August 15, 1941, in Cleveland, Ohio; daughter of Paul (a psychoanalyst) and Ellen (Ascher) Bergman; married Phillip Lopate, January 31, 1964 (divorced June, 1970); married Robert Pittenger, June 19, 1982. *Education:* Attended Vassar College, 1959-61; Barnard College, B.A., 1963; attended School of Visual Arts, 1968-69; Columbia University, Ph.D., 1974.

ADDRESSES: Home—158 West 23rd St., New York, N.Y. 10011. *Agent*—Malaga Baldi, 541 West 49th St., New York, N.Y. 10019.

CAREER: Free-lance researcher and writer, 1963-68; Columbia University, Teachers College, New York City, writer and researcher for U.S. Offices of Education and Economic Opportunity, 1969-72, researcher at Horace Mann-Lincoln Institute on "Social Organization of High Schools Project," 1972-74; Children's Television Workshop, New York City, senior researcher on program "The Best of Families," 1975-76; Brooklyn Educational and Cultural Alliance, Brooklyn, N.Y., director of research for Brooklyn Rediscovery, 1976-77, researcher and writer of pamphlet, 1978; Fulton Mall Improvement Association, Brooklyn, writer and editor of newsletter, 1978-80; Columbia University, Teachers College, senior research associate and staff writer at ERIC Clearinghouse on Urban Education, 1981—; State University of New York at Purchase, assistant professor of fiction writing, 1988—.

Researcher for Rockland State Hospital and New York State Hospital, 1963-66; writer and researcher for Josiah Macy, Jr., Foundation, 1967-68; story line researcher for Talent Associates,

1977; legal researcher for Time-Life Television Productions, 1979; writer and consultant on evaluation project for Pratt Institute, 1979-80. Instructor at Herbert H. Lehman College, 1970-72, York College, 1972, Staten Island Community College, 1974-75, Empire State College, 1977-78; coordinator of women's studies at Sarah Lawrence College, 1977-79; participant in cultural anthropology workshops at Empire State College, 1981.

MEMBER: PEN, American Writers' Guild, Poets and Writers.

AWARDS, HONORS: PEN/National Endowment for the Arts Syndicated Short Fiction Award, 1983 (two), 1984; New York State Creative Artists' Public Service Award, 1984, for partial manuscript of *The Flood;* PEN/New York State Creative Artists' Award, 1984; *Blueline* award for best short fiction, 1985; *Women's Quarterly Review* honorable mention for best fiction, 1986.

WRITINGS:

UNDER NAME CAROL LOPATE

Six Arguments, Columbia Review Press, 1966.
Women in Medicine, Johns Hopkins University Press, 1968.
A Program for Third World Students (monograph), Teachers College Press, Columbia University, 1969.
(Contributor) David Mermelstein, editor, *Economics: Mainstream Readings and Radical Critiques,* Random House, 1976.
Education and Culture in Brooklyn: A History of Ten Institutions (monograph), Brooklyn Educational and Cultural Alliance, 1979.

UNDER NAME CAROL ASCHER

(Contributor) Gaye Tuchman and others, editors, *Hearth and Home: Images of Women in the Mass Media,* Oxford University Press, 1978.
(Contributor) Edith Hoshimo Altbach, editor, *From Feminism to Liberation,* Schenkman, 1980.
Simone de Beauvoir: A Life of Freedom, Beacon Press, 1981.
(Editor with Sara Ruddick and Louise DeSalvo) *Between Women: Biographers, Novelists, Critics, Teachers, and Artists Write about Their Work on Women,* Beacon Press, 1984.
(Contributor) *The Available Press: PEN Short Story Collection,* Ballantine, 1985.
The Flood (novel), Crossing Press, 1987.
(Contributor) Alice Kessler-Harris and W. McBrien, editors, *Faith of a (Woman) Writer,* Greenwood Press, 1987.
(Contributor) *Woman and Stepfamilies,* Temple, 1989.

OTHER

Contributor, under names Carol Ascher and Carol Lopate, of articles and short stories to magazines, including *ERIC/CUE Fact Sheet, Heresies, Present Tense, Confrontation, Socialist Review, Rooms, Feminist Studies, Liberation Magazine, College English, Ms.,* and others; of poetry to periodicals, such as *Aphra, World,* and *Adventures in Poetry;* of book reviews to *Harper's Bookletter, Social Policy, New Women's Times, Parabola,* and others.

WORK IN PROGRESS: The Reprieve, a novel about the friendship between a middle-aged woman and her young college-student tenant; *Who's Afraid of Red, Yellow, and Blue,* a novel about a triangle of professionals.

SIDELIGHTS: Carol Ascher's *Women in Medicine* (written as Carol Lopate) focuses on the problem of recruiting women in medical careers and is based on the 1966 Macy Conference on Women in Medicine. In her analysis, Ascher attempts to discover why the number of female physicians in the United States pales in comparison to the numbers for other countries. Using personal interviews and field research, Ascher considers the historical background of women as physicians, the contemporary problems and issues peculiar to women in medicine, and the social and cultural factors influencing women in their career choices. Written for those planning medical careers, as well as for career counselors, the book "presents a comprehensive picture of the possible role of women in American medicine," notes a *Choice* reviewer.

Ascher's second book, *Simone de Beauvoir: A Life of Freedom,* is part biography, part literary criticism, and part philosophy of the famous French feminist and author. Using careful documentation and research, as well as personal commentary, Ascher looks at de Beauvoir not only as a writer and philosopher, but also as a person. Ascher focuses on her subject as someone with much to offer the contemporary women's movement, indicating the significance of de Beauvoir's notion of women as both oppressed and free. In the opinion of a *Best Sellers* writer, "Ascher clearly respects her [subject], and equally clearly, describes why [de Beauvoir] is worthy of that respect. On the other hand, Ascher is no apologist for her subject, and she takes persuasive exception to certain of de Beauvoir's insights."

Ascher wrote to *CA:* "Two themes baffle and concern me in most of what I write: being a woman and being the daughter of refugees from the Nazis. I use whatever literary form seems most penetrating at the time to go deeper and deeper into these themes."

BIOGRAPHICAL/CRITICAL SOURCES:

PERIODICALS

Best Sellers, September, 1981.
Choice, February, 1969.
Los Angeles Times Book Review, August 9, 1987.
Science Books and Film, March, 1969.
Washington Post Book World, September 27, 1981.

* * *

ASHBY, Nora
See AFRICANO, Lillian

* * *

ASHTON-WARNER, Sylvia (Constance) 1908-1984
(Sylvia Henderson, Sylvia)

PERSONAL: Born December 17, 1908, in Stratford, New Zealand; died April 28, 1984, in Tauranga, New Zealand; married Keith Dawson Henderson (a teacher). *Education:* Attended Wairarapa College, Masterton, New Zealand, and Teachers' College, Auckland, New Zealand, 1928-29.

ADDRESSES: Home—Whenua, 5-9 Levers Rd., Otumoetai, Tuaranga, New Zealand. *Agent*—International Creative Management, 40 West 57th St., New York, N.Y. 10019.

CAREER: Writer and educator. Taught at several schools in New Zealand; former professor of education at Aspen Community School Teaching Center, Aspen, Colo.

WRITINGS:

Spinster (novel), Simon & Schuster, 1959, reprinted, 1985.
Incense to Idols (novel), Simon & Schuster, 1960.
Teacher (nonfiction), Simon & Schuster, 1963, reprinted, 1986.
Bell Call (novel), Simon & Schuster, 1964.
Greenstone (novel), Simon & Schuster, 1967.

Myself (autobiography), Simon & Schuster, 1967.
Three (novel), Knopf, 1970.
Spearpoint: Teacher in America (autobiography), Knopf, 1972.
I Passed This Way (autobiography), Knopf, 1979.

Contributor of short stories, sometimes under names Sylvia and Sylvia Henderson, and of poetry to *New Zealand Listener, New Zealand Monthly Review,* and other periodicals.

SIDELIGHTS: Sylvia Ashton-Warner's novels are set in her native New Zealand, where she spent most of her career not only writing but also teaching grammar school to white and Maori children. The challenges of teaching and the conflicts among the racial mixture served as points in her books, the most notable of them being Ashton-Warner's debut novel *Spinster,* and *Teacher,* a nonfiction work.

Spinster, the story of a New Zealand schoolteacher struggling with inner doubt, won almost unanimous applause from critics, with John Wain's remarks in a *New Yorker* review summing up many opinions: "The identity at the center of [the story], the woman who somehow preserves each day, and every minute of every day, so as to achieve some sort of two-way relationship with so many people and things, is wonderfully real and moving—a useful reminder that the novel is still a field in which the novice, given inspiration, can produce work beyond the range of the average professional, and in which there are many discoveries to be made."

With *Teacher,* Ashton-Warner examined the way children learn in New Zealand schools, written from the viewpoint of an insider. Especially in her dealings with the Maori children, the author noted the way cultural differences can influence the effectiveness of teachers. According to *New York Times Book Review* critic Katharine Taylor, the book "should have great value not only for those interested in the problems of education in old cultures and new nations, but also for those concerned with the future of civilization."

Ashton-Warner wrote three autobiographical volumes. Her last work, *I Passed This Way,* serves as a look back on a long life of teaching and writing. But Carolyn F. Ruffin saw another side to the book. The *Christian Science Monitor* critic found that "what gives this book its power is Ashton-Warner's scrap with the cautious and the blindly secure. She takes on bureaucracy of the spirit as well as red tape in institutions." Noting how the author's "wide-ranging love gives [the work] its poetry, its humor, and an array of carefully drawn human beings," Ruffin concluded that in *I Passed This Way* Ashton-Warner produced a memoir not only full of answers but brimming with questions. And to *Washington Post* reviewer Linda B. Osborne, Ashton-Warner's final book "builds her self-portrait through a series of images that hold for her a special meaning. It is autobiography as art, selective and visionary, grounded in impressions, memories and dreams as much as fact." What concerned this author, Osborne said, is "what is essential to people, what moves their spirits, fuels their imaginations and encourages their potential to be lively human beings."

MEDIA ADAPTATIONS: Spinster was adapted for film and released as "Two Loves," starring Shirley MacLaine.

BIOGRAPHICAL/CRITICAL SOURCES:

BOOKS

Ashton-Warner, Sylvia, *Teacher,* Simon & Schuster, 1963, reprinted, 1986.
Ashton-Warner, Sylvia, *Myself,* Simon & Schuster, 1967.
Ashton-Warner, Sylvia, *Spearpoint: Teacher in America,* Knopf, 1972.
Ashton-Warner, Sylvia, *I Passed This Way,* Knopf, 1979.
Contemporary Literary Criticism, Volume 19, Gale, 1981.
Hood, Lynley, *Sylvia!: The Biography of Sylvia Ashton-Warner,* Viking, 1989.

PERIODICALS

Christian Science Monitor, April 2, 1959, December 3, 1979.
Commonweal, December 9, 1960.
New Republic, September 23, 1972.
New Yorker, April 11, 1959.
New York Times Book Review, September 8, 1963, February 14, 1965, October 8, 1967.
Saturday Review, November 12, 1960, March 19, 1966.
Washington Post, January 6, 1980.

OBITUARIES:

PERIODICALS

New York Times, April 30, 1984.
Publishers Weekly, May 18, 1984.
Times (London), May 2, 1984.*

* * *

AUCHINCLOSS, Louis (Stanton) 1917- (Andrew Lee)

PERSONAL: Surname is pronounced *Auk*-in-klaus; born September 27, 1917, in New York, N.Y.; son of Joseph Howland (a corporate lawyer) and Priscilla (Stanton) Auchincloss; married Adele Lawrence, 1957; children: John Winthrop, Blake Leay, Andrew Sloane. *Education:* Attended Yale University, 1935-39; University of Virginia Law School, LL.B., 1941. *Religion:* Episcopalian.

ADDRESSES: Home—1111 Park Ave., Apt. 14-D, New York, N.Y. 10128; and Claryville, N.Y. *Agent*—Curtis Brown Ltd., Ten Astor Place, New York, N.Y. 10003.

CAREER: Admitted to the Bar of New York State, 1941; Sullivan & Cromwell (law firm), New York City, associate, 1941-51; Hawkins, Delafield & Wood (law firm), New York City, associate, 1954-58, partner, 1958-86. President, Museum of the City of New York; trustee, Josiah Macy, Jr., Foundation; former trustee, St. Barnard's School and New York Society Library; life fellow, Pierpont Morgan Library; former member of administrative committee, Dumbarton Oaks Research Library. *Military service:* U.S. Navy, 1941-45; served in Naval Intelligence and as gunnery officer; became lieutenant senior grade.

MEMBER: National Institute of Arts and Letters, Association of the Bar of the City of New York (former member of executive committee), Phi Beta Kappa, Century Association.

AWARDS, HONORS: D.Litt., New York University, 1974, Pace University, 1979, University of the South, 1986; New York State Governor's Art Award.

WRITINGS:

NOVELS

(Under pseudonym Andrew Lee) *The Indifferent Children,* Prentice-Hall, 1947.
Sybil, Houghton, 1952, reprinted, Greenwood, 1972.
A Law for the Lion, Houghton, 1953.
The Great World and Timothy Colt, Houghton, 1956, reprinted, McGraw, 1987.

Venus in Sparta, Houghton, 1958.
Pursuit of the Prodigal, Houghton, 1959, reprinted, Avon, 1977.
The House of Five Talents, Houghton, 1960.
Portrait in Brownstone, Houghton, 1962, reprinted, McGraw, 1987.
The Rector of Justin, Houghton, 1964, reprinted, Hill & Co. Press, 1987.
The Embezzler, Houghton, 1966.
A World of Profit, Houghton, 1968.
I Come as a Thief, Houghton, 1972.
The Dark Lady, Houghton, 1977.
The Country Cousin, Houghton, 1978.
The House of the Prophet, Houghton, 1980.
The Cat and the King, Houghton, 1981.
Watchfires, Houghton, 1982.
Exit Lady Masham, Houghton, 1983.
The Book Class, Houghton, 1984.
Honourable Men, Houghton, 1986.
Diary of a Yuppie, Houghton, 1987.
The Golden Calves, Houghton, 1988.
Fellow Passengers: A Novel in Portraits, Houghton, 1989.

SHORT STORIES

The Injustice Collectors, Houghton, 1950.
The Romantic Egoists, Houghton, 1954.
Powers of Attorney, Houghton, 1963.
Tales of Manhattan, Houghton, 1967.
Second Chance: Tales of Two Generations, Houghton, 1970.
The Partners, Houghton, 1974.
The Winthrop Covenant, Houghton, 1976.
Narcissa and Other Fables, Houghton, 1982.
Skinny Island: More Tales of Manhattan, Houghton, 1987.

Contributor of stories to *New Yorker, Harper's, Good Housekeeping, Town and Country,* and *Atlantic.*

BIOGRAPHICAL AND CRITICAL STUDIES

Reflections of a Jacobite (essays), Houghton, 1961.
Pioneers and Caretakers: A Study of Nine American Women Novelists, University of Minnesota Press, 1965, reprinted, G. K. Hall, 1985.
On Sister Carrie, University of Minnesota Press, 1968.
Motiveless Malignity (essays), Houghton, 1969.
Edith Wharton: A Woman in Her Time (biography), Viking, 1972.
Richelieu (biography), Viking, 1972.
A Writer's Capital (autobiography), University of Minnesota Press, 1974.
Reading Henry James (essays), University of Minnesota Press, 1975.
Life, Law and Letters (essays), Houghton, 1979.
Persons of Consequence: Queen Victoria and Her Circle, Random House, 1979.
Three "Perfect Novels" and What They Have in Common (lecture; first delivered at Pierpont Morgan Library, January, 1981), Bruccoli Clark, 1981.
(Editor) Adele Florence Sloane, *Maverick in Mauve: The Diary of a Romantic Age,* Doubleday, 1983.
(Editor) *Quotations from Henry James,* University Press of Virginia, 1984.
False Dawn: Women in the Age of the Sun King, Anchor Press, 1985.
The Vanderbilt Era: Profiles of a Gilded Age, Scribner, 1989.

Also author of pamphlets, *Edith Wharton,* 1961, *Ellen Glasgow,* 1964, and *Henry Adams,* 1971, all published by University of Minnesota Press. Contributor of essays to *Partisan Review* and the *Nation.* Member of advisory board, *Dictionary of Literary Biography.*

OTHER

(Editor) Edith Wharton, *An Edith Wharton Reader,* Scribner, 1965, reprinted, Macmillan, 1989.
"The Club Bedroom" (one-act play; published in *Esquire,* December, 1966), produced on television, 1966, and Off-Off Broadway at The Playwright's Unit, 1967.
(Editor) Anthony Trollope, *The Warden* [and] *Barchester Towers,* Houghton, 1966.
(Editor) *Fables of Wit and Elegance,* Scribner, 1972.

Author of four unproduced full-length plays and several one-act plays.

SIDELIGHTS: Although he also writes short stories and criticism, Louis Auchincloss has established himself as a highly prolific novelist of manners, the chronicler of New York City's "aristocracy." According to *New York Times* contributor Charlotte Curtis, "Louis Auchincloss . . . is the nearest we have to a Henry James or an Edith Wharton of the East Coast's WASP upper classes. . . . Aside from his books' literary quality, their value has always been the detailed sociological reporting of what life inside these largely invisible families, their networks, their clubs and work places is like." Ronald Bryden in the *Spectator* also compares Auchincloss to Wharton, and feels that the "mantle of Edith Wharton, or whatever she wore, is now firmly [Auchincloss's] and only these two have made New York so real a place."

But critics have faulted the author for portraying an outmoded way of life. In the *Dictionary of Literary Biography Yearbook: 1980,* Patricia Kane observes how his choice of genre has affected his popularity: "Auchincloss's reputation as a writer has been influenced by factors somewhat external to it. Both the novel of manners and the fictional characters called WASPs are not fashionable." In the *New York Times Book Review* Webster Schott concurs when he states that Auchincloss "is far from the swarming hot center of American literary intellectualism; he's a museum of all that American writing valued before its World War I baptism of despair. . . . Buried in its own riches, his world exists like Shangri-La, lost to inhabitation." But Gore Vidal, writing in the *New York Review of Books,* disagrees: "The world Auchincloss writes about, the domain of Wall Street bankers and lawyers and stockbrokers, is thought to be irrelevant, a faded and fading genteel-gentile enclave when, in actual fact, this little world comprises the altogether too vigorous and self-renewing ruling class of the United States. . . . Of all our novelists, Auchincloss is the only one who tells us how our rulers behave in their banks and their boardrooms, their law offices and their clubs." And Sandra Salmans reports in the *New York Times* that "some academics and publishers praise him as one of the few authors who write about the business world with a real understanding of its complexities and conflicts."

The family as a social unit is important to Auchincloss's novels, many of which are multigenerational sagas. *The House of Five Talents,* which *New York Herald Tribune Book Review* critic E. C. Dunn calls "the story of human beings, their complexity, their insecurity, [and] their magnificent failure to grasp and hold the full meaning of life," takes an originally middle-class New York family from 1873 to 1948, from a social-climbing grandfather to his heiress granddaughter. In another novel, *Portrait in Brownstone,* the author relates the history of the Denison family from the turn of the century to 1951. Granville Hicks states in the *Saturday Review* that Auchincloss "tells the story in a neat, dry style that repeatedly gives great pleasure. . . . What distinguishes the novel is its subtlety." And Fanny Butcher writes in the *Chicago Sunday Tribune:* "The warmth of the family ties, the family traditions make the novel a happy reading experience. . . . when 'Portrait in Brownstone' is good it is very good. The author has a sensitive eye for human foibles, a sensitive ear for conversation, and a sensitive mind that ferrets out human emotions." Citing an occasionally disjointed plot, however, Butcher adds: "If the book were more technically cohesive, it would be a fine novel instead of just a good one."

With *The Rector of Justin,* which critics regard as one of his best works, Auchincloss relates the story of the dead hero, Francis Prescott, through the testimony of friends, coworkers, and relations. Hicks explains in another issue of the *Saturday Review* that "the subject of *The Rector of Justin* does not seem to promise excitement—the octogenarian headmaster of a small private school—and yet I was swept along by it, for the revelation of Prescott's character is fascinating. . . . We do come to feel the reality, the complicated reality, of Francis Prescott." *The House of the Prophet* also uses the testimony of other characters to portray Felix Leitner (based, some critics claim, on editor and journalist Walter Lippmann), a lawyer, columnist, and public figure, who, in his later years, leaves his wife and betrays his best friend. While admitting that Auchincloss's style and "formal prose [are] so well crafted, so consistent, and so entertaining that you forgive him lapses you wouldn't forgive in a less talented writer," *Christian Science Monitor* reviewer Anne Bernays contends that "the people in this novel . . . don't really breathe; they carry ideas, rather than blood, in their veins." However, *Times Literary Supplement* contributor Charles Wheeler speaks of the novel as "a taut and elegant study of a distinguished American whose closest friends cannot decide whether they like or detest him."

Two of Auchincloss's more recent novels draw on his own background. In *The Book Class,* he exposes the power held by "unliberated" upper-class New York City wives in the early twentieth century. The story shows the inner workings of a book club's members; the tale is related by the son of the now-deceased founder, through the reminiscences of surviving members. *Washington Post Book World* contributor Jonathan Yardley claims that while the women "get affectionate and clear-eyed tribute in *The Book Class* . . . Auchincloss never manages to make the reader care about them; they never seem to matter, to be of real consequence, and thus in the end neither does the book. Intelligent and craftsmanlike though it is, *The Book Class* is Auchincloss going through the motions, sticking to his last." But *Los Angeles Times* contributor Carolyn See, who compares the book favorably to Helen Hooven Santmyer's . . . *And Ladies of the Club,* states: " 'The Book Class' really is a *book class,* a compact history of literature as we use it today. It's dazzling."

With *Honorable Men,* Auchincloss attempted "to come to grips with a long-standing American obsession—how the values, if not the beliefs, of our Puritan forefathers still permeate some of their descendants, and what is won and lost by adhering to them," writes A. R. Gurney in the *New York Times Book Review.* In a *New York Times Book Review* interview with Herbert Mitgang, Auchincloss explained: "I used to say to my father, 'Everything would be all right if only my class at Yale ran the country.' Well, they did run the country during the Vietnam War and look what happened. . . . [*Honorable Men*] is my ultimate explanation of the Puritan ethic in our time." According to Yardley in the *Washington Post, Honorable Men* is "a novel about politics, but in no way is it a political novel. What concerns Auchincloss is . . . what shaped the men who determined the nature of [America's role in Vietnam] and pressed their cause even against clamorous public opinion. He is considering in fiction, in other words, the same men whom David Halberstam analyzed journalistically in 'The Best and the Brightest.' " And while Gurney sees "a tendency toward stuffiness in the writing that can occasionally settle over the book like dust," he adds that with *Honorable Men,* "Mr. Auchincloss adds a significant work to his long and considerable canon."

Diary of a Yuppie focuses on anti-hero Robert Service, a man determined to succeed in the world of corporate takeovers and double crosses. Rory Quirk writes in the *Washington Post Book World:* "Auchincloss unfolds this delightful and disquieting tale with his characteristic deftness, allowing Service to destroy himself in his own words through his damning diary entries. . . . This is contemporary fiction of the absolute first rank. It is fiction, isn't it?" As with some of his other books, *Diary of a Yuppie* has prompted critics to compare Auchincloss to his predecessors. According to London *Times* contributor Andrew Sinclair: "Not since rereading *The Great Gatsby* have I felt a whole new class so economically taken apart. . . . [*Diary of a Yuppie* is] the most significant novel Mr. Auchincloss has written in his distinguished career."

Critics also consider the author a skilled short story writer. *Skinny Island* involves a frequently-implemented Auchincloss technique: that of revolving a collection of short stories around a central theme, in this case the "skinny island" of Manhattan. Paul Gray in *Time* suggests another unifying link: "The pieces are not just connected chronologically and geographically but by a common concern as well: the dilemma faced by comfortable people when they must choose between honor and expediency." And *Washington Post Book World* contributor James K. Glassman feels the work "conveys the insular, claustrophobic, dignified and rigid world that obsesses Auchincloss: Old New York." Glassman continues, "the death of society has always been one of Auchincloss' themes, but regular readers will find him here utterly pessimistic, his irony turned to cynicism. This writing on the edge of despair gives *Skinny Island* an urgency and an emotional kick that bring it close to his best books."

A story collection that also stands as a novel, *Fellow Passengers* reveals that the rich "are no different, emotionally or morally, from the rest of us; they just have money left in their checking accounts at the end of the month," according to Edward Hawley in *Tribune Books. Washington Post* contributor Bruce Bawer calls the stories "witty, charming and economical," and states that "these tales have the pithiness of biblical parables or Aesopian fables," while also delivering a criticism frequently levelled at Auchincloss: "At times the dialogue feels not only formal but unnaturally stilted; and some of the characters' off-the-cuff literary references are hard to buy." Bawer concludes, however: "But no matter. This book—novel, memoir, short-story collection, or what-have-you—is at once a triumph of storytelling and an exemplary meditation upon the standards of conduct by which we live. Auchincloss accomplishes something that's not easy: Even as he delightfully celebrates the voyage of life, he delivers a serious reminder of the responsibilities we all have toward our fellow passengers on the trip." And Hawley advocates: "Readers familiar with Auchincloss' rich body of work will find much pleasure in 'Fellow Passengers,' which is full of his characteristic insight and irony. For those who aren't, this is a good place to start."

CA INTERVIEW

CA interviewed Louis Auchincloss by telephone on October 11, 1988, at his home in New York, New York.

CA: When we talked last, for Dictionary of Literary Biography Yearbook: 1980 *you had just finished* The Cat and the King *and* Watchfires, *and you said you felt you were reaching a new dimension and depth in your writing. How did you come to do those books and other recent ones that are specifically historical?*

AUCHINCLOSS: I had always wanted to do them, but I'd been sort of against historical novels. I'd had a feeling that the historical novel was phony because you couldn't fill in the background; you couldn't really know what had happened. But then I decided that one didn't have to be so afraid of that, that it was possible to use the past to reach other values and interests in the present. Everybody would know it was a novel, so you wouldn't have to have every detail right, and you wouldn't have to have your characters talk exactly the way people talked in the past. You could just use the past to set your stage, and then have new values. In *The Cat and the King,* where I have used the form of the memoirs of the Duc de St. Simon, although it's perfectly evidently a twentieth-century composition, I think I have used some of the insights of the twentieth century against the viewpoints of the seventeenth century with a rather interesting flux.

CA: Has research for the historical books taken you literally in new directions in your travels?

AUCHINCLOSS: No. I had always gone to France, and I'd gone to Versailles, which is the setting for *The Cat and the King,* a good deal.

CA: Since you retired from your law practice, there must be a lot more time for such projects. Has retirement changed your writing patterns accordingly?

AUCHINCLOSS: It's given me a much more time, and I've written a good deal more. I've got two books coming out in 1989. One is a work of nonfiction, a book called *The Vanderbilt Era: Profiles of a Gilded Age,* which has about twenty small portraits of people in New York in the 1890s and early 1900s. It centers around the Vanderbilt family because there were so many of them and I know quite a lot about them, but it also reaches out into the people who knew them: people who built for them, people who liked them, people who disliked them, people who disapproved of them. So it's a little picture of the elegant side of New York in that era. That involved a good deal of reading. And then I have another novel coming out, or really a novel in connected short stories running chronologically. Yes, I have lots more time to write. I have perhaps too much time.

CA: Your books span more than forty years in publication, and many of them remain in print. Do you hear periodically from a new generation of readers, or from new kinds of readers who have just discovered them?

AUCHINCLOSS: I do get a certain number of letters from young people, and young people sometimes call me up to talk to me or stop me in the street to say something, which is always encouraging. I definitely felt that I had reached a younger audience with my *Diary of a Yuppie* because I had a certain amount of reaction from that. I was writing there about younger people.

CA: You've been very comfortable also writing about women, both fictional and real, and doing criticism on female writers. Does that affinity come in part from the friendships with women that you described in A Writer's Capital?

AUCHINCLOSS: It goes all the way back to my childhood. I've never been conscious of temperamental and mental differences between men and women. I was always closer to my mother than I was to my father. I was close to him, too, but it wasn't the same deep intimacy that I had with Mother. I think it goes back very much to her. When an intimacy as solid as that is created, it creates a bond beyond sexual differences that lasts for a lifetime.

CA: Do you think women writers have suffered in critical esteem because of their gender?

AUCHINCLOSS: I wouldn't have thought so, although perhaps that was true in the nineteenth century. When the Brontes took male names and George Eliot took a male name, it may have been because they feared that kind of discrimination. But that's getting very far back. In my lifetime I would have thought not. Reading the masses of material written about Willa Cather and Ellen Glasgow and Edith Wharton, I don't feel that they have suffered at all from being women. I think you see reviews sometimes of books by women reviewed by women where the gender of the writers has been a factor in making the reviewers more favorable than they might otherwise have been. That's rare, but I can think of cases when that's struck me rather definitely. I'm very much against the raising of the gender issue in art. To my mind, it doesn't exist. There are books by women that you can tell instantly are written by women, but there are books that you can't. I can tell, for example, that any book by Jean Stafford was written by a woman. With a Mary McCarthy book, I could never tell. But that has nothing to do with the quality of the book. They're equally good writers.

CA: If you are indeed the last novelist of manners, as some critics would have it, why do you think the novel of manners has all but disappeared in current writing?

AUCHINCLOSS: I don't think it's disappeared nearly as much as people think. Of course, literary critics leave out of consideration most novels that are published today. They don't read the best-seller list. Neither do I. But if you turn the pages of novels that sell in the millions, you find that you could often describe them as novels of manners. What people mean is not that the novel of manners has disappeared, which it hasn't—there are more being sold today than ever before—but that novels of manners have ceased to be written by novelists of the first rank. They have turned from them because literature has so notoriously in the last fifty years become a more subjective matter. But that will change. I think there are already signs of change.

CA: In your lecture "Three 'Perfect Novels' and What They Have in Common," given at the Pierpont Morgan Library in January, 1981, you discussed The Scarlet Letter, Wuthering Heights, *and* The Great Gatsby. *If you had been speaking on five perfect novels, say, what would you add to the list?*

AUCHINCLOSS: I'd certainly add *The Ambassadors* by Henry James, which I regard as the most perfect novel of all, and I would add *Madame Bovary* as a perfect novel. Both of those novels are better than any of the three I mentioned in that lecture, but I didn't pick them to speak on. I just said "perfect novels"; I didn't say the only three perfect novels. I would rather have written *The Ambassadors* than any other novel in the world, including *War and Peace.*

CA: There's a familiar photograph of you, by Duane Michals, in which you're sitting at home with a wall of books stretched across the background. What areas have you concentrated on in your book collection?

AUCHINCLOSS: I haven't. My book collection simply represents first or rare or special or even handsome editions of books that I care very much about. There was a time when I went in for later versions of things, like *King Lear* with a happy ending. But then I realized that I never wanted to read them, so I exchanged them all for other things. Now I have nothing like that. There are two qualifications. One is that I must care for the book very much myself. And secondly, I must be able to read it. Very, very delicate ones that I can't read, I have turned in for stronger copies, even though the ones I gave up were sometimes more valuable. The exception is my first edition of *Swann's Way.* It's in mint condition and really can't be read, but I love it so much I keep it. I don't collect much any more; it's too expensive. The prices have gone very much up, and my income has gone down, so I've pretty much given it up. Every now and then I pick up something I like, something I can't resist. But I haven't bought anything very valuable in a long time.

CA: Your literary criticism has focused on earlier writers rather than current ones. Are there people writing now whose work you follow and admire?

AUCHINCLOSS: Yes. I will read everything of Joan Didion; I can't say I read everything of Philip Roth and Norman Mailer, but I'm very much up to date on them. I pretty much read anything of Nathalie Sarraute, but she hasn't written anything recently. And John Updike. I'm apt to follow the rather obvious ones. I've got on my desk at the moment Alison Lurie's *The Truth about Lorin Jones,* which I'm about to start, and *A Far Cry from Kensington* by Muriel Spark.

CA: Has your legal work ever put you in a potential conflict-of-interest situation as a writer—that is, made you privy to material that would have made great fiction but couldn't be used in that way?

AUCHINCLOSS: I don't know specifically. You always run into things from time to time that you think would be a nice to use, but you think, I'd better not put that in the book. And it happens in the law just as much as in anything else. But I don't remember specifically its happening more in the law. It's just a matter of recognizing situations in day-to-day life that it's a good idea not to use in a book, either because you'll hurt people's feelings or make them angry or it would simply be unkind. Or because it would cause a lawsuit!

CA: And on that topic, what are your thoughts about the proliferation of lawsuits against writers and publishers in recent years?

AUCHINCLOSS: I've never been sued. I've never had a suit threatened except once, almost half-humorously, by a man whose house was photographed for the jacket of *Diary of a Yuppie* and he sort of pretended to object—I don't think he did seriously. I had nothing to do with that anyway; the publishers did that. The proliferation of lawsuits against publishers and writers I deplore, but no more than I deplore the proliferation of lawsuits against doctors and against everybody under the sun. It has been said that litigiousness is a mark of decadence in a culture. When you look at the small number of lawsuits in Japan and the huge increase in the number over here, it gives you food for thought. They have hardly any lawyers; they don't believe in litigating. The recent litigation in this country seems to me a bad thing. But it's a social problem, not a literary one.

CA: Your publishing relationship with Houghton Mifflin goes back to 1950 and still continues, which would seem to indicate that it has been a happy one. Would you like to comment on it?

AUCHINCLOSS: It has been a happy one. Of course it's been with different editors, because it's over such a long period of time, and some of the nearest and dearest have gone, either died or retired or both. But I'm very happy with Joseph Canon, the editor I'm working with now. And they accept the fact that I, like the cuckoo bird, lay my eggs in other nests—but only in the nonfiction. I'm doing this book on the Vanderbilt era with Charlie Scribner III. I've always kept free; I've never given an option on nonfiction, because I've always figured that if I had a nonfiction idea, I wanted to do it with a publisher who wants to do it. Houghton Mifflin would probably, because of their investment in me, say, Oh, we'll do it; and then it might be something that they didn't really want to do. Their heart might not be in it. I like to pick the publisher who's just right for a book. Jackie Onassis was just right for *Maverick in Mauve,* the diary that I edited. It's the kind of thing that she's enormously interested in. Charlie Scribner is descended from Commodore Vanderbilt, as is my wife—they're distant cousins—and he's been asking me for a long time to do this Vanderbilt thing. So I'm doing it with him and dedicating it to him. He loves doing it; his heart's very much in it. Houghton Mifflin might feel the same way or might not. That's the way I've done things. I may be doing a book on the J. P. Morgan collection for Abrams. It would need to be illustrated very heavily, and Abrams is just the right publisher to do a book like that.

CA: Your novels are very deliberately structured. Do you usually outline them carefully before you start to write?

AUCHINCLOSS: Yes. I outline them very carefully.

CA: You've seen New York through many changes over the years. What do you feel still makes it a good place to live, and a great city?

AUCHINCLOSS: I'm not sure it is a good place to live. If I were starting my life over again, I'd have very grave thoughts. I hardly think you can say it's a good place to live when two friends of mine, right outside this apartment house in broad daylight, were mugged and one of them had his arm broken in two places. Look at the homeless spread all over the subway. Look at the drug sales that go on at the bus station, when I go down there to take a bus to go north. It's not a good place to live. But I love it; it's in my blood. Here I am, and I'm stuck.

CA: Is there a single one of your books that you've most enjoyed writing or that you feel fondest of?

AUCHINCLOSS: I think I feel fondest of *The House of Five Talents,* because it seemed to me that in that book not only did I come closest to writing what I thought was a good novel, but it had sociological importance too. It dealt with a subject about which I knew a great deal, the expenditure of a great fortune. I had witnessed that and I thought I had things to say about it that had not been said by anyone else before, and hasn't since. I like the combination there of the fiction and the subject matter. To some extent that was also true of *The Rector of Justin,* which is far and away the most popular of my books. They keep bringing that out in hard cover, as well as in paperback. I've got almost a shelf of editions of *The Rector of Justin.*

BIOGRAPHICAL/CRITICAL SOURCES:

BOOKS

Auchincloss, Louis, *A Writer's Capital,* University of Minnesota Press, 1974.

Contemporary Literary Criticism, Gale, Volume 4, 1975, Volume 6, 1976, Volume 9, 1978, Volume 18, 1981, Volume 45, 1987.
Dictionary of Literary Biography, Volume 2: *American Novelists since World War II,* Gale, 1978.
Dictionary of Literary Biography Yearbook: 1980, Gale, 1981.

PERIODICALS

Chicago Sunday Tribune, July 15, 1962.
Christian Science Monitor, May 7, 1980.
Los Angeles Times, September 3, 1984.
New York Herald Tribune Book Review, September 11, 1960.
New York Review of Books, July 18, 1974.
New York Times, October 28, 1985, April 22, 1986.
New York Times Book Review, March 19, 1967, October 13, 1985.
Saturday Review, July 14, 1962, July 11, 1964.
Spectator, March 4, 1960.
Time, May 11, 1987.
Times (London), January 29, 1987.
Times Literary Supplement, May 2, 1980.
Tribune Books (Chicago), March 19, 1989.
Washington Post, September 11, 1985, September 28, 1986, March 28, 1989.
Washington Post Book World, July 22, 1984, September 28, 1986, May 17, 1987.

—Sketch by Jani Prescott

—Interview by Jean W. Ross

* * *

AVERY, June
See REES, Joan

B

BAGLEY, Desmond 1923-1983

PERSONAL: Born October 29, 1923, in Kendal, England; died April 12, 1983, in Southampton, England; son of John (a miner) and Hannah Marie (Whittle) Bagley; married Joan Margaret Brown (a bookstore manager), September 2, 1960.

ADDRESSES: *Home*—Catel House, Les Rohais de Haut, St. Andrew, Guernsey, Channel Islands, England.

CAREER: Began free-lance writing in South Africa in early 1950s; became novelist in England, beginning 1964. Did radio talks on scientific subjects for Durban studio of South African Broadcasting Corp., 1951-52; edited a house magazine for Masonite (Africa) Ltd., 1953; film critic for *Rand Daily Mail,* Johannesburg, South Africa, 1958-62, and contributor to *Star* (Johannesburg), and other newspapers and magazines; scenario writer for Filmlets Ltd. (subsidiary of Twentieth Century-Fox), Johannesburg, 1960-61.

MEMBER: Society of Authors, Crime Writers Association, Mystery Writers of America, Authors Guild, Authors League of America, Authors' Club (London), Detection Club.

WRITINGS:

The Golden Keel, Collins, 1963, reprinted, Perennial Library, 1986.
High Citadel, Doubleday, 1964, reprinted, Fontana, 1986.
Wyatt's Hurricane, Doubleday, 1966.
Landslide, Doubleday, 1967, reprinted, Fontana, 1987.
The Vivero Letter, Doubleday, 1968, reprinted, Fontana, 1986.
Running Blind, Doubleday, 1969, reprinted, Fontana, 1986.
The Spoilers, Doubleday, 1970, reprinted, Fontana, 1986.
The Freedom Trap, Collins, 1971, published as *The Mackintosh Man,* Doubleday, 1972.
The Tightrope Men, Doubleday, 1973, reprinted, Fontana, 1986.
(Contributor) A. S. Burack, editor, *Techniques of Novel Writing,* Writer, Inc., 1973.
The Snow Tiger, Doubleday, 1975.
The Enemy, Doubleday, 1976.
Flyaway, Doubleday, 1978.
Bahama Crisis, Collins, 1980, Summit Books, 1983.
Windfall, Summit Books, 1982.
The Legacy, Collins, 1982.
Night of Error, Collins, 1984, St. Martin's Press, 1987.
Juggernaut, Collins, 1985, St. Martin's Press, 1987.

Contributor of short stories to publications including *Argosy* and *Magazine of Fantasy and Science Fiction.*

SIDELIGHTS: Desmond Bagley had completed a successful career as a journalist in South Africa when he turned to novel writing in 1963. His fiction debut, a thriller called *The Golden Keel,* was praised by *New York Times Book Review* critic Anthony Boucher as the work of a writer who knew "the secret of grand manner storytelling." Bagley wrote more than a dozen further British-accented detective tales before his death in 1983. In a typical plotline like that of *The Tightrope Men,* an English director of industrial films awakens in Oslo to find that his face has been surgically altered to resemble that of a British government scientist, and that he has amnesia to boot. Now the confused protagonist becomes a decoy in a spy plot that moves from Europe to the Arctic Circle, the U.S., and Russia. "There are [triple]-crosses galore and several puzzles within puzzles, all very tensely handled," reported Louis Finger in a *New Statesman* review. "Bagley comes close to turning the whole thing into a convincing political parable."

In a London *Times* obituary, Bagley was remembered as "a thoroughly professional writer and a credit to the genre he chose. As his books suggest, he was a man of many and varied interests, which included music, photography and wine making. His chief recreation in more recent years, however, was provided by his computer—originally acquired to help him edit his work—on which, chiefly, he played war games."

MEDIA ADAPTATIONS: *The Freedom Trap,* published in America as *The Mackintosh Man,* was adapted into a film called "The Mackintosh Man."

BIOGRAPHICAL/CRITICAL SOURCES:

PERIODICALS

New Statesman, May 25, 1973.
New York Times Book Review, May 3, 1964, July 16, 1967, July 11, 1979, January 16, 1983.
Punch, September 11, 1985.
Time, July 30, 1979.
Times Literary Supplement, April 13, 1973, September 22, 1978, November 30, 1984.
Washington Post, October 9, 1982.

OBITUARIES:

PERIODICALS

Chicago Tribune, April 16, 1983.
Los Angeles Times, April 15, 1983.
Times (London), April 14, 1983.
Washington Post, April 16, 1983.*

* * *

BAGWELL, Philip S(idney) 1914-

PERSONAL: Born February 16, 1914, in Ventnor, Isle of Wight, England; son of Philip William (a bookseller) and Nellie (Aldrich) Bagwell; married Rosemary Burnley Olney (a social worker), July 16, 1953; children: Susan, Alison Jane, Richard Philip. *Education:* University of Southampton, B.Sc. (with second class honors) and Cambridge Teacher's Certificate, 1936; London School of Economics and Political Science, Ph.D., 1950. *Politics:* Christian Socialist.

ADDRESSES: Home—14 Brent Way, Finchley, London N3 1AL, England. *Office*—Department of History, Polytechnic of Central London, 309 Regent St., London W.1, England.

CAREER: University of London, College of Estate Management, London, England, lecturer, 1949-51; Polytechnic of Central London, London, 1951—, became professor of history, 1972-77, part-time teacher, 1977—. Visiting lecturer, London School of Economics and Political Science, University of London, 1975—. Member of house committee, Rehabilitation Centre for Alcoholics, London. *Military service:* British Army, Royal Corps of Signals, 1940-45; became sergeant; mentioned in dispatches.

MEMBER: Economic History Society, Society for the Study of Labour History (secretary, 1965-70).

WRITINGS:

The Railwaymen, Volume 1: *A History of the National Union of Railwaymen,* Fernhill, 1963, Volume 2: *The Beeching Era and After,* Allen & Unwin, 1982.
The Railway Clearing House in the British Economy: 1842-1922, Augustus Kelley, 1968.
(With G. E. Mingay) *Britain and America, 1850-1939: A Study of Economic Change,* Praeger, 1970.
(Contributor) Asa Briggs, editor, *Essays in Labour History: 1886-1923,* Macmillan, 1971.
The Transport Revolution from 1770, Batsford, 1974, revised edition published as *The Transport Revolution, 1770-1988,* Routledge & Kegan Paul, 1988.
Industrial Relations in Nineteenth-Century Britain, Irish University Press, 1974.
(Contributor) Mingay, editor, *The Victorian Countryside,* Volume 1, Routledge & Kegan Paul, 1981.
(Contributor) Chris Wrigley, editor, *A History of British Industrial Relations,* Harvester Press, 1982.
(Contributor with John Armstrong) D. H. Aldcroft and M. J. Freeman, editors, *Transport in the Industrial Revolution,* Manchester University Press, 1983.
End of the Line?: The Fate of Public Transport under Thatcher, Verso Books, 1984.
(Contributor) W. J. Mommsen, editor, *Auf dem Wege zur Massengewerkschaft,* Klett-Cotta, 1984.
Outcast London: A Christian Response, Epworth Press, 1987.
(Contributor) *Transport in Victorian Britain,* Manchester University Press, 1988.
The Transport Revolution, 1770-1988, Routledge & Kegan Paul, 1988.

WORK IN PROGRESS: A history of the Doncaster Railway Plant Works.

* * *

BALABAN, John B. 1943-

PERSONAL: Born December 2, 1943, in Philadelphia, Pa.; son of Phillip and Alice (Georgies) Balaban; married Lana Flanagan (a teacher), November 27, 1970; children: one child. *Education:* Pennsylvania State University, B.A. (with highest honors), 1966; Harvard University, A.M., 1967.

ADDRESSES: Home—720 North Thomas, State College, Pa. 16803. *Office*—Department of English, 117 Burrowes Bldg., Pennsylvania State University, University Park, Pa. 16802.

CAREER: Pennsylvania State University, University Park, instructor, 1970-73, assistant professor, 1973-76, associate professor, 1976-82, professor of English, 1982—. Fulbright senior lecturer in Romania, 1976-77; Fulbright distinguished visiting professor in Romania, 1978. Has given poetry readings at colleges and universities throughout the United States and in England, as well as on radio programs. Member of board of directors, Columbia University Translation Center, 1981—. Poetry judge for Academy of American Poets, 1978—, Pennsylvania Council of the Arts, 1979, and Poetry Society of America, 1980. *Wartime service:* Instructor in literature and descriptive linguistics, International Voluntary Services, University of Can Tho, South Vietnam, 1967-68, and field representative, Committee of Responsibility to Save War-Injured Children, 1968-69, as alternative to military service.

MEMBER: PEN American Center, Association of Asian Scholars, Association of Literary Translators, Poetry Society of America.

AWARDS, HONORS: Woodrow Wilson fellowship from Harvard University, 1966-67; Chris Award at Columbus Film Festival, 1969, for "Children of an Evil Hour"; Fulbright-Hays travel grant to Vietnam, 1971-72; National Endowment for the Humanities younger humanist fellowship, 1972; Pennsylvania State University Faculty Research fellowships, 1974, 1977, 1984, and 1986; PEN American Center and Columbia University translation fellowship, 1974; Lamont Award from Academy of American Poets, 1974, and National Book Award for poetry nomination, 1975, both for *After Our War;* Translation Award from Columbia University Translation Center, 1977; National Endowment for the Arts fellowships, 1978 and 1985; Steaua Prize from Romanian Writers' Union, 1978; National Endowment for the Humanities grant, 1980; Vaptsarov Medal from Union of Bulgarian Writers, 1980; Pennsylvania Council on the Arts Creative Writing fellowship, 1983-84.

WRITINGS:

"Children of the Evil Hour" (film), Committee of Responsibility, Inc., 1969.
Vietnam Poems (chapbook), Carcanet, 1970.
(Editor and translator) *Vietnamese Folk Poetry,* Unicorn Press, 1974.
After Our War (poems), University of Pittsburgh Press, 1974.
Letters from across the Sea/Scrisori de Peste Mare, Dacia Press (Cluj, Romania), 1978.
(Editor and translator) *Ca Dao Vietnam: A Bilingual Anthology of Vietnamese Folk Poetry,* Unicorn Press, 1980.
Blue Mountain (poems), Unicorn Press, 1982.

Coming Down Again (novel), Harcourt, 1985.
The Hawk's Tale (juvenile), Harcourt, 1988.

OTHER

Contributor to several poetry anthologies. General editor, with Teo Savory, of Unicorn Press translation series of lesser known poets, 1984—. Contributor of poems, translations, and reviews to periodicals, including *Sewanee Review, New England Review, Southern Review, Nation, Poetry Now, College English, Translation Review, American Scholar, New York Times, Ploughshares, Triquarterly,* and *Life.*

SIDELIGHTS: According to critics, John B. Balaban's skill as a poet, dexterity with language, and familiarity with South-East Asia all contribute to making his first novel, *Coming Down Again,* a success. The novel, an adventure story set in Vietnam toward the conclusion of U.S. involvement in the war there, is praised, for example, by a *New Yorker* reviewer, who calls it "a Conradian novel, with a Conradian theme of integrity, a novel rich in language of action and of description." In the *Birmingham News* Philip D. Beidler also calls *Coming Down Again* "Conradian" and applauds Balaban's vivid depiction of the novel's setting. "The novel is alive with the strange, garish beauty of the landscape," he writes. "The air is dense with the smells, the sounds, and, perhaps most arrestingly of all . . . the language." *Los Angeles Times* contributor Douglas Sun also comments favorably on the "unusual evocative power" of Balaban's prose.

MEDIA ADAPTATIONS: Ca Dao Vietnam: A Bilingual Anthology of Vietnamese Folk Poetry was made into a film entitled "Ca Dao Vietnam: Vietnamese Folk Poetry," in 1982.

BIOGRAPHICAL/CRITICAL SOURCES:

PERIODICALS

Birmingham News, July 28, 1985.
Los Angeles Times, August 9, 1985.
New Yorker, August 26, 1985.
Poetry, April, 1978.

* * *

BALLARD, P. D.
See BALLARD, (Willis) Todhunter

* * *

BALLARD, (Willis) Todhunter 1903-1980
(W. T. Ballard, Willis T. Ballard; pseudonyms: Brian Agar, P. D. Ballard, Parker Bonner, Sam Bowie, Nick Carter, Hunter D'Allard, Brian Fox, Harrison Hunt, George Hunter, John Hunter, Neil MacNeil, Clint Reno, John Shepherd, Jack Slade, Clay Turner)

PERSONAL: Born December 13, 1903, in Cleveland, Ohio; died in 1980; son of Fredrick Wayne (an electrical engineer) and Cordelia (Todhunter) Ballard; married Phoebe Dwiggins (a writer), February 5, 1936; children: Wayne. *Education:* Wilmington College, B.S., 1926.

ADDRESSES: Home—Canada Lake, N.Y., and Mt. Dora, Fla. *Agent*—August Lenniger, Lenniger Literary Agency, 437 Fifth Ave., New York, N.Y. 10016; and H. M. Swanson, 8523 Sunset Blvd., Los Angeles, Calif. 90069.

CAREER: Writer, 1927-80. F. W. Ballard & Co., Cleveland, Ohio, draftsman, 1926-28; employed by various magazines, newspapers, and film studios, 1929-34; Wright Paterson Field, Ohio, member of production control staff in maintenance division, 1942-45.

MEMBER: Western Writers of America (past vice president), Writers Guild of America West.

AWARDS, HONORS: Spur Award for best historical novel, Western Writers of America, 1965, for *Gold in California!*

WRITINGS:

(Under name W. T. Ballard) *Say Yes to Murder,* Putnam, 1942, published under pseudonym John Shepherd as *The Demise of a Louse,* Belmont, 1962.
Murder Can't Stop, McKay, 1946.
(Under name W. T. Ballard) *Dealing Out Death,* McKay, 1948.
Two-Edged Vengeance (appeared serially in *Esquire* under title "Red Horizon"; also see below), Macmillan, 1951.
The Circle C Feud, Sampson Low (London), 1952.
Incident at Sun Mountain, Houghton, 1952.
(Under name W. T. Ballard) *Walk in Fear,* Gold Medal Books, 1952.
West of Quarantine, Houghton, 1953.
High Iron, Houghton, 1953.
(With James Charles Lynch) *Showdown,* Popular Library, 1953.
Rawhide Gunman, Popular Library, 1954.
Trigger Trail (appeared serially in *Ranch* under title "Empire West"), Popular Library, 1955.
Blizzard Range, Popular Library, 1955.
Gunman from Texas, Popular Library, 1956.
Guns of the Lawless, Popular Library, 1956.
(Under name Willis T. Ballard) *The Package Deal,* Appleton, 1956.
Roundup, Popular Library, 1957.
Trail Town Marshal, Popular Library, 1957.
Saddle Tramp, Popular Library, 1958.
(Under name W. T. Ballard) *Chance Elson,* Pocket Books, 1958.
Trouble on the Massacre, Popular Library, 1959.
(Under name W. T. Ballard) *Fury in the Heart,* Monarch Books, 1959.
The Long Trail Back, Doubleday, 1960.
The Night Riders, Doubleday, 1961.
(Under name W. T. Ballard) *Pretty Miss Murder,* Pocket Books, 1961.
(Under name W. T. Ballard) *The Seven Sisters,* Pocket Books, 1962.
Gopher Gold, Doubleday, 1962 (published in England as *Gold Fever in Gopher,* Jenkins, 1962).
Westward the Monitors Roar, Doubleday, 1963, published as *Fight or Die,* Tower Books, 1977.
(Under name W. T. Ballard) *Three for the Money,* Pocket Books, 1963.
Gold in California!, Doubleday, 1965, reprinted, Ace Books, 1981.
(Under name W. T. Ballard) *Murder Las Vegas Style,* Tower, 1967.
The Californian, Doubleday, 1971.
Nowhere Left to Run, Doubleday, 1972.
Outlaw Brand, Avon, 1972.
Loco and the Wolf, Doubleday, 1973.
Home to Texas, Dell, 1974.
Trails of Rage, Doubleday, 1975.
(Under name W. T. Ballard) *This Range Is Mine,* Doubleday, 1975.
Sheriff of Tombstone, Doubleday, 1977.

UNDER PSEUDONYM BRIAN AGAR

Have Love, Will Share, Monarch Books, 1961.
Land of Promise, Universal Publishing & Distributing, 1967.

UNDER PSEUDONYM P. D. BALLARD

Age of the Junkman, Fawcett, 1963.
End of a Millionaire, Fawcett, 1964.
Brothers in Blood, Fawcett, 1972.
Angel of Death, Fawcett, 1972.
The Death Brokers, Fawcett, 1973.

UNDER PSEUDONYM PARKER BONNER

Superstition Range, Popular Library, 1952.
Outlaw Brand, Popular Library, 1954, reprinted, Avon, 1972.
Tough in the Saddle, Monarch Books, 1964.
Modoc Indian Wars, Monarch Books, 1965.
Plunder Canyon, Avon, 1967.
The Man from Yuma, Berkley Publishing, 1967.
The Town Tamer, Paperback Library, 1968.
Applegate's Gold, Avon, 1969.
Borders to Cross, Paperback Library, 1969.
Look to Your Guns, Paperback Library, 1969.

UNDER PSEUDONYM SAM BOWIE

Thunderhead Range, Monarch Books, 1959.
Chisum, Ace Books, 1970.
The Train Robbers, Ace Books, 1973.
Canyon War, G & D, 1980.

UNDER PSEUDONYM BRIAN FOX

A Dollar to Die For, Universal Publishing & Distributing, 1968.
The Wild Bunch, Universal Publishing & Distributing, 1969.
Sabata, Universal Publishing & Distributing, 1970.
The Outlaw Trail, Universal Publishing & Distributing, 1972.
Unholy Angel, Universal Publishing & Distributing, 1972.
Return of Sabata, Universal Publishing & Distributing, 1972.

UNDER PSEUDONYM JOHN HUNTER

West of Justice, Ballantine, 1954.
Ride the Wind South, Pocket Books, 1957.
Badlands Buccaneer, Pocket Books, 1959.
Marshal from Deadwood, Pocket Books, 1960.
Desperation Valley: A Novel of the Cherokee Strip, Macmillan, 1964.
Duke, Paperback Library, 1965.
Death in the Mountain, Ballantine, 1969.
Lost Valley, Ballantine, 1971.
Hell Hole, Ballantine, 1971.
The Burning Land, Ballantine, 1973.
Gambler's Gun, Ballantine, 1973.
The Higraders, Ballantine, 1974.
Death in the Mountain, Ballantine, 1974.

Also author of *Trouble Range.*

UNDER PSEUDONYM NEIL MacNEIL

Death Takes an Option, Gold Medal Books, 1958.
Third on a Seesaw, Gold Medal Books, 1959.
Two Guns for Hire, Gold Medal Books, 1959.
Hot Dam, Gold Medal Books, 1960.
The Death Ride, Gold Medal Books, 1960.
Mexican Slay Ride, Gold Medal Books, 1962.
The Spy Catchers, Gold Medal Books, 1965.

Also author of memoir "The Highland Heart of Nova Scotia."

UNDER PSEUDONYM JACK SLADE

Bandito, Tower, 1968.
Lassiter, Tower, 1968.

UNDER PSEUDONYM CLAY TURNER

Give a Man a Gun, Paperback Library, 1971.
Go West Ben Gold!, Warner, 1974.
Gold Goes to the Mountain, Warner, 1974.

OTHER

(Under pseudonym Harrison Hunt, with Norbert Davis) *Murder Picks the Jury,* S. Curl for Mystery House, 1947.
(Author of script) "The Outcast" (adapted from Ballard's novel *Two-Edged Vengeance* and short story "Red Horizon," published in *Esquire*), Republic Pictures, 1954.
(Under pseudonym John Shepherd) *Lights, Camera, Murder,* Belmont, 1960.
(Under pseudonym Hunter D'Allard) *The Long Sword,* Avon, 1962.
(Under pseudonym Nick Carter) *The Kremlin File,* Universal Publishing & Distributing, 1963.
(With wife, Phoebe Ballard) *The Man Who Stole a University* (juvenile), Doubleday, 1967.
(Under pseudonym George Hunter) *How to Defend Yourself, Your Family, and Your Home: A Complete Guide to Self-Protection,* McKay, 1967.
(Editor) *A Western Bonanza: Eight Short Novels of the West,* Doubleday, 1969.
(Under pseudonym Clint Reno) *Sun Mountain Slaughter,* Fawcett, 1974.

Also author under pseudonym of Clint Reno of *Silent Massacre,* Fawcett, and author of about fifty motion picture and television scripts. Contributor of over one thousand stories to magazines, beginning 1930, including *Saturday Evening Post, Esquire, This Week, Collier's, Liberty, McCall's,* and the original *Black Mask.*

SIDELIGHTS: Todhunter Ballard indicated in an *Armchair Detective* interview with Stephen Mertz that his career as a writer began at the age of twelve when *Hunter Trader Trapper* published a story in exchange for ten copies of the issue in which it appeared. Temporarily detoured from his ambitions by having to work as a draftsman in his father's electrical engineering firm, Ballard continued to write and submit copy to New York, and moved to the West Coast with only a few dollars in his pocket, when the firm collapsed during the Depression. Chancing upon a Hollywood cigar store newsstand carrying an issue of *Detective Dragnet,* in which one of his stories appeared, Ballard also encountered an acquaintance from Cleveland whose family manufactured movie trailers. Queried by the friend as to what he was doing in Hollywood, Ballard told Mertz that he produced a copy of the magazine and "lied gracefully. 'I'm freelancing, working for magazines. . . .' Why [he] was impressed by a dime pulp I'll never know, but he was. The meeting culminated in his offering me a job writing for the studio at seventy-five bucks a week. A bonanza at that time."

Ballard continued to write for the pulp magazines, however. According to Mertz, Ballard's "importance to the mystery field is that he was one of the original contributors to *Black Mask,* that famous detective pulp which, during the thirties . . . , pioneered the then-revolutionary American hard-boiled detective form." Approximating his average output for the pulps at about a million words per year, Ballard described to Mertz the lifestyle of a pulp writer living in Los Angeles during the thirties and forties: "We all worked hard, played hard, lived modestly, drank but only a few to excess, gambled some when we had extra cash.

Most of our friends were other writers. In the Depression when any of us got a check he climbed in his jalopy and made the rounds to see who was in worse straits than he and loaned up to half what he had just received."

When the market for detective fiction, especially for the studios, weakened, Ballard began to write westerns, using his middle name Todhunter. "But unlike the detective publications the westerns would not absorb enough copy under a single byline to support me . . . ," Ballard related to Mertz. "The houses would take only one a year and a name was tied up solely by one house. Therefore the shift to a long series of pseudonyms under which I could work for several houses at once." Acknowledging a preference for westerns over detective fiction, Ballard told Mertz that his most satisfying book was the Spur-winning *Gold in California!,* a young boy's episodic tale of growing up in California: "It's a good book. It sold over 30,000 copies, which is a huge sale for a western and I am proud of it." Ballard once told *CA* that all his books, "no matter what name they carry, are collaborations with Phoebe Ballard." His manuscripts are collected at the University of Oregon Library in Eugene.

AVOCATIONAL INTERESTS: Western history, metals, oil deposits, mining, fishing, travel.

MEDIA ADAPTATIONS: Film rights to *Applegate's Gold* were sold to Solar Productions in 1969.

BIOGRAPHICAL/CRITICAL SOURCES:

PERIODICALS

Armchair Detective, winter, 1979.
Time, October 24, 1969.
Writer's Digest, August, 1969.*

* * *

BALLARD, W. T.
See BALLARD, (Willis) Todhunter

* * *

BALLARD, Willis T.
See BALLARD, (Willis) Todhunter

* * *

BANTA, Martha 1928-

PERSONAL: Born May 11, 1928, in Muncie, Ind.; daughter of John Cullen (a merchant) and Irma (Purman) Banta. *Education:* Attended Western College, Oxford, Ohio, 1946-48; Indiana University, B.A. (with high honors), 1950, Ph.D., 1964.

ADDRESSES: Home—Pasadena, Calif. *Office*—Department of English, 2225 Rolfe Hall, University of California, 405 Hilgard Ave., Los Angeles, Calif. 90024.

CAREER: L. S. Ayers, Indianapolis, Ind., copywriter, 1950-53; Hockaday Associates, New York City, copywriter and account executive, 1954-58; Batten, Barton, Durstine & Osborne, New York City, copywriter, 1958-59; *Harper's Bazaar,* New York City, copy editor, 1959-60; University of California, Santa Barbara, assistant professor of English, 1964-70; University of Washington, Seattle, associate professor, 1970-75, professor of English, 1975-83; University of California, Los Angeles, professor of English, 1983—.

MEMBER: International Association of University Professors, Modern Language Association of America, American Studies Association, Henry James Society, Archives of American Art.

WRITINGS:

Henry James and the Occult: The Great Extension, Indiana University Press, 1972.
Failure and Success in America: A Literary Debate, Princeton University Press, 1978.
Imaging American Women: Idea and Ideals in Cultural History, Columbia University Press, 1987.
(Editor) *New Essays on "The American,"* Cambridge University Press, 1987.
(Editor with others) *The Harper American Literature,* two volumes, Harper, 1987.
(Editor with others) Emory Elliott, general editor, *Columbia Literary History of the United States,* Columbia University Press, 1988.

* * *

BARCLAY, William 1907-1978

PERSONAL: Born in 1907, in Wick, Caithness, Scotland; died January 24, 1978, in Glasgow, Scotland; married Katherine Barbara Gillespie; children: one son, two daughters (one deceased). *Education:* Earned M.A. and B.D. from University of Glasgow; also attended University of Marburg and Trinity College, Glasgow.

ADDRESSES: Home—32 Holmhead Rd., Cathcart, Glasgow G44 3AR, Scotland.

CAREER: Writer. Ordained minister of Church of Scotland; Trinity Church of Scotland, Renfrew, minister, 1933-46; University of Glasgow, Glasgow, Scotland, lecturer in New Testament language and literature, 1946-63, professor of divinity and biblical criticism, 1963-74. Visiting professor at University of Strathclyde, 1975. Bruce Lecturer, 1935; Croall Lecturer, 1955; Kerr Lecturer, 1956; Baird Lecturer, 1969-70; Sir David Owen Evans and Aberystwyth Lecturer, 1969; James Reid Memorial Lecturer, 1969, 1970. Member of joint committee for New English Bible. Speaker on television and radio.

MEMBER: Society of New Testament Studies, Society of Old Testament Studies, National Institute of Journalists, Royal Overseas League, Royal Scottish Automobile Club.

AWARDS, HONORS: D.D. from University of Edinburgh; named Commander of the Order of the British Empire.

WRITINGS:

Ambassador for Christ: The Life and Teaching of Paul, Church of Scotland Youth Committee, 1951, reprinted, Judson Press, 1974.
And Jesus Said: A Handbook on the Parables of Jesus, Church of Scotland Youth Committee, 1952.
The Daily Study Bible: New Testament, Saint Andrew Press, 1953-59, revised edition, eighteen volumes, Westminster, 1975-76.
A New Testament Wordbook (also see below), S.C.M. Press, 1955.
And He Had Compassion on Them: A Handbook on the Miracles of the Bible, Church of Scotland Youth Committee, 1956, Westminster Press, 1970, revised edition published as *And He Had Compassion,* Saint Andrew Press, 1975, Judson Press, 1976.
Letters to the Seven Churches, S.C.M. Press, 1957, Abingdon, 1958, reprinted, Westminster, 1982.
The Letter to the Hebrews, Saint Andrew Press, 1957.
The Letter to the Romans, Saint Andrew Press, 1957.
More New Testament Words (also see below), Harper, 1958.

The Mind of St. Paul, Harper, 1958, reprinted, 1975.
The Master's Men, Abingdon, 1959.
Educational Ideals in the Ancient World, Collins, 1959, published as *Train Up a Child: Educational Ideals in the Ancient World,* Westminster, 1959.
The Plain Man's Book of Prayers, Fontana, 1959, published as *A Book of Everyday Prayers,* Harper, 1960, published as *Everyday Prayers,* 1982.
The Promise of the Spirit, Westminster, 1960.
The Mind of Jesus (also see below), S.C.M. Press, 1960.
Crucified and Crowned (also see below), S.C.M. Press, 1961.
The Making of the Bible, Abingdon, 1961.
Flesh and Spirit, Abingdon, 1962.
A Guide to Daily Prayer, Harper, 1962.
Jesus as They Saw Him: New Testament Interpretations of Jesus, Harper, 1962.
More Prayers for the Plain Man, Collins, 1962.
The Plain Man Looks at the Beatitudes (also see below), Collins, 1962.
The All-Sufficient Christ: Studies in Paul's Letter to the Colossians, Westminster, 1963.
Epilogues and Prayers, S.C.M. Press, 1963, Abingdon, 1964.
Many Witnesses, One Lord, Westminster, 1963.
Prayers for Young People, Collins, 1963, Harper, 1967.
Turning to God: A Study of Conversion in the Book of Acts and Today, Epworth, 1963, Westminster, 1964.
Prayers for the Christian Year, S.C.M. Press, 1964, Harper, 1965.
Two Minutes a Day: Daily Bible Studies, Westminster, 1964.
The Plain Man Looks at the Lord's Prayer (also see below), Collins, 1964.
Epistle to the Hebrews, Abingdon, 1965.
A New People's Life of Jesus, S.C.M. Press, 1965, published as *The Life of Jesus for Everyman,* Harper, 1966.
(Editor) *The New Testament in Historical and Contemporary Perspective: Essays in Memory of G. H. C. Macgregor,* Basil Blackwell, 1965.
The Gospel and Acts, S.C.M. Press, Volume 1: *The First Three Gospels,* 1966, revised edition published as *Introduction to the First Three Gospels,* Westminster, 1975, Volume 2: *The Fourth Gospel and Acts of the Apostles,* 1976, published separately as *Introduction to John and the Acts of the Apostles,* Westminster, 1976.
Fishers of Men, Westminster, 1966.
Seen in the Passing, compiled by Rita F. Snowden, Collins, 1966, published as *In the Hands of God,* Harper, 1967, reprinted, Westminster, 1981.
The Apostles Creed for Everyman, Harper, 1967 (published in England as *The Plain Man Looks at the Apostles' Creed,* Collins, 1967).
The Lord's Supper, Abingdon, 1967.
Communicating the Gospel, Drummond, 1968.
The King and the Kingdom, Westminster, 1968.
Prayers for Help and Healing, Harper, 1968.
(Editor) *The Bible and History,* Lutterworth, 1968, Abingdon, 1969.
(Contributor) R. E. Davies, editor, *We Believe in God,* Westminster, 1968.
(Author of foreword) *The Bible Speaks Again: A Guide from Holland,* translation by Annebeth Mackie, Augsburg, 1969.
As Jesus Said: A Handbook on the Parables of Jesus, Westminster, 1970.
God's Young Church, Westminster, 1970.
Ethics in a Permissive Society, Harper, 1971, published as *Christian Ethics for Today,* 1984.
Through the Year with William Barclay: Devotional Readings for Every Day, edited by Denis Duncan, Hodder & Stoughton, 1971, published as *Daily Celebration: Devotional Readings for Every Day of the Year,* Word, Inc., 1973.
The Old Law and the New Law, Saint Andrew Press, 1972.
By His Spirit, Washington Review and Herald Publishing, 1972.
Introducing the Bible, Abingdon, 1972.
Jesus Christ for Today, Tidings, 1973.
The Plain Man's Guide to Ethics: Thoughts on the Ten Commandments, Fontana, 1973, published as *The Ten Commandments for Today,* Harper, 1973.
Every Day with William Barclay: Devotional Readings for Every Day, edited by Duncan, Hodder & Stoughton, 1973.
Marching On: Daily Readings for Younger People, edited by Duncan, Westminster, 1974.
By What Authority?, Darton, Longman & Todd, 1974, Judson Press, 1975.
William Barclay: A Spiritual Autobiography, Eerdmans, 1975 (published in England as *Testament of Faith,* Mowbray, 1975).
The Men, the Meaning, the Message of the Books, Westminster, 1976, published as *The Men, the Meaning, the Message of the New Testament Books: A Series of New Testament Studies,* 1978.
Jesus of Nazareth (based on the film by Franco Zeffirelli), Ballantine, 1977.
The Character of God, Denholm House Press, 1977.
A Life of Christ (juvenile), Harper, 1977.
Men and Affairs, Westminster, 1977.
Great Themes of the New Testament, edited by Cyril Rodd, Westminster, 1979.
The Lord Is My Shepherd: Expositions of Selected Psalms, introduction by Allan Galloway, Westminster, 1980.
Arguing about Christianity, Saint Andrew Press, 1980.

OMNIBUS VOLUMES

The Mind of Jesus (contains *The Mind of Jesus* and *Crucified and Crowned*), Harper, 1961.
New Testament Words (contains *A New Testament Wordbook* and *More New Testament Words*), S.C.M. Press, 1964.
The Beatitudes and the Lord's Prayer for Everyman (contains *The Plain Man Looks at the Beatitudes* and *The Plain Man Looks at the Lord's Prayer*), Harper, 1975.

OTHER

Editor with F. F. Bruce of "Bible Guides" series, 22 volumes, Abingdon. Editor and translator of books of the New Testament. Author of "Barclay Introduces the Bible" (cassette set), Abingdon Audio-Graphics, 1973. Contributor to scholarly journals.

WORK IN PROGRESS: Old Testament portion of *Daily Study Bible.*

SIDELIGHTS: William Barclay was a theologian who appealed to the common man. Through his numerous books, and radio and television broadcasts, he succeeded in communicating Christianity in terms that everyone could understand. "Making it interesting is a practice that . . . made William Barclay one of the leading religious authors of all time, from the standpoint of both sales and reader devotion," John Charles Walton wrote in *Christianity Today.* Barclay's *Daily Study Bible: New Testament* had sold more than five million copies at the time of his death.

BIOGRAPHICAL/CRITICAL SOURCES:

BOOKS

Barclay, William, *William Barclay: A Spiritual Autobiography,* Eerdmans, 1975.

Kernohan, R. D., editor, *William Barclay: The Plain Uncommon Man,* Hodder & Stoughton, 1980.

McKay, Johnston R., and James F. Miller, editors, *Biblical Studies: Essays in Honor of William Barclay,* Westminster, 1976.

PERIODICALS

Christianity Today, March 15, 1974, January 16, 1976.

Times Literary Supplement, December 8, 1966, April 1, 1977, June 17, 1977.

OBITUARIES:

PERIODICALS

AB Bookman's Weekly, March 20, 1978.

New York Times, January 25, 1978.*

* * *

BARNABY, (Charles) Frank 1927-

PERSONAL: Born September 27, 1927, in Hampshire, England; son of Charles Hector (in Royal Air Force) and Lilian (Sainsbury) Barnaby; married Sandra Ann McKee (a graphic artist), November 2, 1963 (divorced); married Wendy Elizabeth Field (a journalist), December 19, 1972. *Education:* University of London, B.Sc., 1950, M.Sc., 1953, Ph.D., 1960, Diploma in International Relations, 1967. *Religion:* Anglican.

ADDRESSES: Home & office—Brandreth, Chilbolton, Stockbridge, Hampshire, England.

CAREER: United Kingdom Atomic Energy Authority, Aldermaston, England, member of scientific staff, 1951-57; Medical Research Council, London, England, member of senior scientific staff, 1959-68; Pugwash Conferences on Science and World Affairs, London, executive secretary, 1968-70; Stockholm International Peace Research Institute, Stockholm, Sweden, director, 1971-81; Free University, Amsterdam, Holland, guest professor of peace studies and director of World Disarmament Campaign, 1981—.

MEMBER: Institute of Strategic Studies, National Union of Journalists, Fabian Society.

WRITINGS:

The Nuclear Future, Fabian Society, 1969.

(Editor) *Preventing the Spread of Nuclear Weapons,* Humanities, 1969.

(Editor with Anders Boserup) *Implications of Anti-Ballistic Missile Systems,* Humanities, 1969.

Radionuclides in Medicine, Souvenir Press, 1970.

Man and the Atom: The Uses of Nuclear Energy, Thames & Hudson, 1971, Funk, 1972.

Prospects for Peace, Pergamon, 1980.

(Editor with G. P. Thomas) *Nuclear Arms Race: Control or Catastrophe,* Franin Pinter, 1981.

The Automated Battlefield, Free Press, 1986.

(Editor with Marlies Ter Borg) *Emerging Technologies and Military Doctrine: A Political Assessment,* St. Martin's, 1987.

(Editor with P. Terrence Hopmann) *Rethinking the Nuclear Weapons Dilemma in Europe,* St. Martin's, 1988.

(Editor) *The Gaia Peace Atlas: Survival into the Third Millennium,* Doubleday, 1988.

Also contributor to numerous books. Contributor to scientific journals.

WORK IN PROGRESS: The Invisible Bomb; Star Wars Brought Down to Earth; writing on disarmament, arms control, military technology, and social consequences of science and technology.

* * *

BARR, Alfred H(amilton), Jr. 1902-1981

PERSONAL: Born January 28, 1902, in Detroit, Mich.; died August 15, 1981, in Salisbury, Conn.; son of Alfred Hamilton (a minister and educator) and Annie Elizabeth (Wilson) Barr; married Margaret Scolari-Fitzmaurice (an art historian), May 27, 1930 (died, 1987); children: Victoria Fitzmaurice. *Education:* Princeton University, A.B., 1922, A.M., 1923; Harvard University, Ph.D., 1946; additional study in Europe. *Religion:* Presbyterian.

ADDRESSES: Office—The Museum of Modern Art, 11 West 53rd St., New York, N.Y. 10019.

CAREER: Art historian. Vassar College, Poughkeepsie, N.Y., instructor in art history, 1923-24; Harvard University, Cambridge, Mass., assistant in fine arts, 1924-25; Princeton University, Princeton, N.J., instructor in art and archaeology, 1925-26; Wellesley College, Wellesley, Mass., associate professor of art, 1926-29; Museum of Modern Art, New York, N.Y., director, 1929-43, director of research in painting and sculpture, 1944-46, director of collections, 1947-67, counselor to board of trustees, beginning 1967, member of board of trustees, 1939-67, vice-president, 1939-43. Lecturer in England, Iceland, U.S.S.R., and throughout the United States; Mary Flexner Lecturer, Bryn Mawr College, 1946. Harvard University, member of fine arts visiting committee, 1958-60, chairman, 1965-70, overseer of Harvard College, 1964-70; member of fine arts visiting committees, Columbia University and Princeton University. Advisor to Office of Coordinator of Inter-American Affairs, 1940-43, and to art institutes and societies.

MEMBER: Association of Art Museum Directors (vice-president, 1940-41), College Art Association (director, 1943-48), American Association of Museums (past councillor), American Federation of Arts (trustee, 1948-55), Society for the Arts, Religion and Contemporary Cultures (president, 1962-65; became member of board of directors), American Institute of Architects (honorary member of New York chapter).

AWARDS, HONORS: Lord and Taylor American Design Award, 1947, "for bringing to a large number of Americans their first sample of modern art"; Litt.D., Princeton University, 1949; Ph.D., University of Bonn, 1958; Grand Cross of the Order of Merit, Federal Republic of Germany, 1959; named chevalier of Legion of Honor, Government of France, 1959; American Federation of Arts fiftieth anniversary award, 1959; Philadelphia Museum of Art merit award, 1959; D.F.A., University of Buffalo, 1962, Adelphi University, 1963, Yale University, 1967; Star of Italian Solidarity, Government of Italy, 1962; annual award, *Art in America* magazine, 1962; American Institute of Architects award of merit, 1964; Special Medal from Brandeis University Creative Arts Commission, 1964, for "notable creative achievement"; National Institute of Arts and Letters award, 1968, for distinguished service to the arts; New York State award, 1968; Art Dealers Association of America award, 1968, 1972; L.H.D., Columbia University, 1969; Skowhegan Gertrude Vanderbilt Whitney Award, 1974; European Art Dealers Association award, 1974; a permanent endowed lectureship has been established in Barr's honor at the Modern Museum of Art.

WRITINGS:

(Author of foreword) *First Loan Exhibition: Cezanne, Gauguin, Seurat, Van Gogh,* Museum of Modern Art (New York, N.Y.), 1929, reprinted, Arno for Museum of Modern Art, 1972.

(Author of preface) *Winslow Homer, Albert P. Ryder, Thomas Eakins: Sixth Loan Exhibition,* Museum of Modern Art, 1930, reprinted as *Four American Painters* (contains new material on George Caleb Bingham), Arno for Museum of Modern Art, 1969.

(Author of introduction and notes) *Modern German Painting and Sculpture,* Museum of Modern Art, 1931, reprinted, Arno for Museum of Modern Art, 1972.

(With others) *American Art of the Twenties and Thirties: Paintings by Nineteen Living Americans,* Museum of Modern Art, 1932, reprinted, Arno for Museum of Modern Art, 1969.

A Brief Survey of Modern Painting, Museum of Modern Art, 1932.

(Editor with Holger Cahill) *Art in America in Modern Times,* Reynal & Hitchcock, 1934, reprinted, Books for Libraries, 1969.

(Editor) *Vincent van Gogh,* Museum of Modern Art, 1935, reprinted, Greenwood Press, 1970, published under same title with bibliography by Charles Mattoon Brooks, Jr., 1942, reprinted, Arno for Museum of Modern Art, 1966.

Cubism and Abstract Art (also see below), Museum of Modern Art, 1936, reprinted, Belknap Press, 1986.

(Editor) Georges Hugnet, *Fantastic Art, Dada, Surrealism,* Museum of Modern Art, 1936, 3rd edition, 1947, reprinted, Arno for Museum of Modern Art, 1970.

(Editor) *Art in Our Time: An Exhibition to Celebrate the Tenth Anniversary of the Museum of Modern Art,* Museum of Modern Art, 1939, reprinted, Arno for Museum of Modern Art, 1972.

(Editor) *Picasso: Forty Years of His Art,* Museum of Modern Art, 1939, 4th edition, 1941.

(Contributor) Margaret Miller, editor, *Paul Klee,* Museum of Modern Art, 1941, 2nd edition, 1945, reprinted, Arno for Museum of Modern Art, 1968.

(Editor) *Painting and Sculpture in the Museum of Modern Art,* Museum of Modern Art, 1942, 4th edition published as *Painting and Sculpture in the Museum of Modern Art: 1929-1967,* 1977.

What Is Modern Painting?, Museum of Modern Art, 1943, revised edition, 1975.

(Editor with Dorothy C. Miller) *American Realists and Magic Realists,* Museum of Modern Art, 1943, reprinted, Arno for Museum of Modern Art, 1970.

(Contributor) Dorothy C. Miller, *Lyonel Feininger,* Museum of Modern Art, 1944, reprinted, Arno for Museum of Modern Art, 1966.

Picasso: Fifty Years of His Art, Museum of Modern Art, 1946, 3rd edition, 1955, reprinted, 1974.

(With James Thrall Soby) *Twentieth Century Italian Art,* Museum of Modern Art, 1949, reprinted, Arno for Museum of Modern Art, 1972.

(Editor) *The Museum of Modern Art Painting and Sculpture Collection,* Les Editions Braun, 1950.

Matisse: His Art and His Public, Museum of Modern Art, 1951, reprinted, 1974.

(Editor) *Masters of Modern Art,* Museum of Modern Art, 1954.

(Editor) *Picasso: Seventy-fifth Anniversary Exhibition,* Museum of Modern Art, 1957.

The New American Painting as Shown in Eight European Countries, 1958-1959, Museum of Modern Art, 1959, reprinted, Arno for Museum of Modern Art, 1972.

De Stijl, 1917-1928 (adaptation from *Cubism and Abstract Art;* originally published as introduction to exhibition, 1952-53), Museum of Modern Art, 1961.

(Author of foreword) *Three Generations of Twentieth Century Art: The Sidney and Harriet Janis Collection of the Museum of Modern Art,* Museum of Modern Art, 1972.

Defining Modern Art: Selected Writings of Alfred H. Barr, Jr., edited by Irving Sandler and Amy Newman, introduction by Sandler, Abrams, 1986.

Also author of numerous other exhibition catalogues. Contributor to periodicals in the United States and Europe. Member of editorial boards or committees of *Art Bulletin,* beginning 1939, *Gazette des Beaux-Arts,* beginning 1940, *Magazine of Art,* 1942-52, *Art Quarterly,* beginning 1953, and *Art in America,* beginning 1957.

SIDELIGHTS: In the opinion of *New York Times* writer John Russell, "without Alfred H. Barr, Jr., . . . there quite possibly would never have been a Museum of Modern Art." Barr became the first director of this New York-based museum in 1929 at the age of twenty-seven and he remained director until 1943. After this, Barr was affiliated with the museum in one capacity or another for most of his remaining years.

Of particular importance, Barr has been credited with establishing the Museum of Modern Art as a multidisciplinary museum, with emphasis on far more than just the fine arts. As Russell explains, the museum was "a walkthrough encyclopedia, that is to say, of art, architecture, design, photography and film as they had developed during the first two-thirds of this century. That encyclopedia was [Barr's] dream, and to a considerable extent his creation." By providing the best of all facets of modern art, Barr hoped to appeal to varied tastes, and museums nationwide have since grown under Barr's example.

Barr's eclectic approach to modern art is said to have been influenced, at least in part, by his early travels. In 1927 Barr visited the Bauhaus institute in Dessau, Germany (now the German Democratic Republic), where Walter Gropius's major undertaking was the integration of the arts. Later that same year, Barr acquired firsthand knowledge of the Russian avant-garde movement via a spur-of-the-moment trip to the U.S.S.R. According to Russell, "it was an opportunity that would never recur . . . and when [Barr] came to form the collections of the Modern Museum[,] that knowledge paid off many times over. . . . He made the Museum of Modern Art into something that has long been the envy of the world." Indeed, the museum's core collections of modern European art are considered unparalleled by some, and Barr's use of innovative displays—special lighting, movable walls, and so forth—have become standard practice in museums. Barr also wrote numerous catalogues and studies on modern art and artists, some of his most familiar being *What Is Modern Painting?, Picasso: Fifty Years of His Art,* and *Matisse: His Art and His Public.*

BIOGRAPHICAL/CRITICAL SOURCES:

PERIODICALS

October, winter, 1978.

Saturday Review, September 30, 1967.

OBITUARIES:

PERIODICALS

New York Times, August 23, 1981.*

* * *

BASKETTE, Floyd K(enneth) 1910-1979

PERSONAL: Born July 2, 1910, in Chama, N.M.; died February 10, 1979; son of Alexander H. (an engineer) and Pella (Persson) Baskette; married Carol G. Albright (a teacher), June 7, 1934; children: Kathleen Karen (Mrs. Kent Mollohan), Floyd Kenneth, Jr. *Education:* University of Missouri, B.J., 1932, M.A., 1936; attended University of Wisconsin, 1938-39, 1944-45. *Politics:* Democrat. *Religion:* Protestant.

ADDRESSES: Home—2735 Seventh St., Boulder, Colo. 80302. *Office*—School of Journalism, University of Colorado, Boulder, Colo. 80302.

CAREER: Adams State College, Alamosa, Colo., assistant professor of social studies, 1932-38; University of Wisconsin—Madison, assistant professor of journalism, 1938-39; Syracuse University, Syracuse, N.Y., assistant professor of journalism, 1940-41; Emory University, Atlanta, Ga., associate professor of journalism, 1941-50; University of Colorado, Boulder, associate professor, 1950-52, professor of journalism, 1952-77, professor emeritus, 1977–79. Lecturer, University of Wisconsin, 1944-45; director of journalism training program at Hislop College, Nagpur, 1954-55, and University of Rangoon, 1955-56. Part-time copywriter, *Atlanta Constitution,* 1941-50, and *Denver Post,* summers, 1952-53; copy editor, *Honolulu Advertiser,* summers, 1956-58. Director of Methodist Writers' Workshop.

MEMBER: Association for Education in Journalism, Sigma Delta Chi, Kappa Tau Alpha.

WRITINGS:

Colorado Pronunciation Guide, Pruett, 1943.
(With George C. Bastien and Leland D. Case) *Editing the Day's News,* 4th edition (Baskette was not associated with previous editions), Macmillan, 1956.
(With Jack Z. Sissors) *The Art of Editing,* Macmillan, 1971, 2nd edition, 1977.

Also author of materials for Methodist Publishing House; contributor to journalism and literary periodicals. Associate editor, *Journalism Quarterly,* 1945-50.*

* * *

BAWDEN, Nina (Mary Mabey) 1925- (Nina Mary [Mabey] Kark)

PERSONAL: Born January 19, 1925, in London, England; daughter of Charles and Ellalaine Ursula May (Cushing) Mabey; married Austen Steven Kark (an executive for British Broadcasting Corp.), 1954; children: (prior marriage) Nicholas Bawden (deceased), Robert Humphrey Felix Bawden; (current marriage) Perdita Emily Helena Kark. *Education:* Somerville College, Oxford, B.A., 1946, M.A., 1951; additional graduate study at Salzburg Seminar in American Studies, 1960.

ADDRESSES: Home—22 Noel Rd., London N1 8HA, England. *Agent*—Curtis Brown Ltd., 575 Madison Ave., New York, N.Y. 10022.

CAREER: Writer. Assistant, Town and Country Planning Associates, 1946-47; Justice of the Peace, Surrey, England, 1968-76.

MEMBER: PEN, Royal Society of Literature (fellow), Society of Women Writers and Journalists (president), Authors Lending and Copyright Society, Lansdowne, Ski Club of Great Britain.

AWARDS, HONORS: Guardian Award for Children's Fiction, 1975, for *The Peppermint Pig; Yorkshire Post* Novel of the Year Award, 1977, for *Afternoon of a Good Woman;* Booker Prize nomination, 1987, for *Circles of Deceit.*

WRITINGS:

ADULT NOVELS

Eyes of Green, Morrow, 1953 (published in England as *Who Calls the Tune,* Collins, 1953).
The Odd Flamingo, Collins, 1954, reprinted, Chivers, 1977.
Change Here for Babylon, Collins, 1955.
The Solitary Child, Collins, 1956, Lancer, 1966.
Devil by the Sea, Collins, 1957, Lippincott, 1959, reprinted, Heineman Educational, 1984, abridged edition for children, Lippincott, 1976.
Glass Slippers Always Pinch, Lippincott, 1960 (published in England as *Just Like a Lady,* Longmans, Green, 1960).
In Honour Bound, Longmans, Green, 1961.
Tortoise by Candlelight, Harper, 1963.
Under the Skin, Harper, 1964.
A Little Love, a Little Learning, Longmans, Green, 1965, Harper, 1966.
A Woman of My Age, Harper, 1967.
The Grain of Truth, Harper, 1968.
The Birds on the Trees, Longmans, Green, 1970, Harper, 1971.
Anna Apparent, Harper, 1972.
George beneath a Paper Moon, Harper, 1974.
Afternoon of a Good Woman, Harper, 1976.
Familiar Passions, Morrow, 1979.
Walking Naked, St. Martin's, 1981.
The Ice House, St. Martin's, 1983.
Circles of Deceit, St. Martin's, 1987.

JUVENILES

The Secret Passage, Gollancz, 1963, reprinted, Penguin, 1979, published as *The House of Secrets,* Lippincott, 1964.
On the Run, Gollancz, 1964, published as *Three on the Run,* Lippincott, 1965.
The White Horse Gang, Lippincott, 1966.
The Witch's Daughter, Lippincott, 1966, reprinted, Chivers, 1988.
A Handful of Thieves, Lippincott, 1967.
The Runaway Summer, Lippincott, 1969.
Squib, Lippincott, 1971.
Carrie's War, Lippincott, 1973, reprinted, Dell, 1989.
The Peppermint Pig, Lippincott, 1975.
Rebel on a Rock, Lippincott, 1978.
The Robbers, Lothrop, 1979.
(Adaptor) *William Tell,* illustrated by Pascale Allamand, Lothrop, 1981.
Kept in the Dark, Lothrop, 1982.
St. Francis of Assisi (nonfiction), Lothrop, 1983.
The Finding, Lothrop, 1985.
Princess Alice, Deutsch, 1985.
Henry, Lothrop, 1988 (published in England as *Keeping Henry,* Gollancz, 1988).
The Outside Child, Gollancz, 1989.

OTHER

Contributor to *Evening Standard* and *Daily Telegraph.*

SIDELIGHTS: Author of numerous novels for both children and adults, "Nina Bawden is perhaps best known for her incisive satirical inquiry into the family relationships of the educated middle class," notes Gerda Seaman in a *Dictionary of Literary Biography* essay. Since beginning her career with mystery, gothic, and horror stories, Bawden "has moved toward the psychological investigation of modern middle-class existence," continues the critic. "With an urbane irony and often surprising violence, she exposes the uneasy alliances which keep chaos at bay and provides a circumstantial account of the domesticated brutality at the heart of modern life."

In *The Ice House,* for example, Bawden introduces Daisy Brown and Ruth Perkins, who have been best friends since their childhood. When Daisy's husband is killed in an accident, Ruth comes to realize that her friend's marriage was not as happy as it appeared; indeed, she finds her own in jeopardy after discovering her husband's longtime affair. *Washington Post* contributor Elizabeth Ward finds Bawden's use of this situation ironic: "What [the death] catalyzes is not, as one might expect, the unraveling of Ruth's and Daisy's secure family lives. It is the gradual realization of both families that their lives were pretty unraveled already, shredded by false expectations, misplaced trust and betrayal." In addition, the author's portrayal of Ruth's increasingly perplexing search to discover and oust her husband's mistress leads Ward to comment that "it is impossible not to admire the ease with which Bawden manipulates the intricate elements of her plot."

Bawden creates a similarly tangled group of misleading relationships in *Circles of Deceit,* a novel which was nominated for Britain's prestigious Booker Prize. The story is narrated by an artist who, appropriately, paints fine copies of the Old Masters; his first wife betrayed him by having an affair, while his second wife is hiding the abuse of her own son. "Ms. Bawden makes comic use of these characters' foibles, but there is considerable sadness beneath her evocative scenes and lively dialogue," observes Laurel Graeber in the *New York Times Book Review.* In showing the characters' lies and deceptions, the author also reveals the distress they cause themselves; as Jennifer McKay states in the *Listener,* "emotional pain is something Bawden portrays well, perhaps because she knows it is as likely to show itself in banal words and actions as in heroics." Although the pace of the book is slow, Graeber remarks that Bawden "makes the reader care about these people's trials. However much her characters deceive," concludes the critic, "it's refreshing to see that Nina Bawden's own talent is nothing less than genuine."

Bawden has also written many novels for young adults, and in them "we see a real world," asserts Nicholas Tucker in *Children's Literature in Education,* a world "stretching from junk yards to prim, over-immaculate front parlours. Yet it would be facile to place this author in any simple 'social realist' category, since at the same time she is also taken up with the theme of fantasy, both in her characters' lives and in the stories themselves as she writes them." Explains the critic: "The result, then, is neither fantasy nor realism, but the tension between them." *Carrie's War* is perhaps Bawden's best known children's novel, relating the evacuation of a young girl and her brother to a bleak Welsh mining town during World War II. A *Times Literary Supplement* reviewer observes that while Bawden's work has been "immensely readable and accessible yet often thought-provoking," *Carrie's War* is "altogether more moving, richer and stranger than anything she has achieved before. If it is not partly autobiographical, it certainly feels as if it is." "Miss Bawden has written outstanding books," maintains Catherine Storr in her *New Statesman* review; "it's because she writes with compassion and with insight and above all with honesty." Similarly, Bawden's recent *Henry* (published in England as *Keeping Henry*), a story again set on a Welsh farm during the War, recalls autobiography; Deborah Singmaster writes in the *Times Literary Supplement* that the story is "so artfully remembered and retold that it will charm both children and adults alike." "All Nina Bawden's books have a definite quality," says Tucker; "the humour is abundant and never forced, and there are always moments of great pace and excitement." As Seaman concludes, "to read [Bawden's] work is to encounter a writer of great integrity. . . . Her clear-eyed satiric studies of men, women, and children have always probed the hypocritical motive and the mechanical response. Most recently they have also offered us honest alternatives."

MEDIA ADAPTATIONS: Many of Bawden's children's stories have been adapted for television, including *Carrie's War,* which was broadcast in the United States on PBS.

AVOCATIONAL INTERESTS: Traveling, reading, garden croquet.

BIOGRAPHICAL/CRITICAL SOURCES:

BOOKS

Children's Literature Review, Volume 2, Gale, 1976.

Dictionary of Literary Biography, Volume 14: *British Novelists since 1960,* Gale, 1982.

PERIODICALS

Children's Literature in Education, Number 13, 1974.

Listener, September 10, 1987.

New Statesman, May 25, 1973.

Newsweek, August 29, 1983.

New York Times Book Review, June 3, 1973, November 29, 1987.

Times (London), July 14, 1983.

Times Literary Supplement, April 6, 1973, April 17, 1981, July 22, 1983, July 17, 1987, June 24, 1988.

Washington Post, August 29, 1983.

* * *

BEAR, John (Boris) 1938-

PERSONAL: Born March 14, 1938, in New York; son of John Klempner (a writer) and Tina (a teacher; maiden name, Minsker) Bear; married Marina Constantinova Dobroluboff (a philosopher), August 14, 1963; children: Mariah, Susannah, Tanya. *Education:* Attended Reed College, 1955-58; University of California, Berkeley, B.A., 1959, M.J., 1960; Michigan State University, Ph.D., 1966. *Politics:* Democrat. *Religion:* Jewish.

ADDRESSES: Home—2730 Stuart St., Berkeley, Calif. 94705. *Office*—P.O. Box 7070, Berkeley, Calif. 94707. *Agent*—International Creative Management, 40 West 57th St., New York, N.Y. 10019.

CAREER: Weiner & Gossage, San Francisco, Calif., copywriter, 1960-63; Center for the Gifted Child, Inc., San Francisco, Calif., director, 1963-65; Bell & Howell Co., research director in human development, 1966-68; University of Iowa, Iowa City, associate professor of journalism, 1968-69; Midas-International Corp., Chicago, Ill., director of advertising, 1968-70; consultant, 1970-74; writer, 1974—. President, International Institute for Advanced Studies, 1988—. Director, Mendocino County Big Brothers/Big Sisters Organization, 1979-82. Consultant to Xerox Corp., General Motors, *Encyclopaedia Britannica,* Grateful Dead (rock group), and Teknekron, Inc.

WRITINGS:

(With wife, Marina Bear) *The Something-Went-Wrong-What-Do-I-Do-Now Cookbook: What to Do about Salty Soup, Burned Stew, Fallen Cakes, Overcooked Cauliflower, Runny Eggs, Crusty Pots, and Hundreds of Other Kitchen Catastrophes,* Harcourt, 1970, published as *Common Cooking Crises,* Reader's Digest Press, 1972, published as *The Something Went Wrong What Do I Do Now Cookery Book,* Macdonald & Co., 1973.
San Francisco: An Unusual Guide to Unusual Shopping, Price, Stern, 1972.
Signals and Messages, Macdonald Educational, 1973.
Communication, Macdonald Educational, 1974.
The United States of America: The Land and Its People, Macdonald Educational, 1974.
So You're in Your Teens, Price, Stern, 1975.
So You're in Your Twenties, Price, Stern, 1975.
So You're in Your Thirties, Price, Stern, 1975.
So You're in Your Forties, Price, Stern, 1975.
So You're in Your Fifties, Price, Stern, 1975.
So You're in Your Sixties, Price, Stern, 1975.
College Degrees by Mail: A Comprehensive Guide to Non-Traditional Degree Programs, Rafton & Bear, 1975, 8th edition published as *How to Get the Degree You Want: Bear's Guide to Non-Traditional College Degrees,* Ten Speed Press, 1982, 10th edition, 1989.
The World's Worst Maxims, Price, Stern, 1976.
How to Earn an American University Degree, Mendocino Book Co., 1979.
Bear's Guide to Saving Money on Postage, Wightman Publishing, 1980.
The Alternative Guide to Higher Education, Grosset, 1980.
Computer Wimp: 166 Things I Wish I Had Known before I Bought My First Computer, Ten Speed Press, 1983.
Finding Money for College, Ten Speed Press, 1984.
(With Margaret Fox) *Cafe Beaujolais,* Ten Speed Press, 1984.
The Blackmail Diet: Lose Weight or Else, Ten Speed Press, 1984.
How to Repair Food, Ten Speed Press, 1987.
Morning Food, Ten Speed Press, 1989.
Luba's Bistro, Celestial Arts, 1989.
Evening Food, Ten Speed Press, 1990.
Send This Jerk the Bedbug Letter, Ten Speed Press, 1991.

Contributor of articles to magazines, including *Psychology Today, Business Week, California Magazine,* and *World Tennis.*

SIDELIGHTS: John Bear wrote *CA:* "Perhaps because my father was a successful writer of fiction books in the 1930's and 1940's, I have been disinclined or intimidated from moving in that direction. But I have enough splendid nonfiction ideas to keep me going for the balance of years probably allotted me. After writing about non-traditional higher education for over twenty years, in 1988, I began viewing the process from another perspective, when I was appointed President of America's oldest school offering graduate degrees through external study."

BIOGRAPHICAL/CRITICAL SOURCES:

PERIODICALS

Los Angeles Times, August 29, 1984.
Times Literary Supplement, December 14, 1984.

* * *

BEDARD, Michelle
See FINNIGAN, Joan

BEDFORD, Ann
See REES, Joan

* * *

BEDINI, Silvio A. 1917-

PERSONAL: Born January 17, 1917, in Ridgefield, Conn.; son of Vincent L. S. (a businessman) and Cesira (Stefanelli) Bedini; married Gerda Hintz, October 20, 1951; children: Leandra Anne, Peter David. *Education:* Attended Columbia University, 1935-36, 1937-42. *Religion:* Roman Catholic.

ADDRESSES: Home—4303 47th St. N.W., Washington, D.C. 20016. *Office*—National Museum of History and Technology, Smithsonian Institution, Washington, D.C. 20560.

CAREER: Self-employed in Ridgefield, Conn., 1945-61; Smithsonian Institution, Washington, D.C., curator of Division of Mechanical and Civil Engineering, U.S. National Museum, 1961-65, assistant director of Museum of History of Technology, 1965-71, deputy director, 1971-78, keeper of rare books, 1978-86, research associate, 1986—. *Military service:* U.S. Army, 1942-45.

MEMBER: Society of American Historians, History of Science Society, Society for the History of Technology (member of advisory council), American Historical Association, American Philosophical Society, American Antiquarian Society, Washington Academy of Sciences (fellow).

AWARDS, HONORS: Abbott Payson Usher Award, Society for the History of Technology, 1962; Outstanding Performance Award, Smithsonian Institution, 1965; LL.D., University of Bridgeport, 1970.

WRITINGS:

Ridgefield in Review, Walker-Rackliffe Co., 1958.
The Scent of Time, American Philosophical Society, 1963.
Early American Scientific Instruments and Their Makers, Smithsonian Institution Press, 1964.
(With Francis R. Maddison) *Mechanical Universe,* American Philosophical Society, 1966.
(Contributor) *Saggi su Galileo Galilei,* G. Barbera (Florence), 1967.
(Contributor) Ernan McMullin, editor, *Galileo: Man of Science,* Basic Books, 1968.
(With Wernher von Braun and Fred L. Whipple) *Moon: Man's Greatest Adventure,* edited by C. Davis Thomas, Abrams, 1970.
The Life of Benjamin Banneker, Scribner, 1972.
Thinkers and Tinkers: Early American Men of Science, Scribner, 1975.
The Spotted Stones: A Story about the Game of Dominoes (juvenile), Pantheon, 1978.
Declaration of Independence Desk: Relic of Revolution, Smithsonian Institution Press, 1981.
Thomas Jefferson and His Copying Machines, University Press of Virginia, 1984.
Clockwork Cosmos, Vatican Library, 1985.
At the Sign of the Compass and Quadrant, American Philosophical Society, 1986.
The Trail of Time, Cambridge University Press, in press.

WORK IN PROGRESS: Thomas Jefferson: Statesman of Science.

BEILENSON, Edna 1909-1981 (Elisabeth Deane)

PERSONAL: Surname is pronounced *Bee*-lenson; born June 16, 1909, in New York, N.Y.; died February 28, 1981; daughter of John (an artist) and Anna (Beilenson) Rudolph; married Peter Beilenson (a publisher), July 20, 1930 (died January 20, 1962); married Joseph E. Barmack, June 19, 1966 (divorced, 1975); children: Anthony C., Roger N., Elizabeth R. Beilenson Schildkraut. *Education:* Hunter College (now of the City University of New York), A.B. (cum laude), 1928.

ADDRESSES: Home and office—1035 Fifth Ave., New York, N.Y. 10028.

CAREER: Peter Pauper Press, Inc., Mt. Vernon, N.Y., beginning 1932, worked as bookkeeper, typesetter, cover designer, and at other jobs, became president; free-lance designer of children's books, 1935; Walpole Printing Office, Inc., Mt. Vernon, president, 1962-78. American Institute of Graphic Arts, vice-president, 1956, president, 1958-60; Goudy Society, director, 1965, chairman of board, 1968-74 and 1978, honorary chairman of board, 1974-78, president, 1975-78; president of Distaff Side; trustee of American Printing History Association.

MEMBER: Royal Society of Arts (fellow), Grolier Club (New York City).

AWARDS, HONORS: Woman of the Year in Business, Marquis's *Who's Who,* 1968; Goudy Award, Rochester Institute of Technology, 1980.

WRITINGS:

Holiday Cook Book, Peter Pauper, 1950.
(Compiler) *Festive Cookery,* Peter Pauper, 1951.
Cooking to Kill! The Poison Cook-book: Comic Recipes for the Ghoul, Cannibal, Witch, and Murderer, Peter Pauper, 1951.
(Compiler) *Recipes Mother Used to Make,* Peter Pauper, 1952.
(Compiler) *Holiday Goodies and How to Make Them,* Peter Pauper, 1952.
Holiday Punches, Party Bowls, and Soft Drinks, Peter Pauper, 1953.
(Compiler) *Holiday Candies,* Peter Pauper, 1954.
(Compiler) *Holiday Cookies,* Peter Pauper, 1954.
The Merrie Christmas Cook Book, Peter Pauper, 1955.
Queen of Hearts Cook Book, Peter Pauper, 1955.
The Little Quiz Book, Peter Pauper, 1956.
(Compiler) *Holiday Party Casseroles,* Peter Pauper, 1956.
(Compiler) *Holiday Party Desserts,* Peter Pauper, 1956.
Cupid's Almanack: A Collection of Epigrams Witty and Wise about Love and Marriage, Arranged for Your Delight according to the Seasons of the Year, Peter Pauper, 1956.
Abalone to Zabaglione: Unusual and Exotic Recipes, Peter Pauper, 1957.
The Christmas Stocking Book, Peter Pauper, 1957.
The Melting Pot: A Cookbook of All Nations, Peter Pauper, 1958.
(Compiler) *Festive Seafood Cookery,* Peter Pauper, 1969.
The Zodiac Cook Book, Peter Pauper, 1969.
(Editor) *Friendship Is Forever,* Peter Pauper, 1979.
(Compiler) *Festive Cookies,* Peter Pauper, 1985.
(Compiler) *Golden Treasury of Psalms and Prayers,* Walker, 1986.

"ABC OF COOKERY" SERIES

The ABC of Canapes, Peter Pauper, 1953.
. . . *Chafing Dish Cookery,* Peter Pauper, 1956.
. . . *Gourmet Cookery,* Peter Pauper, 1956.
. . . *Herb and Spice Cookery,* Peter Pauper, 1957.
. . . *Wine Cookery,* Peter Pauper, 1957.

"SIMPLE COOKERY" SERIES; COMPILER

Simple French Cookery, Peter Pauper, 1958.
. . . *Italian Cookery,* Peter Pauper, 1959.
. . . *Oriental Cookery,* Peter Pauper, 1960.
. . . *Viennese Cookery,* Peter Pauper, 1960.
. . . *Jewish Cookery,* Peter Pauper, 1962.
. . . *New England Cookery,* Peter Pauper, 1962.
. . . *Continental Cookery,* Peter Pauper, 1963.
. . . *Hawaiian Cookery,* Peter Pauper, 1964.
. . . *German Cookery,* Peter Pauper, 1965.

"GIFTS OF GOLD" SERIES; COMPILER UNDER PSEUDONYM ELISABETH DEANE

Gentle Thoughts: A Collection of Tender and Wise Sayings from Sundry Authors of Wisdom and Renown, Peter Pauper, 1969.
Gift of Friendship: A Collection of Warm, Beautiful Thoughts about the Love of One Heart for Another, Peter Pauper, 1969.
Words of Love: A Collection of Love Poems, Love Letters, and Meaningful Sayings Pertaining to Love and Loving, Peter Pauper, 1969.
Wisdom of the East: Precious Jewels of Great Wisdom Garnered from the Sages of India and the Far Orient, Peter Pauper, 1970.
A Gift of Mistletoe: Thoughts for a Merrie Christmas, Peter Pauper, 1971.
Gift of Prayer: A Selection of Prayers Designed to Make the Burdens Lighter and the Hours Less Lonely, Peter Pauper, 1971.
The Listening Heart: A Collection of Warm, Discerning Sayings for the Heart That Listens with Sympathy and Understanding, Peter Pauper, 1971.

UNDER PSEUDONYM ELISABETH DEANE

(Compiler) *Smiles, Chuckles, and Chortles,* Peter Pauper, 1971.
The Heart of a Friend, Peter Pauper, 1973.
(Compiler) *A Gift of Tenderness,* Peter Pauper, 1979.

SIDELIGHTS: Peter Pauper Press was founded in 1928 by Edna Beilenson's cousin, Peter Beilenson, whom she later married. His goal was to publish fine books at a low price. Most of the books were small in size, 64 pages long, made of high quality paper, and sold for one dollar. A year later Beilenson also opened the Walpole Printing Office, which printed quality books, including over a dozen for George Macy's Limited Edition Club.

Edna Beilenson joined her husband as a business partner at Peter Pauper and Walpole Printing in 1932. Over the years she worked in bookkeeping, typesetting, promotion and general sales, and general operations, but her largest contribution was in cover designing. She felt that the style and color of the cover were important selling points, and she had a flair for choosing the right design. Her husband once wrote: "She looks at a book as would a dress designer or an interior decorator. Our output soon showed the feminine influence in the use of delightful patterned bindings. She also taught me how much better a book can be when it has color inside, too; when the printed pages, the binding and even the slipcase are in harmony."

After her husband's death in 1962 Edna Beilenson took over the business, which has continued to prosper. She told *Publishers Weekly* writer Chandler B. Grannis her secret of success: "I love people and I love the books I make—which is a good combination when it comes to selling."

Beilenson once told *CA:* "My career at the Peter Pauper Press has been a lifelong romance. Although I was taught to set the early books by hand, we now use machine-set type, but the accent is still on the craft of the book, and it is that aspect of publishing to which I have devoted my life."

BIOGRAPHICAL/CRITICAL SOURCES:

PERIODICALS

Publishers Weekly, November 27, 1978.

OBITUARIES:

PERIODICALS

New York Times, March 4, 1981.
Publishers Weekly, March 13, 1981.

* * *

BELLOW, Saul 1915-

PERSONAL: Born June 10, 1915 (officially recorded as July 10, 1915), in Lachine, Quebec, Canada; came to Chicago at the age of nine; son of Abraham (a Russian emigre and businessman) and Liza (Gordon) Bellow; married Anita Goshkin (a social worker), December 31, 1937 (divorced); married Alexandra Tschacbasov, February 1, 1956 (divorced); married Susan Glassman (a teacher), 1961 (divorced); married Alexandra Ionesco Tuleca (a mathematician), 1974 (divorced); children: (first marriage) Gregory, (second marriage) Adam, (third marriage) Daniel. *Education:* Attended University of Chicago, 1933-35; Northwestern University, B.S. (with honors in sociology and anthropology), 1937; graduate study in anthropology at University of Wisconsin, 1937 (abandoned his studies because "every time I worked on my thesis, it turned out to be a story").

ADDRESSES: Home—Chicago, Ill. *Office*—c/o Committee on Social Thought, University of Chicago, 1126 East 59th St., Chicago, Ill. 60637. *Agent*—Harriet Wasserman Literary Agency, 137 East 36th St., New York, N.Y. 10016.

CAREER: Worked for a time on WPA Writers' Project, writing biographies of authors; Pestalozzi-Froebel Teachers College, Chicago, Ill., instructor, 1938-42; Encyclopaedia Britannica, Inc., Chicago, member of editorial department of "Great Books" project, 1943-46; University of Minnesota, Minneapolis, member of English department, 1946, assistant professor, 1948-49, associate professor of English, 1954-59; New York University, New York, N.Y., visiting lecturer, 1950-52; Princeton University, Princeton, N.J., creative writing fellow, 1952-53; Bard College, Annandale-on-Hudson, N.Y., faculty member, 1953-54; University of Puerto Rico, Rio Piedras, visiting professor of English, 1961; University of Chicago, Chicago, celebrity in residence, 1962, currently Grunier Distinguished Services Professor, member of Committee on Social Thought, 1962—, chairman, 1970-76. Presented Jefferson Lecture for National Endowment for the Humanities in 1977; has presented Tanner Lectures at Oxford University. Fellow, Academy for Policy Study, 1966; fellow, Brandford College of Yale University. *Wartime service:* Merchant Marine, 1944-45.

MEMBER: Authors League, American Academy of Arts and Letters, PEN, Yaddo Corporation.

AWARDS, HONORS: Short stories included in *Best American Short Stories,* 1944, "Notes of a Dangling Man," and 1950, "Sermon by Doctor Pep"; Guggenheim fellowship in Paris and Rome, 1948; National Institute of Arts and Letters grant, 1952; National Book Award, 1954, for *The Adventures of Augie March,* 1964, for *Herzog,* and 1970, for *Mr. Sammler's Planet;* O. Henry Award, 1956, for "The Gonzaga Manuscripts," and 1980, for "A Silver Dish"; Ford grant, 1959, 1960; Friends of Literature Fiction Award, 1960; James L. Dow Award, 1964; Prix International de Litterature (France; $10,000), 1965, for *Herzog;* Jewish Heritage Award, B'nai B'rith, 1968; Croix de Chevalier (France), 1968; Formentor Prize, 1970; Pulitzer Prize and Nobel Prize for Literature, both 1976, for *Humboldt's Gift;* Gold Medal, American Academy of Arts and Letters, 1977; Emerson-Thoreau Medal, American Academy of Arts and Sciences, 1977; Neil Gunn International fellowship, 1977; Brandeis University Creative Arts Award, 1978; Commander, Legion of Honour (France), 1983; Malaparte Prize for Literature (Italy), 1984; Commander, Order of Arts and Letters (France), 1985; National Medal of Arts, 1988, for "outstanding contributions to the excellence, growth, support and availability of the arts in the United States." D.Litt. from Northwestern University, 1962, and Bard College, 1963; Litt.D. from New York University, 1970, Harvard University, 1972, Yale University, 1972, McGill University, 1973, Brandeis University, 1974, Hebrew Union College, 1976, and Trinity College (Dublin), 1976.

WRITINGS:

NOVELS

Dangling Man, Vanguard, 1944, reprinted, Penguin, 1988.

The Victim, Vanguard, 1947, reprinted, Penguin, 1988.

The Adventures of Augie March (also see below), Viking, 1953, published with introduction by Lionel Trilling, Modern Library, 1965, reprinted, Penguin, 1984.

Seize the Day; With Three Short Stories and a One-Act Play (novella; also contains stories "Father-to-Be," "The Gonzaga Manuscripts," and "Looking for Mr. Green," and play, "The Wrecker"; also see below), Viking, 1956, published singly as *Seize the Day,* 1961, published with introduction by Alfred Kazin, Fawcett, 1968.

Henderson the Rain King (also see below), Viking, 1959, reprinted, Penguin, 1984.

Herzog (early drafts published in *Esquire,* July, 1961, and July, 1963, in *Commentary,* July, 1964, and in *Saturday Evening Post,* August 8, 1964; also see below), Viking, 1964, published with criticism, edited by Irving Howe, 1976, reprinted, Penguin, 1984.

Mr. Sammler's Planet (originally appeared in a different form in *Atlantic;* also see below), Viking, 1970.

Humboldt's Gift, Viking, 1975.

The Dean's December, Harper, 1982, limited edition with illustrations by Robert Heindel, Franklin Library, 1982.

More Die of Heartbreak, Morrow, 1987.

A Theft (novella; Quality Paperback Book Club dual main selection), Penguin, 1989.

The Bellarosa Connection (novella), Penguin, 1989.

SHORT STORIES

Mosby's Memoirs, and Other Stories (contains "Leaving the Yellow House," "The Old System," "Looking for Mr. Green," "The Gonzaga Manuscripts," "A Father-to-Be," and "Mosby's Memoirs"; also see below), Viking, 1968, reprinted, 1984.

Him with His Foot in His Mouth, and Other Stories (contains "Cousins," "A Silver Dish," "What Kind of Day Did You Have?," "Zetland: By a Character Witness," and "Him with His Foot in His Mouth"), Harper, 1984.

UNCOLLECTED SHORT STORIES

William Phillips and Philip Rahv, editors, *Partisan Reader: Ten Years of Partisan Review, 1934-1944,* (contains "Two Morning Monologues"), introduction by Lionel Trilling, Dial, 1946.

Nelson Algren, editor, *Nelson Algren's Own Book of Lonesome Monsters,* (contains "Address by Gooley MacDowell to the Hasbeens Club of Chicago"), Geis, 1963.

Penny Chapin Hills and L. Rust Hills, editors, *How We Live: Contemporary Life in Contemporary Fiction,* (contains "Herzog Visits Chicago"), Macmillan, 1968.

Other short stories reprinted in more than twenty anthologies.

PLAYS

"The Wrecker," published in *New World Writing 6,* 1954, published in *Seize the Day; With Three Short Stories and a One-Act Play,* Viking, 1956.

"Under the Weather" (three one-act comedies: "Orange Souffle," published in *Esquire,* January, 1965, "A Wen," published in *Esquire,* October, 1965, and "Out from Under"), first produced in London, June 7, 1966; produced in Spoleto, Italy, at Festival of Two Worlds, July 14, 1966; produced on Broadway at the Cort Theatre, October 27, 1966.

The Last Analysis, a Play (full-length; first produced on Broadway at the Belasco Theatre, October 1, 1964; acting edition of first version of play printed under original title *Bummidge*), rewritten version published by Viking, 1965.

OTHER

(Author of foreword) Feodor Dostoevsky, *Winter Notes on Summer Impressions,* Criterion Books, 1955.

(Translator of title story) Isaac Bashevis Singer, *Gimpel the Fool, and Other Stories,* Noonday, 1957.

(Author of text with C. Zervos) Jesse Reichek, *Dessins,* Editions Cahiers d'Art (Paris), 1960.

(Contributor) Alfred Kazin, editor, *The Open Form: Essays for Our Time,* Harcourt, 1961.

(Editor with Keith Botsford [first three volumes also with Jack Ludwig]) *The Noble Savage,* five volumes, Meridian, 1961-62.

(Contributor) Robert M. Hutchins and Mortimer J. Adler, editors, *The Great Ideas Today,* six volumes, Atheneum, 1961-66.

Recent American Fiction; A Lecture Presented under the Auspices of the Gertrude Clarke Whitall Poetry and Literature Fund, Library of Congress, 1963.

(Editor and author of introduction) *Great Jewish Short Stories,* Dell, 1963, reprinted, 1985.

(Contributor) A. L. Bader, editor, *To the Young Writer,* University of Michigan Press, 1963.

(Contributor) Herbert Gold, editor, *First Person Singular: Essays for the Sixties,* Dial, 1963.

Acceptance Speech by Saul Bellow, Author of "Herzog," Fiction Winner, National Book Awards, March 9, 1965, privately printed, c. 1965.

(Contributor) Irving Malin, editor, *Saul Bellow and the Critics* (contains "Where Do We Go from Here: The Future of Fiction"), New York University Press, 1967.

(Contributor) James E. Miller, Jr., and Paul D. Herring, editors, *The Arts & the Public* (essays), University of Chicago Press, 1967.

The Portable Saul Bellow (contains *Henderson the Rain King* and *Seize the Day,* plus selections from *The Adventures of Augie March, Herzog,* and *Mr. Sammler's Planet,* and "Leaving the Yellow House," "The Old System," and "Mosby's Memoirs" from *Mosby's Memoirs, and Other Stories*), critical introduction by Gabriel Josipovici, Viking, 1974.

(Contributor) *Technology and the Frontiers of Knowledge* (contains "Literature in the Age of Technology"), Doubleday, 1975.

To Jerusalem and Back: A Personal Account (memoirs), Viking, 1976.

Herzog (sound recording of Bellow reading excerpts from novel), Caedmon, 1978.

The Nobel Lecture (first published in *American Scholar,* 1977), Targ Editions, 1979.

Also author of "Deep Readers of the World, Beware!," 1959; *Keynote Address before the Inaugural Session of the XXXIV International P.E.N. Congress, June 13, 1966, at Loeb Student Center, New York University,* 1966; and the Carolyn Benton Cockefair Lecture, "The Novel in a Technological Age," 1973. Contributor to *Partisan Review, Hudson Review, Sewanee Review, New Yorker, New Republic, Nation, New Leader, Saturday Review, Holiday, Reporter, Horizon, Esquire, Commentary, New York Times Book Review,* and other publications. Founder and co-editor of *Noble Savage,* 1960-62. An extensive collection of Bellow's manuscripts, including those from most of the novels, correspondence, and memorabilia, are housed at the Regenstein Library of the University of Chicago. The Humanities Research Center at the University of Texas at Austin holds several manuscripts of *Seize the Day.*

WORK IN PROGRESS: Working on "many things at once."

SIDELIGHTS: Saul Bellow has pursued his career as a writer with a steady commitment to the art of fiction as an indispensable form of knowledge. His canon stands as an eloquent testament to the vital life of the human mind and spirit and to the power of art. "I feel," Bellow explained to Gordon L. Harper in an interview for the *Paris Review,* "that art has something to do with the achievement of stillness in the midst of chaos. A stillness which characterizes prayer, too, and the eye of the storm. I think art has something to do with an arrest of attention in the midst of distraction." Tommy Wilhelm of *Sieze the Day* and Artur Sammler of *Mr. Sammler's Planet* offer prayers out of such still centers amid turbulent emotional storms, and Eugene Henderson exclaims in *Henderson the Rain King* that "this is not a sick and hasty ride, helpless, through a dream into oblivion. No, sir! It can be arrested by a thing or two. By art, for instance. The speed is checked, the time is redivided. Measure! That great thought. Mystery." Bellow took Lionel Trilling and Arthur C. Clarke to task in *Harper's* for claiming that scientific truth, a manifestation of man's "maturity," will redeem society through technology "from the childish need for art," including the telling of stories to one another. "Science and technology," Bellow argued, "are not likely to remove this narrative and spellbinding oddity from the soul." But Bellow acknowledged that technology can be distracting to the artist and threatening to his art: "The present age has a certain rationalizing restlessness or cognitive irritability: a participatory delirium that makes the arresting powers of any work intolerable. . . . Technology has weakened certain points of spiritual rest. Wedding guests and ancient mariners both are deafened by the terrific blaring of the technological band."

In his Nobel Prize for Literature acceptance speech, delivered in Stockholm on December 12, 1976, Bellow reaffirmed his conviction that art is more important than science in exploring significant values in twentieth-century human experience. Following Marcel Proust, Bellow explained, "Only art penetrates what pride, passion, intelligence and habit erect on all sides—the seeming realities of this world. There is another reality, the genuine one, which we lose sight of. This other reality is always sending us hints, which, without art, we can't receive. Proust calls these hints our 'true impressions'. . . . The value of literature lies in these intermittent true impressions. . . . What [Joseph] Conrad said was true: art attempts to find in the universe, in matter as well as in the facts of life, what is fundamental, enduring, essential." To Bellow, the novel is "a sort of latter-day lean-to, a hovel in which the spirit takes shelter"; as such, the novel performs the same function that Robert Frost claimed for poetry; it provides "a momentary stay against confusion," and in a world where confusion has become king, momentary stillnesses and humble sanctuaries for the spirit are not insignificant contributions.

The three National Book Awards, the Pulitzer and Nobel Prizes, and the many other honors Bellow has received attest to the high quality he has established as a literary artist. In his essay "Where Do We Go from Here: The Future of Fiction," he has supplied a central standard for the evaluation of the novel: "It becomes art when the views most opposite to the author's own are allowed to exist in full strength. Without this a novel of ideas is mere self-indulgence, and didacticism is simply axe-grinding. The opposites must be free to range themselves against each other, and they must be passionately expressed on both sides. It is for this reason that I say it doesn't matter much what the writer's personal position is, what he wishes to affirm. He may affirm principles we all approve of and write very bad novels." Or as Philip Bummidge says in a Keatsian observation in Bellow's play *The Last Analysis,* "I am convinced that lies are bad art." Giving fair play to the opposition, working through murkiness to clarity, a novel earns its vision. For half a century, Bellow has striven in his work—his art—to give shape and substance to the abstractions by which human beings live. Although individual works have not always risen to his own highest standard, each contributes to a whole that demonstrates a writer deeply engaged with the complexity of human existence and fully committed to his art as a form of understanding; each work thus contributes to the survival of informed intelligence and humanistic culture. His versatility and willingness to take risks have led Bellow to extend his efforts to the short story (*Mosby's Memoirs, and Other Stories* and *Him with His Foot in His Mouth, and Other Stories*), the familiar essay, literary criticism, the drama, and the philosophical-political travelogue (*To Jerusalem and Back: A Personal Account*), but at the core of his art stand the novels.

Joseph, the Kafkaesque protagonist and Dostoevskian underground figure of *Dangling Man,* Bellow's first novel, dangles between the military nightmare of World War II and civilian economic opportunism, between the material world of action and the ideal world of thought, between detachment and involvement, life and death. A compulsive diarist and a man condemned to an existential freedom without moral precedent, Joseph is, as Tony Tanner describes him in *Saul Bellow,* "a man up to his neck in modern history. Joseph oscillates between corrosive inertia and compulsive self-inquiry, wrestling with irresolvable paradoxes of world and spirit which have a drastically deleterious effect on his character and bring him to the point of futility and exhaustion." As Joseph mismanages his freedom and perceives ever more vividly the disparity between his "ideal constructions" and the "craters of the spirit" that the real world places daily in his path, he grows less confident of his ability to understand the universe or to discern his proper identity in it. Finally, in quasi optimistic desperation, Joseph decides that he will find no answers in his detached state; thus he insists that his draft board subject him immediately to the same fate his countrymen are enduring. Marcus Klein has seen this movement toward community as part of a pattern in the contemporary American novel, a "strategy of accommodation." In *After Alienation: American Novels in Mid-Century* he observes, "Joseph must give himself to idiopathic freedom, and that way is madness, or submit to the community's ordinary, violent reality. He hurries his draft call. He surrenders." The novel records this ironically qualified "progress" from Joseph to G.I. Joe.

The journal form that Bellow employs to reveal Joseph's complexities is derivative and a bit contrived, as are the dialogues Joseph has with *Tu As Raison Aussi,* the Spirit of Alternatives. Joseph, however, is a compulsive—and egotistical—cogitator, and the journal and the dialogues are thus in character; furthermore, they provide useful cages for his cerebral pacings between "ideal constructions" and actual world wars, between "separate destinies" and "craters of the spirit." The intellectual vacillation and Joseph's ambivalent character give ample play to opposing ideas—and both prefigure the character of Moses E. Herzog. Joseph fails to formulate an intellectual construct that will reconcile him to the collapse of his old idealistic plans, but he does demonstrate the resilience to continue the search on other grounds. Although his concluding affirmation "Long live regimentation!" is ironic, he still intends to seek an answer to the basic Bellovian question, "How should a good man live?"

Asa Leventhal of *The Victim* is a good man, a middle-aged, happily married Jew who has unknowingly caused the gentile Kirby Allbee to lose his job. In his subsequent decline, Allbee becomes a drunk, loses his wife in an auto accident, and blames Leventhal—and by extension all Jews—for his wretchedness. Because he has always felt very tentative about his place in the scheme of things, Leventhal is susceptible to Allbee's unwarranted accusations and subsequent persecutions. Determining what he owes to himself and what he owes to others—that is, how he should live as a good man—becomes Leventhal's primary concern and the integrating principle in the novel.

The Victim develops on two levels, the realistic and the symbolic. At the realistic levels, its themes are guilt, fear of failure, anti-Semitism, and existential responsibility; and these themes are vividly embodied in the characterizations, the dialogue, and patterns of metaphor, especially those involving tickets and acting. These matters expand, however, to become questions of Death and Evil at the symbolic level, where Bellow draws heavily on classical mythology for the encounters of Levanthal with death, and on the American myth of guilt and redemption, Nathaniel Hawthorne's *The Scarlet Letter,* for his confrontation with guilt in the person of Allbee. Both realistic and symbolic levels function organically together under taut artistic control, yet the dense texture and symbolic richness have invited wide-ranging critical analyses.

In *Fiction of the Forties,* for example, Chester E. Eisinger sees the main thematic concerns of *The Victim* as anti-Semitism and existential responsibility: Asa is "a man who falls short of love and understanding and humanity. . . . His plight is a function of the anti-Semitism, real and imagined, that he feels engulfs him. Loaded with these disabilities [self-interest and fear of victimization] . . . Asa is asked to consider the nature and extent of one human being's responsibility to another." In *Saul Bellow's Fiction,* Irving Malin interprets *The Victim* as "a novel of fathers and sons." Leventhal rejects his natural father, is tyrannized by business fathers, disturbed by a kind of paternal conscience in Allbee, and becomes, first, a surrogate father to his nephews Mickey and Philip and to his brother Max and, finally, with his wife's pregnancy, a real father, thus achieving a natural and psychological resolution to his ambivalence toward fatherhood. According to Jonathan Baumbach's *The Landscape of Nightmare: Studies in the Contemporary Novel,* Allbee functions as Leventhal's psychological and symbolic double; he "is not the cause but the occasion of Leventhal's victimization—the objectification of his free-floating guilt. . . . Allbee is . . . the personification of his evil possibilities, . . . the grotesque exaggeration of his counterpart. He represents Leventhal's failings carried to their logical insanity." Only by acknowledging that he has such a counterpart can Leventhal come to terms with the evil in himself and thus become fully human. Keith Opdahl reaches a similar conclusion in *The Novels of Saul Bellow: An Introduction:* "Bellow subordinates the theme of man's fear of imaginary evil to that of man's denial of the real evil in the world and himself. Each of the characters, Bellows shows, views the other as a symbol of evil he would deny. The moral issue between the two men becomes an issue concerning the nature of the world and man's ability to face it." John J. Clayton claims in *Saul Bellow: In Defense of Man* that the theme of the book lies in Leventhal's "casting off of his self-imposed burdens by learning to accept himself and others rather than to judge and blame, by learning to have an open heart." Both Opdahl and Clayton mention in their discussions of plot the many parallels between Bellow's novel and Feodor Dostoevsky's *The Eternal Husband,* but James Hall, in *The Lunatic Giant in the Drawing Room,* sees Franz Kafka's *The Trial* and James Joyce's *Ulysses* as the two books "that obviously stand behind *The Victim.*"

The differences in focus and emphasis of these critical views point up the scope of meanings in the multi-layered complexity of Bellow's careful blending of realism and symbolism, a strategy that Bellow employed in both of his first two novels as, in part, a way of paying dues to the literary establishment and the tradition of the well-made novel. With Harper in the *Paris Review* interview, Bellow was explicit about his intent as a novelistic newcomer: "I think when I wrote those early books I was timid. I still felt the incredible effrontery of announcing myself to the world (in part I mean the WASP world) as a writer and an artist. I had to touch a great many bases, demonstrate my abilities, pay my respects to formal requirements. In short, I was afraid to let myself go." During the composition of *The Adventures of Augie March,* however, Bellow experienced a kind of artistic liberation: "When I began *Augie March,* I took off many of these restraints. I think I took off too many, and went too far, but I was feeling the excitement of discovery." In fact, as Bellow explained to Harvey Breit in *The Writer Observed,* "The great pleasure of the book was that it came easily. All I had to do was to be there with buckets to catch it."

A *Bildungsroman,* or novel of education, and a picaresque quest novel, *The Adventures of Augie March* traces Augie's erratic pursuit of a worthwhile fate. Telling his own story "free style," Augie relives his experiences for the reader from his boyhood in Chicago to his wanderings in Michigan, Mexico, and the African Sea to his maturity as a husband and import businessman in Paris. Augie encounters a Chaucerian pilgrimage of Bellovian characters, and from each Augie learns something about "bitterness in his chosen thing" and thus something about his search for a worthwhile fate. He does not find the fate he imagined, but he does affirm the validity of the search: "Columbus too," says Augie, "thought he was a flop, probably, when they sent him back in chains. Which didn't prove there was no America."

Despite Bellow's admission that he went "too far" and violated formal unity, *Augie March* does have a firm organizing principle, the tension of opposites. Refusing to lead a disappointed life, Augie seeks a worthwhile fate in accordance with what he calls the "axial lines of life," which lead one to "Truth, love, peace, bounty, usefulness, harmony." Augie is a free and optimistic spirit, but Bellow exposes him to characters, ideas, and situations inimical to his freedom and his optimism. The figure Kayo Obermark supplies a name for the negative factors, *moha,* the limitations imposed by the finite and imperfect, "the Bronx cheer of the conditioning forces." Einhorn's and Georgie's handicaps, Simon's monomania and loveless marriage, the superficiality of the Magnuses, the varied victimizations of Jimmy Klein and Mimi Villars, the limited love of Stella, the lost children everywhere—all testify to the power of *moha* and assail the fortress of Augie's dream of happiness on the axial lines of life. But Augie stands firm in his optimism, earning the book's affirmative vision through his awareness of life's dark side and his resilience in the face of it. "It is important to keep in mind," observes Brigitte Scheer-Schaezler in her study *Saul Bellow,* "that Augie's desire for life in the sun is not motivated by a shunning of action or a rejection of consciousness but arises from his knowledge of darkness, the darkness which he says has widened his outlook." "Indeed," says Sarah Blacher Cohen in the *Saul Bellow Journal,* "Augie is the picaresque apostle who, meeting up with errant humanity, eagerly listens to their confessions and generously pardons their sins, even blessing them for their antic trespasses."

To move from the sprawling and affirmative *The Adventures of Augie March* to the compact and brooding *Seize the Day* is to leave the circus for the court. One is colorful, spontaneous, cacophonous, alive; the other is formal, confessional, tense, fatalistic. Whereas Augie defines his humanity through his charm, striving, and compassion, Tommy Wilhelm defines his humanity through his slovenliness, selfishness, and suffering—and, most important, through his desire to be better than he is. A reader is drawn to both figures, a tribute to Bellow's powerful portraiture. The power grows to an extent out of a personal dimension of the novel. "The shrill quality of the marriage relationship between Tommy and his wife," writes Robert Detweiler in *Saul Bellow: A Critical Essay,* "may echo Bellow's own situation at the time. He worked on the story while living in a desert shack in Nevada and waiting out the residency requirements for a divorce." Four times divorced, Bellow inevitably allows his personal anguish to imbue his fiction. Herzog, whose "heart has been shat on," cries out, "*Will never understand what women want. . . . They eat green salad and drink human blood.*" Wilhelm's lonely cries about his wife and his life come "howling like a wolf from the city window."

An anti-hero, Wilhelm has messed up his life. By changing his name (Saul Bellow was born Solomon Bellows), dropping out of school, and failing in business, Tommy has embarrassed and alienated his father, Dr. Adler, a selfish retired physician. Out of his foolish pride, Wilhelm has quit a good job and now can find no other. His mismanagement of his life has led to estrangement from his wife and painful separation from his two boys. In loneliness and desperation, Wilhelm has turned for companionship and advice to a kind of surrogate father, Dr. Tamkin, a quack psychologist, aspiring poet, slick operator in the stock market, and mainline Bellovian reality-instructor. On the titular day depicted in *Seize the Day,* Wilhelm's lifelong miscalculations and bad judgments bring him to his knees. His father and wife turn deaf ears to his appeals for help, Tamkin abandons him after misguiding him into losing his last savings in the stock market, and Tommy ends the day crying unceasingly in a funeral home over the body of a stranger. The final scene is the nadir of Wilhelm's personal failure, the culmination in a symbolic drowning of a sustained pattern of water imagery in the story, and the conclusion of one of Bellow's bleakest but most tightly integrated novels.

"Wilhelm's drowning," notes Opdahl, "is first of all the climax of his day of failure. The water in which he drowns is both the world and his masochistic self which have murdered him." The masochistic self here is what Tamkin termed the "pretender soul"; its death at least opens the way for the emergence of Wilhelm's "true soul," but that redemptive possibility is not realized within the pages of the novel. Clinton W. Trowbridge observes in *Critique: Studies in Modern Fiction* that "the image of the drowning Wilhelm is the controlling one, but because of the book's ironic structure it is an image that functions in two ways. On a first reading, and on each rereading on the surface of our experience, it intensifies sympathy for Wilhelm's condition. Even when Wilhelm is being depicted least sympathetically, when he is most in the wrong, most a slob, we are continually made aware that we are witnessing the strugglings of a drowning man and we want to see him rescued." Writing in Earl Rovit's *Saul Bellow: A Collection of Critical Essays,* M. Gilbert Porter observes that "the unity of effect achieved in *Seize the Day* results from the skillful blending of all the elements of fiction in tightly constructed scenic units functioning very much like poetic images built around a controlling metaphor. Each scene extends the central image of Wilhelm's drowning by embodying a particular aspect of his life that has contributed to the pressure that finally overwhelms him in literal failure and symbolic death and rebirth. Unity is enhanced further by cross references between scenes." In its compactness, unity, and intensity, *Seize the Day* approaches the configuration of poetry.

In *Henderson the Rain King,* Bellow recaptured the spirit of *The Adventures of Augie March* in a spin-off verbal and comic riot of picaresque energy. At age fifty-five, the manic gentile Henderson stands six feet four, weighs two hundred and thirty pounds, has an M.A. from a prestigious eastern university, plus a second wife, seven children, a three-million-dollar estate, and a voice within him crying, "I want, I want, I want," which testifies to both his unhappiness and his aspiration. Although he has most of the things that Madison Avenue equates with human happiness, Henderson feels that a central element is missing from his life. His vigorous but bumbling quest to discover that element leads him through whimsical pig-farming, gratuitous violence, and antisocial behavior to Africa, where through exotic experiences with African tribes he determines that he can "burst the spirit's sleep" and still the voice within him by serving others as a physician in emulation of his hero Sir Wilfred Grenfill. In the final scene, his dance around the New York-bound plane with the lion cub and the Persian orphan during the refueling stop in symbolic Newfoundland is a rhapsodic celebration of his movement toward community and his confirmed new vision of the possibilities of life over death: "God does not shoot dice with our souls," cries the joyful Henderson, "and therefore grun-tu-molani. . . . I believe there is justice, and that much is promised." According to Walter Clemons and Jack Kroll in a *Newsweek* interview with the author, "Of all his characters, Bellow has said, Henderson, the quixotic seeker of higher truth, is most like himself."

The theme of the novel is a recurrent one in Bellow's fiction: that the world is tough and mysterious, that man is subject to great errors and subsequent pain, but that he yearns for nobility and joy and feels in his deepest soul that such things are possible. The disparity between the exalted aspiration and the flawed self that aspires is, of course, comic. "*Henderson the Rain King* is clearly Bellow's most full-blown comic novel," writes Cohen in *Saul Bellow's Enigmatic Laughter.* "The dreaded nightmare experiences of the earlier realistic novels are transformed into the playful and dreamlike episodes of romance. The comic flaws which the early heroes were often too obtuse to notice are magnified in Henderson, who both flamboyantly exhibits them and exorcises them through his own jocose language."

The comic development of Henderson assumes many forms. Opdahl has shown that the novel is in part a good-natured satire on Ernest Hemingway and the Code Hero. At least three critics have explored waste land motifs, vegetation myths, and related anthropological matters appropriate for a novelist who holds a bachelor's degree in anthropology: Elsie Leach in *Western Humanities Review,* Detweiler in *Modern Fiction Studies,* and Howard Harper in *Desperate Faith.* Klein has shown in *After Alienation* that Henderson's growth is complemented by a pattern of animal imagery involving cats, camels, frogs, octopuses, cows, and bears as Henderson is transformed from pig farmer to lion-like kingly spirit. His development is also supported by an elaborate matrix of music and musical allusion as Henderson, singer and violinist manque, moves from native drums and flutes to Mozart and Handel. Bellow obviously had fun writing this novel, as he did writing "Deep Readers of the World, Beware!," the warning in the *New York Times Book Review* to symbol hunters that preceded the publication of the book: "Novels are being published today which consist entirely of abstractions, meanings, and while our need for meanings is certainly great our need for concreteness, for particulars, is even greater. . . . We must leave it to inspiration to redeem the concrete and the particular and to recover the value of flesh and bone." In the massive Henderson, whose face is like an "unfinished church," flesh and bones dance a joyful meaning and a defiance of death in the pure snow of Newfoundland.

The ebullience of Henderson is transformed into erudition in his successor, Herzog. "What this country needs," says Herzog, "is a good five-cent synthesis." His frantic attempts to formulate such a synthesis to shore up his disintegrating life is the substance of *Herzog,* Bellow's most well-wrought novel. An older Joseph, a more knowing Henderson, Herzog seeks clarity and justice as a professor of history with a Ph.D. and an impressive professional bibliography. But with the discovery that his wife, Madeleine, and his good friend Gersbach have made him a cuckold and abandoned him to his isolated personal fate, Herzog finds himself lost in the modernist waste land of cynical "reality instructors" and existential nothingness, "down in the mire of post-Renaissance, post-humanistic, post-Cartesian dissolution, next door to the void." Such hostile territory is particularly hard on a sensitive intellectual whose sensibilities are at war with his intellect. With his feelings, he resists the negations of the reality instructors, but the chaotic evidence of his personal life makes an intellectual assent to their conclusions almost irresistible. His final transcendence of their teachings and his own anguish in the pastoral setting of Ludeyville testifies to the power Herzog discovers in simple being and the "law of the heart"; at peace at last, he says, "*I am pretty well satisfied to be, to be just as it is willed, and for as long as I may remain in occupancy.*"

The stress and resolution in *Herzog* is typical of the Bellow canon. "It is this problem," Alfred Kazin says in *Contemporaries,* "first of representing all that a man intends and plans and then of getting him not merely to recognize the countervailing strength of life but to humble himself before it, that is the real situation in all Bellow's novels." Where Kazin sees acceptance and submission, Ihab Hassan, in *Radical Innocence: Studies in the Contemporary American Novel,* sees affirmation in the protagonist as the sequel to his conflict between self and the world: "the movement is from acid defeat to acceptance, and from acceptance to celebration. The querulous and ill-natured hero becomes prodigal and quixotic. In this process something of the dignity that the fictional hero has lost to history is restored to him."

A majority of critics agree, as Harold Bloom observes in the Modern Critical Views collection *Saul Bellow,* that *Herzog* "seems to be Bellow's best and most representative novel." Minority reports have been filed, however. In *Time to Murder and Create,* John W. Aldridge sees the novel "as the Waste Land cliche irrigated and transformed in the Promised Land, while the platitude of Alienation is converted into the even hoarier platitude of Accommodation and Togetherness. For what he finally holds up for our inspection is a new hopeful doctrine of potato love not uncolored by righteous disdain." Richard Poirier, in Rovit's *Saul Bellow: A Collection of Critical Essays,* dismisses the novel as empty rhetoric and its author as intellectually dishonest: "What I call the gap in his novels between their intellectual and historical pretensions, on one side, and the stuff of life as he renders it, on the other, prevents me from believing that he is himself convinced by his snappy contempt for 'the commonplaces of the Waste Land outlook, the cheap mental stimulants of Alienation.' " Such a cavil sounds faint amid the general clamor of praise for *Herzog,* in which Bellow displays his shiniest wares, and whose protagonist seems to represent a culmination of all Bellow's key characters: thinker, victim, sufferer (but a "suffering joker"), quester, struggler, sinner, and, at last, affirmer.

Bellow's seventh novel, *Mr. Sammler's Planet,* is an indignant depiction of contemporary America from the perspective of one of Bellow's most formidable "men thinking," Sammler, Cracow-born Anglophile in his seventies and Jewish survivor of a Nazi pogrom in Poland. His war injuries have left him with a tempered post-grave detachment and vision in only one eye. Thus Sammler sees outward and inward. His good right eye records characters, actions, and events in the world around him. His blind left eye subjects current events to introspective analysis, the historical and philosophical perspective. "The damaged eye seemed to turn in another direction, to be preoccupied separately with different matters." The novel oscillates, then, from action to reflection as Sammler tries to make sense of a planet that seems to be coming unglued. Within that general strategy there are complementary movements from past to present, from public to private, from life to death. Three obliquely related plots provide the structural matrix of the narrative: 1) a Black pickpocket who plies his trade on the Forty-second Street Bus and exposes his penis to Sammler to warn him not to interfere; 2) a book manuscript on space travel and inhabitation of the moon stolen from its author, Dr. Govinda Lal, by Sammler's daughter, Shula; and 3) the slow dying of Dr. Gruner from an aneurysm in his brain. Interspersed are a number of encounters with assorted crazies Sammler must endure.

Bellow told Jane Howard in an interview for *Life* that *Mr. Sammler's Planet* is his own favorite work: "I had a high degree of excitement writing it . . . and finished it in record time. It's my first thoroughly nonapologetic venture into ideas. In *Herzog* . . . and *Henderson the Rain King* I was kidding my way to Jesus, but here I'm baring myself nakedly." The novel and this statement about it marked a shift in proportion in Bellow's art, as abstraction began to overshadow concretion. The change has elicited mixed responses. Robert R. Dutton, in Twayne's *Saul Bellow,* calls the novel "Bellow's highest technical achievement," and Scheer-Schaezler, in support of what she calls "enlarged vision," describes the book as representative of "Bellow's effort to turn the novel into a medium of inquiry. In Bellow's most recent novels, experiences are not so much being undergone as discussed in a probing approach that may well be called essayistic." In the same vein, Nathan A. Scott, Jr., declares approvingly in *Three American Moralists: Mailer, Bellow, Trilling* that Bellow's "insistently didactic intention has had the effect of making rhetoric itself—rather than action and character—the main source of the essential energies in his fiction. And there is perhaps no other comparable body of work in the literature of the contemporary novel so drenched in ideas and speculations and theories, even commandments."

Other critics, however, have felt that Bellow's expository treatment of ideas in *Mr. Sammler's Planet* vitiates his art. David Galloway writes in *Modern Fiction Studies* that Bellow's emphasis on ideas leads to a failure of imagination, a too easy recourse to stock situations and well-worn character pairings. "The central problem in Bellow's novels," contends Galloway, is that "the imaginative structure fails to provide adequate support for the intellectual structure, so that at crucial moments the author's ideas fail to be organically embodied in character, action, or image." In her review in the *Nation,* Beverly Gross describes the scene at Columbia when Sammler is confronted by a heckler, a mere straw man in her view, as symptomatic of the fundamental flaw in the novel: "When an artist who is no blunderer—and Bellow is a supreme artist—furnishes so false a moment, it is something of a revelation. Bellow has failed to give credibility to the opposition." Benjamin DeMott, writing for *Saturday Review,* finds abstractions vivid in the novel but concretions pale. For example, Sammler's detachment, says DeMott, "attains insufficient substance for the reader, seemingly belonging only to the surface structure of Sammler's mind and story . . . whereas his scorn and vituperation come forth strongly as from the center." Baring himself as ideologist and didact in *Mr. Sammler's Planet,* Bellow ran the risk of violating the principle he set forth in "Where Do We Go from Here" of giving fair play to opposing ideas, but perhaps he did so to counter a movement in fiction, like Hemingway's, that represents ideas but forbids thought. "It shows," Bellow explained in the same essay, "a great skepticism of the strength of art. It makes it appear as though ideas openly expressed would be too much for art to bear."

In *Humboldt's Gift,* Bellow managed to check his growing impulse toward abstraction at the expense of concretion. Like *Herzog, Humboldt's Gift* strikes an aesthetically functional symmetry between idea and image. The novel tells the story of intellectual Chicagoan Charlie Citrine, Pulitzer Prize-winning biographer and dramatist, who approaches the completion of his sixth decade in the company of the nimbus of his deceased poetic mentor, Von Humboldt Fleisher, and the nemesis of his self-appointed materialistic advisor, Rinaldo Cantabile, both manic manipulators. The dead poet speaks to Citrine of his obligation to his creative spirit, art as power. The minor-league Mafioso Cantabile urges capitalistic enterprise, art as profit. Citrine ultimately frees himself from both figures, and at the end walks from the new grave he has provided for Humboldt into an ambivalently emerging spring to begin a meditative life away from the distractions of dissident voices and grotesque behavior.

Charlie's compulsive flights into metaphysical explanations have to contend with the corrective pragmatism of his earthy mistress, Renata: "I prefer to take things as billions of people have throughout history. You work, you get bread, you lose a leg, kiss some fellows, have a baby, you live to be eighty and bug hell out of everybody, or you get hung or drowned. But you don't spend years trying to dope your way out of the human condition. . . . I think when you're dead you're dead, and that's that." Such views lead Renata to abandon the hyperintellectual Citrine and choose an undertaker for a husband, a marriage with death.

Charlie resists Renata's reality-instructor text by clinging to a message from the dead poet: "Remember: we are not natural beings but supernatural beings," a spiritual reinforcement of Charlie's natural impulses that represents Humboldt's real gift to his protege.

"The novel therefore explores," says Judie Newman in *Saul Bellow and History,* "different approaches to history and retreats from history: pop history, instant history, history as nightmare, as tragedy, as farce, the retreat into myth or transcendence, or into the eternal present of the crisis mentality. By the novel's various structurings of time, Bellow succeeds in avoiding any one style of approach and thereby liberates the event to be judged in its total context, as it affects its participants, as it is recorded in public records, and as it is inherited, transformed and translated by succeeding generations." Bellow himself says in the *Newsweek* interview, "*Humboldt* is very much a comic book about death," and he sees it as an advance in his own authorial detachment and his function as social historian: "The nice thing about this book, which I was really struggling with in *Herzog,* is that I've really come into a cold air of objectivity about all the people in the book, including Charlie. It really came easily for me to see him as America saw him, and thereby America itself became clearer." Despite Bellow's claim of objectivity, the novel contains several elements of his own personal history—the poker game, for example, and the interest in Steinerian philosophy, which Bellow came to by way of Owen Barfield's *Saving the Appearances.* "Does he mean it?—all this business of the soul and an afterlife, and especially about [Rudolf] Steiner and his anthroposophy [or man-centered religious system]," asks Dutton in his revised *Saul Bellow.* "Yes," he answers, "Bellow does—at least figuratively. As far as Steiner is concerned, he is a figure for an illustration of Bellow's contention, through Charlie, that we must try new ideas, even ideas that are unscientific, and hence, that tend to inhibit us. . . . Charlie triumphs over his inhibitions and is able to go ahead with his irrational studies." Still, several critics have observed that there is a shrugging what-the-hell tone about Charlie's experimental commitment to anthroposophy as well as about his shifty character generally that undermines much of his compulsive philosophizing. The novel plays for laughs—and gets them—but it does so in large measure at the expense of its ostensibly serious purposes.

The humor that dominates *Humboldt's Gift* is conspicuously absent in the ninth novel, *The Dean's December,* in a continuation of the upbeat-downbeat, see-saw pattern of Bellow's fiction. As a journalist turned academic, Dean Albert Corde has accompanied his Romanian-born wife, Minna, to Bucharest to attend her dying mother, Valeria. Isolated in his room or cruising the streets as a "hungry observer" and a "moralist of seeing," Corde observes Bucharest and reflects on Chicago, a city whose "whirling lives" typify the chaotic American reality. The communist and the capitalist cities are grim places of different but related forms of disorder, injustice, repression, and destruction; they are yoked by violence together, for death is everywhere: "I imagine, sometimes," Corde thinks, "that if a film could be made of one's life, every other frame would be death." This macabre mood is sustained throughout the novel even though at the end, after Valeria's death, Corde is comforted briefly by a renewed closeness to his wife that somehow has its counterpart in his closeness to the heavens in the great telescope of the Mount Palomar Observatory. Although he is cold there, he tells his guide, significantly, as they descend, "But I almost mind coming down more"—that is, coming down to earth, where robbery, rape, murder, prejudice, and political injustice mock the human quest for order, beauty, love, and justice. The novel is a dark and brooding ethical statement.

Some of the darkness of *The Dean's December* grew out of Bellow's personal experience. Bellow told William Kennedy in *Esquire* that he wrote the novel "in a year and a half . . . and had no idea it was coming. One of these things that came over me. My wife's mother was dying in Bucharest, and I went with her to give her some support, which in that place one badly needs. The old mother died while we were there." Part of the grimness grew out of actual events, like a sensational Chicago rape case, and out of factual conditions, like the Cabrini Green housing project in Chicago, but most of the pessimism came from Bellow's increasing conviction that the decline of civilization is magnified in American cities. Malcolm Bradbury writes in *The Modern American Novel* that *The Dean's December* "confirms the later Bellow as the novelist of a world which has lost cultural bearings, moved into an age of boredom and terror, violence and indifference, private wealth and public squalor." Bellow himself has been very explicit about his intentions in the novel. He told Matthew C. Roudane in an interview for *Contemporary Literature* that the decaying city has its counterpart in an "inner slum": "What I meant was there is a correspondence between outer and inner, between the brutalized city and the psyche of its citizens. Given their human resources I don't see how people today can experience life at all. Politicians, public figures, professors address 'modern problems' solely in terms of employment. They assume that unemployment causes incoherence, sexual disorders, the abandonment of children, robbery, rape and murder. Plainly, they have no imagination of these evils. They don't even *see* them. And in *The Dean's December* what I did was to say, 'Look!' The first step is to display the facts. But the facts, unless the imagination perceives them, are *not* facts. Perhaps I shouldn't say 'perceives'—I should say 'passionately takes hold.' As an artist does. Mr. Corde, the Dean, passionately takes hold of Chicago and writes his articles like an artist rather than a journalist. . . . It is Corde's conviction that without art, it is impossible to interpret reality, and that the degeneration of art and language leads to the decay of judgment." Ironically, an exchange of styles seems to occur, in effect, between Corde and Bellow, for the passionate intensity that allows Corde's journalism to rise to the status of art—as Bellow describes it here—leads Bellow's prose in the novel as a whole to assume the condition of journalism, the documentary, or, as Roudane observes, "a nonfiction novelistic style," an extension of the essayistic prose that has become more prominent in Bellow's later novels. The result, thematically, is a kind of war correspondent's report on the sobering spectacle of the human race mindlessly consuming its own entrails and indifferent to the art that might save it.

Bellow returns to the comic mode in his tenth novel, *More Die of Heartbreak,* a turgid, almost plotless story of two academics connected less by their blood kinship than by their similarly oblique relations to women and to everyday reality. The narrator is thirty-five-year-old Kenneth Tractenberg, a professor of Russian literature at a university in the Midwest. His beloved uncle, Benn Crader, is an internationally respected botanist whose specialty is Arctic lichens and whose patterns of practical misjudgment make him think of himself as "a phoenix who runs with arsonists." Kenneth, though, admires his uncle for reasons that are not clear. Kenneth's philandering father offers his son a sarcastic but perhaps accurate explanation: "you're one of those continuing-education types and you think Benn still has something to teach you." Although intelligent and ceaselessly introspective, Kenneth and Uncle Benn are curious naifs. Kenneth is at great pains to marry Treckie, the mother of his illegitimate daughter and a woman who rejects him to live with a sadist and travel the flea-market circuits. Uncle Benn marries a spoiled rich girl, Matilda Layamon, whose physician father maneuvers to recover Benn's lost inheritance from crooked Uncle Vilitzer so that Matilda can continue to live a life of pampered ease. Benn escapes both the solicitousness of Kenneth and the machinations of the Layamons, finally, by a Charlie Citrine-like retreat to the North Pole to study lichens.

Kenneth's explicit purpose as narrator is "to relate the strange turns in the life of my Uncle Benn," but his narrative—and Bellow's novel—is glossed by his self-assessment: "I was unusually—that is, emotionally—open to associations. It was esthetically intoxicating to entertain them all. Furthermore, it was characteristic—it was me: me as it excited me to be, fully experiencing the fantastic, the bizarre facts of contemporary reality, making no particular effort to impose my cognitions on them. I didn't especially wish to make sense; I wanted only to follow the intoxicating flow of those facts." The novel abounds with the "bizarre facts of contemporary reality": premarital foreshadowings in Charles Addams cartoons and Alfred Hitchcock movies, a crudely intense Japanese strip show, close-up views of the balding crotches of ancient women, a parade of rapacious relatives, and a plastic azalea that comforts the famous botanist for several weeks because he mistakes it for real. The technique of association, digression, and discursiveness is often amusing, but the focus is blurred, and the intentions of the novel—beyond Kenneth's disclaimer—seem vague and thus unrealized. The novel resembles the plastic azalea; it seems to be the genuine article, but it does not bear up well under close scrutiny.

Although *More Die of Heartbreak* was generally well–received, critical response to *More Die of Heartbreak* has been characterized by qualified praise and reluctantly held reservations. "Kenneth's free-ranging mind allows Bellow to put just about everything real and imaginable into this novel," notes Robert Wilson in *USA Today.* "Even so, Kenneth does not seem to me to be among the best of Bellow's characters, nor this among the best of Bellow's comic novels. Kenneth wore me out, especially when his divagations took us so far from the plot that it was barely a memory." Clemons, in *Newsweek,* finds the supporting characters more appealing than the principals: "It's a slight drawback to *More Die of Heartbreak* that the innocents in the foreground, Uncle Benn and Kenneth, are upstaged by their captivating adversaries. . . . Our time with Benn and Kenneth is well spent for the sake of the rascals to whom they introduce us." Rhoda Koenig, reviewing for *New York,* contends that the sympathy implicit in the title is overshadowed by an intelligence that fails to sustain its own weight: "But Bellow's heart seems to be more with the brutal comedy of the doctor than all his sodden mind games with Kenneth and Benn. In *More Die of Heartbreak,* despite the often voiced concern epitomized by the title, it is the mind that is given center stage, and fails to hold it." On the other hand, in the *New York Times Book Review,* William Gaddis judges the return of the wry Bellovian humor an ample trade-off for a makeshift plot: "In *More Die of Heartbreak* we welcome back the calamitous wit of *The Adventures of Augie March* and *Herzog* among people diligently struggling to rearrange one another's lives in their efforts to rescue or simply to define their own. . . . We hear their voices pour from the pages engulfing a plot that is comparatively simple, or would be if left to itself, a possibility this embattled narrator never entertains for a moment." In sum, Bellow's tenth novel has been received as a pleasant but sometimes trying entertainment; it has generated respectful applause but few bravos and no standing ovations.

But Bellow is not greatly affected by critical opinion. In his Cockefair Lecture "The Novel in a Technological Age," delivered in Kansas City in 1973, he observed with typical drollery that "in the sea of literature, there are more ichthyologists than fish." He is not daunted by occasional detractors; he is not inflated by his constant admirers. Defiance of the one or deference to the other would be destructive to his art, and his art is what concerns him. Rovit's comment in his 1967 study *Saul Bellow* that "the seminal image in all of Bellow's fiction is not the image of a man seeking, but that of a man brooding in the midst of his solitude" seems particularly applicable to Bellow himself as he sits alone with his books and his thoughts in the autumn of his life. His thoughts are, as always, of his work and of his world. Despite the charges that his later novels are repetitious and too essayistic, Bellow feels comfortable with his current creative direction. He told David N. Prescott in *Mature Outlook* that his fiction is improving: "Yeah, I think I am getting better. I can think of any number of writers who got better as they got older. Thomas Harding [Hardy] got very good. Ibsen wrote some of his best things when he was older. The painter Titian got really hot when he was in his 80s. Sophocles also wrote some of his very best things in his 80s." And to Clemons, in *Newsweek,* Bellow said, "a writer in his 60s and 70s always has subjects laid aside. Will they be ripe when I'm 90? It's a good reason to hang in there." And his view of the world? "Maybe civilization *is* dying," Bellow remarked to Howard in the *Life* interview, "but it still exists, and meanwhile we have our choice; we can either rain more blows on it, or try to redeem it." For Bellow, redemptive work is the art of fiction, and he continues to do his work with all his might.

MEDIA ADAPTATIONS: "The Wrecker" was televised in 1964; a sound recording of the Chicago Radio Theatre presentation of the plays "Orange Souffle" and "The Wrecker" was produced by All-Media Dramatic Workshop, 1978; a television adaptation of *Seize the Day,* featuring Robin Williams and a cameo appearance by Bellow, was broadcast by Public Broadcasting Service, May 1, 1987.

BIOGRAPHICAL/CRITICAL SOURCES:

BOOKS

Authors in the News, Volume 2, Gale, 1976.
Aldridge, John W., *Time to Murder and Create,* McKay, 1966.
Bakker, J., *Fiction as Survival Strategy: A Comparative Study of the Major Works of Ernest Hemingway and Saul Bellow,* Humanities Press, 1983.
Baumbach, Jonathan, *The Landscape of Nightmare: Studies in the Contemporary Novel,* New York University Press, 1965.
Bellow, Saul, *Dangling Man,* Vanguard, 1944.
Bellow, *The Victim,* Vanguard, 1947.
Bellow, *The Adventures of Augie March,* Viking, 1953.
Bellow, *Seize the Day,* Viking, 1956.
Bellow, *Henderson the Rain King,* Viking, 1959.
Bellow, *Herzog,* Viking, 1964.
Bellow, *The Last Analysis, a Play,* Viking, 1966.
Bellow, *Mosby's Memoirs, and Other Stories,* Viking, 1968.
Bellow, *Mr. Sammler's Planet,* Viking, 1970.
Bellow, *Humboldt's Gift,* Viking, 1975.
Bellow, *To Jerusalem and Back: A Personal Account,* Viking, 1976.
Bellow, *The Nobel Lecture,* Targ Editions, 1979.
Bellow, *The Dean's December,* Harper, 1982.
Bellow, *Him with His Foot in His Mouth, and Other Stories,* Harper, 1984.
Bellow, *More Die of Heartbreak,* Morrow, 1987.

Bloom, Harold, editor, *Saul Bellow,* Chelsea House, 1986.
Bradbury, Malcolm, *The Modern American Novel,* Oxford University Press, 1983.
Breit, Harvey, *The Writer Observed,* World Publishing, 1956.
Clayton, John J., *Saul Bellow: In Defense of Man,* Indiana University Press, 1968, 2nd edition, 1979.
Cohen, Sarah Blacher, *Saul Bellow's Enigmatic Laughter,* University of Illinois Press, 1974.
Concise Dictionary of American Literary Biography: The New Consciousness, 1941-1968, Gale, 1987.
Contemporary Authors Autobiography Series, Gale, Volume 1, 1984.
Contemporary Fiction in America and England, 1950-1970, Gale, 1976.
Contemporary Literary Criticism, Gale, Volume 1, 1973, Volume 2, 1974, Volume 3, 1975, Volume 6, 1976, Volume 8, 1978, Volume 10, 1979, Volume 13, 1980, Volume 15, 1980, Volume 25, 1983, Volume 33, 1985, Volume 34, 1985.
Detweiler, Robert, *Saul Bellow: A Critical Essay,* Eerdmans, 1967.
Conversations with Contemporary American Writers, Rodopi, 1985.
Cronin, Gloria L. and Blaine H. Hall, *Saul Bellow: An Annotated Bibliography,* 2nd edition, Garland Publishing, 1987.
Dictionary of Literary Biography, Gale, Volume 2: *American Novelists since World War II,* 1978, Volume 28: *Twentieth-Century American Jewish Fiction Writers,* 1984.
Dictionary of Literary Biography Yearbook, 1982, Gale, 1983.
Dutton, Robert R., *Saul Bellow,* Twayne, 1971, revised edition, 1982.
Eisinger, Chester E., *Fiction of the Forties,* University of Chicago Press, 1963.
Fuchs, Daniel, *Saul Bellow: Vision and Revision,* Duke University Press, 1984.
Galloway, David D., *The Absurd Hero in American Fiction: Updike, Styron, Bellow, Salinger,* University of Texas Press, 1966, revised edition, 1970, 2nd revised edition, 1981.
Geismar, Maxwell, *American Moderns: From Rebellion to Conformity,* Hill & Wang, 1958.
Hall, James, *The Lunatic Giant in the Drawing Room,* Indiana University Press, 1968.
Handy, William J., *Modern Fiction: A Formalist Approach,* Southern Illinois University Press, 1971.
Harper, Howard, *Desperate Faith: A Study of Bellow, Salinger, Mailer, Baldwin, and Updike,* University of North Carolina Press, 1967.
Harris, Mark, *Saul Bellow: Drumlin Woodchuck,* University of Georgia Press, 1980.
Hassan, Ihab, *Radical Innocence: Studies in the Contemporary American Novel,* Harper, 1966.
Hendin, Josephine, *Vulnerable People: A View of American Fiction since 1945,* Oxford University Press, 1978.
Howe, Irving, editor, *Saul Bellow: Herzog; Text and Criticism,* Viking, 1976.
Iwayama, Tajiro, editor, *Saul Bellow,* Yamaguchi Shoten (Kyoto, Japan), 1982.
Kazin, Alfred, *Contemporaries,* Little, Brown, 1962.
Kiernan, Robert F., *Saul Bellow,* Continuum, 1989.
Klein, Marcus, *After Alienation: American Novels in Mid-Century,* World Publishing, 1965.
Kulshrestha, Chirantan, *Saul Bellow: The Problem of Affirmation,* Arnold-Heinemann (New Delhi), 1978.
Lercangee, Francine, *Saul Bellow: A Bibliography of Secondary Sources,* Center for American Studies (Brussels), 1977.
Malin, Irving, *Jews and Americans,* Southern Illinois University Press, 1965.
Malin, editor, *Saul Bellow and the Critics,* New York University Press, 1967.
Malin, *Saul Bellow's Fiction,* Southern Illinois University Press, 1969.
McCadden, Joseph F., *The Flight from Women in the Fiction of Saul Bellow,* University Press of America, 1980.
McConnell, Frank D., *Four Post-War American Novelists: Bellow, Mailer, Barth, and Pynchon,* Chicago University Press, 1977.
Moore, Harry T., editor, *Contemporary American Novelists,* Southern Illinois University Press, 1964.
Nault, Marianne, *Saul Bellow: His Works and His Critics; An Annotated International Bibliography,* Garland Publishing, 1977.
Newman, Judie, *Saul Bellow and History,* St. Martin's, 1984.
Noreen, Robert G., *Saul Bellow: A Reference Guide,* G. K. Hall, 1978.
Opdahl, Keith, *The Novels of Saul Bellow: An Introduction,* Pennsylvania State University Press, 1967.
Porter, M. Gilbert, *Whence the Power?: The Artistry and Humanity of Saul Bellow,* University of Missouri Press, 1974.
Rodrigues, Eusebio L., *Quest for the Human: An Exploration of Saul Bellow's Fiction,* Bucknell University Press, 1981.
Rovit, Earl, *Saul Bellow,* University of Minnesota Press, 1967.
Rovit, editor, *Saul Bellow: A Collection of Critical Essays,* Prentice-Hall, 1975.
Rupp, Richard H., *Celebration in Postwar American Fiction,* University of Miami Press, 1970.
Scheer-Schaezler, Brigitte, *Saul Bellow,* Ungar, 1972.
Schraepen, Edmond, editor, *Saul Bellow and His Work,* Free University of Brussels, 1978.
Schultz, Max F., *Radical Sophistication: Studies in Contemporary Jewish/American Novelists,* Ohio University Press, 1969.
Scott, Nathan A., Jr., *Three American Moralists: Mailer, Bellow, Trilling,* University of Notre Dame Press, 1968.
Sokoloff, B. A. and Mark Posner, *Saul Bellow: A Comprehensive Bibliography,* Folcroft Library Editions, 1972.
Tanner, Tony, *Saul Bellow,* Oliver & Boyd, 1965.
Tanner, *City of Words: American Fiction 1950-1970,* Harper, 1971.
Trachtenberg, Stanley, editor, *Critical Essays on Saul Bellow,* G. K. Hall, 1979.
Weinberg, Helen, *The New Novel in America: The Kafkan Mode in Contemporary Fiction,* Cornell University Press, 1970.
Wilson, Jonathan, *On Bellow's Planet: Readings from the Dark Side,* Fairleigh Dickinson University Press, 1986.

PERIODICALS

Accent, Volume 18, 1958.
American Literature, Volume 43, number 2, 1971.
Atlantic, January, 1965.
Centennial Review, Volume 22, 1978.
Chicago Jewish Forum, Volume 28, 1959.
Chicago Review, Volume 23, number 4, 1972.
College English, Volume 34, 1973.
College Language Association Journal, Volume 10, 1967.
Comparative Literature Studies, Volume 3, number 2, 1966.
Contemporary Literature, Volume 25, number 3, 1984.
Critical Quarterly, Volume 15, 1973.
Criticism, Volume 15, number 3, 1973.
Critique: Studies in Modern Fiction, Volume 3, 1960, Volume 7, 1965, Volume 9, 1967, Volume 9, 1968.

Durham University Journal, Volume 72, number 1, 1979.
Encounter, Volume 24, number 2, 1965, Volume 45, number 5, 1975.
Esquire, February, 1982.
Essays in Literature, Volume 5, 1979.
Forum, Volume 7, 1969, Volume 14, number 1, 1976.
Georgia Review, winter, 1978.
Harper's, August, 1974.
Hudson Review, Volume 12, 1959.
Historical Reflections, Volume 3, number 2, 1976.
Indian Journal of American Studies, Volume 8, number 2, 1978.
Journal of American Studies, Volume 7, 1973, Volume 9, 1975, Volume 15, 1981.
Judaism, Volume 22, 1972.
Life, April 3, 1970.
Listener, February 13, 1975.
Literary Times, December, 1964.
Mature Outlook, Volume 1, number 3, 1984.
McNeese Review, Volume 24, 1977-78.
Midstream, Volume 10, number 4, 1964.
Modern Fiction Studies, Volume 12, 1966-67, Volume 17, 1971, Volume 19, 1973, Volume 25, 1979.
Nation, February 9, 1970.
New England Review, Volume 1, 1972.
Newsweek, September 1, 1975, June 8, 1987.
New York, June 8, 1987.
New Yorker, September 15, 1975.
New York Times Book Review, February 15, 1959, May 9, 1971, May 24, 1987.
New York Times Magazine, November 21, 1978.
Notes on Modern American Literature, Volume 2, number 4, 1978.
Paris Review, Volume 9, number 36, 1966.
Partisan Review, Volume 26, number 3, 1959.
People, September 8, 1975.
Rolling Stone, March 4, 1982.
St. Louis Post-Dispatch, November 16, 1986.
Salmagundi, Volume 30, 1975 (special Bellow issue).
Saturday Review, February 7, 1970.
Saturday Review of Literature, August 22, 1953, September 19, 1953, September 19, 1964.
Saul Bellow Journal, Volume 4, number 1, 1985, Volume 5, numbers 1 and 2, 1986, Volume 6, number 1, 1987.
Saul Bellow Newsletter, Volume 1, number 1, 1981.
Show, September, 1964.
South Carolina Review, Volume 6, number 1, 1973.
Southern Review, Volume 3, number 1, 1967.
Southwest Review, Volume 62, 1977.
Studies in the Literary Imagination, Volume 17, number 2, 1984 (special Bellow issue).
Studies in the Novel, Volume 1, number 3, 1969.
Studies in the Twentieth Century, Volume 14, 1974.
Twentieth Century Literature, Volume 18, number 4, 1972.
University Review, Volume 37, number 1, 1970.
USA Today, June 5, 1987.
Wascana Review, Volume 6, number 1, 1971.
Western Humanities Review, Volume 14, 1960.

—Sidelights by M. Gilbert Porter

* * *

BENJAMIN, Lois
See GOULD, Lois

BENSTOCK, Bernard 1930-

PERSONAL: Born March 23, 1930, in New York, N.Y.; son of Sol (a carpenter) and Lily (Garde) Benstock; married Eve Cohen, May 28, 1959; married Shari Gabrielson (an English professor), May 6, 1973; children: (first marriage) Kevin, Erika (daughters). *Education:* Brooklyn College (now Brooklyn College of the City University of New York), A.B., 1950; Columbia University, M.A., 1954; Florida State University, Ph.D., 1957. *Politics:* "Not codifiable in a word or phrase." *Religion:* None.

ADDRESSES: Office—Department of English, University of Miami, Coral Gables, Fla. 33124.

CAREER: Louisiana State University, Baton Rouge, 1957-65, began as instructor, became assistant professor of English; Kent State University, Kent, Ohio, associate professor, 1965-67, professor of English, 1967-74; University of Illinois at Urbana-Champaign, professor of English and comparative literature, 1974-82, director of program in comparative literature, 1978-82; University of Tulsa, Tulsa, Okla., chairman of department of foreign languages and comparative literature, 1982-85, director of program in literature and society, 1985-86; University of Miami, Coral Gables, Fla., professor of English, 1986—. Fulbright lecturer in American literature, University of Tabriz, Tabriz, Iran, 1961-62. Has lectured on James Joyce in United States, Canada, Ireland, France, West Germany, Belgium, Italy, Yugoslavia, and India. *Military service:* U.S. Army, 1951-53; Public Information Office correspondent and editor in Korea, 1952-53.

MEMBER: International James Joyce Foundation (member of board of trustees, 1967—; president, 1971-77), International Association of Professors of English, American Comparative Literature Association, Modern Language Association of America, Popular Culture Association, South Central Modern Language Association (chairman of comparative literature section, 1966; chairman of Anglo-Irish literature, 1988).

WRITINGS:

Joyce-again's Wake: An Analysis of Finnegans Wake, University of Washington Press, 1965.
Sean O'Casey, Bucknell University Press, 1971.
(Editor with Thomas F. Staley) *Approaches to Ulysses: Ten Essays,* University of Pittsburgh Press, 1971.
Paycocks and Others: Sean O'Casey's World, Gill & Macmillan (Dublin), 1976.
(Editor with Staley) *Approaches to James Joyce's Portrait: Ten Essays,* University of Pittsburgh Press, 1977.
James Joyce: The Undiscover'd Country, Gill & Macmillan, 1977.
(With wife, Shari Benstock) *Who's He When He's at Home: A James Joyce Directory,* University of Illinois Press, 1980.
(Editor) *Pomes for James Joyce,* Malton Press (Nass, Ireland), 1981.
(Editor) *The Seventh of Joyce,* Indiana University Press, 1982.
(Editor with Suheil B. Bushrui) *James Joyce: An International Perspective,* Colin Smythe, 1982.
(Editor) *Essays in Detective Fiction,* Macmillan (London), 1983.
(Editor) *Art in Crime Writing,* St. Martin's, 1984.
James Joyce, Ungar, 1985.
Critical Essays on James Joyce, G. K. Hall, 1985.
(Editor with Thomas F. Staley) *Dictionary of Literary Biography,* Volume 70: *British Mystery Writers, 1860-1919,* Gale, 1988.
(Editor) *James Joyce: The Augmented Ninth,* Syracuse University Press, 1988.

Contributor to scholarly journals.

WORK IN PROGRESS: Narrative Con/Texts in Ulysses; (with S. Benstock) *Modernism Made Manifest: The Impact of the Literary Periodicals, 1890-1940.*

* * *

BENSTOCK, Shari 1944-

PERSONAL: Born December 2, 1944, in San Diego, Calif.; daughter of Dan and Myrl (Barth) Gabrielson; married Bernard Benstock (a professor of English), May 6, 1973; children: Eric. *Education:* Drake University, B.A., 1967, M.A., 1970; Kent State University, Ph.D., 1975.

ADDRESSES: Office—Department of English, University of Miami, Coral Gables, Fla. 33124.

CAREER: Drake University, Des Moines, Iowa, instructor in English, 1970-72; Kent State University, Kent, Ohio, instructor in English, 1972-74; University of Illinois at Urbana-Champaign, affiliated with departments of political science, 1975-77, and clinical medicine, 1979-82; University of Tulsa, Tulsa, Okla., associate professor, 1982-86; University of Miami, Coral Gables, Fla., professor of English, 1987—.

MEMBER: International James Joyce Foundation, Modern Language Association of America, American Studies Association, American Association of University Women.

WRITINGS:

(With husband, Bernard Benstock) *Who's He When He's at Home: A James Joyce Directory,* University of Illinois Press, 1980.
Feminist Issues in Literary Scholarship, Indiana University Press, 1987.
The Private Self: Theory and Practice in Women's Autobiographical Writings, University of North Carolina Press, 1987.
Women of the Left Bank: Paris, 1910-1940, University of Texas Press, 1988.
(Co-editor) *Coping with Joyce: Essays from the Copenhagen Symposium,* Ohio State University Press, 1989.

Editor, *Tulsa Studies in Women's Literature,* 1982-86; series editor, *Reading Women Writing,* Cornell University Press, 1987—; member of editorial board of *Journal of Modern Literature, James Joyce Quarterly,* and *Ulysse: Fin de Siecle* (Dijon, France).

WORK IN PROGRESS: Textualizing the Feminine: Essays on the Limits of Genre, for University of Oklahoma Press; (with B. Benstock) *Modernism Made Manifest: The Impact of the Literary Periodicals, 1890-1940.*

AVOCATIONAL INTERESTS: Travel.

BIOGRAPHICAL/CRITICAL SOURCES:

PERIODICALS

Times Literary Supplement, March 11, 1988.

* * *

BENYO, Richard (Stephen) 1946-

PERSONAL: Born April 20, 1946, in Jim Thorpe, Pa.; son of Andrew Joseph, Sr., (a machinist) and Dorothy Rita (Herman) Benyo; married Jill Wapensky, April 29, 1972 (divorced April 2, 1979). *Education:* Bloomsburg State College, B.A., 1968; also attended George Mason University, 1976-77. *Politics:* Democrat. *Religion:* Roman Catholic.

ADDRESSES: Home and office—107 Lilac Lane, St. Helena, Calif. 94574. *Agent*—Angela Miller, I.M.G., 22 East 71st St., New York, N.Y. 10021.

CAREER: Times-News, Lehighton, Pa., managing editor, 1968-72; *Stock Car Racing,* Alexandria, Va., editor, 1972-77; *Runner's World,* Mountain View, Calif., managing editor, 1977-79, executive editor, 1979-84, vice-president of Runner's World Magazine Co., Inc., 1981-84. President, Specific Publications, Inc., 1983—. Member of Union 76 panel of experts.

MEMBER: Association Internationale de la Presse Sportive, International Motor Press Association, American Automobile Racing Writers and Broadcasters Association, Amateur Athletic Union Track and Field Writers of America, Commonwealth Club of San Francisco.

AWARDS, HONORS: Best Local Column award, Pennsylvania Newspaper Publishers Association, 1972; winner of American Automobile Racing Writers and Broadcasters Association writing contests, 1973-77; Young Alumnus Award, Bloomsburg State College, 1985.

WRITINGS:

Superspeedway, Mason/Charter, 1977.
Return to Running, World Publications, 1978.
(With Rhonda Provost) *Indoor Exercise Book,* Runner's World Books, 1979.
(With Provost) *Advanced Indoor Exercise Book,* Runner's World Books, 1980.
(With Kym Herrin) *The Sexercise Book,* Anderson World Books, 1982.
Masters of the Marathon, Atheneum, 1983.
(With Elaine LaLanne) *Fitness after 50,* Stephen Greene Press, 1986.
(With Provost) *Feeling Fit in Your 40s,* Atheneum, 1987.
(With LaLanne) *Dynastride!,* Stephen Green Press, 1988.
The Exercise Fix, Leisure Press, 1989.
(With LaLanne) *The Fitness after 50 Workout,* Stephen Green Press, 1989.
(With Rolla Campbell) *The Senior Golfer's Fitness Program,* Stephen Green Press, 1990.

Also author of *The Grand National Stars,* 1975, and *The Book of Richard Petty,* 1976. Author of regular column in *Stock Car Racing,* 1972, 1982; fitness and running columnist, *San Francisco Chronicle,* 1985—. Editor of *The Complete Woman Runner;* editor-at-large of *Stock Car Racing.*

WORK IN PROGRESS: The Quake Creek Monster, a novel; *Pyramid,* a mystery; *The Marathon: How to Make It Your Event; Slipstream,* a novel; research for a biography of James Farrell.

SIDELIGHTS: Richard Benyo told *CA:* "Almost every beginning writing course advises a would-be writer to begin by writing about something of which he has knowledge or which is of interest to him. This is absolutely good advice. The fun in writing nonfiction comes when opportunities arise to write on subjects on which you know little. Book projects that are somewhat out of your usual realm have several advantages: they are usually more challenging (and therefore ultimately more interesting); they provide the opportunity to broaden your interests (and thereby provide sort of an ongoing 'college education'); and they often lead to opportunities to do books that would have never occurred to you or that would not have been offered to you had you not made a tentative step outside your usual territory. A writer should not overlook the possibilities of collaborating with 'experts' in various fields; in an increasingly complex world, there are any number of 'experts' who possess the knowledge of a subject, but are just unable to tell their story. A nonfiction writer can be the bridge between the 'expert' and his potential public."

AVOCATIONAL INTERESTS: Old rock 'n' roll music, running, photography, airships, bicycling, packratting.

* * *

BERLINER, Franz 1930-

PERSONAL: Born August 10, 1930, in Denmark; married Bibi Noergaard; children: Franz, Peter, Bolette. *Politics:* "As a human being, capable of thinking, I'm a pacifist."

ADDRESSES: *Home*—Alleen 45, 8660 Skanderborg, Denmark.

CAREER: Author and journalist. *Soendags-BT,* Copenhagen, Denmark, weekly columnist writing about children and their parents, 1965-71; *Politiken,* Copenhagen, daily critic on children's programs, 1969-83.

WRITINGS:

Tingelingelater, Nyt Nordisk, 1956.
Godnat Skipper (juvenile), Borgen, 1962.
Maane over fjeldet, Borgen, 1964.
Stederne, Borgen, 1966.
Boernene og vi (child study), Berlingske, 1967.
Menneskenes Land (juvenile), Bonniers, 1967, translation by Louise Orr published as *Summertime,* Collins, 1969.
(With wife, Bibi Berliner) *Derude bag havet* (juvenile), Munksgard, 1968.
Groenland, Carit Andersen, 1968.
Vestgroenland, Carit Andersen, 1970.
Haevneren, Sesam, 1978.
Ulven, Sesam, 1979.
Gaeslingen, Sesam, 1980.
En dag den sommer, Sesam, 1982.
Den Frygtloese, Sesam, 1983.
Ytek, Sesam, 1984.
Ilden paa Bjerget, Det danske Bibelselskab, 1985.
Jeg haaber det gaar godt, Sesam, 1985.
Paa gensyn i Groenland, Sesam, 1986.
Bliver der nu krig?, Hoest, 1987.

PUBLISHED BY GYLDENDAL

Evelyn (short stories), 1954.
Hundene, 1957.
(Contributor) *Boerne-og ungdomsboeger* (children's literature study), 1969.
Soefolket (juvenile), 1970, translation by Lone Thygesen-Blecher published as *The Lake People,* Putnam, 1973.
En anden bog om Soefolket, 1972.
(With B. Berliner) *Alene hjemme* (juvenile), 1972.
Kahinoeen, 1973.
Marinus, 1978.
(With B. Berliner) *Seksten dage i september,* 1980.
Hestestormen, 1980.
(With B. Berliner) *Koeb blomster,* 1981.
Hvalens Aar, 1987.

OTHER

Also author of television adaptation of *Menneskenes Land* for Danmarks Radio, 1969; also has written for Greenland and Denmark radio. Editor, *Refleks* (encyclopedia for school children), 1973-77. Contributor of articles to magazines and newspapers, and of book reviews to *Politiken.*

SIDELIGHTS: Franz Berliner spent five years in Greenland and has visited there several times since. He wrote the text of *Summertime* around drawings of Eskimo children done by Ingrid Vang Nyman, who was Danish but did most of her work in Sweden. When she died in 1959 her son took her unpublished drawings to Berliner.

MEDIA ADAPTATIONS: *Alene hjemme* played as Children's Theatre on *Filuren,* Aarhus, 1975.

BIOGRAPHICAL/CRITICAL SOURCES:

PERIODICALS

Books, October, 1969.
Times Literary Supplement, October 16, 1969.

* * *

BERNSTEIN, Joanne E(ckstein) 1943-

PERSONAL: Born April 21, 1943, in New York; daughter of Murray (a lawyer) and Mildred (a teacher; maiden name, Weckstein) Eckstein; married Michael J. Bernstein (a school administrator and photographer), June 9, 1965; children: Robin, Andrew. *Education:* Brooklyn College of the City University of New York, B.A., 1963; Pratt Institute, M.L.S., 1966; Columbia University, Ed.D., 1971.

ADDRESSES: *Home*—3848 Maple Ave., Brooklyn, N.Y. 11224. *Office*—School of Education, Brooklyn College of the City University of New York, Brooklyn, N.Y. 11210.

CAREER: Kindergarten teacher in a public school in Brooklyn, N.Y., 1963-67; substitute teacher for elementary and secondary schools in New York City, 1967-69; Pace College, New York City, adjunct lecturer in education, 1970; New York Community College, New York City, adjunct lecturer in education, 1971; Brooklyn College of the City University of New York, Brooklyn, 1971—, began as assistant professor, currently professor of education.

MEMBER: National Council of Teachers of English, Society of Children's Book Writers.

WRITINGS:

JUVENILES

Loss: And How to Cope with It, Seabury, 1977.
(With Stephen Gullo) *When People Die,* Dutton, 1977.
Fiddle with a Riddle, Dutton, 1979.
Dimitry: A Young Soviet Immigrant, Clarion, 1981.
(With Paul Cohen) *Un-Frog-Gettable Riddles,* Albert Whitman, 1981.
(With Cohen) *Unidentified Flying Riddles,* Albert Whitman, 1983.
(With Cohen) *More Unidentified Flying Riddles,* Albert Whitman, 1985.
(With Cohen) *Happy Holiday Riddles to You,* Albert Whitman, 1985.
(With Cohen) *What Was the Wicked Witch's Real Name, and Other Character Riddles,* Albert Whitman, 1986.
(With Cohen) *Creepy, Crawly Critter Riddles,* Albert Whitman, 1986.
Taking Off: Travel Tips for a Carefree Trip, Harper, 1986.
(With Cohen) *Riddles To Take On Vacation,* Albert Whitman, 1987.
(With Cohen) *Grand-Slam Riddles,* Albert Whitman, 1987.

(With Cohen) *Out to Pasture,* Lerner Publications, 1988.
(With Rose Blue) *Go Upward, Climb Higher, Touch the Stars: Judith Resnik, Challenger Astronaut,* Dutton, 1989.
(With Cohen) *Sporty Riddles,* Albert Whitman, 1989.
(With Cohen) *Touchdown Riddles,* Albert Whitman, 1989.

OTHER

Books to Help Children Cope with Separation and Loss, Bowker, 1977, 3rd edition, 1988.
(With Bryna Fireside) *Special Parents—Special Children,* Albert Whitman, 1990.

Contributor of more than 100 chapters, articles, and reviews to numerous periodicals, including *Reading Teacher, Language Arts, Young Children,* and *Death Education.*

SIDELIGHTS: Joanne E. Bernstein commented to *CA:* "I enjoy writing for varied age groups, and I'm pleased that my work reflects different sides of my personality, from serious self-help books to lighthearted humor pieces. The most satisfying part of the writing process is coming up with the initial idea—then tracking it down, or, more accurately, being dogged by it, until the idea becomes a fully developed proposal."

* * *

BERRY, Herbert 1922-

PERSONAL: Born May 9, 1922, in New York, N.Y.; son of Herbert M. (a printer) and Mary T. (Brennfleck) Berry; married Elizabeth McHenry (a microbiologist), September 3, 1948; children: Margaret, Thomas, Catherine, Judith. *Education:* Furman University, B.A., 1947; University of Nebraska, M.A., 1948, Ph.D., 1953.

ADDRESSES: Home—1405 Ewart Ave., Saskatoon, Saskatchewan, Canada S7H 2K5; 4, Kingsdon, Near Somerton, Somerset TA11 7JX, England.

CAREER: University of Nebraska, Lincoln, instructor in English, 1950-51; University of Nebraska, Omaha, assistant professor of English, 1951-55; Doane College, Crete, Neb., associate professor and head of English department, 1955-58; University of Western Ontario, London, 1958-67, began as assistant professor, became associate professor of English; University of Saskatchewan, Saskatoon, professor of English, 1967-89, professor emeritus, 1989—, head of department, 1970-71 and 1975-77. *Military service:* U.S. Army, 1943-46.

MEMBER: Renaissance Society of America, Shakespeare Association of America, Faculty Association of University of Saskatchewan (vice-president, 1968-69; president, 1970-71).

WRITINGS:

Sir John Suckling's Poems and Letters from Manuscript, University of Western Ontario, 1960.
(Contributor) D. Galloway, editor, *The Elizabethan Theatre I,* Macmillan, 1969.
(Contributor) C. Leech and J. Margeson, editors, *Shakespeare 1971,* University of Toronto Press, 1972.
(Contributor) Galloway, editor, *The Elizabethan Theatre III,* Macmillan, 1973.
(Editor and contributor) *The First Public Playhouse: The Theatre in Shoreditch, 1576-1598,* McGill-Queens University Press, 1979.
(Contributor) C. W. Hodges, S. Schoenbaum, and L. Leone, editors, *The Third Globe,* Wayne State University Press, 1981.
The Boar's Head Playhouse, Folder Library, 1986.
Shakespeare's Playhouses, AMS Press, 1987.

Contributor to scholarly journals, including *Shakespeare Quarterly, Renaissance and Reformation, Shakespeare Studies, Modern Philology, Studies in English Literature, Studies in Philology, Notes and Queries, Review of English Studies, Modern Language Notes, Essays in Theatre, Medieval and Renaissance Drama in England,* and *Philological Quarterly.* Member of editorial advisory boards of *Essays in Theatre* and *Records of Early English Drama.*

WORK IN PROGRESS: With Glynne Wickham, a documentary history of the theatre, 1540-1642.

SIDELIGHTS: Herbert Berry told *CA:* "I am, I suppose, a literary archaeologist. The soil in which I dig consists of English documents of the sixteenth and seventeenth centuries, and the chief city I try to restore consists of the theatres of that time and their people."

BIOGRAPHICAL/CRITICAL SOURCES:

PERIODICALS

Times Literary Supplement, March 28, 1980.

* * *

BEST, Charles H(erbert) 1899-1978

PERSONAL: Born February 27, 1899, in West Pembroke, Me.; died from a ruptured abdominal blood vessel, March 31, 1978, in Toronto, Ontario, Canada; son of Herbert Huestis (a physician) and Luella May (Fisher) Best; married Margaret Hooper Mahon (a historian and botanist), September 3, 1924; children: Charles Alexander (deceased), Henry Bruce Macleod. *Education:* University of Toronto, B.A., 1921, M.A., 1922, M.D., 1925; University of Freiburg, further study, 1926; University of London, D.Sc., 1928. *Religion:* Presbyterian.

ADDRESSES: Home—105 Woodlawn Ave. W., Toronto, Ontario, Canada M4V 1G6. *Office*—Charles H. Best Institute, 112 College St., Toronto, Ontario, Canada M5G 1LG.

CAREER: University of Toronto, Toronto, Ontario, researcher and discoverer, with Frederick G. Banting, of insulin, 1921, Connaught Laboratories, head of division producing insulin commercially, 1922-25, assistant director, 1925-31, associate director, 1932-41, honorary consultant, beginning 1941, Banting and Best Department of Medical Research, research associate, 1923-41, director emeritus, beginning 1965, Department of Physical Hygiene, assistant professor, 1926-28, chairman, 1928-41, director emeritus and special lecturer, beginning 1965, Department of Physiology, chairman, 1941-67, director emeritus, beginning 1967, Charles H. Best Institute, director, beginning 1951.

Rockefeller Foundation, scientific director of International Health Division, 1941-43, 1946-48, chairman of board of scientific directors, 1943; Canadian Department of National Defense, member of Research Defense Board, 1946-65. Josiah Macy, Jr., Foundation Conference on Liver Injury, chairman, 1947-53; Nutrition Foundation, member of scientific advisory committee, 1950-64, trustee, beginning 1964; Roscoe B. Jackson Memorial Laboratory, Bar Harbor, Me., member of board of scientific directors, beginning 1955; World Health Organization, member of advisory committee on medical research, 1963-68. International Diabetes Foundation, honorary president, beginning 1949; International Union of Physiological Sciences, first president, 1953; Council of International University Foundation, charter member, 1953. Held distinguished lectureships in Canada, United States, and Europe, including Phillips Memorial Lecturer, American College of Physicians, 1953, Croonian Lecturer of Royal Society, 1955, Mitchell Lecturer, Queen's University of Belfast, 1957, 150th Anniversary Lecturer at Karolinska Institute, Sweden, 1960, and Grow Memorial Lecturer, U.S. Air Force, 1964. Member of National Research Council of Canada and research defense board of Department of National Defense; consultant to U.S. Public Health Service. *Military service:* Canadian Army, Tank Corps, 1918-19; became sergeant. Royal Canadian Navy, 1941-46; director of Medical Research Division, became surgeon captain.

MEMBER: Pontifical Academy of Sciences (first Canadian member), International Society of Hematology (charter fellow), Royal Society of Canada (fellow), Royal College of Physicians and Surgeons (fellow), Canadian Physiological Society (past president), Canadian Diabetic Association (first honorary president), Nutrition Society of Canada, Biochemical Society of Canada, Royal Society of London (fellow), Royal College of Physicians (London; fellow), Royal College of Physicians (Edinburgh; honorary fellow), British Diabetic Association (vice president, beginning 1934), Physiological Society, Biochemical Society, Nutrition Society, American College of Gastroenterology (honorary fellow), American Diabetes Association (honorary member since founding, 1940; president, 1948-49; member of council and honorary president), American Association for the Advancement of Science (fellow), American Physiological Society, American Society of Biological Chemists, Society for Experimental Biology and Medicine, American Society for Clinical Investigation, National Academy of Sciences (foreign associate), New York Academy of Medicine (corresponding fellow), American Philosophical Society, American Association for the Study of Liver Disease, Association of American Physicians, Nu Sigma Nu, Alpha Omega Alpha. Member or honorary member of scientific societies in Argentina, Uruguay, Chile, Venezuela, Belgium, France, Italy, Czechoslovakia, Denmark, Germany, Hungary, and Sweden; honorary member of numerous societies in Canada, England, and United States.

AWARDS, HONORS: Reeve Prize of University of Toronto, shared with Frederick G. Banting, for discovery of insulin, 1923; F.N.G. Starr Gold Medal of Canadian Medical Association, 1936; Baly Medal, Royal College of Physicians (England), 1939; Charles Mickle fellowship of Faculty of Medicine, University of Toronto, 1939, for contributing the most to science during the preceding ten years; Commander of Order of British Empire, 1944; King Haakon VII Liberty Cross (Norway), 1947; Legion of Merit (United States), 1947; Medal of University of Louvain, 1947; Medal of Freedom, University of Brussels, 1948; Commander of the Order of the Crown (Belgium), 1948; Gold Medal of Canadian Pharmaceutical Manufacturers Association, 1948; Banting Medal of American Diabetes Association, 1949; Flavelle Medal of Royal Society of Canada, 1950; John Phillips Memorial Medal of American College of Physicians, 1953; Coronation Medal (England), 1953; Queen Elizabeth of the Belgians Gold Medal, 1956; Medal of Royal Netherlands Academy of Sciences and Letters, 1958; La Grande Medaille d'Argent (Paris), 1962; Banting and Best Commemorative Medal of Czechoslovak Society of Physical Medicine, 1962; Humanitarian Award of Canadian B'nai B'rith, 1963; Joslin Medal of New England Diabetes Association (first recipient), 1965; Centennial Medal (Canada), 1967; Companion of the Order of Canada, 1967; Companion of Honour (England), 1971; Brazil Science Biennial Award, 1971; Gairdner International Award, 1971; and other awards.

Honorary degrees, including D.Sc., LL.D., and M.D., from University of Chicago, 1941, University of Paris, 1945, Cambridge University, 1946, Universities of Amsterdam, Louvain, and Liege, and Oxford University, 1947, Dalhousie University, 1949, Queen's University at Kingston, 1950, Universities of Chile, Uruguay, and San Marcos (Peru), 1951, University of Melbourne and Laval University, 1952, University of Maine, 1955, Central University of Venezuela, 1958, University of Edinburgh and Northwestern University, 1959, Aristotelian University of Thessaloniki, 1963, Free University of Berlin, 1966, University of Toronto, 1970, Laurentian University and Hebrew University of Jerusalem, 1971, University of Ottawa, 1972, University of Zagreb, 1976.

WRITINGS:

(With Frederick G. Banting) *The Internal Secretions of the Pancreas* (original publication on insulin, first published in *Journal of Laboratory and Clinical Medicine,* Volume VII, number 251, 1922), University of Toronto Library, 1922.

(With Norman Burke Taylor) *The Human Body and Its Functions: An Elementary Textbook of Physiology,* W. J. Gage & Co. (Toronto), 1932, 3rd edition published as *The Human Body, Its Anatomy and Physiology,* Holt, 1956, 5th edition, 1985.

(With Taylor) *The Physiological Basis of Medical Practice: A University of Toronto Text in Applied Physiology,* W. Wood & Co. (Baltimore), 1937, 5th edition published as *The Physiological Basis of Medical Practice: A Text in Applied Physiology,* 1950, 9th edition published as *Best & Taylor's Physiological Basis of Medical Practice,* edited by John R. Brobeck, 1973, 11th edition published with study guide and self-examination review, 1985.

(With Taylor) *The Living Body: A Text in Human Physiology,* Holt, 1938, 5th edition published as *The Living Body: Its Anatomy and Physiology,* 1970.

Diabetes and Insulin and the Lipotropic Factors (lectures), Thomas (Springfield, Ill.), 1948.

Selected Papers of Charles H. Best, University of Toronto Press, 1963.

Contributor of papers on insulin, histamine, choline, carbohydrate and fat metabolism, and related topics to medical journals and some national magazines, including *Reader's Digest, Today's Health,* and *Newsweek.* Member of board of editors, *Endocrinology,* beginning 1943, *Excerpta Medica* (Amsterdam), beginning 1947, *Medicina Experimentalis* (Bonn), beginning, 1959, *International Journal of Medicine,* beginning 1966. Member of journal committee, Canadian Physiological Society, beginning 1943; honorary editor for Canada, *Journal of Industrial Hygiene and Toxicology,* beginning 1945; member of honorary editorial advisory board, *Journal of Canadian Medical Services,* beginning 1946, and *International Encyclopedia of Nutrition,* 1962; co-editor, *Journal of Vitamin Research,* beginning 1947; chairman of editorial board, *Diabetes,* 1952-58; Canadian member of international board of editors, *Gerontology and Geriatrics,* beginning 1958; member of editorial advisory council, *American Journal of Gastroenterology,* beginning 1959.

SIDELIGHTS: American-born Canadian physician, physiologist, and biochemist Charles H. Best was introduced to the field of medicine by accompanying his father, a country doctor, on house calls. As a twenty-two-year-old graduate student in physiology and biochemistry at the University of Toronto, Best assisted the experiments of Frederick G. Banting, and pioneered the discovery of insulin. According to the *New York Times,* Best and Banting spent the entire summer of 1921 in a laboratory, securing test animals and supplies with their own money, searching for the pancreatic hormone that triggers the transformation of sugar to energy in the body: "After weeks of watching their test animals die, the researchers injected a moribund dog with a substance extracted from a steer's pancreas. The dog soon stood up and licked their hands. Six months later, a dying 14-year-old diabetic boy became the first human to control the disease with insulin." Although the discovery earned international acclaim for Best, the Nobel Prize was awarded only to Banting and J. J. R. MacLeod, chairman of the department. Angered, Banting shared his prize money with Best; and according to the *New York Times,* MacLeod later acknowledged that he was awarded the prize not for his discovery of insulin, but for his "discovery of Best."

In addition to his teaching posts and departmental chairs at the University of Toronto, Best served as director of both the Connaught Laboratories, producing insulin commercially, and the Banting and Best Department of Medical Research, where his contributions to the field of medical research include such significant accomplishments as the isolation of the allergy-producing chemical histamine, and histaminase, which destroys histamine in the body. During the Second World War, he and his associates produced an anti-coagulant vital to cardiac surgery, and devised a method of drying and storing human blood serum. After the war, though, Banting and Best returned to diabetic research.

Best was internationally honored with myriad medals, decorations, degrees, and appointments. In 1968, the American Diabetes Association purchased Best's birthplace in West Pembroke, Maine, as a historical landmark; in 1969, the Delaware Diabetic Association established the Charles H. Best Award; in 1970, the Toronto Diabetes Association established the annual Charles H. Best lectureship; in 1971, a Charles H. Best postdoctoral fellowship was established in the Banting and Best Department of Medical Research at the University of Toronto, and Hoechst Pharmaceuticals initiated the Charles H. Best Prize. As a member of the Pontifical Academy of Sciences, which is composed of only sixty members chosen from all branches of science throughout the world, Best earned a right to the title of His Excellency.

AVOCATIONAL INTERESTS: Oil painting, golf, horseback riding, and watching baseball.

BIOGRAPHICAL/CRITICAL SOURCES:

BOOKS

Leibel, B. S., and G. A. Wrenshall, *Insulin,* University of Toronto Press, 1971.

Wrenshall, G. Heteny, and W. R. Feasby, *The Story of Insulin,* Reinhardt, 1962.

PERIODICALS

Canadian Journal of Physiology and Pharmacology (issue dedicated to Best), May, 1968.

Collier's, August 2, 1941.

New York Times, April 1, 1978.

Saturday Night, June 5, 1951.

Science Digest, December, 1954.

OBITUARIES:

PERIODICALS

Maclean's, April 17, 1978.

Newsweek, April 10, 1978.

New York Times, April 1, 1978.

Time, April 10, 1978.*

BLAINE, John
See GOODWIN, Harold L(eland)

* * *

BONDANELLA, Peter Eugene 1943-

PERSONAL: Born December 20, 1943, in Pinehurst, N.C.; son of Frank Patrick (a teacher) and Dorothy (a librarian; maiden name, McKenzie) Bondanella; married Julia Conaway (a professor), June 13, 1969. *Education:* Davidson College, A.B. (cum laude), 1966; Stanford University, M.A., 1967; University of Oregon, Ph.D., 1970.

ADDRESSES: Home—1030 East Atwater St., Bloomington, Ind. 47401. *Office*—Center for Italian Studies, Indiana University, Bloomington, Ind. 47405.

CAREER: Wayne State University, Detroit, Mich., assistant professor of Italian, 1970-72; Indiana University at Bloomington, professor of French and Italian, 1972—, director of Center for Italian Studies, 1979, 1982-84, director of film studies, 1983-84.

MEMBER: American Association of Teachers of Italian, American Association of University Professors of Italian (president, 1984-87).

AWARDS, HONORS: National Endowment for the Humanities, younger humanist fellowship, 1972-73, senior fellowship, 1980-81; senior fellowship, American Council of Learned Societies, 1987; Ailsa Mellon Bruce senior fellowship, National Gallery of Art, Center for Advanced Studies in the Visual Arts, 1987-88; open fellowship, Lilly Foundation, 1988.

WRITINGS:

Machiavelli and the Art of Renaissance History, Wayne State University Press, 1974.

Francesco Guicciardini, Twayne, 1976.

(Editor and translator with Mark Musa) *The Decameron: A Norton Critical Edition,* Norton, 1977.

(Editor) *Federico Fellini: Essays in Criticism,* Oxford University Press, 1978.

(Editor with wife, Julia Conaway Bondanella) *The Macmillan Dictionary of Italian Literature,* Macmillan, 1979.

(Editor) *Dictionary of Italian Literature,* Greenwood Press, 1979.

(With Musa) *The Portable Machiavelli,* Viking, 1979.

(Editor and translator with Musa) *The Decameron,* New American Library, 1982.

Italian Cinema: From Neorealism to the Present, Ungar, 1983.

(Editor) *Machiavelli's "The Prince,"* Oxford University Press, 1984.

"La Strada": Federico Fellini, Director, Rutgers University Press, 1987.

The Eternal City: Roman Images in the Modern World, University of North Carolina Press, 1987.

Contributor to language, literature, and philology journals.

WORK IN PROGRESS: Completing a second edition of *Italian Cinema;* editing and translating, with wife, Julia Conaway Bondanella, an edition of Giorgio Vasari's *Lives of the Most Famous Artists,* for Oxford University Press; working on a critical study entitled *An Honest Liar: The Cinema of Federico Fellini,* for Princeton University Press.

SIDELIGHTS: Peter Eugene Bondanella told *CA* that his commitment to teaching and research in Italian and comparative literature is based on its "crucial contribution to the formation of the very idea of the humanities itself, beginning with the early humanists and continuing until the present day. This rich cultural continuity is particularly important for an assessment of the role the humanities must play in our modern world. One of my chief concerns is that this legacy from Italy's past not be confined to the museum or the pedagogue's study but, instead, that it be placed in a specifically contemporary context. To that end, I am interested in new critical perspectives on older literatures, as well as examining the mutual illumination of literature and the other arts, especially the Italian cinema. My hope is that Italian language and literature departments in America will broaden their horizons to include such areas of interest as Italian cinema, Italian-American relationships, folklore, and history so that departments of Italian studies will be established."

* * *

BONNER, Parker
See BALLARD, (Willis) Todhunter

* * *

BORROR, Donald J(oyce) 1907-1988

PERSONAL: Born August 24, 1907, in Columbus, Ohio; died of liver cancer, April 28, 1988; son of Charles Herman and Dora A. (Caywood) Borror; married J. Elizabeth Killworth, 1931; children: Arthur Charles. *Education:* Otterbein College, B.S., 1928; Ohio State University, M.S., 1930, Ph.D., 1935.

CAREER: Ohio State University, Columbus, instructor, 1930-42, assistant professor, 1942-44, 1946-47, associate professor, 1947-59, professor of zoology and entomology, 1959-77, professor emeritus, 1977-88. Instructor, Audubon Camp, 1938-41, 1946, 1948-53, 1955-62. *Military service:* U.S. Naval Reserve, 1944-46; became lieutenant.

MEMBER: American Association for the Advancement of Science, Entomology Society of America (fellow), Wildlife Society, Society for Systematic Zoology, Wilson Ornithological Society, American Ornithologists' Union (fellow), Cooper Ornithological Society, Ohio Academy of Science, Sigma Xi, Wheaton Club.

AWARDS, HONORS: Award of Merit, Entomology Society of America, 1974.

WRITINGS:

(With Dwight M. DeLong) *An Introduction to the Study of Insects,* Holt, 1954, 6th edition (also with Charles A. Triplehorn), Saunders College, 1989.

Dictionary of Word Roots and Combining Forms: Compiled from the Greek, Latin, and Other Languages, with Special Reference to Biological Terms and Scientific Names, Mayfield Publications, 1960.

Common Bird Songs, (booklet and recording), Dover, 1967, reprinted, 1984.

(With Richard E. White) *A Field Guide to the Insects of America North of Mexico,* Houghton, 1970.

Songs of Western Birds (booklet and recording), Dover, 1970, new edition, 1984.

Songs of Eastern Birds (booklet and recording), Dover, 1970, new edition, 1984.

(With Maurice L. Glitz) *Florida Bird Songs* (booklet and recording), Dover, 1980.

Also author or co-author of other booklet and recording sets on bird and insect songs. Contributor to professional journals. Assistant managing editor, *Annals of Entomological Society of America,* 1943-44.

SIDELIGHTS: Donald J. Borror once told *CA:* "My research interests are . . . entomology and ornithology. In entomology I am interested principally in the taxonomy, morphology, and ecology of the *Odonata* [order of dragonflies and damselflies]," Borror noted, and added that his "interests in ornithology are principally in bird song."*

[Death date provided by Charles A. Triplehorn]

* * *

BOWIE, Norman E. 1942-

PERSONAL: Born June 6, 1942, in Biddeford, Me.; son of Lawrence Walker (a retail manager) and Helen (Jacobsen) Bowie; married Bonnie Bankert, June 11, 1966 (divorced, 1980); married Maureen Burns, September 19, 1987; children: (first marriage) Brian, Peter. *Education:* Bates College, A.B., 1964; Union Theological Seminary, New York, N.Y., additional study, 1964; University of Rochester, Ph.D., 1968. *Politics:* Democrat.

ADDRESSES: Home—13 Woodshaw Rd., Newark, Del. 19711. *Office*—Center for the Study of Values, University of Delaware, Newark, Del. 19716.

CAREER: Lycoming College, Williamsport, Pa., assistant professor of philosophy, 1968-69; Hamilton College, Clinton, N.Y., assistant professor, 1969-74, associate professor of philosophy, 1974-80; University of Delaware, Newark, director of Center for the Study of Values, 1977—, professor of philosophy, 1980—.

MEMBER: American Philosophical Association (executive secretary, 1972-77), American Association of University Professors, Academy of Management, American Society for Political and Legal Philosophy, American Society for Value Inquiry (president, 1980-81), Society for Business Ethics (president, 1988), Phi Beta Kappa.

WRITINGS:

Towards a New Theory of Distributive Justice, University of Massachusetts Press, 1971.

(With Robert L. Simon) *The Individual and the Political Order,* Prentice-Hall, 1977, 2nd edition, 1985.

(Editor with Thomas Beauchamp) *Ethical Theory and Business,* Prentice-Hall, 1979, revised edition, 1983, 3rd edition, 1988.

(Editor) *Ethical Issues in Government,* Temple University Press, 1981.

Business Ethics, Prentice-Hall, 1982.

(Editor with Frederick Elliston) *Ethics, Public Policy and Criminal Justice,* Oelgeschlager, Gunn & Hain, 1982.

(Editor) *Ethical Theory in the Last Quarter of the 20th Century,* Hackett, 1983.

(Editor) *Making Ethical Decisions,* McGraw, 1985.

(Editor with Harrison Hall) *The Tradition of Philosophy,* Wadsworth, 1986.

(Editor) *Equal Opportunity,* Westview Press, 1988.

Contributor of articles and reviews to professional journals.

* * *

BOWIE, Sam
See BALLARD, (Willis) Todhunter

BOYD, Marion M.
See HAVIGHURST, Marion (M.)

* * *

BOYLE, Kay 1902-

PERSONAL: Born February 19, 1902, in St. Paul, Minn.; daughter of Howard Peterson and Katherine (Evans) Boyle; married Richard Brault, June 24, 1923 (divorced); married Laurence Vail, April 2, 1931 (divorced, 1943); married Baron Joseph von Franckenstein, February 20, 1943 (died, 1963); children: Sharon Walsh; (second marriage) Apple-Joan, Kathe, Clover; (third marriage) Faith Carson, Ian Savin. *Education:* Studied architecture at Parson's School of Fine and Applied Arts in New York and Ohio Mechanics Institute in Cincinnati, 1917-19; took courses at Columbia University and studied violin at Cincinnati Conservatory of Music. *Politics:* Democrat.

ADDRESSES: Home—41 Yosemite, Oakland, Calif. 94611. *Agent*—Gloria Loomis, Watkins, Loomis Agency, Inc., 150 E. 35 St., Suite 530, New York, N.Y. 10016.

CAREER: Writer. Taught night school course in writing, Nyack, N.Y., 1941-43; teacher at Miss Thomas's School in Connecticut during fifties and early sixties; San Francisco State College (now San Francisco State University), San Francisco, Calif., member of English faculty, 1963-79. Member of workshop in the short story, New School for Social Research, 1962; lecturer and writer in residence at various colleges and universities, including Northwestern State University, Spokane, Wash., 1981, and Bowling Green State University, Bowling Green, Ohio, 1986. Fellow at Wesleyan University, Middletown, Conn., 1963, and Radcliffe Institute for Independent Study, 1965.

MEMBER: National Institute of Arts and Letters, American Academy.

AWARDS, HONORS: Guggenheim fellowships, 1934 and 1961; O. Henry Memorial Award for best short story of the year, 1934, for "The White Horses of Vienna," and 1941, for "Defeat"; D. Litt., Columbia College, 1971, Skidmore College, 1977, and Southern Illinois College, 1982; California Literature Medal Award, 1971, for *Testament for My Students;* National Endowment for the Arts Fellowship, 1980, for "extraordinary contribution to American literature over a lifetime of creative work"; Before Columbus Foundation American Book Award, 1984, lifetime achievement; Robert Kirsch Award, *Los Angeles Times,* 1986; French-American Foundation Translation prize, 1986, for "distinguished contribution to French and American letters as author and translator"; nominated for *Los Angeles Times* Book Award in poetry, 1986, for *This Is Not a Letter and Other Poems.*

WRITINGS:

NOVELS

Plagued by the Nightingale, Cape & Smith, 1931, new edition, Southern Illinois University Press, 1969, reprinted with new introduction by the author, Virago, 1981.
Year before Last, H. Smith, 1932, new edition, Southern Illinois University Press, 1969.
Gentlemen, I Address You Privately, Smith & Haas, 1933.
My Next Bride, Harcourt, 1934, reprinted with new introduction by Doris Grumbach, Virago, 1986.
Death of a Man, Harcourt, 1936.
Monday Night, Harcourt, 1938, reprinted, P.P. Appel, 1977.
The Crazy Hunter: Three Short Novels (also see below; includes "The Crazy Hunter," "The Bridegroom's Body," and "Big Fiddle"), Harcourt, 1940 (published in England as *The Crazy Hunter and Other Stories,* Faber, 1940), reprinted with introduction by Margaret Atwood, Penguin, 1982.
Primer for Combat, Simon & Schuster, 1942.
Avalanche, Simon & Schuster, 1944.
A Frenchman Must Die, Simon & Schuster, 1946.
1939, Simon & Schuster, 1948.
His Human Majesty, Whittlesey House, 1949.
The Seagull on the Step, Knopf, 1955.
Three Short Novels (includes "The Crazy Hunter," "The Bridegroom's Body," and "Decision"), Beacon, 1958.
Generation without Farewell, Knopf, 1960.
The Underground Woman, Doubleday, 1975.

SHORT STORIES

Short Stories, Black Sun (Paris), 1929.
Wedding Day and Other Stories, Cape & Smith, 1930, reprinted, Books for Libraries Press, 1972.
The First Lover and Other Stories, Random, 1933.
The White Horses of Vienna and Other Stories, Harcourt, 1936.
Thirty Stories, Simon & Schuster, 1946.
The Smoking Mountain: Stories of Post-War Germany, McGraw, 1951.
Nothing Ever Breaks Except the Heart, Doubleday, 1966.
Fifty Stories, Doubleday, 1980.
Life Being the Best and Other Stories, New Directions, 1988.

POETRY

A Statement, Modern Editions Press, 1932.
A Glad Day, New Directions, 1938.
American Citizen: Naturalized in Leadville, Colorado (long poem), Simon & Schuster, 1944.
The Lost Dogs of Phnom Pehn, Two Windows (Berkeley), 1968.
Testament for My Students and Other Poems, Doubleday, 1970.
A Poem for February First 1975, Quercus Press, 1975.

JUVENILE

The Youngest Camel, Little, Brown, 1939, revised edition published as *The Youngest Camel: Reconsidered and Rewritten,* Harper, 1959.
Pinky, the Cat Who Liked to Sleep, Crowell-Collier, 1966.
Pinky in Persia, Crowell-Collier, 1968.

NONFICTION

Breaking the Silence: Why a Mother Tells Her Son about the Nazi Era (pamphlet), Institute of Human Relations Press (New York), 1962.
The Long Walk at San Francisco State and Other Essays, Grove, 1970.
(With others) *Four Visions of America,* Capra, 1977.
Words that Must Somehow Be Said: Selected Essays of Kay Boyle, 1927-1984, North Point Press, 1985.

TRANSLATOR FROM THE FRENCH

Joseph Delteil, *Don Juan,* Cape & Smith, 1931.
Rene Crevel, *Mr. Knife Miss Fork,* Black Sun, 1931.
Raymond Radiguet, *Devil in the Flesh,* H. Smith, 1932.
(And author of afterword) Crevel, *Babylon,* North Point Press, 1985.

GHOST WRITER

Gladys Palmer Brooke, *Relations & Complications: Being the Recollections of H.H. the Dayang Muda of Sarawak,* Lane, 1929.
Bettina Bedwell, *Yellow Dusk,* Hurst & Blackett, 1937.

EDITOR

Poems and Sonnets by Ernest Walsh, Harcourt, 1934.

(With former husband Laurence Vail and Nina Conarain) *365 Days,* Harcourt, 1936.

The Autobiography of Emanuel Carnevali, Horizon Press, 1967.

(And contributor of supplementary chapters) Robert McAlmon, *Being Geniuses Together, 1920-1930* (memoirs), Doubleday, 1968, revised edition with new afterword by Boyle, Northpoint Press, 1984.

(With Justine Van Gundy) *Enough of Dying! Voices for Peace,* Laurel, 1972.

OTHER

(Author of foreword) Herbert Kubly, *At Large,* Gollancz, 1963, Doubleday, 1964.

(Author of afterword) McAlmon, *A Hasty Bunch,* Southern Illinois University Press, 1977.

Contributor to anthologies, including numerous volumes of *Best American Short Stories,* edited by Edward O'Brien. On staff of *Broom* magazine, 1922; foreign correspondent in Germany for *New Yorker,* 1946-53. Regular contributor to *transition, Saturday Evening Post, Harper's,* and *Nation.*

WORK IN PROGRESS: The Irish Women; revised edition of *Gentlemen, I Address You Privately;* a long poem on Samuel Beckett.

SIDELIGHTS: "The older I grow," novelist, short story writer, poet, and essayist Kay Boyle comments in an interview with Kay Mills of the *Los Angeles Times,* "the more I feel that all writers should be more committed to their times and write of their times and of the issues of their times." According to Mills, both Boyle's narrative style and themes reflect the writer's commitment to her times. Boyle's largely autobiographical fiction is her major vehicle for social commentary. Her short stories—which critics such as Robert E. Kroll in *Prairie Schooner* and Theodore L. Gross in *Saturday Review* describe as her best work—illustrate both the writer's noteworthy style and what Gross calls, "her intention to measure [in her fiction] . . . the central issues of our time."

From the publication of Boyle's first volume of short fiction to her anthology of nearly forty years of writing, *Fifty Stories,* her mastery of style has interested critics. When Katherine Anne Porter examined Boyle's early work in a 1931 review (included in *The Critic as Artist: Essays on Books, 1920-1970),* she noted Boyle's involvement with the experimental Parisian literary monthly, *transition,* and the journal's effect on Boyle's writing. According to Porter, Boyle's prose "sums up the salient qualities of [those writers who regularly contributed to *transition*]: a fighting spirit, freshness of feeling, curiosity, the courage of her own attitude and idiom, a violently dedicated search for the meanings and methods of art."

Critical comment on Boyle's style also comes from other sources, including Richard C. Carpenter and Vance Bourjaily. Both compare Boyle's work to that of more well-known writers of the same period. In *Critique: Studies in Modern Fiction,* Carpenter comments: "Like Faulkner or Virginia Woolf or Joyce, Kay Boyle works largely with interior monologue, sometimes with a stream of consciousness, thus setting the internal states of her characters in contrast to the outer world, or complementary to it." In Bourjaily's *New York Times Book Review* essay the critic finds *Fifty Stories* "a wonderful exhibit of . . . techniques and themes [introduced by writers living in Paris in the twenties] in evolution. Among the techniques we have grammatical simplification, rhythmic repetition, the mixing in of vernacular, stream of consciousness, density of impressions, radical imagery and experiments with surrealism that may have originated with Gertrude Stein and James Joyce but became community property of the group."

Like the others members of the American literary set that flourished in Paris during the early years of the twentieth century, Boyle was committed to resisting traditional forms of writing. But, although her writing may have been her first act of defiance against authority, it wasn't her last. During the fifties she fought the accusations and subsequent black-listing brought against her husband, Joseph von Franckenstein, and herself, by Communist-hunters Senator Joseph McCarthy and his fellow investigators. She has continued to speak out against injustice throughout her life no matter how unpopular her views, speaking out in the sixties against the war in Vietnam and in the eighties protesting the U.S. bombing of Libya.

Like the stylistic elements of her fiction, Boyle's most important theme, which *Saturday Review* contributor Carole Cook cites as "the individual's moral responsibility," dates back to some of her earliest writing. For example, in his introduction to *Fifty Stories* David Daiches notes this moral function in particular in Boyle's stories written during World War II. The stories "read as though they have been *lived through* . . . ," he remarks. "But they are far from being merely 'on the spot' reporting, nor are they 'war stories' in the conventional sense. Their object is not to describe either horror or heroism, but to explore the core of human meaning in desperate situations." Earl Rovit finds the same theme in Boyle's stories. He notes in his *Nation* essay, "A steady passionate concern for social justice and an equally unswerving compassion for the poignancies of human suffering are powerful and noble weapons in any artist's arsenal—and to these Kay Boyle can justly lay claim." *Chicago Tribune Book World* contributor Cyra McFadden similarly notes the "strong moral center" illustrated by Boyle's fiction.

Despite general critical approval for Boyle's work, she has never enjoyed wide-spread popularity. *Dictionary of Literary Biography* contributor David V. Koch theorizes that Boyle "has been so busy writing and acting upon her beliefs . . . that she has had little time to cultivate a following. Indeed, seeking literary fame would be contrary to Boyle's beliefs, for she has consistently sought to speak for those who could not speak for themselves."

Boyle's papers and manuscripts are at the Morris Library, Southern Illinois University, Carbondale.

MEDIA ADAPTATIONS: "The Crazy Hunter," was adapted for television by Desilu Productions, 1958; the short story, "The Ballet of Central Park," was adapted and filmed as a short subject in 1972; the short story, "Maiden, Maiden," was made into a full-length feature film by Highland Films, 1980.

AVOCATIONAL INTERESTS: Riding horses and climbing mountains.

BIOGRAPHICAL/CRITICAL SOURCES:

BOOKS

Boyle, Kay, *Fifty Stories,* with introduction by David Daiches, Doubleday, 1980.

Boyle, Kay, *Life Being the Best & Other Stories,* edited and with an introduction by Sandra Whipple Spanier, New Directions, 1988.

Contemporary Authors Autobiography Series, Volume 1, Gale, 1984.

Contemporary Literary Criticism, Gale, Volume 1, 1973, Volume 5, 1976, Volume 19, 1978.

Dictionary of Literary Biography, Gale, Volume 4: *American Writers in Paris, 1920-1939,* 1980, Volume 9: *American Novelists, 1910-1945,* 1981, Volume 48, *American Poets, 1880-1945, Second Series,* 1986.

Madden, Charles F., *Talks with Authors,* Southern Illinois University Press, 1968.

Moore, Harry T., *Age of the Modern and Other Literary Essays,* Southern Illinois University Press, 1971.

Porter, Katherine Anne, *The Critic as Artist: Essays on Books, 1920-1970,* edited by Gilbert A. Harrison, Liveright, 1972.

Spanier, Sandra Whipple, *Kay Boyle: Artist and Activist,* Southern Illinois University Press, 1986.

Wilson, Edmund, *Classics and Commercials: A Literary Chronicle of the Forties,* Farrar, Straus, 1950.

Yalom, Marilyn, editor, *Women Writers of the West Coast,* Capra Press, 1983.

PERIODICALS

Bookman, June, 1932.

Book World, June 9, 1968.

Chicago Tribune Book World, October 12, 1980.

Christian Science Monitor, January 5, 1971, November 10, 1980.

College English, November, 1953.

Critique: Studies in Modern Fiction, winter, 1964-65.

English Journal, November, 1953.

Kenyon Review, spring, 1960.

London Review of Books, April 15, 1982.

Los Angeles Times, December 10, 1980, June 18, 1984, October 12, 1986.

Los Angeles Times Book Review, August 4, 1985, September 29, 1985, April 13, 1986.

Ms., August, 1985.

Nation, December 24, 1930, October 24, 1936, June 8, 1970, June 15, 1970, April 26, 1971, June 26, 1972, March 22, 1975, September 27, 1980.

New Republic, April 22, 1931, July 13, 1932, December 13, 1933, October 21, 1936, January 24, 1970, February 8, 1975.

Newsweek, January 25, 1960, January 13, 1975.

New Yorker, January 20, 1975.

New York Herald Tribune Books, November 12, 1933, February 9, 1936, March 10, 1940.

New York Times, November 16, 1930, March 26, 1933, November 12, 1933, October 11, 1936, December 1, 1946, June 21, 1966.

New York Times Book Review, July 10, 1966, June 9, 1968, February 2, 1975, September 28, 1980, July 15, 1984, August 25, 1985, September 22, 1985, November 16, 1986, July 3, 1988.

Poetry, November, 1971.

Prairie Schooner, summer, 1963, winter, 1966-67.

Publishers Weekly, October 17, 1980, March 11, 1988.

Saturday Review, March 25, 1933, November 4, 1933, November 30, 1946, April 9, 1949, April 21, 1951, July 16, 1966, January 7, 1978, September, 1980.

Times Literary Supplement, November 30, 1967, April 17, 1981, September 27, 1985.

Washington Post Book World, October 19, 1980, October 5, 1986.

Wilson Library Bulletin, January, 1932.

—Sketch by Marian Gonsior

BRADFORD, James C(hapin) 1945-

PERSONAL: Born April 7, 1945, in Detroit, Mich.; son of Raymond Frederick (a civil servant) and Eleanor Mae (Ritter) Bradford; married Judith Robinson, 1964; children: James C., John F. *Education:* Michigan State University, B.A., 1967, M.A., 1968; University of Virginia, Ph.D., 1976.

ADDRESSES: Home—4205 Nagle, Bryan, Tex. 77801. *Office*—Department of History, Texas A & M University, College Station, Tex. 77843.

CAREER: Thomas Jefferson Memorial Foundation, Charlottesville, Va., research assistant, 1972-73; U.S. Naval Academy, Annapolis, Md., assistant professor of history, 1973-81; Texas A & M University, College Station, 1981—, began as assistant professor, currently associate professor of history. Chairman of Anne Arundel County Historic Preservation Commission, 1976-81, and Londontown Public House Commission, 1980-81.

MEMBER: North American Society for Oceanic History, American Historical Association, Organization of American Historians, Society for Historians of the Early American Republic, Association for Documentary Editing, American Military Institute, Southern Historical Association.

WRITINGS:

(Contributor) Leigh E. Grosenick, editor, *The Administration of the New Federalism,* American Society for Public Administration, 1974.

(Editor and contributor) *Anne Arundel County: A Bicentennial History, 1649-1977,* Anne Arundel Bicentennial Commission, 1978.

(Contributor) Kenneth J. Hagan, editor, *Peace and War: Interpretations of American Naval Policy,* Greenwood Press, 1978.

(With E. B. Potter and others) *Sea Power: A Naval History,* 2nd edition, Naval Institute Press, 1981.

(Editor and contributor) *Command Under Sail,* Naval Institute Press, 1984.

Captains of the Old Steam Navy, Naval Institute Press, 1986.

(Editor) *The Papers of John Paul Jones,* Chadwyck-Healey, 1986.

Admirals of the New Steel Navy, Naval Institute Press, 1989.

Book review editor of *Journal of the Early Republic,* 1980—.

WORK IN PROGRESS: A letterpress edition of John Paul Jones's correspondence; a biography of John Paul Jones; historical dictionaries of the U.S. Navy and Coast Guard.

SIDELIGHTS: James Bradford once told *CA:* "The Continental Navy had fewer colonial precedents to guide it than did the Continental Congress and Army. When I began studying its institutional development, I found that John Paul Jones was one of the few individuals who gave careful consideration to how a navy should be organized, what its roles should be, and what its relationship to the new nation should be. As I sought his papers I found that no one had ever collected or edited an edition of them. I had done some editing at 'Monticello' when I was employed by the Thomas Jefferson Foundation and decided to edit the Jones Papers. Beyond this, I remain committed to biography as both an inherently interesting genre and as a lens through which to view institutions and eras."

BRAUNBURG, Rudolf 1924-

PERSONAL: Born July 19, 1924, in Landsberg, Germany; son of Willy and Hedwig (Schulz) Braunburg; married Annemarie Pohl, September 20, 1969; children: Viola. *Education:* Attended high school in Lueneburg, Germany.

ADDRESSES: Home—Felsenweg 15, D-5520, Waldbroel, West Germany.

CAREER: Rudolf Steiner School, Hamburg, West Germany, teacher, 1949-55; Lufthansa (German national airline), Frankfurt, West Germany, pilot and flight captain, 1955-79; writer, 1979—. *Military service:* German Luftwaffe, fighter pilot, 1943-44.

WRITINGS:

Dem Himmel naeher als der Erde (novel; title means "Nearer to Sky Than to Earth"), Marion V. Schroeder, 1957.
Geh nicht nach Dalaba (novel; title means "Don't Go to Dalaba"), Marion V. Schroeder, 1961.
Zwischenlandung (novel; title means "Intermission-Stop"), Schneekluth-Verlag, 1971.
Der verratene Himmel (novel), [West Germany], 1979, translation by J. Maxwell Brownjohn published as *Betrayed Skies,* Doubleday, 1979.
Kennwort Koenigsberg (novel; title means "Codeword Koenigsberg"), Schneekluth-Verlag, 1980.
Masurengold (novel; title means "The Gold of Masuren"), Schneekluth-Verlag, 1981.
Drachensturz (novel; title means "The Fall of the Dragon"), Schneekluth-Verlag, 1982.
Ein Leben auf Flugeln (autobiography; title means "Life on Wings"), Kindler-Verlag, 1982.
Die schwarze Jagd (novel; title means "The Black Hunt"), Schneekluth-Verlag, 1983.
Jetliner (novel), Hoffmann & Campe, 1983.
Nordlicht (novel; title means "Northern Lights"), Koesler-Verlag, 1985.
Der Engel vom anderen Stern (novel; title means "The Angel from the Other Planet"), Koesler-Verlag, 1986.
Der Abschuss (novel; title means "The Kill"), Rowohlt-Verlag, 1987.
Keine Rueckkehr nach Manila (novel; title means "No Return to Manila"), Wunderlich-Verlag, 1988.

OTHER

Also author of scripts for German television.

WORK IN PROGRESS: The Wall, a novel about a youth in Nazi Germany; *Voices in the Sky,* a mystery novel about an aircraft accident.

SIDELIGHTS: Rudolf Braunburg told *CA:* "The time I have spent as an airline captain for more than twenty years is important to my career as a writer. I began writing as a schoolboy in Nazi Germany, when I couldn't agree with the official line of social and political communication. I considered my notices a protest against this. My style and ability then, however, were too simple and unskilled to have any effect. I was eighteen at the time.

"I write ten hours a day, without relaxing or taking time for vacations, etc. I work standing before my typewriter. As I have been sitting on the lefthand seat of a jetliner for more than twenty years, I am always happy when I can stand. I have written more than twenty-five novels and about twenty nonfiction books which have been translated into Dutch, English, French, Italian, Japanese, and Indonesian. I have also been writing some nonfiction scripts about flying for German television, including 'No Fear of Flying' (Westdeutscher Rundfunk).

"My advice to aspiring writers is: don't talk, just listen. Then, ten years later, try your first work. I have been strongly influenced by Ernest Hemingway, Hermann Hesse, and Henry Miller. I feel I can learn from other writers."

BIOGRAPHICAL/CRITICAL SOURCES:

BOOKS

Braunburg, Rudolf, *Ein Leben auf Flugeln* (autobiography; title means "Life on Wings"), Kindler-Verlag, 1982.

PERIODICALS

Library Journal, October, 1980.

* * *

BRETT, Simon (Anthony Lee) 1945-

PERSONAL: Born October 28, 1945, in Worcester Park, Surrey, England; son of John (a surveyor) and Margaret (a schoolteacher; maiden name, Lee) Brett; married Lucy Victoria McLaren, November 27, 1971; children: Sophie Victoria Margaret McLaren, two sons. *Education:* Wadham College, Oxford, B.A. (first class honors), 1967. *Politics:* None. *Religion:* "Some."

ADDRESSES: Home and office—Frith House, Burpham, Arundel, West Sussex BN18 9RR, England. *Agent*—Michael Motley, 78 Gloucester Ter., London W2 3HH, England.

CAREER: Writer. British Broadcasting Corp. (BBC), London, England, radio producer, 1968-77; London Weekend Television, London, television producer, 1977-79.

AWARDS, HONORS: Award from Writers Guild, 1973, for best radio feature script.

WRITINGS:

MYSTERY NOVELS

Cast, in Order of Disappearance (also see below), Gollancz, 1975, Scribner, 1976.
So Much Blood, Gollancz, 1976, Scribner, 1977.
Star Trap, Gollancz, 1977, Scribner, 1978.
An Amateur Corpse, Scribner, 1978.
A Comedian Dies, Scribner, 1979.
The Dead Side of the Mike, Scribner, 1980.
Situation Tragedy, Scribner, 1981.
Murder Unprompted, Scribner, 1982.
Murder in the Title, Scribner, 1983.
Not Dead, Only Resting, Gollancz, 1984.
A Shock to the System, Macmillan, 1984.
Dead Giveaway, Scribner, 1986.
Dead Romantic, Scribner, 1986.
A Nice Class of Corpse, Scribner, 1987.
What Bloody Man Is That?, Scribner, 1987.
Mrs, Presumed Dead, Scribner, 1989.

JUVENILE MYSTERIES

The Three Detectives and the Missing Superstar, Macmillan, 1986.
The Three Detectives and the Knight in Armor, Macmillan, 1987.

PLAYS

"Mrs. Gladys Moxon" (one-act), first produced in London at the Soho Theatre, May 19, 1970.

"Did You Sleep Well?" and "A Good Day at the Office," first produced together in London, 1971.
"Third Person," first produced in London, 1972.
"Drake's Dream" (musical), first produced in Worthing, Sussex, 1977, produced in London, 1977.

RADIO SCRIPTS

"Semi-Circles" series, 1982, "Gothic Romances," 1982, "A Matter of Life and Death," 1982, and "Cast, in Order of Disappearance" (based on his novel of the same title), 1983.

TELEVISION SCRIPTS

"The Crime of the Dancing Duchess," 1983, and "A Promising Death," 1983.

OTHER

Frank Muir Goes Into . . ., four volumes, Robson, 1978-81.
Frank Muir on Children, Heinemann, 1980.
Molesworth Rites Again, Hutchinson, 1983.
The Child Owner's Handbook, Allen & Unwin, 1983.
People Spotting, Elm Tree Books, 1985.
Tickled to Death, and Other Stories of Crime and Suspense, Scribner, 1985 (published in England as *A Box of Tricks,* Gollancz, 1985).
Waste Paper Basket Archive, Sidgwick & Jackson, 1986.

Contributor of stories to *Ellery Queen's Mystery Magazine.*

EDITOR

The Faber Book of Useful Verse, Faber, 1981.
(With Frank Muir) *Frank Muir Presents the Book of Comedy Sketches,* Elm Tree Books, 1982.
Take a Spare Truss: Tips for Nineteenth-Century Travelers, Elm Tree Books, 1983.
The Faber Book of Parodies, Faber, 1984.
Bad Form: The Etiquette of Bad Taste, David & Charles, 1984.
The Faber Book of Diaries, Faber, 1987.

CONTRIBUTOR

George Hardinge, editor, *Winter's Crimes 11,* St. Martin's, 1979.
John Waite, editor, *Mystery Guild Anthology,* Constable, 1980.
Hilary Watson, editor, *Winter's Crimes 12,* St. Martin's, 1980.
Watson, editor, *Winter's Crimes 14,* St. Martin's, 1982.
Herbert Harris, editor, *John Creasey's Crime Collection, 1982,* St. Martin's, 1982.

WORK IN PROGRESS: "Always."

SIDELIGHTS: Simon Brett's novels concerning the struggling actor and amateur sleuth Charles Paris have brought his work to the attention of mystery fans in both England and America. Brett's witty, ironic style and behind-the-scenes look at the world of English show business have been especially praised by reviewers. "What distinguishes [Paris's] adventures . . .," Richard Schickel writes in *Time,* "is the author's wry observations of Britain's entertainment milieu. Brett has a farceur's eye for crooked agents and egomaniac stars, for performers elbowing their way up or trying to take the slide back down graciously, for network nitwits, [and] for creative geniuses unsung by anyone but themselves." Derrick Murdoch of the Toronto *Globe and Mail* finds that "Brett's urbane humor and caustic observations are consistently entertaining."

Brett's own career as a radio and television producer gives him a thorough knowledge of the entertainment world he writes about in his novels. He has produced and written television comedies, radio dramas, and stage plays, and has also done some amateur acting as well. "My acting experience," Brett told Rosemary Herbert of *Publishers Weekly,* "has helped me with dialogue in that having acted and worked with actors, I *hope* I know which lines are sayable."

Brett's work with actors also gives him an insight into the problems they experience in their careers. His actor-sleuth Charles Paris has experienced the range of actor's problems. A promising star in the 1950s, Paris is now a small-time actor, consigned to character parts in the theatre and reduced to seeking minor television roles in programs that he finds insulting. In *Dead Giveaway,* for example, he is asked to appear as a contestant on a game show similar to "What's My Line," in which panelists must guess who he is and what he does for a living. The unstated insult, of course, is that Paris will be a challenging guest for them, since he is unknown to the general public. Paris "is resigned to the fact," Martha Alderson writes in *Clues: A Journal of Detection,* "that his youthful dreams of fame were mostly just that."

Paris is in his early fifties, drinks a bit too much whiskey, "is cynical, usually depressed, half a step ahead of the Inland Revenue, and concerned about his sexual need for young starlets," as Alderson remarks. He happens upon mysteries in the course of his ongoing efforts to secure and hold acting jobs. These mysteries are of the traditional "puzzle" variety. To solve them, Paris is called upon to use his skills as an actor, often disguising himself in costumes and make-up to secure information from otherwise uncooperative witnesses. His adventures have taken place in a variety of show business settings. In *A Comedian Dies,* Paris investigates the electrocution of a performer at a seaside music hall. In *Dead Giveaway,* he looks into the poisoning of a media celebrity on the set of a popular television game show. And in *The Dead Side of the Mike,* Paris unravels the apparent suicide of a young woman in the radio studios of the British Broadcasting Corporation.

The Paris mysteries are written in a light, entertaining style and are as humorous as they are mysterious. As Herbert remarks, "All of [Brett's] work is brightened by a scintillating sense of humor in the understated British tradition, shot through with irony." Newgate Callendar of the *New York Times Book Review* agrees, noting that "there is a pronounced touch of irony in the Brett books; the author knows how to twist a knife." And, writing in the Toronto *Globe and Mail,* Margaret Cannon observes that Brett's work "is laced with his slyly sneering view of current social values." Brett's usual targets are the more absurd aspects of show business and he uses the voice of Paris, a dedicated patron of the arts despite his relative failure as an actor, to make his ironic points.

Brett's mysteries also present the world of entertainment in an accurate, almost documentary style. In a review of the novel *Situation Tragedy,* in which Paris lands a role on a new television program, James Kaufmann of the *Christian Science Monitor* allows that "the strength of [the novel] is the very accurate picture it gives of the making of television shows. Ex-television producer Brett knows what he's talking about." Speaking of the novel *Murder Unprompted,* dealing with a murder in the West End theatre district, Miranda Seymour of the London *Times* notes that the story is primarily about Paris's efforts to secure a role in a stage play and only gradually becomes a murder mystery. She finds that this approach gives the story "an underlying something extra to make it more satisfying than it might have been. . . . Let us hope the engaging Paris keeps his detective instinct always at least dormant while he reveals to us yet other aspects of the actor's world." In his review of *Dead Giveaway,* a novel set in a television studio, John Gross of the *New York Times* claims that Brett "manages to catch both the inanity of junk television and the amount of intensity that people invest in it, audiences and program-makers alike."

While the Charles Paris mysteries are witty and puzzling affairs, Brett's other mystery novels focus on a darker side of human nature. They feature weak characters who, when they experience an upset in their lives, can do nothing else but turn to crime. In *A Shock to the System,* for example, Brett's character Graham Marshall becomes a murderer when his career as an oil company executive seems threatened. Murdoch finds the novel to be "clearly in a new and more ambitious vein" than the Paris books. Gary A. Steffen, in his review of the book for *Armchair Detective,* finds it "a combination of fast, compelling read on one level and psychological novel on another. . . . This is an excellent novel, very well written, with tight construction and a fast-moving plot. It proves too that Simon Brett does not need his series character Charlie Paris to write effectively."

All of Brett's novels display what Callendar calls "a civilized patina to the writing." Robin Winks of the *New Republic* also describes Brett as "a 'civilized' writer who puts neither a word wrong nor an unnecessary expletive under the nose of the fastidious." In an evaluation of Brett's career as a mystery writer, Winks claims that "it is time to elevate Simon Brett from the Comers to those who have Made It."

BIOGRAPHICAL/CRITICAL SOURCES:

PERIODICALS

Armchair Detective, winter, 1988.
Christian Science Monitor, March 3, 1982.
Clue: A Journal of Detection, fall/winter, 1983.
Globe and Mail (Toronto), January 19, 1985, August 31, 1985.
New Republic, October 27, 1979, February 16, 1980.
New Yorker, September 2, 1985.
New York Times, April 4, 1986.
New York Times Book Review, September 23, 1979, February 22, 1981.
Publishers Weekly, October 25, 1985.
Spectator, February 22, 1986.
Time, October 1, 1979, July 7, 1986.
Times (London), February 18, 1982, May 15, 1986, May 7, 1987.
Times Literary Supplement, September 26, 1975.

—Sketch by Thomas Wiloch

* * *

BREWSTER, Townsend 1924-

PERSONAL: Born July 23, 1924, in Glen Cove, N.Y.; son of Townsend (a postal clerk) and Sara (a teacher; maiden name, Tyler) Brewster. *Education:* Queens College (now of the City University of New York), B.A., 1947; Columbia University, M.A., 1962.

ADDRESSES: Home—171-29 103rd Rd., Jamaica, N.Y. 11433. *Office*—*Harlem Cultural Review,* 1 West 125th St., New York, N.Y. 10027. *Agent*—Ronelda Roberts, 1214 Ridge Blvd., Suite 3F, Brooklyn, N.Y. 11209.

CAREER: Writer, 1947-59; Hicks & Greist (advertising agency), New York City, copywriter, 1959-61; Lennen & Newell (advertising agency), New York City, librarian, 1962-67; writer, 1967-69; City College of the City University of New York, New York City, lecturer in theater, 1969-73; writer, 1974—. Vice-president of Harlem Performance Center; member of board of directors of Frank Silvera Writers Workshop and Harlem Cultural Council. Playwright in residence at University of Denver, 1969. Member of BMI Musical Theater Workshop. *Military service:* U.S. Army, 1943-45.

MEMBER: International Brecht Society, ASCAP, Outer Critics Circle, Dramatists Guild, Maple Leaf Society, Ragtime Society.

AWARDS, HONORS: Fellow of National Theater Conference, 1947; Koussevitzky Foundation scholar, 1947; William Morris scholar, American Theater Wing, 1955; award from *Story,* 1969, for "Please Don't Cry and Say 'No' "; Louise Bogan Memorial Prize in poetry, New York Poetry Forum, 1975, for "Dos Suenos"; grants from Harlem Cultural Council, 1976, and National Endowment for the Arts, 1977; Jonathan Swift Award for satire, Virginia Commonwealth University, 1979, for play "The Ecologists."

WRITINGS:

The Tower (libretto for opera; first produced at Santa Fe Opera, Santa Fe, N.M., August 2, 1957), Boosey & Hawkes, 1958.
(Translator) Plautus, *Rudens,* Continental Play Service, 1963.
(Contributor) *Today's Negro Voices,* Messner, 1970.
Lady Plum Blossom (two-act musical play for young people; first produced in Corvallis, Ore., at Oregon State University, April, 1972), Modern Theatre for Youth, 1973.
(Contributor of translation) Bernard F. Dukore, editor, *Dramatic Theory and Criticism: Greeks to Grotowski,* Holt, 1974.
The Cocktail Sip (opera), music by Noel da Costa, ATSOC Music, 1982.
(Translator) Georges Neveux, "The Bougival Vampire," first produced by Ubu Repertory Theater, 1985.
(Translator) Bernard Binlin Dadie, *Monsieur Thogo-gnini* (first produced by Ubu Repertory Theater at 1st Annual Festival of New Plays from French-Speaking Africa, 1986), Ubu Repertory Theater Publications, 1986.
(Adapter) Jean-Francois Regnard, "Up and Down" (a bill of musicals adapted from two one-act comedies), music by Genovis Albright, first produced by ASCAP Musical Theatre Workshop, 1986.
(Translator) Jean-Claude Germain, "Les Hauts et les bas d'la vie d'une diva: Sarah Menard par eux-memes," first produced by Centre D'Essai des Auteurs Dramatiques, 1986.
(Translator) Maxime N'Debeka, *Equatorium* (first produced by Ubu Repertory Theater at 2nd Annual Festival of New Plays from French-Speaking Africa, 1987), Ubu Repertory Theater Publications, 1987.

Also translator of Joseph Boulogne's "L'Amant anonyme," 1976.

UNPUBLISHED PLAYS

"Little Girl, Big Town" (revue), first produced in New York City at Queens College, May 1, 1953.
"Please Don't Cry and Say 'No' " (one-act), first produced off-Broadway at Downtown Circle in the Square, December 6, 1972.
"Though It's Been Said Many Times, Many Ways" (one-act), first produced in New York City at Harlem Performance Center, December 22, 1976.
"Three by One" (trilogy of one-act plays), first produced in New York City at Harlem Performance Center, December 8, 1977.
"The Girl beneath the Tulip Tree" (one-act), first produced in New York City at Harlem Performance Center, December 8, 1977.

"Black-Belt Bertram" (one-act), first produced in New York City at Double Image Theatre, May, 1979.
"Arthur Ashe and I" (one-act), first produced in New York City at Riverside Church, June 20, 1979.
"There Was Something about Mr. Henderson," first produced by Fourth Friday Playwrights, 1985.
"Mascara and Confetti" (revue), first produced by Broadway Tomorrow, 1987.

Also author of "The Ecologists," and of "Memorials," a tetralogy of one-act plays, consisting of "The Jade Funerary Suit," "Idomeneus," "This Is the Gloaming of the Age of Aquarius," and "Praise Song."

UNPUBLISHED LIBRETTOS FOR OPERAS AND LYRICS FOR MUSICAL PLAYS

"The Choreography of Love" (jazz opera), first broadcast by WNYC-Radio, February 16, 1946.
"Revue Sketches," first produced in Akron, Ohio, at Weathervane Theatre, August 8, 1970.
"Harlequinades for Mourners" (four-act play), first produced in New York City at New Theatre, September 14, 1970.
"a," music by Gregory Forbes, first produced by Ubu Repertory Theater, 1986.

Also author of libretto for the folk opera "Of Angels and Donkeys."

OTHER

Translator, adapter, and continuity writer for "NBC Television Opera," 1950-51. Author of "A Word on Plays," a column appearing in *Big Red,* 1980-. Contributor of stories, poems, and reviews to magazines, including *Players, Pioneer, Oracle, Counterpoint, Classical Outlook, Music Journal,* and *Commonweal,* as well as various newspapers. Television critic for *Show Business;* theater critic for *Amsterdam News, Routes, Players,* and *Harlem Cultural Review;* book critic for *Harlem Cultural Review.* Editor of *Harlem Cultural Review.*

WORK IN PROGRESS: "Songs of Experience," a trilogy of one-act plays, consisting of "The Pavane of the Sleeping Beauty," "That Other Go-Round," and "The Briars That Bind."

SIDELIGHTS: Townsend Brewster told *CA:* "I began writing as a lyric poet. While I was an undergraduate at Queens College, a fellow student, a composer, asked me for a libretto. At first I declined, not considering myself a dramatist, but being a great opera buff allowed myself to be persuaded. The resulting work, 'The Choreography of Love,' was not only a great hit on campus but was also broadcast, and, then and there, the poet became loyal to the stage.

"Opera has continued to loom large in my writing career. In 1947 I was one of the four writers selected to inaugurate the libretto-writing department at Tanglewood, and I made my professional debut as a translator-adapter and continuity writer for the 'NBC Television Opera.' The initial translation, 'Carmen,' was subsequently repeated as the first opera telecast in color, and the 'Gianni Schicchi' was later sung at the Metropolitan Opera. On a grant from the Harlem Cultural Council, I translated 'L'Amant anonyme,' the only fully-surviving opera of eighteenth-century black composer Joseph Boulogne, the Chevalier de Saint-Georges.

"Though I still turn out an occasional *rondeau* or sonnet, most of my current versifying takes the form of lyrics for musicals and of the songs that are the features of most of my plays, a few of which are in meter. I have turned out little fiction.

"With two or three exceptions, my plays are comedies, though for me comedy means Wilde and Wycherley, Moliere and Marivaux (who, along with Brecht, is one of my favorite playwrights), rather than Neil Simon. For a definition of comedy, I turn to Victor Hugo, who saw it as 'criticism of human nature.' Most of my comedies fall into the category of 'This is a dream of happiness' or 'This is the way of the world.' I sometimes refer to the former as my *L'Elisir d'amore* vein.

"If Joseph Papp is correct in observing that Afro-American playwrights derive from television and films rather than from literature and drama, then I am one of the exceptions. I feel that I have had the chronological advantage of being able to realize when I encountered the works of Bullins and Baraka that they shared the African heritage not only with Wole Soyinka and Aime Cesaire, but also with Terence and Pushkin."

* * *

BRINNER, William M(ichael) 1924-

PERSONAL: Born October 6, 1924, in Alameda, Calif.; son of Fred Kohn (in business) and Sadie (Weiser) Brinner; married Lisa Johanna Kraus (a research food scientist), September 23, 1951; children: Benjamin Elon, Leyla Anat, Rafael Jonathan. *Education:* University of California, Berkeley, B.A., 1948, M.A., 1950, Ph.D., 1956. *Religion:* Jewish.

ADDRESSES: Home—753 Santa Barbara Rd., Berkeley, Calif. 94707. *Office*—Department of Near Eastern Studies, 699 Evans Hall, University of California, Berkeley, Calif. 94720.

CAREER: Teacher of humanities at regional high school in Bet Alfa, Israel, 1950-52; University of California, Berkeley, instructor, 1956-57, assistant professor, 1957-61, associate professor, 1961-64, professor of Near Eastern studies, 1964—, chairman of department and director of Near Eastern Language and Area Center, 1965-70, director of Center for Arabic Studies Abroad in Cairo, Egypt, 1967-70, director of University of California Study Center in Jerusalem, 1973-75. Harvard University, research fellow at Center for Middle Eastern Studies, 1960, lecturer, 1960-61; visiting professor at Hebrew University of Jerusalem, 1970-71, 1973-75, and at Tel Aviv University and Haifa University, 1973-75; member of faculty at Graduate Theological Union, Berkeley. Member of executive committee of American Research Center in Egypt and American Institute for Iranian Studies, 1968-70; chairman of Joint Committee on the Near and Middle East, American Council of Learned Societies-Social Science Research Council, 1968-70. Panelist on National Educational Television program "World Press," 1967-73, 1975-77. Consultant to Committee on International Exchange of Persons and National Endowment for the Humanities.

MEMBER: Middle East Studies Association of North America (member of board of directors, 1967-68; president, 1976), American Oriental Society (member of board of directors, 1967-70; vice-president, 1975; president, 1976), Mediaeval Academy of America, American Professors for Peace in the Middle East (vice-president, 1977—), Association of Teachers of Arabic (chairman, 1967-68), Institute for Jewish Life (member of board of trustees, 1972-73).

AWARDS, HONORS: Grants from American Council of Learned Societies and Social Science Research Council, 1961-62, and National Endowment for the Humanities, 1977-80; Guggenheim fellowship, 1965-66; Fulbright fellowship, 1970-71; Rabbi Jacob Freedman Award from Jewish Book Council of America, 1979, for translating *An Elegant Composition Concerning Relief after Adversity.*

WRITINGS:

(Editor with Mounah Abdallah Khouri) *Advanced Arabic Readers,* University of California Press, Volume 1, 1961, Volume 2, 1962.

(Editor and translator) Muhammad ibn Muhammad ibn Sasra, *A Chronicle of Damascus, 1389-97: The Unique Bodleian Library Manuscript, Al-Durra Al-Mudi' a Fi l'Dawkla Al-Zahiriya,* University of California Press, Volume 1: *The English Translation,* 1963, Volume 2: *The Arabic Text,* 1963.

Sutro Library Hebraica: A Handlist, California State Library, 1966.

(Editor with Khouri) *Readings in Modern Arabic Literature,* Volume 1, E. J. Brill, 1971.

(Translator and author of introduction) Nissim ben Jacob ben Nissim ibn Shahin, *An Elegant Composition Concerning Relief after Adversity,* Yale University Press, 1978.

(Editor with Stephen D. Ricks) *Studies in Islamic and Judaic Traditions,* Scholars Press, 1986.

(Translator and annotator) *Prophets and Patriarchs,* State University of New York Press, 1987.

(Editor with Moses Rischin) *Like All the Nations?: The Life and Legacy of Judah L. Magnes,* State University of New York Press, 1987.

Contributor to history and Middle East studies journals. Member of editorial board of *International Journal of Middle East Studies,* 1968-79; chairman of editorial board of *Middle East Review,* 1977—.

WORK IN PROGRESS: Research on biblical figures mentioned in the Koran; a study of the role of the prophet Muhammad in Islamic piety.

SIDELIGHTS: William M. Brinner told *CA:* "My interest and involvement in Arabic language and literature were, to me, logical extensions of similar interest and involvement in Hebrew language and literature. While the latter developed naturally out of my own cultural background, the former grew and developed as I became increasingly aware of the historical interrelationships between the two different yet related cultures. The present-day animosities and conflicts only strengthened my resolve to find, in my own life and work, a way to present what unites as well as what divides, what is shared, and what each culture has contributed to the other as well as to civilization at large.

"The [book] *An Elegant Composition Concerning Relief after Adversity,* the title being a literal translation of the Arabic and Hebrew original, is a perfect example of what I have mentioned above. It is a collection of Jewish tales, originally written in Judeo-Arabic, the language of Jews living in an Arabic-speaking environment, in this case Tunisia in the tenth and eleventh centuries. Some of the stories come from the Talmud, some from Islamic sources, but translated into Hebrew by the fifteenth century and later into Yiddish, the origins were forgotten and they spread throughout the Jewish diaspora.

"The Islamic tales about biblical figures mentioned in the Koran are the reverse side of the coin. These stories, in many instances of obviously Jewish origin, became a part of medieval folk Islam and have survived until today, often in a sort of pious folklore throughout the Muslim world."

* * *

BRODSKY, Stanley L. 1939-

PERSONAL: Born July 22, 1939, in Boston, Mass.; son of Harry and Selma (Cohen) Brodsky; married Annette Ratner, February 6, 1962 (divorced, 1981); children: Michael, Rachel. *Education:* University of New Hampshire, B.A., 1960; University of Florida, M.A., 1962, Ph.D., 1964. *Politics:* Democrat.

ADDRESSES: Home—22 Caplewood Dr., Tuscaloosa, Ala. 35401. *Office*—Department of Psychology, P.O. Box 870348, University of Alabama, University, Ala. 35487-0348.

CAREER: U.S. Army, 1963-67, served as chief of Psychology Division, U.S. Disciplinary Barracks, Fort Leavenworth, Kan., 1964-67, left service as captain; Southern Illinois University, Center for the Study of Crime, Delinquency and Corrections, Carbondale, assistant professor, 1967-70, associate professor of psychology, 1971-72; University of Alabama, University, 1972—, began as associate professor, currently professor of psychology. Visiting fellow, Institute of Criminology, Cambridge University, 1979; visiting professor, National Institute of Mental Health and Neurosciences, India, 1988.

MEMBER: American Association of Correctional Psychologists (president, 1969-71), American Psychological Association (secretary-treasurer, 1975-78, president, 1983-84, of Division of Psychologists in Public Service).

WRITINGS:

(Editor with Norman Eggleston) *The Military Prison: Theory, Research, and Practice,* Southern Illinois University Press, 1970.

Psychologists in the Criminal Justice System, University of Illinois Press, 1973.

Families and Friends of Men in Prison, Lexington Books, 1975.

(Editor with Marcia Walker) *Sexual Assault: The Victim and Rapist,* Lexington Books, 1976.

(Editor with Kenneth B. Melvin and Raymond D. Fowler) *Psy-Fi One,* Random House, 1977.

(Editor with Constance Fischer) *Informed Participation in Human Services,* Transaction Books, 1978.

(With H. O'Neal Smitherman) *Handbook of Scales for Research in Crime and Delinquency,* Plenum, 1983.

The Psychology of Adjustment and Well-Being, Holt, 1988.

* * *

BRYANT, Al
See BRYANT, T(homas) Alton

* * *

BRYANT, T(homas) Alton 1926-
(Thomas Alton, Al Bryant)

PERSONAL: Born April 16, 1926, in Grand Rapids, Mich.; son of Harry and Marie (Townsend) Bryant; married Jeanne Carlson, September 10, 1949; children: Thomas A., Jr., Donald Sanford, John Kenneth, Ann Elizabeth. *Education:* University of Michigan, B.A., 1951.

ADDRESSES: Home—9412 Blue Jay Way, Irving, Tex. 75063. *Office*—Word, Inc., 5221 North O'Connor Blvd., Suite 1000, Irving, Tex. 75039.

CAREER: Zondervan Publishing House, Grand Rapids, Mich., editor-in-chief, 1951-76; Word, Inc., Waco, Tex., managing editor, 1977—. *Military service:* U.S. Army, Cavalry, 1944-46; became staff sergeant.

WRITINGS:

Climbing the Heights, Zondervan, 1956.

Keep in Touch, Word, Inc., 1980.

Today, Lord, I Will, Word, Inc., 1982.

UNDER NAME AL BRYANT

Time Out, Zondervan, 1961.
Love Songs: Daily Meditations for Married Couples, Word, Inc., 1978.
The John Wesley Reader, Word, Inc., 1983.
Day by Day with C. H. Spurgeon, Word, Inc., 1985.
(Editor) *New Every Morning: Three Hundred Sixty-Six Daily Meditations from Your Favorite Christian Writers,* Word, Inc., 1985.

COMPILER

Religious Plays That Click, Zondervan, 1954.
Favorite Poems, Zondervan, 1957.
Pocket Treasury of Daily Devotions, Zondervan, c. 1960.
Poems That Bless, Zondervan, 1963.
(Under name Thomas Alton) *The New Compact Bible Dictionary,* Zondervan, 1967.
Sourcebook of Poetry, Zondervan, 1968.
Today's Dictionary of the Bible, Bethany House, 1982.
Songs of My Soul: Devotional Thoughts from the Writings of W. Phillip Keller, Word, Inc., 1989.

OTHER

Author of children's stories and sermon outlines. Editor of *Christian Digest.*

* * *

BULTMANN, Rudolf Karl 1884-1976

PERSONAL: Born August 20, 1884, in Wiefelstede, Germany (now West Germany); died July 30, 1976, in Marburg, West Germany; son of Arthur (a parson) and Helene (Stern) Bultmann; married Helene Feldmann, August 6, 1917; children: Antje (Mrs. B. Lemke), Gesine (Mrs. Malte Diesselhorst), Heilke. *Education:* Studied at Universities of Tuebingen, Berlin, Marburg, Lic. theol., 1910. *Religion:* Evangelical.

ADDRESSES: Home—Calvin St. 14, Marburg on the Lahn, West Germany.

CAREER: University of Marburg, Marburg, Germany (now West Germany), instructor in New Testament science, 1912-16; University of Breslau, Breslau, Germany (now Wroclaw, Poland), assistant professor of New Testament science, 1916-20; University of Giessen, Giessen, Germany (now West Germany), professor, 1920-21; University of Marburg, professor, 1921-51, became professor emeritus.

MEMBER: Society of Biblical Literature (honorary), Academies of Oslo, Heidelberg, and Goettingen (corresponding member), Academia Goethena (Sao Paolo, Brazil; corresponding member).

AWARDS, HONORS: D.Theol. from University of Marburg, 1920; D.D. from University of St. Andrews, 1935; D.S.Th. from Syracuse University, 1959; Dr.Phil. from University of Marburg, 1959.

WRITINGS:

Der Stil der paulinischen Predigt und die kynischstoische Diatribe, Vandenhoeck & Ruprecht (Goettingen), 1910.
Die Geschichte der synoptischen Tradition, Vandenhoeck & Ruprecht, 1921, 5th edition, 1961, English translation by John Marsh of the 3rd German edition published as *The History of the Synoptic Tradition,* Harper, 1963.
Jesus, Deutsche Bibliothek (Berlin), 1926, revised edition, Mohr (Tuebingen), 1961, English translation by Louise Pettibone Smith and Erminie Huntress published as *Jesus and the Word,* Scribner, 1934.
Krisis des Glaubens, Krisis der Kirche, Krisis der Religion (lectures delivered at the University of Marburg), A. Toepelmann (Giessen), 1931.
Glauben und Verstehen, Mohr, Volume I, 1933, Volume II, 1954, Volume III, 1960, Volume IV, 1965, English translation by J. C. G. Greig of Volume II published as *Essays: Philosophical and Theological,* Macmillan, 1955.
(Contributor) F. C. Grant, editor and translator, *Form Criticism* (contains "The Study of the Synoptic Gospels"), Willett, 1934, Harper, 1962.
Offenbarung und Heilsgeschehen, A. Lempp (Munich), 1941.
(Contributor) Hans Werner Bartsch, editor, *Kerygma und Mythos: Ein theologisches Gespraech,* two volumes, Reich & Heidrich (Hamburg), 1948-52, English translation by Reginald H. Fuller published as *Kerygma and Myth: A Theological Debate,* S.P.C.K., 1953.
Das Christentum als orientalische und als abendlaendische Religion, F. Truejen (Bremen) 1949.
Das Urchristentum im Rahmen der antiken Religionen, Artemis-Verlag (Zurich), 1949, reprinted, Rowohlt, 1962, English translation by Fuller published as *Primitive Christianity in Its Contemporary Setting,* Meridian, 1956, reprinted, New American Library, 1974.
Theologie des Neuen Testaments, Mohr, 1950, reprinted, 1977, English translation by Kendrick Grobel published as *Theology of the New Testament,* two volumes, Scribner, 1951-55, reprinted as one volume, 1965.
Das Evangelium des Johannes, Vandenhoeck & Ruprecht, 1952.
(With Karl Jaspers) *Die Frage der Entmythologisierung,* R. Piper (Munich), 1954, English translation published as *Myth and Christianity: An Inquiry into the Possibility of Religion without Myth,* Noonday, 1958.
Marburger Predigten, Mohr, 1956, English translation by Harold Knight published as *This World and the Beyond: Marburg Sermons,* Scribner, 1960.
(Editor) *Die Reden des Johannesevangeliums und der Stil der gnostischen Offenbarungsrede,* Vandenhoeck & Ruprecht, 1956.
History and Eschatology (Gifford lectures at University of Edinburgh, 1955), University Press, Edinburgh, 1957, reprinted, Harper, 1962, published as *The Presence of Eternity: History and Eschatology,* Harper, 1957, published as *The Presence of Eternity,* Greenwood, 1975, German version published as *Geschichte und Eschatologie,* Mohr, 1958.
Gnosis (Bible key words), Harper, 1958.
Jesus Christ and Mythology, Scribner, 1958, German version published as *Jesus Christus und die Mythologie: Das Neue Testament im Licht der Bibelkritik,* Furche (Hamburg), 1964.
Das Verhaeltnis der urchristlichen Christusbotschaft zum historischen Jesus, C. Winter (Heidelberg), 1960.
Existence and Faith: Shorter Writings of Rudolf Bultmann, selected, translated, and introduced by Schubert M. Ogden, Meridian, 1960.
Die Erforschung der synoptischen Evangelien, Toepelman (Berlin), 1960.
(With Artur Weiser) *Faith* (Bible key words), translated by Dorothea M. Barton, edited by P. R. Ackroyd, A. & C. Black, 1961.
(With Friedrich Gogarten and Eduard Thurneysen) *Anfaenge der dialektischen Theologie,* C. Kaiser (Munich), 1963.

Exegetische Probleme des zweiten Korintherbriefes, Wissenschaftliche Buchgesellschaft (Darmstadt), 1963.
(With Karl Heinrich Rengstorf) *Hope* (Bible key words), translated by Barton, edited by Ackroyd, A. & C. Black, 1963.
Der alte und der neue Mensch in der Theologie des Paulus, Wissenschaftliche Buchgesellschaft, 1964, English translation by Keith R. Crim published as *The Old and the New Man in the Letters of Paul,* John Knox, 1967.
(Author of introduction) Adolf von Harnack, *Das Wesen des Christentums,* Siebenstern Taschenbuch Verlag (Munich), 1964.
(With others) *Life and Death* (Bible key words), translated by P. H. Ballard and others, edited by Ackroyd, A. & C. Black, 1965.
(With others) *Translating Theology into the Modern Age,* Volume II, edited by Robert W. Funk and G. Ebeling, Harper Torchbook, 1965.
Beitraege zum Verstaendis der Jenseitigkeit Gottes im Neuen Testament, Wissenschaftliche Buchgesellschaft, 1965.
(With Ebeling) *Theology and Proclamation: A Dialogue with Bultmann,* translated by John Riches, Fortress, 1966.
Die drei Johannesbriefe, Vandenhoeck & Ruprecht, 1967, English translation By R. Philip O'Hara with Lane C. McGaughy and Funk published as *The Johannine Epistles: A Commentary,* Fortress, 1973.
Exegetics, Mohr, 1967.
The Gospel of John: A Commentary, Westminster, 1971.
The Future of Our Religious Past: Essays in Honour of Rudolf Bultmann, S.C.M. Press, 1972.
Rudolf Bultmann, edited with an introduction and notes by E. J. Tinsley, Epworth Press, 1973.
Gesammelte Aufsaetze, Evangelische Verlagsanstalt, 1973.
Der zweite Brief an die Korinther, Vandenhoeck & Ruprecht, 1976, English translation by Wilhelm Linss published as *The Second Letter to the Corinthians,* Augsburg, 1983.
Gedenken an Rudolf Bultmann, Mohr, 1977.
Christ without Myth, translated by Ogden, Southern Methodist University Press, 1979.
Karl Barth-Rudolf Bultmann Letters 1922-1966, translated and edited by Geoffrey W. Bromiley, Eerdmans, 1981.
(With Jaspers) *Die Frage der Entmythologisierung,* R. Piper (Munich), 1981.
The New Testament and Mythology, and Other Basic Writings, translated and edited by Ogden, Fortress, 1984.
A Translation of the Greek Expressions in the Text of the Gospel of John: A Commentary by Rudolf Bultmann, University Press of America, 1985.

Former editor of *Theologische Rundschau.*

SIDELIGHTS: Rudolf Karl Bultmann, one of Europe's leading theologians, was often included among the ranks of the "crisis theologians," who follow the example set by Karl Barth. Bultmann's principle concern, in the words of a *Times Literary Supplement* contributor, was to "commend what he [regarded] as the essential Christian gospel to people whose mental outlook, moulded by modern influences, is utterly different from that of the first and early Christian centuries, which was mythological and is completely unacceptable to our age." In a *Times Literary Supplement* review of *The History of Synoptic Tradition,* another contributor noted that "Bultmann's work is important because it represents the extreme left wing of historical scepticism. . . . Granted the presuppositions, there is a formidable and ruthless logic about the process, a massive consistency in the detailed analysis of every phrase of the Greek text." The critic also remarked that British students "will not find the substitution of an existential confrontation for the Christ of Galilee much to their taste—and who can blame them? But it is as well that they should know in their own tongue how formidable the opposition is."

BIOGRAPHICAL/CRITICAL SOURCES:

BOOKS

Kegley, C. W., editor, *The Theology of Rudolf Bultmann,* Harper, 1966.
Macquarrie, John, *Existentialist Theology: A Comparison of Heidegger and Bultmann,* Macmillan, 1955.
Miegge, G., *Gospel and Myth in the Thought of Rudolf Bultmann,* John Knox, 1960.
Owen, H. P., *Revelation and Existence: A Study in the Theology of Rudolf Bultmann,* University of Wales Press, 1957.
Robinson, J. M., *New Quest of the Historical Jesus,* Allenson, 1959.

PERIODICALS

Crozer Quarterly, April, 1952.
Encounter, summer, 1968.
Hibbert Journal, April, 1956, January, 1958.
Times Literary Supplement, August 30, 1957, April 15, 1960, February 27, 1964.

OBITUARIES:

PERIODICALS

New York Times, August 1, 1976.
Time, August 9, 1976.
Washington Post, August 2, 1976.*

* * *

BUNKER, Linda K. 1947-

PERSONAL: Born January 25, 1947, in Kankakee, Ill.; daughter of Francis M. (an athlete and engineer) and Wilahmine (Kammann) Bunker. *Education:* University of Illinois, B.A. (with highest honors), 1973.

ADDRESSES: Home—525 Gillum's Ridge Rd., Charlottesville, Va. 22901. *Office*—Department of Health and Physical Education, University of Virginia, Charlottesville, Va. 22903.

CAREER: University of Illinois at Urbana-Champaign, instructor in physical education and assistant director of Human Movement Research Laboratory, 1969-73; University of Virginia, Charlottesville, assistant professor, 1973-77, associate professor of health and physical education and chairperson of department, 1977—, director of Motor Learning Laboratory, 1973—, associate dean for academic and student affairs, 1984—. Consultant to National Golf Foundation, Women's Sports Foundation, and Melpomeme Institute for Women's Health.

MEMBER: North American Society for Psychology of Sport and Physical Activity, American Alliance of Health, Physical Education, Recreation, and Dance (member of Research Consortium, Sport Psychology Academy, and Motor Development Academy), National Association of Physical Education for College Women (chairperson of research committee, 1978-80), Southern District Association for Health, Physical Education, and Recreation (member of research council, 1975—), Virginia Association of Health, Physical Education, Recreation, and Dance (member of research council, 1975—; member of executive committee, 1978-80; president), Kappa Delta Pi, Phi Kappa Phi, Phi Delta Kappa, Alpha Sigma Nu.

AWARDS, HONORS: Grants from National Bureau of Standards, 1973-74, National Science Foundation, 1974-75, National Institutes of Health, 1977-78, and U.S. Department of Education, 1980-81, 1981-82; Mabel Lee Award, American Alliance of Health, Physical Education, Recreation, and Dance, 1979; named outstanding alumna, University of Illinois, 1984.

WRITINGS:

(With M. M. Mann) *Sequences of Perceptual-Motor Development with Implications for Child Safety* (monograph), Product Safety Division, National Bureau of Standards, 1974.
(With Mann and C. L. Beers) *Motor Development Module XI* (monograph), U.S. Office of Education, 1974.
(Contributor) J. R. Thomas, editor, *Youth Sport Guide for Coaches and Parents,* American Alliance of Health, Physical Education, Recreation, and Dance, 1977.
An Approach to Movement Education, J. L. Hammett Co., 1978.
(With Robert J. Rotella) *Sport Psychology: From Theory into Practice,* Department of Health and Physical Education, University of Virginia, Volume 1, 1978, Volume 2, 1979, Volume 3, 1980.
(Contributor) W. F. Straub, editor, *Sport Psychology: An Analysis of Athletic Behavior,* Mouvement, 1980.
(With Rotella) *Mind Mastery for Winning Golf,* Prentice-Hall, 1981.
(With Candine E. Johnson and Jane E. Parker) *Motivating Kids through Play,* Leisure Press, 1982.
(With Rotella) *Mind, Set, and Match,* Prentice-Hall, 1982.
(With DeDe Owens) *Golf: Better Practice for Better Play,* Leisure Press, 1984.
(With Rotella) *Parenting Your Superstar,* Human Kinetics, 1988.
(With Owens) *Golf: Steps to Success,* Human Kinetics, 1989.

Also contributor to physical education and psychology journals.

WORK IN PROGRESS: Research on achievement motivation in young children and sport, anxiety management, and maximizing sport performance through mental control; continued interest in issues related to women in sport.

SIDELIGHTS: Linda K. Bunker once told *CA:* "Mind mastery is the key to success. It is essential that you know your strengths and weaknesses and can capitalize upon them. Be willing to risk failure in order to attain success. Set your goals carefully and work diligently toward them. Decide on a strategy for success: choose a motto, such as 'Committed to excellence and excellence in each commitment.' "

* * *

BURLEY, W(illiam) J(ohn) 1914-

PERSONAL: Born August 1, 1914, in Falmouth, England; son of William John (a builder) and Annie (Curnow) Burley; married Muriel Wolsey (a school secretary), April 10, 1938; children: Alan John, Nigel Philip. *Education:* Oxford University, degree in zoology (with honors), 1953. *Politics:* Ex-Socialist. *Religion:* "None (Humanist)."

ADDRESSES: *Home*—St. Patrick's, Holywell, Newquay, Cornwall TR8 5PT, England.

CAREER: Gas engineer, 1933-49, served as assistant manager and manager of gas undertakings in southwest England; Newquay School, Newquay, Cornwall, England, head of biology department and sixth form tutor, 1953-74; full-time writer, 1974—.

MEMBER: Crime Writers Association.

WRITINGS:

A Taste of Power, Gollancz, 1966.
Three Toed Pussy, Gollancz, 1968.
Death in Willow Pattern, Walker & Co., 1969.
To Kill a Cat, Walker & Co., 1970.
Guilt Edged, Gollancz, 1971, Walker & Co., 1972.
Death in a Salubrious Place, Gollancz, 1972.
Death in Stanley Street, Gollancz, 1974, Walker & Co., 1975.
Wycliffe and the Peagreen Boat, Walker & Co., 1976.
The Schoolmaster, Walker & Co., 1977.
Wycliffe and the Scapegoat, Gollancz, 1978, Doubleday, 1979.
The Sixth Day, Gollancz, 1978.
Charles and Elizabeth, Gollancz, 1979, Walker & Co., 1981.
Wycliffe in Paul's Court, Doubleday, 1980.
The House of Care, Gollancz, 1981, Walker & Co., 1982.
Wycliffe's Wild Goose Chase, Doubleday, 1982.
Wycliffe and the Beales, Doubleday, 1983.
Wycliffe and the Four Jacks, Doubleday, 1985.
Wycliffe and the Quiet Virgin, Doubleday, 1986.
Wycliffe and the Winsor Blue, Doubleday, 1987.
Wycliffe and the Tangled Web, Doubleday, 1988.
Wycliffe and the Little Hut, Doubleday, 1989.

SIDELIGHTS: W. J. Burley, whose work has also been published in Germany, Switzerland, Denmark, Sweden, France, Holland, Spain, and Italy, told *CA:* "I started to write at the age of 51 and my intention was to try to write interesting detective fiction which did not exploit extreme forms of violence or sex and was relatively free of 'four-letter' words. In doing this I thought I might help fill a gap that was left in the market by the gradual disappearance of the Traditional Whodunnit."

BIOGRAPHICAL/CRITICAL SOURCES:

PERIODICALS

New York Times Book Review, September 12, 1982.
Times (London), January 14, 1982.
Times Literary Supplement, March 12, 1982, September 11, 1987.

* * *

BURTON, Jane 1933-

PERSONAL: Born 1933, in England; daughter of Maurice (a zoologist and author) and Margaret Rosalie (Maclean) Burton; married Kim Taylor (a biologist and photographer); children: Mark, Hazel.

ADDRESSES: *Home*—Warren House, Albury Heath, Albury, Guildford, Surrey GU5 9DB, England.

CAREER: Photographer and writer.

WRITINGS:

AUTHOR AND PHOTOGRAPHER

Animals of the African Year: The Ecology of East Africa, Holt, 1972.
Wondrous World of Fishes, Colour Library International, 1976.
(With David Gibbon) *Wondrous World of Horses,* Colour Library International, 1976.
(With husband, Kim Taylor) *Your Cat's First Year,* Simon & Schuster, 1985.
(With Michael Allaby) *Nine Lives: Year of the Cat,* photography with Taylor, Ebury Press, 1985.
(With Allaby) *A Dog's Life: A Year in the Life of a Dog Family,* Howell Book, 1986.

(With Allaby) *A Pony's Tale: A Year in the Life of a Foal,* Half Halt Press, 1987.

PHOTOGRAPHER

(And editor) *In Praise of Animals: An Anthology for Friends,* Muller, 1956.
(With Douglas Charles Gohn) *Tropical Fish,* revised edition, Hamlyn, 1971.
(With father, Maurice Burton) *The Sixth Sense of Animals,* Taplinger, 1972.
(With M. Burton) *The Colorful World of Animals,* Longmeadow Press, 1974 (published in England as *The Colourful World of Animals,* Sundial Press, 1976).
Diane Hughes, *World Encyclopedia of Animals,* Octopus Books, 1978.
(With M. Burton) *The Family of Animals,* Mayflower Books, 1979.
(With Taylor) *Nightwatch: The Natural World from Dusk to Dawn,* contributions to the text by John Cloudsley-Thompson and others, Facts on File, 1983.
(With Taylor) Robert Burton, *The Book of the Year: A Natural History of Britain through the Seasons,* Warne, 1983.
(With Dougal Dixon) *Time Exposure: A Photographic Record of the Dinosaur Age,* Beaufort Books, 1984.
(With Taylor) R. Burton, *Bird Behavior,* Knopf, 1985.
Dixon, *The Age of Dinosaurs: A Photographic Record,* Beaufort Books, 1986.
(With Taylor) R. Burton, *Eggs: Nature's Perfect Package,* Facts on File, 1987 (published in England as *Egg: Nature's Miracle of Packaging,* Collins, 1987).
Hunting the Dinosaurs and Other Prehistoric Animals (juvenile), Gareth Stevens, 1988.
The Jurassic Dinosaurs (juvenile), Gareth Stevens, 1988.
The First Dinosaurs (juvenile), Gareth Stevens, 1988.
The Last Dinosaurs (juvenile), Gareth Stevens, 1988.
Nicola McClure, *A Baby's Story: A Remarkable Photographic Account of a Baby's First Year,* M. Joseph, 1989.

"NATURE" SERIES

(Author and photographer) *Wild Animals,* Colour Library International, 1977.
(Author and photographer) *Baby Animals,* Colour Library International, 1977, Crescent Books, 1978.
(Author and photographer) *Small Animals,* Colour Library International, 1977.
(Photographer) R. Burton, *Venomous Animals,* Colour Library International, 1977.
(Author and photographer) *Aquarium Fishes,* Colour Library International, 1978.
(Author and photographer) *Horses,* Crescent Books, 1978.
(Author and photographer) *Pets,* Colour Library International, 1978.
(Photographer) M. Burton, *Sea Life,* Colour Library International, 1978.

JUVENILE; "HOW YOUR PET GROWS!" SERIES

Caper the Kid, Random House, 1988.
Dabble the Duckling, Random House, 1988.
Fancy the Fox, Random House, 1988.
Gipper the Guinea Pig, Random House, 1988.
Chester the Chick, Random House, 1988.
Freckles the Rabbit, Random House, 1988.
Ginger the Kitten, Random House, 1988.
Jack the Puppy, Random House, 1988.

WORK IN PROGRESS: Surfer the Seal, Hoppy the Toad, Snowy the Barn Owl, and *Pacer the Pony,* all for the "How Your Pet Grows!" series.

SIDELIGHTS: Jane Burton once told *CA:* "I am only persuaded to write if, by wrapping a text around them, a batch of photographs will be most readily sold." However, she later added: "Now that I am writing children's books about *real* animals, I find I thoroughly enjoy the writing, almost as much as the photography!"

* * *

BURTON, Maurice 1898-

PERSONAL: Born March 28, 1898, in London, England; son of William Francis and Jane Burton; married Margaret Rosalie Maclean, 1928; children: Richard Francis, Jane Mary (Mrs. Kim Taylor), Robert Wellesley. *Education:* University of London, D.Sc., 1934.

ADDRESSES: Home—Weston House, Albury, Guildford, Surrey GU5 9AE, England.

CAREER: Latymer Foundation, Hammersmith, London, England, biology master, 1924-27; British Museum of Natural History, London, 1927-58, began as assistant keeper, became deputy keeper in zoology department; free-lance writer, 1928—. Science editor, *Illustrated London News,* 1946-64; nature correspondent for *Daily Telegraph,* 1949—.

MEMBER: Zoological Society (fellow).

WRITINGS:

FOR ADULTS

(Co-author) *The Science of Living Things,* Odhams, 1928.
(Co-editor and contributor) *Standard Natural History,* Warne, 1931.
(Editor) Jan Vlasak and Josef Seget, *Snow White: Story of a Polar Bear Cub,* Hodge, 1949, published as *Snowy: Story of a Polar Bear Cub,* Schuman, 1951.
The Story of Animal Life, two volumes, Elsevier, 1949.
Curiosities of Animal Life, Ward Lock, 1952, R. M. McBride, 1956, revised edition, 1959.
Animal Courtship, Hutchinson, 1953, Praeger, 1954.
Margins of the Sea, Harper, 1954.
Living Fossils, Thames & Hudson, 1954.
Animal Legends, Muller, 1955, Coward, 1957.
Infancy in Animals, Roy, 1956.
Phoenix Re-Born, Hutchinson, 1959.
More Animal Legends, Muller, 1959.
Sponges, British Museum, 1959.
Under the Sea, F. Watts, 1960.
Wild Animals of the British Isles: A Guide to the Mammals, Reptiles, and Batrachians of Wayside and Woodland, Warne, 1960.
(Co-author) *The Glorious Oyster,* Sidgwick & Jackson, 1960.
Animal Senses, Routledge & Kegan Paul, 1961.
The Elusive Monster: An Analysis of the Evidence from Loch Ness, Hart-Davis, 1961.
Introducing Life under the Sea, Spring Books, 1961.
Systematic Dictionary of Mammals of the World, Crowell, 1962, published as *University Dictionary of Mammals of the World,* 1968 (2nd edition published in England as *Dictionary of the World's Mammals,* Sphere, 1970).
(With K. Nixon) *Bird Families,* Warne, 1962.

A Revision of the Classification of the Calcareous Sponges: With a Catalogue of the Specimens in the British Museum, British Museum of Natural History, 1963.
Meadows and the Forest Margin, Doubleday, 1965.
Nature in Motion, Doubleday, 1966.
(Editor and contributor) *Nature: The Realm of Animals and Plants,* Grolier, 1966.
Weapons, Doubleday, 1966.
Nature's Architects, Doubleday, 1967.
(Co-editor and contributor) *Larousse Encyclopedia of Animal Life,* Hamlyn, 1967.
Wild Animals of the British Isles, Warne, 1968.
The Hedgehog, Deutsch, 1969, Transatlantic, 1970.
(Editor) *The Shell Natural History of Britain,* Rainbird, 1970.
Observer's Book of Wild Animals, Warne, 1971.
(Editor) *World of Wildlife,* Orbis, 1971.
(Editor) *Encyclopedia of the Animal World,* Elsevier, 1972.
(Editor) *Encyclopedia of Animals in Colour,* Octopus Books, 1972.
The Sixth Sense of Animals, photographs by daughter, Jane Burton, Taplinger, 1972.
Animals of Europe: The Ecology of the Wildlife, Holt, 1973.
The World of Reptiles and Amphibians, Crown, 1973.
(With son, Robert Burton) *World of Nature,* Purnell, 1974.
(Editor with R. Burton and author of introduction) *Encyclopedia of Reptiles, Amphibians, and Other Cold-blooded Animals,* Octopus Books, 1975.
(With R. Burton) *Encyclopedia of Fish,* introduction by Gareth Nelson, Octopus Books, 1975.
How Mammals Live, Elsevier, 1975.
(With R. Burton) *Encyclopedia of Mammals,* introduction by L. Harrison Matthews, Octopus Books, 1975.
Maurice Burton's The Daily Telegraph of Nature Book, David & Charles, 1975.
(Editor with R. Burton) *Encyclopedia of the Animal Kingdom,* Octopus Books, 1976.
(With R. Burton) *Encyclopedia of Insects and Arachnids,* introduction by Michael Tweedie, Octopus Books, 1976.
(With R. Burton) *Inside the Animal World: An Encyclopedia of Animal Behavior,* Quadrangle/New York Times, 1977 (published in England as *The Animal World: An Encyclopedia of Animal Behavior,* Macmillan, 1977).
Just Like an Animal, Dent, 1978.
The Family of Animals, Artus, 1978.
(With R. Burton) *The World's Disappearing Wildlife,* Marshall Cavendish, 1978.
Sea Life, photographs by J. Burton, Colour Library International, 1978.
A Zoo at Home, Dent, 1979.
(Editor with R. Burton) *The New Funk and Wagnalls Illustrated Wildlife Encyclopedia,* Funk & Wagnalls, 1980.
British Wild Flowers, Octopus Books, 1982.
Guide to the Mammals of Britain and Europe, Treasure Press, 1983.
(Editor with R. Burton) Felix R. de La Fuente, *Animals of South America,* translated by John Gilbert, International Specialized Book Services, 1986.

FOR CHILDREN

Animals and Their Behavior, Arnold, 1950.
The Elephant, Gawthorn Press, 1951.
The Ox, Gawthorn Press, 1951.
The Reindeer, Gawthorn Press, 1951.
The Camel, Gawthorn Press, 1951.
The Ass, Gawthorn Press, 1951.
The Sheep, Gawthorn Press, 1951.
When Dumb Animals Talk, Hutchinson, 1955.
The True Book about Animals, Muller, 1956.
Animal Families, Routledge & Kegan Paul, 1958.
British Mammals, Oxford University Press, 1958.
Life in the Deep, Roy, 1958.
The True Book about the Seas, Muller, 1959.
(Editor and contributor) *The Wonder Book of Animals,* Ward Lock, 1960.
In Their Element: The Story of Water Mammals, Abelard, 1960.
Mammals of the Countryside, Wheaton, 1960.
Wild Animals and Birds of the World, Longacre Press, 1960.
Birds and Beasts of Field and Jungle, Odhams, 1960.
The True Book about Prehistoric Animals, Muller, 1961, 2nd edition published as *Prehistoric Animals,* International Publications Service, 1974.
The True Book about Deserts, Muller, 1961, 2nd edition published as *Deserts,* International Publications Service, 1974.
More Mammals of the Countryside, Wheaton, 1961.
Water Creatures, Longacre Press, 1961.
Baby Animals, Longacre Press, 1961.
Birds, Gawthorn Press, 1961.
Mammals, Gawthorn Press, 1961.
(With E. W. Groves) *The Wonder Book of Nature,* Ward Lock, 1961.
Reptiles and Amphibians of the World, Longacre Press, 1962, 2nd edition, 1971.
Birds of Britain, Odhams, 1962, 2nd edition, 1971.
Mammals of Great Britain, Odhams, 1962.
The True Book of the Seashore, Muller, 1963.
(With W. B. Shepherd) *The Wonder Book of Our Earth,* Ward Lock, 1963.
Young Animals, Hamlyn, 1964.
The Zoo Book, Bancroft, 1966.
(Editor) *Animal World in Colour,* Odhams, 1966, Children's Press, 1969, Volume 1: *Artists and Entertainers,* Volume 2: *Explorers and Wanderers,* Volume 3: *Animal Eccentrics,* Volume 4: *Animal Oddities,* Volume 5: *Builders and Breakers,* Volume 6: *Comrades and Companions,* Volume 7: *Hunters: Mammals,* Volume 8: *Hunters: Birds, Fish, and Amphibians,* Volume 9: *Hunters: Reptiles, Insects, and Invertebrates,* Volume 10: *Animal Specialists,* Volume 11: *Unusual Feeders,* Volume 12: *Sleep and Hibernation.*
Animals, Oxford University Press, 1966, F. Watts, 1968.
The Animal World: Birds, Fish, Reptiles [and] *Insects,* F. Watts, 1968.
The Sea's Inhabitants, Golden Press, 1968.
More Animals, F. Watts, 1968.
Animal Partnerships, Warne, 1969.
Animals of Australia, Abelard, 1969.
Maurice Burton's Book of Nature, Purnell, 1971, 3rd edition, 1974.
The Life of Birds, edited by Angela Littler, Macdonald, 1972, Golden Press, 1974.
The Life of Fishes, edited by Littler, Macdonald, 1972, Golden Press, 1974.
The Life of Insects, Macdonald, 1972, Golden Press, 1974.
(With R. Burton) *The Life of Meat Eaters,* Macdonald, 1973, Golden Press, 1974.
The Colorful World of Animals, photography by J. Burton, Longmeadow Press, 1974 (published in England as *The Colourful World of Animals,* Sundial Press, 1976).
The Life of Reptiles and Amphibians, Golden Press, 1974.
First Encyclopedia of Animals, Purnell, 1974.

(With J. Burton) *The Family of Animals,* Mayflower Books, 1979.
Warm-blooded Animals, Facts on File, 1984.
Insects and Their Relatives, Facts on File, 1984.
Cold-blooded Animals, Facts on File, 1985.
Birds, Facts on File, 1985.
(With R. Burton) *The Beginnings of Life,* Facts on File, 1986.

OTHER

Contributor to *Junior Science Encyclopedia;* general editor, *Oxford Junior Encyclopaedia,* Volume 2: *Natural History,* 1949; general editor with R. Burton and contributor, *Purnell's Encyclopedia of Animal Life,* BPC Publishing, 1968-70, published as *The International Wildlife Encyclopedia,* 1970, four volume edition, Octopus Books, 1974, revised edition published as *The New International Wildlife Encyclopedia,* Purnell, 1980; general editor, *The World Encyclopedia of Animals,* 1972; general editor with R. Burton, *The Marshall Cavendish International Wildlife Encyclopedia,* Marshall Cavendish, 1988; contributor to scientific journals.

AVOCATIONAL INTERESTS: Gardening.

BIOGRAPHICAL/CRITICAL SOURCES:

PERIODICALS

Observer, February 8, 1970.*

* * *

BURTON, Robert (Wellesley) 1941-

PERSONAL: Born June 18, 1941, in Sherbourne, Dorset, England; son of Maurice (a zoologist and author) and Margaret Rosalie (Maclean) Burton. *Education:* Attended Downing College, Cambridge, 1960-63.

ADDRESSES: Home and office—80 Caxton End, Eltisley, Huntingdon, Cambridgeshire PE19 4TJ, England. *Agent*—Murray Pollinger, 4 Garrick St., London WC2E 9BH, England.

CAREER: Writer, 1967—. Meteorologist and biologist for British Antarctic Survey, 1963-66; biologist, 1971-72.

MEMBER: Society of Authors, Institute of Biology, Zoological Society of London.

WRITINGS:

Animals of the Antarctic, Abelard Schuman, 1970.
Animal Senses, David & Charles, 1970.
The Life and Death of Whales, Deutsch, 1973, 2nd edition, revised and enlarged, Universe Books, 1980.
How Birds Live, Elsevier Phaidon, 1975.
The Mating Game, Elsevier Phaidon, 1976.
Ponds: Their Wildlife and Upkeep, David & Charles, 1976.
The Cat Family, illustrated by Richard Hook, Silver Burdett, 1976.
The Language of Smell, Routledge & Kegan Paul, 1976.
The Love of Baby Animals, Octopus Books, 1976.
Exploring Hills and Moors, Elsevier Phaidon, 1976.
(With Carole Devaney and Tony Long) *The Living Sea: An Illustrated Encyclopedia of Marine Life,* Putnam, 1976.
Wildlife by the Roadside, Educational Publishing, 1977 (published in England as *Nature by the Roadside,* Educational Publishing, 1977).
The Seashore and Its Wildlife, Putnam, 1977.
Venomous Animals, photographs by sister, Jane Burton, Colour Library International, 1977.
First Nature Book, St. Michael, 1977.
Seals, Bodley Head, 1978.
Carnivores of Europe, Batsford, 1979.
Horses and Ponies, Macmillan, 1979.
Nature's Night Life, Blandford, 1982.
The Book of the Year: A Natural History of Britain through the Seasons, photography by Kim Taylor and J. Burton, Warne, 1983.
Bird Behavior, photography by Taylor and J. Burton, Knopf, 1985.
Look It Up (juvenile), Macmillan Children's Books, Volume 9: *Cold-blooded Animals,* 1985, Volume 10: *Warm-blooded Animals,* 1985.
Eggs: Nature's Perfect Package, photography by Taylor and J. Burton, Facts on File, 1987 (published in England as *Egg: Nature's Miracle of Packaging,* Collins, 1987).
The Mouse in the Barn (juvenile), Stevens, 1988.

WITH FATHER, MAURICE BURTON

The Life of Meat Eaters (juvenile), Macdonald, 1973, Golden Press, 1974.
World of Nature, Purnell, 1974.
(Editor) *Encyclopedia of Reptiles, Amphibians, and Other Cold-blooded Animals,* introduction by M. Burton, Octopus Books, 1975.
Encyclopedia of Fish, introduction by Gareth Nelson, Octopus Books, 1975.
Encyclopedia of Mammals, introduction by L. Harrison Matthews, Octopus Books, 1975.
Encyclopedia of Insects and Arachnids, introduction by Michael Tweedie, Octopus Books, 1976.
(Editor) *Encyclopedia of the Animal Kingdom,* Octopus Books, 1976.
Inside the Animal World: An Encyclopedia of Animal Behavior, Quadrangle/New York Times, 1977 (published in England as *The Animal World: An Encyclopedia of Animal Behaviour,* Macmillan, 1977).
The World's Disappearing Wildlife, Marshall Cavendish, 1978.
The New Funk & Wagnalls Illustrated Wildlife Encyclopedia, Funk & Wagnalls, 1980.
The Beginnings of Life (juvenile), Facts on File, 1985.
(Editor) Felix R. de La Fuente, *Animals of South America,* translated by John Gilbert, International Specialized Book Services, 1986.

OTHER

Contributor to *BBC Wildlife, Guardian, Daily Telegraph, Natural World, World Birds, Country Life, Wildlife News,* and *Sea Frontiers.* General editor, with M. Burton, of *Purnell's Encyclopedia of Animal Life,* BPC Publishing, 1968-70, published in the United States as *The International Wildlife Encyclopedia,* 1970, four-volume edition, Octopus, 1974, revised edition published as *The New International Wildlife Encyclopedia,* Purnell, 1980; general editor, with M. Burton, of *The Marshall Cavendish International Wildlife Encyclopedia,* 24 volumes, Marshall Cavendish, 1988.

AVOCATIONAL INTERESTS: History of whaling, history of polar expeditions, visiting the Arctic.

BIOGRAPHICAL/CRITICAL SOURCES:

PERIODICALS

New York Times Book Review, August 18, 1985.

BUSH, Sargent, Jr. 1937-

PERSONAL: Born September 22, 1937, in Flemington, N.J.; son of Sargent (a clergyman) and Marion L. (Roberts) Bush; married Cynthia Bird Greig, June 18, 1960; children: Charles Sargent, James Jonathan. *Education:* Princeton University, A.B., 1959; University of Iowa, M.A., 1964, Ph.D., 1967. *Religion:* Presbyterian.

ADDRESSES: Home—Madison, Wis. *Office*—Department of English, University of Wisconsin, Madison, Wis. 53706.

CAREER: Washington & Lee University, Lexington, Va., assistant professor of English, 1967-71; University of Wisconsin—Madison, assistant professor, 1971-73, associate professor, 1973-79, professor of English, 1979—, chairman of department, 1980—. Visiting professor, University of Warwick, Coventry, England, 1983-84. *Military service:* U.S. Army Reserve, active duty, 1959-60, 1961-62.

MEMBER: Cambridge Bibliographical Society, Modern Language Association, American Literature Section, Nathaniel Hawthorne Society, Melville Society.

AWARDS, HONORS: National Endowment for the Humanities grant, summers, 1969, 1986; Cooperative Program in the Humanities fellow, 1969-70; American Council of Learned Societies fellowship, 1974; Institute for Research in the Humanities fellow, 1978; American Philosophical Society grant-in-aid, 1979; Vilas Associate, University of Wisconsin, 1988-90.

WRITINGS:

(Editor and contributor) *Thomas Hooker: Writings in England and Holland, 1626-1633,* Harvard University Press, 1975.

The Writings of Thomas Hooker: Spiritual Adventure in Two Worlds, University of Wisconsin Press, 1980.

(With Carl J. Rasmussen) *The Library of Emmanuel College, Cambridge, 1584-1637,* Cambridge University Press, 1987.

Contributor to literature and history journals. Member of editorial advisory board, *Literary Monographs,* 1972-78, *Early American Literature,* 1977-1980, *Resources for American Literary Study,* 1975—, and *American Literary History.*

WORK IN PROGRESS: Research on American Puritan literature and thought, including a complete edition of the letters of John Cotton.

C

CABRERA INFANTE, G(uillermo) 1929-
(G. Cain, Guillermo Cain)

PERSONAL: Born April 22, 1929, in Gibara, Cuba; immigrated to London, England, 1966; naturalized British citizen; son of Guillermo Cabrera Lopez (a journalist) and Zoila Infante; married Marta Calvo, August 18, 1953 (divorced, October, 1961); married Miriam Gomez, December 9, 1961; children: (first marriage) Ana, Carola. *Education:* Graduated from University of Havana, Cuba, 1956. *Politics:* "Reactionary on the left." *Religion:* Catholic.

ADDRESSES: Home—53 Gloucester Rd., London SW7, England. *Agent*—Carmen Balcells, Diagonal 580, Barcelona, 21, Spain.

CAREER: Writer. School of Journalism, Havana, Cuba, professor of English literature, 1960-61; Government of Cuba, Cuban embassy, Brussels, Belgium, cultural attache, 1962-64, charge d'affairs, 1964-65; scriptwriter for Twentieth-Century Fox and Cupid Productions, 1967-72. Visiting professor, University of Virginia, spring, 1982.

MEMBER: Writers Guild of Great Britain.

AWARDS, HONORS: Asi en paz como en la guerra was nominated for Prix International de Literature (France), 1962; unpublished manuscript version of *Tres tristes tigres* won Biblioteca Breve Prize (Spain), 1964, and was nominated for Prix Formentor—International Publishers Prize, 1965; Guggenheim fellowship for creative writing, 1970; Prix du Meilleur Livre Etranger (France), 1971, for *Tres tristes tigres.*

WRITINGS:

FICTION

Asi en la paz como en la guerra: Cuentos (title means "In Peace as in War: Stories"), Revolucion (Havana), 1960.

Vista del amanacer en el tropico, Seix Barral (Barcelona, Spain), 1965, translation by Suzanne Jill Levine published as *View of Dawn in the Tropics,* Harper, 1978.

Tres tristes tigres (novel), Seix Barral, 1967, translation by Donald Gardner, Levine, and the author published as *Three Trapped Tigers,* Harper, 1971.

La Habana para un infante difunto, Seix Barral, 1979, translation by Levine and the author published as *Infante's Inferno,* Harper, 1984.

FILM CRITICISM

(Under pseudonym G. Cain) *Un oficio del siglo veinte* (title means "A Twentieth-Century Job"; film reviews originally published in magazine, *Carteles;* also see below), Revolucion, 1963.

Arcadia todas las noches (title means "Arcadia Every Night"), Seix Barral, 1978.

OTHER

(Editor) *Mensajes de libertad: La Espana rebelde—Ensayos selectos,* Movimiento Universitario Revolucionario (Lima, Peru), 1961.

"Vanishing Point" (screenplay), Twentieth-Century Fox, 1970.

(Translator into Spanish) James Joyce, *Dublineses* (title means "The Dubliners"), Lumen (Barcelona), 1972.

O, Seix Barral, 1975.

Exorcismos del esti(l)o (title means "Summer Exorcisms" and "Exorcising Style"; English, French, and Spanish text), Seix Barral, 1976.

Holy Smoke (English text), Harper, 1985.

Also author of screenplay, "Wonderwall," 1968, and of unfilmed screenplay, "Under the Volcano," based on Malcolm Lowry's novel of the same title. Also translator of stories by Mark Twain, Ambrose Bierce, Sherwood Anderson, Ernest Hemingway, William Faulkner, Dashiell Hammett, J. D. Salinger, Vladimir Nabokov, and others. Work is represented in many anthologies. Contributor to periodicals, including *New Yorker, New Republic, El Pais* (Spain), and *Plural* (Mexico). *Carteles* (Cuban magazine), film reviewer under pseudonym G. Cain, 1954-60, fiction editor, 1957-60; editor of *Lunes* (weekly literary supplement of Cuban newspaper, *Revolucion*), 1959-61.

WORK IN PROGRESS: Cuerpos divinos (title means "Heavenly Bodies"), a novel about women and writing.

SIDELIGHTS: Talking about his award-winning first novel, *Three Trapped Tigers,* Cuban-born Guillermo Cabrera Infante tells Rita Guibert in *Seven Voices:* "I would prefer everyone to consider the book solely as a joke lasting about five hundred pages. Latin American literature errs on the side of excessive seriousness, sometimes solemnity. It is like a mask of solemn words, which writers and readers put up with by mutual consent."

In the novel, we hear the voices of a group of friends as they take part in the nightlife of pre-Castro Havana. The friends take turns narrating the story using the colloquial speech of the lower-class inhabitants of that city. Told from so many perspectives and using the language of such a small population group, the narrative is not always easy to follow. Elias L. Rivers explains in *Modern Language Notes:* "While some passages are readily accessible to any reader, others are obscured by Cuban vernaculars in phonetic transcription and by word-plays and allusions of many different kinds. A multiplicity of 'voices' engage in narrative, dialogue and soliloquy. [The novel] is a test which fascinates as it eludes and frustrates; the over-all narrative sense is by no-means obvious."

The importance of spoken language in *Three Trapped Tigers* is apparent even in the book's title, which in its English version repeats only the alliteration found in the Spanish title and not the title's actual meaning. Inside the book, the emphasis on sound continues as the characters pun relentlessly. There are so many puns in the book that *New Republic* contributor Gregory Rabassa maintains that in it Cabrera Infante "established himself as the punmaster of Spanish-American literature." Appearing most often are literary puns, including such examples as "Shame's Choice" used to refer to James Joyce, "Scotch Fizzgerald" for Scott Fitzgerald and "Somersault Mom" for Somerset Maugham. In another example, a bongo player—a member of the group of friends whose exploits are followed in the novel—is called "Vincent Bon Gogh."

If the emphasis on spoken rather than written language makes complete understanding of the novel difficult, it has made translating nearly impossible. Comparison of the Spanish, English and French editions of the book prove that readers of each language are not reading the same text. "What Cabrera [Infante] has really done," comments Roger Sale in the *New York Review of Books,* "is to write, presumably with the help of his translators, three similar but different novels." Because of the word play, Sale continues, "quite obviously no translation can work if it attempts word-for-word equivalents."

Playing with words is also an important part of Cabrera Infante's next novel, *Infante's Inferno,* and his nonfiction work, *Holy Smoke.* The latter—Cabrera Infante's first book written originally in English—tells the history of the cigar and describes famous smoking scenes from literature and film. Unlike the nearly universal acclaim received for *Three Trapped Tigers,* critics were unable to reach a consensus on these two works. While some praised Cabrera Infante's continued use of puns as innovative, other had grown tired of the Cuban's verbal contortions.

Commenting on *Infante's Inferno* in the *New York Review of Books,* Michael Wood complains that Cabrera Infante's relentless punning "unrepentedly mangles language and hops from one tongue to another like a frog released from the throat. Some of the jokes are . . . terrible. . . . Others are so cumbersome, so fiendlishly worked for, that the noise of grinding machinery deafens all the chance of laughter." *New York Review of Books* contributor Josh Rubins has similar problems with *Holy Smoke.* He comments: "In *Holy Smoke* . . . the surfeit of puns seems to arise not from mania . . . , but from mere tic. Or, worse yet, from a computer program."

Other reviewers are not so harsh in their criticism. In Enrique Fernandez's *Voice Literary Supplement* review of *Infante's Inferno,* for example, the critic observes that the novel is written in "an everyday Cuban voice, unaffected, untrammeled [and], authentic." John Gross of the *New York Times* hails Cabrera Infante as a master in the use of language. Commenting on *Holy Smoke,* he claims: "Conrad and Nabokov apart, no other writer for whom English is a second language can ever have used it with more virtuousity. He is a master of idiomatic echoes and glancing allusions; he keeps up a constant barrage of wordplay, which is often outrageous, but no more outrageous than he intends it to be."

Three Trapped Tigers established Cabrera Infante's reputation as a writer of innovative fiction, a reputation that some critics find justified by his later work. Cabrera Infante once described his literary beginnings to *CA:* "It all began with parody. If it were not for a parody I wrote on a Latin American writer who was later to win the Nobel Prize, I wouldn't have become a professional writer and I wouldn't qualify to be here at all. My parents wanted me to go to University and I would have liked to become a doctor. But somehow that dreadful novel crossed my path. After reading a few pages (I just couldn't stomach it all, of course) and being only seventeen at the time, I said to myself, 'Why, if that's what writing is all about—*anch'io sono scrittore* [I am also a writer]!' To prove I too was a writer I wrote a parody of the pages I had read. It was a dreadfully serious parody and unfortunately the short story I wrote was taken by what was then the most widely-read publication in Latin America, the Cuban magazine, *Bohemia.* They paid me what at the time I considered a fortune and I was hooked: probably hooked by fortune, probably hooked by fame but certainly hooked by writing."

AVOCATIONAL INTERESTS: Birdwatching, old movies.

BIOGRAPHICAL/CRITICAL SOURCES:

BOOKS

Contemporary Literary Criticism, Gale, Volume 5, 1976, Volume 25, 1983, Volume 45, 1987.

Gallagher, David Patrick, *Modern Latin American Literature,* Oxford University Press, 1973.

Guibert, Rita, *Seven Voices,* Knopf, 1973.

Nelson, Ardis L., *Cabrera Infante in the Menippean Tradition,* Juan de la Cuesta (Newark, Delaware), 1983.

Souza, Raymond D., *Major Cuban Novelists: Innovation and Tradition,* University of Missouri Press, 1976.

Tittler, Jonathan, *Narrative Irony in the Contemporary Spanish-American Novel,* Cornell University Press, 1984.

PERIODICALS

Book World, October 3, 1971.

Commonweal, November 12, 1971.

London Review of Books, October 4-17, 1984, February 6, 1986.

Los Angeles Times, June 6, 1984.

Modern Language Notes, March, 1977.

Nation, November 4, 1978.

New Republic, July 9, 1984.

Newsweek, October 25, 1971.

New Yorker, September 19, 1977.

New York Review of Books, December 16, 1971, June 28, 1984, May 8, 1986.

New York Times, February 7, 1986.

New York Times Book Review, October 17, 1971, May 6, 1984, March 2, 1986.

Observer, September 2, 1984, October 13, 1985, December 21, 1986.

Paris Review, spring, 1983.

Review, January/April, 1981.

Time, January 10, 1972.

Times Literary Supplement, April 18, 1968, October 12, 1984, August 26, 1986.

Village Voice, March 25, 1986.

Voice Literary Supplement, April, 1984.
Washington Post Book World, January 28, 1979, May 27, 1984.
World Literature Today, spring, 1977, summer, 1981.*

—*Sketch by Marian Gonsior*

* * *

CAHN, Steven M. 1942-

PERSONAL: Born August 6, 1942, in Springfield, Mass.; son of Judah (an educator) and Evelyn (an educator; maiden name, Baum) Cahn; married Marilyn Ross (a physician). *Education:* Columbia University, A.B., 1963, Ph.D., 1966. *Religion:* Jewish.

ADDRESSES: Office—Graduate School and University Center, City University of New York, 33 West 42nd St., New York, N.Y. 10036.

CAREER: Vassar College, Poughkeepsie, N.Y., assistant professor of philosophy, 1966-68; New York University, New York City, assistant professor, 1968-71, associate professor of philosophy, 1971-73; University of Vermont, Burlington, professor of philosophy and chairman of department, 1973-80, adjunct professor, 1980-83; City University of New York, Graduate School and University Center, New York City, professor of philosophy, 1983—, dean of graduate studies, 1983-84, provost and vice president for academic affairs, 1984—. Visiting instructor in philosophy, Dartmouth College, 1966; visiting professor, University of Rochester, 1967. Program officer, Exxon Education Foundation, 1977-79; Rockefeller Foundation, associate director of humanities, 1979-81, acting director, 1981-82. National Endowment for the Humanities, director of Division of General Programs, 1982-83, consultant panelist, Division of Fellowships and Stipends. Concert pianist.

MEMBER: American Philosophical Association, American Association of University Professors, Phi Beta Kappa.

WRITINGS:

Fate, Logic and Time, Yale University Press, 1967.
An Introduction to Philosophy, Harper, 1971.
The Eclipse of Excellence, Public Affairs Press, 1973.
Education and the Democratic Idea, Nelson-Hall, 1979.
Saints and Scamps: Ethics in Academia, Rowman & Littlefield, 1986.
Philosophical Explorations: Freedom, God, and Goodness, Prometheus Books, 1989.

EDITOR

(With Frank A. Tillman) *Philosophy of Art and Aesthetics,* Harper, 1969.
The Philosophical Foundations of Education, Harper, 1970.
Classics of Western Philosophy, Hackett, 1977.
New Studies in the Philosophy of John Dewey, University Press of New England, 1977.
Scholars Who Teach: The Art of College Teaching, Nelson-Hall, 1978.
(With David Shatz) *Contemporary Philosophy of Religion,* Oxford University Press, 1982.
(With Patricia Kitcher and George Sher) *Reason at Work: Introductory Readings in Philosophy,* Harcourt, 1984.
Studies in Academic Ethics, Temple University Press, 1990.

OTHER

Contributor to *Encyclopedia of Philosophy.* Contributor to periodicals, including *Journal of Philosophy, American Philosophical Quarterly, New Republic,* and *New York Times.*

WORK IN PROGRESS: Research on the philosophy of education, metaphysics, and the philosophy of religion.

* * *

CAIN, G.
See CABRERA INFANTE, G(uillermo)

* * *

CAIN, Guillermo
See CABRERA INFANTE, G(uillermo)

* * *

CALVERT, John
See LEAF, (Wilbur) Munro

* * *

CAMPBELL, Ewing 1940-

PERSONAL: Born December 26, 1940, in Alice, Tex.; son of James Vernon and Marie (Crofford) Campbell; married Lois R. Glenn (an editor), April, 1972 (divorced, 1980). *Education:* North Texas State University, B.B.A., 1968; University of Southern Mississippi, M.A., 1972; Oklahoma State University, Ph.D., 1980.

ADDRESSES: Office—Department of English, Texas A & M University, College Station, Tex. 77843.

CAREER: Writer, 1967—; lecturer, University of Texas, 1981-82; Oklahoma State University, Stillwater, lecturer, 1982-83; Wharton County Junior College, Wharton, Tex., lecturer, 1983-84; Texas A & M University, College Station, assistant professor, 1984—. *Military service:* U.S. Army, 1959-62.

WRITINGS:

Weave It Like Nightfall (novel; also see below), Nefertiti Head Press, 1977.
(Translator) Julio Ortega, *The Land in the Day (Tierra en el dia),* New Latin Quarter Editions, 1978.
(Editor with Ortega) *The Plaza of Encounters,* Latitudes Press, 1981.
The Way of Sequestered Places (novel; also see below), Nefertiti Head Press, 1982.
The Rincon Triptych (includes *Weave It Like Nightfall, A Cameo Illusion,* and *The Way of Sequestered Places*), Latitudes Press, 1984.
Piranesi's Dream: Stories, Nefertiti Head Press, 1986.

Frequent contributor to literary journals, including *Chicago Review, Kenyon Review,* and *New England Review/Bread Loaf Quarterly.*

* * *

CAMPBELL, Jeremy 1931-

PERSONAL: Born November 7, 1931, in Fareham, England; came to United States in 1965; son of Robert C. (a salesman) and Alfreda R. (Way) Campbell; married Edwina Dorothy Esme George, January 19, 1963. *Education:* Keble College, Oxford, B.A., 1955.

ADDRESSES: Home and office—4312 Fessenden St. N.W., Washington, D.C. 20016. *Agent*—Richard A. Balkin, The Balkin Agency, 880 West 181st St., New York, N.Y. 10033.

CAREER: Metal Box Co., London, England, management trainee, 1955-57; *London Evening Standard,* London, England, staff journalist, 1957, reporter, 1957-61, chief editorial writer, 1961-65, correspondent in Washington, D.C., 1965—.

WRITINGS:

Grammatical Man: Information, Entropy, Language, and Life, Simon & Schuster, 1982.

Winston Churchill's Afternoon Nap: A Wide Awake Inquiry into the Human Nature of Time, Simon & Schuster, 1987.

The Improbable Machine, Simon & Schuster, 1989.

SIDELIGHTS: Jeremy Campbell's field is information theory, the study of how seemingly random structures in everyday phenomena can be interpreted as a greater entity of information that might change the way we think about science itself. In his first book, *Grammatical Man: Information, Entropy, Language, and Life,* the British-born writer assesses "some of the rules . . . that underlie our use of words and other tools of communication," according to Joseph McLellan in a *Washington Post* review. "In each of the many areas he reports," says Jack Miles in the *Los Angeles Times Book Review,* "Campbell concentrates on researchers who either have made use of or *could well make use* of information theory. The resulting synoptic view of many scientists simultaneously and independently at work is science journalism of the [forward-thinking] kind, and whatever it proves or fails to prove, it is powerfully suggestive."

Times Literary Supplement critic P. N. Johnson-Laird sees two sides to *Grammatical Man.* On one hand, the work "has some flaws. It embraces so much that readers may begin to feel the author is educating himself at their expense. He seems to have learned little more than he needed in order to write the book, as is betrayed by the cumulation of small errors of fact and emphasis, and by the tell-tale signs of assertions that are almost right and sentences that almost make sense." But at the same time, Johnson-Laird lauds the study as one that "contributes to order in the world rather than to disorder. Its signal-to-noise ratio is satisfactory and would have been higher had its text been filtered through the minds of some of the people whom its author interviewed. None the less, a welcome should be extended to a new scientific writer and to an entertaining book."

Campbell's second book, *Winston Churchill's Afternoon Nap: A Wide Awake Inquiry into the Human Nature of Time,* examines such timely questions as why a watched kettle never boils: The author concludes "that it is because all one is doing while waiting for the kettle to boil is paying attention to the passage of time, and this attention . . . itself makes it seem as if time has slowed down," as *Los Angeles Times* writer Lee Dembart describes. The volume's title refers to the way the renowned British statesman napped faithfully each day after lunch, a regimen that Campbell says subscribes to "a powerful ancient biological rhythm, an artifact of an earlier evolutionary era when, for whatever reason, afternoon napping served to help the species survive," notes Wray Herbert. Writing in *Washington Post Book World,* Herbert finds that the author shows, "in addition to the obvious biological rhythms—the daily sleep-wake cycle, the monthly menstrual cycle—our bodies and minds are under the influence of many, and even subtler, rhythms: predictable rhythms in core body temperature, levels of stress hormones, blood levels of iron, blood pressure."

"In developing his thesis, [Campbell] accumulates an impressive array of facts, many little known beyond specialized circles," states *New York Times Book Review* critic F. Gonzalez-Crussi. "To feel no gratitude for so much [research] effort would make us, to say the least, ill-bred folk. But it would be untrue to say that all is pleasant jaunt and balmy breezes. The trip is at times marred by [the author's] compulsion to tell all." But Gonzalez-Crussi concludes that in *Winston Churchill's Afternoon Nap,* Campbell has written "an intelligent, carefully researched and instructive book. I know of no work of scientific exposition that packs between two covers so much information on chronobiology [the study of time]. The reader will also find many richly suggestive ideas, as is congruous with the ambitious choice of subject matter." And to Herbert, *Winston Churchill's Afternoon Nap* proves the author's "convincing case, [and in doing so] Campbell provides some excellent science reporting on this relatively obscure area of research, and he provides context for his findings by drawing on a wide range of sources in philosophy and world literature. The result is a valuable resource for any serious student of human nature."

CA INTERVIEW

CA interviewed Jeremy Campbell by telephone on October 27, 1988, at his home in Washington, D.C.

CA: You've nicely meshed a writing career with an avid interest in science. Was the combination something you planned early on to work with?

CAMPBELL: Not really. I came to science very late. I've been a journalist for a lot of years, and I've never been a science journalist. I came to America in 1965 from London for my paper, the *London Evening Standard.* I had read English at Oxford, which tends to be a little bit pro-humanist studies, and I'd felt then that scientists were people in a little ghetto, almost a separate society. C. S. Lewis once or twice in his writings refers to scientists as uneducated, and there is a kind of tradition that reflects that trend of thinking. But that may be entirely different now. I know that Baliol, for example, has just appointed as its next master an American scientist. That caused, as you can imagine, a great sensation.

When I came here, I was almost anti-science and very pro-arts. But the longer I stayed here, the more that changed. I think in this country—maybe partly because of the scientists who came here in the thirties—there is a very strong scientific culture which is not closed off and inaccessible. I find many of the scientists I meet here have immensely broad interests; they're not just technical people, but they see how science fits into the rest of culture and other ideas. That took me by surprise and stirred my interest greatly. I realized that, in fact, just taking ideas as ideas, a lot of the most exciting ideas now are not going on in philosophy and maybe not even in the arts (which I think are stagnating a little bit) but in science, where there's a great fountain of ideas coming out. And scientists are so open to change and new ways of looking at old problems here.

Also, I think this particular time is one in which a lot of disciplines converge—for example, in cognitive science, which is an umbrella term for computer scientists, anthropologists, biologists, psychologists, a whole lot of people whose interests converge in this group of studies, and each discipline feeds other disciplines with new ideas. A tremendous ferment seems to be going on, and things are enormously exciting.

But this excitement may be a Washington phenomenon. A lot of Americans, especially those who've spent time in Europe, tend to think that America is a cultural desert and Europe is a kind of Athens. In some ways that's true, but not in all ways. I think people take that view because the part of culture that I find exciting here is going on in disciplines which may put people off a bit: linguistics, logic, computer science. They interest many people, but others think they're anti-humanist activities and therefore don't feel they're really part of culture. I think maybe that's the reason some Americans say to me, "How can you live in this country when you could live in that marvelous Europe?" And I have trouble persuading them out of that view.

CA: Your first book, Grammatical Man: Information, Entropy, Language, and Life, *is concerned with information theory, a science that began during World War II and has applications in many other sciences and disciplines. How did your interest in information theory begin?*

CAMPBELL: It began because of that kind of convergence of ideas I just mentioned. Because I had to read a lot for my newspaper work, I almost couldn't avoid noticing where there seemed to be a convergence of biology, computer science, linguistics, psychology—all these things coming together, unified by a common theme, which is information theory. It's exciting to think how broad that is: in one sense it is a means of seeing that messages are sent along radio channels in the most economic way, and yet at the other end of the spectrum it gives us a fresh way of looking at evolution. Those very things that seem to have absolutely nothing to do with each other are brought together by this unifying idea, and to me that was something very fascinating.

CA: Since the book's publication in 1982, do you see signs that information theory is being incorporated more into various fields of study?

CAMPBELL: It's been put to one side at the moment. Information theory deals with the structure of information, just as syntax deals with the structure of language and not with the meaning of language and the way language is used. I think at the moment we're going through a period when people are very interested in the meaning and use of information and knowledge rather than its structure, which is independent of those things. In artificial intelligence particularly we've moved from an early concern with logic. It is the hallmark of logic that it doesn't have anything to do with meaning, that it just has to do with form. That approach wasn't getting artificial intelligence anywhere very fast. Now the concern is much more with specific knowledge, specific content, expert systems which are things that have very specific knowledge about a very narrow domain, like medicine or geology or something like that. To make these things work, to make them commercially successful, people have had to concern themselves very much with content and meaning. The question of structure, which is what information theory deals with, hasn't been superceded, but it has been put aside.

CA: Did your work on information theory lead you somehow to chronobiology, the broad subject of your second book, Winston Churchill's Afternoon Nap?

CAMPBELL: I don't want to give the impression that everything is related to everything else, but if there's a common theme to those books, it is that what goes on inside us is underdetermined by what goes on outside. In *Grammatical Man* I talk about Noam Chomsky's theory of language. The interesting thing about his theory of language is the suggestion that we are born with a device in our heads that enables us to take sketchy information and construct a theory from it. When adults are talking to a very young child, they don't especially take trouble to train and coach the child in language as we might do in mathematics. The language they speak may be very casual, careless, compressed, maybe inaccurate. And yet from this surprisingly meager and perhaps faulty information, the child manages to construct a theory of language. The idea is that there is a very complex device inside the child's head that allows it to produce this fantastically complex knowledge system, which is a language, out of such a small amount of data and with such little effort and deliberate training.

Chronobiology, a little bit of that same theme is there because we have inside us biological clocks which are very complex devices. There are enormous numbers of them and they're not completely understood, but a brief flash of light from outside into our eyes can reset these inner clocks so that they are synchronized with the time of the outside world. There is another example of a very small amount of information producing an enormously complex time information system inside the body, which means that our bodily functions are synchronized with the day-and-night cycle. This means that the mechanisms we have inside us for making us behave in very intricate ways depend on a fairly small amount of information from the outside world. So there's a similarity; again we bring in the topic of information.

CA: It occurred to me that both topics have to do with a concern for order, and we have these incredible mechanisms for imposing order on things or finding order in them.

CAMPBELL: We probably see more order in the world than there really is. In fact, people have an awful lot of trouble in accepting something completely random. If they're shown a random series of dots, or a random series of numbers, they will find some sort of structure in it. We tend to impose structure on the world.

CA: You pointed out in Winston Churchill's Afternoon Nap *that a knowledge of chronobiology can be useful in medicine; for example, you noted, "the toxic effects of at least eleven widely used anticancer drugs have been found to depend on the hour at which they are given." Is chronobiology being used widely in medicinal practice?*

CAMPBELL: I think it will be, though it's a little bit controversial at the moment. Some biological rhythms are very robust and clear. Others are a bit noisy and they have to be analyzed with computers to find the order in them. I found when I wrote the book that some biologists and medical people tended to say that these latter rhythms were too subtle, and they weren't sure whether they were worth changing our whole drug-giving procedure for. But I have the strong feeling that that's going to change. I think that because of the successes that have already been shown with anticancer drugs given with regard to biological rhythms, someday it will be standard practice to give them that way.

CA: Do you foresee any areas of science in which manipulation of natural rhythms could raise ethical questions?

CAMPBELL: I think these rhythms are extremely adaptable. We wouldn't have survived all these millions of years if some untoward alterations of the rhythms could have had serious bad effects on us. It's much more likely, then, that these rhythms are sufficiently flexible that you can manipulate them to quite a large extent without producing any serious harm. And I think our sleep rhythm is a good example of that. You can't abuse it beyond a certain point. On the other hand, if you do miss a night's sleep or sleep at strange hours, it very soon snaps back. These rhythms, like most things in the body, have their built-in defenses against manipulation and distortion. I would think the beneficial effects of manipulating rhythms, as in the case of depression, would far outweigh the dangers.

CA: Surely one of the most universally interesting things you talked about in the book is the business of morning people, whom you call "larks," and night people, or "owls." How much do you think owls should try to behave like larks, and vice versa?

CAMPBELL: Well, I thought I was an owl, and I behaved like an owl. But now I behave like a lark. I quite liked being an owl; I think being a lark is rather dull. But I can't say that it's really been a terrific problem for me. So if you have good reasons to behave like the one you're not, I wouldn't think it would be a problem to change. Again, this is an example of the flexibility of the rhythms. They're not very rigid like instincts. Also, many of them are in a very ancient part of the brain, and on top of that, more recent evolutionary parts of the brain have superceded them. So these rhythms can be easily overridden by the more modern devices. We have a very, very ancient natural rhythm that makes us want to have a nap in the afternoon, which is the reason for the title of the book. But if you say, "No, I can't nap this afternoon; I've got this important work to do," you can override that tendency to want to nap and you don't do yourself any harm. It's a little bit of an effort, perhaps. But one shouldn't take these rhythms as being ironclad or strict constraints on behavior. Within limits, we can override them.

CA: Music is often mentioned in your writing. Are you by chance an amateur musician?

CAMPBELL: I don't play an instrument, but I'm very fond of music. I also think that it is a wonderful illustration of how our sense of order and our liking for order are demonstrated in a domain other than language, a more abstract domain. That's an interesting relationship, and of course the relationship between our internal rhythms and the rhythms of music is a very interesting subject.

CA: In Diana McLellan's article "Massaging the Muse," in the Washingtonian, *you described how you like to write in noisy places like cafes, and were pictured looking very happy with your writing materials spread out in a corner booth of a local McDonald's. Has your newspaper work so habituated you to a lot of contact with people that you need the bustle for all your writing?*

CAMPBELL: Of course newspaper work puts me continually in contact with other people. It's just that the business of actually writing, of putting words down on paper, is to me something that demands an effort, and I don't like all the time being solitary and quiet and sitting alone in a room to write. That makes a dull process more burdensome. If I'm in a place where there's bustle and the world's affairs are being carried out, I feel happier. I really don't like sitting alone in a quiet room.

CA: You seem to manage the combination of newspaper work and writing books quite ably. Is there ever a conflict between them, or a time when you feel tempted to ditch one and concentrate wholly on the other?

CAMPBELL: I try to make my book writing as different as possible from my newspaper work, so the switch from one to the other is often a refreshing change. The pleasure of newspaper work is the quick results, and the immediate feedback.

CA: What science periodicals or columns do you read regularly?

CAMPBELL: Probably the one I read most often is *Science.* I think *Nature* is must reading for most people who write about science. I think the British-American magazine *New Scientist* is also a great source of ideas. And I find *Discover* magazine awfully good, and the Tuesday science section of the *New York Times.* I think—and many scientists say this—that newspaper coverage of scientific matters has become very good, has improved enormously. Whereas in the past I wouldn't have paid so much attention to newspaper coverage of science, I do much more now.

CA: Do you ever find it hard to write about somewhat complex and often technical subjects in language that a lay reader can understand and enjoy?

CAMPBELL: That's the hardest part; to make it appetizing is absolutely the hardest part. But on the other hand, you get a nice feeling of satisfaction if you have expressed a complicated idea plainly, because that means you have understood it. If you're writing in technical language and not being concerned to make it intelligible for the layman, I think it's possible to fool yourself into thinking that you understand everything. But the discipline of making sure that every part of it is clear, I think, is good for one's own understanding. Tim Ferris, who wrote a book on astronomy recently, said that the best way to understand a subject is to write a book about it, and I think that's absolutely true.

CA: What sort of response have your books brought from scientists whose work is related to your subjects?

CAMPBELL: Really a surprisingly good response, especially to *Grammatical Man.* I was invited to speak at several universities. I thought since I was a journalist and I'd written a popular book, maybe they would look down on me. But I was very pleasantly surprised.

CA: What's next for you that it isn't too early to talk about?

CAMPBELL: I'm writing a book on thinking, and probably I will finish that sometime next year. That's a broad enough topic! I find if you take a really big subject, then there's always something you can say about it. I think that's true in this case too.

CA: I think it's lovely to have a subject you can ramble around in.

CAMPBELL: I agree. You can draw in various related topics. For me, as a newspaper man, the concern always is to keep the reader awake on every page. If you're too specialized on a certain topic, that's difficult.

BIOGRAPHICAL/CRITICAL SOURCES:

BOOKS

Campbell, Jeremy, *Winston Churchill's Afternoon Nap: A Wide Awake Inquiry into the Human Nature of Time,* Simon & Schuster, 1987.

PERIODICALS

Los Angeles Times, February 24, 1987.
Los Angeles Times Book Review, September 26, 1982.
New York Times Book Review, March 8, 1987.
Psychology Today, January, 1987.
Times Educational Supplement, October 12, 1984.
Times Literary Supplement, November 4, 1983.
Voice Literary Supplement, June, 1987.
Washingtonian, August, 1987.

Washington Post, September 1, 1982.
Washington Post Book World, March 1, 1987.

—*Interview by Jean W. Ross*

* * *

CARLSON, Harry Gilbert 1930-

PERSONAL: Born September 27, 1930, in New York, N.Y.; married Carolyn L. Peterson (an architect), March 22, 1957. *Education:* Brooklyn College (now Brooklyn College of the City University of New York), B.A., 1952; Ohio State University, M.A., 1955, Ph.D., 1958.

ADDRESSES: Home—P.O. Box 1297, East Hampton, N.Y. 11937. *Office*—Department of Theatre-Drama, Graduate Center, Queens College and the Graduate Center of the City University of New York, Flushing, N.Y. 11367.

CAREER: Southwest Missouri State College, Springfield, assistant professor of drama, 1957-59; Valparaiso University, Valparaiso, Ind., assistant professor of drama, 1959-61; Northern Illinois University, DeKalb, assistant professor of drama and speech, 1961-64; University of Georgia, Athens, associate professor of theatre and drama, 1964-66; Queens College of the City University of New York, Flushing, N.Y., associate professor, 1967-72, professor of theatre and drama, 1972—, member of Faculty-in-Residence, 1987-88. Member of board of trustees of American Scandinavian Foundation. Chairman of theatre arts screening committee of Committee for International Exchange of Persons, 1971-72.

MEMBER: American Theatre Association, Society for the Advancement of Scandinavian Studies, Strindberg Society.

AWARDS, HONORS: Guggenheim fellowship, 1966-67; grants from Research Foundation of the City University of New York, 1970-71, 1980-81, 1985-86; translation prize from Artur Lundkvist Foundation, 1976; travel grant from Swedish government, 1984; travel grant from American Council of Learned Societies, 1984; fellowship from National Endowment for the Humanities, 1985.

WRITINGS:

(Editor and translator) Martin Lamm, *August Strindberg,* Blom, 1971.
(Co-editor and contributor) *Handbook of Contemporary Drama,* Crowell, 1971.
(Co-editor and contributor) *Encyclopedia of World Drama,* McGraw, 1972.
(Translator) Strindberg, "The Father" (two-act play), first produced in New York, N.Y., at Circle in the Square, 1981.
Strindberg and the Poetry of Myth, University of California Press, 1982.
(Translator) *Strindberg: Five Plays,* University of California Press, 1983.
(Translator) Lars Noren, "Night Is Mother to the Day" (play), first produced by Yale Repertory Theatre, New Haven, Conn., 1984.
(Translator) Per Olov Enquist, "Rain Snakes" (play), first produced by Long Wharf Theatre, New Haven, Conn., 1984.

Contributor to drama and Scandinavian studies journals.

WORK IN PROGRESS: A book on Strindberg and the Romantic tradition; a new volume of Strindberg translations.

SIDELIGHTS: Harry G. Carlson's *Strindberg and the Poetry of Myth* explores the similarities between the Swedish playwright's naturalist works and the dream plays of his later years. Carlson concentrates on Strindberg's use of myths in plays such as "Master Olaf" and "The Ghost Sonata" to reveal the wide range of materials that seem to have inspired the bleak and frequently eerie works. About Carlson's book, Peter Engel writes in the *New York Times Book Review,* "While mythological allusions of diverse origin underlie all of Strindberg's work, Mr. Carlson astutely discerns a general progression over time." Engel adds that Carlson "convincingly demonstrates the importance of mythology—not only in the late dream plays, where the mythical allusions are overt, but in the earlier plays, where the use of mythology is masked by realist technique."

BIOGRAPHICAL/CRITICAL SOURCES:

PERIODICALS

New York Times Book Review, February 20, 1983.

* * *

CARR, Jess(e Crowe, Jr.) 1930-

PERSONAL: Born July 27, 1930, in Bland County, Va.; son of Jesse Crowe and Flossie (Mitchell) Carr; married Lois Domazet (a choir director), June 17, 1955; children: Marsha Ainslie, Susan Kay, Catherine Rae. *Education:* Coyne Technical School, Chicago, Ill., graduate. *Politics:* Independent. *Religion:* Baptist.

ADDRESSES: Home—1401 Madison St., Radford, Va. 24141.

CAREER: Self-employed businessman in southwestern Virginia, 1949-51, 1953-56; Commonwealth Press, Inc., Radford, Va., sales manager, 1956-62, vice president and general manager, 1962-71, chairman of the board, 1977—; full-time writer, 1971—. Owner, Woodland Heights Sub-Division Co.; builder of homes and commercial buildings. *Military service:* U.S. Marine Corps, 1951-52.

MEMBER: Printing Industries of the Virginias (vice president, 1967).

WRITINGS:

A Creature Was Stirring, and Other Stories, Commonwealth Press, 1970.
The Second Oldest Profession: An Informal History of Moonshining in America, Prentice-Hall, 1972.
The Falls of Rabbor, Moore Publishing, 1973.
The Saint of the Wilderness, Commonwealth Press, 1974.
Birth of a Book, Commonwealth Press, 1974.
The Frost of Summer, Moore Publishing, 1975.
The Moonshiners, Aurora, 1977.
Ship Ride down the Spring Branch, and Other Stories, Moore Publishing, 1978.
How a Book Is Born, Moore Publishing, 1978.
Millie and Cleve, Leisure Books, 1979.
A Star Rising, Tower, 1980.
Murder on the Appalachian Trail, Pocket Books, 1986.
The Midas Touch, Commonwealth Press, 1986.
Intruder in the Wind, Pocket Books, 1989.

WORK IN PROGRESS: Echo, a fantasy/science fiction novel; *The Prince of Kusadasi* and *A Gift for a Princess,* travel romance novels; five picture books for children.

AVOCATIONAL INTERESTS: Fishing, water skiing, boating, photography, playing folk guitar, collecting books.

CARSBERG, Bryan Victor 1939-

PERSONAL: Born January 3, 1939, in London, England; son of Alfred Victor (a chartered secretary) and Maryllia (Collins) Carsberg; married Margaret Graham, December 10, 1960; children: Debbie Anne, Sarah Jane. *Education:* London School of Economics and Political Science, M.Sc., 1967. *Religion:* None.

ADDRESSES: Home—14, The Great Quarry, Guildford, Surrey, England. *Office*—Office of Telecommunications, London, England.

CAREER: Bryan Carsberg & Co. (public accounting firm), Amersham, England, public accountant, 1962-64; University of London, London School of Economics and Political Science, London, England, lecturer in accounting, 1964-69; University of Manchester, Manchester, England, professor of accounting, 1969-78; assistant director, Financial Accounting Standards Board, 1978-81; University of London, London School of Economics and Political Science, Arthur Anderson Professor of Accounting, 1981-87; Office of Telecommunications, London, director-general, 1984—. Visiting professor of business administration, University of California, Berkeley, 1974. Visiting lecturer in accounting, Graduate School of Business, University of Chicago, 1968-69.

MEMBER: Institute of Chartered Accountants in England and Wales (director of research, 1981-87).

AWARDS, HONORS: W. B. Peat Medal and Prize from Institute of Chartered Accountants in England and Wales, 1960; Centenary Award for Founding Societies, 1988.

WRITINGS:

An Introduction to Mathematical Programming for Accountants, Augustus M. Kelley, 1969.

(Editor with H. C. Edey) *Modern Financial Management,* Penguin, 1969.

Analysis for Investment Decisions, Haymarket, 1974.

(With E. V. Morgan and M. Parkin) *Indexation and Inflation,* Financial Times, 1975.

Economics of Business Decisions, Penguin, 1975.

(With A. Hope) *Investment Decision under Inflation,* Institute of Chartered Accountants in England and Wales, 1976.

(Editor with Hope) *Current Issues in Accounting,* P. Allen, 1977, 2nd edition, 1984.

(Editor with J. Arnold and R. Seapens) *Topics in Management Accounting,* P. Allen, 1980.

(With S. Lumby) *The Evaluation of Financial Performance in the Water Industry,* CIPFA, 1983.

(With M. Page) *Current Cost Accounting,* Prentice-Hall, 1984.

(With Page and others) *Small Company Financial Reporting,* Prentice-Hall, 1985.

Contributor to accounting, finance, and telecommunications journals.

* * *

CARTER, Nick

See BALLARD, (Willis) Todhunter

* * *

CAVALIERO, Glen 1927-

PERSONAL: Born June 7, 1927, in Eastbourne, England; son of Clarence John (a stockbroker) and Mildred (Tilburn) Cavaliero. *Education:* Oxford University, M.A., 1967, Ph.D., 1972.

ADDRESSES: Home—29 Portugal Pl., Cambridge, England.

CAREER: Curate of Church of England parishes in Margate, 1952-55, and Canterbury, England, 1955-56; chaplain at Lincoln Theological College, 1956-60, and Edinburgh University, 1960-64; Cambridge University, Cambridge, England, fellow of St. Catharine's College, 1967-71, member of faculty of English, 1971—, fellow commoner, 1986; writer. *Military service:* Royal Air Force, 1948-50.

WRITINGS:

John Cowper Powys: Novelist, Oxford University Press, 1973.

The Ancient People (poems), Carcanet, 1973.

The Rural Tradition in the English Novel, 1900-1939, Macmillan, 1977.

Paradise Stairway (poems), Carcanet, 1977.

A Reading of E. M. Forster, Macmillan, 1979.

(Author of introduction) Charles Williams, *Witchcraft,* Aquarian Press, 1980.

(Contributor) Belinda Humphrey, editor, *Recollections of the Powys Brothers,* Peter Owen, 1980.

Elegy for St. Anne's (poems), Warren House, 1982.

(Author of introduction) Edward Thomas, *The Happy-Go-Lucky Morgans,* Boydell & Brewer, 1983.

Charles Williams: Poet of Theology, Macmillan, 1983.

(Author of introduction) E. Lewis, *Dew on the Grass,* Boydell & Brewer, 1983.

(Author of introduction) *The Collected Poems of Gamel Woolsey,* Warren House, 1984.

(Author of afterword) John Cowper Powys, *Three Fantasies,* Carcanet, 1985.

(Contributor) Philip Dodd, editor, *Modern Selves,* Frank Cass, 1986.

(Author of introduction, abridgement, and notes) *Beatrix Potter's Journal,* Frederick Warne, 1986.

Out of Season, Olive Press, 1987.

SIDELIGHTS: "Glen Cavaliero in his excellent study [*Charles Williams: Poet of Theology*]," says *Times Literary Supplement* critic Stephen Medcalf, "traces [the British author's] understanding that our lives are always bound up with an impossibility, from his personal life through his criticism to his theology of the Atonement, and indeed to the quality of his belief in God. . . . Each of [Williams's] novels, as Dr. Cavaliero well points out, is about paying the price: 'in each one the supernatural threatens to overwhelm the natural order, and equilibrium is only restored by those who can accept *both* aspects of reality.' "

BIOGRAPHICAL/CRITICAL SOURCES:

BOOKS

Cavaliero, Glen, *Charles Williams: Poet of Theology,* Macmillan, 1983.

PERIODICALS

Times Literary Supplement, March 7, 1980, April 8, 1983, October 21, 1983, June 14, 1985.

* * *

CHAMBERS, Frances 1940-

PERSONAL: Born May 23, 1940, in Wilkes-Barre, Pa.; daughter of Frank and Victoria (Buynoski) Banko; married Stephen Chambers, 1966. *Education:* College Misericordia, A.B., 1962; Rutgers University, M.L.S., 1965; Hunter College of the City

University of New York, M.A., 1969; Teachers College, Columbia University, M.A., 1985.

ADDRESSES: Home—79 MacDougal St., New York, N.Y. 10012. *Office*—Library Department, City College of the City University of New York, Convent Ave. at 138th St., New York, N.Y. 10031.

CAREER: City College of the City University of New York, New York, N.Y., assistant professor, 1965-88, associate professor in library department, 1989—.

MEMBER: American Library Association, Teachers of English to Speakers of Other Languages.

AWARDS, HONORS: France was named an outstanding academic book by *Choice* in 1981; Fulbright award for University of Kosova, Yugoslavia, 1986-87.

WRITINGS:

France, American Bibliographical Center-Clio Press, 1980, revised edition, 1990.
Haiti, American Bibliographical Center-Clio Press, 1983.
Trinidad and Tobago, American Bibliographical Center-Clio Press, 1986.
Guyana, American Bibliographical Center-Clio Press, 1989.

* * *

CHANDLER, David Porter 1933-

PERSONAL: Born February 7, 1933, in New York, N.Y.; son of Porter R. (a lawyer) and Gabrielle (Chanler) Chandler; married Susan Saunders (a teacher), June 3, 1967; children: Elizabeth, Margaret, Thomas. *Education:* Harvard University, B.A., 1954; Yale University, M.A., 1968; University of Michigan, Ph.D., 1973. *Politics:* Democrat.

ADDRESSES: Home—6 Orford Rd., Ashburton, Victoria 3147, Australia. *Office*—Centre of Southeast Asian Studies, Monash University, Clayton, Victoria 3168, Australia.

CAREER: Department of State, Washington, D.C., foreign service officer, 1958-66; Monash University, Clayton, Australia, lecturer in history, 1972-81, associate professor, 1981—, Centre of Southeast Asian Studies, research director, 1978—. *Military service:* U.S. Army, 1955-57.

MEMBER: Australian Historical Association, Association for Asian Studies, Siam Society, Australian-Cambodian Association.

WRITINGS:

(Contributor) David Joel Steinberg, editor, *In Search of Southeast Asia,* Praeger, 1971, revised edition, University of Hawaii, 1987.
The Land and People of Cambodia, Lippincott, 1972.
(Translator) *The Friends Who Tried to Empty the Sea: Eleven Cambodian Folk Stories,* Monash University, 1976.
(With Ben Kiernan and Muy Hong Lim) *The Early Phases of Liberation in Northwestern Cambodia* (booklet), Centre of Southeast Asian Studies, Monash University, 1977.
(Translator) *Favorite Stories from Cambodia,* Heinemann, 1978.
A History of Cambodia, Westview, 1983.
(Editor with Kiernan) *Revolution and Its Aftermath in Kampuchea: Eight Essays,* Yale University Southeast Asia Studies, 1983.
(Editor and translator with Kiernan and Chanthou Boua) *Pol Pot Plans the Future: Confidential Leadership Documents from Democratic Kampuchea, 1976-1977,* Yale University Southeast Asian Studies, 1988.

Contributor to *World Book Encyclopedia* and *Encyclopaedia Britannica;* also contributor to periodicals, including *Current History, Journal of the Siam Society, Pacific Affairs,* and *Commonweal.*

WORK IN PROGRESS: A History of Cambodia, 1945-1979; a political biography of Pol Pot; a history of Southeast Asia.

SIDELIGHTS: History contributor Ian Brown notes that David Porter Chandler's *A History of Cambodia* "is the first scholarly history of Cambodia to appear in English, and the first in any European language for some seventy years." In a *Times Literary Supplement* review of the same title, Anthony Barnett recommends the book's second section, which deals with Cambodian history from the late eighteenth century through the end of French control of the area. In this part of the book, according to Barnett, Chandler "writes as someone whose own primary researches . . . have made him a foremost authority."

BIOGRAPHICAL/CRITICAL SOURCES:

PERIODICALS

History, June, 1985.
Times Literary Supplement, September 14, 1984.

* * *

CHANDLER, Jennifer
See WESTWOOD, Jennifer

* * *

CHANNING, Steven A. 1940-

PERSONAL: Born December 18, 1940, in Brooklyn, N.Y.; married Rhoda Kramer (a library administrator), August 11, 1963 (divorced July, 1979); married Nancy Clapp (a medical researcher), August 27, 1983; children: (first marriage) Laura Hope. *Education:* Brooklyn College of the City University of New York, B.A., 1962; New York University, M.A., 1965; University of North Carolina at Chapel Hill, Ph.D., 1968.

ADDRESSES: Home—47 Circle Dr., Chapel Hill, N.C. 27516. *Office*—P.O. Box 3552, Chapel Hill, N.C. 27515.

CAREER: University of Kentucky, Lexington, assistant professor, 1968-71, associate professor of American history, 1972-82; independent film and television producer and writer, 1982—. Senior postdoctoral research fellow, Institute of Southern History, Johns Hopkins University, 1971-72; visiting associate professor, Stanford University, 1972-73; Fulbright senior lecturer, University of Genova, Italy, 1977-78.

MEMBER: American Historical Association, Organization of American Historians, American Civil Liberties Union, Southern Historical Association.

AWARDS, HONORS: Allen Nevins Award, Society of American Historians, 1968, for *Crisis of Fear: Secession in South Carolina;* research grants from American Philosophical Society and American Council of Learned Societies, 1971; research fellowships from American Council of Learned Societies, 1973-74, and Guggenheim Foundation, 1977; awards from Ohio State University and Corporation for Public Broadcasting, both 1987, both for "Arkansas Heritage"; International Television Association award, 1989, for "Of Men and Machines."

WRITINGS:

Crisis of Fear: Secession in South Carolina, Simon & Schuster, 1970.
Kentucky: A Bicentennial History, Norton, 1977.
"This Other Eden" (film), Kentucky Education Television, 1979.
"Upon This Rock: The Black Religious Experience" (film), Kentucky Education Television, 1981.
The Confederate Ordeal, Time-Life, 1984.
"And Still I Rise: Maya Angelou" (film), Public Broadcasting Service, 1985.
Fulbright Experience, United States Information Agency, 1986.
"The Roanoke Voyages" (film), North Carolina Public Television, 1987.
Safety's No Accident, Media Guild, 1989.

Author of *The Peaceful Rebel,* 1988; and of television films "Arkansas Heritage," 1987, and "Of Men and Machines," 1989. Also author of "We Remember: America's 400th Anniversary—Historical Minutes," North Carolina Public Television, 1984-87. Contributor to *Biographical Encyclopedia of American History, Encyclopedia of Southern History, Biographical Directory of the Governors of the United States,* and *Review in American History.*

WORK IN PROGRESS: Historical and information/instructional film and video projects.

SIDELIGHTS: Steven A. Channing told *CA:* "After a satisfying career as an academic historian I had the opportunity to begin writing and producing programs for television. I enjoy the challenge of communicating to a wider audience through my independent production company, Video Dialog, Inc."

* * *

CHANT, Barry (Mostyn) 1938-

PERSONAL: Born October 23, 1938, in Adelaide, Australia; son of James Oswald (a teacher) and Vera (Penno) Chant; married Vanessa Bennett, January 23, 1960; children: Rebekah, Michael, Clinton. *Education:* University of Adelaide, B.A. (with honors), 1959, diploma in education, 1962; Melbourne College of Divinity, B.D., 1968.

ADDRESSES: Home and office—House of Tabor, 84 Northgate St., Unley Park, South Australia, Australia 5061.

CAREER: Teacher of English, history, and social studies in secondary school in Murray Bridge, South Australia, 1960-63; ordained to ministry, 1961; pastor of Pentecostal church in Adelaide, South Australia, 1964-75; Crusade Bible College, Adelaide, dean, 1964—; House of Tabor (Christian education center), Unley Park, South Australia, director, 1979—. Partner of Luke Publications, 1974—; chairman of Christian Revival Crusade (South Australia), 1974-81; president, *New Day International,* 1980—.

WRITINGS:

Upon Dry Ground, Crusade Publications, 1969, published as *Your Pocket Guide to the Power of God,* 1975, published as *Your Guide to God's Power,* House of Tabor, 1981.
Fact or Fantasy, Crusade Publications, 1970.
The Secret Is Out, Crusade Publications, 1971.
Heart of Fire: The Story of Australian Pentecostalism, Luke Publications, 1974, revised edition, 1984.
Spindles of the Dusty Range (children's stories), Luke Publications, 1975.
Straight Talk about Sex, Luke Publications, 1976.
Spindles and Eagles, Luke Publications, 1976.
Spindles and the Wombat, Luke Publications, 1978.
Spindles and the Orphan, House of Tabor, 1980.
Miracle of Calvary, House of Tabor, 1980.
(With Fred Grice) *Spindles and the Lamb* (stage musical), House of Tabor, 1982.
Spindles and the Children, House of Tabor, 1983.
Straight Talk about Marriage, House of Tabor, 1983.
(With Grice) *Jack-in-the-Box* (stage musical), House of Tabor, 1987.
Spillebeen en de stoffige Heuvels, Gideon (Holland), 1987.
How to Live the Kind of Life You've Always Wanted to Live, House of Tabor, 1988.
The Return, Sovereign World, 1988.

Associate editor and feature writer, *Impact* (formerly *Revivalist*), 1964—.

SIDELIGHTS: Barry Chant told *CA:* "I am an incurable writer. I seem to find it easier to crystallize my thinking and to be accurate when I put words on paper. But it is not just that. I guess I am also an incurable communicator. The acquisition of a word processor has been a wonderful boon. It enables me to play with words in a way I have never been able to do before.

"I like to teach. I find that ignorance, misunderstanding, or prejudice are problems which really aggravate me. Other people are aggravated by other things. It seems to me, however, that when people think properly and when their ideas are clear, that many other problems are automatically solved. I see this especially in regard to the Scriptures. When people really know and understand the Bible, the rest of their lives begins to become whole. So, I write with this in mind."

He adds: "I enjoy writing stories most of all. Our Lord Jesus Christ set the pattern for this, and it is an example I enjoy following."

* * *

CHARNEY, Hanna (Kurz) 1931-

PERSONAL: Born January 8, 1931, in Vienna, Austria; naturalized U.S. citizen; daughter of Leopold and Frida (Wolf) Kurz; married Maurice M. Charney (a professor and author), June 20, 1954; children: Leopold Joseph, Paul Robert. *Education:* Hunter College (now Hunter College of the City University of New York), B.A., 1951; Smith College, M.A., 1952; Columbia University, Ph.D., 1956.

ADDRESSES: Home—168 West 86th St., New York, N.Y. 10024. *Office*—Department of Romance Languages, Hunter College of the City University of New York, 695 Park Ave., New York, N.Y. 10021.

CAREER: Hunter College of the City University of New York, New York, N.Y., lecturer and instructor, 1952-60, assistant professor, 1960-63, associate professor, 1963-69, professor of French and of comparative literature, 1969—, chairman of department of Romance languages, 1967-70, executive officer of French Ph.D. program, 1986-87. Academic director of baccalaureate program, City University of New York, 1988—.

MEMBER: Modern Language Association of America, American Association of Teachers of French, Academy of Literary Studies (charter member), Phi Beta Kappa.

AWARDS, HONORS: Fulbright grant, 1960-61; Shirley Farr Fellowship, American Association of University Women, 1960-61; PSC-CUNY faculty research award, 1984, 1986; Schuster Faculty Award, Hunter College of the City University of New York, 1986.

WRITINGS:

Le Scepticisme de Valery (title means "Valery's Skepticism"), Didier, 1969.

(Editor with Jeanine Parisier Plottel) *Intertextuality: New Perspectives in Criticism,* New York Literary Forum, 1978.

The Detective Novel of Manners: Hedonism, Morality, and the Life of Reason, Fairleigh Dickinson University Press, 1981.

(Editor with Bettina L. Knapp) Rene Taupin, *Essais indifferents pour une esthetique,* Peter Lang, 1989.

Contributor to journals. Consultant to Doubleday & Co. and several university presses.

WORK IN PROGRESS: Motion and Narrative Time in Novel and Film; research into musical structures in fiction.

* * *

CHIARENZA, Carl 1935-

PERSONAL: Surname is pronounced Kee-a-*ren*-za; born September 5, 1935, in Rochester, N.Y.; son of Charles (a cabinetmaker) and Mary Rose (a seamstress; maiden name, Russo) Chiarenza; married Anne Spencer Thurman, September 1, 1961 (divorced, 1972); married Heidi Faith Katz, August 13, 1978; children: Suzanne Mari, Jonah Katz, Gabriella Christine. *Education:* Rochester Institute of Technology, B.F.A., 1957; Boston University, M.S., 1959, M.A., 1964; Harvard University, Ph.D., 1972.

ADDRESSES: Office—Department of Art and Art History, University of Rochester, 424 Morey Hall, Rochester, N.Y. 14627.

CAREER: Boston University, Boston, Mass., lecturer, 1963-64, instructor, 1964-68, assistant professor, 1968-72, associate professor, 1973-80, professor of art history, 1980-86, chairman of department, 1976-81; University of Rochester, Rochester, N.Y., Fanny Knapp Allen Professor of Art History, 1986—. Harnish Visiting Artist, Smith College, 1983-84; Massachusetts Council of the Arts visiting artist at School of Museum of Fine Arts, Boston, 1983, 1986. Guest curator at Boston's Institute for Contemporary Art, 1980-81; member of board of trustees of Visual Studies Workshop of State University of New York (adjunct visiting professor, 1972-73) and Photographic Resource Center; member of advisory council of International Center for Photography. Photographs exhibited in nearly one hundred and fifty solo and group shows; represented in numerous permanent collections, including International Museum of Photography, Fogg Art Museum, Center for Creative Photography, and Minneapolis Institute of Art. *Military service:* U.S. Army, 1960-62.

MEMBER: Society for Photographic Education, American Association of University Professors, College Art Association of America, Association of Historians of American Art.

AWARDS, HONORS: Danforth Foundation grants, 1966-67, 1967-68; Kress Foundation grant, 1970-71; fellow of Massachusetts Art and Humanities Foundation, 1975-76, and National Endowment for the Arts, 1977-78; Merit Award, American Photographic Historical Society, 1983, for *Aaron Siskind: Pleasures and Terrors.*

WRITINGS:

Aaron Siskind: Pleasures and Terrors, New York Graphic Society/Little, Brown, 1982.

Landscapes of the Mind (monograph), Godine, 1988.

CONTRIBUTOR

Photographs by Aaron Siskind in Homage to Franz Kline, David and Alfred Smart Gallery, University of Chicago, 1975.

Van Deren Coke, editor, *One Hundred Years of Photographic History,* University of New Mexico Press, 1975.

Siskind's Critics: 1946-1966, Center for Creative Photography, University of Arizona, 1978.

Jerome Liebling, editor, *Photography: Current Perspectives,* Light Impressions (Rochester, N.Y.), 1979.

Robert Heinecken, *Vary Cliche,* Light Gallery (New York City), 1979.

James Enyeart, editor, *Heinecken,* Light Gallery/Friends of Photography (Carmel, Calif.), 1980.

Lee Lockwood, *A Photographic Patron: The Carl Siembab Gallery,* Institute of Contemporary Art (Boston), 1981.

Kelly Wise, editor, *Photo Facts and Opinions,* Addison Gallery of American Art (Andover, Mass.), 1981.

Thomas F. Barrow and others, editors, *Reading into Photography: Selected Essays, 1959-1980,* University of New Mexico Press, 1982.

Kenneth Josephson, Museum of Contemporary Art (Chicago), 1983.

Aaron Siskind, *Chicago Facades,* Palm Press (Littleton, Mass.), 1985.

Books for College Libraries, 3rd edition, American Library Association, 1988.

OTHER

Also contributor of photographs to numerous books and catalogs. Contributor of articles and reviews to magazines, including *Afterimage.* Past editor of *Contemporary Photographer.*

WORK IN PROGRESS: Pictures for exhibitions and publications; book reviews; essays; a book of essays on photographic history; *Garry Winogrand,* for the Center for Creative Photography, University of Arizona; "Photography in the 60s in America," an introduction to an anthology.

SIDELIGHTS: Carl Chiarenza told *CA:* "I'm a switch-hitter. I have been making pictures and writing about pictures since high school. Because I seem to do both best when working in concentrated spurts on each, I sometimes feel torn between the two. I work intuitively and in what seems to me to be a constant state of agitation until things find their rightful place on a page or in a picture. Thus the subtitle 'Pleasures and Terrors,' while borrowed from a series of pictures by Siskind ('Pleasures and Terrors of Levitation'), applies to me as well as to him: it's about reaching for a sense of equilibrium, a place of understanding, for the individual as he or she moves through the world in a state of essential ignorance about the meaning of life.

"I wrote about Siskind's life and work for many reasons, but primarily because Siskind brought together a complex web of twentieth-century American issues. Born in 1903, the son of Jewish immigrants, he fought his way through significantly modern and American personal and societal problems. He produced a vast body of work which in its progression reflects the history of twentieth-century American art from figurative and social to abstract and personal. It seemed to me that his story and a critical analysis of his work had much to say about finding and expressing selfness to my own and to succeeding generations of Americans. I wrote, then, to learn about myself, and I hope that my readers read for the same reason.

"My own pictures are about my experience of this quest of self within a complex enviornment. It is difficult today to dwell for long on the notion of an external picturesque world. Much of what we see depends upon it first being pictured in the mind. Our landscape is indeed in the mind, but the mind now survives in an environment which is neither the natural one of the nineteenth century and earlier nor the urban one of the first half of the twentieth century. It is a more thoroughly technological landscape, yet it remains as mysterious and full of unknown forces as any landscape of the past.

"My photographs 'document' this contemporary landscape. For source material I use the discarded products of man's technological work. These tend to be inorganic and inhospitable, yet as they reenter the world as shapes and tones of a photograph, they become for me organic and inviting. References to traditional aesthetics in landscape appear in my work, but they are now pictured as abstract and imaginary structures—places which are as real as any field for stretch of mountain but which can exist only in one's private visual and mental ordering."

* * *

CHIARI, Joseph 1911-

PERSONAL: Born January 12, 1911, on the island of Corsica, France; son of Nicolas and Marie-Claire (Dominici) Chiari; married Margaret Allan Henderson, May 11, 1940 (deceased); married Joyce Hancock Cannon, 1970; children: (first marriage) Jean-Antoine, Margaret, Nicholas-Joseph, Alain-Dominique. *Education:* University of Aix-en-Provence, Licence-es-Lettres and Diplome d'Etudes Superieures, Docteur-es-Lettres.

ADDRESSES: Home—15A Westleigh Ave., London SW15 6RF, England.

CAREER: Free French envoy in Scotland during World War II; French consul, Edinburgh, Scotland, 1944-49; University of Manchester, Manchester, England, special lecturer in French literature, 1949-53; University of London, London, England, tutor in adult education department, 1953-56; French Consulate, Southampton, England, vice-consul, 1956-70.

MEMBER: European Academy of Science, Arts and Letters (corresponding member).

AWARDS, HONORS: First prize for dramatic art, Biennale Azureenne, 1970; literature prize, Academy of Lyons, 1985, for *Hier, c'est aujourd'hui.*

WRITINGS:

France and the War, Moray Press (Edinburgh), 1942.
France and Peace, Moray Press, 1944.
Impressions of People and Literature, Moray Press, 1945, published as *Impressions of People and Literature: On Scottish Life and Literature,* Richard West, 1973.
Corsica, the Scented Isle, Moray Press, 1946.
The Scented Isle: A Parallel between Corsica and the Scottish Highlands, W. MacLellan (Glasgow), 1948.
White Temple by the Sea: Poems, foreword by Pierre Emmanuel, Moray Press, 1949.
Contemporary French Poetry, preface by T. S. Eliot, Manchester University Press, 1952, reprinted, Books for Libraries Press, 1968.
The Eagle of Prometheus (poems), Hand and Flower Press (Aldington), 1953.
The Poetic Drama of Paul Claudel, preface by Eliot, P. J. Kenedy, 1954, reprinted, Gordian, 1969.
Mary Stuart: A Verse Play (produced in Edinburgh, Scotland, at Edinburgh International Festival, 1954; produced in Linlithgow, Scotland, 1987; French version produced in Monaco at Princess Grace Theatre, 1989), Oxford University Press, 1954.
Symbolism from Poe to Mallarme: The Growth of a Myth, preface by Eliot, Macmillan, 1956, 2nd edition, Gordian, 1970.
The Contemporary French Theatre: The Flight from Naturalism, Rockliff, 1958, Macmillan, 1959.
(Editor) *The Harrap Anthology of French Poetry,* Harrap, 1958.
Realism and Imagination, Barrie & Rockliff, 1960, Gordian, 1970.
Corsica: Columbus's Isle, Barrie & Rockliff, 1960.
(Translator) J. L. Barrault, *New Reflections on the Theatre,* Barrie & Rockliff, 1962.
Paradoxes (poems), Villiers, 1962.
Religion and Modern Society, Jenkins, 1964.
Landmarks of the Contemporary Theatre, Jenkins, 1965.
Aesthetics and Modernism, Humanities Press, 1970 (published in England as *The Aesthetics of Modernism,* Vision Press, 1970).
Lights in the Distance, Gordian, 1971.
Britain and France: The Unruly Twins, preface by Lord Robert Boothby, Vision Press, 1971.
T. S. Eliot: Poet and Dramatist, Vision Press, 1972, Barnes & Noble, 1973, 2nd edition, Gordian, 1979.
The Necessity of Being, Gordian, 1973.
The Time of the Rising Sea (poems), Gordian, 1975.
Twentieth Century French Thought: From Bergson to Levi-Strauss, Gordian, 1975.
Reflections on Life and Death, Gordian, 1977.
Art and Knowledge, Gordian, 1977.
Collected Poems: Joseph Chiari, preface by Hugh MacDiarmid, Gordian, 1978.
Christopher Columbus: A Play (produced in Calvi, Corsica, France, 1988), Gordian, 1979.
Slanting Lights: Poems, Enitharmon Press, 1981.
Picasso, l'homme et l'oeuvre, Buchet/Chastel, 1981.
T. S. Eliot: A Memoir, Enitharmon Press, 1982.
Hier, c'est aujourd'hui, Editions du Cerf, 1984.
Questions Unanswered (poems), Enitharmon Press, 1986.
The Need for the Absolute (in French), L'Age d'Homme, 1989.

Contributor to periodicals, including *Guardian, Spectator,* and *Times Literary Supplement.*

WORK IN PROGRESS: With Linda Stewart, a book on the Corsican origins of Christopher Columbus; a book on Greek, Shakespearean, and French tragedy; *Corsica, the Isle of Unrest.*

SIDELIGHTS: Born on the French island of Corsica and a resident for much of his life in Scotland and England, author Joseph Chiari draws from both France and Great Britain in many of his writings. His 1971 book, *Britain and France: The Unruly Twins,* examines "the similarities and differences that exist between Britain and France and between the British and the French," writes a reviewer for the *Times Literary Supplement.* The reviewer notes that Chiari's "deep knowledge of [Britain and France's] literature and languages makes him an ideally interesting person to do this, and even when he is playing the old game of comparing supposed national characters, he does this with assurance and subtlety." Chiari's *Collected Poems,* published in 1978, shows both French and Scottish influences; Anne Stevenson comments in the *Times Literary Supplement* that while the tone of the collection is French, Chiari's poems are "also the poems of a man who loves Scotland and is acquainted with its landscape and its limitations." Stevenson adds: "Chiari's poems will doubtless appeal to readers who are lost among contemporary poets and want to turn the pages of history back to a time when literature was less taxing to the intelligence, and love and death more acceptable as simple poetic themes."

Chiari's historical plays *Mary Stuart* and *Christopher Columbus* further reflect the author's affinity to both his native and adopted cultures. Both plays have been honored by performances in the birthplace of their subject: *Mary Stuart,* first produced in 1954, was staged in 1987 in Linlithgow, Scotland, to commemorate the 400th anniversary of the Scottish monarch's death. *Christopher Columbus,* first published in 1979, was staged in 1988 in Calvi, Corsica, France, in a performance given in the Corsican language. The Corsican production will be repeated yearly through the year 1992.

In addition to his poetry and plays, Chiari is the author of several books of philosophic interest that touch upon various areas of aesthetic theory. Regarding *Symbolism from Poe to Mallarme: The Growth of a Myth,* a reviewer in the *Times Literary Supplement* describes Chiari as "himself a poet, agitated by a restless philosophic curiosity, but he keeps his categories as clear as it is possible to keep them where thought and feeling, idea and form, so closely penetrate one another." Chiari's assessment of modern French philosophy and philosophers, *Twentieth-Century French Thought: From Bergson to Levi-Strauss,* does "not give automatic approval to recent French philosophical fashion, and thereby show[s] a laudable independence of judgement," writes Colin Smith in the *Times Literary Supplement.* Smith adds that Chiari is also "able to bring into interesting prominence some affinities between philosophical and poetic expression." The nature of such affinities are explored at greater length in Chiari's 1977 book *Art and Knowledge* which, according to a reviewer in *Choice,* "explores the intimate and often complex inner connections of aesthetic creation and philosophical thought and attempts to demonstrate how each strives to grasp 'the essence' of human reality."

AVOCATIONAL INTERESTS: The theatre, music, country walks.

BIOGRAPHICAL/CRITICAL SOURCES:

PERIODICALS

Commonweal, December 3, 1954.
Guardian, December 23, 1960.
Modern Language Review, April, 1977.
New York Times, June 22, 1952.
Poetry, May, 1955.
Sewanee Review, January, 1986.
Spectator, December 10, 1954, December 16, 1960, November 12, 1965.
Times Literary Supplement, September 5, 1952, October 15, 1954, January 18, 1957, January 20, 1961, July 1, 1965, February 26, 1971, August 13, 1971, December 14, 1973, October 10, 1975, October 6, 1978.

* * *

CIGLER, Allan J(ames) 1943-

PERSONAL: Born May 29, 1943, in Braddock, Pa.; son of Albert (a toolmaker) and Anne (Vomacha) Cigler; married Beth Ellen Ralston (a teacher), August 29, 1967; children: Kristen Elizabeth. *Education:* Thiel College, B.A., 1965; University of Maryland, M.A., 1967; Indiana University, Ph.D., 1973.

ADDRESSES: Home—R.F.D. 2, Lawrence, Kan. 66044. *Office*—Department of Political Science, University of Kansas, Lawrence, Kan. 66045.

CAREER: University of Kansas, Lawrence, assistant professor, 1970-76, associate professor of political science, 1976—.

WRITINGS:

(With Burdett A. Loomis) *Interest Group Politics,* Congressional Quarterly, 1983, 2nd edition, 1986.
(With William Brown) *Agriculture Interests,* Greenwood Press, 1989.

SIDELIGHTS: Allan J. Cigler wrote *CA:* "The great proliferation of interest groups since the early 1960's has had a tremendously significant impact upon the nature and character of American politics. Yet, we are just at the early stages of learning why some groups survive and others fail. The American Agriculture Movement is a group in the midst of attempting to evolve from an *ad hoc* protest group into a stable interest group, and provides an excellent subject for the study of the 'becoming' stage of an interest group. The group clearly demonstrates the difficulties issue-based 'expressive' groups confront when they try to retain the support of programmatic activists, while simultaneously attempting to provide the tangible membership incentives (like insurance) necessary to attract additional members."

* * *

CLAMPITT, Amy 1920-

PERSONAL: Born in 1920 in New Providence, Iowa; daughter of Roy Justin and Pauline (Felt) Clampitt. *Education:* Grinnell College, B.A. (with honors); attended Columbia University and New School for Social Research.

ADDRESSES: c/o Alfred A. Knopf, Inc., 201 East 50th St., New York, N.Y. 10022.

CAREER: National Audubon Society, New York City, reference librarian, 1952-59; free-lance writer, editor, and researcher, 1960—; E. P. Dutton (publisher), New York City, editor, 1977-82. Writer in residence, College of William and Mary, 1984-85; visiting writer, Amherst College, 1986-87; visiting Hurst Professor, Washington University, 1988.

MEMBER: PEN, National Institute of Arts and Letters, Authors Guild, Authors League of America, Editorial Freelancers Association, Phi Beta Kappa.

AWARDS, HONORS: Bernice Kavinoky Isaacson Award for poetry, New School for Social Research, 1977, for *The Isthmus;* Guggenheim fellowship, 1982; D.H.L., Grinnell College, 1984; Award in Literature, American Academy and Institute of Arts and Letters, 1984; fellowship award for distinguished poetic achievement, Academy of American Poets, 1984.

WRITINGS:

POEMS

Multitudes, Multitudes, limited edition, Washington Street Press, 1974.
The Isthmus, limited edition, Coalition of Publishers for Employment, 1981.
The Summer Solstice, limited edition, Sarabande Press, 1983.
The Kingfisher, Knopf, 1983.
A Homage to John Keats, limited edition, Sarabande Press, 1984.
What the Light Was Like, Knopf, 1985.
Archaic Figure, Knopf, 1987.

OTHER

(Author of introduction) *The Essential Donne,* Ecco Press, 1988.

Contributor of poems to magazines, including *Kenyon Review, Grand Street, Poetry, New Republic, Antaeus,* and *New Yorker.* Contributor of essays and reviews to magazines and newspapers, including *Cream City Review, Verse, Parnassus, Boston Review,* and *Boston Globe.*

WORK IN PROGRESS: "The Three of Us," a play about the Wordsworth family.

SIDELIGHTS: A late bloomer as a published poet, Amy Clampitt's first full-length poetry collection, *The Kingfisher,* came out when she was 63 years old. Her poetry is characterized by a "baroque profusion, the romance of the adjective, labyrinthine syntax, a festival lexicon," says *New York Times Book Review* contributor Alfred Corn in an article about Clampitt's second important collection, *What the Light Was Like.* Indeed, the poet's use of vocabulary and syntax is elaborate. "When you read Amy Clampitt," suggests Richard Tillinghast in the *New York Times Book Review,* "have a dictionary or two at your elbow." The poet has, Tillinghast continues, a "virtuoso command of vocabulary, [a] gift for playing the English language like a musical instrument and [a] startling and delightful ability to create metaphor." Her ability as a poet quickly gained Clampitt recognition as "the most refreshing new American poet to appear in many years," according to one *Times Literary Supplement* reviewer.

Clampitt's work is also characterized by erudite allusions, for which she provides detailed footnotes. *Times Literary Supplement* critic Lachlan Mackinnon compares her "finical accuracy of description and the provision of copious notes at the end of a volume," to a similar tendency in the work of Marianne Moore. "She is as 'literary' and allusive as Eliot and Pound, as filled with grubby realia as William Carlos Williams, as ornamented as Wallace Stevens and as descriptive as Marianne Moore," observes Corn. *Washington Post* reviewer Joel Conarroe adds Walt Whitman and Hart Crane to this list of comparable poets. "Like Whitman, she is attracted to proliferating lists as well as to 'the old thought of likenesses,' " writes Conarroe. "And as in Crane her compressed images create multiple resonances of sound and sense."

What the Light Was Like centers around images of light and darkness. This book is "more chastely restrained than *The Kingfisher,*" according to *Times Literary Supplement* contributor Neil Corcoran. Conarroe believes that the poet's "own imagery throughout [the book] is sensuous (even lush) and specific—in short, Keatsian." Corn similarly comments that "there are stirring moments in each poem, and an authentic sense of Keats' psychology." He opines, however, that "her sequence ['Voyages: A Homage to John Keats'] isn't effective throughout, the reason no doubt being that her high-lyric mode" does not suit narrative as well as a plainer style would.

Archaic Figure, which followed *What the Light Was Like* in 1987, continues in the vein of Clampitt's "idiosyncratic style," as William Logan calls it in the *Chicago Tribune.* But he adds that in this volume "style occasionally lapses into mannerism: the long, sometimes wearying sentences; the sharp enjambments that seem a nervous mania; the vocabulary whirled through a Waring Blender." *New York Times Book Review* contributor Mark Rudman maintains, however, that the collection "gets better as it goes along—as it becomes less archaic, less mythy, less Grecian and moves into cooler climes and grassier realms." Rudman also approves of the poet's "spontaneity and humor; she is quick to react, hasty, impulsive, responsive to place—and to space." In the London *Sunday Times,* David Profumo further praises *Archaic Figure.* Taking the example of the poem "Hippocrene," the critic asserts that this work "demonstrates her new powers of economy, the sureness of her rhythmic touch and the sheer readability of her magnificent narrative skills."

Although her collections since *The Kingfisher* have received many positive reviews, the most enthusiastic responses have been to this first major book. Joseph Parisi, a *Chicago Tribune Book World* reviewer, calls the poet's sudden success "one of the most stunning debuts in recent memory." Parisi continues: "throughout this bountiful book, her wit, sensibility and stylish wordplay seldom disappoint." In one of the first articles to appear after *The Kingfisher*'s debut, *New York Review of Books* critic Helen Vendler avers that "Amy Clampitt writes a beautiful, taxing poetry. In it, thinking uncoils and coils again, embodying its perpetual argument with itself." *Georgia Review* contributor Peter Stitt also feels that "*The Kingfisher* is . . . in many ways an almost dazzling performance." The poetic naissance demonstrated by Clampitt in this collection and the works which followed has been noted by several critics. "She is a virtuoso of the here and the palpable," writes Peter Porter in the *Observer,* who ranks her with the likes of Emily Dickinson and Elizabeth Bishop. "Amy Clampitt," concludes Logan, "has become one of our poetry's necessary imaginations."

BIOGRAPHICAL/CRITICAL SOURCES:

PERIODICALS

Chicago Tribune, May 26, 1987.
Chicago Tribune Book World, June 10, 1984.
Georgia Review, summer, 1983.
New York Review of Books, May 3, 1983.
New York Times Book Review, August 7, 1983, May 19, 1985, December 20, 1987.
Observer, June 17, 1984.
Parnassus, spring-summer, 1983.
Prairie Schooner, spring, 1983.
Sunday Times (London), February 21, 1988.
Times Literary Supplement, June 10, 1983.
Washington Post, July 28, 1985.
Washington Post Book World, March 20, 1983, April 3, 1983.

* * *

CLAYTON, Richard Henry Michael 1907- (William Haggard)

PERSONAL: Born August 11, 1907, in Croydon, Surrey, England; son of Henry James and Mabel Sarah (Haggard) Clayton; married Barbara Myfanwy Sant, 1939; children: Michael Edward, Julia Katharine. *Education:* Attended Lancing College; Christ Church, Oxford, B.A., 1929, M.A., 1947.

ADDRESSES: Home—3 Linkside, Holland Rd., Frinton-on-Sea, Essex C013 9EN, England. *Agent*—John Farquharson, 250 West 57th St., New York, N.Y. 10107.

CAREER: Indian Civil Service, magistrate, 1931, sessions judge, 1937; British Civil Service, controller, Enemy Property Branch of Board of Trade, 1957-69. *Military service:* Indian Army, 1939-45; became lieutenant colonel.

MEMBER: Travellers' Club (London).

WRITINGS:

"COLONEL CHARLES RUSSELL" SERIES; UNDER PSEUDONYM WILLIAM HAGGARD

Slow Burner (also see below), Little, Brown, 1958.
Venetian Blind (also see below), Washburn, 1959.
The Arena (also see below), Washburn, 1961.
The Unquiet Sleep (also see below), Washburn, 1962.

The High Wire (Detective Book Club Selection), Washburn, 1963.
The Antagonists, Washburn, 1964.
The Powder Barrel, Washburn, 1965.
The Hard Sell (also see below), Cassell, 1965, Washburn, 1966.
The Power House, Cassell, 1966, Washburn, 1967.
The Conspirators, Cassell, 1967, Walker & Co., 1968.
A Cool Day for Killing, Walker & Co., 1968, reprinted, 1983.
The Doubtful Disciple, Cassell, 1969.
The Hard Liners, Walker & Co., 1970.
The Bitter Harvest, Cassell, 1971, published as *Too Many Enemies,* Walker & Co., 1972.
The Old Masters, Cassell, 1973, published as *The Notch on the Knife,* Walker & Co., 1973.
The Scorpion's Tail, Walker & Co., 1975.
Yesterday's Enemy, Walker & Co., 1976.
Visa to Limbo, Cassell, 1978, Walker & Co., 1979.
The Poison People, Walker & Co., 1979.
The Median Line, Cassell, 1979, Walker & Co., 1981.
The Mischief Makers, Hodder & Stoughton, 1982, Walker & Co., 1983 (bound with *The Golden Creep* by George Bagby and *Endgame* by Michael Gilbert, W. J. Black, 1982).
The Need to Know, Hodder & Stoughton, 1984.
The Meritocrats, Hodder & Stoughton, 1985.

OTHER; UNDER PSEUDONYM WILLIAM HAGGARD

The Telemann Touch (suspense novel), Little, Brown, 1958, reprinted, Hodder & Stoughton, 1984.
Closed Circuit (suspense novel; also see below), Washburn, 1960.
(Contributor) John Welcome, editor, *Best Secret Service Stories No. 2,* Faber, 1965.
The Haggard Omnibus (contains *Slow Burner, Venetian Blind* and *Closed Circuit*), Cassell, 1967.
Haggard for Your Holiday: Three Complete Novels by William Haggard (contains *The Arena, The Unquiet Sleep,* and *The Hard Sell*), Cassell, 1969.
(Contributor) *Blood on My Mind,* Macmillan (London), 1972.
(Contributor) George Hardinge, editor, *Winter's Crimes No. 4,* Macmillan, 1972.
The Little Rug Book (nonfiction), Cassell, 1972.
The Protectors (suspense novel), Walker & Co., 1972.
The Kinsmen (suspense novel), Walker & Co., 1974.
(Contributor) Hilary Watson, editor, *Winter's Crimes No. 8,* Macmillan, 1976.
The Money Men (suspense novel), Walker & Co., 1981.
The Heirloom (suspense novel), Hodder & Stoughton, 1983.
The Martello Tower (suspense novel), Hodder & Stoughton, 1986.
The Diplomatist (suspense novel), Hodder & Stoughton, 1987.
The Expatriates, Hodder & Stoughton, 1989.

SIDELIGHTS: William Haggard's suspense novels involve nefarious plots and counterplots in the highest levels of government and behind the scenes of international affairs. Called by Anthony Boucher of the *New York Times Book Review* a "strikingly individual novelist," Haggard most often writes about Colonel Charles Russell of the Security Executive, a fictional high-level branch of the English intelligence establishment.

Colonel Russell enjoys a great popularity among readers of spy fiction. Writing in the *New York Times,* Anatole Broyard describes Russell as "a fine character . . . . Urbane, autocratic, ironical, he carries not a gun but a personality into his work." Jean M. White of the *Washington Post Book World* notes that Russell "operates in a very civilized yet undeniably effective manner. He is an urbane man, having about him the air of a mature James Bond." In a review of *A Cool Day for Killing,* Allen J. Hubin of the *New York Times Book Review* judges Russell as "surely one of the most effectively developed characters in spy fiction." In later books, such as *The Mischief Makers,* Haggard allows the senior sleuth to be "very nearly upstaged" by black Englishman Willy Smith, who is "equally urbane," reports Robin W. Winks in the *New Republic.* Smith makes "a perfectly acceptable substitute" for the retired Russell in the suspense novel *The Diplomatist,* says Tim Heald of the London *Times.*

"I always anticipate savouring the delights of William Haggard's writing," Maurice Prior of *Books and Bookmen* states. Prior appreciates Haggard's "mastery and expertise in handling a plot" and his "skill and positiveness plus an almost indefinable air of assurance and atmosphere-cultivation which keeps one absorbed and fascinated from first to last." Newgate Callender notes in the *New York Times Book Review* that Haggard "has been compared as a stylist to C. P. Snow, and there is indeed something of that admirable author in Haggard's deliberate, British upper-class, stiff-lipped understatement." Winks of the *New Republic* esteems Haggard as "a thoroughgoing professional who writes as he wishes to, convincingly, cleverly, and with acid."

BIOGRAPHICAL/CRITICAL SOURCES:

PERIODICALS

Books and Bookmen, November 1968, November, 1969, October, 1970, September, 1973.
Globe and Mail (Toronto), April 21, 1984.
New Republic, March 19, 1977, June 10, 1978, June 13, 1983.
New Yorker, February 1, 1969.
New York Herald Tribune Book Review, August 18, 1963.
New York Times, January 14, 1972, March 10, 1979.
New York Times Book Review, July 23, 1961, March 13, 1966, November 17, 1968, January 14, 1972, April 23, 1972, September 16, 1973, December 28, 1976.
Observer, August 24, 1969, September 12, 1971, September 10, 1972, November 25, 1979.
San Francisco Chronicle, August 20, 1961.
Spectator, September 4, 1971.
Times (London), December 24, 1987.
Times Literary Supplement, September 18, 1969, October 22, 1971, September 29, 1972.
Washington Post Book World, March 18, 1979.

* * *

CLIFFORD, Martin
See HAMILTON, Charles (Harold St. John)

* * *

CLIFTON, Harry
See HAMILTON, Charles (Harold St. John)

* * *

CLIVE, Clifford
See HAMILTON, Charles (Harold St. John)

* * *

CLOUD, Patricia
See STROTHER, Pat Wallace

COBHAM, Sir Alan
See HAMILTON, Charles (Harold St. John)

* * *

COHEN, Morris L(eo) 1927-

PERSONAL: Born November 2, 1927, in New York, N.Y.; son of Emanuel (a manufacturer) and Anna (Frank) Cohen; married Gloria Weitzner (a computer programmer) February 1, 1953; children: Havi, Daniel Asher. *Education:* University of Chicago, B.A., 1947; Columbia University, J.D., 1951; Pratt Institute, M.L.S., 1959. *Religion:* Jewish.

ADDRESSES: Home—84 McKinley Ave., New Haven, Conn. 06515. *Office*—Law School, Yale University, New Haven, Conn. 06520.

CAREER: Admitted to Bar of New York State, 1951; private practice in New York City, 1951-58; Rutgers University, New Brunswick, N.J., assistant law librarian, 1958-59; Columbia University, New York City, assistant law librarian, 1959-61; State University of New York at Buffalo, law librarian and associate professor of law, 1961-63; University of Pennsylvania, Philadelphia, Biddle Law Librarian, 1963-71, associate professor, 1963-67, professor of law, 1967-71; Harvard University, Cambridge, Mass., law librarian and professor of law, 1971-81; Yale University, New Haven, Conn., law librarian and professor of law, 1981—. Lecturer at library school, Columbia University, 1963-70, and Drexel University, 1963-71; adjunct professor at library school, Simmons College, beginning 1976. Member of board of visitors, law school, Columbia University, beginning 1977, and library school, Pratt Institute, beginning 1980. Consultant on law libraries to law schools and legal organizations.

MEMBER: International Association of Law Libraries, American Association of Law Libraries (president, 1970-71), American Library Association, American Civil Liberties Union (member of executive board, Philadelphia chapter, 1965-71), American Bar Association, Bibliographical Society of America, American Association of University Professors, Jewish Publications Society.

AWARDS, HONORS: Grants from National Endowment for the Humanities, 1968-71, 1975-78.

WRITINGS:

Legal Bibliography Briefed, Graduate School of Library Sciences, Drexel Institute of Technology, 1965.
Legal Research in a Nutshell, West Publishing, 1968, 4th edition, 1985.
(General editor) *How to Find the Law,* West Publishing, 7th edition, 1976, 8th edition (also see below), 1983.
(Compiler with Naomi Ronen and Jan Stepan; also author of introduction) *Law and Science: A Selected Bibliography,* Science, Technology, and Human Values, Harvard University, 1978, revised edition (with Ronen), MIT Press, 1980.
(With Robert C. Berring) *Finding the Law: An Abridged Edition of How to Find the Law, 8th Edition,* West Publishing, 1983.
(Editor) *Bibliography of Early American Law,* five volumes, Kraus International, 1988.

* * *

COHEN, Ronald 1930-

PERSONAL: Born January 22, 1930, in Canada; came to the United States in 1963; son of Maxwell B. and Pauline (Golant) Cohen; married Diana Barbara Williams, June 21, 1955; children: Paul Yerima, Stephen Benjamin. *Education:* University of Toronto, B.A., 1951; University of Wisconsin, M.Sc., 1954, Ph.D., 1960.

ADDRESSES: Home—P.O. Box 75, Micanopy, Fla. 32667. *Office*—Department of Anthropology, University of Florida, Gainesville, Fla. 32611.

CAREER: University of Toronto, Toronto, Ontario, lecturer in anthropology, 1958-61; McGill University, Montreal, Quebec, assistant professor of anthropology, 1961-63; Northwestern University, Evanston, Ill., associate professor, 1963-68, professor of anthropology and political science, 1968-81, chairman of the department of anthropology, 1971-72, director of program in ethnography and public policy, 1979-81; Ahmadu Bello University, Zaria, Nigeria, professor of sociology and head of department, 1972-74; University of Florida, Gainesville, professor of anthropology, 1981—. Chairman, Committee on African Studies in Canada, 1962-63; member of review board, National Institute of Mental Health research grants, 1968; member, National Science Foundation Anthropology Panel, 1978-81. Member, planning team for Abuja, Nigeria's new capital city, 1977-79; has done field work in Nigeria and Canada. Consulting director, Canadian Centre for Research in Anthropology, 1962—.

MEMBER: International African Institute of London, Association of Social Anthropologists, Association of Political and Legal Anthropology (president-elect, 1988), African Studies Association (fellow), Committee on African Studies, Rhodes-Livingston Institute of Zambia, Society of Social Anthropologists of Great Britain, African Studies Association of Canada, African Students Foundation of Canada (chairman, 1961-63), American Anthropological Association (fellow), Central States Anthropological Association.

WRITINGS:

An Anthropological Survey of Communities of the Mackenzie-Slave Lake Region of Canada, Department of Northern Affairs and Natural Resources (Ottawa), 1962.
(With Helgi Osterreich) *Good Hope Tales,* National Museum of Canada, 1965.
The Kanuri of Bornu, Holt, 1967.
(With John Middleton) *Comparative Political Systems: Studies in the Politics of Pre-Industrial Societies,* Natural History Press, 1967.
(Editor and contributor with R. Naroll) *Handbook of Methodology in Cultural Anthropology,* Natural History Press, 1970.
(Editor with Middleton, and contributor) *Tribe to Nation in Africa,* Chandler Publishing, 1970.
Dominance and Defiance, American Anthropological Association, 1971.
(Editor) *The Origins of the State: A Symposium,* Institute for the Study of Human Issues, 1977.
(With G. Britan) *Hierarchy and Society,* Institute for the Study of Human Values, 1981.
(Editor with J. Toland) *State Formation and Political Legitimacy,* Transaction Press, 1988.
(Editor) *Satisfying Africa's Food Needs,* Lynne Reiner Press, 1988.

CONTRIBUTOR

G. Zollschan and D. Hirsch, editors, *Explorations in Social Change,* Houghton, 1964.
J. Butler, editor, *Boston University Publications in African History,* Volume II, Boston University Press, 1966.

M. Swartz, V. Turner, and A. Tuden, editors, *Political Anthropology,* Aldine, 1966.

S. M. Lipset, editor, *Politics and the Social Sciences,* Oxford University Press, 1967.

(With A. Schlegel) J. Helm, editor, *American Ethnological Society, Essays on the Problem of the Tribe,* University of Washington Press, 1968.

Tuden and L. Plotnicov, editors, *Class and Status in Sub-Saharan Africa,* Free Press, 1970.

P. J. Bohannan, editor, *Divorce and After,* Natural History Press, 1970.

M. Crowder, editor, *West African Chiefs,* Faber, 1970.

J. Paden and E. Soja, editors, *The African Experience,* Northwestern University Press, 1970.

(With L. Brenner) A. Ajayi and Crowder, editors, *The History of West Africa,* Volume I, Clarendon Press, 1971, Volume II, Longman, 1973.

Turner, editor, *The Impact of Colonialism,* Hoover Institution, 1971.

H. Volpe and R. Melson, editors, *Communalism in Nigeria,* Michigan State University Press, 1971.

B. Ferguson, editor, *Warfare and State Formation,* Academic Press, 1984.

Also contributor to *Research Techniques in Africa,* edited by Tessler, Spain, and O'Barr, 1971, *Sociology in Africa,* edited by P. Wilmot, 1973, *Power Structure and Social Transformation,* edited by T. R. Burns and W. Buckley, 1976, and *The Early States,* edited by H. J. H. Claessen and P. Skalnik, 1977.

OTHER

Contributor to *American Anthropologist, Anthropologica, Canadian Journal of African Studies, Current Anthropology, Human Organization, International Journal, Journal of Social Issues,* and other professional journals. Assistant editor, *Anthropologica,* 1962—, *American Anthropologist,* 1970-72; abstractor in charge of anthropology and related fields, *African Abstracts,* 1966-70; member of editorial board, *Journal of Social History,* 1967—.

SIDELIGHTS: Ronald Cohen told *CA:* "I write books and articles slowly, and without stopping, unless I am doing fieldwork in Africa which is a totally different way of life. Why? First, there is an obligation to do so. I learn as much as I can, but it doesn't really exist in a tangible way unless I can sit down and put it into a form that can be read. Secondly, and over the years, this has meant that I do not really come to grips with my understanding of African societies, and other topics, unless I go through the long and often arduous process of trying to put experience and my claim to knowledge into written form. This forces the ordering and questioning of experience, organizes it, and makes me ask multitudes of questions that need answering before the writing is possible. And then, often as not, the answers change because the writing shows up their superficiality and I'm forced to start over, ask more questions, writing and rewriting until it finally says things 'right.' Thirdly, I write because it joins me to the idea of a university, an age-old institution given over to seeking and disseminating knowledge through teaching and research. Like countless other scholars I absorb the experiences of others who write, adding them to my own efforts at gaining new insights, then passing it all on after it has been stamped by my own personality. If it wasn't there—writing and the idea of a university—we'd have to invent it, it's so awesomely useful, so deeply human."

COHN, Roy M(arcus) 1927-1986

PERSONAL: Born February 20, 1927, in New York, N.Y.; died August 6, 1986, in Bethesda, Md., of cardio-pulmonary arrest brought on by AIDS; son of Albert (a New York state supreme court judge) and Dora (Marcus) Cohn. *Education:* Columbia University, B.A., 1946, LL.B., 1947. *Politics:* "Conservative; registered Democrat." *Religion:* Jewish.

CAREER: Lawyer. Admitted to New York State Bar, 1948. Law clerk and photostat operator for U.S. Attorney for Southern District of New York John F. X. McGohey, 1947; U.S. District Attorney's Office, New York City, assistant U.S. district attorney, 1948-50, confidential assistant to U.S. Attorney Irving Saypol, 1950-52; U.S. Department of Justice, Washington, D.C., special assistant to Attorney General James McGranery, 1952; U.S. Senate, Washington, D.C., chief counsel to Senate Permanent Investigations Subcommittee, 1953-54; New York Law School, New York City, adjunct professor, 1957–86; Saxe, Bacon & Bolan (law firm), New York City, partner, 1959-86. Chairman of board of Prisoner's Art Program; member of board of directors of Western Goals, Washington, D.C.; advisory board member of East Side Conservative Club, New York City. Regent of St. Francis College, Brooklyn, N.Y. Trustee of Roy M. Cohn Foundation. *Military service:* N.Y. State National Guard, 1947-57; became captain.

MEMBER: American Bar Association, American Jewish League against Communism (president), New York Humane Society (chairman of special projects), Bronx County Bar Association, Lafayette Yacht Club, Manhattan Club, Studio 54 (New York City), Regine's (Paris), St. James (London).

AWARDS, HONORS: Federation of Jewish Philanthropies lawyers division award, 1952; American Legion of New York State Americanism Award, 1955; Catholic War Veterans patriotism award, 1970, award of merit, 1975; New York County Conservative Party leadership award, 1975, annual award, 1980; Trial Advocacy Award, Columbia Law Alumni of California, 1981; Jewish National Fund achievement award, 1981; Disabled Veterans Association award, 1982.

WRITINGS:

McCarthy, New American Library, 1968, revised edition published as *McCarthy: The Answer to "Tail Gunner Joe,"* Manor Books, 1977.

A Fool for a Client: My Struggle against the Power of a Public Prosecutor, Hawthorn, 1971.

How to Stand Up for Your Rights—And Win!, Simon & Schuster, 1981.

(With Sidney Zion) *The Autobiography of Roy Cohn,* Lyle Stuart, 1988.

Contributor to magazines, including *Parade, Esquire, Penthouse, Interview,* and *People,* and to legal journals.

SIDELIGHTS: Despite a long and flamboyant career as a controversial lawyer and close friend to many prominent politicians, celebrities, business people, and media figures, Roy Cohn was always best known for his work with Senator Joseph McCarthy in the early 1950s. Still in his early twenties at that time, Cohn served as McCarthy's chief counsel on the Senate Permanent Investigations Subcommittee, a group then probing communist influence in the United States government. Cohn's role in this highly publicized investigation made him a host of life-long friends and enemies, as did his later legal work with many of the nation's most prominent and famous people.

The only child of a respected New York state supreme court judge, Cohn began at an early age to associate with the politically powerful. His father, according to a writer for *Time,* was "a one-time protege of the late Boss Ed Flynn, and a power in the Democratic Party." Cohn frequented Democratic Party fund raising parties while still a child. At the age of ten his father introduced him to President Franklin Delano Roosevelt at one such affair; Cohn reportedly praised Roosevelt for his attempted packing of the United States Supreme Court.

After attending Columbia University, where he graduated with a law degree at the age of twenty, Cohn found himself too young to qualify as a lawyer in the state of New York. He was obliged to wait a year. His family friends and contacts got him a job with the U.S. Attorney for the Southern District of New York until he turned twenty-one. The same day he was admitted to the bar, Cohn was sworn in as an assistant district attorney.

By the early 1950s Cohn was working in Washington, D.C., specializing in the investigation of subversive activities. He played a role in the trial and execution of Julius and Ethel Rosenberg, who were accused of passing on vital A-bomb secrets to the Soviet Union. As an Assistant U.S. Attorney, Cohn was a member of the government's prosecution team that successfully argued the case against the accused couple. Robert Sherrill of the *Nation* claimed that Cohn was also instrumental in convincing the judge in the case to demand the death penalty for both defendants. Cohn argued, according to Sherrill, that "the death penalty was the right penalty." The conviction and execution of the Rosenbergs is still a matter of debate among those on the political Left, who see the couple as political martyrs and continue to call for a reopening of the case.

During 1953 and 1954, Cohn worked with Senator Joseph McCarthy on his ongoing investigation of covert communist activities. McCarthy had drawn criticism from some quarters for his allegedly reckless accusations, guilt-by-association tactics, and headline grabbing charges. His probing of communist influence in several government departments, including the State Department, was seen by some as unfair and exaggerated. Cohn, as McCarthy's special counsel, was also a target of such criticism. But McCarthy defended his assistant. Cohn was, according to McCarthy, "the most brilliant young fellow I've ever seen." A writer for *Time* described Cohn as a "precocious, brilliant, arrogant young man" and the subcommittee's "real brain."

The televised Army-McCarthy hearings, in which the senator looked into allegations of lax security at several military installations, proved to be McCarthy's downfall. His insistence that the military was infiltrated by communists due to inadequate security procedures irked many influential people, including President Dwight D. Eisenhower, himself a former Army general. And Cohn's behind-the-scenes attempt to secure special privileges for his friend G. David Schine, an Army private, also provoked military wrath. The Army issued a report denouncing McCarthy and his investigation. The senator was soon censured by the U.S. Congress and his investigations ended. Yet William A. Rusher in the *National Review* noted that when McCarthy investigated the Signal Corps radar-research installation at Fort Monmouth, New Jersey, he did uncover serious breaches of security. And "two technicians who worked there," Rusher wrote, "subsequently fled to the Soviet Union."

After McCarthy was censured, Cohn moved from Washington, D.C. to New York City and entered into the private practice of law. He quickly established himself as what Albin Krebs of the *New York Times* called "a political power broker, a friend of the rich and the fashionable, one of the city's most sought-after legal talents and probably a very wealthy man." His friends included many media figures, including newspaper columnists Walter Winchell and George Sokolsky. These friends provided Cohn with favorable publicity in the press, and gave Cohn's opponents bad publicity. According to Sherrill, "sometimes lawyers settled cases with Cohn not because they couldn't whip him in court but because they feared that Cohn would smear them and their clients through easy manipulation of the press."

Other critics charged that Cohn's business and personal life was ruled by some questionable ethics: judges were bribed, mob bosses befriended, clients defrauded, estates mishandled. (Just months before his death in 1986, Cohn was disbarred for several such abuses.) Nicholas von Hoffman, in his book *Citizen Cohn,* also claimed that Cohn routinely failed to pay his debts, telling bill collectors to sue him, an expensive course of action. When the Internal Revenue Service tried to collect several million dollars in back taxes from Cohn, they discovered that he had no bank account, and that his Manhattan townhouse, his several houses, and his limousines were all owned by either his law firm or by friends. They were unable to collect any money. Sherrill claimed that Cohn, a Jew, was also known to frequently use such terms as "kike" and to associate with anti-semites. Cohn's openly homosexual lifestyle alienated yet other observers. But Ken Auletta in *Esquire* noted that Cohn's "notoriety hasn't hurt a bit. . . . The more publicity Roy generates, the more clients he attracts."

Cohn was a man who inspired either strong hatred or love, and who could boast of many influential and highly respected friends, among them J. Edgar Hoover, Cardinal Spellman, Calvin Klein, Barbara Walters, Geraldine Ferraro, Donald Trump, William Safire, and Si Newhouse. At his annual birthday party, Cohn invited some of the most prominent people in politics, business, and the arts. His reputation as a flamboyant, daring "character" appealed to many people. Kinder observers noted that Cohn was invariably loyal to his friends, a quality they greatly admired. Many, too, saw Cohn's strong anticommunism, evident since his work with Senator McCarthy, as the primary reason he was sometimes painted in an unfavorable light.

In a memorial service in October of 1986, many of Cohn's friends gathered to pay tribute to him. Among the more than 500 people present were former New York mayor Abraham Beame, Estee Lauder, William Safire, Rupert Murdoch, and Senator Chic Hecht. They called Cohn, according to Joseph Berger in the *New York Times,* "a complicated man whose dedication to fighting Communism inspired liberals to a 'lust for revenge' that persisted throughout his turbulent career."

While Cohn's political work drew fire from his opponents on the Left, Victor Gold in the *American Spectator* doubted Cohn's conservative credentials. Cohn's conservatism, Gold wrote, "became full-blown only after Nixon and Reagan went to the White House; . . . in 1964, when conservatives were in the trenches with Barry Goldwater, our good friend Roy was front-running with Lyndon Johnson." Writing in the *Spectator,* Anthony Holden remarked that Cohn's clients included "the rich and famous, regardless of any political affiliation on their part, and of any ideological or ethical considerations on his. . . . Warmly received by the Reagan White House, he was meanwhile handling the affairs of countless powerful (and supposedly liberal) East Coast dynasties."

Towards the end of his career, when Cohn knew he was dying of AIDS (but publicly insisted it was cancer), he began to write his autobiography. He died before it could be completed. Sidney Zion, a close friend, completed the book and it was published in

1988 as *The Autobiography of Roy Cohn.* Zion was quoted by Beth Levine of *Publishers Weekly* as saying about Cohn: "He made 'ghastly' look a little banal, but . . . he took care of his friends and he took care of his enemies. I grew to like him personally very much. He was a loyal guy." Rusher remembered Cohn in similar terms. He had, Rusher noted, "a gift for warm and loyal friendship, and he evoked it in others. His sheer audacity amused and captivated people. . . . There were 750 people at his memorial service. . . . There should have been an organ playing 'My Way.' " Auletta found Cohn to be "the toughest, meanest, loyalest, vilest, and one of the most brilliant lawyers in America."

BIOGRAPHICAL/CRITICAL SOURCES:

BOOKS

Cohn, Roy and Sidney Zion, *The Autobiography of Roy Cohn,* Lyle Stuart, 1988.
Morgan, Thomas B., *Self-Creations,* Holt, 1965.
Nizer, Louis, *The Implosion Conspiracy,* Doubleday, 1973.
Von Hoffman, Nicholas, *Citizen Cohn,* Doubleday, 1988.

PERIODICALS

American Spectator, February, 1982, July, 1988.
Columbia Journalism Review, May/June, 1980.
Detroit Free Press, June 24, 1986, April 17, 1988.
Esquire, December 5, 1978.
Life, March 22, 1954.
Nation, December 28, 1957, May 21, 1988.
National Review, June 24, 1988.
New Republic, February 28, 1949, June 14, 1954, April 20, 1963, July 6, 1968.
New York Times, November 17, 1985, October 23, 1986.
Publishers Weekly, April 1, 1988.
Spectator, September 17, 1988.
Time, March 22, 1954, September 13, 1963, April 4, 1988.
Times Literary Supplement, June 24, 1988.

OBITUARIES:

PERIODICALS

Chicago Tribune, August 4, 1986.
Los Angeles Times, August 3, 1986.
New York Times, August 3, 1986, August 4, 1986.
Time, August 11, 1986.
Times (London), August 4, 1986.
Washington Post, August 3, 1986.*

—Sketch by Thomas Wiloch

* * *

COLSON, Charles W(endell) 1931-

PERSONAL: Born October 16, 1931, in Boston, Mass.; son of Wendell Ball (a lawyer) and Inez (Ducrow) Colson; married Nancy Billings, June 3, 1953 (divorced); married Patricia Ann Hughes, April 4, 1964; children: (first marriage) Wendell Ball II, Christian Billings, Emily Ann. *Education:* Brown University, A.B. (with distinction), 1953; George Washington University, J.D., 1959. *Religion:* Baptist.

ADDRESSES: Office—Prison Fellowship, P.O. Box 17500, Washington, D.C., 20041.

CAREER: Admitted to the Bar of Virginia, 1959, the Bar of Washington, D.C., 1961, and the Bar of Massachusetts, 1964; assistant to assistant secretary of Navy, 1955-56; administrative assistant to Senator Leverett Saltonstall, 1956-61; Gadsby & Hannah, Boston, Mass., senior partner, 1961-69; special counsel to president of the United States, White House, Washington, D.C., 1969-73; Colson & Shapiro, Washington, D.C., partner, 1973-74; Fellowship House, Washington, D.C., associate, 1975-76; Prison Fellowship, Washington, D.C., president, 1976-84, chairman of the board, Prison Fellowship International, 1979—, Justice Fellowship, 1983-84, and Prison Fellowship Ministries, 1984—, vice chairman of the board, Justice Fellowship, 1984—. Associate member, Fellowship House, Washington, D.C., 1975; member of board of directors, Voice of Calvary and Ligonier Valley Study Center, both 1980—. Speaker on social issues, 1975—. *Military service:* U.S. Marine Corps, 1953-55; became captain; served during Korean conflict.

MEMBER: Christianity Today Institute fellow, 1985—, Beta Theta Pi.

AWARDS, HONORS: Order of Coif; Religious Heritage of America Award, 1977; *Born Again* was named outstanding evangelical book of 1976 by *Eternity* magazine; Layman of the Year award, 1983, from National Association of Evangelicals; Abe Lincoln Award, 1984, from Southern Baptist Radio and TV Commission; L.L.D., Wheaton College, 1982, Houghton College, 1983, Eastern College, 1983, Anderson College, 1984, and Taylor University, 1985.

WRITINGS:

Born Again (autobiography), Chosen Books, 1976.
Life Sentence (autobiography), Chosen Books, 1979.
(Contributor) John Stott and Nicholas Miller, editors, *Crime and the Responsible Community,* Hodder & Stoughton, 1980, Eerdmans, 1981.
Loving God, Zondervan, 1983.
Who Speaks for God?, Crossway, 1985.
Kingdoms in Conflict: An Insider's Challenging View of Politics, Power, and the Pulpit, Morrow, 1987.

Contributor of articles on prison reform to *Policy Review* and other periodicals. Contributing editor, *Christianity Today,* 1983—.

SIDELIGHTS: As a special counsel to President Nixon, Charles Colson earned a reputation as an "arrogant" and "ruthless" hatchet man. He has been described as one of the "original back room boys—the operators and brokers, the guys who fix things when they break down and do the dirty work when necessary." Devoted to Nixon, Colson willingly carried out these unpleasant duties. "I rarely questioned a Presidential order," he explained. Colson, who supposedly established Nixon's "enemies list," was also reported as saying, "I would walk over my grandmother if necessary to get Nixon re-elected." One of Colson's tasks was to discredit Daniel Ellsberg, the man who supplied the "Pentagon Papers" to the *New York Times* and the *Washington Post* during his trial in 1971. Colson's smear tactics indirectly led to the burglary of the office of Ellsberg's ex-psychiatrist in an effort to obtain damaging information.

When the Watergate scandal broke, which brought Nixon and his advisors under fire, Colson was charged with conspiracy for allegedly concealing evidence about the Watergate break-in. While awaiting trial, Colson met an old business associate who had been converted to Christ and also read C. S. Lewis's book, *Mere Christianity.* Under these influences, he soon became a born-again Christian. Bouyed by the support of members of his prayer group, Colson decided to enter a plea of guilty to the obstruction of justice in the trial of Daniel Ellsberg if all other charges against him were dropped. The bargain was accepted, and Colson was convicted and sentenced in 1974. "I have watched with a heavy heart the country I love being torn apart these past months," he said, explaining his actions. "The prompt and just resolution of other proceedings, far more important than my trial, is vital to our democratic process. I want to be free to contribute to that resolution no matter who it may help or hurt—me or others."

After spending seven months in prison, Colson began working with the Christian ministry organization known as Fellowship House. He also published his first book, *Born Again,* which details his spiritual conversion. Many people were skeptical about Colson's convenient change of heart in 1974. Molly Ivins of the *New York Times Book Review* conceded that when "his conversion was made public in mid-Watergate, it produced a spell of coast-to-coast sniggering." But Ivins judged that Colson in *Born Again* "is not only serious, but also . . . manages to make his conversion entirely credible." She added, "There is no doubting his sincerity."

Since 1974, Colson has become a leading spokesman for criminal justice reforms, encouraging Christians in particular to become actively involved with this and other social issues. Prison Fellowship Ministries, which he founded in 1976, "is today the largest evangelical outreach into prisons in America. It has spread to England, Australia, New Zealand, and Canada," Colson once told *CA.* The organization includes three subsidiaries: Prison Fellowship, U.S.A. (with a network of more than thirty-thousand volunteers and affiliated with Prison Fellowship International, a larger network connecting prison ministries in more than thirty countries); Justice Fellowship (formed in 1983, to assist government officials and private sector groups working for change in the nation's criminal justice system); and Fellowship Communications (developed in 1984 to produce publications to mobilize the Christian church for social action). To continue serving in these ministries at all levels, from subsidiary board chairman to speaker at inmate seminars, Colson has turned down offers to head other publishing companies and the PTL ministry (formerly featuring television evangelist Jim Bakker), reports Jon Anderson in the *Chicago Tribune.*

Colson's second book, *Life Sentence,* describes his experiences after he left prison and began to organize Prison Fellowship. Later books, such as *Kingdoms in Conflict: An Insider's Challenging View of Politics, Power, and the Pulpit,* warn American Christians to re-evaluate the proper relationship of faith and politics. A believer who has never identified "with any one camp," Colson, reports Kathleen Hendrix in the *Los Angeles Times,* is equally concerned about "those who see religion as a completely private affair that should have no influence in public life, and those who would use political power to play God, dominating society through legislation and court decisions, taking it upon themselves to fulfill Biblical prophecies." Reading current events as elements of Armageddon, for instance, could lead us prematurely into conflict with other nations, he argues in the book. Hendrix concurs with Colman McCarthy of the *Washington Post* that Colson's assertions qualify him to be placed with the "Christian right" since they present the state as "God's instrument" for restraining evil by force, when necessary. But the right may not welcome Colson, he told Anderson, since he has criticized televised ministries that broadcast "a false message, promising people 'two chickens in every pot.' I don't know why people want to save some of them. Perhaps God wants them destroyed." Hendrix cites Colson's statement in *Kingdoms in Conflict* that sums up the challenge: "The real issue for Christians is not whether they should be involved in politics or contend for laws that affect moral behavior. The question is how."

BIOGRAPHICAL/CRITICAL SOURCES:

BOOKS

Colson, Charles W., *Born Again* (autobiography), Chosen Books, 1976.

Colson, Charles W., *Life Sentence* (autobiography), Chosen Books, 1979.

Colson, Charles W., *Kingdoms in Conflict,* Morrow, 1987.

PERIODICALS

Chicago Tribune, November 3, 1987, January 26, 1988.

Commonweal, July 1, 1976.

Los Angeles Times, October 28, 1987.

National Review, August 6, 1976.

Newsweek, June 17, 1974, July 1, 1974, September 9, 1974, February 17, 1975, October 25, 1976, October 8, 1984.

New York Times, March 29, 1973, March 2, 1974, March 28, 1976.

New York Times Book Review, March 28, 1976.

Time, June 17, 1974, July 8, 1974, February 2, 1976.

USA Today, October 27, 1982.

Washington Post, July 24, 1983, December 25, 1987.

* * *

COMITO, Terry (Allen) 1935-

PERSONAL: Born December 17, 1935, in Santa Ana, Calif.; son of William (a bookkeeper) and Barbara (Allen) Comito. *Education:* Stanford University, A.B., 1957, A.M., 1958; Harvard University, Ph.D., 1968.

ADDRESSES: Home—1789 Lanier Pl. N.W., Apt. 4, Washington, D.C. 20009. *Office*—Department of English, George Mason University, Fairfax, Va. 22030.

CAREER: Rutgers University, New Brunswick, N.J., assistant professor of English, 1963-71; Hunter College of the City University of New York, New York City, assistant professor of English, 1971-76; Stanford University, Stanford, Calif., visiting assistant professor of English, 1977-80; George Mason University, Fairfax, Va., associate professor, 1980-86, professor of English, 1986—.

MEMBER: Modern Language Association of America, Renaissance Society of America, Society for Cinema Studies, Shakespeare Association of America, Phi Beta Kappa.

WRITINGS:

(Contributor) Richard Scowcroft and Wallace Stegner, editors, *Stanford Short Stories, 1957,* Stanford University Press, 1957.

(Author of introduction) Henry James, *The Princess Casamassima,* Crowell, 1976.

The Idea of the Garden in the Renaissance, Rutgers University Press, 1978.

(Contributor) Elisabeth MacDougall, editor, *Fons Sapientiae: Renaissance Garden Fountains,* Dumbarton Oaks, 1979.

(Contributor) Victor Carrabino, editor, *The Power of Myth in Literature and Film,* University Presses of Florida, 1980.

(Editor) *Touch of Evil: Orson Welles, Director,* Rutgers University Press, 1985.

In Defense of Winters: The Poetry and Prose of Yvor Winters, University of Wisconsin Press, 1986.

Contributor to *Dictionary of Literary Biography* and *Spenser Encyclopedia.* Contributor of articles and reviews to periodicals.

WORK IN PROGRESS: Space and Place in Renaissance Romance.

BIOGRAPHICAL/CRITICAL SOURCES:

PERIODICALS

Christian Science Monitor, May 28, 1986.

* * *

CONFORD, Ellen 1942-

PERSONAL: Born March 20, 1942, in New York, N.Y.; daughter of Harry and Lillian (Pfeffer) Schaffer; married David Conford (a professor of English), November 23, 1960; children: Michael. *Education:* Attended Hofstra College (now Hofstra University), 1959-62.

ADDRESSES: Home—26 Strathmore Rd., Great Neck, N.Y. 11023.

CAREER: Writer of books for children and young adults.

AWARDS, HONORS: The Alfred G. Graebner Memorial High School Handbook of Rules and Regulations was chosen Notable Young Adult Book of 1976 by the American Library Association; Pacific Northwest Young Reader's Choice Award, 1981, and California Young Reader's Medal, 1982, both for *Hail, Hail, Camp Timberwood; Lenny Kandell, Smart Aleck* was named one of *School Library Journal*'s Best Books of the Year, 1983.

WRITINGS:

Impossible, Possum (Junior Literary Guild selection), Little, Brown, 1971.
Why Can't I Be William?, Little, Brown, 1972.
Dreams of Victory (Junior Literary Guild selection), Little, Brown, 1973.
Felicia, the Critic (Junior Literary Guild selection), Little, Brown, 1973.
Just the Thing for Geraldine, Little, Brown, 1974.
Me and the Terrible Two, Little, Brown, 1974.
The Luck of Pokey Bloom, Little, Brown, 1975.
Dear Lovey Hart: I Am Desperate, Little, Brown, 1975.
The Alfred G. Graebner Memorial High School Handbook of Rules and Regulations, Little, Brown, 1976.
And This Is Laura, Little, Brown, 1977.
Eugene the Brave, Little, Brown, 1978.
Hail, Hail, Camp Timberwood (Junior Literary Guild selection), Little, Brown, 1978.
Anything for a Friend, Little, Brown, 1979.
We Interrupt This Semester for an Important Bulletin, Little, Brown, 1979.
The Revenge of the Incredible Dr. Rancid and His Youthful Assistant, Jeffrey, Little, Brown, 1980.
Seven Days to a Brand New Me, Little, Brown, 1982.
To All My Fans, with Love, from Sylvie, Little, Brown, 1982.
Lenny Kandell, Smart Aleck, Little, Brown, 1983.
If This Is Love, I'll Take Spaghetti (story collection), Scholastic Book Services, 1983.
You Never Can Tell (Junior Literary Guild selection), Little, Brown, 1984.
Why Me?, Little, Brown, 1985.
Strictly for Laughs, Putnam, 1985.
A Royal Pain, Scholastic Book Services, 1986.
The Things I Did for Love, Bantam, 1987.
A Job for Jenny Archer, Little, Brown, 1988.
A Case for Jenny Archer, Little, Brown, 1988.
Genie with the Light Blue Hair, Bantam, 1989.
Jenny Archer, Author, Little, Brown, 1989.
What's Cooking, Jenny Archer?, Little, Brown, 1989.

Contributor of stories and poems to *Teen, Reader's Digest, Modern Bride,* and other periodicals, and of reviews to *New York Times* and *American Record Guide.*

SIDELIGHTS: Ellen Conford is "a very clever, very intelligent young writer of children's books whose reputation as a writer children like to read and who teachers, librarians and parents like to have children like to read, is growing at a steady rate," states John G. Keller, her editor at Little, Brown, in *Elementary English.* Critics appreciate Conford's ability to understand young adults and the problems they face. Her books for children and young adults, which are hallmarked by a sprightly style and much witty dialogue, are characterized by Conford's "ability to make everyday events interesting and amusing," writes Harriet McClain in *School Library Journal.* Noting that Conford writes quickly once the idea for a story is formulated, Keller suggests that there is a thematic unity of optimism in her work: "Believe in yourself. You are worthwhile and have something to contribute. You may have a problem, but we all have problems and, basically, life is good and people care what happens to you."

Conford told *CA:* "The reason I write for children is probably because I was a kid who loved to read. I turned into an adult who loves to read. I am disturbed by the number of children *and* adults who have never experienced the joys of reading a book just for pleasure. Therefore, I write the kinds of books for children and teenagers that *I* liked to read at their age, books meant purely to entertain, to amuse, to divert. I feel that I am competing with the television set for a child's mind and attention, and if I receive a letter that says, 'I never used to like to read until I read one of your books, and now I really enjoy reading,' I feel I've won a great victory. A child who discovers that reading can be pleasurable may become an educated, literate, well-informed adult. I like to think I'm doing what I can to help the cause."

MEDIA ADAPTATIONS: Dear Lovey Hart, I Am Desperate, And This is Laura, and *The Alfred G. Graebner Memorial High School Handbook of Rules and Regulations* have been filmed for television.

BIOGRAPHICAL/CRITICAL SOURCES:

BOOKS

Children's Literature Review, Volume 10, Gale, 1986.

PERIODICALS

Elementary English, September, 1974.
New York Times Book Review, June 24, 1973, November 4, 1973, April 17, 1983.
School Library Journal, March, 1981.

* * *

CONIL, Jean 1917-

PERSONAL: Born August 28, 1917, in Fontenay-le-Comte, France; son of Octave (a restaurateur) and Marie-Josephine (Gorriez) Conil; married October 10, 1942; children: Patricia, Christopher. *Education:* Attended Stanislas College, Paris, France. *Politics:* Socialist-Liberal. *Religion:* Spiritualist.

ADDRESSES: Home—282 Dollis Hill Ln., London NW2 6HH, England. *Office*—Arts Club, 40 Dover St., London, England.

CAREER: Executive master chef and senior manager, Fortnum & Mason, 1950-55; Atheneum Court Hotel, London, England, catering director, 1955-58; Hurlingham Club, London, senior catering manager, 1962-64; food and cookery lecturer, Hendon College of Hotel Administration, 1965-70; Arts Club, London, currently executive chef; principal, Academy of Gastronomy. Lecturer. *Military service:* Served in British and French navies.

MEMBER: International Academy of Chefs (president), Society of Master Chefs (president, 1982—), Cercle Epicurien (president), Academie Culinaire de France (corresponding).

AWARDS, HONORS: Silver Medal, Berne Exhibition, 1950, and Gold Medal, London Exhibition, 1951, 1952, all for cookery.

WRITINGS:

For Epicures Only, Laurie, 1953.
Haute Cuisine, Faber, 1955.
The Home Cookery, Methuen, 1956.
The Jean Conil Cookery Classes, P. Owen, 1957.
The Gastronomic Tour de France, Allen & Unwin, 1959.
The Epicurean Book, Allen & Unwin, 1961.
Oriental Cookery, Croom Helm, 1978.
(With Daphne MacCarthy) *Vegetarian Dishes,* Thorsons, 1980.
(With Hugh Williams) *Variations on a Starter,* Piatkus Books, 1980.
(With Williams) *Variations on a Recipe: How to Create Your Own Original Dishes,* Piatkus Books, 1980.
(With Williams) *Variations on a Dessert,* Piatkus Books, 1981.
(With Williams) *Variations on a Main Course: How to Create Your Own Original Dishes,* Piatkus Books, 1981.
The French Vegetarian Cookery, Thorsons, 1985.
Cuisine Fraicheur, Aurum Press, 1987.
Fabulous Fruit Cuisine, Thorsons, 1988.
Dishes from the Great Chefs of the World, Epicurean Circle, 1989.

Also executive cookery editor, *Look 'n' Cook* (encyclopedia), sixty volumes, Bay Books. Also author of *French Home Cookery,* Methuen, *Magnum Cookery,* Methuen, *European Cookery,* and *Arab Cookery.* Author of column, *Sunday Times,* 1951-56, *Daily Sketch,* 1955-56, and *Modern Woman,* 1955-56. Contributor to magazines.

* * *

CONQUEST, Owen
See HAMILTON, Charles (Harold St. John)

* * *

CONWAY, Gordon
See HAMILTON, Charles (Harold St. John)

* * *

COOK, Lila
See AFRICANO, Lillian

* * *

COOPER, Sandi E. 1936-

PERSONAL: Born May 11, 1936, in New York, N.Y.; daughter of Irving (a decorator) and Claire (Ditzion) Cooper; married John M. Cammett (a professor), December 22, 1967; children: Melani Claire. *Education:* City College (now City College of the City University of New York), B.S. (summa cum laude), 1957; New York University, M.A., 1959, Ph.D. (with honors), 1967. *Politics:* Independent. *Religion:* None.

ADDRESSES: Home—905 West End Ave., New York, N.Y. 10025. *Office*—Department of History, College of Staten Island of the City University of New York, Staten Island, N.Y. 10301.

CAREER: Rutgers University, Douglass College, New Brunswick, N.J., instructor in history, 1961-65, lecturer, 1966-67, assistant professor, 1967-71, associate professor, 1971-79; College of Staten Island of the City University of New York, Staten Island, N.Y., professor of history, 1979—.

MEMBER: American Historical Association, Conference on Peace Research in History (council member, 1969-74; vice-president, 1974-76), Coordinating Committee on Women in the Historical Profession (president, 1971-73), Society for French Historical Studies, Institute for Research in History, Berkshire Conference of Women Historians (president, 1978-81).

WRITINGS:

(Editor, translator from the French, and author of foreword) *Peace and Civilization: Selections from the Writings of Jacques Novicow, 1849-1912,* Garland Publishing, 1976.
Internationalism in Nineteenth-Century Europe, Garland Publishing, 1976.
Patriotic Pacifism: The Political Vision of Italian Peace Movements, 1867-1915, California State University, 1985.
(Co-editor) *The Biographical Dictionary of Modern Peace Leaders,* Greenwood Press, 1986.

Co-editor, with Charles Chatfield and Blanche W. Cook, *Garland Library of War/Peace,* Garland Publishing, 1972-76. Contributor of numerous essays, articles, and reviews to journals and edited collections.

* * *

COPPA, Frank John 1937-

PERSONAL: Born July 18, 1937, in New York, N.Y.; son of Peter Paul and Fanny Coppa; married Rosina Genovese (an educator), August 7, 1965; children: Francesca, Melina. *Education:* Brooklyn College (now Brooklyn College of the City University of New York), B.A., 1960; Catholic University of America, M.A., 1962, Ph.D., 1966. *Religion:* Roman Catholic.

ADDRESSES: Office—Department of History, St. John's University, Jamaica, N.Y. 11432.

CAREER: St. John's University, Jamaica, N.Y., instructor, 1965-66, assistant professor, 1966-70, associate professor, 1970-79, professor of history, 1979—. Member of Columbia University's Seminar on Modern Italy.

MEMBER: American Historical Association, Catholic Historical Association, Society for Italian Historical Studies, Inter-university Center for European Studies, New York State Association of European Historians.

AWARDS, HONORS: Fulbright grant to Italy, 1964-65; U.S. Educational Foundation grant, 1965; received various university grants, 1967, 1969, 1974; National Endowment for the Humanities grant, summer, 1977.

WRITINGS:

(Contributor) Gaetano L. Vincitorio, editor, *Studies in Modern History,* St. John's University Press, 1968.
(Co-editor and contributor) *From Vienna to Vietnam: War and Peace in the Modern World,* W. C. Brown, 1969.

Planning, Protectionism, and Politics in Liberal Italy: Economics and Politics in Liberal Italy, Catholic University Press, 1971.
Camillo di Cavour, Twayne, 1973.
Cities in Transition: From the Ancient World to Urban America, Nelson-Hall, 1974.
Religion in the Making of Western Man, St. John's University Press, 1974.
The Immigrant Experience in America, [Boston], 1976.
(Contributor) Philip C. Dolce and George Skau, editors, *Power and the Presidency,* Scribner, 1976.
(Contributor) Dolce, editor, *Suburbia,* Doubleday, 1976.
Pope Pius IX: Crusader in a Secular Age, Twayne, 1979.
Screen and Society: The Image of Television upon Aspects of Contemporary Civilization, Nelson-Hall, 1979.
Technology in the Twentieth Century, Kendall/Hunt, 1983.
(Editor and contributor) *Studies in Modern Italian History: From the Risorgimento to the Republic,* Peter Lang, 1986.
(Contributor) Rocco Coporale, editor, *The Italian-Americans through the Generations,* American-Italian Historical Association, 1986.
(Contributor) R. Wolf and Hoensch, editors, *Catholics, the State, and the European Radical Right, 1919-1945,* Social Science Monographs, 1987.
(Contributor) Pastor, editor, *Revolutions and Interventions in Hungary and Its Neighbor States, 1918-1919,* Social Science Monographs, 1988.
Cardinal Giacomo Antonelli: Villain of the Counter-Risorgimento, State University of New York Press, 1989.

Contributor to *Catholic Historical Review, Journal of Modern History, Journal of Economic History, American Historical Review, Clio, La Popolo,* and other publications.

* * *

COREN, Alan 1938-

PERSONAL: Born June 27, 1938, in London, England; son of Samuel (a builder) and Martha (Phelps-Cholmondeley) Coren; married Anne Kasriel (a doctor), October 14, 1963; children: Giles, Victoria. *Education:* Wadham College, Oxford University, B.A., 1960, M.A., 1970; attended University of Minnesota, 1961, Yale University, 1962, and University of California, Berkeley, 1962-63.

ADDRESSES: Home—26 Ranulf Rd., London, England. *Agent*—A. D. Peters & Co., 10 Buckingham St., London WC2N 4DD, England.

CAREER: Punch magazine, London, England, assistant editor, 1963-67, literary editor, 1967-69, deputy editor, 1969-77, editor, 1977-87. Television critic for the *Times* (London), beginning 1971. Author of columns for *Daily Mail,* 1972-77, and *Evening Standard,* beginning 1977. Rector of St. Andrew's University, 1973-76.

WRITINGS:

FICTION FOR ADULTS

The Dog It Was That Died, Hutchinson, 1965.
All except the Bastard, Gollancz, 1969.
The Sanity Inspector, Robson, 1974, St. Martin's, 1975.
The Collected Bulletins of Idi Amin, Robson, 1974.
The Further Bulletins of Idi Amin, Robson, 1975.
Golfing for Cats, Robson, 1975, St. Martin's, 1976.
(Editor) *The Punch Book of Crime,* Robson, 1976.
The Lady from Stalingrad Mansions, St. Martin's, 1977.
The Peanut Papers: In Which Miz Lillian Writes, St. Martin's, 1977.
(Editor) *Pick of Punch,* Hutchinson, 1978, Beaufort Books, 1985.
A Rhinestone As Big As the Ritz, Robson, 1979.
Tissues for Men, Robson, 1980.
(Editor) *Punch Book of Short Stories,* Robson, 1980, St. Martin's, 1982.
(Editor) *Punch Book of Short Stories II,* St. Martin's, 1981, published as *The Second Punch Book of Short Stories,* Penguin, 1982.
The Best of Alan Coren, St. Martin's, 1981.
The Cricklewood Diet, Robson, 1982, Parkwest, 1984.
(Editor) *Present Laughter: A Personal Anthology of Modern Humour,* Robson, 1982.
(Editor) *Penguin Book of Modern Humour,* Penguin, 1984.
Bumf, Robson, 1984, Parkwest, 1985.
Something for the Weekend, Robson, 1986.

FICTION FOR CHILDREN

Buffalo Arthur, Robson, 1976, Little, Brown, 1978.
Arthur the Kid, Robson, 1976, Little, Brown, 1978.
The Lone Arthur, Robson, 1976, Little, Brown, 1978.
Railroad Arthur, Robson, 1977, Little, Brown, 1978.
Klondike Arthur, Robson, 1977, Little, Brown, 1978.
Arthur's Last Stand, Robson, 1977, Little, Brown, 1979.
Arthur and the Great Detective, Little, Brown, 1979.
Arthur and the Bellybutton Diamond, Robson, 1979.
Arthur and the Purple Panic, Robson, 1981, Parkwest, 1984.
Arthur Versus the Rest, Robson, 1981, Parkwest, 1985.

TELEVISION SCRIPTS

"That Was the Week That Was," BBC-TV, 1963-64.
"Not So Much a Programme," BBC-TV, 1965-66.
"At the Eleventh Hour," BBC-TV, 1967.
"The Punch Review," BBC-TV, 1976-77.
"Every Day in Every Way" (play), BBC-TV, 1977.
"Nuts" (situation comedy), Yorkshire TV, 1977.
"The Losers," 1978.

RADIO PLAYS

"The Shelter," BBC-Radio, 1965.
"End As a Man," BBC-Radio, 1965.
"Black and White and Red All Over," BBC-Radio, 1966.

SIDELIGHTS: The venerable English humor magazine *Punch* had seen but eleven editors in its 146 years. Alan Coren, who began his career at the weekly at the age of 24, became *Punch*'s twelfth editor in 1977, a post he inherited after serving as assistant, literary, and deputy editors. Despite his success at the helm of the magazine, however, Coren announced his retirement from full-time work at *Punch* in 1987. Libby Purves, a contributor to the periodical under Coren's leadership, recalls in a London *Times* article that the humorist's qualifications "lay not in management . . . , but strictly on the printed page. Here was a joker, a parodist, a savage but romantic clown, the sort of man who shut himself in his office, banging his typewriter, frowning and laughing maniacally to himself."

Coren stated that he was leaving *Punch* to pursue his writing career. In the same *Times* article, he added that his stint as editor contributed to the decision: "I came to *Punch* because I loved comedy. I wanted to be in a place surrounded by comic writers. Being an editor has changed me: it took a long while, but it has." Purves adds that Coren "can be crusty, short and woundingly decisive (he once rejected an idea of mine with the syllable

'Naah!'), but he is generous and perceptive, and worth rewriting anything to please. And in conversation, it is still blessedly easy to make him laugh immoderately. Not bad after 25 years laughing for a living."

MEDIA ADAPTATIONS: Some of Coren's *Arthur* books have been adapted into children's television features.

BIOGRAPHICAL/CRITICAL SOURCES:

BOOKS

James, Clive, *The Metropolitan Critic,* Faber, 1974.

PERIODICALS

New Yorker, December 19, 1977.
New York Times Book Review, March 21, 1976.
Times (London), June 10, 1987.*

* * *

COSLOW, Sam(son) 1905-1982

PERSONAL: Born December 12, 1905, in New York, N.Y.; died April 2, 1982, in Bronxville, N.Y.; son of Harry (a textile designer) and Rebecca (Novitch) Coslow; married Frances King (a singer), October 30, 1953; children: Laurence, Jacqueline Eliopoulis, Cara. *Education:* Educated in Brooklyn, N.Y.

CAREER: Composer and lyricist. Co-founder, Spier & Coslow, Inc., 1927, "Soundie" Industry, 1940, and, with James Roosevelt, RCM Productions, Inc. (now Famous Music Co.), 1941; producer, Paramount Pictures, 1944-45, Mary Pickford Productions, 1945-47; wrote for film and stage musicals in London, England, 1954-55. Stock market analyst, beginning 1961. Founder, *Indicator Digest* (investment-advisory newsletter).

MEMBER: American Society of Composers, Authors, and Publishers (ASCAP), American Guild of Authors and Composers.

AWARDS, HONORS: (With Jerry Bresler) Academy Award for producing best musical short, Academy of Motion Picture Arts and Sciences, 1943, for "Heavenly Music"; elected to Songwriters Hall of Fame, 1974.

WRITINGS:

Super Yields: How to Get the Highest Possible Returns on Your Savings and Investments, Hirsch Organization (Old Tappan, N.J.), 1975.
Cocktails for Two: The Many Lives of Giant Songwriter Sam Coslow (autobiography), Arlington House, 1977.
Make Money on the Interest Rate Roller Coaster: A Proven Method for Profitable Investment in a Rising or Falling Market, Coward, 1982.

COMPOSER AND LYRICIST OF SCREENPLAYS WITH OTHERS

"College Humor," Paramount, 1933.
"Murder at the Vanities," Paramount, 1934.
"Belle of the Nineties," Paramount, 1934.
"One Hundred Men and a Girl," Universal, 1936.
"Double or Nothing," Paramount, 1937.
"Thrill of a Lifetime," Paramount, 1937.
"True Confession," Paramount, 1937.
"Out of This World," Paramount, 1945.

Also composer and lyricist for numerous other screenplays.

OTHER

(Lyricist) "Artists and Models" (musical), produced on Broadway at the Winter Garden Theatre, October 15, 1924.
(Screenwriter and producer) "Copacabana," United Artists, 1947.

Composer and lyricist, with others, of songs, including "True Blue Lou," 1929, "Just One More Chance," 1931, "Sing You Sinners," 1931, "Moon Song," 1931, "Learn to Crow," 1932, "Down the Old Ox Road," 1933, "This Little Piggie," 1936, "Mister Paganini," 1936, "Blue Mirage," 1955, and numerous others; composer and lyricist with Arthur Johnston of "My Old Flame," 1934, and "Cocktails for Two," 1934.

WORK IN PROGRESS: An untitled musical comedy.

BIOGRAPHICAL/CRITICAL SOURCES:

BOOKS

Coslow, Sam, *Cocktails for Two: The Many Lives of Giant Songwriter Sam Coslow,* Arlington House, 1977.

OBITUARIES:

PERIODICALS

New York Times, April 6, 1982.*

* * *

COWAN, James C(ostello) 1927-

PERSONAL: Born September 16, 1927, in Albany, Ga.; son of James C. (a pecan farmer) and Elizabeth B. (Browne) Cowan; married Judith H. Ryder (a psychiatrist), January 29, 1960; children: Catherine Nancy, Cynthia Mary, Christina Judith, Michael James. *Education:* Mercer University, A.B., 1950; Oklahoma State University, M.A., 1956; University of Oklahoma, Ph.D., 1964. *Religion:* Episcopalian.

ADDRESSES: Office—Department of English, University of North Carolina, Chapel Hill, N.C. 27514.

CAREER: Tulane University, New Orleans, La., instructor, 1963-64, assistant professor of English, 1964-66; University of Arkansas, Fayetteville, assistant professor, 1966-67, associate professor, 1967-72, professor of English, 1972-83; University of North Carolina—Chapel Hill, department of social and administrative medicine, research professor, 1983-86, department of English, adjunct professor, 1983—. *Military service:* U.S. Army, 1952-54.

MEMBER: Modern Language Association of America, South Central Modern Language Association (vice-president, 1976-77, president, 1977-78).

WRITINGS:

D. H. Lawrence's American Journey: A Study in Literature and Myth, Press of Case Western Reserve University, 1970.
D. H. Lawrence: An Annotated Bibliography of Writings about Him, Northern Illinois University Press, Volume 1, 1982, Volume 2, 1985.
D. H. Lawrence and the Trembling Balance, Pensylvania State University Press, 1990.

Contributor of articles to literary journals. Founding editor, *D. H. Lawrence Review,* 1968-83.

WORK IN PROGRESS: Further considerations of D. H. Lawrence.

SIDELIGHTS: James C. Cowan told *CA:* "D. H. Lawrence wrote more honestly about human existence and human feelings, including his own being and feelings, than anyone else I know. Other modern writers have conveyed better than he the sense of deadness, futility, and ennui that pervades much of the modern world. No others have expressed so well as he a reverence for life and a sense of being alive. I write about literature, in general, because I care about human thought, art, and culture. I write about D. H. Lawrence, in particular, because I care about staying alive."

* * *

CRAIG, Brian
See STABLEFORD, Brian (Michael)

* * *

CRAIG, Jasmine
See CRESSWELL, Jasmine (Rosemary)

* * *

CRAIG, Lee
See SANDS, Leo G(eorge)

* * *

CRANE, Barbara (Joyce) 1934-
(Cathy O'Day)

PERSONAL: Born June 2, 1934, in Trenton, N.J.; daughter of Herman (a surgeon) and Elizabeth (a teacher; maiden name, Stein) Cohen; married Stuart G. Crane (in finance), August 27, 1956; children: Susan Jill, Patricia Lynne. *Education:* Vassar College, B.A., 1956.

ADDRESSES: Home—1909 Yardley Rd., Yardley, Pa. 19067. *Office*—Crane Publishing Co., 1301 Hamilton Ave., P.O. Box 3713, Trenton, N.J. 08629.

CAREER: Writer and publisher. Teacher in public schools, Trenton, N.J., 1956-58; Little People's Reading School, Yardley, Pa., principal, 1964-66; Newton Friends School, Newton, Pa., reading consultant, 1967-68; Crane Publishing Co., Trenton, president, 1968—. Trenton State College, lecturer in English, linguistics, Spanish, reading, and child psychology and reading consultant, 1968-69; director of Demonstration School for Center City Five Years Olds, 1969. Member of board of Institute of New World Archaelogy.

MEMBER: International Reading Association, National Association of Bilingual Education, Vassar Club.

WRITINGS:

"CRANE READING SYSTEM—ENGLISH" SERIES; ALL WITH PRACTICE AND SKILL BOOKLETS

Apple and the Ax, Crane Publishing, 1977.
The Baby Nay, Crane Publishing, 1977.
The Bee Book, Crane Publishing, 1977.
A Head Start through Reading, Crane Publishing, 1977.
I'm Late, Crane Publishing, 1977.
Me, Crane Publishing, 1977.
My New Friends, Crane Publishing, 1977.
Only for a Day, Crane Publishing, 1977.
Over the Top, Crane Publishing, 1977.
Playmates, Crane Publishing, 1977.
The Queen and I, Crane Publishing, 1977.

COMPREHENSIVE, BASIC READING PROGRAMS

"Categorical Sound System," Motivational Learning Program, 1964, revised edition, Crane Publishing, 1977.
"Trenton State Kindergarten Study of Categorical Sound System," Crane Publishing, 1969.
"Crane Oral Dominance Test," Crane Publishing, 1976.
"Crane Reading System: BASIC Program," Crane Publishing, 1977-82.
"Crane System in Spanish," Crane Publishing, 1978-87.
"Crane Reading System: PACER Program," Crane Publishing, 1981-87.

OTHER

Contributor to periodicals, including *Vassar Alumnae, Educational Leadership, Reading Instruction Journal, Perspectives,* and, under pseudonym Cathy O'Day, *Today's Catholic Teacher.*

WORK IN PROGRESS: A basic reading/literature program for kindergarten through sixth grade; support materials for basic reading and bilingual education programs.

SIDELIGHTS: Barbara Crane told *CA:* "I began my teaching career in 1956 in Trenton, N.J. The majority of my students were Hispanic and black with an age span of six to ten years. Although I tried to reach these students with traditional materials and teaching methods, I failed. By the end of my first year as a teacher, I was creating my own materials. The Crane philosophy took form: simplify the learning-to-read process by reducing the memory load, reducing the timeline to reach independent reading level, and therefore increasing success. These materials resulted in an outstanding performance record.

"In 1968 I received a grant from the state of New Jersey to field-test my materials. The Crane program was field-tested in a study involving 2,000 pupils from four segments of the population: center city, semi-rural, suburban, and private school. The experimental population (using Crane materials) of each segment significantly outperformed the control population. Young five-year-olds learned to read; ten-year-olds, with a past history of failure, learned to read. The program that was developed to teach the hard-to-reach proved to have merit with average and bright students who reached an independent reading level earlier than what was traditionally expected. When the field-testing grant expired there was a demand for the Crane materials, and I was instrumental in founding a publishing company to make these materials available.

"When bilingual education became a reality in the 1970s, I became a major influence in the avant-garde movement of bilingual education in the United States. I designed the first basic, bilingual materials to be published by an American publishing company. (Programs were being imported that were not meeting the needs of students in the United States.) I have continued to develop materials that represent the latest trends in education. The structure of the Crane materials also reflects child orientation, self-motivation, logical sequencing, and success orientation.

"I enjoy public speaking and take part in talk shows on national radio and television. Frequently, I am the luncheon speaker and/or keynote speaker at conferences. I also give mini-courses at the college level and teacher-training sessions at the elementary school level. Although much of my time is devoted to the running of Crane Publishing Co., public speaking and writing are very much a part of my life."

BIOGRAPHICAL/CRITICAL SOURCES:

PERIODICALS

Early Years, October, 1973.
Instructor, September, 1973, August, 1980, August, 1981, August, 1982.

Reading News Report, February, 1973.
Reading Teacher, November, 1973.

* * *

CRAWFORD, Robert
See RAE, Hugh C(rauford)

* * *

CREMIN, Lawrence A(rthur) 1925-

PERSONAL: Born October 31, 1925, in New York, N.Y.; son of Arthur T. and Theresa (Borowick) Cremin; married Charlotte Raup (a mathematics teacher), September 19, 1956; children: Joanne Laura, David Lawrence. *Education:* City College (now City College of the City University of New York), B.S.S., 1946; Columbia University, A.M., 1947, Ph.D., 1949.

ADDRESSES: Home—35 East 85th St., New York, N.Y. 10028. *Office*—Teachers College, Columbia University, New York, N.Y. 10027; Spencer Foundation, 875 North Michigan Ave., Chicago, Ill. 60611.

CAREER: Columbia University, Teachers College, New York, N.Y., instructor, 1949-51, assistant professor, 1951-54, associate professor, 1954-57, professor, 1957, Frederick A. P. Barnard Professor of Education, 1961—, director of Division of Philosophy, Social Sciences, and Education, 1958-74, director of Institute of Philosophy and Politics of Education, 1965-74, president of Teachers College, 1974-84. President, Spencer Foundation, Chicago, 1985—. Horace Mann Lecturer, University of Pittsburgh, 1965, Sir John Adams Memorial Lecturer, University of London, 1966, Cecil H. Green Visiting Professor, University of British Columbia, 1972, Merle Curti Lecturer, University of Wisconsin, 1976, Sir John Adams Memorial Lecturer, University of California at Los Angeles, 1976, Vera Brown Memorial Lecturer, National Institute of Education, 1978, Distinguished Visiting Lecturer, Simon Fraser University, 1982, and Irving R. Melbo Visiting Professor, University of Southern California, 1982. Visiting associate professor of education, University of California, Los Angeles, 1956, Harvard University, 1957. Visiting professor of education, Seminar in American Studies, Salzburg, 1956, Harvard University, 1961, Stanford University, 1973. Visiting instructor, University of Wisconsin, and Bank Street College of Education. Center for Advanced Study in the Behavioral Sciences, fellow, 1964-65, visiting scholar, 1971-72, 1984-85, trustee. U.S. Office of Education, chairman of Curriculum Improvement Panel, 1963-65, chairman of Regional Laboratories Panel, 1965-66; vice-chairman of White House Conference on Education, 1965; chairman, Carnegie Commission on the Education of Educators, 1966-70. Trustee, Spencer Foundation, Charles F. Kettering Foundation, and John and Mary Markle Foundation. *Military service:* U.S. Army Air Forces, 1944-45.

MEMBER: National Academy of Education (president, 1969-73), History of Education Society (president, 1959), National Society of College Teachers of Education (president, 1961), American Academy of Arts and Sciences, American Antiquarian Society, American Philosophical Society, Council on Foreign Relations, Society of American Historians, Phi Beta Kappa.

AWARDS, HONORS: Guggenheim fellowship, 1957-58; Bancroft Prize in American history, 1962, for *The Transformation of the School;* American Educational Research Association award for distinguished contributions to education research, 1969; Creative Educational Leadership award, New York University, 1971; Butler Medal, Columbia University, 1972; Townsend Harris Medal, College of the City of New York, 1974; Litt.D., Columbia University, 1975, Rider College, 1979; L.H.D. from various colleges and universities, including Ohio State University, 1975, Kalamazoo College, 1976, Widener University, 1983, and George Washington University, 1985; LL.D., University of Bridgeport, 1975, University of Rochester, 1980, Miami University, 1983; Pulitzer Prize in history, 1981, for *American Education: The National Experience, 1783-1876;* Medal for Distinguished Service to Public Education, New York Academy of Public Education, 1982; President's Medal, Hunter College, 1984; Carnegie Corporation of New York Medal, 1988.

WRITINGS:

The American Common School: An Historic Conception, Teachers College Press, 1951.

(With R Freeman Butts) *A History of Education in American Culture,* Holt, 1953.

(With D. A. Shannon and M. E. Townsend) *History of Teachers College, Columbia University,* Columbia University Press, 1954.

(Co-author) *Public Education and the Future of America,* National Education Association, 1955.

(With M. L. Borrowman) *Public Schools in Our Democracy,* Macmillan, 1956.

(Editor) *The Republic and the School: Horace Mann on the Education of Free Men,* Teachers College Press, 1957.

The Transformation of the School, Knopf, 1961.

The Genius of American Education, University of Pittsburgh Press, 1965.

The Wonderful World of Ellwood Patterson Cubberley, Teachers College Press, 1965.

(With Lee J. Cronbach, Patrick Suppes, and others) *Research for Tomorrow's Schools: Disciplined Inquiry for Education,* Macmillan, 1969.

American Education, Harper, Volume I: *The Colonial Experience, 1607-1783,* 1970, Volume II: *The National Experience, 1783-1876,* 1980, Volume III: *The Metropolitan Experience, 1876-1980,* 1988.

Public Education, Basic Books, 1976.

Traditions of American Education, Basic Books, 1977.

Editor, "Classics in Education" series, Teachers College Press. Associate editor, *Teachers College Record,* 1952-59; member of editorial board, *History of Education* (England), *Journal of Family History,* and *Education Research and Perspectives* (Australia).

SIDELIGHTS: Lawrence A. Cremin is "one of our foremost historians of American education, and certainly one of the most readable," writes Edward B. Fiske in the *New York Times.* The author of over a dozen educational studies, Cremin has been affiliated with Columbia University's Teachers College since 1949, and is currently Frederick A. P. Barnard Professor of Education at the college. He also serves as president of the Spencer Foundation, which gives grants in support of educational research to scholars throughout the world.

Cremin's best known work is a three-volume study entitled *American Education.* In all three of the volumes, subtitled *The Colonial Experience, 1607-1783, The National Experience, 1783-1876,* and *The Metropolitan Experience, 1876-1980,* Cremin proposes a broad view of education that includes not only the work of schools and colleges, but also the efforts of families, churches and synagogues, libraries and museums, and the media to convey knowledge and advance certain values. While reviewers in general admire the scope and scholarship of Cremin's study, some state that Cremin, in trying to reconcile such a large number of educative forces, sometimes loses his focus.

For example, in a review of *The National Experience, 1783-1876,* for which Cremin was awarded the Pulitzer Prize in history, *New York Times Book Review* contributor Kenneth S. Lynn writes: "Mr. Cremin discusses, among other things, religious revivals, the popular press, the slavery controversy, the Mormon hegira, the rise of industrialism and the spread of voluntary associations, all of which indubitably contributed to the education of the American people. One of the many unfortunate consequences of this quixotic effort at comprehensiveness is that neither the child nor the schoolhouse receives adequate attention." Reviewing *The Metropolitan Experience, 1876-1980* in the *Washington Post Book World,* Timothy Foote similary notes: "One sees how good the book might have been if Cremin had confined himself to education as it is generally understood, a process conducted at schools and colleges in fairly measurable terms following specific curricula that can be debated and modified."

America reviewer John F. Roche, on the other hand, maintains that "there is perhaps no historian of American culture who has done more than Lawrence Cremin . . . to demonstrate with convincing scholarship that education involves much more than schooling." In his *Washington Post Book World* review of *The National Experience, 1783-1876,* Chester E. Finn, Jr. concurs that "Cremin has wrestled his way clear from the straitjacket that confines most accounts of American education history, an obsession with the invention and institutionalization of the public school, and has reached out to embrace the full range of organization, ideas, events and individuals that constitute the American educational experience." In a review of *The Metropolitan Experience, 1876-1980, New York Times Book Review* contributor Amy Gutmann concludes: "Rather than fully articulating what an American educational ideal should be or what better circumstances would be, Mr. Cremin's history celebrates the continuing search. Within these limits, Mr. Cremin has written a liberating history. For its staggering scope, meticulous scholarship and subtle understanding, his account of American education should elicit admiration, even if it does not command agreement."

BIOGRAPHICAL/CRITICAL SOURCES:

PERIODICALS

America, November 1, 1980.
Atlantic, November, 1980.
Commentary, November, 1971, June, 1977.
Commonweal, April 16, 1971.
Los Angeles Times, December 15, 1980.
Nation, June 9, 1962.
New Republic, December 3, 1977.
New York Times, April 16, 1977.
New York Times Book Review, July 9, 1961, November 21, 1976, January 25, 1981, May 8, 1988.
Saturday Review, April 15, 1961, June 20, 1970, March 20, 1971, June 12, 1976.
Washington Post Book World, August 10, 1980, March 27, 1988.

* * *

CRESSWELL, Jasmine (Rosemary) 1941- (Jasmine Craig)

PERSONAL: Born January 14, 1941, in Dolgelly, Wales; came to United States in 1963, naturalized in 1983; daughter of John Frederick (a singer) and Glenys (Young) Steger; married Malcolm Candlish (a business executive), April 15, 1963; children: Fiona Jane, Vanessa Cresswell, Sarah Siobhan, John Malcolm. *Education:* University of Melbourne, B.A., 1972; Macquarie University, B.A. (with honors), 1973; Case Western Reserve University, M.A, 1975.

ADDRESSES: Home—5241 South Race St., Littleton, Colo. 80121. *Agent*—Maureen Walters, Curtis Brown Ltd., 575 Madison Ave., New York, N.Y. 10022.

CAREER: Foreign Office, London, England, trainee, 1961; British Embassy, Rio de Janeiro, Brazil, assistant to head of chancery, 1962-63; writer, 1976—.

MEMBER: Authors Guild, Authors League of America, Romance Writers of America, Romantic Novelists Association (England), Colorado Authors League (president, 1986-88).

AWARDS, HONORS: Rocky Mountain Romance Writer of the Year, 1986; Golden Rose Award, Romance Writers of America, 1988.

WRITINGS:

CONTEMPORARY ROMANCES

Forgotten Marriage, R. Hale, 1977.
The Substitute Bride, R. Hale, 1978.
The Rossiter Arrangement, R. Hale, 1979.
Mixed Doubles, Silhouette, 1984.
Hunter's Prey, Harlequin, 1986.

HISTORICAL ROMANCES

The Abducted Heiress, R. Hale, 1978, Harlequin, 1980.
Tarrisbroke Hall, R. Hale, 1979, Harlequin, 1981.
The Blackwood Bride, R. Hale, 1980, Harlequin, 1982.
Caroline, R. Hale, 1980, published as *Lord Carrisford's Mistress,* Fawcett, 1982.
The Danewood Legacy, R. Hale, 1981, Fawcett, 1982.
The Reluctant Viscountess, R. Hale, 1981, Fawcett, 1982.
The Princess, R. Hale, 1982.
Lord Rutherford's Affair, Mills & Boon, 1984.
Traitor's Heir, Mills & Boon, 1984.
The Moreton Scandal, Mills & Boon, 1986.

UNDER PSEUDONYM JASMINE CRAIG; CONTEMPORARY ROMANCES

Tender Triumph, Jove, 1982.
Runaway Love, Jove, 1982.
Stormy Reunion, Jove, 1982.
Imprisoned Heart, Jove, 1983.
Refuge in His Arms, Jove, 1984.
Surprised by Love, Jove, 1984.
Under Cover of Night, Jove, 1984.
Dear Adam, Jove, 1985.
Master Touch, Jove, 1985.
This Side of Paradise, Jove, 1986.
For Love of Christy, Jove, 1987.
Knave of Hearts, Jove, 1988.

OTHER

Undercover (romantic suspense), Harlequin, 1986.
Chase the Past (romantic suspense), Harlequin, 1987.
(Under pseudonym Jasmine Craig) *The Devil's Envoy* (mainstream historical), Berkley Jove, 1988.
(Under pseudonym Jasmine Craig) *Empire of the Heart* (mainstream historical), Berkley Jove, 1989.
Free Fall (romantic suspense), Harlequin, 1989.

Editor, *Romance Writers' Report,* 1986-88.

WORK IN PROGRESS: Co-authoring a suspense novel, the third in a trilogy, set in the Colorado mountains.

SIDELIGHTS: Jasmine Cresswell once told *CA:* "Romance novels are often condemned as escapist reading for the male-dominated, housebound female. I write romantic fiction, and yet I consider myself a feminist. (I define a feminist as somebody who thinks society functions better when all human beings are given the opportunity to develop their talents regardless of sex, race, or class).

"I see no contradiction in being a feminist and a romance writer. I enjoy creating heroines who in the course of the book learn to be strong, independent human beings. It is *because* my heroines are eventually sure of themselves and their place in the world that they are able to develop a deep, happy relationship with the hero."

* * *

CROWE, Frederick Ernest 1915-

PERSONAL: Born July 5, 1915, in Jeffries Corner, New Brunswick, Canada; son of Jeremiah Chesley (a merchant in a country store) and Margaret Lucinda (a teacher; maiden name, Mahoney) Crowe. *Education:* University of New Brunswick, B.Sc., 1934; Loyola College, Montreal, Quebec, B.A., 1943; Gregorian University of Rome, S.T.D., 1953; College de l'Immaculee-Conception, Lic.Phil., 1962.

ADDRESSES: Home—94 Isabella St., Toronto, Ontario, Canada M4Y 1N4. *Office*—Lonergan Research Institute, 10 St. Mary St., Toronto, Ontario, Canada M4Y 1P9.

CAREER: Entered Society of Jesus (Jesuits), 1936, ordained Roman Catholic priest, 1949; St. Mary's College (now University), Halifax, Nova Scotia, assistant professor of philosophy, 1943-44, language teacher at university high school, 1943-46; Regis College, University of Toronto, Toronto, Ontario, associate professor, 1953-58, professor of theology, 1958-75, research professor of theology, 1975-80, professor emeritus, 1980—, president of college, 1969-72, founder of Lonergan Research Center, 1972, director of Lonergan Research Institute, 1985—. Visiting professor, Gregorian University of Rome, 1953 and 1984.

MEMBER: Canadian Theological Society (president, 1974-75), Catholic Theological Society of America, Jesuit Philosophical Association, American Catholic Philosophical Association.

AWARDS, HONORS: D.Litt., St. Mary's University, 1971; John Courtney Murray Award, Catholic Theological Society of America, 1977; D.D., Trinity College, Toronto, Ontario, 1977; LL.D., Saint Thomas University, Fredericton, New Brunswick, 1982; D.D., University of St. Michael's College, Toronto, 1986.

WRITINGS:

(Editor) *Spirit as Inquiry: Studies in Honor of Bernard Lonergan,* St. Xavier College, 1964.

A Time of Change, Bruce, 1967.

(Editor) *Collection: Papers by Bernard Lonergan,* Herder & Herder, 1967.

Excatologia e missione terrena in Gesu di Nazareth (title means "Eschaton and Worldly Mission in the Mind and Heart of Jesus"), Paoline, 1976.

Theology of the Christian Word: A Study in History, Paulist/Newman, 1978.

Method in Theology: An Organon for Our Time, Marquette University Press, 1980.

The Lonergan Enterprise, Cowley, 1980.

Old Things and New: A Strategy for Education, Scholars Press, 1984.

(Editor) *A Third Collection: Papers by Bernard Lonergan,* Paulist, 1985.

Appropriating the Lonergan Idea (collection of articles and papers), edited by Michael Vertin, Catholic University of America Press, 1989.

Contributor to *New Catholic Encyclopedia;* contributor to theology journals and religious magazines, including *Science et Esprit, Theological Studies, Canadian Journal of Theology,* and *Ultimate Reality and Meaning.*

WORK IN PROGRESS: Editing, with Robert Doran, the *Collected Works of Bernard Lonergan,* 22 volumes, for University of Toronto Press; research on the thought of Bernard Lonergan.

SIDELIGHTS: Frederick Ernest Crowe once told *CA:* "In the Middle Ages, Bernard of Chartres said, 'We are dwarfs standing on the shoulders of giants.' The trick is to reach the level of the giants' shoulders, and then to add your own vision. It was my good fortune early in life, when I was a theology student at Regis College, to meet a modern giant in the person of Bernard Lonergan, at that time a professor there, but I am still trying to reach up to the level of his mind. This involves a great deal of research and interpretation of his writings—work which is now my main occupation. I try to add my own vision, which consists of a reconstruction of theology as implementation of his methods (mainly in the areas of the Trinity, Christology, and grace)."

BIOGRAPHICAL/CRITICAL SOURCES:

BOOKS

Dunne, Thomas A., and Jean-Marc Laporte, editors, *Trinification of the World: A Festschrift in Honour of Frederick E. Crowe in Celebration of His Sixtieth Birthday,* Regis College Press, 1978.

* * *

CURRAN, Charles A(rthur) 1913-1978

PERSONAL: Born October 9, 1913, in Philadelphia, Pa.; died July 25, 1978; son of Michael and Mary (Daugherty) Curran. *Education:* St. Charles College, Columbus, Ohio, B.A., 1935; Ohio State University, M.A., 1941, Ph.D., 1944; additional study at St. Mary's Seminary, Cincinnati.

ADDRESSES: Office—Department of Psychology, Loyola University, Lewis Towers, 820 North Michigan Ave., Chicago, Ill. 60611.

CAREER: Ordained Roman Catholic priest, 1939. St. Charles College, Columbus, Ohio, professor of psychology, 1944-53; Loyola University, Graduate School, Chicago, Ill., professor of psychology, 1955-78. Visiting professor at Catholic University of Louvain, 1953-54, and Menninger Foundation, Topeka, Kan., 1960-64. Served as *peritus* (expert) at Second Vatican Council, Rome. Consultant to Veterans' Administration Hospital and U.S. Army, 1960-65.

MEMBER: American Psychological Association, American Academy of Psychotherapy, American Personnel and Guidance Association, Academy of Religion and Health (member of advisory council).

AWARDS, HONORS: Society for Human Relations grant, 1955-64; Pope Paul VI Medal, 1968, for distinguished contribution to the Catholic priesthood; Pastoral Psychology Prize, 1969, for *Religious Values in Counseling and Psychotherapy.*

WRITINGS:

Personality Factors in Counseling, Grune, 1945.
Counseling in Catholic Life and Education, Macmillan, 1952.
Counseling and Psychotherapy: The Pursuit of Values, Sheed, 1968, 2nd edition, 1976.
Religious Values in Counseling and Psychotherapy, Sheed, 1969.
Psychological Dynamics in Religious Living, Herder & Herder, 1971.
Counseling-Learning: A Whole-Person Model for Education, Grune, 1972.
The Word Becomes Flesh: A Psychodynamic Approach to Homiletics and Catechetics and Meditation, Apple River Press, 1973.
Understanding: A Necessary Ingredient in Human Belonging, Apple River Press, 1978.
The Cognitive Client, Counseling-Learning Publications, 1982.

Also author of *Counseling-Learning in Second Languages,* 1976.

CONTRIBUTOR

R. J. Deferrari, editor, *Guidance in Catholic Colleges and Universities,* Catholic University of America Press, 1949.
A. H. Brayfield, editor, *Readings in Modern Methods of Counseling,* Appleton, 1950.
Magda Arnold and John Gasson, editors, *The Human Person,* Ronald, 1954.
W. C. Bier, editor, *Perception,* Fordham University Press, 1957.
J. E. Haley, editor, *Proceedings of the 1959 Sisters' Institute of Spirituality,* University of Notre Dame Press, 1960.
Haley, editor, *Proceedings of the 1960 Sisters' Institute of Spirituality,* University of Notre Dame Press, 1961.
Systems of Human Guidance: Religion and Psychotherapy, C. C Thomas, 1972.

OTHER

Contributor of numerous articles to religion and psychology journals. Member of editorial board of *Journal of Pastoral Counseling.*

WORK IN PROGRESS: Community Language Learning; Achieving Understanding.

OBITUARIES:

PERIODICALS

Language Learning, December, 1978.*

* * *

CURTIS, (Hubert) Arnold 1917-

PERSONAL: Born May 20, 1917, in London, England; son of Frank Hubert and Elizabeth Ethel (Ward) Curtis; married Almaria Daphne Wingfield Digby, March 9, 1948; children: Stephanie, Jill. *Education:* New College, Oxford, B.A., 1939, M.A., 1959.

ADDRESSES: Home—P.O. Box 10, Limuru, Kenya.

CAREER: Chief of East Africa Mission, International Refugee Organization, 1947-50; staff member, British Council for Aid to Refugees, 1951; Kenya Ministry of Education, Nairobi, 1952-73, secretary of Institute of Education, 1964-66, inspector of teacher education, 1966-73. *Wartime service:* Friends Ambulance Unit, 1940-44; United Nations Relief and Rehabilitation Administration, Middle East and Greece, 1944-47.

WRITINGS:

(Co-author) "New Peak" juvenile series, Oxford University Press, 1962-65.
(Co-author) "Pivot English Course" series, Longmans (Kenya), 1965-69.
Africa (youth book), Oxford University Press, 1969.
Conversation Practice, East Africa Publishing House, 1970.
Write Well (junior composition textbook), Oxford University Press, 1975.
(Editor) "Kenya Primary Geography" series, ten volumes, Evans Brothers (London), 1977-81.
(Co-editor) *Pioneers Scrapbook,* Evans Brothers, 1980.
"Know Your English" series, three volumes, East Africa Publishing House, 1983.
Kenya: A Visitor's Guide, Evans Brothers, 1985.
(Co-author) "Four Skills English" juvenile series, five volumes, Oxford University Press, 1985-88.
(Editor) *Memories of Kenya,* Evans Brothers, 1986.

D

DABNEY, Virginius 1901-

PERSONAL: Born February 8, 1901, in University (now Charlottesville), Va.; son of Richard Heath (a professor) and Lily Heth (Davis) Dabney; married Douglas Harrison Chelf, October 10, 1923; children: Douglas Gibson (Mrs. James S. Watkinson), Lucy Davis (Mrs. Alexander P. Leverty II), Richard Heath II. *Education:* University of Virginia, B.A., 1920, M.A., 1921. *Politics:* Independent. *Religion:* Episcopalian.

ADDRESSES: Home—5621 Cary Street Rd., No. 213, Richmond, Va. 23226.

CAREER: Episcopal High School, Alexandria, Va., teacher of French and algebra, 1921-22; *Richmond News Leader,* Richmond, Va., reporter, 1922-28; *Richmond Times-Dispatch,* Richmond, member of editorial staff, 1928-34, chief editorial writer, 1934-36, editor, 1936-69. Member of board of trustees, Episcopal High School, 1935-38, 1940-43, 1944-54, and Institute of Early American History and Culture, 1940s; member of board of directors, Richmond Public Library, 1943-61, and University Press of Virginia, 1966-70; chairman of board of directors, Southern Education Reporting Service, 1954-57. Chairman of Virginia Governor's Statewide Conference on Education, 1966; Virginia Commonwealth University, first rector, 1968-69, trustee, 1969-79. Visiting lecturer, Princeton University, 1939-40, and Cambridge University, 1954.

MEMBER: American Society of Newspaper Editors (member of board of directors, 1946-59; president, 1957-58), U.S. Historical Society (chairman of advisory board), Authors League, Southern Academy of Letters, Arts, and Sciences, Virginia Historical Society (president, 1969-72), Raven Society, Phi Beta Kappa, Omicron Delta Kappa, Delta Kappa Epsilon, Sigma Delta Chi (fellow), Society of the Cincinnati, Jamestowne Society, Country Club of Virginia (member of board of directors).

AWARDS, HONORS: Oberlaender Trust grant, 1934, for travel and study in Central Europe; Lee Award, Virginia Press Association and Washington and Lee School of Journalism, 1937, for distinguished editorial writing; D.Litt., University of Richmond, 1940; LL.D., Lynchburg College and College of William and Mary, both 1944; Pulitzer Prize, 1947, for editorial writing; National Editorial Award, Sigma Delta Chi, 1948, 1952; Medallion of Honor, Virginians of Maryland Society, 1961; B'nai B'rith (Richmond) Man of the Year Award, 1963; Guggenheim fellow, 1968; George Mason Award, Sigma Delta Chi, 1969, for outstanding contribution to journalism; National Endowment for the Humanities grant, 1970; Brotherhood Award, National Conference of Christians and Jews, 1971; Raven Society award, 1972, for service to the University of Virginia; Thomas Jefferson Award for public service, 1972; Distinguished Service Award, Virginia Social Science Association, 1975; Jackson Davis Medal, 1975, for service to higher education; Virginia State Chamber of Commerce special award, 1975; Liberty Bell Award, Richmond Bar Association, 1976; L.H.D., Virginia Commonwealth University, 1976; Douglas Southall Freeman Literary Award, 1985, for *The Last Review: The Confederate Reunion, Richmond 1932.*

WRITINGS:

Liberalism in the South, University of North Carolina Press, 1932, reprinted, AMS Press, 1970.

Below the Potomac: A Book about the New South, Appleton, 1942, reprinted, Kennikat, 1969.

Dry Messiah: The Life of Bishop Cannon, Knopf, 1949, reprinted, Greenwood Press, 1970.

Virginia: The New Dominion, a History from 1607 to the Present, Doubleday, 1971.

(Editor) *The Patriots: The American Revolution Generation of Genius,* Atheneum, 1975.

Richmond: The Story of a City, Doubleday, 1976.

Across the Years: Memories of a Virginian, Doubleday, 1978.

Mr. Jefferson's University: A History, University Press of Virginia, 1981.

The Jefferson Scandals: A Rebuttal, Dodd, 1981.

(Editor) Robert P. Winthrop, *Architecture in Downtown Richmond,* Junior Board of Historic Richmond Foundation, 1982.

Bicentennial History and Roster of the Society of Cincinnati in the State of Virginia, 1783-1983, The Society, 1983.

The Last Review: The Confederate Reunion, Richmond 1932, Algonquin Books, 1984.

(Editor with others) *New Virginia Review Anthology Three,* New Virginia Review, 1984.

Virginius Dabney's Virginia: Writings about the Old Dominion, Algonquin Books, 1986.

Virginia Commonwealth University: A Sesquicentennial History, University Press of Virginia, 1987.

Pistols and Pointed Pens: The Dueling Editors of Old Virginia, Algonquin Books, 1987.

Contributor to *Dictionary of American Biography* and *Encyclopaedia Britannica,* and to numerous periodicals, including *Atlantic, Economist, Foreign Affairs, Harper's, Life, Nation, New Republic, New York Times Magazine, Reader's Digest, Saturday Evening Post, Saturday Review,* and *Virginia Quarterly Review.*

SIDELIGHTS: "In the long, long catalogue of [Virginia state] histories," Virginius Dabney's *Virginia: The New Dominion, a History from 1607 to the Present* "must surely stand for many years to come as one of the most thorough and conscientious in modern times," claims Cabell Phillips in the *New York Times Book Review.* "In detail, it appears that the author . . . [has] missed nothing of importance that occurred between the 1607 landing" and the early 1970s when the book was published. The critic adds that Dabney's qualifications for the writing of this history are "excellent," for Dabney is a native Virginian, a Pulitzer Prize-winning journalist, and was editor of the state's "most influential" newspaper, the *Richmond Times-Dispatch,* for over thirty years. While histories of Virginia are numerous, Phillips notes that "the book retraces this well-worn literary trail with absorbing detail and insight." *Virginia Quarterly Review* contributor Allen W. Moger concurs, explaining that "the narrative is woven around men and events, ideas and accomplishments, and Virginia is made a vital part of the nation's history." Concludes the critic: "[Dabney] demonstrates that his personal skill and long experience as a journalist have made him the master of writing, and he has a distinctive appreciation for the facts and trends of history."

Dabney has also chronicled the history of Virginia through his own memoirs, *Across the Year: Memories of a Virginian,* and through the collection *Virginius Dabney's Virginia: Writings about the Old Dominion.* In *Across the Years,* which a *New Yorker* reviewer calls "one of the least self-centered autobiographies imaginable," Dabney recalls his attachment to his home state and his observations of the political and social changes that took place during his lifetime. *Virginius Dabney's Virginia* provides a different kind of retrospective, collecting journalistic pieces from over six decades which deal with subjects ranging from early state history to famous Virginians to current events. "All these pieces," notes *Washington Post* writer Edwin M. Yoder, Jr., "show Dabney to be an ingratiating and urbane writer with an eye for the telling detail." In addition, the critic remarks that "in the last analysis, the appeal of Virginius Dabney's graceful and good-humored writing is inseparable from qualities of character. . . . You will find it stamped on everything he writes and thinks. Read Dabney. You will learn a lot about Virginia and, in the process, a lot about the unusual man who was named for her."

In addition to his more personal surveys of Virginia, Dabney has authored several scholarly studies about his home state and her natives. His most noted, perhaps, is *The Jefferson Scandals: A Rebuttal.* Written in response to two popular and widely-publicized accounts of Thomas Jefferson's alleged affair with a family slave, one fiction and one nonfiction, *The Jefferson Scandals* "assembles the sources of the story, assesses the evidence and appraises the uses made of it pro and con," describes C. Vann Woodward in the *New York Times Book Review.* Tracing the accusations of Jefferson's indiscretions to a disgruntled political adversary, Dabney asserts that the rumors were blown out of proportion and that the woman's children were in all likelihood fathered by Jefferson's nephews, not the Virginian himself. While he finds the book "a valuable corrective to the uncritical acceptance of this irrepressible rumor," Charles W. Akers observes in the *Washington Post Book World* that "Dabney's polemical tone may lead some readers to think that he 'doth protest too much.' " Woodward similarly faults the author for drawing " 'quite definite conclusions' about matters that more cautious and informed scholars find inconclusive." Nevertheless, the critic admits that "responsible historians have found Mr. Dabney's rebuttal so forceful and persuasive as to say that it will dispose of the story for good and all." And a *New Yorker* reviewer concludes that while *The Jefferson Scandals* is primarily interested in exonerating Jefferson, this "brief, sensible, and readable work is really devoted to vindicating something like a rational historical method."

BIOGRAPHICAL/CRITICAL SOURCES:

BOOKS

Dabney, Virginius, *Across the Years: Memories of a Virginian,* Doubleday, 1978.

PERIODICALS

Atlantic, December, 1975.
Commentary, November, 1981.
New Yorker, September 4, 1978, August 17, 1981.
New York Times, August 11, 1981.
New York Times Book Review, February 27, 1972, July 5, 1981, September 9, 1984, December 14, 1986.
South Atlantic Quarterly, summer, 1979.
Virginia Quarterly Review, spring, 1972, spring, 1976, winter, 1979.
Washington Post, September 26, 1978, November 29, 1986, November 25, 1987.
Washington Post Book World, July 5, 1981, July 22, 1984.

* * *

DAICHES, David 1912-

PERSONAL: Born September 2, 1912, in Sunderland, England; son of Salis and Flora (Levin) Daiches; married Isobel Janet Mackay, July 28, 1937 (died, 1977); married Hazel Neville, 1978 (died, 1986); children: (first marriage) Alan H., Jennifer R. (Mrs. Angus Calder), Elizabeth M. *Education:* University of Edinburgh, M.A. (with first class honors), 1934; Balliol College, Oxford, M.A., 1937, D.Phil., 1939; Cambridge University, Ph.D., 1939.

ADDRESSES: Home—12 Rothesay Pl., Edinburgh EH3 7SQ, Scotland.

CAREER: Oxford University, Balliol College, Oxford, England, fellow, 1936-37; University of Chicago, Chicago, Ill., assistant professor of English, 1939-43; British Embassy, Washington, D.C., second secretary, 1944-46; Cornell University, Ithaca, N.Y., professor of English, 1946-51, chairman of Division of Literature, 1948-51; Cambridge University, Cambridge, England, university lecturer, 1951-61, fellow of Jesus College, 1957-62; University of Sussex, Brighton, England, professor of English, 1961-77, dean of School of English and American Studies, 1961-67. Visiting professor, University of Indiana, 1956-57; Hill Foundation visiting professor, University of Minnesota, spring, 1966. Fellow, Center for Humanities, Wesleyan University, 1970. Elliston Lecturer, University of Cincinnati, spring, 1960; Whidden Lecturer, McMaster University, 1964; Ewing Lecturer, University of California at Los Angeles, 1967; Carpenter Memorial Lecturer, Ohio Wesleyan University, 1970; Alexander Lecturer, University of Toronto, 1980; Gifford Lecturer, University of Edinburgh, 1983; lecturer at the Sorbonne. Lecturer on tours in America, Germany, India, Finland, Norway, Italy, Holland, and Denmark.

MEMBER: Royal Society of Literature (fellow), Royal Society of Edinburgh (fellow), Scottish Arts Club.

AWARDS, HONORS: Brotherhood Award, 1957, for *Two Worlds: An Edinburgh Jewish Childhood;* Litt.D., Brown University, 1964; Abe Prize, Tokyo, 1965, for best educational television programme; doctor honoris causa, Sorbonne, Paris, 1973; D.Litt., University of Edinburgh, 1976, University of Sussex, 1978, University of Stirling, 1980, University of Glasgow, 1987; teaching prize, University of Chicago.

WRITINGS:

CRITICISM

The Place of Meaning in Poetry, Oliver & Boyd, 1935.
New Literary Values: Studies in Modern Literature, Oliver & Boyd, 1936.
Literature and Society, Gollancz, 1938.
The Novel and the Modern World, University of Chicago Press, 1939, revised edition, 1960.
Poetry and the Modern World, University of Chicago Press, 1940, reprinted, Octagon Books, 1978.
Virginia Woolf, New Directions, 1942, revised edition, 1963, reprinted, Greenwood Press, 1979.
Robert Louis Stevenson, New Directions, 1947.
A Study of Literature for Readers and Critics, Cornell University Press, 1948, reprinted, Norton, 1964.
Robert Burns, Rinehart, 1950, revised edition, Macmillan, 1966, reprinted, Spurbooks (Edinburgh), 1981.
Willa Cather: A Critical Introduction, Cornell University Press, 1951, reprinted, Greenwood Press, 1971.
Stevenson and the Art of Fiction, privately printed, 1951, reprinted, Darby Books, 1980.
Walt Whitman: Man, Poet, Philosopher, Library of Congress, 1955.
Critical Approaches to Literature, Prentice-Hall, 1956.
Literary Essays, Oliver & Boyd, 1956, Philosophical Library, 1957.
Milton, Hutchinson, 1957, revised edition, Norton, 1966.
The Present Age in British Literature, Indiana University Press, 1958 (published in England as *The Present Age: After 1920,* Cresset Press, 1958).
A Critical History of English Literature, two volumes, Ronald Press, 1960, 2nd edition, 1970.
George Eliot: Middlemarch, Edward Arnold, 1962, Barron's, 1963.
Carlyle and the Victorian Dilemma, Carlyle Society, 1963.
English Literature, Prentice-Hall, 1964.
Time and the Poet, University of Swansea College, 1965.
More Literary Essays, Oliver & Boyd, 1967, University of Chicago Press, 1968.
The Teaching of Literature in American Universities, Leicester University Press, 1968.
Some Late Victorian Attitudes, Norton, 1969.
Shakespeare: Julius Caesar, Edward Arnold, 1976.

EDITOR

(With William Charvat) *Poems in English, 1530-1940,* Ronald Press, 1950.
A Century of the Essay, British and American, Harcourt, 1951.
(With others) *The Norton Anthology of English Literature,* two volumes, Norton, 1962, revised edition, 1974.
Joseph Conrad and Robert Louis Stevenson, *White Man in the Tropics: Two Moral Tales,* Harcourt, 1962.
The Idea of a New University: An Experiment in Sussex, Deutsch, 1964, 2nd edition, 1970, MIT Press, 1970.
Emily Bronte, *Wuthering Heights,* Penguin, 1965.
Sir Walter Scott, *Kenilworth,* Limited Editions Club, 1966.
The Penguin Companion to Literature, Volume 1: *Britain and the Commonwealth,* Allen Lane, 1971.
(With others) *Literature and Western Civilization,* six volumes, Aldus Books, 1972-75.
Andrew Fletcher of Saltoun: Selected Political Writings and Speeches, Scottish Academic Press, 1979.
(And author of introduction) *The Selected Poems of Robert Burns,* Deutsch, 1980.
A Companion to Scottish Culture, Edward Arnold, 1981.

OTHER

The King James Version of the English Bible: A Study of Its Sources and Development, University of Chicago Press, 1941, reprinted, Archon Books, 1968.
Two Worlds: An Edinburgh Jewish Childhood (autobiography), Harcourt, 1956, 2nd edition, Sussex University Press, 1971.
The Paradox of Scottish Culture: The Eighteenth Century Experience, Oxford University Press, 1964.
(Author of introduction) Robert Burns, *Commonplace Book, 1783-1785,* Centaur Press, 1965.
Scotch Whisky: Its Past and Present, Deutsch, 1969, 3rd edition, 1978.
A Third World (autobiography), Sussex University Press, 1971.
Robert Burns and His World, Thames & Hudson, 1971, Viking, 1972.
Sir Walter Scott and His World, Viking, 1971.
Robert Louis Stevenson and His World, Thames & Hudson, 1973.
The Last Stuart: The Life and Times of Bonnie Prince Charlie, Putnam, 1973 (published in England as *Charles Edward Stuart: The Life and Times of Bonnie Prince Charlie,* Thames & Hudson, 1973).
The Quest for the Historical Moses (booklet), The Council of Christians and Jews, c. 1975.
Was: A Pastime from Time Past, Thames & Hudson, 1975.
James Boswell and His World, Thames & Hudson, 1975, Braziller, 1976.
Moses: The Man and His Vision, Praeger, 1976 (published in England as *Moses: Man in the Wilderness,* Weidenfeld & Nicolson, 1976).
Scotland and the Union, J. Murray, 1977.
Glasgow, Deutsch, 1977.
Edinburgh, Hamish Hamilton, 1978.
(With John Flower) *Literary Landscapes of the British Isles: A Narrative Atlas,* Paddington Press, 1979.
Literature and Gentility in Scotland, Edinburgh University Press, 1982.
Robert Fergusson, Scottish Academic Press, 1982.
God and the Poets, Oxford University Press, 1984.
Edinburgh: A Traveller's Companion, Constable, 1986.

SIDELIGHTS: Published in 1942, David Daiches's *Virginia Woolf* has long been considered an excellent introduction to that author's work. Howard Doughty, writing in *Books,* calls it a "competent and intelligent guide" that is "informed with insight into the relation of technical problems to currents of thought and feeling in the writer's time." In a *Canadian Forum* article, Robert Finch commends Daiches for his "brilliance that illuminates more often than it dazzles."

Daiches's 1950 study of Robert Burns has been recognized as one of the best modern books on the subject. A critic for the *Economist* considers *Robert Burns* one of "the most perceptive books about Scottish literature." Writing in *Commonweal,* Virginia Mercier voices a similar opinion: "[Daiches] deserves a nobler title than scholar—that of humanist. . . . No critical study has done fuller justice to Burns' work as a song-writer or supplied more information about it." The *New York Herald Tribune Book Review*'s G. F. Whicher believes that the book "is notable for its vigorous grasp of crucial issues and for its success in clearing the air of misapprehensions that have often blurred the understanding of Robert Burns' position and achievement."

Robert Alter, a reviewer for *Commentary,* offers this summation of Daiches as a literary critic: "He commands a very impressive range of English and American literature, with a minutely-informed sense of its classical and Continental backgrounds, and he uses all this knowledge gracefully, relevantly, without a trace of pedantry. . . . Virtually everything he writes is sane, lucid, and tactful, and in an age when the language of most literary people is tainted with learned barbarism or stylistic exhibitionism, he writes an eminently civilized prose that seems effortless in its clarity and directness."

Book World writer Joel Sayre notes that while Daiches's "vocation is English . . . his avocation [is] Pot-Still Highland Malt Scotch Whisky." In *Scotch Whisky: Its Past and Present,* Daiches contends: "The proper drinking of Scotch whisky is more than an indulgence. It is a toast to civilization, a tribute to the continuity of culture, a manifesto of man's determination to use the resources of nature to refresh mind and body and enjoy to the full the senses with which he has been endowed."

Daiches points out that the United States leads the world in Scotch consumption and that approximately ninety-nine percent of all Scotch consumed there is a blended rather than a single malt whisky. He laments that too many Scotch drinkers are unaware that the single malts can be obtained. Sayre relates the following anecdote: "When he was a member of the Cornell faculty, Daiches once casually mentioned in a lecture . . . that Mortlach [a single malt] was to be had at Macy's in New York. On his next trip to Manhattan he dropped in at Macy's to stock up his Mortlach supply. 'Sorry, but some damn fool prof up at Ithaca recommended it to his students, and we're all out.' "

BIOGRAPHICAL/CRITICAL SOURCES:

BOOKS

Daiches, David, *Two Worlds: An Edinburgh Jewish Childhood,* Harcourt, 1956, 2nd edition, Sussex University Press, 1971.
Daiches, David, *A Third World,* Sussex University Press, 1971.

PERIODICALS

Books, September 27, 1942.
Book World, March 8, 1970.
Canadian Forum, November, 1942.
Commentary, May, 1969.
Commonweal, February 23, 1951.
Economist, May 28, 1977.
Newsweek, March 26, 1956.
New York Herald Tribune Book Review, August 26, 1951.
New York Times Book Review, April 12, 1970.
Washington Post, March 30, 1979.
Yale Review, winter, 1970.

* * *

D'ALLARD, Hunter
See BALLARD, (Willis) Todhunter

DANIELS, Jonathan (Worth) 1902-1981

PERSONAL: Born April 26, 1902, in Raleigh, N.C.; died November 6, 1981, in Hilton Head Island, S.C.; son of Josephus (an editor and statesman) and Addie Worth (Bagley) Daniels; married Elizabeth Bridgers, September 5, 1923 (died, 1929); married Lucy Billing Cathcart (an editorial researcher), April 30, 1932 (died, 1979); children: (first marriage) Elizabeth (Mrs. C. B. Squire); (second marriage) Lucy (Mrs. Thomas Inman), Adelaide (Mrs. B. J. Key), Mary Cleves (Mrs. Steven Weber). *Education:* University of North Carolina, A.B., 1921, M.A., 1922; graduate study at Columbia University Law School, 1923. *Politics:* Democrat. *Religion:* Episcopalian.

ADDRESSES: Home—Hilton Head Island, S.C. *Office—News and Observer,* Box 191, Raleigh, N.C. 27602. *Agent*—Brandt & Brandt, 101 Park Ave., New York, N.Y. 10017.

CAREER: Louisville Times, Louisville, Ky., reporter, 1922-23; *News and Observer,* Raleigh, N.C., reporter and sports editor, 1923-25, Washington correspondent, 1925-28; *Fortune,* New York, N.Y., staff writer, 1930-31; *News and Observer,* associate editor, 1932, editor, 1933-42; Office of Civilian Defense, Washington, D.C., associate director, 1942; administrative assistant and press secretary to President Franklin D. Roosevelt, 1943-45; *News and Observer,* executive editor, 1947-48, editor, 1948-69, editor emeritus, 1969-1981. U.S. representative to U.N. Subcommission on Prevention of Discrimination and Protection of Minorities, 1947-53; member of Federal Hospital Council of U.S. Public Health Service, 1950-53. Democratic National committeeman from North Carolina, 1949-52; active in presidential campaigns of Harry S Truman in 1948 and Adlai Stevenson in 1952.

MEMBER: Delta Kappa Epsilon, National Press Club (Washington, D.C.).

AWARDS, HONORS: Guggenheim fellowship for study in France, Italy, and Switzerland, 1930; American Association of University Women Juvenile Award, 1960, for *Stonewall Jackson.*

WRITINGS:

Clash of Angels (novel), Brewer & Warren, 1930.
A Southerner Discovers the South, Macmillan, 1938, reprinted, Da Capo Press, 1970.
A Southerner Discovers New England, Macmillan, 1940.
Tar Heels: A Portrait of North Carolina, Dodd, 1941.
Frontier on the Potomac, Macmillan, 1946, reprinted, Da Capo Press, 1972.
The Man of Independence, Lippincott, 1950, reprinted, 1971.
The End of Innocence, Lippincott, 1954.
The Forest Is the Future, International Paper Co., 1957.
Prince of the Carpetbaggers, Lippincott, 1959, reprinted, Greenwood Press, 1974.
Stonewall Jackson, Random House, 1959.
Mosby, Gray Ghost of the Confederacy, Lippincott, 1959.
Robert E. Lee, Houghton, 1960.
October Recollections, Bostick & Thornley, 1961.
The Devil's Backbone: The Story of the Natchez Trace, McGraw, 1962.
They Will Be Heard, McGraw, 1964.
The Time between the Wars: Armistice to Pearl Harbor, Doubleday, 1966.
Washington Quadrille: The Dance beside the Documents, Doubleday, 1967.
Ordeal of Ambition: Jefferson, Hamilton, Burr, Doubleday, 1970.
The Randolphs of Virginia, Doubleday, 1972.

The Gentlemanly Serpent and Other Columns from a Newspaperman in Paradise: From the Pages of the Hilton Head Island Packet, 1970-73, University of South Carolina Press, 1974.
White House Witness: 1942-1945, Doubleday, 1975.

Contributor of weekly page, "A Native at Large," to *Nation,* 1941-42; founding editor and contributor, *Island Packet,* Hilton Head Island, S.C., beginning 1970.

OBITUARIES:

PERIODICALS

Newsweek, November 16, 1981.
New York Times, November 7, 1981.
Time, November 16, 1981.*

* * *

DARY, David A. 1934-

PERSONAL: Born August 21, 1934, in Manhattan, Kan.; son of Milton Russell and Ruth (Long) Dary; married Carolyn Sue Russum, June 2, 1956; children: Cathy, Carol, Cindy, Cris. *Education:* Kansas State University, B.S., 1956; University of Kansas, M.S., 1970. *Religion:* Episcopalian.

ADDRESSES: Home—Norman, Okla. *Office*—H. H. Herbert School of Journalism and Mass Communication, University of Oklahoma, Norman, Okla. 73019. *Agent*—Lurton Blassingame, Blassingame, McCauley & Wood, 432 Park Ave. S., New York, N.Y. 10016.

CAREER: Columbia Broadcasting System, Inc., Washington, D.C., reporter and editor, 1960-63; National Broadcasting Company, Inc., Washington, D.C., manager of local news, 1963-67; free-lance writer, Topeka, Kan., 1967-69; University of Kansas, William Allen White School of Journalism, Lawrence, assistant professor, 1969-75, associate professor, beginning 1975, professor of journalism, 1981-89; University of Oklahoma, School of Journalism and Mass Communication, Norman, director and professor, 1989—. Newsman for KWFT-Radio in Wichita Falls, Tex., and KLIF in Dallas, Tex.

MEMBER: Westerners International (president, 1986-88), Radio and Television News Directors Association, Association for Education in Journalism, Western Writers of America (president, 1988-90), Western History Association, Kansas State Historical Society (member of board of directors, 1972—), Kansas Corral of the Westerners, Kaw Valley Corral of the Westerners, Sigma Delta Chi, Kappa Tau Alpha, Masons.

AWARDS, HONORS: Golden Spur Award from Western Writers of America, 1982, for *Cowboy Culture;* Wrangler Award from National Cowboy Hall of Fame, 1982.

WRITINGS:

Radio News Handbook, TAB Books, 1967, 2nd edition, 1970.
Television News Handbook, TAB Books, 1971.
The Buffalo Book, Swallow Press, 1971.
How to Write News for Print and Broadcast, TAB Books, 1973.
Comanche, Museum of Natural History, University of Kansas, 1976.
True Tales of the Old-Time Plains, Crown, 1979.
Cowboy Culture—A Saga of Five Centuries, Knopf, 1981.
Lawrence Douglas County, Kansas: An Informal History, Allen Books, 1982.
True Tales of Old-Time Kansas, University Press of Kansas, 1984.
Kanzana, 1854-1900, Allen Press, 1986.
Entrepreneurs of the Old-West: The Silent Army, Knopf, 1986.
More True Tales of Old-Time Kansas, University Press of Kansas, 1987.

Contributor of newspaper and magazine articles dealing with the Old West and articles and book reviews related to journalism.

SIDELIGHTS: Among David Dary's many books on the Old West, his *Cowboy Culture* and *Entrepreneurs of the Old West: The Silent Army* have attracted attention from critics for their combination of scholarly history and popular folklore. "*Cowboy Culture* takes us all the way," notes a *Detroit News* contributor, "from the early, stringy longhorn bulls right down to the Wild West shows, dime novels, rodeos, and movies. It untangles the myths. It exposes the Spanish and European roots of the cowboys, cattle, and horses. It connects the raw and reckless frontier to history." Dary asserts that the cowboy's secure place in the American consciousness is as much a product of legend as of historical fact. According to J. D. Reed's *Time* review, Dary "deflates the mythic machismo of the bunkhouse and the open range. His real cowpoke is hardly an existential drifter on the Plains. Rather, he is a common laborer beset by the pressures of a hard life and slim wages." Similarly, in *Entrepreneurs of the Old West: The Silent Army,* Dary unmasks the myth surrounding the early settlers of the West. Wray Herbert observes in the *Washington Post* that in the book Dary asserts that despite fanciful portrayals in popular films and novels "it was the search for personal wealth rather than any romantic urge or sense of adventure . . . that was the driving force behind the move west" by the early pioneers.

BIOGRAPHICAL/CRITICAL SOURCES:

PERIODICALS

Detroit News, September 13, 1981.
Time, September 7, 1981.
Washington Post, August 10, 1986.

* * *

d'AULAIRE, Edgar Parin 1898-1986

PERSONAL: Surname originally Parin, took mother's maiden name as professional name; born September 30, 1898, in Munich, Germany (now West Germany); came to the United States, 1929; naturalized, 1939; died May 1, 1986, in Georgetown, Conn.; son of Gino (an artist) and Ella (an artist; maiden name, d'Aulaire) Parin; married Ingri Mortenson (an artist and author of children's books), July 24, 1925 (died October 24, 1980); children: Per Ola, Nils Maarten. *Education:* Attended Technological Institute of Munich, 1917-1919, Schule Hans Hofman, Munich, Germany (now West Germany), 1922-24, and art schools in Paris, France.

ADDRESSES: Home—Lia Farm, 74 Mather Rd., Georgetown, Conn. 06829; and Upper Lea Farm, Royalton Hill, South Royalton, Vt. 05068 (summer).

CAREER: Artist, lecturer, author and illustrator of children's books in collaboration with wife, Ingri d'Aulaire, beginning 1930. Worked as book illustrator in Germany, 1922-26; exhibited artwork in Norway, France, Italy, Czechoslovakia, and the United States.

MEMBER: Authors Guild, Authors League of America.

AWARDS, HONORS: American Library Association's Caldecott Medal, with wife, Ingri d'Aulaire, 1940, for *Abraham Lincoln;* Catholic Library Association Regina Medal, 1970, for "continued distinguished contribution to children's literature";

D'Aulaires' Trolls was selected by the *New York Times Book Review* as one of the "outstanding books" of 1972, and was nominated for the National Book Award, 1973.

WRITINGS:

AUTHOR AND ILLUSTRATOR WITH WIFE, INGRI d'AULAIRE; JUVENILES

The Magic Rug, Doubleday, Doran, 1931.
Ola, Doubleday, Doran, 1932.
Ola and Blakken and Line, Sine, Trine, Doubleday, Doran, 1933, revised edition published as *The Terrible Troll-Bird,* Doubleday, 1976.
The Conquest of the Atlantic, Viking, 1933.
The Lord's Prayer, Doubleday, Doran, 1934.
Children of the Northlights, Viking, 1935, revised edition, 1963.
George Washington: A Biography for Children, Doubleday, Doran, 1936, reprinted, Doubleday, 1987.
Abraham Lincoln, Doubleday, Doran, 1939, revised edition, Doubleday, 1957, reprinted, 1987.
Animals Everywhere, Doubleday, Doran, 1940.
Leif the Lucky, Doubleday, Doran, 1941, revised edition, Doubleday, 1951.
The Star Spangled Banner, Doubleday, Doran, 1942.
Don't Count Your Chicks, Doubleday, Doran, 1943.
Wings for Per, Doubleday, Doran, 1944.
Too Big, Doubleday, Doran, 1945.
Pocahontas, Doubleday, 1946.
Nils, Doubleday, 1948.
Foxie, Doubleday, 1949, revised edition published as *Foxie the Singing Dog,* 1969.
Benjamin Franklin, Doubleday, 1950, reprinted, 1987.
Buffalo Bill, Doubleday, 1952.
The Two Cars, Doubleday, 1955.
Columbus, Doubleday, 1955, reprinted, 1986.
The Magic Meadow, Doubleday, 1958.
Ingri and Edgar Parin d'Aulaire's Book of Greek Myths, Doubleday, 1962.
Norse Gods and Giants, Doubleday, 1967, published as *D'Aulaires' Norse Gods and Giants,* 1986.
D'Aulaires' Trolls, Doubleday, 1972.

ILLUSTRATOR

John Matheson, *Needle in the Haystack,* Morrow, 1930.
Katie Seabrook, *Gao of the Ivory Coast,* Coward, 1930.
Dhan Gopal Mukerji, *Rama, the Hero of India,* Dutton, 1930.
Hanns H. Ewers, *Blood,* Heron Press, 1930.
Florence McClurg Everson and Howard Everson, *Coming of the Dragon Ships,* Dutton, 1931.
Nora Burglon, *Children of the Soil,* Doubleday, 1932.

Also illustrator of seventeen books in Germany, 1922-26, and of Dmitri Merejkowski's *Leonardo de Vinci,* 1931.

OTHER

(Translator and illustrator with I. d'Aulaire) Peter Christen Asbjoernsen and J. E. Moe, *East of the Sun and West of the Moon: Twenty-one Norwegian Folktales,* Viking, 1938, reprinted, 1969.
(Contributor with I. d'Aulaire) Bertha Mahony Miller and Elinor Whitney Field, editors, *Caldecott Medal Books: 1938-1957,* Horn Book, 1957.

SIDELIGHTS: Describing the beginnings of his career as a writer and illustrator of children's books, Edgar Parin d'Aulaire once told *CA:* "Both my parents were artists, it never occurred to me to be anything but an artist. I grew up in the art centres of Europe—Paris, Florence, Munich, mostly Munich. I made my first picture book when I was 12—it described the adventures of my grandmother as she drove in a buggy across the prairie, pursued by Indians. It was very favorably received—by my family. As a grown-up I never thought of doing children's books. I painted frescoes and did lithographs for sophisticated limited editions. I married an art student who was very fond of children and planned to specialize in children's portraits. When we came to the U.S. we met the most outstanding authorities in books for children. [They] persuaded us to do books for children."

In Hugh Crago's *Dictionary of Literary Biography* essay about d'Aulaire and his wife, Ingri, the critic commented: "The d'Aulaires' reputation today remains high: many of their books have been reprinted and appear again and again in listings of 'best books for children.' " Crago continued: "In America, uncritical superlatives marked most of their early reviews, with favorable comments focusing especially on the amount of work that had gone into researching and creating the books and on the childlike quality of the artwork. Few of their books have been published by British houses, and they appear to have little impact there, though several have been translated into seven languages for publication outside the English-speaking world."

AVOCATIONAL INTERESTS: Landscaping, forestry, and working a large farm in Vermont.

BIOGRAPHICAL/CRITICAL SOURCES:

BOOKS

Dictionary of Literary Biography, Volume 22: *American Writers for Children, 1900-1960,* Gale, 1983.

OBITUARIES:

PERIODICALS

Publishers Weekly, May 23, 1986.*

* * *

d'AULAIRE, Ingri (Mortenson Parin) 1904-1980

PERSONAL: Given name originally Ingrid; born December 27, 1904, in Kongsberg, Norway; came to United States, 1929; naturalized, 1939; died October 24, 1980, of cancer in Wilton, Conn.; daughter of Per (director of Royal Norwegian Silver Mines) and Oline (Sandsmark) Mortenson; married Edgar Parin d'Aulaire (an artist and author of children's books), July 24, 1925 (died May 1, 1986); children: Per Ola, Nils Maarten. *Education:* Attended Konsberg Junior College, and several art schools in Norway, Germany, and France.

ADDRESSES: Home—Lia Farm, 74 Mather Rd., Georgetown, Conn. 06829; and Upper Lea Farm, Royalton Hill, South Royalton, Vt. 05068 (summer).

CAREER: Artist, lecturer, author and illustrator of children's books in collaboration with husband, Edgar Parin d'Aulaire, beginning 1930.

MEMBER: Authors Guild, Authors League of America, Scandinavian-American Foundation.

AWARDS, HONORS: American Library Association's Caldecott Medal, with husband, Edgar Parin d'Aulaire, 1940, for *Abraham Lincoln;* Catholic Library Association Regina Medal, 1970, for "continued distinguished contribution to children's literature"; *D'Aulaires' Trolls* was selected by the *New York Times Book Review* as one of the "outstanding books" of 1972, and was nominated for the National Book Award, 1973.

WRITINGS:

AUTHOR AND ILLUSTRATOR WITH HUSBAND, EDGAR PARIN d'AULAIRE; JUVENILES

The Magic Rug, Doubleday, Doran, 1931.
Ola, Doubleday, Doran, 1932.
Ola and Blakken and Line, Sine, Trine, Doubleday, Doran, 1933, revised edition published as *The Terrible Troll-Bird,* Doubleday, 1976.
The Conquest of the Atlantic, Viking, 1933.
The Lord's Prayer, Doubleday, Doran, 1934.
Children of the Northlights, Viking, 1935, revised edition, 1963.
George Washington: A Biography for Children, Doubleday, Doran, 1936, reprinted, Doubleday, 1987.
Abraham Lincoln, Doubleday, Doran, 1939, revised edition, Doubleday, 1957, reprinted, 1987.
Animals Everywhere, Doubleday, Doran, 1940.
Leif the Lucky, Doubleday, Doran, 1941, revised edition, Doubleday, 1951.
The Star Spangled Banner, Doubleday, Doran, 1942.
Don't Count Your Chicks, Doubleday, Doran, 1943.
Wings for Per, Doubleday, Doran, 1944.
Too Big, Doubleday, Doran, 1945.
Pocahontas, Doubleday, 1946.
Nils, Doubleday, 1948.
Foxie, Doubleday, 1949, revised edition published as *Foxie the Singing Dog,* 1969.
Benjamin Franklin, Doubleday, 1950, reprinted, 1987.
Buffalo Bill, Doubleday, 1952.
The Two Cars, Doubleday, 1955.
Columbus, Doubleday, 1955, reprinted, 1986.
The Magic Meadow, Doubleday, 1958.
Ingri and Edgar Parin d'Aulaire's Book of Greek Myths, Doubleday, 1962.
Norse Gods and Giants, Doubleday, 1967, published as *D'Aulaires' Norse Gods and Giants,* 1986.
D'Aulaires' Trolls, Doubleday, 1972.

OTHER

(Illustrator) Hans Aanrud, *Sidsel Longskirt: A Girl of Norway,* Winston, 1935.
(Illustrator) Aanrud, *Solve Suntrap,* Winston, 1936.
(Translator and illustrator with E. P. d'Aulaire) Peter Christen Asbjoernsen and J. E. Moe, *East of the Sun and West of the Moon: Twenty-One Norwegian Folktales,* Viking, 1938, reprinted, 1969.
(Illustrator) Dikken Zwilgmeyer, *Johnny Blossom,* Pilgrim Press, 1948.
(Contributor with E. P. d'Aulaire) Bertha Mahony Miller and Elinor Whitney Field, editors, *Caldecott Medal Books: 1938-1957,* Horn Book, 1957.

SIDELIGHTS: Ingri d'Aulaire once told *CA:* "In 1930 my husband, Edgar Parin d'Aulaire, and I decided to go into partnership and write and draw childrens' books. He was a fine illustrator of sophisticated limited editions, I loved children, loved to paint them, and tell them stories. The combination has worked out very well, for fifty years now. And we both think that the very best we can do as artists is to give our very best to children."

Dartmouth College, University of Oregon, University of Minnesota, and University of Southern Mississippi hold collections of the d'Aulaires' papers.

AVOCATIONAL INTERESTS: Traveling, walking, gardening, cooking, playing with children, family.

BIOGRAPHICAL/CRITICAL SOURCES:

BOOKS

Dictionary of Literary Biography, Volume 22: *American Writers for Children, 1900-1960,* Gale, 1983.

OBITUARIES:

PERIODICALS

New York Times, October 28, 1980.
Publishers Weekly, November 14, 1980.*

* * *

DAVIES, R(obert) W(illiam) 1925-

PERSONAL: Born April 23, 1925, in London, England; son of William and Gladys Hilda (Hall) Davies; married Frances Rebecca Moscow (a researcher and teacher), December 29, 1953; children: Maurice William, Catherine Gladys Anne. *Education:* University of London, B.A., 1950; University of Birmingham, Ph.D., 1954.

ADDRESSES: *Office*—Center for Russian and East European Studies, University of Birmingham, Birmingham B15 2TT, England.

CAREER: University of Glasgow, Glasgow, Scotland, senior research scholar and assistant in department of Soviet institutions, 1954-56; University of Birmingham, Birmingham, England, research fellow, 1956-59, lecturer, 1959-62, senior lecturer in department of economics and institutions of the U.S.S.R., 1962-63, director of Center for Russian and East European Studies, 1963-79, professor of Soviet economic studies, 1965—. Member of British academic committee for liaison with Soviet archives. *Military service:* Royal Air Force, 1943-46; served as aircraftsman.

MEMBER: National Association of Soviet and East European Studies (member of National Committee, 1965-76).

WRITINGS:

The Development of the Soviet Budgetary System, Cambridge University Press, 1958.
(With E. Zaleski and others) *Science Policy in the U.S.S.R.,* Organisation for Economic Cooperation and Development, 1969.
(With E. H. Carr) *Foundations of a Planned Economy, 1926-1929,* Volume I, two parts, Macmillan, 1969.
(Editor with R. Amann and J. Cooper) *The Technological Level of Soviet Industry,* Yale University Press, 1977.
(Editor) *The Soviet Union,* Allen & Unwin, 1977, 2nd edition, 1989.
The Socialist Offensive: The Collectivization of Soviet Agriculture, 1929-1930, Harvard University Press, 1980.
(Editor) *Soviet Investment for Planned Industrialization, 1929-1937: Policy and Practice,* Berkeley Slavic, 1983.
(Co-editor) *Materials for a Balance of the Soviet National Economy, 1928-1930,* Cambridge University Press, 1985.
(Editor) E. H. Carr, *What is History?,* 2nd edition, Macmillan, 1986.
The Soviet Economy in Turmoil, 1929-1930, Harvard University Press, 1989.
Soviet History in the Gorbachev Revolution, Macmillan, 1989.

Contributor of articles on Soviet science and technology, and history of Soviet economic institutions, to periodicals. Member of editorial board, *Economics of Planning.*

WORK IN PROGRESS: A multivolume history of Soviet industrialization, 1929-1937; research on Soviet economic officials.

* * *

DAVIS, Peter (Frank) 1937-

PERSONAL: Born January 2, 1937, in Santa Monica, Calif.; son of Frank (a screenwriter) and Tess (a writer; maiden name, Slesinger) Davis; married Johanna Mankiewicz, September 13, 1959 (died, 1974); married Karen Zehring (in publishing), June 10, 1979; children: Timothy, Nicholas, Jesse, Antonia. *Education:* Harvard University, A.B. (magna cum laude), 1957. *Politics:* Independent Democrat.

ADDRESSES: Home and office—320 Central Park W., New York, N.Y. 10025. *Agent*—Lynn Nesbit, International Creative Management, 40 West 57th St., New York, N.Y. 10019.

CAREER: New York Times, New York City, copyboy, 1958-59; Columbia Broadcasting System, Inc. (CBS-TV), New York City, producer and writer of documentary films, 1968-72; screenwriter and director of documentary films, 1972—. Associated with Yale University, 1972. *Military service:* U.S. Army, 1959-60.

MEMBER: Writers Guild of America.

AWARDS, HONORS: Award from Writers Guild of America, 1968, for "Hunger in America"; award from *Saturday Review,* 1970, for "The Battle of East St. Louis"; Emmy Award, National Academy of Television Arts and Sciences, Peabody Award, George Polk Award, and awards from Writers Guild of America and *Saturday Review,* all 1971, all for "The Selling of the Pentagon"; Academy Award for best documentary film, Academy of Motion Picture Arts and Sciences, 1975, for "Hearts and Minds."

WRITINGS:

Hometown (nonfiction), Simon & Schuster, 1982.
Where Is Nicaragua? (nonfiction), Simon & Schuster, 1987.

DOCUMENTARIES; WRITER AND DIRECTOR

"The Heritage of Slavery," Columbia Broadcasting System (CBS-TV), 1968.
(With Martin Carr) "Hunger in America," CBS-TV, 1968.
"Once upon a Wall," CBS-TV, 1969.
"The Battle of East St. Louis," CBS-TV, 1969.
"The Selling of the Pentagon," CBS-TV, 1971.
"Hearts and Minds," Warner Brothers, 1975.
"Middletown," Public Broadcasting Service (PBS-TV), 1982.

OTHER

Also co-author of screenplay for made-for-television film "Haywire," adapted from the book by Brooke Hayward. Contributor to periodicals, including *Esquire, Nation, New York Times,* and *New York Woman.*

SIDELIGHTS: Peter Davis received a great deal of attention in the mid-1970s as the director of the controversial documentary "Hearts and Minds." The film is an examination, according to Paul D. Zimmerman for *Newsweek,* of "loss, both personal and national, of ideals and illusion, sons and brothers, lives, limbs, liberties, and, finally, of a collective ability to connect with human suffering" during the Vietnam War. Davis created "Hearts and Minds" using film footage featuring President Johnson and General Westmoreland making, respectively, pro-war and racist statements; the documentary also uses interviews and sequences of actual encounters between American troops and the Viet Cong and North Vietnamese Army.

Supporters of "Hearts and Minds" praise its impassioned plea for peace and its expose of war as folly. Zimmerman calls it a "thoroughly committed, brilliantly executed and profoundly moving document," and further observes: "Unlike our leaders who encourage us to put Vietnam behind us, Davis wants us to confront our feelings about it first and to understand the experience before we bury it. We turn away from this portrait of ourselves at our peril."

The film's detractors, however, contend that it is too disorganized and too eager to elicit an emotional response. *Time*'s Stefan Kanfer writes: "Throughout, *Hearts and Minds* displays more than enough heart. It is mind that is missing. Perhaps the deepest flaw lies in the method: the Viet Nam War is too convoluted, too devious to be examined in a style of compilation without comment. And righteous indignation may tend to blind the documentary film maker to his prime task: the representation of life in all its fullness, not only those incidents that conform to the thesis." But Kanfer quotes Davis's conviction that the film "is not a chronology of war so much as a study of people's feelings." Davis further responded to charges that the film slighted the anti-war movement by declaring: "I wasn't puzzled as to why 3 million Americans turned against the war. . . . I was *very* puzzled why 197 million American didn't turn against the war," quotes Zimmerman.

Davis's book *Hometown* is an account of his six years of observations and experiences in Hamilton, Ohio. He was led to the town by the Census Bureau after asking for a location where he could "understand America by going into one community and penetrating its society as deeply and widely as possible," records Susan Allen Toth in the *New York Times Book Review.* The book is full of lively characters, including a Mayor Witt and a Congressman Kindness, and exciting events, such as a basketball game between rival high schools, a murder between brothers-in-law, and a sex scandal that causes the entire town to reexamine its morals.

Hometown has received enthusiastic praise from several critics. The *Los Angeles Times*'s Elaine Kendall calls it "social science with heart and soul," and adds that "such attempts to straddle fact and fiction can easily fall between them in a no-man's land: 'Hometown' strikes a precarious balance." While Toth concedes that "no single 'hometown' could reveal it all," she feels that "Davis has made an honorable effort, and the stories he tells so effectively in 'Hometown' will doubtless resonate in other American hometowns as well." Christopher Lehmann-Haupt similarly remarks in the *New York Times* that "one doesn't absolutely have to make anything symbolic" of the characters in *Hometown.* "That they stand intensely and dramatically for themselves," Lehmann-Haupt concludes, "is really satisfying enough."

Davis wrote *Where Is Nicaragua?* after visiting that nation in 1983 and then again in 1986, during which time he spoke with individuals from all classes, religions, and political affiliations, including Americans in the country. In a *New York Times* assessment, Lehmann-Haupt explains that "the question in [Davis's] title is not intended to insult our geographical intelligence, but rather to ask, 'Where is Nicaragua in relation to our fantasies of it?' " According to Lehmann-Haupt, Davis is particularly interested in presenting the context of Nicaragua and does so by relating many of its contradictions and by not taking sides: "almost to a fault he keeps his feelings and opinions to himself, trying instead to give us a camera's-eye view of Nicaragua." The critic also points out Davis's success at bringing understanding to American-Nicaraguan relations. In a somewhat lengthier *New*

York Times Book Review commentary on *Where Is Nicaragua?*, Jefferson Morely explains that "amateurs like Mr. Davis seem to be able to capture Central America in a way that Central American professionals rarely do. . . . 'Where Is Nicaragua?' is part of this modest tradition, the log of a curious gringo." Like Lehmann-Haupt, Morely feels Davis's analysis gives insight into the United States's role in Nicaragua. Writes Morley: "Where is . . . Nicaragua in the plans and policies of the United States? Mr. Davis implies that it isn't in our plans yet because we refuse to see [Nicaragua as it really is]. We are still fixed on . . . the particular Nicaragua that we want to believe in." Concludes the critic: "Davis suggests instead that we take Nicaragua seriously and at face value." Although *Washington Post Book World* critic Lloyd Grove wishes Davis had spent more time interviewing, he finds Davis's work "seldom tendentious, and often refreshingly clear-headed. . . . He has the sharp eye of a film maker, and a sharp pen as well."

BIOGRAPHICAL/CRITICAL SOURCES:

PERIODICALS

Boston Globe, May 2, 1982.
Los Angeles Times, March 8, 1982, March 20, 1982.
Newsweek, March 3, 1975, March 29, 1982.
New York Times, March 14, 1982, March 18, 1982, April 6, 1987.
New York Times Book Review, April 4, 1982, April 12, 1987.
People, March 29, 1982.
Time, March 17, 1975.
USA Today, March 27, 1987.
Washington Post Book World, April 4, 1982, April 19, 1987.

* * *

DAY, Stacey B(iswas) 1927-

PERSONAL: Born December 31, 1927, in London, England; became naturalized U.S. citizen; son of Satis Biswas (a barrister) and Emma Lenora (Camp) Day; married Noor Kassim Kanji (a microbiologist), May 6, 1952 (divorced, 1969); married Nasreen Y. Fazalbhoy (a psychologist), June 7, 1970 (divorced, 1973); married Ivana Podvalova (a research neuropharmacologist), October 20, 1973; children: (first marriage) Kahlil Amyn, Selim. *Education:* Attended University of Birmingham; Royal College of Surgeons, Dublin, Ireland, M.D., 1955; McGill University, Ph.D., 1964; University of Cincinnati, D.Sc., 1971. *Politics:* "Stevensonian Democrat."

ADDRESSES: Home—6 Lomond Ave., South Spring Valley, N.Y. 10977. *Office*—World Health Organization Collaborating Center, Nashville, Tenn. *Agent*—Robert Faher, c/o Cultural and Educational Productions, 310 Craig St. E., Montreal, Quebec, Canada.

CAREER: University of Minnesota Hospitals, Minneapolis, surgeon, 1956-60; St. George's Hospital, London, England, honorary clinical assistant in surgery, 1960-61; McGill University, Montreal, Quebec, surgeon in Experimental Division, 1961-65; Hoffman La Roche (pharmaceutical manufacturer), Nutley, N.J., medical director for New England, 1966-68; Shriners Hospital Burns Institute, University of Cincinnati, Cincinnati, Ohio, associate director of basic medical research, 1969-70; University of Minnesota, Minneapolis, associate professor in pathology department, assistant professor of research surgery in the medical school, and conservator at the Bell Museum of Pathobiology, 1971-73; Cornell University, School of Medical Sciences, New York City, professor of biology in Sloan-Kettering Division and member and director of biomedical communication and medical education at Sloan-Kettering Institute for Cancer Research, 1974-80; New York Medical College, Valhalla, N.Y., clinical professor of medicine in division of behavioral medicine, 1980—; University of Arizona, Tucson, adjunct professor of family and community medicine, 1985-89.

Canadian Heart Association, research associate, 1964-66, senior research associate, 1966-67; research director for Phase I and Phase II, Federal Drug Administration, 1966-68; clinical investigator, Department of Medical Research, Hoechst Pharmaceutical Co., Cincinnati, Ohio, 1966-67; professor of biopsychosocial medicine, and professor and chairman of department of community health, College of Medical Sciences, University of Calabar, Nigeria, 1982-84, and at University of Maiduguri, Borno State, Nigeria, 1984; international health director and visiting professor, International Center for Health Sciences, Meharry Medical College, Nashville, Tenn., 1985; distinguished visiting professor of international health, University of Calabar, Nigeria, 1989—. Arris and Gale Lecturer, Royal College of Surgeons, England, 1972; Sama Foundation Lecturer, Hope Waddell College and Training Institute, Calabar, Nigeria, 1982. Visiting professor to numerous institutions, including Royal College of Surgeons, Dublin, Ireland, 1972, National Academy of Science, New Delhi, India, 1976, and University of California, Irvine, 1981. Exchange scientist to the Soviet Union for the National Cancer Institute, USA-USSR Exchange, 1976.

President and chairman, Cultural and Educational Productions Publishing, Montreal, Quebec, 1966-86; director and vice-president for research and American scientific affairs, Mario Negri Foundation, New York City, 1974-80; member of board of directors and honorary chairman, Lambo Foundation, 1985; founding director and professor of international health, World Health Organization for Community Based and Multiprofessional Education for Health Personnel, Nashville, Tenn., 1985—; founding director, Project to Develop Oban Research Institute, Cross River State, Nigeria, 1988; founder of four Self-Health Primary Care Centers, Cross River State, Nigeria; former president, India League, Dublin, Ireland. Organizer and director of interdisciplinary conference education radio programs in Minnesota and Nigeria. Consultant to various organizations, including Pan American Health Organization, Brazil, 1974, Sama Foundation, Nigeria, 1983—, U.S. Agency for International Development/African Regional Organization (USAID/AFRO), 1985-88, African Research Foundation, Lagos, 1986—, and World Health Organization.

MEMBER: World Academy of Arts and Sciences (fellow), International Communication Association, Institute International de Medicine Biologique, International Foundation for Biosocial Development and Human Health (founder; president, 1977-86), American Institute of Stress (founding member, consultant, and member of board of directors, 1979-82), American Rural Health Association (founding member; director and vice-president of international affairs, 1977-81), American Medical Association, American Association for the Advancement of Science, American Anthropological Association, American Cybernetics Society, Society for Anthropology of Visual Communication, Society for Medicine and Anthropology, Council of Biology Editors, Japanese Foundation of Biopsychosocial Health (international honorary fellow and most distinguished member), Zoological Society of London (fellow), Medical Geographers of the USSR Geographic Society (honorary member), Harvey Society, New York Historical Society, Bombay Society of Natural History, University of Minnesota Alumni Club (charter member), Sigma Xi.

AWARDS, HONORS: Royal College of Surgeons in Ireland, first prize and silver medal in biology, 1950, Biology Society, silver medal for best scientific paper of academic year, 1953 and 1954, Triennial Reuben Harvey Memorial Prize and Medal, 1957; second prize in clinical surgery, St. Laurence's Richmond Hospital, Dublin, 1955; Moynihan Prize and Medal, Association of Surgeons of Great Britain and Ireland, 1960; Ciba fellow in Canada, 1963; Gold Key, University of Minnesota Medical School, Bell Museum of Pathobiology, 1973; *Behavioral Medicine* selection for one of the best books of the year, 1979, for *Cancer, Stress, and Death;* distinguished scholar award, International Communication Association, Division of Health Communications, 1980. Sama Foundation Award, Nigeria, 1982; initiation into the Mgbe (Ekpe) Society, and conferment of the chieftaincy title, Ntufam Ajan of Oban (title means "King of Medicines"), by the people of Oban, Cross River State, Nigeria, 1983; commendation from H. R. H. the Obong of Calabar, Edidem Bassey Eyo Ephraim Adam III, King of Calabar, 1983, in honor of World Health Day; decoration with chieftaincy costumes and conferment of chieftaincy title, Obong Nsong Idem Ibibio, by the people of Ikot Imo, Cross River State, Nigeria, 1983; Day was awarded the Key to the City of Nashville, Tennessee, by Mayor Bill Boner, 1987; commendation from President Ronald Reagan, 1987, for the establishment of the World Health Organization Center in Nashville; Day was proclaimed "ambassador for the State of Tennessee" by Governor Ned McWherter, 1987; outstanding citizen citation, the Assembly State of New York, 1987; citation in the U. S. Congressional Record, 1987; Maestro Honorario, Universidad Autonoma Agraria Antonio Narro, 1987. Fellowships from Minnesota Heart Association, 1958-59, American Heart Association, 1959-60, American Cancer Society, 1961-62, Canadian Defense Board, 1962-63, Canadian Heart Association, 1964-66, and other organizations.

WRITINGS:

SCIENTIFIC NONFICTION

The Idle Thoughts of a Surgical Fellow: Being an Account of Experimental Surgical Studies, 1956-1966, foreword by Robert A. Good, Cultural and Educational Productions, 1968.

(Consultant and contributor) *Dictionary of Scientific Biography,* Scribner, 1968.

Edward Stevens—Gastric Physiologist: Physician and American Statesman, Cultural and Educational Productions, 1969.

(With Bruce G. MacMillan and William A. Altemier) *Curling's Ulcer: An Experiment of Nature,* foreword by Owen H. Wangensteen, C. C Thomas, 1971.

(Editor) *Death and Attitudes toward Death,* Bell Museum of Pathobiology, 1972.

(Editor with Good) *Membranes, Viruses, and Immune Mechanisms in Experimental and Clinical Diseases,* Academic Press, 1972.

(Editor with Good) *The Bulletin of the Bell Museum of Pathobiology,* Volumes 1-4, University of Minnesota Medical School, 1972-75.

(Author of introduction) Joseph Black, *De Humore Acido a Cibis Orto et Magnesia Albo,* translation by Thomas Hanson, Bell Museum of Pathobiology, 1973.

(Editor) *Proceedings: Ethics in Medicine in a Changing Society,* Bell Museum of Pathobiology, 1973.

(Editor and contributor with Good and Ellis S. Benson) *Miscellaneous Papers of the Bell Museum of Pathobiology,* University of Minnesota Medical School, 1973.

Tuluak and Amaulik: Dialogues on Death and Mourning with the Inuit Eskimo of Point Barrow and Wainwright, Alaska, Bell Museum of Pathobiology, 1973.

(Editor with Good and J. Yunis) *Molecular Pathology,* C. C Thomas, 1975.

(Editor) *Trauma: Clinical and Biological Aspects,* Plenum, 1975.

(Editor) *Communication of Scientific Information,* S. Karger, 1975.

(With E. Teischoly) *Computer Graphics: Application of Computer Graphics in Medicine and Health Care Science,* S. Karger, 1975.

(Editor with W. P. Myers, W. P. Laird, P. Stanley, S. Garattini, and M. C. Lewis) *Cancer Invasion and Metastases: Biologic Mechanisms and Therapy,* Raven Press, 1976.

Report of a Visit to the Soviet Union in January, 1976, as an Exchange Scientist for Three Weeks under the Aegis of the U.S.-U.S.S.R. Agreement for Health Cooperation, Biomedical Communications, Oncology, Education, and Cancer Research Imperatives in the Soviet Union, Day, 1976.

(Editor with Good) *Comprehensive Immunology,* nine volumes, Plenum, 1976-80.

The Image of Science and Society, S. Karger, 1977.

(With R. V. Cuddihy and H. H. Fudenberg) *The American Biomedical Network: Health Care Systems in America, Present and Future,* Scripta Medica, 1977.

Some Systems of Biological Communication, S. Karger, 1977.

(Editor) *Companion to the Life Sciences,* Volume I, Van Nostrand, 1978.

What Is a Scientist?, S. Karger, 1979.

(With Jean Tache and Hans Selye) *Cancer, Stress, and Death,* Plenum, 1979, 2nd edition, 1985.

Health Communications, International Foundation for Biosocial Development and Human Health, 1979.

(With Everett Sugarbarker, Bruce A. Warren, and Paul J. Rosch) *Readings in Oncology,* International Foundation of Biosocial Development and Human Health, 1980.

(Editor with Fernando Lolas and Marc Kusinitz) *Biopsychosocial Health,* International Foundation for Biosocial Development and Human Health, 1980.

(Editor) *Integrated Medicine: Volume II of the Companion to the Life Sciences,* Van Nostrand, 1981.

(Editor with Jan F. Brandejs) *Computers for Medical Office and Patient Management,* Van Nostrand, 1982.

(Editor and author of introduction) *Life Stress: Volume III of the Companion to the Life Sciences,* Van Nostrand, 1982.

(Editor with Emmanuel Aban Oddaye and Habteab Zerit) *Primary Health Care Guide Lines: A Training Manual; Field Training Programs and Education for Health,* introduction by H. L. Mays, International Center for Health Sciences at Meharry Medical College, 2nd edition, 1986.

Also author with L. H. Schloen, *Sloan-Kettering Institute of Cancer Research Annual Report,* 1973.

NONFICTION

Ten Poems and a Letter from America for Mr. Sinha (cultural anthropology essay), Cultural and Educational Productions, 1970.

(Author of introduction) George Dahl, *Of Physicians and Fairies,* Cultural and Educational Productions, 1973.

(With Satis Biswas Day) *A Hindu Interpretation of the Hand and Its Portents as Practiced by Palmists of India,* Bell Museum of Pathobiology, 1973.

East of the Navel and Afterbirth: Reflections and Song Poetry from Rapa Nui—Mysterious Easter Island, Cultural and Educational Productions, 1975.

Also author of *Introduction to Poems and Masks by Vera Stacey Wainwright,* 1969, and *A Leaf of the Chaatim,* 1970.

FICTION

Collected Lines (verse), Cultural and Educational Productions, 1966.

By the Waters of Babylon (four-act play), Cultural and Educational Productions, 1966.

East and West: A Play in Three Acts, Cultural and Educational Productions, 1967.

American Lines (verse), Cultural and Educational Productions, 1967.

The Music Box (three-act play), Cultural and Educational Productions, 1967.

Poems and Etudes (verse), Cultural and Educational Productions, 1968.

Rosalita (novella), Cultural and Educational Productions, 1968.

Three One-Act Plays for Reading: Presenting Portland en Passant, The Cricket Cage, and Little Boy on a Red Horse, Cultural and Educational Productions, 1968.

Bellechasse (novella), Cultural and Educational Productions, 1970.

(Contributor) *The Broken Glass Factory* (poetry anthology), edited by Louis Safer, University of Minnesota, 1974.

OTHER

Author of monographs for the International Foundation of Biosocial Development and Human Health, including *The Biopsychosocial Imperative: Understanding the Biologos and General Systems Theory Approach to Bio-Communications as the Psychospiritual Anatomy of Good Health,* 1981, *Creative Health and Health Enhancement: Individual Initiative and Responsibility for Self Health and Wellness,* 1982, and *The Way of a Physician: The Biologos, Biopsychosocial Way; Survival and the Parasympathetic towards an Ethic and a Way of Life,* 1982; author of *Three Folk Songs Set to Music* (guitar and harmonica music), 1967. Editor, narrator and author of script for the documentary films "AKAMPA 1983" and "Oban under the Mountain" which aired in 1983 on Nigerian Television Authority (NTA-TV), Calabar, Nigeria. Contributing editor, *Postgraduate Medicine,* 1971; editor, member of editorial board, *University of Minnesota Medical Bulletin,* 1972-74; founder, editor-in-chief, contributor, and member of editorial board, *Health Communications and Informatics* (Basle, Switzerland; formerly, *Biosciences Communications*), 1974-80; consulting editor, *Life Sciences,* 1976—; editor, *Foundation One,* and *Monographs in Biopsychosocial Health,* 1980-84; member of editorial board, *Psyche et Cancer* [Switzerland], 1980—; editor, *Contemporary International Health,* 1986; editor-in-chief, *Health Communications and Biopsychosocial Health;* member of editorial board for *Psychooncology, Kosmos, Annual Reviews on Stress, Nambo Foundation Newsletter,* and *Current Selected Research in Human Stress.*

Contributor to journals, including *Surgery, Gynecology and Obstetrics, Surgery,* and *Journal of the History of Medicine.*

SIDELIGHTS: Stacey Day is a poet-playwright-surgeon-philosopher who "feels that man should not follow a career or profession to the point of boredom," according to a writer for the Montreal *Weekly Post.* Medical writer and journalist Walter S. Alvarez considers him "one of the most remarkable physicians of today . . . [with] a great flair for doing splendid literary research." Initially calling himself a "perspective humanitarian," Day has come to view himself in terms of what he calls the "psychospiritual concept of the pastoral physician." Day told *CA* that over the last twenty years he has had an increasing intellectual curiosity for people, places, and events, which he visualizes "within a biopsychosocial space-time continuum." He further remarked that he is especially interested in the region between Europe and Asia, feudal economies coping with advanced technological societies, and the social, moral, and health problems of indigent inhabitants. The upsurge of political and social unrest in the Near East during the 1970s and 1980s has increased Day's concern for this area of the world even more.

Born in England of an English mother and Indian father, Day has traveled widely in Europe, Africa, Asia, and the Americas. Although his education originally trained him for a career in India, Day decided after his military service to learn about Russia and its economic history, studying at the University of Birmingham under the tutelage of the late Russian expatriate and economic historian, Alexander M. Baykov. Continuing his studies abroad, Day later completed his doctorate degrees in Ireland, Canada and the United States.

Concerning his mixed ancestry, Day has written: "The possibility of fusing two esthetic modes so different in culture and religio-politic traditions . . . is by no means easy." Nevertheless, he is fascinated by the contrasts that are part of his heritage and which exist between cultures both within and between countries. With regard to the latter, the writer's novella, *Rosalita,* is described as "a post-Ulysses Joycean psychoanalytic treatment of the generation gap and contemporary . . . living" in the United States during the 1960s. In comparing the lifestyle of the West to that of the East, Day observes that the "West is an external society, while the East is internal, more spiritual." Day continues, "I have tried to assimilate things of goodness from many cultures and to bring about synthesis of these expressions to my own life and writings."

Day's medical writings include studies on heart and circulatory disease and on the extinct Irish elk; and his research has led him to pioneer the studies of community based education, health communications and informatics, and biopsychosocial health. As a poet and philosopher he has studied the American hippie subculture, appeared on radio and television programs (including "60 Minutes"), and given poetry readings in Africa, England, Canada, India, and the United States. In addition to appearances in these countries, he has lectured, led workshops, and been a guest speaker in Germany, Italy, Japan, Czechoslovakia, Ireland, and the U.S.S.R., where he appeared at the 13th International Congress of the History of Science in Moscow in 1971. His work in the United States includes the development of the World Health Organization at the Meharry Medical College in Tennessee. President Ronald Reagan awarded Day a commendation for this achievement, which begins: "The vision of Dr. Stacey Day, and his fine team at the Center, builds on a community approach to medicine which is truly international in scope."

The goodness that Day sees in all cultures is, for him, made manifest in the common people. One of the physician's main concerns involves the way in which scientists often forget humanity in their pursuit of knowledge, or worse, fame. About his observations of those who tutored him and their struggles to win the Nobel Prize, Day told *CA:* "It was always the research, never the patient." He believes that "salvation, greatness, and importance exude from elegant self deception, the crown of the 'successful' life." In a *Hindustan Times* article, he told writer Nandini Chandra: "We doctors and scientists are autocratic and live in ivory towers. We don't spread our knowledge." In order to raze these towers "we need a new system with scientists trained as communicators," he explained in the same article. According to Day, not only do doctors need to communicate better with others, they also need to focus more on sociology, cultural anthropology, and psychology, instead of only on the biology of change.

"After all," he concludes, "we are dealing with people, not only with rats and guinea pigs."

BIOGRAPHICAL/CRITICAL SOURCES:

PERIODICALS

Ananda Bazar Patrika (Calcutta), March, 1968.
Cincinnati Enquirer, November 26, 1967.
East African Standard (Nairobi), February, 1968.
Gastroenterology, Number 6, 1969.
Hindustan Times, December 26, 1976.
Los Angeles Times, September 19, 1967.
Meharry Reporter, November 12, 1985.
Nashville Banner, October 26, 1987, November 27, 1987.
Nigerian Chronicle, June 1, 1983, June 3, 1983.
Tennessean, January 8, 1987.
Weekly Post (Montreal), September 7, 1967.

* * *

DEANE, Elisabeth
See BEILENSON, Edna

* * *

DeCOSTER, Cyrus C(ole) 1914-

PERSONAL: Born September 21, 1914, in Leesburg, Va.; son of Cyrus C. (a businessman) and Jeanne (Brulay) DeCoster; married Barbara Krause, December 28, 1948; children: Janine, David, Kenneth, James. *Education:* Harvard University, A.B., 1937; additional study at Sorbonne, University of Paris, 1937-38; University of Chicago, M.A., 1940, Ph.D., 1951.

ADDRESSES: Home—17 Martha Lane, Evanston, Ill. 60201. *Office*—Department of Hispanic Languages, Northwestern University, Evanston, Ill. 60201.

CAREER: Carleton College, Northfield, Minn., instructor, 1946-48, assistant professor, 1948-56, associate professor of Romance languages, 1956-57; University of Kansas, Lawrence, professor of Romance languages, 1957-69, head of department, 1962-65; Northwestern University, Evanston, Ill., professor of Spanish, 1969-85, professor emeritus, 1985—, chairman of department of Spanish and Portuguese, 1973-76, 1979-83. *Military service:* U.S. Naval Reserve, 1941-46; became lieutenant.

MEMBER: Modern Language Association of America, American Association of Teachers of Spanish and Portuguese, American Association of University Professors, Midwest Modern Language Association.

AWARDS, HONORS: Fulbright research fellow in Madrid, 1963-64.

WRITINGS:

(Editor) Juan Valera, *Correspondencia inedita de Juan Valera,* Castalia, 1956.
(Editor) *Obras desconocidas de Juan Valera,* Castalia, 1965.
(Editor) Valera, *Articulos de "El Contemporaneo,"* Castalia, 1966.
(Editor) Valera, *Las ilusiones del Doctor Faustino,* Castalia, 1970.
Bibliografia critica de Juan Valera, Consejo Superior de Investigaciones Cientificas, 1970.
Juan Valera, Twayne, 1974.
(Editor) Valera, *Genio y figura,* Catedra, 1975.
Pedro Antonio de Alarcon, Twayne, 1979.
(Editor) Pedro Antonio de Alarcon, *Obras olvidadas,* Studia Humanitatis, 1984.

de KAY, Ormonde (Jr.) 1923-

PERSONAL: Born December 17, 1923, in New York, N.Y.; son of Ormonde and Margaret (McClure) de Kay; married Barbara Ellen Scott Roosevelt, January 20, 1967; children: Thomas Scott. *Education:* Harvard University, A.B., 1947. *Politics:* Democrat. *Religion:* Episcopalian.

ADDRESSES: Home—1225 Park Ave., New York, N.Y. 10128.

CAREER: Louis de Rochemont Associates, Inc., New York City, screenwriter, 1948-49; free-lance screenwriter in New York City, Rome, Italy, Munich, West Germany, and Paris, France, 1950-57; Central Office of Information, London, England, radio producer, 1958-60; free-lance writer in New York City, 1961-66; *Interplay,* New York City, special projects editor, 1967-69; *Horizon,* New York City, articles editor, 1970-75; free-lance writer, 1975—. *Military service:* U.S. Naval Reserve, active duty, 1943-46, 1951-52.

MEMBER: Poetry Society of America, PEN American Center, Housing Conservation Coordinators (secretary, 1974-79; director), Century Club (New York), Harvard Club (New York).

AWARDS, HONORS: Cannes Film Festival Award for best scenario (with M. J. Furlaud), 1949, for "Lost Boundaries."

WRITINGS:

Universal History of the World, Volume V: *The East in the Middle Ages,* Volume XIII: *Imperialism and World War I,* Western Publishing, 1964.
Meet Theodore Roosevelt (juvenile), Random House, 1967.
Meet Andrew Jackson (juvenile), Random House, 1967.
The Adventures of Lewis and Clark (juvenile), Random House, 1968.
Rimes de la Mere Oie: Mother Goose Rhymes Rendered into French, Little, Brown, 1971.
(Contributor) *Mysteries of the Deep,* American Heritage Publishing, 1980.
(Editor and translator) *N'Heures Souris Rames: The Coucy Castle Manuscript,* C. N. Potter, 1980.
Three Centuries of Notable American Architects, American Heritage Publishing, 1981.
Fractured French Encore, illustrations by Frank Modell, Doubleday, 1983.
(Adaptor) *The Snorks and the Waterwitch* (juvenile), illustrations by George Wildman, Random House, 1983.

Also translator of Jean Larteguy's *The Walls of Israel,* 1969. Author of film scripts, including "Lost Boundaries." Contributor of poems and articles to *Harper's, Atlantic, New Yorker, Mademoiselle, Horizon, American Heritage, Cosmopolitan, Quest,* and other magazines. Editor, *Manuscripts,* 1977-79; contributing editor, *Art World,* 1979—, *Harvard Magazine,* 1981-87.

* * *

DELACORTA
See ODIER, Daniel

* * *

DELBANCO, Nicholas (Franklin) 1942-

PERSONAL: Born August 27, 1942, in London, England; brought to United States in 1948; son of Kurt (a businessman) and Barbara (Bernstein) Delbanco; married Elena Greenhouse, September 12, 1970; children: Francesca Barbara, Andrea Katherine. *Education:* Harvard University, B.A. (magna cum laude), 1963; Columbia University, M.A., 1966.

ADDRESSES: Home—428 Concord St., Ann Arbor, Mich. 48104. *Office*—Department of English, University of Michigan, 7611 Haven Hall, Ann Arbor, Mich. 48109. *Agent*—Brandt & Brandt Literary Agents, Inc., 1501 Broadway, New York, N.Y. 10036.

CAREER: Bennington College, Bennington, Vt., member of department of language and literature, 1966-84, writing workshop director, 1977-84; Skidmore College, Saratoga Springs, N.Y., professor of English, 1984-85; University of Michigan, Ann Arbor, professor of English, 1985—. Visiting adjunct professor, Columbia University School of the Arts, 1979; visiting professor, Williams College, 1982. Visiting lecturer, University of Iowa, 1979; writer in residence, Trinity College, 1980. Director, the Hopwood Awards, University of Michigan, 1988—.

MEMBER: PEN, Authors Guild, Authors League of America, Signet Society, New York State Writers Institute, Phi Beta Kappa.

AWARDS, HONORS: National Endowment for the Arts creative writing award, 1973 and 1982; National Endowment of Composers and Librettists fellowship, 1976; Guggenheim fellowship, 1980; Woodrow Wilson fellowship; Edward John Noble fellowship; New York State CAPS Award; Vermont Council of the Arts Award; Michigan Council of the Arts Award.

WRITINGS:

NOVELS

The Martlet's Tale, Lippincott, 1966.
Grasse, 3/23/66, Lippincott, 1968.
Consider Sappho Burning, Morrow, 1969.
News, Morrow, 1970.
In the Middle Distance, Morrow, 1971.
Fathering, Morrow, 1973.
Small Rain, Morrow, 1975.
Possession (first novel in trilogy), Morrow, 1977.
Sherbrookes (second novel in trilogy), Morrow, 1978.
Stillness (third novel in trilogy), Morrow, 1980.

OTHER

(Contributor) Peter Simon, *On the Vineyard,* Doubleday, 1980.
Group Portrait: Joseph Conrad, Stephen Crane, Ford Madox Ford, Henry James, and H. G. Wells (nonfiction), Morrow, 1982.
About My Table, and Other Stories, Morrow, 1983.
The Beaux Arts Trio: A Portrait (nonfiction), Morrow, 1985.
(Editor and author of introduction) John Gardner, *Stillness* [and] *Shadows,* Knopf, 1986.
Running in Place: Scenes from the South of France (nonfiction), Atlantic Monthly, 1989.
The Writer's Trade, and Other Stories, Morrow, 1990.

Contributor to periodicals, including *Atlantic Monthly, Esquire,* and *New Republic.* Contributor of articles to the *New York Times Book Review.*

SIDELIGHTS: Nicholas Delbanco "wrestles with the abundance of his gifts as a novelist the way other men wrestle with their deficiencies," says John Updike in a *Dictionary of Literary Biography* entry by Alan Cheuse. Mostly recognized for his poetic, modernistic novels, the author is nevertheless "one of those consistently highly acclaimed writers who remains relatively unknown to the general public," according to one *Publishers Weekly* review. Born of German Jewish parents who had fled to England before World War II began, Delbanco was brought to the United States at the age of six. His initial childhood attraction for such writers as Lewis Carroll and Ogden Nash ignited an interest that eventually would lead him to study literature at Harvard and Columbia. With the encouragement of one of his professors, Theodore Morrison, and former teacher Updike, Delbanco published *The Martlet's Tale,* a novel set in Greece and based on the Prodigal Son fable. His next books, *Grasse 3/23/66* and *Consider Sappho Burning,* are experimental works, which employ a "very poetic kind of fiction," as Stanley G. Eskin calls it in *Mainstream.* Eskin continues: "Delbanco's novels are clearly in the modernist mainstream; his affinities (whether or not of direct influence) are with such writers as Joyce, Faulkner, Beckett, and the French 'new novelists.' "

The author's next three novels after *Consider Sappho Burning, News, In the Middle Distance,* and *Fathering* have what Eskin considers "an important public and political dimension which makes him very much a writer of his time." "*News* is probably the most fully realized and yet most neglected political novel in recent decades," remarks Cheuse. The book concerns the efforts of several men to improve society and how three of them are destroyed in the process. *In the Middle Distance* and *Fathering* also touch on political issues, though the former is primarily "a fictive autobiography," says Delbanco in his entry in the *Contemporary Authors Autobiography Series,* "and *Fathering* [is] a truncate version of the Theban trilogy" (Sophocles' plays about Oedipus and Antigone).

A former Vermont resident, Delbanco's best-known works are *Possession, Sherbrookes,* and *Stillness,* which comprise a trilogy concerning a New England family. In the *Contemporary Authors Autobiography Series* he remarks that he considers the trilogy to mark "the transition from apprentice to journeyman laborer. These books are built around no previous structure, nor modelled consciously on the work of others; they take place where I've come to call home." The novels tell of the declining years of an elite Vermont family, the Sherbrookes, and depicts what *Washington Post Book World* contributor Garrett Epps calls "the underside of family life."

The Sherbrookes are a family struggling between the past and the present. Richard Bausch's *Washington Post Book World* article on *Stillness* explains how the character of "Maggie retains the past in the memory and spirit of Judah, her dead husband, from whom, in life and death, she has tried to break free." While she struggles with these memories, her son Ian is strongly affected by "the whole weight of Sherbrooke ancestry," says Bausch. Unlike his aunt Hattie, who eventually kills herself, or his mother, whose sanity is seriously threatened, the lessons of the family's past actually help Ian. He learns, Bausch explains, "to love without the will to possess—which is what Judah never learned to do."

In *Chicago Tribune Book World* reviewer Ann Grimes' opinion, the author portrays a present in these works that "is extraordinarily bleak. . . . But in 'Stillness' Delbanco brings history to the fore and casts it in heroic light. He lashes out at the present with bits from the past." However, in a *New York Times Book Review* article Katherine Pollitt states that "the reverence [Delbanco] feels for the Sherbrookes seems to have paralyzed his literary will." Because of this, Pollitt believes "he lets the story bog down in ruminations on Sherbrooke specialness." In keeping with the style of many of his other novels, the author's trilogy is written so that it "is more in the fashion of a long poem, or a series of vibrant images held in rigid frames," explains Epps in a review of *Stillness. New York Times Book Review* critic Frederick Busch feels "the prose, as ever, is offered with the precision of heavy, precious coins being counted on the palm." Concerning the last book in the trilogy, Bausch asserts, "he is never poetic merely for the sake of a turn of phrase, yet there is poetry in 'Stillness.' "

After completion of the Sherbrooke trilogy, Delbanco's interests began to move away from the novel and toward the publication of nonfiction works and short stories, including *Group Portrait: Joseph Conrad, Stephen Crane, Ford Madox Ford, Henry James, and H. G. Wells, The Beaux Arts Trio: A Portrait,* and *About My Table, and Other Stories.* The latter, which contains nine stories linked by a common theme and a New England setting, has received the approval of many critics. In the *Los Angeles Times Book Review* Richard Eder says the stories are "written with breathtaking technique and an uncanny ability to bring a penetrating emotion up out of a gesture, a pause, or a random thought."

The tales are all related in that they tell about aging men suffering a crisis as they make the transition from youth to old age. The tone of these stories towards present-day life is similar to that of the Sherbrookes novels. "Taken together," comments *New York Times Book Review* critic Edith Milton, "the stories in 'About My Table' provide a warm yet despairing view of contemporary life." Eder also recognizes a tone of despair in the tales. "But," he adds, "his stories are only tangentially bleak. He writes warmly about cold things. His tormented heroes are priggish and winning at the same time, and sometimes comical. The author's gift for comedy is considerable, in fact." In a *Detroit News* article Peter Ross sums up *About My Table* as being "a thoughtful, extraordinarily intelligent journey in nine directions that promises to coalesce at some distant and ever-mysterious point, delineating just what we do, how we do it, and why."

As for Delbanco, the explanation for what he does is answered in the last chapter of *Group Portrait. Los Angeles Times* reviewer Carolyn See believes this part of the book, which discusses the lives of several famous authors and their relationships with one another, is "by far the most beautiful and interesting part of the book. It addresses itself to the question (indirectly, wittily) of why would one want to write in the first place? The answer, modestly put, is that . . . writing is a calling, maybe the most sacred one there is." Offering an additional reason, Delbanco says in the *Contemporary Authors Autobiography Series:* "It's easy to inveigh against the writer's rotten lot, . . . and most professional wordsmiths could find some other job. They don't; they won't; why not? One answer is, it's fun."

In his early years as a writer, Delbanco was considered by some to be "a prodigy of a novelist whose early parables were dazzling in their language," writes Cheuse in the *Dictionary of Literary Biography.* Now in his middle years, he describes himself two ways in the *Contemporary Authors Autobiography Series.* He writes, "The first: I was a startling, prodigious child who has been declining steadily and will, at sixty, be worthless. The second: I was a boastful egotist who has been gaining in the attributes of manhood and who may amount to something by the age of sixty. Truth resides between."

MEDIA ADAPTATIONS: The Martlet's Tale was made into a film in 1970.

BIOGRAPHICAL/CRITICAL SOURCES:

BOOKS

Contemporary Authors Autobiography Series, Volume 2, Gale, 1985.
Contemporary Literary Criticism, Gale, Volume 6, 1976, Volume 13, 1980.
Dictionary of Literary Biography, Volume 6: *American Novelists since World War II, Second Series,* Gale, 1980.

PERIODICALS

Chicago Tribune Book World, November 23, 1980.
Detroit News, September 23, 1983.
Hudson Review, summer, 1974.
Los Angeles Times Book Review, May 10, 1982, August 7, 1983.
Mainstream, October, 1974.
New York Times Book Review, January 29, 1979, November 9, 1980, September 18, 1983.
Publishers Weekly, November 6, 1978.
Village Voice, January 3, 1974.
Washington Post Book World, December 31, 1978, September 29, 1980.

—*Sketch by Kevin S. Hile*

* * *

DESPLAND, Michel 1936-

PERSONAL: Born July 25, 1936, in Lausanne, Switzerland; son of Amy and Lisette (Vuagniaux) Despland; married Sheila McDonough, September 13, 1979 (divorced, 1985); married Francine Lichtert, 1986; children: (first marriage) Emma, Alexis; (second marriage) Joachim. *Education:* Universite de Lausanne, Lic.Theol., 1958; Harvard University, Th.D., 1966.

ADDRESSES: Office—Department of Religion, Concordia University, 1455 De Maisonneuve W., Montreal, Quebec, Canada H3G 1M8.

CAREER: Concordia University, Montreal, Quebec, assistant professor, 1965-70, associate professor, beginning 1970, currently professor of religion.

WRITINGS:

Le Choc des morales, L'Age d'Homme, 1973.
Kant on History and Religion, McGill-Queen's University Press, 1973.
La Religion en occident, Fides/Cerf, 1979.
The Education of Desire: Plato and the Philosophy of Religion, University of Toronto Press, 1985.
Christianisme: Dossier corps, Cerf, 1986.
(With Louis Rousseau) *Sciences religieuses au Quebec 1972-1982,* Wilfred Laurier University Press, 1988.

* * *

DEW, Charles B(urgess) 1937-

PERSONAL: Born January 5, 1937, in St. Petersburg, Fla.; son of Jack Carlos and Amy (Meek) Dew; married Robb Reavill Forman (a novelist), January 26, 1968; children: Charles Stephen, John Forman. *Education:* Williams College, A.B., 1958; Johns Hopkins University, Ph.D., 1964.

ADDRESSES: Office—Department of History, Williams College, Main St., Williamstown, Mass. 01267.

CAREER: Wayne State University, Detroit, Mich., instructor, 1963-64, assistant professor of history, 1964-65; Louisiana State

University, Baton Rouge, assistant professor of history, 1965-68; University of Missouri, Columbia, associate professor, 1968-72, professor of history, 1972-78; Williams College, Williamstown, Mass., professor of history, 1978—. Visiting associate professor, University of Virginia, 1970-71; visiting professor, Williams College, 1977-78.

MEMBER: American Historical Association, Organization of American Historians, Southern Historical Association (member of executive council, 1975-78), Virginia Historical Society, Phi Beta Kappa.

AWARDS, HONORS: Award of merit, American Association for State and Local History, 1966; Fletcher Pratt Award, Civil War Round Table of New York, 1967, for *Ironmaker to the Confederacy: Joseph R. Anderson and the Tredegar Ironworks.*

WRITINGS:

Ironmaker to the Confederacy: Joseph R. Anderson and the Tredegar Ironworks, Yale University Press, 1966.
(Contributor) *Origins of the New South, 1877-1913,* Louisiana State University Press, 1971.
(Editor with T. C. Cochran and T. H. Williams) *The Meanings of American History: Interpretations of Events, Ideas, and Institutions,* Volume 2: *Civil War to the Present,* Scott, Foresman, 1972.
(Contributor) *Race, Region, and Reconstruction: Essays in Honor of C. Vann Woodward,* revised edition, Oxford University Press, 1982.

Contributor to *South Atlantic Quarterly, Louisiana History, Civil War History, American Historical Review, Journal of Southern History,* and *William and Mary Quarterly.* *

* * *

DEW, Robb (Reavill) Forman 1946-

PERSONAL: Born October 26, 1946, in Mt. Vernon, Ohio; daughter of Oliver Duane (a neurosurgeon) and Helen (Ransom) Forman; married Charles Burgess Dew (a professor of history), January 26, 1968; children: Charles Stephen, John Forman. *Education:* Attended Louisiana State University.

ADDRESSES: Agent—Virginia Barber, c/o Virginia Barber Literary Agency, Inc., 353 West 21st St., New York, N.Y. 10011.

CAREER: Writer. Teacher at Iowa Writers' Workshop, University of Iowa, spring, 1984.

AWARDS, HONORS: American Book Award for first novel, Association of American Publishers, 1982, for *Dale Loves Sophie to Death.*

WRITINGS:

Dale Loves Sophie to Death (novel), Farrar, 1981.
The Time of Her Life (novel), Morrow, 1984.

Contributor of stories to periodicals, including *Mississippi Quarterly, Southern Review, Virginia Quarterly,* and *New Yorker.*

WORK IN PROGRESS: A novel with the tentative title *Agnes and Anna.*

SIDELIGHTS: In Robb Forman Dew's two novels, *The Time of Her Life* and the American Book Award-winning *Dale Loves Sophie to Death,* of central importance is the contemporary family. According to Dew in a *Publishers Weekly* interview conducted by Sybil Steinberg, the environment she encountered as a child was an unhappy one: "What I understood with the deepest part of my compassion and with an abiding sense of irony was the unconscious harm people can do to each other, with the best of intentions." In her writing, Dew gets at this unconscious harm, and also at the sometimes insurmountable, inexplicable pleasures and love associated with family life. Overall, critics feel she does this well, as evidenced by Lisa Schwarzbaum's comment in the *Detroit News:* "In *The Time of Her Life,* Dew . . . puts her sensitive ear to a family's heart. And . . . she comes up with a beautiful, personal language with which to describe its pulse."

Dew's highly acclaimed first novel, *Dale Loves Sophie to Death,* is characterized by reviewers as a quiet, domestic, mildly passionate piece of literature. Katha Pollitt remarks in the *New York Times Book Review* that, for the most part, this novel is "a mosaic of small events and inner reflections," because its principal action takes place in the minds of Dinah and Martin Howells. At the outset, Dinah and the three Howells children return to Dinah's hometown of Enfield, Ohio, for the summer, a routine they have undertaken for the past eight years. As usual, Martin stays behind in the Berkshires to teach and edit a literary journal. Although the separation is an increasingly difficult one for this couple, Dinah's dependency on this annual ritual suggests that she has not come to terms with her past. Indeed, *Ms.* contributor Joan Silber views this perennial undertaking as Dinah's plea for an apology from her parents and her brother for neglecting her when she was growing up. In turn, *Washington Post Book World*'s Robert Wilson interprets the action as Dinah's attempt to extend her own adolescence. Although, as in summers past, Dinah engages in the same summertime activities at the same summertime pace, this summer, at age thirty-six, she is fraught with heightened sensitivities. Only when her middle child becomes sick do certain realities of life become solidified for her, thereby allowing her to reckon with her past. According to Wilson, "what Dinah realizes, simply and awfully, is that she is grown up, 'and because she was grownup she had . . . to contend with a terrible fate—she had *mortal* children, and she had to recognize it and deal with it every moment of her days.' " During these same months, Martin, after experiencing a displeasing extramarital affair and other circumstances, makes his own personal discoveries, and when husband and wife are reunited at summer's end, they come together with a greater appreciation of the enduring nature of marital and familial love.

According to Wilson, *Dale Loves Sophie to Death* is the type of novel that grows richer with each reading: "Dew's gift is to transform the ordinary, to charge it with interest," and yet, he explains, Dew is never sentimental about children nor about family life in general. To Wilson, Dew has taken a difficult subject for a novel, "because familial love is not as vivid as first love or adulterous love or homosexual love. . . ., [and] has shaped a novel that profoundly satisfies both the mind and the heart." Similarly, Pollitt gives Dew credit for having the "courage to write the traditional novel of domestic feeling today, the novel with no violence, no million-dollar deals, no weird sex. . . . The rewards of 'Dale Loves Sophie to Death' are quiet but rich, and prove once again that in fiction there are no automatically compelling subjects. There are only compelling writers."

In contrast to *Dale Loves Sophie to Death,* in which Dew affirms the goodness of family life, *The Time of Her Life* is Dew's testament to the family unit as a potential perpetrator of "unconscious harm." According to Jonathan Yardley in the *Washington Post Book World, The Time of Her Life* examines "the fragility of [family] ties, the ease with which they can be broken, the carelessness of what passes for 'love,' and the terrible, lasting damage that can result. . . . It is a dark novel. . . . There's no artificial uplift in *The Time of Her Life*. . . . Dew offers what life itself offers: no easy way out."

As Yardley maintains, the central character in *The Time of Her Life* is a family. This family, a threesome, consists of Claudia, the well-educated yet unambitious, indecisive wife; Avery, the boyish, cheerful husband who hides behind his countenance and his drinking because he has not achieved his dreams; and, finally, Jane, the eleven-year-old daughter of "pre-adolescent sweetness and stubbornness, intelligence and mood," writes Schwarzbaum. In the space of this novel, Avery moves out on Claudia (not for the first time) and eventually has an affair with Jane's violin teacher; in due time, Claudia slips into a state of dormancy. After a lengthy separation, the Parkses reconcile, but even this is inconclusive and takes place after Jane has suffered terribly from the actions and inactions of her insensitive parents.

According to reviewers, Dew's capacities as a writer are well at work in *The Time of Her Life.* In his *New York Times* assessment, Michiko Kakutani marvels at Dew's ability to "convey, with a skill matched by few writers today, the quick, peculiar shifts in feelings that we experience, moment to moment, day to day—how, in an instant, love can sour into irritation; anxiety dissolve into affection; attraction subside into nostalgia. . . . In 'The Time of Her Life,' [Dew] uses this ability to map out the ambiguities of the Parks' marriage, and to show the devastating consequences that this unstable alliance has on their daughter. . . . Jane is treated by her parents as a miniature adult. Claudia confides to Jane her fears that Avery is a closet homosexual. Avery uses Jane as a go-between in his affair with her violin teacher. . . . As readers[,] we watch with growing trepidation as [Jane] gradually becomes infected with the violence of her parents' emotions." Yardley likewise describes Jane as the chief victim in this work: "It is a heartbreaking descent. . . . Nothing is spared us: none of the terrible things Avery and Claudia say, to each other and to Jane. . . . It is not easy to read *The Time of Her Life,* because it cuts so close to the bone that the reader feels the blade. . . . Everything about this novel is right: the characters . . . , the interplay of plot and theme, the wonderful prose, and the depiction of the world of children—a world Dew seems to know better, and to convey with greater understanding, than any American writer since Carson McCullers. *The Time of Her Life* is the work of that rarest of people, a *real* writer, and it will knock your socks off."

Dew told *CA:* "I grew up as a Southerner and I believe that background is the source of my interest in the intricacies of family life. My grandfather, with whom I lived for a portion of my adolescence, was the poet and critic John Crowe Ransom, and his voice has certainly shaped my style."

BIOGRAPHICAL/CRITICAL SOURCES:

BOOKS

Dew, Robb Forman, *Dale Loves Sophie to Death,* Farrar, 1981.

PERIODICALS

Detroit News, September 23, 1984.
Los Angeles Times, September 27, 1984.
Ms., July, 1981.
New Republic, April 4, 1981.
Newsweek, May 4, 1981.
New York Times, September 4, 1984.
New York Times Book Review, April 26, 1981, October 7, 1984.
Publishers Weekly, September 7, 1984.
Washington Post Book World, June 7, 1981, August 26, 1984.*

—Sketch by Cheryl Gottler

DINER, Steven J(ay) 1944-

PERSONAL: Born December 14, 1944, in New York, N.Y.; son of Dave (a garment worker) and Helen (a garment worker; maiden name, Fenster) Diner; married Hasia R. Schwartzman (a writer and historian); children: Shira Miriam, Eli Moshe. *Education:* State University of New York at Binghamton, B.A., 1966, M.A., 1968; University of Chicago, Ph.D., 1972.

ADDRESSES: Home—3825 Veazey St. N.W., Washington, D.C. 20016. *Office*—Office of the Provost, George Mason University, 4400 University Dr., Fairfax, Va. 22030.

CAREER: University of Chicago, Chicago, Ill., instructor at Metropolitan Institute, 1970-72; University of the District of Columbia, Washington, D.C., assistant professor, 1972-76, associate professor, 1976-81, professor of urban studies, 1981-85, chairperson of department; George Mason University, Fairfax, Va., vice-provost for academic programs and professor of history, 1985—. Lecturer in American studies at University of Maryland, 1975; American Council on Education fellow in academic administration at George Mason University, 1983-84. President of North Cleveland Park Citizens Association, 1980-81, and Phoebe Hearst Elementary School PTA, 1981-84; American Jewish Committee, member of executive board, 1981-86, co-chairman of domestic affairs committee, 1982-85; member of executive board of Jewish Community Council of Greater Washington, 1983-85. Member, District of Columbia Community Humanities Council, 1983-87, District of Columbia Educational Institution Licensure Commission, 1988—, and Washington Jewish Campus Activities Board, 1988—. Public speaker; guest on television programs. Consultant to Educational Development Corp., Washington "Ear" Historical Project, and Associates for Renewal in Education.

MEMBER: American Historical Association, Organization of American Historians, American Studies Association, Immigration History Group, Urban Affairs Association.

WRITINGS:

A City and Its Universities: Public Policy in Chicago, 1892-1919, University of North Carolina Press, 1980.

(Editor with Frank R. Breul) *Compassion and Responsibility: Readings in the History of Social Welfare Policy,* University of Chicago Press, 1980.

The Center of a Metropolis: Washington since 1954, Associates for Renewal in Education, 1980.

Crisis of Confidence: The Reputation of Washington's Public Schools in the Twentieth Century, University of the District of Columbia, 1982.

The Governance of Education in the District of Columbia: An Historical Analysis of Current Issues, University of the District of Columbia, 1982.

The Regulation of Housing in the District of Columbia: An Historical Analysis of Policy Issues, University of the District of Columbia, 1983.

(Editor with Helen Young) *Housing Washington's People: Public Policy in Retrospect,* University of the District of Columbia, 1983.

(Editor with Young) *Managing the Nation's Capital,* University of the District of Columbia, 1986.

Democracy, Federalism and the Governance of the Nation's Capital, 1790-1974, University of the District of Columbia, 1987.

Also contributor to *Encyclopedia of Social Work.* Contributor of approximately twenty articles and reviews to scholarly journals and newspapers.

BIOGRAPHICAL/CRITICAL SOURCES:

PERIODICALS

American Historical Review, June, 1981.

* * *

DORIAN, Harry
See HAMILTON, Charles (Harold St. John)

* * *

DOVER, K(enneth) J(ames) 1920-

PERSONAL: Born March 11, 1920, in Croydon, England; son of Percy Henry James (a civil servant) and Dorothy (Healey) Dover; married Audrey Latimer, March 17, 1947; children: Alan Hugh, Catherine Ruth. *Education:* Balliol College, Oxford, M.A., 1947; Merton College, Oxford, additional study, 1948. *Politics:* "Left of center." *Religion:* Agnostic.

ADDRESSES: Home—49 Hepburn Gardens, St. Andrews, Fife KY16 9LS, Scotland. *Office*—Office of Chancellor, University of St. Andrews, St. Andrews, Scotland.

CAREER: Oxford University, Balliol College, Oxford, England, fellow and tutor in classics, 1948-55; University of St. Andrews, St. Andrews, Scotland, professor of Greek, 1955-76, dean of faculty of arts, 1960-63, 1973-75; Oxford University, Corpus Christi College, president, 1976-86; University of St. Andrews, chancellor, 1986—. Visiting lecturer, Harvard University, 1960; Sather Visiting Professor of Classics, University of California, Berkeley, 1967; visiting professor of classics, Stanford University, 1988—. *Military service:* British Army, 1940-45; served in Africa and Italy; became lieutenant; mentioned in dispatches.

MEMBER: British Academy (fellow; president, 1978-81), Royal Society of Edinburgh (fellow), Society for the Promotion of Hellenic Studies (president, 1971-74), Society for the Promotion of Roman Studies, Classical Association (president, 1976), Linguistics Association of Great Britain.

AWARDS, HONORS: Knighted, 1977.

WRITINGS:

Greek Word Order, Cambridge University Press, 1960.
(Author of commentary) Thucydides, *History of the Peloponnesian War,* Books 6 and 7, Clarendon Press, 1965.
(Editor and author of introduction and commentary) Aristophanes, *Clouds,* Clarendon Press, 1968.
Lysias and the Corpus Lysiacum, University of California Press, 1968.
(Editor and author of introduction and commentary) Theocritus, *Selected Poems,* Macmillan, 1971.
Aristophanic Comedy, University of California Press, 1972.
Greek Homosexuality, Duckworth, 1978.
The Greeks, BBC Publications, 1980.
(Co-author and editor) *Ancient Greek Literature,* Oxford University Press, 1980.
(Editor and author of commentary with A. W. Gomme and A. Andrewes) *Historical Commentary on Thucydides,* Clarendon Press, 1981.
Greek and the Greeks, Blackwell, 1988.
The Greeks and Their Legacy, Blackwell, 1989.

Co-editor, *Classical Quarterly,* 1962-68.

WORK IN PROGRESS: Writing on the language of Greek prose literature; an edition of Aristophanes' *Frogs,* with commentary; an autobiography.

SIDELIGHTS: K. J. Dover is "a Hellenist of unimpeachable credentials," writes Erich Segal in the *New York Times Book Review.* Segal's remarks occur in a review of Dover's groundbreaking text on Hellenic society, *Greek Homosexuality.* Long recognized as a historically important aspect of Greek society during the classical period, the topic of homosexuality has in Segal's words "been all but ignored" by historians. "Clearly," he remarks, "this has been a difficult subject for scholars to deal with." *Greek Homosexuality* is thus an attempt to shed light on an important issue. The book outlines the role of male sexual relations in Greek education, sport, and philosophy, drawing on classical art and literature for examples. *Greek Homosexuality* is a "sound, scholarly . . . work," according to a reviewer for the *Christian Century.* And Segal summarizes: "One cannot underestimate the importance of Mr. Dover's book. With philological brilliance and scholarly objectivity, he presents facts that can no longer be ignored. It is a step toward understanding the complex nature of the Greeks, whom we claim as cultural fathers."

In addition to Greek, Dover is competent in Latin, Italian, Spanish, German, Dutch, French, and modern Greek.

AVOCATIONAL INTERESTS: "Unspoilt natural scenery, fauna and flora, comparative and historical linguistics, the processes of change in ethics, religion and society."

BIOGRAPHICAL/CRITICAL SOURCES:

PERIODICALS

Christian Century, July 16, 1980.
New York Times Book Review, April 8, 1979.
Times Literary Supplement, April 3, 1981.

* * *

DRAKE, Frank
See HAMILTON, Charles (Harold St. John)

* * *

DRAPER, Alfred 1924-

PERSONAL: Born October 26, 1924, in London, England; son of Richard and Florence (Wills) Draper; married Barbara Pilcher, March 31, 1951; children: Nicholas, Antony. *Education:* Studied four years at North West Polytechnic, London.

ADDRESSES: Home—31 Oakridge Ave., Radlett, Hertfordshire, England.

CAREER: Daily Express and *Daily Mail,* London, England, journalist specializing in crime and murder trials at home and reporting from abroad, 1950-1972. *Military service:* Royal Navy; served in Atlantic and Pacific theaters; became sub-lieutenant.

MEMBER: Society of Authors, National Union of Journalists.

AWARDS, HONORS: Runner-up in Macmillan/Panther first crime novel competition, 1970, for *Swansong for a Rare Bird.*

WRITINGS:

Swansong for a Rare Bird, Coward, 1969.
The Death Penalty, Macmillan, 1972.
Smoke without Fire, Arlington Books, 1974.
The Prince of Wales, New English Library, 1975.
The Story of the Goons, Everest, 1976.
Operation Fish, Cassell, 1978.
Amritsar: The Massacre that Ended the Raj, Cassell, 1981, reprinted as *The Amritsar Massacre: Twilight of the Raj,* Buchan & Enright, 1987.

Dawns like Thunder, Arrow Books, 1987.
Scoops and Swindles, Buchan & Enright, 1988.
The Con Man, Piatkus Books, 1987, Doubleday, 1988.

"GREY SEAL" SERIES

Grey Seal, Macdonald Futura, 1981.
. . . *: The Restless Waves,* Macdonald Futura, 1983.
. . . *: The Raging of the Deep,* Piatkus Books, 1985.
. . . *: Storm over Singapore,* Piatkus Books, 1986.
. . . *: The Great Avenging Day,* Piatkus Book, 1988.

OTHER

Contributor to British dailies and numerous magazines. Some novels also translated into German, French, and Dutch.

WORK IN PROGRESS: A nonfiction account of SAS activities behind German lines in World War II, to be published in 1990; a novel about Burma.

MEDIA ADAPTATIONS: The Death Penalty was made into a film shown in France.

* * *

DRUCKER, H. M.
See DRUCKER, Henry M(atthew)

* * *

DRUCKER, Henry M(atthew) 1942-
(H. M. Drucker)

PERSONAL: Born April 29, 1942, in Paterson, N.J.; son of Arthur (a merchant) and Frances (Katz) Drucker; married Nancy Newman (a lecturer), March 29, 1975. *Education:* Allegheny College, B.A., 1964; London School of Economics and Political Science, Ph.D., 1967.

ADDRESSES: Home—33 Bainton Rd., Oxford, England. *Office*—Oxford University, University Offices, Wellington Square, Oxford OX1 2JD, England.

CAREER: University of Edinburgh, Edinburgh, Scotland, assistant lecturer, 1967, lecturer, 1967-78, senior lecturer in politics, 1978-86; Oxford University, Oxford, England, director of University Development Office, 1987—.

WRITINGS:

The Political Uses of Ideology, Macmillan, 1974.
(Editor with others) *The Scottish Government Yearbook,* six volumes, Unit for Study of Government in Scotland, Edinburgh University, 1976-82.
Breakaway: The Scottish Labour Party, EUSPB (Edinburgh), 1978.
Doctrine and Ethos in the Labour Party, Allen & Unwin, 1979.
(Editor) *Multi-Party Britain,* Macmillan, 1980.
(With Gordon Brown) *The Politics of Nationalism and Devolution,* Longman, 1980.
(Editor and author of introduction) *John P. Mackintosh on Scotland,* Longman, 1982.
(General editor) *Developments in British Politics,* Macmillan, 1983.
(General editor) *Developments in British Politics 2,* Macmillan, 1986.

DUKORE, Bernard F. 1931-

PERSONAL: Born July 11, 1931, in New York, N.Y.; married second wife, Barbara Cromwell, 1986. *Education:* Brooklyn College (now Brooklyn College of the City University of New York), A.B., 1952; Ohio State University, M.A., 1953; University of Illinois, Ph.D., 1957.

ADDRESSES: Office—Humanities Center, Virginia Polytechnic and State University, Blacksburg, Va. 24061.

CAREER: Hunter College in the Bronx (now Herbert H. Lehman College of the City University of New York), Bronx, N.Y., instructor in drama, 1957-60; University of Southern California, Los Angeles, assistant professor of drama, 1960-62; California State College at Los Angeles (now California State University, Los Angeles), 1962-66, began as assistant professor, became associate professor of drama; City University of New York, New York, N.Y., 1966-72, began as associate professor, became professor of drama; University of Hawaii, Honolulu, professor of drama, 1972-86; Virginia Polytechnic and State University, Blacksburg, university distinguished professor of theatre arts and humanities, 1986—. Visiting fellow at Humanities Research Centre, Australian National University, 1979. *Military service:* U.S. Army, 1954-56; became sergeant.

MEMBER: American Educational Theatre Association, American Society for Theatre Research.

AWARDS, HONORS: Guggenheim fellow, 1969-70; American Theatre Association fellow, 1975; National Endowment for the Humanities fellow, 1976-77, 1984-85.

WRITINGS:

(Editor and author of introduction) George Etherege, *The Man of Mode,* Chandler Publishing, 1962.
(Editor with Ruby Cohn) *Twentieth Century Drama: England, Ireland, United States,* Random House, 1966.
Saint Joan: A Screenplay by Bernard Shaw, University of Washington Press, 1968.
(Editor with Daniel C. Gerould) *Avant-Garde Drama: Major Plays and Documents, Post World War I,* Bantam, 1969.
(Editor with Robert O'Brien) *Tragedy: Ten Major Plays,* Bantam, 1969.
Bernard Shaw, Director, University of Washington Press, 1970.
(Editor) John Gassner, *A Treasury of the Theatre,* Volume 2, revised edition, Simon & Schuster, 1970.
(Compiler) *Drama and Revolution,* Holt, 1970.
(Compiler) *Documents for Drama and Revolution,* Holt, 1970.
Bernard Shaw, Playwright: Aspects of Shavian Drama, University of Missouri Press, 1973.
Dramatic Theory and Criticism, Holt, 1974.
Seventeen Plays: Sophocles to Baraka, Crowell, 1976.
Where Laughter Stops: Pinter's Tragicomedy, University of Missouri Press, 1976.
Money and Politics in Ibsen, Shaw, and Brecht, University of Missouri Press, 1980.
(Editor and author of introduction) *The Collected Screenplays of Bernard Shaw,* University of Georgia Press, 1980.
The Theatre of Peter Barnes, Heinemann Educational, 1981.
(Compiler) *Bernard Shaw's "Arms and the Man": A Composite Production Book,* Southern Illinois University Press, 1982.
Harold Pinter, Grove, 1982.
American Dramatists, 1918-1945, Grove, 1984.
"Death of a Salesman" and "The Crucible": Text and Performance, Macmillan, 1989.

Contributor to *Tulane Drama Review, Educational Theatre Journal, Modern Drama, Theatre Survey,* and other drama journals.

* * *

DUMAS, Andre 1918-

PERSONAL: Born December 7, 1918, in Montauban, France; son of Andre (a doctor) and Therese (a professor; maiden name, Maury) Dumas; married Francine Buss (a social worker), July 11, 1944; children: Michel, Annick (Mrs. Christian Guillemot). *Education:* University of Montpellier, license (philosophy), 1939, doctorate (Protestant theology), 1941. *Religion:* Protestant.

ADDRESSES: Home—45 rue de Sevres, 75006 Paris, France. *Office*—Faculte de Theologie, 83 blvd. Arago, 75014 Paris, France.

CAREER: Social worker in internment camps in southern France, 1942-43; general secretary of the French student movement in Paris, France, 1943-49; pastor of the French Reformed Church in Pau, France, 1949-56; student chaplain in Strasbourg, France, 1959-61; University of Paris, professor of Protestant theology, 1961-84.

MEMBER: World Council of Churches.

AWARDS, HONORS: Doctorate honoris causa from University of Lausanne, 1979; doctorate state from University of Strasbourg, 1982.

WRITINGS:

La Guerre d'Algerie (title means "The Algerian War"), Zollikon (Zurich), 1959.

Le Controle de naissances (title means "Birth Control"), Bergers & Mages (Paris), 1965.

Foi et ideologie (title means "Faith and Ideology"), Tempoe Presenca (Rio de Janeiro), 1968.

Une Theologie de la realite: Dietrich Bonhoeffer, Labor (Geneva), 1968, translation by Robert McAfee Brown published as *Dietrich Bonhoeffer: Theologian of Reality,* Macmillan, 1971.

Croire et douter (title means "Believing and Doubting"), Saint-Paul (Paris), 1971.

Prospective et prophetie (title means "Futurology and Prophecy"), Cerf (Paris), 1971.

Theologies politiques et vie de l'eglise, Chalet (Paris), 1977, translation by John Bowden published as *Political Theology and the Life of the Church,* Westminster, 1978.

Nommer Dieu (title means "Names for God"), Cerf, 1978.

Cent prieres possibles (title means "Hundred Possible Prayers"), Cana (Paris), 1982.

L'Amour et la mort au cinema: 1945-1982 (title means "Love and Death in Movies: 1945-1982"), Labor, 1982.

Protestants, Bergers & Mages, 1987.

Marie de Nazareth, Labor, 1989.

SIDELIGHTS: Andre Dumas told *CA:* "My interest has been to look at the consistency of biblical analogy in confrontation with actual questioning situations, like sexuality, industrial society, the common good and the battle of classes, epistomological shifts."

BIOGRAPHICAL/CRITICAL SOURCES:

PERIODICALS

Christian Century, December 1, 1971.

Commonweal, September 29, 1972.

E

EBON, Martin 1917-
(Eric Ward)

PERSONAL: Born May 27, 1917, in Hamburg, Germany; came to United States in 1938; son of Julius (a manufacturer) and Martha (Ludwig) Ebon; married Chariklia S. Baltazzi, April 25, 1949; children: Andrew Richard. *Education:* University of Hamburg, M.A., 1934.

ADDRESSES: Home—5616 Netherland Ave., Riverdale, N.Y. 10471.

CAREER: Held various positions in book and magazine retailing and was managing editor of foreign language division, Overseas News Agency; U.S. Information Agency, New York City, information officer on Far Eastern desks, 1950-52; Hill & Knowlton, Inc. (public relations), New York City, account executive, 1952-53; Parapsychology Foundation, Inc., New York City, administrative secretary and editor, 1953-65; Lombard Associates, Inc. (public relations and publications consultants), New York City, president, 1962-82. Consulting editor, New American Library (publishers), 1966-83; executive editor of hardcover book division, Playboy Press, 1971-72. Lecturer in Division of Social Sciences, New School for Social Research, 1949-50, 1955-56, 1967. Consultant, Foundation for Research on the Nature of Man, 1966-67. *Wartime service:* Member of staff, U.S. Office of War Information, and, for a short time, information officer with U.S. Department of State, both during World War II.

MEMBER: American Association for the Advancement of Science, American Sociological Association, American Academy of Political and Social Science, American Society for Psychical Research.

AWARDS, HONORS: Freedoms Foundation Award for editorials in *Saturday Evening Post,* 1948-62.

WRITINGS:

World Communism Today, McGraw, 1948.
Malenkov: Stalin's Successor, McGraw, 1953.
Svetlana: The Story of Stalin's Daughter, New American Library, 1967.
Prophecy in Our Time, New American Library, 1968.
Che: The Making of a Legend, Universe Books, 1969.
Lin Piao: The Life and Writings of China's New Ruler, Stein & Day, 1970.
Witchcraft Today, New American Library, 1971.
Every Woman's Guide to Abortion, Universe Books, 1971.
They Knew the Unknown, World Publishing, 1971.
The Truth about Vitamin E, Bantam, 1972.
(Under pseudonym Eric Ward; with Ursala Russell) *The President's Daughter,* Bantam, 1973.
The Devil's Bride: Exorcism, Past and Present, Harper, 1974.
The Essential Vitamin Counter, Bantam, 1974.
Which Vitamins Do You Need?, Bantam, 1974.
Saint Nicholas: Life and Legend, Harper, 1975.
The Satan Trap: Dangers of the Occult, Doubleday, 1976.
The Relaxation Controversy, New American Library, 1976.
The Evidence for Life after Death, New American Library, 1977.
Miracles, Signet, 1981.
Psychic Warfare: Threat or Illusion?, McGraw, 1983.
The Andropov File, McGraw, 1983.
Nikita Khrushchev, Chelsea House, 1986.
The Soviet Propaganda Machine, McGraw, 1987.

COMPILER OR EDITOR

True Experiences in Prophecy (also see below), New American Library, 1967.
True Experiences in Telepathy (also see below), New American Library, 1967.
Beyond Space and Time: An ESP Casebook (contains *True Experiences in Prophecy* and *True Experiences in Telepathy*), New American Library, 1967.
(And author of introduction) *Communicating with the Dead,* New American Library, 1968.
(And contributor) *Maharishi, the Guru: An International Symposium,* Pearl Books, 1968, published as *Maharishi: The Founder of Transcendental Meditation,* New American Library, 1975.
True Experiences with Ghosts, New American Library, 1968.
True Experiences in Exotic ESP, New American Library, 1968.
The Psychic Reader, World Publishing, 1969.
(And contributor) *Reincarnation in the Twentieth Century,* New American Library, 1969.
(And author of introduction) Danton M. Walker, *I Believe in Ghosts: True Stories of Some Haunted Celebrities and Their Celebrated Haunts,* Taplinger, 1969.
Test Your ESP, World Publishing, 1970.
Psychic Discoveries by the Russians, New American Library, 1971.

(And author of introduction) *Exorcism: Fact Not Fiction,* New American Library, 1974.

(And contributor) *The Amazing Uri Geller,* New American Library, 1975.

The Riddle of the Bermuda Triangle, New American Library, 1975.

Five Chinese Communist Plays, John Day, 1975.

TM: How to Find Peace of Mind through Meditation, New American Library, 1976.

Mysterious Pyramid Power, New American Library, 1976.

The Cloning of Man: A Brave New Hope—or Horror?, New American Library, 1978.

Demon Children, New American Library, 1978.

The Signet Handbook of Parapsychology, New American Library, 1978.

The World's Weirdest Cults, New American Library, 1979.

The World's Great Unsolved Mysteries, New American Library, 1981.

TRANSLATOR

(And author of introduction) Justin Jonas and others, *The Last Days of Luther,* Doubleday, 1970.

Johannes Lehmann, *The Jesus Establishment,* Doubleday, 1974.

Demosthenes Savramis, *Satanizing of Woman: Religion versus Sexuality,* Doubleday, 1974.

Adolf Rodewyk, *Possessed by Satan: The Church's Teaching of the Devil, Possession and Exorcism,* Doubleday, 1975.

OTHER

Contributor of articles and editorials to magazines, including *Saturday Evening Post.* Managing editor, *Tomorrow,* 1953-62; executive editor, *International Journal of Parapsychology,* 1959-62, and *Spiritual Frontiers* (quarterly), 1969-71, 1976-78; member of editorial board, *International Reports,* 1960-67.

WORK IN PROGRESS: Biographical research; psychology of economics and public affairs; contemporary events.

SIDELIGHTS: Martin Ebon once told *CA:* "From the very first, I have written books primarily for myself. When I came out of the Office of War Information after World War II, I looked for a one-volume encyclopedia-type book that would tell me all about communism. There was no such book, and so I wrote it." That first book, the successful *World Communism Today,* was praised in the *New York Times* by Arthur M. Schlesinger, Jr., as a "highly intelligent compilation of the crucial facts [about communism]." Written at the beginning of the Cold War era when fear of communism and the "Soviet threat" was escalating in the United States, *World Communism Today* provided "a patient, judicious and dispassionate report, country by country, of the present state and significance of communist activity throughout the world," said Schlesinger.

When *World Communism Today* was published, few Americans were informed about the actual beliefs, strengths, and goals of communist parties throughout the world; and Ebon pointed out in his book that many people were unreasonably afraid of the threat communism posed to the United States. According to Schlesinger, "One way to reduce the hysteria [caused by fear of communism] is to slap it in the face with facts. . . . [*World Communism Today*] is a valuable analysis of the nature of the Communist challenge—and [one] which those concerned about Soviet totalitarianism should take into account." In a *Nation* review, McAlister Coleman suggests that "Ebon's book rates a place on the shelves of anyone interested in knowing what means are employed by the Communists everywhere to achieve their professional ends." Finding that the book presents several perspectives—social, political, economic, as well as psychological—of what constitutes a communist, *Saturday Review of Literature* contributor Louis Fischer observes that Ebon "seems sweetly reasonable and factual, not very original or passionate, but solid, careful, eager to be safe. This book . . . contains no strident tones, no denunciations." And considering *World Communism Today* "a valuable corrective," Schlesinger comments that "its moderate tone and its hard factual substance should commend it to all serious students of foreign policy."

Ebon's abiding interest in the Soviet Union is reflected in several of his numerous other books; however, more than a few of his subjects died soon after Ebon wrote about them. Ebon explains in a *Newsday* interview with Leslie Hanscom: "I wrote a book about Malenkov (a brief successor to Stalin) and he didn't last very long. Then I wrote about Lin Piao (antagonist of Mao) and he was shot down over Manchuria. I wrote a book about Che Guevara and he was dead already." Dubbing it the "Ebon curse," the author was unaware that this unlucky coincidence would continue with *The Andropov File,* a profile of Leonid Brezhnev's successor Yuri Andropov: Hanscom questioned Ebon if "the Ebon curse brings his power to an early end, who will replace him?"; to which Ebon prophetically replied: "I have my eye on a man named Mikhail Gorbachev."

Ebon recently told *CA:* "To myself, and to aspiring writers, the most striking factor in being an author today is the lasting element of independence. Publishers come and go, and while there is much big-time consolidation of the publishing industry, there remains a varied and constantly changing market. As I look back on a half-century of writing, editing and administrative duties, I feel that these three aspects express the same essential skills: as authors, we are our own first editors, and much of our time is basically administrative, in that it consists of keeping files, organizing material, presenting outlines and negotiating agreements.

"Among the variety of books I have written, my interest in Soviet affairs and in parapsychology are most apparent. They came together in my book *Psychic Warfare: Threat or Illusion?,* which dealt with Soviet research in the potential of such fields as telepathy and clairvoyance. Among my recent books, my biography of Yuri Andropov, who was the top Soviet leader from late 1982 to early 1984, took only six weeks to write—but I had been collecting material on Andropov for about five years, so that virtually all the research was done when I sat down to do the actual writing. By contrast, my book on *The Soviet Propaganda Machine* took about three years of research and writing, on top of a lifetime of working in the vineyards of Sovietology." In a *New York City Tribune* review of this work, Ellsworth Raymond calls it "encyclopedic in scope and sparkling in style . . . the best popular study of Soviet propaganda to appear in many years." Acknowledging that "the influence of propaganda is almost impossible to measure," Raymond concludes that "this book vividly describes the enormous efforts of the Kremlin to mold the minds of mankind."

Indicating his plans to write "three future books, on disparate topics, including an autobiographical one," Ebon told *CA:* "After that, I hope to devote myself entirely to reading other people's books, of which there are, happily, an enormous number of splendid and admirable works."

BIOGRAPHICAL/CRITICAL SOURCES:

PERIODICALS

American Political Science Review, October, 1948.

Chicago Sun, February 5, 1948.

Los Angeles Times, September 8, 1983.
Los Angeles Times Book Review, January 31, 1982.
Nation, July 10, 1948.
Newsday, June 19, 1983.
New York City Tribune, August 19, 1987.
New Yorker, February 7, 1948.
New York Herald Tribune Weekly Book Review, February 15, 1948.
New York Times, February 1, 1948.
New York Times Book Review, November 6, 1983.
San Francisco Chronicle, March 21, 1948.
Saturday Review of Literature, February 14, 1948.
Times Literary Supplement, July 6, 1984.

* * *

EDWARDS, David L(awrence) 1929-

PERSONAL: Born January 20, 1929, in Cairo, Egypt; son of Lawrence Wright (a civil servant) and Phyllis Edwards; married Hilary Phillips; children: Helen, Katharine, Clare, Martin. *Education:* Magdalen College, Oxford, B.A., 1952, M.A., 1959.

ADDRESSES: Office—51 Bankside, London SE1 9JE, England.

CAREER: Ordained a priest of the Church of England. S.C.M. Press, London, England, managing director and editor, 1959-66; Cambridge University, Cambridge, England, fellow and dean of King's College, 1966-70; canon of Westminster and rector of St. Margaret's, London, 1970-78; Norwich Cathedral, Norwich, England, dean, 1978-83; Southwark Cathedral, London, provost, 1983—. Curate, St. Martin-in-the-Fields, London, 1958-66.

WRITINGS:

Not Angels but Anglicans, S.C.M. Press, 1958.
This Church of England, Church Information Office, 1962.
God's Cross in Our World, Westminster, 1963.
(Editor) *The Honest to God Debate: Some Reactions to the Book "Honest to God,"* Westminster, 1963.
(Editor) *Preparing for the Ministry of the 1970s: Essays on the British Churches by H. G. G. Herklots, James Whyte and Robin Sharp,* S.C.M. Press, 1964.
(Editor) *Christians in a New World,* S.C.M. Press, 1966.
F. J. Shirley: An Extraordinary Headmaster, S.P.C.K., 1969.
The Last Things Now, S.C.M. Press, 1969.
Religion and Change, Harper, 1969, revised edition, Hodder & Stoughton, 1974.
Leaders of the Church of England, 1828-1944, Oxford University Press, 1971, revised edition published as *Leaders of the Church of England, 1828-1978,* Hodder & Stoughton, 1978.
St. Margaret's, Westminster, Pitkin, 1972.
What Is Real in Christianity?, Westminster, 1972.
(Editor) *Unity: The Next Step?,* S.P.C.K., 1972.
The British Churches Turn to the Future: One Man's View of the Church Leaders' Conference, Birmingham, 1972, S.C.M. Press, 1973.
Ian Ramsey, Bishop of Durham: A Memoir, Oxford University Press, 1973.
What Anglicans Believe, Mowbray, 1974, published as *What Anglicans (Episcopalians) Believe,* Forward Movement Publications, 1975.
Jesus for Modern Man: An Introduction to the Gospels in Today's English Version, Fontana for the Bible Reading Fellowship, 1975.
A Key to the Old Testament, Collins, 1976.
Your Faith, Mowbray, 1978.
A Reason to Hope, Collins & World, 1978.
Christian England, Volume 1: *Its Story to the Reformation,* Oxford University Press, 1981, Volume 2: *From the Reformation to the Eighteenth Century,* Eerdmans, 1983, Volume 3: *From the Eighteenth Century to the First World War,* Eerdmans, 1984.
The Futures of Christianity, Morehouse, 1988.
(With John R. W. Stott) *Evangelical Essentials: A Liberal-Evangelical Dialogue,* Inter-Varsity Press, 1988.
The Cathedrals of Britain, Pitkin, 1989.

Also author of *A History of King's School, Canterbury,* Faber, and *Movements into Tomorrow,* S.C.M. Press. Compiler of abridgements from *Good News Bible in Today's English* version, for Collins: *Good News in Acts,* 1974; *Today's Story of Jesus,* 1976; *The Catholic Children's Bible,* 1979; and *The Children's Bible,* 1979.

SIDELIGHTS: In his 1969 work *Religion and Change,* David L. Edwards considers the challenges to religion which have arisen during the twentieth century. As John H. Wright observes in his *Commonweal* review, Edwards "has attempted to survey and evaluate the social and intellectual forces operating in twentieth-century Christianity and to project both a new shape for the Christian church and a new statement of Christian belief." While Edwards himself has described the book's purpose as "absurdly audacious," many reviewers find the study a success. "Here," remarks a *Times Literary Supplement* contributor, "is a quite superb account of the present scene combining a scholarly depth with a breadth of vision. While it is a masterly survey, brilliant in its detail," continues the critic, "there are excellent summaries and many constructive insights. It should be prescribed reading for all concerned with the Christian faith and its institutions as well as with the well-being of humanity."

In addition, Edwards has written a continuing series on the history of Christianity in Britain, *Christian England,* and it has received similar praise. In Volume II, for example, *From the Reformation to the Eighteenth Century,* Edwards "has brought to his task a remarkable acquaintance with recent historical writing on a two-hundred-year period," comments Eamon Duffy in the *Times Literary Supplement.* "His narrative never flags, and for all its compression is never clotted with mere brute fact. . . . Difficult theological issues are sketched out with remarkably little distortion, and all this with an admirable breadth of comprehension." Although Duffy faults the author for neglecting the popular aspect of religious development, he notes that "within its own terms of reference, it is difficult to see how this [volume] could have been better done." Duffy presents a similar assessment of Volume III, *From the Eighteenth Century to the First World War,* which he calls "a wide-ranging and lively book." While the critic notes in the London *Times* that "the book is not so much an analysis of a period as a gallery of significant characters," he admits that "this is a perfectly legitimate approach, [and] indeed it is difficult to see how [Edwards] could in any other way have produced so comprehensive and so entertaining a book."

BIOGRAPHICAL/CRITICAL SOURCES:

PERIODICALS

Commentary, January, 1970.
Commonweal, December 26, 1969.
Times (London), August 16, 1984.
Times Literary Supplement, August 21, 1969, February 5, 1982, February 24, 1984, September 21, 1984, January 8, 1988.

EDWARDS, Philip 1923-

PERSONAL: Born February 7, 1923, in Barrow-in-Furness, England; son of Robert Henry (in politics) and Bessie (Pritchard) Edwards; married Hazel Valentine, July 8, 1947 (deceased); married Sheila Wilkes, May 8, 1952; children: (second marriage) Matthew, Charles, Richard, Catherine. *Education:* University of Birmingham, B.A., 1942, M.A., 1946, Ph.D., 1960.

ADDRESSES: Home—12 South Bank, Oxton, Birkenhead L43 5UP, England. *Office*—Department of English Language and Literature, University of Liverpool, P.O. Box 147, Liverpool L69 3BX, England.

CAREER: University of Birmingham, Birmingham, England, lecturer in English, 1946-60; University of Dublin, Trinity College, Dublin, Ireland, professor of English literature, 1960-66; University of Essex, Colchester, England, professor of literature, 1966-74; University of Liverpool, Liverpool, England, professor of English literature, 1974—. Visiting professor, University of Michigan, 1964-65, Williams College, 1969, and Otago University, New Zealand, 1980. *Military service:* British Navy, 1942-45; became sub-lieutenant.

AWARDS, HONORS: Fellow, Harvard University, 1954-55; Fellow of the British Academy, 1986.

WRITINGS:

Sir Walter Ralegh, Longmans, Green, 1953.
(Editor) Thomas Kyd, *The Spanish Tragedy,* Methuen, 1958.
Thomas Kyd and Early Elizabethan Tragedy, Longmans, Green, 1965.
(With Roger Joseph McHugh) *Jonathan Swift, 1667-1967: A Dublin Tercentary Tribute,* Dolmen Press, 1967.
Shakespeare and the Confines of Art, Barnes & Noble, 1968.
(Editor) William Shakespeare, *King Lear,* Macmillan, 1975.
(Editor) Shakespeare, *Pericles, Prince of Tyre,* Penguin, 1976.
(Editor with Colin Gibson) *The Plays and Poems of Philip Massinger,* Oxford University Press, 1976.
Threshold of a Nation: A Study in English and Irish Drama, Cambridge University Press, 1979.
(Editor with Inga-Stine Ewbank and G. K. Hunter) *Shakespeare's Styles: Essays in Honour of Kenneth Muir,* Cambridge University Press, 1980.
(Editor) Shakespeare, *Hamlet,* Cambridge University Press, 1985.
Shakespeare: A Writer's Progress, Oxford University Press, 1986.
Last Voyages: Cavendish, Hudson, Ralegh, Oxford University Press, 1988.

Contributor to *Shakespeare Survey* and other journals.

SIDELIGHTS: The Plays and Poems of Philip Massinger, edited by Philip Edwards and Colin Gibson, "is a model of what such things should be: a splendid, scholarly achievement that is intelligent, thorough and humane," writes *Times Literary Supplement* contributor Ann Barton. "It does Massinger himself a great service, and it is also of incalculable value to students of Jacobean and Caroline drama generally. . . . The editors offer an excellent general introduction concerned with Massinger's life and theatrical career, and with some of the fluctuations of his literary reputation." She concludes: "There are a number of significant new discoveries recorded here." In *Threshold of a Nation: A Study in English and Irish Drama,* "Philip Edwards has had the original and interesting idea of examining the English drama of Shakespeare's time and the Irish drama of Yeats's time under the same light," explains Katharine Worth in the *Times Literary Supplement.* "His approach is so fruitful that one can only wonder why it was never tried before." Overall, Worth finds the book "a spirited, scholarly, and absorbing study." And Edwards' book *Shakespeare's Styles: Essays in Honour of Kenneth Muir* has also received praise. *Times Literary Supplement* contributor Katherine Duncan-Jones says the collection offers "a high level of originality and interest" and believes that "the book deserves to become a critical classic."

Edwards wrote *CA* in the preface to the 1981 edition of *Shakespeare and the Confines of Art,* that he has "continued to put forward the thesis basic to [*Shakespeare and the Confines of Art*], that a main strand in Shakespeare's greatness is the way in which his works so frequently question their own right to exist."

BIOGRAPHICAL/CRITICAL SOURCES:

BOOKS

Edwards, Philip, *Shakespeare and the Confines of Art,* Barnes & Noble, 1968.

PERIODICALS

Times Literary Supplement, May 20, 1977, February 29, 1980, October 3, 1980.

* * *

EIBLING, Harold Henry 1905-1976

PERSONAL: Born August 5, 1905, in Dola, Ohio; died January 2, 1976; son of Henry Williams (a civil servant) and Sarah (Stanyer) Eibling; married Evelyn Agner, August 14, 1929; children: Judith Anne (Mrs. Robert C. Ackerman), Stephen Harold, David Michael. *Education:* Ohio Northern University, B.Sc., 1926; Ohio State University, M.A., 1932, Ph.D., 1950. *Religion:* Presbyterian.

CAREER: Liberty Township Schools, Findlay, Ohio, teacher, principal, and superintendent of schools, 1926-36; superintendent of schools in Maumee, Ohio, 1936-47, Elyria, Ohio, 1947-49, Akron, Ohio, 1949-50, Canton, Ohio, 1950-56, and Columbus, Ohio, 1956-71; educational consultant, 1971-76. Member of board of trustees, Ohio Northern University, beginning 1960; board member of several reading organizations, banks, and civic organizations.

MEMBER: American Association of School Administrators (president, 1970-71), Central Ohio Teachers Association (president, 1959), Phi Delta Kappa, Alpha Phi Gamma, Kappa Phi Kappa, Masons, Rotary Club.

AWARDS, HONORS: D.Sc. in Ed., Mount Union College, 1953; Ph.D., Northern Ohio University, 1959; Freedoms Foundation educator's medal, 1963; LL.D., Miami University, Oxford, Ohio, 1963; Liberty Bell Award, Columbus Bar Association, 1964; Superintendent of the Year award, Ohio Education Association, 1966; honor award, State of Ohio Department of Education, 1971; also recipient of many awards from civic groups and institutions in the Columbus, Ohio, area.

WRITINGS:

Our United States: A Bulwark of Freedom, Laidlaw Brothers, 1960, published as *History of Our United States,* 1965.
(With Fred M. King and James Harlow) *Great Names in American History,* Laidlaw Brothers, 1965.
Our Country, Laidlaw Brothers, 1965.
Our Beginnings in the Old World, Laidlaw Brothers, 1965.
The Story of America, Laidlaw Brothers, 1965.

(With Carlton Jackson and Vito Perrone) *Foundations of Freedom: United States History to 1877,* Laidlaw Brothers, 1973, 2nd edition, 1977.
(With Jackson and Perrone) *Challenge and Change, United States History: The Second Century,* Laidlaw Brothers, 1973.
(With Jackson and Perrone) *Two Centuries of Progress: United States History,* Laidlaw Brothers, 1974.

Also author of *World Background for American History,* 1968. Contributor of articles to educational journals.

WORK IN PROGRESS: A historical novel on man's achievements through the ages.

AVOCATIONAL INTERESTS: Travel (to Europe, Australia, and New Zealand).*

* * *

EINSTEIN, Charles 1926-

PERSONAL: Born August 2, 1926, in Boston, Mass.; son of Harry (the radio comedian "Parkyakarkas") and Lillian (Anshen) Einstein; married Corrine Pendlebury, April 18, 1947; children: David, Michael, Jeffrey, Laurie. *Education:* University of Chicago, Ph.B., 1945.

CAREER: International News Service, New York City and Chicago, Ill., reporter, sports and feature writer, 1945-53; *San Francisco Examiner,* San Francisco, Calif., general columnist, entertainment editor, and baseball writer, 1958-61; *San Francisco Chronicle,* San Francisco, baseball columnist, 1965-70; *Sport,* New York City, columnist, 1968-70; writer. Editor of first wire-service news report specifically designed for television, 1950; chief writer, Goddard for governor, Arizona, 1964 and 1966; Northern California campaign director, Unruh for governor, 1970.

MEMBER: Authors League of America, Writers Guild of America, American Newspaper Guild, Baseball Writers Association of America.

AWARDS, HONORS: Benjamin Franklin citation, University of Illinois, 1957, for short story; American Cancer Society journalism citation, 1957; Junior Book Award, Boys' Clubs of America, 1964.

WRITINGS:

NONFICTION

(With Willie Mays) *Born to Play Ball,* Putnam, 1955.
(Editor) *The Fireside Book of Baseball,* Simon & Schuster, 1956.
(Editor) *The Second Fireside Book of Baseball,* Simon & Schuster, 1958.
A Flag for San Francisco, Simon & Schuster, 1962.
Willie Mays: Coast to Coast Giant, Putnam, 1963.
(With Mays) *My Life in and out of Baseball,* Dutton, 1966.
(With Juan Marichal) *A Pitcher's Story,* Doubleday, 1967.
(With Orlando Cepeda) *My Ups and Downs in Baseball,* Putnam, 1968.
(Editor) *The Third Fireside Book of Baseball,* introduction by Stan Musial, Simon & Schuster, 1968.
How to Coach, Manage, and Play Little League Baseball, Simon & Schuster, 1968, reprinted, 1986.
How to Win at Blackjack: The Einstein System, Cornerstone Library, 1968.
(With Art Fisher and Neal Marshall) *Garden of Innocents,* Dutton, 1972.
(With Mary Ann Harbert) *Captivity: How I Survived 44 Months as a Prisoner of the Red Chinese,* Delacorte, 1973.
The San Francisco Forty-Niners, Macmillan, 1974.
Willie's Time: A Memoir, edited by Jean Ervin, Lippincott, 1979.
(Editor) *The Baseball Reader: Favorites from the Fireside Books of Baseball,* Harper, 1980.
Basic Blackjack Betting, Gamblers Book Shelf, 1980.
How to Communicate: The Manning, Selvage & Lee Guide to Clear Writing and Speech, McGraw, 1985.
(Editor) *The Fireside Book of Baseball,* 4th edition, introduction by Reggie Jackson, Simon & Schuster, 1987.

OTHER

The Bloody Spur (novel), Dell, 1953.
The Only Game in Town (novel), Dell, 1955.
Wiretap! (novel), Dell, 1955.
The Last Laugh (novel), Dell, 1956.
No Time at All (novel; also see below), Simon & Schuster, 1957.
"Key Location" (play), first produced in Phoenix, Ariz., by Arizona Repertory Theatre, 1958.
(Adaptor from television series) *Naked City,* Dell, 1958.
The Day New York Went Dry (novel), Fawcett, 1965.
(Adaptor from motion picture) *Woman Times Seven,* Fawcett, 1967.
The Blackjack Hijack (novel), Random House, 1976.

Also author of "No Time at All," a teleplay based on his novel, 1957; author of three hundred radio scripts. Contributor to *Playboy, Sport, True, Argosy, Atlantic, Colliers, Esquire, Saturday Evening Post,* and other periodicals.

SIDELIGHTS: Although he has written several novels and screenplays, Charles Einstein is best known for his collections of anecdotes and memoirs about baseball. A sports writer since the mid-1940s, Einstein has edited several volumes of the popular "Fireside" collections of baseball literature. The 1980 compilation *The Baseball Reader: Favorites from the Fireside Books of Baseball* "contains some of the choicest examples of this pairing [of writers and baseball]," notes V. K. Burg in the *Christian Science Monitor.* Containing poems, autobiography, newspaper and magazine articles and columns, fiction, and even radio transcripts, *The Baseball Reader* "covers a broad miscellany of the game's moments, real and imagined, from baseball's roughly organized, salty origins after the Civil War to the sixth game of the 1977 World Series," describes Burg. Einstein's collection is the "baseball book [of the year] to read if you can read only one," asserts *Times Literary Supplement* contributor Donald Hall. Calling the book "well-edited," Hall adds that "the book continually surprises, as we turn each corner to find the unexpected: H. L. Mencken, Grantland Rice, Kenneth Patchen, 'Casey at the Bat. . . .' " As Burg concludes, the quality of this compilation is such that "the only thing that might have improved this book is twice as much of it."

Einstein similarly applies a broad spectrum of baseball happenings in *Willie's Time: A Memoir,* a reminiscence which *Los Angeles Times Book Review* contributor Grover Sales terms a "breezy, engaging pastiche of statistics, anecdotes and socio-political history spanning [Willie] May's active career from Truman to Nixon." Recalling both the state of the country and of the sport during the Hall of Famer's era, *Willie's Time* "is a superb blend of sports lore and American history," notes Marc Ongiman in the *Christian Science Monitor.* "Where others might have tried to concoct tenuous connections or cause-effect relationships between Mays's life and the course of America in the '50s, '60s, and early '70s, Einstein has chosen merely to select and intertwine the most important—at least in his mind, and it is a memoir—

events of the two stories." Calling Einstein's account "authentically evocative of Mays's career," the *New York Times*'s Christopher Lehmann-Haupt similarly observes that while "the connections [Einstein] makes between Mays and history sometimes seem subjective ones, there is one important sense in which they do not. That is Mays's significance in the history of civil rights." In recounting Mays's legend through statistics, anecdotes, and opinions, "Einstein has swallowed the myth whole, and we are the winners for it," comments Joel Oppenheimer in the *New York Times Book Review.* The critic adds that while there is an emphasis on Mays' career, "what makes this book work is that the myth is inextricably entwined with Mr. Einstein's life and our times, so that it becomes much more than a simple collection of anecdotes."

MEDIA ADAPTATIONS: Einstein's novel *The Bloody Spur* was the basis for the 1956 RKO Pictures film, "While the City Sleeps."

BIOGRAPHICAL/CRITICAL SOURCES:

BOOKS

Einstein, Charles, *Willie's Time: A Memoir,* edited by Jean Ervin, Lippincott, 1979.

PERIODICALS

Christian Science Monitor, July 9, 1979, August 27, 1980.
Los Angeles Times Book Review, July 8, 1979.
New York Times, June 18, 1979.
New York Times Book Review, May 30, 1976, June 17, 1979.
Times Literary Supplement, February 27, 1981.*

* * *

ELCOCK, Howard J(ames) 1942-

PERSONAL: Born June 6, 1942, in Shrewsbury, England; son of George (a coal merchant) and Marion S. (Edge) Elcock. *Education:* Queen's College, Oxford, B.A., 1964, B.Phil., 1966, M.A., 1968. *Politics:* Labour Party. *Religion:* Anglican.

ADDRESSES: Home—23, Wolsingham Rd., Gosforth, Newcastle-upon-Tyne NE3 4RP, England. *Office*—Department of Economics and Government, Newcastle-upon-Tyne Polytechnic, Newcastle-upon-Tyne NE1 8ST, England.

CAREER: University of Hull, Hull, Yorkshire, England, lecturer, 1966-77, senior lecturer in politics, 1977-81; Newcastle-upon-Tyne Polytechnic, Newcastle-upon-Tyne, England, head of School of Government, 1981-87, professor of government, 1984—. Member of Humberside County Council, 1973-81.

MEMBER: Political Studies Association, Royal Institute of Public Administration, Royal Yachting Association, Yorkshire Ouse Sailing Club, Tynemouth Sailing Club.

WRITINGS:

Administrative Justice, Longmans, Green, 1969.
Portrait of a Decision: The Council of Four and the Treaty of Versailles, Methuen, 1972.
Political Behaviour, Methuen, 1976.
(With Stuart Haywood) *The Buck Stops Where? Accountability and Control in the NHS,* University of Hull, 1980.
(With Michael Wheaton) *Local Government: Politicians, Professionals and the Public in Local Authorities,* Methuen, 1982, 2nd edition, 1986.
(With others) *What Sort of Society? Economic and Social Policy in Modern Britain,* Martin Robertson & Co., 1982.
(Editor with M. Stephenson) *Public Policy and Management,* Polytechnic Products, 1985.
(Editor G. Jordan) *Learning from Local Authority Budgeting,* Avebury Press, 1987.
(With Jordan) *Policy, Politics and Budgets,* Longman, 1989.

WORK IN PROGRESS: A book on public administration in the 1990s; an essay on the Fire Service and local authorities for a volume on the Fire Brigades Union.

AVOCATIONAL INTERESTS: Dingy sailing, music.

* * *

ELLIOTT, Janice 1931-

PERSONAL: Born October 14, 1931, in Derby, England; daughter of Douglas John (an advertising executive) and Dorothy (Wilson) Elliott; married Robert Cooper (a public affairs adviser for an oil company), April 11, 1959; children: Alexander. *Education:* Oxford University, B.A. (with honors), 1953.

ADDRESSES: Home—England. *Agent*—Richard Scott Simon, Ltd., 32 College Cross, London N1 1PR, England.

CAREER: Journalist in London, England, 1954-62; novelist, free-lance journalist, and critic, 1962—.

MEMBER: PEN (England), Society of Authors.

AWARDS, HONORS: Secret Places was awarded the Southern Arts Award for Literature.

WRITINGS:

NOVELS

Cave with Echoes, Secker & Warburg, 1962.
The Somnambulists, Secker & Warburg, 1964.
The Godmother, Secker & Warburg, 1966, Holt, 1967.
The Buttercup Chain, Secker & Warburg, 1967.
The Singing Head, Secker & Warburg, 1968.
Angels Falling, Knopf, 1969.
The Kindling, Knopf, 1970.
The Birthday Unicorn (children's novel), Gollancz, 1970.
A State of Peace (first novel in trilogy), Knopf, 1971.
Private Life (second novel in trilogy), Hodder & Stoughton, 1972.
Alexander in the Land of Mog (children's novel), Brockhampton Press, 1973.
Heaven on Earth (third novel in trilogy), Hodder & Stoughton, 1975.
A Loving Eye, Hodder & Stoughton, 1977.
The Honey Tree, Hodder & Stoughton, 1978.
Summer People, Hodder & Stoughton, 1980.
Secret Places, Hodder & Stoughton, 1981, St. James Press, 1982.
The Country of Her Dreams, Hodder & Stoughton, 1982.
The Incompetent Dragon (children's novel), Blackie & Son, 1982.
Magic, Hodder & Stoughton, 1983.
The Italian Lesson, Hodder & Stoughton, 1985.
Dr. Gruber's Daughter, Hodder & Stoughton, 1986.
The Sadness of Witches, Hodder & Stoughton, 1987.
The King Awakes (children's novel), Walker Books, 1987.
Life on the Nile, Hodder & Stoughton, 1989.

CONTRIBUTOR TO ANTHOLOGIES

A. D. Maclean, editor, *Winter's Tales,* Macmillan, 1966.
Derwent May, editor, *Good Talk,* Gollancz, 1968.
Judith Burnley, editor, *Penguin Modern Stories 10,* Penguin, 1972.

A. S. Burack, editor, *Techniques of Novel Writing,* Writer, Inc., 1973.

James Hale, editor, *The Midnight Ghost Book,* Barrie & Jenkins, 1978.

Caroline Hobhouse, editor, *Winter's Tales 25,* Macmillan, 1979.

Hale, editor, *The After Midnight Ghost Book,* Hutchinson, 1980.

Hale, editor, *The Twilight Book,* Gollancz, 1981.

Judy Cooke and Elizabeth Bunster, editors, *The Best of the Fiction Magazines,* Dent, 1986.

OTHER

Regular book reviewer for *Sunday Telegraph,* 1969—. Contributor of short stories to *Harper's Bazaar, Transatlantic Review, Nova,* and *Queen;* contributor of articles to newspapers and magazines, including *Sunday Times* and *Twentieth Century;* contributor of book reviews to *Sunday Times, London Times, New York Times,* and *New Statesman.* Former member of editorial staff, *House and Garden, House Beautiful, Harper's Bazaar,* and *Sunday Times.*

WORK IN PROGRESS: A novel.

SIDELIGHTS: Janice Elliott's novels have been praised by many reviewers for the authenticity of their atmosphere and mood. According to a *Times Literary Supplement* review of *A State of Peace,* Elliott's first novel in a trilogy that explores the aftermath of World War II, she is "now firmly establishing herself as a novelist with notable talent for recreating times past. . . . [Her books] capture a remarkably authentic, solid and evocative background." David Haworth, reviewing the same book for *New Statesman,* comments on the difficulties of writing about recent history and adds that "Elliott is not in the least daunted. . . . She evokes the immediate postwar world with accuracy and panache." Piers Brendon, in *Books and Bookmen,* describes the novel as "an imaginative and deeply felt account of the vicissitudes of an upper middle class family in the London of the immediate post-war years. The atmosphere of demob drabness, poverty and points, bomb-sites and black marketeers is well conveyed. . . . I found this an involving and moving book—one which transmits life instead of trying to explain it."

In the *Dictionary of Literary Biography,* Virginia Briggs describes *Summer People* as a novel of "social criticism." And while William Boyd commends Elliott for her "sure, deft touch," he is puzzled by the novel's futuristic setting, continuing in the *Times Literary Supplement:* "The book's post-1984 world consists of a few layabout hippies on the beach, wandering stray dogs, hints that essential services are not all they could be, and dark talk of violence in the cities. The apocalyptic doom-laden atmosphere that's so patently striven for just doesn't emerge." John Mellors, however, is more impressed with Elliott's scenario, noting in the *Listener* that she creates "a sultry, threatening atmosphere, like the lull before a cosmic storm." Similarly, Peter Tinniswood of the London *Times* believes the book is "perfection," and adds: "Gradually a complex and beautifully modulated picture is built up of a society crumbling in on itself. . . . It is a brilliantly imaginative work. Everything about it shimmers with quality of the highest order."

Several critics have commented on Elliott's economical use of language and images in conveying theme. "She builds meaning from snatches of conversation, exact portrayals of scene and mood," Mary Borg says in the *New Statesman.* In a review of *The Kindling,* Borg writes: "One is deeply impressed with the reverberations of the story. The effect is of gradual osmosis." And in an appraisal of *Secret Places* for the *Listener,* John Naughton asserts that "Elliott has succeeded in etching her characters, and their story, with a gossamer touch. Her book is full of eloquent understatement."

In the *Times Literary Supplement,* Lindsay Duguid describes Elliott's *Magic* as an impressionistic novel in which "parallel streams-of-consciousness" and "bits and pieces of information are slyly smuggled in" to establish a complex plot and "to encompass a generous notion of magic." Duguid continues: "By means of tight control and a contrastingly lavish use of irony, Elliott gives us a picture of human powers which is highly wrought but harmonious; the unequivocally fictional becomes the really real." And of *The Italian Lesson,* a novel set in Tuscany, Julia O'Faolain notes in the *Times Literary Supplement* that Elliott "plays variations on themes from E. M. Forster's Italian novels." O'Faolain speaks of the "economy" in the novel typical of Elliott, and believes that she "unfolds her story with wit and irony, keeping to the present tense and using short, affirmative sentences which build up tension."

Mansel Stimpson suggests in the *Times Literary Supplement* that the success of *Dr. Gruber's Daughter,* Elliott's novel about the daughter of Adolph Hitler by a niece, "lies in its strikingly individual and daring combination of comedy and drama." Stimpson adds, however, that "the book's comedy is not a denial of its seriousness." Calling the book a "splendid" novel, Stimpson concludes: "Remembering the Nazi past, the book confidently asserts that people will be caught by history in the same way in the future: there will be other monsters, other victims, other passengers." Anita Brookner, who discusses the novel's "voluminous" plot, remarks in the *Spectator,* "I finished the book with considerable admiration for her insight." And John Nicholson observes in the London *Times* that "Elliott is one of the most accomplished literary stylists at work in this country, with an imagination second to none and an extraordinarily consistent output." "Elliott writes like an angel," says Nicholson. "Her imagination is diabolical."

MEDIA ADAPTATIONS: "The Buttercup Chain," based on Elliot's novel of the same title, was produced by Columbia Pictures in 1969. "Secret Places," an award-winning film based on the novel of the same title, was produced by Skreba in 1984 and released by Twentieth Century-Fox/TLC Films in 1985.

AVOCATIONAL INTERESTS: Sailing.

BIOGRAPHICAL/CRITICAL SOURCES:

BOOKS

Dictionary of Literary Biography, Volume 14: *British Novelists since 1960,* Gale, 1983.

PERIODICALS

Books and Bookmen, September, 1971.

Book World, November 8, 1970.

Chicago Tribune, October 23, 1985.

Listener, April 10, 1980, March 5, 1981.

Nation, September 11, 1967.

New Statesman, June 12, 1970, July 16, 1971.

New Yorker, March 23, 1987.

Saturday Review, April 8, 1967.

Spectator, March 15, 1975, March 28, 1981, September 17, 1983, September 6, 1986.

Times (London), April 30, 1980, March 18, 1982, September 15, 1983, April 18, 1985, September 4, 1986.

Times Literary Supplement, July 21, 1966, July 11, 1970, July 23, 1971, October 13, 1978, April 18, 1980, March 13, 1981, March 19, 1982, September 9, 1983, April 19, 1985, September 19, 1986, March 31, 1989.

ELLIS, William Donahue 1918-

PERSONAL: Born September 23, 1918, in Concord, Mass.; son of William Otterbein (a chemist, botanist, and entomologist) and Maude (Donahue) Ellis; married Dorothy Ann Naiden (a school library coordinator), June 13, 1942; children: William Naiden, Sarah Elizabeth. *Education:* Wesleyan University, Middletown, Conn., B.A., 1941.

ADDRESSES: *Home*—1060 Richmar Dr., Westlake, Ohio 44145. *Office*—1276 West 3rd St., Cleveland, Ohio 44113.

CAREER: Beaumont & Hohman, Cleveland, Ohio, writer, 1946-47; Storycraft, Inc., Cleveland, vice president, 1947-52; Editorial Services, Inc. (scriptwriters), Cleveland, president, 1952—. Member, Staff Writers Conference, University of New Hampshire, 1958—; member of advisory committee, Westlake School Board. *Military service:* U.S. Army, Infantry, 1941-46; served in Philippines and Guam; became captain; received Bronze Star and Purple Heart.

MEMBER: Authors Guild, Authors League of America.

AWARDS, HONORS: Ohioana Literary Award for fiction and Western Reserve Historical Society Award, both 1952, both for *The Bounty Lands;* Pulitzer Prize nomination and *Saturday Review* top fiction of the year listing, both 1954, both for *Jonathan Blair: Bounty Land Lawyer;* literature award, Cleveland Arts Council, 1967, for *The Cuyahoga.*

WRITINGS:

The Bounty Lands (first novel of a trilogy), World Publishing, 1952, reprinted, Landfall Press, 1981.
The Fabulous Dustpan (business biography), World Publishing, 1953.
Jonathan Blair: Bounty Land Lawyer (second novel of a trilogy), World Publishing, 1954.
(With Frank Siedel) *How to Win the Conference,* Prentice-Hall, 1955.
The Brooks Legend (third novel of a trilogy), Crowell, 1958.
The Cuyahoga ("Rivers of America" series), Holt, 1967.
(With Thomas J. Cunningham, Jr.) *Clarke of St. Vith: The Sergeant's General* (biography), Dillon-Liederbach, 1974.
Land of the Inland Seas, Crown, 1974.
Early Settlers of Cleveland, Cleveland State University, 1976.
On the Oil Lands with City Service, Service Oil and Gas Corp., 1981.
(With R. Q. Armington) *More: The Rediscovery of American Common Sense,* Regnery Gateway, 1984.
(Editor with Armington) *This Way Up: The Local Official's Handbook for Privatization and Contracting Out,* Regnery Gateway, 1985.
With a Name Like—, J. M. Smucker Co., 1987.
The Ordinance of 1787: The Nation Begins, Landfall Press, 1987.

Co-author, "The Ohio Story," radio-TV series, 1947—. Contributor of fiction to *Saturday Evening Post,* and of nonfiction to *Reader's Digest, True, Harper's, Rotarian, Atlanta Constitution, Frontiers,* and other periodicals. Editor, *Inland Seas Quarterly.*

WORK IN PROGRESS: *The Canal Lands,* a novel; *Concord Revisited,* nonfiction.

MEDIA ADAPTATIONS: Edward Lasker Productions has bought the motion picture rights to *The Bounty Lands;* Alwyn Productions has bought the television rights to *The Brooks Legend.* *

EMERY, Gary 1942-

PERSONAL: Born April 8, 1942, in Omaha, Neb.; son of Dale and Josephine (Rice) Emery; married Patsy Day, October 23, 1969; children: Zachary. *Education:* California State University, Long Beach, B.A., 1966, M.A., 1969; Creighton University, M.S., 1972; University of Pennsylvania, Ph.D., 1977.

ADDRESSES: *Home*—630 South Wilton Pl., Los Angeles, Calif. 90005. *Office*—Los Angeles Center for Cognitive Therapy, 630 South Wilton Pl., Los Angeles, Calif. 90005. *Agent*—Richard S. Pine, Arthur Pine Associates, Inc., 1780 Broadway, New York, N.Y. 10019.

CAREER: Los Angeles Center for Cognitive Therapy, Los Angeles, Calif., director, 1979—. Assistant clinical professor at University of California, Los Angeles, 1981—; clinical associate in psychology at University of Southern California, 1982—. Consultant to public and private agencies.

MEMBER: American Psychological Association, Association for the Advancement of Behavior Therapy.

WRITINGS:

(With A. T. Beck, A. J. Rush, and B. F. Shaw) *Cognitive Therapy of Depression,* Guilford Press, 1979.
(Contributor) D. Rathjen and J. Foreyt, editors, *Social Competence: Interventions for Children and Adults,* Pergamon, 1980.
(With Beck) *Cognitive Therapy: A Guide to Therapy and Training,* University of Pennsylvania, 1980.
(Editor with S. Hollon and R. Bedrosian, and contributor) *New Directions in Cognitive Therapy,* Guilford Press, 1981.
A New Beginning: How You Can Change Your Life through Cognitive Therapy, Simon & Schuster, 1981.
(With Beck) *Cognitive Therapy of Alcohol and Drug Dependency,* University of Pennsylvania, 1981.
Controlling Your Depression through Cognitive Therapy (tapes and workbook), BMA, 1982.
Own Your Own Life: How the New Cognitive Therapy Can Make You Feel Wonderful, New American Library, 1982.
(With Beck) *Cognitive Therapy of Anxiety and Phobic Disorders,* Basic Books, 1985.
(With James Campbell) *Rapid Relief from Emotional Distress,* Rawson, Wade, 1986.
Rapid Cognitive Therapy for the Treatment of Stress, Los Angeles Center for Cognitive Therapy, 1987.
Stress Free Home Study Course, Los Angeles Center for Cognitive Therapy, 1987.
Overcoming Anxiety: A Program for Self-Management (tapes and workbook), BMA, 1987.

Also author of tape, "Becoming More Self-Reliant," Psychology Today, 1985. Contributor to periodicals, including *Psychological Report, Complete Woman, Self, Cosmopolitan,* and *Beauty Digest.*

WORK IN PROGRESS: *Stop Defeating Yourself.*

SIDELIGHTS: Gary Emery told *CA:* "Cognitive therapy is a treatment that's based on the thinking model of emotional problems. The model holds that how you evaluate or think about your experiences and yourself determines how you feel and behave. Recent research has found that people with emotional disorders systematically distort their experiences. Cognitive therapy teaches the patient how to correct his distortions.

"*Rapid Relief from Emotional Distress* is based on rapid cognitive therapy and features thirty-eight tests and exercises to help pinpoint problems and find immediate relief. It is based on the ACT formula: Accept your current reality, Choose to create what you want in your life, Take action to create it."

* * *

EPP, Frank, H(enry) 1929-1986

PERSONAL: Born May 26, 1929, in Lena, Manitoba, Canada; died January 22, 1986; son of Henry Martin (a minister) and Anna (Enns) Epp; married Helen Louise Dick (a secretary), June 27, 1953; children: Marianne Louise, Esther Ruth, Marlene Gay. *Education:* Attended Vancouver Teachers College, 1948-49; Canadian Mennonite Bible College, B.Th., 1953; Bethel College, North Newton, Kan., B.A., 1956; University of Minnesota, M.A., 1960; Brandon University, LL.D., 1975.

ADDRESSES: Office—Department of History, Conrad Grebel College, University of Waterloo, Waterloo, Ontario, Canada N2L 3G6.

CAREER: Elementary school teacher in British Columbia, 1949-50; *Canadian Mennonite,* Winnepeg, Manitoba, founding editor and general manager, 1953-67; free-lance writer and lecturer, Ottawa, Ontario, 1967-71; University of Waterloo, Conrad Grebel College, Waterloo, Ontario, associate professor of history and communications, 1971-86, president of college, 1973-79. Editor, *Mennonite Reporter,* 1971-73. Mennonite Central Committee, director of studies with special assignment in the Middle East, 1968-71, chairman, 1979-86, member of executive board; president, United Nations Association (Waterloo Region), 1980-86. Member of advisory board for the Adjustment of Immigrants of the Minister for Manpower and Immigration, 1968-78. Has been a part-time pastor in several cities in Canada and United States; has lectured at colleges throughout Canada, United States, and eight foreign countries, including University of Ottawa and St. Paul's University, and for civic and religious organizations.

MEMBER: World Federalists of Canada, Canadian Consultation Council on Multiculturalism, Canadian Historical Association, Institute of Mennonite Studies.

AWARDS, HONORS: Canadian Council awards, 1972, 1973, 1975, 1976, 1978, 1979, 1980.

WRITINGS:

Mennonite Exodus: The Rescue and Resettlement of the Russian Mennonites since the Communist Revolution, D. W. Frieson, 1962.

(Contributor) Cornelius J. Dyck, editor, *An Introduction to Mennonite History: A Popular History of the Anabaptists and the Mennonites,* Herald Press, 1967.

Your Neighbour as Yourself: A Study on Responsibility in Immigration, Mennonite Central Committee, 1968.

The Glory and the Shame: Editorials on the Past, Present, and Future of the Mennonite Church, Canadian Mennonite Publishing Co., 1968.

(Contributor) John A. Lapp, editor, *Peacemakers in a Broken World,* Herald Press, 1969.

(Contributor) Richard Marshall, editor, *Aspects of Religion in the Soviet Union,* University of Chicago Press, 1970.

I Would Like to Dodge the Draft-Dodgers, but. . . , [Winnipeg], 1970.

Whose Land Is Palestine?: The Middle East Problem in Historical Perspective, Eerdmans, 1970.

Strategy for Peace: Reflections of a Christian Pacifist, Eerdmans, 1970.

(Contributor) John H. Redekop, editor, *Canada and the United States,* Peter Martin, 1971.

Mennonites in Canada, Volume 1, *1786-1920: The History of a Separate People,* Macmillan, 1974, Volume 2, *1920-1940: A People's Struggle for Survival,* Herald Press, 1982.

Education with a Plus, Conrad Press, 1975.

The Palestinians: Portrait of a People in Conflict, McClelland & Stewart, 1976.

Mennonite Peoplehood: A Plea for New Initiatives, Conrad Press, 1977.

The Israelis: Portrait of a People in Conflict, photographs by John Goddard, Herald Press, 1980.

Partners in Service: The Story of Mennonite Central Committee Canada, Mennonite Central Committee, 1983.

Also author of *Stories with Meaning,* 1978. Contributor to *Canadian Mennonite, Mennonite Quarterly Review, Mennonite Life, World Federalist, Winnipeg Free Press, Ottawa Citizen,* and other publications.

SIDELIGHTS: Frank H. Epp was interested in twentieth-century issues, including Canadian immigration minorities, the U.S.S.R., the Middle East, and the mass media. Beginning in 1966 he traveled every year, visiting various countries in Asia, Europe, the Middle East, Latin America, and the Far East.*

* * *

ERHARD, Thomas A. 1923-

PERSONAL: Born June 11, 1923, in West Hoboken, N.J.; son of Herbert Charles and Grace (Agnew) Erhard; married first wife, Jean M. Beebe, July 21, 1945 (divorced); married third wife, Evelyn Madrid, July 14, 1979; children: (first marriage) Bruce, Lawrence, Daniel. *Education:* Hofstra University, B.A., 1947; University of New Mexico, M.A., 1950, Ph.D., 1960; University of Denver, summer graduate study, 1951.

ADDRESSES: Home—2110 Rosedale Dr., Las Cruces, N.M. 88001. *Office*—Department of Theatre Arts, Box 3072, New Mexico State University, Las, Cruces, N.M. 88033.

CAREER: Albuquerque (N.M.) public schools, publications sponsor at high school, 1949-53, public information director for the school system, 1953-57; National Education Association, Washington, D.C., assistant director of Press, Radio, and Television Division, 1957-58; New Mexico State University, Las Cruces, assistant professor, 1960-64, associate professor, 1964-68, professor of English, 1968—. Conducts annual creative writing awards program which reaches more than five hundred high schools in six southwestern states. *Military service:* U.S. Army, 1943-47; became sergeant.

MEMBER: National Education Association, National Council of Teachers of English, American Association for Higher Education, American Association of University Professors, Sigma Delta Chi.

AWARDS, HONORS: Received a first and a third prize in national play writing contests conducted by community theaters.

WRITINGS:

Your Town, on the Map, National Education Association, 1957.

Lynn Riggs: Southwestern Playwright, Steck, 1970.

Nine Hundred Plays: A Synopsis-History of American Theatre, Richards Rosen, 1977.

COMEDY PLAYS

For the Love of Pete (three-act), Heuer, 1953.

The High White Star (three-act), Eldridge Publishing, 1957.

Memory, Marlyn, Memory! (one-act), Ivan Bloom Hardin, 1957.
Tex, Two Knuckles, and a Note (one-act), National Education Association, 1957.
Command Performance (one-act), National Education Association, 1959.
Standing Room Only (one-act), National Education Association, 1959.
After the Honeymoon (one-act), National Education Association, 1959.
Rocket in His Pocket (three-act), Row, Peterson, 1960.
Eleventy Percent (one-act), National Education Association, 1960.
Instant Education, (one-act), National Education Association, 1961.
The Electronovac Gasser (three-act), Eldridge Publishing, 1962.
Vacation on the Moon (one-act), National Education Association, 1962.
Reach for the Stars (one-act), National Education Association, 1963.
The Greatest American (one-act), National Education Association, 1963.
The Payoff! (one-act), National Education Association, 1964.
Cathy's Choice (one-act), National Education Association, 1964.
Two Million Heroes (one-act), National Education Association, 1964.
A Wild Fight for Spring (three-act), Baker's Plays, 1966.
The Cataclysmic Loves of Cooper and Looper and Their Friend Who Was Squashed by a Moving Van (three-act), Eldridge Publishing, 1969.
Francis Asbury: America, Accent on Youth Magazine, 1974.
But I Know I Saw Gypsies, Dramatic Publishing, 1982.
Pomp and Circumstances, Baker's Plays, 1982.
(With wife, Evelyn Madrid Erhard) *A Merry Medieval Christmas!,* Dramatic Publishing, 1984.
I Saved Winter Just for You, Dramatic Publishing, 1984.
Laughing Once More, Dramatic Publishing, 1986.

OTHER

Assistant editor, *Current Issues in Higher Education,* Association for Higher Education, 1960, 1964, and associate editor of other A.H.E. yearbooks published under various titles, 1965-71. Contributor of over 30 entries on American and European playwrights to *Worldbook Encyclopedia.* Contributor of short stories, about 130 articles to magazines, and about 6,000 articles to newspapers.

WORK IN PROGRESS: Several plays.

* * *

ERISMAN, Fred (Raymond) 1937-

PERSONAL: Born August 30, 1937, in Longview, Tex.; son of Fred Raymond (an attorney) and Dorothy (a teacher; maiden name, Barnhart) Erisman; married Patricia Ann Longley, August 28, 1961; children: Wendy Elizabeth. *Education:* Rice Institute, B.A., 1958; Duke University, M.A., 1960; University of Minnesota, Ph.D., 1966.

ADDRESSES: Office—Department of English, Texas Christian University, Fort Worth, Tex. 76129.

CAREER: Texas Christian University, Fort Worth, instructor, 1965-67, assistant professor, 1967-72, associate professor, 1972-77, professor of English, 1977—, Lorraine Sherley Professor of Literature, 1985—, chairman of department, 1983—, director of honors program, 1972-74, acting dean of arts and sciences, 1970-71, 1972-73.

MEMBER: International Research Society for Children's Literature (publications editor, 1981—; member of executive board, 1981-85), American Studies Association, Modern Language Association of America, Organization of American Historians, Popular Culture Association, Western Social Science Association (member of executive council, 1986-89), Western Literature Association, Phi Beta Kappa (honorary member).

AWARDS, HONORS: Hess fellow at University of Minnesota, 1981; Kinnucan Arms Chair fellow at Buffalo Bill Historical Center, 1982.

WRITINGS:

Frederic Remington, Boise State University Press, 1975.
(Editor with Richard W. Etulain) *Fifty Western Writers,* Greenwood Press, 1982.
(With Zena Sutherland) *Barnboken i USA,* Raben & Sjogren (Stockholm), 1986.
(Contributor) Thomas J. Lyon, editor, *A Literary History of the American West,* Texas Christian University Press, 1987.
(Contributor) Jane M. Bingham, editor, *Writers for Children,* Scribner, 1988.
Tony Hillerman, Boise State University Press, 1989.

Contributor to scholarly journals and popular magazines, including *Armchair Detective, Extrapolation,* and *Phaedrus.* Editor, *French-American Review Journal,* 1976-84; *Social Science Journal,* book review editor, 1978-82, associate editor, 1983-85.

WORK IN PROGRESS: A study of emotional realism in fantasy literature for children; a study of the aesthetic effects of technology.

SIDELIGHTS: Fred Erisman told *CA:* "For me, the aims of scholarship are two-fold: first, to identify and explore the cultural, emotional, and intellectual bonds that link persons of all eras and societies; second, to shed additional light on that most absorbing and fascinating of all topics, the human condition. When we at last come to know ourselves, we are all the better equipped to know our times and our place in history.

"My interest in children's literature dates from 1958, the fiftieth anniversary of Kenneth Grahame's *The Wind in the Willows.* Attracted to the book by the publicity surrounding its anniversary, I began to investigate its background, discovering two fascinating things in the process. First, children's literature had been largely ignored by literary scholars. And second, children's literature provides an uncommonly revealing insight into the dreams and ambitions of a culture. In the works that a society 'authorizes' as suitable for its youth, one finds expressed in their purest form the values that the society holds as ideals. Children's literature reveals what a society believes *ought* to be; history reveals what *is.* And the two together work as a complementary team to present a society in its efforts to grow and endure.

"From children's literature to other forms of popular writing (e.g., detective and suspense fiction, science fiction, the Western) is only a short step, and one I've taken readily. In these widely-read literary forms I find other fascinating and revealing evidence of how a culture works, how it evaluates itself, and how it looks to the future. More accessible to more persons than the acknowledged 'classics' of literature, these genre publications form a valuable aid to any investigator wanting to understand just *how* a society goes about its day-to-day affairs."

EVANS, C(harles) Stephen 1948-

PERSONAL: Born May 26, 1948, in Atlanta, Ga.; son of Charles Hinton (a transit operator) and Pearline (a teacher; maiden name, Prewett) Evans; married Jan Walter (a high school teacher), September 6, 1969. *Education:* Wheaton College, Wheaton, Ill., B.A., 1969; Yale University, M.Ph., 1971, Ph.D., 1974. *Politics:* Independent. *Religion:* Protestant.

ADDRESSES: Home—816 Ivanhoe Dr., Northfield, Minn. 55057. *Office*—Department of Philosophy, St. Olaf College, Northfield, Minn. 55057.

CAREER: Trinity College, Deerfield, Ill., assistant professor of philosophy, 1972-74; Wheaton College, Wheaton, Ill., assistant professor, 1974-78, associate professor, 1978-83, professor of philosophy, 1983-84; St. Olaf College, Northfield, Minn., professor of philosophy and curator of Hong Kierkegaard Library, 1984—.

MEMBER: American Philosophical Association, Society for Values in Higher Education (fellow), Society of Christian Philosophers.

AWARDS, HONORS: Danforth fellowship, 1969-74; Marshall fellowship, 1977-78; National Endowment for the Humanities fellowship, 1988-89.

WRITINGS:

Despair: A Moment or a Way of Life? An Existential Quest for Hope, Inter-Varsity Press, 1971.

Preserving the Person: A Look at the Human Sciences, Inter-Varsity Press, 1977.

Subjectivity and Religious Belief, Eerdmans, 1978.

Kierkegaard's "Fragments" and "Postscript": The Religious Philosophy of Johannes Climacus, Humanities, 1983.

Philosophy of Religion: Thinking about Faith, Inter-Varsity Press, 1984.

The Quest for Faith: Reason and Mystery as Pointers to God, Inter-Varsity Press, 1986.

Wisdom and Humanness in Psychology, Baker Book, 1989.

Editor of "Contours of Christian Philosophy" series, Inter-Varsity Press.

F

FABER, Harold 1919-

PERSONAL: Born September 12, 1919, in New York, N.Y.; son of Charles and Anna (Glassman) Faber; married Doris Greenberg (a writer), June 21, 1951; children: Alice, Marjorie. *Education:* City College (now City College of the City University of New York), B.S., 1940.

ADDRESSES: Home—R.D. 1, Ancram, N.Y. 12502. *Office*—*New York Times,* 229 West 43rd St., New York, N.Y. 10036.

CAREER: New York Times, New York, N.Y., reporter and war correspondent, 1940-52, day national news editor, 1952-68, editorial director of Book and Educational Division, 1968-72, upstate New York correspondent, 1972—. *Military service:* U.S. Army, 1942-46; awarded Purple Heart for war injuries received as correspondent in Korea, 1950-51.

WRITINGS:

(Editor) *New York Times Election Handbook—1964,* McGraw, 1964.

George C. Marshall, Soldier and Statesman, Farrar, Straus, 1964.

(Editor) *The Kennedy Years,* Viking, 1964.

(Editor) *The Road to the White House: The Story of the 1964 Election by the Staff of the "New York Times,"* McGraw, 1965.

(With wife, Doris Faber) *American Heroes of the 20th Century,* Random House, 1967.

From Sea to Sea: The Growth of the United States, Farrar, Straus, 1967.

(Editor) *New York Times Election Handbook—1968,* New American Library, 1968.

(Editor) *New York Times Guide for New Voters,* Quadrangle Books, 1972.

(Editor) *Luftwaffe: A History,* Times Books, 1977.

(With D. Faber) *The Assassination of Martin Luther King, Jr.,* F. Watts, 1978.

The Book of Laws, Times Books, 1979.

(With D. Faber) *Martin Luther King, Jr.* (young adult), Messner, 1986.

(With D. Faber) *Mahatma Gandhi* (juvenile), Messner, 1986.

(With D. Faber) *We the People,* Scribner, 1987.

(With D. Faber) *Great Lives: American Government* (juvenile), Scribner, 1988.

(With D. Faber) *The Birth of a Nation: The First Years of the United States,* Scribner, 1989.

SIDELIGHTS: While an editor at the *New York Times,* Harold Faber worked with other staff members to assemble an account of the 1964 presidential campaign. As Tom Wicker states in the introduction to *The Road to the White House,* the campaign was "an important event because never before had a Presidential election so dramatically and so fully disclosed the nature of American politics. Never before had the rules of the game or even its cliches been so sharply challenged, and probably never again will a candidate be more thoroughly rebuked and penalized for such transgressions." According to *Saturday Review* contributor Margaret L. Coit, the book is "a brisk, readable account of the making and election of the president in 1964. It is well-documented, rich with political guidelines and folklore." *The Road to the White House* is also "a remarkable feat of useful book-making, of shaping a vast amount of detailed material . . . into a coherent and fascinating narrative," writes Eliot Fremont-Smith in the *New York Times.* He continues, "The great merit of 'The Road to the White House' is not simply that it brings back to memory the facts and feel of the election . . . but that it corrects distorted emphasis. Goldwater still holds center stage, but others, including the voters, are very much there, and in focus. After all, Lyndon Johnson and Hubert Humphrey did win. The book is also as 'objective' an account as we are likely to get."

Faber has also collected a variety of life's "rules," called *The Book of Laws.* Faber quotes Brecht ("The ideal amount of rehearsal time is always one week more"), Bok ("If you think education is expensive, try ignorance"), and of course, Murphy ("If anything can go wrong, it will"). *Los Angeles Times* reviewer Robert Kirsch states: "The whole point of these laws is that they quickly become universal. . . . There are fun and wit here." And a *New York Times Book Review* contributor believes that "taken together, these laws provide the reader with a quotable collection of witty comments on the way we think, live and operate."

BIOGRAPHICAL/CRITICAL SOURCES:

BOOKS

Faber, Harold, editor, *The Road to the White House: The Story of the 1964 Election by the Staff of the "New York Times,"* McGraw, 1965.

Faber, Harold, *The Book of Laws,* Times Books, 1979.

PERIODICALS

Los Angeles Times, March 23, 1979.
New York Times, May 29, 1965, February 12, 1979.
New York Times Book Review, June 13, 1965, March 18, 1979.
Saturday Review, July 10, 1965.

* * *

FAHY, Christopher 1937-

PERSONAL: Surname is pronounced "Fay"; born November 15, 1937, in Philadelphia, Pa.; son of William J. (a teacher) and Dorothy (a teacher; maiden name, Kitsch) Fahy; married Davene Sernoff (a director of a program for preschool handicapped children), January 25, 1960; children: Gregory, Benjamin. *Education:* Temple University, B.A., 1959, M.A., 1962. *Politics:* "Declining." *Religion:* "Stable."

ADDRESSES: Home—6 Mechanic St., Thomaston, Me. 04861.

CAREER: Speech therapist in public schools in New Jersey, 1961-62; Bancroft School, Haddonfield, N.J., speech therapist, 1962-65, director of speech clinic and coordinator of clinical services, 1967-72; free-lance writer, 1972—. Maine state vocational rehabilitation counselor for the blind and visually impaired, 1985—; coordinator of Supplemental Security Income Disabled Children's Program, Knox and Lincoln Counties, Me., 1979-81. Vice-president of Friends of Jackson Library, Tenants Harbor, Me., 1975-76, and Jackson Memorial Library League, 1982-83; member of literature advisory panel, Maine Arts Commission, 1983-87.

MEMBER: International Society for General Semantics, National Rehabilitation Association, Association for the Education and Rehabilitation of the Blind and Visually Impaired, American Speech and Hearing Association, Authors Guild, Authors League of America, Maine Writers and Publishers Alliance.

AWARDS, HONORS: Winner, Maine Arts Commission Fiction Competition, 1987, for *One Day in the Short Happy Life of Anna Banana.*

WRITINGS:

The Compost Heap (novel), Outerbridge & Dienstfrey, 1970.
Home Remedies (on home repair), Scribner, 1975.
Greengroundtown (short stories), Puckerbush Press, 1978.
The End Beginning (poetry), Red Earth, 1978.
Nightflyer (novel), Jove, 1982.
Dream House (novel), Zebra Books, 1987.
One Day in the Short Happy Life of Anna Banana (short stories), Coastwise Press, 1988.

Contributor of stories, poems, and articles to periodicals, including *Beloit Poetry Journal, Twilight Zone Magazine, Fiction Review,* and *Down East Magazine.*

WORK IN PROGRESS: Two novels, *Stalking Bliss* and *Fever 42.*

SIDELIGHTS: Christopher Fahy told *CA:* "Maine is the best place in the world for a writer to be these days. Plenty of stimulation, plenty of isolation. Hard, but intimate and nurturing. Lots of small press activity, and my god, the writers: Ruth Moore, Elizabeth Ogilvie, May Sarton, Mary McCarthy, Philip Booth, Stephen and Tabitha King, Rick Hautala, Michael Kimball, Carolyn Chute, Susan Kenney, Willis Johnson, William Kotzwinkle, Jan Willem van de Vettering, Martin Dibner, Helen Yglesias, Robert Creeley—the list goes on and on. I feel lucky to live here."

AVOCATIONAL INTERESTS: Fixing old houses, gardening.

* * *

FARLEY, Walter (Lorimer) 1915-1989

PERSONAL: Born June 26, 1915, in Syracuse, N.Y.; died October 16, 1989, in Sarasota, Fla., of a heart attack; son of Walter (assistant manager in hotel) and Isabelle (Vermilyea) Farley; married Rosemary Lutz, 1945; children: Pamela, Alice, Steven, Time. *Education:* Attended Mercersburg Academy and Columbia Unversity.

ADDRESSES: Home—Pennsylvania and Florida. *Office*—c/o Random House Inc., 201 E. 50th St., New York, N.Y. 10022.

CAREER: Writer and Arabian horse breeder. Copywriter for a New York advertising agency, 1941. Consultant and promoter for films, "The Black Stallion" and "The Black Stallion Returns." *Military service:* U.S. Army, Fourth Armoured Division, 1942-46; reporter for *Yank,* an army publication.

AWARDS, HONORS: Pacific Northwest Library Association's Young Reader's Choice Award, 1944, for *The Black Stallion,* and 1948, for *The Black Stallion Returns;* Boys Club Junior Book Award, 1948, for *The Black Stallion Returns;* literary landmark established in Farley's honor by Venice Area Public Library, Venice, Fla.

WRITINGS:

YOUNG ADULT; PUBLISHED BY RANDOM HOUSE, EXCEPT AS NOTED

The Black Stallion, (Junior Literary Guild selection; also see below), illustrations by Keith Ward, 1941, new edition, 1982.
Larry and the Undersea Raider, illustrations by P. K. Jackson, 1942.
The Black Stallion Returns (Junior Literary Guild selection; also see below), illustrations by Harold Eldridge, 1945, revised edition, 1982.
Son of the Black Stallion (Junior Literary Guild selection), illustrations by Milton Menasco, 1947, 2nd edition with drawings by Hofbauer, Collins, 1950, Hodder and Stoughton, 1973.
The Island Stallion (Junior Literary Guild selection), illustrations by K. Ward, 1948, Hodder and Stoughton, 1973.
The Black Stallion and Satan (Junior Literary Guild selection; also see below), illustrations by M. Menasco, 1949, revised edition, Hodder and Stoughton, 1974.
The Blood Bay Colt, illustrations by M. Menasco, 1950, published as *The Black Stallion's Blood Bay Colt,* 1978.
The Island Stallion's Fury, illustrations by H. Eldridge, 1951, Hodder and Stoughton, 1975.
The Black Stallion's Filly, illustrations by M. Menasco, 1952, new edition, Hodder and Stoughton, 1980.
The Black Stallion Revolts (Junior Literary Guild selection), illustrations by H. Eldridge, 1953, Hodder and Stoughton, 1978.
The Black Stallion's Sulky Colt, illustrations by H. Eldridge, 1954.
The Island Stallion Races, illustrations by Eldridge, 1955.
The Black Stallion's Courage, illustrations by Allen F. Brewer, Jr., 1956, Hodder and Stoughton, 1978.
The Black Stallion Mystery (also see below), illustrations by Mal Singer, 1957, Severn House (London), 1982.
The Horse-Tamer, illustrations by James Schucker, 1958, reprinted, 1980.

The Black Stallion and Flame, illustrations by H. Eldridge, 1960, revised edition, Hodder and Stoughton, 1974.

Man o'War, illustrations by Angie Draper, 1962, new edition, 1983.

The Black Stallion Challenged!, illustrations by A. Draper, 1964, published in England as *The Black Stallion's Challenge,* Hodder and Stoughton, 1983.

The Great Dane, Thor, illustrations by Joseph Cellini, 1966.

The Black Stallion's Ghost, illustrations by A. Draper, 1969.

The Black Stallion and the Girl, illustrations by A. Draper, 1971.

Walter Farley's Black Stallion Books, four volumes (includes *The Black Stallion, The Black Stallion Returns, The Black Stallion and Satan,* and *The Black Stallion Mystery*), 1979.

The Black Stallion Legend, 1983.

(With son, Steven Farley) *The Young Black Stallion,* 1989.

JUVENILES

(With Josette Frank) *Big Black Horse* (adaptation of *The Black Stallion*), illustrations by P. K. Jackson, Random House, 1953, 2nd edition with illustrations by James Schucker, Publicity Products, 1955.

Little Black, a Pony, illustrations by J. Schucker, Random House, 1961.

Little Black Goes to the Circus, illustrations by J. Schucker, Random House, 1963.

The Horse That Swam Away, illustrations by Leo Summers, Random House, 1965.

The Little Black Pony Races, illustrations by J. Schucker, Random House, 1968.

The Black Stallion Picture Book, illustrated with photographs from the motion picture, Random House, 1979.

The Black Stallion Returns: A Storybook Based on the Movie, edited by Stephanie Spinner, Random House, 1982.

The Black Stallion: An Easy-to-Read Adaptation, illustrations by Sandy Rabinowitz, Random House, 1986.

The Black Stallion Beginner Book, Random House, 1987.

OTHER

Many of Farley's early manuscripts and papers have been collected by the Butler Library at Columbia University.

SIDELIGHTS: Juvenile novelist Walter Farley was known worldwide as the creator of the Black Stallion, a wild horse that appeared in the 1940s young adult novel of the same title. Since then, the popularity of *The Black Stallion* with children and young teenagers has led to a series of books and two movies. "In the field of publishing, where 'phenomenal' authors appear with the regularity of the spring lilacs and the autumn asters (and disappear just as regularly), Walter Farley is a genuine phenomenon," claims *Christian Science Monitor* contributor Richard Brunner. Philip A. Sadler writes in the *Dictionary of Literary Biography* that "Farley is a leader in the field of books about horses, sharing his popularity possibly only with Marguerite Henry and Lynn Hall." And *Atlantic Monthly* contributor Martha Bacon thinks Farley's horse, affectionately known as "the Black," continues "in the satisfactory tradition of Black Beauty." Even though librarians and critics have at times ignored the books or criticized them as improbable and melodramatic, Farley's tales have sold over twelve million copies in the United States and are in print in fifteen countries.

The Black Stallion "did not emerge all of a sudden, over a single evening and bottle of beer," relates Lewis Nichols in *Young Wings.* The writer "began it as a student at Erasmus High, wrote another version while a student at Mercersburg, . . .wrote other versions as class assignments at Columbia. His first editor told him he never could make a living writing children's books, which was one of the misstatements of the age." Brunner continues, "Walter Farley has proved the literary, academic, and publishing experts wrong, and in doing so has proved to himself and others that his personal philosophy of making one's avocation one's vocation cannot only work but can work handsomely." While Farley later felt that the first book of the series compared poorly to its successors, his publisher would not allow him to revise it. But John Strassburger writes in *Chronicle of the Horse* that "the original book *The Black Stallion* is quite a remarkable work for one so young. The research is excellent, the characterization strong, and the descriptions vivid." And while *Growing Point* contributor Margery Fisher thinks "Walter Farley's style is not innocent of cliche and it is not particularly polished," she allows "it works admirably as a medium for fast event, for the speed of a race or a trial gallop or the chases and escapes in the desert."

The Black's human companion is Alec Ramsey. In *The Black Stallion* the boy is shipwrecked on a desert island with the half-wild horse. Although the animal distrusts people, Alec's patient care finally wins the stallion's confidence. Alec starts the series as a teenager but ages and matures through the sequels. Fisher maintains that the stories, however, generally highlight the stallion: "these are essentially tales of a horse and its fortunes and at times Alec seems little more than a necessary link in the narrative. . . . This is as it should be, of course. In these linked adventure stories, action comes first." But Sadler sees the boy become a more essential element as the stories gain in emotional depth: "Alec Ramsey begins to develop as a character as the Black Stallion books continue. . . . Perhaps this is what sets this series a few steps above some of the others." In the *New York Herald Tribune Books,* Louise Bechtel notes, "In each Farley stallion story, the material has become more adult, and the style more tense and emotional." Strassburger also writes that the growing depth of these apparently simple tales of horses and adventure makes them transcend the usual limitations of their genre: "Walter Farley's 16 Black Stallion books are more than just an ordinary collection of stories about a boy and his horse growing up together in America. Carried in those scores of pages are strong moral themes, messages to children about life. Farley's books weren't originally intended to carry a message. No, the stories about Alec Ramsay and the Black Stallion were an escape for him that became an escape for his readers. But as Farley has gotten older, the messages have become stronger."

Not all of Farley's books deal with the Black Stallion or his descendents. In *The Great Dane Thor,* "Farley exhibits almost as much knowledge of dogs and wildlife as he does about horses," Sadler observes. But *New York Times Book Review* contributor Andrea DiNoto feels that Farley makes a mistake in forgoing "an atmosphere of sheer animal excitement in favor of object lessons in loneliness, courage, fear and ethics." Still, the book is noteworthy, Taliaferro Boatwright maintains in *Book Week,* as it "is not a boy-animal love affair, as so many children's books about horses and dogs tend to be. Lars Newton, its fifteen-year-old hero, does not like his father's Great Dane, Thor, and is happy when their new colt outwits the dog. . . .Nevertheless, the knowledge and the love of nature that permeate the book and the understanding of a boy's behavior and wellsprings, as well as those of horses and dogs, make it well worthwhile."

Farley once wrote *CA,* "My greatest love was, and still is, horses. I wanted a pony as much as any boy or girl could possibly want anything—but I never owned one. I tried selling subscriptions to win a pony, which was offered as a prize to the kid who sold the most subscriptions. Then my uncle with a flock of show horses and jumpers moved from the West Coast to Syracuse, and

I was deliriously happy. I was at the stables every chance I could get."

Farley's books on horses have remained his best sellers. The reason for this, Sadler claims is Farley's belief "that children today are little different from the children of forty years ago." Sadler continues, "He may be right, because the children of today love the Black and continue to read about him, just as did those children of the 1940s." Strassburger confirms this, writing, "Some three generations of readers have now experienced the Black Stallion because the books are healthy and enjoyable reading for children. They stir the imagination, they evoke emotion, they teach children to care and to dream." And Brunner concludes, "Today children starting the series may not realize they are reading a 'modern classic' but they are as enthusiastic as their parents or their grandparents were when they embarked on this adventure."

MEDIA ADAPTATIONS: *The Black Stallion* was released by United Artists in 1979, and also was produced as a filmstrip with cassette by Media Basics in 1982; *The Black Stallion Returns* was released by United Artists in 1983.

BIOGRAPHICAL/CRITICAL SOURCES:

BOOKS

Contemporary Literary Criticism, Volume 17, Gale, 1981.
Dictionary of Literary Biography, Volume 22: *American Writers for Children, 1900-1960,* Gale, 1983.
Hopkins, Lee Bennett, *More Books by More People,* Citation, 1974.

PERIODICALS

Atlantic Monthly, December, 1969.
Best Sellers, December, 1978, January, 1983.
Booklist, January 1, 1980, June 1, 1983, February 1, 1987.
Book Week, April 30, 1967.
Children's Book Review Service, December, 1983.
Christian Science Monitor, February 1, 1971.
Chronicle of the Horse, November 13, 1987.
Growing Point, November, 1978.
Los Angeles Times, March 28, 1983.
New York Herald Tribune Books, October 4, 1953.
New York Times, March 27, 1983.
New York Times Book Review, November 2, 1947, May 9, 1965, November 6, 1966.
School Library Journal, February, 1984, February, 1987.
Young Wings, September, 1945.

OBITUARIES:

PERIODICALS

Washington Post, October 19, 1989.

[Sketch reviewed by wife, Rosemary Farley]

* * *

FAXON, Alicia Craig 1931-

PERSONAL: Born July 27, 1931, in New York, N.Y.; daughter of William Donald and Alicia (Harnecker) Craig; married Richard Bremer Faxon (a clergyman), February 21, 1953; children: Richard Paul, Thomas Hardwick. *Education:* Vassar College, B.A. (magna cum laude), 1952; Radcliffe College, M.A., 1953; Boston University, M.A., 1971, Ph.D., 1979. *Religion:* Episcopal.

ADDRESSES: *Office*—Department of Art History, Simmons College, 300 The Fenway, Boston, Mass. 02115.

CAREER: Mt. Vernon High School, Washington, D.C., teacher of English, 1955-56; American Historical Association, Washington, D.C., research assistant, 1958; University of Maryland, College Park, instructor in American history, 1961-63; Boston University, Boston, Mass., teaching fellow, 1970-71; DeCordova Museum School, Lincoln, Mass., teacher of art history, 1972, 1973; New England School of Art, Boston, lecturer in art history, 1974-77; Massachusetts College of Art, Boston, instructor, 1975—; Simmons College, Boston, instructor, 1979-80, assistant professor, 1980-86, associate professor of art history, 1987—, department chair, 1987—. Member of print council, DeCordova Museum, 1968-69; Danforth Museum, trustee, 1974-77, guest curator, 1975, acting director, 1977. Visiting lecturer, Tufts University, 1973.

MEMBER: College Art Association, National Society for Literature and the Arts, National League of American Penwomen, Women's Caucus of Art, Boston Authors Club, Vassar Club (Boston; seminar chairman), Rectory Club (Washington, D.C.; president, 1960-61), Phi Beta Kappa.

WRITINGS:

Collecting Art on a Shoestring, Barre, 1969.
Women and Jesus, United Church Press, 1973.
(With Yves Brayer) *Jean-Louis Forain: Artist, Realist, Humanist,* C. E. Tuttle, 1982.
Jean-Louis Forain: A Catalogue Raisonne of the Prints, Garland Publishing, 1982.
(Editor with Sylvia Moore) *Pilgrims and Pioneers: New England Women in the Arts,* Midmarch Arts-WAN, 1987.
Dante Gabriel Rossetti as Artist, Abbeville Press, 1989.

Contributor to local magazines and newspapers. Art critic, *Boston Phoenix,* 1970-71, Minute-Man Publications, 1971-73, *Real Paper,* 1975-76, and *Art New England,* 1985—; art writer, *Boston Globe,* 1971-73.

SIDELIGHTS: Alicia Craig Faxon once wrote *CA:* "My interest at present in art history seems to be taking top priority over all forms of writing."

* * *

FEINBERG, Beatrice Cynthia Freeman 1915(?)-1988 (Cynthia Freeman)

PERSONAL: Born c. 1915, in New York, N.Y.; died of cancer, October 22, 1988, in San Francisco, Calif.; daughter of Albert C. and Sylvia Jeannette (Hack) Freeman; married Herbert Feinberg (a physician), 1938; children: one son, one daughter. *Education:* Attended University of California.

ADDRESSES: *Home*—San Francisco, Calif.

CAREER: Writer. Worked as an interior decorator until she was 50 years old.

WRITINGS:

NOVELS; UNDER NAME CYNTHIA FREEMAN

A World Full of Strangers (also see below), Arbor House, 1975.
Fairytales, Arbor House, 1977.
The Days of Winter (also see below), Arbor House, 1978.
Portraits (also see below), Arbor House, 1979.
Come Pour the Wine (also see below), Arbor House, 1980.
No Time for Tears, Arbor House, 1981.
Cynthia Freeman: A World Full of Strangers, The Days of Winter, Portraits, [and] *Come Pour the Wine* (boxed set), Arbor House, 1981.

Catch the Gentle Dawn, Arbor House, 1983.
Illusions of Love, Putnam, 1984.
Seasons of the Heart, Putnam, 1986.
The Last Princess (Doubleday Book Club selection; Literary Guild alternate selection), Putnam, 1987.

SIDELIGHTS: Beatrice Cynthia Freeman Feinberg's novels, published under the name Cynthia Freeman, have appealed to many readers. *New York Times Book Review* writer Merin Wexler pointed to Feinberg's deft storytelling, her understanding of family dynamics, and her sometimes "vivid" writing as elements that have sold over ten million copies of such novels as *Portraits, Come Pour the Wine,* and *Catch the Gentle Dawn.* Feinberg professed a lifelong affinity for writing, but she never seriously considered writing a novel until she was idled by a five-year illness. To amuse herself during that period, she wrote *A World Full of Strangers,* a multi-generational novel focusing on a Jew from New York's Lower East Side who goes to great lengths to conceal his ethnic background. Not only does he change his name and forbid his wife to tell their son about their heritage, he indulges in some anti-Semitism himself.

Gilbert Millstein was not generous with *A World Full of Strangers* in his *New York Times Book Review* appraisal. Dubbing it a "Jewish soap opera," he dismissed its plot as "preposterous": "Many Jews have, indeed, changed their names and concealed the fact that they are Jewish. But I never heard of one carrying on against the Jews in the manner of David Resinetsky-Reid." Of the book's mood and style, Millstein wrote: "It is a novel of singular, if not intentional, innocence. Its writing is of a primitive directness—lush here, bromidic there and so heartfelt that it wore me out." The reading public responded more favorably to Feinberg's first effort than Millstein, buying over one million copies of *A World Full of Strangers.*

Feinberg's subsequent novels have been as eagerly received as her first. Maude McDaniel commented on the author's appeal in the *Washington Post Book World.* Although McDaniel described *Come Pour the Wine* as "written in 10th-grade English for simple minds and girlish hearts," she readily admitted that "it is, like all Freeman's books, compulsively readable. . . . You have learned to like these silly, one-dimensional people, and you want to be in on everything that happens to them."

No Time for Tears was Feinberg's most "ambitious" novel, according to Mona E. Simpson in the *Los Angeles Times Book Review. New York Times Book Review* contributor Mel Watkins agreed that *No Time For Tears* is "more than a generational saga; Miss Freeman has attempted to depict the struggle for a Jewish state in Palestine through the lives of her characters." Watkins felt that the book was hampered by its ambitious scope, but declared that "Miss Freeman relates this tale of struggle and courage in heartfelt, almost inspirational prose." She concluded that especially in its personal scenes, "the novel has some poignancy."

Feinberg described herself to *Los Angeles Times* interviewer Harriet Stix as "hooked" on writing, explaining that she wrote because she enjoyed it. "It has nothing to do with fame or fortune or celebrity—nothing. . . . I just do what's comfortable for me. I don't believe there are any rules—that's why it's called creative writing." She told Stix that her novels usually featured Jewish characters simply because "it is easier for me to write about the Jewish experience. They are Jewish themes, but they could be universal—love, hate, peace, war, cradle, grave, self-hatred."

Feinberg shared these insights in a *Parade* essay: "You know, all of us are gifted in some unique way. All of us harbor some dream we never had time to fulfill, some treasured hobby we never had enough time for. Whether it's writing or interior design, painting or caring for the very young or the very old, there is in each of us the key to open the door to the great need we have to acquire satisfaction and bestow satisfaction. Imagination is forever young; dreams don't turn gray. And remember, a royalty check never hurt, either."

BIOGRAPHICAL/CRITICAL SOURCES:

PERIODICALS

Los Angeles Times, June 12, 1986.
Los Angeles Times Book Review, December 20, 1981, February 21, 1988.
New York Times Book Review, November 14, 1976, February 17, 1980, November 22, 1981, January 13, 1985, April 27, 1986.
Parade, March 3, 1985.
Publishers Weekly, May 30, 1977.
Washington Post Book World, April 3, 1980, November 28, 1980.

OBITUARIES:

PERIODICALS

Chicago Tribune, October 27, 1988.
Los Angeles Times, October 27, 1988.
New York Times, October 26, 1988.*

* * *

FENSCH, Thomas 1943-
(Lander Moore)

PERSONAL: Born November 29, 1943, in Ashland, Ohio; son of Edwin A. Fensch (an educator) and stepson of Flossie (Hoover) Fensch; married Jean Robinson, December 27, 1977; stepchildren: Bill, Susan, LynnMarie. *Education:* Ashland College, B.A., 1965; University of Iowa, M.A., 1967, additional study, 1967-70; Syracuse University, Ph.D., 1977.

ADDRESSES: Home—6202 Olympic Overlook, Austin, Tex. 78746. *Office*—Department of Journalism, University of Texas, Austin, Tex. 78712.

CAREER: Writer and educator. Shippensburg State College, Shippensburg, Pa., associate professor of English and journalism, 1970-71; Ohio State University, Columbus, instructor in journalism, 1971-73; University of Texas at Austin, associate professor of journalism, 1977—.

MEMBER: American Society of Journalists and Authors.

AWARDS, HONORS: Received honorable mention in *Story, the Yearbook of Discovery,* 1968-70; Book of the Year in Biography award, Martha Kinney Cooper Ohioana Library Association, 1980, for *Steinbeck and Covici;* honorable mention, Texas Institute of Letters, 1980, for *Steinbeck and Covici.*

WRITINGS:

The Lions and the Lambs (illustrated with his own photographs), A.S. Barnes, 1970.
Alice in Acidland, A.S. Barnes, 1970.
Films on the Campus (illustrated with his own photographs), A.S. Barnes, 1970.
Smokeys, Truckers, C.B. Radios and You, Fawcett, 1976.
Steinbeck and Covici: The Story of a Friendship, Paul Eriksson, 1979.
Skydiving, Anderson-World, 1980.
The Hardest Parts: Techniques for Effective Non-fiction, Lander Moore Books, 1984.

(Editor) *Conversations with John Steinbeck,* University Press of Mississippi, 1988.
The Sports Writing Handbook, Lawrence Erlbaum, 1988.
Writing Solutions: Beginnings, Middles and Endings, Lawrence Erlbaum, 1988.

Contributor to magazines under pseudonym Lander Moore.

WORK IN PROGRESS: Four additional nonfiction books.

SIDELIGHTS: Thomas Fensch told *CA:* "When I was young, I recall reading and keeping great stacks of *Time, Newsweek, Life,* and other magazines. I wondered then who the people were who knew the *secrets,* who knew things before I did—later I discovered they were reporters and editors and writers. I wanted to be someone who *knew the secrets*—who knew facts and stories—before anyone else did. Writing nonfiction is one of the most satisfying preoccupations in the world: dealing with real people, their fears, hopes, dreams, lives. As a writer and college educator, it is satisfying to know the secrets about people and to pass on the techniques of nonfiction writing to young writers."

AVOCATIONAL INTERESTS: Antiquing, swimming, jogging.

BIOGRAPHICAL/CRITICAL SOURCES:

PERIODICALS

Chicago Tribune Book World, August 19, 1979.
Des Moines Register, March 30, 1969.
Los Angeles Times, August 24, 1979.
New York Times, August 31, 1979.
New York Times Book Review, December 16, 1979.
Washington Post Book World, September 16, 1979.

* * *

FERICANO, Paul 1951-

PERSONAL: Born January 16, 1951, in San Francisco, Calif.; son of Frank Paul and Josephine (Anello) Fericano; married Katherine Judeen Daly, October 14, 1972; children: Kate. *Education:* Attended various universities in California, 1969-75. *Politics:* "Stoogism." *Religion:* "Catholic Stoogism."

ADDRESSES: Home—P.O. Box 236, Millbrae, Calif. 94030. *Agent*—Elizabeth Trupin, JET Literary Associates, Inc., 125 East 84th St., Suite 4A, New York, N.Y. 10028.

CAREER: Satirist and poet. Has worked as a dishwasher, waiter, washing machine repairman, gardener, carpenter, clown, playground supervisor, truck driver, warehouseman, disc jockey, house painter, Santa Claus, and in various other occupations; publisher, Scarecrow Books, 1974-78; publisher, Poor Souls Press, 1978—; co-founder/editor, Yossarian Universal News Service (YU), 1984—. Worked for California Poetry-in-the-Schools program, 1978-79; conducted poetry workshops at Western Federal Penitentiary, Pittsburgh, Pa., 1980.

AWARDS, HONORS: American Association of University Women fiction award, 1969; Creative Artists Award for poetry, 1976; International Poet award, 1982; Howitzer Prize, 1982.

WRITINGS:

POETRY

Beneath the Smoke Rings, Dithyramb Poetry Series, 1976.
The Cancer Quiz, Scarecrow Books, 1977.
Loading the Revolver with Real Bullets, Second Coming Press, 1977.
The Ventriloquist, Poetry Exchange, 1978.
The Answer, Hearthstone Press, 1979.
Sinatra, Sinatra, Poor Souls Press, 1982.
Commercial Break, Poor Souls Press, 1982.

OTHER

(Editor) *Stoogism Anthology,* Scarecrow Books, 1977.
The Condition of Poetry in the Modern World: A Stoogist Manifesto, Poor Souls Press, 1982.
(With E. Ligi) *The One Minute President* (fiction), Stroessner & Shultz Verlag, 1986, Poor Souls Press, 1987.

Contributor to periodicals, including *Realist, Harper's, LA Weekly, Krokodil, Private Eye,* and *3 Stooges Journal.* Editor, *West Conscious Review* and *Crow's Nest Magazine,* 1974-77.

WORK IN PROGRESS: A Quantum Theory of Gravity (poetry); *Universal Times* (novel); "News from Alien Places" (screenplay).

SIDELIGHTS: Paul Fericano wrote *CA:* "As an investigative satirist, I lead a glamorous but often dangerous life. The only consideration that keeps me doing this kind of work is the money. Frankly, there's so much money to be made in this satire business that I'm surprised at how few satirists there really are in America today. I guess I'm just lucky. But the job is not without its risks. For instance, last year, in an attempt to get backstage during a Sinatra concert to get the singer's reaction to my story about South Africa renaming Sun City 'Frank's Town,' I nearly lost my life. Ironically, it was Sinatra himself who actually saved my life. Six guys began beating me with fists and clubs before Frank finally stepped in and said, 'Okay fellas, that's enough.' I later attributed the entire episode to comedian Shecky Greene who hasn't been heard from since.

"Another time I crashed a CIA fundraiser for Latin American military intelligence and woke up the next morning in a court-ordered, seventy-two hour observation cell in Dallas. The only identification on me was a business card for a plumbing supply outfit in Miami with George Bush's name and home phone number scrawled on the back. And just recently, another lawsuit was brought against me, this one by Jerry Lewis concerning a story I had reported about English housewives who were concerned about possible exposure to the AIDS virus while watching old Jerry Lewis movies on TV. When Mr. Lewis died unexpectedly from complications caused by appearing too often in public without Wayne Newton's permission, the suit was duly dismissed. I am presently at work on exposing an illegal drug cartel in which millions of drugs are being smuggled into this country disguised as daily editions from the Hearst newspaper chain."

* * *

FERNEA, Elizabeth Warnock 1927-

PERSONAL: Surname is pronounced *Fur*-nee-ah; born October 21, 1927, in Milwaukee, Wis.; daughter of David Wallace (a chemist) and Elizabeth (Meshynsky) Warnock; married Robert Alan Fernea (a social anthropologist), June 8, 1956; children: Laura Ann, David Karim, Laila Catherine. *Education:* Reed College, B.A., 1949; graduate study, Mount Holyoke College, 1949-50, and University of Chicago. *Politics:* Democrat. *Religion:* Roman Catholic.

ADDRESSES: Home—3003 Bowman Rd., Austin, Tex. 78703. *Office*—Center for Middle Eastern Studies, University of Texas, Austin, Tex. 78712. *Agent*—Watkins-Loomis Agency, 150 E. 35th St., New York, N.Y. 10014.

CAREER: Reed College, Portland, Ore., director of public relations, 1950-54; University of Chicago, Chicago, Ill., admissions counselor and promotion assistant, 1954-56; U.S. Information Agency, contract reporter and writer in Baghdad, Iraq, 1956-58; University of Chicago, member of public relations staff, 1958-59; University of Texas at Austin, Center for Middle Eastern Studies, research associate, 1973—, instructor, 1975-86, senior lecturer, 1986—. Lecturer on women in the Middle East at numerous conferences and symposia in the United Sates and abroad. Ethnographer for film, "Some Women of Marrakech," 1977; associate producer for film, "Saints and Spirits," 1979; producer of films, "A Veiled Revolution," 1982, "The Price of Change," 1982, and "Women under Siege," 1982. Member, board of directors, America-Mideast Educational and Training Services, Middle East Institute, and Georgetown University Center for Arabic Studies. Chairman of film and media committee, Center for Middle Eastern Studies; coordinator, Resource Sharing Program, 1979—. Member, Travis County Democratic Women's Committee and Lay Citizen Advisory Committee on Textbooks, Austin Independent School District. Faculty advisor; consultant.

MEMBER: Middle Eastern Studies Association of North America (president), Texas Institute of Letters (council member, 1985-86).

AWARDS, HONORS: Outstanding Woman in Literature, Texas America Association of University Women, 1978; National Endowment for the Humanities film grants, 1978, 1980; recipient with husband, Robert Alan Fernea, of Carr P. Collins Award for best nonfiction book, Texas Institute of Letters, 1985, for *The Arab World: Personal Encounters;* Fulbright study grant, 1988.

WRITINGS:

Guests of the Sheik, Doubleday, 1965, published as *Guests of the Sheik: An Ethnography of an Iraqi Village,* 1969.

A View of the Nile, Doubleday, 1970.

(Contributor with husband, Robert A. Fernea) Alice Taylor, editor, *Focus on the Middle East,* Praeger, 1971.

(Contributor with R. A. Fernea) Nikki Keddie, editor, *Scholars, Saints and Sufis,* University of California Press, 1972.

A Street in Marrakech, Doubleday, 1975.

(Editor with Marilyn Duncan) *Texas Women in Politics,* Foundation for Women's Resources (Austin, Tex.), 1977.

(Editor and translator with Basima Qattan Bezirgan) *Middle Eastern Muslim Women Speak,* University of Texas Press, 1977.

(Contributor of translation with Bezirgan) Jacques Berque, *Cultural Expressions in Arab Society,* University of Texas Press, 1978.

(Contributor with James Malarkey and Sara Webber) *History of the Family and Kinship: A Select International Bibliography,* Kraus, 1979.

(With R. A. Fernea) *The Arab World: Personal Encounters,* Doubleday, 1985.

(Editor) *Women and Family in the Middle East: New Voices of Change,* University of Texas Press, 1985.

Also author of filmscripts, "Saints and Spirits," 1979, "A Veiled Revolution," 1982, "The Price of Change," 1982, and "Women under Siege," 1982. Contributor of reviews to periodicals. Contributing editor, *Texas Books in Review.*

WORK IN PROGRESS: A book about children in the Arab world.

SIDELIGHTS: Elizabeth Warnock Fernea and her family have lived in various locations in the Middle East. In the 1970s, Fernea, her husband, and their three children spent a year in the old section of Marrakech in Morocco. Fernea spoke Arabic and was familiar with the culture, but found life in Marrakech difficult and frustrating. "Mrs. Fernea made an interesting and intelligent attempt to get inside the life of Marrakech," reports Anatole Broyard in the *New York Times.* He also comments on Fernea's attempts to disguise herself and gain access to religious services forbidden to foreigners: "Though the author tries to give a sympathetic portrait of these religious excursions, she sounds . . . like a shopper who is determined to buy something as a souvenir of her stay. In spite of herself, she does give us, in 'A Street in Marrakech,' a most unglamorous picture."

In *Women and the Family in the Middle East,* Fernea ties together and presents the disparate voices of women facing a changing world and rigid cultures. According to Amal Rassam in the *New York Times Book Review,* "Faced with the exigencies of a rapidly changing environment . . . Moslem women have started to articulate their ideas and to formulate solutions to the problems facing them and their society. . . . [Fernea] has brought together poems, short stories, essays and reports by women and about women to illustrate these developments." Mervat Hatem in the *Women's Review of Books* thinks that the editor does not fully present the difficulties experienced by her subjects: "In her introduction, Fernea stresses that nationalism provides the framework that influences the way Arab women think of themselves and their families. Yet the poems, short stories and articles in this book tell a different story. The Middle Eastern families presented are not cohesive or harmonious. On the contrary, they are very *tense* institutions." However, Hatem also approves that "Fernea tries to allow those women to speak for themselves. The result is nothing less than spectacular. The diversity of voices shatters the problematic Orientalist assumption about the monolithic conditions and views of women in that part of the world." Rassam also feels the book's diversity defies old stereotypes: "The popular image of Middle Eastern women generally take one of two forms—there is the Western fantasy of the passive yet sensual odalisque, and there is the image of a silent and exploited beast of burden. This collection should help to erase both caricatures."

The Arab World is "an excellent cultural travelogue by Elizabeth and Robert Fernea," writes Zuhair Kashmeri in the Toronto *Globe and Mail.* " It is more than 300 pages of a political, non-headline material that introduces us to the common people of the Middle East and avoids the Sheikh Yamanis and their custom-built Boeing jetliners. . . . [The Fernea's experiences are] described with incredible detail in a personal and moving account." Kashmeri continues, "The Arab World brings the region to life. People and events begin to fall into place and even the violence takes on a new meaning. . . . The view offered in The Arab World begs comparison with the recalcitrant western stand on the Arab-Israeli question." And *Los Angeles Times Book Review* critic Alex Raskin believes that while the book "won't lift the shroud of mystery that seems to envelop people in the Middle East, but by humanizing the Arab world, it might mitigate prejudice."

Fernea's films have been shown on Public Broadcasting Service (PBS-TV), Channel 4 (London), at the Margaret Mead Film Festival of the American Museum of Natural History, and in classrooms all over the United States and Canada. Two have been translated back into Arabic and shown in the Middle East.

BIOGRAPHICAL/CRITICAL SOURCES:

PERIODICALS

Globe and Mail (Toronto), July 13, 1985.

Los Angeles Times Book Review, June 7, 1987.

Ms., January, 1978.
New York Times, October 27, 1975.
New York Times Book Review, September 29, 1985.
Women's Review of Books, Vol. 2, no. 10.

* * *

FERNEA, Robert Alan 1932-

PERSONAL: Surname is pronounced *Fur*-nee-ah; born January 25, 1932, in Vancouver, Wash.; son of George Jacob and Alta (Carter) Fernea; married Elizabeth Warnock (a writer), June 8, 1956; children; Laura Ann, David Karim, Laila Catherine. *Education:* Reed College, B.A., 1954; University of Chicago, M.A., 1957, Ph.D., 1959.

ADDRESSES: Home—3003 Bowman Rd., Austin, Tex. 78703. *Office*—Department of Anthropology, University of Texas, Austin, Tex. 78712.

CAREER: American University, Cairo, Egypt, assistant professor, 1959-63, associate professor, 1963-65; Harvard University, Cambridge, Mass., postdoctoral fellow at Center for Middle Eastern Studies, 1965-66; University of Texas at Austin, associate professor, 1966-69, professor of anthropology, 1969—, director of Center for Middle Eastern Studies, 1966-73. Visiting lecturer, University of Alexandria, Egypt, 1963-65; visiting professor, University of California, Los Angeles, 1968, and University of Washington, summers, 1970, 1988. Researcher in Marrakesh, Morocco, 1972-72; director, summer program in Middle East studies, for HEW and University of Texas, 1971; member of board of governors and president, American Research Center in Egypt, 1984-87; Council for American Overseas Research Centers, Smithsonian Institution, chairman, 1985, member of board of governors, 1987-91. Chairman, Austin Ballet Academy, 1971. Consultant.

MEMBER: Society for Cultural Anthropology (fellow; elected to executive board, 1987-91), American Anthropological Association (fellow; elected to ethics committee, 1986-89), Middle East Studies Association (founding fellow), Sigma Xi.

AWARDS, HONORS: Fulbright postdoctoral awards for study in Afghanistan and Morocco; chosen "Texas Writer of the Year," 1970; French government scholar, Paris and Aix-en-Provence, 1976; recipient with wife, Elizabeth Warnock Fernea, of Carr P. Collins Award for best nonfiction book, Texas Institute of Letters, 1985, for *The Arab World: Personal Encounters.*

WRITINGS:

(Editor) *Contemporary Egyptian Nubia,* Volumes 1 and 2, Human Relations Area File Press, 1966.
Shaykh and Effendi: Changing Patterns of Authority among the El Shabana of Southern Iraq, Harvard University Press, 1970.
(Contributor with wife, Elizabeth Warnock Fernea) Alice Taylor, editor, *Focus on the Middle East,* Praeger, 1971.
(Contributor with E. W. Fernea) Nikki Keddie, editor, *Scholars, Saints and Sufis,* University of California Press, 1972.
(With Georg Gerster) *Nubians in Egypt: Peaceful People,* University of Texas Press, 1973.
(With E. W. Fernea) *The Arab World: Personal Encounters,* Doubleday, 1985.

Contributor of articles and reviews to academic journals.

WORK IN PROGRESS: Research in Middle East; problems of developing countries; ideology of poverty; symbolic anthropology; culture and materialism.

SIDELIGHTS: The Arab World: Personal Encounters is "an excellent cultural travelogue by Elizabeth and Robert Fernea," writes Zuhair Kashmeri in the Toronto *Globe and Mail.* "It is more than 300 pages of a political, non-headline material that introduces us to the common people of the Middle East and avoids the Sheikh Yamanis and their custom-built Boeing jetliners. . . . [The Ferneas' experiences are] described with incredible detail in a personal and moving account." Kashmeri continues that *The Arab World* "brings the region to life. People and events begin to fall into place and even the violence takes on a new meaning. . . . The view offered in The Arab World begs comparison with the recalcitrant western stand on the Arab-Israeli question." And *Los Angeles Times Book Review* critic Alex Raskin believes that while the book "won't lift the shroud of mystery that seems to envelop people in the Middle East, but by humanizing the Arab world, it might mitigate prejudice."

BIOGRAPHICAL/CRITICAL SOURCES:

PERIODICALS

Globe and Mail (Toronto), July 13, 1985.
Los Angeles Times Book Review, June 7, 1987.

* * *

FERRATER-MORA, Jose 1912-

PERSONAL: Born October 30, 1912, in Barcelona, Spain; came to United States, 1947; became naturalized citizen, 1960; son of Maximiliano and Carmen (Mora) Ferrater; married, 1940; children: James. *Education:* Institute of Maragall, Barcelona, B.A., 1932; University of Barcelona, Licenciado en Filosofia, 1936.

ADDRESSES: Home—1518 Willowbrook Lane, Villanova, Pa. 19085. *Office*—Department of Philosophy, Bryn Mawr College, Bryn Mawr, Pa. 19010.

CAREER: University of Chile, Santiago, professor, 1943-47; Bryn Mawr College, Bryn Mawr, Pa., lecturer, 1949-51, associate professor, 1951-56, professor of philosophy, 1956-75, Fairbank Professor of Humanities, 1975-81, professor emeritus, 1981—, chairman of philosophy department, 1971. Visiting professor, Princeton University, 1951-52, Johns Hopkins University, 1955-56, and Temple University, 1970-71.

MEMBER: Institute Internationale de Philosophie, American Philosophical Association, Association for Symbolic Logic, Hispanic Society of America (honorary member).

AWARDS, HONORS: Guggenheim fellowship, 1947-49; American Council of Learned Societies fellowship, 1963-64; D.Litt., Autonomous University of Barcelona, Universidad Nacional de Educacion a Distancia, University of Colombia, National University of Uruguay, University of Mendoza, University of Tucuman, University of Salta, and Central University of Barcelona.

WRITINGS:

Coctel de verdad, Ediciones Literatura (Madrid), 1935.
Diccionario de filosofia, four volumes, Editorial Atlante, (Mexico), 1941, 6th edition, 1979.
Unamuno: Bosquejo de una filosofia, Editorial Losada (Buenos Aires), 1944, Alianza Editorial, 1985, translation by Philip Silver published as *Unamuno: A Philosophy of Tragedy,* University of California Press, 1962, reprinted, Greenwood Press, 1981.
Las formas de la vida catalana, Ediciones de la Agrupacio, 1944, 4th edition, 1972.
Variaciones sobre el espiritu, Editorial Sudamericana (Buenos Aires), 1945.

La ironia, la muerte y la admiracion, Cruz del Sur (Mexico), 1946.

El hombre en la encrucijada, Editorial Sudamericana, 1952, 2nd edition, 1965.

Cuatro visiones de la historia universal: San Agustin, Vico, Voltaire, Hegel, Editorial Sudamericana, 1952, 6th edition, 1971.

Logica matematica, Fondo de Cultura Economica (Buenos Aires), 1955, 4th edition, 1967.

Cuestiones disputadas: Ensayos de filosofia, Revista de Occidente (Madrid), 1955.

Ortega y Gasset: An Outline of His Philosophy, Bowes & Bowes, 1956, Yale University Press, 1957, revised edition, 1963.

Que es la logica?, Editorial Columbia (Buenos Aires), 1957, 3rd edition, 1965.

Man at the Crossroads, translation by Willard R. Trask, Beacon, 1957.

La filosofia en el mundo de hoy, Revista de Occidente, 1959, 2nd edition, c. 1963.

Philosophy Today: Conflicting Tendencies in Contemporary Thought, Columbia University Press, 1960.

Una mica de tot, Editorial Moll (Palma de Mallorca), 1961.

El ser y la muerta: Bosquejo de filosofia integrationista, Aguilar (Madrid), 1962, translation published as *Being and Death: An Outline of Integrationist Philosophy,* University of California Press, 1965.

(With T. A. Brody, J. D. Garcia Bacca, and Henry Margenau) *Symposium sobre informacion y comunicacion,* Universidad Nacional Autonoma de Mexico, 1963.

Obras selectas, two volumes, Ediciones de la Revista de Occidente, 1967.

El ser y el sentido, Ediciones de la Revista de Occidente, 1967.

La filosofia actual, Alianza Editorial, 1969, 4th edition, 1982.

De Joan Oliver a Pere Quart, Ediciones 62 (Barcelona), 1969.

Indagaciones sobre el lenguaje, Alianza Editorial, 1970.

Els mots i els homes, Ediciones 62, 1970.

El hombre y su medio y otros ensayos, Veinteuno de Espana (Madrid), 1971.

Las palabras y los hombres, Ediciones Peninsul, 1972.

Las crisis humanas, Salvat, 1972, reprinted, Alainza Editorial, 1983.

Cambio de marcha en la filosofia, Alianza Editorial, 1974.

Cine sin filosofia, Esti-Arte Ediciones, c. 1974.

De la materia a la razon, Alianza Editorial, 1979.

Siete relatos capitales, Editorial Planeta, 1979.

Etica aplicada: Del aborto a la violencia, Alianza Editorial, 1981.

Claudia, mi Claudia, Alianza Editorial, 1982.

El mundo del escritor, Editorial Critica, 1983.

Fundamentos de filosofia, Alianza Editorial, 1985.

Modos de hacer filosofia, Critica (Barcelona), 1985.

Voltaire en Nueva York, Alianza Editorial, 1985.

Ventana al mundo, Anthropos, 1986.

Hecho en Corona, Alianza Editorial, 1986.

El juego de la verdad, Destino, 1988.

Regreso del infierno, Destino, 1989.

BIOGRAPHICAL/CRITICAL SOURCES:

BOOKS

Cohn, Priscilla, editor, *Transparencies: Philosophical Essays in Honor of J. Ferrater-Mora,* Humanities, 1981.

FETTIG, Art(hur John) 1929-

PERSONAL: Born July 5, 1929, in Detroit, Mich.; son of Arthur J., Sr. (an inventor) and Jenny (Sands) Fettig; married Ruth R. Zepke (a registered nurse), September 11, 1955; children: Nancy Lou, Daniel, Amy, David. *Education:* Attended high school in Detroit, Mich. *Religion:* Roman Catholic.

ADDRESSES: Home—31 East Ave. S., Battle Creek, Mich. 49017. *Office*—Growth Unlimited, Inc., 36 Fairview Dr., Battle Creek, Mich. 49017.

CAREER: Grand Trunk Western Railroad Co., Battle Creek, Mich., railroad claim agent in Detroit, 1948-60, and in Battle Creek, 1960-73, company relations officer, 1973-83; Growth Unlimited (publishers), Battle Creek, president, 1983—. President of True-Fettig & Associates, 1975-78. Conductor of seminars on personal growth, sales management, safety, public speaking, and creative writing, 1973—. *Military service:* U.S. Army, combat rifleman, 1951-53; served in Korea; received Purple Heart and five battle stars.

MEMBER: National Speakers Association, Professional Speakers Association of Michigan.

AWARDS, HONORS: Awards from American Association of Railroads, 1959, 1960; award from National Public Relations Association, 1977; designated certified speaking professional by National Speakers Association, 1980.

WRITINGS:

It Only Hurts When I Frown (humor), Liguori Publications, 1973, revised edition, Growth Unlimited, 1986.

Selling Lucky (true stories) Ovations Unlimited, 1977.

(Co-editor) Herb True, *Funny Bone,* Humor Guild of America, 1977.

(Contributor) Sylvia Costa, editor, *A Manager's Guide to Audio Visuals,* Peterson, 1978.

How to Hold an Audience in the Hollow of Your Hand, Fell, 1979, revised edition, Growth Unlimited, 1988.

The Santa Train, Grand Trunk Western Railroad, 1980.

(Contributor) Donald M. Dible, *Build a Better You, Starting Now,* Volume 7, Dutton, 1981.

Mentor: Secret of the Ages, Fell, 1981.

Remembering, Growth Unlimited, 1982.

The Pos Activity Book, Growth Unlimited, 1984.

"Pos" Parenting: A Guide to Greatness with Twenty-five Keys for Building Your Child's Self-Esteem, Growth Unlimited, 1986.

(With True) *How Funny Are You?: The Humor Game,* Growth Unlimited, 1986.

Selling Luckier Yet, Growth Unlimited, 1987.

Unfit for Glory, Growth Unlimited, 1987.

The Pos "Just Say Yes" Activity Book, Growth Unlimited, 1987.

The Platinum Rule, Growth Unlimited, 1988.

"THE THREE ROBOTS" SERIES

The Three Robots, Growth Unlimited, 1980.

. . . *and the Sandstorm,* Growth Unlimited, 1983.

. . . *Find a Grandpa,* Growth Unlimited, 1984.

. . . *Discover Their Pos-Abilities,* Growth Unlimited, 1984.

. . . *Learn about Drugs,* Growth Unlimited, 1987.

OTHER

Also author of three filmstrips, "They Can't Stop," for Grand Trunk Western Railroad, 1976, "Stages," 1976, and "No Place to Play," 1978. Work has been anthologized in *Forty Salutes to Michigan,* for Poetry Society of Michigan. Contributor of more than a thousand articles, stories, and poems to a variety of magazines in the United States and abroad.

WORK IN PROGRESS: *Rally,* a book for parents and teachers about teaching children to say "yes" to positive values; videotapes on safety.

SIDELIGHTS: Art Fettig told *CA:* "As I travel around America speaking to audiences of all ages, I am becoming alarmed that unless we learn how to instill a sense of values into the lives of our young people, we will be faced with greater problems with our youth. . . . In Woody Wirt's book *The Inner Life of the Believer,* he states that 'TV, which is making the greatest single impact on our culture, is doing its best to convince the human race that love will not work. Instead, it offers revenge, greed, pride and lust as correct motivators of human behavior. I guess if we want to say that love is the key, then we must be willing to stand against the world.' I'll accept that challenge. . . . These are critical times in America. I guess that my job as an author and as a professional speaker is to do my best to bring love into the lives of our children. I believe that love is the answer and if I write books or articles or poems or give speeches to the young or the old, that will be my continuing theme. And if that separates me from the throng, then I will go my way alone and at peace."

* * *

FINKEL, Donald 1929-

PERSONAL: Born October 21, 1929, in New York, N.Y.; son of Saul Aaron (an attorney) and Meta (Rosenthal) Finkel; married Constance Urdang (a writer), August 14, 1956; children: Liza, Thomas Noah, Amy Mariah. *Education:* Columbia University, B.S., 1952, M.A., 1953.

ADDRESSES: *Office*—The Writing Program, Washington University, St. Louis, Mo. 63130.

CAREER: University of Iowa, Iowa City, instructor, 1957-58; Bard College, Annandale-on-Hudson, N.Y., instructor, 1958-60; Washington University, St. Louis, Mo., poet in residence, 1960—. Visiting professor, Bennington College, 1966-67; visiting lecturer, Princeton University, 1985.

MEMBER: Antarctican Society, Cave Research Foundation, Phi Beta Kappa.

AWARDS, HONORS: Helen Bullis Prize, 1964, for *Simeon;* Guggenheim fellow, 1967; *The Garbage Wars* was nominated for a National Book Award, 1970; Ingram Merrill Foundation grant, 1972; National Endowment for the Arts grant, 1973; Theodore Roethke Memorial Award, 1974, for *Adequate Earth; A Mote in Heaven's Eye* and *What Manner of Beast* were nominated for National Book Critics Circle awards, 1975 and 1981, respectively; Morton Dauwen Zabel Award, 1980, for *Endurance: An Antarctic Idyll* [and] *Going Under.*

WRITINGS:

POETRY

The Clothing's New Emperor, edited by John Hall Wheelock, Scribner, 1959.
Simeon, Atheneum, 1964.
A Joyful Noise, Atheneum, 1966.
Answer Back, Atheneum, 1968.
The Garbage Wars, Atheneum, 1970.
Adequate Earth, Atheneum, 1972.
A Mote in Heaven's Eye, Atheneum, 1975.
Endurance: An Antarctic Idyll [and] *Going Under,* Atheneum, 1978.
What Manner of Beast, Atheneum, 1981.
The Detachable Man, Atheneum, 1984.
(With others) *Reading Ourselves to Sleep,* Pterodactyl Press, 1985.
Selected Shorter Poems, Atheneum, 1987.
The Wake of the Electron, Atheneum, 1987.
Time of My Life, Knopf, 1989.

OTHER

Contributor to *Poetry, New Yorker,* and other publications.

WORK IN PROGRESS: *This Child,* a book-length poem on the Wild Child of Aveyron, for Knopf; a collection of translations of contemporary Chinese poetry.

SIDELIGHTS: Donald Finkel, says Peter Meinke in the *St. Petersburgh Times,* "is one of the few Americans trying to extend poetry past the internal into the external world." Finkel is also the recipient of a number of prizes for his poetry: the Helen Bullis Prize in 1964, for *Simeon;* the Theodore Roethke Memorial Award ten years later for *Adequate Earth;* the Morton Dauwen Zabel Award in 1980 for *Endurance: An Antarctic Idyll* [and] *Going Under;* and a National Book Award nomination for *The Garbage Wars* in 1970. As Robert Pack of the *Saturday Review* explains, "Finkel's is not a glib and instant art; it is not, as is so much poetry today, designed for self-destruction after a single reading." Finkel's forte, in the opinion of *Nation* contributor Mary Kinzie, is "finding eloquent and credible language for the speechless and the alien"—a feat accomplished by "extraordinary leaps of insight." His "poetic method," she notes, "has been likened to collage—the interleaving of found, quoted and overheard material with his own dramatic, unpunctuated free verse." *Saturday Review* critic Chad Walsh applauds Finkel's "impressive sense of poetic architecture," noting that "an unsolemn but not frivolous vitality charges through much of his verse."

This vitality is evident in Finkel's 1966 publication, *A Joyful Noise,* which reveals the author to be "a creator of comic extravagance, of an imagination which responds to the seemingly chance, grotesque and unreal nature of present-day life in its own terms," according to *Poetry* reviewer R. J. Mills. Finkel's poems are grimly and outrageously funny, bawdy, satirical, and dreamlike. His characters comprise "a Jewish-French-Irish stew whose chefs might be [Yiddish storyteller] Isaac Singer, [surrealist poet] Andre Breton, and [theater-of-the-absurd playwright] Samuel Beckett," Mills says. Finkel's "poems will last for the raisins in their chocolate," for startling images such as " 'the iron-faced virgin . . . with a thumbtack in her forehead,' " Joseph Bennett suggests in the *New York Times Book Review.* He also feels that Finkel is "so gifted he does not need subjects for his poems. . . . He has, above all, the gift of wonderment."

In *Answer Back,* his 1968 volume of poems, Finkel is "T. S. Eliot reborn, so far as much of the technique is concerned," writes Walsh. The book is actually one long poem which, "zig-zagging between the neolithic past and the napalm present, creates a sense of the human condition in which all times are blended into a dimension of external experience. This poet is worthy grist for the scholarly commentators, but meanwhile I pause to celebrate his extraordinary sense of language and acuteness of observation," Walsh says. Pack appreciates that the quotes and allusions in the poem are carried "by its own strong rhythm, its discrete images, and above all, by its courage to make affirmations seem possible and true in a difficult world." *The Garbage Wars,* says Richard Howard in the *New York Times Book Review,* continues in the same vein, "cheerfully acknowledging indebtedness to just about everything—the Old Testament and Roget's Thesaurus,

Heraclitus and Stokely Carmichael—for the poet insists he is a part of whatever he has read." Again, the reviewer praises Finkel's command of rhythm, calling him a "master of phrasing."

In *Adequate Earth,* Finkel not only "weaves syntactical patterns" skillfully, he also demonstrates the ability to make the reader "see," remarks Louis Coxe in a *New Republic* review. Finkel's vision of the remote continent's alien landscape, informed by his experience as the member of a scientific expedition to Antarctica in 1970, reveals its beauty and mystery. Coxe, the author of a long narrative poem "Middle Passage," recommends *Adequate Earth,* calling it "a splendid piece of work . . . [which is] rich, complex, resonant and—simple, in the best sense." Finkel records another view of antarctic wastelands in *Endurance: An Antarctic Idyll* [and] *Going Under.* Two tales of "the inhospitality of the earth," the first describes the shipwreck and rescue of a 1914 expedition led by Ernest Shackleton, notes John Fuller in the *Times Literary Supplement;* in the second, Finkel borrows the voices of two men who explored Kentucky's Mammoth Caves, where one of them died. Finkel uses the narrative to search "the dark beyond the dark," as it is named in the poem. An encounter with "moral conflict" or "the external verities" such as is available in similar works is lacking here, says Fuller, since the book casts man as "nothing more than a kind of biological rust clinging to the surface of our small planet." G. E. Murray, writing in the *Nation,* feels that *Endurance* is the stronger of the two poems, since its story "of shipwreck and blind treks across glaciers build to an incantation of survival." Murray concludes, "Finkel's detailed pacing and breadth of voice make this a poetry of considerable scope and spirit."

The National Book Critics Circle considered *A Mote in Heaven's Eye* eligible for an award when it was published in 1975. Though it did not win the award, the volume was generally well-received. "Finkel has, as he has always had, an authentic rhythm, a colloquial and jeering tone, a surrealist humor and a gift for childlike diminution of life to cartoon dimensions. But these tricks are laid aside for a harsher outline in his . . . poems about Mexico, beautiful and clearly seen," writes Helen Vendler in the *New York Times Book Review.* Finkel's far-reaching surreal imagery at times requires more imagination than the *Western Humanities Review* contributor could muster; but when successful, says the reviewer, those images make the poems "memorable." The same reviewer comments, "[Finkel's] tone is often absurdly grave and gravely ironic . . . . He controls a mixed style with a faultless ear."

For the poems in *What Manner of Beast* (also nominated for the National Book Critics Circle award), Finkel returns to the collage method of organization. Using quotes from "a bizarre miscellany of sources," Finkel concentrates on bizarre relationships between animals and humans to reflect on the perhaps arbitrary distinctions between the two forms of life, says Jay Parini in the *Times Literary Supplement.* "The boundaries between humans and the other creatures, he seems to be saying, grow ever hazier," observes Phoebe Pettingell. In the *New Leader,* she continues, "Ultimately humans and animals communicate affection and need—a universal connective according to [Finkel]. He sees all creatures as sojourners in a strange land, wandering bewildered and delighted among half-understood objects." Kinzie summarizes in the *Nation:* "Owing to the correspondence between these two realms, every cruel act by a beast (for example, rival apes tearing each other's infants to bits) is matched with equally gratuitous acts committed by men. . . . For every dark intention within primitive men alluded to in his sources, he excerpts yet more chilling and indefensible motives on the part of men presumed civilized."

Particularly bestial, as Finkel casts them, are the actions of scientists and psychologists who subject animals to isolation and sexual deprivation in the process of studying or training them to communicate with humans. A number of Finkel's human characters in this series of poems fall unexpectedly into the same kinds of frustration and agony they have observed in their animal subjects. "It should take a great mind and stout heart to remove oneself into the flesh and minds of other men, other beasts, so deeply as Finkel does," remarks *Best Sellers* reviewer Russ Williams, who regrets what he feels are diffusive humorous ending lines in the poems. Taking a different view, Pettingell states, "A man less sure of his purpose might rely too much on the pathos of the predicament. [Finkel] uses his compassion and humor to poke our sensitive spots and our loneliness, binding us close to our fellow inhabitants on this earth."

Coxe places Finkel among poets who "know their craft and . . . have something to say." According to Richard Howard in *Alone with America: The Art of Poetry in the United States since 1950,* "Finkel's purpose is to establish the poem in a world without myth, on the surface . . . . The poem becomes Finkel's direct experience of what surrounds him—imperfect, but continuing—without his being able to shield himself by a mythology or a metaphysic in his combat with the damages of a lifetime, the disgraces of a death." His creed, concludes Howard, is stated in these lines from *Answer Back:* "My angel is mortal, for which, by the gods, / I believe in him the more."

BIOGRAPHICAL/CRITICAL SOURCES:

BOOKS

Finkel, Donald, *Answer Back,* Atheneum, 1968.
Finkel, Donald, *Endurance: An Antarctic Idyll* [and] *Going Under,* Atheneum, 1978.
Howard, Richard, *Alone with America: The Art of Poetry in the United States since 1950,* Atheneum, 1969.

PERIODICALS

Best Sellers, March, 1982.
Booklist, April 1, 1973.
Georgia Review, fall, 1979.
Hudson Review, spring, 1976.
Nation, May 19, 1979, December 12, 1981.
New Leader, March 8, 1982.
New Republic, February 3, 1973.
New York Times, March 1, 1966.
New York Times Book Review, December 20, 1964, September 4, 1966, November 22, 1970, September 7, 1975.
Parnassus, fall/winter, 1973, spring/summer, 1979.
Poetry, November, 1966, February, 1969, September, 1973, February, 1976, December, 1982.
St. Petersburgh Times, April 3, 1988.
Saturday Review, January 2, 1965, August 24, 1968.
Times Literary Supplement, January 18, 1980, July 2, 1982.
Virginia Quarterly Review, autumn, 1982.
Western Humanities Review, autumn, 1976.
Yale Review, March, 1976.

* * *

FINNERAN, Richard J(ohn) 1943-

PERSONAL: Born December 19, 1943, in New York, N.Y.; son of Edward G. and Maude Florence (Rudden) Finneran; married Mary M. FitzGerald, December 29, 1976; children: two. *Education:* New York University, B.A., 1964; University of North Carolina at Chapel Hill, Ph.D., 1968.

ADDRESSES: Home—243 Evangeline Dr., Mandeville, La. 70448-1875. *Office*—Department of English, University of Tennessee, Knoxville, Tenn. 37996-0430.

CAREER: University of Florida, Gainesville, instructor in English, 1967-68; New York University, New York, N.Y., instructor in English, 1968-70; Tulane University, New Orleans, La., assistant professor, 1970-74, associate professor, 1974-77, professor of English, 1977-88; University of Tennessee, Knoxville, Hodges Chair of Excellence in English Professor, 1988—. Visiting professor, Ohio State University, 1985. Lecturer, Yeats International Summer School, 1972, 1976.

MEMBER: International Association for the Study of Anglo-Irish Literature (executive committee member, 1973-82), American Association of University Professors, Modern Language Association of America (Celtic group chair, 1972, and Anglo-Irish group chair, 1979), South Atlantic Modern Language Association (Irish studies section, program committee chair, 1977, nominating committee chair, 1980 and 1990, executive committee chair, 1987), South Central Modern Language Association (chairman of Anglo-Irish group, 1972).

AWARDS, HONORS: Centenary fellowship to Yeats International Summer School at Sligo, Ireland, 1965; National Endowment for the Humanities summer stipend, 1975 and 1987; American Philosophical Society grant, 1976 and 1980; Huntington Library fellowship, 1978.

WRITINGS:

The Prose Fiction of W. B. Yeats: The Search for "Those Simple Forms," Dolmen Press (Dublin), 1973.
The Olympian and the Leprechaun: W. B. Yeats and James Stephens, Dolmen Press, 1978.
Editing Yeats's Poems, St. Martin's, 1983.
Editing Yeats's Poems: A Reconsideration, St. Martin's, 1989.

EDITOR

W. B. Yeats, *John Sherman and Dhoya,* Wayne State University Press, 1969.
W. B. Yeats: The Byzantium Poems, C. E. Merrill, 1970.
Letters of James Stephens, Macmillan, 1974.
(And contributor) *Anglo-Irish Literature: A Review of Research,* Modern Language Association, 1976, supplement published as *Recent Research on Anglo-Writers: A Supplement,* 1983.
The Correspondence of Robert Bridges and W. B. Yeats, Macmillan, 1977.
(With George Mills Harper and William M. Murphy) *Letters to W. B. Yeats,* two volumes, Columbia University Press, 1977.
(With wife, Mary M. FitzGerald) *Some Unpublished Letters from AE to James Stephens,* Cuala Press (Dalkey, Ireland), 1979.
The Poems of W. B. Yeats: A New Edition, Macmillan, 1983, revised edition, 1989.
Critical Essays on W. B. Yeats, G. K. Hall, 1986.
W. B. Yeats, *The Collected Poems,* Macmillan, 1989.

OTHER

Contributor of essays and reviews to language journals. Founding editor, *Yeats Annual,* 1982-83, and *Yeats: An Annual of Critical and Textual Studies,* 1983—. Editor, with Patricia McFate, of James Stephens number of *Journal of Irish Literature,* 1975. General editor, with George Mills Harper, of the fourteen-volume *Collected Works of W. B. Yeats,* Macmillan; series editor of the ten-volume *Manuscripts of the Poems of W. B. Yeats,* Cornell University Press. Member of editorial/advisory boards for *Irish Renaissance Annual,* 1978-79, *South Atlantic Review,* 1979-82, *Southern Humanities Review,* 1979—, and *TEXT,* 1980—.

WORK IN PROGRESS: Editor and contributor of *Anglo-Irish Literature: A Guide to Research* for Modern Language Association.

SIDELIGHTS: Educator and W. B. Yeats scholar Richard J. Finneran is especially recognized for his editorial efforts on several volumes of work by and about the Irish poet. His recent new edition of Yeats's poetry, *The Poems: A New Edition,* though, has drawn mixed critical response. Delving into the multifarious problems inherent in preparing a definitive edition of Yeats's poetry, citing in particular earlier abandoned attempts by both Macmillan and Scribners, Warwick Gould writes in the *Times Literary Supplement,* for instance: "Finneran has contrived to evade full examination of the archive which stands behind both [of these projects]. . . . As a result, *The Poems: A New Edition* . . . is unsatisfactory in canon, in order and in text. I do not question Finneran's 'eclectic' methodology, as far as it goes. I do question his judgment and his lack of a full perspective on the relation of poet, widow, publisher and publisher's assistant." Conversely, though, in a *New York Times Book Review* assessment, poet Seamus Heaney lauds Finneran's "meticulous and awesome" efforts, stating: "The editor . . . has done prodigious work. Not only has he provided more than 100 pages of 'Explanatory Notes,' which guarantee this publication a double life, textbook and sacred text in one, but in a companion volume on 'Editing Yeats's Poems' he has uncovered the prehistory of the previous standard edition, offered a comma-by-comma critique of it, and established his reasons for the changes he has made in the order, wording and punctuation of many familiar poems." Declaring, moreover, that "all readers of Yeats will need this book," Heaney remarks that "when they open it they will feel a surprise like that experienced by St. Brendan the Navigator and his crew when they disembarked upon an island that turned out to be the back of a dormant sea monster."

AVOCATIONAL INTERESTS: Tennis, basketball, football, music.

BIOGRAPHICAL/CRITICAL SOURCES:

PERIODICALS

New York Times Book Review, March 18, 1984.
Times Literary Supplement, June 29, 1984.

* * *

FINNIGAN, Joan 1925-
(Michelle Bedard)

PERSONAL: Born November 23, 1925, in Ottawa, Ontario, Canada; daughter of Frank (a former National Hockey League player) and Maye (Horner) Finnigan; married Charles Grant MacKenzie (a psychiatrist), May 23, 1949 (died August, 1965); children: Jonathan Alexander, Christopher Roderick, Martha Ruth. *Education:* Queen's University, B.A. *Religion:* "Homegrown."

ADDRESSES: Home—Moore Farm, Hambly Lake, Harrington, Ontario, Canada K0H 1W0.

CAREER: Former school teacher and reporter for the Ottawa *Journal,* Ottawa, Ontario; free-lance writer for the National Film Board of Canada and the Canadian Broadcasting Corporation, Toronto, Ontario, 1965—.

AWARDS, HONORS: Borestone Mountain Poetry Prize, 1959, 1961, 1963; Centennial Prize for Poetry, 1967; President's Prize for Poetry, University of Western Ontario, 1969; Canadian Film Award (Genie) for best screenplay, 1969, for "The Best Damn Fiddler from Calabogie to Kaladar"; six Canada Council grants, including senior grant, 1973-74; Philemon Wright Award for History and Research in the Outaouais; Ottawa-Carleton Literary Award; Explorations Grant from Canada Council; Multiculturalism Grant; Ontario Heritage Foundation grant; Historical Society of the Gatineau grants.

WRITINGS:

POETRY

Through the Glass, Darkly, Ryerson, 1957.
A Dream of Lilies, University of New Brunswick Press, 1965.
Entrance to the Greenhouse, Ryerson, 1968.
It Was Warm and Sunny When We Set Out, Ryerson, 1970.
In the Brown Cottage on Loughborough Lake, CBC Learning Systems, 1970.
Living Together, Fiddlehead Poetry Books, 1976.
A Reminder of Familiar Faces, NC Press, 1978.
This Series Has Been Discontinued, University of New Brunswick Press, 1981.
The Watershed Collection, edited and introduced by Robert Weaver, Quarry Press, 1988.
Wintering Over, Quarry Press, in press.

PROSE

(Under pseudonym Michelle Bedard) *Canada in Bed,* Pagurian Press, 1969.
Kingston: Celebrate This City, McClelland & Stewart, 1976.
"I Come from the Valley," (also see below), NC Press, 1976.
Canadian Colonial Cooking, NC Press, 1976.
Canada: Country of the Giants, General Store Publishing, 1981.
Some of the Stories I Told You Were True, Deneau Publishers, 1981.
Look! The Land Is Growing Giants, Tundra Press, 1983.
Laughing All the Way Home, Deneau Publishers, 1984.
Legacies, Legends and Lies, Deneau Publishers, 1985.
Finnigan's Guide to the Ottawa Valley, Quarry Press, 1988.
Tell Me Another Story (oral history), McGraw-Hill Ryerson, 1988.
The Dog Who Wouldn't Be Left Behind, Douglas & McIntyre, 1989.
Tallying the Tales of the Old-Timers (oral history), McGraw-Hill Ryerson, 1990.
Growing Up and Leaving Town (memoir), General Publishing, in press.

PLAYS AND SCREENPLAYS

"The Best Damn Fiddler from Calabogie to Kaladar" (screenplay; also see below), produced by National Film Board of Canada and shown on Canadian television, 1969.
"Up the Vallee!" (play), produced in Toronto at Tarragon Theatre, 1978.
The Best Damn Fiddler from Calabogie to Kaladar (collection), Quarry Press, 1990.

Also author of play "A Prince of Good Fellows," (first produced on CBC-TV), published in *"I Come from the Valley";* author of plays "Songs from Both Sides of the River," produced in Ottawa at National Art Centre, "A Night on the Black River," and "Abigail Edey on the Ottawa," both produced in Ottawa at Museum of Civilization.

OTHER

Author of *A Final Understanding,* a collection of short stories, 1989, *The Opeongo Line,* a literary history, 1989. Contributor to magazines.

* * *

FORSYTH (OUTRAM), Anne 1933-

PERSONAL: Born March 17, 1933, in Dunfermline, Scotland; daughter of James Whyte and Catherine (Marshall) Forsyth; married D.H. Outram. *Education:* University of St. Andrews, M.A., 1953.

ADDRESSES: Home—4 East Ridgeway, Cuffley, Hertfordshire, England.

CAREER: Fife Herald, Cupar, Fife, Scotland, reporter, 1953-55; *Manchester Evening News,* Manchester, England, reporter, 1955-57; Halle Concerts Society, Manchester, secretary to Sir John Barbirolli, 1957-59; *Woman's Own,* London, England, 1959-64, began as sub-editor, became assistant home editor; Macmillan & Co., London, editor in overseas department, 1964-69; Routledge & Kegan Paul Ltd., London, editorial manager, 1969-70; Evans Brothers Ltd., London, managing editor of Overseas and English Language Teaching Books, 1970-78; Bell & Hyman Ltd., London, editorial manager, 1979-81; free-lance editor.

WRITINGS:

English for Everyone, Macmillan, 1969.
Cheap and Cheerful, Homemaking on a Budget, Mills & Boon, 1973.
Table Settings for All Occasions, Mills & Boon, 1975.
Your Own Place, Oliver & Boyd, 1976.
(With others) *Practical Homemaking,* Bell & Hyman, 1980.
Baxter the Travelling Cat, Hodder & Stoughton, 1981.
(Co-author) *Beginning Cookery,* Bell & Hyman, 1981.
Sam's Wonderful Shell, Hamish Hamilton, 1982.
Monster Monday, Hamish Hamilton, 1983.
Baxter and the Golden Pavements, Hodder & Stoughton, 1984.
The Money Makers, Hamish Hamilton, 1984.
The Spitfire Secret, Hamish Hamilton, 1985.
The Wedding-Day Scramble, Hamish Hamilton, 1985.
Mostly Magic, Hamish Hamilton, 1986.
Baxter by the Sea, Hodder & Stoughton, 1987.
The Monster Flower Show, Hamish Hamilton, 1987.
The Library Monster, Hamish Hamilton, 1988.
The Digger, Macdonald, 1988.

BIOGRAPHICAL/CRITICAL SOURCES:

PERIODICALS

Books and Bookmen, September, 1969.

* * *

FOX, Brian
See BALLARD, (Willis) Todhunter

* * *

FOX, C(arol) Lynn 1948-

PERSONAL: Born June 22, 1948, in Louisville, Ky.; daughter of Charles Fremont and Gladys Ruth (Williams) Fox; married Dean H. Nafziger, October 11, 1986. *Education:* University of

Louisville, B.A., 1970, M.A., 1971; University of California, Los Angeles, Ph.D., 1978. *Politics:* Republican. *Religion:* Baptist.

ADDRESSES: Home—128 Sugar Loaf Dr., Tiburon, Calif. 94920. *Office*—College of Education, San Diego State University, San Diego, Calif. 92182.

CAREER: Substitute teacher at public schools in Louisville, Ky., 1968-70, teacher of learning-disabled children, 1970-71; resource teacher at public schools in Atlanta, Ga., 1971-73; teacher at Center for the Educationally Handicapped, 1973-74; itinerant learning disabilities teacher, 1974-75; California State University, Los Angeles, assistant professor of special education, 1978-79; San Diego State University, School of Teacher Education, San Diego, Calif., assistant professor, 1979-82, associate professor, 1982—. Educational therapist for Valley Psychological and Learning Group, 1978-79; private educational consultant, 1979—; gives workshops nationally; guest on television and radio programs. Member of Arthritis Foundation of California, 1977-80, and San Diego Area Chapter of National Multiple Sclerosis Society Committee, 1986. Balboa Park Concert Committee, vice-chairman, 1982-84, chairperson, 1984—. Member of San Diego Very Special Arts Festival, 1982, and San Diego World Affairs Council, 1982. Member of board, East County Neighborhood Recovery Center, 1984-86. Co-director of Project STOP (Standing Together to Offer Prevention).

MEMBER: International Association of Learning Disabilities, National Council for Exceptional Children, Association for Children with Learning Disabilities, Association of Teacher Educators, National Federation for Drug-Free Youth, California Association of Professors in Special Education, California Association of Vocational Education, California Reading Association, California State Federation/Council for Exceptional Children, California State Division of Children with Learning Disabilities, California Association of Teacher Educators, Californians for Drug-Free Youth, Pi Lambda Theta, Kappa Delta Pi.

AWARDS, HONORS: Second prize from International Rehabilitation Film Festival, 1982, for "Making Special Friends"; Special Merit Award for Informational Public Television from Western Educational Society for Telecommunications, 1983; named Outstanding Faculty Member at San Diego State University, 1983; media development grant from Ilan Lael Foundation, 1986; award of merit and award of excellence for education from International Television association, both 1986; Best of the West Award for Elementary Education Video from Western Education Society, 1986; Emmy from National Academy of Television Arts and Sciences, 1987, for children's program "Poems of Wonder and Magic"; U.S. Department of Education grant for Project STOP, 1987-88; Colby Award from Sigma Kappa, 1988.

WRITINGS:

Guidelines for Setting Differential Standards for the Handicapped (monograph), California State Department of Education, 1979.

(With Susan Hocevar) *Understanding Handicapping Conditions: Strategies for Improving Awareness and Acceptance of Handicapped Students in the Regular Classroom* (training manual), California Regional Resource Center, 1979.

Communicating to Make Friends: A Program for the Classroom Teacher, B. L. Winch & Associates, 1980.

(With I. M. Malian) *Social Acceptance: Key to Mainstreaming,* B. L. Winch & Associates, 1983.

(With F. L. Weaver) *Unlocking Doors to Friendship,* B. L. Winch & Associates, 1983.

(Contributor) Thomas N. Fairchild, editor, *Crisis Intervention Strategies for School-Based Helpers,* C. C Thomas, 1986.

(With S. E. Forbing and P. S. Anderson) *Model for Drug-Free Schools* (monograph), Northwest Regional Educational Laboratory, 1987.

(Editor with Anderson and J. R. Salmon) *Curricula and Programs for Drug and Alcohol Education,* Northwest Regional Educational Laboratory, 1987.

(With Forbing) *Fighting Substance Abuse in Our Schools,* Scott, Foresman, 1988.

EDUCATIONAL MEDIA/VIDEOTAPES

"Peer Acceptance of Exceptional Children," released by Los Angeles Unified School District, 1978.

"Making Special Friends," released by Learning Resource Center at San Diego State University, 1981.

"Unlocking Doors to Friendship," released by Learning Resource Center at San Diego State University, 1983.

"Work and Motherhood: The Dilemma of the New Professional Women," released by Learning Resource Center at San Diego State University, 1985.

"Poems of Wonder and Magic," released by Learning Resource Center at San Diego State University, 1986.

OTHER

Author of instructional activity packets, "Handicapped: How Does It Feel?," for elementary and secondary schools, B. L. Winch & Associates, 1982. Contributor to many education journals and newspapers. Guest editor of *UCLA Educator,* 1978.

WORK IN PROGRESS: With Kettner, *The Success-Maker Formula; The "Work Smarter, Not Harder" Program for Organizing a Successful Classroom.*

SIDELIGHTS: C. Lynn Fox commented: "I have worked with both regular education and special education students at elementary and secondary levels. I find it an exciting challenge to help special needs students (especially the learning disabled, behavior disordered, and mildly retarded children) meet their full potential. With the correct assistance and understanding, these children can become productive members of society.

"I am especially interested in the areas of social acceptance and self-concept enhancement of all children. I have chosen to focus my writing on these areas. My first book, *Communicating to Make Friends,* was my initial contribution to directing elementary-school-age children to communicate with others more effectively. The direction at this age is of a preventive nature. My book *Unlocking Doors to Friendship* carries the concepts of building strong self-concepts and interpersonal skills to adolescents. It was developed because of direct requests from teachers and parents who feel there is more to living and learning than academic instruction alone. There is a strong need to deal with the social and emotional problems of adolescents in order to be able to teach them academic skills.

"Now I feel that I need to carry these concepts to the adult population. This will be the focus of a future book.

"As for mainstreaming—the practice of placing handicapped students in the regular classroom—I feel an ultra-strong commitment to making sure that it works for all involved. I feel that everyone wins if the social environment is properly set. My research and writing will continue to assist teachers, parents, and children in establishing the right environment for the mainstreamed student. Handicapped individuals have come a long way since 1975, when they received their Bill of Rights in the schools.

"My workshops and conferences have allowed me to travel extensively throughout the United States. I have spent quite a bit of time in Alaska, have traveled in Europe, and plan some workshops in the Arab countries. People all over the world are interested in better educating the handicapped. I'm proud to be involved in this positive movement."

Fox continued: "In the last five years my professional focus has been in fighting drugs and alcohol abuse among our youth. It continues to be a challenge as there is so much new information being disseminated in the area. I believe teacher training and parent and community cooperation are the keys to success."

BIOGRAPHICAL/CRITICAL SOURCES:

PERIODICALS

Chula Vista Star News, December 27, 1981.
Mainstream, September, 1981.
Rochester Times-Union, August 16, 1979.
San Diego Evening Tribune, September 15, 1980.
San Diego Sentinel, June 4, 1980.
San Diego Union, December 22, 1981.

* * *

FOX, Connie
See FOX, Hugh (Bernard, Jr.)

* * *

FOX, Freeman
See HAMILTON, Charles (Harold St. John)

* * *

FOX, Hugh (Bernard, Jr.) 1932-
(Connie Fox)

PERSONAL: Born February 12, 1932, in Chicago, Ill.; son of Hugh Bernard (a physician) and Helen M. (Mangan) Fox; married Lucia Alicia Ungaro (a Peruvian poet and critic), June 9, 1957 (divorced, 1969); married Nona W. Werner (a professor and writer), June, 1970; children: (first marriage) Hugh Bernard III, Cecilia, Marcella; (second marriage) Margaret, Alexandra, Christopher. *Education:* Loyola University, Chicago, B.A., 1954, M.A., 1955; University of Illinois, Ph.D., 1958. *Politics:* None. *Religion:* None.

ADDRESSES: Office—Department of American Thought and Language, Michigan State University, East Lansing, Mich. 48823.

CAREER: Loyola University of Los Angeles (now Loyola Marymount University), Los Angeles, Calif., professor of American literature, 1958-68; Michigan State University, East Lansing, professor of American thought and language, 1968—. U.S. Information Service lecturer throughout Latin America, 1958—. Fulbright Professor in Mexico, 1961, in Caracas, Venezuela, 1964-66, and in Brazil at Federal University of Santa Catarina, 1978-80.

MEMBER: Committee of Small Magazine Editors and Publishers (member of board of directors, 1968-76).

AWARDS, HONORS: John Carter Brown Library magazines grant, 1968; Organization of American States research grant, 1969-70, for study in Buenos Aires, Argentina, 1987, for archaeological fieldwork in the Atacama Desert, Chile.

WRITINGS:

America Today (lectures), [Caracas, Venezuela], 1965.
Problems of Our Time (essays), [Caracas], 1966.
A Night with Hugh Fox (three one-act plays), [Caracas], 1966.
Henry James: A Critical Introduction, J. Westburg (Conesville, Iowa), 1968.
Countdown on an Empty Streetcar (novel), Abyss Publications, 1969.
Charles Bukowski: A Critical and Bibliographical Study, Abyss Publications, 1969.
Gnosis Knows Best: A Radiography of the North American Subconsciousness (novella), [East Lansing, Mich.], 1969, reprinted, Semiotext, 1988.
(Editor with Sam Cornish) *The Living Underground: An Anthology of Contemporary American Poetry,* Ghost Dance, 1969, revised edition, Whitston, 1973.
The Living Underground: A Critical Overview, Whitston, 1970.
The Omega Scriptures, Ghost Dance, 1971.
Peeple (short stories), Dustbooks, 1972.
The Gods of the Cataclysm: A Revolutionary Investigation of Man and His Gods before and after the Great Cataclysm (anthropology), Harper's Magazine Press, 1976.
The Invisibles (novel), The Smith, 1976.
The Face of Guy Lombardo (short stories), Fault, 1976.
(Contributor) John Bennett, editor, *Happy Deathday,* Vagabond, 1977.
(Editor) *First Fire* (anthology of Amerindian poetry), Doubleday-Anchor, 1978.
Honeymoon (semi-autobiographical novel), December Press, 1978.
Mom (semi-autobiographical novel), December Press, 1978.
The Poetry of Charles Potts (criticism), Dustbooks, 1979.
Leviathan (novel), Carpenter Press, 1981.
The Guernica Cycle: The Year Franco Died (diary), Cherry Valley, 1983.
(Contributor) *Fiction 84,* Paycock Press, 1984.
Lyn Lifshin: A Critical Study, Whitston, 1985.
The Mythological Foundations of the Epic Genre: The Solar Voyage and the Hero's Journey, Edwin Mellen, 1988.
Song of Christopher, Clock Radio Press, 1988.
(Under pseudonym Connie Fox) *The Dream of the Black Topaze Chamber: The Portfolio* (contains selections from Fox's unpublished novel *The Dream of the Black Topaze Chamber*), Trout Creek Press, 1988.

POETRY

Soul-Catcher Songs, Ediciones de la Frontera, 1967, 2nd edition, 1968.
Eye into Now, Ediciones de la Frontera, 1967.
Apotheosis of Olde Towne, Fat Frog Press, 1968.
Glyphs, Fat Frog Press, 1969.
The Permeable Man, Black Sun Press, 1969.
Son of Camelot Meets the Wolf Man, Quixote Press, 1969.
Waca, Ghost Dance, 1975.
Almazora 42, Laughing Bear Press, 1982.
Papa Funk (chapbook), Brian C. Clark, 1986.

UNDER PSEUDONYM CONNIE FOX; POETRY

Blood Cocoon, Zahir, 1980.
The Dream of the Black Topaze Chamber: The Poem Cycle, Ghost Pony, 1983.
Oma, Implosion Press, 1985.
Nachthymnen, Mudborn, 1986.
Ten to the One Hundred Seventieth Power, Trout Creek Press, 1986.

Babicka, Kangaroo Court Press, 1986.
Skull Worship, Applezaba, 1988.
Our Lady of Laussel, Spectacular Diseases Press (England), 1988.
Noria, Plain View, 1988.

OTHER

Also author of *The Living Underground: The Prose Anthology,* Whitston. Author of several screenplays, including "The Laundromat." Unpublished works include: the novels *Shaman, Mandala, Sketches toward the Definition of a False Brazilian Messiah,* and, under pseudonym Connie Fox, *The Dream of the Black Topaze Chamber;* the prose piece "Dialogue"; and the play "Voices." Editor, "Ghost Dance Portfolio" series, 1968—. Contributor of poetry, criticism, fiction, and articles on cultural history to periodicals, including *Transatlantic Review, TriQuarterly, Pan American Review, Prairie Schooner, Western Humanities Review, Choice, Long Story,* and *West Coast Review.* Founder and editor, *Ghost Dance: The International Quarterly of Experimental Poetry.*

WORK IN PROGRESS: 666: The Case of the Screaming Torch, a murder mystery based on Sherlock Holmes; *The Voyage to the House of Yama,* a fantasy novel with roots in C. S. Lewis; *The Thirteen Keys to Talmud,* which "begins as a science fiction novel in the Stanislaw Lem tradition but changes into a novel about a psychotic child."

SIDELIGHTS: Hugh Fox once told *CA:* "The most 'releasing' experiences I've had were trips to Spain (1975-76) and Brazil (1978-80). While in Spain I fell under the influence of contemporary Spanish authors like Juan Bennett and Camilo Jose Cela. While in Spain I wrote a nonstop diary *The Guernica Cycle: The Year Franco Died.* I also did some poetry in Spain . . . [published] as *Almazora 42* (my address in Valencia). When I came back to the United States in 1976, I went into a fit of depression and wrote a whole book of death meditations that John Bennett excerpted from to produce *Happy Deathday.* I also did three essays that came out as a special issue of *Camels Coming.*

"The Brazil trip activated everything. I fell in love with Brazilian *Modernismo,* especially the work of Oswald de Andrade, his 'mural novels,' which triggered my own [as yet unpublished] novel *Sketches toward the Definition of a False Brazilian Messiah* . . . and my first [as yet unpublished] novel as Connie Fox, *The Dream of the Black Topaze Chamber* . . . . I found Brazil itself a huge experiment, romantic, surrealistic, magical, a complicated syncretic blend of the African, the Portuguese, the Indian. Never stopped writing."

Fox later wrote to *CA* that "all during the 1980s I worked on prehistory, both European and American, wrote a number of articles for *Pulpsmith,* and in 1987 got a grant from the Organization of American States as an archaeologist to spend the winter in San Pedro de Atacama in the Chilean desert right *on* the Tropic of Capricorn, following up the work of Belgian Jesuit Gustavo le Page. . . . The conclusion I came to was that Atacama was a sun-worship point for ancient world peoples going back as far as 60,000 B.C. or earlier, which more or less agrees with le Page's theories.

"One by-product of these anthropological-archaeological books was *Our Lady of Laussel,* a poem-cycle (accompanied by prose meditations) attempting to use prehistoric (mainly European) ideas linked up with modern life to show that under the facade of The Modern, we are essentially the same as prehistoric man."

MEDIA ADAPTATIONS: The poetry volume *Babicka* is available on cassette, Suburban Wilderness Aural Library, 1988; *Song of Christopher* is available on cassette, Suburban Wilderness Aural Library.

* * *

FREEDLAND, Michael 1934-

PERSONAL: Born December 18, 1934, in London, England; son of David (a sales manager) and Lily (Mindel) Freedland; married Sara Hockerman (a secretary), July 3, 1960; children: Fiona Anne, Danielle Ruth, Jonathan Saul. *Education:* National Council for Training of Journalists, proficiency certificate, 1955. *Religion:* Jewish.

ADDRESSES: Home and office—35 Hartfield Ave., Elstree, Hertfordshire WD6 3JB, England.

CAREER: Luton News, Luton, England, journalist, 1951-60; *Daily Sketch,* London, England, journalist, 1960-61; British Broadcasting Corp., London, executive producer and presenter of radio show "You Don't Have to Be Jewish," 1971—. Member of board of deputies, British Jews, 1969-72.

WRITINGS:

Jolson, Stein & Day, 1972 (published in England as *Al Jolson,* W. H. Allen, 1972), revised and updated edition published as *"Jolie": The Story of Al Jolson, 1885-1985,* W. H. Allen, 1986.
Irving Berlin, Stein & Day, 1974, new edition published as *A Salute to Irving Berlin,* W. H. Allen, 1986.
James Cagney, W. H. Allen, 1974, published as *Cagney,* Stein & Day, 1975.
Fred Astaire, W. H. Allen, 1976, Grosset, 1978.
Sophie: The Sophie Tucker Story, Woburn Press, 1976.
The Two Lives of Errol Flynn, Morrow, 1978 (published in England as *Errol Flynn,* Arthur Barker, 1978).
Jerome Kern, Robson Books, 1978, Stein & Day, 1981.
Gregory Peck: A Biography, Morrow, 1980.
Maurice Chevalier, Arthur Barker, 1981, Morrow, 1982.
(With Eric Morecambe and Ernie Wise) *There's No Answer to That!: An Autobiography,* Arthur Barker, 1981.
Peter O'Toole: A Biography, St. Martin's, 1983.
The Warner Brothers, Harrap, 1983.
So Let's Hear the Applause: A Tribute to the Jewish Entertainer, Vallentine, Mitchell, 1984.
Jack Lemmon, St. Martin's, 1985.
Katharine Hepburn, Comet, 1985.
Shirley MacLaine, W. H. Allen, 1986.
The Secret Life of Danny Kaye, St. Martin's, 1986.
The Goldwyn Touch: A Biography of Sam Goldwyn, Harrap, 1986.
Linda Evans, St. Martin's, 1986.
Leonard Bernstein, Harrap, 1987.
Jane Fonda, St. Martin's, 1987.
Liza with a Z, W. H. Allen, 1988.
(With Walter Scharf) *Composed and Conducted,* Vallentine, Mitchell, 1988.

Contributor to the London *Times, Evening Standard,* and national magazines.

WORK IN PROGRESS: Three biographies.

SIDELIGHTS: Michael Freedland wrote *CA:* "There are too many attempts at pop psychiatry among so-called biographers. I never try to put myself in some Freudian chair, but I do try to see a person from the point of view of those who know him or her well; to be able to tell the true story that perhaps even the subjects themselves never know—the stories behind the newspaper pieces. Too many other writers, I believe, forget that their principal task should simply be that of story teller."

* * *

FREEMAN, Cynthia
See FEINBERG, Beatrice Cynthia Freeman

* * *

FRIEDENBERG, Edgar Zodiag 1921-

PERSONAL: Born March 18, 1921, in New York, N.Y.; son of Edgar M. and Arline (Zodiag) Friedenberg. *Education:* Centenary College, B.S., 1938; Stanford University, M.A., 1939; University of Chicago, Ph.D., 1946.

ADDRESSES: Home—Conrad Rd., Hubbards, Nova Scotia, Canada. *Office*—Department of Education, Dalhousie University, Halifax, Nova Scotia, Canada.

CAREER: University of Chicago, Chicago, Ill., instructor, 1946-49, assistant professor of education, 1949-53; Brooklyn College (now of the City University of New York), Brooklyn, N.Y., assistant professor, 1953-60, associate professor of education, 1960-64; University of California, Davis, professor of sociology, 1964-67; State University of New York at Buffalo, professor of sociology and education, 1967-70; Dalhousie University, Halifax, Nova Scotia, professor of education, 1970-86, professor emeritus, 1986—. R. Freeman Butts lecturer, American Educational Studies Association, 1978; George M. Duck lecturer, University of Windsor Faculty of Law, 1979; Aquinas lecturer, St. Thomas University, 1981; Weiner distinguished visitor, University of Manitoba, 1982; visiting professor of law, State University of New York at Buffalo, fall, 1986; speaker, American Society for Adolescent Psychiatry, Montreal, 1988.

MEMBER: American Civil Liberties Union, Canadian Civil Liberties Association, Authors Guild, Authors League of America, Society for the Study of Social Problems, Sociologists Gay Caucus, Dalhousie University Faculty Association (president, 1980-81).

WRITINGS:

A Technique for Developing Courses in Physical Science Adapted to the Needs of Students at the Junior College Level, University of Chicago Press, 1946.

(With Julius A. Roth) *Self-Perception in the University: A Study of Successful and Unsuccessful Graduate Students,* University of Chicago Press, 1954.

The Vanishing Adolescent, Beacon Press, 1959, reprinted, Greenwood Press, 1985.

(With Carl Nordstrom) *Why Successful Students of the Natural Sciences Abandon Careers in Science,* Brooklyn College of the City University of New York, 1961.

(With Nordstrom) *Influence of Resentment on Student Experience in Secondary School,* Brooklyn College of the City University of New York, 1965.

Coming of Age in America: Growth and Acquiescence, Random House, 1965.

The Dignity of Youth and Other Atavisms, Beacon Press, 1965.

(With Nordstrom and A. Hilary Gold) *Society's Children,* Random House, 1967.

Adolescence as America's Last Minority (sound recording), Jeffrey Norton, 1969.

(Editor) *The Anti-American Generation,* Aldine, 1971, 2nd edition, Transaction Books, 1972.

Laing, Fontana, 1973, published as *R. D. Laing,* Viking, 1974.

The Disposal of Liberty and Other Industrial Wastes, Doubleday, 1975.

Deference to Authority: The Case of Canada, M. E. Sharpe, 1980, published in part as "Deference to Authority: Education in Canada and the United States," in *Poverty, Power, and Authority in Education,* edited by Edgar B. Gumbert, Center for Cross-Cultural Education, College of Education, Georgia State University, 1981.

WORK IN PROGRESS: Screw Your Courage.

SIDELIGHTS: Social and educational critic Edgar Zodiag Friedenberg is of a group "far too independent and cantankerous to develop a consistent voice or anything that could be considered a program, but their common defense of children and adolescents and their fundamental attacks on established practices have given them a place apart from the conventional critics," describes Peter Schrag in the *Saturday Review.* In evaluating the condition of American education, Friedenberg is "more interested in the processes of growing up, in learning and experience, than [he is] in the formalities of educational programs, the design of curricula, or the planning of administrative conveniences," adds Schrag. In *Coming of Age in America: Growth and Acquiescence,* Friedenberg investigates some of these processes and programs, "conduct[ing] us on a harrowing tour of what it means to be an adolescent in America today and, more specifically, what it means to be a student in an American high school today," relates Eliot Fremont-Smith in a *New York Times* review. The critic further comments that the work is "an ambitious and useful synthesis of current criticism of American education and the dubious conformist values it reflects." As the author asserts in his book, "Adolescents are among the last social groups in the world to be given the full nineteenth-century colonial treatment. Our colonial administrators . . . study the young with a view to understanding them, not for their own sake but in order to learn how to induce them to abandon their barbarism and assimilate the folkways of normal adult life." As Miriam L. Goldberg maintains in her *Saturday Review* article, the "immediate effect" of Friedenberg's argument "is to engage the reader in an intense dialogue on crucial social and educational issues and to force him to clarify his own beliefs and commitments."

Although Friedenberg "has great gifts in reporting how children feel" about education and conformity, *New York Review of Books* contributor Morton White believes that "like so many behavioral scientists who study values, he tries to rise to a higher level on which he begins to use the terminology of philosophy, and here is where the reader begins to have a certain amount of difficulty in understanding or believing what he has to say." Goldberg also finds fault with the author's thesis, claiming that by blaming schools for "the distorted values of the majority of adolescents, Friedenberg joins the ranks of other social critics who unwittingly compliment the school by endowing it with power it doesn't have and then castigate it for failing to exercise these powers." While he calls *Coming of Age in America* "a rich and provocative book," Fremont-Smith also admits that "there are points of weakness and possible disagreement," including "an anachronistic tendency to romanticize." Despite these problems, Jonathan Kozol terms the work in the *Christian Science Monitor* "one of the most insightful condemnations of American education that I have ever read." The critic concludes that Friedenberg's essays are "consistently eloquent and they rise on many occasions . . . to something like an inspired social tract." "The book is itself a model of the qualities the author cherishes and finds wanting in our schools," claims Goldberg; "it has style and charm and it boldly presents ideas that diverge in all directions from any standard point of view."

In *The Disposal of Liberty and Other Industrial Wastes,* "Friedenberg develops themes which he has examined in prior work on youth and schools and the shaping of values and behaviors in American society," recounts Steven Deutsch in *Contemporary Sociology.* In this work Friedenberg defines and explores the idea of *ressentiment,* a concept first proposed by Nietzsche: "Ressentiment is a free-floating disposition to visit upon others the bitterness that accumulates from one's own subordination and existential guilt at allowing oneself to be used by other people for their own purposes, while one's life rusts away unnoticed." It is due to this ressentiment, claims the author, that people "are outraged by the proposal of a direct subvention of [or support for] the poor," and thus "fear that the poor may get a little more than they deserve." While Deutsch feels that at times "Friedenberg is wonderfully insightful and in few words makes solid points," he feels that the author is lacking "some structural analysis that [would] document . . . the process of *ressentiment* and mass political psychology." And Wilson Carey McWilliams accuses the book of being "itself a lengthy example of bourgeois *ressentiment,* characterized by an indignation so extreme as to lack moral discrimination." But Kenneth F. Kister, in a *Library Journal* review, calls the book both "a brilliant exercise in conservative reductionism" and a "thoughtful exposition of why our social and political verities have broken down." "If nothing else," comments Schrag, "people like Friedenberg have raised the current level of discourse from its programmatic, managerial plateau to a level in which individual human beings are restored to the argument." In the case of education, Schrag concludes, "[Friedenberg and other] critics have reminded us . . . that if [relevant education] does not deal with the humanity of its students, it is not dealing with anything."

BIOGRAPHICAL/CRITICAL SOURCES:

BOOKS

Contemporary Issues Criticism, Volume 1, Gale, 1981.
Friedenberg, Edgar Zodiag, *Coming of Age in America: Growth and Acquiescence,* Random House, 1965.
Friedenberg, Edgar Zodiag, *The Disposal of Liberty and Other Industrial Wastes,* Doubleday, 1975.

PERIODICALS

Christian Science Monitor, September 9, 1965.
Contemporary Sociology, May, 1978.
Dalhousie Review, Number 1, 1986-87.
Library Journal, September 1, 1975.
Nation, March 28, 1966.
New York Review of Books, June 17, 1965, July 17, 1980.
New York Times, June 19, 1965.
New York Times Book Review, August 15, 1965, October 12, 1975, May 18, 1980.
Saturday Night, March, 1976.
Saturday Review, November 20, 1965, February 18, 1967.

* * *

FROMM, Erich 1900-1980

PERSONAL: Born March 23, 1900, in Frankfurt, Germany; died of a heart attack March 18, 1980, in Muralto, Switzerland; came to United States in 1934; naturalized citizen, 1940; son of Naphtali (a wine merchant) and Rosa (Krause) Fromm; married Frieda Reichmann, June 16, 1926 (divorced); married Henny Gurland, July 24, 1944 (died, 1952); married Annis Freeman, December 18, 1953. *Education:* University of Heidelberg, Ph.D., 1922; attended University of Munich, 1923-24, Institute of the German Psychoanalytic Society, 1928-31, Psychoanalytic Institute (Berlin), and University of Frankfurt.

ADDRESSES: Home—180 Riverside Dr., New York, N.Y. 10024; and Locarno, Switzerland.

CAREER: Psychoanalyst, philosopher, and writer, 1925-80. Psychoanalytic Institute and University of Frankfurt, Frankfurt, Germany, lecturer in social psychology at Institute for Social Research, 1929-32; Columbia University, International Institute for Social Research, New York City, lecturer, 1934-39, guest lecturer, 1940-41; Bennington College, Bennington, Vt., member of faculty, 1941-50; William Alanson White Institute for Psychiatry, Psychoanalysis and Psychology, New York City, cofounder, member of faculty, 1946-50, chairman of faculty, 1947-50; National Autonomous University of Mexico, Medical School, Frontera, professor of psychoanalysis, 1951-80, head of department, 1955-80; Mexican Institute for Psychoanalysis, Mexico City, Mexico, director, 1955-65; Michigan State University, East Lansing, professor, 1957-61, founder of Institute of Psychology; New York University, New York City, adjutant professor of psychology, 1962-80. Lecturer, American Institute for Psychoanalysis, 1941-42, and New School for Social Research, 1946-56; Terry Lecturer, Yale University, 1949-50. Diplomate in clinical psychology, American Psychological Association.

MEMBER: Mexican National Academy of Medicine (honorary member), New York Academy of Science (fellow), Washington Psychoanalytic Society.

AWARDS, HONORS: Fellow at Washington School of Psychiatry, 1940, and at William Alanson White Institute for Psychiatry, Psychoanalysis and Psychology, 1945.

WRITINGS:

Die Entwicklung des Christusdogmas (title means "The Development of the Dogma of Christ"), Internationaler Psychoanalytischer Verlag (Vienna), 1931.
Escape from Freedom, Farrar & Rinehart, 1941, Avon, 1971 (published in England as *The Fear of Freedom,* Kegan Paul, Trench, Trubner & Co., 1942).
Man for Himself: An Inquiry into the Psychology of Ethics, Rinehart, 1947, reprinted, Fawcett, 1978.
Psychoanalysis and Religion, Yale University Press, 1950.
The Forgotten Language: An Introduction to the Understanding of Dreams, Fairy Tales, and Myths, Rinehart, 1951.
The Sane Society, Rinehart, 1955, reprinted, Fawcett, 1977.
The Art of Loving: An Enquiry into the Nature of Love, Harper, 1956, reprinted, 1974.
Sigmund Freud's Mission: An Analysis of His Personality and Influence, Harper, 1959.
(Editor with Daisetz T. Suzuki and Richard De Martino) *Zen Buddhism and Psychoanalysis,* Harper, 1960.
Let Man Prevail: A Socialist Manifesto and Program (booklet), Lambert Schneider (Heidelberg), 1961.
(Editor with Hans Herzfeld) *Der Friede: Idee und Verwirklichung* (title means "Peace: Theory and Reality"), Lambert Schneider, 1961.
(Editor) *Marx's Concept of Man,* Ungar, 1961.
Is World Peace Still Possible?: An Enquiry into the Facts and Fictions of Foreign Policy, [New York], c. 1962.
Beyond the Chains of Illusion: My Encounter with Marx and Freud, Simon & Schuster, 1962, reprinted, 1985.

War within Man: A Psychological Enquiry into the Roots of Destructiveness, American Friends Service Committee, 1963.
The Dogma of Christ and Other Essays on Religion, Psychology, and Culture, Holt, 1963.
May Man Prevail?: An Enquiry into the Facts and Fictions of Foreign Policy, Doubleday, 1964.
The Heart of Man: Its Genius for Good and Evil, Harper, 1964, reprinted, 1980.
(Editor) *Socialist Humanism: An International Symposium,* Doubleday, 1965.
You Shall Be as Gods: A Radical Interpretation of the Old Testament and Its Tradition, Holt, 1966.
(Editor with Raymond Xirau) *The Nature of Man,* Macmillan, 1968.
The Revolution of Hope: Toward a Humanized Technology, Harper, 1968.
(With Michael Maccoby) *Social Character in a Mexican Village: A Socio-Psychoanalytic Study,* Prentice-Hall, 1970.
The Crisis of Psychoanalysis (essays), J. Cape, 1970, Fawcett, 1971.
The Anatomy of Human Destructiveness, Holt, 1973.
(With Hans Juergen Schultz) *Im Namen des Lebens: Ein Portraet im Gespraech mit Hans Juergen Schultz* (booklet; title means "In the Name of Life: A Portrait in Conversation with Hans Juergen Schultz"), Deutsche Verlags-Anstalt, 1974.
To Have or To Be?, Harper, 1976.
Greatness and Limitations of Freud's Thought, Harper, 1980.
Gesamtsausgabe (title means "Complete Works"), Deutsche Verlags-Anstalt, 1980-81.
On Disobedience and Other Essays, Seabury, 1981.
The Working Class in Weimar Germany: A Psychological and Sociological Study, edited by Wolfgang Bonss, translated by Barbara Weinberger, Harvard University Press, 1984.
For the Love of Life, translated by Robert and Rita Kimber, Free Press, 1985.

CONTRIBUTOR

Ruth N. Anshen, *Moral Principle of Action: Man's Ethical Imperative,* Harper, 1952.
James R. Newman, editor, *What Is Science?,* Simon & Schuster, 1955.
Clark E. Moustakas, editor, *The Self: Explorations in Personal Growth,* Harper, 1956.
Anshen, editor, *Language: An Enquiry into Its Meaning and Function,* Harper, 1957.
William Phillips, editor, *Art and Psychoanalysis,* Criterion, 1957.
Abraham H. Maslow, editor, *New Knowledge in Human Values,* Harper, 1959.
Anshen, editor, *Family: Its Function and Destiny,* revised edition, Harper, 1959.
Michael Harrington and Paul Jacobs, editors, *Labor in a Free Society,* University of California Press, 1959.
Huston Smith, editor, *Search for America,* Prentice-Hall, 1959.
Richard A. Condon and Burton O. Kurth, editors, *Writing from Experience,* Harper, 1960.
Hiram Collins Haydn and Betsy Saunders, editors, *The American Scholar Reader,* Atheneum, 1960.
Donald G. Brennan, editor, *Arms Control, Disarmament, and National Security,* Braziller, 1961.
Irving Louis Horowitz, editor, *The New Sociology: Essays in Social Science and Social Theory in Honor of C. Wright Mills,* Oxford University Press, 1964.
Steven E. Deutsch and John Howard, editors, *Where It's At: Radical Perspective in Sociology,* Harper, 1969.
Summerhill: For and Against, Hart Publishing, 1970.

Contributor of articles to professional journals.

WORK IN PROGRESS: A sequel to *To Have or To Be?;* a book on "godless religion," a study of religious experience in which the concept of god is "unnecessary and undesirable"; a book on self-analysis.

SIDELIGHTS: Critics, disciples, and objective analysts alike have been hard pressed to define Erich Fromm's role in the world of letters. As John Dollard pointed out in the *New York Herald Tribune,* Fromm was "at once sociologist, philosopher, historian, psychoanalyst, economist, and anthropologist—and, one is tempted to add, lover of human life, poet, and prophet." Fromm himself indicated the vast scope of his concerns in the foreword to his most famous book, *Escape from Freedom,* when he wrote that "this book is part of a broad study concerning the character structure of modern man and the problems of the interaction between psychological and sociological factors which I have been working on for several years."

Throughout his career Fromm strove toward an understanding of human existence based upon the breaking down of barriers—between individuals as well as between schools of thought. In a *Los Angeles Times* obituary article of the famous psychologist, a reviewer summarizes: "Fromm's lifelong concern was how people could come to terms with their isolation, insignificance and doubts about life's meaning." As his theories developed over the decades into what would later be collectively labeled "social humanism," he incorporated knowledge and information culled from such diverse fields as Marxist socialism and Freudian psychology. The psychologist used these schools of thought as building blocks for developing original theories which, like his idiosyncratic life, often ran against popular beliefs.

A descendent of a Jewish family whose members had often become rabbis, Fromm ceased practicing Judaism when he was 26. In a quote from the *New York Times,* he once told a reporter, "I gave up my religious convictions and practices because I just didn't want to participate in any division of the human race, whether religious or political." As a pacifist, Fromm protested against the use of military force during World War I, helped organize the National Committee for a Sane Nuclear Policy (SANE) in 1957, and strove to encourage understanding between the Soviet Union and the United States. As a psychologist, he diverged from the Freudian school, in which the unconscious was the main factor in understanding human actions, by pointing out the importance of the influence of social and economic factors.

Fromm's numerous and varied interests are revealed in the over twenty publications which he completed during his lifetime. For instance, *May Man Prevail? An Enquiry into the Facts and Fictions of Foreign Policy* is an analysis of the cold war between the United States and the Soviet Union, while *The Forgotten Language: An Introduction to the Understanding of Dreams, Fairy Tales, and Myths* is an early examination of the role of fantasy and myth in the interplay between social control and individual imaginative freedom. In 1956, he published *The Art of Loving: An Enquiry into the Nature of Love,* in which he maintained that "love is the only sane and satisfactory answer to the problem of human existence" and examined the many varieties and forms of the emotion. *The Art of Loving* enjoyed enormous popularity during the 1960s, and many sociologists believe it has had a significant influence on the lifestyles of Americans. Within these pages, the psychologist asserted that "love is not primarily a relationship to a specific person; it is an attitude, an orientation of character, which determines the relatedness of a person to the world as a whole, not toward one 'object' of love." Fromm believed that love could only be called a mature emotion when it "preserves one's integrity."

Most of Fromm's work has been an application of psychoanalysis, sociology, philosophy, and religion to the peculiar problems of man in modern industrialized society. In *Escape from Freedom* he postulated that "modern man, freed from the bonds of pre-individualistic society, which simultaneously gave him security and limited him, has not gained freedom in the positive sense of the realization of his individual self; that is, the expression of his intellectual, emotional and sensuous potentialities. Freedom, though it has brought him independence and rationality, has made him isolated and, thereby, anxious and powerless." This problem, the individual's tenuous relationship to institutions and society, became the core of such later works as *Man for Himself: An Enquiry into the Psychology of Ethics* and *The Sane Society.*

Fromm's penultimate book, *To Have or To Be?,* presents "the viewpoint and challenge of 'radical humanistic psychoanalysis,' " explains Paul Roazen in *Nation.* The volume has been seen as the culmination of Fromm's work at that time and maintains, according to a publisher's note, "that two modes of existence are struggling for the spirit of humankind; the *having* mode, which concentrates on material possession, acquisitiveness, power, and aggression and is the basis of such universal evils as greed, envy, and violence; and the *being* mode, which is based in love, in the pleasure of sharing, and in meaningful and productive rather than wasteful activity. Dr. Fromm sees the *having* mode bringing the world to the brink of psychological and ecological disaster, and he outlines a program for socio-economic change [to] turn the world away from its catastrophic course."

Although some of Fromm's work has been collected and published since his death, the last book to be completed during his lifetime is *Greatness and Limitations of Freud's Thought.* This work echoes the sentiment of his 1962 publication, *Beyond the Chains of Illusion: My Encounter with Marx and Freud,* in which he wrote that Marx was superior to Freud because he believed in the possibility that mankind could be perfected. As the author said in a *Spectator* article by Hans Keller, "If Freud could have imagined a classless and free society he would have dispensed with the ego and id as universal categories of the human mind." Because of this lack of confidence in Freud's theories as well as his methods, Fromm developed a new approach to psychoanalysis. Dr. Earl G. Witenberg, director of the William Alanson White Institute for Psychiatry, Psychoanalysis and Psychology that Fromm co-founded in 1946, related in a *New York Times* article by Dava Sobel that Fromm was interested in "working face to face with [his patient] and dynamically engaging him with insights about his condition and working actively toward the goal of getting those things clarified."

This method of psychoanalysis which Fromm devised was never described by him in print, however. His theories in this area are instead preserved only in the memories of his colleagues. Nevertheless, the psychoanalyst and philosopher will be remembered as one "who sought to apply the lessons of psychology to the social and political problems of the 20th century," according to J. Y. Smith of the *Washington Post.* "His theory of human nature cut a middle path between the instinctivists, who held that innate qualities were fixed at birth, and the behaviorists, who taught that all responses are the result of learning," says Sobel. Erich Fromm, concludes Dr. Witenberg in Sobel's article, "was a great man, both by his presence and his firm ideas."

BIOGRAPHICAL/CRITICAL SOURCES:

BOOKS

Butz, Otto, editor, *To Make a Difference,* Harper, 1967.

Evans, Richard I., *Dialogue with Erich Fromm,* Harper, 1966.

Fromm, Erich, *Escape from Freedom,* Farrar & Rinehart, 1941.

Fromm, Erich *The Art of Loving: An Enquiry into the Nature of Love,* Harper, 1956, reprinted, 1974.

Fromm, Erich *Greatness and Limitations of Freud's Thought,* Harper, 1980.

Glen, J. S., *Erich Fromm: A Protestant Critique,* Westminster, 1966.

Gotesky, Rubin, *Personality: The Need for Liberty and Rights,* Libra, 1967.

Hammond, G. B., *Man in Estrangement,* Vanderbilt University Press, 1965.

Hausdorff, Don, *Erich Fromm,* Twayne, 1972.

Landis, Bernard, and Edward S. Tauber, editors, *In the Name of Life: Essays in Honor of Erich Fromm,* Holt, 1971.

Montague, Ashley, editor, *Culture and the Evolution of Man,* Oxford University Press, 1962.

Schaar, J. H., *Escape from Authority: The Perspectives of Erich Fromm,* Basic Books, 1961.

PERIODICALS

Book World, November 10, 1968.

Choice, October, 1984.

Commonweal, March 14, 1969, March 15, 1974, May 19, 1976.

Kirkus Reviews, November 15, 1985.

Nation, September 1, 1969.

New Republic, December 7, 1968.

New York Herald Tribune, September 4, 1955.

Publishers Weekly, September 13, 1976.

Saturday Review, April 11, 1959, December 14, 1968.

Spectator, January 10, 1981.

Times Literary Supplement, December 7, 1969, April 28, 1972, December 27, 1974.

OTHER

"Focus on Erich Fromm; the Eminent Psychologist Talks with Heywood Hale Broun" (cassette recording), Center for Cassette Studies, c. 1976.

"Childhood" (cassette recording), Pacifica Tape Library, c. 1980.

OBITUARIES:

PERIODICALS

AB Bookman's Weekly, April 14, 1980.

Chicago Tribune, March 19, 1980.

Los Angeles Times, March 19, 1980.

Newsweek, March 31, 1980.

New York Times, March 19, 1980.

Publishers Weekly, April 4, 1980.

Time, March 31, 1980.

Times (London), March 19, 1980.

Washington Post, March 19, 1980.*

* * *

FULDHEIM, Dorothy (Violet Snell) 1893-

PERSONAL: Born June 26, 1893, in Passaic, N.J.; daughter of Herman and Bertha (Wishner) Snell; married Milton Fuldheim (deceased); married W. L. Ulmer (deceased); children: (first marriage) Dorothy Fuldheim Urman (deceased). *Education:* Milwaukee Normal College, A.S., 1914.

ADDRESSES: Home—13900 Shaker Blvd., #216, Cleveland, Ohio 44118. *Office*—WEWS-TV, 3001 Euclid Ave., Cleveland, Ohio 44115.

CAREER: Author, interviewer, and television commentator. Taught briefly before turning to the stage and appearing in plays in Milwaukee and Chicago. Affiliated with Scripps-Howard, Inc., 1924—; WEWS-TV, Cleveland, Ohio, news analyst, 1946—. Former host of live television variety program, "The One O'Clock Club." Has appeared as a guest on numerous television talk shows, including "Tonight," "Merv Griffin," "Donahue," and "Good Morning America." Member of board of directors, Crippled and Disabled Children, 1948-58, Cleveland Women's Symphony, 1948—, and Society for the Blind.

MEMBER: Women's City Club, Men's City Club, Play House Club, Theta Sigma Phi.

AWARDS, HONORS: Ohio Firemen and Police awards, 1955, 1972; Overseas Press Club award, 1959; Theta Sigma Phi national award, 1964; Israeli Freedom award, 1967; Ohio AFL-CIO award, 1973; D.H.L., 1975 and 1977; UPI award, 1978; Ohio State Senate award, 1979; Woman of the Year Award, Radio and Television Broadcasters Association, 1984. Ohio Governor's award; Distinguished Daughters of Ohio award; Variety Club Super Citizen award.

WRITINGS:

I Laughed, I Loved, I Cried: A News Analyst's Love Affair with the World (autobiography), World Publishing, 1966.
Where Were the Arabs?, World Publishing, 1967.
A Thousand Friends (autobiography), Doubleday, 1974.
Three and a Half Husbands (novel), Simon & Schuster, 1976.
The House I Live In, limited signed edition, Friends of the Kent State University Libraries, 1981.

SIDELIGHTS: "Dorothy Fuldheim has lived through the major technological innovations of the twentieth century—the invention of the telephone, the automobile, the airplane, the television, and the computer," writes Patricia Burstein in a *Savvy* profile. An inspiration to those who might equate aging solely with degeneration, Fuldheim continues to pursue an active professional career in her middle nineties. Best known as an interviewer, reviewer, and news analyst, she has recounted the experiences of her long, extraordinarily interesting, and varied life in *I Laughed, I Loved, I Cried: A News Analyst's Love Affair with the World* and *A Thousand Friends.* Praised by many for her drive and intelligence, especially at her age, "Fuldheim shrugs off such praise," notes Burstein: " 'It gets my goat when people say it's remarkable how bright I am at my age,' she says. 'I was bright forty years ago. And the more I use my brain, the sharper it gets.' "

Originally trained as a teacher, she became an actress in her early twenties. She appeared in several Chicago productions, one of which was attended by "social reformer Jane Addams, who knew of Fuldheim's ability as a public speaker, [and] asked her to share a lecture platform on a world tour," notes Burstein. At the age of 24, she joined Addams's worldwide speaking tour and lectured on peace. Fourteen years later in 1932, she interviewed Adolph Hitler in Munich; and although few took heed of her warnings about the imminent fuehrer, Fuldheim was frequently sought thereafter as a lecturer. "Her ability to extemporize informed and lively lectures soon enabled her to command audiences of 2,000 nightly," writes Nancy K. Gray in *Ms.* That "exposure on the lecture circuit led to radio commentaries," adds Gray, which in turn led to a network radio show that immediately followed the Metropolitan Opera broadcasts. Soon thereafter, in 1947, Fuldheim was offered an opportunity to present her commentaries on television. Although she was "skeptical of television's future," says Burstein, and continued broadcasting her commentaries on the radio and lecturing to groups, Fuldheim eventually accepted the offer and made television history by becoming the country's first female anchor person of a news program. In *Newsweek,* Harry F. Waters and John Lowell call Fuldheim "the nation's dean of broadcast journalism—and the personality with more on-camera hours than anyone else in the industry."

Fuldheim also hosted one of the industry's pioneer live variety programs, "The One O'Clock Club," and Waters and Lowell remark that she "has interviewed as many celebrities as anyone else in the business." Not only has she interviewed every president since Franklin D. Roosevelt, her list of interviewees is as diverse as it is extensive, and includes such names as Albert Einstein, Martin Luther King, Jr., Albert Speer, Helen Keller, Jane Fonda, the Duke of Windsor, the Shah of Iran, Jimmy Hoffa, and Barbara Walters, who is quoted by Burstein as saying, "Her drive, her intelligence, her audience appeal give us all hope that we can go on forever."

"The biggest coup of Fuldheim's career," states Gray, occurred in 1955 when she was able to obtain exclusive interviews with the two Americans who had been released from Chinese communist prisons. Gray relates that while Fuldheim was in Hong Kong on assignment, she heard that the American prisoners were to be released and rushed to where they were staying. Upon arrival, she discovered that while she was not the only journalist there, she was the only one with a tape recorder. "Fuldheim sent the tape back, and it created a sensation," says Gray. "It was obvious by the prisoners' rote responses that they had been brainwashed. The record is now in the Library of Congress." An incident that Fuldheim particularly enjoys talking about though, according to Burstein, is when she threw activist Jerry Rubin off the set in 1971. Burstein explains that "when Rubin started talking about 'eliminating pigs' and his support of the Black Panther party, Fuldheim ripped the microphone off him. 'Out!' she shouted, pushing him off the seat during a live interview. 'The interview is over!' "

Fuldheim prepares and delivers editorial commentaries that are featured twice daily on Cleveland's WEWS-TV, but she acknowledges to Gray that her "great trouble is finding two different subjects a day. It exhausts my intellectual resources. No editor of a newspaper would write two editorials a day. But I have finally arrived at the place where I don't flagellate myself because I think a commentary is bad." In 1970, however, after she went on the air and condemned the Kent State University killings as "murder, then cried over the dead students," says Burstein, "the station was flooded with letters and calls protesting her show of emotion." And although she offered to resign from the station, the offer was refused.

Because of her positions on social issues, notes Burstein, Fuldheim earned an early reputation in her adopted Cleveland as a "militant." But according to Waters and Lowell, that city now regards her as a veritable institution: " 'Dorothy is a fascinating conversationalist,' notes a local lawyer. 'Even at her age, she can dominate a room.' Predictably, that kind of flattery does not send Fuldheim into ecstasy. 'Listen,' she retorts. 'I still win awards, and not one of them says anything about how old I am.' " Expressing to Gray that she has little intention of retiring from her active schedule, Fuldheim remarks: "I've carved a unique place for myself. Also, this is a youth-oriented society and anyone over forty has a hell of a job trying to get a job, and if you're sixty, you're over the hill. . . . retaining this dominant position is a satisfaction to me."

MEDIA ADAPTATIONS: Fuldheim's novel *Three-and-a-Half Husbands* has been adapted as a musical comedy.

BIOGRAPHICAL/CRITICAL SOURCES:

BOOKS

Fuldheim, Dorothy Snell, *A Thousand Friends,* Doubleday, 1974.

Hayes, Helen, and Marion Glasserow Gladney, *Our Best Years,* Doubleday, 1984.

PERIODICALS

Best Sellers, November 15, 1975.

Ms., December, 1976.

Newsweek, June 11, 1979.

Savvy, July, 1984.*

—*Sketch by Sharon Malinowski*

* * *

FULLER, Lois Hamilton 1915-

PERSONAL: Born August 13, 1915, in Bayonne, N.J.; daughter of Emmett S. (a banker) and Mabel (a musician; maiden name, Havens) Hamilton; married Donald L. Fuller (a scientist), October 15, 1938; children: Margaret, John. *Education:* Smith College, A.B., 1937; additional study at University of California, Berkeley, 1939, Churchman Business College, 1945, and University of Maryland, 1960. *Politics:* Independent. *Religion:* Presbyterian.

ADDRESSES: Home—1310 Shoshone St., Boise, Idaho 83705.

CAREER: Briarcliff Junior College, Briarcliff Manor, N.Y., English teacher, 1937-38; Churchman Business College, Easton, Pa., English and shorthand teacher, 1945-46; substitute teacher in Ridgewood, N.J., public schools, 1957, and Montgomery County, Md., elementary schools, 1958-63.

MEMBER: Authors Guild, Authors League of America, Mystery Writers of America, American Association of University Women, Children's Book Guild, Society of Children's Book Writers.

WRITINGS:

(With Mary Shiverick Fishler) *The Mystery of the Old Fisk House,* Abingdon, 1960.

Keo, the Cave Boy, Abingdon, 1961.

The Jade Jaguar Mystery, Abingdon, 1962.

Fire in the Sky: Story of a Boy of Pompeii, Abingdon, 1965.

Swarup Returns (English and Hindi edition), Children's Book Trust (New Delhi), 1968.

Little Tiger, Big Tiger (English and Hindi edition), Children's Book Trust, 1970.

WORK IN PROGRESS: Picture books.

SIDELIGHTS: Lois Hamilton Fuller has traveled in the United States, Canada, Mexico, Europe, and Asia. She has learned about people through her studies in philosophy, psychology, sociology, and comparative religions.

AVOCATIONAL INTERESTS: Swimming, bridge, fishing.

FULLER, Maud
See PETERSHAM, Maud (Sylvia Fuller)

* * *

FULLMER, Daniel W(arren) 1922-

PERSONAL: Born December 12, 1922, in London Mills, Ill.; son of Daniel Floyd and Sarah Louisa (Essex) Fullmer; married Janet Saito, June 11, 1980; children: (first marriage) Daniel William, Mark Warren. *Education:* Western Illinois University, B.S., 1947, M.S., 1952; University of Denver, Ph.D., 1955.

ADDRESSES: Office—Department of Counselor Education, University of Hawaii 96822.

CAREER: University of Oregon, Eugene, assistant professor, 1955-57, associate professor of education, 1957-60, professor of psychology, 1960-66; University of Hawaii, Honolulu, professor of educational psychology, 1966—. Specialist in counseling, U.S. Office of Education, Washington, D.C., 1962-63. Consultant and advisor to Grambling State University. Member of State Board for Certification of Psychologists, Hawaii, 1970-79; president, Sussannah Wesley Community Center, Honolulu, 1972. *Military service:* U.S. Navy, Submarine Service, 1944-46.

MEMBER: American Association for Counseling and Development, American Psychological Association.

AWARDS, HONORS: Nancy C. Wimmer Award for outstanding contribution to field of counseling and guidance from American Personnel and Guidance Association, 1963; Francis E. Clark Award from Hawaii Personnel and Guidance Association, 1972; inducted into Grambling State University's Hall of Fame, 1987.

WRITINGS:

(With H. W. Bernard) *Counseling: Content and Process,* Science Research Associates, 1964.

(Editor with Daniel Schrieber and B. A. Kaplan) *Guidance and the School Dropout,* National Education Association and American Personnel and Guidance Association, 1964.

(With Bernard) *Family Consultation,* Houghton, 1968.

(With Bernard) *Principles of Guidance: A Basic Text,* Harper, 1969, 2nd edition, 1977.

(Editor with G. M. Gazda) *Theory and Methods of Group Counseling,* C. C Thomas, 1969.

Counseling: Group Theory and System, Carroll Press, 1971, 2nd edition, 1977.

(With Bernard) *The School Counselor-Consultant,* Houghton, 1972.

(Contributor) Gazda, editor, *Theories and Methods of Group Counseling in the Schools,* C. C Thomas, 1976.

(With Carlson) *Focus on Guidance,* Love Publishing, 1977.

The Peer Counselor-Consultant Training Manual, Carroll Press, 1982.

Conflict Resolution, Carroll Press, 1982.

Crisis Intervention and Child Abuse, Carroll Press, 1982.

Values Clarification, Carroll Press, 1982.

Family Group Consultation, Carroll Press, 1982.

Elementary Schools, Carroll Press, 1982.

(With Janet Ishikawa) *The Family Therapy Dictionary and Text,* Carroll Press, 1989.

Manabu: Life in a Different Dimension, H.R.D.C. Press, 1989.

(With Ishikawa) *Manual for Child and Family Practice,* Carroll Press, 1990.

(With Ishikawa) *Parents Who Kill: Beyond Abuse and Neglect,* Carroll Press, 1990.

SIDELIGHTS: Daniel W. Fullmer wrote *CA:* "My home in academe has been the Universities of Denver, Oregon, and Hawaii. I spent almost thirty years as a consultant to Grambling State University. Predominantly Black state colleges and universities had a tough time justifying a continuing existence. I found Grambling to be a national treasure. It changed my life. Helping people is my life's work as a psychologist and educator. I found those same skills could help an institution. Writing is the most productive way to share the new discoveries derived from a life of service. My goal is to become an author."

* * *

FURNISS, Tim 1948-

PERSONAL: Born April 14, 1948, in Epsom, England; son of John (a businessman) and Marnie (Battersby) Furniss; married Susan Jacob (a trampoline instructor), January 6, 1979; children: Tom. *Education:* Attended private school in Guildford, England. *Politics:* Conservative. *Religion:* Methodist.

ADDRESSES: Home and office—23 Downs Way, Epsom, Surrey KT18 5LU, England.

CAREER: Publisher's assistant, 1966-68; public relations manager, 1970-73; advertising manager, Air Products, 1973-82; freelance public relations consultant, 1982-85; writer and broadcaster on space subjects, 1982—; spaceflight correspondent, *Flight International,* 1985—.

MEMBER: British Interplanetary Society (fellow).

AWARDS, HONORS: Space was selected as one of the Child Study Association's Children's Books of the Year, 1985.

WRITINGS:

A Trip to the Moon (juvenile), Pitman, 1971.
A Source Book of Rockets, Spacecraft, and Spacemen, Ward, Lock, 1973.
UFOs, World, 1978.
Space Today, Kaye & Ward, 1979.
The Story of the Space Shuttle, Hodder & Stoughton, 1979, 3rd edition, 1986.
Space Satellites (juvenile), Hodder & Stoughton, 1980.
The Sun (juvenile), F. Watts, 1980.
Man in Space (juvenile), David & Charles, 1981.
Space Stowaway, Kaye & Ward, 1982.
Manned Spaceflight Log, Jane's Publishing, 1983, new edition, 1987.
Space Exploitation (juvenile), David & Charles, 1984.
Aliens, Granada, 1984.
Shuttle to Mars (juvenile novel), Kaye & Ward, 1984.
Space Flight: The Records, Guinness Superlatives, 1985.
Space (juvenile), F. Watts, 1985.
Space Technology, F. Watts, 1985.
Our Future in Space (juvenile), Bookwright Press, 1985.
Space Shuttle Log, Jane's Publishing, 1986.
Let's Look at Outer Space (juvenile), Bookwright Press, 1987.
Space Rocket (juvenile), Gloucester Press, 1988.

Writer for radio and television; contributor to magazines. European correspondent, *Space World,* 1984.

SIDELIGHTS: Tim Furniss told *CA:* "I have been interested in space since Gagarin's adventure in 1961. It has been my ambition to write and broadcast on space ever since I was fourteen, when John Glenn's flight inspired me. From then on I collected news cuttings, magazine articles, pictures, and books on space. I was quite simply a 'space nut.' The sixties, culminating with Apollo on the moon, was a most exciting period for me, and then as I was beginning to write about space professionally (two small books and some local radio), interest in the seventies dwindled to such an extent that I spent a very frustrating time waiting for the shuttle to arrive. Then pow! Everything started to happen. From 1979 onwards I wrote more books and did national radio and television, including a regular 'space spot' on national radio for kids.

"In the early seventies I went to the Cape to see *Apollo XIII* and *XV* launched and met a number of the astronauts, including some that landed on the moon. I even got to wear a moon suit. I return[ed] to cover a shuttle launch in a more professional capacity for *Flight International.* I would like to fly on a shuttle one day but the possibility is more remote now than it was before Challenger.

"I have a long way to go yet to achieve my ultimate objective, but sometimes do allow myself a smile of pride at what my perseverance, determination, enthusiasm, and luck have earned me since those days when I used to sit during school breaks trying to pick up a news station on the radio during a launch. I well remember listening in awe to Gordon Cooper's launch on my faithful blue transistor radio in 1963. I remember quite clearly thinking to myself then how good it would be to write and broadcast about space when I grew up."

G

GACH, Michael Reed 1952-

PERSONAL: Born August 19, 1952, in Los Angeles, Calif.; son of Theodore Irving (in furniture sales) and Muriel Lee (a program director) Gach. *Education:* Immaculate Heart College, B.A., 1975; University of California, Berkeley, graduate study, 1976-77.

ADDRESSES: *Office*—Acupressure Institute, 1533 Shattuck Ave., Berkeley, Calif. 94709.

CAREER: Acupressure Workshop and Institute (now Acupressure Institute), Berkeley, Calif., director, 1976—. Founder of state-approved vocational training school in acupressure; gives stress management, back pain, and weight loss seminars.

WRITINGS:

(With Carolyn Marco) *Acu-Yoga: Self-Help Techniques to Relieve Tension,* Kodansha, 1981.
The Bum Back Book, Celestial Arts, 1985.
Greater Energy at Your Fingertips, Celestial Arts, 1987.
Arthritis Relief at Your Fingertips, Warner Books, 1989.
Acupressure for Weight Loss and Dietary Therapy, Acu Press, in press.

WORK IN PROGRESS: Potent Points; Headaches and Eyestrain Relief at Your Fingertips; The Complete Acupressure Training Book.

SIDELIGHTS: Michael Gach told *CA:* "It is the birthright of every American to learn natural ways to relieve stress and maintain well-being. With our fast pace of life we need ways to release stress now more than ever before. I know effective techniques for relieving asthma, headaches, ulcers, cramps, and backaches that are safe and easy to do anywhere. Through my books and seminars I intend to make these methods—acupressure points, exercises, and dietary considerations—available to the public.

"In college while studying humanistic psychology, sociology, organizational development, and gestalt therapy, I got the idea of connecting the mind and body in my work. I thought there must be a way to physically work with people as well as psychologically with a touch therapy that serves as an adjunct to counseling. When I first heard about acupressure I had no idea what it was and therefore felt rather skeptical. I received an acupressure treatment to find out what it was all about. It was tremendously relaxing. Simply by holding a series of points it released my tension far more deeply than anything I had ever experienced.

"When I began to study acupressure I practiced on many friends and family, anyone I could get my hands on. I was fascinated by the results that people reported. I began to realize how important and effective acupressure is in dealing with stress-related problems.

"Although my acupressure practice was very successful, I was frustrated by the limited number of people that I could help. Since thousands of people needed my services and hundreds more wanted to learn how to do acupressure, I developed a professional training program. Established in 1976, the Acupressure Institute in Berkeley has been approved by the Board of Registered Nurses for continuing education credit and the California Department of Education. The 150-hour comprehensive training program, which can be completed in one month, teaches over seventy-five points and acupressure techniques especially effective for relieving stress and related disorders.

"I teach acupressure as an adjunct to Western medicine, not as a substitute. For instance, if you break a bone it's important to see a doctor. Acupressure is not going to set a broken bone. If you have internal bleeding or a tumor you should see a medical doctor. Acupressure would not be the treatment of choice in such instances.

"There are many cases where acupressure and Western medicine can be used together. Let's look at cancer. I don't have any evidence that acupressure can treat cancer, but I know it can help a cancer patient in many ways. It can help reduce a cancer patient's physical discomfort and emotional distress.

"My first book, *Acu-Yoga: Self-Help Techniques,* is an integration of acupressure and yoga designed to relieve tension. Yoga postures naturally stress or press certain acupuncture points. This self-help stress management manual, filled with over 250 photos and drawings, illustrates practical techniques for dealing with many common complaints, from headaches to insomnia. Increased effectiveness is the result of combining these two holistic practices for self-treatment.

"Back pain is often accompanied by muscular tension. Pain, pressure, or stiffness tends to accumulate around acupressure points. *The Bum Back Book* shows you how to help yourself and others to relieve sciatica, backaches, and neck pains. I introduced many alternative therapies in the book, including Reflexology, Shiatsu, Jin Shin back releases, acupressure massage for the lower back, easy breathing exercises, compresses, and instructions on how to design your own custom back roller.

"Many people are curious about how acupressure works to help them lose weight. There are specific 'trigger points' that balance the appetite and digestive system. Other points help to eliminate excess water weight. Once you learn how to reduce your stress and anxieties with acupressure, the frustrations that once caused you to overeat eventually fade away.

"There is now an alternative to using drugs for relieving arthritic pain. All it takes is your fingertips, twenty minutes two or three times daily. This self-help workbook, *Arthritis Relief at Your Fingertips,* is fully illustrated with over 350 line drawings and photographs.

"My greatest interest in using acupressure is to empower people with greater awareness and trust in themselves that they may lead more pain-free and healthy lives. I have found that holding these points enhances the results of behavior therapy. Mental and emotional problems become physically stored in the body. The acupressure points are keys for relieving psychosomatic obstacles. I have seen this ancient touch therapy work wonders for relieving trauma in women who have been raped and people who have been in car accidents. Acupressure therapy, along with exercise and a natural whole foods diet, is also an effective treatment for depression and for children with emotional difficulties, including learning disabilities.

"During the past eighteen years of my professional practice, I have seen acupressure work wonders, time and time again. Hence, I dedicated my life to teaching people how to apply this ancient art of healing to the common stress-related problems we all face today."

* * *

GAEDDERT, Lou Ann (Bigge) 1931-

PERSONAL: Surname is pronounced *Gad*-ert; born June 20, 1931, in Garden City, Kan.; married Orlan M. Gaeddert; children: Andrew, Martha. *Education:* Attended Phillips University; University of Washington, B.A., 1952.

ADDRESSES: *Agent*—Robert Lewis, 65 East 96th St., New York, N.Y. 10128.

CAREER: Author. *West Seattle Herald,* Seattle, Wash., writer and editor, 1952-54; worked in publicity departments of T. Y. Crowell, 1954-55, and Doubleday, 1956-61.

WRITINGS:

Noisy Nancy Norris, illustrations by Gioia Fiammenghi, Doubleday, 1965.
The Split-Level Cookbook: Family Meals to Cook Once and Serve Twice, Crowell, 1967.
Noisy Nancy and Nick, illustrations by Fiammenghi, Doubleday, 1970.
Too Many Girls, illustrations by Marylin Hafner, Coward, McCann, 1972.
All-in-All: A Biography of George Eliot, Dutton, 1976.
Gustav the Gourmet Giant, illustrations by Steven Kellogg, Dial, 1976.
Your Night to Make Dinner, illustrations by Ellen Weiss, Watts, 1977.
A New England Love Story: Nathaniel Hawthorne and Sophia Peabody, Dial, 1980.
Just Like Sisters, Dutton, 1981.
Survival Cooking for the Busy and Broke, Milk and Honey Press, 1981.
The Kid with the Red Suspenders, Dutton, 1983.
Your Former Friend, Matthew (a Junior Literary Guild selection), Dutton, 1984.
Daffodils in the Snow, Dutton, 1984.
A Summer Like Turnips, Holt, 1989.
Perfect Strangers (adult romance), St. Martin's Paperback, 1989.

WORK IN PROGRESS: An adult romance for St. Martin's Paperback, 1990.

SIDELIGHTS: Lou Ann Gaeddert's first book, *Noisy Nancy Norris,* grew out of her concern and experience with raising children in an apartment building. In 1967, the Communications Laboratory of Bank Street College of Education produced a motion picture based on *Noisy Nancy Norris* that was narrated by Shirley MacLaine.

BIOGRAPHICAL/CRITICAL SOURCES:

BOOKS

Hopkins, Lee Bennett, *Books Are by People,* Citation, 1969.

PERIODICALS

Horn Book, December, 1976.

* * *

GALBRAITH, Vivian Hunter 1889-1976

PERSONAL: Born December 15, 1889, in Sheffield, England; died November 25, 1976, in Oxford, England; son of David (a secretary) and Eliza Davidson (McIntosh) Galbraith; married Georgina Rosalie Cole Baker, 1921; children: one son, two daughters. *Education:* Attended Manchester University, 1907-10 (first class honors) and Balliol College, Oxford (first class honors).

ADDRESSES: *Home*—20A Bradmore Rd., Oxford OX2 6QP, England.

CAREER: Manchester University, Manchester, England, Langton research fellow; assistant lecturer, 1920-21; Assistant Keeper of the Public Records, London, England, 1921-28; Balliol College, Oxford, England, fellow, tutor, and university reader in diplomatic, 1928-37; Edinburgh University, Edinburgh, Scotland, professor, 1937-44; University of London, London, director of Institute of Historical Research, 1944-48; Oxford, Regius Professor of Modern History, 1947-57. Ford's Lecturer in English History at Oxford, 1940-41; David Murray Lecturer, Glasgow University, 1943-44; James Bryce Memorial Lecturer, Somerville College, 1944; Creighton Lecturer, University of London, 1949; Purington Lecturer, Mount Holyoke College, 1965; Penrose Lecturer, American Philosophical Society, 1966. *Military service:* Queen's Regiment, 1915-1918; served in Palestine (now Israel) and France; became company commander.

MEMBER: Royal Commission on Ancient and Historical Monuments of England and Scotland, American Philosophical Society.

AWARDS, HONORS: Honorary doctorates from University of Manchester, University of Edinburgh, University of Belfast, and Emory University; elected fellow, British Academy, 1939; honorary fellow, Balliol College, Oxford, 1957, and Oriel College, Oxford, 1958.

WRITINGS:

An Introduction to the Use of the Public Records, Clarendon Press, 1934, reprinted with corrections by Oxford University Press, 1963.

The Literacy of the Medieval English Kings (Raleigh lectures), Longwood, 1935.

(Editor with James Tait) *Herefordshire Domesday, circa 1160-1170: Reproduced by Collotype from Facsimile Photographs of Balliol College Manuscript 350,* [London], 1947-48, reprinted, Kraus Reprint, 1974.

Studies in the Public Records, Thomas Nelson, 1948.

(Editor with Tait) *Domesday Book,* J. W. Ruddock, 1950.

The Making of Domesday Book, Clarendon Press, 1961, reprinted, AMS Press, 1961.

The Historian at Work, BBC Publications, 1962.

An Introduction to the Study of History (includes 1938 Edinburgh inaugural lecture), C. A. Watts, 1964.

A Draft of the Magna Carta, Oxford University Press, 1967.

(Editor) *The Anonimalle Chronicle, 1333 to 1381,* Manchester University Press, 1970.

Domesday Book: Its Place in Administrative History, Clarendon Press, 1974.

Historical Research in Medieval England, Gordon, 1977.

Kings and Chroniclers: Essays in English Medieval History, Hambledon, 1982.

Also editor of pamphlet, *Roger Wendover and Matthew Paris,* Jackson (Glasgow, Scotland), reprinted, University of Glasgow Press, 1970. Contributor to *English Historical Review.*

OBITUARIES:

PERIODICALS

Times (London), November 26, 1976.*

* * *

GALLANT, Mavis 1922-

PERSONAL: Born Mavis de Trafford Young, August 11, 1922, in Montreal, Quebec, Canada. *Education:* Attended secondary schools in the United States and Canada.

ADDRESSES: *Home*—Paris, France. *Agent*—Georges Borchardt, 136 East 57th St., New York, N.Y. 10022.

CAREER: *The Standard,* Montreal, Quebec, feature writer and critic, 1944-50; free-lance writer, 1950—. Writer in residence at University of Toronto, 1983-84.

MEMBER: PEN, Authors Guild, Authors League of America.

AWARDS, HONORS: Named Officer of the Order of Canada, 1981; Governor General's Award, 1981, for *Home Truths: Selected Canadian Stories;* honorary doctorates from University of St. Anne, Nova Scotia, and York University, Ontario, both 1984; Canada-Australia Literary Prize, 1985.

WRITINGS:

FICTION

The Other Paris (short stories), Houghton, 1956, reprinted, G. K. Hall, 1986.

Green Water, Green Sky (novel), Houghton, 1959, reprinted, Macmillan, 1982.

My Heart Is Broken: Eight Stories and a Short Novel, Random House, 1964, reprinted, General Publishing Company (Toronto), 1982 (published in England as *An Unmarried Man's Summer,* Heinemann, 1965).

A Fairly Good Time (novel), Random House, 1970, reprinted, G. K. Hall, 1986.

The Pegnitz Junction: A Novella and Five Short Stories, Random House, 1973.

The End of the World and Other Stories, McClelland & Stewart, 1974.

From the Fifteenth District: A Novella and Eight Short Stories, Random House, 1979.

Home Truths: Selected Canadian Stories, Macmillan, 1981.

Overhead in a Balloon: Stories of Paris, Macmillan, 1985.

In Transit (short stories), Viking, 1988.

OTHER

(Author of introduction) Gabrielle Russier, *The Affair of Gabrielle Russier,* Knopf, 1971.

(Author of introduction) J. Hibbert, *The War Brides,* PMA (Toronto), 1978.

What Is To Be Done? (play; first produced in Toronto at Tarragon Theatre, November 11, 1982), Quadrant, 1983.

Paris Notebooks: Essays and Reviews, Macmillan, 1986.

Contributor of essays, short stories, and reviews to numerous periodicals, including *New Yorker, New York Times Book Review, New Republic,* and *New York Review of Books.*

WORK IN PROGRESS: A novel.

SIDELIGHTS: Canadian-born Mavis Gallant is widely considered one of the finest crafters of short stories in the English language. Her works, most of which appear initially in the *New Yorker* magazine, are praised for sensitive evocation of setting and penetrating delineation of character. In the words of *Maclean's* magazine contributor Mark Abley, Gallant "is virtually unrivalled at the art of short fiction," an exacting artist whose pieces reveal "an ability to press a lifetime into a few resonant pages as well as a desire to show the dark side of comedy and the humor that lurks behind despair." *Time* magazine correspondent Timothy Foote calls Gallant "one of the prose masters of the age," and adds that no modern writer "casts a colder eye on life, on death and all the angst and eccentricity in between." Since 1950 Gallant has lived primarily in Paris, but she has also spent extended periods of time in the United States, Canada, and other parts of Europe. Not surprisingly, her stories and novellas show a wide range of place and period; many feature refugees and expatriates forced into self-discernment by rootlessness. As Anne Tyler notes in the *New York Times Book Review,* each Gallant fiction "is densely-woven, . . . rich in people and plots—a miniature world, more satisfying than many full-scale novels. . . . There is a sense of limitlessness: each story is like a peephole opening out into a very wide landscape."

Dictionary of Literary Biography essayist Ronald B. Hatch observes that the subject of children, "alone, frightened, or unloved," recurs often in Gallant's work. This, he notes, reflects Gallant's own difficult youth. The author underwent a solitary and transient childhood, attending seventeen different schools in the United States and Canada. Her father died while she was in grade school, and her mother, soon remarried, moved to the United States, leaving the child with strangers. Speaking to how her formative years influenced her writing, Gallant told the *New York Times:* "I think it's true that in many, many of the things I write, someone has vanished. And it's often the father. And there is often a sense that nothing is very safe, and you're often walking on a very thin crust." One advantage of Gallant's far-flung education has endured, however. As a primary schooler in her native Montreal, she learned French, and she remained bilingual into adulthood.

Gallant matured into a resourceful young woman determined to be a writer. At the age of twenty-one she became a reporter with the Montreal *Standard,* a position that honed her writing talents while it widened her variety of experiences. Journalism, she told the *New York Times,* "turned out to be so valuable, because I saw the interiors of houses I wouldn't have seen otherwise. And a great many of the things, particularly in . . . [fiction] about Montreal, that I was able to describe later, it was because I had seen them, I had gone into them as a journalist. If I got on with the people, I had no hesitation about seeing them again. . . . I went right back and took them to lunch. I could see some of those rooms, and see the wallpaper, and what they ate, and what they wore, and how they spoke, . . . and the way they treated their children. I drew it all in like blotting paper." From these encounters Gallant began to write stories. In 1950 she decided to leave Montreal and begin a new life as a serious fiction writer in Paris. At the same time she began to send stories to the *New Yorker* for publication. Her second submission, a piece called "Madeline's Birthday," was accepted, beginning a four-decade relationship with the prestigious periodical. Gallant used the six hundred dollar check for her story to finance her move abroad. Paris has been her permanent home ever since.

Expatriation provided Gallant with new challenges and insights that have formed central themes in her fiction. In *The Other Paris* and subsequent story collections, her characters are "the refugee, the rootless, the emotionally disinherited," to quote a *Times Literary Supplement* reviewer, who adds: "It is a world of displacement where journeys are allegorical and love is inadequate." Gallant portrays postwar people locked into archaic cultural presuppositions; often dispossessed of their homes by haphazard circumstances, they are bewildered and insecure, seeking refuge in etiquette and other shallow symbols of tradition. *Time* correspondent Patricia Blake maintains that Gallant's "natural subject is the varieties of spiritual exile. . . . All [her characters] are bearers of a metaphorical 'true passport' that transcends nationality and signifies internal freedom. For some this serves as a safe-conduct to independence. For others it is a guarantee of loneliness and despair." Gallant also presents the corollary theme of the past's inexorable grip on its survivors. In her stories, *New York Review of Books* essayist V. S. Pritchett contends, "we are among the victims of the wars in Europe which have left behind pockets of feckless exiles. . . . History has got its teeth into them and has regurgitated them and left them bizarre and perplexed." Whether immersed in the past or on the run from it, vainly trying to "turn over a new leaf," Gallant's characters "convey with remarkable success a sense of the amorphousness, the mess of life," to quote *Books and Bookmen* contributor James Brockway. Spiritually and physically marginal, they yearn paradoxically for safety, order, and freedom. "Hearts are not broken in Mavis Gallant's stories . . .," concludes Eve Auchincloss in the *New York Review of Books.* "Roots are cut, and her subject is the nature of the life that is led when the roots are not fed."

Most critics applaud Gallant's ability to inhabit the minds of her characters without resort to condescension or sentimentality. Abley claims that the author "can write with curiosity and perceptiveness about the kind of people who would never read a word of her work—a rarer achievement than it might sound. She is famous for not forgiving and not forgetting; her unkindness is usually focused on women and men who have grown complacent, never reflecting on their experience, no longer caring about their world. With such people she is merciless, yet with others, especially children bruised by neglect, she is patient and even kind. In the end, perhaps, understanding can be a means of forgiveness. One hopes so, because Mavis Gallant understands us terribly well." In the *Chicago Tribune Book World* Civia Tamarkin suggests that Gallant's works "impose a haunting vision of man trapped in an existential world. Each of the stories is a sensitive, though admirably understated, treatment of isolation, loneliness, and despair. Together they build an accumulating sense of the frustrating indifference of the cosmos to human hopes."

Gallant is best known for her short stories and novellas, but she has also written two novels, *Green Water, Green Sky* and *A Fairly Good Time.* Hatch contends that these works continue the author's "exploration of the interaction between an individual's thoughts and his external world." In *Green Water, Green Sky,* according to Constance Pendergast in the *Saturday Review,* Gallant "writes of the disaster that results from a relationship founded on the mutual need and antagonism of a woman and her daughter, where love turns inward and festers, bringing about inevitably the disintegration of both characters." Lighter in tone, *A Fairly Good Time* follows the blundering adventures of a Canadian, Shirley Perrigny, who lives in France. Hatch notes that the novel "may well be the funniest of all her works. . . . As a satire on the self-satisfied habits of the French, *A Fairly Good Time* proves enormously high-spirited. Yet the novel offers more than satire. As the reader becomes intimately acquainted with Shirley, her attempts to defeat the rigidity of French logic by living in the moment come to seem zany but commendable."

Home Truths: Selected Canadian Stories, first published in 1981, has proven to be one of Gallant's most popular collections. In Abley's view, the volume "bears repeated witness to the efforts made by this solitary, distant writer to come to terms with her own past and her own country." The stories focus on footloose Canadians who are alienated from their families or cultures; the characters try "to puzzle out the ground rules of their situations, which are often senseless, joyless and contradictory," to quote *Nation* reviewer Barbara Fisher Williamson. *New York Times Book Review* contributor Maureen Howard observes that in *Home Truths,* Canada "is not a setting, a backdrop; it is an adversary, a constraint, a comfort, the home that is almost understandable, if not understanding. It is at once deadly real and haunting, phantasmagoric." Phyllis Grosskurth elaborates in *Saturday Night:* "Clearly [Gallant] is still fighting a battle with the Canada she left many years ago. Whether or not that country has long since vanished is irrelevant, for it has continued to furnish the world of her imagination. . . . She knows that whatever she writes will be in the language that shaped her sensibility, though the Canada of her youth imposed restraints from which she could free herself only by geographic separation. Wherever she is, she writes out of her roots. . . . Her Montreal is a state of mind, an emotion recalled, an apprenticeship for life." *Home Truths* won the 1981 Governor General's Award, Canada's highest literary honor. *Books in Canada* correspondent Wayne Grady concludes that it is not a vision of Gallant's native country that emerges in the book, but rather "a vision of the world, of life: it is in that nameless country of the mind inhabited by all real writers, regardless of nativity, that Mavis Gallant lives. We are here privileged intruders."

The *New Yorker* has been the initial forum for almost all of Gallant's short fiction—and much of her nonfiction, too—since 1950. Critics, among them *Los Angeles Times* reviewer Elaine Kendall, feel that Gallant's work meets the periodical's high literary standards; in Kendall's words, Gallant's stories "seem the epitome of the magazine's traditional style." Readers of the *New Yorker* expect to find challenging stories, and according to Hatch, Gallant offers such challenges. "The reader finds that he cannot comprehend the fictional world as something given, but must engage with the text to bring its meanings into being," Hatch writes. "As in life, so in a Gallant story, no handy editor exists ready to point the moral." Foote expresses a similar opinion. "Gallant rarely leaves helpful signs and messages that readers tend to expect of 'literature': This way to the Meaning or This story is about the Folly of Love . . .," the critic concludes. "In the end the stories are simply there—haunting, enigmatic, printed with images as sharp and durable as the edge of a new coin, relentlessly specific."

The critical reception for Gallant's work has been very positive, indeed. *Washington Post Book World* reviewer Elizabeth Spencer suggests that there is "no writer in English anywhere able to set Mavis Gallant in second place. Her style alone places her in the first rank. Gallant's firmly drafted prose neglects nothing, leaves no dangling ends for the reader to tack up. . . . She is hospitable to the metaphysics of experience as well as to the homeliest social detail." Grosskurth writes: "Gallant's particular power as a writer is the sureness with which she catches the ephemeral; it is a wry vision, a blend of the sad and the tragi-comic. She is a born writer who happens to have been born in Canada, and her gift has been able to develop as it has only because she could look back in anger, love, and nostalgia." *New York Times Book Review* contributor Phyllis Rose praises Gallant for her "wicked humor that misses nothing, combined with sophistication so great it amounts to forgiveness." The critic concludes: "To take up residence in the mind of Mavis Gallant, as one does in reading her stories, is a privilege and delight."

BIOGRAPHICAL/CRITICAL SOURCES:

BOOKS

Contemporary Literary Criticism, Gale, Volume 7, 1977, Volume 18, 1981, Volume 38, 1986.

Dictionary of Literary Biography, Volume 53: *Canadian Writers since 1960, First Series,* Gale, 1986.

Lecker, Robert and Jack David, editors, *The Annotated Bibliography of Canada's Major Authors,* Volume 5, ECW (Ontario), 1984.

Merler, Grazia, *Mavis Gallant: Narrative Patterns and Devices,* Tecumseh, 1978.

Moss, John, editor, *Present Tense,* NC Press (Toronto), 1985.

PERIODICALS

Atlantis, autumn, 1978.

Books and Bookmen, July, 1974.

Books in Canada, October, 1979, October, 1981, April, 1984, October, 1985.

Canadian Fiction Magazine, Number 28, 1978, Number 43, 1982.

Canadian Forum, February, 1982, November, 1985.

Canadian Literature, spring, 1973, spring, 1985.

Chicago Tribune Book World, November 11, 1979.

Christian Science Monitor, June 4, 1970.

Globe and Mail (Toronto), October 11, 1986, October 15, 1988.

Los Angeles Times, April 15, 1985.

Los Angeles Times Book Review, November 4, 1979, May 24, 1987.

Maclean's, September 5, 1964, November 9, 1981, November 22, 1982.

Nation, June 15, 1985.

New Republic, August 25, 1979, May 13, 1985.

New York Review of Books, June 25, 1964, January 24, 1980.

New York Times, June 5, 1970, October 2, 1979, April 20, 1985, July 9, 1985, March 4, 1987.

New York Times Book Review, February 26, 1956, September 16, 1979, May 5, 1985, March 15, 1987.

Quill and Quire, October, 1981, June, 1984.

Rubicon, winter, 1984-85.

Saturday Night, September, 1973, November, 1981.

Saturday Review, October 17, 1959, August 25, 1979, October 13, 1979.

Spectator, August 29, 1987, February 20, 1988.

Time, November 26, 1979, May 27, 1985.

Times (London), February 28, 1980.

Times Literary Supplement, March 14, 1980, February 28, 1986, September 25-October 1, 1987, January 22-28, 1988.

Virginia Quarterly Review, spring, 1980.

Washington Post Book World, April 14, 1985, March 29, 1987.

—*Sketch by Anne Janette Johnson*

* * *

GALLANT, Roy A(rthur) 1924-

PERSONAL: Born April 17, 1924, Portland, Me.; children: Jonathan Roy, James Christopher. *Education:* Bowdoin College, B.A., 1948; Columbia University, M.S., 1949, and additional study.

ADDRESSES: *Home*—Beaver Mountain Lake, Rangely, Me. 04970. *Office*—Office of the Director, Southworth Planetarium, University of Southern Maine, 96 Falmouth St., Portland, Me. 04103.

CAREER: *Retailing Daily,* reporter, and *Boys' Life,* New York City, staff writer, 1949-51; *Scholastic Teacher,* New York City, managing editor, 1954-57; Doubleday & Co., Inc., New York City, author in residence, 1957-59; Aldus Books Ltd., London, England, executive editor, 1959-62; Natural History Press, New York City, editor in chief, 1962-65; member of faculty, Hayden Planetarium, American Museum, 1972-79; owner, publisher, and editor of *The Rangeley Highlander* (a weekly newspaper), 1977-78; University of Southern Maine, Portland, director of Southworth Planetarium, 1980—, adjunct professor, 1980-81, professor of English, 1981—; free-lance author. Instructor, Teachers College, Columbia University, 1958, and University of Maine, Farmington, 1975-76; guest lecturer, University of Illinois, 1964, 1965, and 1966. Science commentator, WCSH-TV, Portland, Me., 1985-86. Lecturer to professional, special interest and school groups on social problems associated with science and technology. Member of advisory board, Center for the Study of the First Americans. Consultant (temporary appointment) to President's Committee for Scientists and Engineers. *Military service:* U.S. Army Air Forces, navigator, 1943-46; Military Intelligence, member of faculty and staff, Psychological Warfare School, Fort Riley, Kan., and psychological warfare officer, Tokyo, Japan, during Korean War.

MEMBER: PEN, Authors Guild, Authors League of America, American Association for the Advancement of Science, Aircraft Owners and Pilots Association, Royal Astronomical Society (fellow), New York Academy of Sciences.

AWARDS, HONORS: Co-recipient of Thomas Alva Edison Foundation Award for best children's science book of the year, 1959, for *Exploring the Universe;* Boys' Clubs of America junior book award certificate, 1959, for *Exploring Chemistry;* National Science Teachers Association outstanding science book for children awards, 1980, for *Memory: How It Works and How to Improve It,* 1982, for *The Planets,* 1983, for *Once around the Galaxy,* 1984, for *101 Questions and Answers about the Universe,*

1986, for *The Macmillan Book of Astronomy,* and 1987, for *Rainbows, Mirages, and Sundogs;* Publication Award, Geographic Society of Chicago, 1980, for *Our Universe;* Distinguished Achievement Award, University of Southern Maine, 1981; Outstanding Science Trade Book for Children award, Children's Book Council, 1987, for *Rainbows, Mirages, and Sundogs.*

WRITINGS:

Exploring the Moon, Doubleday, 1955, revised edition, 1966.
Exploring the Universe, Doubleday, 1956, revised edition, 1968, published as *The Nature of the Universe,* Doubleday, 1956.
Exploring Mars, Doubleday, 1956, revised edition, 1968.
Exploring the Weather, Doubleday, 1957, 2nd revised edition, 1969, published as *The Nature of the Weather,* 1959.
Exploring the Planets, Doubleday, 1958, revised edition, 1967.
Exploring Chemistry, Doubleday, 1958.
Exploring the Sun, Doubleday, 1958.
Man's Reach into Space, Doubleday, 1959, revised edition, 1964.
Exploring under the Earth, Doubleday, 1960.
(Editor with F. Debenham) *Discovery and Exploration,* Doubleday, 1960.
The ABC's of Astronomy: An Illustrated Dictionary, Doubleday, 1962.
Antarctica, Doubleday, 1962.
The ABC's of Chemistry: An Illustrated Dictionary, Doubleday, 1963.
(Editor with G. E. R. Deacon) *Seas, Maps and Men,* Doubleday, 1963.
Universe, Doubleday, 1964.
(Editor with T. F. Gaskill) *World beneath the Oceans,* Natural History Press, 1964.
(Editor with C. A. Ronan) *Man Probes the Universe,* Natural History Press, 1964.
Weather, Doubleday, 1966.
(With C. J. Schuberth) *Discovering Rocks and Minerals: A Nature and Science Guide to Their Collection and Identification,* Natural History Press, 1967.
(With Clifford Swartz) *Measure and Find Out: A Quantitative Approach to Science* (textbook series for grades 4-6), Scott, Foresman, 1969.
Man Must Speak: The Story of Language and How We Use It, Random House, 1969.
(Editor with McElroy) *Foundations of Biology,* Prentice-Hall, 1969.
(Editor) *The Universe in Motion,* Harper, 1969.
(Co-author and editor) *Gravitation,* Harper, 1969.
(Co-author and editor) *The Message of Starlight,* Harper, 1969.
Man's Reach for the Stars, Doubleday, 1971.
Me and My Bones, Doubleday, 1971.
Man the Measurer: Our Units of Measure and How They Grew, Doubleday, 1972.
Charles Darwin: The Making of a Scientist, Doubleday, 1972.
(With Roderick A. Suthers) *Biology: The Behavioral View,* Xerox Publishing, 1973.
Explorers of the Atom, Doubleday, 1973.
Astrology: Sense or Nonsense?, Doubleday, 1974.
How Life Began: Creation versus Evolution, Four Winds Press, 1975.
Beyond Earth: The Search for Extraterrestrial Life, Four Winds Press, 1977.
Fires in the Sky: The Birth and Death of Stars, Four Winds Press, 1978.
Earth's Changing Climate, Four Winds Press, 1978.
National Geographic Picture Atlas of Our Universe, National Geographic Society, 1980, revised edition, 1986.
Our Universe, National Geographic Society, 1980, revised edition, 1986.
Memory: How It Works and How to Improve It, Macmillan, 1980.
The Constellations: How They Came to Be, Four Winds Press, 1980.
The Planets: Exploring the Solar System, Four Winds Press, 1982.
The Jungmann Concept and Technique of Anti-Gravity Leverage, Institute for Gravitational Strain Pathology, 1982.
Once around the Galaxy, Watts, 1983.
(Contributor) Ashley Montague, editor, *Science and Creationism,* Oxford University Press, 1983.
101 Questions and Answers about the Universe, Macmillan, 1985.
Fossils, Watts, 1985.
The Ice Ages, Watts, 1985.
Lost Cities, Watts, 1985.
The Macmillan Book of Astronomy, Macmillan, 1986.
Private Lives of the Stars, Macmillan, 1986.
The Solar System, Macmillan, 1986.
From Living Cells to Dinosaurs, Watts, 1986.
Our Restless Earth, Watts, 1986.
The Rise of Mammals, Watts, 1986.
Rainbows, Mirages, and Sundogs (Junior Literary Guild selection), Macmillan, 1987.
Ancient Indians: The First Americans, Enslow Publishers, 1989.
Before the Sun Dies: The Story of Evolution, Macmillan, 1989.
The Peopling of Planet Earth: From Neanderthal to the Present, Macmillan, 1990.
Language Families of the World, Enslow, 1990.

Also co-author with Isaac Asimov and Jeanne Bendick of volumes in "The Ginn Science Program" series, Ginn, 1973-80. Author of study guides and instructors' manuals for science textbooks. Contributor to *Book of Knowledge* and to *Science-86, Omni, Reporter, American Biology Teacher, Science and Children,* and other magazines. Editorial advisor, Doubleday's "Pictorial Library" series and Prentice-Hall's high school biology textbook program. Member of editorial board, *Natural History,* 1962-64; consulting editor, *Nature and Science,* 1965-68; consultant in earth and space science to *Science and Children,* National Science Teacher's Association, 1980—.

SIDELIGHTS: In the realm of physical science, Roy A. Gallant's special interest is astronomy. As a science writer and editor, he believes that few subjects are too complex to present to children. "If a writer has command of the scientific concept he is dealing with," Gallant comments, "he can operate on the level of abstraction he chooses; and if he knows the capabilities of his audience, he can communicate with them."

AVOCATIONAL INTERESTS: Photography, oil painting, flying, horseback riding.

BIOGRAPHICAL/CRITICAL SOURCES:

BOOKS

Contemporary Literary Criticism, Volume 17, Gale, 1981.

PERIODICALS

New York Times Book Review, August 1, 1982.
Washington Post Book World, May 12, 1985.

* * *

GAZDA, George M(ichael) 1931-

PERSONAL: Born March 6, 1931, in Thayer, Ill.; son of Thomas A. and Mary (Wargo) Gazda; married Barbara Boyd,

July 3, 1954; children: David Andrew. *Education:* Western Illinois University, B.S., 1952, M.S., 1953; University of Illinois, Ed.D., 1959. *Politics:* Democrat. *Religion:* Roman Catholic.

ADDRESSES: Office—Office of the Dean, College of Education, University of Georgia, Athens, Ga. 30602.

CAREER: Teacher in Hopedale, Ill., School District, 1953-54; teacher in Auburn, Ill., School District, 1954-57; University of Illinois, Urbana, assistant professor of counselor education, 1959-62; University of Missouri, Columbia, assistant professor of counselor education, 1962-63; University of Georgia, Athens, associate professor, 1963-67, professor, 1967-75, research professor of education, 1976—, director of counseling psychology program, 1980—, acting associate dean for research, College of Education, 1984—; Medical College of Georgia, consulting professor of psychiatry, 1967—, clinical professor of psychiatry, 1980—. President, Human Relations Consultants, Inc., 1970—. Consultant, U.S. Office of Education, Veterans Administration Hospital, Augusta, Ga., and Bureau of Indian Affairs.

MEMBER: American School Counselor Association, American Psychological Association (fellow; president of counseling psychology division), American Personnel and Guidance Association (member of board, 1972—; chairperson of committee to revise ethical standards, 1974—; president, 1976-77), American Society of Group Psychotherapy and Psychodrama (fellow), Association for Counselor Education and Supervision (president, 1972—), American Group Psychotherapy Association, Association for Religious and Values Issues in Education, Association for Humanistic Education and Development, Georgia Psychological Association (fellow), Georgia School Counselors.

AWARDS, HONORS: Research award, American Personnel and Guidance Association, 1968-70; award, Association for Specialists in Group Work Services, 1976, 1982; research award, Association for Humanistic Education and Development, 1985.

WRITINGS:

(Editor with Robert Clever) *Guidance Readings and Annotated Bibliography,* Superintendent of Public Instruction (Springfield, Ill.), 1961.

(With Jonell H. Folds) *Handbook of Guidance Services,* R. W. Parkinson, 1966.

(Editor and contributor) *Basic Approaches to Group Psychotherapy and Group Counseling,* C. C Thomas, 1968, 2nd edition, 1981.

(With Folds) *Group Guidance: A Critical Incidents Approach,* Follett, 1968.

(Editor) *Theories and Methods of Group Counseling in the Schools,* C. C Thomas, 1969, 2nd edition, 1976.

Group Counseling: A Developmental Approach, Allyn & Bacon, 1971, 4th edition, 1989.

(With others) *Human Relations Development: A Manual for Educators,* Allyn & Bacon, 1973, 3rd edition, 1984.

(Contributor) M. M. Ohlsen, editor, *Counseling Children in Groups,* Holt, 1973.

Human Relations Development: A Manual for Health Sciences, Allyn & Bacon, 1975.

(With Calvin D. Caterall) *Strategies for Helping Students,* C. C Thomas, 1978.

(Editor with Raymond J. Corsini) *Theories of Learning: A Comparative Approach,* F. E. Peacock, 1980.

(With William C. Childers and Richard Walters) *Interpersonal Communication: A Handbook for Health Professionals,* Aspen Systems Corporation, 1982.

Editor, "Group Procedure Symposium" proceedings, University of Georgia, 1967-73. Contributor of more than one hundred articles and monographs to journals in his field. Editor, *Student Personnel Association for Teacher Education Journal,* 1966-68, and American Personnel and Guidance Association *Newsletter,* 1967-73; member of editorial board, *Together: Journal of the Association for Specialists in Group Work, Journal of Counseling and Development,* and *Small Group Behavior Journal.* Co-executive editor, *Journal of Group Psychotherapy, Psychodrama, and Sociometry,* 1982-1988.

WORK IN PROGRESS: Foundations of Counseling and Human Services.

* * *

GEISMAR, L(udwig) L(eo) 1921-

PERSONAL: Born February 25, 1921, in Mannheim, Germany; son of Heinrich (a salesman) and Lina Geismar; married Shirley Ann Cooperman (an editor), September 18, 1948; children: Layah, Deborah, Aviva. *Education:* University of Minnesota, B.A. (cum laude), 1947, M.A., 1950; Hebrew University of Jerusalem, Ph.D., 1956. *Religion:* Jewish.

ADDRESSES: Home—347 Valentine St., Highland Park, N.J. 08904. *Office*—Graduate School of Social Work, Rutgers University, New Brunswick, N.J. 08903.

CAREER: Ministry of Social Welfare, Jerusalem, Israel, coordinator of social research, 1954-56; Family Centered Project, St. Paul, Minn., director, 1956-59; Rutgers University, New Brunswick, N.J., associate professor, 1959-62, professor of social work and sociology, 1962-74, distinguished professor of social work and sociology, 1974—, director of Rutgers University Social Work Research Center. Visiting professor and director of a cross-national family study, University of Melbourne, 1975-76; lecturer at Columbia University School of Social Work, summers, 1963-66, 1968, and at Brandeis University, University of Sydney, University of New South Wales, and Flinders University. Project director of a cross-national family study in Stockholm, 1969-73. Member of review team in Mediterranean countries, United Nations, 1955; member of Social Welfare Administration grant review panel, U.S. Department of Health, Education, and Welfare, 1963. Member of Raritan Valley Community Welfare Council, 1960-62, and Middlesex County Mental Health Board, 1962-64. Consultant, Area Development Project, Vancouver, 1962-67. *Military service:* U.S. Army, 1942-45; served in North Africa and Europe; became sergeant.

MEMBER: American Sociological Association (fellow), National Association of Social Workers, Council on Social Work Education (member of accreditation commission, 1965—), National Council on Family Relations, Society for the Study of Social Problems, American Association of University Professors.

AWARDS, HONORS: Research grants from U.S. Department of Health, Education, and Welfare, Ford Foundation, Buckland Foundation (Australia), Victorian Family Council (Australia), U.S. Social and Rehabilitation Service, National Institute of Mental Health, New Haven Foundation, Tri-Centennial Fund of the Bank of Sweden, Rutgers Research Council, and Australian Department of Social Security.

WRITINGS:

Community Organization in Israel, Israel Ministry of Social Welfare, 1955.

Family Centered Project, Family Centered Project (St. Paul, Minn.), 1957.

Report on a Check List Survey, Family Centered Project, 1957.
(With Beverly Ayres) *Families in Trouble,* Family Centered Project, 1958.
(With Ayres) *Patterns of Change in Problem Families,* Family Centered Project, 1959.
(With Ayres) *Measuring Family Functioning,* Family Centered Project, 1960.
(With Michael La Sorte) *Understanding the Multi-Problem Family: A Conceptual Analysis and Exploration in Identification,* Association Press, 1964.
(With Jane Krisberg) *The Forgotten Neighborhood: Site of an Early Skirmish in the War on Poverty,* Scarecrow, 1967.
Preventive Intervention in Social Work, Scarecrow, 1968.
Family and Community Functioning, Scarecrow, 1971, revised edition, 1980.
(With Bruce Lagey and others) *Early Supports for Family Life,* Scarecrow, 1972.
555 Families: A Social Psychological Study of Young Families in Transition, Transaction Books, 1973.
(With wife, Shirley Geismar) *Families in an Urban Mold,* Pergamon, 1979.
(Co-editor and contributor) *A Quarter Century of Social Work Education,* National Association of Social Workers and ABC-Clio, 1984.
(With Katherine Wood) *Family and Delinquency,* Human Sciences, 1986.

CONTRIBUTOR

The Social Welfare Forum 1960, Columbia University Press, 1960.
Ellen B. Hill, editor, *Ricerche applicate al Servizio Sociale negli Stati Uniti,* Instituto per Gli Studi de Servizio Sociale (Rome), 1964.
(With Lagey) *Social Welfare Practice 1965,* Columbia University Press, 1965.
Gordon E. Brown, editor, *The Multi-Problem Dilemma,* Scarecrow, 1968.
Hadden and Borgatta, editors, *Marriage and the Family,* F.E. Peacock, 1969.
Edward J. Mullen and James R. Dumpson, editors, *Evaluation of Social Intervention,* Jossey-Bass, 1972.
Sheila Maybanks and Marvin Bryce, editors, *Home-Based Services for Children and Families,* C. C Thomas, 1979.

OTHER

Contributor to professional journals. Member of editorial committee, *Social Casework,* 1964-75.

* * *

GETZ, Gene A(rnold) 1932-

PERSONAL: Born March 15, 1932, in Francesville, Ind.; son of John A. (a farmer) and Matilda (Honegger) Getz; married Elaine Holmquist, June 11, 1956; children: Renee Elaine, Robyn Lynn, Kenton Gene. *Education:* Moody Bible Institute, diploma, 1952; attended Eastern Montana College of Education (now Eastern Montana College), 1952-53; Rocky Mountain College, B.A., 1954; Wheaton College, Wheaton Ill., M.A., 1958; New York University, Ph.D., 1969.

ADDRESSES: Home—2822 Woods Lane, Garland, Tex. 75042. *Office*—Center for Church Renewal, 200 Chisholm Pl., No. 234, Plano, Tex. 75075.

CAREER: Engaged in radio ministry with Montana Gospel Crusade and youth director of Church of the Air, Billings, Mont., 1952-54; assistant pastor of community church in Hinsdale, Ill., 1954; director of Christian education at Bible church in Lisle, Ill., 1956-58; Moody Bible Institute, Chicago, Ill., instructor in Christian education, 1956-68, director of evening school, 1963-68; Dallas Theological Seminary, Dallas, Tex., associate professor of Christian education, beginning 1968; Fellowship Bible Church, Dallas, pastor, 1972-81; Center for Church Renewal, Plano, Tex., director, 1978—. Visiting professor, Word of Life Summer Institute of Camping, Schroon Lake, N.Y., 1964-68. President, Space Age Communications, Dallas.

MEMBER: National Association of Professors of Christian Education, National Sunday School Association (former president of research commission).

WRITINGS:

Audio-Visuals in the Church, Moody, 1959, revised edition published as *Audiovisual Media in Christian Education,* 1972.
The Vacation Bible School in the Local Church, Moody, 1962.
The Christian Home, Moody, 1967.
(With Roy B. Zuck) *Christian Youth: An In-Depth Study,* Moody, 1968.
The History of the Moody Bible Institute, Moody, 1969.
The Story of the Moody Bible Institute, Moody, 1969.
(Editor with Zuck) *Adult Education the Church,* Moody, 1970.
(With Zuck) *Ventures in Family Living,* Moody, 1971.
Sharpening the Focus of the Church, Moody, 1974, revised edition, Victor Books, 1984.
The Measure of a Man, Regal Books, 1974.
The Measure of a Church, Regal Books, 1975.
The Measure of a Family, Regal Books, 1976.
Building Up One Another, Victor Books, 1976.
When You're Confused and Uncertain, Regal Books, 1976.
When You Feel Like You Haven't Got It, Regal Books, 1976.
The Measure of a Woman, Regal Books, 1977.
Loving One Another, Victor Books, 1979.
When You Feel Like a Failure, Regal Books, 1979.
When the Job Seems Too Big, Regal Books, 1979.
Encouraging One Another, Victor Books, 1981.
When Your Goals Seem Out of Reach, Regal Books, 1981.
Joseph: From Prison to Palace, Regal Books, 1983.
Pressing On When You'd Rather Turn Back, Regal Books, 1983.
Saying No When You'd Rather Say Yes, Regal Books, 1983.
Serving One Another, Victor Books, 1984.
When the Pressure's On, Regal Books, 1984.
Believing God When You're Tempted to Doubt, Regal Books, 1984.
Doing Your Part When You'd Rather Let God Do It All, Regal Books, 1984.
Looking Up When You Feel Down, Regal Books, 1985.
Living for Others When You'd Rather Live for Yourself, Regal Books, 1985.
Standing Firm When You'd Rather Retreat, Regal Books, 1986.
God's Plan for Building a Good Reputation, Victor Books, 1987.
Partners for Life, Regal Books, 1988.

WORK IN PROGRESS: An exposition on Romans; books on leadership in the local church, on financial freedom, and on biblical renewal.

SIDELIGHTS: Gene A. Getz wrote *CA:* "One of the unique surprises for me is the way in which a number of my books have been translated into foreign languages. To date, over fifty titles have been translated into at least twelve different languages. Several of my titles are scheduled for translation and release in all of the Eastern European languages. This is encouraging in that I have attempted to write with a supracultural perspective."

GIBBS, James A.
See GIBBS, James Atwood

* * *

GIBBS, James Atwood 1922-
(James A. Gibbs, Jim Gibbs)

PERSONAL: Born January 17, 1922, in Seattle, Wash.; son of A. James (in investments) and Vera (Smith) Gibbs; married Cherie Lola Norman, May 26, 1950; children: Debbie Ann Gibbs Pedrick. *Education:* Attended University of Washington, Seattle. *Politics:* Independent. *Religion:* Baptist.

ADDRESSES: Home—Cleft of the Rock Lighthouse, P.O. Box 93, Yachats, Ore. 97498.

CAREER: Marine Digest, Seattle, Wash., assistant editor, 1948-55, editor, 1959-72; G.E.B. Properties, Seattle, partner, 1964—. *Military service:* U.S. Coast Guard, 1942-46.

MEMBER: Puget Sound Maritime Historical Society (cofounder; charter member).

AWARDS, HONORS: Twelve Anchor Award from Port of Seattle, 1954-72; award of merit from Seattle Historical Society, 1955, for *Sentinels of the North Pacific: The Story of Pacific Coast Lighthouses and Lightships.*

WRITINGS:

Pacific Graveyard: A Narrative of the Ships Lost Where the Columbia River Meets the Pacific Ocean, Binford & Mort, 1950, 3rd edition (under name James A. Gibbs), 1964.
Tillamook Light, Binford & Mort, 1953, published as *Tillamook Light: A True Narrative of Oregon's Tillamook Rock Lighthouse,* 1979.
Sentinels of the North Pacific: The Story of Pacific Coast Lighthouses and Lightships, Binford & Mort, 1955.
Shipwrecks of the Pacific Coast, Binford & Mort, 1957.
(Under name James A. Gibbs) *Shipwrecks off Juan de Fuca,* Binford & Mort, 1968.
(With Joe Williamson) *Maritime Memories of Puget Sound,* Superior, 1977, revised edition, Schiffer, 1987.

UNDER NAME JIM GIBBS

West Coast Windjammers in Story and Pictures, Superior, 1968.
Pacific Square-Riggers: Pictorial History of the Great Windships of Yesteryear, Superior, 1969, revised edition, Schiffer, 1987.
The Unusual Side of the Sea: A Slop Chest of Sea Lore, Windward Publishing, 1971.
Disaster Log of Ships, Superior, 1971.
West Coast Lighthouses: A Pictorial History of the Guiding Lights of the Sea, Superior, 1974.
Shipwrecks in Paradise, Superior, 1977.
Oregon's Salty Coast, Superior, 1978.
Sentinels of Solitude: West Coast Lighthouses, Graphic Arts Center, 1981.
Lighthouses of the Pacific, Schiffer, 1986.
Peril at Sea, Schiffer, 1986.
Windjammers of the Pacific Rim, Schiffer, 1987.

SIDELIGHTS: James Atwood Gibbs told *CA:* "One should write about the things he enjoys most; then, even if nobody else likes his work, he feels satisfied. If people enjoy his work, he's doubly satisfied. Everything comes from the good Lord, and to him all basic credit must go for any works. Without him one has a missing ingredient."

GIBBS, Jim
See GIBBS, James Atwood

* * *

GILLESPIE, Robert B(yrne) 1917-

PERSONAL: Born December 31, 1917, in Brooklyn, N.Y.; son of John F. (a veterinarian) and Lillian S. (a teacher; maiden name, Blankley) Gillespie; married Marianna Albert (a researcher), June 26, 1957 (died, 1987); children: Laura. *Education:* Attended Brooklyn College (now Brooklyn College of the City University of New York), 1935-37; St. Johns University, LL.B., 1940.

ADDRESSES: Home and office—226 Bay Ave., Douglaston, N.Y. 11363. *Agent*—Albert Zuckerman, Writers House, Inc., 21 West 26th St., New York, N.Y. 10010.

CAREER: Boocheever, McManus, & Regosin, New York City, attorney, 1940-41; Poletti, Diamond, Roosevelt, Freidin & McKay, New York City, attorney, 1947-49; private law practice in New York City, 1949-54; New York Herald-Tribune Syndicate, New York City, promotion manager, 1954-64; Newsday Specials Syndicate, Garden City, N.Y., promotion director, 1964-71, acting director and editor, 1970-71; Chicago Tribune-New York News Syndicate, New York City, promotion director, 1971-75; Los Angeles Times Syndicate, New York City, promotion director and eastern manager, 1975-77; free-lance writer and editor, 1977—. *Military service:* U.S. Army, 1942-46; became staff sergeant; received Croix de Guerre.

WRITINGS:

SUSPENSE NOVELS

The Crossword Mystery, Constable, 1979, Raven House, 1982.
Little Sally Does It Again, Raven House, 1982.
Print-Out (a Detective Book Club selection), Dodd, 1983.
Heads You Lose, Dodd, 1985.
Empress of Coney Island (a Detective Book Club selection), Dodd, 1986.
The Hell's Kitchen Connection (a Detective Book Club selection), Dodd, 1987.
The Last of the Honeywells, Dodd, 1988.

PUZZLE BOOKS

The Daily Crosswords, Grosset, Numbers 1-6, 1975, Numbers 7-8, 1977.
Jumbo Crossword Treasury, Sunridge Press, 1978.
Ace Daily Crosswords, Ace Books, Number 2, 1981, Number 6, 1981, Number 7, 1982.
All-New Crosswords, Pocket Books, Numbers 1-3, 1983.
Cryptopic Crosswords, Prentice-Hall, 1983.

OTHER

Work represented in anthologies, including *Discovery Six,* edited by Vance Bourjaily, 1954.

WORK IN PROGRESS: Another mystery novel.

SIDELIGHTS: "Because I was the son of a veterinarian," Robert B. Gillespie told *CA,* "I spent my otherwise sheltered childhood assisting him in the repairing of damaged animals and cleaning out the kennels. I was in further protective custody for four years at Cathedral College, a preparatory seminary in Brooklyn where one, presumably, prepared for the priesthood by withdrawing from the secular world—that is, by going to school on Saturday and getting Thursday off. I dropped out because I figured I'd make a lousy priest, if not a scandalous one. My mind meandered.

"A four-year hitch as a medic in World War II thoroughly fragmented a legal career that wasn't going anywhere anyway. I was a lousy lawyer because I always sympathized with the other fellow's point of view. Lawyers shouldn't do that.

"During my law years I wrote scores of short stories and collected scores of rejection slips, including many from *Story* magazine which began: 'This, alas, is a rejection slip.' Those stories were so bad that Hallie Burnett should have burned them instead of sending them back! During those years I also wrote a lousy novel, based partly on my legal career. I even acquired a literary agent at that time, Naomi Burton of Curtis Brown Limited. That valiant lady tried hard to get a publisher for the novel and succeeded in getting me a few words of encouragement and requests to see the *next* book. There wasn't a next book for twenty-four years.

"A segment of the novel was accepted by Vance Bourjaily for inclusion in *Discovery Six* as a short story. I had had some writings in the *St. John's Law Review,* but this was my first piece of fiction to be published, and I'll always be grateful to Bourjaily for that. He said he took the story because it was the only one he had ever come across in which a poem was successfully integrated in the narration.

"The next piece of fiction was published when I was sixty. Miles Huddleston, astute editor of Constable and Company, saw merit in *The Crossword Mystery* where others had not. For that I have erected a plaque to him in my heart.

"The intervening years were spent in what is known as earning a living—writing volumes of promotion copy, editing columns and comic strips, introducing to the newspaper public such worthy comics as 'Miss Peach' by Mel Lazarus and 'B.C.' by Johnny Hart and such profound columnists as Art Buchwald, Erma Bombeck, and Jeane Dixon. I was surprised and delighted that the commercial world had a place for a misfit. They paid me money for having fun. (Of course, the beloved *New York Herald-Tribune* eventually died, which shows that you shouldn't pay people for having fun.) At one time I ghosted an exercise column and at another abruptly became crossword editor when the previous editor died rather suddenly at his retirement home on Majorca, which shows that you shouldn't retire to a tropical island if you want to go on living.

"The crossword chore put a severe strain on my marriage, since the only time I could work at it included evenings, weekends, and while commuting on the Long Island Railroad. The extra money helped to soothe the savage bride, however, and at least a dozen books came out of the syndicated puzzles. The experience led to *The Crossword Mystery,* in which the reader had to solve a crossword puzzle for the final solution; it also led to added careers as a puzzle editor and constructor. For *Cryptopic Crosswords* I created fifty-five British-Style crosswords, each constructed around a theme.

"There's not much money in all this. The best advance I received was for a book that was never published—an 'adult' western for a series that petered out."

Empress of Coney Island was also published in France.

BIOGRAPHICAL/CRITICAL SOURCES:

PERIODICALS

Observer, June 17, 1979.

GILMAN, J. D.
See ORGILL, Douglas

* * *

GITTELL, Marilyn 1931-

PERSONAL: Born April 3, 1931, in New York, N.Y.; daughter of Julius and Rose (Meyerson) Jacobs; married Irwin Gittell (a certified public accountant), August 20, 1950; children: Amy, Ross. *Education:* Brooklyn College (now Brooklyn College of the City University of New York), A.B., 1952; New York University, M.P.A., 1953, Ph.D., 1960.

ADDRESSES: Home—70 East 10th St., New York, N.Y. 10003. *Office*—Graduate School and University Center of the City University of New York, New York, N.Y. 10036.

CAREER: Tax Foundation, New York City, research assistant, 1952-55; Government Affairs Foundation, Albany, N.Y., research associate, 1955-60; Queens College of the City University of New York, Flushing, Long Island, N.Y., instructor, 1960-62, assistant professor, 1962-65, associate professor, 1965-67, professor of political science, 1967-71, professor of urban studies and chairman of department, 1971-73, director of Institute for Community Studies and director of honors program, 1967-73; Brooklyn College of the City University of New York, Brooklyn, N.Y., professor of political science, 1973-78, assistant vice-president and associate provost, 1973-78; Graduate School and University Center of the City University of New York, New York City, professor of political science, 1978—.

Visiting distinguished professor, University of Texas at Arlington, 1981. Consulting editor, Praeger Publishers, 1968-73. Chairperson, Citizens Committee for Robert Kennedy, Queens County, N.Y., 1968; member of planning committee, White House Conference on Children and Youth, 1970; member of Task Force on Democratic Forms for New Towns, Twentieth Century Fund, 1970-71, Associate Task Force on Manpower, U.S. Department of Labor, 1970-74, community connittee for New York Metropolitan Museum of Art, 1971-78, New York State Task Force on Post Secondary Education, 1971—, National Study Commission on Undergraduate and Teacher Education, 1972-76, and of New York State Regents Committee on Examinations, 1974-78; member of board of trustees, Interface, 1975—; member of board of directors, Research Foundation of the City University of New York, 1980—. Member of advisory board, Legal Research and Services for the Elderly, 1969-73, Puerto Rican Research Center, 1971-75, and Queens Lay Advocate Service, 1972-78; member of New York State Advisory Committee for Resource Center for Women, 1975-77. Consultant to numerous organizations, including New York State Constitutional Revision Commission, 1958-59, United Nations, 1966, Ford Foundation, 1967, and to New Jersey Chancellor of Higher Education, 1978-79. Conductor of series of forty radio programs, "Megalopolis: U.S.A.," for WNYC, 1960.

MEMBER: American Political Science Association, American Society for Public Administration, Northeastern Regional Political Science Association (member of executive committee, 1972), New York State Political Science Association (member of executive board, 1966-67), Phi Beta Kappa.

AWARDS, HONORS: Grants from Ford Foundation, 1967-70, 1975-76, City University of New York, 1970-71, New York Foundation, 1971, New World Foundation, 1971-72, Carnegie Foundation, 1972-74, 1981, and from several other public and private sources.

WRITINGS:

(Co-editor) *Metropolitan Communities: A Bibliography,* Public Administration Service, 1956.

(Co-author) *Metropolitan Surveys: A Digest,* Public Administration Service, 1958.

(Editor) *Educating an Urban Population,* Sage Publications, 1967.

Participants and Participation: A Study of School Policy in New York City, Praeger, 1967.

(With T. Edward Hollander) *Six Urban School Systems: A Comparative Study of Institutional Response,* Praeger, 1968.

(Editor with Alan Hevesi) *The Politics of Urban Education,* Praeger, 1969.

(Editor with Maurice Berube) *Confrontation at Ocean Hill-Brownsville:The New York School Strikes of 1968,* Praeger, 1969.

(With Mario Fantini and Richard Magat) *Community Control and the Urban School,* introduction by Kenneth B. Clarke, Praeger, 1970.

(With Berube and others) *Demonstration for Social Change: An Experiment in Local Control,* Institute for Community Studies, Queens College of the City University of New York, 1971.

(With Berube and others) *Local Control in Education: Three Demonstration School Districts in New York City,* Praeger, 1972.

(With Fantini) *Decentralization: Achieving Reform,* Praeger, 1973.

(With Berube and others) *School Boards and School Policy: An Evaluation of Decentralization in New York City,* Praeger, 1973.

(Editor with Ann Cook and Herb Mack) *City Life, 1865-1900: Views of Urban America,* Praeger, 1973.

(Editor with Cook and Mack) *What Was It Like?: When Your Grandparents Were Your Age,* Pantheon, 1976.

(With Bruce Hoffacker and others) *Limits of Participation: The Decline of Community Organizations,* Sage Publications, 1980.

(Editor) *State Politics and the New Federalism: Readings and Commentary,* Longman, 1986.

MONOGRAPHS

Megalopolis, U.S.A.: A Radio Course, Queens College Press, 1960.

(With William L. Frederick) *State Technical Assistance to Local Government: A Review of Selected State Services,* Council of State Governments, 1962.

Governing the Public Schools: Educational Decision-Making and Its Financial Implications in New York City, Temporary Commission on City Finances (New York), 1966.

(With Hollander and William S. Vincent) *Investigations of Fiscally Independent and Dependent City School Districts,* U.S. Office of Education, 1967.

The Community School in the Nation, Institute for Community Studies, Queens College of the City University of New York, 1970.

School Decentralization and School Policy in New York City, Institute for Community Studies, Queens College of the City University of New York, 1971.

Evaluation of the Impact of the Emergency Employment in New York City, Institute for Community Studies, Queens College of the City University of New York, 1972.

Citizen Organizations: Citizen Participation in Educational Decision-making, two volumes, Institute for Responsive Education, 1979.

CONTRIBUTOR

Louis Masotti and Dan Bowen, editors, *Civil Violence in the Urban Community,* Sage Publications, 1968.

Alan Rosenthal, editor, *Governing Education: A Reader on Politics, Power and Public School Policy,* Doubleday, 1969.

H. R. Mahodd and Edward L. Angus, editors, *Urban Politics and Problems,* Scribner, 1969.

Needs of Elementary and Secondary Education for the Seventies, U. S. Government Printing Office, 1970.

Henry M. Levin, editor, *Community Control of Schools,* Brookings Institution, 1970.

Annette Rubinstein, editor, *Schools against Children: The Case for Community Control,* Monthly Review Press, 1970.

Jewel Bellush and Stephen David, editors, *Race and Politics in New York City: Six Case Studies in Decentralization,* Praeger, 1971.

Freedom, Bureaucracy and Schooling, National Education Association, 1971.

Susan Fainstein and Norman Fainstein, editors, *The View from Below: Urban Politics and Social Policy,* Little, Brown, 1972.

Allan Gartner, Colin Greer, and Frank Riessman, editors, *What Nixon Is Doing to Us,* Harrow Books, 1974.

Sar A. Levitan and Robert Taggart, editors, *Emergency Employment Act,* Olympus, 1974.

(With Bruce Dollar) Antonia Pantoja, Barbara Blourock, and James Bowman, editors, *Badges and Indicia of Slavery: Cultural Pluralism Redefined,* Study Commission on Undergraduate Education and the Education of Teachers, 1975.

Maynard C. Reynolds, editor, *Special Education in School System Decentralization,* Leadership Training Institute, University of Minnesota, 1975.

Frederick B. Rough, editor, *Milliken vs. Bradley: Implication for Metropolitan Desegregation,* U. S. Government Printing Office, 1975.

Carl A. Grant, editor, *Community Participation in Education: What Is/What Should Be,* Pendell, 1976.

Charles Brecher and Raymond D. Horton, editors, *Setting Municipal Priorities, 1981,* Allanheld, Osmun, 1980.

Choosing Equality, Temple University Press, 1987.

OTHER

Author of *Studying the Community: A Research Handbook,* with Constancia Warren, 1980; author of *Final Evaluation Report on Syracuse Youth Community Service* and *Final Evaluation Report on Syracuse Youth Community Service: Ethnographic Research,* both with Marguerite Beardsley and Marsha Weissman, 1981. Contributor to *Hearings of 92nd Congress,* U. S. Government Printing Office, 1971; contributor to *Encyclopedia Americana,* 1964, *Proceedings of the Academy of Political Science,* 1968, and *Encyclopedia of Education,* 1971. Contributor of articles to professional journals, including *Change, Social Policy, Public Administration Review, Journal of Negro Education, New Generations,* and *American Behaviorial Scientist.* Editor, *Urban Affairs Quarterly,* 1965-70; member of editorial advisory board, *Urban Affairs Annual Review,* 1966-74, and *Journal of Education,* 1977-79; member of editorial board, *Social Policy,* 1969—.

* * *

GODWIN, Joscelyn 1945-

PERSONAL: Born January 16, 1945, in Kelmscott, Oxford, England; came to the United States in 1966, naturalized in 1980; son of Edward (an artist and writer) and Stephanie (an artist and writer; maiden name, Allfree) Scott-Snell, later Godwin; married

Sharyn Louise Cook (a musician), July 31, 1971 (divorced, 1979); married Janet Matthews, November 21, 1979; children: (second marriage) Ariel. *Education:* Attended Radley College; Magdalene College, Cambridge, B.A., 1965, Mus.B., 1966, M.A., 1970; Cornell University, Ph.D., 1969.

ADDRESSES: Home—R.D. 1, Earlville, N.Y. 13332. *Office*—Department of Music, Colgate University, Hamilton, N.Y. 13346.

CAREER: Cleveland State University, Cleveland, Ohio, instructor in music, 1969-71; Colgate University, Hamilton, N.Y., assistant professor, 1971-76, associate professor, 1976-82, professor of music, 1982—. Church organist, 1969-75.

MEMBER: American Musicological Society, Royal College of Organists (fellow).

AWARDS, HONORS: Harding Prize from Royal College of Organists, 1965; Abingdon Prize from Cambridge University, 1966, for "String Trio"; grant from American Council of Learned Societies, 1985.

WRITINGS:

(Author of preface and notes) Henry Cowell, *New Musical Resources,* Something Else Press, 1969.

(Translator) Werner Walcker-Meyer, *The Roman Organ of Aquincum,* Musikwissenschaftliche Verlagsgesellschaft, 1973.

(Editor) *Schirmer Scores: A Repertory of Western Music,* Schirmer Books, 1975.

(Editor) Alessandro Scarlatti, *Marco Attilio Regolo,* Harvard University Press, 1975.

Robert Fludd: Hermetic Philosopher and Surveyor of Two Worlds, Thames & Hudson, 1979.

Athanasius Kircher: A Renaissance Man and the Quest for Lost Knowledge, Thames & Hudson, 1979.

Mystery Religions in the Ancient World, Thames & Hudson, 1981.

(Translator) Salomon Trismosin, *Splendor Solis,* Magnum Opus Hermetic Sourceworks, 1981.

(Translator) Rene Guenon, *The Multiple States of Being,* Larson, 1984.

(Editor) *Music, Mysticism and Magic: A Sourcebook,* Routledge & Kegan Paul, 1986.

(Editor) Michael Maier, *Atalanta Fugiens,* Magnum Opus Hermetic Sourceworks, 1987.

(Author of foreword) *The Pythagorean Sourcebook,* Phanes Press, 1987.

Harmonies of Heaven and Earth: The Spiritual Dimension of Music from Antiquity to the Avant-Garde, Thames & Hudson, 1987.

(Author of foreword) D. P. Walker, *La Magie spirituelle et angelique de Ficin a Campanella,* Albin Michel, 1987.

(Translator) Fabre d'Olivet, *Music Explained as Science and Art,* Inner Traditions, 1988.

(Editor) *Cosmic Music: Three Musical Keys to the Interpretation of Reality,* Lindisfarne, 1988.

Also contributor to *Dictionary of Twentieth-Century Music* and *Dictionary of the Middle Ages.* Composer of "String Trio," "Epistle to Harmodius," and "A Few Thoughts for Treble Recorder." Contributor to music, religion, and esoteric journals.

WORK IN PROGRESS: L'Esoterisme musical en France: 1750-1950; research into the history of esoteric movements.

SIDELIGHTS: Author, composer, and organist Joscelyn Godwin told *CA* that his work "describes the circuitous route I am having to take in order to reach a better understanding of music in the light of my philosophical interests." Those interests encompass a broad range of time and thought, and include such subjects as hermeticism (the study of the astrological and occult writings attributed to Hermes Trismegistus), the role of music in the universe, and the "Perennial Philosophy," a concept central to Godwin's work that attempts to unify and find a common purpose in man's religious experience.

One of Godwin's most widely reviewed works, *Mystery Religions in the Ancient World,* is described by Mary Beard in the *Times Literary Supplement* as "a book not of history, but of theosophy. Ancient religion has been rescued from the hands of 'unbelieving academics' and 'Christian chauvinists,' and the Mysteries are seen to play their part in the 'Perennial Philosophy,' as 'attempts, each valid for its time and place, to point the way to the true goal of human existence!' "

Godwin defined for *CA* the relationship between *Mystery Religions in the Ancient World* and two of his previous works, *Robert Fludd: Hermetic Philosopher and Surveyor of Two Worlds* and *Athanasius Kircher: A Renaissance Man and the Quest for Knowledge:* "Fludd and Kircher were two universal men of the Renaissance for whom music was a fundamental element of their attempt to grasp the cosmos as a whole. Both were deeply concerned with hermeticism, and Kircher especially with the mystery religions of antiquity. Hence [*Mystery Religions in the Ancient World*], which approaches these religions with the question, 'how are we to empathize with these believers?' "

Although Beard faults Godwin's approach, she nevertheless points out the value of his purpose, declaring of *Mystery Religions in the Ancient World:* "There is something of interest here. [As a work of mysticism] this book is, I suspect, quite par for the course. Moreover, the recurring and shifting notion of the 'Perennial Philosophy,' from its inception in sixteenth-century Italy, through Leitniz, Huxley, and beyond, is certainly worth attention; as is also . . . the intellectual make-up of Godwin himself."

Having explored the religious implications of his earlier work through the writing of *Mystery Religions in the Ancient World,* Godwin has returned to music. He explains the present and future course of his work: "I have assembled in my sourcebook a continuous stream of 'musical hermeticism' as it appears in the West, Judaism, and Islam. *Harmonies of Heaven and Earth: The Spiritual Dimensions of Music from Antiquity to the Avant-Garde* presents my own ideas about this material. Although I have written exclusively about Western esotericism, I hope to move in spirit to the East, where I feel more at home philosophically. My current research focuses on the meeting of the Western and Eastern esoteric streams around 1900."

BIOGRAPHICAL/CRITICAL SOURCES:

PERIODICALS

A.R.I.E.S., Number 7, 1988.
Gnosis Magazine, summer, 1988.
Literary Review, August, 1988.
New York Times, April 23, 1987.
Temenos (London), Number 10, 1988.
Times Literary Supplement, January 15, 1982, July 31, 1987.

* * *

GOLD, Barbara K(irk) 1945-

PERSONAL: Born March 23, 1945, in Brooklyn, N.Y.; daughter of Alfred Kurtzhalls (a stockbroker) and Dorothy Temple

(Kirk) Simpson; married Paul E. Gold, August 26, 1967 (divorced); married Carl A. Rubino, December 21, 1986; children: Scott David. *Education:* University of Michigan, B.A., 1966; University of North Carolina, M.A., 1968, Ph.D., 1975.

ADDRESSES: Home—170 Las Astas Dr., Los Gatos, Calif. 95030. *Office*—Department of Classics, Santa Clara University, Santa Clara, Calif. 95053.

CAREER: University of California, Irvine, lecturer, 1971-73, assistant professor of classics, 1973-76; University of Virginia, Charlottesville, assistant professor of classics, 1977-78; University of Texas at Austin, assistant professor of classics, 1978-86; Santa Clara University, Santa Clara, Calif., associate professor of classics, 1986—.

MEMBER: American Philological Association, American Institute of Archaeology, American Classical League, Vergilian Society, Classics Association of the Middle West and South, Philological Association of the Pacific Coast.

AWARDS, HONORS: Mellon fellowship, 1979-80.

WRITINGS:

(Editor) *Literary and Artistic Patronage in Ancient Rome,* University of Texas Press, 1982.

Literary Patronage in Greece and Rome, University of North Carolina Press, 1987.

Contributor to philology and classical studies journals, including *American Journal of Philology, Classical Journal,* and *Renaissance Quarterly.*

WORK IN PROGRESS: A book on Roman satire; commentary on Juvenal's *Satire 6.*

SIDELIGHTS: Barbara K. Gold's *Literary and Artistic Patronage in Ancient Rome* is a collection of seven essays on various aspects of patronage. In her introduction, Gold discusses the modern replacement of the individual by the institutional patron. The essays, which explore the lives of such ancient writers as Horace, Virgil, Propertius, and Ovid, demonstrate, according to N. M. Horsfall in the *Times Literary Supplement,* that "the correct rituals of good behavior between Romans of unequal status determine[d] the realities of patronage."

Gold told *CA* that *Literary Patronage in Greece and Rome* "traces the institution of patronage from the time of Homer down to the Roman empire and demonstrates its importance for social relations and literary relationships and products." She adds: "I have done work on many kinds of literature, from Greek and Roman poetry (mainly elegy and lyric) to the Argentine writer Jorge Luis Borges. My main interests—or the things that I seem to return to regardless of the period or genre about which I am writing—are the interrelationship of literature and society, the theme of order and disorder, and the place of women in Greek and Roman society and literature. It is rewarding to be able to work these interests into university teaching and to communicate the excitement of new ideas to my students. For research to be important and vital, it must form a part of the rest of one's life and interests."

BIOGRAPHICAL/CRITICAL SOURCES:

PERIODICALS

Times Literary Supplement, August 13, 1982.

GOLDMAN, William (W.) 1931-
(Harry Longbaugh, S. Morgenstern)

PERSONAL: Born August 12, 1931, in Chicago, Ill.; son of Maurice Clarence (a businessman) and Marion (Weil) Goldman; married Ilene Jones, April 15, 1961; children: Jenny Rebecca, Susanna. *Education:* Oberlin College, B.A., 1952; Columbia University, M.A., 1956.

ADDRESSES: Home—50 East 77th St., New York, N.Y. 10021. *Agent*—Morton Janklow Associates, 598 Madison Ave., New York, N.Y. 10022 (books); Creative Artists Agency, 1888 Century Park East, 14th Floor, Los Angeles, Calif. 90067 (films).

CAREER: Novelist, 1956—; playwright and screenwriter, 1961—. *Military service:* U.S. Army, 1952-54.

AWARDS, HONORS: Academy of Motion Picture Arts and Sciences Award (Oscar) for best original screenplay, 1970, for "Butch Cassidy and the Sundance Kid"; Academy of Motion Picture Arts and Sciences Award (Oscar) for best screenplay based on material from another medium, 1976, for "All the President's Men"; Laurel Award, 1983, for lifetime achievement in screenwriting.

WRITINGS:

NOVELS

The Temple of Gold, Knopf, 1957.

Your Turn To Curtsy, My Turn To Bow, Doubleday, 1958.

Soldier in the Rain, Atheneum, 1960.

Boys and Girls Together, Atheneum, 1964.

(Under pseudonym Harry Longbaugh) *No Way To Treat a Lady,* Gold Medal, 1964, published under own name, Harcourt, 1968.

The Thing of It Is . . . , Harcourt, 1967.

Father's Day, Harcourt, 1971.

The Princess Bride: S. Morgenstern's Classic Tale of True Love and High Adventure, the "Good Parts" Version, Abridged by William Goldman (also see below), Harcourt, 1974.

Marathon Man (also see below), Macmillan, 1975.

Wigger (juvenile), Harcourt, 1974.

Magic (also see below), Delacorte, 1976.

Tinsel, Delacorte, 1979.

Control, Delacorte, 1982.

(Under pseudonym S. Morgenstern) *The Silent Gondoliers,* Ballantine, 1983.

The Color of Light, Warner Books, 1984.

Heat (also see below), Warner Books, 1985.

Brothers, Warner Books, 1987.

NONFICTION

The Season: A Candid Look at Broadway (an excerpt; originally appeared in *Esquire,* January, 1969), Harcourt, 1969.

Adventures in the Screen Trade: A Personal View of Hollywood and Screenwriting, Warner Books, 1983.

(With Mike Lupica) *Wait till Next Year: The Story of a Season When What Should've Happened Didn't & What Could've Gone Wrong Did!,* Bantam, 1988.

PLAYS

(With brother, James Goldman) *Blood, Sweat and Stanley Poole* (produced on Broadway at Morosco Theatre, October 5, 1961), Dramatists Play Service, 1962.

(With Goldman and John Kander) "A Family Affair" (musical), produced on Broadway at Billy Rose Theatre, January 27, 1962.

"Mr. Horn" (teleplay), produced by Columbia Broadcasting System (CBS), 1979.

SCREENPLAYS

(With Michael Relph) "Masquerade," United Artists, 1965.
"Harper," Warner Brothers, 1966.
Butch Cassidy and the Sundance Kid, (20th Century-Fox, 1969), Bantam, 1971.
"The Hot Rock," 20th Century-Fox, 1972.
"The Stepford Wives," Fadsior/Palomar, 1974.
The Great Waldo Pepper, (Universal, 1975), Dell, 1975.
"All the President's Men" (based on book of same title by Bob Woodward and Carl Bernstein), Warner Brothers, 1976.
"Marathon Man" (based on Goldman's novel of same title), Paramount, 1976.
"A Bridge Too Far," (United Artists, 1977), published as *William Goldman's Story of A Bridge Too Far,* Dell, 1977.
"Magic" (based on Goldman's novel of same title), Twentieth Century-Fox, 1978.
"The Princess Bride" (based on Goldman's novel of same title), Twentieth Century-Fox, 1987.
"Heat" (based on Goldman's novel of same title), New Century/Vista, 1987.

OTHER

Contributor to periodicals, including *Transatlantic Review, Esquire,* and *New World Writing.*

SIDELIGHTS: William Goldman is "just about the biggest, the best, the most successful writer in movies today," according to Bruce Cook in the *Chicago Tribune Book World.* Goldman, who has won two Academy Awards for his screenplays, prefers to think of himself as a novelist who happens to write for films; indeed, his fiction has found as wide an audience as any movie he has written. As Ralph Tyler notes in the *New York Times,* Goldman has the "enviable ability to move freely back and forth between big-selling novels and big-attendance films. . . . The author has never climbed from the great plains of popular art to the mountains where the literary laurels bloom. But that doesn't mean his knack is negligible." In the *Dictionary of Literary Biography,* Botham Stone calls Goldman "an instinctive writer who works very quickly and with little revision. His extremely popular screenplays and books have a quality of humanity that sets them apart from formula best-sellers and other, more calculated 'blockbuster' films. . . . There is no small amount of skill in [his works'] creation." Goldman is "not only prolific and versatile," concludes Bob Ellison in the *Chicago Tribune Book World,* "he's one of only a handful of earthlings who can write screenplays and novels—and excel at both."

Summing up his career for *CA,* Goldman said: "I've only been a writer. My first novel was taken the summer I finished graduate school, so I've never known anything else." Part of the reason for Goldman's consistent success through thirty years of writing is his rather unconventional attitude toward his work. He goes to an office every day, even though his home is quiet and comfortable, because an office environment encourages him to apply himself. "I grew up in a businessman's town [Chicago]," he told the *New York Times,* "and it's essential that I maintain a sense that what I'm doing is as important as what an insurance man or businessman is doing. That's why I have an office." Stone describes Goldman as "normally unenthusiastic about his work, no matter how flamboyant or comic it might appear." While this may not necessarily be the case, Goldman is satisfied to leave his projects behind at the end of a working day while he relaxes elsewhere. "The sooner I'm done," he told Stone, "the sooner I can go to the movies."

Goldman enjoyed attending films as a youngster, so it is perhaps not surprising that he also claims to enjoy writing for the medium. In the *New York Times* he said: "I have a theory that we gravitate toward affection. I have a facility for screenwriting. It's gone very well. I needed something else to write besides novels, which are physically hard and take time. Since nobody wanted my stories and people seemed to want my screenplays, I gravitated toward that affection." Before he ventured into screenwriting, however, Goldman had established himself as an author of "well-crafted, moderately interesting, psychological novels [with] a distinctive talent for creating characters through dialogue," to quote *New York Times Book Review* contributor Sheldon Frank. Between 1957, when he published his first novel, *The Temple of Gold,* until 1966, when he penned his first solo screenplay, Goldman wrote five full-length works of fiction and two Broadway plays.

According to Stone, Goldman's novels are "blunt and direct, and he avoids symbolism and elaborate detail. His narrative voice is rarely intrusive, but he will occasionally step away from his omniscient stance and deliver a few words of his own. . . . He constructs scenes efficiently and with a deliberate punch line, as if determining the weight and flow of scenes from the very start of the writing process. He very rarely thinks in visual terms, preferring to work with plot and character action as a way of building his themes." Cook also observes that Goldman's adventure stories "are written rather casually, as though shot from the hip right onto the page." This is not to suggest, though, that Goldman's work lacks psychological depth. In a full-length study entitled *William Goldman,* Richard Andersen describes the author's main theme as an investigation of "the illusions men and women live by, which often make human existence more miserable than it need be." Andersen detects a tendency for Goldman's protagonists to seek escape from a society that encroaches on their desire for personal freedom. Ironically, he adds, "what they escape to is more often than not other illusions."

In *Season of Promise: Spring Fiction 1967,* Warren French contends that Goldman's fiction is "particularly timely, because [it deals] with conditions that are specifically characteristic of our affluent time. The depression and World War II caught Americans unprepared. To survive, they were forced to develop psychological expedients for dealing with these catastrophic events. By the time, however, that these expedients have hardened into conventions—as expedients have a way of doing—conditions have changed enough so that people are once again unprepared to deal with their immediate situation." Goldman's protagonists often survive the bewildering times by developing bonds of camaraderie—a "closeness that transcends individual backgrounds and differences," to quote Stone. Otherwise, in Andersen's view, what slight affirmation Goldman's heroes can achieve "seems to be the small but valuable awareness that life is simply better than death."

Goldman entered the screenwriting business quite by chance when actor Cliff Robertson saw the typescript for one of Goldman's novels, *No Way to Treat a Lady.* Unexpectedly, Robertson offered Goldman some screen work; a first project, an adaptation of the short story "Flowers for Algernon," was eventually turned over to someone else. Goldman did earn a screen credit, however, for his contribution to the British film "Masquerade," released in 1965. Armed with that experience, Goldman was able to land other film work relatively easily. In 1966 he wrote his first solo screenplay, "Harper," a detective story based on a Ross Macdonald novel. Paul Newman starred in the film, and Stone notes that the association between Newman and Goldman "signaled the start of an acting/writing collaboration that would perfectly mesh."

Newman also starred with Robert Redford in the film from Goldman's second solo screenplay, *Butch Cassidy and the Sundance Kid.* The movie follows the adventures of two affable bank robbers who must outrun a posse hired to track and kill them. Stone states that the film "was one of the best received in the 1960s. Goldman won his first Academy Award for the screenplay, which continues to be one of the most influential works in Hollywood, still defining a standard for entertainment movies." Stone adds: "It was a breakthrough film, not just for Goldman, but for screenwriters in general; Goldman received $400,000 for his script, the first time a screenwriter had ever received so high a payment." With the success of *Butch Cassidy and the Sundance Kid,* Goldman began to alternate between novels and screenplays; several of his subsequent films, including "The Hot Rock," "A Bridge Too Far," "The Great Waldo Pepper," and "All the President's Men," featured the popular Redford in leading roles. Goldman won his second Oscar for "All the President's Men," a script he based on the Watergate-era book by Bob Woodward and Carl Bernstein.

Stone writes: "Goldman has often suggested in his work that friendship is the only comfort in an absurd universe in which individual lives are ultimately meaningless, but for commercial reasons this darker slant to the material is usually missing from the final product on the screen. Two of Goldman's scripts do deal effectively with this darker theme, however." Stone is referring to "Marathon Man" and "Magic," two movies Goldman adapted from his own novels. In the novel and film *Marathon Man,* a meek graduate student becomes the target of a brutal team of ex-Nazi diamond smugglers simply because his murdered brother had been a spy. Eventually the student adopts the ruthless techniques of his tormentors in order to free himself from their grasp. Addressing his comments to the novel, *Best Sellers* contributor William R. Evans states: "Unlike many thrillers, *Marathon Man* has some serious implications. Upon finishing it, the reader finds that the issues of hatred, war, destruction, and revenge focus in the mind. Are these things naturally part of humankind? Are we condemned to go on making the same mistakes, year after year, decade after decade? If such a thing as a timely, relevant, thoughtful novel of suspense exists, this is it." *Magic* explores the psychological dangers of an uncontrollable alter ego through the person of a ventriloquist who is dominated by his puppet. *Best Sellers* reviewer Edward F. Warner finds the novel "a fascinating [work] about the dark world of a man's mind driven to its inevitable end." As films, both "Marathon Man" and "Magic" did well at the box office, and as books they signalled a new direction for Goldman's writing: the adventure-thriller with psychological or satirical undertones.

Goldman's more recent screenplays include "The Princess Bride," based on a fractured fairy tale he wrote in 1973. The film, like the book, is framed around an old adventure story by "S. Morgenstern" (actually a Goldman pseudonym), from which the "boring parts" have been extracted. What remains is a simple tale of swashbuckling rescue and true romance, peopled by evil princes, giants, and miracle workers. According to S. K. Oberbeck in *Newsweek,* Goldman has concocted "a 'classic' medieval melodrama that sounds like all the Saturday serials you ever saw feverishly reworked by the Marx brothers." Most reviewers have praised the film treatment for its balance of sincerity and tongue-in-cheek parody. *New York Times* contributor Janet Maslin writes: "The material might easily have lent itself to broad parody or become too cute for its own good. But Mr. Reiner [the director] presents it as a bedtime story, pure and simple. The film's style is gentle, even fragile, with none of the bold flourishes that might be expected but with none of the silliness either. . . . Mr. Reiner seems to understand exactly what Mr. Goldman loves about stories of this kind, and he conveys it with clarity and affection."

Many writers who have worked for Hollywood have subsequently written about life and business there. Goldman is no exception. His novel *Tinsel* and his nonfiction memoir *Adventures in the Screen Trade: A Personal View of Hollywood and Screenwriting* detail "how Hollywood [has] alchemied literary gold into commercial dross," to quote *Los Angeles Times Book Review* correspondent Nancy Yanes Hoffman. In *Film Comment,* John Sayles observes that *Adventures in the Screen Trade* is "split between descriptions of studio and star politics and discussions of writing technique. In this way it mirrors the life of the screenwriter. Ask any screenwriter why a certain moment exists in a movie he's worked on and you're as likely to hear an anecdote about the producer's wife or the cost of camel wranglers as you are to hear about plot, dialogue, or pacing. The tension between these two—between what you hope for when you start a screenplay and what you settle for when it smacks up against the reality of film production—runs up and down the spine of Goldman's book." Maslin explains in the *New York Times Book Review* that the work "is not the most complex or sophisticated analysis of movie-making," but that it "does take a nuts-and-bolts approach very like Hollywood's own. This is a savvy, gossipy book by someone with considerable insight into the tricks of the trade." Sayles concludes: "Like listening to a much-traveled sailor before your first time at sea, Goldman offers horror stories, tales of hardship, and plenty of warnings, but through it all he weighs anchor in the exhilaration and transcendent moments that get you hooked on the idea in the first place."

When he himself talks about screenwriting, Goldman does not tend to dwell upon the "exhilaration and transcendent moments." His approach to the work is both modest and pragmatic. "No one has ever heard me use the word 'good' about any of my screenplays," he said in *Esquire.* "I would never attribute that kind of quality—good, bad, or beautiful—to a screenplay. A screenplay is a piece of carpentry, and except in the case of Ingmar Bergman, it's not an art, it's a craft. And you want to be as good as you can at your craft, and you want to give them what they need within the limits of your talents—and the only reason I am 'hot' now has nothing to do with the quality of the films that I have been involved with. It has to do with two things: some of the films have been successful, but more important, *they have been made.*" Goldman has also expressed relief that screenwriting is not his sole professional and creative outlet—too many people, he says, have a hand in producing a finished movie script. "My feeling is that you must have something else, something you create that won't get altered for reasons that have nothing to do with quality," he told *Publishers Weekly.* "If what you want to do is to bring something into being, and you want to have control over the final product, you must have another outlet." That outlet for Goldman is fiction. Assessing that aspect of Goldman's career, Andersen concludes: "Goldman may be considered an accomplished and inventive storyteller, and, in thematic terms, a serious artist. Though his angle of vision has become increasingly more violent and absurd, he has not given way to despair or cynicism, but has managed to deal with his resignation about the human condition without losing his sense of humor or concern for humanity. . . . Goldman's works provide an unassailable argument against the novel-is-dead critics and effectively contribute to the life span of our literature's most popular and therefore most important genre."

MEDIA ADAPTATIONS: Soldier in the Rain was filmed by Allied Artists, 1963; *No Way To Treat a Lady* was filmed by Paramount, 1968; a musical play based on *No Way To Treat a Lady* was produced on Broadway at the Hudson Guild theatre, May 27, 1987.

AVOCATIONAL INTERESTS: Tennis, swimming, mysteries, basketball, and baseball.

BIOGRAPHICAL/CRITICAL SOURCES:

BOOKS

Andersen, Richard, *William Goldman,* Twayne, 1979.
Brady, John, *The Craft of the Screenwriter,* Touchstone, 1982.
Contemporary Literary Criticism, Gale, Volume 1, 1973, Volume 48, 1988.
Dictionary of Literary Biography, Volume 44: *American Screenwriters, Second Series,* Gale, 1986.
French, Warren, *Season of Promise: Spring Fiction 1967,* University of Missouri Press, 1968.
Goldman, William, *Adventures in the Screen Trade: A Personal View of Hollywood and Screenwriting,* Warner Books, 1983.
Kael, Pauline, *Reeling,* Little, Brown, 1972.

PERIODICALS

Atlantic Monthly, August, 1960.
Best Sellers, May 1, 1967, September 15, 1969, March 15, 1971, November 1, 1974, December, 1976.
Books and Bookmen, January, 1968.
Book World, April 18, 1971.
Chicago Sunday Tribune, October 13, 1957.
Chicago Tribune, November 13, 1978, March 13, 1987, October 9, 1987.
Chicago Tribune Books, February 15, 1987, February 28, 1988.
Chicago Tribune Book World, August 12, 1979, May 16, 1982, June 30, 1985.
Christian Science Monitor, April 27, 1967, October 9, 1969.
Commonweal, November 29, 1957.
Detroit News, May 20, 1984.
Esquire, October, 1981.
Film Comment, June, 1983.
Globe and Mail (Toronto), July 4, 1987.
Life, October 31, 1969.
Los Angeles Times, March 13, 1987, September 25, 1987.
Los Angeles Times Book Review, July 15, 1979, June 6, 1982, April 3, 1983, May 20, 1984, June 2, 1985, May 17, 1987.
New Leader, September 15, 1969.
Newsweek, September 17, 1973, August 13, 1979, October 5, 1987.
New Yorker, May 20, 1967.
New York Herald Tribune Book Review, November 3, 1957.
New York Times, November 17, 1957, August 31, 1969, September 19, 1969, November 8, 1978, November 12, 1978, July 24, 1979, April 12, 1982, March 17, 1983, February 5, 1987, March 13, 1987, June 12, 1987, September 25, 1987.
New York Times Book Review, November 17, 1957, July 17, 1960, July 26, 1964, April 19, 1967, April 14, 1968, September 28, 1969, January 31, 1971, December 23, 1973, October 27, 1974, September 12, 1976, August 26, 1979, September 16, 1979, April 25, 1982, March 20, 1983, April 15, 1984, May 19, 1985, February 15, 1987.
People, August 20, 1979, March 30, 1987, September 28, 1987.
Publishers Weekly, March 18, 1983.
Saturday Review, October 19, 1957, July 25, 1964, September 13, 1969.
Spectator, March 12, 1965, October 16, 1982.
Time, April 4, 1983, September 12, 1987.
Variety, August 13, 1969.
Washington Post, November 11, 1978, May 1, 1982, April 14, 1984, October 9, 1987.
Washington Post Book World, August 19, 1979, June 5, 1983, June 16, 1985, February 15, 1987.

—*Sketch by Anne Janette Johnson*

* * *

GOLDSTEIN, Abraham S(amuel) 1925-

PERSONAL: Born July 27, 1925, in New York, N.Y.; son of Isidore and Yetta (Crystal) Goldstein; married Ruth Tessler, August 31, 1947; children: William Ira, Marianne Susan. *Education:* City College (now of the City University of New York), B.B.A., 1946; Yale University, LL.B., 1949.

ADDRESSES: Home—175 Ford Rd., Woodbridge, Conn. 06525. *Office*—Law School, Yale University, 127 Wall St., New Haven, Conn. 06520.

CAREER: Admitted to District of Columbia Bar, 1949. Cook & Berger (law firm), Washington, D.C., associate, 1949; U.S. Court of Appeals, Washington, D.C., clerk to circuit judge, 1949-51; Donohue & Kaufmann (law firm), Washington, D.C., partner specializing in civil and criminal litigation, 1951-56; Yale University, New Haven, Conn., associate professor, 1956-61, professor of law, 1961-67, William Nelson Cromwell Professor of Law, 1967-75, Sterling Professor of Law, 1975—, dean of Law School, 1970-75. Visiting professor and fellow at universities and institutes in Europe, Japan, and Israel. Member of numerous commissions and committees on law and legal education; consultant to President's Commission on Law Enforcement and Administration of Criminal Justice, 1966-67, and to Procurador-General of Colombia, 1968. *Military service:* U.S. Army, 1943-46.

MEMBER: American Academy of Arts and Sciences, American Association of University Professors, Beta Gamma Sigma.

AWARDS, HONORS: M.A., Yale University, 1961, Cambridge University, 1964; Guggenheim fellow, 1964-65, 1975-76; LL.D., New York Law School, 1978, DePaul University, 1987.

WRITINGS:

The Insanity Defense, Yale University Press, 1967.
(Editor with Joseph Goldstein) *Crime, Law and Society* (readings), Free Press, 1971.
(With L. Orland) *Criminal Procedure,* Little, Brown, 1974.
The Passive Judiciary: Prosecutional Discretion and the Guilty Plea, Louisiana State University Press, 1981.

Contributor of articles to legal and other journals.

SIDELIGHTS: In his seminal study *The Insanity Defense,* Abraham S. Goldstein filters through the profuse amount of research on the legal premise that mentally ill people should not be held responsible for criminal actions and provides a concise analysis of the history and controversy surrounding this concept. Goldstein's "inspection of 'the gritty managerial detail' of the insanity defense is thorough and revealing, yet remarkably succinct and readable," notes a *Yale Review* contributor. "He probes through the mounds of accumulated rhetorical dust to find . . . the real insanity defense lying beneath a practically insignificant part of the criminal legal process, unworthy of the fuss that has been made over it." As Leon Radzinowicz describes in *Commentary,* "Goldstein cuts his way through any remaining illusions that there are clearly definable categories of the normal, the psychotic, the psychopathic, or the neurotic, which the psychiatrist can identify on purely medical grounds," thus making the practice of the insanity defense difficult to implement.

Goldstein observes that the great majority of criminal defendants plead guilty; those criminals who are clearly insane are generally found incompetent to stand trial, and are immediately placed in the appropriate mental or corrective institution. As a result, it is a few borderline cases which use the insanity defense, leading to questions about the appropriate detention or punishment for these criminals. As Herbert L. Packer points out in the *New York Review of Books,* "Goldstein recognizes that *the* central problem of the insanity defense arises when, as inevitably occurs, the defense does not win release [for the defendant] but rather confinement in a mental institution." While the author recognizes that the insanity defense is necessary for those individuals who are genuinely ill, "he ends his book with a cogent plea for retention . . . of the concepts of blame and responsibility in the criminal law," summarizes the *Yale Review* writer. The critic explains: "Men's conduct may well be determined by forces outside themselves, he seems to be saying, but those external forces include not only the threat of the law's sanctions, but also the fruit of its teachings in the form of the quasi-instructional notions of responsibility." *The Insanity Defense* "is plainly the definitive book on its subject," states Packer. "It will be read by serious lawyers but not by feckless behaviorists or their camp followers."

While Goldstein's treatise offers a complete portrait of the insanity defense, critics also praise it for doing so in an engaging fashion. "The attractiveness of this book lies in the way it is presented and written," notes Radzinowicz. "It deals with a somber subject, yet it is a pleasure to read. Casebooks, digests, technical dissertations, are inexorably killing the art of writing; it is good to know that Professor Goldstein has escaped such influences," the critic continues. "*The Insanity Defense,* then, fulfills a double function. It can be understood and appreciated by any intelligent reader. Yet it should also be recommended to advanced students, both in law and psychiatry." The *Yale Review* critic similarly concludes that "Goldstein's book is the first and probably the last treatise on the insanity defense. He both blankets the field and reveals how small a field it is. But *The Insanity Defense* is more than the definitive work on the insanity defense," the critic elaborates. "It is also a deftly and sparely painted portrait of the modern criminal law, its procedures, problems, doctrines, and rationalizations. In both respects it should enlighten the sick and the bad, the well and the good, alike."

BIOGRAPHICAL/CRITICAL SOURCES:

PERIODICALS

Commentary, May, 1969.
National Review, March 12, 1968.
New York Review of Books, October 23, 1969.
Yale Review, spring, 1968.

* * *

GOMERY, Douglas 1945-

PERSONAL: Born April 5, 1945, in New York, N.Y.; son of John E., Jr. (self-employed) and Julia (Halsted) Gomery; married Marilyn L. Moon (an economist and public policy analyst), January 13, 1973. *Education:* Lehigh University, B.S. (cum laude), 1967; University of Wisconsin—Madison, M.A., 1970, Ph.D., 1975.

ADDRESSES: Home—4817 Drummond Ave., Chevy Chase, Md. 20815. *Office*—Department of Communication Arts and Theatre, University of Maryland, 0208 Tawes Hall, College Park, Md. 20742.

CAREER: University of Wisconsin—Milwaukee, instructor, 1974-75, assistant professor, 1975-80, associate professor of mass communication, 1980-81; University of Maryland, College Park, associate professor, 1981-86, professor of broadcasting and film, 1987—. Visiting professor at University of Wisconsin—Madison, 1977, Northwestern University, 1981, and University of Iowa, 1982. Producer of "Focus on Film," on WUWM-FM radio, 1975, 1979. Member of National Gallery of Art Film Advisory Board, 1987—; member of Society for Cinema Studies Task Force on Moving Image Archives Policy, 1986—. Consultant to numerous organizations, including Voice of America, British Broadcasting Corporation (BBC), Paramount Pictures, Federal Communications Commission, Smithsonian Institution, Bozell & Jacobs Advertising Agency, Marcus Theatres, and State of Wisconsin Department of Revenue.

MEMBER: American Film Institute (member of board of trustees, 1986—; chair of education committee, 1986—), Organization of American Historians, Theatre Historical Society (member of board of directors, 1987-88), Society for Education in Film and Television, Association for Cultural Economics, University Film and Video Association, Speech Communication Association, Broadcast Education Association, Society for Cinema Studies, Domitar, Phi Beta Kappa, Beta Gamma Sigma, Phi Kappa Phi.

AWARDS, HONORS: Fellowship, Center for Twentieth Century Studies, University of Wisconsin—Milwaukee, 1976; Bernhart C. Korn grant, Milwaukee County Historical Society, 1980-81; fellow, Center for Arts and Humanities, University of Maryland, 1988.

WRITINGS:

High Sierra: Screenplay and Analysis, University of Wisconsin Press, 1979.
(With Robert C. Allen) *Film History: Theory and Practice,* Addison-Wesley, 1985.
The Golden Age of the Hollywood Studio System, 1925-1950, St. Martin's, 1986.
(Editor) *The Papers of Will H. Hays,* University Publications of America, 1987.
(Editor with Phillip Cook and Lawrence W. Lichty) *The Wilson Quarterly Media Reader,* Woodrow Wilson Center Press (Washington, D.C.), 1988.

CONTRIBUTOR

Benefit-Cost Analysis of Federal Programs, Joint Economic Committee, U.S. Congress, 1972.
Todd McCarthy and Charles Flynn, editors, *King of the B's: Working within the Hollywood System,* Dutton, 1975.
Film Studies Annual, Purdue University Press, 1976.
Tino Balio, editor, *The American Film Industry: An Historical Anthology of Readings,* University of Wisconsin Press, 1976, revised edition, 1989.
The Film Annual, Volume 2, Redgrave, 1978.
Gerald Peary and Roger Shatzhin, editors, *The Modern American Novel and the Movies,* Ungar, 1979.

John A. Garraty, editor, *Dictionary of American Biography,* Scribner, 1980.

Stephen Heath, editor, *The Cinematic Apparatus: Technology as Historical and Ideological Form,* St. Martin's, 1980.

Evan William Cameron, editor, *Sound and the Cinema,* Redgrave, 1980.

James H. Soltow, editor, *Essays in Economic and Business History,* Graduate School of Business Administration, Michigan State University, 1981.

Gorham A. Kindem, editor, *American Film Industry: A Case Studies Approach,* Southern Illinois University Press, 1982.

Gerald Mast, editor, *The Movies in Our Midst,* University of Chicago Press, 1982.

Sari Thomas, editor, *Film/Culture: Explorations of Cinema and Its Social Context,* Scarecrow, 1982.

Richard Dyer MacCann and Jack C. Ellis, editors, *Cinema Examined,* Dutton, 1982.

Adriano Apra, editor, *Hollywood: Lo Studio System,* Marsilo (Rome), 1982.

E. Ann Kaplan, editor, *Perspectives on Television,* University Publications of America, 1983.

Peter Rollins, editor, *Hollywood as Historian: American Film in a Cultural Context,* University Press of Kentucky, 1983.

John E. O'Connor, editor, *American History/American Television,* Ungar, 1983.

Lino Micciche, Vito Zagarrio, and Steven J. Ricci, editors, *Hollywood Verso La Televisione,* Marsilio, 1983.

Thomas Elsaessar, editor, *Space/Frame/Narrative,* University of East Anglia, 1983.

Christopher Lyon, editor, *Films: An International Dictionary,* Macmillan, 1984.

Lyon, editor, *Directors/Filmmakers: An International Dictionary,* Macmillan, 1984.

John Belton and Elisabeth Weis, editors, *Film Sound: Theory and Practice,* Columbia University Press, 1985.

William S. Hendon, Nancy K. Grant, and Douglas V. Shaw, editors, *The Economics of Cultural Industries,* Association for Cultural Economics, 1985.

Bill Nichols, editor, *Movies and Methods,* Volume 2, University of California Press, 1985.

Colin MacCabe, editor, *High Theory/Low Culture: Analysing Popular Film and Television,* Manchester University Press, 1986.

Patricia Erens, editor, *College Course Files,* University Film and Video Association (Chicago), 1986.

Lyon, editor, *Film Actors and Actresses: An International Dictionary,* St. James Press, 1986.

Horace Newcomb, editor, *Television: The Critical View,* Oxford University Press, 1987.

Paul Kerr, editor, *The Hollywood Film Industry,* Routledge & Kegan Paul, 1987.

James Vinson, editor, *Film Writers and Production Artists: An International Dictionary,* St. James Press, 1987.

Michael Emery and Ted Curtis Smythe, editors, *Readings in Mass Communication,* 6th edition, W. C. Brown, 1988.

Gary Crowdus, editor, *The Political Companion to Film,* Pantheon, 1988.

Peter Lehman, editor, *Close Viewings: Understanding Films,* Florida State University Press, 1988.

Lyon, editor, *Film Writers and Production Artists: An International Dictionary,* St. James Press, 1988.

Richard Butsch, editor, *For Fun and Profit: The Historical Transformation of Leisure into Consumption,* University of North Carolina Press, 1988.

Erik S. Lunde and Douglas A. Noverr, editors, *Film History: Selected Course Outlines and Reading Lists,* Markus Wiener, 1988.

OTHER

Contributing editor, *Purdue Film Studies Annual,* 1977-80, and "Communication Booknotes," George Washington University, 1979—; member of advisory board, "Films and Filmmakers" reference series, St. James Press; member of editorial board, *Mass Communications Yearbook,* Sage Publications, 1987, and "Film and Television" series, Wayne State University Press, 1988—. Contributor of numerous articles and reviews to periodicals, including *Wilson Quarterly, Marquee, Film Reader, Screen, Wide Angle, Velvet Light Trap,* and *Mediapourvoirs.* Contributing editor, *Film Studies Annual,* 1977-80; guest editor, *Cinema Journal,* 1979, *Milwaukee History,* 1979, *Marquee,* 1984, *Journal of Film and Video,* 1985, and *Wilson Quarterly,* 1986; book review editor, *Cinema Journal,* 1980-82; member of editorial board, *IRIS* (Paris), 1982—; associate editor, *Journal of Film and Video,* 1983—, *Cinema Journal,* 1983—, and *Marquee,* 1986—; corresponding editor, *Screen* (London), 1985—.

WORK IN PROGRESS: Movie History: A Survey, for Wadsworth Publishing; *Shared Pleasures: A History of Motion Picture Presentation,* for University of Wisconsin Press.

SIDELIGHTS: Douglas Gomery told *CA:* "I came to film studies by a somewhat unique route. My B.S. and M.A. are in economics. But when I went to the University of Wisconsin—Madison to study economics (and provide a career alternative to being a soldier in Vietnam), I became heavily involved in the movie scene in Madison. [I became involved in] committees that helped select films, writings for the student newspaper, and some activity with the creation and publication of the magazine the *Velvet Light Trap.* Since the university had just acquired the corporate papers of the United Artists Corporation, this gave me a chance to work for a Ph.D. in communications and use my knowledge in economics. I made the switch in 1972.

"My interest in writing about the motion picture industry comes from a desire to fill an obvious gap in the field. The motion picture industry has always been that—an industry made up of profit-seeking corporations. But scholars, by and large, look beyond that goal and concentrate only on the films themselves, directors, or stars. Interesting, but hardly the whole story. Happily, others have joined in the effort to investigate the history of the American film industry. I believe that what we need now are quality monographs, and I have concentrated on this form."

BIOGRAPHICAL/CRITICAL SOURCES:

BOOKS

Hanson, Patricia King, Philip L. Hanson, and Anthony Slide, *Dramatic Arts Sourcebook,* Greenwood Press, 1988.

PERIODICALS

Washington Post, December 16, 1987, December 21, 1988.

* * *

GOOCH, Bob
See GOOCH, Robert M(iletus)

GOOCH, Robert M(iletus) 1919-
(Bob Gooch)

PERSONAL: Born November 20, 1919, in Troy, Va.; son of Octavious Price (a farmer) and Lola (Williams) Gooch; married Virginia Winn (a teacher), October 24, 1943; children: Pamela Gooch Hallissy, Patricia Ann Gooch. *Education:* University of Virginia, B.A., 1943. *Politics:* Independent. *Religion:* Southern Baptist.

ADDRESSES: Home and office—P.O. Box 265, Troy, Va. 22974.

CAREER: Gooch & Winn, Inc. (insurance company), Charlottesville, Va., president and insurance agent, 1947-73; writer, 1973—. Vice-president of Fluvanna County Development Corp. *Military service:* U.S. Marine Corps Reserve, 1947-65; became lieutenant colonel.

MEMBER: Outdoor Writers Association of America, Mason-Dixon Outdoor Writers Association (past president), Virginia Outdoor Writers Association (past president), Ruritan Club (president).

AWARDS, HONORS: Awards from Mason-Dixon Outdoor Writers Association, 1974, for "Stripers the Santee-Cooper Way" in *Outdoors,* July, 1974, and 1976, for "Wildlife Refuge Crisis" in *Virginia Wildlife,* May, 1976; award from Safari Club, 1975, for "Turkey Dogs and Fall Hunting: A Family Tradition" in *Field and Stream,* September, 1975; Ducks Unlimited Award, 1988, for "Steel Shot Works for Me."

WRITINGS:

UNDER NAME BOB GOOCH

The Weedy World of the Pickerels, A. S. Barnes, 1970.
Squirrels and Squirrel Hunting, Tidewater, 1972.
Bass Fishing, Tidewater, 1975.
In Search of the Wild Turkey, Greatlakes Living Press, 1978.
Coveys and Singles, A. S. Barnes, 1980.
Land You Can Hunt, A. S. Barnes, 1980.
Spinning for Trout, Scribner, 1981.
Virginia Hunting Guide, University Press of Virginia, 1985.
Virginia Fishing Guide, University Press of Virginia, 1988.
The Bird Hunter's Book, Atlantic Publishing, 1988.
Hunting Boar, Hogs, and Javelina, Atlantic Publishing, 1989.

Author of "Virginia Afield," syndicated column appearing in about thirty newspapers, 1962—; also author of column "Virginia Report and West Virginia Report" in *Outdoor Life,* 1970—. Outdoor columnist for United Press International. Contributor of more than four thousand articles to major outdoor magazines.

WORK IN PROGRESS: Bass Fishing Simplified.

SIDELIGHTS: Robert M. Gooch writes *CA:* "My current production schedule is a weekly newspaper column, a weekly magazine article, a monthly column, an article for *Turkey Call* twice a year, and a book each two years. I shoot all my own photographs for illustrations and travel regularly all over the North American continent. I am primarily a rod and gun writer, but touch on outdoors generally."

* * *

GOODRICK, Edward W(illiam) 1913-

PERSONAL: Born March 11, 1913, in Appleton, Wis.; son of John B. (a bookkeeper) and Mary Althea (Wood) Goodrick; married Gwendolyn Helen Davidson, 1940 (died, 1984); children: Janet M., John B., Cynthia L., Lynda D., James W. *Education:* Biola College, Th.B., 1940; Westmont College, B.A., 1943; University of Montana, Dillon, M.S., 1956; further graduate studies at Hebrew Union College, Jerusalem, 1964, American Institute of Holy Land Studies, Jerusalem, 1964, and University of Manchester, 1965.

ADDRESSES: Home—16321 Northeast Oregon St., Portland, Ore. 97230.

CAREER: Ordained Baptist minister, 1944; pastor of community church in Mossyrock, Wash., 1944-50, and of Baptist churches in Sandy, Ore., 1950, and Dillon, Mont., 1950-56; Multnomah School of the Bible, Portland, Ore., teacher of Greek and the Bible, 1956-83. *Military service:* U.S. Navy, 1932-36; became fireman first class.

MEMBER: Evangelical Theological Society (regional chairman, 1982-83), American Schools of Oriental Research.

AWARDS, HONORS: D.D. from Western Conservative Baptist Theological Seminary, 1980.

WRITINGS:

Do It Yourself Hebrew and Greek, Zondervan, 1976.
NIV Complete Concordance, Zondervan, 1981.
NIV Handyman's Concordance, Zondervan, 1982.
(Contributor) *The Thompson Chain-Reference Bible: New International Version,* Kirkbride-Zondervan, 1983.
(Contributor) *The Oxford NIV Scofield Study Bible: New International Version,* Oxford University Press, 1984.
(Contributor) *The NIV Study Bible,* Zondervan, 1985.
(Contributor) *The Ryrie Study Bible: New International Version,* Moody, 1986.
Is My Bible the Inspired Word of God?, Multnomah, 1988.
Your Bible: From Beginning to Now, Multnomah, 1990.
NIV Exhaustive Concordance, Zondervan, 1990.

Contributor to periodicals, including *Evangelical Theological Quarterly, Moody Monthly,* and *Christian Life.*

WORK IN PROGRESS: NIV Englishman's Greek Concordance, NIV Interlinear Greek New Testament, and *NIV Analytical Concordance,* all for Zondervan.

SIDELIGHTS: Edward W. Goodrick told *CA:* "The NIV is the New International Version of the Bible, which was published by Zondervan in 1978 and is one of the better, if not the best, of modern translations. It was mentioned in *Time* magazine as the translation most likely to be the replacement for the King James Version. As with the concordances for the King James Version, different kinds are needed for different users of the NIV. There is a 'compact' one printed in the back of the Bible, a larger 'complete' one for more thorough study, and an 'exhaustive' one that identifies the Greek or Hebrew word from which each English word has been translated."

* * *

GOODWIN, Hal
See GOODWIN, Harold L(eland)

* * *

GOODWIN, Harold L(eland) 1914-
(Hal Goodwin; pseudonyms: Hal Gordon, Blake Savage; John Blaine, a joint pseudonym)

PERSONAL: Born November 20, 1914, in Ellenburg, N.Y.; son of Frank Elmer (a salesman) and Imogene (Van Arman) Goodwin; married Elizabeth Swensk, April 12, 1947; children: Alan, Christopher, Derek. *Education:* Attended Elliot Radio School, 1934-35.

ADDRESSES: Home and office—6212 Verne St., Bethesda, Md. 20817.

CAREER: WNBC-Radio, New Britain, Conn., announcer, writer, and program director, 1934-37; WHAI-Radio, Greenfield, Mass., announcer, continuity director, writer, and commentator, 1937-40; Blackett-Sample-Hummert (advertising agency), New York, N.Y., copywriter, 1940; TransRadio News Service, New York and Washington, reporter and writer, 1941-53; free-lance writer, 1945—; U.S. Foreign Service, Philippines, member of staff, 1947-50; Federal Civil Defense Administration, Washington, D.C., director of atomic test operations, 1951-58; U.S. Information Agency, Washington, D.C., science advisor, 1958-61; National Aeronautics and Space Administration, Washington, D.C., member of staff, 1961-67; National Science Foundation, Washington, D.C., planning officer and deputy director of National Sea Grant Program, 1967-70; U.S. Department of Commerce, National Oceanic and Atmospheric Administration, Washington, D.C., deputy director of National Sea Grant Program, 1970-74; self-employed with wife, Elizabeth S. Goodwin, in marine services and education, Bethesda, Md., 1974—. Lecturer at American University Business Council for International Understanding (BCIU), Washington, D.C. *Military service:* U.S. Marine Corps, 1942-45; became first lieutenant; received Air Medal.

MEMBER: World Aquaculture Society (vice-president, 1977; honorary life member), Antarctican Society, American Science Film Association (editor; board member), Marine Technology Society, National Marine Education Association (honorary life member), American Littoral Society (board member), Professional Association of Diving Instructors (PADI; member of international board), National Association of Underwater Instructors (NAUI), Boston Sea Rovers (associate), Washington Children's Book Guild.

AWARDS, HONORS: Flemming Award, U.S. Junior Chamber of Commerce, 1953, for outstanding young man in federal service; Federal Civil Defense Administration Meritorious Service Award, 1958; U.S. Information Agency Meritorious Service Award, 1959; U.S. Department of Commerce Silver Medal, 1971; James Dugan Award, American Littoral Society, 1973, for contributions to aquatic science; National Sea Grant Award, 1983.

WRITINGS:

(Under name Hal Goodwin) *A Microphone for David,* William Penn Publishing Corp., 1939.
(Under name Hal Goodwin) *Aerial Warfare: The Story of the Aeroplane as a Weapon,* Garden City, 1943.
(Under name Hal Goodwin) *The Feathered Cape,* Westminster, 1947.
(Under name Hal Goodwin) *The Real Book about Stars,* Garden City, 1951.
(Under pseudonym Blake Savage) *Rip Foster Rides the Gray Planet,* Whitman, 1952, published as *Adventure in Outer Space,* 1952, published as *Assignment in Space,* 1958.
(Under name Hal Goodwin) *The Real Book about Space Travel,* Garden City, 1952.
The Science Book of Space Travel, F. Watts, 1954.
Space: Frontier Unlimited, Van Nostrand, 1962.
All about Rockets and Space Flight, Random House, 1964.
The Images of Space, Holt, 1965.
(With Claiborne Pell) *Challenge of the Seven Seas,* Morrow, 1966.
(Under pseudonym Hal Gordon) *Divers Down,* Whitman, 1971.
(With Joe A. Hanson) *The Aquaculture of Freshwater Prawns (Macrobrachium Species),* Oceanic Institute (Wainalo, Hawaii), 1975.
(Editor with Hanson) *Shrimp and Prawn Farming in the Western Hemisphere: State-of-the-Art Reviews and Status Assessments,* Dowden, Hutchinson & Ross, 1977.
(Editor and annotator) *Americans and the World of Water,* Delaware University Sea Grant Press, 1978.
(Under name Hal Goodwin) *Seafaring with Hal Goodwin,* Review Press, 1985.

"RICK BRANT ELECTRONIC ADVENTURE" SERIES; UNDER PSEUDONYM JOHN BLAINE

(With Peter Harkins) *The Rocket's Shadow,* Grosset & Dunlap, 1947.
(With Harkins) *The Lost City,* Grosset & Dunlap, 1947.
(With Harkins) *Sea Gold,* Grosset & Dunlap, 1947.
100 Fathoms Under, Grosset & Dunlap, 1947.
The Whispering Box Mystery, Grosset & Dunlap, 1948.
The Phantom Shark, Grosset & Dunlap, 1949.
Smuggler's Reef, Grosset & Dunlap, 1950.
The Caves of Fear, Grosset & Dunlap, 1951.
Stairway to Danger, Grosset & Dunlap, 1952.
The Golden Skull, Grosset & Dunlap, 1954.
The Wailing Octopus, Grosset & Dunlap, 1956.
The Electronic Mind Reader, Grosset & Dunlap, 1957.
The Scarlet Lake Mystery, Grosset & Dunlap, 1958.
The Pirates of Shan, Grosset & Dunlap, 1959.
The Blue Ghost Mystery, Grosset & Dunlap, 1960.
The Egyptian Cat Mystery, Grosset & Dunlap, 1961.
The Flaming Mountain, Grosset & Dunlap, 1962.
The Flying Stingaree, Grosset & Dunlap, 1963.
The Ruby Ray Mystery, Grosset & Dunlap, 1964.
The Veiled Raiders, Grosset & Dunlap, 1965.
Rocket Jumper, Grosset & Dunlap, 1966.
The Deadly Dutchman, Grosset & Dunlap, 1967.
Danger Below!, Grosset & Dunlap, 1968.

OTHER

(Under pseudonym John Blaine) *Rick Brant's Science Projects* (nonfiction), Grosset & Dunlap, 1960.

Contributor to *World Book Encyclopedia* and *Book of Knowledge.* Contributor to periodicals and journals, including *Liberty, Post, New York Times Magazine, Blue Book,* and *Journal of Marine Education.*

WORK IN PROGRESS: The Young Captains, stories of the very young men who captained American ships between 1790-1890; technical papers on problems in the environment and aquaculture; *The Magic Talisman,* the "lost" twenty-fourth volume of the "Rick Brant" series, "because of continuing requests by (now adult) readers of the series."

SIDELIGHTS: Harold L. Goodwin, writing under the pseudonym John Blaine, produced one "of the best series ever," according to a *Mystery and Adventure Series Review* contributor. His "Rick Brant Electronic Adventures" and Sam Epstein's "Ken Holt Mysteries" (written under the pseudonym Bruce Campbell) are fondly remembered by readers as some of the most exciting juvenile fiction ever produced. "These two series, along with Tom Quest, had an appeal well beyond the manufactured lure of the professional merchandisers," the contributor continues. "Excellent writing, thoughtful attention to characterization, imaginative plots and a very evident familiarity with most of the regions and places they wrote about, injected a sense of excitement into these books."

Rick's adventures anticipated many scientific advances. An experiment in "moon-bounce" communications chronicled in *The Lost City* preceded Navy experiments by some ten years, and the Submobile of *100 Fathoms Under* predated the free submersible *Alvin* which discovered the wreck of the *Titanic* in 1985 by almost thirty years. Other books envisioned mobile robots, proton magnetometers, and surgical lasers. Before the last series volume was published in 1968, Rick, his ex-Marine pal Scotty, and the scientists of the Spindrift Foundation had traveled the world over with their machines in pursuit of knowledge.

"I regret the passing of Rick," Goodwin writes in the *Mystery and Adventure Series Review.* "What Ken, Rick, Tom Quest, and some of the series did was to stimulate both curiosity and imagination. They were the stuff of constructive fantasy, and I'm committed to the view that such fantasy in the young is the wellspring of adult creativity. . . . My reader mail from kids who've grown up and finished college, and who have taken time to write, includes several budding scientists and at least five budding authors. I'm proudest of letters, some dozens of them, from such readers who have reread the series and who tell me that time hasn't faded their pleasure."

Recently Harold L. Goodwin told *CA:* "I've been fortunate in reaching that stage in a writer's life when writing becomes not only a vocation but a pleasurable hobby because I can choose my subject, take as much time as needed to do research or experience some aspects of it, and write and rewrite until completely pleased with the product.

"During the past three years I've focused on sea history, and especially the vital roles of young men and women in the great days of American sail. By young, I mean under age twenty. Their stories are marvelous adventure, and there were dozens who captained their own ships by the age of eighteen, trading around the world. There were young women, too, married to their captains at the age of sixteen, who learned to navigate and used their skills in grave emergencies. Some of these yarns became columns in the *Journal of Marine Education* and were later printed in *Seafaring.* Others are coming together in a book manuscript. The purpose is not only to share exciting sea yarns, but to show both youth and adults that young people, given responsibility, can rise to great heights."

Harold L. Goodwin's books have been translated into many different languages, including several of the major dialects of India and South Asia. Individual volumes of the "Rick Brant Electronic Adventures" have appeared in French, Dutch, Norwegian, Finnish, and Japanese.

AVOCATIONAL INTERESTS: Boating, archery, scuba diving.

BIOGRAPHICAL/CRITICAL SOURCES:

PERIODICALS

Mystery and Adventures Series Review, number 19, 1987.
Times Literary Supplement, May 19, 1966.

* * *

GOODWIN, R(ichard) M(urphey) 1913-

PERSONAL: Born February 24, 1913, in New Castle, Ind.; son of William Murphey (a farmer) and Mary (Florea) Goodwin; married Jacqueline Wynmalen, June 24, 1937. *Education:* Harvard University, B.A. (summa cum laude), 1934, Ph.D., 1941; Oxford University, B.A., 1936, B.Litt., 1937. *Politics:* "Formerly Communist, now Socialist (member, British Labour Party)." *Religion:* None.

ADDRESSES: Home—Dorvis's Ashdon, Essex, England. *Office*—Instituto di Economia, Piazza S. Francesco, 53100 Siena, Italy.

CAREER: Harvard University, Cambridge, Mass., instructor, 1942-45, assistant professor of economics, 1945-50; Cambridge University, Cambridge, England, lecturer and fellow, 1952-67, reader in economics, 1967-79; University of Siena, Siena, Italy, professor of economics, 1979—. Painter.

MEMBER: Econometric Society (fellow), Royal Economic Society.

AWARDS, HONORS: Rhodes scholar.

WRITINGS:

Elementary Economics from the Higher Standpoint, Cambridge University Press, 1970.
Essays in Economic Dynamics, Macmillan, 1982.
Essays in Linear Economic Structures, Macmillan, 1983.
(Editor with M. Krueger and A. Vercelli) *Nonlinear Models of Fluctuating Growth,* Springer Verlag, 1984.
(Editor with L.F. Punzo) *The Dynamics of a Capitalist Economy,* Polity Press, 1987.
Essays in Nonlinear Economic Dynamics, Peter Lang Verlag, 1988.

SIDELIGHTS: R.M. Goodwin spends approximately half his time painting, pointing out that "this is not an avocation but of equal importance in my life to the writing and teaching of economics."

BIOGRAPHICAL/CRITICAL SOURCES:

BOOKS

Velupillai, K., editor, *Essays in Honour of R.M. Goodwin,* Macmillan, 1989.

* * *

GORDON, Hal
See GOODWIN, Harold L(eland)

* * *

GORDON, Lois G. 1938-

PERSONAL: Born November 13, 1938, in Englewood, N.J.; daughter of Irving David and Betty (Davis) Goldfein; married Alan Lee Gordon (a psychiatrist), November 13, 1961; children: Robert Michael. *Education:* University of Michigan, B.A. (with honors), 1960; University of Wisconsin, M.A., 1962, Ph.D., 1966. *Religion:* Jewish.

ADDRESSES: Home—300 Central Park W., New York, N.Y. 10024. *Office*—Department of English, Fairleigh Dickinson University, Teaneck, N.J. 07666.

CAREER: City College of the City University of New York, New York, N.Y., lecturer in English, 1964-66; University of Missouri at Kansas City, assistant professor of English, 1966-68; Fairleigh Dickinson University, Teaneck, N.J., assistant professor, 1968-71, associate professor, 1971-75, professor of English, 1975—, chairman of department of English and comparative literature, 1982—.

MEMBER: International League for Human Rights, Modern Language Association of America, Academy of American Poets, PEN.

WRITINGS:

Stratagems to Uncover Nakedness: The Dreams of Harold Pinter, University of Missouri Press, 1969.
Donald Barthelme, Twayne, 1981.
Robert Coover: The Universal Fictionmaking Process, Southern Illinois University Press, 1983.
American Chronicle: Six Decades in American Life, 1920-1980, Atheneum, 1987.
American Chronicle: Seven Decades in American Life, 1920-1990, Crown, 1990.
Harold Pinter Casebook, Garland Publishing, 1990.

Also author and narrator of educational tapes on modern drama for Everett Edwards. Contributor to literature journals. Assistant editor, *Literature and Psychology,* 1968-70.

WORK IN PROGRESS: Samuel Beckett; The New Mimesis.

AVOCATIONAL INTERESTS: Piano.

* * *

GOULD, Lois (Lois Benjamin)

PERSONAL: Daughter of E. J. Regensburg (a cigar company executive) and Jo Copeland (a fashion designer); married first husband Philip Benjamin (a reporter and novelist), 1959 (deceased); married second husband Robert E. Gould (a psychiatrist and psychoanalyst), September 14, 1967; children: (first marriage) Anthony, Roger. *Education:* Wellesley College, B.A.

ADDRESSES: Home—144 East End Ave., New York, N.Y. 10028. *Agent*—Brandt and Brandt Literary Agency, 1501 Broadway, New York, N.Y. 10036.

CAREER: Journalist and writer. *New York Times,* New York, N.Y., columnist, 1977. Former reporter, *Long Island Star Journal;* former executive editor and columnist, *Ladies Home Journal;* columnist and senior editor, *McCall's;* founder and editor, *Insider's Newsletter* (*Look* Magazine). Lecturer and teacher at Wesleyan University, Northwestern University, and New York University. Board member, Wesleyan Writers Conference.

WRITINGS:

(Under name Lois Benjamin; with Waldo L. Fielding) *Sensible Childbirth: The Case Against Natural Childbirth* (nonfiction), Viking, 1962.
(Under name Lois Benjamin) *So You Want To Be a Working Mother!* (nonfiction), McGraw, 1966.
Such Good Friends (novel), Random House, 1970, reissued, Farrar, Straus, 1988.
Necessary Objects (novel), Random House, 1972.
Final Analysis (novel), Random House, 1974.
A Sea-Change (novel), Simon & Schuster, 1976.
Not Responsible for Personal Articles (essays), Random House, 1978.
X: A Fabulous Child's Story (fiction), illustrated by Jacqueline Chwast, Daughters Publishing, 1978.
La Presidenta (novel), The Linden Press/Simon & Schuster, 1981.
Subject to Change (novel), Farrar, Straus, 1988.

Author of column "Hers" for the *New York Times;* contributor of articles to *New York, Newsday, Ms., New York Times* magazine, and the North American Newspaper Alliance.

SIDELIGHTS: Despite Lois Gould's reputation for giving a "sharply etched presentation of a female viewpoint" in her writing, as *Publishers Weekly* contributor John F. Baker calls it, Gould told *CA:* "My fiction works represent neither a popularization of feminism nor a politicization of literature, nor are they intended to achieve either of these dubious purposes. I have been reviewed by feminist critics who say my work is anti-feminist and by anti-feminist critics who say the reverse." She is interested in gender roles in society and how these roles are formed, but not to the exclusion of exploring other ideas about which to write. In addition to her works about gender role and society with which she is often associated, she has written everything from nonfiction to adult fairy tales.

Her book *X: A Fabulous Child's Story* is an example of the author's handling of the gender role issue in allegorical form. The plot involves a government experiment in which a child named X is raised to be androgynous, and relates how the frustration of not being able to identify X's sex reveals people's gender prejudices. Although the illustrations by Jacqueline Chwast suggest the book is for children, a *New York Times Book Review* critic says "the message of Lois Gould's narrative is very grown-up." Some adult readers, remarks Susan Jacoby in the *Washington Post,* "are disturbed by the serious questions about gender identity that are woven throughout 'X.' The book has already been criticized on grounds that it evokes fantasies of 'genital mutilation,' that it is authoritarian because the scientists are government scientists, and that it is too upper-middle-class" because so many toys are bought for X. *Village Voice* contributor Eliot Fremont-Smith realizes, however, that "the book is intended to be sunny and cheerful. . . . It's less against sexist toys and gender roles than for all toys and roles; kids' psyches shouldn't be stupidly restricted by these things."

On a more serious note, Gould's *A Sea-Change* is also an allegorical story, but one meant exclusively for adults. Like her earlier books *Such Good Friends* and *Final Analysis, A Sea-Change* deals with a relationship between two adults, but uses more direct imagery in describing the sexual identity changes that the woman character, Jessie Waterman, goes through. In this novel, explains *Chicago Tribune Book World* critic Doris Grumbach, the woman undergoes "a curious and fascinating [female to male] metamorphosis effected not only from within, but also from the external, masculine cultural pressures upon her." Grumbach concludes that *A Sea-Change* is "an entirely meaningful study, in contemporary terms, of the problem of being a woman." However, to critics like Anne Tyler, who discusses the book in the *New York Times Book Review,* the novel's maze of symbols makes it difficult to understand. Tyler also objects to what she feels is Gould's generalization that "men are brutal, and women love it." In *Harper's,* reviewer Ella Leffland says that the book's central idea is that of "the concept of exploitee-turning-exploiter"; beyond this point she feels that "clarity ends." But the idea, Leffland adds, "is a good one, psychologically valid."

Gould does not limit herself to fictional works about gender roles in society, though. She has written nonfiction books about subjects such as childbirth and the working woman, as well as fiction dealing with politics and other social issues. *La Presidenta,* for example, is "an evocative study of sex and politics based loosely on the Perons of Argentina," summarizes Baker in his *Publishers Weekly* interview with Gould. The novel is also interested in the role of the media in society. Rosa, whose life in the book reflects that of Eva Peron, begins her career as an actress and radio personality before becoming a political figure, her elevation in status being aided by "key political developments touched off by hints in newspaper gossip columns," says Baker. "Gould sees the media's role in America today as similar." She tells Baker: "It's hardly just a Latin thing. We now have a movie star as a President."

Although *Washington Post Book World* contributor Anita Desai feels that the author's language "wears cinematic make-up too heavy for daylight and employs smooth, silken strings of cliches," *Chicago Tribune Book Review* contributor Diane M. Ross believes the strength of *La Presidenta* lies in its ability to raise itself above the "merely . . . historical novel, or worse, a thinly disguised celebrity life." Ross maintains that Gould "holds the uncertain facts of history and the trivial rumors of celebrity at arm's length, uncovering for study the skeleton of fear and aspiration beneath the artificial flesh of legend."

In 1988, seven years after *La Presidenta,* Gould published *Subject to Change,* an adult fairy tale which marked an even greater departure from the author's early novels. MacDonald Harris describes it in the *New York Times Book Review* as a "fantasy, but hard-minded, ironic and concise." It is a tale about a "30-year old child-king . . . [and a] frigid young queen," says *Washington Post Book World* reviewer Octavia E. Butler. They live in an imaginary Renaissance kingdom in need of an heir and finances. The cast of characters includes a female dwarf and a scheming sorcerer who involve themselves in the royal couple's problems.

The style of the book, notes Richard Eder in the *Los Angeles Times Book Review,* is "dreamlike," so that "what happens precisely is not precisely clear." Eder continues: "The book is a carousel; importance lies not in what or where each figure is itself, but in its ornamental revolutions. . . . The book stops but the carousel doesn't. The last line tells us that 'the ending is subject to change.' " Butler finds that not only the ending, but also the tense and narrative voices are "subject to change," and remarks that this is a distracting feature of the novel. She also believes that the characters "are never permitted quite enough humanity to be liked or cared about in any way for more than a few minutes at a time." The most significant feature of the novel, says Butler, is the book's tone, which is "cool, clever, and distant." Harris categorizes the author's work as "an erudite book." Furthermore, he writes, the story is meant "to exercise not our liberal sentiments, but our power of laughter." It is, he concludes, "curiously wise."

Subject to Change demonstrates Gould's willingness to try new things. "Gould is a writer who determinedly resists pigeonholing and in each new book strikes out in fresh directions," remarks a *Publishers Weekly* reviewer. Over the years, the author has concerned herself less with the issue of gender roles in society in order to explore other issues; and sometimes she abandons issues altogether in favor of pure storytelling. "After each book I've always felt that this was not what I was trying to do," Gould tells Baker in her interview. "I think that each time I've had a change of viewpoint, and I like to think I've always moved on."

BIOGRAPHICAL/CRITICAL SOURCES:

BOOKS

Contemporary Literary Criticism, Gale, Volume 4, 1975, Volume 10, 1979.

PERIODICALS

Chicago Tribune Book Review, September 19, 1976, May 31, 1981.
Harper's, October, 1976.
Los Angeles Times Book Review, July 17, 1988.
New York Times Book Review, September 19, 1976, June 29, 1980, May 31, 1981, July 10, 1988.
Publishers Weekly, April 17, 1981, May 27, 1988.
Village Voice, July 10, 1978.
Washington Post, July 29, 1978.
Washington Post Book World, May 24, 1981, July 17, 1988.*

—Sketch by Kevin S. Hile

* * *

GRAFF, (S.) Stewart 1908-

PERSONAL: Born May 8, 1908, in Worthington, Pa.; son of John Francis and Martha Grier (Stewart) Graff; married Polly Anne Colver (a free-lance writer and author of children's books), March 3, 1945; children: Jeremy Markham Harris (stepson), Kate Stewart (Mrs. Donald S. Miller). *Education:* Harvard University, A.B., 1930, LL.B., 1936. *Politics:* Independent. *Religion:* Lutheran.

ADDRESSES: Home—157 West Clinton Ave., Irvington, N.Y. 10533.

CAREER: Brown, Cross & Hamilton (law firm), New York City, associate attorney, 1936-48; Synthetic Organic Chemical Manufacturers Association, New York City, executive secretary, 1948-68; writer of children's books, 1961—. *Military service:* U.S. Army Air Forces, 1942-46; became captain.

WRITINGS:

JUVENILES

John Paul Jones, Garrard, 1961.
George Washington: Father of Freedom, Garrard, 1964.
Theodore Roosevelt's Boys, Garrard, 1967.
Hernando Cortes, Garrard, 1970.
The Story of World War II, Dutton, 1978.

WITH WIFE, POLLY ANNE GRAFF; JUVENILES

Squanto: Indian Adventurer, Garrard, 1965.
Helen Keller: Toward the Light, Garrard, 1965.
The Wayfarer's Tree, Dutton, 1973.

OTHER

(Co-editor with P. A. Graff) *Wolfert's Roost,* Washington Irving Press, 1971, revised edition, 1979.

WORK IN PROGRESS: Research on family records from Civil War period; specialized studies in history and biography.

AVOCATIONAL INTERESTS: Travel.*

* * *

GREEN, Martin (Burgess) 1927-

PERSONAL: Born September 21, 1927, in London, England; son of Joseph William Elias (a shopkeeper) and Hilda (Brewster) Green; married Carol Elizabeth Hurd, 1967; children: Martin Michael, Miriam. *Education:* St. John's College, Cambridge, B.A. (with English honours), 1948, M.A., 1952; King's College, London, teacher's diploma, 1951; Sorbonne, University of Paris, Certificat d'Etudes Francaises, 1952; University of Michigan, Ph.D., 1957. *Politics:* Labour. *Religion:* Roman Catholic.

ADDRESSES: Office—Department of English, Tufts University, Medford, Mass. 02155.

CAREER: Teacher at College Moderne, Fourmies, France, 1951-52, and at Konya Koleji, Konya, Turkey, 1955-56; Wellesley College, Wellesley, Mass., instructor in modern literature, 1957-61; Tufts University, Medford, Mass., assistant professor of American literature, 1963-65; University of Birmingham, Birmingham, England, lecturer in American literature, 1965-68; Tufts University, professor of English, 1968—. *Military service:* Royal Air Force, 1948-50; became sergeant.

AWARDS, HONORS: Three major Avery and Jule Hopwood Creative Writing Awards, University of Michigan, 1954.

WRITINGS:

Mirror for Anglo-Saxons, Harper, 1960.
Reappraisals, Hugh Evelyn, 1963, Norton, 1965.
Science and the Shabby Curate of Poetry, Norton, 1965.
The Problem of Boston, Norton, 1966.
Yeats's Blessings on von Hugel: Essays in Literature and Religion, Longmans, Green, 1967, Norton, 1968.
Cities of Light and Sons of the Morning, Little, Brown, 1972.
The von Richthofen Sisters: The Triumphant and the Tragic Modes of Love—Else and Frieda von Richthofen, Otto Gross, Max Weber, and D. H. Lawrence in the Years 1870-1970, Basic Books, 1974, 2nd edition, University of New Mexico Press, 1988.
(Editor with Philip C. Ritterbush) *Technology as Institutionally Related to Human Values,* Acropolis Books, 1974.
Children of the Sun: A Narrative of "Decadence" in England after 1918, Basic Books, 1976, revised edition, Constable, 1977.
Transatlantic Patterns: Cultural Comparisons of England with America, Basic Books, 1977.
The Earth Again Redeemed: May 26 to July 1, 1984 (science fiction), Basic Books, 1977.
The Challenge of the Mahatmas (first book in "The Lust for Power" trilogy), Basic Books, 1978.
Dreams of Adventure, Deeds of Empire (second book in "The Lust for Power" trilogy), Basic Books, 1979.
Tolstoy and Gandhi: Men of Peace (third book in "The Lust for Power" trilogy), Basic Books, 1983.
The Great American Adventure, Beacon Press, 1984.
The English Novel in the Twentieth Century: The Doom of Empire, Routledge & Kegan Paul, 1985, Pennsylvania State University Press, 1987.
(With John Swan) *The Triumph of Pierrot: The Commedia dell'Arte and the Modern Imagination,* Macmillan, 1986.
The Origins of Non-Violence: Tolstoy and Gandhi in Their Historical Setting, Pennsylvania State University Press, 1986.
Mountain of Truth: The Counterculture Begins—Ascona, 1900-1920, University Press of New England, 1986.
(Editor) Mahatma Gandhi, *Gandhi in India: In His Own Words,* University Press of New England, 1987.
New York 1913: The Armory Show and the Paterson Strike Pageant, Scribner, 1988.

SIDELIGHTS: Scholar Martin Green is, according to Jonathan Raban in the *New York Times Book Review,* a "merchant venturer in the commerce of ideas, a wickedly clever cultural historian at whose approach disciplinary frontiers seem to melt into thin air. He has the gift of making himself appear equally at home in literature, anthropology, social history, politics and gossip." Green, a British expatriate, has written several books on English cultural and social history, often using literary figures to illustrate his point. In *Children of the Sun: A Narrative of "Decadence" in England after 1918,* for example, Green explores the post-World War I cultural phenomenon of dandyism among the young, wealthy socialites and artists of the period. Focusing on such writers as Evelyn Waugh, Christopher Isherwood, and Harold Acton, Green sets out "to describe the imaginative life of English [high] culture after 1918 and to trace the prominence within it, the partial dominance over it, established by men of one intellectual temperament," Gerry C. Gunnin quotes Green in his *World Literature Today* article. According to Hilton Kramer in his *New York Times Book Review* contribution, "among much else that Mr. Green's book accomplishes, it gives us a new and vivid understanding of what the concept of the Establishment in England truly signified. . . . He has . . . written a very important book."

In *Transatlantic Patterns: Cultural Comparisons of England with America,* Green discusses the contemporary cultural differences between the two countries on the basis of their literature. Examining writers as diverse as Dorothy Sayers and John D. MacDonald, Norman Mailer and Doris Lessing, Green tries "to define the difference between England and America in terms of attitudes toward marriage, humor, detective stories, Marx and Freud. . . . What he is after is extremely subtle and pertinent—not cultural—caricature," explains Christopher Lehmann-Haupt of the *New York Times.* Lehmann-Haupt goes on to say that this book "will not come as much of a surprise to anyone who has followed Mr. Green's lively and original intellectual career."

Green focuses on two revolutionary events in what Chicago *Tribune Books* critic Ron Grossman calls a "masterly study of America's earliest rebels-with-a-cause" entitled *New York 1913: The Armory Show and the Paterson Strike Pageant.* In February, 1913, Greenwich Villagers presented the first exhibition of modern art in the United States at the 69th Regiment Armory. For the first time, Americans encountered modern paintings by such artists as Matisse, Duchamp, and Picasso. A few months later some of these same revolutionaries helped demonstrate with striking textile workers of Paterson, New Jersey. Although neither of these events was a critical success, Green illustrates that "once upon a time in a certain place, revolutionary art and politics did appear to go hand in hand . . . ," notes Lehmann-Haupt; "their leaders knew one another, being of the same class and sometimes sharing the rebellious culture of Greenwich Village. They were saying no to certain things. . . . [Green] traces the tangled thread connecting the events and the people who figured prominently in them. . . . He makes us see what these people shared, where they came from and why they wanted to overthrow the old order in its various forms." In the opinion of Richard Snow for the *New York Times Book Review, New York 1913* is a "complex and intriguing book. . . . [It] is sometimes repetitive, and one may quail a bit at the outset when Susan Sontag's esthetic vocabulary is introduced to help clarify the analysis to follow. But the book is full of fascinating things, and alive with the vigor of the eloquent men and women who were so sure they were about to create a renaissance through the fusion of art and politics. It is greatly to Mr. Green's credit that he never patronizes them in their ardent certainties, and that he is able to resurrect so sympathetically an era whose 'gay, inclusive, experimental spirit' seems as distant from us today as the Greenwich Village that fomented it."

BIOGRAPHICAL/CRITICAL SOURCES:

BOOKS

Green, Martin, *New York 1913: The Armory Show and the Paterson Strike Pageant,* Scribner, 1988.

PERIODICALS

Globe and Mail (Toronto), July 21, 1984.
New York Review of Books, April 15, 1976.
New York Times, June 29, 1977, June 11, 1986, December 8, 1988.
New York Times Book Review, January 25, 1976, August 7, 1977, May 27, 1979, August 28, 1983, June 29, 1986, July 13, 1986, December 11, 1988.
Spectator, June 4, 1977.
Times Literary Supplement, July 18, 1980, February 22, 1985, February 6, 1987.
Tribune Books (Chicago), January 18, 1989.
Washington Post Book World, November 27, 1988.
World Literature Today, spring, 1977.

* * *

GREENING, Hamilton
See HAMILTON, Charles (Harold St. John)

* * *

GREY, Anthony 1938-

PERSONAL: Born July 5, 1938, in Norwich, England; son of Alfred (a tradesman) and Agnes (Bullent) Grey; married Shirley McGuinn (a college lecturer), April 4, 1970; children: Clarissa, Lucy-Emma. *Education:* Attended grammar school in England.

ADDRESSES: Home—Kensington, London W8, England. *Agent*—Michael Sissons, A. D. Peters, 5th Floor, The Chambers, Chelsea Harbour, Lots Rd., London SW10 0XF, England; and Peter Matson, Literistic Ltd., 1 Madison Ave., New York, N.Y. 10010.

CAREER: Reporter for *Eastern Daily Press,* England, 1960-64; correspondent for Reuters News Agency in East Berlin, 1965-67, and in Peking, China, 1967-69, where he was interned by the Chinese; host of daily international current affairs program, "Twenty-Four Hours," for British Broadcasting Corp. World Service, 1974-79; writer. Also host of such television documentaries as "One Man's Freedom," broadcast in England, 1972, "The Lure of the Dolphins," broadcast in England and United States, 1976, and "Witness of the Long March," "Return to Saigon," and "Return to Peking," all broadcast in England in 1988.

AWARDS, HONORS: Member, Order of the British Empire, 1969; International Publishing Corporation Journalist of the Year Award, 1970.

WRITINGS:

Hostage in Peking (autobiography), M. Joseph, 1970, Doubleday, 1971, reprinted, Weidenfeld & Nicolson, 1988.
A Man Alone (short stories), M. Joseph, 1971.
Crosswords from Peking, Penguin, 1971.
Some Put Their Trust in Chariots, M. Joseph, 1973.
The Bulgarian Exclusive, M. Joseph, 1976, Dial Press, 1977.
The Chinese Assassin (novel), M. Joseph, 1978.
Saigon (novel; Book-of-the-Month Club alternate selection), Little, Brown, 1982.
The Prime Minister Was a Spy (nonfiction), Weidenfeld & Nicolson, 1983.
Peking (novel), Little, Brown, 1988.

Author of radio play, "Himself," broadcast in England, Australia, New Zealand, and Switzerland. Contributor of short stories and articles to publications, including *Playboy, Listener, China Review, Punch, New York Times Book Review, Times* (London), and *Illustrated London News.*

SIDELIGHTS: During the 1960s, Anthony Grey, a reporter in Asia for England's Reuters News Agency, was held prisoner in his Peking flat for more than 800 days while Chinese nationals pressured for the release of thirteen Chinese journalists jailed in Hong Kong. "Imprisonment is usually rent-free . . . [but during Grey's internment] Reuters had to keep up payments for his flat," notes a *Times Literary Supplement* critic on Grey's book *Hostage in Peking.* "This is one of the many ironies mentioned in an attempt to make something of what must have been an appallingly negative experience." *Hostage in Peking* is based on the diary that Grey was forced to keep secret from his captors. "When I felt self-pity beginning even slightly to assert its influence, I deliberately tried to counteract this with a rational appraisal of my plight," he writes in the volume. "Nobody had forced me into China. I was not a soldier who had been drafted there. All Reuters correspondents are offered their assignments and may refuse them if they wish."

Nevertheless, the effects of such a long and confusing imprisonment were bound to take their toll. "Most of the book is devoted to the inspiring account of how Grey overcame the terrors that invaded his mind and being," says Harry Schwartz in *Saturday Review.* "The key element was his essential emotional health, the outgrowth, one gathers, of his somewhat Victorian upbringing and values. Prayer helped to sustain him, as did thoughts of his mother and girlfriend. He was lucky enough to have a short book on yoga that gave him a routine of physical exercises and meditation, which proved invaluable in bolstering his determination not to surrender to the extreme psychological pressure put on him." Grey's triumph over adversity "was a virtuoso performance," concludes Schwartz. "*Hostage in Peking* deserves to be read and remembered as the latest in a long line of sagas of British courage [and] endurance."

Grey has also published several novels, most notably *Saigon,* an epic retelling of Asian history from 1925 through 1975. The book reached the bestseller lists in Australia, where Danielle Robinson of *Weekend Australian* reports that *Saigon* "is undoubtably one of the richest, most fascinating, yet factual novels ever written about Vietnam and one which completely exhausted the seemingly inexhaustible Anthony Grey." In that article, the author says of the four years of research that went into the novel: "It nearly killed me, that book. I am pleased to survive it."

BIOGRAPHICAL/CRITICAL SOURCES:

BOOKS

Grey, Anthony, *Hostage in Peking,* M. Joseph, 1970, Doubleday, 1971, reprinted, Weidenfeld & Nicolson, 1988.

PERIODICALS

Chattanooga News-Free Press, October 31, 1982.
China Review, December, 1988.
Saturday Review, June 26, 1971.
Time, March 29, 1971.
Times Literary Supplement, September 11, 1970.
Washington Post, September 5, 1970, November 1, 1982.
Weekend Australian, September 17, 1983.

* * *

GUNN, John (Charles) 1937-

PERSONAL: Born June 6, 1937, in Hove, Sussex, England; son of Albert Charles (a grocer) and Lily (Edwards) Gunn; married

Celia Ann Frances Willis, September 9, 1959 (marriage ended, 1987); children: Richard, Frances. *Education:* University of Birmingham, M.B., Ch.B., 1961, M.D., 1969; Institute of Psychiatry, London, Academ DPM, 1966, M.R.C.Psych., 1971.

ADDRESSES: Office—Institute of Psychiatry, De Crespigny Park, Camberwell, London SE5 8AF, England.

CAREER: University of London, London, England, senior registrar at Maudsley Hospital, 1967-71, senior lecturer, 1971-78, currently professor of forensic psychiatry at Institute of Psychiatry and consultant to Maudsley Hospital. Williams Travelling Professor in Australia and New Zealand, 1985; member of house staff or registrar at various British hospitals. Advisor to numerous national and international organizations, including House of Commons select committee, 1975 and 1985, and World Health Organization, 1987.

MEMBER: Royal College of Psychiatrists (member of court of electors), Royal Society of Medicine, British Society of Criminology, Council for Science and Society.

AWARDS, HONORS: Brackenbury Prize in forensic psychiatry, British Medical Association, 1969; Bronze Medal, Royal Medico-Psychological Association, 1970.

WRITINGS:

(Editor with others) Aubrey Lewis, *Inquiries in Psychiatry: Clinical and Social Investigations,* Routledge & Kegan Paul, 1967.

(Editor with others) Lewis, *The State of Psychiatry: Essays and Addresses,* Science House, 1967.

(Compiler) *A Directory of World Psychiatry,* World Psychiatric Association, 1971.

Violence, Praeger, 1973.

Epileptics in Prison, Academic Press, 1977.

(With others) *Psychiatric Aspects of Imprisonment,* Academic Press, 1978.

(Editor with David P. Farrington) *Abnormal Offenders, Delinquency, and the Criminal Justice System,* Wiley, 1982.

(With Farrington) *Aggression and Dangerousness,* Wiley, 1985.

(Editor with Farrington) *Reactions to Crime: The Public, the Police, Courts and Prisons,* Wiley, 1985.

Assistant editor and book review editor, *British Journal of Psychiatry,* 1967-71; member of editorial board, *British Journal of Criminology,* 1988—.

WORK IN PROGRESS: A textbook of forensic psychiatry; recent advances in forensic psychology and psychiatry.

H

HADAS, Rachel 1948-

PERSONAL: Born November 8, 1948, in New York, N.Y.; daughter of Moses (a classical scholar) and Elizabeth (Chamberlayne) Hadas; married George Edwards (a composer and teacher), July 22, 1978. *Education:* Harvard University, B.A. (magna cum laude), 1969; Johns Hopkins University, M.A., 1977; Princeton University, Ph.D. (with special distinction), 1981.

ADDRESSES: Home—838 West End Ave., No. 3A, New York, N.Y. 10025. *Office*—Department of English, Newark College of Arts and Sciences, Rutgers University, Hill Hall, Newark, N.J. 07102.

CAREER: Rutgers University, Newark, N.J., assistant professor, 1980-87, associate professor of English, 1987—.

MEMBER: Poetry Society of America (member of governing board, 1983-84), Modern Language Association of America, Modern Greek Studies Association, National Council of Teachers of English, Phi Beta Kappa.

AWARDS, HONORS: Fellow of MacDowell Colony and scholar at Bread Loaf Writers Conference, both 1976.

WRITINGS:

Starting from Troy (poems), David Godine, 1975.
(Translator) Stephanos Xenos, *Trelles* (poems; title means "Follies"), [Athens], 1978.
(Co-editor with Charlotte Mandel and Maxine Silverman) *Saturday's Women: Eileen W. Barnes Award Anthology,* introduction by Mandel, Saturday Press, 1982.
Slow Transparency (poems), Wesleyan University Press, 1983.
Form, Cycle, Infinity: Landscape Imagery in the Poetry of Robert Frost and George Seferis, Bucknell University Press, 1985.
A Son from Sleep (poems), Wesleyan University Press, 1987.
Pass It On (poems), Princeton University Press, 1989.

Work represented in anthologies, including *Ardis Anthology of American Poetry.* Contributor of poems, articles, translations, and reviews to magazines, including *Atlantic Monthly, National Forum, Harper's, New Yorker, New Republic,* and *Ploughshares.*

WORK IN PROGRESS: A book of essays, *In and Out of Books.*

SIDELIGHTS: Rachel Hadas's book of poems *Slow Transparency* moves in time from childhood into adulthood and in location from a Greek island to rural New England. While *Times Literary Supplement* contributor Anne Stevenson believes that Hadas's "poems suffer from being worked on for too long under the shadow of Wallace Stevens," she adds that "there is intelligence here, and imagination which augurs well for the future." Jorie Graham in the *New York Times Book Review* points out the poet's tendency to over-editorialize, but also states that "in those poems where thinking is not inflated to fit shapeliness, Miss Hadas confronts the details of her life with some genuine power."

Rachel Hadas once told *CA:* "All my work—writing poems, teaching, writing criticism—comes from the same source of energy: the point where language and world, or inner and outer, feeling and landscape, converge."

BIOGRAPHICAL/CRITICAL SOURCES:

PERIODICALS

New York Times Book Review, March 4, 1984.
Times Literary Supplement, July 20, 1984.

* * *

HAEBERLE, Erwin J(akob) 1936-

PERSONAL: Born March 30, 1936, in Dortmund, Germany (now West Germany); son of Erwin Clemens (a salesman) and Hedwig (Hertling) Haeberle. *Education:* Attended University of Cologne, 1956-57, University of Freiburg, 1957-60, and University of Glasgow, 1960-61; Cornell University, M.A., 1964; University of Heidelberg, Ph.D. (magna cum laude), 1966; Institute for Advanced Study of Human Sexuality, San Francisco, Calif., D.A., 1976.

ADDRESSES: Office—AIDS-Zentrum, Reichpietschufer 74–76, D–1000 Berlin 30, West Germany; and Institute for Advanced Study of Human Sexuality, 1523 Franklin St., San Francisco, Calif. 94109.

CAREER: Private tutor for the family of the late Prince of Hohenzollern, 1961-62; University of Heidelberg, Heidelberg, West Germany, lecturer in English, 1964-66; Yale University, New Haven, Conn., research fellow in American studies, 1966-68, 1970-71; University of California, Berkeley, Center for Japanese and Korean Studies, research fellow, 1968-69, 1971-72; Herder & Herder, New York, N.Y., editor, 1969-70; Institute for Advanced Study of Human Sexuality, San Francisco, Calif., director of historical research, 1976—; Indiana University, Alfred C. Kinsey Institute for Sex Research, Bloomington, research associate, 1981–84; AIDS–Zentrum, Berlin, West Germany, director of department of information and documentation, 1988—.

WRITINGS:

Das szenische Werk Thornton Wilders, Carl Winter Universitaetsverlag (Heidelberg), 1967.

(With Martin Goldstein and Will McBride) *The Sex Book,* Herder & Herder, 1971.

(Contributor) H.-J. Lang, editor, *Der Amerikanische Roman,* [Duesseldorf], 1972.

(Contributor) K. Schubert and U. Mueller-Richter, editors, *Geschichte und Gesellschaft in der Amerikanischen Literatur,* Quelle & Meyer, 1975.

(Contributor) H. Gochros and J. Gochros, editors, *The Sexually Oppressed,* Association Press, 1977.

(Editor of English language edition) *The Collected Works of Karl May,* Seabury, 1977—.

The Sex Atlas: A New Illustrated Guide, Seabury, 1978, new revised and expanded popular reference edition, Continuum, 1983.

Die Sexualitaet der Menschen: Handbuch und Atlas, De Gruyter, 1983.

Anfaenge der Sexualwissenschaft, de Gruyter, 1983.

(Editor with R. Taylor Segraves) *Emerging Dimensions of Sexology: Selected Papers from the Sixth World Congress of Sexology,* Praeger, 1984.

(Author of introduction) Magnus Hirschfeld, *Die Homosexualitaet des Mannes und des Weibes,* De Gruyter, 1984.

(Editor with Axel Beduerftig) *AIDS—Beratung, Betreuung, Vorbeugung,* de Gruyter, 1987.

Contributor to *Jahrbuch fuer Amerikastudien* and *Neue Rundschau.*

* * *

HAGGARD, William
See CLAYTON, Richard Henry Michael

* * *

HALEVI, Z'ev ben Shimon
See KENTON, Warren

* * *

HAMILTON, Charles (Harold St. John) 1876-1961 (Martin Clifford, Harry Clifton, Clifford Clive, Sir Alan Cobham, Owen Conquest, Gordon Conway, Harry Dorian, Frank Drake, Freeman Fox, Hamilton Greening, Cecil Herbert, Prosper Howard, Robert Jennings, Gillingham Jones, T. Harcourt Llewelyn, Clifford Owen, Ralph Redway, Ridley Redway, Frank Richards, Hilda Richards, Raleigh Robbins, Robert Rogers, Eric Stanhope, Robert Stanley, Peter Todd, Nigel Wallace, Talbot Wynyard)

PERSONAL: Born August 8, 1876, in Ealing, Middlesex (now in London), England; died December 24, 1961, in Kent, England; son of John (a journalist and bookseller), and Marian Hannah (Trinder) Hamilton. *Education:* Attended a local private school.

ADDRESSES: Home—"Rose Lawn," Kingsgate, Broadstairs, Kent, England.

CAREER: Author of stories for children. Creator of series of school and adventure series for numerous boys' magazines, 1906-40.

WRITINGS:

"On the Ball" (song), Woodford, (Canvey Island, Essex), 1908.

(Contributor under own name and pseudonyms Martin Clifford, Owen Conquest, and Frank Richards) *The Schoolboys Own Library,* Amalgamated Press, 1925-40.

(Under pseudonym Hilda Richards) *Bessie Bunter of Cliff House School,* illustrated by Macdonald, C. Skilton, 1949.

(Under pseudonym Owen Conquest) *The Rivals of Rockwood School,* Mandeville, 1951.

(Under pseudonym Frank Richards) *The Autobiography of Frank Richards* (nonfiction), C. Skilton, 1952, memorial edition, 1962.

(Under pseudonym Peter Todd) *The Adventures of Herlock Sholmes,* introduction by Philip Jose Farmer, Mysterious Press, 1976.

A New Anthology from the Works of Charles Hamilton, edited by John Wernham, Museum Press (Maidstone, Kent), 1977.

UNDER PSEUDONYM MARTIN CLIFFORD

The Secret of the Study, Mandeville, 1949.

Tom Merry and Co. of St. Jim's, Mandeville, 1949.

Rallying around Gussy, Mandeville, 1950.

The Scapegrace of St. Jim's, Mandeville, 1951.

Talbot's Secret, Mandeville, 1951.

"GOLD HAWK" SERIES; UNDER PSEUDONYM MARTIN CLIFFORD

Tom Merry's Secret, Mandeville, 1952.

Tom Merry's Rival, Mandeville, 1952.

The Man from the Past, Mandeville, 1952.

Who Ragged Railton?, Mandeville, 1952.

Skimpole's Snapshot, Mandeville, 1952.

Trouble for Trimble, Mandeville, 1952.

D'Arcy in Danger, Mandeville, 1952.

D'Arcy on the Warpath, Mandeville, 1952.

D'Arcy's Disappearance, Mandeville, 1952.

D'Arcy the Reformer, Mandeville, 1952.

D'Arcy's Day Off, Mandeville, 1952.

UNDER PSEUDONYM FRANK RICHARDS

Billy Bunter of Greyfriars School, illustrated by R. J. Macdonald, C. Skilton, 1947, reprinted, edited by Kay King and illustrated by Victor Ambrus, Granada, 1983.

Billy Bunter's Banknote, C. Skilton, 1948, reprinted, Howard Baker, 1977.

Billy Bunter's Barring-Out, illustrated by Macdonald, C. Skilton, 1948.

Billy Bunter in Brazil, C. Skilton, 1949, 2nd edition, Cassell, 1952, reprinted, Howard Baker, 1976.

Billy Bunter's Christmas Party, illustrated by Macdonald, C. Skilton, 1949, 2nd edition, Cassell, 1952, published as *Bunter's Christmas Party,* Howard Baker, 1976.

Billy Bunter among the Cannibals, illustrated by Macdonald, C. Skilton, 1950.

Billy Bunter's Benefit, illustrated by Macdonald, C. Skilton, 1950, new edition edited by King, Dragon, 1984.

Jack of All Trades, Mandeville, 1950.

Billy Bunter Butts In, illustrated by Macdonald, C. Skilton, 1951.

Billy Bunter's Postal Order, illustrated by Macdonald, C. Skilton, 1951, new edition, edited by King, Quiller, 1983.

Billy Bunter and the Blue Mauritius, illustrated by Macdonald, C. Skilton, 1952.
Billy Bunter's Beanfeast, illustrated by Macdonald, Cassell, 1952.
Billy Bunter's Brain-Wave, illustrated by Macdonald, Cassell, 1953.
Billy Bunter's First Case, illustrated by Macdonald, C. Skilton, 1953.
Billy Bunter the Bold, illustrated by Macdonald, Cassell, 1954.
Bunter Does His Best!, illustrated by Macdonald, Cassell, 1954, reprinted, edited by King and illustrated by Ambrus, Granada, 1983.
The Lone Texan, Atlantic, 1954.
Backing Up Billy Bunter, illustrated by Charles H. Chapman, Cassell, 1955.
Billy Bunter's Double, illustrated by Macdonald, Cassell, 1955, new edition, edited by King and illustrated by Ambrus, Quiller, 1982.
The Banishing of Billy Bunter, illustrated by Chapman, Cassell, 1956.
Lord Billy Bunter, Cassell, 1956.
Billy Bunter Afloat, illustrated by Chapman, Cassell, 1957.
Billy Bunter's Bolt, illustrated by Chapman, Cassell, 1957.
Billy Bunter the Hiker, illustrated by Chapman, Cassell, 1958.
Billy Bunter's Bargain, illustrated by Chapman, Cassell, 1958.
Bunter Comes for Christmas, illustrated by Chapman, Cassell, 1959, reprinted, edited by King and illustrated by Ambrus, Granada, 1983.
Bunter Out of Bounds, illustrated by Chapman, Cassell, 1959.
Bunter the Bad Lad, Cassell, 1960.
Bunter Keeps It Dark, illustrated by Chapman, Cassell, 1960.
Billy Bunter at Butlin's, illustrated by Chapman, Cassell, 1961.
Billy Bunter's Treasure-Hunt, illustrated by Chapman, Cassell, 1961.
Bunter the Ventriloquist, illustrated by Chapman, Cassell, 1961.
Just Like Bunter, illustrated by Chapman, Cassell, 1961.
Billy Bunter's Bodyguard, illustrated by Chapman, Cassell, 1962.
Bunter the Caravanner, illustrated by Chapman, Cassell, 1962.
Big Chief Bunter, illustrated by Chapman, Cassell, 1963.
Bunter the Stowaway, illustrated by Chapman, Cassell, 1964.
Thanks to Bunter, illustrated by Chapman, Cassell, 1964.
Bunter and the Phantom of the Towers, May Fair Books, 1965.
Bunter's Holiday Cruise, May Fair Books, 1965.
Bunter's Last Fling, illustrated by Chapman, Cassell, 1965.
Bunter the Racketeer, May Fair Books, 1965.
Bunter the Sportsman, illustrated by Chapman, Cassell, 1965.
Bunter the Tough Guy of Greyfriars, May Fair Books, 1965.
Billy Bunter and the Man from South America, Hamlyn, 1967.
Billy Bunter and the School Rebellion, Hamlyn, 1967.
Billy Bunter and the Secret Enemy, Hamlyn, 1967.
Billy Bunter's Big Top, Hamlyn, 1967.
Billy Bunter and the Bank Robber, Hamlyn, 1968.
Billy Bunter and the Crooked Captain, Hamlyn, 1968.
The Billy Bunter Picture Book, Charles Hamilton Museum, 1968.
Billy Bunter Sportsman!, Hamlyn, 1968.
Billy Bunter's Convict, Howard Baker, 1968.
Billy Bunter in the Land of the Pyramids, Howard Baker, 1969.
Billy Bunter of Bunter Court, Howard Baker, 1969.
The Rebellion of Harry Wharton, Howard Baker, 1969.
Billy Bunter and the Courtfield Cracksman, Howard Baker, 1970.
Billy Bunter and the Terror of the Form, Howard Baker, 1970.
The Mystery of Wharton Lodge, Greyfriars Press, 1971.
Bunter and the Greyfriars Mutiny, Howard Baker, 1972.
My Lord Bunter, Greyfriars Press, 1972.
The Schemer of the Remove, Howard Baker, 1972.
Six Boys in a Boat, Greyfriars Press, 1972.
Alonzo the Great, Greyfriars Press, 1973.
Billy Bunter's Christmas, Greyfriars Press, 1973.
The Black Sheep of Greyfriars, Greyfriars Press, 1973.
Calling Mr. Quelch, Greyfriars Press, 1973.
The Greyfriars Hikers, Greyfriars Press, 1973.
Harry Wharton's Enemy, Greyfriars Press, 1973.
The Tyrant of Greyfriars, Greyfriars Press, 1973.
A Bargain for Bunter, Greyfriars Press, 1974.
Billy Bunter in China, Greyfriars Press, 1974.
Billy Bunter's Circus, Greyfriars Press, 1974.
The Joker of Greyfriars, Greyfriars Press, 1974.
The Kidnapped Schoolboys, Greyfriars Press, 1974.
The Mystery of the Moat House, Howard Baker, 1974.
The Shadow over Harry Wharton, Greyfriars Press, 1974.
Billy Bunter's Coronation Party, Greyfriars Press, 1975
Billy Bunter's Hat Trick, Greyfriars Press, 1975.
Billy Bunter's Lucky Day, Howard Baker, 1975.
Bob Cherry's Big Bargain, Howard Baker, 1975.
Bunter Tells the Truth, Howard Baker, 1975.
Bunter's Seaside Caper, Howard Baker, 1975.
The Burglar of Greyfriars, Howard Baker, 1975.
The Ghost of Polpelly, Howard Baker, 1975.
The Greyfriars Cowboys, Howard Baker, 1975.
The Sit-In Strike at Greyfriars, Howard Baker, 1975.
The Sleuth of Greyfriars, Greyfriars Press, 1975.
Billy Bunter's Hair Raid, Howard Baker, 1976.
The Dictator of Greyfriars, Howard Baker, 1976.
Gunmen at Greyfriars, Howard Baker, 1976.
The Popper Island Rebels, Howard Baker, 1976.
The Schoolboy Smuggler, Howard Baker, 1976.
Yarooh!: A Feast of Frank Richards, edited by Gyles Brandreth, Eyre Methuen, 1976.
The Bounder's Rebellion, Howard Baker, 1977.
Bunter the Lion Tamer, Howard Baker, 1977.
Bunter's Funny Turn, Howard Baker, 1977.
The Mystery Man of Greyfriars, Howard Baker, 1977.
Vernon-Smith's Rival, Howard Baker, 1977.
The Big Bang at Greyfriars, Howard Baker, 1978.
Bunter's Orders, Howard Baker, 1978.
The Schoolboy Tourists, Howard Baker, 1978.
The Bully of Greyfriars, Howard Baker, 1979.
The Greyfriars Second Eleven, Howard Baker, 1979.
The Rogue of the Remove, Howard Baker, 1979.
The Shylock of Greyfriars, Howard Baker, 1979.
The Greyfriars Mysteries, Howard Baker, 1981.
The Odd Fellows of Greyfriars, Howard Baker, 1981.
Billy Bunter Expelled, Howard Baker, 1982.

"SCHOOLBOY" SERIES; UNDER PSEUDONYM FRANK RICHARDS

The Secret of the School, W. C. Merrett, 1946.
The Black Sheep of Sparshott, W. C. Merrett, 1946.
First Man In, W. C. Merrett, 1946.
Looking After Lamb, W. C. Merrett, 1946.
The Hero of Sparshott, W. C. Merrett, 1946.
Pluck Will Tell, W. C. Merrett, 1946.

"MASCOT SCHOOLBOY" SERIES; UNDER PSEUDONYM FRANK RICHARDS

Top Study at Topham, John Matthew, 1947.
Bunny Binks on the War-Path, John Matthew, 1947.
The Dandy of Topham, John Matthew, 1947.

Sent to Coventry, John Matthew, 1947.

"HEADLAND HOUSE" SERIES; UNDER PSEUDONYM HILDA RICHARDS

Winifred on the Warpath, W. C. Merrett, 1946.
The Girls of Headland House, W. C. Merrett, 1946.
Under Becky's Thumb, W. C. Merrett, 1946.

"MASCOT SCHOOLGIRL" SERIES; UNDER PSEUDONYM HILDA RICHARDS

Pamela of St. Olive's, John Matthews, 1947.
The Stranded Schoolgirls, John Matthews, 1947.
The Jape of the Term, John Matthews, 1947.

OTHER

Also author of radio play, "Plus ca Change; or, The 8:45 from Surbiton," 1945, and of Billy Bunter scripts for television. Contributor of stories about the adventures of Ken King of the Islands to *Modern Boy,* and of stories under various pseudonyms to numerous periodicals: As Martin Clifford contributed to *Boys Friend, Gem, Greyfriars Holiday Annual, Pluck,* and *Triumph;* as Harry Clifton to *Chuckles;* as Clifford Clive to *School and Sport;* as Sir Alan Cobham to *Modern Boy;* as Owen Conquest to *Boys Friend, Gem, Greyfriars Herald, Magnet,* and *Popular;* as Gordon Conway to *Funny Cuts, Vanguard,* and *Smiles;* as Harry Dorian to *Gem* and *Pluck;* as Frank Drake to *Funny Cuts, Picture Fun,* and *Vanguard;* as Freeman Fox to *Coloured Comic* and *Worlds Comic;* as Hamilton Greening to *Funny Cuts;* as Cecil Herbert to *Picture Fun* and *Vanguard;* as Prosper Howard to *Boys Friend, Chuckles, Empire,* and *Gem;* as Robert Jennings to *Picture Fun;* as Gillingham Jones to *Funny Cuts, Picture Fun,* and *Vanguard;* as T. Harcourt Llewelyn to *Smiles;* as Clifford Owen to *Diamond;* as Ralph Redway, stories about "Rio Kid" to *Boys Friend, Modern Boy, Ranger,* and *Popular;* as Ridley Redway to *Funny Cuts, Picture Fun, Smiles,* and *Vanguard;* as Frank Richards to *Billy Bunter's Own, Boys Friend, Chuckles, Dreadnought, Gem, Greyfriars Holiday Annual, Magnet, Popular, Ranger, Tom Merry's Own, Wonder Book of Comics,* and other post-war publications; as Hilda Richards, stories about Bessie Bunter (Billy's sister) and the girls of Cliff House to *Schoolfriend;* as Raleigh Robbins to *Funny Cuts;* as Robert Rogers, to *Funny Cuts* and *Picture Fun;* as Eric Stanhope to *Picture Fun* and *Vanguard;* as Robert Stanley to *Best Budget, Funny Cuts, Larks,* and *Vanguard;* as Nigel Wallace to *Vanguard;* and as Talbot Wynyard to *Picture Fun.*

SIDELIGHTS: "Charles Hamilton was not only the best-loved of all school-story writers, but easily the most prolific," wrote W. O. G. Lofts and D. J. Adley in *The Men behind Boys' Fiction.* He published his first story at the age of seventeen and launched an astonishing writing career that spanned nearly seventy years and included more than twenty known pseudonyms. He created more than one hundred fictional schools as a backdrop for the more than six thousand stories he contributed to the boys' weeklies that flourished in England prior to World War II. In an annual output that was estimated at more than one and a half million words, Hamilton was credited with having created dozens of memorable and well-liked characters, none more popular than Billy Bunter whose adventures provided material for scores of stories and books. Contributing stories under various pseudonyms to several periodicals simultaneously, Hamilton turned to writing books when the outbreak of the war brought a close to many juvenile magazines. However, a renewed interest in his fictional characters after World War II encouraged him to write a new series of stories at the age of seventy. He identified most closely with the pseudonym Frank Richards, however, and published *The Autobiography of Frank Richards* in 1953, written in the third person. Although Hamilton suffered from ill health and failing eyesight toward the end of his life, he continued to write stories and correspond with his many readers, both young and old.

AVOCATIONAL INTERESTS: Chess, music.

BIOGRAPHICAL/CRITICAL SOURCES:

BOOKS

Lofts, W. O. G., and D. J. Adley, *The Men behind Boys' Fiction,* Howard Baker, 1970.
Richards, Frank, *The Autobiography of Frank Richards,* C. Skilton, 1952.
Wernham, John, Mary Codogan, Eric Fayne, and Roger Jenkins, *The Charles Hamilton Companion,* six volumes, Museum Press (Maidstone, Kent), 1972-82.*

* * *

HARBERT, Earl N(orman) 1934-

PERSONAL: Born April 1, 1934, in Cleveland, Ohio; son of Elmer William and Elsie (Francis) Harbert; married Ellen Mayo, May 24, 1971. *Education:* Hamilton College, A.B., 1956; Johns Hopkins University, M.A., 1961; University of Wisconsin, Ph.D., 1966.

ADDRESSES: Home—42 Calvin Rd., Newtonville, Mass. 02160. *Office*—Department of English, Northeastern University, Boston, Mass. 02115.

CAREER: George Washington University, Washington, D.C., instructor in English, 1961-62; Tulane University, New Orleans, La., 1966-80, began as assistant professor, became professor of English; Northeastern University, Boston, Mass., professor of English, 1980—. Visiting professor, University of Wisconsin—Madison, 1974, and Harvard University, 1980. Fulbright-Hayes lecturer, 1967-68. *Military service:* U.S. Navy, 1957-60.

MEMBER: Modern Language Association of America, American Studies Association, Association for Documentary Editing.

AWARDS, HONORS: American Philosophical Society research grants, 1972, 1979; Kellogg Essay Prize from Hamilton College.

WRITINGS:

(Editor with Robert A. Rees) *Fifteen American Authors before 1900,* University of Wisconsin Press, 1971, revised edition, 1974.
The Force So Much Closer Home: Henry Adams and the Adams Family, New York University Press, 1977.
Henry Adams: A Reference Guide, G. K. Hall, 1977.
Critical Essays on Henry Adams, G. K. Hall, 1981.
(Editor with Donald Pizer) *Dictionary of Literary Biography,* Volume 12: *American Realists and Naturalists,* Gale, 1982.
(With Jon DiGaetani) *Writing Out Loud,* Dow Jones-Irwin, 1983.
Writing for Action, Dow Jones-Irwin, 1984.
(Editor) Henry Adams, *History of the U.S. during the Administrations of Jefferson and Madison,* Library of America, 1986.
Handbook of Executive Communication, Dow Jones-Irwin, 1986.
(Editor) Washington Irving, *A Chronicle of the Conquest of Granada,* G. K. Hall, 1988.
(Editor) Bennett G. Wall, *Growth in a Changing Environment: A History of Standard Oil Company (New Jersey) and Exxon Corporation, 1950-1975,* McGraw-Hill, 1988.

Also author of *John T. Hayward: Creative Engineer* and *Tulane University Accreditation Study: The Professional Schools.* Contributor to *American Literature, Journal of American Studies, Tulane Studies in English,* and other publications.

* * *

HARTSHORNE, Charles 1897-

PERSONAL: Surname is pronounced *Harts*-horn; born June 5, 1897, in Kittanning, Pa.; son of Francis Cope (an Episcopal clergyman) and Marguerite (Haughton) Hartshorne; married Dorothy Eleanore Cooper, December 22, 1928; children: Emily Lawrence (Mrs. Nicholas D. Goodman). *Education:* Attended Haverford College, 1915-17; Harvard University, A.B., 1921, A.M., 1922, Ph.D., 1923. *Politics:* Independent.

ADDRESSES: Home—724 Sparks Ave., Austin, Tex. 78705. *Office*—University of Texas, 313 Waggener Hall, Austin, Tex. 78712.

CAREER: Harvard University, Cambridge, Mass., Sheldon traveling fellow, 1923-25, instructor in philosophy and research fellow, 1925-28; University of Chicago, Chicago, Ill., 1928-55, began as instructor, became professor of philosophy, 1945-55; Emory University, Atlanta, Ga., professor of philosophy, 1955-62; University of Texas at Austin, Ashbel Smith Professor, 1962—. Visiting professor at Stanford University, 1937, New School for Social Research, 1941-42, Goethe University, 1948-49, University of Washington, Seattle, 1958, and Banaras Hindu University, 1966. Fulbright professor, Melbourne, Australia, 1952, and Kyoto, Japan, 1958, 1966; Terry Lecturer, Yale University, 1947; Matchette Lecturer, Wesleyan University, 1964; Dudleian Lecturer, Harvard University, 1964; Morse Lecturer, Union Theological Seminary, 1964.

MEMBER: American Philosophical Association (president, Western division, 1949), C. S. Peirce Society (president, 1951), Metaphysical Society of America (president, 1955), Southern Society for Philosophy of Religion (president, 1963), Southern Society for Philosophy and Psychology (president, 1965), Phi Beta Kappa, Phi Kappa Phi.

AWARDS, HONORS: Pierre Lecomte du Nouey Award, 1963, for *The Logic of Perfection, and Other Essays in Neoclassical Metaphysics;* L.H.D., Haverford College, 1967; Litt.D., Emory University, 1969.

WRITINGS:

(Editor with Paul Weiss) *The Collected Papers of Charles Sanders Peirce,* six volumes, Harvard University Press, 1931-35.

The Philosophy and Psychology of Sensation, University of Chicago Press, 1934.

Beyond Humanism: Essays in the New Philosophy of Nature, Willett, Clark & Co., 1937.

Man's Vision of God and the Logic of Theism, Willett, Clark, & Co., 1941, Harper, 1948.

The Divine Relativity: A Social Conception of God (Terry Lectures), Yale University Press, 1948.

(With Victor Lowe and A. H. Johnson) *Whitehead and the Modern World,* Beacon Press, 1950.

Reality as Social Process: Studies in Metaphysics and Religion, Free Press of Glencoe, 1953.

(Editor with William L. Reese) *Philosophers Speak of God,* University of Chicago Press, 1953.

The Logic of Perfection, and Other Essays in Neoclassical Metaphysics, Open Court, 1962.

Anselm's Rediscovery: A Re-examination of the Ontological Proof for God's Existence, Open Court, 1965.

A Natural Theology for Our Time, Open Court, 1967.

Creative Synthesis and Philosophic Method, Open Court, 1970.

Whitehead's Philosophy: Selected Essays, 1935-1970, University of Nebraska Press, 1972.

Born to Sing: An Interpretation and World Survey of Bird Song, Indiana University Press, 1973.

Aquinas to Whitehead: Seven Centuries of Metaphysics of Religion, Marquette University Press, 1976.

Insights and Oversights of Great Thinkers: An Evaluation of Western Philosophy, State University of New York Press, 1983.

Omnipotence and Other Philosophical Mistakes, State University of New York Press, 1983.

Creativity in American Philosophy, State University of New York Press, 1984.

Wisdom as Moderation: A Philosophy of the Middle Way, State University of New York Press, 1987.

CONTRIBUTOR

Philosophical Essays for Alfred North Whitehead, Longmans, Green, 1936.

Marvin Farber, editor, *Philosophical Essays in Memory of Edmund Usserl,* Harvard University Press, 1940.

P. A. Schlipp, editor, *The Philosophy of George Santayana,* Northwestern University Press, 1940.

Schlipp, editor, *The Philosophy of Alfred North Whitehead,* Northwestern University Press, 1941.

Sydney Rome and Beatrice Rome, editors, *Philosophical Interrogations,* Holt, 1964.

John Hick, editor, *Faith and the Philosophers,* St. Martin's, 1964.

Leroy S. Rouner, editor, *Philosophy, Religion, and the Coming World Civilization,* Nijhoff, 1966.

John Lachs, editor, *Animal Faith and Spiritual Life,* Appleton, 1967.

Perry Le Fevre, editor, *Philosophical Resources for Christian Thought,* Abingdon, 1968.

Hick and Arthur McGill, editors, *The Many-Faced Argument,* Macmillan, 1968.

George L. Abernathy and Thomas A. Langford, editors, *Philosophy of Religion,* 2nd edition, Macmillan, 1968.

Paul G. Kuntz, editor, *The Concept of Order,* University of Washington Press, 1968.

Jerry H. Gill, editor, *Philosophy and Religion: Some Contemporary Perspectives,* Burgess, 1968.

Dwight Van de Vate, Jr., editor, *Persons, Privacy, and Feeling: Essays in the Philosophy of Mind,* Memphis State University Press, 1970.

H. J. Cargas and B. Lee, editors, *Religious Experience and Process Theology,* Paulist Press, 1976.

F. H. Hetzler and A. H. Kutscher, editors, *Philosophical Aspects of Thanatology,* two volumes, Arno, 1978.

E. Wolf-Gazo, editor, *Whitehead: Einfuehrung in seine Kosmologie,* Verlag Karl Alber, 1980.

J. J. E. Garcia, editor, *Philosophical Essays in Honor of Risieri Frondisi,* Editoria Universitaria, 1980.

OTHER

Contributor of more than 150 articles and more than 100 book reviews to philosophy and religion journals; contributor of articles on ornithology to *Victorian Naturalist* (Australia), *Elepaio* (Hawaii), *Emu* (Australia), *Ibis* (Great Britain), *Oriole, Wilson Library Bulletin,* and *Auk.*

SIDELIGHTS: Charles Hartshorne wrote to *CA:* "The principal motivation of all my books is the desire to call attention to neglected or hitherto undiscovered truths or cogent reasonings in philosophy, theology, or ornithology."

Hartshorne has pursued his hobby of bird-song study on five trips to Europe, and also in Hawaii, the Philippines, Taiwan, Japan, Central America, South America, Africa, India, Nepal, Malaya, Thailand, Hong Kong, Mexico, Fiji, and Jamaica.

* * *

HARVEY, Earle (Sherburn) 1906-

PERSONAL: Born February 21, 1906, in Marshfield, Wis.; son of Jesse H. (a baker) and Nellie Bell (Bartle) Harvey; married Adelaide T. Karp, October 11, 1933 (died October 1, 1982); children: Paul E., James H. *Education:* Attended high school in Marshfield, Wis. *Politics:* Independent. *Religion:* Roman Catholic.

ADDRESSES: Home—1623 Ashland, Unit 5-D, Des Plaines, Ill. 60016. *Office*—(Summer) P.O. Box 56, Wallace, Mich. 49893.

CAREER: Milwaukee Sentinel, Milwaukee, Wis., staff artist, 1931-38; associated with *Waukegan Post,* Waukegan, Ill., 1939-41; *Chicago American* (now *Chicago Today*), Chicago, Ill., staff artist, 1941-48, assistant editorial art director, 1948-58, editorial art director, 1958-71.

MEMBER: Association of American Editorial Cartoonists, Chicago Press Veterans.

AWARDS, HONORS: Award from *Cartoons Magazine,* 1926.

WRITINGS:

Funny Laws (cartoons), New American Library, 1982.
More Funny Laws, New American Library, 1985.
Still More Funny Laws, New American Library, 1987.

Author of "Wisconsin Historic Oddities," a cartoon feature in *Milwaukee Sentinel,* 1933-36, "Chicago Firsts," in *Chicago American,* 1955-60, and "Speaking of the Law," syndicated by Associated Court and Commercial Newspapers News Service, 1963—.

SIDELIGHTS: Earle Harvey told *CA:* "Even before finishing grade school I had completed three cartoon and illustration correspondence courses. I didn't finish high school in Marshfield because I couldn't pass up an offer to join the *Milwaukee Herald,* a German language daily paper published in Milwaukee. The editor was surprised to find me so young, but we got along beautifully, and with his coaching I was soon doing editorial cartoons in German. Many of the cartoons were reprinted in papers in Germany.

"In 1926 I won the annual, worldwide *Cartoons Magazine* contest. It opened a few doors for me. I joined a studio and went into commercial art. After a few years, illustrating advertising matter, drawing radios, furniture, etc., became boring to me. One day Frank Marasco called and asked if I would like to join his staff on the editorial art department of the *Milwaukee Sentinel.* That was in 1931, and I was to spend the rest of my art career on newspapers.

"After a year or so I developed a cartoon panel called 'Wisconsin Historic Oddities.' It was an instant success—letters poured in, and school kids all over Wisconsin were making scrap books. In 1936 I transferred to the *Wisconsin News,* serving there until the paper had labor troubles and folded in 1938.

"Hearing that a new daily newspaper was going to start publishing in Waukegan, Illinois, I went there and got a job with the *Waukegan Post.* Tough luck followed again: the *Post* folded in 1941. A few weeks later, however, I accepted a job with the *Chicago American.* I was assigned to making daily war maps during World War II, but told the editor that I would like to get back to cartooning. One day editor Ted Doyle called me into his office and asked if I would like to do a series on Chicago 'firsts.' I jumped at the opportunity. Again it was a success, and school kids were pasting them in scrap books. I really enjoyed working on this feature. I was named editorial art director in 1958 and continued in that position when the paper's name changed to *Chicago Today* [in 1960]. I retired in 1971.

"While my son Jim was an editor for the *Chicago Daily Law Bulletin* he was in charge of national news and front page layout. One day in 1963 he mentioned to me that he wished he had better art to liven up a dull page of type. I suggested a cartoon, 'Speaking of the Law.' During all my years on the newspapers my one hobby was collecting stories and clips regarding odd laws. I had a box full of them. The first cartoon Jim ran was a hit. Lawyers and judges called asking for more. It became a regular feature. Other law papers asked to run them, and soon the cartoon was syndicated to all Associated Court and Commercial Newspapers. *Funny Laws* is a collection of these cartoons."

AVOCATIONAL INTERESTS: Travel, baseball, photography, painting.

* * *

HASZARD, Patricia Moyes 1923- (Patricia Moyes)

PERSONAL: Born January 19, 1923, in Bray, Ireland; daughter of Ernst (a judge in the Indian Civil Service) and Marion (Boyd) Pakenham-Walsh; married John Moyes (a photographer), 1951 (divorced, 1959); married John S. Haszard (an official of the International Monetary Fund), October 13, 1962. *Politics:* Liberal (non-party). *Religion:* Church of England.

ADDRESSES: Home—P.O. Box 1, Virgin Gorda, British Virgin Islands, West Indies. *Agent*—Curtis Brown, Ltd., 162-168 Regent St., London W1, England.

CAREER: Writer. Peter Ustinov Productions, Ltd., London, England, secretary, 1947-53; *Vogue,* London, assistant editor, 1954-58. *Military service:* British Women's Auxiliary Air Force, Radar Section, 1940-45; became flight officer.

AWARDS, HONORS: Edgar Allan Poe Award from Mystery Writers of America, 1970, for *Many Deadly Returns.*

WRITINGS:

UNDER NAME PATRICIA MOYES

Time Remembered (play; first produced in London, 1954; produced in New York, 1957), Methuen, 1955.
Dead Men Don't Ski (mystery novel), Collins, 1959, Rinehart, 1960.
(With Peter Ustinov and Hal E. Chester) "School for Scoundrels" (screenplay), Continental Pictures, 1960.
Down among the Dead Men (mystery novel), Holt, 1961 (published in England as *The Sunken Sailor,* Collins, 1961).
Death on the Agenda (mystery novel), Holt, 1962.
Murder a la Mode (mystery novel), Holt, 1963.
Falling Star (mystery novel), Holt, 1964.
Johnny under Ground (mystery novel), Collins, 1965, Holt, 1966.
Murder by 3's (omnibus volume of mystery novels), Holt, 1965.
Murder Fantastical (mystery novel), Holt, 1967.
Death and the Dutch Uncle (mystery novel), Holt, 1968.

Helter-Skelter (juvenile), Holt, 1968.
Many Deadly Returns (mystery novel), Holt, 1970 (published in England as *Who Saw Her Die?*, Collins, 1970).
Seasons of Snows and Sins (mystery novel), Holt, 1971.
(Contributor) *Techniques of Novel Writing,* Writer, Inc., 1973.
The Curious Affair of the Third Dog (mystery novel), Holt, 1973.
After All, They're Only Cats, Curtis Books, 1973.
Black Widower (mystery novel), Holt, 1975.
The Coconut Killings (mystery novel), Holt, 1977 (published in England as *To Kill A Coconut,* Collins, 1977).
How to Talk to Your Cat, Holt, 1978.
Who Is Simon Warwick? (mystery novel), Collins, 1978, Holt, 1979.
Angel Death (mystery novel), Holt, 1980.
A Six-Letter Word for Death (mystery novel), Holt, 1983.
Night Ferry to Death (mystery novel), Holt, 1985.
Black Girl, White Girl (mystery novel), Holt, 1989.

Contributor of short stories and articles to *Women's Mirror, Evening News* (London), *Writer, Ellery Queen's Mystery Magazine,* and other publications. Moyes's books have been translated into fifteen languages.

WORK IN PROGRESS: A mystery novel.

SIDELIGHTS: "One of the brightest contemporary practitioners of the puzzle-and-plot whodunit," as a *New York Times Book Review* critic describes her, Patricia Moyes writes mystery novels about Inspector Henry Tibbett of Scotland Yard and his wife, Emmy. Jean M. White of the *Washington Post Book World* calls them a "thoroughly engaging couple" and praises Moyes's "talent for overlaying mystery with witty, sophisticated social comment." Writing in the *New York Times Book Review,* Newgate Callendar sees Moyes as "carrying on the traditions of the classical British mystery." Similarly, Anthony Boucher, writing for the same publication, states that "Moyes is so good with people and professions and milieus that her books . . . keep reminding one more and more of the best work of [Ngaio] Marsh and [Margery] Allingham and other exemplary products of the Golden Thirties."

MEDIA ADAPTATIONS: The short stories "A Sad Loss" and "Hit and Run" were made into episodes of the British television program "Tales of the Unexpected."

AVOCATIONAL INTERESTS: Skiing, sailing, good food and wine, travel.

BIOGRAPHICAL/CRITICAL SOURCES:

PERIODICALS

Listener, April 7, 1977, January 11, 1979.
Los Angeles Times Book Review, October 6, 1985.
New York Times Book Review, July 26, 1964, May 31, 1970, February 22, 1981, May 16, 1982.
Observer, July 5, 1970, February 6, 1977.
Saturday Review, December 25, 1971.
Spectator, August 18, 1973.
Times Literary Supplement, August 13, 1964, July 16, 1970, November 12, 1971, October 3, 1980, June 20, 1986.
Washington Post Book World, November 18, 1973, July 20, 1975, January 21, 1979.

HAVIGHURST, Marion (M.) 1894-1974 (Marion M. Boyd)

PERSONAL: Born January 6, 1894, in Marietta, Ohio; died February 24, 1974, in Oxford, Ohio; daughter of William Waddell (a college president) and Mary (Gates) Boyd; married Walter Havighurst (a writer and college English professor), December 22, 1930. *Education:* Smith College, A.B., 1916; Yale University, M.A., 1926. *Politics:* Independent. *Religion:* Presbyterian.

CAREER: Western College for Women (now Western College of Miami University), Oxford, Ohio, instructor in English, 1920-23; Miami University, Oxford, Ohio, instructor in English, 1926-34; author and poet.

MEMBER: Ohio Valley Poetry Association, Martha Kinney Cooper Ohioana Library Association, Women's Faculty Club (Miami University).

AWARDS, HONORS: Ohioana Book Award (with Walter Havighurst), 1949, for *Song of the Pines: A Story of Norwegian Lumbering in Wisconsin.*

WRITINGS:

(Under name Marion M. Boyd) *Silver Wands* (poetry), Yale University Press, 1923, reprinted, AMS Press, 1971.
Murder in the Stacks, Lothrop, 1934.
(With husband, Walter Havighurst) *High Prairie,* Farrar, Rinehart, 1944.
(With W. Havighurst) *Song of the Pines: A Story of Norwegian Lumbering in Wisconsin,* Winston, 1949, reprinted, Holt, 1966.
(With W. Havighurst) *Climb a Lofty Ladder: A Story of Swedish Settlement in Minnesota,* Winston, 1952.
Strange Island, World Publishing, 1957.
The Sycamore Tree, World Publishing, 1960.

Contributor of poetry and stories to magazines.

[Sketch reviewed by husband, Walter Havighurst]

* * *

HAVIGHURST, Walter (Edwin) 1901-

PERSONAL: Born November 28, 1901, in Appleton, Wis.; son of Freeman Alfred and Winifred (Weter) Havighurst; married Marion Boyd (a writer), December 22, 1930 (died, 1974). *Education:* University of Denver, A.B., 1924; attended King's College, London, 1925-26; Columbia University, A.M., 1928.

ADDRESSES: Home—163 Shadowy Hills Dr., Oxford, Ohio 45056. *Office*—King Library, Miami University, Oxford, Ohio 45056. *Agent*—McIntosh and Otis, Inc., 475 Fifth Ave., New York, N.Y. 10017.

CAREER: Worked for a time as a merchant seaman; Miami University, Oxford, Ohio, assistant professor, 1928-35, associate professor, 1935-42, professor of English, 1942-49, research professor, 1949-68, Regents professor, 1968-69, research professor emeritus, 1969—.

MEMBER: Society of American Historians, Ohio Historical Society (member of board of editors, 1956—).

AWARDS, HONORS: Ohioana Library Association Medal, 1946-50; Friends of American Writers award, 1947, for *Land of Promise: The Story of the Northwest Territory;* D.Litt., Lawrence University and Ohio Wesleyan University, both 1947; Ohioana Book Award (with Marion Havighurst), 1949, for *Song of the Pines: A Story of Norwegian Lumbering in Wisconsin;* Association for State and Local History award, 1956, for *Wilderness for Sale: The First Wisconsin Land Rush,* and 1964, for *Voices on the River: The Story of the Mississippi Waterways;* L.H.D., Miami University, 1960, and Marietta College, 1961; History Prize, Society of Midland Authors, 1971, for *River to the West: Three Centuries of the Ohio;* elected to Ohio Hall of Fame, 1981.

WRITINGS:

Pier 17: A Novel, Macmillan, 1935.
The Quiet Shore, Macmillan, 1937.
Upper Mississippi: A Wilderness Saga, Farrar, Rinehart, 1937, revised edition, 1944.
(Editor with Harold L. Haley) *Designs for Writing,* Dryden, 1939.
The Winds of Spring, Macmillan, 1940.
No Homeward Course, Doubleday, 1941.
The Long Ships Passing: The Story of the Great Lakes, Macmillan, 1942, reprinted, 1961, revised and enlarged edition, 1975.
(Editor with Robert F. Almy and Joseph M. Bachelor) *Approach to America,* Odyssey, 1942.
(With wife, Marion Havighurst) *High Prairie,* Farrar, Rinehart, 1944.
Land of Promise: The Story of the Northwest Territory, Macmillan, 1946.
(Editor) *Masters of the Modern Short Story,* Harcourt, 1949, 2nd edition, 1955.
Signature of Time, Macmillan, 1949.
(With M. Havighurst) *Song of the Pines: A Story of Norwegian Lumbering in Wisconsin,* Winston, 1949, reprinted, Holt, 1966.
Life in America: The Great Plains (juvenile; teaching aid), Fideler, 1951, published as *Great Plains States,* 1964 revised edition published as *Great Plains States: A Geography,* 1967.
Life in America: The Midwest (juvenile; teaching aid), Fideler, 1951, published as *The Midwest,* 1965, revised edition, 1967.
Life in America: The Northeast (juvenile; teaching aid), Fideler, 1952, published as *The Northeast,* 1964, revised edition, 1967.
George Rogers Clark: Soldier in the West, McGraw, 1952.
(With M. Havighurst) *Climb a Lofty Ladder: A Story of Swedish Settlement in Minnesota,* Winston, 1952.
Annie Oakley of the Wild West, Macmillan, 1954.
(Editor with others) *Selection: A Reader for College Writing,* Dryden, 1955.
Wilderness for Sale: The First Western Land Rush, Hastings House, 1956.
Buffalo Bill's Wild West Show, Random House, 1957.
Vein of Iron: The Pickens Mather Story, World, 1958.
The Miami Years: 1809-1959, Putnam, 1959, 2nd edition published as *The Miami Years: 1809-1969,* 1969, 3rd edition published as *The Miami Years: 1809-1984,* 1984.
The First Book of Pioneers: Northwest Territory (juvenile), F. Watts, 1959.
The First Book of the Oregon Trail (juvenile), F. Watts, 1960.
(Editor) *Land of the Long Horizons,* Coward, 1960.
The Heartland: Ohio, Indiana, Illinois, Harper, 1962, revised edition, 1974.
The First Book of the California Gold Rush (juvenile), F. Watts, 1962.
Voices on the River: The Story of the Mississippi Waterways, Macmillan, 1964.
Proud Prisoner (juvenile), Holt, 1964.
(Editor) *The Great Lakes Reader,* Macmillan, 1966.
The Upper Mississippi Valley: A Student's Guide to Localized History, Teachers College Press, 1966.
Three Flags at the Straits: The Forts of Mackinac, Prentice-Hall, 1966.
(Editor) *Midwest and Great Plains* (juvenile), Fideler, 1967.
Alexander Spotswood: Portrait of a Governor, Holt, 1967.
(Editor with others) *Exploring Literature,* Houghton, 1968.
River to the West: Three Centuries of the Ohio, Putnam, 1970.
Men of Old Miami, 1809-1873: A Book of Portraits, Putnam, 1974.
From Six at First: A History of Phi Delta Theta, 1848-1973, G. Banta, 1975.
Ohio: A Bicentennial History, Norton, 1976.
(Editor with Jerry E. Jennings and Marion H. Smith) *The United States* (juvenile), Fideler, 1979.
(Author of text) *Miami Album,* King Library, Miami University, 1981.
The Dolibois Years: To These Things You Must Return, Miami University Alumni Association, 1982.
(Contributor) *A Sense of History: The Best Writing from the Pages of American Heritage,* American Heritage Press/Houghton, 1985.

Contributor to scholarly and popular magazines.

SIDELIGHTS: Although the majority of Walter Havighurst's books have focused on the old Northwest Territory—the region between the Ohio River and the Great Lakes—his earlier work draws on his experiences as a merchant seaman in such diverse locations as London, Alaska, and Hong Kong. Havighurst told *CA* that he attributes these earlier writings to the groping most authors undergo before they find their essential material. Eventually, he says, "I realized that my own background, of midland America, was for me the inexhaustible subject." Havighurst was born next to Wisconsin's Fox River, along the path French explorers took on their way to the Mississippi River from Canada. This, he states, gave rise to a "dual curiousity, wanting to recall the Midwest of past times while trying to understand its ever-changing present. This is the background I am most at home with," he continues, "and toward which my writing seems to gravitate."

* * *

HEEZEN, Bruce C(harles) 1924-1977

PERSONAL: Born April 11, 1924, in Vinton, Iowa; died of a heart attack, June 21, 1977, on a submarine off the coast of Iceland; buried in Greenwood Cemetary, Muscatine, Iowa; son of Charles Christian (engaged in farming) and Esther (Schirding) Heezen. *Education:* University of Iowa, B.A., 1948; Columbia University, M.A., 1952, Ph.D., 1957. *Religion:* Unitarian Universalist.

ADDRESSES: Home—747 River Rd., Piermont, N.Y. 10968. *Office*—Lamont Doherty Geological Observatory, Palisades, N.Y. 10964.

CAREER: Woods Hole Oceanographic Institute, Woods Hole, Mass., geologist, 1947-48; Columbia University, New York, N.Y., fellow in geology, 1948-51, assistant, 1951-53, lecturer, 1953-55, research associate, 1955-57, assistant professor, 1960-64, associate professor of geology, 1964-77; Lamont Doherty Geological Observatory, Palisades, N.Y., senior research scientist, 1957-60. Explorer and charter of ocean floors. Chairman of panel on ocean-wide survey, National Academy of Sciences, 1964-68; president of Commission for Marine Geology, International Union of Geological Sciences, 1965-70; secretary,

International Commission on Marine Geophysics, 1969. Consultant, U.S. Naval Oceanographic Office and Naval Research Laboratory; member, U.S. Department of State advisory committee, Law of the Sea Task Force.

MEMBER: International Association of the Physical Sciences of the Oceans, American Geographical Society (fellow), Geological Society of America (fellow), American Association for the Advancement of Science (fellow), Marine Biology Association (U.K.; fellow), Royal Astronomical Society (fellow), American Geophysical Union, Geochemical Society, Seismological Society of America, American Society of Limnology and Oceanography, American Association of Petroleum Geologists, Socitea Limnologae Internalis, Society of Exploration Geophysicists, Iowa Academy of Sciences (fellow), New York Academy of Sciences, Sigma Xi.

AWARDS, HONORS: Henry Bryant Bigelow Medal and Prize, Woods Hole Oceanographic Institute, 1964, for physiographic studies of the deep ocean; National Book Award nomination, 1972, for *The Face of the Deep;* Cullum Geographical Medal, American Geographical Society, 1973, for contributions to knowledge of the earth beneath the oceans; Francis A Shepard Medal, American Association of Petroleum Geologists, 1975; Walter Bucher Medal, American Geophysical Union, 1977; Hubbard Medal (posthumous), National Geographic Society, 1978.

WRITINGS:

(With Marie Tharp and Maurice Ewing) *The Floors of the Oceans* (also see below), Geological Society of America, 1959.

Geologie sous-marine et deplacements des continents, [Paris], 1959.

(With Ewing and G. Leonard Johnson) *Cable Failures in the Gulf of Corinth: A Case History,* Lamont Geological Observatory, Columbia University, 1960.

(Compiler) *The Quaternary History of the Ocean Basins,* Pergamon, 1967.

(With others) *A Coast to Coast Tectonic Study of the United States,* University of Missouri at Rolla, 1968.

(Editor with Irina Petrovna Kosminskaya) *The Structure of the Crust and Mantle beneath Inland and Marginal Seas,* Elsevier Science, 1969.

(Editor with Leon Knopoff and Gordon James Fraser MacDonald) *The World Rift System,* Elsevier Science, 1969.

(With Johnson) *Mediterranean Undercurrent and Microphysiology West of Gibraltar,* [Monaco], 1969.

(With Charles D. Hollister) *The Face of the Deep,* Oxford University Press, 1971.

(With others) *Initial Reports of the Deep Sea Drilling Project,* Volume 6: *Hawaii to Guam,* National Science Foundation, 1971, Volume 20: *Japan to Fiji,* U.S. Government Printing Office, 1973.

(Editor) *Influence of Abyssal Circulation on Sedimentary Accumulations in Time and Space,* Elsevier Science, 1977.

The Ocean Floor: Bruce Heezen Commemorative Volume, edited by R. A. Scrutton and Manik Talwani, Wiley, 1982.

PHYSIOGRAPHIC DIAGRAMS AND MAPS

(With Tharp) "Physiographic Diagram, Atlantic Ocean," Geological Society of America, 1959.

(With Tharp) "Physiographic Diagram of the South Atlantic Ocean, the Caribbean Sea, the Scotia Sea, and the Eastern Margin of the South Pacific Ocean" (originally published with text as *The Floors of the Oceans*), Geological Society of America, 1961.

(With Tharp) "Physiographical Diagram of the Indian Ocean, the Red Sea, the South China Sea, the Sulu Sea, and the Celebes Sea," Geological Society of America, 1964.

(With Tharp) "Physiographic Diagram of the North Atlantic Ocean," Geological Society of America, 1968.

(With Tharp) "Physiographic Diagram of the Western Pacific Ocean," Geological Society of America, 1971.

(With Tharp and Charles R. Bentley) "Morphology of the Earth in the Antarctic and Subantarctic," American Geographical Society, 1972.

(With Tharp) "World Ocean Floor," United States Navy Office of Naval Research, 1977.

(With Raymond P. Lynde, Jr., and Daniel J. Fornari) "Geological Map of the Indian Ocean," American Geophysical Union, 1978.

(With Tharp) "Bathymetric Map of the Northeast Equitorial Pacific Ocean," U.S. Geological Survey, 1978.

CONTRIBUTOR

Lewis G. Weeks, editor, *Habitat of Oil,* American Association of Petroleum Geologists, 1958.

G. O. Raasch, editor, *The Geology of the Arctic,* University of Toronto Press, 1960.

Mary Sears, editor, *Oceanography,* American Association for the Advancement of Science, 1961.

S. K. Runhorn, editor, *Continental Drift,* Academic Press, 1962.

Maurice N. Hill, editor, *The Sea,* Volume 3: *The Earth beneath the Sea,* Wiley, 1963.

Askell Love and Doris Love, editors, *The North Atlantic Biota and Their History,* Pergamon, 1963.

Alan E. Nairn, editor, *Problems in Paleoclimatology,* Wiley, 1964.

S. W. Carey, editor, *Syntaphral Tectonics,* University of Tasmania, 1965.

W. F. Whittard and R. Bradshaw, editors, *Submarine Geology and Geophysics,* Shoe String, 1965.

John B. Hersey, editor, *Deep Sea Photography,* Johns Hopkins Press, 1967.

Menachem Dishon, *Digital Deep-Sea Sounding Library: Description and Index List,* International Hydrographic Bureau (Monaco), 1969.

A. I. Gordon, editor, *Studies in Physical Oceanography,* Volume 2, Gordon & Breach, 1972.

OTHER

Contributor to *Encyclopedia of Oceanography, International Dictionary of Geophysics,* and *Encyclopaedia Britannica.* Author of over three hundred scientific papers for journals and proceedings published in the United States, Colombia, France, England, Canada, Germany, and other countries; also contributor of popular articles to *Saturday Review* and *Paris Match.* Coordinator for Atlantic, Indian, and Pacific Oceans, *Geologic Atlas of the World.* President of editorial committee, General Bathymetric Chart of the Oceans, beginning 1959; member of editorial committee, International Tectonic Map of the World, and convenor for oceans, beginning 1965.

SIDELIGHTS: Bruce C. Heezen, "a pioneer in mapping the ocean floors," according to Walter Sullivan of the *New York Times,* researched many areas of oceanography. Among his interests were the study of tektites, small glassy particles in the ocean sediments, which he theorized were remnants of the collision of meteorites or comets with the earth. He also discovered an extensive layer of ash on the bottom of the Mediterranean, thought to be laid down when the island of Thera exploded around 1400 B.C., an event that may have been the origin of the legend of Atlantis.

Heezen once said that, although he and his longtime associate Marie Tharp recognized the power of verbal expression, they as frequently used the economical graphic media of maps and diagrams to record their explorations. Many maps based on their work, including ones of the floors of the Indian, Atlantic, Pacific, and Arctic Oceans, have been issued as special supplements to the *National Geographic* magazine. All of them were painted by Heinrich C. Berann.

BIOGRAPHICAL/CRITICAL SOURCES:

BOOKS

Scrutton, R. A., and Manik Talwani, editors, *The Ocean Floor: Bruce C. Heezen Commemorative Volume,* Wiley, 1982.

OBITUARIES:

PERIODICALS

New York Times, June 23, 1977.
Time, July 4, 1977.

* * *

HELMHOLZ, R(ichard) H(enry) 1940-

PERSONAL: Born July 1, 1940, in Pasadena, Calif.; son of Lindsay (a professor) and Alice (Bean) Helmholz; married Marilyn Palmer, 1980. *Education:* Princeton University, A.B., 1962; Harvard University, LL.B., 1965; University of California, Berkeley, Ph.D., 1970. *Religion:* Episcopalian.

ADDRESSES: Home—1222 East 49th St., Chicago, Ill. 60615. *Office*—University of Chicago, Law School, 1111 East 60th St., Chicago, Ill. 60637.

CAREER: Washington University, School of Law, St. Louis, Mo., professor of law and history, 1970-81; University of Chicago, Law School, Chicago, Ill., professor of law, 1981—. Maitland lecturer, Cambridge University, 1987.

MEMBER: American Bar Association, American Society for Legal History, Selden Society (vice president, 1984—), University Club of Chicago, Reform Club (London).

AWARDS, HONORS: Guggenheim fellow, 1986.

WRITINGS:

Marriage Litigation in Medieval England, Cambridge University Press, 1974.
Select Cases on Defamation, Selden Society, 1985.
(Editor with Bernard J. Reams, Jr.) *Historical Writings in Law and Jurisprudence,* 2nd series, 23 volumes, W. S. Hein, 1986.
Canon Law and the Law of England, Hambledon Press, 1987.
Roman Canon Law in Reformation England, Cambridge University Press, in press.

Contributor to *Law Quarterly Review, American Journal of Legal History,* and other journals.

* * *

HELMI, Jack
See SANDS, Leo G(eorge)

HEMPHILL, Paul 1936-

PERSONAL: Born February 18, 1936, in Birmingham, Ala.; son of Paul (a truck driver) and Velma Rebecca (an employee of the U.S. Government; maiden name, Nelson) Hemphill; married Susan Milliage Olive, September 23, 1961 (divorced, 1975); married Susan Farran Percy (a writer and editor for *Atlanta*), November 6, 1976; children: (first marriage) Lisa, David, Molly; (second marriage) Martha. *Education:* Auburn University, B.A., 1959.

ADDRESSES: Home—1353 Fama Dr. N.E., Atlanta, Ga. 30329. *Agent*—Sterling Lord Literistic, Inc., One Madison Ave., New York, N.Y. 10010.

CAREER: Sportswriter for newspapers in Birmingham, Ala., Augusta, Ga., and Tampa, Fla., 1958-64; *Atlanta Journal,* Atlanta, Ga., columnist, 1964-69; free-lance writer, 1969—. Writer in residence, Brenau College, 1984—. Visiting lecturer at University of Georgia, fall, 1973; instructor in journalism at Florida A & M University, beginning 1975. Commentator on "All Things Considered" radio show; guest on "Today" and "McNeill-Lehrer Report" television shows. *Military service:* Alabama Air National Guard, active duty, 1961-62; served in France.

AWARDS, HONORS: Nieman fellow at Harvard University, 1968-69; literary achievement award from Georgia Writers Association, 1970, for *The Nashville Sound: Bright Lights and Country Music.*

WRITINGS:

The Nashville Sound: Bright Lights and Country Music, Simon & Schuster, 1970.
(Ghostwriter) Ivan Allen, Jr., *Mayor: Notes on the Sixties* (autobiography), Simon & Schuster, 1971.
The Good Old Boys (collection of Hemphill's newspaper columns), Simon & Schuster, 1974.
Long Gone: A Novel, Viking, 1979.
Too Old to Cry (collection of Hemphill's newspaper columns), Viking, 1981.
The Sixkiller Chronicles (novel), Macmillan, 1985.
Me and the Boy: Journey of Discovery—Father and Son on the Appalachian Trail (autobiographical), Macmillan, 1986.

Author of columns appearing in *San Francisco Examiner, Baltimore Sun, USA Today, Atlanta Constitution, Sport,* and *Country Music.* Contributor to periodicals, including *Life, Playboy, Cosmopolitan, Mademoiselle, Atlantic, New York Times Magazine, True, Sports Illustrated, Southern,* and *TV Guide.* Senior editor, *Atlanta* (magazine), 1980.

WORK IN PROGRESS: King of the Road, a novel for Houghton.

SIDELIGHTS: In his life and in his writing, Paul Hemphill is committed to the South. Upon reviewing Hemphill's complete body of work in an essay for the *Dictionary of Literary Biography Yearbook: 1987,* Stephen Whited finds that Hemphill "has consistently produced some of the most carefully pictured views of southern American life." Although Hemphill moved west at one point in his life, he is back in the midst of the foothills he calls home: "Yes, right here on this dinky little old street that hardly anybody in Atlanta knows about, I have found it. I'm home," Hemphill told a *Goodlife* interviewer.

As both a journalist and a fiction author, Hemphill's writings have emerged from the Southern experience. His first book, *The Nashville Sound: Bright Lights and Country Music,* is a journalistic overview of the rise to popularity of country and western music. Christopher Lehmann-Haupt of the *New York Times* writes that Hemphill describes this phenomenon "delightfully, by mixing together history and spot interviews and on-the-scene reportage in a book that reads as smoothly and sparklingly as a bluegrass breakdown." Craig McGregor similarly comments on the book in his *New York Times Book Review* article: "Hemphill describes the scene in a racy, impressionistic style, mixing profiles of singers . . . with on-the-spot accounts of Friday night at Tootsie's Orchid Lounge, Saturday night at the Grand Ole Opry and several nights on the road with Bill Anderson and the Po' Boys. . . . His book is like a huge pop star collage." Even so, Whited maintains that *The Nashville Sound* is "more than a collection of star biographies. Hemphill gives the reader an understanding of how the country music business is run, what it had to overcome, who (Chet Atkins) make it what it is today, when it all got started, and where it all came from."

In a later autobiographical work called *Me and the Boy: Journey of Discovery—Father and Son on the Appalachian Trail,* Hemphill presents his rendering of the several hundred-mile hike through southern Appalachia that he and his son undertook. The purpose of the journey was for Hemphill to amend his relationship with the nineteen-year-old David, whom he had abandoned almost ten years earlier because of divorce. The two set out to walk the entire 2,100 miles of the Appalachian Trail, from Georgia to Maine, but were beset with problems from the start. As Dennis Drabelle in the *Washington Post Book World* records: "In some ways the hike was a fiasco. Paul's knees gave out early and often, David sulked and usually hiked miles ahead of his father, and they covered only about a fourth of the total mileage," not to mention the fact that Hemphill's drinking developed a strain between the two. However, as both Drabelle and Chicago *Tribune Books* reviewer Paul Perry explain, what arises between father and son during the latter part of the journey and book is a "greater understanding of each other and a sort of acceptance that, in an imperfect world, we have no reason to expect perfection from one another," writes Perry. Whited views the eventual reconciliation between father and son as the re-establishment of "the bond between generations, between Hemphill and his son, between Hemphill and his father, between Hemphill and his heritage."

Southern heritage is the focal point of Hemphill's novel *The Sixkiller Chronicles,* as well. Whereas *Los Angeles Times* reviewer Frank Levering is of the opinion that literature often reduces Southern culture to stereotypes and one-dimensionality, he claims "Hemphill [in *The Sixkiller Chronicles*] doesn't spit on the region; in a sympathetic, folksy narrative that harbors supremely good intentions, Hemphill has grasped many of the essentials and much of the cussed complication of this elusive, contemporary culture." Accordingly, Hemphill takes the reader into the lives of three generations of the Clay family as they venture out from the mountains of their heritage in Sixkiller Gap and then return. Although Levering feels Hemphill has not succeeded in actually conveying specificity of place, he nevertheless feels "the central drama of a man trying to raise his son, preserve his land, express his values . . . and ensure their continuity in succeeding generations remains as potent as good corn liquor." In turn, critic Bruce Cook for the *Detroit News* charges that "the people in [*The Sixkiller Chronicles*] breathe life and whoop and holler just like real people. You want to spend more time with them, know all about them, discover what they have been up to in the years [Hemphill] leaves unchronicled. . . . Hemphill is growing stronger with each novel he writes. One or two books down the line he may well emerge as the next truly important Southern novelist."

BIOGRAPHICAL/CRITICAL SOURCES:

BOOKS

Dictionary of Literary Biography Yearbook: 1987, Gale, 1988.

PERIODICALS

Chicago Tribune Book World, October 7, 1979, May 11, 1986.
Detroit News, July 7, 1985.
Goodlife, June-July, 1985.
Los Angeles Times, September 18, 1985.
Miami Herald, November 30, 1975.
New Republic, June 27, 1970.
Newsweek, August 20, 1979.
New York Review of Books, November 4, 1971.
New York Times, April 27, 1970, January 26, 1981.
New York Times Book Review, July 19, 1970, September 22, 1974, January 18, 1981.
Washington Post, August 27, 1979, February 14, 1981, April 20, 1986.
Washington Post Book World, April 7, 1985.

* * *

HENDERSON, Sylvia
See ASHTON-WARNER, Sylvia (Constance)

* * *

HENKES, Robert 1922-

PERSONAL: Born October 28, 1922, in Kalamazoo, Mich.; son of Peter John (a policeman) and Veronica (Itsenhuiser) Henkes; married Frances Malerney, April 21, 1956; children: Catherine, Anne, Susan, Jane. *Education:* Drake University, B.F.A., 1948; University of Wisconsin, M.A., 1950; attended summer painting workshops at University of Michigan, 1955, and Michigan State University, 1956. *Religion:* Roman Catholic.

ADDRESSES: Home—1124 Bretton Dr., Kalamazoo, Mich. 49007. *Office*—Department of Art, Kalamazoo Institute of Arts, Kalamazoo, Mich. 49001.

CAREER: Kalamazoo Institute of Arts, Kalamazoo, Mich., instructor in painting, 1954—; Nazareth College, Kalamazoo, professor of art, 1966-72. Instructor in art, Barbour Hall Boys School, Kalamazoo, 1968—; director of community art education workshops for children and painting instructor at Adult Community Center, Kalamazoo. Has had one-man shows in Des Moines, Milwaukee, Racine, Wis., and at Nazareth College, Kalamazoo College, Western Michigan University, and Luther College.

MEMBER: National Art Education Association, Western Arts Association, Michigan Art Education Association, Kalamazoo Council of the Arts, Delta Phi Delta.

AWARDS, HONORS: Awards for painting from South Bend Art Association, Grand Rapids Art Association, Detroit Artists, and Kalamazoo Institute of Arts.

WRITINGS:

Orientation to Drawing and Painting, International Textbook, 1965.

Notes on Art and Art Education, MSS Educational Publishing, 1969.

Eight American Women Painters, Gordon Press, 1977.

(Contributor) *Great Men,* Dial, 1978.
The Crucifixion in American Painting, Gordon Press, 1979.
Insights in Art and Education, Gordon Press, 1979.
300 Lessons in Art, J. Weston Walch, 1980.
American Art Activity Book, J. Weston Walch, 1982.
Sport in Art, Prentice Hall, 1986.
New Vision in Art, International University Press, 1989.

FILMSTRIPS

Open Your Eyes to Art, J. Weston Walch, 1981.
Twentieth Century American Painting, J. Weston Walch, 1983.
Hispanic Art, J. Weston Walch, 1984.

OTHER

Contributor of more than two hundred articles to art and education journals.

WORK IN PROGRESS: Ten American Humanist Painters; Painting Styles; Drawing in the Junior High School; The Clown in American Art; Ten American Religious Painters; The Art Experience; The Crucifixion; Christ in Art; Spirituality of Abraham Rattner; Community Art Projects; Ten American Women Artists of the Depression; Art of Drawing; Art Activities Around the Calendar.

SIDELIGHTS: Robert Henkes told *CA:* "Writing is essential to teaching and painting as the latter are essential to my writing. Successful teaching only reaches a small segment of society while the printed word reaches thousands in a single moment. Aside from contribution, work manipulation arouses the aesthetic experience. It is quite similar to composing a painting. Words can change man's spiritual condition as much as the color images of a canvas. My interest in art and sports led to the publication of *Sport in Art.* Other works centered upon my religious background have produced *The Spirituality of Abraham Rattner, Christ in Art,* and *Crucifixion.*

"Correspondence with contemporary artists has been a great research technique for my writing and has led to memorable friendships. My writing day includes the reading of art and religious books and periodicals. I have been influenced by such writers as Thomas Merton and Fulton Sheen, and have been named as a religious writer by American painters, Umberto Romano and Abraham Rattner. I continue to paint religious themes which affect the tone of some of my writing."

AVOCATIONAL INTERESTS: Track (member of national collegiate cross-country championship team, 1944-45), collecting antique glass, collecting original etchings and lithographs by American artists of the Depression decade.

* * *

HEPBURN, James Gordon 1922-

PERSONAL: Born December 13, 1922, in Montgomeryville, Pa.; son of William Wallace and Ethel Remington (Morton) Hepburn; married Margaret Mary Doorey, December 29, 1947; children: James. *Education:* Yale University, B.A., 1944; University of Pennsylvania, M.A., 1949, Ph.D., 1957.

ADDRESSES: Home—Smoke Tree Cottage, Amberly, Arundel, Sussex, England.

CAREER: Lafayette College, Easton, Pa., instructor in English, 1952-54; Cornell University, Ithaca, N.Y., instructor in English, 1957-61; University of Rhode Island, Kingston, assistant professor, 1961-64, associate professor of English, 1965-67; University of Leicester, Leicester, England, research fellow in English, 1969-72; Bates College, Lewiston, Me., Dana Professor of English and head of department, 1972-88. *Military service:* U.S. Army, 1944-46.

WRITINGS:

(Editor with Robert A. Greenberg) *Robert Frost: An Introduction,* Holt, 1961.
(Editor with Greenberg) *Modern Essays: A Rhetorical Approach,* Macmillan, 1962, 2nd edition, 1968.
The Art of Arnold Bennett, Indiana University Press, 1963.
College Composition: Rhetoric, Grammar, Research, Macmillan, 1964.
Poetic Design: Handbook and Anthology, Macmillan, 1966.
(Editor) *Letters of Arnold Bennett,* Oxford University Press, Volume 1, 1966, Volume 2: *1889-1915,* 1968, Volume 3: *1916-1931,* 1970, Volume 4: *Family Letters,* 1986.
The Author's Empty Purse and the Rise of the Literary Agent, Oxford University Press, 1968.
Confessions of an American Scholar, University of Minnesota Press, 1971.
My Fierce Tiger (juvenile), Platt, 1971.
(Editor) Edmund Gosse, *Father and Son,* Oxford University Press, 1974.
(Editor) *Sketches for Autobiography,* Allen & Unwin, 1980.
Arnold Bennett, the Critical Heritage, Routledge & Kegan Paul, 1981.
Critic into Anti-Critic, Camden House, 1984.

PLAYS; ALL FIRST PRODUCED IN EALING, ENGLAND, AT QUESTORS THEATRE

"Poor Dumb Animals" (three-act), June, 1971.
"Time, Life, Sex, and You Know What" (three-act), June, 1972.
"Magic 'n Tragic" (two-act), June, 1975.
"Deaf, Dumb, and Blind" (two-act), June, 1975.
"Moonship Moonshot" (three-act), May, 1977.
"Men and Women" (three-act), October, 1984.

BIOGRAPHICAL/CRITICAL SOURCES:

PERIODICALS

New Statesman, January 24, 1969.
Observer Review, May 24, 1970.
Punch, July 3, 1968.
Times Literary Supplement, May 2, 1980, March 13, 1981, July 31, 1987.

* * *

HEPPENSTALL, (John) Rayner 1911-1981

PERSONAL: Born July 27, 1911, in Huddlesfield, Yorkshire, England; died May 23, 1981, shortly after a stroke in Kent, England; son of Edgar and Lizzie (Rayner) Heppenstall; married Margaret Harwood Edwards, 1937; children: Lindy Foord, Adam Justinian. *Education:* University of Leeds, B.A., 1933; graduate study, University of Strasbourg.

ADDRESSES: Home—Coach Cottage, 2 Gilford Rd., Deal, Kent, England.

CAREER: Schoolmaster, 1934; free-lance writer, 1935-39; British Broadcasting Corp., London, England, feature writer and producer, 1945-65, drama producer, 1965-67. *Military service:* British Army, Royal Artillery and Royal Army Pay Corps, 1940-45; released on psychiatric grounds.

AWARDS, HONORS: Arts Council Prize, 1966, for *The Blaze of Noon.*

WRITINGS:

POEMS

Patins, privately printed, 1931.
First Poems, Heinemann, 1935.
Sebastian, Dent, 1937.
Blind Men's Flowers Are Green, Secker & Warburg, 1940.
Poems, 1933-45, Secker & Warburg, 1945.

NOVELS

The Blaze of Noon, with foreword by Elizabeth Bowen, Secker & Warburg, 1939, Alliance, 1940, reprinted, Secker & Warburg, 1980.
Saturnine (also see below), Secker & Warburg, 1943.
The Lesser Infortune (also see below), J. Cape, 1953.
The Greater Infortune (includes most of *Saturnine* and the last chapter of *The Lesser Infortune*), P. Owen, 1960, New Directions, 1961.
The Connecting Door, Barrie & Rockliff, 1962, Dufour, 1968.
The Woodshed, J. Calder, 1962.
The Shearers, Hamish Hamilton, 1969.
Two Moons, Allison & Busby, 1977.
The Pier, Allison & Busby, 1986.

NONFICTION

Middleton Murry: A Study in Excellent Normality, J. Cape, 1934.
Apology for Dancing, Faber, 1936.
(Editor and author of introduction) Guido de Ruggierio, *Existentialism,* Secker & Warburg, 1946, Social Sciences, 1948.
The Double Image: Mutations of Christian Mythology in the Works of Four French Catholic Writers of Today and Yesterday, Secker & Warburg, 1947, reprinted, R. West, 1973.
(Editor and author of introduction) *Imaginary Conversations,* Secker & Warburg, 1948.
(With J. I. M. Stewart) *Three Tales of Hamlet,* Gollancz, 1949.
Leon Bloy, Bowes, 1954.
(Translator and author of introduction) F. Cali and others, *Architecture and Truth,* Thames and Hudson, 1957.
Four Absentees: Eric Gill, George Orwell, Dylan Thomas and J. Middleton Murry, (memoirs), Barrie & Rockliff, 1960, reprinted, Arden Library, 1979.
The Fourfold Tradition: Notes on the French and English Literatures, with Some Ethnic and Historical Asides, New Directions, 1961.
(Translator) Chateaubriand, *Atala* [and] *Rene,* Oxford University Press, 1963.
(Author of introduction) Claude Prosper Jolyot de Crebillion, *The Wayward Head and Heart,* Oxford University Press, 1963.
The Intellectual Part (autobiography), Barrie & Rockliff, 1964.
Raymond Roussel: A Critical Guide, J. Calder, 1966, University of California Press, 1967.
(Translator with daughter, Lindy Foord) Raymond Roussel, *Impressions of Africa,* J. Calder, 1966, reprinted, Riverrun Press, 1984.
Portrait of the Artist as a Professional Man, P. Owen, 1969.
A Little Pattern of French Crime, Hamish Hamilton, 1969.
(Translator) Honore De Balzac, *A Harlot High and Low,* Penguin, 1970.
French Crime in the Romantic Age, Hamish Hamilton, 1970.
(Editor and translator) Rene Floriot, *When Justice Falters,* Harrap, 1972.
Bluebeard and After: Three Decades of Murder in France, P. Owen, 1972.
The Sex War and Others: Survey of Recent Murder Principally in France, P. Owen, 1973.
Reflections on the Newgate Calendar, W. H. Allen, 1975.
The Master Eccentric: The Journals of Rayner Heppenstall, 1969-1981, edited by Jonathan Goodman, Allison & Busby, 1986, Schocken, 1987.

OTHER

Also author of plays, including "A Clean Break" and "Daily Bread," both adapted from plays of Jules Renard, 1969, and radio plays, including "The Death of the Prophet," "The Rising in the North," "The Battle for St. David's," "The Green Bay Tree" (adapted from novel by Paul Desjardins), "The Generations," "Renard," "The Literate Killer," "Vaurin" (adapted from Balzac), "The General's Daughter," "A Pretty Liar," "Dr. Satan," "A Tidy Little Man," "The Case of Eugene Weidmann," and "The Murder of Jean Jaures." Author of television plays, "The Seventh Juror," 1972, and "The Bells," 1974. Contributor of feature articles to *Times Literary Supplement* and other periodicals.

SIDELIGHTS: Rayner Heppenstall was a radio producer for the British Broadcasting Corp., a composer, conversationalist, poet, and specialist on French literature. He was also a distinguished novelist, critic and criminal historian whose work was neglected largely because his writing techniques and critical stances were seen as "highly eccentric," a London *Times* writer reports. According to a *Times Literary Supplement* reviewer, the autobiography *Portrait of the Artist as a Professional Man* reveals a man "wilfully opposed to received opinion, amusing, catty, often witty, sometimes perceptive, and always obstinately his own man and courageous in defence of his eccentricities."

Critical reaction to his works in all genre was sharply divided. For example, *Observer Review* contributor Maurice Richardson called *A Little Pattern of French Crime* "a distinctly original crime study written with zest and a minimum of cliche, quite different from the average rehash." In contrast, Richard Cobb of the *Listener* called it "slightly disturbing and vaguely distasteful" for presenting "murder as if it were some sort of parlour game." Richard Wittington-Egan's comment in *Books and Bookmen* offered a mixed assessment, saying that it was "frankly belletristic" yet "irresistable, even to those who are not normally addicted to . . . 'true life crime.' "

Heppenstall's characteristically unconventional critical studies of French literature were also admired. At various times "outrageously and . . . charmingly original," according to a *New Yorker* reviewer, Heppenstall's *The Fourfold Tradition: Notes on the French and English Literatures, with Some Ethnological and Historical Asides,* struck some reviewers as a subjective and perhaps intentionally playful commentary. V. S. Pritchett, writing in the *New Statesman,* saw in the collection of essays the critic's central concern: "He is, I think, excessively concerned with literary manoeuvres. . . . He is always on the lookout for intrigue and manipulation. . . . The attractive things in Mr Heppenstall are his bursts of gaiety, his intelligence, his edge and his pleasure in literature, especially in language."

Heppenstall's most important contribution as a critic was his studies of French novelist Raymond Roussel. The *Times* writer reported that Heppenstall was "one of the few English critics to have seen the joke in the jokes of *Raymond Roussel,*" a writer who made novels out of complex word games. George Steiner remarked in the *New Yorker,* "[Heppenstall] is seeking to give Roussel a wider echo. . . . Winks at 'my fellow Rousselians' abound, and the transcription of French . . . is not always accurate. Nevertheless, these irritants would be trivial if we owed to Mr. Heppenstall's enthusiasm the rediscovery of a body of major work."

Heppenstall's talents were best suited to fiction, suggests the *Times* writer. In eight novels written over a forty-year period Heppenstall emerges "as an original and skillful writer, rather more adventurous than most of his contemporaries" whose experiments with fiction generally distanced him from the appreciation of critics. His first novel *The Blaze of Noon* drew a number of negative reviews, but won an Arts Council Award for a neglected major work nearly thirty years after it was published.

Heppenstall's awareness that cinema and television had in some ways taken the place of realistic fiction led him to write narratives that turned the writer's eye inward. Making the narrator of *The Blaze of Noon* a blind man allowed the author to present this "fresh approach to ordinary experience" with "absolute consistency and vividness. It is a remarkable achievement," stated *Spectator* reviewer Derek Verschoye. Charles Marriott of the *Manchester Guardian* commented, "Out of a simple story, [Heppenstall] has raised innumerable questions about human nature, and it may well be, as Miss [Elizabeth] Bowen says in her foreword, that 'The Blaze of Noon' is the beginning of something new in fiction." Later novels kept their focus on the writer's inner life by incorporating self-expressions and attending to the structure of the narrative, the method of storytelling, and the process of working with language. The *Times* reviewer concludes that because Heppenstall "thoroughly absorbed French modernism," he "will perhaps be seen to have made a notable contribution to the history of the modern novel in Britain."

AVOCATIONAL INTERESTS: Public affairs, music.

BIOGRAPHICAL/CRITICAL SOURCES:

BOOKS

Contemporary Literary Criticism, Volume 10, Gale, 1979.
Heppenstall, Rayner, *Four Absentees: Eric Gill, George Orwell, Dylan Thomas, and J. Middleton Murry,* Barrie & Rockliff, 1960.
Heppenstall, Rayner, *The Intellectual Part,* Barrie & Rockliff, 1964.
Heppenstall, Rayner, *Portrait of the Artist as a Professional Man,* P. Owen, 1969.

PERIODICALS

Books Abroad, Autumn, 1967.
Books and Bookmen, September, 1969.
Listener, March 12, 1970.
Manchester Guardian, November 28, 1939.
New Republic, December 4, 1961.
New Statesman, April 7, 1961.
New Yorker, December 2, 1961, October 28, 1967.
New York Times, May 19, 1940, August 8, 1954.
New York Times Book Review, October 29, 1967.
Observer Review, July 19, 1970.
Saturday Review, May 25, 1940.
Spectator, December 15, 1939, March 24, 1961.
Time, April 22, 1940.
Times (London), December 4, 1986.
Times Literary Supplement, March 31, 1966, November 24, 1966, July 24, 1969, July 31, 1969, June 3, 1977, February 13, 1981.
Yale Review, March, 1962.

OBITUARIES:

PERIODICALS

Times (London), May 25, 1981.*

* * *

HERBERT, Cecil
See HAMILTON, Charles (Harold St. John)

* * *

HERMAN, Donald L. 1928-

PERSONAL: Born October 13, 1928, in New York. *Education:* University of Michigan, B.A., 1950, Ph.D., 1964; Wayne State University, M.A., 1958.

ADDRESSES: Office—Suite 407, Waters Bldg., Grand Rapids, Mich. 49503.

CAREER: Grand Valley State College, Allendale, Mich., professor of political science and director of Latin American Studies Program until 1981; Michigan State University, East Lansing, adjunct professor of political science and in the Center for Latin American and Caribbean Studies, 1981—.

WRITINGS:

(Editor and contributor) *The Communist Tide in Latin America,* University of Texas Press, 1973.
The Comintern in Mexico, Public Affairs Press, 1974.
Christian Democracy in Venezuela, University of North Carolina Press, 1980.
(Contributor) Howard R. Penniman, editor, *Venezuela at the Polls: The Election of 1978,* American Enterprise Institute (Washington, D.C.), 1981.
The Latin American Community of Israel, Praeger, 1984.
(Contributor) John D. Martz and David J. Myers, editors, *Venezuela: The Democratic Experience,* Praeger, 1986.
(Contributor) *The World Votes,* American Enterprise Institute, 1986.
(Editor and contributor) *Democracy in Latin America: Colombia and Venezuela,* Praeger, 1988.

Contributor to *Hoover Institution's 1980 Yearbook on International Communist Affairs.*

WORK IN PROGRESS: U.S. Military Intervention and Democracy in Latin America: The Dominican Republic and Grenada.

* * *

HERRON, Don 1952-

PERSONAL: Born January 22, 1952, in Detroit, Mich.; son of Huston and Jimmie Louise (Ray) Herron. *Education:* Attended Middle Tennessee State University, 1970-73.

ADDRESSES: Home—Box 982, Glen Ellen, Calif. 95442.

CAREER: Dashiell Hammett Tour and Literary Walks, San Francisco, Calif., owner and operator, 1977—; Underwood/Miller Publishers, San Francisco, editor, 1988—.

WRITINGS:

Echoes from the Vaults of Yoh-Vombis (biography), privately printed, 1976.
Dashiell Hammett Tour, privately printed, 1979, new edition, 1984.
(Contributor) Tim Underwood and Chuck Miller, editors, *Fear Itself: The Horror Fiction of Stephen King,* Underwood/Miller, 1982.

(Editor) *The Dark Barbarian: The Writings of Robert E. Howard,* Greenwood Press, 1984.
The Literary World of San Francisco and Its Environs, City Lights, 1985.
(Contributor) Underwood and Miller, editors, *Kingdom of Fear: The World of Stephen King,* Underwood/Miller, 1986.
(Contributor) Jack Sullivan, editor, *The Penguin Encyclopedia of Horror and the Supernatural,* Viking, 1986.
(Contributor of bibliography) Charles Willeford, *Everybody's Metamorphosis,* Dennis McMillan, 1988.
(Editor) *Reign of Fear: Fiction and Film of Stephen King,* Underwood/Miller, 1988.

WORK IN PROGRESS: Editing *The Selected Letters of Philip K. Dick,* for Underwood/Miller.

BIOGRAPHICAL/CRITICAL SOURCES:

PERIODICALS

Choice, January, 1985.
Los Angeles Times Calendar, September 26, 1982.
New York Times, October 23, 1981.
Wall Street Journal, December 1, 1982.
Washington Post, January 29, 1989.

* * *

HIGGINS, Dick
See HIGGINS, Richard C(arter)

* * *

HIGGINS, Richard C(arter) 1938-
(Dick Higgins)

PERSONAL: Born March 15, 1938, in Cambridge, England; son of Carter Chapin Higgins (a steel manufacturer) and Katharine (Bigelow) Higgins Doman; married Alison Knowles (a silk screen technician and artist), May 31, 1960 (divorced, 1970; remarried, 1984); children: Hannah and Jessica (twins). *Education:* Attended Yale University, 1955-57; studied music with John Cage, Henry Cowell, and others, 1957-59; Columbia University, B.S., 1960; Manhattan School of Printing, C.P.O. certificate, 1961; New York University, M.A., 1977. *Politics:* Progressive Republican.

ADDRESSES: Home—P.O. Box 27, Station Hill Rd., Barrytown, N.Y. 12507-0027.

CAREER: Writer, publisher, graphics designer. Zaccar Offset (printers), New York City, cameraman, 1963; Book Press, New York City, technician and member of production staff, 1963-64; Russell & Russell (publishers), New York City, member of production staff, beginning 1964; Something Else Press, New York City, founder, designer, and U.S. manager, 1964-73; Printed Editions (formerly Unpublished Editions), New York City, founder, 1973-85. Visiting Clark Professor in Art, Williams College, autumn, 1987. Instructor in publishing, California Institute of the Arts, 1970-71; fellow of Center for Twentieth-Century Studies, University of Wisconsin—Milwaukee, 1977; member of literature panel, New York State Council on the Arts, 1979-81; research associate, State University of New York at Purchase, 1983—; lecturer. Operator of Something Else Gallery, 1966-69; has had one-man shows, in a number of media, in the the United States, Canada, Brazil, Argentina, Germany, Sweden, Iceland, and Italy; has participated in many other shows, festivals, and exhibitions in the United States and abroad.

MEMBER: Modern Language Association, Renaissance Society, Film Makers' Co-op, New York Audio-Visual Society (cofounder; vice-president), Broadway Opera Company.

AWARDS, HONORS: New York State Council on the Arts grant, 1968; Deutscher Akademischer Austauschdienst grants to Berlin, 1975, 1981-82; State University of New York at Purchase foundation grant, 1984-86.

WRITINGS:

What Are Legends (essay), Bern Porter, 1960.
Jefferson's Birthday (plays) [and] *Postface* (essay; also see below), Something Else Press, 1964.
A Book about Love and War and Death, Canto 1, Something Else Press, 1965, Cantos 2 and 3, Nova Broadcast Press, 1969, Cantos 1-3, Something Else Press, 1972.
Towards the 1970s, Abyss Publications, 1969.
foew&ombwhnw: A Grammar of the Mind and a Phenomenology of Love and a Science of the Arts as Seen by a Stalker of the Wild Mushroom, Something Else Press, 1969.
(Editor with Wolf Vostell) *Pop Architektur,* Droste Verlag (Duesseldorf), 1969, translation published as *Fantastic Architecture,* Something Else Press, 1971.
Die fabelhafte Getraeume von Taifun-Willi, Reflexion Press (Stuttgart), 1969, Abyss Publications, 1970.
Computers for the Arts, Abyss Publications, 1970.
Amigo, Unpublished Editions, 1972.
The Ladder to the Moon, Unpublished Editions, 1973.
For Eugene in Germany, Unpublished Editions, 1973.
Le Petit Cirque au Fin du Monde: Un Opera Arabasque, Aarevue/Aafondation (Liege, Belgium), 1973.
Spring Game, Unpublished Editions, 1973.
City with All the Angles, Unpublished Editions, 1974.
Modular Poems, Unpublished Editions, 1975.
Classic Plays, Unpublished Editions, 1976.
Legends and Fishnets, Unpublished Editions, 1976.
Cat Alley, Tuumba Press, 1976.
The Epitaphs, Studio Morra (Naples), 1977.
Everyone Has Sher Favorite (His or Hers), Unpublished Editions, 1977.
George Herbert's Pattern Poems: In Their Tradition, Unpublished Editions, 1977.
The Epickall Quest of the Brothers Dichtung and Other Outrages, Unpublished Editions, 1977.
A Dialectic of Centuries: Notes towards a Theory of the New Arts, Printed Editions, 1978, 2nd edition, 1979.
(Translator) Novalis, *Hymns to the Night,* Treacle Press, 1978, bilingual 2nd edition, McPherson, 1984.
Some Recent Snowflakes (and Other Things), Printed Editions, 1979.
Of Celebration of Morning, Printed Editions, 1980.
Ten Ways of Looking at a Bird, Printed Editions, 1981.
(Author of introduction) Venantius Fortunatus, *A Basket of Cherries,* Cherry Valley, 1981.
Twenty-six Mountains for Viewing the Sunset From, Printed Editions, 1981.
1959/60, Edizioni Francesco Conz (Verona, Italy), 1982.
Selected Early Works, Galerie Ars Viva, 1982.
Horizons: The Poetics and Theory of the Intermedia, Southern Illinois University Press, 1983.
Intermedia, Akademia Ruchu (Warsaw), 1985.
Poems: Plain and Fancy, Station Hill, 1986.
Czternascie tlumaczen telefonicznych dla Steve'a McCaffery (title means "Fourteen Telephone Translations for Steve McCaffery"), edited by Piotr Rypson, WitrynArtystow (Klodzko, Poland), 1987.

Fluxus: Theory and Reception, Inkblot, 1987.
Five Hear-Plays, Inkblot, 1987.
Pattern Poetry: Guide to an Unknown Literature, State University of New York Press, 1988.

MUSICAL COMPOSITIONS

Graphis 144: "Wipeout for Orchestra" [and] *Graphis 143: "Softly for Orchestra,"* Something Else Press, 1967.
Suggested by Small Swallows, Dorn Editions, 1973.
Emmett Williams's Ear, Pari & Dispari (Italy), 1978.
Piano Album: Short Pieces, 1962-1984, Printed Editions, 1980.
Sonata for Prepared Piano, Printed Editions, 1981.
Variations on a Natural Theme: For Orchestra, Printed Editions, 1981.
Sonata No. 2 for Piano, Printed Editions, 1983.
Song for Any Voice(s) and Instrument(s), Printed Editions, 1983.

Also author of "Stacked Deck," the first electronic opera, with music by Richard Maxfield, 1958. Also composer of music for records, reel-to-reel tapes, and cassettes.

CONTRIBUTOR

Fred McDarrah, editor, *The Beat Scene,* Corinth Books, 1959.
La Monte Young, editor, *An Anthology,* La Monte Young & Jackson Mac Low, 1963, 2nd edition, Heiner Friedrich Gallery, 1970.
Vostell and Juergen Becker, editors, *Happenings,* Rowohlt Verlag (Hamburg), 1966.
Richard Kostelanetz, editor, *The Young American Writers,* Funk, 1967.
Eugene Wildman, editor, *An Anthology of Concretism,* Swallow Press, 1968.
Mary Ellen Solt, editor, *Concrete Poetry: A World View,* Indiana University Press, 1968.
Jean-Francois Bory, editor, *Once Again,* New Directions, 1968.
Andre Balthazar and Pol Bory, editors, *Qui Who Etes Are Vous You?,* Daily Bul (Brussels), 1968.
Jean-Jacques Lebel, editor, *El Happening,* Ediciones Nueva Vision (Buenos Aires), 1968.
John Cage, editor, *Notations,* Something Else Press, 1969.
Dieter Roth, editor, *Anekdoten zu einer Topographie des Zufalls von Daniel Spoerri mit Emmett Williams,* Luchterhand Verlag (Neuwied, West Germany), 1969.
Kostelanetz, *John Cage,* Praeger, 1970.
Vostell, *Aktionen,* Rowohlt Verlag, 1970.
Dana Atchley, editor, *Space Atlas,* Ace Space Co. (Victoria, B.C.), 1971.
Jean-Marc Poinsot, editor, *Mailart Communications: A Distance Concept,* Editions Cedic (Paris), 1971.
Barry McCallion, *Prepare to Publish,* Aleatory Press, 1971.
David Mayor, editor, *Fluxshoe,* Beau Geste Press, 1972.
Kostelanetz, editor, *Breakthrough Fictioneers,* Something Else Press, 1973.
Rothenberg and George Quasha, editors, *America, a Prophecy: A New Reading of American Poetry from Pre-Columbian Times to the Present,* Random House, 1973.
Ronald Gross and others, editors, *Open Poetry: Four Anthologies of Expanded Poems,* Simon & Schuster, 1973.
Bill Henderson, editor, *The Publish-It-Yourself Handbook,* Pushcart, 1973, revised edition, 1979.
Bill Katz, editor, *Library Lit 4: The Best of 1973,* Scarecrow, 1974.
Jan Herman, editor, *Something Else Yearbook,* Something Else Press, 1974.
Milton Klonsky, editor, *Speaking Pictures,* Harmony Books, 1975.
Kostelanetz and Beth Learn, editors, *Language and Structure in North America,* Kensington Arts Association (Toronto), 1975.
Endre Tot, *Total Questions by Tot,* Edition Hundertmark (Berlin), 1976.
Kostelanetz, editor, *Essaying Essays,* Out of London Press, 1976.
Harry Smith, editor, *X-1,* The Smith, 1976.
Terry Reid, editor, *Mask Media Profile,* Sunnyland Press, 1976.
Arthur Daigon and Rita S. Weisskoff, editors, *Live and Learn,* Prentice-Hall, 1977.
Walter Zanini and Julio Plaza, editors, *Poeticas Visuais,* Museu de Arte Contemporanea da Universidade de Sao Paulo (Brazil), 1977.
Kostelanetz, editor, *Esthetics Contemporary,* Prometheus Books, 1978.
Sarenco, editor, *Poesia e Prosa della Avanguardia,* Museo del Castelvecchio (Verona), 1978.
Michael Gibbs, editor, *Deciphering America,* Contexts Publications (Amsterdam), 1978.
Gabor Toth, editor, *Reflections,* Onga Press (Budapest), 1978.
Steve McCaffery and B. P. Nichol, editors, *Sound Poetry: A Catalogue,* Underwhich Editions (Toronto), 1978.
Robert Filliou, *Six Fillious,* Membrane Press, 1978.
Michael Tarachow, *Fire and Immense Decorum,* Grand View, 1978.
Jonathan Greene, editor, *A Fiftieth Birthday Celebration for Jonathan Williams,* Truck/Gnomon, 1979.
James Laughlin, editor, *New Directions 38,* New Directions, 1979.
Carollee Schneemann, *More Than Meat Joy,* edited by Bruce McPherson, DocumenText, 1979.
Nichol, *Translating Translating Apollinaire,* Membrane Press, 1979.
Umberto Romano, editor, *Great Men,* Dial, 1979.
Sarenco, *In Support of Fine Arts,* Edizioni Factotum-Art (Verona), 1979.
A. A. Bronson and Peggy Gale, editors, *Performance by Artists,* Art Metropole (Toronto), 1979.
Milli Graffi, editor, *Readings in English,* C. P. Paravia (Torino, Italy), 1979.
Hugh Fox, editor, *Ilha do destere: "Poesia tambem e literatura,"* Universidade de Santa Caterina (Brazil), 1979.
Henri Chopin, *Poesie sonore internationale,* Jean-Michel Place (Paris), 1979.
Rene Block, editor, *Fuer Augen und Ohren,* Berliner Kunstakademie (Berlin), 1980.
Kostelanetz, editor, *Text-Sound Texts,* Morrow, 1980.
Luciano Caruso and others, editors, *Il golpo de glottide,* Valecchi (Florence, Italy), 1980.
Sarenco and others, editors, *Practice internazionale del libro d'artista,* Edizioni Factotum-Art, 1980.
Melody Sumner, editor, *1970-1979,* Burning Books, 1980.
Tom Beckett and Earl Meikerk, editors, *The Difficulties,* privately printed, 1980.
Kostelanetz and David Cole, editors, *Tenth Assembly,* Assembling Press, 1980.
Peter Van Beveren, editor, *The Archives,* Provincial Museum (Hasselt, Netherlands), 1981.
Roger Johnson, editor, *Scores,* Schirmer Books, 1981.
Kostelanetz, editor, *Scenarios,* Assembling Press, 1981.
Gregory Battcock, editor, *Breaking the Sound Barrier,* Dutton, 1981.
Michael Morris, *Pret-a-porter,* Ars Viva Edition (Berlin), 1982.
The Word and Beyond: Four Literary Cosmologists (contains *Paleface*), The Smith, 1982.

Daniele Lombardi, editor, *To Gather Together #10,* Multhipla (Milan, Italy), 1982.
Kostelanetz, *The Avant-Garde Tradition in Literature,* Prometheus Books, 1982.
Donald Hall, *Claims for Poetry,* University of Michigan Press, 1982.
Hermann Gabler, *Statistiche Fragmente,* AKI (Netherlands), 1982.
Lombardi, *Il rumor del tempo,* Centro Di (Florence), 1983.
Bruce Andrews and Charles Bernstein, editors, *The L-A-N-G-U-A-G-E Book,* Southern Illinois University Press, 1984.
Peter Frank, editor, *Re-dact 1,* Willis, Locker, & Owens, 1984.
Michel Crane and Mary Stoffler, editors, *Correspondence Art: Source Book for the Network of International Postal Art Activity,* Contemporary Arts Press, 1984.
Francoise Janicot, editor, *Poesie en action,* Edition Loques, 1984.
Nam June Paik, *Art and Satellite,* DAAD (Berlin), 1984.
Visuelle Poesie, Saarlaendischer Rundfunk (West Germany), 1984.
Barbara Haskell, *Blam,* Whitney Museum, 1984.
Rothenberg, *Technicians of the Sacred,* 2nd edition, University of California Press, 1985.
Joan Lyons, editor, *Artists' Books: A Critical Anthology and Sourcebook,* Peregrine Smith, 1985.
Barbara Moore, editor, *Cookpot,* Reflux Editions, 1985.
Stefano Mecatti, *Fone: La voce e la traccia,* la Casa Usher (Florence), 1985.
Jacques Donguy, *Une generation,* Henri Vegrier (Paris), 1985.
Fred Truck, *The Memory Bank,* Electronic Bank, 1986.
Matthew Hogan, editor, *Concrete Poetry: The Early Years,* Metropolitan Museum of Art, 1986.

OTHER

Translator, with Doria, of Giordano Bruno's *On the Composition of Images, Signs, and Ideas.* Also author of a number of films, including "A Tiny Movie," "The Flight of the Florence Bird," "The Flaming City," "Invocation of Canyons and Boulders for Stan Brakhage," "Plunk," "For the Dead," "Scenario," "Hank and Mary without Apologies," "Mysteries," and "Men and Women and Bells." Creator of graphics, "multiples," "postcards and miniatures," and "sound poems." Contributor to numerous periodicals, including *Chelsea Review, Arts in Society, Los Angeles Free Press, Panache, General Schmuck, West Coast Review, Performing Arts Journal,* and *Mouth of the Dragon.* U.S. editor of *Fluxus,* beginning 1961, and *De-collage,* 1962—; editor of *Something Else Newsletter,* 1964—.

SIDELIGHTS: Dick Higgins was one of the founders and early promoters of the "Happenings" movement, other noteworthy proponents being Allan Kaprow, who coined the term, Claes Oldenburg, Robert Whitman, and John Cage. "Happenings" are staged events that are intended to bring drama and reality as close together as possible. They have little formal structure: groups of participants assemble—on stages, in lofts, at galleries, on streetcorners, or in parking lots—and react to each other and to stimuli provided by the organizers of the Happening or by other persons or occurrences.

The object of a Happening is to affect participants and spectators on an unconscious rather than a rational level. They are not improvisations, since a good deal of the necessary stimulation—usually visual and oral—is planned and provided by the organizers, but, like improvisations, Happenings are meant to be single-performance phenomena; they are not usually recorded or preserved (although a number of them have been described in scholarly works).

Early Happenings were somewhat elitist events, consisting of a rather small group of participants and performed before small audiences. Eventually, however, the term Happening came to be applied to mass gatherings in which everyone present participated: "Love-ins" or "Be-ins."

In addition to being involved in the founding of the Fluxus movement, Higgins participated in Fluxus Festivals, 1962-64, which introduced the new art form to Europe.

BIOGRAPHICAL/CRITICAL SOURCES:

BOOKS

Frank, Peter, *Something Else Press,* DocumenText/McPherson, 1983.
Kostelanetz, Richard, *The End of Intelligent Writing,* Sheed, 1975.
Kostelanetz, Richard, *Metamorphosis in the Arts,* Assembling Press, 1980.
Kostelanetz, Richard, *Twenties in the Sixties,* Assembling Press, 1980.
Nyman, Michael, *Experimental Music: Cage and Beyond,* Studio Vista (London), 1974.
Sohm, Hanns, editor, *Happenings and Fluxus,* Koelner Kunstverein (Cologne), 1970.

PERIODICALS

Rolling Stone, April 27, 1972.
Times Literary Supplement, May 27-June 2, 1988.
Village Voice, August 17, 1967.
West Coast Poetry Review, Number 18, 1977.

* * *

HILL, Adrian Keith Graham 1895-1977

PERSONAL: Born March 24, 1895, in Charlton, Kent, England; died 1977; son of Graham Hill; married Dorothy Margaret Whitley; children: one son. *Education:* Attended Royal College of Art.

ADDRESSES: Home—Old Laundry Cottage, Midhurst, Sussex, England.

CAREER: Artist and writer. Life master and lecturer in anatomy, Westminster School of Art, 1935-38; external examiner for teachers certificate, University of Durham, 1938-39; appointed under the Pilgrim Trust grant to depict the changing face of Britain, 1940; art lecturer to Her Majesty's Forces, 1943-44; vice-president, St. James Art School, 1947; governor of Chichester School of Art, 1951-62, Midhurst Grammar School, 1957-67, and Federation of British Artists, beginning 1968. Presenter of the television program, "Sketch Club," British Broadcasting Corporation (BBC-TV), London, 1955-63. Works represented in Victoria and Albert Museum, Bradford Corporation Art Gallery, and various municipal galleries; held one-man exhibitions in 1938, 1940, 1961, 1964, 1966, and 1968. President, Royal Institute of Oil Painters. *Military service:* Honorable Artillery Company (HAC), 1914-19; became lieutenant; official War Artist.

MEMBER: British Association of Art Therapists (president, 1966), British Society of Aesthetics (founding member), Chichester Art Society (president, 1969), Midhurst Art Society (president, 1972), National League of Hospital Friends (vice-president, 1950), Ancient Monuments Society (vice-president, 1960).

AWARDS, HONORS: Awarded De Lasizo Silver and Bronze Medals by Royal Society of British Artists; Prix Catherine-Hadot from Academie Nationale de Medicine, 1947.

WRITINGS:

On Drawing Trees, Pitman, 1936, revised edition, 1957.
On the Mastery of Water Colour Painting, Pitman, 1939, new edition, 1961.
Art Versus Illness: A Story of Art Therapy, foreword by Geoffrey Marshall, Allen & Unwin, 1945.
On Drawing and Painting Trees, Pitman, 1947, revised edition, 1957, abridged edition, 1964, published as *Drawing and Painting Trees,* Blandford, 1977.
Trees Have Names, Faber, 1949.
A Book of Trees, Faber, 1951.
Painting Out Illness, Williams & Norgate, 1951.
The Pleasures of Painting: With Practical Demonstrations, Pitman, 1953.
Adventures in Line and Tone, Allen & Unwin, 1955.
What Shall We Draw?, Blandford, 1957, Emerson, 1959, reprinted, Sterling, 1986.
(And illustrator) *The Beginner's Book of Oil Painting,* Blandford, 1958, Emerson, 1959, reprinted, Sterling, 1986.
The Beginner's Book of Watercolour Painting, Emerson, 1959, reprinted, Sterling, 1986.
Painting as a Hobby, Stanley Paul, 1959.
(And illustrator) *Knowing and Drawing Trees,* Faber, 1960, 2nd edition, Blandford, 1969.
(And illustrator) *Sketching and Painting Indoors,* Pitman, 1961.
Sketching and Painting Out of Doors, Pitman, 1961.
Countryside, Longacre, 1961.
Adventures in Painting with Adrian Hill and BBC Television 'Sketch Club,' Blandford, 1962.
The Beginners' Book of Basic Anatomy, Reinhold, 1962 (published in England as *The Studio Handbook of Basic Anatomy,* Studio Books, 1962).
(And illustrator) *Faces and Figures,* Blandford, 1962.
How to Draw, Pan Books, 1963, published as *You Can Draw,* Hart, 1966.
The Handbook of Learning to Draw, Barker, 1964.
(And illustrator) *How to Paint Landscapes and Seascapes,* Blandford, 1964.
The Beginner's Book of Drawing and Painting Flowers, Blandford, 1965.
Drawing and Painting Architecture in Landscape, Blandford, 1966.
How to Paint in Water Colour, Pitman, 1967.
(And illustrator) *Further Steps in Oil Painting,* Blandford, 1970, reprinted, Sterling, 1986.
(And illustrator) *Further Steps in Drawing and Sketching,* Blandford, 1972.

* * *

HILL, Susan (Elizabeth) 1942-

PERSONAL: Born February 5, 1942, in Scarborough, England; daughter of R. H. and Doris Hill; married Stanley W. Wells (a Shakespearean scholar), April 23, 1975; children: Jessica, Clemency. *Education:* King's College, University of London, B.A. (with honors), 1963. *Religion:* Anglican.

ADDRESSES: *Home*—Midsummer Cottage, Church Lane, Beckley, Oxford, England. *Agent*—Curtis Brown, Ltd., 1 Crave Hill, London W2 3EW, England; and John Cushman Associates, Inc., 25 West 43rd St., New York, N.Y. 10036.

CAREER: Novelist, playwright, and critic, 1960—. *Coventry Evening Telegraph,* Coventry, England, 1963-68; *Daily Telegraph,* London, England, monthly columnist, 1977—.

MEMBER: King's College (fellow).

AWARDS, HONORS: Somerset Maugham Award, 1971, for *I'm the King of the Castle;* Whitbread Literary Award for fiction, 1972, for *The Bird of Night;* John Llewelyn Rhys Memorial Prize, 1972, for *The Albatross;* fellow of the Royal Society of Literature, 1972.

WRITINGS:

The Albatross (short stories), Hamish Hamilton, 1971, published as *The Albatross and Other Stories,* Saturday Review Press, 1975.
The Custodian (short stories), Covent Garden Press, 1972.
A Bit of Singing and Dancing (short stories), Hamish Hamilton, 1973.
(Contributor) A. D. Maclean, editor, *Winter's Tales 20,* Macmillan (London), 1974, St. Martin's, 1975.
The Elephant Man, Cambridge University Press, 1975.
(Editor and author of introduction) Thomas Hardy, *The Distracted Preacher and Other Tales,* Penguin, 1980.
(Editor with Isabel Quigly) *New Stories 5,* Hutchinson, 1980.
(Translator with Jonathan Tittler) *Juyungo: The First Black Ecuadorian Novel,* Three Continents, 1982.
The Magic Apple Tree: A Country Year, Hamish Hamilton, 1982, Holt, 1983.
(Editor) *People: Essays and Poems,* Chatto & Windus, 1983.
(Editor) *Ghost Stories,* Hamish Hamilton, 1983.
Through the Kitchen Window, illustrated by Angela Barrett, Hamish Hamilton, 1984, Stemmer House, 1986.
One Night at a Time (juvenile), illustrated by Vanessa Julian-Ottie, Hamish Hamilton, 1984.
Go Away, Bad Dreams! (juvenile), illustrated by Julian-Ottie, Random House, 1985.
The Lighting of the Lamps, David & Charles, 1986.
Shakespeare Country, photographs by Rod Talbot, Penguin, 1987.
(Editor with Joelie Hancock) *Literature-Based Reading Programs at Work,* Heinemann Educational, 1988.
Can It Be True? A Christmas Story, illustrated by Barrett, Viking, 1988.
Lanterns across the Snow, Crown, 1988.
Mother's Magic, illustrated by Alan Marks, David & Charles, 1988.
Through the Garden Gate, David & Charles, 1988.

NOVELS

The Enclosure, Hutchinson, 1961.
Do Me a Favour, Hutchinson, 1963.
Gentleman and Ladies, Hamish Hamilton, 1968, Walker & Co., 1969.
A Change for the Better, Hamish Hamilton, 1969, Penguin, 1980.
I'm the King of the Castle, Viking, 1970.
Strange Meetings, Saturday Review Press, 1972.
The Bird of the Night, Saturday Review Press, 1972.
In the Springtime of the Year, Saturday Review Press, 1974.
The Woman in Black: A Ghost Story, Hamish Hamilton, 1983, Godine, 1986.

RADIO PLAYS

"Miss Lavender Is Dead," British Broadcasting Corp. (BBC Radio), 1970.
"Taking Leave," BBC Radio, 1971.

"The End of the Summer" (also see below), BBC Radio, 1971.
"Lizard in the Grass" (also see below), BBC Radio, 1971.
"The Cold Country" (also see below), BBC Radio, 1972.
"Winter Elegy," BBC Radio, 1973.
"Consider the Lilies" (also see below), BBC Radio, 1973.
"A Window on the World," BBC Radio, 1974.
"Strip Jack Naked" (also see below), BBC Radio, 1974.
"Mr. Proudham and Mr. Sleight," BBC Radio, 1974.
"On the Face of It," BBC Radio, 1975, published in *Act 1,* edited by David Self and Ray Speakman, Hutchinson, 1979.
The Cold Country and Other Plays for Radio (includes "The Cold Country," "The End of Summer," "Lizard in the Grass," "Consider the Lilies," and "Strip Jack Naked"), BBC Publications, 1975.
"The Summer of the Giant Sunflower," BBC Radio, 1977.
"The Sound that Time Makes," BBC Radio, 1980.
"Here Comes the Bride," BBC Radio, 1980.
"Chances," BBC Radio, 1981, stage adaptation first produced in London, 1983.
"Out in the Cold," BBC Radio, 1982.
"Autumn," BBC Radio, 1985.
"Winter," BBC Radio, 1985.

OTHER

Author of "The Badness within Him," a television play, first broadcasted in 1980, and "The Ramshackle Company," a children's play, first produced in London in 1981. Contributor of two stories to *Penguin New Short Stories.*

MEDIA ADAPTATIONS: Gentleman and Ladies was adapted as a radio play in 1970.

SIDELIGHTS: Susan Hill's novels tend to deal with people who live outside what is considered to be the mainstream lifestyle. She tends to place these characters in isolated spots, characterizing them with her use of language and portraying their situations with a strong emphasis on atmosphere. For example, Jonathan Raban writes in *London Magazine* that Hill's *A Change for the Better* "is artfully composed of the dead and rotting language of Westbourne itself; a destitute society finds its linguistic correlative in a dialect of sad cliches. . . . The language of the narrative strictly follows the airless corridors of the characters' own thoughts, reproduced in every colourless detail—mean, complaining, platitudinous. . . . But the tone of *A Change for the Better* is rooted in its dialogue: Miss Hill has created a stylized, yet brilliantly accurate grammar and vocabulary for her distressed gentlefolk—an entirely authentic idiom to be spoken by the living dead as they inhabit their shabby-genteel wasteland. Their language is rigid, archaic, and metrical, a mixture of drab proverbs, oratorical flourishes borrowed from popular romance, and catch phrases from the more sober varieties of adman's English." Raban finds that Miss Hill has "a fine sense of pace and timing and a delicious eye for incongruous detail."

In keeping with the tradition of the horror story, the author's *The Woman in Black: A Ghost Story,* first published in 1983, "could almost pass for a Victorian ghost novel," remarks E. F. Bleiler in the *Washington Post Book World.* Outside of its setting in the early twentieth century, the novel may seem like "a routine horror story" of the late nineteenth century, suggests Bleiler. However, the reviewer continues, "the sustained mood and the depth of emotion that the author evokes with minimal means" make it atypical. Similarly, *Times Literary Supplement* contributor Patricia Craig feels that "the fullest flavour is extracted from every ingredient that goes into *The Woman in Black.*" Bleiler's only objections to the story are its initially slow plot development and the somewhat "confusing, perhaps even unnecessary" circumstances of the main character's situation. But the story as a whole, Bleiler concludes, "is certainly memorable, one of the strongest stories of supernatural horror that I have read in many years."

Other critics have also noted, while reviewing Hill's books, the author's special ability in creating an atmosphere to help set a novel's mood. In one case, *Books and Bookmen* contributor J. A. Cuddon remarks that the title story of *The Albatross and Other Stories* is "about fear, anxiety and inadequacy in which the atmosphere and environment are evoked with great skill and feeling and the characters are presented and developed with a kind of austere compassion." Cuddon later continues: "The language is spare, the dialogue terse and the tone beautifully adjusted to the severe vision. . . . The narrative, the events, are simple enough, but long after one has read these stories one is left with a curious, hard-edged almost physical sensation; a feeling of chill and desolation. But not depression. Miss Hill's art brings an elation of its own."

In a review of *Strange Meetings* in *Books and Bookmen,* Diane Leclercq writes: "Coming hard on the heels of Susan Hill's very considerable achievements in her most recent work, one expects great things from [this book]. In many respects one gets them: the hard-edged prose, the painstaking detail, some aspects of the portrayal of Hilliard, and many of the minor characters. But the book has inbuilt defects that make it, in the final analysis, a failure. . . . The radical weakness is, perhaps, a failure to realize any of the attitudes that people must have had in the situation at the Western Front."

New Republic reviewer Michele Murray believes that "*The Bird of the Night* lacks all those elements that automatically stamp a new novel as 'profound' or 'important,' and worth noticing. What it has instead are qualities rarely found in contemporary fiction and apparently not much valued, which is a pity. It is a thoroughly *created* piece of work, a novel wrought of language carefully designed to tell a story drawn, not from the surface of the author's life or fragments of her autobiography, but from the heart of the imagination. . . . The careful shaping of material to make its effect with the utmost economy, adhered to and practiced by such modern masters as Gide, Woolf, Colette, and Pavese, seems to have fallen into abeyance, and it is good to see it once again employed with such great skill."

Murray calls *In the Springtime of the Year* "another triumph by an artist who, in her quiet, steady way, is fast becoming one of the outstanding novelists of our time." She goes on to say that Susan Hill "has already demonstrated her mastery of character-drawing and fictional technique in her earlier novels, but *In the Springtime of the Year,* with its deliberate stripping away of almost all the elements of conventional fiction, represents a remarkable advance in what is turning out to be a considerable *oeuvre* for such a young writer. . . ." Margaret Atwood concludes in a *New York Times Book Review* article that despite "lapses into simplemindedness, *In the Springtime of the Year* justifies itself by the intensity of those things it does well: moments of genuine feeling, moments of vision. It is less a novel than the portrait of an emotion, and as this it is poignant and convincing."

BIOGRAPHICAL/CRITICAL SOURCES:

PERIODICALS

Best Sellers, October 1, 1970.
Books and Bookmen, April, 1971, January, 1972, June, 1974.
Bookseller, October 23, 1971.
Listener, October 8, 1970.
London Magazine, November, 1969.

New Republic, February 16, 1974, May 18, 1974.
New Statesman, January 31, 1969, January 25, 1974.
New York Times Book Review, March 30, 1969, May 27, 1973, May 18, 1974.
Times Literary Supplement, October 14, 1983.
Washington Post, May 19, 1974.
Washington Post Book World, August 24, 1986.*

* * *

HOBSBAUM, Philip (Dennis) 1932-

PERSONAL: Born June 29, 1932, in London, England; son of Joseph (an engineer) and Rachel (Sapera) Hobsbaum; married Hannah Kelly, August 7, 1957 (marriage dissolved, 1968); married Rosemary Phillips Singleton, July 20, 1976. *Education:* Downing College, Cambridge, B.A., 1955, M.A., 1961; Royal Academy of Music, licentiate, 1956; Guildhall School of Music, licentiate, 1957; research at University of Sheffield, 1959, Ph.D., 1968.

ADDRESSES: Home—156 Wilton St., Glasgow G20, Scotland. *Office*—Department of English, University of Glasgow, Glasgow G12 8QQ, Scotland.

CAREER: Writer, 1955—; part-time lecturer and teacher, 1955-59; Queen's University, Belfast, Northern Ireland, lecturer in English, 1962-66; University of Glasgow, Glasgow, Scotland, lecturer in English, 1966-72, senior lecturer, 1972-79, reader, 1979-85, Titular Professor of English Literature, 1985—. Member of Northern Ireland Civic Theatre Committee, 1963-64; chairman, Glasgow Schools-Universities Liaison Committee for the Teaching of English, 1980-84.

MEMBER: Association of University Teachers, BBC Club (Glasgow).

WRITINGS:

(Editor with Edward Lucie-Smith) *A Group Anthology,* Oxford University Press, 1963.
The Place's Fault, and Other Poems, Macmillan, 1964.
Snapshots, Festival Publications, 1965.
In Retreat, and Other Poems, Macmillan, 1966, Dufour, 1968.
Coming Out Fighting (poems), Macmillan, 1969, Dufour, 1969.
(Editor) *Ten Elizabethan Poets,* Longmans, Green, 1969.
Some Lovely Glorious Nothing: A Poem, Sceptre Press, 1969.
A Theory of Communication, Macmillan, 1970, published as *A Theory of Criticism,* Indiana University Press, 1970.
A Reader's Guide to Charles Dickens, Thames & Hudson, 1972, Farrar, Straus, 1973.
Women and Animals (poems), Macmillan, 1972.
Tradition and Experiment in English Poetry, Macmillan, 1979.
A Reader's Guide to D. H. Lawrence, Thames & Hudson, 1981.
Essentials of Literary Criticism, Thames & Hudson, 1983.
A Reader's Guide to Robert Lowell, Thames & Hudson, 1987.
(Editor) *Wordsworth: Selected Poetry and Prose,* Routledge, 1989.
Post-Structuralist Discourse and Analysis, in press.

Contributor to more than a dozen poetry anthologies, including *Poetry for You,* 1986, *Appreciative Poetry,* 1986, *Of Caterpillars, Cats and Cattle,* 1987, and *Oxford Book of Twentieth Century Verse.* Contributor to literary journals and newspapers in the United States and Great Britain, including *Scottish International, New York Times, Hutchinson Review, Poetry Review,* and *Times Higher Education Supplement.* Editor, *Delta,* 1954-55; co-editor, *Poetry from Sheffield,* 1959-61; member of editorial board, *Northern Review,* 1964-66.

WORK IN PROGRESS: Poems for several voices.

SIDELIGHTS: Philip Hobsbaum, poet, critic, and workshop organizer, draws consistently mixed responses from reviewers on both sides of the Atlantic. Christopher Levenson's survey of reviews in the *Dictionary of Literary Biography: Poets of Great Britain and Ireland since 1960* leads him to conclude that critics "approved of the subject matter and the attitudes, but sometimes deplored the tone and the manner in which [the poems] were presented." In a representative response, Alan Brownjohn of the *New Statesman* explains in his review of *Coming Out Fighting* that Hobsbaum "writes with . . . honesty, but the confessional rawness of [this book] is pretty difficult to take; and one hopes that it is only an interim stage in an enterprising poet's progress. . . . The content of most of the love poems is curiously untender and crude, the manner brutally banal. . . . He is rather better (though much too indulgently anecdotal) when he is being stridently rancorous and hearty in the pub verses."

Critics generally find more to praise in Hobsbaum's books of literary criticism, which include the major works *A Theory of Communication, Tradition and Experiment in English Poetry,* and *Essentials of Literary Criticism.* Of *A Reader's Guide to D. H. Lawrence,* for example, *America* commentator R. F. Walch writes, "Here, in one brief volume is a complete, concise, literate overview of one of the century's most remarkable writers." Boyd M. Tonkin, writing in the *Times Literary Supplement,* recommends all but the final section of *Essentials of Literary Criticism* as a fine introduction to the literary canon: "Hobsbaum's genial initiation into critical method approaches its subject as a craft and not a mystery. He attends to critical writing as an ally of the literary text, not as its competition or usurper, and in doing so strives to span the gulf between work and reader that the teaching of literature often serves only to widen. . . . *Essentials of Literary Criticism* displays an unusual sensitivity to the fragmented and rootless way in which prescribed literature drifts into the lives of students." Reviews of Hobsbaum's prose, like reviews of the poetry, include a wide range of comment. In the *New Statesman,* Blake Morrison remarks that *Tradition and Experiment* "is little short of a disaster. . . .Some of [Hobsbaum's] critical observations . . . would hardly pass muster in an O-level essay." On the other hand, Morrison goes on, "the vivid forcefulness with which Hobsbaum makes [his] different cases is the forcefulness which has made him such an important encourager of young British poets over the last 20 years."

Hobsbaum's editing and communication skills, combined with his energetic and pointed style of commentary, have made him the leader of several lively writing workshops in Great Britain. Hobsbaum founded "The Group," a creative writing seminar in 1955, which has since become a movement in contemporary poetry, and similar groups in Belfast (in 1963) and Glasgow (in 1966 and 1972). In an *Honest Ulsterman* article, writers who had benefitted from association with Hobsbaum give him tribute. Seamus Heaney credits Hobsbaum for giving a generation of poets "a sense of themselves."

According to Levenson, Hobsbaum finds the writing of criticism somewhat more rewarding than writing poetry. Levenson cites the poet's comment that while his poetry does not yet convey as wide a range of voice, the criticism allows him access to the minds of others. Thus, records Levenson, Hobsbaum says, "I have my best work still to do."

BIOGRAPHICAL/CRITICAL SOURCES:

BOOKS

Bergonzi, Bernard, editor, *Sphere History of Life: The Twentieth Century,* Sphere Books, 1970.
Dictionary of Literary Biography, Volume 40: *Poets of Great Britain and Ireland since 1960,* Gale, 1985.
Fraser, G. S., *The Writer and the Modern World,* Penguin, 1964.
Williams, John, *Reading Poetry,* Edward Arnold, 1985.

PERIODICALS

America, June 20, 1981.
Books and Bookmen, December, 1972.
Encounter, March, 1967.
Honest Ulsterman, Number 53, 1976.
Hudson Review, summer, 1972.
Kenyon Review, Volume 30, number 5, 1968.
New Statesman, April 25, 1969, September 18, 1970, April 20, 1979.
Poetry, July, 1969.
Review of English Studies, February, 1973.
Times Literary Supplement, July 24, 1969, October 20, 1972, September 23, 1983.
Twentieth Century, June, 1960.

* * *

HOFFMANN, Erik P(eter) 1939-

PERSONAL: Born August 7, 1939, in New York, N.Y.; son of William H. (a management consultant) and Helene (a writer; maiden name, Grasshoff) Hoffmann. *Education:* Haverford College, B.A., 1961; Indiana University, M.A., 1965, Ph.D., 1967.

ADDRESSES: Office—Department of Political Science, State University of New York, Albany, N.Y. 12222.

CAREER: Temple University, Philadelphia, Pa., instructor, 1965-67, assistant professor of political science, 1967-69; State University of New York at Albany, assistant professor, 1969-72, associate professor, 1972-85, professor of political science, 1985—. Columbia University, seminar associate, 1972—, senior research fellow, 1975-76, 1982-83; Institute for East-West Security Studies, American scholar in residence, 1987-89. Project director, United States Information Agency affiliation grant, State University of New York at Albany/University of Belgrade, 1984-89. Member of board of trustees, Citizen Exchange Corps.

AWARDS, HONORS: American Council of Learned Societies and Social Science Research Council grant for Soviet studies, 1975-76; National Science Foundation grant, 1980-82.

WRITINGS:

(Editor with Frederic J. Fleron, Jr.) *The Conduct of Soviet Foreign Policy,* Aldine-Atherton, 1971, 2nd edition, Aldine, 1980.
(With Robbin F. Laird) *"The Scientific-Technological Revolution" and Soviet Foreign Policy,* Pergamon, 1982.
(With Laird) *The Politics of Economic Modernization in the Soviet Union,* Cornell University Press, 1982.
(Editor with Laird) *The Soviet Polity in the Modern Era,* Aldine, 1984.
(Editor) *The Soviet Union in the 1980s,* Academy of Political Science, 1984.
(With Laird) *Technocratic Socialism: The Soviet Union in the Advanced Industrial Era,* Duke Press, 1985.
(Editor with Laird) *Soviet Foreign Policy in a Changing World,* Aldine, 1986.

Contributor of chapters to numerous scholarly books. Contributor to professional journals, including *World Politics, Problems of Communism,* and *Bulletin of the Atomic Scientists.*

WORK IN PROGRESS: Research on Soviet domestic politics and foreign policy.

* * *

HOLCOMBE, Randall G(regory) 1950-

PERSONAL: Born June 4, 1950, in Bridgeport, Conn.; son of L. M. Holcombe and R. E. Ledbetter; married. *Education:* University of Florida, B.S. and B.A. (with honors), 1972; Virginia Polytechnic Institute and State University, M.A., 1974, Ph.D., 1976.

ADDRESSES: Home—3514 Limerick Dr., Tallahassee, Fla. 32308. *Office*—Department of Economics, Florida State University, Tallahassee, Fla. 32306.

CAREER: Texas A & M University, College Station, assistant professor of economics, 1975-77; Auburn University, Auburn, Ala., assistant professor, 1977-81, associate professor, 1981-85, professor of economics, 1985-88; Florida State University, Tallahassee, professor of economics, 1988—. Member of staff, Center for Naval Analyses, 1973-75; member of staff of Republican Senator William Brock of Tennessee, 1974; member of synthetic fuels review panel, U.S. Synthetic Fuels Corp., 1982; consultant to Resource Planning Associates, Federal Energy Administration, and U.S. Department of Energy. Member of board of advisors, James Madison Institute, 1988—.

AWARDS, HONORS: Earhart Foundation fellow, summers, 1979-80, 1983, 1989.

WRITINGS:

Public Finance and the Political Process, Southern Illinois University Press, 1983.
An Economic Analysis of Democracy, Southern Illinois University Press, 1985.
Public Sector Economics, Wadsworth Publishing, 1988.
Economic Models and Methodology, Greenwood Press, 1989.

Contributor of more than eighty articles and reviews to economics and political science journals.

WORK IN PROGRESS: The Economic Foundations of Government; research on the economics of government.

SIDELIGHTS: Randall G. Holcombe told *CA:* "Most of my writing has been analyzing the effects of decision making by majority rule. The government is a major factor in modern economies, but the way in which democracies make economic decisions is not well enough understood. Too often, the result has been government policies that are well intentioned but are unable to accomplish. I hope that my writing can contribute to this understanding."

* * *

HOLMES, John
See SOUSTER, (Holmes) Raymond

* * *

HOLMES, Raymond
See SOUSTER, (Holmes) Raymond

HOLT, Andrew
See ANHALT, Edward

* * *

HOPKINS, Lee Bennett 1938-

PERSONAL: Born April 13, 1938, in Scranton, Pa.; son of Gertrude (Thomas) and Leon Hall Hopkins. *Education:* Newark State Teachers College (now Kean College), Union, N.J., B.A., 1960; Bank Street College of Education, M.Sc., 1964; Hunter College of the City University of New York, Professional Diploma in Educational Supervision and Administration, 1967.

ADDRESSES: *Home*—Kemeys Cove, Scarborough, N.Y. 10510.

CAREER: Public school teacher in Fair Lawn, N.J., 1960-66; Bank Street College of Education, New York City, senior consultant, 1966-68; Scholastic Magazines, Inc., New York City, curriculum and editorial specialist, 1968-74. Lecturer on children's literature; host and consultant to children's television series, "Zebra Wings," Agency for Instructional Television, beginning 1976. Consultant to school systems on elementary curriculum; literature consultant, Harper & Row, Text Division.

MEMBER: International Reading Association, American Library Association, American Association of School Librarians, National Council of Teachers of English (member of board of directors, 1975-78; chair of 1978 Poetry Award Committee; member of Commission on Literature, 1983-85; member of Children's Literature Assembly, 1985-88), Authors Guild, Authors League of America.

AWARDS, HONORS: *Don't You Turn Back* was chosen as an American Library Association notable book; Outstanding Alumnus in the Arts award, Kean College, 1972; *Mama* was chosen as a National Council for Social Studies notable book; *To Look at Any Thing* was chosen as choice book of the 1978 International Youth Library exhibition, Munich, Germany; *Wonder Wheels* received a children's choice award, 1980, International Reading Association/Children's Book Council; honorary doctor of laws, Kean College, 1980; Phi Delta Kappa Educational Leadership Award, 1980; International Reading Association Broadcast Media Award for Radio, 1982; Ambassador Extraordinary in the Order of the Long Leaf Pine, presented by Governor James B. Hunt of North Carolina, 1982; International Reading Association Manhattan Council Literacy Award, 1983; National Children's Book Week Poet, 1985; *Side by Side: Poems to Read Together* and *Voyages: Poems by Walt Whitman* were chosen as American Booksellers Pick-of-the-List books in 1988.

WRITINGS:

(With Annette F. Shapiro) *Creative Activities for Gifted Children,* Fearon, 1968.
Books Are by People, Citation Press, 1969.
Let Them Be Themselves: Language Arts Enrichment for Disadvantaged Children in Elementary Schools, Citation Press, 1969, 2nd edition published as *Let Them Be Themselves: Language Arts for Children in Elementary Schools,* 1974.
(With Misha Arenstein) *Partners in Learning: A Child-Centered Approach to Teaching the Social Studies,* Citation Press, 1971.
Pass the Poetry, Please!: Bringing Poetry into the Minds and Hearts of Children, Citation Press, 1972, revised edition, Harper, 1987.
More Books by More People, Citation Press, 1974.
(With Arenstein) *Do You Know What Day Tomorrow Is?: A Teacher's Almanac,* Citation Press, 1975.
The Best of Book Bonanza (Instructor Book-of-the-Month Club selection), Holt, 1980.

YOUNG ADULT NOVELS

Mama, Dell, 1977.
Wonder Wheels, Dell, 1980.
Mama and Her Boys, Harper, 1981.

JUVENILES

Important Dates in Afro-American History, F. Watts, 1969.
This Street's for Me (poetry), illustrated by Ann Grifalconi, Crown, 1970.
(With Arenstein) *Faces and Places: Poems for You,* illustrated by Lisl Weil, Scholastic Book Services, 1970.
Happy Birthday to Me!, Scholastic Book Services, 1972.
When I Am All Alone: A Book of Poems, Scholastic Book Services, 1972.
Charlie's World: A Book of Poems, Bobbs-Merrill, 1972.
Kim's Place and Other Poems, Holt, 1974.
I Loved Rose Ann, illustrated by Ingrid Fetz, Knopf, 1976.
A Haunting We Will Go: Ghostly Stories and Poems, illustrated by Vera Rosenberry, Albert Whitman, 1976.
Witching Time: Mischievous Stories and Poems, illustrated by Rosenberry, Albert Whitman, 1976.
Kits, Cats, Lions, and Tigers: Stories, Poems, and Verse, illustrated by Rosenberry, Albert Whitman, 1979.
Pups, Dogs, Foxes, and Wolves: Stories, Poems, and Verse, illustrated by Rosenberry, Albert Whitman, 1979.
How Do You Make an Elephant Float and Other Delicious Food Riddles, illustrated by Rosekranz Hoffman, Albert Whitman, 1983.

COMPILER

I Think I Saw a Snail: Young Poems for City Seasons, illustrated by Harold James, Crown, 1969.
Don't You Turn Back: Poems by Langston Hughes, forward by Arna Bontemps, Knopf, 1969.
City Talk, illustrated by Roy Arnella, Knopf, 1970.
The City Spreads Its Wings, illustrated by Moneta Barnett, F. Watts, 1970.
Me!: A Book of Poems (Junior Literary Guild selection), illustrated by Talavaldis Stubis, Seabury, 1970.
Zoo!: A Book of Poems, illustrated by Robert Frankenberg, Crown, 1971.
Girls Can Too!: A Book of Poems, illustrated by Emily McCully, F. Watts, 1972.
(With Arenstein) *Time to Shout: Poems for You,* illustrated by Weil, Scholastic, Inc., 1973.
(With Sunna Rasch) *I Really Want to Feel Good about Myself: Poems by Former Addicts,* Thomas Nelson, 1974.
On Our Way: Poems of Pride and Love, illustrated by David Parks, Knopf, 1974.
Hey-How for Halloween, illustrated by Janet McCaffery, Harcourt, 1974.
Take Hold!: An Anthology of Pulitzer Prize Winning Poems, Thomas Nelson, 1974.
Poetry on Wheels, illustrated by Frank Aloise, Garrard, 1974.
Sing Hey for Christmas Day, illustrated by Laura Jean Allen, Harcourt, 1975.
Good Morning to You, Valentine, illustrated by Tomie de Paola, Harcourt, 1976.
Merrily Comes Our Harvest In, illustrated by Ben Shecter, Harcourt, 1976.

(With Arenstein) *Thread One to a Star,* Four Winds, 1976.
(With Arenstein) *Potato Chips and a Slice of Moon: Poems You'll Like,* illustrated by Wayne Blickenstaff, Scholastic Inc., 1976.
Beat the Drum! Independence Day Has Come, illustrated by de Paola, Harcourt, 1977.
Monsters, Ghoulies, and Creepy Creatures: Fantastic Stories and Poems, illustrated by Rosenberry, Albert Whitman, 1977.
To Look at Any Thing, illustrated by John Earl, Harcourt, 1978.
Easter Buds Are Springing: Poems for Easter, illustrated by de Paola, Harcourt, 1979.
Merely Players: An Anthology of Life Poems, Thomas Nelson, 1979.
My Mane Catches the Wind: Poems about Horses, illustrated by Sam Savitt, Harcourt, 1979.
By Myself, illustrated by Glo Coalson, Crowell, 1980.
Elves, Fairies and Gnomes, illustrated by Hoffman, Knopf, 1980.
Moments: Poems about the Seasons, illustrated by Michael Hague, Harcourt, 1980.
Morning, Noon, and Nighttime, Too!, illustrated by Nancy Hannans, Harper, 1980.
I Am the Cat, illustrated by Linda Rochester Richards, Harcourt, 1981.
And God Bless Me: Prayers, Lullabies and Dream-Poems, illustrated by Patricia Henderson Lincoln, Knopf, 1982.
Circus! Circus!, illustrated by John O'Brien, Knopf, 1982.
Rainbows Are Made: Poems by Carl Sandburg, illustrated by Fritz Eichenberg, Harcourt, 1982.
A Dog's Life, illustrated by Rochester Richards, Harcourt, 1983.
The Sky Is Full of Song, illustrated by Dirk Zimmer, Charlotte Zolotow/Harper, 1983.
A Song in Stone: City Poems, illustrated by Anna Held Audette, Crowell, 1983.
Crickets and Bullfrogs and Whispers of Thunder: Poems and Pictures by Harry Behn, Harcourt, 1984.
Love and Kisses (poems), illustrated by Kris Boyd, Houghton, 1984.
Surprises: An I Can Read Book of Poems, illustrated by Meagan Lloyd, Charlotte Zolotow/Harper, 1984.
Creatures, illustrated by Stella Ormai, Harcourt, 1985.
Munching: Poems about Eating, illustrated by Nelle Davis, Little, Brown, 1985.
Best Friends, illustrated by James Watts, Charlotte Zolotow/Harper, 1986.
The Sea Is Calling Me, illustrated by Walter Gaffney-Kessel, Harcourt, 1986.
Click, Rumble, Roar: Poems about Machines, illustrated by Audette, Crowell, 1987.
Dinosaurs, illustrated by Murray Tinkelman, Harcourt, 1987.
More Surprises: An I Can Read Book, illustrated by Lloyd, Charlotte Zolotow/Harper, 1987.
Voyages: Poems by Walt Whitman, illustrated by Charles Mikolaycak, Harcourt, 1988.
Side by Side: Poems to Read Together (Book-of-the-Month Club selection), illustrated by Hilary Knight, Simon & Schuster, 1988.
Still as a Star: Nighttime Poems, illustrated by Karen Malone, Little, Brown, 1988.

OTHER

Also author of columns, "Poetry Place," in *Instructor* magazine, and "Book Sharing," in *School Library Media Quarterly.* Associate editor, *School Library Media Quarterly,* 1982—.

SIDELIGHTS: Poetry enthusiast Lee Bennett Hopkins is the compiler of over forty-five children's verse collections. His collections encompass a variety of topics, including animals, holidays, the seasons, and the works of noted poets like Walt Whitman and Carl Sandburg. Poetry, Hopkins states in *Instructor* magazine, "should come to [children] as naturally as breathing, for nothing—*no thing*—can ring and rage through hearts and minds as does this genre of literature."

One of Hopkins seasonal collections, *The Sky Is Full of Song,* is described by a *Language Arts* reviewer as a "rare gem [that] poetically radiates the unique sense of each season." The reviewer adds that each poem is "short, crisp, and in tune with the quartet of seasons." Steven Ratiner comments in the *Christian Science Monitor* that *The Sky Is Full of Song* "is an attractive packet of poetry for a young reader, pleasing to both the ear and eye."

BIOGRAPHICAL/CRITICAL SOURCES:

BOOKS

Roginski, James W., *Behind the Covers: Interviews with Authors and Illustrators of Books for Children and Young Adults,* Libraries Unlimited, 1985.
Something about the Author Autobiography Series, Volume 4, Gale, 1987.

PERIODICALS

Best Sellers, August, 1979.
Christian Science Monitor, June 29, 1983.
Early Years, January, 1982.
Instructor, March, 1982.
Language Arts, November/December, 1978, September, 1983, December, 1984, September, 1986.
New York Times Book Review, April 8, 1979, October 5, 1986.
Washington Post Book World, May 11, 1980.

* * *

HOUSTON, James D. 1933-

PERSONAL: Born November 10, 1933, in San Francisco, Calif.; son of Albert Dudley and Alice Loretta (Wilson) Houston; married Jeanne Toyo Wakatsuki, 1957; children: Corinne, Joshua, Gabrielle. *Education:* San Jose State College (now University), B.A., 1956; Stanford University, M.A., 1962.

ADDRESSES: Home—2-1130 East Cliff Dr., Santa Cruz, Calif. 95062. *Office*—University of California, Santa Cruz, Calif. 95064.

CAREER: Cabrillo College, Aptos, Calif., instructor in English, 1962-64; guitar instructor in Santa Cruz, Calif., 1964-66; Stanford University, Stanford, Calif., lecturer in English, 1967-68; University of California, Santa Cruz, lecturer in writing, 1969—. Writer in residence, Villa Montalvo, Saratoga, Calif., spring, 1980; distinguished visiting writer, University of Hawaii at Manoa, spring, 1983; visiting writer, University of Michigan, fall, 1985; Allen T. Gilliland Chair in Telecommunications, San Jose State University, 1985. Member of California Council for the Humanities, 1983-87. *Military service:* U.S. Air Force, 1957-60; became lieutenant.

MEMBER: PEN, Writers Guild of America, West.

AWARDS, HONORS: U.S. Air Force Short Story Contest, winner, 1959; Wallace Stegner creative writing fellow at Stanford University, 1966-67; Joseph Henry Jackson Award, San Francisco Foundation, 1967, for *Gig;* University of California faculty research grant, 1972; Humanitas Prize, 1976, and Christopher Award, both for screenplay "Farewell to Manzanar"; National Endowment for the Arts creative writing grant, 1976-77; National Endowment for the Arts small press grant, 1977; travel grant to Asia, Arts America Program, fall, 1981 and 1984; Before Columbus Foundation American Book Award, 1983, for *Californians: Searching for the Golden State.*

WRITINGS:

Between Battles (novel), Dial, 1968.
Gig (novel), Dial, 1969.
A Native Son of the Golden West (novel), Dial, 1971.
The Adventures of Charlie Bates (short stories), Capra, 1973, enlarged edition published as *Gasoline: The Automotive Adventures of Charlie Bates,* 1980.
(With wife, Jeanne Wakatsuki Houston) *Farewell to Manzanar: A True Story of Japanese American Experience during and After the World War II Internment* (nonfiction; also see below), Houghton, 1973.
Writing from the Inside (textbook), Addison-Wesley, 1973.
(With John R. Brodie) *Open Field* (biography), Houghton, 1974.
Three Songs for My Father (essays), Capra, 1974.
(With J. W. Houston and John Korty) "Farewell to Manzanar" (screenplay), Universal and MCA-TV, 1976.
Continental Drift (novel), Knopf, 1978.
(Editor with Gerald Haslam) *California Heartland: Writings from the Great Central Valley,* Capra, 1978.
(Editor and contributor) *West Coast Fiction: Modern Writing from California, Oregon and Washington,* Bantam, 1979.
Californians: Searching for the Golden State (nonfiction), Knopf, 1982.
Love Life (novel), Knopf, 1985.
One Can Think about Life after the Fish Is in the Canoe and Other Coastal Sketches (bound with *Beyond Manzanar and other Views of Asian–American Womanhood,* by J. W. Houston), Capra, 1985.
The Men in My Life, and Other More or Less True Recollections of Kinship (personal stories), Creative Arts, 1987.

CONTRIBUTOR TO ANTHOLOGIES

Year's Best Science Fiction, Delacorte, 1965.
Stanford Stories 1968, Stanford University Press, 1968.
Voices of Man, Addison-Wesley, 1970.
Capra Chapbook Anthology, Capra, 1977.
Yardbird Lives, Grove Press, 1978.
Borzoi College Reader, Knopf, 1980.
Unknown California, Collier/Macmillan, 1985.
California Childhood, Creative Arts, 1988.

OTHER

Also author of a teleplay "Barrio," with J. W. Houston, developed by National Broadcasting Co. (NBC). Contributor of short stories and articles to *Playboy, Rolling Stone, New York Times, Los Angeles Times,* and *Mother Jones.*

SIDELIGHTS: James D. Houston is a native Californian whose works of fiction and nonfiction reflect his interest in the literature and people of this region. Among his nonfiction works he is notable for *Californians: Searching for the Golden State,* which received the Before Columbus Foundation American Book Award. *Californians* is structured as a travel narrative, and contains interviews with various residents, including an ecological activist, a playwright, a winemaker, and a psychic. "Taken together these lives make a prism through which the multilfaceted California dream can be viewed at every angle," writes a *Wilson Library Bulletin* reviewer.

Critics praise Houston's objective, balanced, thorough handling of his subject. *Boston Globe* contributor Mark Muro writes: "California unhinges us, makes us lose all proportion. But in 'Californians . . . ,' James D. Houston gives us something different, for he summons us to join him in a reexploration of his home state that manages to stir an admirable course between the twin seductions of California Boosterism and Acopalypse Gnaw." *National Review* contributor Lee Hopkins notes: "A genial, lyrical, and rational man, James Houston avoids extremes, and in his fair-minded, very equitable way is the ideal observer and chronicler." Concurs a *Western American Literature* critic: "This book is really a love story by native-son Houston, a distinguished novelist, but it is a mature love, not uncritical, one that accepts the beloved complete with warts."

Los Angeles Times Book Review contributor Bill Stout concludes: "Whether in a Hollywood film studio or an Asian grocery in San Francisco, [Houston] found himself fascinated by the swirl of this wondrous place we share, and so often fail to notice or even try to understand. His journey makes one want to try harder; for a book, it is difficult to imagine anything better that could be said."

One of Houston's most widely-reviewed novels is *Love Life,* a contemporary work set in northern California. The narrator is Holly Doyle, a wife, mother, and occasional country and western singer. On her thirty-second birthday Holly discovers that Grover, her husband of ten years, is having an affair with a twenty-year-old feminist. Holly reacts by flying to New York, where she intends to get revenge by having a fling with a former lover. Instead, she has a five-minute affair with a stranger, which activates a desire to repair her marriage. Shortly after her return home, California is hit with a torrential rainstorm, and the family's enforced isolation enables Holly and Grover to reconcile.

"This may sound like the stuff of another 'divorce novel,' as the genre seems to be known, but there is much more to 'Love Life' than that," writes *Washington Post* book critic Jonathan Yardley, who adds, "They're ordinary [characters] but Houston makes them interesting, because they talk and think in ways that we immediately recognize as authentic." Elizabeth Chamish concurs in the *Christian Science Monitor:* "[Holly's] is not a new story; there is no surprise ending, no mystery, but an admirable unraveling of how she gets from here to there."

Several reviewers comment that one of the novel's distinguishing characteristics is the engaging and convincing quality of Holly's narration. *New Republic* contributor Jamie Baylis, for example, observes: "The pat story line is salvaged . . . by Holly's first-person narrative. A spirited, sturdy, intuitive woman, she turns to wide-ranging introspection as she recounts this 'Unidentified Flying Object' stage, when obstacles seemed to appear from every direction." A *Publishers Weekly* contributor similarly notes that "the special joy of this warm and wonderful book is the narrator, Holly, whose voice . . . rings with resonating implications."

New York Times Book Review contributor Sheila Ballantine, on the other hand, detects random shifts in Holly's voice from first to third person. These inconsistencies, Ballantine claims, "seem to reflect uncertainty on the part of a man who has decided to speak through a female persona. They undermine the integrity of an otherwise compelling character." Chamish likewise points out: "As often as it is accurate, fair and likable, Houston's female perspective is also weak, detached, and essentially untrue."

On the whole, however, critics praise the novel. *Los Angeles Times Book Review* contributor Taffy Cannon writes: "Houston's characters are carefully drawn, intelligent, funny and beguiling. 'Love Life' is a charming novel, an insightful and marvelously fresh examination of a good marriage in sudden disarray." Baylis writes: "[Holly] expresses her worldview with such wit and force that it's hard to resist being taken in. James Houston's foray into the female psyche is entirely convincing to this reviewer (a woman), who bristled only once." *Detroit News* critic Ruth Pollack Coughlin urges, "Try *Love Life.* Houston is a storyteller's storyteller. This tale is told by Holly Doyle and it is much to Houston's credit that the voice rings true—no easy feat for a male writer. Houston's people are enormously real and alive; you can't help but be with them at every step."

BIOGRAPHICAL/CRITICAL SOURCES:

PERIODICALS

Best Sellers, January, 1979.
Boston Globe, November 14, 1982.
Christian Science Monitor, December 9, 1985.
Detroit News, October 6, 1985.
Los Angeles Times Book Review, March 20, 1983, November 3, 1985.
National Review, September 30, 1983.
New Republic, September 30, 1978, November 11, 1985.
New York Times Book Review, September 29, 1985.
Publishers Weekly, September 4, 1978, July 12, 1985.
San Francisco Review of Books, March/April, 1983.
Washington Post, October 2, 1985.
Washington Post Book World, July 26, 1987.
Western American Literature, winter, 1984, summer, 1986.
Wilson Library Bulletin, January, 1983.

—Sketch by Melissa Gaiownik

* * *

HOUSTON, Jeanne (Toyo) Wakatsuki 1934-

PERSONAL: Born September 26, 1934, in California; daughter of Ko (a fisherman) and Riku (Sugai) Wakatsuki; married James D. Houston (a writer), 1957; children: Corinne, Joshua, Gabrielle. *Education:* University of San Jose, B.A., 1956; also attended Sorbonne, University of Paris.

ADDRESSES: Home—2-1130 East Cliff Dr., Santa Cruz, Calif. 95062. *Agent*—George Diskant, Diskant and Associates, 1033 Gayley Ave., Suite 202, Los Angeles, Calif. 90024.

CAREER: Writer. Group worker and juvenile probation officer in San Mateo, Calif., 1955-57.

MEMBER: Writers Guild, Screen Writers Guild.

AWARDS, HONORS: Humanitas Prize, 1976, and Christopher Award, both for screenplay "Farewell to Manzanar"; award from National Women's Political Caucus; Wonder Woman Award, 1984.

WRITINGS:

(With husband, James D. Houston) *Farewell to Manzanar: A True Story of Japanese American Experience during and After the World War II Internment* (nonfiction; also see below), Houghton, 1973.

(With J. D. Houston and John Korty) "Farewell to Manzanar" (screenplay), Universal and MCA-TV, 1976.

(With Paul G. Hensler) *Don't Cry, It's Only Thunder* (nonfiction), Doubleday, 1984.

Beyond Manzanar and Other Views of Asian-American Womanhood (bound with *One Can Think about Life after the Fish Is in the Canoe and Other Coastal Sketches,* by J. D. Houston), Capra, 1985.

Also author of teleplay "Barrio," with J. D. Houston, developed by National Broadcasting Co. (NBC). Contributor to magazines.

WORK IN PROGRESS: Fire Horse Woman, a novel about a picture bride at the turn of the century.

SIDELIGHTS: With the publication of Jeanne Wakatsuki Houston's book *Farewell to Manzanar,* coauthored with her husband James D. Houston, she "became, quite unintentionally, a voice for a heretofore silent segment of society," observes a *Los Angeles Times* reporter. The daughter of first and second generation Japanese-American parents, Houston describes herself in the *Los Angeles Times* as "almost third-generation American." Yet she and her family, along with thousands of other Japanese-Americans, were interned at a work camp during World War II.

Silenced by guilt and shame, Houston was thirty-seven years old before she felt comfortable articulating her feelings about the internment. Houston explains in the *Los Angeles Times* that she felt "sullied, like when you are a rape victim. . . . You feel you must have *done* something. You feel you are part of the act."

The Wakatsukis were one of the first families interned at the Manzanar camp, and one of the last to be released. *Farewell to Manzanar* describes the indignities of the camp experience and the harmful effects it had on Houston's family, particularly her father. As a *New Yorker* critic observes, "Her father was too old to bend with the humiliations of the camp. . . . His story is at the heart of this book, and his daughter tells it with great dignity." Dorothy Rabinowitz writes in *Saturday Review,* "Mrs. Houston and her husband have recorded a tale of many complexities in a straightforward manner, a tale remarkably lacking in either self-pity or solemnity." A *New York Times Book Review* critic concludes that *Farewell to Manzanar* is "a dramatic, telling account of one of the most reprehensible events in the history of America's treatment of its minorities."

BIOGRAPHICAL/CRITICAL SOURCES:

BOOKS

Houston, Jeanne Wakatsuki and James D. Houston, *Farewell to Manzanar: A True Story of Japanese American Experience during and After the World War II Internment,* Houghton, 1973.

PERIODICALS

Los Angeles Times, November 15, 1984.
New Yorker, November 5, 1973.
New York Times Book Review, January 13, 1974.
Saturday Review, November 6, 1973.
Washington Post, February 27, 1984.

* * *

HOUSTON, R. B.

See RAE, Hugh C(rauford)

* * *

HOWARD, Prosper

See HAMILTON, Charles (Harold St. John)

* * *

HOYLE, Fred 1915-

PERSONAL: Born June 24, 1915, in Bingley, Yorkshire, England; son of Ben and Mabel (Pickard) Hoyle; married Barbara

Clark, December 28, 1939; children: Geoffrey, Elizabeth Jeanne (Mrs. N. J. Butler). *Education:* Emmanuel College, Cambridge, M.A., 1939.

ADDRESSES: Office—St. John's College, Cambridge University, Cambridge, England.

CAREER: Cambridge University, Cambridge, England, research fellow of St. John's College, 1939-72, honorary fellow, 1973—, university lecturer in mathematics, 1945-58, Plumian Professor of Theoretical Astronomy and Experimental Philosophy, 1958-73, director of Institute of Theoretical Astronomy, 1966-72. California Institute of Technology, visiting professor of astrophysics, 1953 and 1954, visiting associate in physics, 1963—, and Sherman Fairchild Distinguished Scholar, 1974-75. Professor of astronomy, Royal Institution, 1969-72; Andrew D. White Professor-at-Large, Cornell University, 1972-78. Honorary research professor, University of Manchester, 1972—, and University of Cardiff, 1975—; honorary fellow, Emmanuel College, Cambridge, 1983. Member of staff, Mount Wilson and Palomar Observatories in California, 1956-58. Senior exhibitioner of the Royal Commission of the Exhibition of 1851, 1939; member of science research council, 1967-72. *Wartime service:* British Admiralty, wartime research, 1940-45.

MEMBER: Royal Astronomical Society (fellow; president, 1971-73), Royal Society (fellow; vice-president, 1970-71), American Academy of Arts and Sciences (honorary member), American Philosophical Society, National Academy of Sciences (foreign associate).

AWARDS, HONORS: Smith Prize, 1939; D.Sc. from University of Norwich, 1967, University of Leeds, 1969, University of Bradford, 1975, and University of Newcastle, 1976; received Gold Medal from Royal Astronomical Society, 1968; Kalinga Prize, 1968; Bruce Medal, Astronomical Society of the Pacific, 1970; knighted, 1972; Royal Medal from Royal Society, 1974; Dorothea Klumpke-Roberts Award, Astronomical Society of the Pacific, 1977.

WRITINGS:

Some Recent Researches in Solar Physics, Cambridge University Press, 1949.
The Nature of the Universe, Harper, 1951, revised edition, 1960.
A Decade of Decision, Heinemann, 1953, published as *Man and Materialism,* Harper, 1956.
Frontiers of Astronomy, Heinemann, 1955, New American Library, 1957.
The Black Cloud (science fiction), Harper, 1957.
Ossian's Ride (science fiction), Harper, 1959.
(With John Elliott) *A for Andromeda,* Harper, 1962, reprinted, Avon, 1985.
Astronomy, Doubleday, 1962.
Star Formation, H.M.S.O., 1963.
Contradiction in the Argument of Malthus, University of Hull, 1963.
Of Men and Galaxies, University of Washington Press, 1964.
(With Elliott) *Andromeda Breakthrough* (science fiction), Harper, 1964.
Encounter with the Future, Trident, 1965.
Galaxies, Nuclei, and Quasars, Harper, 1965.
Man in the Universe, Columbia University Press, 1966.
October the First Is Too Late (science fiction), Harper, 1966.
Element 79 (science fiction), New American Library, 1967.
From Stonehenge to Modern Cosmology, W. H. Freeman, 1972.
Copernicus, Harper, 1973.
The Relation of Physics and Cosmology, W. H. Freeman, 1973.
(With J. V. Narlikar) *Action-at-a-Distance in Physics and Cosmology,* W. H. Freeman, 1973.
Astronomy and Cosmology, W. H. Freeman, 1975.
Highlights in Astronomy, W. H. Freeman, 1975, (published in England as *Astronomy Today,* Heinemann, 1975).
Ten Faces of the Universe, W. H. Freeman, 1977.
Stonehenge: A High Peak of Prehistoric Culture, W. H. Freeman, 1977.
On Stonehenge, W. H. Freeman, 1977.
Energy or Extinction?, Heinemann, 1977, 2nd edition, 1980.
(With Chandra Wickramasinghe) *Lifecloud,* Harper, 1978.
The Cosmogony of the Solar System, Enslow, 1978.
(With Wickramasinghe) *Diseases from Space,* Harper, 1979.
(With son, Geoffrey Hoyle) *Commonsense in Nuclear Energy,* Heinemann, 1979, W. H. Freeman, 1980.
(With Narlikar) *The Physics-Astronomy Frontier,* W. H. Freeman, 1980.
Steady-State Cosmology Re-Visited, Longwood, 1980.
Space Travellers, University College Cardiff Press, 1981.
The Quasar Controversy Resolved, Longwood, 1981.
Facts and Dogmas in Cosmology and Elsewhere, Cambridge University Press, 1982.
Ice, New English Library, 1982.
Evolution from Space and Other Papers on the Origin of Life (also see below), Enslow Publishers, 1982.
The Intelligent Universe: A New View of Creation and Evolution, Holt, 1984.
(With Wickramasinghe) *Evolution from Space: A Theory of Cosmic Creationism,* Simon & Schuster, 1984.
From Grains to Bacteria, Longwood, 1984.
(Editor with Wickramasinghe) *Fundamental Studies and the Future of Science,* University College of Cardiff Press, 1984.
Comet Halley, St. Martin's, 1985.
Living Comets, Longwood, 1985.
(With others) *Viruses from Space,* University College Cardiff Press, 1986.
The Small World of Fred Hoyle (autobiography), Joseph, 1986.
(With Wickramasinghe) *Archaeopteryx, the Primordial Bird: A Case of Fossil Forgery,* Longwood, 1987.

SCIENCE FICTION NOVELS; WITH GEOFFREY HOYLE

Fifth Planet, Harper, 1963.
Rockets in Ursa Major, Harper, 1969.
Seven Steps to the Sun, Harper, 1970.
The Molecule Man: Two Short Novels, Harper, 1971.
The Inferno, Harper, 1973.
Into Deepest Space, Harper, 1974.
The Incandescent Ones, Harper, 1977.
The Westminster Disaster, Harper, 1978.
The Energy Pirate, illustrated by Martin Aitchison, Ladybird, 1982.
The Frozen Planet of Azuron, illustrated by Aitchison, Ladybird, 1982.
The Giants of Universal Park, illustrated by Aitchison, Ladybird, 1982.
The Planet of Death, illustrated by Aitchison, Ladybird, 1982.

BOOKLETS

The Origin of Life, University College Cardiff Press, 1980.
(With Wickramasinghe) *Why Neo-Darwinism Does Not Work,* University College Cardiff Press, 1982.
Evolution from Space, University College Cardiff Press, 1982.
The Anglo-Austrian Telescope, University College Cardiff Press, 1982.

OTHER

Author of libretto, "The Alchemy of Love." Contributor of numerous articles to scientific and professional journals.

SIDELIGHTS: Internationally renowned astronomer and professor Fred Hoyle has "published a string of books challenging first one and then another of the basic tenets of modern cosmology," writes John Durant in the *Times Literary Supplement.* In his 1951 book *The Nature of the Universe,* for example, Hoyle rejects the long-standing big bang theory of the origin of the universe in favor of the steady state theory developed by him and his colleagues at Cambridge University.

Hoyle expounds further upon the steady state and other theories in *The Intelligent Universe,* published in 1977. "Writing with the moral indignation of one who believes himself to be up against a conservative and conspiratorial establishment, and who consequently does not expect a fair hearing, Hoyle dismisses one piece of 'orthodox science' after another, replacing each with ingenious alternatives that pop up from page to page like so many rabbits out of a conjurer's hat," writes Durant. In *The Intelligent Universe,* writes *Science Fiction Review* critic Gene Deweese, Hoyle "presents both old and new evidence for [his steady state theory] and shows how the Big Bang has at least as many shortcomings and problems as the Steady State is supposed to have." Hoyle also presents an argument against Darwin's theory of evolution, claiming that "living organisms are too complex to have been produced by chance," relates Durant. Hoyle suggests, instead, that "we owe our existence to another intelligence which created a structure for life as part of a deliberate plan," writes John R. Kalafut in *Best Sellers,* adding that "in describing the attributes of an intelligence superior to ourselves, [Hoyle] admits that we may have to use the word forbidden in science, 'God.' " Durant finds Hoyle's argument inadequate, stating that the chapter on Darwinism reads "more like the feeble meanderings of a latter-day fundamentalist than like the work of a major scientist." Kalafut, on the other hand, maintains that "this part of the book is extremely well done and the case against traditional evolution is argued most persuasively."

Hoyle and co-author Chandra Wickramasinghe's 1981 book *Diseases from Space* introduced a similarly controversial theory. The authors hypothesize that viruses and bacteria fall into the atmosphere after being incubated in the interiors of comet heads, and that people become ill by breathing the infected air. They support their theory by stating that the spread of disease is frequently far too rapid to attribute to person-to-person contact. Several reviewers express skepticism that Hoyle and Wickramasinghe's thesis will be accepted by the medical profession. *Science Books and Films* contributor George Podgorny, for instance, comments that their "hypothesis, though engaging, is most likely farfetched." Expressing a like opinion in the *Antioch Review,* Robert Bieri writes, "This is a fascinating, humorous, challenging book, but few biologists will buy the thesis."

Reviewers do, however, express their admiration for the author's statistical data. Maddox writes: "Like everything Hoyle writes, this book is a splendid read. It is rich in classical quotations . . . , in data gathered from old shipping records, with the outcome of a questionnaire survey among British schools in 1978 on the incidence of influenza, and with simple explanations of statistical arguments well worth reading for their own sake." Bieri concludes, "Even if one can't follow all of their arguments, the almost offhand historical comments throughout the book are amusing, challenging, enlightening."

Hoyle has also authored over a dozen science fiction novels, more than half of which were co-written with his son Geoffrey Hoyle. Several critics suggest that Hoyle's highly technical and scientific background enhances the credibility and appeal of his novels. For example, *Listener* reviewer Robert Garioch comments that *Seven Steps to the Sun* "is a remarkable story, well-told, and too credible for comfort. . . . The science in *Seven Steps to the Sun* is correct, as a middle-aged reviewer may learn by consulting his 15-year-old son. The main interest, however, is in the anthropology. . . . It is not at all far-fetched."

Jeanne Cavallini concurs with Garioch and explains in *Library Journal* that "Fred Hoyle is considered one of the world's foremost astrophysicists . . . ; his distinguished scientific background is evident in [*The Molecule Man: Two Short Novels*]. Science fiction buffs who like their science fiction to take place in the present and to have the stamp of scientific accuracy will enjoy these stories."

BIOGRAPHICAL/CRITICAL SOURCES:

BOOKS

The Small World of Fred Hoyle (autobiography), Joseph, 1986.

PERIODICALS

Antioch Review, spring, 1981.
Best Sellers, April, 1984.
Books and Bookmen, December, 1979.
Books of the Times, September, 1980.
British Book News, September, 1986.
Listener, September 13, 1979.
New York Review of Books, October 23, 1980.
New York Times Book Review, April 29, 1984.
Observer, August 10, 1986.
Science Books and Films, March, 1981.
Science Fiction Review, February, 1986.
Spectator, August 23, 1986.
Times Literary Supplement, February 10, 1978, December 9, 1983.

* * *

HOYLE, Geoffrey 1942-

PERSONAL: Born January 12, 1942, in Scunthorpe, Lancashire, England; son of Fred (a scientist and author) and Barbara (Clark) Hoyle; married Valerie Jane Coope (an accountant), April 21, 1971. *Education:* Attended St. John's College, Cambridge, 1961-62.

ADDRESSES: *Home*—West Wissett 8, Milner Rd., Bournemouth PR4 0TJ, England.

CAREER: Writer. Worked in documentary film production, 1963-67; magazine editor, 1980-83.

WRITINGS:

SCIENCE FICTION NOVELS; WITH FATHER, FRED HOYLE

Fifth Planet, Harper, 1963.
Rockets in Ursa Major, Harper, 1969.
Seven Steps to the Sun, Harper, 1970.
The Molecule Man: Two Short Novels, Harper, 1971.
The Inferno, Harper, 1973.
Into Deepest Space, Harper, 1974.
The Incandescent Ones, Harper, 1977.
The Westminster Disaster, Harper, 1978.
The Energy Pirate, illustrated by Martin Aitchison, Ladybird, 1982.

The Frozen Planet of Azuron, illustrated by Aitchison, Ladybird, 1982.
The Giants of Universal Park, illustrated by Aitchison, Ladybird, 1982.
The Planet of Death, illustrated by Aitchison, Ladybird, 1982.

FOR CHILDREN

2010: Living in the Future, Parents Magazine Press, 1972.
Disaster, Heinemann Educational, 1975.
(With Janice Robertson) *Ask Me Why,* PAN, 1976.

OTHER

(With F. Hoyle) *Commonsense in Nuclear Energy,* Heinemann, 1979, W.H. Freeman, 1980.
Flight, Ladybird, 1984.

SIDELIGHTS: See entry for father, Fred Hoyle, in this volume.

AVOCATIONAL INTERESTS: Skiing, sailing, target-shooting.

* * *

HUBLEY, Faith Elliot 1924-

PERSONAL: Born September 16, 1924, in New York, N.Y.; daughter of Irving and Sally (Rosenblatt) Chestman; married John Hubley (a film producer and animator), June 24, 1955 (died, 1977); children: Mark, Ray, Emily, Georgia. *Education:* Attended Actor's Lab in California.

CAREER: Worked as editor, script supervisor, and music editor of motion pictures in Hollywood, Calif., and New York City, 1944-55; animated motion picture producer, 1955—, writer and director, 1975—. Producer with husband, John Hubley, of animated motion pictures, including "Adventures of an *," 1956, "Moonbird," 1959, "The Hole," 1963, "The Hat," 1964, "Windy Day," 1968, "Of Men and Demons," 1969, "Voyage to Next," 1974, "People, People, People," 1975, and "A Doonesbury Special," 1977; producer of animated motion picture "Whither Weather," 1977. Founder, with John Hubley, of production company, Storyboard (now Hubley Studio, Inc.), 1955. Visiting lecturer at Yale University, 1972-85. Artist; paintings displayed in over twenty exhibits in New York, California, and Europe.

MEMBER: International Animated Film Society, Academy of Motion Picture Arts and Sciences, Motion Picture Editors, Art Students League of New York (life member).

AWARDS, HONORS: (With husband, John Hubley) Diploma Speciale, 1956, for "Adventures of an *," honorable mention, 1957, for "Harlem Wednesday," Silver Lion Award, 1958, for "Tender Game," Special Jury Prize, 1964, for "The Hat," and Golden Lion Award, 1968, for "Windy Day," all from Venice Film Festival; (with J. Hubley) Academy Award, Academy of Motion Picture Arts and Sciences, 1959, for "Moonbird," 1963, for "The Hole," and 1966, for "Herb Alpert and the Tijuana Brass Double Feature"; (with J. Hubley) Venice Documentary Festival first prize award, 1960, for "Children of the Sun"; (with J. Hubley) Prix Speciale du Jury, Annecy Film Festival, 1962, for "Of Stars and Men"; (with J. Hubley) CINE Golden Eagle award, Council on International Nontheatrical Events, 1966, for "Urbanissimo," 1970, for "Eggs," 1972, for "Dig," 1975, for "People, People, People"; nomination from Academy of Motion Picture Arts and Sciences, 1968, for "Windy Day," 1969, for "Men and Demons," and 1974, for "Voyage to Next"; CINE Golden Eagle award, Council on International Nontheatrical Events, 1975, for "WOW (Women of the World)," 1976, for "Second Chance: Sea," 1978, for "A Doonesbury Special," 1978, for "Whither Weather," 1979, for "Step by Step," 1980, for "Sky Dance," 1981, for "The Big Bang and Other Creation Myths," and 1985, for "Hello" and "Starlore"; Blue Ribbon Award, American Film Festival, 1975, for "Everybody Rides the Carousel"; Special Jury Prize, Cannes Film Festival, 1978, for "A Doonesbury Special"; Best Film award, Dallas USA Film Festival, 1978, for "Whither Weather"; Best Children's Film award, Annecy Film Festival, 1979, and Outstanding Achievement award, San Francisco Film Festival, 1979, both for "Step by Step"; Diploma of Merit, Tampere Film Festival, 1982, for "Enter Life"; Special Jury Prize, Houston International Film Festival, 1983, and inclusion in Best of Annecy 1983 Traveling Film Festival, both for "Starlore"; Silver Award, Houston International Film Festival, 1984, for "Hello."

WRITINGS:

(With husband, John Hubley, and Gary Trudeau) *John and Faith Hubley's "A Doonesbury Special": A Director's Notebook,* Sheed, Ward, & McMeel, 1977.

ADAPTATIONS FROM SCREENPLAYS

(Illustrator with J. Hubley) Robert M. Hutchins, *Zuckerlandl!* (also see below), Grove, 1968.
(With J. Hubley) *Dig: A Journey Under the Earth's Crust* (also see below), Harcourt, 1973.
(With J. Hubley) *The Hat* (also see below), Harcourt, 1974.
Lullaby (based on screenplay "Step by Step"), Harper, 1980.
Sky Dance (also see below), Harper, 1981.
(With Kenneth M. Towe) *Enter Life* (also see below), illustrated by F. Hubley, Delacorte, 1982.

SCREENPLAYS

"Adventures of an *" (also see below), Films, Inc., 1956.
"Harlem Wednesday" (also see below), Films, Inc., 1957.
"Tender Game" (also see below), Films, Inc., 1958.
"A Date with Dizzy," Films, Inc., 1958.
(Creator) "Moonbird" (also see below), Films, Inc.,1959.
"Seven Lively Arts," Films, Inc., 1959.
"Children of the Sun" (also see below), Films, Inc., 1960.
"Of Stars and Men" (adapted from the book by Harlow Shapley), Museum of Modern Art, 1962.
"The Hole" (also see below), Films, Inc., 1963.
"The Hat" (also see below), Films, Inc./Museum of Modern Art, 1964.
"Urbanissimo" (also see below), Films, Inc., 1966.
"Herb Alpert and the Tijuana Brass Double Feature," A & M Records, 1966.
"Gulliver's Troubles," Films, Inc., 1967.
"The Cruise," National Film Board of Canada, 1967.
"Zuckerlandl!" (also see below), Films, Inc., 1968.
(Creator) "Windy Day" (also see below), Films, Inc., 1968.
"Of Men and Demons" (also see below), Films, Inc., 1969.
"Eggs" (also see below), Films, Inc., 1970.
"Dig" (also see below), Films, Inc., 1972.
"Cockaboody" (also see below), Pyramid Films/Museum of Modern Art, 1974.
"Voyage to Next," Films, Inc./Museum of Modern Art, 1974.
"People, People, People" (also see below), Pyramid Films, 1975.
"WOW (Women of the World)" (also see below), Pyramid Films, 1975.
(With J. Hubley) "Everybody Rides the Carousel" (adapted from the works of Erik H. Erikson), Pyramid Films, 1975.
"In Quest of Cockaboody," Films, Inc., 1975.
"Second Chance: Sea" (also see below), Films, Inc., 1976.

(With Gary Trudeau) "A Doonesbury Special," Pyramid Films, 1977.
(And producer) "Whither Weather," Pyramid Films, 1977.
"Step by Step," Pyramid Films/Museum of Modern Art, 1978.
"Sky Dance," Pyramid Films/Museum of Modern Art, 1979.
"The Big Bang and Other Creation Myths," Pyramid Films/ Museum of Modern Art, 1979.
"Enter Life," Pyramid Films, 1981.
"Starlore," Pyramid Films, 1982.
"Hello," Pyramid Films, 1984.
"The Cosmic Eye," Pyramid Films, 1985.
"Academy Award Winners: Animated Short Films" (videocassette; contains "The Hole" and "Moonbird"), Vestron Video, 1985.
"The Ages of Humankind" (videocassette; contains "Tender Game," "Dig," "WOW (Women of the World)," "People, People, People," and "Cockaboody"), Disney, 1986.
"Flights of Fancy" (videocassette; contains "The Adventures of an *," "Moonbird," "Windy Day," and "Zuckerlandl!"), Disney, 1986.
"Urbanscape," (videocassette; contains "Of Men and Demons," "Harlem Wednesday," "Urbanissimo," and "The Hole"), Disney, 1986.
"A Delicate Thread" (videocassette; contains "Eggs," "Children of the Sun," "The Hat," and "Second Chance: Sea"), Disney, 1986.

All of Hubley's films are available on videocassette from Pyramid Films and Video.

WORK IN PROGRESS: "Amazonia," a screenplay.

SIDELIGHTS: Along with her husband John, Faith Hubley began a small studio in New York "making animated films in an anti-Disney visual style that was closer in form and spirit to European surrealism and impressionism," writes Pat McGilligan in *Film Quarterly.* McGilligan continues: "They pioneered the use of name performers and of their own children with improvised dialogue. They sponsored marvelous jazz and new-music sound tracks." Instead of catering to a young audience, the Hubley's animated films addressed such issues as war, the environment, feminism, and spirituality. About the unorthodoxy of her films, Hubley tells McGilligan: "I am a bit of a slob and I like a free-flowing line and texture. That was our contribution . . . to liberate animation from itself, and to go to watercolors and to paint pastels. It was a big, big liberation and resisted by the [movie] industry." Despite this resistance, Hubley concludes: "My choice as a working artist is not to play to the marketplace. It's not because I don't know how. I've chosen another path. As hard as my life is, and it is hard without Johnny, I wake up every morning and I can't wait to get to work."

AVOCATIONAL INTERESTS: Painting, playing the cello.

BIOGRAPHICAL/CRITICAL SOURCES:

PERIODICALS

Film Quarterly, winter, 1988-89.*

* * *

HUNT, Harrison
See BALLARD, (Willis) Todhunter

HUNTER, George
See BALLARD, (Willis) Todhunter

* * *

HUNTER, Jack D(ayton) 1921-

PERSONAL: Born June 4, 1921, in Hamilton, Ohio; son of Whitney Guy (a business executive) and Mary Irene (Dayton) Hunter; married Shirley Thompson, October 31, 1944; children: Lee and Lyn (twin daughters), Jill, Jack Dayton, Jr. *Education:* Pennsylvania State University, B.A., 1943. *Politics:* Independent. *Religion:* Presbyterian.

ADDRESSES: Home—22 Hypolita St., St. Augustine, Fla. 32084. *Office*—20 Hypolita St., St. Augustine, Fla. 32084. *Agent*—Blassingame, McCauley & Wood, 432 Park Ave. S., New York, N.Y. 10016; Ralph Vicinanza, Ltd., 432 Park Ave. S., New York, N.Y. 10016; and Joel Gotler, Los Angeles Literary Associates, 8955 Norma Place, Los Angeles, Calif. 90069.

CAREER: Chester Times, Chester, Pa., news reporter, 1939-40; Station WILM, Wilmington, Del., newscaster, 1946-47; *Evening Journal,* Wilmington, Del., news reporter, 1947-50; U.S. House of Representatives, Washington, D.C., executive secretary to member from Delaware, 1950-52; E. I. du Pont de Nemours & Co., Wilmington, affiliated with public relations and advertising department, 1952-75; *Sunday Journal,* Wilmington, columnist, 1975-77; U.S. Senate, Washington, D.C., special counsel to member from Delaware, 1977-79; Flagler College, St. Augustine, Fla., adjunct professor, 1980-82. Writing coach, *Florida Times-Union, Jacksonville Journal,* and *St. Augustine Record,* 1981—. Public relations consultant to small firms. *Military service:* U.S. Army, 1943-46; special agent in Counter Intelligence Corps; received Bronze Star and six campaign ribbons. U.S. Air Force Reserve; retired as captain.

MEMBER: Authors Guild, Authors League of America, Sigma Delta Chi, Sigma Alpha Epsilon.

AWARDS, HONORS: Edgar Award for best first novel, Mystery Writers of America, 1966, for *The Expendable Spy.*

WRITINGS:

The Blue Max, Dutton, 1964.
The Expendable Spy, Dutton, 1965.
One of Us Works for Them, Dutton, 1967.
Spies Incorporated, Dutton, 1969.
Word of Life, Simon & Schuster, 1976.
The Blood Order, Times Books, 1979.
The Terror Alliance, Leisure Books, 1980.
The Tin Cravat, Harper, 1981.
Florida Is Closed Today, Tower, 1982.
Judgment in Blood, Avon, 1986.
The Flying Cross, Avon, 1987.
"Aktion Achtung," Tor Books, 1989.

WORK IN PROGRESS: The Potsdam Bluff, for Tor Books.

SIDELIGHTS: Jack D. Hunter told *CA:* "I play jazz piano. As a water colorist, I specialize in action scenes of World War I and II aircraft and have sold many paintings to galleries and collectors in recent years. As a major hobby I pursue every shred of information to be found on aircraft of the 1914-1918 period. I am deeply involved in architectural restoration and preservation and have in fact restored two historic homes in Maryland, two in Florida, and one in Vermont."

MEDIA ADAPTATIONS: The Blue Max was produced as a film by Twentieth Century-Fox in 1965. The film rights to *The Ex-*

pendable Spy were optioned by International Film Traders, and the film rights to *One of Us Works for Them* were acquired by Bristol Productions.

* * *

HUNTER, John
See BALLARD, (Willis) Todhunter

* * *

HYMAN, Harold M(elvin) 1924-

PERSONAL: Born July 24, 1924, in New York, N.Y.; son of Abraham and Beatrice (Herman) Hyman; married Ferne Beverly Handelsman, March 22, 1946; children: Lee, Ann, William. *Education:* University of California, Los Angeles, B.A., 1948; Columbia University, M.A., 1950, Ph.D., 1952. *Politics:* Democrat. *Religion:* Jewish.

ADDRESSES: Home—4823 Creekbend, Houston, Tex. 77035. *Office*—Department of History, Rice University, Houston, Tex. 77001.

CAREER: U.S. Veterans Administration, Los Angeles, Calif., rehabilitation officer, 1946-48; City College (now City College of the City University of New York), New York, N.Y., instructor in modern history, 1950-52; Earlham College, Richmond, Ind., assistant professor of history, 1952-55; University of California, Los Angeles, visiting assistant professor of American history, 1955-56; Arizona State University, Tempe, associate professor of American history, 1956-57; University of California, Los Angeles, professor of history, 1963-68; Rice University, Houston, Tex., William P. Hobby Professor of History, 1968—, chairman of history department, 1968-70. *Military service:* U.S. Marine Corps, 1941-45; became master technical sergeant.

MEMBER: American Historical Association, Organization of American Historians, Illinois State Historical Society, Los Angeles Civil War Round Table.

AWARDS, HONORS: Albert J. Beveridge award, American Historical Association, 1952; Sidney Hillman award for *Era of the Oath: Northern Loyalty Tests During the Civil War and Reconstruction* and *To Try Men's Souls: Loyalty Tests in American History.*

WRITINGS:

Era of the Oath: Northern Loyalty Tests during the Civil War and Reconstruction, University of Pennsylvania Press, 1954, reprinted, Hippocrene Books, 1978.

To Try Men's Souls: Loyalty Tests in American History, University of California Press, 1959, reprinted, Greenwood Press, 1981.

(With Benjamin P. Thomas) *Stanton: The Life and Times of Lincoln's Secretary of War,* Knopf, 1962, reprinted, Greenwood Press, 1980.

Soldiers and Spruce: The Loyal Legion of Loggers and Lumbermen, the Army's Labor Union of World War I, University of California Press, 1963.

A More Perfect Union: The Impact of the Civil War and Reconstruction on the Constitution, Knopf, 1973.

Union and Confidence: The 1860s, Crowell, 1976.

(With William Wiecek) *Equal Justice under Law: Constitutional History, 1835-1875,* Harper, 1982.

Quiet Past and Stormy Present?: War Powers in American History, American History Association, 1986.

American Singularity: The 1787 Northwest Ordinance, the 1862 Homestead-Morrill Acts, and the 1944 G.I. Bill, University of Georgia Press, 1986.

EDITOR

The Radical Republicans and Reconstruction Policy, 1861-1870, Bobbs-Merrill, 1966.

New Frontiers of the American Reconstruction, University of Illinois Press, 1966.

(With Leonard W. Levy) *Freedom and Reform: Essays in Honor of Henry Steele Commager,* Harper, 1967.

H. C. Allen and others, *Heard 'round the World: The Impact Abroad of the Civil War,* Knopf, 1969.

(And author of introduction) Carleton Parker, *The Casual Laborer and Other Essays,* new edition of 1919 original, University of Washington Press, 1972.

(And author of introduction, with wife, Ferne Hyman) *The Circuit Court Opinions of Salmon Portland Chase,* new edition of 1875 original, Da Capo Press, 1972.

(And author of introduction) Sidney George Fisher, *The Trial of the Constitution,* new edition of 1862 original, Da Capo Press, 1972.

Edward McPherson, *The Political History of the United States of America during the Great Rebellion, 1860-1865,* new edition of 1865 original, Da Capo Press, 1972.

(With Hans L. Trefousse) McPherson, *Handbook of Politics,* six volumes, new edition of 1894 original, Da Capo Press, 1972-73.

(With Trefousse) McPherson, *The Political History of the United States of America during the Period of Reconstruction,* new edition of 1871 original, Da Capo Press, 1973.

(With Kermit L. Hall and Leon V. Sigal) *The Constitutional Convention as an Amending Device,* American Historical Association/American Political Science Association, 1981.

OTHER

Editor, with Stuart Bruchey, of the "American Legal and Constitutional History Series," Garland Publishing, 1986-87. Member of board of editors, *Reviews in American History,* 1964—, Ulysses S. Grant Association, 1968—, *American Journal of Legal History,* 1970—, and *Journal of American History,* 1970-74.*

I

IMFELD, Al 1935-

PERSONAL: Born January 14, 1935, in Galgenen, Switzerland; son of Alois (a farmer) and Franziska (Hunkeler) Imfeld. *Education:* Attended Seminary Schoeneck, 1954-60, and Gregoriana University, 1961-62; Fordham University, M.A., 1964; Northwestern University, M.S.J., 1966. *Politics:* "Independent, but on the side of underprivileged."

ADDRESSES: *Home and office*—Konradstrasse 23, 8005 Zurich, Switzerland.

CAREER: Ordained Roman Catholic priest in Missionary Society of Bethlehem Fathers, 1960; journalist in Asia, 1966; conducted research in Rhodesia on the Shona people, 1967-68; taught courses in the sociology of development and rural journalism in Malawi, Tanzania, and Kenya, 1969-71; i3w (Information Third World), Berne, Switzerland, founder and team member, 1971-76; development consultant in Tanzania, 1976-77, and at Gottlieb Duttweiler-Institute, 1977-79; *epd Entwicklungspolitik,* Frankfort, Germany, editor, 1979-83; free-lance writer, 1984—.

WRITINGS:

China als Entwicklungsmodel, Laetare Verlag, 1974, English translation by Matthew J. O'Connell published as *China as a Model of Development,* Orbis, 1976.

Women on the African Continent: From the Kraal to the Nightclub, from Humiliation to Power, Waldgut Verlag, 1989.

The Daily Bread: Between Religious Symbols and Agro-Business, Unionsverlag, 1990.

IN GERMAN

Die Dritte Welt im Jahr 2000 (title means "Third World in the Year 2000: Prophecies"), Benziger (Zurich), 1973.

Suedafrika: Ende des Dialogs? (title means "South Africa: End of Dialogue?"), CETIM (Geneva), 1974.

Thema, Entwicklungspolitik: Eine bibliographische Einfuehrung mit mehr als 6000 Titeln, Laetare-Verlag, 1978.

Verlernen, was mich stumm macht (reader on African culture), Unionsverlag (Zurich), 1980.

Afrika den Afrikanern, Ullstein Buch, 1980.

(Contributor) *Der schwarze Fuerst,* Hammer, 1980.

Vision und Waffe: Afrikanische Autoren, Themen, Traditionen, (title means "African Authors, Topics, and Traditions"), Unionsverlag, 1981.

Zucker (title means "Sugar"), Unionsverlag, 1983.

(With Gerhard S. Schuerch) *Die Wueste erobert uns* (poems), Dendron (Lugnorre), 1984.

(With Schuerch) *Zerstreut liegen die Steine des Heiligtums* (poems), Dendron, 1984.

(With Maja Zuercher) *Afrika—Der langsame Marsch der Entkolonialisierung: 22 Gedichte aus dem suedlichen Afrika der Bantu* (poems), Dendron, 1984.

Hunger und Hilfe: Provokationen (a radical treatise on hunger), Unionsverlag, 1985.

(With Peter Meyns and others) *Mit Bauerngruppen arbeiten: Burkina Faso, Ein-Sichten in ein Ausbildungsprojekt,* Weltfriedensdienst, 1985.

(With Verena M. Gerber) *Zorn und Traurigkeit: Aphorismen—Anstoesse zu einer Medienphilosophie; Plastiken—Begegnungen auf der Suche nach Raum,* Dendron, 1985.

(With C. F. Beyers Naude) *Widerstand in Sudafrika: Apartheid, kirchliche Opposition, Solidaritaet,* Exodus (Freiburg), 1986.

(With Bernd Merzenich) *Tee: Gewohnheit und Konsequenz,* Edition dia/PRO, 1986.

(Contributor) *Wer hat Angst vorm Schwarzen Mann?: Asylpolitik in der Schweiz,* Limmat/VVA, 1986.

Die Schatten kann man nicht begraben (reader on African politics and economics), Unionsverlag, 1989.

Also author of a book of South African photography and poetry, *Nichts wird uns trennen,* for Benteli Verlag; author of introductions to several German translations of African novels. Contributor of poetry to small publications.

WORK IN PROGRESS: A poetry collection, for Dendron; a reader on African liberation theology, for Exodus; *20,000 Years of African Agriculture.*

SIDELIGHTS: Al Imfeld told *CA:* "After I learned demythologizing in scripture theology I started to apply the very same methods also to economics and politics and our way of life." Since 1984 Imfeld has specialized in writings on African culture and agriculture.

* * *

IRELAND, David 1927-

PERSONAL: Born August 24, 1927, in Lakemba, New South Wales, Australia; son of John and Lillian (Stroud) Ireland; married Elizabeth Ruth Morris, October 29, 1955; children: Stephen, Christine, Alison, David.

ADDRESSES: Home—Box 101, Darlinghurst, NSW 2010, Australia. *Agent*—Curtis Brown Ltd. (Australia), 27 Union St., Paddington, NSW 2021, Australia.

CAREER: Writer.

MEMBER: Australian Society of Authors.

AWARDS, HONORS: First prize, *Adelaide Advertiser* literary competition, 1966; New South Wales literary fellowship, 1968-69; Miles Franklin Award, 1972, 1977, 1980; *The Age* Book of the Year Award, 1980, for *A Woman of the Future.*

WRITINGS:

Image in the Clay (play; produced in Sydney, 1962), University of Queensland Press, 1964, 2nd edition, 1987.
The Chantic Bird (novel), Scribner, 1968.
The Unknown Industrial Prisoner (novel), Angus & Robertson, 1971.
Burn (novel), Angus & Robertson, 1974.
The Flesheaters (novel), Angus & Robertson, 1975.
The Glass Canoe (novel), Macmillan, 1976.
A Woman of the Future (novel), Braziller, 1979.
(Contributor) Caroline Hobhouse, editor, *Winter's Tales 25,* Macmillan (London), 1979, St. Martin's, 1980.
City of Women (novel), Allen Lane, 1981.
Archimedes and the Seagle (novel), Viking, 1984.
Bloodfather, Hamish Hamilton, 1988.

SIDELIGHTS: "David Ireland is Australia's most mature and astute political novelist, and one of the nation's most innovative prose stylists," Van Ikin asserts in a *Contemporary Novelists* essay. Ireland's earliest works depict an Australian society consumed with industry and production, and frequently demonstrate the denigration of people who are perceived as detriments to progress. His recent novels, however, "have moved more clearly in the direction of fable, the prose style has become remarkably agile and witty, and the author's earlier concern with specific political issues has broadened into a preoccupation with the inner world of the imagination," as Ikin describes. One such novel is Ireland's most celebrated, *A Woman of the Future,* which confronts Australia's self-image through the science fictional story of a young woman's coming of age. The result, as Judith Gies summarizes in the *Saturday Review,* is "a strange, disturbing, and ferociously funny novel in the form of diaries and notes left behind by 18-year-old Alethea Hunt before her escape from a harsh, surrealistic society."

Alethea is the daughter of two Servants, members of the ruling class who are respected because they are productively employed; those who do not work are termed the "Free," and frequently fall victim to a series of metamorphoses, producing spare body parts, plants, and other items out of their own flesh. The novel portrays this world through Alethea's perceptions, and concludes with her disappearance. "The true power of *A Woman of the Future* is in the more naturalistic elements of David Ireland's portrayal of Alethea Hunt," remarks *Washington Post Book World* contributor Doug Lang, from the girl's early learning experiences "to her final evaluation of the world she has inherited and her abandonment of both that world and of her human form. It is here," the critic explains, "with the impact of an intelligent young woman's recognition of the disturbing and distressing nature of life on this planet, that the novel is most convincing."

While critics note that Ireland's novel works on one level as "an extraordinary memoire of adolescence," as the *New York Times*'s John Leonard comments, it also serves an allegorical function. Leonard elaborates: "On another level, 'A Woman of the Future' is a meditation on the mechanized welfare state, on the nature of freedom and responsibility, of work and love. . . . On the third and deepest level, it deploys the continent of Australia in the service of myth." An *Atlantic* reviewer concurs, observing that while the novel can be classified as science fiction, "this is a book that easily transcends such labels. Written with a wit as dry as the Australian outback . . ., it has much to say about the nature of our future, and our innate abilities." "Bursting with energy and ideas, *A Woman of the Future* is a stinging, original, and mercilessly rendered vision of a system in which social promises are as broken and useless as the people to whom they are made," Gies concludes. "More than the record of a personal odyssey, Alethea Hunt's diary is a song of protest and affirmation."

BIOGRAPHICAL/CRITICAL SOURCES:

BOOKS

Contemporary Novelists, St. James Press/St. Martin's, 1986.

PERIODICALS

Atlantic, September, 1979.
New Statesman, September 25, 1981, March 1, 1985.
New York Times, September 3, 1979.
New York Times Book Review, May 3, 1987.
Saturday Review, September 29, 1979.
Washington Post Book World, September 9, 1979.*

J

JACKMAN, Leslie (Arthur James) 1919-

PERSONAL: Born December 23, 1919, in London, England; son of Arthur James and Lilian (Abrey) Jackman; married Cynthia Rudge, July, 1942; children: Diane, Paul, Rodger, Lynne. *Education:* Attended Weymouth Training College, 1946-47.

ADDRESSES: Home—44 Old Torquay Rd., Paignton, Devonshire, England.

CAREER: Schoolmaster in Torquay, Devonshire, England, 1947-63; Devonshire County Council, Devonshire, schools museum officer, 1963—. Maker of natural history films for British Broadcasting Corp. "Look" series, and producer of other educational television films for BBC-TV. *Military service:* British Army, 1939-46.

MEMBER: Zoological Society (London; fellow), Marine Biological Association.

WRITINGS:

(Editor) *The Angler's Guide (South Devon): Sea Fishing, Salmon and Trout Rivers, Coarse Fishing,* Torquay Times, 1953.

Marine Aquaria, Cassell, 1957, new edition, David and Charles, 1968, Transatlantic, 1969.

(Editor) *Hobbies for Boys,* drawings by Brian Denyer, Evans Brothers, 1968.

Exploring the Woodland, Evans Brothers, 1970, reprinted with new illustrations, 1976.

Exploring the Park, Evans Brothers, 1970, reprinted with new illustrations, 1976.

Exploring the Hedgerow, Evans Brothers, 1970, reprinted with new illustrations, 1976.

Exploring the Seashore, Evans Brothers, 1970, new edition published as *Exploring Seashore,* 1976.

The Field: Its Wildlife and Plants through the Year, photographs by the author, Evans Brothers, 1972.

The Beach, photographs by the author, Evans Brothers, 1974.

Sea Water Aquaria, David and Charles, 1974.

Exploring the Pond, photographs by the author and son, Rodger Jackman, Evans Brothers, 1976.

Exploring the Garden, photographs by the author and daughter, Lynne Jackman, Evans Brothers, 1976.

Life in Ponds and Streams, illustrations by Fred Anderson and Vanessa Luff, Macmillan (London), 1978.

The Seashore Naturalist's Handbook, Hamlyn, 1981.

Freila Finds a Nest, State Mutual Books, 1985.

WORK IN PROGRESS: Laurus; The Herring Gull; Exploring a Canal; Exploring the Town.

BIOGRAPHICAL/CRITICAL SOURCES:

PERIODICALS

Books and Bookmen, November, 1968.*

*   *   *

JACKSON, Edgar (Newman) 1910-

PERSONAL: Born July 10, 1910, in Cold Spring Harbor, N.Y.; son of Edgar Starkey (a clergyman) and Abbie (Newman) Jackson; married Estelle Miller, 1934; children: Edgar D. (deceased), James W. (deceased), Lois Estelle. *Education:* Ohio Wesleyan University, A.B., 1932; graduate study at Drew Theological Seminary, 1932-34, and Union Theological Seminary, New York, N.Y., 1934-35; earned B.D. and M.Div. from Yale University; graduate study at Postgraduate Center for Psychotherapy, 1949-52, and Columbia University, 1954.

ADDRESSES: Home—Washington Rd., Corinth, Vt. 05039. *Agent*—Ann Elmo Agency, Inc., 52 Vanderbilt Ave., New York, N.Y. 10017.

CAREER: Ordained Methodist minister, 1933; pastor of Methodist churches in Centerport, N.Y., Thomaston, Conn., New Haven, Conn., Winsted, Conn., Bridgeport, Conn., and Mamaroneck, N.Y. Visiting professor at University of Minnesota, 1964-66; professor at Royalton College, 1968-72; adjunct professor at Union Graduate School, 1972—; Danforth lecturer at Brooklyn College of the City University of New York; Ritter Lecturer at Congregational School of Theology; lecturer at numerous universities, seminaries, religious and medical conferences, and military schools in the United States, Japan, the Philippines, England, Germany, Italy, Greece, and Iceland, including Columbia University and St. John's University, Collegeville, Minn. Clinical psychologist at Veterans Administration Hospital; chaplain at U.S. Air Force General Hospital; director and chairman of advisory board of New Rochelle Guidance Center; member of board of trustees of New England Institute. Guest on several hundred local and national television and radio programs; consultant to medical, religious, and military groups.

MEMBER: Association for Humanistic Psychology, National Council on Family Relations, Hastings Institute.

AWARDS, HONORS: D.D., Ohio Wesleyan University, 1959; essay award, National Cancer Society; Freedoms Foundations award; named honorary chaplain of U.S. House of Representatives.

WRITINGS:

This Is My Faith, Abingdon, 1951.
How to Preach to People's Needs, Abingdon, 1956.
Understanding Grief: Its Roots, Dynamics, and Treatment, Abingdon, 1957.
(With Russell Dicks) *Facing Ourselves,* Abingdon, 1961.
Green Mountain Hero (juvenile historical novel), Lantern Press, 1961, reprinted, New England Press, 1988.
You and Your Grief, Channel Press, 1961.
The Pastor and His People, Channel Press, 1963.
For the Living, Channel Press, 1963.
(With M. K. Bowers, Lawrence LeShan, and Knight) *Counseling the Dying,* Thomas Nelson, 1963.
The Christian Funeral, Channel Press, 1967.
Understanding Prayer: Its Roots, Disciplines, and Growth, World Publishing, 1968.
Group Counseling: Possibilities for Small Groups, Pilgrim Publications, 1969.
Though We Suffer, Graded Press, 1971.
When Someone Dies, Fortress, 1971.
Coping with the Crises in Your Life, Hawthorn, 1974.
Parish Counseling, Jason Aronson, 1975.
The Many Faces of Grief, Abingdon, 1977.
Understanding Loneliness, Fortress, 1980.
A Psychology for Preaching, Harper, 1981.
The Role of Faith in the Process of Healing, Fortress, 1982.
Your Health and You, Augsburg, 1986.
Conquering Disability, Augsburg/Fortress, 1989.
Understanding Health: An Introduction to the Holistic Approach, SCM Press, 1989.

Also author of *Doubting Is Not Enough,* 1982.

CONTRIBUTOR

Herman Feifel, editor, *The Meaning of Death,* McGraw, 1959.
Catastrophic Illness, National Cancer Institution, 1966.
Earl Grollman, editor, *Explaining Death to Children,* Beacon Press, 1967.
Growth through Grief (monograph), Forest Hospital, 1968.
Sociologia de la Muerte (title means "The Sociology of Death"), Tribuna Medica, 1974.

Also contributor to *But Not to Lose,* 1968, *Death and Bereavement,* 1969, *Religion and Bereavement,* 1972, and *Children and Dying,* 1974, all edited by Austin Kutscher, and to *Concerning Death,* 1974. Contributor of more than three hundred articles to religious and professional journals, and a wide variety of popular magazines, including *Modern Bride, Successful Farmer, Adult Student,* and *Yankee.* Member of editorial advisory boards.

WORK IN PROGRESS: Mobilizing the Life Force, with Lawrence LeShan; *With Further Ado: A Guide for Program Chairpersons; Mysticism, Man, and Meaning; The Varieties of Pastoral Language; Pastoral Care of Children and Their Families; A Mystic Looks at Life,* autobiographical essays.

JAHAN, Rounaq 1944-

PERSONAL: Born March 2, 1944, in Naokhali, Bangladesh; daughter of Ahmad (a government employee) and Razia (Begum) Ullah. *Education:* University of Dacca, B.A. (with honors), 1962, M.A., 1963; Harvard University, M.A., 1968, Ph.D., 1970.

ADDRESSES: Home—4 Elephant Rd., Dacca, Bangladesh. *Office*—Department of Political Science, University of Dacca, Ramna, Dacca 2, Bangladesh.

CAREER: University of Dacca, Dacca, Bangladesh, associate professor, 1970-78, professor of political science, 1978—.

MEMBER: American Political Science Association.

WRITINGS:

Pakistan: Failure in National Integration, Columbia University Press, 1972.
Women in Bangladesh, Ford Foundation (Dacca), 1974.
(Contributor) Lebow and Henderson, editors, *Divided Countries in a Divided World,* McKay, 1974.
(Contributor) Dana Raphael, editor, *Being Female,* Mouton, 1975.
(Contributor) Ruby Rohrlich-Leavitt, editor, *Women Cross-Culturally: Change and Challenge,* Mouton, 1975.
(Editor with Hanna Papanek) *Women and Development: Perspectives from South and Southeast Asia,* Bangladesh Institute of Law and International Affairs (Dacca), 1979.
Bangladesh Politics: Problems and Issues, University Press (Dacca), 1980.
(Editor) *Women in Asia,* Minority Rights Group (London), 1980.

Contributor to journals.

WORK IN PROGRESS: Research on problems of political development, and on the political system of Bangladesh.

* * *

JAMES, Preston E(verett) 1899-1986

PERSONAL: Born February 14, 1899, in Brookline, Mass.; died, 1986; son of Frank Everett (a banker) and Gertrude (Woodworth) James; married Dorothy Tenney Upham, April 3, 1922 (divorced, 1943); married Eileen Woodbury Bowles, July 23, 1943; children: (second marriage) Everett Woodbury. *Education:* Harvard University, B.A., 1920, M.A., 1921; Clark University, Ph.D., 1923. *Politics:* Independent. *Religion:* Unitarian Universalist.

ADDRESSES: Home—379 Villa Dr. S., Atlantis, Fla. 33462.

CAREER: Clark University, Worcester, Mass., instructor in geography, 1921-23; University of Michigan, Ann Arbor, instructor, 1923-24, assistant professor, 1924-28, associate professor, 1928-34, professor of geography, 1934-45; Syracuse University, Syracuse, N.Y., professor of geography, 1945-61, Frank Smalley Professor of Geography, 1961-64, Maxwell Professor of Geography, 1964-69, Maxwell Professor Emeritus, 1970-86, chairman of department, 1951-1970. Fulbright professor, University of Edinburgh, 1957. Visiting professor, University of Brazil, 1949-50, University of Puerto Rico, 1971. Adjunct professor, Florida Atlantic University, Boca Raton. Member, National Research Council, 1937-40; member of Committee on Geophysics and Geography, Research and Development Board, 1948-53; member of Commission on Geography, Pan American Institute of Geography and History, 1949-57. Member of U.S. delegation to International Geographical Congress in Rio de Janeiro, 1956, London, 1964, New Delhi, 1968, and Montreal, 1972. *Military service:* U.S. Army, Infantry, 1918. U.S. Army Reserve, Military Intelligence Reserve, 1923-41; recalled to active duty, Office of Strategic Services (OSS), 1941-45; became colonel.

MEMBER: American Academy of Arts and Sciences, Association of American Geographers (secretary, 1936-41; president, 1951-52; honorary president, 1966), Council for Latin American Affairs (president, 1957), American Geographical Society, National Council on Geography Education, American Meteorological Society, Sigma Xi, Phi Kappa Phi, Cosmos Club (Washington, D.C.), Rotary Club of Syracuse.

AWARDS, HONORS: National Council for Geographic Education, Distinguished Writing Award, 1963, and distinguished service award, 1964; George Morgan Ward Medal, Rollins College, 1964; Pan American Medal, Pan American Institute of Geography and History, 1965; David Livingstone Centenary Medal, American Geographical Society, 1966; Sc.D., Eastern Michigan University, 1967; LL.D., Clark University, 1968, University of Michigan, 1974; Helen Culver Gold Medal, Geographic Society of Chicago, 1973; L.H.D., Syracuse University, 1973.

WRITINGS:

An Outline of Geography, Ginn, 1935.
Latin America, Odyssey, 1942, 5th edition, Wiley, 1986.
Brazil, Odyssey, 1946.
A Geography of Man, Blaisdell, 1949, 3rd edition, Xerox College Publishing, 1966.
(Editor with Clarence F. Jones) *American Geography: Inventory and Prospect,* Syracuse University Press for Association of American Geographers, 1954.
(With Nelda Davis) *The Wide World: A Geography,* Macmillan, 1959, 4th edition, 1972.
(Editor and contributor) *New Viewpoints in Geography,* National Council for the Social Studies, 1959.
One World Divided: A Geologist Looks at the Modern World, Ginn, 1964, 3rd edition, Wiley, 1980.
Introduction to Latin America, Odyssey, 1964.
One World Perspective, Blaisdell, 1964.
(Editor with Lorrin Kennamer) *Geography as a Professional Field,* U.S. Office of Education, 1966.
(With Gertrude Whipple and Morris Weiss) *Man on the Earth,* Macmillan, 1971.
On Geography: Selected Writings of Preston E. James, edited by D. W. Meinig, Syracuse University Press, 1971.
All Possible Worlds: A History of Geographical Ideas, Bobbs-Merrill, 1972, 2nd edition, Wiley, 1981.
(With Geoffrey J. Martin) *The Association of American Geographers, the First Seventy-five Years, 1904-1979,* The Association of American Geographers, 1978.
(With Davis) *Global Geography* (textbook with teacher's edition), Macmillan, 1981.

Contributor to about a dozen books on geography, world affairs, and Latin America.

ELEMENTARY GEOGRAPHIES; WITH GERTRUDE WHIPPLE

Our Earth, Macmillan, 1947.
Using Our Earth, Macmillan, 1947.
Living on Our Earth, Macmillan, 1948.
At Home on Our Earth, Macmillan, 1949.
Neighbors on Our Earth, Macmillan, 1950.
Our Earth and Man, Macmillan, 1951.
Our Changing Earth, Macmillan, 1954.

OTHER

Contributor to encyclopedias, annals, and yearbooks of learned societies. Contributor of more than one hundred papers and articles to professional journals in the United States, Europe, and South America.

OBITUARIES:

PERIODICALS

Journal of Geography, November/December, 1986.*

* * *

JEFFERSON, Alan 1921-

PERSONAL: Born March 20, 1921, in Surrey, England; son of H. E. and Dorothy (Clark) Jefferson; married Elisabeth Ann Grogan (a dancer), 1944 (divorced, 1949); married Joan Pamela Bailey (a singer), July 22, 1955 (divorced, 1976); married Antonia Raeburn (an author), 1976; children: (first marriage) one son; (second marriage) two sons, one daughter; (third marriage) two sons. *Education:* Attended Rydal School, 1935-37, and Old Vic Theatre School, 1947-48.

ADDRESSES: *Home*—Deviock Farm House, Deviock, Torpoint, Cornwall PL11 3DL, England. *Agent*—Watson & Little, Ltd., 26 Charing Cross Rd., London WC2H 0DG, England.

CAREER: Stage manager and producer in theatres in London and Stratford-on-Avon, England, 1948-54; worked for various advertising agencies in London, 1954-62, and for Shell-Mex and B. P. Ltd., London, 1962-66; London Symphony Orchestra, London, administrator, 1967-68; British Broadcasting Corp. (BBC), London, orchestral and concerts manager, 1968-73. Professor of vocal interpretation, Guildhall School of Music and Drama, 1967-74. Deputy registrar of births and deaths, 1974-84. *Military service:* British Army, Duke of Cornwall's Light Infantry, Reconnaissance Corps, Parachute Regiment, 1939-46; became captain.

WRITINGS:

The Operas of Richard Strauss in Great Britain: 1910-1963, Putnam, 1964.
The Leider of Richard Strauss, Praeger, 1971.
Delius, Octagon, 1972.
Inside the Orchestra, Reid, 1974.
The Life of Richard Strauss (biography), David & Charles, 1975.
The Glory of Opera, Putnam, 1976.
Sir Thomas Beecham: A Centenary Tribute, Macdonald & Jane's Publishers, 1979.
The Complete Gilbert and Sullivan Opera Guide, Webb & Bower, 1984.
Richard Strauss: Der Rosenkavalier, Cambridge University Press, 1986.
Assault of the Guns of Merville: D-Day and After, J. Murray, 1987.
Lotte Lehman: A Centenary Biography, Julia Macrae Books, 1988.

* * *

JENNINGS, Gary (Gayne) 1928-

PERSONAL: Born September 20, 1928, in Buena Vista, Va.; son of Glen Edward (a printer) and Vaughnye May (Bays) Jennings; children: Jesse G. *Education:* Studied with New York Art Students League, 1949-51.

ADDRESSES: *Home*—Lexington, Va. *Agent*—McIntosh & Otis, Inc., 310 Madison Ave., New York, N.Y. 10017.

CAREER: Writer. Copywriter and account executive for advertising agencies, New York, N.Y., 1947-58; newspaper reporter in California and Virginia, 1958-61; managing editor, *Dude* and *Gent*, 1962-63. *Military service:* U.S. Army, Infantry, 1952-54; served as correspondent in Korea; awarded Bronze Star, citation from Republic of Korea Ministry of Information.

MEMBER: PEN International, Authors Guild, Authors League of America, Pocaliers Club.

WRITINGS:

Personalities of Language, Crowell, 1965, revised and updated edition published as *World of Words: The Personalities of Language,* Atheneum, 1984.

The Treasure of the Superstition Mountains (nonfiction), Norton, 1973.

The Terrible Teague Bunch (novel), Norton, 1975.

Sow the Seeds of Hemp (novel), Norton, 1976.

Aztec (novel; Literary Guild selection), Atheneum, 1980.

The Journeyer (novel; Literary Guild selection), Atheneum, 1984.

Spangle (novel; Literary Guild selection), Atheneum, 1987.

NONFICTION FOR YOUNG ADULTS

March of the Robots, Dial, 1962.

The Movie Book, Dial, 1963.

Black Magic, White Magic, Dial, 1964.

Parades!, Lippincott, 1966.

The Killer Storms: Hurricanes, Typhoons, and Tornadoes, Lippincott, 1970.

The Shrinking Outdoors, Lippincott, 1972.

The Earth Book, Lippincott, 1974.

March of the Heroes, Association Press, 1975.

March of the Gods, Association Press, 1976.

March of the Demons, Association Press, 1978.

OTHER

The Rope in the Jungle (novel for young adults), Lippincott, 1976.

Contributor to numerous anthologies and textbooks. Contributor of articles, short stories, and essays to periodicals, including *American Heritage, Cosmopolitan, Fantasy & Science Fiction, Harper's, National Geographic, New York Times Book Review, Reader's Digest, Redbook,* and *Ellery Queen's Mystery Magazine.*

WORK IN PROGRESS: a novel dealing with the Ostrogoths in the time of Theodoric the Great.

SIDELIGHTS: "In rubbing the myths of each race to their common bones, Gary Jennings has produced in *Aztec* a monumental novel" about the Spanish conquest of Mexico in the sixteenth century, notes Nicholas Shakespeare in the London *Times.* Jennings unfolds the story of the overthrow of the natives "through the voice of the amiable Mixtli," writes Judith Matloff in *Saturday Review.* "In picaresque fashion, Mixtli travels the length and breadth of Mexico, working as scribe, merchant, warrior, and ambassador to Montezuma," thus becoming involved in various aspects of the war against the conquistadores. In addition, the novel contains an abundance of details about the Aztecs—their culture, their religion, their customs, their daily life.

In preparing to write the novel, Jennings lived for ten years in Mexico while conducting research on Aztec culture and the Spanish conquest. He read many accounts about the wars, but found many of them biased against the Indians. So, as Jennings told John F. Baker in a *Publishers Weekly* interview, "I began to study the Nahuatl language [of the Aztecs], and it shows them as people who had a sense of the bawdy, and who had all sorts of human reactions. I wanted to bring them alive as flesh-and-blood people." The author traveled about the country, seeking primary sources and "trying to get a sense, from living Indians, of their legendary past," recounts Baker. Jennings's research pays off, for the voice of his narrator Mixtli is filled with resonances of the Nahuatl speech. As *Times Literary Supplement* contributor Gordon Brotherston comments, "Much of the novel's power stems from Nahua sources transcribed into the alphabet after the Spanish invasion, not just the direct quotations from Nahua poems and of set pieces . . . but the whole range of devices used by Mixtli to keep his audience alert."

"Historical novels are most often praised or dismissed as novels," observes Thomas M. Disch in the *Washington Post Book World,* "but surely it is their power as narrative history that is their main strength, the power to evoke the *feel* of ages lost to memory. . . . So it is with Gary Jennings's *Aztec,*" adds Disch. The novel "has everything that makes a story vulgarly appealing, in the best sense of the phrase," remarks Christopher Lehmann-Haupt of the *New York Times.* "It has sex—my goodness, does it have sex! . . . [and] it has violence," enumerates the critic. While these elements may be appealing, "the violence usually serves a constructive storytelling purpose . . . and the sexual passages almost always relate to the book's most fascinating and subtle aspect, which is the way the hero, Mixtli, unconsciously re-enacts the life of the Indian god Quetzalcoatl," continues Lehmann-Haupt. "It is this particular dimension of 'Aztec' which raises it above the level of a mere historical potboiler."

In *The Journeyer,* Jennings relates the "other half" of Marco Polo's adventures, the half the famous explorer supposedly withheld so as not to offend European sensibilities. The author recreated much of Polo's route for his research, traveling through Italy, the Middle East, and Central and Southeast Asia by various modes of transport—including camel and elephant. "Thus he enlivens his picaresque story with wonderfully detailed descriptions of the landscape, climate, flora and fauna Polo encountered along the way," writes Gene Lyons in *Newsweek.* "As Jennings did for pre-Hispanic Mexico in 'Aztec,' " comments Grover Sales in the *Los Angeles Times Book Review,* "he has enriched 'The Journeyer' with an anthropologist's knowledge of diverse lands and cultures." Adds the critic: "Jennings combines inexhaustible research with the yarn-spinner's art, drawing indelible portraits of Marco and his companions on the long journey."

Chicago Tribune Book World contributor Jack Dierks similarly finds the novel engrossing, explaining that "employing both great sweep and meticulous detail, Jennings has produced an impressively learned gem of the astounding and the titillating. As pure travelogue it is impeccable," says the critic, "and the adventures that befall our heroes come like tales spun out by some erudite and prurient Scheherazade, heaping wonder onto oddity." Lehmann-Haupt, however, expresses some reservations about the work: "For all the wonders of 'The Journeyer'—its sweep, its humor, its vivid scenery, its sustained narrative drive—I found it ever so faintly disappointing after the brilliance of 'Aztec.' Part of the problem may be the predictability" of the novel, for "many of the deeper patterns of 'Aztec' are repeated in 'The Journeyer,' " observes Lehmann-Haupt. But Sales believes that "with astonishing speed and consummate skill, novelist Gary Jennings has capped his 1980 'Aztec,' " while Dierks considers it an "even more compelling work of derring-do."

For *Spangle,* his third and largest historical work, Jennings's research involved traveling with nine different circuses in America and Europe. The novel follows the adventures of "Florian's Flourishing Florilegium" and Zachary Edge, a Southern Civil War veteran who joins the circus troupe after the war. Like the author's previous works, *Spangle* contains the same elements of the spectacle, sex, violence, and detail that mark most historical fiction. "Yet for Gary Jennings," notes Lehmann-Haupt, "the formula seems to work uniquely. There is something mesmerizing about the world he creates." *Los Angeles Times Book Review* contributor MacDonald Harris feels the work "is impressive in its sheer mass and richness, in the enthusiasm and energy of its telling, in the obvious pleasure the author takes in the work." This enthusiasm, asserts Harris, "is contagious. Before the novel is over we develop, along with the characters, a contempt for non-circus people and a conviction that the only sensible and reasonable thing to do . . . is to run away and join a circus."

While some critics consider the amount of detail and breadth of scope in Jennings's work enriching, Donna Olendorf finds it distracting. Writing in the *Detroit Free Press,* Olendorf remarks that "if only [Jennings] had restricted his focus to the performing arena, 'Spangle' might have shone. Instead, Jennings changes gears as the caravan rumbles along, shifting from history into romantic tragedy. . . . This tangled tale has more contortions than the Florilegium's acrobat." And Lehmann-Haupt points out that one "disappointment about 'Spangle' is that, like 'The Journeyer,' it lacks the multiple layers of meaning that made 'Aztec,' with its re-enactment by the hero of the life of the god Quetzalcoatl, so unusual." But Harris thinks that the setting, more contemporary than Jennings's previous work, makes it "a realistic novel, not a romance. . . . It is also the great strength of 'Spangle' and its superiority over his first two books." Similarly, H. J. Kirchhoff states in the Toronto *Globe and Mail* that the protagonists "are picaresque triumphs, and the supporting cast . . . is strong from top to bottom." Kirchhoff concludes by commenting that any faults "that blemished the earlier books seem to have been overcome; Spangle is simply excellent."

Aztec, The Journeyer, and *Spangle* have been published in ten countries abroad.

BIOGRAPHICAL/CRITICAL SOURCES:

PERIODICALS

Chicago Tribune Book World, November 30, 1980, March 25, 1984.
Detroit Free Press, January 10, 1988.
Globe and Mail (Toronto), February 25, 1984, April 16, 1988.
Los Angeles Times, March 26, 1985.
Los Angeles Times Book Review, January 29, 1984, November 1, 1987.
Newsweek, January 9, 1984.
New York Times, February 5, 1981, January 10, 1984, November 16, 1987.
New York Times Book Review, December 14, 1980.
Publishers Weekly, December 12, 1980.
Saturday Review, November, 1980.
Times (London), July 9, 1981.
Times Literary Supplement, July 24, 1981.
Washington Post, November 30, 1987.
Washington Post Book World, November 30, 1980, November 29, 1984.

JENNINGS, Robert
See HAMILTON, Charles (Harold St. John)

* * *

JHABVALA, Ruth Prawer 1927-

PERSONAL: Born May 7, 1927, in Cologne, Germany (now West Germany); came to England, 1939; naturalized British citizen, 1948; naturalized U.S. citizen, 1986; daughter of Marcus (owner of a clothing business) and Eleonora (Cohn) Prawer; married Cyrus S. H. Jhabvala (an architect), 1951; children: Renana, Ava, Firoza. *Education:* Queen Mary College, London, M.A., 1951.

ADDRESSES: Home and office—400 East 52nd St., New York, N.Y. 10022. *Agent*—Harriet Wasserman, 137 East 36th St., New York, N.Y. 10016.

CAREER: Full-time writer, 1951—.

AWARDS, HONORS: Booker Award for Fiction, National Book League, 1975, for *Heat and Dust;* Guggenheim fellow, 1976; Neil Gunn International fellow, 1979; MacArthur Foundation fellow, 1986-89; Writers Guild of America Award for best adapted screenplay, 1986, and Academy Award (Oscar) for best screenplay adapted from another medium, 1987, both for "A Room with a View"; D.Litt., London University.

WRITINGS:

FICTION

To Whom She Will, Allen & Unwin, 1955, reprinted, Penguin, 1985, published as *Amrita,* Norton, 1956, reprinted, Fireside Paperbacks, 1989.
The Nature of Passion, Allen & Unwin, 1956, Norton, 1957, reprinted, Penguin, 1986.
Esmond in India, Allen & Unwin, 1957, Norton, 1958, reprinted, Penguin, 1980.
The Householder (also see below), Norton, 1960, reprinted, 1985.
Get Ready for Battle, J. Murray, 1962, Norton, 1963, reprinted, Fireside Paperbacks, 1989.
Like Birds, Like Fishes and Other Stories, J. Murray, 1963, Norton, 1964, reprinted, Granada, 1984.
A Backward Place, Norton, 1965, reprinted, Penguin, 1980.
A Stronger Climate: Nine Stories, J. Murray, 1968, Norton, 1969, reprinted, Granada, 1983.
An Experience of India (stories), J. Murray, 1971, Norton, 1972.
A New Dominion, J. Murray, 1972, published as *Travelers,* Harper, 1973.
Heat and Dust (also see below), J. Murray, 1975, Harper, 1976.
How I Became a Holy Mother and Other Stories, J. Murray, 1975, Harper, 1976.
In Search of Love and Beauty, Morrow, 1983.
Out of India: Selected Stories, Morrow, 1986.
Three Continents, Morrow, 1987.

SCREENPLAYS

"The Householder" (based on her novel), Royal, 1963.
(With James Ivory) *Shakespeare Wallah* (produced by Merchant-Ivory Productions, 1966), Grove, 1973.
(With Ivory) "The Guru," Twentieth Century-Fox, 1968.
"Bombay Talkie," Merchant-Ivory Productions, 1970.
Autobiography of a Princess, Harper, 1975.
"Roseland," Merchant-Ivory Productions, 1977.
"Hullabaloo over Georgie and Bonnie's Pictures," Contemporary, 1978.

(With Ivory) "The Europeans" (based on the novel by Henry James), Levitt-Pickman, 1979.

"Jane Austen in Manhattan," Contemporary, 1980.

(With Ivory) "Quartet" (based on the novel by Jean Rhys), Lyric International/New World, 1981.

"Heat and Dust" (based on her novel), Merchant-Ivory Productions, 1983.

"The Bostonians" (based on the novel by James), Merchant-Ivory Productions, 1984.

"The Courtesans of Bombay," Channel 4, England/New Yorker Films, 1985.

"A Room with a View" (based on the novel by E. M. Forster), Merchant-Ivory Productions, 1986.

(With John Schlesinger) "Madame Sousatzka" (based on the novel by Bernice Rubens), Universal, 1988.

WORK IN PROGRESS: A screenplay adaptation of Evan S. Connell's *Mr. Bridge* and *Mrs. Bridge;* a novel.

SIDELIGHTS: Although Ruth Prawer Jhabvala has long been celebrated in Europe and India for her quality fiction and screenplays, it was not until she captured an Academy Award for her adaptation of "A Room with a View" that she began winning widespread attention in the United States for her work. As a German-born, British citizen living in India for over twenty years, and as a New Yorker for over a decade, Jhabvala brings a unique perspective to her novels and stories of East-West conflict. "With a cool, ironic eye and a feeling for social nuance," asserts Bernard Weinraub in a *New York Times Magazine* article, Jhabvala "[has] developed a series of themes—families battered by change in present-day India, the timeless European fascination with the subcontinent—that were probably both incomprehensible and inconsequential to readers who were not intrigued with India in the first place. And yet," continues the critic, "as Mrs. Jhabvala's work darkened and turned more melancholy, as her detachment grew chilling in her later work, critics began to notice that the writer's India had become as universal as Faulkner's Yoknapatawpha and Chekhov's czarist Russia." "Like Jane Austen," notes *Saturday Review* contributor Katha Pollitt, Jhabvala "treats satirically and intimately a world in which conventions are precisely defined and widely accepted, even by those who are most harmed by them."

Indeed, since the appearance of her first work in 1955, *Amrita* (published in England as *To Whom She Will*), Jhabvala has frequently been compared to the great English writer, due to her cutting portrayals of the foibles of the Indian middle-class. In *Amrita,* comments Nancy Wilson Ross in the *New York Herald Tribune Book Review,* Jhabvala "has written a fresh and witty novel about modern India. It is not necessary to know anything about the customs and habits of . . . New Delhi—the setting of Mrs. Jhabvala's lively comedy of manners—to enjoy her ironic social commentary." And in a *Times Literary Supplement* review of *A Backward Place,* one critic maintains that while Jhabvala "has not the sustained brilliance that Jane Austen often rises to . . . all the same her many excellent qualities are nearly all Austenish ones, and they make her a most interesting and satisfactory writer." "At least three British reviewers have compared her to Jane Austen," observes J. F. Muehl in his *Saturday Review* account of Jhabvala's debut novel, "and the comparison is not only just; it is inevitable."

Jhabvala's later fiction, while still set in India, has focused more on the differences and resultant conflicts between Eastern and Western cultures, and has led to comparison with the work of yet another great English novelist. Jhabvala's Booker Prize-winner *Heat and Dust,* for example, which *Washington Post Book World* contributor calls "crafted with a technical skill as assured as it is unobtrusive," is, "because of its setting and its theme of Anglo-Indian relationships, reminiscent of E. M. Forster's great novel, *A Passage to India.*" The story of a young British woman who is journeying through India in imitation of her grandfather's first wife Olivia, *Heat and Dust* contains "social comedy . . . as funny and as sympathetic as it is in Mrs. Jhabvala's earlier novels, even though she has departed from her more usual theme of middle-class Indian life," states Brigid Allen in the *Times Literary Supplement.* The account presents the parallel experiences of the two women by moving between the journal of the elder and the story of the younger; Pearl K. Bell says in the *New York Times Book Review* that "Jhabvala moves nimbly between the two generations and the divergent points of time and sentiment." The critic elaborates: "Writing with austere emphatic economy, [Jhabvala] does not belabor the parallels between the two levels of narrative—at least not until the end. Like Forster, she renders the barriers of incomprehension and futility that persist between English and Indians with witty precision."

While *New York Review of Books* contributor Frank Kermode agrees that Jhabvala's "two narratives are quite subtly plaited, with magical chiming between the two," he believes that the author writes "impassively, almost incuriously," about her characters' failures. But Julian Barnes finds this distancing appropriate and deliberate, noting in the *New Statesman* that Jhabvala "offers no comment except through the subsequent experiences of the narrator, which gradually flow into a distorted, parallel version of Olivia's life." Barnes adds that "the two halves make up a stylish and gentle exploration of the theme of Anglo-Indian interpenetration, confirming Aziz's prophetic remarks in *A Passage to India* about the relationship between the two nations." Calling *Heat and Dust* "distinguished by a rapier wit and subtlety," Dorothy Rabinowitz likewise concludes in the *Saturday Review* that Jhabvala's novel "is, particularly in its delicate chartings of passion and of the growth of consciousness, a superb story, a gift to those who care for the novel, and to the art of fiction itself."

Although Jhabvala had been securing a name for herself as one of the foremost modern writers about India after the publication of *Heat and Dust,* she was finding it difficult both to remain in and write about her adopted country. Critics began observing an increasing amount of ambivalence toward India in Jhabvala's writing, a change evident in her retrospective collection of stories, *Out of India.* The *New York Times*'s Michiko Kakutani, for example, comments that "bit by bit, . . . the stories in 'Out of India' darken, grow denser and more ambiguous. In choosing narrative strategies that are increasingly ambitious," explains the reviewer, "Mrs. Jhabvala gradually moves beyond the tidy formulations of the comedy of manners, and a strain of melancholy also begins to creep into her writing."

Village Voice contributor Vivian Gornick similarly sees a sense of "oppressiveness" in Jhabvala's writing, and speculates that "Jhabvala is driven to separate herself from India." The critic believes that this need undermines the author's work: "That drive deprives her of empathy and, inevitably, it deprives her characters of full humanness." In contrast, Paul Gray claims in his *Time* review that the stories in *Out of India* "do not demystify India; they pay the place tributes of empathy and grace." "Reading [these stories] is like watching a scene through an exceptionally clear telescope," states Rumer Godden in the *New York Times Book Review.* This distance, however, "does not take away from the stories' sureness of touch," Godden continues. "They have a beginning, middle and end, but fused so subtly we drift into them—and are immediately at home—and drift out again."

Jhabvala's most recent works, while eschewing the familiar Indian setting, still explore some of her usual themes, such as the search for spiritual fulfillment. *Three Continents,* for example, relates the story of 19-year-old twins Michael and Harriet Wishwell, heirs to a large fortune who are drawn to the promises of a trio of supposed spiritual philosophers. The twins become obsessed with the Rawul, his consort the Rani, and their "adopted son" Crishi, and turn over control of their lives and fortune to the swindlers. "In its geographical scope, its large and far-flung cast and its relentless scrutiny of both sexual and intellectual thralldom," maintains Laura Shapiro in *Newsweek, Three Continents* "is Jhabvala's most ambitious and impressive work." The *Los Angeles Times*'s Elaine Kendall similarly calls the novel "perhaps [Jhabvala's] most ambitious work," remarking that it "not only confronts these issues [from her previous work] directly but in a more contemporary context."

Despite these assessments of Jhabvala's novel as "ambitious," some critics fault the author for her narrative method. "The narrative belongs to Harriet," Nancy Wigston notes in the Toronto *Globe and Mail,* "and therein lies much of the frustration of the book. Harriet may not be a phony," the reviewer explains, "but she is somewhat of an airhead . . . [and] her insights are limited." Kendall likewise observes that "while the youth and naivete of the narrator help our credulity, ultimately we're left with an inescapable skepticism." "This is an intelligent but unsatisfactory novel," Anita Brookner asserts in the *Spectator,* "intelligent because the author is and cannot help but be so, unsatisfactory because the effort of staying inside Harriet's stupid head conveys a certain tedium." Victoria Glendinning, however, believes that Harriet's narration provides an added dimension: "One of the cleverest things about the writing is the way Ruth Prawer Jhabvala shows how on one level Harriet is aware of everything that is happening, while never admitting it to herself," as the critic writes in the London *Times. Three Continents,* she adds, "[is] a book full of urgent messages about the East and West, about the need to belong somewhere, and the sinister pressures of the modern world." "As a meditation on the twin themes of inheritance and family, 'Three Continents' is a significant achievement," comments *New York Times Book Review* contributor Peter Ackroyd, concluding that "as a guidebook to the inner recesses of idealism and desire it is undoubtedly a success."

While Jhabvala has been a consistent force on the literary scene, she is also a member of the longest producer-director-writer partnership in film history. Along with Ismail Merchant and James Ivory, Jhabvala has helped create numerous movies that, while not hits at the box office, have been praised by critics for their consistent literary quality. Although the author was initially reluctant to attempt screenplays, the dramatic qualities necessary for films have always been present in Jhabvala's work, thinks critic Yasmine Gooneratne. Writing in *World Literature Written in English,* Gooneratne states that the author's early novels have "the tight structure of stage plays, and even [contain] casts of characters. The process by which the comparative simplicities of satiric drama yield to the complexity of ironic fiction is hastened, it would appear, through her experience of working repeatedly within the narrow limits of a screenplay." The critic cites the film-like structure of *Heat and Dust* as an example, and adds that "despite the fact that Mrs. Jhabvala's increasing technical skill as a writer of screenplays has helped her to devise ways and means to make the cinema screen yield workable equivalents for her established fictional techniques, it is probable that her artistry as a fiction-writer still outstrips her achievement as a writer for film. So rapid has her development been, however," Gooneratne continues, "that this is unlikely to be the case for very long." This prediction has proved accurate, for recent Merchant-Ivory-Jhabvala productions have been popular as well as critical successes.

For example, about "The Bostonians," the 1984 adaptation of Henry James's novel, Vincent Canby of the *New York Times* remarks that "it's now apparent [that the trio has] enriched and refined their individual talents to the point where they have now made what must be one of their best films as well as one of the best adaptations of a major literary work ever to come onto the screen." The best—until Jhabvala and her collaborators produced the film that would earn the author an Oscar, 1986's "A Room with a View." Director Ivory and screenwriter Jhabvala "have taken E. M. Forster's 1908 novel and preserved its wit, irony and brilliant observation of character," states Lawrence O'Toole in *Maclean's.* "And they never allow its theme—the importance of choosing passion over propriety—to escape their grasp." Calling the trio's film "an exceptionally faithful, ebullient screen equivalent to a literary work that lesser talents would embalm," Canby notes that "maybe more important than anything else [in the film] is the narrative tone." He explains that Ivory and Jhabvala "have somehow found a voice for the film not unlike that of Forster, who tells the story of 'A Room with a View' with as much genuine concern as astonished amusement. That's quite an achievement." Audiences found the film entertaining as well, for "A Room with a View" became the most popular Merchant-Ivory-Jhabvala collaboration ever, setting house records at many theaters.

While she has been compared to several classic writers, Jhabvala has achieved a prominent literary standing with her consistently excellent work, and critics no longer need comparisons to describe its quality. "How does one know when one is in the grip of art, of a literary power?" asks Rabinowitz in the *New York Times Book Review.* "One feels, amongst other things, the force of personality behind the cadence of each line, the sensibility behind the twist of the syllable. One feels the texture of the unspoken, the very accents of a writer's reticence." Jhabvala, maintains the critic, "seems to come naturally by a good deal of that reticence." Godden similarly praises the author for her original voice: "Time has proved [her unique]; she has written [numerous works] . . . and I could wager there is not in any of them one shoddy line or unnecessary word, a standard few writers achieve. Each book," Godden continues, "has her hallmark of balance, subtlety, wry humor and beauty." And Weinraub, in assessing Jhabvala's reputation in the literary community, quotes the late novelist C. P. Snow: "Someone once said that the definition of the highest art is that one should feel that life is this and not otherwise. I do not know of a writer living who gives that feeling with more unqualified certainty than Mrs. Jhabvala."

CA INTERVIEW

CA interviewed Ruth Prawer Jhabvala by telephone on September 2, 1988, at her home in New York, New York.

CA: After living in India for twenty-four years, you moved in 1975 to New York City, where you spend most of your time, visiting India for a part of each year. Does New York continue to provide amply both the stimuli and the more necessary solitude you need for your writing?

JHABVALA: Solitude, certainly. Stimuli? I don't really need outside stimuli that much anymore. It doesn't make that much difference to me now.

CA: In the often-quoted introduction to Out of India, *you described the ambivalence of your feelings about that country. Now that you see India as a non-resident, though still on a regular basis, has your outlook on it changed at all?*

JHABVALA: The attitude hasn't really changed, but the emotional pressure certainly has. I'm no longer in that situation, and I'm calmer about it.

CA: Is India easier for you to write about from a distance?

JHABVALA: If I were writing about India as I used to, as the center of my interest, then I would want to be there. But as I am no longer doing that, as it isn't the central subject anymore that obsesses me, I'm better off outside, I think. When I do write about India, it's in a much more objective way, though probably I don't write about it in such a committed way as I did.

CA: In Search of Love and Beauty *revolved around the guru figure Leo Kellerman. In* Three Continents, *there's the much more sinister Crishi. The concern with charismatic men and the women who flock around them goes way back in your work, yet you continue to examine it with fresh interest. Would you comment on the fascination it holds for you—and obviously for your readers?*

JHABVALA: It's something that I first saw and learned about in India in the sixties. Then it became so interesting to me, so important to me, I saw it over and over again; I felt it was something that was happening to people, and especially to women, very much nowadays, the need to have a kind of higher authority figure.

CA: Certainly the charismatic is topical, given all the activities of evangelical groups and personalities in this country right now, which are very much in the news.

JHABVALA: Yes. People seem to need something like that. I suppose they had an entity like the church in their lives before, as well as stronger family relationships that they could depend and lean on. But now both the family relationships and the priest relationship, the church relationship, are gone, and there's this absolute need people seem to have for that kind of passionate personal and super-personal fulfillment. I suppose there is a physical need tied up with it too, besides the spiritual need—there are so many facets of it. But it does seem to be a tremendous *want* within the human being.

CA: Would you talk about the connections between Three Continents *and* In Search of Love and Beauty? *Some are apparent to the reader, but perhaps there are more in your mind that might not be.*

JHABVALA: I never thought of them as connected except in that they are my first two non-Indian novels—that is, they're not centered in India; they're much more concerned with European characters, and set largely outside India. That is my principal connection between them. They're my own return to Europe, in a way, but of course dragging with me everything I had in India, all the same questions and the same personality. I can't get away from myself.

CA: When you finished the earlier book, had Three Continents *already taken shape in your imagination?*

JHABVALA: Not at all. I always think each novel is the last—not that I think it's a final statement, but I think, I just can't go through this again. But then, after a period of not writing (I wouldn't call it lying fallow, but just after some time), quite naturally a new book comes up; I have something more I want to write about.

CA: You talked with Bernard Weinraub for the New York Times Magazine *about the irony of your creating such characters as the large, passionate Louise and the flamboyant Regi in* In Search of Love and Beauty, *whom you regard as the opposite of you. Do you find such characters hard to get a writer's grasp on because of their difference?*

JHABVALA: No. On the contrary, they're much easier. You step back and you get a much easier view. In India, people were so far removed from me. I could see them much more objectively because they weren't me at all.

CA: Out of India *brings together stories from four previous collections, going back to 1963 with* Like Birds, Like Fishes. *How did you go about making the selection of stories?*

JHABVALA: I didn't reread them. I just put in the ones that I remembered the most vividly, or the ones that struck me first. Those must be the ones that have the most significance for me, so they must be the ones that somehow came out the best. I didn't have to think twice; they were just my own favorites as I remembered them. I think many writers don't reread their work, so what was written five, ten, twenty, thirty years ago you have only the vaguest idea of. There are some things, some novels and some stories, that I have completely forgotten. When it comes to selecting, I assume the things I happen to remember are the ones that are the strongest, that mean the most to me, so I trust they are the ones that would have the most meaning for potential readers.

CA: Have any of your novels had their genesis directly from short stories?

JHABVALA: With *Heat and Dust* I thought I was writing a short story and found that I was writing a novel. That was the only time it happened to me. Usually I'm absolutely sure whether I'm writing a story or a novel.

CA: Your husband did the lovely endpaper drawings for Travelers, In Search of Love and Beauty, *and* Out of India—*and maybe for other books that I haven't seen.*

JHABVALA: He's done all the covers of the new Simon & Schuster Fireside paperback editions: *Out of India, Heat and Dust, Travelers,* and *Three Continents.*

CA: You've also said that he was your translator when you first went to India, "literally and in other ways." How else does he play a part in your work?

JHABVALA: Just like that. When we were in India, I wouldn't have been able to make head or tail of anything without him. He himself is so witty and perceptive, I just learned from him. I couldn't speak Hindi for years and years. He spoke fluently, and somehow through him I knew what people were saying.

CA: Does he read your work while it's in progress?

JHABVALA: Not so much now, but in the early days he was always the first reader.

CA: Your three daughters grew up in India. How does their perspective on that country differ from your own, which was formed when you were an adult and more an outsider?

JHABVALA: Theirs is much more straightforward. They were born in India; they all stayed there until they were eighteen and went to school; and they think of themselves as completely and absolutely Indian, although two of them live abroad, now married to non-Indians. Before they were married, they went back to India whenever they could. Now that they're married with a child each, it's more difficult for them. The eldest had no doubt that she wanted to go back and stay. She's a trade union leader. She wanted to go back and work among the poorest of the poor, and that's what she's doing.

CA: Though you've been writing screenplays for Ismail Merchant and James Ivory since 1963, when they persuaded you to do the script for your book The Householder, *surely the most publicized movie you have done as a team is "A Room with a View." Did that work have the crossover effect of bringing some new readers to your fiction?*

JHABVALA: I think the two audiences are completely different. I suppose people who see films may also read books, but to me it's either one or the other. But I may be wrong. Quite recently my books have been more available in America, and I may be getting more readers. But one doesn't really know about these things.

CA: You've called the screenwriting a hobby, indicating that you feel it's definitely secondary, for you, to writing fiction. Do you find the two kinds of writing mutually enriching?

JHABVALA: Yes, I do. I certainly don't think I could write screenplays very well if I didn't, most of the time, work at creating characters and dialogue and situations of my own in my fiction. Then whatever I've accumulated of experience in that, I bring to the screenplays. And in writing novels you also get a certain feel for structure which you have to have in constructing a screenplay. But I also think the screenwriting has definitely influenced my fiction. For instance, I think you can see it in *Heat and Dust,* and in *In Search of Love and Beauty* in the way I've juggled scenes and time sequences around. That's something I learned in films. They certainly are mutually enriching, but one is so much more difficult than the other—writing fiction is much harder.

CA: With filmscripts for books like E. M. Forster's A Room with a View *and Henry James's* The Bostonians, *the atmosphere and setting are particularly important. How much of that must you get into the script?*

JHABVALA: What I think of first of all in writing a script is how to present the story in the most economical terms possible. That includes the characters and the whole ambience, but the ambience is not going to be my job. What I have to do myself in fiction, like actually dressing the characters and furnishing the rooms, somebody else is obviously doing in the film. But, on the other hand, I have to give them the opportunity to do that. I have to give a sense of how the characters are interacting with their setting and why there should be this particular setting and how it will enhance what is going on in their minds and in the dialogue. So I do have to think about all these things, although I don't actually do them in screenwriting as I do in fiction.

CA: Do you find your own books generally easier or harder to adapt to screen than those of other writers?

JHABVALA: I've only done two of mine, *Heat and Dust* and *The Householder.* I'd rather do somebody else's. With my own, I've been over all that and I don't want to do it again. I kept trying to postpone *Heat and Dust,* thinking, Do I have to do this again? In that way you might say your own is more difficult.

CA: Your writing pattern has been described in the past as ten in the morning until one, then usually rest and reading in the afternoons. Is that still the case?

JHABVALA: That's still the case except that I now find it difficult to do a whole ten-to-one stretch. I get tired after an hour and a half or two hours. Sometimes I can still do three, but I do get tired much more quickly now.

CA: What writers, past or present, do you particularly enjoy reading?

JHABVALA: When I'm in India, which is in the winter, I read all the people I've been nurtured on, or nurtured myself on, all the great classics that I so much love. When I'm here, and when I'm working, which is most of the time, then I just read what I have to read that feeds me. For instance, doing a filmscript for a book like *The Bostonians,* obviously I'll read lots of Henry James. And I'll also read whatever else I can that would help, such as material on the feminist movement for that particular book. But for pleasure, and only in India, I read the Russians, Dostoevski and Chekhov, and I read Proust over and over again—and the stalwarts.

CA: There's been a shift in your work from the early comic view to a more pessimistic tone in the later books, as some reviewers have noted. Do you have any feelings about that change?

JHABVALA: I think it happens to many writers. You're lighthearted in your youth and less so as you get older, shadows descend. It seems to be a natural process. You can't stay the same as you were in your early twenties, or view the world in the same way.

CA: What's in progress or planned for the future that you'd like to mention?

JHABVALA: I'm writing another screenplay at the moment. You never know with films, but it's supposed to start next year. It's two books by Evan S. Connell, *Mr. Bridge* and *Mrs. Bridge.* I like the project very much; it's wonderful to do a really good book. I will write another novel. I'm vaguely thinking about it. You know, these things start off like sound waves. It's a long time before they become anything more.

BIOGRAPHICAL/CRITICAL SOURCES:

BOOKS

Contemporary Literary Criticism, Gale, Volume 4, 1975, Volume 8, 1978, Volume 29, 1984.

Gooneratne, Yasmine, *Silence, Exile, and Cunning: The Fiction of Ruth Prawer Jhabvala,* Orient Longman (New Delhi), 1983.

Pritchett, V. S., *The Tale Bearers: Literary Essays,* Random House, 1980.

Sucher, Laurie, *The Fiction of Ruth Prawer Jhabvala,* St. Martin's, 1988.

PERIODICALS

Globe and Mail (Toronto), July 26, 1986, October 17, 1987.

Los Angeles Times, November 9, 1983, September 4, 1987.

Maclean's, March 31, 1986.

Modern Fiction Studies, winter, 1984.

New Statesman, October 31, 1975, April 15, 1983.
Newsweek, April 19, 1976, March 10, 1986, August 24, 1987.
New York Herald Tribune Book Review, January 15, 1956.
New York Review of Books, July 15, 1976.
New York Times, August 30, 1973, July 19, 1983, September 15, 1983, August 2, 1984, August 5, 1984, March 7, 1986, May 17, 1986, July 5, 1986, August 6, 1987.
New York Times Book Review, January 15, 1956, February 2, 1969, July 8, 1973, April 4, 1976, June 12, 1983, May 25, 1986, August 23, 1987.
New York Times Magazine, September 11, 1983.
People, March 17, 1986, September 28, 1987.
Publishers Weekly, June 6, 1986.
Saturday Review, January 14, 1956, March 1, 1969, April 3, 1976, October 30, 1976.
Spectator, April 23, 1983, October 24, 1987.
Time, May 12, 1986, October 6, 1986.
Times (London), February 4, 1983, April 14, 1983, October 15, 1987.
Times Literary Supplement, May 20, 1965, November 7, 1975, April 15, 1983, April 24, 1987, November 13, 1987.
Twentieth Century Literature, July, 1969.
Village Voice, August 2, 1983, May 8, 1986, September 30, 1986.
Washington Post, October 7, 1983, September 22, 1984, April 5, 1986.
Washington Post Book World, September 12, 1976, September 18, 1983, May 25, 1986.
World Literature Written in English, April, 1978, November, 1979.

—*Sketch by Diane Telgen*

—*Interview by Jean W. Ross*

* * *

JOHANNSEN, Hano D. 1933-

PERSONAL: Born December 26, 1933, in Hamburg, Germany (now West Germany); son of Ernst (an author and playwright) and Roselotte (Blank) Johannsen; married Grace Blaker, December, 1958; children: Helen, Paul, Ruth, Naomi. *Education:* Attended Polytechnic Management School, London, 1954-57.

ADDRESSES: *Office*—British Institute of Management, Africa House, 64-78 Kingsway, London WC2B 5PT, England.

CAREER: British Institute of Management, London, England, research officer, 1961-64, head of information department, 1964-68, manager of surveys and publications, 1968-77, head of research and publications, 1977—.

MEMBER: Organisation and Methods Society, Institute of Linguists.

WRITINGS:

(Compiler with A. B. Robertson) *Management Glossary,* Longmans, Green, 1968, American Elsevier, 1969, English-Arabic edition, International Book Centre, 1972.
Inside Information on Careers in Management, Dickens Press, 1969.
Company Organization Structure, British Institute of Management, 1970.
(With G. Terry Page) *The International Dictionary of Management,* Houghton, 1975, 3rd revised edition, Nichols Publishing, 1986.
(Editor) *Business Relocation: Management Checklist and Guide,* State Mutual Book, 1983.
(Editor) *Know Your Training Films: Directory and Reviews of Business and Management Training Films, Videos and Audio-Visual Materials,* two volumes, State Mutual Book, 1985.
(Editor) *The Business Fact Finder,* Kogan Page, 1986.

Editor, *Management Abstracts.*

AVOCATIONAL INTERESTS: Gardening, ceramics, German, mountains.*

* * *

JOHN PAUL I, Pope 1912-1978

PERSONAL: Birth-given name, Albino Luciani; born October 17, 1912, in Forno di Canale (now Canale d'Agordo), Italy; died September 28, 1978, of a heart attack; son of Giovanni (a bricklayer, stonemason, metalsmith, and glassworker) and Bertola (a scullery maid) Luciani. *Education:* Belluno Seminary, degree in philosophy and theology, 1935; Pontifical Gregorian University, graduate study, 1936, laureate in theology, 1947.

ADDRESSES: *Home*—Vatican City, Rome, Italy.

CAREER: Ordained Roman Catholic priest, July 7, 1935; assistant parish priest, Canale d'Agordo, Italy, 1935-37; religion teacher in mining technicians school, Canale d'Agordo, 1935-37; Belluno Seminary, Belluno, Italy, professor of dogmatic theology, canon law, and became deputy director, 1937-47; deputy to bishop of Belluno, 1948-54, Belluno diocese, director of catechism teaching, 1948-54, vicar general, 1954-58; appointed bishop of Vittorio Veneto diocese, Venice, Italy, December 27, 1958; named patriarch of Venice, December 15, 1969; named cardinal of Vittorio Veneto, March 5, 1973; elected pope, August 26, 1978, coronation ceremony, September 3, 1978, papal reign until September 28, 1978. Metropolita of Ecclesiastical Province of Venice; president of Episcopal Conference Triveneta; named by Pope Paul VI to participate in third synod of bishops, 1971; vice-president of Episcopal Conference in Italy, 1972; member, Sacred Congregation for Sacraments and Divine Worship. Consultant for Pope Paul VI, 1963.

WRITINGS:

Catechism Crumbs, [Italy], 1949.
L'origine dell'anima umana secondo Antonio Rosmini: Esposizione e critica, Tip. Vescovile, 1950.
Illustrissimi (title means "Most Illustrious"), Edizioni Messaggero di S. Antonio, 1976, translation by William Weaver published under same title, Little, Brown, 1978.
Il Carisma della semplicita, Logos (Rome), 1978.
Il tempo d'un sorriso, Logos, 1978.
Il dono della chiarezza, Logos, 1979.
The Teachings of Pope John Paul I, Libreria Editirice Vaticana, 1979.
Nauczanie spoteczne (speeches), Osrodek Dokumentacj i Studio Spotecznych (Warsaw), 1980.
The Family, St. Paul Editions, 1981.
To the Church in America, St. Paul Editions, 1981.
La casa sulla roccia, EMP, 1981.
Un Vescovo al Concilio, Citta Nuova (Rome), 1983.

Contributor of numerous articles on church affairs to newspapers and Italian journals.

SIDELIGHTS: Pope John Paul I was distinguished by being the first Holy Father to come from the working classes, and to serve the shortest amount of time as Pope in 373 years. Although highly respected in his own diocese, Albino Luciani was barely considered as a candidate after Pope Paul VI's death on August 6, 1978. However, the electors found in him qualities they thought important to the papacy. He was an Italian, which they felt would enable him to more easily handle the Church's delicate role in Italian politics; he was a pastoral leader, a humble man who could touch the average parishioner with his deep faith; and finally, he was not controversial, but quite conservative on doctrinal issues.

John Paul I's book *Illustrissimi* is a compilation of imaginary letters to illustrious people through the ages, including some of his favorite authors, such as Charles Dickens and Sir Walter Scott. To Mark Twain he wrote: "My students were always excited when I told them 'now I will tell you another story about Mark Twain.' However, I fear my superiors were scandalized—'A bishop who quotes Mark Twain!' Perhaps one should explain to them that bishops are as varied as books are." *Christian Century* contributor David Delaney wrote that *Illustrissimi* "is not a scholarly or devotional classic. . . . The book is worth reading, however, for its insights into a man from a working-class family who seemed genuinely bemused by his election as pope."

BIOGRAPHICAL/CRITICAL SOURCES:

BOOKS

Luciani, Albino, *Illustrissimi,* Little Brown, 1978.

PERIODICALS

Christian Century, March 28, 1979.*

* * *

JOHNSON, Harry G(ordon) 1923-1977

PERSONAL: Born May 26, 1923, in Toronto, Ontario, Canada; died May 8, 1977, in Geneva, Switzerland; son of Henry Herbert and Frances Lily (Muat) Johnson; married Elizabeth Scott (a journalist), May 28, 1948; children: Steven Ragnar, Karen Eve. *Education:* University of Toronto, B.A., 1943, M.A., 1947; Cambridge University, B.A., 1946, M.A., 1951; Harvard University, M.A., 1948, Ph.D., 1958; University of Manchester, M.A., 1960; St. Francis Xavier University, LL.D., 1965.

ADDRESSES: Home—5628 South Dorchester Ave., Chicago, Ill. *Office*—Department of Economics, University of Chicago, 1126 East 59th St., Chicago, Ill. 60637.

CAREER: Cambridge University, Cambridge, England, lecturer, 1950-56, King's College, fellow, 1950-56; University of Manchester, Manchester, England, professor of economic theory, 1956-59; University of Chicago, Chicago, Ill., professor of economics, beginning 1959, became Charles F. Grey Distinguished Service Professor of Economics. Professor, London School of Economics and Political Science, beginning 1966, and Graduate School of International Relations, Geneva, Switzerland.

MEMBER: Royal Economic Society, Econometric Society, Canadian Political Science Association (former president), American Economic Association, Association of University Teachers of Economics (former chairman), Society for Economic Studies, American Academy of Arts and Sciences (fellow), American Association for the Advancement of Science (fellow), Japanese Economic Research Center (honorary member).

AWARDS, HONORS: Prix Mondial Nessim Habif, University of Geneva; Bernhard Harms Prize, University of Kiel.

WRITINGS:

International Trade and Economic Growth, Allen & Unwin, 1958.

Money, Trade and Economic Growth, Allen & Unwin, 1962.

Canada in a Changing World Economy, University of Toronto Press, 1962.

(Editor with Earl J. Hamilton and Albert E. Rees) *Landmarks in Political Economy,* University of Chicago Press, 1962.

(With John W. L. Winder) *Lags in the Effect of Monetary Policy in Canada,* Royal Commission on Banking and Finance, 1962.

The Canadian Quandary, McGraw, 1963.

The World Economy at the Crossroads, Clarendon, 1965.

Economic Policies towards Less Developed Countries, Bookings, 1967.

(Editor) *Economic Nationalism in Old and New States,* University of Chicago Press, 1967.

Essays in Monetary Economics, Allen & Unwin, 1967.

U.S. Economic Policy toward the Developing Countries, Brookings Institution, 1968.

Harmonization of National Economic Policies under Free Trade, University of Toronto Press, 1968.

Economic Approach to Social Questions, Fernhill, 1969.

(Editor) *New Trade Strategy for the World Economy,* University of Toronto Press, 1969.

(With John E. Nash) *United Kingdom and Floating Exchanges: A Debate on the Theoretical and Practical Implications,* Institute of Economic Affairs, 1969.

Crisis of Aid and the Pearson Report, Edinburgh University Press, 1970.

(With A. R. Nobay) *The Current Inflation,* St. Martin's, 1971.

Aspects of the Theory of Tariffs, Harvard University Press, 1971.

Two-Sector Model of General Equilibrium, Beresford Book Service, 1971.

Macroeconomics and Monetary Theory, Gray-Mills Publishing (London), 1971, Aldine, 1972.

Trade Strategy for Rich and Poor Nations, Allen & Unwin, 1971.

Readings in British Monetary Economics, Clarendon, 1972.

Further Essays in Monetary Economics, Allen & Unwin, 1972, Harvard University Press, 1973.

Inflation and the Monetarist Controversy, North-Holland, 1972.

The Theory of Income Distribution, Basil Blackwell, 1973.

(With Alexander K. Swobody) *The Economics of Common Currencies,* Harvard University Press, 1973.

(Editor with Burton A. Weisbrod) *The Daily Economist: A Chronicle of Contemporary Subjects Showing the Scope and Originality of Economic Research and Its Application to Real-World Issues,* Prentice-Hall, 1973.

(Editor with Nobay) *Issues in Monetary Economics: Conference Proceedings,* Oxford University Press, 1974.

(With Melvyn Krauss) *General Equilibrium Analysis,* Allen & Unwin, 1974, Aldine, 1975.

On Economics and Society, University of Chicago Press, 1975, new edition, 1983.

Technology and Economic Interdependence, Macmillan (London), 1975, St. Martin's, 1976.

(Editor) *The New Mercantilism: Some Problems in International Trade, Money and Investment,* St. Martin's, 1975.

(Editor with Jacob A. Frenkel) *The Monetary Approach to Balance of Payment,* University of Toronto Press, 1976.

Selected Essays in Monetary Economics, Allen & Unwin, 1978.

(Editor with Frenkel) *Economics of Exchange Rates,* Addison-Wesley, 1978.

(Editor with Elizabeth S. Johnson) *The Shadow of Keynes: Understanding Keynes, Cambridge, and Keynesian Economics,*

Blackwell Scientific Publications, 1978, Unviersity of Chicago Press, 1979.
(Editor with Richard E. Caves) *Readings in International Economics,* Allen & Unwin, 1978.
(With Austin Whittan) *A Practical Foundation in Accounting,* Allen & Unwin, 1982.

Contributor of articles to economic journals in the United States, Canada, Europe, India, Malaya, and to other publications. Assistant editor, *Review of Economic Studies,* 1950-59; editor, *Manchester School,* 1956-59, *Journal of Political Economy,* beginning 1960. Member of editorial board, *Journal of International Economics.*

SIDELIGHTS: Harry G. Johnson "crowded an extraordinary amount of work and unusually broad academic experience into a relatively short professional career," wrote a *New York Times* reporter on the occasion of Johnson's death in 1977. A Keynesian economist, Johnson postulated that "unemployment was a greater social problem than inflation," as a *Time* obituary put it, and he also predicted the economic effects of the devaluation of the dollar and a guaranteed minimum income. Johnson's many books and hundreds of scholarly articles cover aspects of economy, international finance, and fiscal history.

BIOGRAPHICAL/CRITICAL SOURCES:

PERIODICALS

Commonweal, March 8, 1968.
Economist, September 6, 1975.
Journal of Political Economics, August, 1984.
New Republic, June 3, 1967.
Times Literary Supplement, May 19, 1966, June 15, 1967, December 28, 1967, March 12, 1970, April 18, 1975.

OBITUARIES:

PERIODICALS

New York Times, May 10, 1977.
Time, May 23, 1977.
Washington Post, May 27, 1977.*

* * *

JONES, Gillingham
See HAMILTON, Charles (Harold St. John)

* * *

JONES, W(alton) Glyn 1928-

PERSONAL: Born October 29, 1928, in Manchester, England; son of Emrys (an engineer) and Dorothy Ada (North) Jones; married Karen Ruth Fleischer, June 12, 1953 (divorced, August, 1981); married Kirsten Gade, November 30, 1981; children: (first marriage) Stephen Francis, Olaf Emrys Robert, Catherine Monica, Anna Elizabeth. *Education:* Pembroke College, Cambridge, B.A., 1952, M.A. and Ph.D., 1956.

ADDRESSES: Home—The Gardener's Cottage, South Burlingham Rd, Lingwood, Norwich NR13 4ET, England. *Office*—School of Modern Languages and European History, University of East Anglia, Norwich NR4 7TJ, England.

CAREER: University of London, University College, London, England, assistant lecturer, 1956-58, lecturer, 1958-66, reader in Danish, 1966-73; University of Newcastle-upon-Tyne, Newcastle-upon-Tyne, England, professor of Scandinavian studies, 1973-86; University of East Anglia, Norwich, England, professor of European literature, 1986—. Visiting professor, University of Iceland, 1971; visiting professor of Scandinavian literature, Faroese Academy, 1979-81. Member of British-Danish Cultural Commission, 1975—.

WRITINGS:

Johannes Joergensen's Modne Aar (title means "Johannes Joergensen's Mature Years"), Gyldendal (Copenhagen), 1963.
Johannes Joergensen, Twayne, 1969.
Denmark: A Modern History, Praeger, 1970, 2nd edition, Methuen, 1986.
William Heinesen, Twayne, 1974.
Faeroe og Kosmos (title means "Faroe and Cosmos"), Gyldendal, 1974.
(With wife, Kirsten Gade) *Danish: A Grammar with Exercises,* two volumes, Gyldendal, 1980.
Tove Jansson, Twayne, 1984.
(Translator) Villy Sorensen, *Seneca: The Humanist at the Court of Nero,* University of Chicago Press, 1984.
(Translator) Bodil Wamberg, *Out of Denmark: Isak Dinesen, Karen Blixen, and Danish Women Writers Today,* Nordic Books, 1985.
(Translator) Knud J. Krogh, *Kirkiubour Bench Ends and the Cathedral,* Bokagardur, 1988.
(Editor) *Selected Letters of Georg Brandes, with Introduction and Notes,* Norvik Press, 1989.
(Co-editor) *Edith Soedergran Studies,* SSEES (London), 1989.

Contributor to *Scandinavian Studies, Scandinavica, Nordisk Tidskrift, Month, World Literature Today, Skandinavistik,* and *Times Literary Supplement.* Member of advisory editorial board, *Scandinavica,* 1979—; member of British editorial board, *Books from Finland,* 1980-85; member of editorial advisory board, *Nordica,* 1986—.

AVOCATIONAL INTERESTS: Music.

* * *

JOSEFSBERG, Milt 1911-1987

PERSONAL: Born June 29, 1911, in New York, N.Y.; died after a stroke, December 14, 1987, in Burbank, Calif.; son of Jacob (a merchant) and Dinah (Fruchter) Josefsberg; married Hilda Wolarsky, January 26, 1936; children: Alan Roy, Steven Kent. *Education:* Attended City College of the City University of New York. *Religion:* Jewish.

ADDRESSES: Home—Encino, Calif. *Agent*—Scott Meredith Literary Agency, Inc., 845 Third Ave., New York, N.Y. 10022.

CAREER: Worked as a press agent, 1933-38; radio writer, "The Bob Hope Show," 1938-43; radio and television writer, "The Jack Benny Show," 1943-55; National Broadcasting Corp., New York, N.Y., programming executive, 1955-57; television script consultant, "The Bob Hope Show," 1957-59; television writer, "The Milton Berle Show," 1959-60; television script consultant, "The Danny Thomas Show," 1960-61; television script consultant, "Joey Bishop," 1962-63; television script consultant and head writer, "The Lucy Show" and "Here's Lucy," 1964-73; television script consultant, "The Odd Couple," 1972-73; writer for various television specials, 1973-75; television writer, script supervisor, and producer, "All in the Family," beginning 1975. Executive script consultant, "You Can't Take It with You"; creator of television series, "Here's Lucy"; also affiliated with television programs "Happy Days" and "Laverne and Shirley."

AWARDS, HONORS: Emmy Award nominations for best comedy writing, Academy of Television Arts and Sciences, 1955, for

"The Jack Benny Show," and 1968, for "Here's Lucy"; Emmy Award for best comedy series, 1978, for "All in the Family"; also nominated for Humanities Award, Population Zero Award, Critics Circle Award, and awards from Writers Guild of America.

WRITINGS:

The Jack Benny Show: The Life and Times of America's Best Loved Entertainer, Arlington House, 1977.
Comedy Writing: For Television and Hollywood, foreword by Norman Lear, Harper, 1987.

Author of numerous scripts for radio and television programs.

SIDELIGHTS: When Milt Josefsberg began submitting gags to a gossip column in the 1930s, it was only the beginning of a comedy writing career that would span almost fifty years, from "The Bob Hope Show" to "All in the Family." Josefsberg wrote for radio programs and with the advent of television became involved in some of the medium's best-loved comedy series. "He was probably the dean of American comedy writers in broadcasting," producer Hal Kanter commented in Josefsberg's *Los Angeles Times* obituary. "He probably had the best track record of any comedy writer I know of." This record included the creation of "Here's Lucy," classic jokes for "The Jack Benny Show," and his Emmy-winning production and scripting for "All in the Family," the controversial and popular show which featured stubborn bigot Archie Bunker. Josefsberg's success and longevity were due to his knowledge of comedy and his ability to create a broad variety of humorous effects, as Norman Lear stated in the foreword to Josefsberg's *Comedy Writing: For Television and Hollywood:* "He has written every type of comedy known to man—from Bob Hope's one-liner monologues and sketches to side-splitting Lucy [Ball] slapstick to some of the most serious and controversial 'All in the Family' episodes ever aired." "[Josefsberg] was essentially a rather shy person but there probably wasn't a joke ever told he hadn't heard or couldn't remember," Kanter explained. "He was literally an encyclopedia of comedy."

BIOGRAPHICAL/CRITICAL SOURCES:

BOOKS

Josefsberg, Milt, *Comedy Writing: For Television and Hollywood,* foreword by Norman Lear, Harper, 1987.

PERIODICALS

Christian Science Monitor, April 6, 1977.
Tribune Books (Chicago), October 11, 1987.

OBITUARIES:

PERIODICALS

Los Angeles Times, December 16, 1987.
Washington Post, December 18, 1987.*

* * *

JOSEPHS, Rebecca
See TALBOT, Toby

* * *

JUSSIM, Estelle 1927-

PERSONAL: Born March 18, 1927, in New York, N.Y.; daughter of Boris Ossipovich (a photographer) and Manya Aaronovna (Glusker) Jussim. *Education:* Queens College (now of the City University of New York), B.A., 1948; Columbia University, M.S., 1963, D.L.S., 1970.

ADDRESSES: Home—P.O. Box 132, Granby, Mass. 01033. *Office*—Graduate School of Library and Information Science, Simmons College, 300 The Fenway, Boston, Mass. 02115.

CAREER: Free-lance art director and graphic designer in New York City, 1948-60; Columbia University libraries, New York City, member of staff, 1963-65; Borough of Manhattan Community College, New York City, executive assistant director of educational resources, 1965-66; Hampshire College, Amherst, Mass., assistant professor of communications media, 1969-72; Simmons College, Boston, Mass., professor of film, photography, and visual communication, 1972—. Lecturer on history of photography, film, mass media, and visual communications theory. Member of board of trustees, Massachusetts State Library, 1971-73, and Visual Studies Workshop, Rochester, N.Y., 1980—; member of visiting committee, International Museum of Photography.

MEMBER: Society for Photographic Education, Friends of Photography, American Photographic Historical Society (honorary fellow), Deutsches Gesellschaft fuer Photographie (honorary member).

AWARDS, HONORS: Award for distinguished achievement in the history of photography, New York Photographic Historical Society, 1974, for *Visual Communication and the Graphic Arts;* Guggenheim fellowship, 1982-83; Laurence R. Winship Award for Best Book of 1981, *Boston Globe,* 1982, and first prize for distinction in the history of photography, American Photographic Historical Society, 1983, both for *Slave to Beauty: The Eccentric Life and Controversial Career of F. Holland Day, Photographer, Publisher, Aesthete.*

WRITINGS:

Visual Communication and the Graphic Arts, Bowker, 1974.
Jerome Liebling, Friends of Photography, 1979.
Barbara Crane: Photographs 1948-1980, Center for Creative Photography, University of Arizona, 1980.
Slave to Beauty: The Eccentric Life and Controversial Career of F. Holland Day, Photographer, Publisher, Aesthete, David Godine, 1981.
Frederic Remington, the Camera, and the Old West, Amon Carter Museum of Western Art, 1983.
(With Elizabeth Lindquist-Cock) *Landscape as Photograph: Reflections on Nature, Art, and Ideology,* Yale University Press, 1985.
Stopping Time: The Photographs of Harold Edgerton, Abrams, 1988.
The Eternal Moment: Essays on the Photographic Image, Aperture, 1989.

Contributor to photographic texts and anthologies; contributor to photographic history and communications media journals and encyclopedias, and to *Boston Review* and *Massachusetts Review.* Member of international advisory board, *History of Photography* (London), 1980—; member of editorial board, *Exposure.*

WORK IN PROGRESS: A work on photographer Alvin Langdon Coburn and his literary circle; essays on Paul Strand, John Pfahl, and women in the arts.

SIDELIGHTS: Although F. Holland Day, the subject of Estelle Jussim's biography *Slave to Beauty: The Eccentric Life and Controversial Career of F. Holland Day, Photographer, Publisher, Aesthete,* was a celebrated and influential literary figure in the 1890s, his place in the history of modern arts has been somewhat neglected. "How odd this seems in light of the fascinating material presented in Estelle Jussim's book," Tom Zito observes in the *Washington Post Book World,* for *Slave to Beauty* is "one [of] those stranger-than-fiction baroque American biographies that helps to define the interplay between visionary art and solipsistic madness." In rescuing Day from "this undeserved obscurity," notes *New York Times Book Review* contributor Alan Fern, Jussim uses a wide variety of sources and "has interwoven her biography with an account of the esthetic trends that shaped [Day's] work and has produced a fascinating glimpse into the worlds of literature and the visual arts between 1890 and the First World War." While the critic remarks that *Slave to Beauty* has some shortcomings, they "do not obscure [Jussim's] considerable contribution to the history of American arts and letters." "In general," concludes Zito, the author "has created a biography that not only provides an absorbing glimpse of a delightful quirk in American cultural history, but also stands as one of the more literate and beautifully crafted photo books of the past several years."

Jussim told *CA:* "The ideologies underlying the visual arts, visual communication, visual information—these continue to be my major obsessions. At the same time, I am increasingly interested in writing about the Southwest—landscape, people, history. My sometimes irrepressible sense of humor is also seeking new outlets, but is being overwhelmed by the many recent environmental tragedies which sadden me beyond words.

"My [1985] work, *Landscape as Photograph,* co-authored by a pioneering art historian (Elizabeth Lindquist-Cock), was destined for controversy. In attempting to review American ideas concerning nature and picture-making, we discovered that the history of painting and the history of photography are even more closely connected than is usually believed. Understanding the impact of politics and economics, as well as aesthetics, on both the ideas and the realities of 'landscape' is crucial to any understanding of photography in that genre.

"I want to write well. . . . I have been accused, in academic circles, of being *clear* and sometimes even entertaining. I hope I can continue this obviously sinful behavior while I also continue to pursue a sense of style. I have found I have a hard time translating what seems to be my natural flamboyance as a lecturer (to large museum audiences) to what works on the printed page. To counterbalance the influence of years of scholarly research, I am reading everyone from Cynthia Ozick to John Updike, and re-reading, enjoying her even in translation, that master of clarity, Colette."

AVOCATIONAL INTERESTS: The Southwest, various breeds of dogs, environmental politics, popular culture.

BIOGRAPHICAL/CRITICAL SOURCES:

PERIODICALS

Christian Science Monitor, September 26, 1985.
Los Angeles Times Book Review, August 11, 1985.
New York Times Book Review, April 12, 1981.
Times Literary Supplement, February 12, 1982.
Washington Post Book World, May 10, 1981.

K

KAMINSKY, Stuart M(elvin) 1934-

PERSONAL: Born September 29, 1934, in Chicago, Ill.; son of Leo and Dorothy (Zelac) Kaminsky; married first wife, Merle Gordon, August 30, 1959; married second wife, Enid Lisa Perll, January 7, 1986; children: (first marriage) Peter Michael, Toby Arthur, Lucy Irene; (second marriage) Natasha Melisa Perll. *Education:* University of Illinois, B.S., 1957, M.A., 1959; Northwestern University, Ph.D., 1972.

ADDRESSES: Home—7644 North Keduale, Skokie, Ill. 60016. *Office*—Northwestern University School of Speech, Evanston, Ill. 60208. *Agent*—Dominick Abel Literary Agency, Inc., 498 West End Ave., New York, N.Y. 10024.

CAREER: University of Illinois at Urbana-Champaign, Champaign, science writer, 1962-64; University of Illinois at Chicago, medical writer, 1965-68; University of Michigan, Ann Arbor, editor of News Service, 1968-69; University of Chicago, Ill., director of public relations and assistant to the vice-president for public affairs, 1969-72; Northwestern University, Evanston, Ill., assistant professor, 1973-75, associate professor of speech, 1975-77, professor, 1977—, currently head of Radio/Television/Film Department. *Military service:* U.S. Army, 1957-59.

MEMBER: International Crime Writers Association, Writers Guild of America, Private Eye Writers of America, Mystery Writers of America, Popular Culture Association of America, Society for Cinema Studies.

WRITINGS:

MYSTERY NOVELS

Bullet for a Star, St. Martin's, 1977.
Murder on the Yellow Brick Road, St. Martin's, 1978.
You Bet Your Life, St. Martin's, 1979.
The Howard Hughes Affair, St. Martin's, 1980.
Never Cross a Vampire, St. Martin's, 1980.
Death of a Dissident, Ace Books/Charter Books, 1981.
High Midnight, St. Martin's, 1981.
Catch a Falling Clown, St. Martin's, 1982.
He Done Her Wrong: A Toby Peters Mystery, St. Martin's, 1983.
When the Dark Man Calls (also see below), St. Martin's, 1983.
The Fala Factor, St. Martin's, 1984.
Black Knight in Red Square, Charter Books, 1984.
Down for the Count, G. K. Hall, 1985.
Red Chameleon, Scribner, 1985.
Exercise in Terror, St. Martin's, 1985.
Smart Moves, St. Martin's, 1986.
The Man Who Shot Lewis Vance, St. Martin's, 1986.
Think Fast, Mr. Peters, St. Martin's, 1987.
A Fine, Red Rain, Scribner, 1987.
A Cold Red Sunrise, Scribner, 1988.
Buried Caesars, Mysterious Press, 1989.

OTHER

"Here Comes the Interesting Part" (one-act play), first produced in New York City at New York Academy of Arts and Sciences, 1968.
Don Siegel, Director (biography), Curtis Books, 1974.
American Film Genres (textbook), Pflaum/Standard, 1974, 2nd revised edition, Nelson-Hall, 1984.
Clint Eastwood (biography), New American Library, 1975.
(Contributor) Ralph Amelio, editor, *Hal in the Classroom,* Pflaum/Standard, 1976.
(Contributor) Thomas Atkins, editor, *Graphic Violence on the Screen,* Simon & Schuster, 1976.
(Contributor) Atkins, editor, *Science Fiction Film,* Simon & Schuster, 1976.
(Editor with Joseph Hill) *Ingmar Bergman: Essays in Criticism,* Oxford University Press, 1976.
John Huston: Maker of Magic (biography), Houghton, 1978.
Coop: The Life and Legend of Gary Cooper (biography), St. Martin's, 1980.
(With Dana Hodgdon) *Basic Filmmaking* (textbook), Arco, 1981.
(With Jeffrey Mahan) *American Television Genres* (textbook), Nelson-Hall, 1985.
Writing for Television, Dell, 1988.

Also author of dialogue for the film "Once upon a Time in America," 1984; author of story and screenplay for the film "Enemy Territory," 1987; author of screenplay for the film "A Woman in the Wind," 1988. Contributor to cinema journals and other magazines, including *U.N.C.L.E., Positif, Take One, Journal of Popular Film, Journal of the Literary Imagination, The Wooster Review,* and *New Mexico Quarterly.*

WORK IN PROGRESS: A mystery novel set in contemporary Chicago; a novel featuring the character Porfiry Rostnikov; another novel featuring Toby Peters; a screenplay for Metro-Goldwyn-Mayer.

SIDELIGHTS: A film historian and head of the Radio/Television/Film Department at Northwestern University in Illinois, Stuart M. Kaminsky is best known for his mystery novels featuring detective Toby Peters. The Peters books, including among others *Murder on the Yellow Brick Road, Catch a Falling Clown,* and *Think Fast, Mr. Peters,* involve famous real-life characters (often of Hollywood renown) in fictional situations during the 1930s and 1940s. Kaminsky uses his interest in trivia about this time period to fill his books with nostalgic references to things past, such as Beechnut Gum and the Dagwood and Blondie radio show. Concerning his interest in radio, television, and film history, the author told *CA:* "I am interested in fostering a concern for serious study of those aspects of our cultural life which are seldom considered seriously. I think our objects of nostalgia and entertainment merit serious attention."

In a review of *Catch a Falling Clown, Los Angeles Times* book editor Art Seidenbaum remarks that "the fun of Kaminsky comes in dollops of nostalgia and sometimes drops of literary insights." *Catch a Falling Clown* concerns a series of murders at a circus. The famous clown Emmett Kelley is portrayed as Toby Peters' client, while one of the suspects is none other than Alfred Hitchcock. Other novels by Kaminsky feature film stars like Mae West, in *He Done Her Wrong,* and Judy Garland, in *Murder on the Yellow Brick Road.* Well-known names like Howard Hughes, Joe Louis, and Albert Einstein also become victims of plots against their lives or reputations in the Peters novels.

Remarking on the author's use of characterization, Seidebaum believes that "Kaminsky creates people who perform a nice balancing act, between sympathy and cynicism," adding that the author's portrayal of Emmett Kelley is "credible and engaging." *New York Times Book Review* critic Newgate Callendar, however, thinks that "Kaminsky is too obvious in his nostalgia kick." Margaret Cannon also objects to the author's frequent use of trivia. In a *Globe and Mail* article Cannon says that Kaminsky "has a talent for nicely developed plot, but he buries it under in-group jokes and period references." In a later review, Cannon notes: "This is not the case in *Think Fast, Mr. Peters.* Kaminsky serves up a nice plot. . . . The pace is fast, the story is clean and there are only two or three brand names to the page."

Although Kaminsky is better known for his books which have Peters as the main character, he has written a series of novels about Russian inspector Porfiry Rostnikov, too, including *Death of a Dissident, Red Chameleon,* and *A Cold Red Sunrise.* Also, he has written screenplays, textbooks, and four biographies. Regarding his writing in general, Kaminsky once told *CA:* "In my fiction writing, I am particularly interested in avoiding pretension. In my nonfiction, I am particularly concerned with being provocative and readable."

MEDIA ADAPTATIONS: *When the Dark Man Calls* was adapted as a film entitled "Frequence Meurtre" for Geuville Pictures in 1988.

AVOCATIONAL INTERESTS: Athletics (especially basketball and football), reading detective fiction and media history/criticism.

BIOGRAPHICAL/CRITICAL SOURCES:

PERIODICALS

Globe and Mail (Toronto), April 11, 1987, April 9, 1988.
Los Angeles Times, January 20, 1982.
New York Times Book Review, April 22, 1979.

KAPOOR, Sukhbir Singh 1937-

PERSONAL: Born November 21, 1937, in Amritsar, India; son of Kulwant Singh (a company director) and Lakhinder (Kaur) Kapoor; married Mohinder Kaur (a bank officer), September 21, 1958; children: Preetbir Singh (son), Ramanbir Singh (son). *Education:* City of London Polytechnic, M.A., 1982; Panjab University, Ph.D., 1983; University of London, Ph.D. *Religion:* Sikh.

ADDRESSES: *Home*—Bir Villa, 26 St. Thomas Dr., Pinner, Greater London HA5 4SX, England. *Office*—Faculty of Accounting and Finance, City of London Polytechnic, 84 Moorgate, London, E.C.2M., England.

CAREER: University of Delhi, Delhi, India, lecturer, 1957-65, senior lecturer in accounting, 1969-70; Glasgow College of Technology, Glasgow, Scotland, lecturer in accounting, 1971-77; City of London Polytechnic, London, England, senior lecturer in accounting, 1977—; Khalsa College, London, principal, 1985—.

MEMBER: Chartered Institute of Cost and Management Accounting (London; fellow), British Institute of Management, Chartered Association of Certified Accountants (fellow).

WRITINGS:

Lectures on Business Organisation, Aryan, 1964.
Elements of Book-Keeping and Accountancy, two volumes, Aryan, 1965.
Dynamic Approach to Economics, Holmes & McDougal, 1976.
Sikhs and Sikhism, Wayland, 1982.
Sikh Festivals, Wayland, 1984.
The Ideal Man, KEL Publications, 1987.

Contributor to accounting journals. Editor, *Sikh Courier International* (London).

WORK IN PROGRESS: Research on Guru Gobind Singh's concept of an ideal man.

* * *

KARK, Nina Mary (Mabey)
See BAWDEN, Nina (Mary Mabey)

* * *

KASUYA, Masahiro 1937-

PERSONAL: Born July 18, 1937, in Hyogo, Japan; son of Kichisuke and Toshie (Arai) Kasuya; married Yoko Watari (a poet), January 28, 1966; children: Kimiko (daughter), Nami (daughter). *Education:* Attended public schools in Japan. *Politics:* "Let it be." *Religion:* Roman Catholic.

ADDRESSES: *Home*—577 Ishiki, Hayama-cho, Miura-gun, Kanagawa Prefecture, Japan 240-01.

CAREER: Illustrator, artist, and author of books for children. Worked for a printing company, a papermaker, an advertising agency, and as a producer of plays, movies, and television programs for children.

AWARDS, HONORS: Winner of West Japan Cross-Country Motorcycle Event.

WRITINGS:

SELF-ILLUSTRATED JUVENILES; ORIGINALLY PUBLISHED IN JAPANESE BY SHIKO-SHA

Little Mole and His World, 1970.
White Blossom, 1972.

Kurisumasu, 1973, translation by Chieko Funakoshi published as *The Way Christmas Came,* edited by Mildred Schell, Judson, 1973 (translation by Peggy Blakely published in England as *Long Ago in Bethlehem,* A. & C. Black, 1973).
A Tower Too Tall, 1975, translation by Shona McKellar published in England as *Tower of Babel,* Evans Brothers, 1978, original retold by Schell, Judson, 1979.
The Beginning of the Rainbow, 1976, translation by McKellar published in England by Evans Brothers, 1977.
The Tiniest Christmas Star, 1977, adaptation by Schell, Judson, 1979.
Swim and Swim like a Fish, 1978.
Creation, 1979.
The Smallest Christmas Tree, 1979, Judson, 1981.
David Sings, 1980.
Martin the Cobbler, 1980.

IN GERMAN

Regenbogenschatten (title means "I Have Never Thought It"), Friedrich Wittig Verlag, 1982.
Jan wundert sich (title means "The Wide World of Wonders"), Friedrich Wittig Verlag, 1983.
Rotkehlchens feuerrote Federn (title means "Robin's Christmas"), Friedrich Wittig Verlag, 1985.
Es werde Licht!, Friedrich Wittig Verlag, 1985.

IN ENGLISH

The Beginning of the World, Abingdon, 1982.
The Shoemaker's Dream, Judson, 1982.

SIDELIGHTS: Masahiro Kasuya told *CA:* "Works that 'show' the artist's feelings are best. When my illustrations are printed and take the form of a book, it is an exhibition in itself. The customary exhibition, with framed pictures expressing only one theme and no continuing story, does not appeal to me. I am most happy when my own song is expressed (sung) through my works. For me, illustration should be as such. I hope to someday realize the 'communion of the inner and the outer.' "

AVOCATIONAL INTERESTS: Motorcycling.

* * *

KELLER, Allan 1904-1981

PERSONAL: Born August 3, 1904, in South Windham, Conn.; died November 24, 1981, in Columbus, Ohio; son of Harry Howard (an engineer) and Anna (Stedman) Keller; married Ima Elberfeld, May 10, 1926; children: Barbara (Mrs. Gerald Dolan), Katherine (Mrs. Roger A. Hood). *Education:* Columbia University, B.Litt., 1926; New York University, M.A., 1953. *Religion:* Congregationalist.

ADDRESSES: Home—Tuppers Plains, Ohio.

CAREER: New York World-Telegram, New York, N.Y., reporter, columnist, and city editor, 1933-67; also writer and city editor, *Sun.* Adjunct professor, Columbia University Graduate School of Journalism, 1947-74. *Military service:* U.S. Navy, 1942-46; became commander.

MEMBER: Confrerie de la Chaine des Rotisseurs (member of board of directors), Civil War Round Table (Fairfield, Conn.; president).

WRITINGS:

(With Anne Putnam) *Madami,* Prentice-Hall, 1954.
Grandma's Cooking, Prentice-Hall, 1955.
Thunder at Harper's Ferry, Prentice-Hall, 1958.
Morgan's Raid, Bobbs-Merrill, 1961.
The Spanish-American War: A Compact History, Hawthorn, 1969.
Colonial America: A Compact History, Hawthorn, 1971.
Life along the Hudson, Sleepy Hollow Restorations, 1976.
(With Charles Howell) *The Mill at Philipsburg Manor, Upper Mills, and a Brief History of Milling,* Sleepy Hollow Restorations, 1977.
Scandalous Lady: The Life and Times of Madame Restell, New York's Most Notorious Abortionist, Atheneum, 1981.

Author of weekly column, "The Roving Gourmet." Contributor to magazines and newspapers. Editorial consultant, Sleepy Hollow Restorations, Inc.

WORK IN PROGRESS: A novel set in West Virginia.

AVOCATIONAL INTERESTS: Travel, gourmet food, wines.

OBITUARIES:

PERIODICALS

New York Times, December 3, 1981.*

* * *

KELLERMAN, Jonathan 1949-

PERSONAL: Born August 9, 1949, in New York, N.Y.; son of David (an electrical engineer) and Sylvia (Fiacre) Kellerman; married Faye Marilyn Marder (an author), July, 1972; children: Jesse, Rachel, Ilana. *Education:* University of California, Los Angeles, B.A., 1971; University of Southern California, M.A., 1973, Ph.D., 1974. *Religion:* Jewish.

ADDRESSES: Agent—Barney Karpfinger, 500 Fifth Ave., Suite 2800, New York, N.Y. 10110.

CAREER: Writer. University of California, Los Angeles, *Daily Bruin,* editorial cartoonist, editor, and political satirist, 1967-71; Children's Hospital, Los Angeles, Calif., director of psychosocial program, 1976-80; University of Southern California, Los Angeles, assistant clinical professor, 1978-80, clinical associate professor, 1980-89. Free-lance illustrator, 1966-1972.

AWARDS, HONORS: Samuel Goldwyn literary award, University of California, Los Angeles/Metro-Goldwyn-Mayer, 1971, for *Poor Lieber;* Edgar Allan Poe Award for first novel, Mystery Writers of America, and Anthony Boucher Award, both 1986, both for *When the Bough Breaks.*

WRITINGS:

Psychological Aspects of Childhood Cancer, C. C Thomas, 1980.
Helping the Fearful Child: A Parent's Guide to Everyday and Problem Anxieties, Norton, 1981.
When the Bough Breaks (mystery), Atheneum, 1985 (published in England as *Shrunken Heads,* Macdonald & Co., 1986).
Blood Test (mystery), Atheneum, 1986.
Over the Edge (mystery; Literary Guild selection; Mystery Guild main selection), Atheneum, 1987.
The Butcher's Theater (mystery; Literary Guild selection; Mystery Guild main selection), Bantam, 1988.
Silent Partner (mystery; Literary Guild featured alternate; Mystery Guild main selection), Bantam, 1989.
Time Bomb (mystery), Bantam, 1990.

Also co-author of *Poor Lieber,* an unpublished comic novel. Contributor to anthologies; contributor of stories to *Alfred Hitchcock's Mystery Magazine;* contributor to *Newsweek* and *Los Angeles Times.*

WORK IN PROGRESS: Two more mystery novels for Bantam featuring psychologist Alex Delaware.

SIDELIGHTS: Working as a child psychologist for ten years before he became a full-time writer, Jonathan Kellerman now bases his popular mystery novels on the experience he gained while in practice. The hero of his first three mysteries, Dr. Alex Delaware, is also a child psychologist and somewhat similar to Kellerman in that they both have worked with cancer-stricken children, a subject about which the author wrote professionally in his *Psychological Aspects of Childhood Cancer.* "The novels reflect [this] experience," observes *Publishers Weekly* contributor William C. Brisick. Fellow mystery writer Dick Lochte elaborates in the *Los Angeles Times Book Review* that Kellerman's previous professional work places him "on firm ground when discussing the workings of the mind. But his expertise doesn't stop there. I have no idea how much of the material he feeds us is based on research or how much he has made up whole cloth."

Kellerman's first published novel, *When the Bough Breaks,* won him the Edgar Allan Poe Award and Anthony Boucher Award in 1986, and was also made into a television movie. John Gross evaluates the merits of this book in his *New York Times* article this way: *When the Bough Breaks* "marks an assured and more than promising debut. Some of the ingredients may have a familiar look—memories of 100 television programs hover somewhere in the background—but they have been whipped together with skill and conviction, and the result is an exceptionally exciting story." In this first novel to feature Alex Delaware, the 33-year-old retired psychologist is introduced while recuperating from the stress of his job. But his newly found, relaxing lifestyle is interrupted when Sergeant Milo Sturgis, a friend of his who is also a homosexual homicide detective, enlists the psychologist's help to solve a double-homicide. The only witness is an abused and uncommunicative little girl from whom Delaware must get a testimony.

Because *When the Bough Breaks* was published soon after the highly publicized child molestation case against the McMartin Preschool workers in California, "there is . . . the niggling suspicion that [Kellerman] had cashed in on the most unspeakable crime of the year," writes *Los Angeles Times Book Review* critic Mary Dryden. But, Dryden assures, "These doubts are quickly dispelled. The reader rapidly will gather that neither the child molesters nor the children themselves are exploited. Further, the author . . . had written and submitted this novel for publication many months before the McMartin case surfaced." The subjects about which Kellerman writes, however, are indeed topical. In addition to the subject of child molestation in his first mystery, he addresses the issues of child abduction in *Blood Test* and child persecution in *Over the Edge,* doing so "with authority and humor, sensitivity and more than considerable skill," says one *Publishers Weekly* reviewer.

Critics have also lauded the author's depiction of life on the West Coast and his skills at characterization. For example, *Newsweek* contributor David Lehman comments that *Blood Test,* which, like the other Delaware novels, is set in Los Angeles, "renders this atmosphere of nouveau depravity and trendy nuttiness vividly but not ostentatiously. It's a relentlessly intelligent thriller." "Kellerman is also unusually good at making his characters seem [genuinely human]," adds Tony Hillerman in a *Washington Post Book World* review, "and at telling a story of multiple murder which holds your attention." But one weakness in the author's thrillers, note several critics, is his portrayal of the relationship between Delaware and his girlfriend, "who remains stubbornly uninteresting," attests Dryden. In his review of *Over the Edge,* Gross also expresses a certain disappointment with the book's "gothic superabundance of revelations, and a sentimental finale." Gross qualifies, however, that "this is the kind of letdown that readers of mysteries learn to live with, and it doesn't cancel out the excitement of what has gone before." But in general, critics like Lochte and others feel that Kellerman "gets better with each book, refining his style, replacing melodrama with credible situations, discovering new ways to say more with less."

In a more recent book, *The Butcher's Theater,* the author has decided to break away from the Alex Delaware series in Los Angeles and take his readers to Jerusalem. About this move Mort Kamins remarks in the *Los Angeles Times Book Review* that "it's good to see Kellerman break a mold that threatened to straitjacket his creativity. And Jerusalem as a setting was an inspired choice." Having lived in that city in 1968 and 1969, Kellerman is able to write about it from the same kind of experience that lent realism to his earlier novels. In his interview with Brisick, he reveals: "[Jerusalem is] almost a second home to me, and I feel comfortable writing about places that I know." Several reviewers have praised the book for this authenticity. As Edward Hawley asserts in a *Chicago Tribune* article, "The author does a superb job of evoking the sights, sounds and smells of Jerusalem." And Kamins concludes that "Kellerman has written a compelling story full of idiosyncratic characters in a beautifully rendered setting." Within this setting, the author weaves a tale about a serial murderer who targets young Arab women in Jerusalem, a city in which the homicide rate is normally very low. Avoiding the temptation to dwell on the political aspects that such a situation could inspire, Kellerman instead provides his readers with an action-packed plot which, according to Hawley, "is constructed like a good movie, . . . with episode after episode that keeps the pace moving swiftly."

The Butcher's Theater has sold more copies than any of Kellerman's previous books. Nevertheless, the popularity of the Alex Delaware mysteries remains high, and the author tells Briswick: "I still like Alex, and I'll go back to him." The quality of Kellerman's first thrillers has established him as one of the most talented writers of this genre in recent times, according to *Los Angeles Times* reviewer Carolyn See, who asserts: "He's as morose as Kem Nunn, as outrageously sexual as T. Jefferson Parker; he creates characters as blithely as Mark Schorr or Dick Lochte; and he plots as well as Roger Simon or Wayne Warga." What separates Kellerman from these others, though, is his experience in probing the horrors that can dwell within the human mind. As See remarks, the author "has intimately known terror, not in any abstract sense, but as a constant professional adversary." Brisick adds that it is the "humanistic strain, especially a concern for families and family pathology, . . . [that is] a departure from the more traditional, hard-boiled detective fiction."

MEDIA ADAPTATIONS: When the Bough Breaks was adapted for television in 1986; audiotapes have been recorded of Kellerman's first four novels.

AVOCATIONAL INTERESTS: Painting, book collecting, art collecting, playing and collecting guitars.

CA INTERVIEW

CA interviewed Jonathan Kellerman by telephone on November 14, 1988, at his home in Los Angeles, California.

CA: With your 1988 novel, The Butcher's Theater, *you've moved away from serial hero Alex Delaware and away from Atheneum to Bantam. What are the implications of these new directions in your work?*

KELLERMAN: Switching publishers was a business decision. I have a two-book deal with Bantam. The first was *Butcher's Theater,* and the second one is another Alex Delaware novel, which probably answers the other part of your question. It's called *Silent Partner;* it's finished and coming out in October, 1989. And I'm about four chapters into the fifth Delaware novel, which is called *Time Bomb.* Obviously *Butcher's Theater* was a temporary vacation. I think of myself as a storyteller; the story leads me. *The Butcher's Theater* was something that had been percolating in my mind for many, many years—not in the sense of having a complete story, but just as the concept of doing a crime thriller set in Jerusalem. I'd been thinking about it back into the seventies. When it finally coalesced, I sat down and wrote the book, and I enjoyed it.

After *Time Bomb,* I don't know. I find that the idea for a new book starts to come about three-quarters through the book I'm working on. And I see Delaware books as something I'll do quite a few of—as long as I can keep getting the shrink into trouble, I'm OK. There are other books that I want to do. I see in the long term doing another book with Daniel Sharavi, the hero of *The Butcher's Theater.* One gets affection for the character, of course, but the base of everything is that there's a particular story I want to tell, and I just go from book to book. I'm not one of those guys who sits down and plans his whole life in advance.

CA: Did you do a lot of the actual writing of The Butcher's Theater *in Jerusalem?*

KELLERMAN: No, I did some of the research there, but I did the writing here. I had planned the book for two or three years, and I had lived there, so I knew it very well—not only the place, but the people and the language. I'm too much of a coward to write about something I don't know well; I'm always afraid of being inauthentic. As a final capper, about a year before I wrote the book—right after I'd finished *Over the Edge*—the family went to Jerusalem for six or seven weeks with the explicit intention of doing research, and I had some very specific assignments as opposed to just collecting local color. Returning here to write it was a challenge; it was the first time I'd done that. The Delaware books are Los Angeles novels. I'm sitting here and the atmosphere just soaks in. With *The Butcher's Theater,* I had to bring home voluminous notes on specifics. And I'm an artist, so I did a lot of sketches, because I write visually. But fortunately it was something I knew very well, and I was able to pull it off.

CA: You do convey a sense of place very convincingly. I was aware that you were an artist, and I'd wondered if your art was in some way related to your writing.

KELLERMAN: It probably is, because I'm a visual person. The thing that I intentionally do always is try to make the book almost a hypnotic experience. I think for a book to read very well, to be very enjoyable, you should be able to immerse yourself in it as sensually as possible without having that aspect of it overtake the story. You should be able to get lost in it. That's what I want to do as a reader, so I try to make that possible in the books I write.

CA: Your work as a child psychologist provided the subject matter for your first books, Helping the Fearful Child *and* Psychological Aspects of Childhood Cancer, *and a concern for children is often central to your fiction as now. I'm interested in the dual nature of your work.*

KELLERMAN: I've always wanted to be a doctor of some kind, since I was a kid. But I always wanted to be a writer too. I guess I never really saw writing as a reasonable way to make a living. And my background was kind of middle-class; even though my folks were of an intellectual bent, the social impetus was clearly toward the professions. My friends became doctors and lawyers and scientists. When I went to college at UCLA, I worked on the school paper. I did a lot of journalism and I was a cartoonist and a columnist. In my senior year, a friend and I co-wrote a book that won a Goldwyn writing award, and we had a lot of our stuff collected for anthologies. For the next ten years I proceeded to write bad novels that didn't get published—learning my craft as a writer, really—while I was going to grad school, getting a doctorate, and working with children.

Children have always appealed to me. Before I was a psychologist I worked as a teacher and a youth director. I had my own kids, and I've just always enjoyed working with kids. I don't know why, really. I guess I like the honesty, and of course they're very cute. Also, I think that if you can help someone at an early stage, you can prevent later problems. The other thing is that I like to see a positive outcome. A lot of psych is very long-term, but with children one tends to see more cures. A friend of mine who is a psychiatrist and child therapist said to me, "Let's face it; we do this kind of work because we like to feel effective." I think I always had that personal need to be effective rather than just talk to adults about their problems for years and years and years. Child therapy is generally shorter-term; the goals are clearer; you're dealing with specific problems. A child would come in with a sleep disorder, a nightmare, a bed-wetting, something you could deal with.

I recall that when I won the Goldwyn award, this Hollywood agent called me in. There he sat smoking a big cigar, and he said, "Well, kid, what do you want to do?" I said, "I want to be a psychologist." He looked at me like, Are you nuts? That award was really an entree to the movie business, to screenwriting, which never appealed to me and still doesn't. I always wanted to write novels, and only novels. So I proceeded through grad school just to keep churning this crap out, and having it rejected and rejected and rejected and not understanding why. Looking back, I can see that obviously it was trash. It really is a matter of learning your craft.

Also, I didn't have enough to say. In psych, I was fortunate in a sense in that I saw a lot in the jobs I had. It wasn't just a Beverly Hills couch practice; I really saw everything—murder and suicide and cancer. And I was very, very young. I was twenty-four when I got a Ph.D. and was working as a therapist when I was twenty-five, twenty-six. It was a baptism of fire. I didn't know what I was doing, and I got involved in a lot of heavy stuff. Finally, when I was thirty-one or so, I said to myself, I've got to take this novel business seriously. I quit my job and went into full-time private practice, thinking it was going to be very slow building up. I had read about Arthur Conan Doyle, who had had a slow practice and started writing Sherlock Holmes, so I thought maybe I could do something like that. But my practice built up very fast—in a week and a half, actually. I still managed, though, because I was really driven to write *When the Bough Breaks.* I didn't expect what happened to happen. But I think it was the first time I really took fiction seriously. I outlined and rewrote. I think I really had something burning to say that time.

CA: You're obviously a man of incredible energy to have done both jobs and to have accomplished so much at an early age.

KELLERMAN: It was a manic-depressive situation! I've always been very driven to write. I got turned down and got upset and quit many times, but I found experientially that when I quit writing I got depressed. I learned that I needed to write whether I was going to get published or not. I did have tremendous energy, and I still do. Of course now I don't practice, I just write, so it's not quite as crazy. The first two or three novels were done while I was still in practice. Trying to wind down, I was still quite busy.

CA: Was it hard to break away from your practice?

KELLERMAN: It wasn't hard in a psychological sense, but it was hard in a technical sense because you can't walk away from your patients. I think you have an obligation to them; you're not like a dentist who can transfer a patient to someone else. There's a relationship. What I did, back when I was writing *Over the Edge* and had started to see that I could make a living as a writer, was say, Let me give it a shot, and I stopped taking any new patients. I had three associates—it was a big office—so I would give them all the new patients; I was very firm about not taking any more. Then it took two or three years to finish up with the ones I had. In fact, it's not totally over, because my old patients still have the option to come back and see me, and last week a teenager whom I had treated as a child came by the house to chat about something. I don't think a therapist is ever really finished as long as his patients are still around. I'm constantly getting people who want me to see them, and I have to resist. But it's not really difficult; I'm thirty-nine now, and I've been doing it for fourteen or fifteen years very intensely. Writing is legalized theft if you can make a living at it. I do love it, and it's a different type of life.

CA: Alex Delaware, ex-clinical psychologist like his creator, is an unusual protagonist for mystery novels, as is his friend and sidekick, the gay police detective Milo Sturgis. How did they develop in your mind?

KELLERMAN: I think my inspiration is clearly the hard-boiled Southern California novels, those of Ross Macdonald and Raymond Chandler specifically. Once I started to read Macdonald, that really gave me direction because I realized that what he was writing about was family pathology, and I saw that, as a psychologist, I had access to that kind of material—not in the sense of divulging confidential client stuff, but in the sense of having an understanding of the way families get out of control. But I thought, I want to do it differently. And I want to write what I know: I don't know how to be a detective, and it's a cliche to some extent, so I'll write about a psychologist who gets into trouble. I never even thought I would get published, let alone be creating a series character, or I might have chickened out.

With Milo, the thought was, OK, I'm writing a crime novel, and you can't have a crime without a cop. I don't like the books where the amateur comes in and shows the pros how to do it. But I didn't want the cliched homicide cop; I wanted to make him different. I had friends who were doctors and policemen who were in the closet and were macho types, but they just happened to be gay; it wasn't a big thing. So I thought, Let's make a character who's very tough, a hard-boiled homicide cop who happens to be gay. These people really do exist, and they make the books interesting, which is what I always try to do first of all. I am a reader too. I feel if something gets my interest, it will get other people's. But in another sense I write for myself; I never write for an audience. So I was just trying to keep myself interested most of all, and that's how it came out. I had no intention of making a political or philosophical point. I've said many times that, had I known Milo was going to be a series character, I might not have done it, because it's boxed me into all sorts of trouble. I really was very naive.

CA: There's a lot of information in your books that must require considerable research—police procedure and history, for example. Do you know in advance of writing what you'll need, and go out and do the digging before you start writing?

KELLERMAN: I was a researcher when I was in academic medicine, and I'm still a professor at USC Medical School. I stayed with academic medicine because I love research. I know other novelists who love to write but hate to do the research. I love both, so for me it's really a dual process. It takes me three to six months to conceive a novel. During that time I'm writing down notes, thinking, taking walks—it looks as if I'm loafing, but of course we all know it's work, right? Before I sit down to write, I have an outline, chapter-by-chapter. Often I won't look at the outline, and often I will deviate from it, but I do know where I'm going, which means I never block.

In terms of research, *When the Bough Breaks* and *Blood Test* required none at all. *Over the Edge* required a little bit of psychopharmaceutical research, but mostly it was stuff that I knew because it was my field, so I wasn't like a layman going in and starting from scratch. I knew where to look, and it was just a matter of going after the fine details. *Butcher's Theater* required a little more research. In the case of the police stuff, I've been an expert witness in court; I've associated with the police and the police system. *Blood Test* has a scene where Alex Delaware is testifying in court as an expert witness in a custody case. I did that for a couple of years until I got burned out and told the judge to stop sending these cases to me. Fortunately I have had a lot of life experience that keeps me from having to do heavy research. And I'm also not obsessed with getting all the details. To me the characterization of a story is more important, although I do want things to be accurate. And it's very easy to get the material if you know where to look.

CA: Do you think you reached a broader audience with The Butcher's Theater?

KELLERMAN: It sold more books. Whether it's a broader audience or just more of the same kind of people, I don't know. From what I can tell—though it's hard to get good data in the publishing business—my readership tends to be primarily women, we think seventy percent. I was a little concerned that the violence in *Butcher's Theater* would turn them off, but I haven't gotten too much response to that effect. Each book has sold more than the previous one, and *Butcher* sold more than *Over the Edge* did in hardcover. I'd like to think my audience is broadening, but there's no way to tell.

CA: Were you happy with the television movie that was made from When the Bough Breaks?

KELLERMAN: As TV movies go, I think it was very good. They had to take out about half the plot. I never saw my writing as all that adaptable to a movie, especially a television movie. My books are loaded with story, and a two-hour TV movie is really about an hour and a half of screen time. But what they left in was true to the book, and I was consulted on the project; they treated me very well. I'm not one of these guys who says, Oh, they've ruined my book. I think it was James N. Cain who made a wonderful remark about that. He was asked, "How do you feel about the fact that Hollywood has ruined all your books?" and he replied, "They haven't. They're right there on the shelf." I believe people are sufficiently sophisticated to know that a book's a book and a movie's a movie. Readers will say to me, "I loved the book more." Well, I hope so. It's got a lot more depth and motivation and character. When you take a book and abstract it, you boil it down to action and broad images; you lose a lot of the nuances and the subplots.

Audio tapes have been done of all four of my novels. I've read the scripts, and *Butcher* especially suffered in the translation. But that's the nature of the beast. You want to reach the people who use audiotapes. I've had blind people say that they wish they could read the books, but they're not in Braille. So they get the audiotapes. Bantam has done the tapes, and they've done a good job. I've approved the scripts; I think they've been excellent. They've had good people read them: John Rubinstein did the Delaware books, and Ben Kingsley did *Butcher's Theater.* I spoke to Ben, and he wants to do the movie. But you know the movie business. I live in Los Angeles, and I want nothing to do with the movie business. I have no desire to write screenplays; I think I'd rather have to go back and see patients. But I love writing novels. All I want to do is write a novel a year; that's my sole goal in life.

CA: You told William C. Brisick for Publishers Weekly *that your ideas for fiction come "in nebulous ways—in imagery, sometimes in dreams." Are there specific ways you have of cultivating a state of mind in which ideas can develop and speak to you?*

KELLERMAN: No, I've never had to. And I hope it never comes to that. I've been very lucky in that the ideas keep coming. As I said, as I'm finishing one book, the ideas for the next one seem to come. I don't know how long this will happen, but so far it's been very good. It's almost like a seance in which I am the medium. I think it's really difficult to say you're going to try and get an idea. Stephen King once talked about the difference between getting an idea and having an idea. It's like a Chinese finger puzzle: the tighter you pull, the worse it gets. I think it took me so long to get published, all this stuff had time to get pent up in me that I'm now releasing in an orgy of fiction writing.

CA: Your wife, Faye Kellerman, is also a successful writer. What are the ups and downs of having two writers in the house?

KELLERMAN: It's been mostly up. Faye and I have been married for sixteen years. We were very young when we got married; she was nineteen and I was twenty-two. She was just out of high school, starting college, and I was in grad school. We were adamant about not being in the same profession, because both her parents and mine had worked together, with disastrous consequences. She was a mathematics major and she became a dentist, which she really didn't like; I think dentistry was not stimulating enough for her. I was the artsy type. She watched me struggle with the writing, and when I finally got published, she said, "I'm going to try that." I said, "Sure. Great." I had no idea—and she had no idea—that she had any talent.

Then she started to write, and when she showed her work to me, I said, "This is very, very good." I read a lot of garbage—people send me their stuff all the time—but here's my own wife, someone I'd known at that time for thirteen or fourteen years, and I had no idea she had this talent. I was very surprised. I called my agent and said, "Listen, Barney, I know what it sounds like, but my wife wrote a book, and. . . . " He told me later that his eyes rolled back in his head when he heard this, but he said, "Oh, sure. Send it along." About a month later he sold it.

I think what Faye has going for her, first of all, is a fantastic imagination. She was always a daydreamer and fantasizer, but she had never put it on paper before. Second, she has a golden ear for dialogue. She's a gifted mimic; she could be a female Rich Little. (My oldest child can do that too.) Faye's first-draft dialogue is brilliant. Like Elmore Leonard, she knows what people sound like, and she can put it down on paper. That's something you can't learn. The third thing is that she's very self-disciplined, much more than I am, and she has tremendously high energy. She has the perseverance to sit down and do the work, and she's done very well. She's published two mysteries and has a big historical adventure called *The Quality of Mercy* coming out in April. Beyond that she's sold two more thrillers. She has ideas for ten books, many more ideas than I do.

Despite all the fears we had, it's worked out very, very well. The only down side was that right in the beginning we started to critique each other's stuff, and, you know, the egos are fragile. It took us a year or two to learn how to do it, but we've been through much tougher stuff in our marriage. We have an unusually good marriage: we're best friends as well as lovers and spouses. If we can go through three kids and deaths in the family and all sorts of crises, we can go through editing each other's writing.

CA: Do you think we're in a great renaissance of the mystery genre?

KELLERMAN: We talk now about a Golden Age of mysteries, the second Golden Age. I think that's overblown to some extent; I think we're getting a few very good writers, and in five or ten years a lot of what's coming out now will fade away. But it will prove to be a Golden Age at the end in the sense that a handful of very good people will endure.

I'm not touchy about the literary-versus-the-mystery issue; I have no pretensions of being a great literary novelist. But I do think to some extent that American fiction took a wrong turn around the turn of the century by getting away from story line. I'm just an old-fashioned person as a reader; I think there's an awful lot of emperor's clothing in fiction, stories about nothing. I still like something that has a beginning, a middle, and an end, that has some conflict and has people we can identify with. I think a lot of the books we look at as classics now would have been classified today as mysteries or thrillers—look at the writing of Robert Louis Stevenson, Victor Hugo, Dumas, Poe, Twain, Dickens. Those are the kinds of writers I enjoy. And I never tried to write a message book. People may think I set out to write about child molestation, but that's not true. I just did the old saw of writing what I knew. I'm not trying to make any political points or hype a big message. I just want to tell an engrossing story that captivates the reader.

BIOGRAPHICAL/CRITICAL SOURCES:

BOOKS

Contemporary Literary Criticism, Volume 44, Gale, 1987.

PERIODICALS

Chicago Tribune, May 6, 1988.
Chicago Tribune Book World, April 20, 1986.
Detroit News, April 26, 1987.
Los Angeles Times, December 2, 1985, March 20, 1986.
Los Angeles Times Book Review, September 8, 1985, April 26, 1987, March 13, 1988.
Newsweek, June 9, 1986.
New York Times, March 12, 1985, April 4, 1986, April 24, 1987.

Publishers Weekly, January 25, 1985, February 19, 1988.
Times (London), December 31, 1987.
Times Literary Supplement, January 30, 1987.
Washington Post Book World, March 16, 1986, July 5, 1987.

—*Sketch by Kevin S. Hile*

—*Interview by Jean W. Ross*

* * *

KELLMAN, Steven G. 1947-

PERSONAL: Born November 15, 1947, in Brooklyn, N.Y.; son of Max (an electronics technician) and Pearl (an insurance broker; maiden name, Pomerantz) Kellman. *Education:* State University of New York at Binghamton, B.A. (summa cum laude), 1967; University of California Berkeley, M.A., 1969, Ph.D., 1972.

ADDRESSES: Home—302 Fawn Dr., San Antonio, Tex. 78231. *Office*—Division of Foreign Languages, University of Texas at San Antonio, San Antonio, Tex. 78285-0644.

CAREER: University of California, Berkeley, acting instructor in comparative literature, 1972; Bemidji State College (now University), Bemidji, Minn., assistant professor of English, 1972-73; Tel-Aviv University, Tel-Aviv, Israel, lecturer in poetics and comparative literature, 1973-75; University of California, Irvine, visiting lecturer in English and comparative literature, 1975-76; University of Texas at San Antonio, assistant professor, 1976-80, associate professor, 1980-85, professor of comparative literature, 1985—. Fulbright senior lecturer at Tbilisi State University, U.S.S.R., and at other Soviet institutions, 1980; visiting associate professor at University of California, Berkeley, 1982; Partners of the Americas lecturer in Peru, 1985. Member of numerous committees at University of Texas at San Antonio. Guest on television and radio programs; advisor and juror, CineFestival; workshop leader and guest speaker. Editorial consultant; consultant to Israel Institute for Poetics and Semiotics.

MEMBER: Popular Culture Association, PEN American Center, National Book Critics Circle, Modern Language Association of America (Romance Literary Relations executive committee), South Central Modern Language Association (secretary of Comparative Literature Section, 1981-82, chairman, 1982-83), National Society of Arts and Letters.

AWARDS, HONORS: Shrout Short Story Award, University of California, 1972; Danforth Teaching Associate, 1981-86; American Council of Learned Societies Travel Grant, 1984; Finalist, National Book Critics Circle Citation for Excellence in Reviewing, 1984; Amoco Teaching Award, 1985-86; H. L. Mencken Writing Award, *Baltimore Sun,* 1986; first place award, San Antonio Sigma Delta Chi magazine column competition, 1987.

WRITINGS:

(Translator) Jean Anouilh, "Antigone," first produced in New York by Gallery Players of Park Slope, March, 1979.
The Self-Begetting Novel, Columbia University Press, 1980.
(Editor) *Approaches to Teaching Camus's "The Plague,"* Modern Language Association of America, 1985.
Loving Reading: Erotics of the Text, Archon Books, 1985.

CONTRIBUTOR

Walton Beacham, editor, *Critical Survey of Long Fiction,* Salem Press, 1983.
George E. Toles, editor, *Film/Literature,* Mosaic, 1983.
Frank N. Magill, editor, *Critical Survey of Long Fiction: Foreign Language Series,* Salem Press, 1983.
Marjorie Smelstor, editor, *Nineteen Eighty-Four in 1984: Perspectives on George Orwell's Novel,* UTSA, 1984.
Daniel Walden, editor, *Studies in American Jewish Literature 5,* SUNY Press, 1986.
Masterplots II: Short Story Series, Salem Press, 1986.
Magill, editor, *Masterplots II: American Fiction Series,* Salem Press, 1986.
Magill, editor, *Masterplots II: British and Commonwealth Fiction Series,* Salem Press, 1987.
Beacham, editor, *Popular American Fiction,* Research Publishing, 1987.
Magill, editor, *Great Lives from History: A Biographical Survey, American Series,* Salem Press, 1987.
Magill, editor, *Winners of the Nobel Prize for Literature,* Salem Press, 1988.

Contributor to anthologies. Contributor to *Dictionary of Literary Biography,* Volume 9, Gale, 1981; contributing editor, *Contemporary Authors,* 1987. Contributor of more than one hundred articles, poems, stories, translations, and reviews to magazines and newspapers, including *Newsweek, USA Today, Nation, Saturday Review, Washington Post, New Republic.*

OTHER

Translator of poetry, drama, and essays. Arts columnist and reviewer, for *San Antonio Light,* 1983—; film critic for *San Antonio Current,* 1986—. *Occident* magazine, member of editorial board, 1967-68, assistant editor, 1968-69, editor in chief, 1969-70, advisory editor, 1970-72; staff contributor to *Abstracts of English Studies,* 1971—; editorial secretary, *Poetics and Theory of Literature,* 1973-75; member of editorial board, *Newark Review,* 1982-85, and *Jewish Journal of San Antonio,* 1987—; literary scene editor, *USA Today* magazine, 1985—.

SIDELIGHTS: Steven G. Kellman once told *CA:* "*The Self-Begetting Novel* is an account of how so much of the most compelling fiction is a record of its own invention. All sentences are an attempt to re-invent the real, a further contribution to consciousness's vast reclamation project. Though I would not want Aeolus, the god of wind, as my patron, I would contribute to that project.

"I admit to writing for recognition, and what I recognize is the enormity of the task for both reader and writer. My weekly newspaper column has provided me the precious opportunity to discuss whatever in the arts and culture tackles my fancy. Whether I am writing for a deadline or for eternity, for a mass audience or for specialists, I dread the dead line. I suppose I write, like a prospector, for acclaim, but I am willing to settle for wisdom."

* * *

KENNEDY, Richard S(ylvester) 1920-

PERSONAL: Born October 13, 1920, in St. Paul, Minn.; son of William W. (a chemist) and Ellen (Foley) Kennedy; married Ella Dickinson, March 31, 1943; children: Elizabeth, Catherine, James. *Education:* Attended University of Southern California, 1938-39; University of California, Los Angeles, B.A., 1942; University of Chicago, M.A., 1947; Harvard University, Ph.D., 1953. *Politics:* Democrat. *Religion:* Unitarian Universalist.

ADDRESSES: Home—120 Merbrook Lane, Merion, Pa. *Office*—Department of English, Temple University, Philadelphia, Pa. 19122.

CAREER: Harvard University, Cambridge, Mass., teaching fellow, 1948-50; University of Rochester, Rochester, N.Y., assistant professor of English, 1950-57; University of Wichita, Wichita, Kan., associate professor, 1957-63, professor of English, 1963-64; Temple University, Philadelphia, Pa., professor of English, 1964—. Fulbright fellow, University of Nijmegen, Netherlands, 1989. *Military service:* U.S. Navy, 1942-46; became lieutenant; awarded Bronze Star Medal and Purple Heart.

MEMBER: Modern Language Association of America, American Studies Association, Thomas Wolfe Society (president, 1983-85), E. E. Cummings Society, NAACP, New York Browning Society.

WRITINGS:

The Window of Memory: The Literary Career of Thomas Wolfe, University of North Carolina Press, 1962.

The Notebooks of Thomas Wolfe, two volumes, University of North Carolina Press, 1970.

Dreams in the Mirror: A Biography of E. E. Cummings, Liveright, 1980.

(Editor) *Beyond Love and Loyalty: The Letters of Thomas Wolfe and Elizabeth Nowell, together with "No More Rivers," a Story by Thomas Wolfe,* University of North Carolina Press, 1983.

(Editor with George James Firmage) *Etcetera: The Unpublished Poems of E. E. Cummings,* Liveright, 1983.

(Editor and author of introduction) *Thomas Wolfe: A Harvard Perspective,* Croissant, 1983.

(Editor) Thomas Wolfe, *Welcome to Our City: A Play in Ten Scenes,* Louisiana State University Press, 1983.

(Editor) Thomas Wolfe, *The Train and the City,* Thomas Wolfe Society, 1984.

(Editor) *The Starwick Episodes: Unpublished Fictional Characterization by Thomas Wolfe,* Thomas Wolfe Society, 1989.

Contributor to *Dictionary of American Biography* and to professional journals.

WORK IN PROGRESS: A book on the early career of Robert Browning; a critical study of the fiction of the modern American South; a study of Thomas Hardy.

SIDELIGHTS: Richard S. Kennedy's biographies have drawn strong praise from several critics. C. H. Holman of the *Virginia Quarterly Review* calls Kennedy's first book, *The Window of Memory: The Literary Career of Thomas Wolfe,* "a work of impressive scope and critical importance, the first fully detailed, exhaustive, and truly first-rate study of a major writer the unevenness and seeming formlessness of whose work has been a serious challenge to American criticism." Although a *Times Literary Supplement* reviewer finds that the critical aspect of the book falls short of his expectations, he still affirms that of all the books available on Thomas Wolfe, "Kennedy's is certainly the most painstaking, consistently enlightening and elegant." *Saturday Review*'s R. E. Spiller similarly notes that "never before has the evidence [of Thomas Wolfe's creative processes] been so carefully sifted and presented. This is the scholar's workbook for all future study of Wolfe."

Like *The Window of Memory,* Kennedy's third publication, *Dreams in the Mirror: A Biography of E. E. Cummings,* does not rely heavily on past criticism for its emphasis. As London *Times* critic Richard Holmes points out, Kennedy's "warmhearted and psychologically acute biography is content to leave the larger literary questions alone, and locate Cummings vividly within his American inheritance." Holmes later continues: "The success of Kennedy's biography is shown most distinctly in the places where he links . . . psychological interpretations with Cummings' uniquely established literary identity." *Dreams in the Mirror,* unlike earlier biographies of Cummings that were closely controlled by the poet, presents previously suppressed information "tastefully but in satisfying detail," writes Joseph McLellan in the *Washington Post.* "Kennedy handles his subject with an understanding and sympathy that could not automatically be expected," the reviewer continues. McLellan also adds that the author "ventures discreetly and convincingly into psychological analysis, and his examination of some of the poems uncovers details that might have been missed previously even by avid admirers."

Kennedy once told *CA* that his strong interest in biography has influenced his work in progress as well. What he originally intended to be a history of twentieth-century American fiction, "may turn out to be 'The Lives of the Modern American Novelist' " instead.

AVOCATIONAL INTERESTS: Pottery-making, photography.

BIOGRAPHICAL/CRITICAL SOURCES:

PERIODICALS

Los Angeles Times, January 27, 1980.
Los Angeles Times Book Review, March 4, 1984.
Newsweek, February 4, 1980.
New York Times, January 18, 1980.
New York Times Book Review, January 13, 1980.
Saturday Review, January 12, 1963.
Times (London), June 5, 1980, November 22, 1984.
Times Literary Supplement, July 26, 1963, March 5, 1982.
Virginia Quarterly Review, winter, 1963.
Washington Post, February 3, 1980.
Washington Post Book World, February 3, 1980.

* * *

KENTON, Warren 1933-
(Z'ev ben Shimon Halevi)

PERSONAL: Born January 8, 1933; son of Simon and Esther (Barnet) Kenton. *Education:* Attended St. Martins School of Art, London, 1950-54, and Royal Academy Schools, London, 1956-58.

ADDRESSES: c/o Gateway Books, The Hollies, Wellow, Bath BA2 8QK, England; also c/o Samuel Weiser Inc., P.O. Box 612, York Beach, Me. 03910.

CAREER: Free-lance writer and lecturer. Early in career worked as a hospital worker, teacher, graphic designer, and spent three years in a theater workshop; Royal Academy of Dramatic Art, London, England, lecturer, 1963-78. Tutor, Architectural Association School of Architecture, 1966-71. Lecturer for Wrekin Trust; lecturer at New York Open Center, Omego Institute (New York), and Interface (Boston); lecturer in the United Kingdom, Israel, Canada, Mexico, the Netherlands, and Belgium.

WRITINGS:

Stage Properties and How to Make Them, Pitman, 1964, Drama Book Specialists, 1974, 2nd edition, 1978.

As Above So Below: A Study in Cosmic Progression, Stuart & Watkins, 1969.

Introducing Stagecraft (novel), Drake Publishers, 1971 (published in England as *The Play Begins: A Documentary-Novel upon the Mounting of a Play,* Elek, 1971).

Astrology: The Celestial Mirror, Avon, 1974, reprinted, Thames & Hudson, 1989.

UNDER NAME Z'EV BEN SHIMON HALEVI

An Introduction to the Cabala: Tree of Life, Samuel Weiser, 1972 (published in England as *Tree of Life: An Introduction to the Cabala,* Rider, 1972).
Adam and the Kabbalistic Tree, Samuel Weiser, 1974.
The Way of Kabbalah, Samuel Weiser, 1976.
A Kabbalistic Universe, Samuel Weiser, 1977.
Kabbalah: Tradition of Hidden Knowledge, Thames & Hudson, 1979.
Kabbalah and Exodus, Shambhala, 1980.
The Work of the Kabbalist, Gateway Books, 1984, Samuel Weiser, 1985.
The School of Kabbalah, Samuel Weiser, 1985.
Kabbalah and Psychology, Samuel Weiser, 1986.
The Anointed: A Kabbalistic Novel, Arkana, 1987.

OTHER

The Anatomy of Fate: Kabbalistic Astrology, Rider, 1978, 2nd edition (under name Z'ev ben Shimon Halevi), Gateway Books, 1986.

Kenton's books have been published in seven foreign languages.

WORK IN PROGRESS: A novel, *The White Ship;* a play, "Don Immanuel."

* * *

KLINGER, Eric 1933-

PERSONAL: Born May 23, 1933, in Vienna, Austria; came to United States in 1943, naturalized in 1946; son of Alfred (a lawyer and wholesaler) and Auguste (Stiasny) Klinger; married Karla A. Michelke, April 11, 1960; children: Heather Jill, Roderick Michael, Benjamin Karl. *Education:* Harvard University, A.B., 1954; University of Chicago, Ph.D., 1960.

ADDRESSES: Home—307 East Fifth St., Morris, Minn. 56267. *Office*—Division of Social Sciences, University of Minnesota, Morris, Minn. 56267.

CAREER: Association of American Medical Colleges, Evanston, Ill., research assistant, 1954-57, research associate, 1957-60; Veterans Administration Hospitals at Hines and Chicago, Ill., clinical psychology trainee, 1957-60; University of Wisconsin—Madison, instructor in psychology, 1960-62; University of Minnesota, Morris, assistant professor, 1962-63, associate professor, 1963-69, professor of psychology, 1969—, vice-chairman of Division of Social Sciences, 1969-73. Adjunct professor of psychology, University of Minnesota, Morris, 1978—.

MEMBER: American Psychological Society (fellow), American Psychological Association (fellow), American Association for the Study of Mental Imagery (president, 1980-81), American Association for the Advancement of Science (fellow), Society for Personology, Psychonomic Society, American Association of University Professors, Sigma Xi.

WRITINGS:

Structure and Functions of Fantasy, Wiley, 1971.
Meaning and Void: Inner Experience and the Incentives in People's Lives, University of Minnesota Press, 1977.
(Contributor) K. S. Pope and J. L. Singer, editors, *The Stream of Consciousness: Scientific Investigations into the Flow of Human Experience,* Plenum, 1978.
(Editor and contributor) *Imagery: Concepts, Results, and Applications,* Volume 2, Plenum, 1981.
(Contributor) P. C. Kendall and S. D. Hollon, editors, *Assessment Strategies for Cognitive-Behavioral Interventions,* Academic Press, 1981.
(Contributor) P. Karoly and F. H. Kanfer, editors, *The Psychology of Self-Management: From Theory to Practice,* Pergamon, 1982.
(Contributor) W. M. Cox, editor, *Treatment and Prevention of Alcohol Problems: A Resources Manual,* Academic Press, 1987.
(Contributor) J. N. Butcher and C. D. Spielberger, editors, *Advances in Personality Assessment,* Volume 6, Lawrence Erlbaum, 1987.
(Contributor) F. Halisch and J. Kuhl, editors, *Motivation, Intention, and Volition,* Springer Publishing, 1987.
(Contributor) Cox, editor, *Why People Drink: Parameters of Alcohol as a Reinforcer,* Gardner Press, in press.
(Contributor) T. K. Srull and R. S. Wyer, editors, *Advances in Social Cognition,* Volume 2, Lawrence Erlbaum, in press.
Daydreaming, J. P. Tarcher, in press.

Contributor of articles to psychology journals.

WORK IN PROGRESS: Research on fantasy processes, thought flow, incentive motivation and personality, and personality theory and measurement.

* * *

KNOEPFLE, John 1923-

PERSONAL: Surname pronounced "Know-full"; born February 4, 1923, in Cincinnati, Ohio; son of Rudolph (a salesman) and Catherine (Brickley) Knoepfle; married Margaret Godfrey Sower, December 26, 1956; children: John Michael, Mary Catherine, David Edmund, James Girard (deceased), Christopher Brickley. *Education:* Xavier University, Cincinnati, Ohio, Ph.B., 1947, M.A., 1949; St. Louis University, Ph.D., 1967. *Politics:* Democrat. *Religion:* Catholic.

ADDRESSES: Office—Brookens 390, Sangamon State University, Springfield, Ill. 62708.

CAREER: WCET (educational television), Cincinnati, Ohio, producer-director, 1953-55; Ohio State University, Columbus, assistant instructor, 1956-57; Southern Illinois University, East St. Louis, lecturer, 1957-61; St. Louis University High School, St. Louis, Mo., lecturer in English, 1961-62; Maryville College of the Sacred Heart, St. Louis, Mo., assistant professor of English, 1962-66; St. Louis University, St. Louis, Mo., associate professor and director for creative writing, 1967-71; Sangamon State University, Springfield, Ill., professor of literature, 1972—. Also affiliated with Mark Twain Summer Institute, 1962-64, and Washington University College, 1963-66. Consultant to Project Upward Bound, 1965-70. Collector of "The Knoepfle Collection," fifty one-hour recordings of steamboat men of the inland rivers, Division of Inland Rivers, Public Library of Cincinnati and Hamilton County, 1954-60. *Military service:* U.S. Navy, 1942-46; became lieutenant junior grade; received Purple Heart.

MEMBER: Modern Language Association, American Studies Association.

AWARDS, HONORS: Rockefeller Foundation fellowship, 1967; National Endowment for the Arts fellowship, 1980; Mark Twain Award, Society for the Study of Midwestern Literature, 1986, for distinguished contributions to Midwestern literature; Illinois Author of the Year, Illinois Association of Teachers of English, 1986; Illinois Arts Council fellowship, 1986.

WRITINGS:

(Translator with James Wright and Robert Bly) *Twenty Poems of Cesar Vallejo,* Sixties Press, 1961, published as *Neruda and Vallejo: Selected Poems,* Beacon Press, 1971.
Rivers into Islands, University of Chicago Press, 1965.
An Affair of Culture and Other Poems, Juniper, 1969.
After Gray Days and Other Poems, Crabgrass Press, 1969.
Songs for Gail Guidry's Guitar, New Rivers Press, 1969.
The Intricate Land, New Rivers Press, 1970.
Dogs and Cats and Things like That: A Book of Poems for Children, McGraw, 1971.
The Ten-Fifteen Community Poems, Back Door, 1971.
Our Street Feels Good: A Book of Poems for Children, McGraw, 1972.
Whetstone: A Book of Poems, BkMk, 1972.
Deep Winter Poems, Three Sheets, 1972.
Thinking of Offerings: Poems 1970-1973, Juniper, 1975.
A Box of Sandalwood: Love Poems, Juniper, 1978.
A Gathering of Voices, Rook, 1978.
(Editor with Dan Jaffe) *Frontier Literature: Images of the American West,* McGraw, 1979.
Poems for the Hours, Uzzano, 1979.
Selected Poems, BkMk, 1985.
Poems from the Sangamon, University of Illinois Press, 1985.
(With Wang Shouyi) *T'ang Dynasty Poems,* Spoon River Poetry Press, 1985.
(With Shouyi) *Song Dynasty Poems,* Spoon River Poetry Press, 1985.

CONTRIBUTOR

David Ray, editor, *From the Hungarian Revolution,* Cornell University Press, 1967.
Lucien Stryk, editor, *Heartland: Poets of the Midwest,* Northern Illinois University Press, 1967.
John Judson, editor, *Voyages to the Inland Sea,* Juniper, 1971.
Messages, Little, Brown, 1972.
John Gordon Blake, editor, *Regional Perspectives: America's Literary Heritage,* American Library, 1973.
Late Harvest: Plains and Prairie Poets, BkMk, 1977.
Jim Barnes, editor, *Five Missouri Poets,* Chariton Press, 1979.
Stryk, editor, *Prairie Voices: A Collection of Illinois Poets,* Illinois Arts Council Foundation, 1980.
A Reader's Guide to Illinois Literature, Read Illinois Program, 1985.

OTHER

Also contributor to anthologies, including *Poems at the Gate,* 1964. Contributor of essays and articles to periodicals, including *Minnesota Review.*

SIDELIGHTS: John Knoepfle's poetry speaks of his life in the Midwest. Because Midwestern poets are rarely recognized by modern critics, says Dan Jaffe in *Great Lakes Review,* Knoepfle, who "has been producing poems of enormous resonance," remains generally unknown.

The poet, writes Jaffe, "does not write one or two kinds of poems. One of the indications of his strength is the variety of textures, attitudes, subjects, and tactics found in his poems. He can be cryptically epigrammatic, journalistically surreal, and religiously sardonic. So those sound like paradoxes? He is a landscape poet and a political poet. At times he searches our history and our folklore, at others creates nightmares. He is a poet of gentleness who probes the inhumane. He lays it out without comment in one poem; the next poem is a riddle. To be sure there is a Knoepfle personality, a quality of language and concern that marks all of the poems, but I hesitate to label it."

BIOGRAPHICAL/CRITICAL SOURCES:

PERIODICALS

Focus Midwest, number 14, 1980.
Great Lakes Review, number 3, 1976.
Minnesota Review, number 3, 1968.

* * *

KNOWLES, Alison 1933-

PERSONAL: Born April 29, 1933, in New York, N.Y.; daughter of Edwin B. (a professor) and Helen Lois (Beckwith) Knowles; married James Ericson, 1955; married Richard Carter Higgins (a writer and publisher), May 31, 1960 (divorced, 1970; remarried, 1984); children: (second marriage) Hannah and Jessica (twins). *Education:* Attended Middlebury College, 1950-52; Pratt Institute, B.F.A., 1955; attended Manhattan School of Printing, 1962. *Politics:* Liberal. *Religion:* "?"

ADDRESSES: Home—P.O. Box 27, Station Hill Rd., Barrytown, N.Y. 12507-0027. *Office*—122 Spring St., New York, N.Y. 10012.

CAREER: Visual and performance artist. Free-lance silk screen artist, New York City, 1959—, including work for Something Else Press, New York City; California Institute of the Arts, Los Angeles, associate professor of art, 1970-72. Sole female performer in the original Fluxus Festivals, 1962-64, in such cities as London, England; Weisbaden, West Germany; Copenhagen, Denmark; Stockholm, Sweden; Paris, France; Madrid, Spain; and New York City. One-woman exhibitions include Nonagon Gallery, New York, 1958, Judson Gallery, New York, 1962, Galerie Inge Baeker, Bochum, West Germany, 1973, Galerie Rene Block, Berlin, West Germany, 1974, De Appel Galerie, Amsterdam, Netherlands, 1974, Centre Beaubourg, Paris, 1977, Walter Art Center, Minneapolis, Minn., 1980, Galerie Ars Viva, Berlin, West Germany, 1984, and Emily Harvey Gallery, New York, 1987. Has also done radio performances, video performances, and group shows throughout the United States and abroad.

AWARDS, HONORS: Guggenheim fellowship, 1968; National Endowment for the Arts grant, 1981, 1985; Karl Sczuka Radio Award from Station WDR (West Germany), 1982, for the play "The Bean Sequences"; Deutscher Akademischer Austauschdienst grant (West Germany), 1984.

WRITINGS:

The Bean Rolls, Fluxus, 1963.
(Contributor) *The Four Suits,* Something Else Press, 1965.
By Alison Knowles, Something Else Press, 1965.
The Big Book, Something Else Press, 1967, 2nd edition, 1969.
The House of Dust (computer poem), Verlag Gebrueder Koenig, 1968.
(With John Cage) *Notations,* Something Else Press, 1968.
Journal of the Identical Lunch, Nova Broadcast Press, 1970.
(Editor with Anna Lockwood) *Women's Work* (anthology of performance pieces), Unpublished Editions, 1975.
More by Alison Knowles, Unpublished Editions, 1976, 2nd edition, 1979.
Gem Duck, Pari & Dispari (Italy), 1977, Printed Editions, 1978.
Seven Days Running, Edition after Hand (Copenhagen), 1978.
Natural Assemblages and the True Cow, Printed Editions, 1980.
(With George Brecht) *The Red, the Green, the Yellow, the Black, and the White,* Edition Lebeer-Hossman (Brussels), 1983.

(Compiler) *A Bean Concordance,* Volume 1, Printed Editions, 1983.

(Contributor) Barbara Moore, editor, *Cookpot,* Reflux Editions, 1985.

(Contributor) Jerome Rothenberg, editor, *Technicians of the Sacred,* 2nd edition, University of California Press, 1985.

(Contributor) Charles Doria, editor, *Assembling,* Assembling Press, 1986.

(Contributor) Michael Erlhoff, editor, *Schwitters* (anthology), Zweitschrift, 1988.

Also author of *The Book of Bean,* 1981, *A Finger Book,* Volume 1, 1985, Volume 2, 1987, and the play "The Bean Sequences." Contributor to magazines, including *Yam, CC V TRE, V TRE,* and *Fluxus.*

SIDELIGHTS: Since the late 1950s Alison Knowles has been active in performance art, in which sound, images, and text are united into a new, creative whole. According to Knowles, one of her major contributions to twentieth-century art is her restructuring of the book form. *The Big Book,* for instance, is an eight-foot tall, one-ton reading structure equipped with a telephone, toilet, hot plate, art gallery, graffiti wall, and a four-foot sleeping tunnel lined with artificial grass. *The Bean Rolls* is a tin can full of bean recipes and lore written on scrolls.

BIOGRAPHICAL/CRITICAL SOURCES:

BOOKS

Roth, Moira, editor, *The Amazing Decade: Woman and Performance Art in America, 1970-1980,* Astro Artz, 1983.

Shapiro, Miriam, editor, *Art: A Woman's Sensibility,* California Institute of the Arts, 1975.

PERIODICALS

Whitewalls, spring, 1987.

* * *

KUHN, Annette 1945-

PERSONAL: Born September 29, 1945, in London, England; daughter of Henry Philip Kuhn (a bus conductor) and Betty Saunders (a bus conductor); married Broadnax Moore (divorced). *Education:* University of Sheffield, B.A. (with honors), 1969, M.A., 1975; University of London, Ph.D., 1985.

ADDRESSES: Home—London, England. *Office*—Department of Theatre, Film and TV Studies, University of Glasgow, Glasgow G12 8QF, Scotland.

CAREER: University of Sheffield, Sheffield, England, independent research worker in sociology, 1969-73; University of London, Goldsmith's College, London, England, lecturer in sociology, 1974-77; free-lance writer and teacher of film studies, 1977-88; University of Glasgow, Glasgow, Scotland, lecturer in film and TV studies, 1989—. Visiting professor at University of Iowa and University of Wisconsin—Madison, 1979-80.

MEMBER: British Sociological Association, Society for Education in Film and Television, Society for Cinema Studies.

WRITINGS:

(Editor with AnneMarie Wolpe) *Feminism and Materialism: Women and Modes of Production,* Routledge & Kegan Paul, 1978.

(Editor with Michele Barrett, Philip Corrigan, and Janet Wolff) *Ideology and Cultural Production,* Croom Helm, 1979.

Women's Pictures: Feminism and Cinema, Routledge & Kegan Paul, 1982.

The Power of the Image: Essays on Representation and Sexuality, Routledge & Kegan Paul, 1985.

Cinema, Censorship and Sexuality, 1909-1925, Routledge & Kegan Paul, 1988.

(Co-editor) *The Feminist Companion Guide to Cinema,* Virago and Ballantine, 1990.

Contributor to magazines, including *Signs* and *Wide Angle.* Member of editorial board of *Screen,* 1976-1985, and *Feminist Review,* 1977-80.

WORK IN PROGRESS: An anthology of essays on science fiction cinema and film theory for Verso.

SIDELIGHTS: Annette Kuhn told *CA:* "To be described as an author is rather strange, perhaps because I feel a little uneasy with the author-ity the title confers. For, to the extent that the work I do is best motivated by a will to knowledge, scholarship rather than authorship is what lies behind it. That is, I enjoy trying to understand—a curiosity that goes in all sorts of directions, not the least of which is cinema. Aside from its continuing importance as a medium of communication, writing is but a moment in the will to knowledge. A crucial moment, though: a writing project provides both the opportunity and the necessity to question, to work ideas through as nothing else—except possibly the best kind of teaching relationship—can."

BIOGRAPHICAL/CRITICAL SOURCES:

PERIODICALS

New Society, November 9, 1978.

New Statesman, August 20, 1982.

San Francisco Examiner-Chronicle, October 10, 1982.

Signs, Volume 5, 1980.

L

LAMBERT-LAGACE, Louise 1941-

PERSONAL: Born August 20, 1941, in Montreal, Quebec, Canada; daughter of Paul (an architect) and Lucille (a graphoanalyst; maiden name, Blais) Lambert; married Maurice Lagace (a supreme court judge), August 5, 1961; children: Pascale, Janique, Marie-Claire. *Education:* University of Montreal, B.Sc., 1961.

ADDRESSES: *Home*—Montreal, Quebec, Canada. *Office*—3550 Cote des Neiges, Suite 490, Montreal, Quebec, Canada, H3H 1V4.

CAREER: Nutrition consultant, 1971—. Consulting dietician in private practice, 1975—. Lecturer, Adult Education Department, University of Montreal, 1981—. Appeared on "Menus de Sante," weekly program on CFTM-TV, 1972-75, "A Votre Sante," weekly program on Canadian Broadcasting Corp. (CBC-TV), 1978-81, "Lifetime," on CTV-TV, "Sante la vie," on CFTM-TV, 1988, and weekly program "Visa Sante," on Radio Quebec, 1988-89. Public speaker and guest lecturer on health issues, 1977—. Advisory Committee on Science and Technology, CBC-TV, member, 1979-82, chair, 1982-85; member, Canadian Science Committee on Food and Nutrition, 1975-78; member of board of directors and vice-chair, Montreal Diet Dispensary, 1983—; member, Montreal Heart Institute Research Fund, 1984-86; vice-chair, National Institute of Nutrition, 1984—; member, Quebec Professional Corporation of Dietitians and Union des Artistes.

MEMBER: Society for Emotional Development of Children (professional advisory committee member, 1983-84), Society for Nutrition Education (member of board of directors, 1982-85; member of Select Committee on International Nutrition Education, 1984-86, chair, 1986-88), RAPSI (co-founder and chair, 1983-88), Canadian Dietetic Association, Quebec Science Writers Association.

AWARDS, HONORS: General Foods award, 1977, for excellence in nutrition education in written materials for media; Food Writer of the Year, Nabisco Brands, 1985; Silver Award, National Magazine Awards Foundation, for text on nutrition, 1986.

WRITINGS:

IN ENGLISH TRANSLATION

Comment nourrir son enfant, Editions de l'Homme, 1974, translation published as *Feeding Your Child: From Infancy to Six Years Old,* Habitex, 1976, revised edition, Stoddart, 1982, Beaufort Book, 1983.

Le Defi alimentaire de la femme, Editions de l'Homme, 1988, translation published as *The Nutrition Challenge for Women,* Stoddart, 1989.

Also author of "An Infant Feeding Counselling Guide," 1983-84, for health professionals across Canada.

IN FRENCH

La Dietetique dans la vie quotidienne (title means "Dietetics in Your Daily Life"), Editions de l'Homme, 1973.

La Boite a lunch (title means "Box Lunches"), Editions de l'Homme, 1973.

Menu de Sante (title means "Healthy Menus"), Editions de l'Homme, 1977.

Une Cuisine sage (title means "Wisdom in the Kitchen"), Editions de l'Homme, 1981.

J'allaite mon enfant (title means "Breastfeeding Your Child"), Editions Opuscule, 1981.

La Sage Bouffe de 2 a 6 ans, Editions de l'Homme, 1984.

Also author of "A votre sante," a weekly column in *Montreal Matin,* 1971-73. Contributor to nutrition journals and popular magazines. Nutrition editor for French edition, *Chatelaine* magazine, 1975-85; nutrition consultant, *Le Devoir,* 1976-82.

SIDELIGHTS: Louise Lambert-Lagace once told *CA:* "My best seller, *Feeding Your Child,* reflects a very strong conviction that eating habits are formed in very early childhood. Good nutrition then can help bypass many, if not all, health problems in later years. Most of all, it can eliminate the 'diet obsession' in adulthood. Good nutrition during childhood is not only eating the right nutrients in sufficient amounts. In my opinion, it goes beyond the food itself and can be described as the establishment of a 'happy relation' with healthy foods through all kinds of daily eating experiences. Good nutrition is having fun biting into a branch of broccoli, tasting a new dish, smelling an exciting spice, eating an apple for dessert. It is not a set of rigid rules nor a list of foods to avoid. Parents, grandparents, and day care personnel must share this philosophy and the responsibility, and perhaps change their own eating habits before they can facilitate the development of this 'happy relation.' Good nutrition is important at all ages and is one way of achieving greater respect of one's body and soul!"

AVOCATIONAL INTERESTS: Cooking and eating, bird watching, tennis, skiing, travel.

* * *

LANE, Margaret 1907-

PERSONAL: Born June 23, 1907, in Cheshire, England; daughter of Harry George (a newspaper editor) and Edith (Webb) Lane; married Bryan Edgar Wallace, June 23, 1934 (divorced, 1939); married Francis John Clarence Westenra Plantagenet Hastings, fifteenth earl of Huntingdon (an artist), becoming countess of Huntingdon, February, 1944; children: (second marriage) Selina, Harriet. *Education:* St. Hugh's College, Oxford, M.A., 1928.

ADDRESSES: Home—Blackbridge House, Beaulieu, Hampshire, England.

CAREER: Novelist, biographer, and book reviewer for *Daily Telegraph. Daily Express,* London, England, reporter, 1928-31; special correspondent in New York and for International News Service in the United States, 1931-32; *Daily Mail,* London, special correspondent, 1932-38.

MEMBER: Women's Press Club (president, 1958-60), Society of Authors, Bronte Society (president, 1976), Dickens Fellowship (president, 1959-61 and 1970), Johnson Society (president, 1971), Jane Austen Society (president, 1983).

AWARDS, HONORS: Prix Femina-Vie Heureuse, 1935, for *Faith, Hope, No Charity.*

WRITINGS:

Faith, Hope, No Charity, Harper, 1935.
At Last the Island, Harper, 1937.
Edgar Wallace: The Biography of a Phenomenon, Harper, 1938, revised edition, with introduction by Graham Greene, Hamish Hamilton, 1965, reprinted, Arden Library, 1980.
Walk into My Parlor, Harper, 1941.
Where Helen Lies, Duell, Sloan & Pearce, 1944.
The Tale of Beatrix Potter, Warne, 1946, published as *The Tale of Beatrix Potter: A Biography,* 1959, revised and enlarged edition, 1968.
The Bronte Story: A Reconsideration of Mrs. Gaskell's "Life of Charlotte Bronte," Duell, Sloan & Pearce, 1953, Greenwood Press, 1971.
A Crown of Convolvulus, Heinemann, 1954.
A Calabash of Diamonds, Duell, Sloan & Pearce, 1961 (published in England as *A Calabash of Diamonds: An African Treasure Hunt,* Heinemann, 1961).
Life with Ionides, Viking, 1963.
A Night at Sea: A Novel, Hamish Hamilton, 1964, published as *A Night at Sea,* Knopf, 1965.
A Smell of Burning: A Novel, Hamish Hamilton, 1965, published as *A Smell of Burning,* Knopf, 1966.
Purely for Pleasure (literary-biographical essays), Hamish Hamilton, 1966, Knopf, 1967.
The Day of the Feast, Knopf, 1968 (published in England as *The Day of the Feast: A Novel,* Hamish Hamilton, 1968).
Frances Wright and "The Great Experiment," Rowman & Littlefield, 1972.
Samuel Johnson and His World, Harper, 1975.
The Magic Years of Beatrix Potter, Warne, 1978.
(Editor) Flora Thompson, *A Country Calendar,* Oxford University Press, 1980.
The Drug-Like Bronte Dream, Humanities, 1981.
The Beatrix Potter Country Cookery Book, Warne, 1982.
Literary Daughters (essays), St. Martin's, 1989.

JUVENILES

The Squirrel, Dial, 1981.
The Beaver, Dial, 1982.
The Fish: The Story of the Stickleback, Dial, 1982.
The Fox, Dial, 1982.
The Frog, Dial, 1982.
The Spider, Dial, 1982.
The Lion, Walker Books, 1985.
The Chimpanzee, Walker Books, 1985.
The Elephant, Walker Books, 1985.
The Giraffe, Walker Books, 1985.

OTHER

Contributor to periodicals, including *Punch, Cornhill,* and *Times Literary Supplement.*

SIDELIGHTS: Margaret Lane's *Edgar Wallace: The Biography of a Phenomenon* is "an admirable biography in a field where good biographies are rare," writes V. S. Pritchett in the *Christian Science Monitor.* According to Robert Van Gelder in the *New York Times,* the book "is witty, brisk, and serenely sensible. The eager, high-spirited little poseur whose gritty determination to live beyond his income helped make him the most popular writer of his time is neither overpraised nor undervalued. [Lane's] study is friendly but objective, factual and most engagingly presented. It is built upon an uncommonly solid job of research."

Lane's *Samuel Johnson and His World* has also elicited praise. Elizabeth Longford calls it in the *New Statesman* a "very satisfying, . . . evocative biography" of the English lexicographer, critic, and conversationalist. Reviewing the book in *America,* J. B. Breslin believes Lane "proves a competent guide to [Johnson's *Preface to Shakespeare,* his *Rambler* and *Idler* essays, and his *Lives of the Poets*], and she fits them into a narrative that gives us the man as well."

BIOGRAPHICAL/CRITICAL SOURCES:

PERIODICALS

America, February 28, 1976.
Christian Science Monitor, January 4, 1939, March 15, 1967.
Manchester Guardian, December 16, 1938.
New Statesman, January 23, 1976.
New York Times, March 19, 1939.
New York Times Book Review, December 12, 1965, October 13, 1968.
Times Literary Supplement, December 3, 1938, July 2, 1964, November 25, 1965, January 5, 1967, March 28, 1968, March 17, 1972, March 27, 1981, August 2, 1985.

* * *

LANGSTAFF, J(ohn) Brett 1889-1985

PERSONAL: Born March 22, 1889, in New York, N.Y.; died February 12, 1985, in Morristown, N.J.; son of John Elliot and Sarah Josephine (Meredith) Langstaff; married Phyllis Bard McVickar, 1931 (deceased); children: John McVickar, Brett Elliot, Bard Hoffman. *Education:* Attended Columbia University, 1908-09; Harvard University, A.B., 1913; attended General

Theological Seminary, 1913-14; Magdalen College, Oxford, Litt.B., 1916.

ADDRESSES: Home and office—49 Macculloch Ave., Morristown, N.J.

CAREER: Ordained deacon and priest, Protestant Episcopal Church, 1917. St. Mary and St. John Cathedral, Manila, Philippines, assistant dean, 1917-18; St. Mark's Church, London, England, assistant vicar, 1918-20; Magdalen College Mission, London, president, 1921-22; president, Children's Libraries Movement, England, 1921-23; affiliated with St. John's Church, Yonkers, N.Y., 1923-24, St. Andrew's Church, Walden, N.Y., 1924-29, and Christ Church, Indianapolis, Ind., 1930; St. Edmund's Church, New York, N.Y., rector, 1930-58, rector emeritus, 1958-85. Member of board of managers, Episcopalian Diocese of New York. Founder of a cathedral for children in Walden, 1926; founder of the David Copperfield Library for Children, London. Former Republican candidate for mayor of Morristown, N.J. *Military service:* British Army, Scots Guard, during World War I; received Silver Badge.

MEMBER: Knights Templar (eminent grand prelate, New York state, 1958-60), Red Cross of Constantine (grand high prelate, 1958-59), Household Brigade Association of North America, Morris County Historical Society (president, 1958-62), Harvard-Yale-Princeton Association (president, 1963-66), Royal Societies Club (London), Harvard Club (New York), Pilgrims (New York).

AWARDS, HONORS: Named honorary citizen of New Orleans, La., 1962; author award in history, New Jersey Association of Teachers of English, 1964.

WRITINGS:

Harvard of Today, Harvard University Press, 1913.
The Holy Communion Service in Great Britain and America, Oxford University Press, 1919.
(Editor) *Not So Bad As We Seem,* Spottiswoode, 1921.
David Copperfield's Library, Stokes, 1924.
From Now to Adam, Harper, 1928.
The American Communion Service, Morehouse, 1937.
Dr. Bard of Hyde Park, Dutton, 1942.
(Self-illustrated) *Man and Christmas Verse,* Emmerson, 1947.
In Her Own Right (biography), Emmerson, 1957.
The Enterprising Life, John McVickar, 1787-1868, St. Martin's, 1961.
New Jersey Generations, Macculloch Hall, Vantage, 1964.
Oxford 1914, Vantage, 1965.
Likeable People Who Changed a World, Vantage, 1970.
God and Man, privately printed, 1972.
Cadena de amor (title means "Chain of Love"), Vantage, 1979.

Also author of privately printed poetry; contributor to children's books on nursery rhymes.

AVOCATIONAL INTERESTS: Oriental gardening, sculpture, acting, singing.

OBITUARIES:

PERIODICALS

New York Times, February 14, 1985.*

* * *

LANSKY, Bruce 1941-

PERSONAL: Born June 1, 1941, in New York, N.Y.; son of David (a business executive) and Lorretta (a librarian; maiden name, Berkowitz) Lansky; married Vicki Rogosin (an author), May 14, 1967 (divorced); children: Douglas, Dana. *Education:* Attended St. John's College, 1958-60; New York University, B.A., 1963; University of Chicago, graduate study, 1963-64.

ADDRESSES: Home—16648 Meadowbrook Ln., Wayzata, Minn. 55391. *Office*—Meadowbrook Press, 18318 Minnetonka Blvd., Wayzata, Minn. 55391.

CAREER: Cunningham & Walsh (advertisers), New York, N.Y., account executive, 1965-68; Candy Corp. of America, Brooklyn, N.Y., marketing manager, 1968-70; Pillsbury Co., Minneapolis, Minn., manager of new products, 1970-72; Lansky & Associates (advertising agency), Wayzata, Minn., president, 1973—; Meadowbrook Press, Wayzata, publisher, 1975—. Director of Rational Life Center, 1982—.

WRITINGS:

ALL PUBLISHED BY MEADOWBROOK

The Best Baby Name Book in the Whole Wide World, 1979.
(Editor) *Free Stuff for Kids,* 1979.
Successful Dieting Tips, 1981.
Make Your Own Greeting Cards, 1981.
Make Your Own Crazy Minerals, 1982.
Make Your Own Crazy Monsters, 1982.
Baby and Child Medical Care, 1982.
First Year Baby Care, 1983.
10,000 Baby Names, 1984.
The Best Baby Shower Book, 1986.
Mother Murphy's Law, 1986.
Baby Talk, 1986.
The Best Wedding Shower Book, 1987.
Mother Murphy's 2nd Law, 1987.
Webster's Dictionary Game, 1987.
Wall Street Bull, 1987.
Mother's Memories, 1988.

OTHER

Editor, "Can You Solve the Mystery?" series, 14 volumes, 1984-85.

SIDELIGHTS: Bruce Lansky told *CA:* "As the president and publisher of Meadowbrook Press, I am in the position of being able to create books that interest me and seem to have market potential, and get them published. My creative work includes books that I write, cover to cover, and books that I conceive of, create an outline and style guide for, and whose data collection/writing I closely supervise. I am 'author' of all these books, but in many cases some of the writing is done by others, and my name does not necessarily appear on the cover. As much as I enjoy the act of writing, particularly humor writing, my role as president and publisher keeps me quite busy editing and shaping the work of other authors, too.

"It may interest you to note that books I've authored have sold nearly four million copies. *The Best Baby Name Book in the Whole Wide World* is now up to 1.5MM copies in print, while *Free Stuff for Kids* is up to 1.2MM copies in print. Several others, including the 'Can You Solve the Mystery?' series, *Baby and Child Medical Care,* and *First Year Baby Care* have sold over 100,000 copies."

BIOGRAPHICAL/CRITICAL SOURCES:

PERIODICALS

Washington Post Book World, August 22, 1982.

LATNER, Pat Wallace
See STROTHER, Pat Wallace

* * *

LAZARSFELD, Paul F(elix) 1901-1976

PERSONAL: Born February 13, 1901, in Vienna, Austria; died August 30, 1976, in New York, N.Y.; came to United States in 1933, naturalized in 1943; son of Robert and Sofie (a lay analyst; maiden name, Munk) Lazarsfeld; married second wife, Herta Herzog, February 29, 1936; married third wife, Patricia L. Kendall (a professor), November 21, 1949; children: (first marriage) Lotte Lazarsfeld Bailyn; (third marriage) Robert Kendall. *Education:* University of Vienna, Ph.D., 1924.

ADDRESSES: Home—50 West 96th St., New York, N.Y. 10025.

CAREER: Teacher of mathematics at junior college in Vienna, Austria, 1929; University of Vienna, Vienna, Austria, 1929-33, began as instructor in psychology at Psychological Institute, became director of division of applied psychology; psychological researcher in the United States, 1933-37; Princeton University, Princeton, N.J., director of Office of Radio Research, 1937-40; Columbia University, New York, N.Y., associate professor, 1940-62, Quetelet Professor of Social Science, 1963-76, director of bureau of applied social research, 1940-50, chairman of graduate sociology department, 1949-59; University of Pittsburgh, Pittsburgh, Pa., distinguished professor, 1970-76. Visiting professor at University of Oslo, 1948-49, and the Sorbonne, University of Paris, 1962-63, 1967-68. Consultant to government organizations and business.

MEMBER: American Statistical Association (fellow), American Sociological Association (past president), American Marketing Association, American Psychological Association, American Association for Public Opinion Research (past president), National Academy of Science, National Academy of Education, Academy of Arts and Sciences.

AWARDS, HONORS: Grant from Rockefeller Foundation for psychological research, 1933-37; award from Sigma Delta Chi, 1941, and from Kappa Tau Alpha, 1948, for research in journalism; award from American Association for Public Opinion Research, 1955; award from Conference on Enlightened Public Opinion, 1958; L.H.D., Yeshiva University, 1966; LL.D., University of Chicago, 1966, and Columbia University, 1970; Eastern Sociological Society award, 1975; awarded only honorary degree ever conferred upon an American sociologist by the Sorbonne; received Golden Cross of the Republic of Austria for his contributions to Austrian culture.

WRITINGS:

Statistisches praktikum fuer Psychologen und Lehrer, G. Fischer, 1929.

(With others) *Jugend und Beruf: Kritik und Material,* G. Fischer, 1931, reprinted, Arno, 1975.

Radio and the Printed Page: An Introduction to the Study of Radio and Its Role in the Communication of Ideas, Duell, Sloan & Pearce, 1940, 3rd edition, Columbia University Press, 1968.

(With Bernard Berelson and Hazel Gaudet) *The People's Choice,* Duell, Sloan & Pearce, 1944, 3rd edition, Columbia University Press, 1968.

(With Harry H. Field) *The People Look at Radio,* University of North Carolina Press, 1946.

(With wife, Patricia L. Kendall) *Radio Listening in America: The People Look at Radio—Again,* edited by Lewis A. Coser and Walter W. Powell, Prentice-Hall, 1948, reprinted, Ayer, 1979.

(With Wagner Thielens, Jr.) *The Academic Mind: Social Scientists in Time of Crisis,* edited by Walter P. Metzger, Free Press of Glencoe, 1958, reprinted, Arno, 1977.

Non-Intellectual Factors in the Prediction of College Success, [Princeton, N.J.], 1959.

(With Sam D. Sieber) *Organizing Educational Research,* Prentice-Hall, 1964.

(With Jane Z. Hauser) *The Admissions Officer in the American College,* Columbia University Press, 1964.

(With Elihu Katz) *Personal Influence: The Part Played by People in the Flow of Mass Communications,* foreword by Elmo Roeper, Free Press of Glencoe, 1965.

(With Sieber) *The Organization of Educational Research in the United States,* Columbia University Press, 1966.

Metodologie e ricerca sociologica (title means "Methodology and Social Research"), Il Mulino, 1967.

An Episode in the History of Social Research: A Memoir, Charles Warren Center for Studies in American History, 1968.

(With Neil W. Henry) *Latent Structure Analysis,* Houghton, 1968.

Am Puls der Gesellschaft, Europa Verlag, 1968.

L'Analyse des processus sociaux (title means "The Analysis of Social Processes"), Mouton, 1970.

(With Jeffrey G. Reitz) *Toward a Theory of Applied Sociology: A Progress Report,* Columbia University Bureau of Applied Social Research, 1970.

(With Marie Jahoda) *Marienthal: The Sociography of an Unemployed Community,* Aldine, 1971.

(With Sieber) *Reforming the University,* Columbia University Bureau of Applied Social Research, 1971.

Qualitative Analysis: Historical and Critical Essays, Allyn & Bacon, 1972.

(With Samuel A. Stouffer) *Research Memorandum on the Family in the Depression,* Arno, 1972.

Main Trends in Sociology, Harper, 1973.

(Contributor) *Views from the Socially Sensitive Seventies,* American Telephone and Telegraph Co., 1973.

(With Douglas C. McDonald) *Some Problems of Research Organization,* Columbia University Bureau of Applied Social Research, 1973.

(With Reitz) *An Introduction to Applied Sociology,* Elsevier, 1975.

Radio Research: Nineteen Hundred Forty-One, Ayer, 1979.

Radio Research: Nineteen Hundred Forty-Two to Nineteen Hundred Forty-Three, Ayer, 1979.

Communications Research, Nineteen Forty-Eight to Nineteen Forty-Nine, Arno, 1979.

The Varied Sociology of Paul F. Lazarsfeld: Writings, collected and edited by P. L. Kendall, Columbia University Press, 1982.

Voting, University of Chicago Press, 1986.

EDITOR

Communications Research, Harper, 1941.

(With Frank N. Stanton) *Radio Research,* Duell, Sloan & Pearce, 1941, reprinted, Ayer, 1979.

(With Robert K. Merton) *Studies in the Scope and Method of "The American Soldier,"* Free Press, 1950, reprinted as *Continuities in Social Research: Studies in the Scope and Method of the American Soldier,* Ayer, 1974.

Mathematical Thinking in the Social Sciences, Free Press, 1954.

(With Morris Rosenberg) *The Language of Social Research: A Reader in the Methodology of Social Research,* Free Press, 1955.
(With Raymond Boudon) *Methodes de la sociologie* (title means "Sociological Methods"), Mouton, 1965.
(With Boudon) *Le Vocabulaire des sciences sociales* (title means "The Vocabulary of the Social Sciences"), Mouton, 1965, 3rd edition, 1971.
(With Boudon) *L'Analyse empirique de la causalite* (title means "The Empirical Analysis of Causality"), Mouton, 1966, 3rd edition, 1976.
(With Henry) *Readings in Mathematical Social Science,* Science Research Associates, 1966.
(With William H. Sewell and Harold L. Wilensky) *The Uses of Sociology,* Basic Books, 1967.
(With Ann K. Pasanella and Rosenberg) *Continuities in the Language of Social Research,* Free Press, 1972.
(With Merton) *Continuities in Social Research,* Arno Press, 1974.

OTHER

Also author of *The People's Choice: How the Voter Makes up His Mind in a Presidential Campaign,* published by Columbia University Press. Author of booklets published by Columbia University Bureau of Applied Social Research. Contributor to journals on social research techniques.

OBITUARIES:

PERIODICALS

New York Times, September 1, 1976.*

* * *

LEAF, (Wilbur) Munro 1905-1976
(John Calvert, Mun)

PERSONAL: Born December 4, 1905, in Hamilton (now part of Baltimore), Md.; died December 21, 1976, of cancer in Garrett Park, Md.; son of Charles Wilbur (a painter) and Emma India (Gillespie) Leaf; married Margaret Butler Pope, December 29, 1926; children: Andrew Munro, James Gillespie. *Education:* University of Maryland, A.B., 1927, Harvard University, M.A., 1931; graduate of Army Staff and Command School, 1943.

ADDRESSES: Home—11121 Rokeby Ave., Garrett Park, Md. 20766.

CAREER: Belmont Hill School, Belmont, Mass., teacher and football coach, 1929-30; Montgomery School, Wynnewood, Pa., teacher and football coach, 1931; Bobbs-Merrill Co., Inc., New York City, manuscript reader, 1932-33; F. A. Stokes, Co., New York City, editor and director, 1933-39; author and illustrator, 1934-76. Made three cultural and educational exchange program tours for U.S. State Department, 1961-64. *Military service:* U.S. Army, 1942-46; became major.

MEMBER: Kappa Alpha, Cosmos Club (Washington, D.C.), Players Club, Dutch Treat Club, Century Association (New York City).

WRITINGS:

JUVENILES; SELF-ILLUSTRATED

(Under pseudonym Mun) *Lo, the Poor Indian,* Lead, Mahony, 1934.
Grammar Can Be Fun (also see below), Stokes Publishing, 1934, revised edition, Lippincott, 1958.
Robert Francis Weatherbee, Stokes Publishing, 1935.
Manners Can Be Fun (also see below), Stokes Publishing, 1936, revised edition, Lippincott, 1958.
Safety Can Be Fun (also see below), Stokes Publishing, 1938, revised edition, Lippincott, 1961.
The Watchbirds: A Picture Book of Behavior (also see below), Stokes Publishing, 1939.
Fair Play, Stokes Publishing, 1939, reprinted, Lippincott, 1967.
More Watchbirds: A Picture Book of Behavior (also see below), Stokes Publishing, 1940.
John Henry Davis, Stokes Publishing, 1940.
Fly Away, Watchbirds!: A Picture Book of Behavior (also see below), Stokes Publishing, 1941.
Fun Book: The Munro Leaf Big Three—Manners Can Be Fun, Grammar Can Be Fun, Safety Can Be Fun, Stokes Publishing, 1941.
A War-Time Handbook for Young Americans, Stokes Publishing, 1942.
Health Can Be Fun, Stokes Publishing, 1943.
Three and Thirty Watchbirds: A Picture Book of Behavior, Lippincott, 1944.
Gordon the Goat, Lippincott, 1944.
Let's Do Better, Lippincott, 1945.
Flock of Watchbirds (includes *Watchbirds, More Watchbirds,* and *Fly Away, Watchbirds!*), Lippincott, 1946.
How to Behave and Why, Lippincott, 1946.
Sam the Superdroop, Viking, 1948.
Arithmetic Can Be Fun, Lippincott, 1949.
History Can Be Fun, Lippincott, 1950.
Geography Can Be Fun, Lippincott, 1952, revised edition, 1962.
Reading Can Be Fun, Lippincott, 1953.
Lucky You, Lippincott, 1955.
Three Promises to You, Lippincott, 1957.
Science Can Be Fun, Lippincott, 1958.
The Wishing Pool, Lippincott, 1960.
Being an American Can Be Fun, Lippincott, 1964.
Turnabout, Lippincott, 1967.
Who Cares? I Do, Lippincott, 1971.
Metric Can Be Fun, Lippincott, 1976.

JUVENILES; ILLUSTRATED BY OTHERS

The Story of Ferdinand, illustrated by Robert Lawson, Viking, 1936, reprinted, 1966.
Noodle, illustrated by Ludwig Bemelmans, Stokes Publishing, 1937, reprinted, Four Winds, 1969.
Wee Gillis, illustrated by Lawson, Viking, 1938, reprinted, 1967.
The Story of Simpson and Sampson, illustrated by Lawson, Viking, 1941.
(Reteller) *Aesop's Fables,* illustrated by Lawson, Heritage, 1941.
(Under pseudonym John Calvert) *Gwendolyn the Goose,* illustrated by Garrett Price, Random House, 1946.
Boo, Who Used to Be Scared of the Dark, illustrated by Francis Tipton Hunter, Random House, 1948.

OTHER

Listen, Little Girl, Before You Come to New York, illustrated by Dick Rose, Stokes Publishing, 1938.
(With William C. Menninger) *You and Psychiatry,* Scribner, 1948.

Also author of an army field manual on malaria, *This Is Ann* (short for anopheles mosquito), illustrated by Dr. Seuss, 1934, and of a self-illustrated booklet, *I Hate You! I Hate You!,* 1968; also author of *Who Is the Man,* an explanation of the Marshall Plan. Author of monthly column, "Watchwords," for *Ladies' Home Journal,* 1931-67.

SIDELIGHTS: Munro Leaf's *The Story of Ferdinand,* the tale of a Spanish bull who preferred sniffing flowers to fighting in a bull ring, secured for its author a place of renown in the world of children's literature. Published in December of 1936, the book soon became both a literary and cultural phenomenon. Margaret Leaf, Munro Leaf's widow, wrote about the success of her husband's children's book in a *Publishers Weekly* article. "What happened with *Ferdinand* is still a mystery. After Christmas, sales increased every week, and within thirteen months eight editions had been published. Ferdinand appeared as a giant balloon in the Macy's Thanksgiving Day Parade; a Ferdinand song made the hit parade; and in December of 1938, *The Story of Ferdinand* nudged *Gone with the Wind* off the top of the bestseller lists." The book was published in fifty foreign editions in sixteen languages and had sold 2.5 million copies in the United States at the time of Leaf's death in 1976.

Controversy over the little book's true meaning helped boost its popularity. Published in an era marked by the beginning of the Spanish Civil War and rising tensions in Europe, according to *New York Times* contributor Ben A. Franklin, *The Story of Ferdinand* "was . . . variously attacked . . . as 'red propaganda' or a bitter satire of pacifism, on the one hand, and as a 'pro-Fascist tract' on the other." Book burnings were even held in Germany where it was viewed as a product of U.S. propaganda. Through all this, Leaf insisted he had merely written the book as children's entertainment, choosing to tell the story of a bull only so it would stand out among the countless juvenile books already written about dogs, cats, or other common animals.

MEDIA ADAPTATIONS: The Story of Ferdinand was made into an animated film, "Ferdinand, the Bull," by Disney Studios, in 1938.

BIOGRAPHICAL/CRITICAL SOURCES:

PERIODICALS

New York Times, November 15, 1936, September 19, 1937.
Publishers Weekly, October 31, 1986.
Washington Post, September 18, 1986.

OBITUARIES:

PERIODICALS

New York Times, December 22, 1976.
Publishers Weekly, January 17, 1977.
Time, January 3, 1977.*

* * *

LEAHY, Syrell Rogovin 1935-

PERSONAL: Given and middle names are accented on second syllable; surname is pronounced *Lay*-he; born January 4, 1935, in Brooklyn, N.Y.; daughter of Samuel (an optometrist) and Dora (a teacher; maiden name, Cedar) Rogovin; married Daniel J. Leahy (a professor of mathematics), August 25, 1963; children: Joshua, Melinda. *Education:* Cornell University, B.A., 1956; Phillipps Universitat, graduate study, 1956-57; Columbia University, M.A., 1959, additional study, 1959-61. *Politics:* "Frequently Democrat." *Religion:* Jewish.

ADDRESSES: Home and office—74 Highwood Ave., Tenafly, N.J. 07670. *Agent*—Claire Smith, Harold Ober Associates, Inc., 40 East 49th St., New York, N.Y. 10017.

CAREER: Textbook writer in New York City, 1961-62; International Business Machines Corp., Yorktown Heights, N.Y., linguistic researcher, 1962-65; teacher of remedial courses for adults in New York City, 1966-69; American Telephone and Telegraph Co., New York City, writer of training materials, 1970—.

MEMBER: Linguistic Society of America, Authors Guild, Authors League of America.

WRITINGS:

Modern English Sentence Structure, Random House, 1964.
Baby Care, McGraw, 1966.
(With Harry Huffman) *Programmed College English,* McGraw, 1968.
A Book of Ruth (novel), Simon & Schuster, 1975.
Circle of Love (novel), Putnam, 1980.
Family Ties (novel), Putnam, 1982.
Family Truths (novel), Putnam, 1984.
Love Affair (novel), Putnam, 1986.

WORK IN PROGRESS: The Friends of Molly Gross.

SIDELIGHTS: Syrell Rogovin Leahy told *CA:* "As writing has become an increasingly important and time-consuming part of my life, I have relinquished more and more of the outside work I used to do. Now I accept only the occasional, short-term job, partly to get out of the house for a brief period to see what the world is doing. What I have learned is that the work that I do—alone and quietly, with only my typewriter and the people I have invented—is the most fun I have ever had."

* * *

LEE, Andrew
See AUCHINCLOSS, Louis (Stanton)

* * *

LEE, David 1944-

PERSONAL: Born August 13, 1944, in Matador, Tex.; son of Chant D. and Ruth (Rushing) Lee; married Jan Miller, August 13, 1971; children: Jon Dee, Jodee Duree. *Education:* Colorado State University, B.A., 1967; Idaho State University, M.A., 1970, University of Utah, Ph.D., 1973. *Religion:* "Christianity approached through Buddhism."

ADDRESSES: Home—P.O. Box 62, Paragonah, Utah 84760. *Office*—Department of English, Southern Utah State College, Cedar City, Utah 84760.

CAREER: Lobo Lodge, Chama, N.M., cowhand, 1964-67; Southern Utah State College, Cedar City, instructor, 1971-73, assistant professor, 1973-76, associate professor, 1976-79, professor of English, 1979—, chairman of department, 1973-82. Coordinator of special events at Centrum Writing Conference, Port Townsend, Wash.; member of advisory panel and peer group panel of Utah Endowment for the Arts. *Military service:* U.S. Army, 1967-69.

AWARDS, HONORS: Elliston Award honoree by University of Cincinnati, 1978; first prize for serious poetry from Utah Creative Writing Contests, 1983, for "The Muffler and the Law"; first place for book-length poetry manuscript from Utah Arts Council, 1988, for *Days Work.*

WRITINGS:

The Porcine Legacy (poetry), Copper Canyon Press, 1978.
Driving and Drinking (long poem), Copper Canyon Press, 1979, 2nd edition, 1982.
Shadow Weaver (poetry), Jawbone, 1984.
The Porcine Canticles (poetry), Copper Canyon Press, 1984.

Days Work, Copper Canyon Press, 1990.
Paragonak Canyon, Autumn, Brooding Heron Press, in press.

Work represented in anthologies, including *Anthology of Magazine Verse and Yearbook of American Poetry,* edited by Alan F. Pater, Monitor Book, 1981; *The Southwest: A Contemporary Anthology,* Red Earth Press; *Seven Poets;* and *Writing Poems,* edited by Robert Wallace. Contributor to magazines, including *West Coast Poetry Review, Kayak, Midwest Quarterly, Chowder Review, Willow Springs, Elkhorn Review,* and *Western Humanities Review.*

WORK IN PROGRESS: Penance in Seseret, a book of poems; a fantasy novel; a novel for children.

SIDELIGHTS: David Lee told *CA:* "My first interest is my family. I'm a full-time husband and father. I am also a teacher, a part-time pig farmer, constant scribbler, and long distance runner. I write about whatever catches my mind's eye. I've been called an eclectic reader, I suppose I'm an eclectic writer. I'm interested in the concentration and distillation of language and experience. I've also been told I have the cleanest mind in all of Utah: I change it daily. My writing reflects that change. I do not write to express a philosophy; I write to try and recreate the dance of the mind."

* * *

LEECH, Geoffrey N(eil) 1936-

PERSONAL: Born January 16, 1936, in Gloucester, England; son of Charles Richard (a bank employee) and Dorothy (Foster) Leech; married Frances Berman, July 29, 1961; children: Thomas, Camilla. *Education:* University College, London, B.A., 1959, M.A., 1962, Ph.D., 1969; additional study, Massachusetts Institute of Technology, 1964-65. *Religion:* Church of England.

ADDRESSES: Home—Old Manor House, Mill Brow, Kirkby Lonsdale, Cumbria, England. *Office*—Department of Linguistics and Modern English Language, University of Lancaster, Bailrigg, Lancaster, England.

CAREER: Clarendon School, South Oxhey, Hertfordshire, England, assistant schoolmaster, 1960-61; University of London, University College, London, England, assistant lecturer, 1962-65, lecturer in English, 1965-69; University of Lancaster, Bailrigg, Lancaster, England, reader in English, 1969-74, professor of linguistics and modern English languages, 1974—. Harkness fellow, Massachusetts Institue of Technology, 1964-65. *Military service:* Royal Air Force, 1954-56; became senior aircraftsman.

MEMBER: Philological Society, Linguistic Association of Great Britain.

AWARDS, HONORS: Honorary Doctor of Philosophy, Lund University, Sweden, 1987; fellow of British Academy, 1987.

WRITINGS:

English in Advertising: A Linguistic Study of Advertising in Great Britain, Longmans, Green, 1966.
A Linguistic Guide to English Poetry, Longmans, Green, 1969.
Towards a Semantic Description of English, Longmans, Green, 1969, Indiana University Press, 1970.
Meaning and the English Verb, Longman, 1971.
(With Randolph Quirk, Sidney Greenbaum, and Jan Svartvik) *A Grammar of Contemporary English,* Longman, 1972.
Semantics, Penguin Books, 1974, revised edition, 1981.
(With Svartvik) *A Communicative Grammar of English,* Longman, 1975.
Explorations in Semantics and Pragmatics, Benjamins, 1980.
(Editor with Greenbaum and Svartvik) *Studies in English Linguistics: For Randolph Quirk,* Longman, 1980.
(With Michael H. Short) *Style in Fiction,* Longman, 1981.
(With Margaret Deuchar and Robert Hoogenraad) *English Grammar for Today,* Macmillan, 1982.
Principles of Pragmatics, Longman, 1983.
(With Quirk, Greenbaum, and Svartvik) *A Comprehensive Grammar of the English Language,* Longman, 1985.
(Editor with Christopher N. Candlin) *Computers in English Language Teaching and Research,* Longman, 1986.
(Editor with Roger Garside and Geoffrey Sampson) *The Computational Analysis of English: A Corpus-based Approach,* Longman, 1987.
An A-Z Guide to English Grammar and Usage, Edward Arnold, 1989.

Contributor of articles and essays to journals.

AVOCATIONAL INTERESTS: Music (playing piano and organ).

* * *

LEVERTOV, Denise 1923-

PERSONAL: Born October 24, 1923, in Ilford, Essex, England; came to the United States in 1948, naturalized in 1955; daughter of Paul Philip (an Anglican priest) and Beatrice Adelaide (Spooner-Jones) Levertoff; married Mitchell Goodman (a writer), December 2, 1947 (divorced, 1972); children: Nikolai Gregory. *Education:* Privately educated; also studied ballet.

ADDRESSES: Home—4 Glover Circle, West Somerville, Mass. 02144.

CAREER: Poet, essayist, editor, translator, and educator. Worked in an antique store and a bookstore in London, England, 1946; taught English in Holland, three months; Young Men and Women's Christian Association (YM-YWCA) poetry center, New York City, teacher of poetry craft, 1964; Drew University, Madison, N.J., visiting lecturer, 1965; City College of the City University of New York, New York City, writer in residence, 1965-66; Vassar College, Poughkeepsie, N.Y., visiting lecturer, 1966-67; University of California, Berkeley, visiting professor, 1969; Massachusetts Institute of Technology, Cambridge, visiting professor and poet in residence, 1969-70; Kirkland College, Clinton, N.Y., visiting professor, 1970-71; University of Cincinnati, Cincinnati, Ohio, Elliston Lecturer, 1973; Tufts University, Medford, Mass., professor, 1973-79; Brandeis University, Waltham, Mass., Fannie Hurst Professor, 1981-83; Stanford University, Stanford, Calif., professor of English, 1981—. Co-initiator of Writers and Artists Protest against the War in Vietnam, 1965; active in the anti-nuclear movement. *Wartime service:* Nurse for Britain, 1943-45.

MEMBER: American Academy and Institute of Arts and Letters.

AWARDS, HONORS: Bess Hokin Prize from *Poetry,* 1959, for poem "With Eyes at the Back of Our Heads"; Longview Award, 1961; Guggenheim fellowship, 1962; Harriet Monroe Memorial Prize, 1964; Inez Boulton Prize, 1964; American Academy and Institute of Arts and Letters grant, 1965; Morton Dauwen Zabel Memorial Prize from *Poetry,* 1965; D.Litt., Colby College, 1970, University of Cincinnati, 1973, Bates College, 1984, Saint Lawrence University, 1984; Lenore Marshall Poetry Prize, 1976; Elmer Holmes Bobst Award in poetry, 1983; Shelley Memorial Award from Poetry Society of America, 1984.

WRITINGS:

POETRY

The Double Image, Cresset, 1946.
Here and Now, City Lights, 1957.
Overland to the Islands, Jargon, 1958.
Five Poems, White Rabbit, 1958.
With Eyes at the Back of Our Heads, New Directions Press, 1959.
The Jacob's Ladder, New Directions Press, 1961.
O Taste and See: New Poems, New Directions Press, 1964.
City Psalm, Oyez, 1964.
Psalm Concerning the Castle, Perishable Press, 1966.
The Sorrow Dance, New Directions Press, 1967.
(With Kenneth Rexroth and William Carlos Williams) *Penguin Modern Poets 9,* Penguin (London), 1967.
(Editor) *Out of the War Shadow: An Anthology of Current Poetry,* War Resisters League, 1967.
A Tree Telling of Orpheus, Black Sparrow Press, 1968.
A Marigold from North Vietnam, Albondocani Press-Ampersand, 1968.
Three Poems, Perishable Press, 1968.
The Cold Spring and Other Poems, New Directions Press, 1969.
Embroideries, Black Sparrow Press, 1969.
Relearning the Alphabet, New Directions Press, 1970.
Summer Poems 1969, Oyez, 1970.
A New Year's Garland for My Students, MIT 1969-1970, Perishable Press, 1970.
To Stay Alive, New Directions Press, 1971.
Footprints, New Directions Press, 1972.
The Freeing of the Dust, New Directions Press, 1975.
Chekhov on the West Heath, Woolmer/Brotherston, 1977.
Modulations for Solo Voice, Five Trees Press, 1977.
Life in the Forest, New Directions Press, 1978.
Collected Earlier Poems, 1940-1960, New Directions Press, 1979.
Pig Dreams: Scenes from the Life of Sylvia, Countryman Press, 1981.
Wanderer's Daysong, Copper Canyon Press, 1981.
Candles in Babylon, New Directions Press, 1982.
Poems, 1960-1967, New Directions Press, 1983.
Oblique Prayers: New Poems with Fourteen Translations from Jean Joubert, New Directions Press, 1984.
El Salvador: Requiem and Invocation, William B. Ewert, 1984.
The Menaced World, William B. Ewert, 1984.
Selected Poems, Bloodaxe Books, 1986.
Breathing the Water, New Directions Press, 1987.
Poems, 1968-1972, New Directions Press, 1987.

OTHER

(Translator and editor with Edward C. Dimock, Jr.) *In Praise of Krishna: Songs from the Bengali,* Doubleday, 1967.
In the Night: A Story, Albondocani Press, 1968.
(Contributor of translations) Jules Supervielle, *Selected Writings,* New Directions Press, 1968.
(Translator from French) Eugene Guillevic, *Selected Poems,* New Directions Press, 1969.
The Poet in the World (essays), New Directions Press, 1973.
Light Up the Cave (essays), New Directions Press, 1981.
(Translator with others from Bulgarian) William Meredith, editor, *Poets of Bulgaria,* Unicorn Press, 1985.
(Translator from French) Jean Joubert, *Black Iris,* Copper Canyon Press, 1988.

Also contributor to poetry anthologies, such as *The New American Poetry, Poet's Choice, Poets of Today,* and *New Poets of England and America.* Sound recordings of Levertov's poetry include "Today's Poets 3," Folkways, and "The Acolyte," Watershed, 1985. Contributor to numerous journals. Poetry editor, *Nation,* 1961-62, and *Mother Jones,* 1976-78.

Manuscript collections are housed in the following locations: Humanities Research Center, University of Texas at Austin; Washington University, St. Louis, Mo.; Indiana University, Bloomington; Fales Library, New York University, New York City; Beinecke Library, Yale University, New Haven, Conn.; Brown University, Providence, R.I.; University of Connecticut, Storrs, Conn.; Columbia University, New York City; State University of New York at Stony Brook.

SIDELIGHTS: As *World Literature Today* contributor Doris Earnshaw explains, poet and essayist "Denise Levertov was fitted by birth and political destiny to voice the terrors and pleasures of the twentieth century. . . . She has published poetry since the 1940s that speaks of the great contemporary themes: Eros, solitude, community, war." Although born and raised in England, Levertov came to the United States when she was twenty-five years old and all but her first few poetry collections have been described as thoroughly American. Early on, critics and colleagues alike detected an American idiom and style to her work, noting the influences of writers like William Carlos Williams, H. D. (Hilda Doolittle), Kenneth Rexroth, Wallace Stevens, and the projectivist Black Mountain poets. With the onset of the turbulent 1960s, Levertov delved into socio-political poetry and has continued writing in this sphere; in *Modern American Women Poets,* for instance, Jean Gould calls her "a poet of definite political and social consciousness." In the end, however, Levertov refuses to be labeled, and Rexroth in *With Eye and Ear* says she is "in fact classically independent."

Because Levertov never received a formal education, her earliest literary influences can be traced to her home life in Ilford, England, a suburb of London. Levertov and her older sister, Olga, were educated by their Welsh mother Beatrice Adelaide Spooner-Jones until the age of thirteen. The girls further received sporadic religious training from their father Paul Peter Levertoff, a Russian Jew who converted to Christianity and subsequently moved to England to become an Anglican minister. In the *Dictionary of Literary Biography,* Carolyn Matalene explains that "the education [Levertov] did receive seems, like Robert Browning's, made to order. Her mother read aloud to the family the great works of nineteenth-century fiction, and she read poetry, especially the lyrics of Tennyson. . . . Her father, a prolific writer in Hebrew, Russian, German, and English, used to buy secondhand books by the lot to obtain particular volumes. Levertov grew up surrounded by books and people talking about them in many languages." Many of Levertov's readers favor her lack of formal education because they see it as an impetus to verse that is consistently clear, precise, and accessible. According to Earnshaw, "Levertov seems never to have had to shake loose from an academic style of extreme ellipses and literary allusion, the self-conscious obscurity that the Provencal poets called 'closed.' " Since Levertov decided at age five to become a poet and wrote poems as a child, it is apparent that her home environment has been integral to the success she has become.

Levertov had confidence in her poetic abilities from the beginning, and several well-respected literary figures believed in her talents, as well. Gould records Levertov's "temerity" at the age of twelve when she sent several of her poems directly to T. S. Eliot: "She received a two-page typewritten letter from him, offering her 'excellent advice'. . . . His letter gave her renewed impetus for making poems and sending them out." Other early supporters included critic Herbert Read, editor Charles Wrey Gardiner, and author Kenneth Rexroth. When Levertov had her first poem published in *Poetry Quarterly* in 1940, Rexroth professed: "In no time at all Herbert Read, Tambi Mutti, Charles Wrey Gardiner, and incidentally myself, were all in excited correspondence about her. She was the baby of the new Romanticism. Her poetry had about it a wistful *Schwarmerei* unlike anything in English except perhaps Matthew Arnold's 'Dover Beach.' It could be compared to the earliest poems of Rilke or some of the more melancholy songs of Brahms."

During World War II, Levertov pursued nurse's training and spent three years as a civilian nurse at St. Luke's Hospital in London helping to rehabilitate returning war veterans. She wrote poetry in the evenings. Her first book of poems, *The Double Image,* was published just after the war in 1946. Although many poems in this collection focused on the war, there was no evidence of the immediacy of the death and desperation of the time. Instead, as noted above by Rexroth, the work was very much in keeping with the British neo-romanticism of the 1940s, for it contained formal verse that some considered artificial and overly sentimental. Some critics detect the same propensity for sentimentality in Levertov's second collection, *Here and Now.* In the *National Review,* N. E. Condini comments in retrospect on both of these volumes: "In *The Double Image,* a recurrent sense of loss prompts [Levertov] to extemporize on death as not a threat but a rite to be accepted gladly and honored. This germ of personal mythology burgeons in *Here and Now* with a fable-like aura added to it. . . . [*Here and Now*] is a hymn to 'idiot' joy, which the poet still considers the best protection against the aridity of war and war's memories. Her weakness lies in a childish romanticism, which will be replaced later by a more substantial concision. Here the language is a bit too ornate, too flowery." Criticism aside, Gould says *The Double Image* revealed one thing for certain: "the young poet possessed a strong social consciousness and . . . showed indications of the militant pacifist she was to become."

Levertov came to the United States in 1948, after marrying American writer Mitchell Goodman, and began developing the style that was to make her an internationally respected American poet. Some critics maintain that her first American poetry collection, *Here and Now,* contains vestiges of the bathos that characterized her first book, but for some, *Here and Now* displays Levertov's newly-found American voice. Rexroth, for one, insists in his 1961 collection of essays entitled *Assays* that "the *Schwarmerei* and lassitude are gone. Their place has been taken by a kind of animal grace of the word, a pulse like the footfalls of a cat or the wingbeats of a gull. It is the intense aliveness of an alert domestic love—the wedding of form and content. . . . What more do you want of poetry? You can't ask much more." By the time her third poetry collection, *With Eyes at the Back of Our Heads,* was published, Gould claims Levertov was "regarded as a bona fide American poet."

Levertov's American poetic voice is, in one sense, indebted to the simple, concrete language and imagery, and also the immediacy, characteristic of Williams Carlos Williams' art. Accordingly, Ralph J. Mills, Jr., remarks in his essay in *Poets in Progress* that Levertov's verse "is frequently a tour through the familiar and the mundane until their unfamiliarity and otherworldliness suddenly strike us. . . . The quotidian reality we ignore or try to escape, . . . Levertov revels in, carves and hammers into lyric poems of precise beauty." In turn, *Midwest Quarterly* reviewer Julian Gitzen explains that Levertov's "attention to physical details permits [her] to develop a considerable range of poetic subject, for, like Williams, she is often inspired by the humble, the commonplace, or the small, and she composes remarkably perceptive poems about a single flower, a man walking two dogs in the rain, and even sunlight glittering on rubbish in a street."

In another sense, Levertov's verse exhibits the influence of the Black Mountain poets, such as Robert Duncan, Charles Olson, and Robert Creeley, whom Levertov met through her husband. Creeley was among the first to publish Levertov's poetry in the United States in *Origin* and *Black Mountain Review* in the 1950s. Unlike her early formalized verse, Levertov now gave homage to the projectivist verse of the Black Mountain era, whereby the poet "projects" himself or herself through content rather than through strict meter or form. Although Levertov was assuredly influenced by several renowned American writers of the time, Matalene believes Levertov's "development as a poet has certainly proceeded more according to her own themes, her own sense of place, and her own sensitivities to the music of poetry than to poetic manifestos." Indeed, when Levertov became a New Directions author in 1959, Matalene explains that this came to be because the editor James Laughlin had detected in Levertov's work her own unique voice.

With the onset of U.S. involvement in the Vietnam War in the 1960s, Levertov's social consciousness began to more completely inform both her poetry and her private life. With poet Muriel Rukeyser and several fellow poets, Levertov founded the Writers and Artists Protest against the War in Vietnam. She took part in several anti-war demonstrations in Berkeley, California, and elsewhere, and was jailed at least once for protesting. More recently she has spoken out against nuclear weaponry and U.S. aid to El Salvador. *The Sorrow Dance, Relearning the Alphabet, To Stay Alive,* and to an extent *Candles in Babylon,* as well as other poetry collections, address many socio-political themes, like the Vietnam War, the Detroit riots, and nuclear disarmament. Her goal has been to motivate others into an awareness on these various issues, particularly the Vietnam War.

In contrast with the generally favorable criticism of her work, commentators tend to view the socio-political poems with a degree of distaste, often noting that they resemble prose more than poetry. In *Contemporary Literature,* Marjorie G. Perloff writes: "It is distressing to report that . . . Levertov's new book, *To Stay Alive,* contains a quantity of bad confessional verse. Her anti-Vietnam War poems, written in casual diary form, sound rather like a versified *New York Review of Books.*" Gould mentions that some consider these poems "preachy," and Matalene notes that in *Relearning the Alphabet* Levertov's "plight is certainly understandable, but her poetry suffers here from weariness and from a tendency toward sentimentality. . . . *To Stay Alive* is a historical document and does record and preserve the persons, conversations, and events of those years. Perhaps, as the events recede in time, these poems will seem true and just, rather than inchoate, bombastic, and superficial. History, after all, does prefer those who take stands."

In an interview with *Los Angeles Times Book Review* contributor Penelope Moffet just prior to the publication of *Candles in Babylon,* Moffet explains that "the poet probably would not go so far as to describe any of her own political work as 'doggerel,' but she does acknowledge that some pieces are only 'sort-of' poems." Moffet then quotes Levertov: "If any reviewer wants to criticize [*Candles in Babylon*] when it comes out, they've got an obvious place to begin—'well, it's not poetry, this ranting and roaring and speech-making.' It [the 1980 anti-draft speech included in *Candles in Babylon*] *was* a speech." Nevertheless, others are not so quick to find fault with these "sort-of" poems. In the opinion of Hayden Carruth for the *Hudson Review, Staying Alive* "contains, what so annoys the critics, highly lyric passages next to passages of prose—letters and documents. But is it, after *Paterson,* necessary to defend this? The fact is, I think Levertov has used her prose bits better than Williams did, more prudently and economically . . . . I also think that 'Staying Alive' is one of the best products of the recent period of politically oriented vision among American poets." In turn, James F. Mersmann's lengthy analysis of several years of Levertov's poetry in *Out of the Vietnam Vortex: A Study of Poets and Poetry against the War* contains remarkable praise for the social protest poems. For contrast, Mersmann first analyzes Levertov's early poetry: "*Balanced* and *whole* are words that have perhaps best characterized the work and the person of Denise Levertov—at least until the late sixties. . . . There are no excesses of ecstasy or despair, celebration or denigration, naivete or cynicism; there is instead an acute ability to find simple beauties in the heart of squalor and something to relish even in negative experiences. . . . Through poetry she reaches to the heart of things, finds out what their centers are. If the reader can follow, he is welcomed along, but although the poetry is mindful of communication and expression, its primary concern is discovery." However, claims Mersmann, the chaos of the war disrupted the balance, the wholeness, and the fundamental concern for discovery apparent in her work—"the shadow of the Vietnam War comes to alter all this: vision is clouded, form is broken, balance is impossible, and the psyche is unable to throw off its illness and sorrow. . . . A few notes of *The Sorrow Dance* sound something like hysteria, and later poems move beyond desperation, through mild catatonia toward intransigent rebellion. . . . In some sense the early poems are undoubtedly more perfect and enduring works of art, more timeless and less datable, but they are, for all their fineness, only teacups, and of sorely limited capacities. The war-shadowed poems are less clean and symmetrical but are moral and philosophical schooners of some size. . . . The war, by offering much that was distasteful and unsightly, prompted a poetry that asks the poet to add the light and weight of her moral and spiritual powers to the fine sensibility of her palate and eye."

In addition to being a poet, Levertov has taught her craft at several colleges and universities nationwide; she has translated a number of works, particularly those of the French poet Jean Joubert; she was poetry editor of *Nation* from 1961-62 and *Mother Jones* from 1976-78; and she has authored two essay collections, *The Poet in the World* and *Light Up the Cave.* With respect to the essay collections, both were generally very well-received. According to Carruth, *The Poet in the World* is "a miscellaneous volume, springing from many miscellaneous occasions, and its tone ranges from spritely to gracious to, occasionally, pedantic. It contains a number of pieces about the poet's work as a teacher; it contains her beautiful impromptu obituary for William Carlos Williams, as well as reviews and appreciations of other writers. But chiefly the book is about poetry, its mystery and its craft, and about the relationship between poetry and life. . . . It should be read by everyone who takes poetry seriously." Other reviewers also recommend the work to those interested in the craft of poetry since, as *New Republic* commentator Josephine Jacobsen puts it, "Levertov speaks for the reach and dignity of poetry. . . . [The book] makes . . . large claims for an art form so often hamstrung in practice by the trivial, the fake and the chic. It is impossible to read this book, to listen to its immediacy, without a quickening."

The essays in *Light Up the Cave,* in turn, are considered "a diary of our neglected soul," by *American Book Review* critic Daniel Berrigan: "Norman Mailer did something like this in the sixties; but since those heady days and nights, he, like most such makers and writers, has turned to other matters. . . . Levertov is still marching, still recording the march. . . . The entire book is beyond praise. I think of how, in a sane time, such a book and those who preceded it . . . would form a university course entitled something like: A Renaissance Woman of the Late Twentieth Century. But this is dreaming; it would mean crossing jealous frontiers, violating 'expertise.' " *Library Journal* contributor Rochelle Ratner detects much maturation since the earlier *Poet in the World* and Ingrid Rimland, in the *Los Angeles Times Book Review,* remarks that "the strong impression remains that here speaks a poet intensely loyal to her craft, abiding by an artist's inner rules and deserving attention and respect. . . . This volume is a potpourri: assorted musings, subtle insights, tender memories of youth and strength, political passions, gentle but respectful accolades to other writers. The prose is utterly free of restraints, save those demanded by a fierce, independent spirit insisting at all times on honesty."

Into the 1970s and the 1980s Levertov has continued to produce volume after volume of poetry. She has devoted her writing talents to myriad topics, including the childhood and adolescence of her son, Nikolai Gregory; her female perspective on the world; and her sister, Olga, who died at the age of fifty, her health depleted by an activist career. The disruption of balance that infused her poetry during the 1960s and early 1970s war era is also evidenced in the confessional poems she wrote about her 1972 divorce from Mitchell Goodman in *The Freeing of the Dust.* With regard to her 1982 volume *Candles in Babylon, World Literature Today* reviewer John Martone is fond of Levertov's "consciously encyclopedic scope" and believes "she remains in this book one of the most vitally innovative of contemporary poets." Although in his *World Literature Today* review of the 1984 *Oblique Prayers,* George Economou expresses regret that Levertov has not taken any new risks or ventured into a new direction, other critics praise her consistency in providing good art. And all along, Levertov's social and political consciousness rings strong. In summary, according to Berrigan, "our options [in a tremulous world], as they say, are no longer large. . . . [We] may choose to do nothing; which is to say, to go discreetly or wildly mad, letting fear possess us and frivolity rule our days. Or we may, along with admirable spirits like Denise Levertov, be driven sane; by community, by conscience, by treading the human crucible."

CA INTERVIEW

CA interviewed Denise Levertov by telephone on August 1, 1988, at her home in West Somerville, Massachusetts.

CA: In "Some Notes on Organic Form," collected in The Poet in the World, *you wrote about how, in the making of a poem, "content and form are in a state of dynamic interaction," form being discovered in the work rather than determined beforehand. Does at least some idea of its form usually become apparent early in the writing of a poem?*

LEVERTOV: Yes. It varies from one poem to another, particularly in relation to the length of the poem. But of course, yes—it does. One is not writing in a literal trance.

CA: Usually, though, there's that interaction between content and form going on until the poem is really finished and tidy?

LEVERTOV: That's right. It isn't that you start off not knowing and then you abruptly know and then you go along knowing until you get it finished. It is an ongoing, extended process, with not knowing blending imperceptibly into knowing.

CA: You had an unusual education, not in schools, and you seem always to have come upon just the right influences at the right times. Do you have any thoughts about whether this good fortune might have been more than luck?

LEVERTOV: The fact that I didn't go to school was a kind of luck. I happened to have had the kind of parents who didn't send me to school. As for things that happened later on, I think one thing leads to another. The kind of thing you're referring to as good fortune or luck—I don't mean every kind of good luck, like winning bets at the racetrack, but the kind of life-history good luck—is a matter of a sort of accretion, the influence of one event upon another so that a context occurs which is a lucky context. Once you're in it, then things happen which don't really happen out of the blue; they happen because you're in a particular place at a particular time.

CA: It's lovely that you sent some of your poems to T. S. Eliot when you were twelve, too young to be shy about doing such a thing. What sort of advice did he offer in his reply to you?

LEVERTOV: How I wish I hadn't lost that letter! He said to learn to read poetry in some language other than one's own; that was one good piece of advice. Basically, I think, it was just sort of *keep on keepin' on.*

CA: Coming to the United States in 1948, at a time of other big changes in your life, you were faced with the differences in spoken language that you've said the poetry of William Carlos Williams especially helped you to adapt to. Was there a period then of mainly learning and adjusting before you were writing as much as before?

LEVERTOV: I don't know whether the actual quantity of writing was particularly different. I think during the first two or three years of my son's life I was writing less, as most women find who are writers and who have a child—they don't get very much writing done in that time.

CA: How would you assess the influence of that change in the speech you were hearing, coupled with reading American poets, on your own poetic use of language?

LEVERTOV: It's plain to see in my poems of that period, I think! They begin to sound less "literary," the diction broadens, the rhythms come closer to speech, and there are fewer echoes of other poets—except, for a while, of Williams himself.

CA: You're very concerned that readers approach poetry with their hearing attuned to its musical qualities. Does music—the kind that comes from instruments and voices—play some real part in your writing or in setting a mood for it?

LEVERTOV: I listen to a lot of music, but I don't know that I can say it plays any direct part in my writing. Occasionally while writing I put on a record of something that has the "feel" of what I'm trying to do. My poem about the death of Chausson (in *Breathing the Water*) did emerge from listening to some of his music while picturing his death in a bicycling accident.

CA: You've written about dreams and their relationship to your poetry. Have the dreams that seem to figure in your work changed in any way—in intensity or clarity or pattern, for example—over the years?

LEVERTOV: There was a period of my life when my poems were much more directly related to dreaming than in recent years, because I was remembering and writing down my dreams a lot, which I haven't done in recent years. They haven't been playing such a large part in my work the last few years, though that's not to say they might not again.

CA: One of your poems I especially like is "By Rail through the Earthly Paradise, Perhaps Bedfordshire," from Footprints. *Do you feel a special excitement in traveling?*

LEVERTOV: I do like traveling, but the poem's not about travel as such but about England—ordinary common or garden dear England—in particular. I don't think that poem was written the first time I went back to England after a long absence; I believe it was a later trip. But I grew up there (not in Bedfordshire, however!) and I have very particular feelings about it.

CA: In "Goodbye to Tolerance," written in 1973 while you were very actively protesting the U.S. involvement in Vietnam, you criticized poets who were not doing likewise. You continue to use your poetry as a voice against social and political injustice. Have your feelings softened at all towards those poets who do not?

LEVERTOV: I never demanded of other poets that they write anti-war poems, but that they activate themselves in whatever way they were able. If they were *able* to write poems about it, fine. But if they stood apart from everything—never signed any protest, never demonstrated, never took a stand—that is what I criticized, not that they didn't write anti-war poems. I think there was a certain mealy-mouthed kind of poem which poets who weren't doing any of those things were sometimes publishing at that time, just as if nothing were happening. That certainly irritated me. But I would never demand of anyone that they write a politically-engaged poem, because you cannot write well to order, though you may sincerely wish to. You may not be inspired. I've never demanded on-tap inspiration of anyone.

CA: I think you included in your criticism in that essay not just poets but people at large who were taking what they considered a sort of objective, reasoned stance about the war.

LEVERTOV: That's right. What sort of objectivity can you have about the deliberate maiming (by napalm, by fragmentation bombs, and various "antipersonnel weapons") of civilians as an attempted strategy of demoralization? It was not a game of chess.

CA: Are you in touch currently with poets from countries where writers are censored?

LEVERTOV: Not particularly, no.

CA: You mentioned earlier Eliot's advice about becoming familiar with poetry in another language. How do you feel your own translations of other poets's work have affected your original writing, if indeed they have?

LEVERTOV: Translations are an excellent thing to be working on when you're not in a very productive phase yourself. As for other ways, I can't really think of any particularly. I don't feel my work in translations has been of direct influence on my own creative work. They are an extension of it, rather—and I think this is probably true for most poets who translate (except when a translation is undertaken as a sort of commission or obligation, and then it is a literary task to be done as well as possible, but cannot have the same charge).

CA: You have bemoaned, in the good company of many other people, the erosion of language by misuse, the growing general ignorance of language, and the lack of knowledge of history on the part of many younger people today. Do you sometimes feel because of these conditions that you are writing for a diminishing readership?

LEVERTOV: Yes!

CA: You must confront this especially in your teaching. Any idea about remedies?

LEVERTOV: The remedies have to start at a very early age, and they have to do, really, with the condition of the whole society. Everything else is Band-Aids.

CA: Through the years your work has elicited a good bit of written response from academic critics. Have you found much of it to be perceptive and useful to readers and students?

LEVERTOV: The poet can never really answer that question, because the poet isn't the reader, but the writer. However, not to quibble, I must say I have found some of it has been perceptive. When the writer says that something is perceptive, he or she means that the critic understood what the writer was trying to do. One is not, obviously, the best person to evaluate one's own work. Whether something in praising or dispraising the writer's work is perceptive or not is not for the writer to say; he cannot be objective in that way. But certainly I have come across things which got it all wrong, and I've come across others which were gratifying in that the response one might hope for seemed to have occurred.

CA: You care very much not only about the form of individual poems, but about unity and order in your collections. Is it usually readily apparent to you when you have enough poems, or the right combination of poems, to make a good book?

LEVERTOV: Absolutely not. Usually I've got enough numerically, and I therefore think, Oh, maybe I've got a book here. So I start looking at what I've got. At first it seems to me as if it's hopelessly disparate. It isn't until I've laid everything out on a large surface like a floor and shifted things around into groups that, if I am in fact ready for a book, the pattern begins to emerge.

CA: Have experience and time made the process of writing poems in any way easier for you, or harder, or otherwise different?

LEVERTOV: There are certain skills that anybody acquires as they go on doing something. But to say that writing a poem is easier for me at this stage of my life than it was thirty years ago would certainly not be true. In fact, it's probably more difficult because one is that much more cautious and demanding of one's self.

CA: You teach at Stanford part of the year and spend part of the year at your home in Massachusetts. How is your writing affected by living in two places and by moving between them?

LEVERTOV: It doesn't seem to be adversely affected. I write in both places.

CA: Does the teaching affect your writing in any way?

LEVERTOV: It would if I were teaching all year. Since I'm only teaching one quarter a year, it doesn't seem to get in the way of writing that much. In fact, this year while I was at Stanford I was more productive than I have been during the summer here at home when I'm living a busy but unscheduled life. So I can't really say with certainty. I know, because I did it for many years, that I don't want to teach full-time anymore. I wouldn't get enough writing done if I did. But sometimes I'm quite productive even at a period when I am teaching. However, if I could afford to, I'd give up all the racing around the country giving readings that I do in order to make up the rest of my income. I love going to Stanford, but ideally I guess I'd give that up too if I won the Irish sweepstakes or something.

CA: Many people say that teaching takes the same kind of energy as writing, and that makes it hard for them to do both things at the same time.

LEVERTOV: I think it takes an entirely different kind of energy. It's just that one's time gets chopped up into so many obligations. My crushing burden of mail, always backlogged, is a much worse problem than my teaching has ever been. When one sees that one probably has ten to twenty years left, at the most, it gets pretty scary.

CA: Does the community of writers in each place you live differ considerably?

LEVERTOV: I have a circle of friends in both places, but they are by no means all writers. Here particularly I avoid the literary scene. I know too many people, and it's too much social bother. And out there I have lots of academic friends who are writers of one kind or another, but I don't see many poets. Some of my friends are poets, but I don't live in a literary community in either place.

CA: In a larger sense of community, what kinds of audiences do you see at readings now, what sort of response to poetry in such a public setting?

LEVERTOV: I read all over this country. I read a lot in the Midwest, for example, Texas, all over. There are regional differences in audiences, almost state by state. In university or college settings, the institution usually determines the nature of the audience and the degree of enthusiasm.

CA: In "An Approach to Public Poetry Listening" you wrote about the business we spoke of earlier of hearing the music of the poem, and about bringing the whole self, not just the reasoning mind, to poetry. In that regard, how did you feel about the recent public television series on poets, "Voices and Visions"?

LEVERTOV: I only saw a few of the segments. They varied; some were better than others. They were all pretty skimpy, actually. I don't think they particularly helped people approach poetry in the way you've mentioned. It would be more useful if we had more radio poetry.

CA: Do you have any particular thoughts about the poetry that's being written currently? Any directions you'd like to see change or continue?

LEVERTOV: I dislike L-A-N-G-U-A-G-E poetry, which ignores the consensus of understanding of what words denote; I find that arrogant, a kind of elitism that denies the human communion. Of the poets I've gotten the most from this year, 1988, quite a few of them are translated. One is Polish, one is Estonian, and there are several other European ones. Those happen to be the poets I've found the most stimulating, along with a handful of English-language poets.

CA: What are your greatest social and political concerns now?

LEVERTOV: That's a big question. Central America . . . trying to stop the trade embargo on Nicaragua, not to speak of stopping more funding of the contras, which Reagan is still trying to obtain . . . South Africa. . . . I am praying for a Democratic victory—not that I think it will solve all problems, but four more years of the Republicans would certainly be a catastrophe. Hoping that Jesse Jackson's influence will be felt after a Democratic victory, as it has been during the campaign. The usual things about the arms race, about the environment. Today I was talking to the fishmonger: I bought some fish from him that's farm-raised, and he was pointing out to me which fish comes from the deepest sea, and far out at sea. He's in the business, and yet he's concerned. He is avoiding fish from coastal waters, even though he knows the fishermen that the store buys from and they don't buy anything that was caught in the harbor. All the environmental problems . . . and then AIDS . . . cocaine-addicted newborn babies . . . the destruction of the rain forests. . . . Maybe as people begin to feel the effects in their own lives there is beginning to be a ground swell of protest? Unless there is, we haven't a hope—if we don't do ourselves in in one way, we'll do it another. But I still hope for change, and believe work and prayer can produce results. I have a button that says Picket and Pray. There's still a chance to turn things around. *Glasnost* and *perestroika* are what we need in the USA, just as much as in the Soviet Union—especially *perestroika!*

BIOGRAPHICAL/CRITICAL SOURCES:

BOOKS

Breslin, James E. B., *From Modern to Contemporary American Poetry, 1945-1965,* University of Chicago Press, 1984.

Dictionary of Literary Biography, Volume 5: *American Poets since World War II,* Gale, 1980.

Gould, Jean, *Modern American Women Poets,* Dodd, 1985.

Hungerford, Edward, editor, *Poets in Progress,* Northwestern University Press, 2nd edition, 1967.

Mersmann, James, *Out of the Vietnam Vortex: A Study of Poets and Poetry against the War,* University Press of Kansas, 1974.

Rexroth, Kenneth, *Assays,* New Directions Press, 1961.

Rexroth, Kenneth, *With Eye and Ear,* Herder & Herder, 1970.

Slaughter, William, *The Imagination's Tongue: Denise Levertov's Poetic,* Aquila, 1981.

Wagner, Linda W., *Denise Levertov,* Twayne, 1967.

Wagner, Linda W., editor, *Denise Levertov: In Her Own Province,* New Directions Press, 1979.

PERIODICALS

American Book Review, January-February, 1983.

Contemporary Literature, winter, 1973.

Library Journal, September 1, 1981.

Los Angeles Times Book Review, June 6, 1982, July 18, 1982.

Michigan Quarterly, fall, 1985.

Midwest Quarterly, spring, 1975.

Nation, August 14, 1976.

National Review, March 21, 1980.

New Republic, January 26, 1974.

New York Times Book Review, January 7, 1973, November 30, 1975.

Village Voice, September 29, 1987.

World Literature Today, winter, 1981, spring, 1983, summer, 1985.*

—*Sketch by Cheryl Gottler*

—*Interview by Jean W. Ross*

* * *

LEVINE, Murray 1928-

PERSONAL: Born February 24, 1928, in Brooklyn, N.Y.; son of Israel and Birdie (Cutler) Levine; married Adeline Gordon (a professor of sociology), June 15, 1952; children: David, Zachary. *Education:* City College (now City College of the City University of New York), B.S., 1949; University of Pennsylvania, M.A., 1951, Ph.D., 1954; State University of New York at Buffalo, J.D., 1983.

ADDRESSES: Home—74 Colonial Circle, Buffalo, N.Y. 14213. *Office*—Department of Psychology, State University of New York at Buffalo, 228 Park Hall, Buffalo, N.Y. 14260.

CAREER: Certified diplomate in clinical psychology of American Board of Professional Examiners in Psychology, 1959; licensed in psychology in New York, 1971; admitted to New York State Bar, 1984. Veterans Administration Mental Hygiene Clinic, Philadelphia, Pa., clinical psychologist, 1954-56; Devereux Schools, Devon, Pa., research clinical psychologist, 1956-63; Yale University, New Haven, Conn., assistant professor, 1963-64, associate professor of psychology and director of clinical training program, 1964-68; State University of New York at Buffalo, professor of psychology, 1968—, adjunct professor of law, 1986—, director of clinical/community graduate psychology program, 1968-74, 1978—, director of Research Center for Children and Youth, 1985—. Associate in psychology, University of Pennsylvania, 1959; lecturer, Beaver College, Glenside, Pa., 1962-63. Consultant for Southeastern Pennsylvania Heart Association, 1957-59, Community Progress, Inc., 1963-68, and Veterans Administration, 1963—.

MEMBER: American Association for the Advancement of Science, American Psychological Association (president of division 27, 1977-78), American Orthopsychiatric Association, American Public Health Association, American Association of University Professors, National Society for the Study of Education, Eastern Psychological Association (member of board of directors, 1985-88).

AWARDS, HONORS: Henry Box Prize for Academic Excellence, State University of New York at Buffalo, School of Law and Jurisprudence, 1980; Distinguished Achievement Award, Psychological Association of Western New York, 1987; Community Psychology Distinguished Contribution Award, American Psychological Association Division 27, 1987.

WRITINGS:

(With George Spivack) *The Rorschach Index of Repressive Style,* C. C Thomas, 1964.

(With S. B. Sarason, I. I. Goldenberg, D. L. Cherlin, and E. M. Bennett) *Psychology in Community Settings: Clinical, Educational, Vocational, Social Aspects,* Wiley, 1966.

(With wife, Adeline Levine) *A Social History of Helping Services: Clinic, Court, School, and Community,* Appleton, 1970.

(Editor and author of introduction with A. Levine) Randolph Bourne, *The Gary Schools,* MIT Press, 1970.

(Editor and author of introduction with Barbara B. Bunker) *Mutual Criticism,* Syracuse University Press, 1975.

From State Hospital to Psychiatric Center: The Implementation of Planned Organizational Change, Heath, 1980.

The History and Politics of Community Mental Health, Oxford University Press, 1981.

(With Lois Marie Gibbs) *Love Canal: My Story,* State University of New York Press, 1981.

(With David Perkins) *Principles of Community Psychology,* Oxford University Press, 1987.

Contributor to State University of New York at Buffalo's *Studies in Psychotherapy and Behavioral Change,* and to professional journals, including *Journal of Psychiatry and Law* and *Law & Policy.* Member of editorial board of several periodicals, including *Law and Human Behavior, Journal of Applied Developmental Psychology,* and *Evaluation and Program Planning.*

* * *

LEVINSON, Harry 1922-

PERSONAL: Born January 16, 1922, in Port Jervis, N. Y.; son of David (a tailor) and Gussie (Nudell) Levinson; married Roberta Freiman, January 11, 1946 (divorced, 1970); children: Marc Richard, Kathy, Anne, Brian Thomas. *Education:* Kansas State Teachers College (now Emporia State University), B.S. in education, 1943, M.S., 1947; University of Kansas, Ph.D., 1952. *Religion:* Jewish.

ADDRESSES: Home—225 Brattle St., Cambridge, Mass. 02138. *Office*—Levinson Institute, P.O. Box 95, Cambridge, Mass. 02138.

CAREER: Topeka Veterans Administration Hospital, Topeka, Kan., psychological intern, 1946-50; Topeka State Hospital, Topeka, coordinator of professional education, 1950-54; Menninger Foundation, Topeka, psychologist, 1954-55, director, division of industrial mental health, 1955-68; Levinson Institute, Cambridge, Mass., president, 1968—; Harvard University, Medical School, Boston, Mass., lecturer, 1972-85, clinical professor, 1985—. Adjunct professor at Boston University, 1972-74, and Pace University, 1973-84. Visiting professor at business schools of Massachusetts Institute of Technology, 1961-62, University of Kansas, 1967, Harvard University, 1968-72, and Texas A & M University, 1976. Diplomate, American Board of Professional Examiners in Psychology; past president, American Board of Professional Psychology. Consultant to business and industry. *Military service:* U.S. Army, Field Artillery, 1943-46; became staff sergeant.

MEMBER: American Psychological Association (fellow), American Association for Advancement of Science, New York Academy of Science.

AWARDS, HONORS: Distinguished Alumnus Award, Kansas State Teachers College (now Emporia State University), 1968; Perry L. Rohrer Consulting Psychology Practice Award, American Psychological Association, 1984; Association of Psychologists in Management award, 1985, for contributions in the psychology of management; Career Contribution Award, Massachusetts Psychological Association, 1985; distinguished service citation from Hadassah for contribution to public education in mental health.

WRITINGS:

(With William C. Menninger) *Human Understanding in Industry,* Science Research Associates, 1956.

(Editor) *Toward Understanding Men,* Menninger Foundation, 1956.

(With Charlton R. Price, Kenneth J. Munden, Harold J. Mandl, and Charles M. Solley) *Men, Management and Mental Health,* Harvard University Press, 1962.

Emotional Health in the World of Work, Harper, 1964, revised edition, Levinson Institute, 1980.

The Exceptional Executive, Harvard University Press, 1968, revised edition published as *Executive,* Harvard University Press, 1981.

Executive Stress, Harper, 1970, revised edition, New American Library, 1975.

Organizational Diagnosis, Harvard University Press, 1972.

The Great Jackass Fallacy, Harvard University Press, 1973.

Psychological Man, Levinson Institute, 1976.

(With Stuart Rosenthal) *CEO: Corporate Leadership in Action,* Basic Books, 1984.

(With Janet Robinson) *Ready, Fire, Aim,* Levinson Institute, 1986.

(Editor) *Designing and Managing Your Career,* Harvard Business School Press, 1988.

Contributor to professional journals and popular periodicals.

WORK IN PROGRESS: Organizational Intervention.

* * *

LEWIS, Janet 1899-
(Janet Lewis Winters)

PERSONAL: Born August 17, 1899, in Chicago, Ill.; daughter of Edwin Herbert (a novelist, poet, and teacher) and Elizabeth (Taylor) Lewis; married Yvor Winters (a poet and professor of English), June 22, 1926 (died January, 1968); children: Joanna Winters Thompson, Daniel Lewis. *Education:* Lewis Institute, A.A., 1918; University of Chicago, Ph.B., 1920.

ADDRESSES: Home—West 143 Portola Ave., Los Altos, Calif. 94022. *Agent*—Joanne Kellock and Associates, Ltd., 11019-80 Ave., Edmonton, Alberta, Canada T6G OR2.

CAREER: Novelist, poet, editor, and librettist. Has worked at the American consulate in Paris, France, as a proofreader for *Redbook* in Chicago, Ill., and as a teacher at Lewis Institute, Chicago, Ill. Lecturer, University of California, Berkeley, 1978—; lecturer, St. John's College, Santa Fe, N.M., 1984. Visiting lecturer in creative writing, Stanford University, 1960, 1966, 1967, 1969, 1970; lecturer at writers' workshops at University of Missouri, 1952, University of Denver, 1956, and in Aspen, Colo., 1987.

MEMBER: PEN, American Society of Composers, Authors and Publishers, NAACP (life member).

AWARDS, HONORS: Friends of American Writers award, 1932, for *The Invasion: A Narrative of Events Concerning the Johnston Family of St. Mary's;* Shelley Memorial Award for poetry, 1948; Gold Medal, Commonwealth Club of California, 1948, for *The Trial of Soren Qvist;* Guggenheim fellowship in creative writing for research in Paris, 1950-51; Horace Gregory Foundation award, 1977; Silver Medal, Commonwealth Club of California, 1982, for *Poems Old and New, 1918-1978;* University of Chicago Alumni Association Award for Professional Achievement, 1982; Discovery Award, PEN (West), 1982; Robert Kirsch Award for Body of Work, *Los Angeles Times,* 1985.

WRITINGS:

The Indians in the Woods (poetry), Monroe Wheeler Manikin I (series), 1922, reprinted, with new introduction by Lewis, Matrix Press, 1980.

The Friendly Adventures of Ollie Ostrich (juvenile), illustrated by Fay Turpin, Doubleday, 1923.

The Wheel in Midsummer (poetry), Lone Gull, 1927.

The Invasion: A Narrative of Events Concerning the Johnston Family of St. Mary's (also see below), Harcourt, 1932, reprinted, Alan Swallow, 1964.

The Wife of Martin Guerre (novel; also see below), Colt, 1941, reprinted, Swallow Press, 1970.

Against a Darkening Sky (novel), Doubleday, 1943, Ohio University Press, 1985.

The Earth-Bound, 1924-1944 (poetry), Wells College Press, 1946.

Good-Bye, Son, and Other Stories, Doubleday, 1946, revised edition, Ohio University Press, 1986.

The Trial of Soren Qvist (novel), Doubleday, 1947, reprinted, Ohio University Press, 1989.

Poems, 1924-1944, Swallow Press, 1950.

(Librettist) *The Wife of Martin Guerre: An Opera* (first produced at the Julliard School of Music, 1956), music by William Bergsma, Alan Swallow, 1958, reprinted as *The Wife: A Libretto (For an Opera in Three Acts),* John Daniel, 1988.

The Ghost of Monsieur Scarron (novel), Doubleday, 1959.

Keiko's Bubble (juvenile), illustrated by Kazue Mizumura, Doubleday, 1961.

(Librettist with Alva Henderson) *The Last of the Mohicans* (three-act opera; first produced in Wilmington, Del., June, 1976), Wilmington Opera Society, 1978.

(Librettist with Malcolm Seagrave) *The Birthday of the Infanta: An Opera in One Act* (first produced by the Hidden Valley Opera Ensemble, April 2, 1977), music by Seagrave, Symposium Press, 1979.

The Ancient Ones: Poems (also see below), drawings by Daniel M. Mendelowitz, No Dead Lines, 1979.

Poems Old and New, 1918-1978, Ohio University Press, 1981.

(Librettist) *Mulberry Street: An Opera,* music by Henderson, Dermont, 1981, published as Act II of *West of Washington Square,* Opera San Jose, 1988.

(Librettist) *The Swans: An Opera in Three Acts,* music by Henderson, John Daniel, 1986.

(Librettist) *The Legend, the Story of Neengay, an Ojibway War Chief's Daughter, and the Irishman John Johnston: An Opera Oratorio* (based on *The Invasion: A Narrative of Events concerning the Johnston Family of St. Mary's;* first performed at Cleveland State University, May 8, 1987), music by Bain Murray, John Daniel, 1987.

Late Offerings (poems; chapbook), Robert Barth, 1988.

Librettist for "Easter Laudate," 1977, and "A Christmas Canticle," 1978, music for both by Henderson; librettist for cantata adaptation of *The Ancient Ones,* music by Henderson, 1981. Contributor of short stories, poetry, and reviews to *New Yorker, New Republic, McCall's, Poetry, Revue de Paris, Southern Review,* and other magazines. Co-editor, *Gyroscope,* 1929-30.

SIDELIGHTS: "Being a writer has meant nearly everything to me beyond my marriage and children," says Janet Lewis in *Women Writers of the West Coast: Speaking of Their Lives and Careers.* Lewis, whose father and husband both taught college-level English, credits her father "with being the first to teach her the rudiments of good prose and poetic style," according to Donald E. Stanford in the *Dictionary of Literary Biography Yearbook.* "[Her] first wish was to be a poet," Stanford later remarks, "and, as did her husband, she considers poetry to be superior to prose." Because of this, Lewis's prose works are suffused with what *New York Times Book Review* contributor Eugene Gay-Tifft calls: "Exquisite craftsmanship, a cool perfection of utterance." Discussing her work in general, Lewis informs Brigitte Carnochan in *Women Writers of the West Coast:* "[writing] has concerned the way I have thought and the friends I have made. I've noticed that whenever writing, I'm . . . interested in everything, because I'm still waiting for the answer for the next page. I don't pay as much attention, when I'm not writing, to living in general."

The poet's first published collection of verse, entitled *The Indians in the Woods,* stems from a childhood fascination with the American Indian, whose tales she had heard while vacationing on Neebish Island off the coast of northern Michigan. "The early Indian poems," remarks Suzanne J. Doyle in the *Southern Review,* "owe much to the imagists, whose intention was to capture the isolated perception with such precision, clarity, and harmony that it would suggest a considerable depth of conceptual content." As in her later poetry collections, such as *The Ancient Ones,* Doyle believes that Lewis's work shows "a temperamental affinity of the poet for the Indian consciousness." This is also the case for the author's first novel, *The Invasion: A Narrative of Events Concerning the Johnston Family of St. Mary's,* which relates the story of an 18th century Irish fur trader who marries the daughter of an Ojibway chief. Lewis's honest portrayal of the Indian has been praised by several critics. "Hers is the only book I know which treats the Indian as casually as the white," writes *Bookman* contributor J. V. Cunningham.

Besides her preoccupation with the American Indian, Lewis has written several historical novels set in Europe and based on the 1873 text *Famous Cases of Circumstantial Evidence with an Introduction of the Theory of Presumptive Guilt by S. M. Phillips.* The author's interest in legal cases involving circumstantial evidence was kindled when one of her family's friends was narrowly convicted of murdering his wife. After this experience Lewis wrote *The Wife of Martin Guerre, The Trial of Soren Qvist,* and *The Ghost of Monsieur Scarron,* all of which involve plots revolving around the misinterpretation of circumstantial evidence. *Atlantic Monthly* reviewer Evan S. Connell, Jr., feels that Lewis's best-known book of the three, *The Wife of Martin Guerre,* is "one of the most significant short novels in English," although he hesitates to label it a "masterpiece."

Discussing all these three novels together, Fred Inglis asserts in *Critique: Studies in Modern Fiction,* "It is a small body of work and it may be unspectacular and unsensual, so it is never likely to be fashionable. But in three novels it is sane, honest and courageous and, as I think, more enduring than most of the novels of the last thirty-five years." These books also demonstrate "the excellence and purity of [Lewis's] style and her rare ability to translate the mustier aspects of historical research into clear and shining prose," declares *Chicago Sunday Tribune Magazine of Books* contributor Joan Brace. Inglis sees an influence in her prose from "poets like Jonson and perhaps Horace, Valery and Landor—though without any of the latter's petrified self-indulgence."

Focusing once again on her poetry after a hiatus of almost 30 years, Lewis, who is "by talent and temperament primarily a lyric poet," according to Stanford, not only returned to her free verse works about the Indians, but also began to write compositions for music. She has penned six librettos for operas since 1956, two of which are based her own works *The Wife of Martin Guerre* and *The Invasion.* Stanford considers *The Legend, The Story of Neengay, an Ojibway War Chief's Daughter, and the Irishman John Johnston: An Opera Oratorio,* which is based upon *The Invasion,* to be "probably the most successful [libretto by Lewis] from a literary point of view—that is, it can stand on its own as a dramatic poem."

In an overview of the author's work, Timothy Steele concludes in a *Los Angeles Times Book Review* article: "The excellence of [Lewis's] work results partly from the simple fact that she writes very well, hers being a style that combines clear speech with distinctive and personal inflection and perception." The author's historical works reveal that "she is a realist in the straightforward and now rather rare sense that she uses her art to embellish history and to clarify it . . . , but not at all to supplant the historian's truth by the allegedly superior truth of art," asserts *Southern Review* critic Donald Davie; her poetry, Theodore Roethke describes in *Poetry,* "is marked by an absolute integrity of spirit and often by the finality in phrasing that can accompany such integrity." Steele concludes that "to read her is to read someone who has been a child, sibling, friend, spouse and parent, and who has clearly cared as deeply about those aspects connected with her art."

BIOGRAPHICAL/CRITICAL SOURCES:

BOOKS

Contemporary Literary Criticism, Volume 41, Gale, 1987.
Dictionary of Literary Biography Yearbook: 1987, Gale, 1988.
Yalom, Marilyn, editor, *Women Writers of the West Coast: Speaking of Their Lives and Careers,* Capra Press, 1983.

PERIODICALS

American Poetry Review, November/December, 1981.
Bookman, November, 1932.
Chicago Sunday Tribune Magazine of Books, February 22, 1959.
Critique: Studies in Modern Fiction, winter, 1964-65.
Los Angeles Times Book Review, November 3, 1985.
New York Times Book Review, October 2, 1932, January 24, 1943, April 8, 1951.
Poetry, January, 1947.
Southern Review, winter, 1966, spring, 1980, spring, 1982.
Times Literary Supplement, April 10, 1987.

—Sketch by Kevin S. Hile

* * *

LINCOLN, W(illiam) Bruce 1938-

PERSONAL: Born September 6, 1938, in Stafford Springs, Conn.; son of William Albert and Ruth (a nurse; maiden name, Drake) Lincoln; married Mary Lynda Eagle Livingston, March 27, 1984. *Education:* College of William and Mary, A.B. (cum laude), 1960; University of Chicago, M.A. (honors), 1962, Ph.D., 1966.

ADDRESSES: Office—Department of History, Northern Illinois University, DeKalb, Ill. 60115. *Agent*—Robert Gottlieb, William Morris Agency, 1350 Ave. of the Americas, New York, N.Y. 10019.

CAREER: Memphis State University, Memphis, Tenn., assistant professor of history, 1966-67; Northern Illinois University, DeKalb, assistant professor, 1967-70, associate professor, 1970-78, professor of history, 1978-82, Presidential Research Professor, 1982-86, University Research Professor, 1986—. Visiting associate professor, University of Illinois at Chicago Circle, 1971-72, and University of Chicago, 1977-78; associate of University of Illinois Russian and East European Studies Center, summers, 1975-84; visiting fellow, St. Antony's College, Oxford University, 1983. Speaker on Russian and Soviet affairs.

MEMBER: American Association for the Advancement of Slavic Studies (member of board of directors, 1986-89), Mid-West Slavic Association (member of executive committee, 1976-77), Phi Beta Kappa.

AWARDS, HONORS: Dissertation exchange research fellowship, Inter-University Committee on Travel Grants, 1964-65, for the Soviet Union; American Council of Learned Societies and Social Science Research Council grant, 1967; visiting scholar at Columbia University's Russian Institute, summer, 1967, senior fellowship, 1978; American Philosophical Society grants, 1968, 1970; International Research and Exchanges Board exchange research fellowship, 1970-71, for the Soviet Union, senior fellowships, 1973-74, 1978-79, 1982, 1986; Fulbright-Hays fellowships, 1970-71, 1974 (for Poland), 1978-79, 1982-83; American Council of Learned Societies grants, 1973, 1978, 1978-79; Guggenheim fellowship, 1982-83; winner of numerous other grants and awards.

WRITINGS:

(Editor) *Documents in World History, 1945-67,* Chandler Publishing, 1968.
Nikolai Miliutin: An Enlightened Russian Bureaucrat, Oriental Research Partners, 1977.
Nicholas I: Emperor and Autocrat of All the Russias, Indiana University Press, 1978.
(Editor and author of introduction) *Vospominaniia Generala Fel'dmarshala Grafa Dmitriia Alekseevicha Miliutina,* Oriental Research Partners, 1979.
Petr Petrovich Semenov-Tian-Shanskii: The Life of a Russian Geographer, Oriental Research Partners, 1980.
The Romanovs: Autocrats of All the Russias (Macmillan Library of World History Book Club selection; Book-of-the-Month Club alternate selection), Dial Press, 1981.
In the Vanguard of Reform: Russia's Enlightened Bureaucrats, 1825-1861, Northern Illinois University Press, 1982.
In War's Dark Shadow: Russians before the Great War (Book-of-the-Month Club selection; History Book Club selection), Dial Press, 1983.
Passage through Armageddon: Russia in the Great War, 1914-1918 (Book-of-the-Month Club alternate selection; History Book Club alternate selection), Simon & Schuster, 1986.
Red against White: Civil War among the Russians, Simon & Schuster, in press.

Contributor of over 90 articles, essays, and reviews to journals, including *American Historical Review, Slavic Review, Oxford Slavonic Papers, Journal of Modern History,* and *History Today;* contributor to *Chicago Tribune* and *Los Angeles Times.* Editor, Northern Illinois University Press Russian Studies series, 1982—.

WORK IN PROGRESS: Russia's Great Reforms, to be published by Northern Illinois University Press; *Siberia,* to be published by Morrow.

SIDELIGHTS: W. Bruce Lincoln once told *CA:* "My work has been most influenced by the writings and personalities of three great contemporary historians whose vast knowledge about Russia's past cannot but inspire awe in one who knows them and has read their works: professors Leopold Haimson, Marc Raeff, and Petr Andreevich Zaionchkovskii. It was more years ago than I care to remember when they taught me that the writing of history is an all-consuming craft that demands not sporadic attention but daily devotion. This is the dictum I have sought to follow since I began to study Russia's history. . . . More recently, I have become convinced that the historian who writes only for other specialists neglects an important part of an historian's broader task. Therefore, beginning with my book about Nicholas I, I have begun to write for a broader audience in the hope that my efforts to explain Russia's past may enable readers to better understand Russia's present. I like to think that I have succeeded in that broader effort, at least to some extent."

Lincoln, who is fluent in Russian and has spent four years in that country as an exchange scholar, has concentrated most of his writings upon the reign of the Romanov dynasty, which ruled Russia from 1613 to 1917. His books discuss the lives of the Romanovs, their political policies, and the difficulties they faced in struggling to modernize their backward country. Lincoln's *In the Vanguard of Reform: Russia's Enlightened Bureaucrats, 1825-1861,* for example, includes the earliest historical study of *glasnost* and its impact on Russian politics in the nineteenth century. Reviewers of the historian's books, such as Alden Whitman, often note the skill with which Lincoln brings his subject to life. Whitman writes in the *Chicago Tribune Book World:* "[Lincoln] makes history not only vivid but accessible." F. D. Reeve comments in a *New York Times Books Review* article on the author's *Passage through Armageddon: The Russians in War and Revolution, 1914-1918,* "he manipulates his extensive Russian sources with imaginative zeal, animates diary entries and, like a novelist, turns crucial episodes into mini-dramas."

BIOGRAPHICAL/CRITICAL SOURCES:

PERIODICALS

British Book News, September, 1978.
Chicago Tribune, November 5, 1987.
Chicago Tribune Book World, September 6, 1981, May 8, 1983.
History Today, September, 1978.
Los Angeles Times Book Review, December 28, 1986.
New Statesman, July 7, 1978.
New York Times Book Review, December 28, 1986.
Times Literary Supplement, October 6, 1978, March 19, 1982.
Washington Post Book World, September 20, 1981, October 5, 1986.

* * *

LINDOP, Grevel 1948-

PERSONAL: Born October 6, 1948, in Liverpool, England; son of John Neale (a solicitor) and Winifred (Garrett) Lindop. *Education:* Wadham College, Oxford, B.A., 1970; attended Wolfson College, Oxford, 1970-71. *Religion:* Theravada Buddhist.

ADDRESSES: Office—Department of English, University of Manchester, Manchester M13 9PL, England.

CAREER: University of Manchester, Manchester, England, lecturer in English, 1971-85, senior lecturer, 1985—.

WRITINGS:

Against the Sea (poems), Carcanet, 1970.
(Editor with Michael Schmidt and contributor) *British Poetry since 1960: A Critical Survey,* Carcanet, 1972, Dufour, 1973.
(Editor) *Thomas Chatterton: Selected Poems,* Carcanet, 1972, Dufour, 1973.
Fool's Paradise, Carcanet, 1977.
The Opium-Eater: A Life of Thomas De Quincey, Dent, 1981, Taplinger, 1982.
Thomas De Quincey: Confessions of an English Opium-Eater and Other Writings, Oxford, 1985.
Tourists (poems), Carcanet, 1987.
Moon's Palette (poems), Words Press, 1988.

Contributor to literary magazines, including *Poetry, Nation, Critical Quarterly* and *Times Literary Supplement.*

WORK IN PROGRESS: A Literary Guide to the English Lake District.

SIDELIGHTS: According to Michael Ratcliffe in the London *Times,* Grevel Lindop's *The Opium-Eater: A Life of Thomas De Quincey* is "both scholarly and entertaining, and if Lindop declines to persuade us why we should start reading De Quincey again, he does succeed, and handsomely, in a biographer's first task. *The Opium Eater* brings its extraordinary subject back to life and, having done so, assures for him, despite a glittering supporting cast, . . . the centre of the stage. It is the first biography of Thomas De Quincey since 1936 and all amateurs of the marvellous age in which he lived will relish the thoroughness with which the gap has been filled."

BIOGRAPHICAL/CRITICAL SOURCES:

PERIODICALS

Times (London), July 23, 1981.
Times Literary Supplement, September 11, 1981, November 20, 1987.
Village Voice Literary Supplement, April, 1982.

* * *

LIVELY, Penelope (Margaret) 1933-

PERSONAL: Born March 17, 1933, in Cairo, Egypt; daughter of Roger Low (a bank manager) and Vera Greer; taken to England in 1945; married Jack Lively (a university teacher), June 27, 1957; children: Josephine, Adam. *Education:* St. Anne's College, Oxford, B.A., 1956.

ADDRESSES: Home and office—Duck End, Great Rollright, Chipping, Norton, Oxfordshire OX7 55B, England. *Agent*—Murray Pollinger, 4 Garrick St., London WC2E 9BH, England.

CAREER: Free-lance writer.

MEMBER: Society of Authors.

AWARDS, HONORS: Children's Spring Book Festival Award, *Book World,* 1973, for *The Driftway;* Carnegie Medal, 1973, and Hans Christian Anderson Award List, 1973, both for *The Ghost of Thomas Kempe;* Whitbread Award, 1976, for *A Stitch in Time;* named to Booker-McConnell Prize shortlist, 1977, for *The Road to Lichfield,* and 1984, for *According to Mark: A Novel;* Southern Arts Literary Prize, 1978, for *Nothing Missing but the Samovar and Other Stories;* Arts Council of Great Britain National Book Award, 1979, for *Treasures of Time;* Booker-McConnell Prize, 1987, for *Moon Tiger.*

WRITINGS:

FOR CHILDREN

Astercote, illustrated by Antony Maitland, Heinemann, 1970, Dutton, 1971.
The Whispering Knights, illustrated by Gareth Floyd, Heinemann, 1971, Dutton, 1976.
The Wild Hunt of Hagworthy, illustrated by Juliet Mozley, Heinemann, 1971, new edition illustrated by Robert Payne, Pan Books, 1975, published as *The Wild Hunt of the Ghost Hounds,* Dutton, 1972, new edition illustrated by Jeremy Ford, Puffin Books, 1984.
The Driftway, Heinemann, 1972, Dutton, 1973.
The Ghost of Thomas Kempe, illustrated by Maitland, Dutton, 1973.
The House in Norham Gardens, Dutton, 1974.
Boy without a Name, illustrated by Ann Dalton, Parnassus Press, 1975.
Going Back, Dutton, 1975.
A Stitch in Time, Dutton, 1976.
The Stained Glass Window, illustrated by Michael Pollard, Abelard-Schumann, 1976.

Fanny's Sister (also see below), illustrated by John Lawrence, Heinemann, 1976, new edition, illustrated by Anita Lobel, Dutton, 1980.

The Presence of the Past: An Introduction to Landscape History, Collins, 1976.

The Voyage of QV66, illustrated by Harold Jones, Heinemann, 1978, Dutton, 1979.

Fanny and the Monsters (also see below), illustrated by Lawrence, Heinemann, 1979, enlarged edition, 1983.

Fanny and the Battle of Potter's Piece (also see below), illustrated by Lawrence, Heinemann, 1980.

The Revenge of Samuel Stokes, Dutton, 1981.

Fanny and the Monsters and Other Stories (contains *Fanny's Sister, Fanny and the Monsters,* and *Fanny and the Battle of Potter's Piece*), Puffin Books, 1982.

Uninvited Ghosts and Other Stories, illustrated by Lawrence, Heinemann, 1984, Dutton, 1985.

Dragon Trouble, illustrated by Valerie Littlewood, Heinemann, 1984.

A House Inside Out, illustrated by David Parkins, Deutsch, 1987, Dutton, 1988.

FOR ADULTS

The Road to Lichfield, Heinemann, 1977, Penguin, 1983.

Nothing Missing but the Samovar and Other Stories, Heinemann, 1978.

Treasures of Time, Heinemann, 1979, Doubleday, 1980.

Judgement Day, Heinemann, 1980, Doubleday, 1981.

Next to Nature, Art, Heinemann, 1982, Penguin, 1984.

Perfect Happiness, Heinemann, 1983, Dial Press, 1984.

Corruption and Other Stories, Heinemann, 1984.

According to Mark: A Novel, Beaufort Books, 1984.

Pack of Cards (short stories, including "Nothing Missing but the Samovar" and "Corruption"), Heinemann, 1986, Penguin, 1988.

Moon Tiger, Deutsch, 1987, Grove, 1988.

Passing On (novel), Deutsch, 1989.

OTHER

Contributor to periodicals, including *Encounter.*

SIDELIGHTS: Penelope Lively has distinguished herself as a writer of both juvenile and adult books, winning such prestigious awards as the Booker-McConnell Prize and the Whitbread Award. *Publishers Weekly* contributor Amanda Smith remarks that "'Lively is one of England's finest writers," and adds that her novels are "characterized by intelligence, precision and wit." Sheila A. Egoff, author of *Thursday's Child: Trends and Patterns in Contemporary Children's Literature,* writes that Lively "has an uncannily accurate and honest recall of what it is like to be a child in a world made for adults." As to her adult fiction, a *Times Literary Supplement* reviewer comments that Lively conveys "a prose that is invariably as precise as it is unostentatious."

Born in Cairo, Egypt, Lively received no formal education until she was taken to England at the age of twelve and placed in a boarding school, one she was later to condemn in a *Dictionary of Literary Biography* article as a "barbaric institution." The school was "aimed at turning out competent hockey and lacrosse players and did not encourage other activities," writes Lively. Once, she was even reprimanded by her headmistress for reading *The Oxford Book of English Verse* on her own time. Despite this discouragement, her curiosity about the past, which had developed in Egypt, was nourished by England's historical richness. "I need to write with a very strong sense of topography and place," remarks Lively in a *Publishers Weekly* interview, and her new home well satisfied this need. In the same article she recalls that her studies in modern history at St. Anne's College, where she received a B.A. in 1954, were "wonderful" compared to her earlier education. With her degree completed, the author "originally intended to write social history, but turned to stories for children as a convenient way of exploring her own particular interests," according to Alec Ellis, editor of *Chosen for Children: An Account of the Books Which Have Been Awarded the Library Association Carnegie Medal, 1936-1975.*

In a public speech that was revised to appear in *Horn Book,* Lively writes: "My particular preoccupation as a writer, is with memory. Both with memory in the wide historical sense and memory in the personal sense." Children's literature, with its strong element of imagination, has provided an appropriate means for her study of memory, since, in her view, there is a large amount of fantasy involved in the way people remember the past. Whether it is world history or our own personal history, "we like the past gutted and nicely cleaned up," says Lively; "then we know where we are with it." The relationship between our conceptions of the past and the actual past is a subject the author likes to explore "without presuming to come up with any answers."

Writing juvenile fiction, however, is also a type of mission for Lively that can provide enlightenment. In *A Sounding of Storytellers: New and Revised Essays on Contemporary Writers for Children,* John Rowe Townsend comments: "Penelope Lively sees a sense of continuity as essential to the life of the imagination. In an article in the *Horn Book* for August, 1973, she regretted that modern children were in danger of losing the personal memory that came from contact with the old ('the grandmother at the fireside')." She suggests in this article: "It may be that books attending to memory . . . are more important than ever before." While discussing *The Ghost of Thomas Kempe* in *Junior Bookshelf,* Lively notes that children are not aware of memory simply because they have not lived long enough to become well acquainted with it. It is hard for them to understand how people and their viewpoints change over time. "The point at which children extend this unimaginable truth" towards others, explains Lively, is "an important moment in the growing-up process." It is through her books, then, that she seeks to "introduce children to the art of memory so that they can observe its possibilities and effects and wonder about them," as the author does herself.

It is this process which Lively attempts to describe in *The Driftway.* The story follows Paul and his tag-along sister as he runs away from his stepmother and a charge of shoplifting. He comes across an old road which has been used for thousands of years by various travellers. They have left messages from the past which Paul is able to see and interpret with the help of a cart-driver named Bill. Margery Fisher, editor of *Growing Point,* explains that each "interlude reflects part of Paul's situation and brings him a step nearer to understanding himself and his family." The characters from the past make him aware that "there is more than one point of view to every story, and he takes the first steps away from the morbid self-absorption of childhood towards feeling sympathy for others," concludes a *Times Literary Supplement* reviewer. Some writers such as John Townsend feel that the point of the story is weakened because the book as a whole lacks a strong storyline—the reader never does find out what happens to Paul and his sister. However, *Junior Bookshelf* contributor Aneurin R. Williams expresses her belief that, overall, "Lively writes well, exceeding by far the style and effect of" her earlier work.

Lively's best-received juvenile book, *The Ghost of Thomas Kempe,* offers a much lighter approach to the coming-of-age theme. But, a *Times Literary Supplement* critic qualifies, "the gaiety and high spirits of Penelope Lively's story do not disguise its essentially sober wisdom." In this book the author uses one of her favorite devices: the ghost. The purpose of Thomas Kempe's character, explains Lively in *Junior Bookshelf,* is to explore "the memory of places and the memory of people, and the curious business that we are all of us not just what we are now but what we have been." Putting this another way, *Children's Literature in Education* contributor Judith Armstrong writes that this book "is concerned with different aspects of the same person, the person [James] might have been, or might still become, had he not encountered the ghost of his potential self." The story involves a boy's visitation by the spirit of a sorcerer from Stuart England. At first, the ghost seems only mischievious, but slowly becomes more and more menacing. James learns through the ghost what wickedness is, and is only able to put Kempe to rest by learning to recognize and cope with the wickedness within himself. Many critics agree that *The Ghost of Thomas Kempe* is a well written children's book. "The expert blend of humour and historical imagination is at once more mature and more skillful than anything Penelope Lively has so far written," claims Margery Fisher. David Rees, author of *The Marble in the Water: Essays on Contemporary Writers of Fiction for Children and Young Adults,* feels that the book is of such high quality because for the first time "the author is completely sure of her own abilities, and the writing has a positiveness that derives from the author's pleasure in her awareness of these abilities."

Rees has even higher praise for *A Stitch in Time,* Lively's Whitbread Award winner. "*A Stitch in Time* is probably Penelope Lively's most important and memorable book," he declares. "Not only is its exploration of the significance of history and memory more profound than in any other of her novels, but the unfolding of the story is very fine." As *Times Literary Supplement* reviewer Ann Thwait notes, the story does not have a great deal of plot action, since most of this action occurs unobtrusively within the mind of Marie, the main character. Marie, who is spending her vacation with her parents in an old Victorian house in Lyme Regis, discovers a sampler made in 1865 by a girl named Harriet. The sampler provides a link to the past which Marie senses through such things as the squeaking of a swing and the barking of a dog, neither of which exist near the house at the present; they are only echoes of the past. The tension in the story lies in Marie's suspicion that something tragic has happened to Harriet, a belief supported by the lack of any pictures in the house of Harriet as an adult. Though the mystery is eventually solved, the real message of the book is summarized by the owner of the old house when he sagely remarks: "Things always could have been otherwise. The fact of the matter is that they are not." This declaration, explains Terry Jones, a contributor to *Children's Literature in Education,* "finally ends Maria's 'vague imaginings' and completes one part of her education. . . . She leaves the Regency house determined to acquire 'some new wisdom about the way things are.' She grows, and the reader grows with her."

In the late 1970s, after writing children's books for almost a decade, Lively decided it was time for a change. "I began to feel that I was in danger of writing the same children's books over and over again," she says in *Publishers Weekly.* "More than that, I'd exhausted the ways in which I could explore my own preoccupations and interests within children's books.' " In writing for this new audience, the author has maintained her interest in the past and memory, but has followed a different approach. Her adult characters consider memory "in the context of a lifetime rather than in the context of history," explains Lively in *Horn Book.* These later works no longer deal with how the past can teach one to mature so much as how it can change one's perspective or philosophy of life.

Lively's first novel for adults, *The Road to Lichfield,* is a complex tale about what happens to a married history teacher named Anne Linton when her conceptions about her childhood family life are suddenly altered. While going through her dying father's papers, she discovers that he was involved in an affair similar to her own extramarital relationship. "As everything in her life swings and changes, her father dies, her love is choked off, and only the road [between her present life in Cuxing and her childhood memories of Lichfield] remains permanent," summarizes Jane Langton in the *Dictionary of Literary Biography.* "There is nothing very original about the plot [of *The Road to Lichfield*]," notes John Mellors of *Listener,* but the "book is lifted out of the ordinary by the author's treatment of her two main themes: continuity and memory." Lively "has an easy, unobtrusive style," adds Mellors, which "throws light from unexpected angles" upon questions like whether or not memory actually distorts or preserves the past.

History is not clouded by memory at all in Lively's more cynical book, *Judgement Day.* In this novel, the violent history of an ancient church nags at the thoughts of the main character, Clare, as she witnesses similarly senseless acts occuring in her own life. From the vicar of the church she receives only muddled, unsatisfactory answers to her doubts that a loving and omnipotent God could allow such atrocities. Her experiences in the book eventually compel her to believe "that we are quite fortuitously here, and that the world is a cruel and terrible place, but inexplicably and bewilderingly beautiful." Francis King of *Spectator* wonders if it is "presumptuous to assume that it is also Clare's creator who is speaking here." Stating her beliefs in a *Publishers Weekly* article, Lively appears to confirm King's suspicion: "Life is governed by Fate—Fate being another word for history—governed by outside forces over which one has no control. This is one of the things that most people find unacceptable about life and therefore try to camouflage." Although *Times Literary Supplement* contributor William Boyd questions the effectiveness of "fate's visitations" in *Judgement Day, Encounter* contributor Alan Brownjohn feels that Lively handles this premise well. *Listener* reviewer John Naughton asserts that this novel "is an impressive work, sharp and surefooted on the nuances of class and of personal conflict."

In Lively's Booker-McConnell Award-winning story *Moon Tiger,* a novel which presents a perspective on life similar to that of *Judgement Day,* the "true center is no less than history itself—the abiding backdrop across which mere human beings flutter," says Ann Tyler in the *New York Times Book Review.* It is "the transitoriness of all human happiness and indeed of all human life" which is the concern of a respected historian, Claudia Hampton, as she considers her life from the vantage point of her deathbed, explains Francis King in a *Spectator* article. In this book a complex interweaving of flashbacks takes the reader on a voyage through the dying historian's life, including a sojourn in World War II Egypt, where Claudia finds brief happiness with a tank commander, who is later killed in action. "Her image for their love," writes Richard Eder of the *Los Angeles Times Book Review,* "is the moon tiger—a spiral coil of punk that burns slowly through the night beside their bed to keep away mosquitos and that leaves only ash in the morning."

Parallel to this image are the last lines of the book in which Claudia passes away: "The sun sinks and the glittering tree is extinguished. The room darkens again. . . . And within the room a change has taken place. It is empty. Void. It has the stillness of a place in which there are only inanimate objects; metal, wood, glass, plastic. No Life." The denoument marks the end of, in Eder's words, Claudia's "long postponed search for herself." For some critics, like Martha Duffy of *Time* magazine, the flashbacks involved in her search become "overdrawn" after a while. However, many reviewers concur with *Times Literary Supplement* contributor J. K. L. Walker, who writes: "Penelope Lively's ingenious, historically informed handling of [the story] is a considerable achievement and Claudia Hampton herself a formidably reflective and articulate protagonist." It is a tale told from the most widely encompassing perspective possible for a human being, a study of one character's entire lifetime memory and how she regards it.

Although Lively bases most of *Moon Tiger* upon the memory of a single character, exploring this favorite subject in depth, the author admits to herself in *Horn Book:* "I don't imagine that I am ever going to find the answer to the questions prompted by the workings of memory; all I can do is pose these questions in fictional form and see what happens." Nevertheless, Penelope Lively has achieved "something unique" in her novels, according to David Rees, "a kind of book that is neither history nor fantasy but has something of both, and that cannot be labeled conveniently—a book . . . where 'history is now.' " Ultimately, the purpose of writing, explains Lively in *Horn Book,* is "to provide plunder for the reader's imagination." Books should give the reader "something to take away and mull over on his own and maybe develop and enlarge and breed from." In this way, Lively hopes her books will help illustrate "what it is like to be a human being."

BIOGRAPHICAL/CRITICAL SOURCES:

BOOKS

Children's Literature Review, Volume 7, Gale, 1984.

Contemporary Literary Criticism, Volume 32, Gale, 1985.

Dictionary of Literary Biography, Volume 14: *British Novelists Since 1960,* Gale, 1983.

Egoff, Sheila A., *Thursday's Child: Trends and Patterns in Contemporary Children's Literature,* American Library Association, 1981.

Ellis, Alec, and Marcus Crouch, editors, *Chosen for Children: An Account of the Books Which Have Been Awarded the Library Association Carnegie Medal, 1936-1975,* 3rd edition, American Library Association, 1977.

Rees, David, *The Marble in the Water: Essays on Contemporary Writers of Fiction for Children and Young Adults,* Horn Book, 1980.

Townsend, John Rowe, *A Sounding of Storytellers: New and Revised Essays on Contemporary Writers for Children,* Lippincott, 1979.

PERIODICALS

Chicago Tribune Book World, August 9, 1981, May 15, 1988.

Children's Literature in Education, summer, 1978, autumn, 1981.

Encounter, May, 1981.

Globe and Mail (Toronto), November 14, 1987.

Growing Point, July, 1972, July, 1973.

Horn Book, June, 1973, August, 1973, February, 1978, April, 1978.

Junior Bookshelf, September, 1972, June, 1974.

Listener, August 4, 1977.

Los Angeles Times Book Review, April 17, 1988.

New York Times Book Review, April 17, 1988.

Publishers Weekly, November 13, 1987, March 25, 1988.

Spectator, November 22, 1980, May 23, 1987.

Time, May 2, 1988.

Times (London), October 30, 1987.

Times Literary Supplement, July 14, 1972, April 6, 1973, July 16, 1976, November 21, 1980, May 23, 1986, May 15, 1987.

Washington Post Book World, August 2, 1981, September 13, 1988.*

—*Sketch by Kevin S. Hile*

* * *

LLEWELYN, T. Harcourt
See HAMILTON, Charles (Harold St. John)

* * *

LOBLEY, Robert (John) 1934-

PERSONAL: Born May 17, 1934, in London, England; son of Robert William (a surveyor) and Winifred (Duffy) Lobley; married Priscilla Elmore-Jones (a writer and designer), July 28, 1956; children: Benjamin. *Education:* St. Martin's College of Art, National Diploma in Design, 1954; University of London, Art Teacher's Certificate, 1955. *Religion:* None.

ADDRESSES: Home—12 The Common, Ealing, London W5, England.

CAREER: John Kelly Boys' School, London, England, head of art department, 1958-68; Chiswick School, London, head of art department, beginning 1968; Latymer Upper School, London, head of art department, 1976—. Partner, Priscilla Lobley Flower Kits, 1968—. *Wartime service:* Hospital worker as "humanitarian objector" to military service, 1956-58.

MEMBER: National Union of Teachers.

WRITINGS:

(Self-illustrated) *Circus* (children's book), privately printed, 1961.

(Self-illustrated) *Farm* (children's book), privately printed, 1961.

(Self-illustrated) *Toys* (children's book), privately printed, 1961.

(Self-illustrated) *Tom and Peter* (children's book), Faber, 1968.

(With wife, Priscilla Lobley) *Your Book of Patchwork,* Faber, 1974.

Your Book of Painting, Faber, 1977.

(With P. Lobley) *Your Book of English Country Dancing,* Faber, 1980.

Designer of Christmas and birthday cards for Magpie Press, 1960-64. Contributor to *Visual Education.* Contributor to children's television.

WORK IN PROGRESS: A book on film-making for children; *The Grubblings,* a children's book.

AVOCATIONAL INTERESTS: English canals, mountain walking, industrial architecture.*

LOEWENSTEIN, Prince Hubertus (F. zu)
See LOEWENSTEIN(-WERTHEIM-FREUDENBERG), Hubertus (Friedrich Maria Johannes Leopold Ludwig) zu

* * *

LOEWENSTEIN(-WERTHEIM-FREUDENBERG), Hubertus (Friedrich Maria Johannes Leopold Ludwig) zu 1906-1984
(Prince Hubertus [F. zu] Loewenstein)

PERSONAL: Born October 14, 1906, in Schoenwoerth Castle, near Kufstein, Tirol, Austria; died November 28, 1984, in Bonn, West Germany; son of Maximilian, Prince zu Loewenstein-Wertheim-Freudenberg and Constance, daughter of Lord Pirbright; married Helga Schuylenburg, April 4, 1929; children: Maria Elisabeth, Konstanza Maria, Margareta Maria. *Education:* Attended University of Munich, University of Geneva, University of Berlin, and University of Florence; University of Hamburg, Doctor of Law, 1931. *Religion:* Catholic.

ADDRESSES: Home—Lahnstrasse 50, D-5300 Bonn, Bad Godesberg, West Germany.

CAREER: Editorial writer for democratic German newspapers, including *Berliner Tageblatt* and *Vossische Zeitung,* prior to 1933; leader of Republican Youth in Germany, 1933; political exile in United States, 1933-46, serving as visiting Carnegie Professor of History and Government, 1937-46; University of Heidelberg, Heidelberg, Germany (now West Germany), guest professor, 1947; member of German Bundestag (Lower House), 1953-57; special adviser to Office of Press and Information, German Federal Government, 1959-73. Co-founder, German Academy of Arts and Sciences in Exile, 1936; founder and general secretary, American Guild for German Cultural Freedom.

MEMBER: German Authors' Council, Free German Authors' Association (president), Gallery of Living Catholic Authors (United States).

AWARDS, HONORS: D.Litt., Hamline University, 1943; Golden Grand Cross of Athos, presented by the Ecumenical Patriarch, Athenagoras I, 1966; Commander of the German Order of Merit, 1968; Commander of the Italian Order of Merit, 1970; honorary professor, War Academy of the Republic of China, 1975; Knight Commander's Cross (Badge and Star) of the German Order of Merit, 1982; Papal Order of St. Gregorius (Badge and Star), 1982.

WRITINGS:

Umrisse der Idee des faschistischen Staates und ihre Verwirklichung, unter Vergleichung mit den wichtigsten Gebieten des deutschen Staatsrechts, Kirchhain N.L., 1931.

Die Tragoedie eines Volkes: Deutschland 1918-1934, Steenuil-Verlag, 1934, translation published as *The Tragedy of a Nation,* Faber, 1934.

After Hitler's Fall: Germany's Coming Reich, translated by Denis Waldock, Faber, 1934.

A Catholic in Republican Spain, Gollancz, 1937.

Conquest of the Past (autobiography), Houghton, 1938.

A Catholic Looks at Fascism, Modern Age, 1940.

On Borrowed Peace, Doubleday, 1942.

The Germans in History, Columbia University Press, 1945, reprinted, AMS Press, 1969.

The Child and the Emperor (first book of a legend trilogy), Macmillan, 1945.

The Lance of Longinus (second book of a legend trilogy), Macmillan, 1946.

The Eagle and the Cross (third book of a legend trilogy), Macmillan, 1947.

Von des deutschen Reiches Erneuerung: Eine Rede in Heidelberg, Amorbacher Buchhandlung, 1949.

Deutsche Geschichte: Der Weg des Reiches in zwei Jahrausenden, Scheffler, 1950, 6th edition, Herbig, 1978.

Stresemann: Das deutsche Schicksal im Spiegel seines Lebens, Scheffler, 1951.

Kleine deutsche Geschichte, Scheffler, 1953, 3rd edition, 1962, translation published as *A Basic History of Germany,* Inter Nationes, 1965.

Die roemishchen Tagebuecher des Privatdozenten Dr. Remigius von Molitor (novel), Norddeutsche Verlagsanstalt O. Goedel, 1956.

(With Volkmar von Zuehlsdorff) *Deutschlands Schicksal, 1945-1957,* Athenaeum-Verlag, 1957.

(With von Zuehlsdorff) *Die Verteidigung des Westens,* Athenaeum-Verlag, 1960, translation by Edward Fitzgerald published as *NATO and the Defense of the West,* Praeger, 1963.

Der rote Imperialismus: Die Strategie Moskaus und Pekings im Kampf um die Weltherrschaft, Westdeutscher Verlag, 1965.

Was war die deutsche Widerstandsbewegung?, Grafes, 1965, translation published as *What Was the German Resistance Movement?,* Grafes, 1965.

Towards the Further Shore (autobiography), Gollancz, 1968.

Botschafter ohne Auftrag, Droste Verlag, 1973.

Seneca, Langen Mueller, 1975.

Tiberius, Langen Mueller, 1977.

Capri fuer Kenner, Langen Mueller, 1979.

Rom, Reich ohne Ende, Propylaen, 1979.

Trajanus, Langen Mueller, 1980.

Abenteurer der Freiheit, Ullstein, 1983.

Konstantin der Grosse, Langen Mueller, 1983.

Alabanda; oder, der deutsche Juengling in Griechenland, Langen Mueller, 1986.

Contributor to magazines and newspapers in Germany, England, and the United States, including *Atlantic, American Mercury, Commonweal, American Scholar, This Week, New York Herald Tribune, Saturday Evening Post, Spectator,* and *Nineteenth-Century Review.*

SIDELIGHTS: Hubertus zu Loewenstein once told *CA* that his main interest was the propagation of "the basic truth that freedom is indivisible." During his lifetime he strove to make people conscious of the need for defense of freedom and emphasized the importance of enlightening the youth of all nations.

[Sketch reviewed by author's friend, Volkmar von Zuehlsdorff]

* * *

LOHNES, Walter F. W. 1925-

PERSONAL: Born February 8, 1925, in Frankfurt, Germany; immigrated to United States, 1948; naturalized United States citizen, 1954; son of Hans (a civil engineer) and Dina (Koch) Lohnes; married Claire Shane, February 6, 1950; children: Kristen, Peter, Claudia. *Education:* Studied at University of Frankfurt, 1945-48, Ohio Wesleyan University, 1948-49, and University of Missouri, 1949-50; Harvard University, Ph.D., 1961.

ADDRESSES: Home—733 Covington Rd., Los Altos, Calif. 94022. *Office*—Department of German Studies, Stanford University, Stanford, Calif. 94305.

CAREER: University of Missouri, Columbia, instructor in German, 1949-50; Phillips Academy, Andover, Mass., head of German department, 1951-61; Stanford University, Stanford, Calif., assistant professor, 1961-65, associate professor, 1965-69, professor of German, 1969—, chairman of department of German studies, 1973-79. Visiting professor, Woehler-Gymnasium, Frankfurt, 1956-57, Middlebury College, 1959, and University of New Mexico, 1980, 1981, 1986. Director, NDEA (National Defense Education Act) Institute of Advanced Study, 1961-68; director, Institute of Basic German. Examiner for College Entrance Examination Board, Graduate Record Examination Board, and Educational Testing Service.

MEMBER: American Association of Teachers of German (vice-president, 1960, 1970-71), Modern Language Association of America, American Council on the Teaching of Foreign Languages, American Association of Applied Linguistics, German Studies Association, Internationale Vereinigung fuer Germanische Sprach- und Literaturwissenschaft.

AWARDS, HONORS: Federal Order of Merit, Federal Republic of Germany, 1989.

WRITINGS:

(With F. W. Strothmann) *German: A Structural Approach,* Norton, 1967, 4th edition (with W. E. Petig), 1988.
(Editor with V. Nollendorfs) *German Studies in the United States: Assessment and Outlook,* University of Wisconsin Press, 1976.
(With E. A. Hopkins) *The Contrastive Grammar of English and German,* Karoma, 1982.
(With Martha Woodmansee) *Erkennen und Deuten,* E. Schmidt Verlag, 1983.
(With J. A. Pfeffer) *Grunddeutsch: Texte zur gesprochenen deutschen gegenwartssprache,* three volumes, M. Niemeyer, 1984.
(With David P. Benselev and V. Nollendorfs) *Teaching German in America: Prolegomena to a History,* University of Wisconsin Press, 1988.

Contributor of numerous articles to professional journals. Editor, *Unterrichtspraxis,* 1971-74.

* * *

LONG, A(nthony) A(rthur) 1937-

PERSONAL: Born August 17, 1937, in Manchester, England; son of Tom Arthur (a teacher) and Joan (LeGrice) Long; married Janice Calloway (a teacher), 1960; married second wife, Kay Flavell (a university lecturer), 1970; children: Stephen Arthur, Rebecca Jane. *Education:* University College, London, B.A., 1960, Ph.D., 1964.

ADDRESSES: Office—Department of Classics, Dwinelle Hall, University of California, Berkeley, Calif. 94720.

CAREER: University of Otago, Dunedin, New Zealand, lecturer in classics, 1961-64; University of Nottingham, Nottingham, England, lecturer in classics, 1964-66; University of London, University College, London, England, lecturer, 1966-71, reader in Greek and Latin, 1971-73; University of Liverpool, Liverpool, England, Gladstone Professor of Greek, 1973-83; University of California, Berkeley, professor of classics, 1983—. Visiting professor of classical philology, University of Munich, 1973; public orator, University of Liverpool, 1981-83; visiting professor of classics, University of California, Berkeley, 1982. Treasurer, Council of University Classical Departments, 1970-75; member, Institute for Advanced Study, Princeton, N.J., 1970, 1979. *Military service:* British Army, 1955-57; became lieutenant.

MEMBER: Aristotelian Society, Classical Association (member of council, 1974-77), Society for Promotion of Hellenic Studies (member of council, 1972-75), Institute of Classical Studies (member of board of management, 1970-73, 1982-83), American Philological Association.

AWARDS, HONORS: Cromer Greek Prize, British Academy, 1968, for *Language and Thought in Sophocles: A Study of Abstract Nouns and Poetic Technique;* Guggenheim fellowship, 1986.

WRITINGS:

Language and Thought in Sophocles: A Study of Abstract Nouns and Poetic Technique, Athlone Press, 1968.
(Editor) *Problems in Stoicism,* Athlone Press, 1971.
Hellenistic Philosophy, Scribner, 1974, 2nd edition, University of California Press, 1986.
(Co-editor) *Studies in Theophrastus,* Rutgers University Press, 1985.
(With D. N. Sedley) *The Hellenistic Philosophers,* 2 volumes, Cambridge University Press, 1987.
(Co-editor) *The Question of Eclecticism,* University of California Press, 1988.

CONTRIBUTOR

Dictionary of the History of Ideas, Scribner, 1973.
A. P. D. Mourelatos, editor, *The Pre-Socratics,* Doubleday, 1974.
R. E. Allen and D. J. Furley, editors, *Studies in Presocratic Philosophy,* Routledge & Kegan Paul, 1975.
F. Bossier and others, editors, *Images of Man in Ancient and Medieval Thought,* Leuven University Press, 1976.
J. Brunschwig, editor, *Les Stoiciens et leur logique,* Vrins, 1978.
J. M. Rist, editor, *The Stoics,* University of California Press, 1978.
D. J. O'Meara, editor, *Studies in Aristotle,* Catholic University of America Press, 1981.
J. Barnes and others, editors, *Science and Speculation,* Cambridge University Press, 1982.
J. Luce, editor, *Ancient Writers,* Scribner, 1982.
W. W. Fortenbaugh, editor, *On Stoic and Peripatetic Ethics,* Rutgers University Press, 1983.
R. Browning, editor, *The World of Greece,* Thames & Hudson, 1984.
P. Easterling and B. Knox, editors, *The Cambridge History of Greek Literature,* Cambridge University Press, 1985.

OTHER

Contributor to *Classical Review, Classical Quarterly, Journal of Hellenic Studies, Philosophical Quarterly, Phronesis,* and other scholarly journals. Editor, *Bulletin* of University College, London, 1971-73, and *Classical Quarterly,* 1975-81; co-editor, *Classical Antiquity,* 1987—.

WORK IN PROGRESS: Co-editing *The Cambridge History of Hellenistic Philosophy; Arcesilaus,* for Bibliopolis; *Greek Models of Mind,* for Harvard University Press.

AVOCATIONAL INTERESTS: Music, talking, travel, cricket.

BIOGRAPHICAL/CRITICAL SOURCES:

PERIODICALS

New York Times, May 28, 1971.

LONG, Naomi Cornelia
See MADGETT, Naomi Long

* * *

LONGBAUGH, Harry
See GOLDMAN, William W.

* * *

LOPATE, Carol
See ASCHER, Carol

* * *

LORD, Phillips H.
See YOLEN, Will(iam Hyatt)

* * *

LORD, Vivian
See STROTHER, Pat Wallace

* * *

LOWBURY, Edward (Joseph Lister) 1913-

PERSONAL: Born December 6, 1913, in London, England; son of Benjamin William (a physician) and Alice (Halle) Lowbury; married Alison Young (a musician), June 12, 1954; children: Ruth, Pauline, Miriam. *Education:* University College, Oxford, B.A., 1936, B.M. and B.Ch., 1939; London Hospital Medical College, London, M.A., 1940; Oxford University, D.M., 1957.

ADDRESSES: Home—79 Vernon Rd., Birmingham B16 9SQ, England.

CAREER: Member of scientific staff, Medical Research Council of Great Britain, 1947—; Birmingham Accident Hospital, Birmingham, England, bacteriologist in Medical Research Council Burns Research Unit, 1949-79; University of Aston, Birmingham, honorary professor of medical microbiology, 1979—. Honorary research fellow, University of Birmingham, 1950—. Consultant in bacteriology, Birmingham Regional Hospital Board, 1960—; founder and honorary director, Hospital Infectional Research Laboratory, Birmingham, 1966-79. Consultant to United States on hospital-acquired infection, World Health Organization, 1965. *Military service:* Royal Army Medical Corps, 1943-47; became major.

MEMBER: Royal College of Pathologists (fellow), Royal College of Physicians (honorary fellow), Royal College of Surgeons (honorary fellow), Royal Society of Literature (fellow), Society for General Microbiology, Society for Applied Bacteriology, Pathological Society of Great Britain and Ireland, British Medical Association, Hospital Infection Society (president, 1980-82).

AWARDS, HONORS: Newdigate Prize, 1934, for *Fire;* John Keats Memorial Lecturer award, 1973; Everett Evans Memorial Lecturer award, 1977; D.Sc., University of Aston, 1977; A.B. Wallace Memorial Lecturer and Medal, 1978; LL.D., University of Birmingham, 1980; Officer, Order of the British Empire.

WRITINGS:

POETRY

Fire, Blackwell, 1934.
Crossing the Line, Hutchinson, 1947.
(With Terence Heywood) *Facing North,* Mitre Press, 1957.
Metamorphoses, Keepsake Press, 1960.
Time for Sale, Chatto & Windus, 1961.
New Poems, Keepsake Press, 1965.
Daylight Astronomy, Wesleyan University Press, 1968.
Figures of Eight, Keepsake Press, 1969.
Green Magic (for young people), Chatto & Windus, 1972.
Two Confessions, Keepsake Press, 1973.
The Night Watchman, Chatto & Windus, 1974.
Poetry and Paradox: Poems and an Essay, Keepsake Press, 1976.
(With others) *Troika: A Selection of Poems,* Daedalus Press, 1977.
Selected Poems, Celtion Press, 1978.
A Letter from Masada, Keepsake Press, 1982.
Goldrush, Celandine Press, 1983.
Apocryphal Letters, Sceptre Press, 1985.
Birmingham! Birmingham!, Keepsake Press, 1985, enlarged 2nd edition, 1989.
Flowering Cypress, Pointing Finger Press, 1986.
A Letter from Hampstead, Keepsake Press, 1987.
Variations on Aldeburgh, Mandeville Press, 1987, 2nd edition, 1989.

OTHER

(With wife, Alison Young, and Timothy Salter) *Thomas Campion: Poet, Composer, Physician* (biography and critical study), Barnes & Noble, 1970.
(With G. A. Ayliffe) *Drug Resistance in Antimicrobal Therapy,* C. C Thomas, 1974.
(Editor with others) *Control of Hospital Infection: A Practical Handbook,* Chapman & Hall, 1975, 2nd edition, 1981.
(Editor with Alison Young) Andrew Young, *The Poetical Works of Andrew Young,* Secker & Warburg, 1985.

Also contributor of chapters and articles to numerous books, including *The Scientific Basis of Medicine, Textbook of British Surgery, Recent Advances in Surgery, Recent Advances in Clinical Pathology, Chambers Encyclopedia,* and *Encyclopedia of Poets.* Contributor to *Widening Circles,* 1976, *Night Ride and Sunrise,* 1978, *Golden Treasury, A Map of Modern Verse,* "The Poet Speaks" (recordings), and other collections. Contributor of poetry and medical and scientific articles to periodicals, including *British Medical Journal, Encounter, Lancet, London Magazine, Nature, New York Times, Times Literary Supplement,* and *Southern Review.* Editor, *Equator* (Nairobi), 1945-46.

WORK IN PROGRESS: With Alison Young, *To Shirk No Idleness: A Critical Biography of Andrew Young; One Might Live Twice,* an autobiography; *Apollo: An Anthology of Poems by Medical Men and Women,* for the 150th anniversary of the British Medical Journal.

SIDELIGHTS: The two sides of Edward Lowbury's life as a medical man and a poet are "excitingly contrasted," he noted to *CA,* adding: "I write at weekends and on holiday, but store up memories and experiences for use at these times. The collaborative study on Thomas Campion reflects an interest of many years in Elizabethan music and poetry, and incidentally gave me an insight into the divided life of a seventeenth-century doctor-poet who was also a fine composer."

BIOGRAPHICAL/CRITICAL SOURCES:

BOOKS

My Medical School, Robson Books, 1978.

PERIODICALS

Agenda, Volume 21, number 4, 1989.

Southern Review, Volume 6, 1970.
Times Literary Supplement, June 13, 1986.

* * *

LOWE, David A(llan) 1948-

PERSONAL: Born January 15, 1948, in Carlinville, Ill.; son of Harold Sager (a teacher) and Martha Jane (Yates) Lowe. *Education:* Macalester College, B.A., 1969; Indiana University, M.A., 1972, Ph.D., 1977.

ADDRESSES: Home— Nashville, Tenn. *Office*—Department of Slavic Languages and Literatures, Vanderbilt University, Box 75, Station B, Nashville, Tenn. 37235.

CAREER: Ardis Publishers, Ann Arbor, Mich., editor, 1974-75, 1981; Macalester College, St. Paul, Minn., instructor in Russian, 1975-77, assistant professor of Slavic languages and literatures and chairman of department, 1978-79; Indiana University at Bloomington, visiting lecturer in Russian, 1977-78; Vanderbilt University, Nashville, Tenn., associate professor of Slavic languages and literatures, 1979—. Member of Soviet-American teacher exchange sponsored by International Research and Exchanges Board, 1976. Director of Slavic workshops.

MEMBER: American Association for the Advancement of Slavic Studies, American Association of Teachers of Slavic and East European Languages, South Eastern Modern Language Association, Southern Conference of Slavic Studies, Phi Beta Kappa.

WRITINGS:

(Contributor) Carl Proffer, editor, *Russian Romantic Prose,* Translation Press, 1979.
Turgenev's "Fathers and Sons," Ardis, 1983.
(Editor and translator) Ivan Turgenev, *Letters,* two volumes, Ardis, 1983.
(Contributor) C. Proffer and Ellendea Proffer, editors, *The Barsukov Triangle, The Two-Toned Blond, and Other Stories,* Ardis, 1983.
(Contributor) Helena Goscilo, editor, *The Peak of Success and Other Stories,* Ardis, 1983.
(Editor and contributor) *Callas As They Saw Her,* Ungar, 1987.
(Translator and editor with Ronald Meyer) *Fyodor Dostoevsky: Complete Letters,* Ardis, Volume 1: *1832-1859,* 1988, Volume 2: *1860-1867,* 1989.
(Translator) Inna Varlamova, *A Counterfeit Life,* Ardis, 1988.
(Translator) Raissa L. Berg, *Acquired Traits,* Viking, 1988.
(Editor and contributor) *Critical Essays on Ivan Turgenev,* Twayne, 1989.

Contributor to *Columbia Dictionary of Modern European Literature* and *Encyclopedia of World Literature in the Twentieth Century.* Contributor of more than a dozen articles and translations to language and literature journals. Associate editor of *Russian Literature Triquarterly.*

* * *

LUMSDEN, Charles J(ohn) 1949-

PERSONAL: Born April 9, 1949, in Hamilton, Ontario, Canada; son of John P. (in business) and Elva M. (Cousins) Lumsden; married Eunice W. Po (in business), June 16, 1973; children: Alexander Peter. *Education:* University of Toronto, B.Sc., 1972, M.Sc., 1974, Ph.D., 1977.

ADDRESSES: Home—Toronto, Ontario, Canada. *Office*—Clinical Science Division, Room 7313, Medical Sciences Building, University of Toronto, Ontario, Canada M5S 1A8.

CAREER: Harvard University, Cambridge, Mass., postdoctoral research fellow in biology, 1979-81; University of Toronto, Toronto, Ontario, associate professor of medicine, 1982—. Career scientist, Medical Research Council of Canada, 1988—.

MEMBER: American Physical Society, Society for Mathematical Biology, Biophysical Society.

AWARDS, HONORS: E. C. Stevens Award in Physics from University of Toronto, 1977; National Research Council of Canada postdoctoral scholar, 1979; North Atlantic Treaty Organization (NATO) postdoctoral scholar, 1981; Medical Research Council of Canada scholar, 1983-88.

WRITINGS:

(With Edward O. Wilson) *Genes, Mind, and Culture: The Coevolutionary Process,* Harvard University Press, 1981.
(With Wilson) *Promethean Fire: Reflections on the Origin of Mind,* Harvard University Press, 1983.
(Contributor) C. J. Brainerd, editor, *Recent Progress in Cognitive-Developmental Theory,* Springer-Verlag, 1983.
(With C. Scott Findlay) *The Creative Mind,* Academic Press, 1988.
(With Catharine I. Whiteside) *Clinical Methods,* Alan Liss, 1988.
(Editor with Derrick de Kerdhove) *The Alphabet and the Brain,* Springer-Verlag, 1988.

Also contributor to *Mathematical Essays on Growth and the Emergence of Form.* Contributor to journals, including *Physics Today, American Journal of Physics, Canadian Journal of Physics, Journal of Statistical Physics, Journal of Theoretical Biology, Journal of Human Evolution,* and *New York Review of Books.* Member of editorial board, *Journal of Social and Biological Structures,* 1982—, and *Human Medicine,* 1984—.

WORK IN PROGRESS: Physical Theory in Biology and *Michelangelo: A Sociobiology of Creative Genius.*

SIDELIGHTS: Sociobiology is the subject of Charles J. Lumsden and Edward O. Wilson's *Genes, Mind, and Culture: The Coevolutionary Process.* According to Howard E. Gruber in the *New York Times Book Review,* Lumsden and Wilson "argue that culture evolves through genetic change and is in good part passed from generation to generation through genetic transmission. Their theory requires that the genetic changes mediating culture would have to be far more rapid than previously thought possible." The book is technical and was written for scientific professionals, but neurologist Richard Restak, writing for the *Washington Post Book World,* indicates that a more popular version of the book is available as *Promethean Fire: Reflections on the Origin of Mind.*

Genes, Mind, and Culture received an uneven reception. Restak commends the authors for avoiding "both hysteria and extravagant claims about evolution" and is of the opinion that the book presents "a powerful, compelling and vigorously reasoned 'attempt to trace development all the way from genes through the mind to culture.' " On the other hand, P. B. Medawar criticizes both the book's style and content in the *New York Review of Books* and insists that the authors' ideas suffer from two great aberrations, historicism and geneticism. A controversial response to the book was also reflected in a *New Republic* review by Oxford University professor of philosophy Paul Seabright. Seabright faults some of Lumsden and Wilson's fundamental assumptions but at the same time acknowledges that their book convinced him "that the possibilities are immense for a sociobiology that is more firmly grounded in a detailed knowledge of the human brain, and can face the fact that human society is a long way from evolutionary equilibrium."

Lumsden told *CA:* "Many of the principle mysteries remaining in science fall in areas between traditional fields like physics, chemistry, biology, and anthropology. Creative work in these areas requires interdisciplinary investigation in which scholars with a grounding in more than one traditional academic discipline pool their enthusiasm and expertise. Much of the research activity that led to my writings in human sociobiology was stimulated by the possibility of better understanding human nature by applying novel ideas and techniques from areas such as evolutionary biology, theoretical physics, and mathematics. . . . To the natural scientist, the variety of hypotheses and competing explanatory schemes within the human sciences and social sciences is colorful, yet somewhat worrisome. Whereas a broad eclecticism has in many cases been tolerated in discussions about human nature, I have tried to bring to my own writings the view that there is one fundamental explanation about the organization and evolution of human nature waiting to be discovered and that the elucidation of these underlying laws and principles (still largely hidden) can be assisted by the utilization of viewpoints that heretofore have been more commonly found in the natural sciences."

AVOCATIONAL INTERESTS: Fine art photography, publishing, running, Arabian horses.

BIOGRAPHICAL/CRITICAL SOURCES:

BOOKS

Lumsden, Charles J. and Edward O. Wilson, *Genes, Mind, and Culture: The Coevolutionary Process,* Harvard University Press, 1981.

PERIODICALS

American Anthropologist, December, 1982.
American Journal of Sociology, January, 1983.
Contemporary Psychology, April, 1982.
Contemporary Sociology, March, 1982.
Dimensions, April, 1987.
Graduate: The University of Toronto Alumni Magazine, March-April, 1985.
New Republic, December 2, 1981.
New York Review of Books, July 16, 1981.
New York Times Book Review, October 18, 1981, April 24, 1983.
Quarterly Journal of Speech, February, 1983.
Science, August 14, 1981.
Technology Review, October, 1981.
Washington Post Book World, June 7, 1981.

* * *

LYLE, Katie Letcher 1938-

PERSONAL: Born May 12, 1938, in Peking, China; daughter of John Seymour (a U.S. Marine Corps brigadier general) and Elizabeth (an artist; maiden name, Marston) Letcher; married Royster Lyle, Jr. (associate director of a research foundation), March 16, 1963; children: Royster Cochran, Virginia. *Education:* Hollins College, B.A., 1959; Johns Hopkins University, M.A., 1960; graduate study at Vanderbilt University, 1961-62.

ADDRESSES: *Home*—110 West McDowell, Lexington, Va. 24450. *Agent*—Elsie K. Miels, 1124 North Coalter St., Staunton, Va. 24401.

CAREER: Teacher in Baltimore, Md., 1960-61, 1962-63; Southern Seminary Junior College, Buena Vista, Va., member of English faculty, 1963-87, chairman of English department, 1968-80, chairman of liberal arts division, 1971-73. Guest instructor, Washington and Lee University, 1987; Hollins College, writer in residence, 1989, guest instructor, 1989-90. Elder hostel instructor, Southern Seminary and Mary Baldwin College, 1984—. Has been a professional folksinger in Baltimore and Nashville.

AWARDS, HONORS: Bread Loaf fellowships, 1973, 1974.

WRITINGS:

(With Maude Rubin and May Miller) *Lyrics of Three Women,* Linden Press, 1964.
On Teaching Creative Writing, National Defense Education Act, 1968.
I Will Go Barefoot All Summer for You (young adult), Lippincott, 1973.
Fair Day, and Another Step Begun (young adult), Lippincott, 1974.
The Golden Shores of Heaven (young adult), Lippincott, 1976.
Scott's Marathon (young adult), Coward, 1980.
Dark but Full of Diamonds (young adult), Coward, 1981.
Finders Weepers (young adult), Coward, 1982.
Scalded to Death by the Steam: Authentic Stories of Railroad Disasters and the Ballads That Were Written about Them, Algonquin Books, 1983.
The Man Who Wanted Seven Wives, Algonquin Books, 1986.

Also author of "Footsteps," a television series. Work represented in anthologies, including *Beyond the Square,* edited by Robert K. Rosenburg, Linden Press, 1972. Author of "A Foreign Flavor," a weekly column on food and humor, for *Roanoke Times,* 1970-74. Contributor to *A Guide to Chessie Trail,* 1988, and to *Virginia Wild Rivers Study,* edited by Paul Dulaney. Contributor of poems and short stories to *Shenandoah* and other literary magazines, and of articles and reviews to newspapers and magazines, including *Newsweek.*

AVOCATIONAL INTERESTS: Acting, European travel, mycology, foreign cooking, and archaeology, particularly Aegean.

M

MacDOUGALL, A(llan) Kent 1931-

PERSONAL: Born December 11, 1931, in Madison, Wis.; son of Curtis D. (an educator and journalist) and Elizabeth (a child psychiatrist; maiden name, Pier) MacDougall; married Kathleen Downing (an editor), March 14, 1970; children: Daniel Grant. *Education:* Knox College, B.A., 1953; Columbia University, M.S., 1956.

ADDRESSES: *Home*—911 Oxford St., Berkeley, Calif. 94707. *Office*—Graduate School of Journalism, University of California, North Gate Hall, Berkeley, Calif. 94720.

CAREER: *Herald-News,* Passaic, N.J., staff reporter, 1956-61; *Wall Street Journal,* New York City, staff reporter, 1961-72; Columbia University, Graduate School of Journalism, New York City, adjunct lecturer, 1971-74; American University, Washington, D.C., associate professor in School of Communication, 1974-77; *Los Angeles Times,* Los Angeles, Calif., staff writer, 1977-87; University of California, Graduate School of Journalism, Berkeley, professor, 1977—; free-lance writer.

AWARDS, HONORS: Professional Journalism Fellowship, Stanford University, 1969-70; John Hancock Award for Excellence in Business and Financial Journalism, and Lowell Mellett Award for Improving Journalism through Critical Evaluation, both 1981, both for 1980 *Los Angeles Times* series on business and the news media.

WRITINGS:

(Editor and contributor) *The Press: A Critical Look from the Inside,* Dow Jones, 1972.

Ninety Seconds to Tell It All: Big Business and the News Media, Dow Jones-Irwin, 1981.

Contributor to *Columbia Journalism Review, MORE,* and *Monthly Review.*

BIOGRAPHICAL/CRITICAL SOURCES:

PERIODICALS

Los Angeles Times, January 31, 1989.

MacDOUGALL, Curtis D(aniel) 1903-1985

PERSONAL: Born February 11, 1903, in Fond du Lac, Wis.; died November 10, 1985, from complications following hip surgery, in Evanston, Ill.; son of Gilbert Thomas (a physician) and Mae Isabella (a bookkeeper; maiden name, McCollum) MacDougall; married Elizabeth Pier, June 11, 1929 (divorced, January 9, 1942); married Genevieve R. Rockwood (a teacher), June 20, 1942; children: (first marriage) Gordon Pier, Allan Kent, Lois Mae (Mrs. Gilbert West); (second marriage) Priscilla Ruth, Bonnie Maurine Cottrell. *Education:* Ripon College, B.A., 1923; Northwestern University, M.S., 1926; University of Wisconsin, Ph.D., 1933. *Politics:* Independent. *Religion:* Humanist.

ADDRESSES: *Home*—537 Judson Ave., Evanston, Ill. 60202.

CAREER: *Commonwealth Reporter,* Fond du Lac, Wis., reporter, 1918-1923; *Two Rivers Chronicle,* Two Rivers, Wis., reporter, 1923-25; United Press (UP), Chicago, Ill., staff correspondent, 1926-27; Lehigh University, Bethlehem, Pa., head of courses in journalism, 1927-31; University of Wisconsin—Madison, lecturer in journalism, 1931-33; *St. Louis Star-Times,* St. Louis, Mo., reporter, 1933-34; *Evanston Daily News-Index,* Evanston, Ill., editor, 1934-37; *National Almanac and Year Book* (formerly *Chicago Daily News Almanac*), Chicago, editor, 1937-38; *News Map of the Week,* Chicago, editor, 1938-40; state supervisor, Illinois Writers Project, Work Projects Administration (WPA), 1940-42; *Chicago Sun,* Chicago, editorial writer, 1942; Northwestern University, Evanston, professor of journalism, 1942-71, professor emeritus, 1971-85. Visiting professor and lecturer at universities in the United States, Canada, Latin America, and Africa. Conductor of "Editorial Page on the Air," radio station WEAW, 1945-48; panelist on "Matters of Opinion," radio station WBBM (CBS), 1973-76. Member of numerous community and civil committees. Democratic candidate for Congress, 1944; Progressive candidate for U.S. Senate, 1948; candidate for Democratic nomination for Congress, 1970. Consultant to numerous newspapers and publishers.

MEMBER: American Association of Teachers of Journalism (past president), Association for Education in Journalism (past second vice-president; head of newspaper division, 1965-70), American Sociological Association (fellow), American Society for the Study of Social Problems, American Society for the Study of Communication, American Association for Public Opinion Research, National Conference of Editorial Writers (life member), Investigative Reporters and Editors, Authors League of America, Council of Teaching Standards, Society of Midland Authors, Chicago Headline Club, Pi Kappa Delta, Pi Delta Epsilon, Alpha Kappa Delta, Sigma Delta Chi, Kappa Tau Alpha, Phi Beta Kappa, Acacia.

AWARDS, HONORS: Research citation, 1946, for *Covering the Courts,* research award, 1953, for *Understanding Public Opinion: A Guide for Newspapermen and Newspaper Readers,* and distinguished teaching in journalism award, 1968, all from Sigma Delta Chi; Chicago Newspaper Guild award, 1947, for *Interpretative Reporting;* American Negro Museum and Historical Foundation citation, 1951; Ripon College alumni citation, 1951; Certificate of Merit, South-Side Community Committee, 1959; distinguished service to journalism awards, Ball State University, 1964, and University of Wisconsin, 1971; Litt.D., Columbia University, 1965; Citizenship Award, Evanston Democratic Club, 1965; Journalism Educator of the Year award, Southern Illinois University, 1972; Pi Delta Epsilon Medal of Merit, 1972; distinguished service award, Chicago association of Phi Beta Kappa, 1983; Medal of Honor, Ripon College, 1985.

WRITINGS:

A College Course in Reporting for Beginners, Macmillan, 1932, revised edition published with teacher's manual as *Interpretative Reporting,* 1938, 9th edition (with Robert D. Reid), 1987.

Hoaxes, Macmillan, 1940, 2nd revised and enlarged edition, Dover, 1958, reprinted, 1982.

Newsroom Problems and Policies, Macmillan, 1941, revised and enlarged edition, Dover, 1963.

Covering the Courts, Prentice-Hall, 1946.

Understanding Public Opinion: A Guide for Newspapermen and Newspaper Readers, Macmillan, 1952, revised edition, W. C. Brown, 1966.

Greater Dead than Alive, Public Affairs Press, 1963.

The Press and Its Problems, W. C. Brown, 1964.

Gideon's Army, Marzani & Munsell, Volume I, 1965, Volumes II and III, 1966.

(Editor) *Reporters Report Reporters,* Iowa State University Press, 1968.

News Pictures Fit to Print . . . Or Are They?: Decision-Making in Photojournalism, Journalistic Services, 1971.

Principles of Editorial Writing, W. C. Brown, 1973.

Superstition and the Press, Prometheus Books, 1983.

Contributor of numerous articles to professional and general periodicals; editorial contributor, *Focus/Midwest.* Columnist, Chicago *Skyline,* 1977-80. Editor of journalism series for W. C. Brown. Associate editor, *Journal of Communication,* 1950-60; member of advisory editorial board, *International Journal of Opinion and Attitude Research,* 1947-51.

SIDELIGHTS: A veteran reporter and long-time professor of journalism, Curtis D. MacDougall was one of the country's leading advocates of interpretative journalism for over fifty years. His classic textbook on reporting the "how" and "why" of news events, *Interpretative Reporting,* has been a mainstay in college journalism classrooms and has gone through nine editions in fifty-five years. Outside of his teaching activities, MacDougall also headed the Illinois Writers Project of the Work Projects Administration from 1939 to 1942, a program in which "the taxpayers got more than their money's worth," as MacDougall was quoted in his *Chicago Tribune* obituary. "It was not a boondoggle as many critics said. It provided a minimum income to indigent writers and helped them continue their own creative activities." Some of these writers included Studs Terkel, Saul Bellow, Nelson Algren, and Richard Wright.

MacDougall wrote *CA* in 1981: "My physician father wanted me to emulate him, my uncle and cousins and be a doctor; my mother yearned for me to become a minister; as a result of my interest in high school debating, I thought I'd like to be a lawyer. Then, during the summer months between my sophomore and junior years, I received an unsolicited telephone call from the editor of one of the daily newspapers asking me if I wanted to cover high school news as his daughter, recently graduated, had done. I accepted and arranged to use the typewriter in the principal's office for one period every day when he taught a class. After about a month the swine flu epidemic closed our schools as it did similar institutions all over the country. I became a full-time reporter and continued as such after school reopened—weekends, holidays, vacations, for six years.

"At Ripon College I took a newly-created elective course in Journalism taught by Harbor (Hank) Allen, brother of Bob Allen of Washington Merry-go-Round fame, who was fresh from the *Chicago Tribune.* He fascinated me with anecdotes of assignments in the Windy City during the Al Capone-William Hale Thompson time. I thought nothing could be more romantic than to be a reporter in the Loop. So, after two years of saving money by teaching and writing, I entered the Medill School of Journalism in Evanston and when I received my master's degree became a reporter for the United Press. Those were the 'Front Page' days and I escaped being eligible for the cast of characters by leaving shortly before [Ben] Hecht and [Charles] MacArthur came."

MacDougall added that he wrote *Reporting for Beginners* and *Interpretative Reporting* "because I was dissatisfied with the reporting textbooks then on the market. Fortunately it caught on, set a new pattern. . . . I didn't invent interpretative reporting, as [is] sometimes contended, but I surely helped popularize it at a time when the oldtime objective reporting was favored.

"To protect myself against becoming a theoretical, ivory-towered professor, I engaged myself heavily in civic and political affairs. My teaching was enriched by my firsthand knowledge of public affairs and I pride myself on having not become a propagandist. I tried to have an atmosphere of complete freedom in my classes.

"All of my other books are really supportive of my basic reporting book. All journalism is reporting and the best journalists are many-sided and thoroughly knowledgeable. The greatest obstacles to a free press—which means democracy—are (1) government censorship and the Supreme Court conservatism; (2) the trend toward monopoly and absentee ownership of the media, meaning public service becomes secondary to money making, counterbalanced only by the adamant skepticism of the reportorial staff; (3) the failure of the school to provide future readers adequate knowledge of American history, including the meaning of the First Amendment, and how to read and/or listen critically. The so-called behavioral scientists have injured education at all levels. The false value placed on a Ph.D. and the lobbying of schools and departments of education have been and continue to be dangerous."

OBITUARIES:

PERIODICALS

Chicago Sun-Times, November 11, 1985, November 12, 1985.
Chicago Tribune, November 12, 1985, November 13, 1985.
Detroit Free Press, November 12, 1985.

Los Angeles Times, November 12, 1985.
New York Times, November 13, 1985.
San Francisco Chronicle, November 11, 1985.
Washington Post, November 12, 1985.

[Sketch reviewed by son, A. Kent MacDougall]

* * *

MacKENZIE, Andrew (Carr) 1911-

PERSONAL: Born May 30, 1911, in Oamaru, New Zealand; son of John Gretton (a municipal park director) and Jeannie (Carr) MacKenzie; married Kaarina Sisko Sihvonen (an agronomist), March 1, 1952; children: Annaliisa Kaarina, Elsa Helena, Donald Ensio. *Education:* Attended Victoria University College, Wellington, New Zealand, 1930-33. *Religion:* Presbyterian.

ADDRESSES: Home—18 Castlebar Park, London W5 1BX, England. *Agent*—A.M.Heath & Co., 70 St. Martins Lane, London WC2N 4AA, England.

CAREER: Evening Post, Wellington, New Zealand, member of editorial staff, 1928-38; Thomson Newspapers Ltd. (formerly Kemsley Newspapers Ltd.), London, England, member of editorial staff, 1946-63; United Newspapers Ltd., London, member of editorial staff, 1963-76. *Military service:* British Army, 1939-45; served in Burma; became captain; mentioned in dispatches.

MEMBER: Society for Psychical Research (member of council, 1970—; chairman of library committee, 1978—; vice-president, 1989—).

WRITINGS:

The Unexplained: Some Strange Case in Psychical Research, Arthur Barker, 1966, Abelard, 1970.
Frontiers of the Unknown, Arthur Barker, 1968, Popular Library, 1970.
Apparitions and Ghosts, Arthur Barker, 1971, Popular Library, 1972.
(Editor) *A Gallery of Ghosts: An Anthology of Reported Experience,* Arthur Barker, 1972, Taplinger, 1973.
The Riddle of the Future: A Modern Study of Precognition, Arthur Barker, 1974, Taplinger, 1975.
Dracula Country: Travels and Folk Beliefs in Romania, Arthur Barker, 1977.
Hauntings and Apparitions: An Investigation of the Evidence, Heinemann, 1982.
Romanian Journey, R. Hale, 1983.
(Editor with Andrei Otetea) *A Concise History of Romania,* R. Hale, 1985.
Archaeology in Romania: Mystery of the Roman Occupation, R. Hale, 1986.
The Seen and the Unseen: Study of Presences, Apparitions and Other Paranormal Phenomena, Weidenfeld & Nicolson, 1987.

Contributor of critical reviews to *Journal of the Society for Psychical Research* and articles to *Fate* magazine. London news editor of Sheffield *Morning Telegraph,* 1958-76, and staff writer for *Yorkshire Post,* 1971-76.

SIDELIGHTS: Andrew MacKenzie told *CA:* "In 1960 I was asked by the then editor of the Sheffield *Morning Telegraph* to write a series of articles on the supernatural. This involved visits to the office of the Society for Psychical Research, and I was so impressed by the quality of the material in the publications and archives [there] that I have remained 'hooked' on psychical research, or parapsychology as it is generally referred to today, ever since. The very large correspondence I get from readers in the United States and Canada is an indication that experiences of the type I describe are fairly common but are often not revealed for fear that the writer might be thought 'mad' or 'abnormal' in some way. This is not so. We know so little about the universe—or ourselves—that we must keep an open mind on reports which involve experiences of apparitions, telepathy, clairvoyance, precognition, and poltergeist-type phenomena. I believe that the only way to make sense of such reports is to present them with arguments for and against the likelihood of the happening described. Often there is a natural explanation."

* * *

MacNEIL, Neil
See BALLARD, (Willis) Todhunter

* * *

MACQUARRIE, John 1919-

PERSONAL: Born June 27, 1919, in Renfrew, Scotland; son of John and Robina (McInnes) Macquarrie; married Jenny Fallow Welsh, 1949; children: John Michael, Catherine Elizabeth, Alan Denis. *Education:* University of Glasgow, M.A., 1940, B.D., 1943, Ph.D., 1954, D.Litt., 1964; Oxford University, D.D., 1981.

ADDRESSES: Home—206 Headley Way, Headington, Oxford OX3 7TA, England.

CAREER: Ordained clergyman in Episcopal Church. St. Ninian's Church, Brechin, Scotland, minister, 1948-53; Glasgow University, Glasgow, Scotland, lecturer, 1953-62; Union Theological Seminary, New York, N.Y., professor of systematic theology, 1962-70; Oxford University, Oxford, England, Lady Margaret Professor of Divinity, and Canon of Christ Church, 1970-86, governor of St. Stephen's House, 1970—, and Pusey House, 1975—. *Military service:* British Army, Chaplains Department, 1945-48; became captain. Territorial Army, thirteen years.

MEMBER: British Academy (fellow).

AWARDS, HONORS: Recipient of numerous honorary degrees from universities and seminaries in the United States and Great Britain.

WRITINGS:

An Existentialist Theology: A Comparison of Heidegger and Bultmann, Macmillan, 1955, reprinted, Greenwood Press, 1979.
The Scope of Demythologizing, Harper, 1960.
(Translator with Edward Robinson) Martin Heidegger, *Being and Time,* Harper, 1962.
Twentieth Century Religious Thought: Frontiers of Philosophy and Theology, Harper, 1963, 2nd revised edition, Scribner, 1981.
Studies in Christian Existentialism, McGill University Press, 1965.
Principles of Christian Theology, Scribner, 1966, revised edition, S.C.M. Press, 1979.
(Editor) *Dictionary of Christian Ethics,* Westminster, 1967, new edition (with James F. Childress) published as *The Westminster Dictionary of Christian Ethics,* 1986.
God-Talk, Harper, 1967.
God and Secularity, Westminster, 1967.
Martin Heidegger, John Knox, 1968.
Mystery and Truth, Marquette University Press, 1969.
Three Issues in Ethics, Harper, 1970.
Paths in Spirituality, Harper, 1972.

Existentialism, Westminster, 1972.
The Faith of the People of God: A Lay Theology, Scribner, 1972.
The Concept of Peace, Harper, 1973.
Thinking about God, Harper, 1975.
Christian Unity and Christian Diversity, Westminster, 1975.
The Humility of God, Westminster, 1978.
Christian Hope, Seabury, 1978.
In Search of Humanity: A Theological and Philosophical Approach, Crossroad Publishing, 1982, revised edition, 1985.
In Search of Deity: An Essay in Dialectical Theism, Crossroad Publishing, 1984.
Theology, Church and Ministry, Crossroad Publishing, 1986.
(With others) *If Christ Be Not Risen: Essays in Resurrection and Survival,* St. Mary's Bourne St., 1986.

Contributor to professional journals.

WORK IN PROGRESS: Jesus Christ in Modern Thought.

SIDELIGHTS: "Unlike some modern theologians, John Macquarrie writes about God as though he believes in Him," asserts N. K. Bruger in the *New York Times Book Review.* "And he has an uncanny knack for making that belief real and meaningful." One of Macquarrie's areas of study is religious existentialism, a philosophical investigation of man's and God's existence in the universe; the scholar frequently employs anthropological axioms in considering these spiritual issues. "John Macquarrie offers us an excellent example of such a theological enquiry in a book whose character shows itself in the title *In Search of Humanity,*" notes *Times Literary Supplement* contributor Stewart R. Sutherland. Using such topics as "Becoming," "Freedom," "Conscience," and "Being," the scholar examines what humanity's spiritual nature is like, and what it can become. "At its best the book is an exploration of ideas theological and philosophical, schooled by insights won by the professionals in the fields of the biological and social sciences," remarks Sutherland. The book concludes with what Macquarrie calls an "anthropological argument for the existence of God," and the critic maintains that "here the author is at his cumulative, scholarly and systematic best, condensing into a few pages the outline of a natural theology for the twentieth century."

BIOGRAPHICAL/CRITICAL SOURCES:

BOOKS

Jenkins, David, *The Scope and Limits of John Macquarrie's Existential Theology,* Acta Universitatis Upsaliensis, 1987.
Long, Eugene T., *Existence, Being and God: An Introduction to the Philosophical Theology of John Macquarrie,* Paragon House, 1985.

PERIODICALS

Los Angeles Times, October 25, 1983.
New York Times Book Review, August 27, 1972.
Times Literary Supplement, September 29, 1972, March 1, 1974, April 1, 1983.

* * *

MADGETT, Naomi Long 1923-
(Naomi Cornelia Long, Naomi Long Witherspoon)

PERSONAL: Born July 5, 1923, in Norfolk, Va.; daughter of Clarence Marcellus (a clergyman) and Maude (a teacher; maiden name, Hilton) Long; married Julian F. Witherspoon, March 31, 1946 (divorced April 27, 1949); married William Harold Madgett, July 29, 1954 (divorced December 21, 1960); married Leonard Patton Andrews (an elementary school principal), March 31, 1972; children: (first marriage) Jill Witherspoon Boyer. *Education:* Virginia State College, B.A. (with honors), 1945; Wayne State University, M.Ed., 1956; International Institute for Advanced Studies, Ph.D., 1980. *Politics:* Independent, but usually Democratic Party. *Religion:* Protestant (Congregational).

ADDRESSES: Home—16886 Inverness St., Detroit, Mich. 48221. *Office*—18080 Santa Barbara Dr., Detroit, Mich. 48221.

CAREER: Michigan Chronicle, Detroit, Mich., reporter and copy reader, 1945-46; Michigan Bell Telephone Co., Detroit, service representative, 1948-54; English teacher in public high schools, Detroit, 1955-65, 1966-68; Oakland University, Rochester, Mich., research associate, 1965-66; Eastern Michigan University, Ypsilanti, Mich., associate professor, 1968-73, professor of English, 1973-84, professor emeritus, 1984—. Visiting lecturer in English, University of Michigan, 1970-71; lecturer on Afro-American literature at colleges and universities. Editor, Lotus Press, 1974—. Conducts poetry readings and writing workshops. Member, trustee board, Plymouth Congregational United Church of Christ.

MEMBER: College Language Association, National Association for the Advancement of Colored People, Langston Hughes Society, Zora Neale Hurston Society, Howard University Stylus Society, Metropolitan Detroit Poetry Resource Center, Detroit Women Writers, Alpha Kappa Alpha, Alpha Rho Omega.

AWARDS, HONORS: Mott fellowship in English, Oakland University, 1965-66; Esther R. Beer poetry award, National Writers Club, 1957, for poem, "Native"; Josephine Nevins Keal Development Fund Award, 1979; Distinguished Service Award, Chesapeake/Virginia Beach Links, Inc., 1981; testimonial resolutions, Michigan State Legislature, 1982, 1984; testimonial resolutions, Detroit City Council, 1982, 1985; citation, Afro-American Museum of Detroit, 1983; citation, National Coalition of Black Women, 1984; citation, Black Caucus, National Council of Teachers of English, 1984; Robert Hayden Runagate Award, Heritage House, 1985; Arts Achievement Award, Wayne State University, 1985; Creative Artist Award, Michigan Council for the Arts, 1987; Creative Achievement Award, College Language Association, 1988, for *Octavia and Other Poems.*

WRITINGS:

(Under name Naomi Cornelia Long) *Songs to a Phantom Nightingale* (poems), Fortuny's, 1941.
One and the Many (poems), Exposition, 1956.
Star by Star (poems), Harlo, 1965, revised edition, 1970.
(With Ethel Tincher and Henry B. Maloney) *Success in Language and Literature—B* (high school textbook), Follett, 1967.
Pink Ladies in the Afternoon (poems), Lotus Press, 1972.
Exits and Entrances (poems), Lotus Press, 1978.
Deep Rivers, A Portfolio: Twenty Contemporary Black American Poets (with teacher's guide), Lotus Press, 1978.
A Student's Guide to Creative Writing (college textbook), Penway Books, 1980.
Phantom Nightingale: Juvenilia (poems), Lotus Press, 1981.
Octavia and Other Poems, Third World Press, 1988.
(Editor) *A Milestone Sampler: Fifteenth Anniversary Anthology,* Lotus Press, 1988.

Poetry represented in nearly a hundred anthologies, including *The Third Woman,* edited by Dexter Fischer, Houghton, 1980, *Refugees: An Anthology of Poems and Songs,* edited by Brian Coleman, Ottowa, 1988, and *Contemporary Michigan Poetry,* edited by Conrad Hilberry, Michael Delp, and Herbert Scott,

Wayne State University Press, 1988. Contributor of poetry to numerous periodicals, including *Michigan Quarterly Review, Argo, World Order, Zora Neale Hurston Forum,* and *Great Lakes Review.* Madgett's papers are being collected in the Special Collections Library at Fisk University.

SIDELIGHTS: Naomi Long Madgett, a poet and educator active in Detroit area schools, told *CA:* "As a child I was motivated by my father's library and the interests and inspiration of literary parents. I discovered Alfred Lord Tennyson and Langston Hughes at about the same time, [while] sitting on the floor of my father's study when I was about seven or eight. I think my poetry represents something of the variety of interest and style that these two widely divergent poets demonstrate. I would rather be a good poet than anything else I can imagine. It pleases me tremendously that my daughter is also a poet and author."

BIOGRAPHICAL/CRITICAL SOURCES:

BOOKS

Arata, Esther Spring, and others, *Black Writers Past and Present,* Morrow, 1975.

Dictionary of Literary Biography, Volume 76: *Afro-American Writers, 1940-1955,* Gale, 1988.

Redmond, Eugene B., editor, *Drumvoices: The Mission of Afro-American Poetry,* Doubleday, 1976.

PERIODICALS

Black American Literature Forum, summer, 1980.
Black Books Bulletin, spring, 1974.
Black Scholar, March-April, 1980.
Black World, September, 1974.
City Arts Quarterly, Volume 3, number 4, 1988.
Ebony, March, 1974.
English Journal, April, 1957.
First World, Volume 2, number 4, 1980.
Michigan Chronicle, January 15, 1966.
Negro Digest, September, 1966.
New Orleans Review, September, 1976.
Phylon, winter, 1956.
Richmond News Leader (Virginia), March 28, 1979.

* * *

MAGARSHACK, David 1899-1977

PERSONAL: Born December 23, 1899, in Riga, Russia (now U.S.S.R.); died, 1977; married Elsie Duella; children: Morris, Stella, John, Christopher. *Education:* University College, London, B.A. (honors in English), 1924.

ADDRESSES: *Home*—49 Willow Rd., Hampstead, London NW3 1TS, England. *Agent*—Curtis Brown, 162-168 Regent St., London W1R 5TA, England.

CAREER: Author and translator.

WRITINGS:

FICTION

Big Ben Strikes Eleven: A Murder Story for Grown-up People, Macmillan (Toronto), 1934.
Death Cuts a Caper, Holt, 1935.
Three Dead, Macmillan, 1937.

BIOGRAPHY

Stanislavsky: A Life, Macgibbon & Kee, 1950, reprinted, Faber, 1986.
Chekhov: The Dramatist, Auvergne, 1952, Hill & Wang, 1960, reprinted, Eyre Methuen, 1980.
Chekhov: A Life, Faber, 1952, Grove, 1953.
Turgenev: A Life, Grove, 1954.
Gogol: A Life, Grove, 1957.
Dostoevsky, Secker & Warburg, 1962, Harcourt, 1963.
Pushkin: A Biography, Chapman & Hall, 1967, Grove, 1968.
The Real Chekhov: An Introduction to Chekhov's Last Plays, Allen & Unwin, 1972.

TRANSLATOR FROM THE RUSSIAN

Aleksandr N. Ostrovsky, *Easy Money, and Two Other Plays: Even a Wise Man Stumbles* [and] *Wolves and Sheep,* Allen & Unwin, 1944, Verry, 1965.
Aleksei K. Iugov, *Immortality,* Hutchinson, 1945.
Nikolai S. Leskov, *The Enchanted Pilgrim, and Other Stories,* Hutchinson, 1946, reprinted, Hyperion Press (Westport, Conn.), 1977, published as *The Enchanted Wanderer: Selected Tales,* Deutsch, 1988.
Mikhail M. Prishvin, *Black Arab, and Other Stories,* Hutchinson, 1947.
Mikhail M. Morozov, *Shakespeare on the Soviet Stage,* Universal Distributors, 1947.
Nikolai V. Gogol, *Tales of Good and Evil,* Lehmann, 1949, Doubleday, 1957, published as *The Overcoat, and Other Tales of Good and Evil,* Norton, 1965.
Leskov, *The Amazon, and Other Stories,* Allen & Unwin, 1949, reprinted, Hyperion Press, 1976.
Dostoevsky, *Gentle Creature, and Other Stories,* Lehmann, 1950.
Stanislavsky on the Art of the Stage, Faber, 1950, Hill & Wang, 1962.
Lidya A. Avilova, *Chekhov in My Life,* Harcourt, 1950 (published in England as *Chekhov in My Life: A Love Story,* Lehmann, 1950), reprinted, Greenwood Press, 1971.
Dostoevsky, *Crime and Punishment,* Penguin, 1951.
Sergei Balukhatyi, *Seagull: Produced by Stanislavsky,* Theatre Arts, 1952.
Dostoevsky, *The Devils,* Penguin, 1954.
Dostoevsky, *Best Short Stories,* Modern Library, 1955.
Ivan S. Turgenev, *Literary Reminiscences and Autobiographical Fragments,* Farrar, Straus, 1958.
Dostoevsky, *The Brothers Karamazov,* Penguin, 1958.
Boris L. Pasternak, *I Remember: Sketch for an Autobiography,* Pantheon, 1959, reprinted, Harvard University Press, 1983.
Turgenev, *Selected Tales,* Doubleday, 1960, published as *First Love, and Other Tales,* Norton, 1968.
(And editor) *The Storm, and Other Russian Plays* (also see below), Hill & Wang, 1960.
Turgenev, *Torrents of Spring,* Farrar, Straus, 1960.
Leskov, *Selected Tales,* Farrar, Straus, 1961.
Gogol, *Dead Souls,* Penguin, 1961.
(And editor) Dostoevsky, *Occasional Writings,* Random, 1963.
Anton P. Chekhov, *Lady with Lapdog, and Other Stories,* Penguin, 1964.
Chekhov, *Platonov* (play), Hill & Wang, 1964.
(And author of introduction) Pasternak, *Letters to Georgian Friends,* Secker & Warburg, 1968.
Chekhov, *Four Plays,* Hill & Wang, 1969.
Ilya I. Schneider, *Isadora Duncan: The Russian Years,* Harcourt, 1969.
Mikhail Saltykor-Shchedrin, *The Pompadours,* Ardis, 1982.
The Storm (originally published in *The Storm, and Other Russian Plays*), Ardis, 1988.

Also translator of *Anna Karenina* by Leo Tolstoy.

OTHER

(Editor and author of notes in English) Chekhov, *Uncle Vanya* (Russian text), Heath, 1965.
(Author of introduction) *Chekhov's Plays and Stories,* Dutton, 1967.

[Sketch verified by wife, Elsie D. Magarshack]

* * *

MAHAJAN, Vidya Dhar 1913-

PERSONAL: Born September 1, 1913, in Punjab, India; son of Hari Ram and Sulakhani (Devi) Mahajan; married wife, Savitri (a school principal), April 13, 1945; children: Mridula, Sucheta, Ajaya. *Education:* Punjab University, Lahore, M.A. (history), 1936, M.A. (politics), 1937, Ph.D., 1945; University of Delhi, LL.B., 1948. *Religion:* Hindu.

ADDRESSES: Home and office—D-805, New Friends Colony, New Delhi 65, India.

CAREER: Punjab University College, New Delhi, India, teacher of history and politics to M.A. candidates, 1950-60; Supreme Court of India, New Delhi, advocate, 1960—. Part-time lecturer in law, University of Delhi, 1962-67. Founder and president, Sulakhani Devi Mahajan Trust and Hari Ram Mahajan Trust.

MEMBER: Indian Law Association (New Delhi; secretary), Cultural League of India (secretary), Servants of People Society (New Delhi), Constitution Club, Indian Council of World Affairs, Bar Association of India, Bar Council of India, Welfare Society (president).

WRITINGS:

Essays in Municipal Administration in the Punjab, with foreword by Beni Prasad, Doaba House (Lahore), c. 1943.
The General Clauses Act, Eastern Book Co. (Lucknow), 1952, 3rd edition, 1968.
Commentaries on Indian Sale of Goods Act: Act III of 1930, Eastern Book Co., 1953, supplement, 1956.
Recent Political Thought, Premier, 1953, 6th edition, S. Chand, 1982.
The Law Relating to Sales Tax in Delhi, Eastern Book Co., 1954.
(With R. R. Sethi) *Constitutional History of India,* 2nd edition, S. Chand, 1954, 11th edition, 1982.
(With Sethi) *Indian Constitution and Administration,* S. Chand, 1954.
English Constitutional Law, Eastern Book Co., 1955, 3rd edition, 1962.
The Constitution of India, Eastern Book Co., 1955, 12th edition, S. Chand, 1988.
Principles of Civics, Modern Publications, 1955.
International Law, Eastern Book Co., 1956, 5th edition, 1974.
(With Sethi) *Mughal Rule in India,* 3rd edition, S. Chand, 1957, 13th edition, 1982.
India since 1956, 3rd edition, S. Chand, 1958, 14th edition, 1983.
(With B. K. Gahrana) *Select Modern Governments,* 3rd edition, S. Chand, 1958, 14th edition, 1983.
Ancient India, S. Chand, 1960, 12th edition, 1988.
(With wife, Savitri Mahajan) *The Muslim Rule in India,* S. Chand, 1962, 7th edition, 1981, 9th edition published as *History of Medieval India,* 1988.
The Nationalist Movement in India and Its Leaders, S. Chand, 1962.
(With B. M. Lalwani and Y. N. Deodhar) *Political and Cultural History of Ancient India,* S. Chand, 1962.
(With S. Mahajan) *The Sultanate of Delhi,* S. Chand, 1962, 6th edition, 1981.
Principles of Jurisprudence, 2nd edition, Eastern Book Co., 1962, 4th edition published as *Principles of Jurisprudence and Legal Theory,* 1980.
(With S. Mahajan) *British Rule in India and After,* 6th edition, S. Chand, 1964, 11th edition, 1974.
International Politics since 1900, 2nd edition, S. Chand, 1964, 3rd edition, 1968.
The Constitution of Pakistan, revised edition, Munawar Book Depot, 1965, 2nd revised edition, S. Chand, 1969.
Early History of India, S. Chand, 1965.
England since 1688, 6th edition, S. Chand, 1965, revised edition, 1976.
England under the Tudors and Stuarts, S. Chand, 1966.
Chief Justice P. B. Gajendragadkar, S. Chand, 1966.
History of Modern Europe since 1789, 4th edition, S. Chand, 1966, 12th edition, 1988.
Chief Justice K. Subba: Defender of Liberties, S. Chand, 1967.
Chief Justice Mehr Chand Mahajan: The Biography of the Great Jurist, Eastern Book Co., 1969.
Fifty Years of Modern India, 1919-1969, S. Chand, 1970, 2nd edition published as *Fifty-Five Years of Modern India, 1919-1974,* 1975.
History of India from the Beginning to 1526, S. Chand, 1970, 5th edition, 1985.
Principles of Political Science, S. Chand, 1970, 3rd edition, 1981, 4th edition published as *Political Theory,* 1988.
International Law, 5th edition, Eastern Book Co., 1974.
Select Foreign Governments, S. Chand, 1975.
Leaders of the Nationalist Movement, Sterling (New Delhi), 1975.
International Politics, S. Chand, 1976.
The Nationalist Movement in India, Sterling, 1976, 2nd edition, 1981.
The British Constitution, S. Chand, 1977.
Early History of India, S. Chand, 1979.
Commentary on the General Clauses Act, 5th edition, Eastern Book Co., 1980.
History of Great Britain, 2nd edition, S. Chand, 1982.
History of Modern India, 1919-1974, two volumes, S. Chand, 1983.
Advanced History of India, 2nd edition, S. Chand, 1983.
Constitutional Law of India, Eastern Book Co., 1983.
Modern Indian Political Thought, S. Chand, 1984.
England since 1485, 5th edition, S. Chand, 1986.
International Relations since 1900, 7th edition, S. Chand, 1986.
Modern Indian History from 1707 up to Date, S. Chand, 1988.

SIDELIGHTS: "I write as I feel inspired to write," Vidya Dhar Mahajan told *CA.* "I write because I want to carry my message to the readers. I find personal satisfaction only when I write something. I do not find the same satisfaction when preparing and arguing cases in courts."

* * *

MALLON, Thomas 1951-

PERSONAL: Born November 2, 1951, in Glen Cove, N.Y.; son of Arthur Vincent (a salesman) and Caroline (Moruzzi) Mallon. *Education:* Brown University, B.A., 1973; Harvard University, M.A., 1974, Ph.D., 1978.

ADDRESSES: Home—321 East 45th St., Apt. 1E, New York, N.Y. 10017. *Office*—Department of English, Vassar College, Poughkeepsie, N.Y. 12601.

CAREER: Vassar College, Poughkeepsie, N.Y., 1979—, began as assistant professor, currently associate professor of English.

WRITINGS:

Edmund Blunden (biography), G. K. Hall, 1983.
A Book of One's Own: People and Their Diaries, Ticknor & Fields, 1984.
Arts and Sciences: A Seventies Seduction (novel), Ticknor & Fields, 1988.
Stolen Words, Ticknor & Fields, 1989.

Contributor of articles and reviews to literature journals, newspapers, and national magazines, including *American Spectator, New York Times, Washington Post,* and *Wall Street Journal.*

WORK IN PROGRESS: A novel about childhood entitled *Aurora 7* which takes place entirely on May 24, 1962, the day Mercury astronaut Scott Carpenter orbited the earth.

SIDELIGHTS: After reading *A Book of One's Own: People and Their Diaries, Los Angeles Times* critic Richard Eder asserts that "Thomas Mallon, who has read hundreds of diaries, has written a marvelous book about them. It is a basket full of good things, and some of the best are his own. . . . [Mallon] has sat in libraries listening to famous and obscure voices. Pepys, Virginia Woolf, Dostoevsky, of course; and also a London spinster who spent her life in a boarding house, and a bed-ridden Boston patrician whose diary runs 30,000 pages. Here we are, they told him. Here they are, he tells us." For the most part, reviewers like Eder are pleased by the broad scope of Mallon's book, noting that he gives equal deference to the famous, the rich, and the noble, as well as the unknown, the poor, and the lowly. In her *New Yorker* assessment, Naomi Bliven describes the work as "inclusive . . . but not a bit long-winded. It is learned but never pedantic. It is also charming, diverting, and exceptionally intelligent. The book is literary criticism, yet it is something more—a knowing, sympathetic, but not soppy commentary on humanity. . . . By bringing together so many diverse people at their most candid[,] . . . Mallon offers us a glimpse of human possibility we could get no other way." In the opinion of *New York Times Book Review* contributor and poet Brad Leithauser, Mallon "lets the diaries speak for themselves" with each chapter of the work devoted to a specific type of diarist, like chroniclers, travelers, creators, confessors, and so forth. To Leithauser, "the book proves winsome and ingratiating. . . . Some of the book's most affecting passages come from diaries of pioneer women whose lives were 'unremarkable' in the sense of not being surprising, given their surroundings. But what surroundings!"

Mallon's first novel, *Arts and Sciences: A Seventies Seduction,* is, according to *Newsday* reviewer Edward Guereschi, "the type of revenge comedy every disenchanted graduate student vows to write once he has passed from the cave into the sunlight." This is a coming-of-age novel about the awkward, youthful Artie as he pursues his graduate degree in literature from Harvard University. Artie's difficult first weeks push him close to a nervous breakdown; indeed, he has the impulse to throw people into oncoming traffic, to destroy rare books from the university library, and the like. Georgia Jones-Davis remarks in the *Los Angeles Times Book Review*: "Imagine if Keats had somehow rematerialized in the fall of 1973 as a . . . graduate student in English at Harvard. That's partly what Thomas Mallon is up to" in *Arts and Sciences.* Jones-Davis adds that Artie, "a Keats worshiper, really is a Keats clone—a 113-pound mass of quivering, nervous energy and sensibility." "Into all of this," notes Roger Davis Friedman for the Chicago *Tribune Books,* "comes Angela Downing, the 28-year-old blonde English divorcee who wins Artie's heart through her knowledge of Greek [since Artie fears failing this subject foremost]. . . . Artie and Angela's romance is far-fetched but more often than not entertaining in a smirky way. Angela is all the things Artie is not: spoiled, rich, unbearably witty, and purposefully dumb. One might call her an intellectual coquette." According to Jones-Davis, at the end of the academic year "Artie finds himself standing a little taller, and Angela . . . is exhibiting signs of emotional wear and tear. This is all *Sturm-und-Drang* in a teacup stuff. . . . 'Arts and Sciences' is a sweet, frothy story that tries to illustrate, as Keats put it, 'how necessary a World of Pains and troubles is to school an Intelligence and make it a Soul.' " Although some reviewers consider the novel slight and merely good for a few laughs, Guereschi believes it "shows it seams with bravado, charm and tenderhearted wit. . . . This is a skillful fictional debut." As for *USA Today* contributor David Guy, he insists "Mallon is a deft writer with a light touch and the sense to let a small subject remain small. He has produced a novel that seems perfectly suited to its theme, its humor shot through with wisdom."

BIOGRAPHICAL/CRITICAL SOURCES:

PERIODICALS

Boston Globe, February 1, 1988.
Los Angeles Times, November 18, 1984.
Los Angeles Times Book Review, February 14, 1988.
Newsday, February 14, 1988.
New Yorker, January 21, 1985.
New York Times, November 17, 1984.
New York Times Book Review, March 31, 1985, March 13, 1988.
People, May 20, 1985.
Tribune Books (Chicago), March 20, 1988.
USA Today, March 4, 1988.
Washington Post, February 3, 1988.
Washington Post Book World, February 3, 1985.

* * *

MANNING, Olivia 1915-1980

PERSONAL: Born in 1915, in Portsmouth, England; died July 23, 1980, in Isle of Wight, England; daughter of Oliver (a commander in Royal Navy) and Olivia (Morrow) Manning; married Reginald Donald Smith (a drama producer for British Broadcasting Corp.), August, 1939.

ADDRESSES: Home—36 Abbey Gardens, London NW8, England.

CAREER: Writer.

AWARDS, HONORS: Commander of the Order of the British Empire, 1976.

WRITINGS:

FICTION

The Wind Changes, Cape, 1937, Knopf, 1938.
Artist among the Missing, Heinemann, 1945, reprinted, 1975.
Growing Up: A Collection of Short Stories, Heinemann, 1948.
School for Love, Heinemann, 1951, reprinted, Penguin, 1982.
A Different Face, Heinemann, 1953, Abelard-Schuman, 1957, reprinted, Heinemann, 1975.
The Doves of Venus, Heinemann, 1955, Abelard-Schuman, 1956, published with a new introduction by Isobel English in an omnibus edition with Rosamond Lehmann's *The Weather in the Streets* and Antonia White's *Frost in May,* Virago, 1984,

My Husband Cartwright, illustrations by Len Deighton, Heinemann, 1956.

The Great Fortune (first novel in "Balkan" trilogy; also see below), Heinemann, 1960, Doubleday, 1961.

The Spoilt City (second novel in "Balkan" trilogy; also see below), Doubleday, 1962.

The Crimson Dawn, Merlin Press, 1963.

Friends and Heroes (third novel in "Balkan" trilogy; also see below), Heinemann, 1965, Doubleday, 1966.

A Romantic Hero and Other Stories, Heinemann, 1967.

The Camperlea Girls, Coward-McCann, 1969.

The Play Room, Heinemann, 1969, published with a new introduction by Isobel English, Virago, 1984.

The Rain Forest, Heinemann, 1974.

The Danger Tree (first novel in "Levant" trilogy; also see below), Atheneum, 1977.

The Battle Lost and Won (second novel in "Levant" trilogy; also see below), Weidenfeld & Nicolson, 1978, Atheneum, 1979.

The Sum of Things (third novel in "Levant" trilogy; also see below), Weidenfeld and Nicolson, 1980, Atheneum, 1981.

The Balkan Trilogy, Volume 1: *The Great Fortune,* Volume 2: *The Spoilt City,* Volume 3: *Friends and Heroes,* Penguin, 1981.

The Levant Trilogy, Volume 1: *The Danger Tree,* Volume 2: *The Battle Lost and Won,* Volume 3: *The Sum of Things,* Penguin, 1982.

NONFICTION

The Reluctant Recluse: The Story of Stanley's Rescue of Emin Pasha from Equatorial Africa, Doubleday, 1947 (published in England as *The Remarkable Expedition: The Story of Stanley's Rescue of Emin Pasha from Equatorial Africa,* Heinemann, 1947), reprinted under English title, Atheneum, 1985.

The Dreaming Shore (travelogue of Ireland), Evans Brothers, 1950.

Extraordinary Cats, Joseph, 1967.

OTHER

(With Ken Annakin) "The Playroom" (screenplay; based on Manning's novel of same title), International Screen Production, 1970.

(Editor) *Romanian Short Stories,* Oxford University Press, 1971.

(Author of introduction and notes) Jane Austen, *Northanger Abbey,* Pan Books, 1979.

Also contributed to newspapers and periodicals, including *Horizon, Spectator, New Statesman, Punch, Observer,* and *Times* (London).

SIDELIGHTS: Olivia Manning, considered "one of the most gifted English writers of her generation" by Eve Auchincloss in *Book World,* was born at the outset of World War I to a British father and an Irish mother in Portsmouth, England. She spent much of her childhood in Northern Ireland; and when she married at the outset of World War II, she travelled abroad with her husband, living in the Balkans before fleeing from the German invasion to Greece and then the Middle East. Despite an early ambition to become a painter, Manning "realized that her artistic tool should be the pen rather than the brush," according to a London *Times* contributor, and she believed that "the novel form seemed 'perfectly adapted to the expression of our bewildered and self-conscious civilization.' " Although she authored several books of fiction and nonfiction during a career that spanned more than forty years, Manning was perhaps best recognized for the six novels about the Second World War that comprise her Balkan and Levant trilogies, which focus upon what Peter Ackroyd described in the *Spectator* as "a world of war, of panic, of violence and isolation." And according to Auchincloss, "Nobody has written better about World War II—the feel of fighting it and its dislocating effects on ordinary, undistinguished lives."

The novels of the Balkan trilogy, *The Great Fortune, The Spoilt City,* and *Friends and Heroes,* recreate the period of impending war and its early years; its sequel, the Levant trilogy, is composed of *The Danger Tree, The Battle Lost and Won,* and *The Sum of Things,* and focuses upon the remaining years of the war. "Obviously rooted in personal experience, the trilogies, centered first in Bucharest, shift South in the face of the advancing Germans, anchor in Athens, decamp in Cairo, and—with stopovers in Beirut, Cairo, and Damascus—end up in Jerusalem," wrote Howard Moss in the *New York Review of Books.* Although Manning's characterizations of Harriet and Guy Pringle were autobiographically inspired, critics such as Auchincloss recognized "this restrained and civilized writer's ability to penetrate mentalities very unlike her own and to infuse a knowledge of circumstances she could never have participated in, or even observed, with an imaginative life that is vivid, rich and precise." In his *Continuance and Change: The Contemporary British Novel,* Robert K. Morris observed: "The series concerns itself neither with abstract or metaphysical theories of time, refashioned or shifting ideologies, nor various plays for power or status; but with the often bare, ironically conditioned facts of living in uncertainty—uncertainty not as accident, but as a constant of life—in a world over which hangs the certainty of ruin."

To Anthony Burgess in his *The Novel Now,* the Balkan trilogy seemed "one of the finest records we have of the impact of that war on Europe." Moreover, Burgess considered it a rarity to find "such a variety of gifts in one contemporary woman writer—humour, poetry, the power of the exact image, the ability to be both hard and compassionate, a sense of place, all the tricks of impersonation and, finally, a historical eye." As historical fiction, the novels are "remarkable," assessed Walter Allen, suggesting in his *Tradition and Dream: The English and American Novel from the Twenties to Our Time* that "the place and the time, the corruption and the sense of doom, seem caught perfectly; and the characters . . . are drawn with delicacy and strength, so that they come alive on the page, often absurd, but even so always as suffering human beings." For against the larger canvas of the war itself, Manning depicted the problems confronted by ordinary individuals; and as a *Times Literary Supplement* reviewer of *The Great Fortune* stated, by "juxtaposing the personal, sometimes trivial, problems of individuals within the great European conflict which distantly threatens all their futures," Manning offers the reader "the consolation that the great fortune is indeed to have preserved life and hope; nothing else really matters." Noting in a *Christian Science Monitor* review of *The Battle Lost and Won* that the war's effect on Manning's protagonists "is the paradigm of a dismal contradiction: that human labor and human affection exist in a universe which makes rather little of either," Edith Milton added that Manning "has a fine, tragic vision of the enormity of our littleness, and she defines that vision with force and with restraint. Her ironies are deep but understated; her prose is totally admirable in its chill clarity."

Manning was regularly praised for her mastery in creating authenticity of scene or sense of place. A *Times Literary Supplement* reviewer of *Friends and Heroes* found the Balkan trilogy "so full of intriguing minor characters . . . , so evocative of both place and mood, and so well proportioned the incidents that provide constant narrative pleasure . . . that one might extract from the trilogy all kinds of meanings and thereby lose the overlying quality, which is simply to have covered an amazingly full and colourful canvas with people and scenes so real and authoritatively recalled that it hardly seems like fiction." And regarding the Levant trilogy, John Mellors stated in the *Listener:* "Place and people are equally real in Olivia Manning's books. She could conjure up a city and a season with a few almost throwaway remarks." Virgilia Peterson indicated in the *New York Times Book Review* about *The Great Fortune* that "Bucharest . . . the way it looked and behaved, its expressions and its probable rumors and improbable characters in those last few months of freedom are boldly drawn." Maurice Richardson concurred in *New Statesman,* "You get such a detailed picture of Rumanian society, haphazard, frivolous, iniquitous and indefensible, that you acquire quite a strong taste for it and regret that you will know what it was like during the German occupation and the sovietisation that followed."

"One of Miss Manning's greatest talents is that she so cleverly conceals the intricate machinery which is needed in organizing so variegated and full a novel," according to a *Times Literary Supplement* reviewer of *The Spoilt City.* "Her often wise and witty comments on the futility of war as it touches ordinary people are always concealed in understatements of fact." Other critics commented about the way in which form complimented content in her work. For instance, in a *New York Times Book Review* assessment of the novel, Martin Levin called its intrigue "the bumbling loosely organized kind, approximating the real thing in those desperate days," adding that the novel's design is one "of a prelude to disaster, which the author's skill resurrects vividly." Describing the trilogies as "the work of a dispassionate moralist who is also an inimitable storyteller," Moss suggested that "Manning's giant six-volume effort is one of those combinations of soap opera and literature that are so rare you'd think it would meet the conditions of two kinds of audiences: those after what the trade calls 'a good read,' and those who want something more." Although finding Manning's prose "often pedestrian, and sometimes so bone-plain we wince a little," Moss nonetheless declared that "as the six novels of the two trilogies accumulate, one reinforcing the other, they ultimately have the effect of a strongly lit tableaux."

"Subtlety, asperity, vividness and ease of manner" distinguish the Levant trilogy, remarked a *Times Literary Supplement* contributor. And Manning was especially credited for the ability, despite her gender, to realistically render scenes of battle. Calling Manning "an adroit technician," Moss observed that her depiction "of desert warfare is chilling and exact; it has the quality of the fantastic that rises from the simultaneous conjunction of the incredibility and believability of fact." Ackroyd echoed this impression about *The Danger Tree:* "I haven't often read battle scenes which come so immediately and horrifyingly to life. And yet they are presented neutrally and even blandly, as if the world were always like this. It all fits very well within the pessimistic vision of the book, but the images which embody it are of an extraordinary power."

"She writes with blessed economy, evoking the sights and smells of the Middle East, the spring-green deserts and a mosque at dawn, with beautiful precision rather than purple passages," commented Charles Champlin in his *Los Angeles Time* review of Manning's final novel, *The Sum of Things.* Although praising Manning's "accurate, superbly economical writing," Jonah Jones felt in the London *Times* that her characterizations inspired little interest, and therefore considered the novel, "further evidence that the reputation she enjoyed during her life may have been inflated." Champlin maintained, however, that "there is in her work as well a calm judiciousness, a special combination of distance and sympathy, of passion described, not celebrated, and of violence serenely depicted, that may have stood in the way of wider sales, but that is individual and very satisfying."

Although loyal, Manning's audience was not large. Remarking that Manning "has been compared with Graham Greene and Anthony Powell," Champlin added that in the United States, she "remains bafflingly little-known . . . , and in England is less a cult figure than a quiet enthusiasm." Explaining that she was "a dedicated professional . . . with a reputation for shyness," the London *Times* contributor pointed out that she "never sought the attention of press or prizegivers." Allen suggested that from the beginning, Manning "possessed an exceedingly pure and exact style, together with what one thinks of as a painter's eye for the visible world, that . . . enabled her to render particularly well the sensual surface of landscapes and places. . . . It is a prose and an eye that seem accurately to take the measure of things." Manning ought to "rank among the very rare writers of our day whose gift of style and story is enlarged to importance by the dimensions of intelligence and moral purpose," said Milton. Victoria Glendinning suggested in the *Times Literary Supplement* that "the 'stray figures' of Olivia Manning's fiction won her a *succes d'estime.* A *succes d'estime* that survives an author's lifetime becomes something more."

MEDIA ADAPTATIONS: Manning's *The Balkan Trilogy* was adapted for British Broadcasting Corp. (BBC-Radio) and for the Public Television Service series, "Masterpiece Theatre."

AVOCATIONAL INTERESTS: Theatre-going, travel, and cats.

BIOGRAPHICAL/CRITICAL SOURCES:

BOOKS

Allen, Walter, *Tradition and Dream: The English and American Novel from the Twenties to Our Time,* J. M. Dent, 1964.

Burgess, Anthony, *The Novel Now,* Norton, 1967.

Contemporary Literary Criticism, Gale, Volume 5, 1976, Volume 19, 1981.

Morris, Robert K., *Continuance and Change: The Contemporary British Novel Sequence,* Southern Illinois University Press, 1972.

PERIODICALS

Book World, May 17, 1981.

Christian Science Monitor, April 9, 1979.

Guardian, February 23, 1960.

Listener, September 25, 1980.

Los Angeles Times, March 23, 1981.

New Statesman, January 30, 1960, November 5, 1965, November 17, 1978, September 26, 1980.

New York Herald Tribune Books, November 25, 1962.

New York Review of Books, April 25, 1985.

New York Times Book Review, July 16, 1961, November 11, 1962, August 28, 1966, October 9, 1977.

Saturday Review, January 22, 1961.

Spectator, January 29, 1960, August 20, 1977, November 25, 1978.

Times (London), July 24, 1980, October 2, 1980.

Times Literary Supplement, January 29, 1960, May 11, 1962, November 4, 1965, August 19, 1977, November 24, 1978, September 19, 1980, January 21, 1983, September 21, 1984.

Washington Post Book World, October 21, 1985.

OBITUARIES:

PERIODICALS

AB Bookman's Weekly, October 6, 1980.
Publishers Weekly, September 5, 1980.
Times (London), July 24, 1980.*

—*Sketch by Sharon Malinowski*

* * *

MANUEL, Frank Edward 1910-

PERSONAL: Born September 12, 1910, in Boston, Mass.; son of Morris and Jessica (Fredson) Manuel; married Fritzie Prigohzy, October 6, 1936. *Education:* Harvard University, A.B., 1930, M.A., 1931, Ph.D., 1933; additional graduate study at Ecole des Hautes Etudes Politiques et Sociales, Paris, France, 1933.

ADDRESSES: Home—10 Emerson Pl., No. 21E, Boston, Mass. 02114.

CAREER: Harvard University, Cambridge, Mass., member of department of history, government, and economics, 1935-37; research and administrative positions with National Defense Commission and Office of Price Administration, 1940-43, 1945-47; Western Reserve University (now Case Western Reserve University), Cleveland, Ohio, professor of history, 1947; Brandeis University, Waltham, Mass., professor of history and moral psychology, 1949-65; New York University, New York, N.Y., professor, 1965-76, Kenan Professor of History, 1970-76; Brandeis University, Alfred and Viola Hart University Professor, 1977-86. Visiting professor at various universities, including Hebrew University of Jerusalem, 1972, and Boston University, 1986-88; visiting lecturer and fellow at various universities. Member of Institute for Advanced Study, 1976-77. *Military service:* U.S. Army, 1943-45; served as combat intelligence officer with Twenty-First Corps; received Bronze Star.

MEMBER: American Academy of Arts and Sciences (fellow), Phi Beta Kappa.

AWARDS, HONORS: Guggenheim fellow, 1957-58; Center for Advanced Study in the Behavioral Sciences fellow, 1962-63; Litt.D., Jewish Theological Seminary, 1979; Melcher Prize, 1980, Phi Beta Kappa Emerson Award, 1980, and American Book Award, paperback history, 1983, all for *Utopian Thought in the Western World;* Doctor of Humane Letters, Brandeis University, 1986.

WRITINGS:

The Politics of Modern Spain, McGraw, 1938.
The Realities of American-Palestine Relations, Public Affairs Press, 1949.
The Age of Reason, Cornell University Press, 1951, reprinted, Greenwood Press, 1982.
The New World of Henri Saint-Simon, Harvard University Press, 1956.
The Eighteenth Century Confronts the Gods, Harvard University Press, 1959.
The Prophets of Paris, Harvard University Press, 1962.
Isaac Newton: Historian, Harvard University Press, 1963.
Shapes of Philosophical History, Stanford University Press, 1965.
(Editor) *The Enlightenment,* Prentice-Hall, 1965.
(Editor) *Utopias and Utopian Thought,* Houghton, 1966.
(Editor, translator, and author of introduction with wife, Fritzie P. Manuel) *French Utopias: An Anthology of Ideal Societies,* Free Press, 1966.
A Portrait of Isaac Newton, Harvard University Press, 1968.
(Editor) Johann Gottfried von Herder, *Reflections on the Philosophy of the History of Mankind,* University of Chicago Press, 1968.
Freedom from History, and Other Untimely Essays, New York University Press, 1971.
The Religion of Isaac Newton, Clarendon Press, 1974.
(With F. P. Manuel) *Utopian Thought in the Western World,* Harvard University Press, 1979.
The Changing of the Gods, University Press of New England, 1983.

Member of board of editors, *Dictionary of the History of Ideas,* 1969-71; consulting editor, *Psychoanalysis and Contemporary Science,* 1970—; advisory editor, *Clio,* 1971—.

SIDELIGHTS: "Frank [Edward] Manuel has long been distinguished for the depth and diversity of his interest in European intellectual history of the eighteenth and nineteenth centuries; and to this we must add his two books on Newton and his various anthologies of thinkers of the Enlightenment and of the classical utopian writers," comments Robert Brown in the *Times Literary Supplement.* "Now he has joined with his wife [Fritzie P. Manuel] to produce" *Utopian Thought in the Western World,* "a highly informative study which is both a summary of, and reflection upon, the results of their many years of shared work on the ideas of utopian writers." "Since the Renaissance, many of the most gifted Western intellectuals . . . have exhibited a striking 'utopian propensity,' " summarizes *New York Times Book Review* contributor Leo Marx, "and the Manuels set out to describe and, if possible, explain that curious habit of mind." The result, asserts Marx, "is a work of monumental scope, written with authority, wit and unfailing lucidity. 'Utopian Thought in the Western World' challenges received ideas about an entire mode of expression and, by implication, about creativity itself." In his *New Republic* review, Robert Nisbet similarly claims that the American Book Award-winning *Utopian Thought in the Western World* "is without any doubt the finest single history of Western utopias to be found anywhere. It is comprehensive, covering the last 2500 years, from early Hebrew and Greek texts, richly detailed, and written with a verve and an unerring eye for the illuminating essence of whatever the authors happen to be dealing with."

In providing such an extensive overview of utopian thought, the Manuels first arrange their subjects into seven "constellations," groups which contain clusters of important writers, with minor writers of the same general area attached to the main cluster. In addition, the Manuels "are interested in bringing to life all of the circumstances, outward, and inward, public and private, that bear upon the making of utopias, and much of this book reads like traditional narrative biography or history," notes Marx. These biographies, adds the critic, "are gems of concise, detached yet sympathetic analysis, never condescending, seldom reductive and invariably engaging. The book's essence lies in these audacious character studies in which a particular life and work and cultural milieu is connected to the overall history of the mode. For all the idiosyncratic diversity of the utopians—and the study is based on many examples," continues Marx, "the Manuels succeed in sketching a compelling profile of their characteristic neurotic style." And Nisbet finds that in particular, "the authors' treatment of Sir Thomas More and his classic [*Utopia*]is masterly and a pure distillation of some of the finest recent scholarship on this complex mind."

Brown, however, while acknowledging the magnitude of *Utopian Thought,* also faults the authors for not presenting enough connections to support their "constellation" groupings: "Useful generalizations about all the members of a given constellation are conspicuously scarce. This is not surprising since the Manuels nowhere give us much reason to believe that they have found common elements of the desired sort." The critic continues by observing that unless the few generalizations that are made "are to be used by the authors in the course of developing an argument or as a test of theory—which they are not—there is no work for them to do." David McLellan similarly remarks in the *New Statesman* that he "get[s] the impression that the book is really a set of separate chapters rather than an overall study within a single, united framework. . . . The book obviously raises a number of difficulties about the whole concept of Utopia—how it is related to political philosophy and social science, and how it should be studied." The critic adds that while "Manuel's almost belletristic style and treatment is extremely readable and at times utterly captivating, nevertheless I feel the lack ultimately of a rigorous framework of analysis."

Nisbet, however, believes that this separation into clusters helps the book achieve overall consistency; he maintains that "it is not simply utopias the authors write about; what they refer to as 'constellations' of utopias are the real subject of the book, its 'underlying pattern.' Thus conventional, linear, event-by-event narrative is happily avoided," concludes the critic, "its place taken by a more comparative and sociological approach to the history of utopias." Marx, while commenting that "the Manuels may have a political blind spot" in their selection of utopians, nevertheless concludes that these reservations "do not drastically diminish my admiration for the Manuels' achievement. 'Utopian Thought' is a triumph of old-fashioned personal scholarship. Anyone who bothers to contemplate the size and complexity of the materials they mastered will have trouble believing, as I do, that it was the work of two people." The critic concludes that "no group effort could possibly produce a work of such force and empathy. What the Manuels accomplish is rooted in self-knowledge, and above all in their profound ambivalence about the imagining and writing of utopias." "What is of overriding and overwhelming importance is that the Manuels have given us a book of ideas and personages, written in a style often brilliant and never less than graceful, and filled with more wit than one usually finds in half a hundred works of scholarship," declares Nisbet. "I repeat: it is by far the best and the grandest of histories of the utopian mind."

BIOGRAPHICAL/CRITICAL SOURCES:

PERIODICALS

New Republic, March 1, 1975, November 10, 1979.

New Statesman, March 21, 1969, January 25, 1980.

New York Review of Books, April 10, 1969, March 6, 1980.

New York Times, December 1, 1979.

New York Times Book Review, February 25, 1968, October 21, 1979.

Spectator, February 2, 1980.

Times Literary Supplement, June 1, 1973, June 20, 1975, June 6, 1980.

* * *

MAQUET, Jacques Jerome Pierre 1919-

PERSONAL: Surname sounds like "McKay"; born August 4, 1919, in Brussels, Belgium; came to United States in 1967, naturalized in 1974; son of Jerome (a state administrator) and Jeanne (Lemoine) Maquet; married Emma de Longree, June 17, 1947 (divorced, 1969); married Gisele Cambresier, November 13, 1970; children: (first marriage) Bernard, Denis. *Education:* University of Louvain, LL.D., 1946, D.Phil., 1948; University of London, Ph.D., 1952.

ADDRESSES: Office—Department of Anthropology, University of California, Los Angeles, Calif. 90024.

CAREER: Institute for Scientific Research in Central Africa, Astrida, Ruanda-Urundi (now Butare, Rwanda), field anthropologist, 1949-51, research director of Social Sciences Center, 1951-57; State University of Congo (now Universite Nationale de Zaire), Elisabethville, Congo (now Lubumbushi, Zaire), professor of anthropology, 1957-60; University of Paris, Ecole Pratique des Hautes Etudes, Paris, France, research director of anthropology, 1961-68; Case Western Reserve University, Cleveland, Ohio, professor of anthropology, 1968-70; University of California, Los Angeles, professor of anthropology, 1971—, chairman of department, 1978-83. Visiting professor, Northwestern University, 1956, University of Brussels, 1963-68, Harvard University, 1964, University of Montreal, 1965, University of Pittsburgh, 1967, Stanford University, 1976, and Princeton University, 1983. Secretary, Inter-African Committee for the Social Sciences, 1953-56; consultant in museology, UNESCO, 1964-65.

MEMBER: Association internationale des sociologues de langue francaise, International Association for Buddhist Studies, Royal Anthropological Institute of Great Britain, Association for Asian Studies, Federation of American Scientists, American Anthropological Association (fellow), Pali Text Society, American Society for the Study of Religion.

AWARDS, HONORS: Emile Waxweiler Award, Royal Academy of Belgium, 1961, for *The Premise of Inequality in Ruanda: A Study of Political Relations in a Central African Kingdom;* Wenner-Gren Foundation grants, 1965 and 1973; best French book on African art award, 1966, for *Afrique: Les Civilisations noires;* D.Litt., University of Paris, 1973.

WRITINGS:

Sociologie de la connaissance, sa structure et ses rapports avec la philosophie de la connaissance: Etude critique des systemes de Karl Mannheim et de Pitirim A. Sorokin, Institut de Recherches Economiques et Sociales (Louvain, Belgium), 1949, 2nd edition, Institut de Sociologie de l'Universite Libre de Bruxelles (Brussels), 1969, translation by John F. Locke published as *The Sociology of Knowledge, Its Structure and Its Relation to the Philosophy of Knowledge: A Critical Analysis of the Systems of Karl Mannheim and Pitirim A. Sorokin,* Beacon Press, 1951, reprinted, Greenwood Press, 1973.

Le Systeme des relations sociales dans le Ruanda ancien, Musee Royal d'Afrique Centrale (Tervuren, Belgium), 1954, translation by the author published as *The Premise of Inequality in Ruanda: A Study of Political Relations in a Central African Kingdom,* Oxford University Press for the International African Institute, 1961.

Aide-memoire d'ethnologie africaine (title means "Photographic Essay on an African Society in Transition"), Elsevier (Brussels), 1957.

(With Marcel d'Hertefelt) *Elections en societe feodale: Une Etude sur l'introduction du vote populaire au Ruanda-Urundi* (title means "Elections in a Feudal Society: A Study of the Introduction of Popular Vote in Ruanda-Urundi"), Academie Royale des Sciences d'Outremer, 1959.

Afrique: Les Civilisations noires, Horizons de France (Paris), 1962, 2nd edition, 1968, published as *Les Civilisations noires: Histoire, techniques, arts, [et] societes,* Gerard (Verviers, Belgium), 1966, translation by Joan Rayfield published as *Civilizations of Black Africa,* Oxford University Press, 1972.

Africanite: Traditionnelle et moderne, Presence Africaine (Paris), 1967, translation by Rayfield published as *Africanity: The Cultural Unity of Black Africa,* Oxford University Press, 1972.

(Editor with Georges Balandier) *Dictionnaire des civilisations africaines,* Hazan (Paris), 1968, translation by Mariska Caroline Peck, Beltina Wadia, and Peninah Heimark published as *Dictionary of Black African Civilization,* Leon Amiel, 1974.

Pouvoir et societe en Afrique, Hachette (Paris), 1971, translation by Jeanette Kupfermann published as *Power and Society in Africa,* McGraw, 1971.

Introduction to Aesthetic Anthropology, Addison-Wesley, 1971, 2nd revised edition, Undena, 1979.

(Editor) *On Linguistic Anthropology,* Undena, 1980.

(Editor) *On Symbols in Anthropology,* Undena, 1982.

(Editor) *On Marxian Perspectives in Anthropology,* Undena, 1984.

The Aesthetic Experience: An Anthropologist Looks at the Visual Arts, Yale University Press, 1986.

CONTRIBUTOR

Daryll Forde, editor, *African Worlds,* Oxford University Press for the International African Institute, 1954.

F. S. C. Northrop and Helen Livingston, editors, *Cross-Cultural Understanding: Epistemology in Anthropology,* Harper, 1964.

Paul Alexandre, editor, *L'Heritage de l'homme,* Editions de la Grange-Bateliere (Geneva, Switzerland), 1967.

Mary Douglas and Phyllis M. Kaberry, editors, *Man in Africa,* Tavistock Publications, 1969.

Philip K. Bock, editor, *Cultural Shock: A Reader in Modern Cultural Anthropology,* Knopf, 1970.

Ronald Cohen and John Middleton, editors, *From Tribe to Nation in Africa,* Chandler Publishing, 1970.

Arthur Tuden and Leonard Plotnicov, editors, *Social Stratification in Africa,* Free Press, 1970.

James A. Clifton, editor, *Applied Anthropology: Readings in the Use of the Science of Man,* Houghton, 1970.

Hubert Deschamps, editor, *Histoire generale de l'Afrique noire,* Presses Universitaires de France (Paris), 1970.

Somaratna Balasooriya, editor, *Buddhist Studies in Honour of Walpola Rahula,* Gordon Fraser (London), 1980.

Also contributor to *International Encyclopedia of the Social Sciences* and *Encyclopaedia Universalis.*

OTHER

Editor of "Other Realities" anthropological series, Undena, 1978-86. Author of screenplay for motion picture, "Ruanda: Tableaux d'une feodalite pastorale," filmed in 1956. Contributor of over 200 articles and reviews to scholarly journals. Editor of *Jeune Afrique,* 1958-60; member of editorial boards of *Journal of African Studies,* 1975—, *Journal of Transpersonal Psychology,* 1981—, *The Mankind Quarterly,* 1981—, and *The Maha Bodhi,* 1986—.

WORK IN PROGRESS: On comparative Buddhist monasticism in South and East Asia, and North America; on aesthetic qualities and symbolic meanings of nonfigurative visual art.

SIDELIGHTS: Jacques Jerome Pierre Maquet told *CA:* "A scholar in the social sciences writes but is not necessarily a writer, and I think I am one. To be a writer does not simply mean 'to write well' (which is what I try to do, but English is a second language for me!); it means that one's professional research and one's life are not two separate compartments. Shifts in my scholarly interests—from sociology to anthropology, from Black Africa to South Asia, from social stratifcation and power to aesthetics and symbolic thinking—reflect and are parallel to the unfolding of my personal itinerary. Commitments and experiences in turn give insight and depth to scholarly endeavors. This dimension makes the difference between a scholar who writes, and a scholar who is a writer."

BIOGRAPHICAL/CRITICAL SOURCES:

PERIODICALS

New York Times Book Review, April 6, 1986.

Times Literary Supplement, August 15, 1986.

* * *

MARCH, Jessica
See AFRICANO, Lillian

* * *

MARCHAK, M(aureen) Patricia 1936-
(Maureen Marchak)

PERSONAL: Born June 22, 1936, in Lethbridge, Alberta, Canada; daughter of Adrian Ebenezer and Wilhelmina Rankin (Hamilton) Russell; married William Marchak, 1956; children: Geordon Eric, Lauren Craig. *Education:* University of British Columbia, B.A., 1958, Ph.D., 1970.

ADDRESSES: Office—Department of Anthropology and Sociology, University of British Columbia, 6303 Northwest Marine Dr., Vancouver, British Columbia, Canada V6T 2B2.

CAREER: Free-lance writer, 1963-65; University of British Columbia, Vancouver, instructor, 1965-67, sessional lecturer, 1968-72, assistant professor, 1973-75, associate professor, 1975-80, professor of sociology, 1980—, head of department, 1987—. Sorokin Lecturer at University of Saskatchewan, 1982; visiting professor of Carleton University, summer, 1986; Shastri-Indo-Canadian Institute Visiting Professor to India, 1987. Director of research on housing in North Vancouver, 1972. Member of Pacific group of Canadian Centre for Policy Alternatives, 1983—; member of committee on Yukon water resources, Westwater Research Institute, 1979-82. Canadian Registrar of Research and Researchers in the Social Sciences, 1981-86. Lecturer and speaker at conferences.

AWARDS, HONORS: Research grant from Institute of Industrial Relations, University of British Columbia, 1969-70; Social Science and Humanities Council of Canada, grants, 1977-78 and 1981-84, fellowships, 1984-85 and 1984-85; *Green Gold: The Forest Industry in British Columbia* was selected as one of the outstanding academic books of the year by American Library Association, 1985; John Porter Memorial Book Prize from Canadian Association of Sociology and Anthropology, 1986, for *Green Gold: The Forest Industry in British Columbia.*

MEMBER: International Sociological Association, Canadian Political Science Association, Canadian Sociology and Anthropology Association (member of advisory board, 1975-81; president, 1979-80), Association for Canadian Studies (member of executive board, 1978-80), Western Anthropology and Sociology Association.

WRITINGS:

Ideological Perspectives on Canada, McGraw, 1975, 2nd revised edition, 1987.

(Editor) *The Working Sexes,* Institute of Industrial Relations, University of British Columbia, 1977.

In Whose Interests: An Essay on Multinational Corporations in a Canadian Context, McClelland & Stewart, 1979.

Green Gold: The Forest Industry in British Columbia, University of British Columbia Press, 1983.

(Co-editor) *Uncommon Property: The Fishing and Fish Processing Industries in British Columbia,* Methuen, 1987.

CONTRIBUTOR

(Under name Maureen Marchak) Elizabeth A. Thorn and M. Irene Richmond, editors, *Comprehension Strategies I,* Gage, 1972.

Marylee Stephenson, editor, *Women in Canada,* New Press, 1973, revised edition, 1977.

James Heap, editor, *Everybody's Canada,* Burns & MacEachern, 1974.

Raymond Breton, editor, *Aspects of Canadian Society,* Canadian Sociology and Anthropology Association, 1974.

Christopher Beattie and Stewart Crysdale, editors, *Sociology Canada: Readings,* 2nd edition, Butterworth, 1977.

Anne Piternick, editor, *National Conference on the State of Canadian Bibliography: Proceedings,* National Library of Canada, 1977.

Paul Cappon, editor, *In Our Own House: Social Perspectives on Canadian Literature,* McClelland & Stewart, 1978.

Beattie, Katherina Lundy, and Barbara Warme, editors, *Work in the Canadian Context,* Butterworth, 1981.

Anne Crichton, editor, *Health Policy Making: Fundamental Issues in the United States, Canada, Great Britain, Australia,* Health Administration Press, 1981.

Michael S. Whittington and Glen Williams, editors, *Canadian Politics in the 1980's,* revised edition, Methuen, 1984.

Robert B. Stouffer, editor, *Transnational Corporations and the State,* University of Sydney, 1985.

Robert J. Brym, *Regionalism in Canada,* Irwin, 1986.

Meg Luxton and Heather Jon Maroney, editors, *Feminism and Political Economy,* Methuen, 1987.

Rennie Warburton and David Coburn, editors, *Workers, Capital, and the State in British Columbia: Selected Papers,* UBC Press, 1988.

OTHER

Contributor of over sixty articles and reviews to professional journals, research reports, and other publications. Book review editor of *Canadian Review of Sociology and Anthropology,* 1971-74; member of editorial board of *Studies in Political Economy,* 1980—, *Current Sociology,* 1982—, *Canadian Journal of Sociology,* 1986—, and *B. C. Studies,* 1988—.

WORK IN PROGRESS: The Integrated Circus: Politics in a Global Economy; research on reorganization of forest industry in Pacific Rim countries.

SIDELIGHTS: M. Patricia Marchak told *CA:* "My research concerns are Canadian studies, with particular interest in industrial organization, social and political ideologies, the labor force, and rural-industrial communities, the sociology of industrial society and industrial organizations, the macro-level theory and political economy theory, and women's studies. Over the past decade I have concentrated on conducting research and writing about the resource industries, resource communities, and labor in forestry and fishing regions of British Columbia.

"I've always felt driven to find an explanation for the kind of society we've created in the twentieth century. North American society seems to be characterized by inequalities, waste, rewards for uncivilized behavior, and other unsavory traits. I'm still trying to figure out why. My own life, even so, has been extremely happy. Most of it has been spent on the British Columbia coast where, not so incidentally, trees grow to legendary heights and fishing is an honorable way of life. What I have done is combine the quest for understanding with my concern for the natural environment and the people who earn their livings in resource regions. It is impossible to understand British Columbia [B. C.] (or Canada, for that matter) without knowing a good deal about our dependence on resource industries and the export of raw materials. My books on forestry and fishing will, I hope, contribute to this understanding.

"While conducting forestry research I learned a bit about inadequate reforestation in B.C. and about some economic policies that are both environmentally damaging and incapable of leading to genuine economic stability for a region such as this. This prompted me to become a candidate in a provincial election, though I do not imagine myself as a politician and will continue to live my life as an academic, researcher, and writer.

"I am deeply concerned about the potential for destruction of the earth, and all who inhabit her, that grows daily with the rhetoric and childish pontifications of our political leaders. The 'cold war' is an idiotic game fueled largely by greed. While Canadians no doubt benefit in many ways from our close association with the United States, I would greatly prefer an independent stance on foreign policy whereby Canadians might express their earnest desire for our neighbors on either side to make peace. I expect that I, like so many other writers and researchers, will devote more of my time in the next years to the cause of peace: we can no longer leave that to politicians."

* * *

MARCHAK, Maureen
See MARCHAK, M(aureen) Patricia

* * *

MARCHANT, Anyda 1911-
(Sarah Aldridge)

PERSONAL: Name is pronounced *Annee*-da *Mar*-chant; born January 27, 1911, in Rio de Janeiro, Brazil; daughter of U.S. citizens Langworthy (an educator and editor) and Maude Henrietta (Annett) Marchant. *Education:* National University (now George Washington University), Washington, D.C., A.B. (with distinction), 1931, M.A., 1933, LL.B., 1936. *Politics:* Democrat. *Religion:* Episcopalian.

ADDRESSES: Home—P.O. Box 283, Rehoboth Beach, Del. 19971. *Office*—c/o Naiad Press, P.O. Box 10543, Tallahassee, Fla. 32302.

CAREER: Admitted to the bars of Virginia, District of Columbia, and U.S. Supreme Court. Former attorney with law firms Schuster & Feuille, New York, N.Y., and Covington & Burling, Washington, D.C.; Library of Congress, Washington, D.C., staff member of Law Library, 1940-45; Light & Power Co., Rio de Janeiro, Brazil, member of legal staff, 1947-48; U.S. Department of Commerce, Washington, D.C., staff member of Bureau of Foreign and Domestic Commerce, 1951-53; International Bank for Reconstruction and Development, Washington, D.C., member of legal staff, 1954-73; writer.

WRITINGS:

NOVELS; UNDER PSEUDONYM SARAH ALDRIDGE

The Latecomer, Naiad Press, 1974.
Tottie: The Tale of the Sixties, Naiad Press, 1975.
Cytherea's Breath, Naiad Press, 1976.
All True Lovers, Naiad Press, 1978.
The Nesting Place, Naiad Press, 1982.
Madame Aurora, Naiad Press, 1983.
Misfortune's Friend, Naiad Press, 1985.
Magdalena, Naiad Press, 1987.
Keep to Me Stranger, Naiad Press, 1989.

OTHER

(Contributor) T. Lynn Smith and Alexander Marchant, editors, *Brazil: Portrait of Half a Continent,* Dryden Press, 1951, revised edition, University of Florida Press, 1966.
Viscount Maua and the Empire of Brazil, University of California Press, 1965.

Contributor to *Hispanic American Historical Review, Frontiers, Americas, Southwest Review,* and other journals.

WORK IN PROGRESS: A social and horticultural history of the introduction of the tea rose from China into England and the United States.

AVOCATIONAL INTERESTS: Popular horticulture and the history of horticultural research in South America.

* * *

MARGOSHES, Dave 1941-

PERSONAL: Born July 8, 1941, in New Brunswick, N.J.; son of Harry (a journalist) and Berte (Shalley) Margoshes; married Ilya Silbar (a potter and librarian), 1963. *Education:* Attended Middlebury College, 1959-61; University of Iowa, B.A., 1963, M.F.A., 1969.

ADDRESSES: Home—2922 19th Ave., Regina, Saskatchewan, Canada S4T 1X5.

CAREER: Writer. Worked as newspaper reporter and editor, 1963-75; Southern Alberta Institute of Technology, Calgary, instructor in journalism, 1975-77; Mount Royal College, Calgary, instructor in journalism, 1975-77 and 1981-84; *Calgary Herald,* Calgary, reporter, 1977-81; *Vancouver Sun,* Vancouver, British Columbia, reporter, 1984-86.

MEMBER: Saskatchewan Writers Guild (board member), Writers Guild of Alberta.

AWARDS, HONORS: Poem of the year award, *Canadian Author and Bookman,* 1982, for "Season of Lilac."

WRITINGS:

Third Impressions (stories), edited by John Metcalf, Oberon, 1982.
(Contributor) Geoff Hancock, editor, *Metavisions,* Quadrant Press, 1984.
Small Regrets (stories), Thistledown Press, 1986.
(Contributor) *86: Best Canadian Stories,* Oberon, 1986.
Walking at Brighton (poetry), Thistledown Press, 1988.
(Contributor) *Open Windows,* Quarry Press, 1988.
(Contributor) *Sky High,* Coteau Books, 1988.

Also contributor of stories and poems to various periodicals, including *Canadian Forum, Canadian Literature, Dalhousie Review, Descant, Fiddlehead, Malahat Review, Prism International, Queen's Quarterly,* and *Wascana Review.*

MARIUS, Richard (Curry) 1933-

PERSONAL: Born July 29, 1933, in Martel, Tenn.; son of Henri (a foundryman) and Eunice (a journalist, maiden name Henck) Marius; married Gail Smith, June 28, 1955 (divorced); married Lanier Smythe, March 21, 1970; children: (first marriage) Richard, Fred; (second marriage) John. *Education:* University of Tennessee, B.S. (summa cum laude), 1954; Southern Baptist Theological Seminary, B.D., 1958; Yale University, M.A., 1959, Ph.D., 1962. *Politics:* Liberal Democrat. *Religion:* Unitarian.

ADDRESSES: Office—Department of Expository Writing, Harvard University, Cambridge, Mass. 02138.

CAREER: Newspaper reporter while attending college, and worked at odd jobs to pay for further education; Gettysburg College, Gettysburg, Pa., assistant professor of history, 1962-64; University of Tennessee, Knoxville, assistant professor, 1964-68, associate professor, 1968-73, professor of history, 1973-78; Harvard University, Cambridge, Mass., director of expository writing, 1978—.

MEMBER: American Association of University Professors, Authors League of America, Authors Guild.

AWARDS, HONORS: The Coming of Rain was designated the best novel of 1969 by Friends of American Writers; *Thomas More: A Biography* was nominated for the 1984 American Book Award in nonfiction.

WRITINGS:

The Coming of Rain (novel; Book-of-the-Month Club alternate selection), Knopf, 1969.
Bound for the Promised Land (novel), Knopf, 1976.

NONFICTION

(Contributor) Michael J. Moore, editor, *Quincentennial Essays on St. Thomas More,* Albion, 1962.
(Co-editor) Thomas More, *Confutations,* three volumes, Yale University Press, 1973.
Luther (biography), Lippincott, 1974.
(Contributor) Dolly Berthelot, editor, *Pioneer Spirit 76: Commemorative BicenTENNial Portrait,* [Knoxville, Tenn.], 1975.
(Editor with Thomas M. C. Lawler and Germain Marc'hadour, and contributor) *The Complete Works of St. Thomas More,* Volume 6, Yale University Press, 1982.
(Editor with others, and contributor) *The Yale Edition of the Complete Works of St. Thomas More,* Volume 8, Yale University Press, 1983.
Thomas More: A Biography, Knopf, 1984.
A Writer's Companion, Knopf, 1985.
(With Harvey S. Wiener) *The McGraw-Hill College Handbook* (with annotated teacher's supplement), McGraw, 1985, 2nd edition, 1988.
(With J. Bean) *The McGraw-Hill Self Study Workbook,* McGraw, 1985.
A Short Guide to Writing about History, Little, Brown, 1987.

OTHER

Featured on the sound recording *The Writer and Human Values,* Tennessee Library Association, 1973. Contributor to scholarly journals and other periodicals, including *Daedalus, Moreana, Traditio, Sewanee Review, Boston Sunday Globe, Christian Century, Esquire,* and *National Forum.*

WORK IN PROGRESS: A novel, tentatively entitled *The Immigrant.*

SIDELIGHTS: As a historian, educator, and distinguished scholar of the Renaissance, Richard Marius has written extensively about that period and its personages; but he is also a novelist who "classifies both fiction and nonfiction as 'creative writing' and applies the same criteria of writing to both: ideas must 'make sense' and be real and 'memorable,' " reports Nancy G. Anderson in the *Dictionary of Literary Biography Yearbook, 1985.* As Marius explains in *National Forum:* "Writers observe in a world of restless change. In setting their observations on paper, all writers create something—a design that makes the observations make sense, something that relates them to the rest of our thought and feeling, something that may make them memorable." As director of expository writing at Harvard University, Marius has also authored student textbooks on the subject which, according to Anderson, are "praised for their commonsensical approach to writing, their readable and even humorous style." Although Marius's stylistic approach is informal and personal, his work is hallmarked by clarity and precision. "The levels of language and tone vary with the subject and audience," observes Anderson, "but readable style, use of memorable details, the sense of drama, and, when appropriate, humor persist."

Luther, Marius's biography of Martin Luther, evolved out of his "opposition to the Vietnam War and his efforts at that time to teach the Reformation," notes Anderson. And while *Christian Science Monitor* contributor J. G. Harrison objects to "gratuitous references to the 'dirty war' in Vietnam," he simultaneously believes that the biography "is a serious, well-written and—most important of all—understandable history of a complex subject and time." Commending its "historical authenticity" and its author's efforts to discover a "relevance for our own times," *Library Journal* contributor J. S. Nelson considers *Luther* "interesting, lively, and informative." However, Anderson mentions that Marius's informal, personal style and the conclusions he draws (that help comes from within the individual rather than from arcane theology, and that life itself is but a process in which one makes peace with death) provoked critical objections. Finding "little admiration expressed by the author for anyone," Roland H. Bainton claims in a *Christian Century* review that *Luther* is "an indictment not so much of a man as of a century." Moreover, says Bainton, "I hear in Marius's book the reverberations of an agonized cry of frustration because the contemporary church has let the author down." Conversely, though, Harrison believes that the biography accomplishes its informative task clearly, simply, and directly: "Luther's struggles, his anguish, his world-upsetting insights, his medieval prejudices, his human shortcomings are set forth without either adulation or prejudice. From here emerges a man, not a symbol."

Marius's scholarly writings about Thomas More, which emanated from his graduate studies and dissertation, analyze "More's beliefs and his place in the political and religious developments of his day," says Anderson; whatever his audience, she continues, Marius's "argument, often complex or abstract, is carefully reasoned and developed with documented evidence from primary sources." *Thomas More: A Biography,* which was nominated for the American Book Award, resulted from his work on the Yale University Press edition of *The Complete Works of St. Thomas More,* and represents "the culmination of Richard Marius's research on More, the Reformation, and the sixteenth century," states Anderson. *Library Journal* contributor Bennett D. Hill asserts that "this sympathetic but judicious, sensitively written work" appeals to the lay person and scholar alike, but "as popular biography, it's absolutely first-rate." Finding that it "sparkles with epigrams," Carl Banks adds in *Christian Century,* "Wry comments and pointed parallels enliven the biography." And as Jack Miles expresses it in the *Los Angeles Times Book Review:* "When smart people talk about other people, this is how they do it. . . . It is as subtle and satisfying a portrait as I have encountered in years."

In contrasting the public figure with the private one, Marius pursues a dual purpose in *Thomas More,* observes Nicolas Barker in the *Times Literary Supplement:* "To peel away the hagiography . . . and to present him in terms that today's reader, unfamiliar with the historic background, will grasp as real and lively. This is not easy." Acknowledging the difficulty Marius faced in crafting such a biography, *New Republic* reviewer Robert M. Adams points out: "Thomas More is one of those historical figures who are easy to take a piece at a time, but hard to assemble." Critics frequently compare *Thomas More* with a 1935 biography by R. W. Chambers, which Adams deems "an elegantly written but patently unctuous piece of sentimental hagiography." Adams suggests that Marius's study of More is "just as hagiographic . . . since he represents More as a lifelong advocate of, and finally a martyr to, a particularly noble ideal of the church." However, unlike that of Chambers, Marius's portrait of More lacks charm, decries Adams, who then summarizes his estimation of Marius's antithetical perspective: "Marius gives us a thoroughly disagreeable More, a domestic tyrant, neurotically afraid of sex, a quarrelsome and self-important writer, a vicious and dishonest controversialist, an obsequious sycophant, a man quite without sympathy for the poor or concern over the slaughter of innocent men in brutally expensive and futile wars."

In *Thomas More,* the subject "receives tremendous sympathy, but without suppression of the dark ambiguities of his life and character," observes Banks. Similarly, *Newsweek*'s Peter S. Prescott finds that Marius considers a wealth of new evidence and, "careful not to reject the prevailing image," he develops another, darker one. "Marius's More is in public an actor, creating his own role on a stage of his own devising," writes Prescott, adding that "the More he gives us is the last medieval man, a failed monk who by necessity chose marriage and a secular career in London, a merciless scourge of heretics who was forever preoccupied with death and fearing for his soul." *Time*'s Melvin Maddocks thinks that "it is Marius's persuasive thesis that, far from being the serene humanist . . . , More was a soul tormented by the little death knells of ticktocking time, and haunted even more by the silences of eternity." But as O. B. Hardison, Jr., explains in *Book World,* although Marius shows us the infallible More, "In the end, and almost in spite of Marius's effort to identify his defects, More the saint eclipses More the man."

Marius's "unrivaled knowledge of More's works . . . serves him very well," declares Paul Johnson in the *New York Times Book Review,* adding that Marius "is the first writer to stress the central importance of More's unfinished biography of Richard III," which, as Johnson posits, "expresses not so much Tudor propaganda as More's political philosophy." Citing Marius's frequent use of "the image of More as an actor on stage," Anderson writes that "Marius records his life against the rich setting of the Renaissance and the nascent Reformation, with the full drama of a fall from power and relative luxury. . . . And, even for an audience that knows the ending, Marius builds to the climax of the final scene of the scaffold, where, having apparently conquered his fear of death, More gave his best performance." Maddocks suggests that "without presuming to answer, the author raises a question: Did More die for what he believed or for what he wanted to believe?" Calling *Thomas More* an "an iconoclastic book which yet recognizes the ultimate greatness of Thomas More," G. R. Elton proclaims in the *New York Review of Books:*

"The debate about More will now continue because Marius has helped to reopen it after More threatened to get embalmed, and that debate will be different through this book."

Agreeing that *Thomas More* is "clearly a work of authority and scholarship," Prescott detects that "it nonetheless contains a multitude of unsupported assertions and misleading generalizations." Elton recognizes that "Marius's achievement is not perfect; with a writer so deeply involved in everything he says it could hardly be." However, acknowledging that "avowed conjecture abounds . . . and not all of that conjecture carries conviction," Elton maintains that "genuine mistakes are very few." And Barker, who believes that "Marius succeeds in forcing his mind into the sixteenth-century mentality, without losing sight of his twentieth-century reader," proposes that "what faults there are come from Marius's determination . . . to see for himself with his own eyes." Moreover, says Elton, "Marius has written a very remarkable book, full of knowledge and understanding. He has written a very personal book, full of wrestling with intractable material and the overwhelming problem of comprehending a man, 450 years dead, who lived in a world and by rules that the present day finds it hard even to contemplate." And, concludes Elton, Marius should be particularly pleased that "he replaces Chambers not only because he knows much more and thinks far more deeply, but also because he writes infinitely better." Prescott also admits that "if Marius too often writes about more than he knows, what he knows is impressive."

"Richard Marius's Renaissance-like interests have developed naturally from his background and education," remarks Anderson, who perceives that just as "history is a focus of Marius's scholarly publications, . . . attitudes toward history are also concerns in his fiction." Marius's novels are set in the fictional city of Bourbonville, based upon the nearby town of his childhood, Lenoir City, Tennessee. *The Coming of Rain,* described by D. C. Taylor in *Library Journal* as an "ambitious and successful first novel about love and violence and family pride and murder and coming of age in post-Civil War eastern Tennessee," explores what Marius describes in "The Middle of the Journey," an autobiographical essay in *Sewanee Review,* as the "Confederate myth of the Lost Cause." The novel recounts the events of only two days in 1885 but, as R. V. Cassill declares in *Book World,* "Threads of action and subplots intertwine so luxuriously that one almost needs a concordance to keep them from entangling hopelessly in his mind." Commenting that the novel "contains multitudes," and is "superbly plotted," a *Times Literary Supplement* contributor especially lauds Marius's ability to "convey vividly the feeling of a rough, sweat-soiled, primitive society overawed by tub-thumping preachers and haunted by the still rankling evils of slavery and civil war." And although Joyce Carol Oates suggests in the *New York Times Book Review,* that the novel is "betrayed by [its] melodramatic complications," she discerns within it, a "slender, tragic, perhaps beautiful story of the ruins of dreams."

"I always ponder history in my fiction," states Marius in *Sewanee Review.* "In *The Coming of Rain* the real conflict is one between good history and bad history." Marius also explains that in his second novel, *Bound for the Promised Land,* "the conflict between illusion and reality is such that one must wonder if writing history is even possible. Nothing in that book is what it first seems to be." In this novel about a family's journey from Tennessee to California forty years earlier during the 1850s, "Marius uses a journey comparable to Chaucer's pilgrimage to bring together disparate, and desperate, characters," explains Anderson, adding that the novel explores "the discrepancy between the appearance of people and things and their reality, and about the meaning—or meaninglessness—of life." While Marius may craft his fiction in multiple layers of meaning, critics also appreciate his ability to tell a story: "It's a good solid story, colorful, lively and authentic," maintains a *Publishers Weekly* contributor about *Bound for the Promised Land.* "A sound if somewhat exhausting read," concurs a *Booklist* reviewer.

"Ultimately, [*The Coming of Rain* and *Bound for the Promised Land*] are quite similar philosophically or thematically," states Anderson, explaining that "characters in both novels search for meaning and purpose in life." Anderson also notes that Marius's unhappy "seminary experiences and the fundamentalist religious environment of his childhood are reflected in both of his novels as religious fanatics cause death and destruction." And although both novels speak about southern lives and the romantic traditions of the South, Marius, whose maternal ancestry can be traced to the American Revolution, and whose grandfather fought for the Union in the Civil War, indicates in *Sewanee Review:* "I bristle when anyone calls me a 'southern' writer. I am a novelist of the border, and in both my novels the romantic traditions of the old South take a good beating. I shall beat those traditions still more in my third."

"As best I can tell," continues Marius, "three things seem to have contributed most to my fiction: a love for the English language, the experiences of a vividly remembered childhood, and my profession as a historian." Anderson suggests that "after a study of his essays, his novels, and his biographies, one must complete the list with the influence of religion." In his autobiographical essay, Marius recalls his family's move to a farm as well as his own happy, if somewhat isolated, childhood. They moved, he says, partly to be nearer his father's work, but also to avoid the "curious and reproachful attention of near neighbors in town" upon his older, mentally impaired brother, whom his mother believed to have been a divine punishment for her failure to become a missionary. Marius describes his mother as having been "cursed by religion"; and although he entered the seminary essentially because of her religiosity, he relates that the isolation of his childhood was relieved by the pleasure of listening to his mother read aloud—especially the Bible—and he credits this with having given him a love for the English language. "To this day I read aloud everything that I write, and if the rhythms are not right, I write again," he says. "I rewrote every page of both my novels at least ten times, and there are some scenes . . . in *The Coming of Rain* that I rewrote as many as thirty times. It is a burden to rewrite so much because it takes me years to finish a book."

"In all of his works, as eclectic as the interests of the Renaissance which he has studied and about which he has written, Marius strives to achieve 'memorability,'" declares Anderson. "He claims that he writes because 'I am going to die, and I don't want to perish completely from this earth.'" And in his autobiographical essay, Marius contemplates his responsibility as a historian, educator, and writer: "Anyone who has taught and written about the past, as I do regularly, must ponder some awesome questions. Any historian is perhaps nothing more than a weaver of glittering illusion as fragile as light and as dangerous as poison." Offering, however, a slight modification to Marius's statement, Anderson concludes: "And a memorable novelist is perhaps nothing more than a good historian with a love of language."

BIOGRAPHICAL/CRITICAL SOURCES:

BOOKS

Dictionary of Literary Biography Yearbook: 1985, Gale, 1986.

PERIODICALS

Best Sellers, November 1, 1969, January 1, 1975.
Booklist, June 1, 1976.
Book World, September 14, 1969.
Boston Globe Magazine, December 11, 1983.
Christian Century, February 19, 1975, October 6, 1976, July 3-10, 1985.
Christian Science Monitor, December 24, 1974.
Commonweal, May 3, 1985.
Library Journal, September 1, 1969, December 1, 1974, September 1, 1984.
Life, September 6, 1969.
Los Angeles Times Book Review, October 28, 1984.
National Forum, fall, 1985.
New Republic, January 21, 1985.
Newsweek, October 29, 1984.
New York Review of Books, January 31, 1985.
New York Times, November 20, 1979, June 16, 1985.
New York Times Book Review, September 21, 1969, January 6, 1985.
Publishers Weekly, April 19, 1976.
Sewanee Review, summer, 1977.
Spectator, February 2, 1985.
Time, December 24, 1984.
Times Literary Supplement, August 21, 1970, April 12, 1985.
USA Today, December 14, 1984.*

—*Sketch by Sharon Malinowski*

* * *

MARRIS, Peter (Horsey) 1927-

PERSONAL: Born July 6, 1927, in London, England; came to United States in 1976; son of George Christopher (an engineer) and Nancy (Eaton) Marris; married Dolores Hayden (a professor), May 17, 1975. *Education:* Cambridge University, B.A., 1951. *Religion:* None.

ADDRESSES: Home—8318 Ridpath Dr., Los Angeles, California. 90046. *Office*—School of Architecture and Urban Planning, University of California, Los Angeles, Calif. 90026.

CAREER: Government of Kenya, Nyeri, district officer, 1953-55; Institute for Community Studies, London, England, research member of institute, 1955-72; Center for Environmental Studies, London, senior research officer, 1972-75; Boston University, Boston, Mass., visiting professor of sociology, 1975-76; University of California, Los Angeles, professor of social planning, 1976—. Visiting lecturer at University of California, Berkeley, 1969-73, Massachusetts Institute of Technology, 1974, and University of Massachusetts, 1975.

MEMBER: International Sociological Association, British Sociological Association.

AWARDS, HONORS: Guggenheim fellow, 1983; German Marshall Fund fellow, 1984.

WRITINGS:

Widows and Their Families, Routledge & Kegan Paul, 1958.
Family and Social Change in an African City: A Study of Rehousing in Lagos, Northwestern University Press, 1962.
The Experience of Higher Education, Routledge & Kegan Paul, 1964.
(With Martin Rein) *Dilemmas of Social Reform: Poverty and Community Action in the United States,* Aldine, 1967, 2nd edition, University of Chicago Press, 1982.
(With Anthony Somerset) *African Entrepreneur: A Study of Entrepreneurship and Development in Kenya,* Africana, 1971 (published in England as *African Businessmen,* Routledge & Kegan Paul, 1971).
Loss and Change, Pantheon, 1974, revised edition, Routledge & Kegan Paul, 1986.
Community Planning and Conceptions of Change: Dilemmas of Inner City Planning, Routledge, Chapman & Hall, 1983, revised edition published as *Meaning and Action,* 1987.
The Dreams of General Jerusalem (novel), Bloomsbury, 1988.

Also contributor to a dozen books on applied sociology in the United States and Africa, including *Uprooting and Development,* edited by George Coehlo and Paul Ahmed, Plenum, 1980, and *The Place of Attachment in Human Behavior,* edited by Colin Murray Parks, Basic Books, 1982. Contributor of more than fifty articles to social science journals.

WORK IN PROGRESS: Research on social policy, especially "the management of uncertainty."

SIDELIGHTS: Peter Marris commented: "Throughout my career I have been concerned with how people respond to social changes, and my research has explored this at many levels—from the individual response to bereavement to the adjustment of an African society to colonization and economic development.

"In *Loss and Change* I tried to explain the common thread that I saw running through the many different experiences of change I had written about—the need to grieve for what we have lost, even in benign changes, and the way grieving enables us to recover the sense of life's meaning that loss has disrupted. Because loss is painful, we are impelled both to try to return, nostalgically, to the past before the loss occurred and to hurry on to a future where it no longer matters. I have tried to show how these contradictory impulses play themselves out, not only in the personal history of the bereaved, but in social organizations like the tribal associations of eastern Nigeria. Out of this ambivalent struggle, new meanings evolve that enable us to make sense of our lives again. In my most recent work, I have been trying to explore the question of how people construct and sustain the meaning of their lives more generally and how this may be relevant to the social policies of complex urban societies like contemporary America.

"I have always been very interested in the craft of making sociological insight accessible to the widest possible range of readers, without oversimplifying it. My book, *The Dreams of General Jerusalem,* extends this endeavor in a work of fiction." *Times Literary Supplement* reviewer Richard Gibson feels this "all-too-credible story of contemporary Africa" retains the flavor of the author's nonfiction prose, but finds the book "a solidly realistic work which should add to the understanding of Africa today." London *Times* critic Stuart Evans values the first novel because "it poses relevant questions" about human responses to wide-scale economic and social change.

BIOGRAPHICAL/CRITICAL SOURCES:

PERIODICALS

Times (London), March 17, 1988.
Times Literary Supplement, July 15, 1988.

* * *

MARSHALL, Herbert (Percival James) 1906-

PERSONAL: Born January 20, 1906, in London, England; son of Percival Charles and Anne (Organ) Marshall; married Fredda

Brilliant (a sculptress and actress), 1935. *Education:* Attended a London County Council school and Higher Institute of Cinematography in Moscow; All-Union State Institute of Cinematography, Moscow, diploma.

ADDRESSES: Home—1204 Chautauqua St., Carbondale, Ill. 62901. *Office*—Center for Soviet and East-European Studies in the Performing Arts, 809 South Forest, Southern Illinois University, Carbondale, Ill. 62901.

CAREER: Theatrical and film director, producer, and consultant on theater architecture. Empire Marketing Board Film Unit, London, England, began as editorial assistant, 1929-30; worked in Soviet Union as assistant director at Moscow Jewish Theater, Moscow Art Theater, and other theaters, 1931-35, and as drama director for Moscow Radio (English), 1933-35; Unity Theater, London, founder and director, 1935-39, principal of training school; Neighbourhood Theatre, South Kensington, London, founder and artistic director, 1939-40; named director of Old Vic, London, 1940, and toured England with the company after the London theater was bombed, 1940-41; advised the British Ministry of Information of Soviet Union films and dubbed films in Slavic languages, 1942-45; independent film producer in England, 1946-50; produced official Mahatma Gandhi documentary and other films for Indian Film Industry, 1951-55; Advision Ltd., London, executive producer for television, 1955-56; film producer and consultant on theater architecture for Government of India, and stage producer for Natya National Theater Company, 1957-60; theater architecture consultant in England and organizer of first all-British Negro theater group, 1962; Southern Illinois University, Carbondale, distinguished visiting professor and director of Center for Soviet and East-European Studies in the Performing Arts, 1967—. Lecturer at Royal Academy of Dramatic Art, 1940-41, American University at Biarritz, 1945-46, New York University, 1964, Royal College of Art, 1965, University of Illinois, 1968, and Oxford University, 1968. Consultant to various theater groups. Productions directed in England include "Plant in the Sun," with Paul Robeson, "The Beggars Opera" for Sadlers Wells Opera Company, "Man and Superman" for Festival of Britain, and "Thunder Rock," starring Michael Redgrave and Alex Guiness; productions in India include "Macbeth" in Marathi, "The Inspector General" in Hindi, and "Pygmalion," "Born Yesterday," and "The Diary of Anne Frank" in English.

MEMBER: Royal Society of Arts (fellow), Association of British Theatre Technicians, British Film Academy, British Actors Equity (member of executive committee), Establishment Club (London).

AWARDS, HONORS: Edinburgh Festival Award for "Tinker."

WRITINGS:

(With wife, Fredda Brilliant) "The Proud Valley" (screenplay), Ealing Studios, 1940.
(Editor with Ivor Montagu) *Soviet Heroes,* Pilot Press, 1942.
(Editor with Montagu) *Soviet Short Stories,* Pilot Press, 1942.
(Translator) E. Shvarts, *Growing Things,* Pilot Press, 1943.
(Editor and translator) *Mayakovsky and His Poetry,* Pilot Press, 1943, 4th edition, Dobson, 1965.
(Translator) S. Marshak, *Play,* Pilot Press, 1943.
(Editor and translator with others) *Soviet One Act Plays,* Pilot Press, 1944.
(Editor with Montagu, and author of foreword) *Soviet Short Stories, 1942-43,* Pilot Press, 1944.
(Editor) Jack Chen, *Soviet Art and Artists,* Pilot Press, c. 1944.
(Editor with Montagu) Igor Boelza, *Handbook of Soviet Musicians,* Pilot Press, c. 1944.
(With Ra Mander and Joe Mitchenson) *Hamlet through the Ages,* Rockliff, 1953.
(With Mildred Stock) *Ira Aldridge: The Negro Tragedian,* Macmillan, 1953, reprinted, Southern Illinois University Press, 1968.
(Translator with Montagu) Sergei Prokofiev and Sergei M. Eisenstein, *Ivan the Terrible* (oratorio), Simon & Schuster, 1961.
(Co-author) "The Bare Evidence" (screenplay), Amber Films, 1962.
(Translator) *Kobzar* (collected poems of Taras Shevchenko), UNESCO World Celebrations, 1964.
(Editor and translator) *Selected Poems of Yevtushenko,* Dutton, 1966.
(Editor and translator) *Voznesensky: Selected Poems,* Hill & Wang, 1966.
(Editor and author of introduction) *Battleship Potemkin: Best Film of All Time,* Avon, 1976.
(Editor) *Pictorial History of Russian Theatre,* Crown, 1976.
(Translator) Eisenstein, *An Autobiography of Sergei Eisenstein,* Volume 1: *Immoral Memories,* Houghton, 1983.
Masters of Soviet Cinema: Crippled Creative Biographies, Routledge & Kegan Paul, 1983.
(Translator) Eisenstein, *Nonindifferent Nature,* Cambridge University Press, 1987.

Also author of comedy screenplays "Method and Madness with Mr. Pastry," c. 1947, and (with Terry Thomas) "What's Cooking?," c. 1947; author of screenplay (with wife, Fredda Brilliant), producer, and director for "Tinker," c. 1948; author of screenplay "The Fabulous Ira Aldridge" (based on *Ira Aldridge: The Negro Tragedian*), 1961, and (with Matthew Finch) "The Naked Island," 1961. Author of *The Stanislavsky Method of Direction,* 1969, and *An Anthology of Soviet Poetry,* 1970; author of lyrics and songs for G. Sviridov's "Oratorio Pathetique"; lyrics for Dmitry Shostakovich's "13th Symphony," "14th Symphony," and "Execution of Stepan Razin"; lyrics of "Sergei Yessenin"; and of other lyrics. Editor, "International Library of Cinema and Theatre," Dobson, 1946-56.

WORK IN PROGRESS: Anthology of Russian and Other Poems; editing and translating *Eisenstein, S. M.: Collected Works,* six volumes; translating *Requiem,* poems by Anna Akhmatova Mikhoels, for the Moscow State Yiddish Theatre.*

* * *

MASTNY, Vojtech 1936-

PERSONAL: Given name is pronounced "Voytekh"; born February 26, 1936, in Prague, Czechoslovakia; son of Antonin and Jindriska (Rybakova) Mastny; married Catherine Louise Kacmarynski, July 25, 1964 (divorced, 1987); children: John Adalbert, Elizabeth Louise. *Education:* Charles University of Prague, Promovany Historik, 1962; Columbia University, Ph.D., 1968. *Politics:* Democrat. *Religion:* Roman Catholic.

ADDRESSES: Home—23 Fifer Lane, Lexington, Mass. 02173. *Office*—Center for International Relations, Boston University, 152 Bay State Rd., Boston, Mass. 02215.

CAREER: California State College (now University), Long Beach, assistant professor of history, 1967-68; Columbia University, New York, N.Y., assistant professor of history, 1968-74, acting director, Institute on East Central Europe, 1970-71; University of Illinois at Urbana-Champaign, 1974-80, began as associate professor, became professor of history; European University Institute, Florence, Italy, guest professor, 1980; distinguished visiting professor of strategy, United States Naval War College, 1982-83; Boston University, Boston, Mass., professor of international relations, 1983—. Visiting professor of Soviet studies, Johns Hopkins University, 1977-88; fellow at Harvard University, 1983; Fulbright senior professor, University of Bonn, West Germany, 1989-90. Lecturer in Europe and the Middle East. Fellow of Netherlands Institute for Advanced Study, 1988-89; international fellow of Federal Institute of Soviet, East European, and International Studies, Cologne, West Germany, 1988-90.

MEMBER: American Association for the Advancement of Slavic Studies, American Committee on the History of the Second World War, Council of European Studies, National Committee on American Foreign Policy, Deutscher Alpenverein.

AWARDS, HONORS: Clarke F. Ansley Award, 1968, for *The Czechs under Nazi Rule;* Alexander von Humboldt faculty fellow, 1972; Lehrman Institute research fellow, 1974-75; Guggenheim fellow and fellow of the Institute for the Study of World Politics, 1977-78; American Council of Learned Societies East European research fellow, 1978-79; Austrian government research grant, 1981; German Academic Exchange Service grant, 1983.

WRITINGS:

(Editor) *Disarmament and Nuclear Tests, 1964-69,* Facts on File, 1970.
The Czechs under Nazi Rule: The Failure of National Resistance, 1939-1942, Columbia University Press, 1971.
(Editor) *Czechoslovakia: Crisis in World Communism,* Facts on File, 1972.
(Editor) *East European Dissent,* Facts on File, Volume I: *1953-1964,* 1972, Volume II: *1965-1970,* 1972.
Russia's Road to the Cold War: Diplomacy, Warfare, and Communism, 1941-1945, Columbia University Press, 1979.
(Editor) *Soviet/East European Survey: Selected Research and Analysis from Radio Free Europe Radio Liberty,* Duke University Press, Volume 1: *1983-84,* 1985, Volume 2: *1984-85,* 1986, Volume 3: *1985-86,* 1987, Volume 3: *1986-87,* 1987, Volume 4: *1987-88,* 1988.
Helsinki, Human Rights, and European Security, 1975-1985, Duke University Press, 1986.

Contributor to *Foreign Affairs, American Historical Review, Journal of Modern History, Problems of Communism, New Leader, Naval War College Review,* and other journals. Book review editor, *Slavic Review,* 1976-77.

WORK IN PROGRESS: The Cold War and Soviet Insecurity: The Last Stalin Years, 1947-53.

SIDELIGHTS: Vojtech Mastny has traveled extensively in Europe. He can speak or read German, French, Russian, Polish, Spanish, and Italian, as well as Czech and English.

AVOCATIONAL INTERESTS: Mountain hiking, cross-country skiing.

* * *

McCLURE, Charles R(obert) 1949-

PERSONAL: Born May 24, 1949, in Syracuse, N.Y.; son of Robert C. and Doris C. (Gordon) McClure; married Victoria Anne (a librarian), 1970; children: Gwendolyn Anne. *Education:* Oklahoma State University, B.A., 1970, M.A., 1971; University of Oklahoma, M.L.S., 1972; Rutgers University, Ph.D., 1977.

ADDRESSES: Home—Manlius, N.Y. *Office*—School of Information Studies, Syracuse University, Syracuse, N.Y. 13244.

CAREER: Oklahoma State University, Stillwater, stack supervisor at university library, 1969-71; University of Oklahoma, Norman, archival assistant in Western History Collection, 1972; University of Texas, El Paso, head of library's history and government department, 1972-74; Rutgers University, New Brunswick, N.J., director of audiovisual laboratory of Graduate School of Library Service, 1974-75, instructor in library service, 1976-77; University of Oklahoma, assistant professor, 1977-81, associate professor, 1981-83, professor of library science, 1983-86; Syracuse University, Syracuse, N.Y., professor of information studies, 1986—. President of Information/Management Consultant Services, Inc., 1978—; consultant to government agencies and to businesses, including National Technical Information Service, Government Printing Office, U.S. International Communication Agency, Benham Blair & Affiliates, and GHK Corporation.

MEMBER: American Library Association, American Society for Information Science, Association of Library Science Information Educators, Association of College and Research Libraries, Library Administration and Management Association, New York Library Association, Beta Phi Mu.

AWARDS, HONORS: Award from American Library Association, 1979, for paper "Evaluation of Information Sources for Library Decision Making"; best research paper of the year, 1985; Best Book of the Year Award in information science from American Society for Information Science, 1988.

WRITINGS:

Information for Academic Library Decision Making: The Case for Organizational Information Management, Greenwood Press, 1980.
(Editor) *Planning for Library Services: A Guide to Utilizing Planning Methods for Library Management,* Haworth Press, 1982.
(Editor with Alan Samuels) *Approaches to Library Administration: Strategies and Concepts,* Libraries Unlimited, 1982.
(With Peter Hernon) *Improving the Quality of Reference Services for Government Publications,* American Library Association, 1983.
Public Access to Government Information, Ablex Publishing, 1984, 2nd edition, 1988.
Action Research for Library Decision Making, American Library Association, 1984.
State Library Services and Issues, Ablex Publishing, 1986.
Unobtrusive Testing of Library Reference Service, Ablex Publishing, 1987.
Planning and Role Setting for Public Libraries, American Library Association, 1987.
Output Measures for Public Libraries, American Library Association, 1987.
Federal Information Policies in the 1980s, Ablex Publishing, 1987.
U.S. Government Information Policies: Views and Perspectives, Ablex Publishing, 1989.
U.S. Scientific and Technical Information Policies: Views and Perspectives, Ablex Publishing, 1989.

Also co-editor of book series "Information Management, Policy, and Services," Ablex Publishing, 1987—. Author or co-author of more than ninety articles and reports on such topics as librarianship, information science, management, and information policy. Co-editor and founder of *Government Information Quarterly,* 1984—.

SIDELIGHTS: Charles R. McClure wrote to *CA:* "The emphasis of my writings is on 1.) increasing the effectiveness with which libraries and other information centers can respond to and resolve the information needs of their clientele, and 2.) increasing the public's access to and use of U.S. government information. As we all struggle to cope with the various impacts of living in the 'information age,' concern for the individual's ability to exploit and access information is essential. Assisting in that process of making necessary information accessible to individuals, managing information resources, and controlling technology to serve *our* needs are themes that I try to stress [with] my publishing activities."

* * *

McCRANK, Lawrence J(oseph) 1945-

PERSONAL: Born April 14, 1945, in Fargo, N.D.; son of James F. and Florence E. (Kloeckner) McCrank; married Ruth Diane Madson, December 23, 1967; children: Kirstin Lea, Jaime Lynn. *Education:* Moorhead State University, B.A. (magna cum laude), 1967; University of Kansas, M.A. (with honors), 1970; University of Virginia, Ph.D., 1974; University of Oregon, M.L.S., 1976.

ADDRESSES: Home—6606 Bella Vista Dr., Rockford, Mich. 49341. *Office*—Library and Instructional Services Administration, Ferris State University, Big Rapids, Mich. 49307.

CAREER: University of Virginia, Charlottesville, instructor in adult education and history, 1971-72, serials acquisitions librarian at Alderman Library, 1972; Whitman College, Walla Walla, Wash., instructor in European history, 1972-73; H.G.E., Inc. (planners and engineers), Portland, Ore., technical writer, 1974; Professional Translators, Inc., Portland, free-lance translator, 1975; Mt. Angel Abbey Library, St. Benedict, Ore., project director, rare books and manuscripts catalog and centennial history, 1975-76; University of Oregon, Eugene, instructor, department of history, 1976; University of Maryland, College Park, assistant professor and advanced studies program director, 1976-82; Indiana State University, Terre Haute, senior librarian and head of department of rare books and special collections of Cunningham Memorial Library, 1982-84; Auburn University at Montgomery, Alabama, librarian and dean, 1984-88; Ferris State University, Big Rapids, Mich., dean of library and instructional services, 1988—.

Secondary social studies teacher at military academy in Fork Union, Va., 1972; scholar-in-residence at Trappist Abbey of Our Lady of Guadalupe, 1974; visiting lecturer, University of Oregon, 1975, University of California, Berkeley, 1976; visiting professor, Indiana University, 1983—, University of Alabama, Tuscaloosa, 1984; faculty member, Information Institute, International Academy, Santa Barbara, Calif., 1987—. Instructor and director of conservation and collection management workshop with Library of Congress, at University of Maryland, 1980-81; workshop instructor at Biblioteca Nacional, Madrid, Spain, 1980. Abstractor for American Bibliographical Center/Clio Press, 1971-82. Guest on radio and educational television programs.

MEMBER: Art Libraries of North America, Society of American Archivists, American Library Association, American Association for State and Local History, American Historical Association, Association for the Bibliography of History (vice president and president, 1987-89), American Academy of Research Historians of Medieval Spain, Association of College and Research Libraries, Society of Spanish and Portuguese Historians, Smithsonian Institution Associates, Mid-Atlantic Archives Conference, Midwest Archives Conference, Mid-Atlantic Regional Libraries Federation, Indiana Society of Archivists, Maryland Library Association, Washington Conservation Guild, Washington Bibliophiles, Maryland Historical Society, Friends of the Cunningham Memorial Library (executive office, 1982-84), Alabama Library Association, Michigan Library Association.

AWARDS, HONORS: Fullbright scholar to Spain, 1971-72; grants from Collins Foundation, 1975-76, Maryland State Department of Education, 1978, American Philosophical Society, 1979-80, Mount Angel Abbey, 1979-81, Art Libraries of North America, 1980, American Society for Information Science, 1980, and Hill Monastic Microfilm Library, 1981; essay award from American Library Association, 1977, for "How a Levy Was Won in the West"; certificate of merit from Maryland Association for Higher Education, 1981; Dupont research grant.

WRITINGS:

(Contributor) John Sommerfeldt, editor, *Studies in Medieval Cistercian History,* Cistercian Publications, 1976.

(Contributor) Hendrick Vervliet, editor, *International Bibliography of the History of the Printed Book and Libraries,* International Federation of Library Associations, 1976-83.

(Contributor) Virginia Jackson, editor, *Museums of the World,* Greenwood Press, 1984-87.

Ladders across Cultures: Instructional Media in the Catholic Mission to the Oregon Frontier, 1835-1885, University Press of America, 1988.

(Contributor) Donald Pitzer, editor, *American Communal Utopias: The Developmental Process,* University of Wisconsin Press, 1988.

Indexing and Thesaurus Control for Archival Information Systems, Society of American Archivists, 1989.

MONOGRAPHS

An Introduction to Basic Information Sources in American History, edited by Paul Wasserman, Library Training Consultants, 1978.

An Introduction to Basic Information Sources in the Humanities, edited by Wasserman, Library Training Consultants, 1978.

Education for Rare Book Librarianship: A Re-Examination of Trends and Problems, edited by R. Stevens, University of Illinois, 1980.

(Editor and contributor) *Automating the Archives: Current Trends and Future Problems,* Knowledge Industry Publications, 1981.

Mt. Angel Abbey: A Centennial History of a Benedictine Community and Its Library, 1882-1982, Scholarly Resources, 1983.

The Rare Book and Manuscript Collections of Mt. Angel Abbey Library: A Catalogue and Index (fiche), Scholarly Resources, 1983.

(Editor and contributor) *Archives and Library Administration: Divergent Traditions and Common Concerns,* Haworth Press, 1986.

(With Jean Caswell) *The Monastic Imprint, 480-1980: A Visual Arts Celebration of the 1500th Birthday of St. Benedict,* St. Anselm's Abbey Press, 1986.

An Introduction to Literature and Research in the Arts and Humanities: A Self-Instruction Text, privately printed, 1986.

OTHER

Contributor to *Historical Periodicals Directory,* 1981-82, *Dictionary of the Middle Ages,* 1986, and *Terminology and Knowledge Engineering,* 1987. Contributor to numerous proceedings of conferences and of more than fifty articles and reviews to scholarly journals. Series editor, *Oryx Sourcebooks,* thirty volumes, Oryx Press, 1987—; editor, *The Primary Source,* 1989—; contributing editor of *Annual Bibliography of the History of Printed Books and Libraries;* member of editorial board of *Computers and Humanities,* and *Encyclopedia of Library History,* 1988.

WORK IN PROGRESS: Reconquest and Restoration in Medieval Catalonia: The Frontier Church and Principality of Tarragona, 971-1177; El Viejo, a novel about Count Ramon Berenguer I of Barcelona; *The Curatorship of Historical Collections; Introduction of Codicology and Analytical Bibliography; The White Monks of Poblet: A Study in Medieval Frontier Monasticism, 1150-1276; The Cistercians in the Crown of Aragon, 1150-1276; Medieval History: A Bibliographic Guide.*

SIDELIGHTS: Lawrence J. McCrank told *CA:* "I work in two distinct fields, history (medieval, early modern European, American western, and frontier studies) and library/archival and information science. I was attracted to the latter by historical bibliography and training in paleography, diplomatics, bibliography and the like as a medievalist, but expanded this to include computer assisted work in bibliographic control or cultural resource management for rare books, archives, historical records, and documentation. I am particularly interested in the interplay between archives, rare book repositories, and museums and the problems of information services in the arts and humanities, especially historical studies, and the whole spectrum of conservation/preservation work.

"My medieval and early modern history interests relate to church history, especially reformed monasticism, and the reconquest of former Christian territory from the Muslims. This concentration on frontier and Iberian studies led to similar interests in the American frontier, western history influenced by Iberian expansion and/or monastic and ecclesiastical institutions.

"A blend of this interest in history and library science is seen in my work with rare book cataloging, library history, and historical bibliography (i.e., history of books, manuscript and printed), which is compatible with my strong leaning toward interdisciplinarity. These interests are tied together by a focus on monastic and ecclesiastical institutions, communications and cultural assimilation, and the spread of Western civilization into non-Western areas. My topics are chosen to reflect these concerns, often for subjects and periods not well known but which deserve to be elucidated because of their intrinsic importance to a larger area of history. Other activities reflect my concern for the information systems which support historical inquiry and preserve important documentation."

* * *

McDOWELL, Michael 1950-
(Nathan Aldyne, Axel Young, joint pseudonyms)

PERSONAL: Born June 1, 1950, in Enterprise, Ala.; son of Thomas Eugene (an accountant) and Marian (a social worker; maiden name, Mulkey) McDowell. *Education:* Harvard University, B.A. (magna cum laude), 1972; Brandeis University, Ph.D., 1978.

ADDRESSES: Home—117 Mystic St., Medford, Mass. 02155. *Agent*—Jane Otte, Otte Co., 9 Goden St., Belmont, Mass. 02178.

CAREER: Writer, 1978—.

WRITINGS:

The Amulet (novel), Avon, 1979.
Cold Moon Over Babylon (novel), Avon, 1980.
Gilded Needles (novel), Avon, 1980.
(With Dennis Schuetz, under joint pseudonym Nathan Aldyne) *Vermilion* (novel), Avon, 1980.
The Elementals (novel), Avon, 1981.
(With Schuetz, under joint pseudonym Nathan Aldyne) *Cobalt* (novel), St. Martin's, 1982.
(With Schuetz, under joint pseudonym Axel Young) *Blood Rubies* (novel), Avon, 1982.
Katie (novel), Avon, 1982.
The Flood (also see below), Avon, 1983.
The Levee (also see below), Avon, 1983.
The House (also see below), Avon, 1983.
The War (also see below), Avon, 1983.
The Fortune (also see below), Avon, 1983.
Rain (also see below), Avon, 1983.
Blackwater (serial novel; contains *The Flood, The Levee, The House, The War, The Fortune,* and *Rain*), Avon, 1983.
(With Schuetz, under joint pseudonym Axel Young) *Wicked Stepmother* (novel), Avon, 1983.
(With Schuetz, under joint pseudonym Nathan Aldyne) *Slate* (novel), Villard, 1984.
Toplin (novel), Scream Press, 1985.
Jack and Susan in 1953 (novel), Ballantine, 1985.
Jack and Susan in 1913 (novel), Ballantine, 1986.
Jack and Susan in 1933 (novel), Ballantine, 1987.
(With Warren Skaaren) "Beetlejuice" (screenplay; based on a story by McDowell and Larry Wilson), Warner Bros., 1988.

SIDELIGHTS: Michael McDowell once told *CA:* "I began writing fiction when I was an undergraduate at Harvard, and had completed six novels before I sold the seventh, *The Amulet,* to Avon, in 1977. The first six had been written more or less to my own taste; *The Amulet,* however, was written specifically with the hope of interesting a publisher. I was gratified that it did, and soon came to see that this commercial property was probably the best written of all my work, if only because the constrictions of writing within a specific form, in this case, the occult novel, had sharpened my literary wits. Now, I am happiest working within a specific genre: detective, occult, historical-adventure, because the constraints discourage my tendencies towards self-indulgence."

BIOGRAPHICAL/CRITICAL SOURCES:

PERIODICALS

Ms., June, 1986.
New York Times Book Review, March 23, 1980, July 22, 1984.
Washington Post Book World, March 16, 1980, July 10, 1983.

* * *

McGAHERN, John 1934-

PERSONAL: Born 1934, in Dublin, Ireland; son of John (a police officer) and Susan (McManus) McGahern. *Education:* Attended Presentation College, Carrick-on-Shannon, Ireland, and University College, Dublin.

ADDRESSES: c/o Viking Press, Inc., 40 West 23rd St., New York, N.Y. 10010.

CAREER: Writer, 1963—. Teacher at St. John the Baptist Boys National School, 1956-63; O'Connor Professor of Literature,

Colgate University, 1969, 1972; British Northern Arts Fellow at University of Newcastle and University of Durham, 1974-76. Visiting professor at numerous colleges in England and Ireland.

AWARDS, HONORS: A. E. Memorial Award, 1962, and Macauley fellowship, 1964, both for *The Barracks;* Society of Authors award, 1967; British Arts Council awards, 1968, 1970, 1973.

WRITINGS:

NOVELS

The Barracks, Faber, 1963, Macmillan, 1964.
The Dark, Faber, 1965, Knopf, 1966.
The Leavetaking, Faber, 1974, Little, Brown, 1975.
The Pornographer, Faber, 1979, Harper, 1980.

SHORT STORIES

Nightlines, Faber, 1970, Atlantic, 1971.
Getting Through, Faber, 1978, Harper, 1980.
High Ground, Faber, 1985, Viking, 1987.

OTHER

Also author of radio play, "Sinclair," 1971, and television play, "Swallows," 1975.

SIDELIGHTS: John McGahern is a contemporary Irish fiction writer whose works explore the vagaries of life in his native land. *Saturday Review* contributor Robert Emmet Long includes McGahern among Ireland's finest living writers, calling him "surefooted, elegiac, graceful when he moves in the confines of the land of his birth, his people speaking in accents of truth as they do." Long also describes McGahern as "an original voice, a writer who works without tricks within carefully controlled limits. . . . In . . . all of his best work, he examines the epiphanies in ordinary Irish lives." McGahern has been praised for his style, which some have compared to that of James Joyce, as well as for his controversial themes. Regardless of his topic, writes Patricia Craig in the *Times Literary Supplement,* McGahern "always writes well about the state of being Irish, its special deprivations and depravities." *Washington Post* correspondent John Breslin likewise concludes that McGahern "poignantly details the abrasions we inflict as well as the brief glimpses of delight we afford one another." According to Julian Moynahan in the *New York Times Book Review,* McGahern is quite simply "the most accomplished novelist of his generation."

The Ireland of McGahern's fiction is often dark and dour, a prison for the soul. His stories reveal the lives of the suffering poor, "human nature at its bitterest," to quote Long. *New York Times Book Review* contributor Joel Conarroe finds McGahern's characters "paralyzed by convention and habit, . . . unable to escape their parochial fates; their powerlessness suggests a central motif in James Joyce." Tom Pavlin elaborates in *Encounter:* "Running through McGahern's work is a fusion of sex, death and hopelessness. They are the presiding trinity of his imagination and are revealed in a series of epiphanies." Indeed, McGahern's work deals forthrightly with several taboo aspects of Irish social life—the Catholic church and its repressive tactics, sexuality, and family turmoil, Shaun O'Connell explains in the *Massachusetts Review.* "To stay within the circle of acceptability is, spiritually and sexually, to starve, but to range outside the province of the predictable in Ireland, particularly for sexual purposes, is to bring about retribution," writes O'Connell. ". . . Repression is the means by which community is sustained." An important theme in McGahern is how his characters overcome this community repression, or conversely, how they are destroyed by it.

In *The Irish Short Story,* Terence Brown notes that McGahern, "while confident and skilled in portraying the provincial world he knows, recognises a need for modern Irish fiction to meet more stringent demands. It must be attentive to the recent major social changes in the country, in an art that more appropriately reflects the complex psychological currents that stir in its turbulent waters. So McGahern is consciously experimental in his work, welcoming the resonance of image and symbol to the enclosed worlds of rural and small-town Ireland, taking his protagonists away from their childhood farms and fields to the confused cultural settings of modern Dublin and London." Much of McGahern's work rests on the strength of his style, a feeling for "things like the everyday ecstasies" to quote Craig. *Newsweek* columnist Peter S. Prescott observes that McGahern "means us to read slowly, to hear the sounds, feel the weight of his words." *Encounter* essayist Jonathan Raban compares McGahern to that other experimental and widely-travelled Irish writer, James Joyce. "McGahern's and Joyce's prose styles bleed imperceptibly into one another like the voices of kissing-cousins," writes Raban. ". . . At his best, McGahern writes so beautifully that he leaves one in no doubt of his equality with Joyce: the similarities between the two writers spring from a sense of tradition which is thoroughly and profoundly shared. And that is something which one is so unused to encountering in 20th-century literature that it is tempting to mistake what is really a glory for a shabby vice."

McGahern was a teacher at the St. John the Baptist Boys National school in Clontarf when his first novel, *The Barracks,* was published in 1963. The novel set the tone for the author's early fiction; it details the last months in the life of Elizabeth Reegan, a rural Irish housewife afflicted with terminal cancer. *Studies* essayist John Cronin writes of Elizabeth: "Life has set her on a collision course and McGahern enters her experience at a point where his philosophy gives him complete and convincing command of her destiny and her doom." Moynahan finds the book memorable "for its dark portrayal of vindictiveness in the hateful feuding of a policeman with his superior, for the unusual sensitivity and fullness with which a stepmother's domestic unhappiness and grave illness were rendered, and for its hell of tedium and of self- and mutual thwarting." In the *Dictionary of Literary Biography,* Patricia Boyle Haberstroh contends that the juxtaposition of life and death, "the need to find a way of getting through the mysterious cycle from birth to death, and the acceptance of life as a series of small deaths leading to the final mystery recur. The death that overshadows every life pervades McGahern's fiction." *The Barracks* won two of Ireland's most prestigious literary awards, the A. E. Memorial Award and the Macauley fellowship. McGahern was thereby enabled to take a leave of absence from his teaching post in order to write full time.

Public acclaim for McGahern's next novel, *The Dark,* came almost entirely from outside Ireland. The controversial book was banned by the Irish Censorship Board, and it ultimately cost McGahern his teaching job as well. A portrait of a confused Catholic adolescent and his abusive father, *The Dark* takes "a sombre, sufferingly malicious view of contemporary Ireland, [dwelling] with fond revulsion on the strange, brutal paradoxes that feed on and are fed by the 'Irish imagination,' " according to a reviewer for the *Times Literary Supplement.* The novel focuses on the young boy's dawning sexuality and his conflicting desire to become a priest. "We think at times we are reading a story of studious success or failure about which the author is excited," writes the *Times Literary Supplement* reviewer. "We discover we are reading grim and terrible farce. The writer who is capable of such a double take deserves esteem." McGahern's well-publicized battles with the Censorship Board and with the Catholic school hierarchy over *The Dark* made him anxious to leave Ireland. For several years he travelled through England and Europe, teaching at universities, lecturing, and writing.

Censorship and marriage outside the church, both experienced by McGahern, form the foundation of his novel *The Leavetaking,* published in London in 1974. In that work, the protagonist comes to know himself through his loss of his teaching job at a Catholic school and his marriage to an American woman. O'Connell suggests that in the novel, and his other recent works, McGahern "leads some of his characters through a door into the light, into a problematic freedom, out to an open field in which they first run free, but from which they eventually seek release, so some return to the familiar confines." McGahern's hero in *The Leavetaking* escapes; his central character in the 1979 book *The Pornographer* chooses to stay after examining his tawdry life and casual sexual encounters. In either case, notes Craig, "the gloom which permeated John McGahern's earlier novels is beginning to lift. It has been transformed into a reasonable despondency and flatness, tempered with irony—no longer a terrible Irish seediness and vacancy of spirit."

McGahern has also published several volumes of short stories. These, like his novels, "deal in love, frustrated or misplaced, and in intimations of mortality," to quote Michael Irwin in the *Times Literary Supplement.* Most of the fiction is set in Ireland, but *New York Times Book Review* contributor David Pryce-Jones finds it "free from the emerald sentiments that have been invested in [McGahern's] native land. He is his own master, and his stories owe nothing to anybody." Irwin feels that each tale "has resonance: some slight incident is made to disclose a mode of living and an attitude to experience." In the *London Review of Books,* Pat Rogers maintains that the author's short works "are unmistakably conservative: their freshness proceeds from close observation, a deep inwardness with the milieu, and a willingness to let events and description do their work unmolested by the urge to be wise about human affairs." Haberstroh concludes that an Irish sensibility informs McGahern's stories, "and the public and fictional history he creates from his personal life testifies to the degree to which art and life intertwine."

McGahern told the *New York Times Book Review:* "In my upbringing, there were very few books, and one would never have met a writer. But there was the pleasure of playing with words, and then you found that, almost without knowing it, you wanted to do this more than anything else." McGahern is widely praised for his prose fiction, and for refusing "the poet laureateship offered by the *status quo,*" according to Anthony C. West in *The Nation.* O'Connell claims that McGahern's "revised version of the Irish pastoral is edged in irony, weighted by expectation and sustained by compelling fictional energies." Raban feels that the author "has a genius—and that word does not overstate what he does—for mediating between the deep currents of feeling which belong to myth and history and the exact texture of the moment, seen so freshly that it comes off the page in a vivid cluster of sensations." Irwin observes that McGahern "writes with unobtrusive concision. So much of his skill lies in selection, or rather in omission, that his terse narrative seems free and full. He has the Irish gift of being able to move fluently and unselfconsciously between a simple and a heightened style. . . . Pace and proportion seem effortlessly adjusted: there is no sense of expository strain." Perhaps the most compelling praise for McGahern's work comes from fellow writer John Updike. In *Hugging the Shore: Essays and Criticism,* Updike concludes that the artist "writes well, and for the usual reasons: he observes well, hears faithfully, and feels keenly."

BIOGRAPHICAL/CRITICAL SOURCES:

BOOKS

Contemporary Literary Criticism, Gale, Volume 5, 1976, Volume 9, 1978, Volume 48, 1988.
Dictionary of Literary Biography, Volume 14: *British Novelists since World War II,* Gale, 1982.
Dunn, Douglas, editor, *Two Decades of Irish Writing,* Carcanet Press, 1975.
Rafroidi, Patrick and Terence Brown, editors, *The Irish Short Story,* Colin Smythe, 1979.
Updike, John, *Hugging the Shore: Essays and Criticism,* Knopf, 1983.

PERIODICALS

Catholic World, January, 1968.
Censorship, spring, 1966.
Chicago Tribune, April 27, 1987.
Critique: Studies in Modern Fiction, Volume XIX, number 1, 1977, Volume XXI, number 1, 1979.
Detroit News, August 3, 1980.
Encounter, June, 1975, June, 1978.
Globe and Mail (Toronto), August 18, 1984.
London Review of Books, October 3, 1985.
Los Angeles Times, February 18, 1987.
Massachusetts Review, summer, 1984.
Nation, November 7, 1966.
New Leader, March 31, 1975.
New Republic, December 15, 1979.
Newsweek, February 17, 1975, November 5, 1979.
New Yorker, December 24, 1979.
New York Review of Books, May 1, 1980.
New York Times, July 12, 1980.
New York Times Book Review, March 6, 1966, February 7, 1971, February 2, 1975, December 2, 1979, July 13, 1980, February 8, 1987.
Saturday Review, May 1, 1971.
Spectator, January 11, 1975, June 17, 1978.
Studies, winter, 1969.
Times Literary Supplement, May 13, 1965, November 27, 1970, January 10, 1975, June 16, 1978, January 11, 1980, September 13, 1985.
Washington Post, March 23, 1987.
Washington Post Book World, December 23, 1979.*

—*Sketch by Anne Janette Johnson*

* * *

McNEISH, James 1931-

PERSONAL: Born October 23, 1931, in Auckland, New Zealand; son of Arthur William (an Army officer) and Geraldine (a violinist; maiden name, Bosworth) McNeish; married Felicity Wily, July 16, 1960 (divorced, August 31, 1964); married Helen Schnitzer (a photographer and author), December 27, 1968; children: (first marriage) Kathryn Ann. *Education:* University of Auckland, B.A., 1952.

ADDRESSES: Home—New Zealand. *Agent*—Vivienne Schuster, John Farquharson Ltd., 162 Regent St., London W1R 5TB, England.

CAREER: Writer. *New Zealand Herald,* Auckland, New Zealand, journalist and arts editor, 1950-58; teacher in London, England, 1960-62; free-lance radio broadcaster and radio documentary producer, 1962—. Founder and director, with wife Helen, of Bridge in New Zealand (private educational travel trust), 1974-82. *Military service:* Territorial Service Army of New Zealand.

MEMBER: PEN International.

AWARDS, HONORS: Katherine Mansfield fellowship, 1973; New Zealand Government scholarship, 1979; Berlin Kuenstler program fellowship, 1983.

WRITINGS:

Fire under the Ashes (biography of Danilo Dolci), Hodder & Stoughton, 1965, Beacon Press, 1966.
Mackenzie (novel), Hodder & Stoughton, 1970.
The Mackenzie Affair (novel), Hodder & Stoughton, 1972.
(With Marti Friedlander) *Larks in a Paradise,* Collins, 1974.
The Glass Zoo (novel), St. Martin's, 1976.
As for the Godwits (autobiographical diary), Hodder & Stoughton, 1977.
(With Brian Brake) *Art of the Pacific,* Oxford University Press, 1979.
Belonging: Conversations in Israel, Holt, 1980.
Joy (novel), Hodder & Stoughton, 1982.
(With wife, Helen McNeish) *Walking on My Feet* (biography), Collins & World, 1983.
Ahnungslos in Berlin (diary), Literarisches Colloquium (Berlin), 1986.
Lovelock (novel), Hodder & Stoughton, 1986.
(Contributor) Michael King, editor, *Salute to New Zealand,* Lansdowne Press, 1990.

Author of plays "1895," "The Rocking Cave," and "The Mouse Man," produced in Auckland, New Zealand, at Mercury Theatre, 1973-76. Also author of penal report to New Zealand Minister of Justice, 1974.

WORK IN PROGRESS: Penelope's Island, a novel set in the French Pacific colony of New Caledonia; a volume of selected prose writings.

SIDELIGHTS: James McNeish told *CA:* "New Zealanders live on the edge of the world looking out. If they go away and stay too long, they usually suffer an identity crisis. If they become celebrities, the crisis is that much worse. Few come through unscathed, and some not at all."

BIOGRAPHICAL/CRITICAL SOURCES:

BOOKS

McNeish, James, *As for the Godwits* (autobiographical diary), Hodder & Stoughton, 1977.

PERIODICALS

Time, April 8, 1966.
Times Literary Supplement, August 12, 1983.

* * *

MEINKE, Peter 1932-

PERSONAL: Surname is pronounced *Mine*-key; born December 29, 1932, in Brooklyn, N.Y.; son of Harry Frederick (a salesman) and Kathleen (McDonald) Meinke; married Jeanne Clark (an artist), December 14, 1957; children: Peri, Peter, Gretchen, Timothy. *Education:* Hamilton College, A.B., 1955; University of Michigan, M.A., 1961; University of Minnesota, Ph.D., 1965.

ADDRESSES: Home—147 Wildwood Lane S.E., St. Petersburg, Fla. 33705. *Office*—Writing Workshop, Eckerd College, St. Petersburg, Fla. 33733.

CAREER: High school English teacher in Mountain Lakes, N.J., 1958-60; Hamline University, St. Paul, Minn., instructor, 1961-65, assistant professor of English, 1965-66, poet in residence, 1973; Eckerd College, St. Petersburg, Fla., assistant professor, 1966-68, associate professor, 1968-72, professor of English literature and director of writing workshop, 1972—. Visiting professor and lecturer at numerous colleges and universities, including term as McGee Writer in Residence at Davidson College, 1989. Director of Mid-Florida Colleges in Neuchatel, Switzerland, and of Emory University Writing Institute, summer, 1982. *Military service:* U.S. Army, 1955-57.

MEMBER: American Association of University Professors.

AWARDS, HONORS: First prize, Olivet National Sonnet Competition, 1965; Gustav Davidson Memorial Award, Poetry Society of America, 1976; First prize in poetry, *Writer's Digest* competition, 1976; Emily Clark Balch Prize for short fiction, *Virginia Quarterly,* 1982; O. Henry Award for short fiction, 1983, for "The Ponoes," and 1986, for "Uncle George and Uncle Stefan"; Flannery O'Connor Award for short fiction, 1986, for *The Piano Tuner.* Also recipient of numerous grants and fellowships, including National Endowment for the Arts fellowships, 1974, 1989.

WRITINGS:

Howard Nemerov, University of Minnesota Press, 1968.
The Legend of Larry the Lizard (children's verse), illustrations by wife, Jeanne Meinke, John Knox, 1968.
Very Seldom Animals (children's verse), Possum Press, 1969.
Lines from Neuchatel (poetry), illustrations by J. Meinke, Konglomerati Press, 1974.
The Night Train and the Golden Bird (poetry), University of Pittsburgh Press, 1977.
The Rat Poems, illustrations by J. Meinke, Bits Press, 1978.
Trying to Surprise God (poetry), University of Pittsburgh Press, 1981.
The Piano Tuner (short stories), University of Georgia Press, 1986.
Night Watch on the Chesapeake (poetry), University of Pittsburgh Press, 1986.
Underneath the Lantern (poetry), illustrations by J. Meinke, Heatherstone Press, 1986.
Far from Home (poetry), illustrations by J. Meinke, Heatherstone Press, 1988.

Contributor of poems, essays, and reviews to periodicals, including *New Yorker, New Republic, Nation, Redbook,* and *Virginia Quarterly Review.*

WORK IN PROGRESS: Liquid Paper: New and Selected Poems.

SIDELIGHTS: "As opposed to much of today's literature, which is experimental, obscure, and even at times shows a conscious disregard for its audience, Peter Meinke's poems are accessible to a broad group of readers," Deno Trakas asserts in the *Dictionary of Literary Biography.* This is the poet's specific intent, for as he told *CA,* clarity is "a chief virtue that my writing strives for, an avoidance of academic bookishness that restricts the audience for serious literature to a handful of similarly trained critics." Trakas describes Meinke's work as "sometimes bright with joy, sometimes pale with despair," and notes that the poems "are rarely abstract or intellectual and never pretentious." Although the poet's verse is both funny and witty, Trakas observes that "Meinke does not write 'light' verse; rather, his talent is in mixing levity with gravity in a single poem." As the critic concludes, Meinke's "poems are not always successful, but despite blemishes, his work . . . is mature, varied, and vigorous."

AVOCATIONAL INTERESTS: Sports, movies, music.

BIOGRAPHICAL/CRITICAL SOURCES:

BOOKS

Berke, Roberta, *Bounds out of Bounds,* Oxford University Press, 1981.

Dictionary of Literary Biography, Volume 5: *American Poets since World War II,* Gale, 1980.

PERIODICALS

Chattahoochie Review, winter, 1988.

Columbus Dispatch, July 12, 1987.

* * *

MEISSNER, W(illiam) W. 1931-

PERSONAL: Born February 13, 1931, in Buffalo, N.Y.; son of William Walter (a surgeon) and Mary (Glauber) Meissner. *Education:* St. Louis University, B.A., 1956, M.A. and Ph.L., 1957; Woodstock College, S.T.L., 1962; Harvard University, M.D., 1967.

ADDRESSES: Office—129 Mount Auburn St., Cambridge, Mass. 02138.

CAREER: Ordained Roman Catholic priest of Society of Jesus (Jesuits), 1951; Mount Auburn Hospital, Cambridge, Mass., psychiatry intern, 1967-68; Massachusetts Mental Health Center, Boston, resident in psychiatry, 1968-71, staff psychiatrist, 1971-87; Cambridge Hospital, Cambridge, staff psychiatrist, 1971-78; Boston Psychoanalytic Institute, Boston, chairman of faculty, 1975-77, training and supervising analyst, 1980—; Harvard University, Medical School, Cambridge, associate clinical professor, 1976-81, clinical professor of psychiatry, 1981-87; Boston College, Boston, professor of psychoanalysis, 1987—.

MEMBER: International Psychoanalytical Association, American Psychiatric Association, American Psychoanalytic Association, Massachusetts Psychiatric Society, Boston Psychoanalytic Institute, Sigma Xi, Psi Chi.

AWARDS, HONORS: Deutsch Prize from Boston Psychoanalytic Institute, 1969.

WRITINGS:

Annotated Bibliography in Religion and Psychology, Academy of Religion and Mental Health, 1961.

Group Dynamics in the Religious Life, University of Notre Dame Press, 1965.

Foundations for a Psychology of Grace, Paulist Press, 1966.

The Assault on Authority: Dialogue or Dilemma?, Orbis Books, 1971.

(With Elizabeth R. Zetzel) *Basic Concepts in Psychoanalytic Psychiatry,* Basic Books, 1973.

The Paranoid Process, Jason Aronson, 1978.

Internalization in Psychoanalysis, International Universities Press, 1981.

The Borderline Spectrum, Jason Aronson, 1984.

Psychoanalysis and Religious Experience, Yale University Press, 1984.

Psychotherapy and the Paranoid Process, Jason Aronson, 1986.

Life and Faith: Psychological Perspectives on Religious Experience, Georgetown University Press, 1987.

Treatment of Patients in the Borderline Spectrum, Jason Aronson, 1988.

Contributor of chapters to over thirty books. Contributor of over one hundred articles to professional journals.

* * *

MELLOW, James R(obert) 1926-

PERSONAL: Born February 28, 1926, in Gloucester, Mass.; son of James R. (a mechanic/engineer) and Cecilia Margaret (Sawyer) Mellow. *Education:* Northwestern University, B.S., 1950.

ADDRESSES: Office—P.O. Box 297, Clinton, Conn. 06413. *Agent*—Georges Borchardt, Inc., 136 East 57th St., New York, N.Y. 10022.

CAREER: Arts (magazine), New York City, reviewer and production manager, 1955-61, editor in chief, 1961-65; *The New Leader,* New York City, art critic, 1964-72; *Industrial Design,* New York City, editor, 1965-69; *Art International,* Lugano, Switzerland, art critic, 1965-69; *New York Times,* New York City, art critic, 1968-74; writer, 1974—. *Military service:* U.S. Army Air Force, 1944-46.

MEMBER: National Book Critics Circle, Authors Guild.

AWARDS, HONORS: National Book Award nomination, biography, 1974, for *Charmed Circle: Gertrude Stein and Company;* American Book Award, paperback biography, 1983, for *Nathaniel Hawthorne in His Times;* Guggenheim fellowship, 1983.

WRITINGS:

(Editor) *The Best in Arts,* Art Digest, Inc., 1962.

(Editor) *New York: The Art World,* Art Digest, Inc., 1964.

Charmed Circle: Gertrude Stein and Company (biography), Praeger, 1974.

Nathaniel Hawthorne in His Times (biography), Houghton, 1980.

Jim Dine, Recent Work (monograph), Pace Gallery Publications, 1980.

Picasso, the Avignon Paintings (monograph), Pace Gallery Publications, 1981.

(Author of introduction) Nathaniel Hawthorne, *The Scarlet Letter* [and] *The House of the Seven Gables,* New American Library, 1981.

Invented Lives: F. Scott and Zelda Fitzgerald (biography), Houghton, 1984.

(Author of introduction) Gertrude Stein, *Three Lives,* New American Library, 1985.

(Author of introduction) Stein, *Operas and Plays,* Station Hill, 1987.

Contributor of articles to magazines and newspapers, including *Architectural Digest, Art News, Gourmet, Horizon, New York Times,* and *Washington Post.*

WORK IN PROGRESS: Hemingway: A Life without Consequences, "a biographical study of Hemingway as a writer and journalist, the third volume in a trilogy, forming a history of the American writers of the so-called Lost Generation period," for Houghton; a study of Greenwich Village in the Twenties, for Thames & Hudson; a biography of Margaret Fuller, "the second volume in a sequence of interlocking biographical studies on nineteenth-century American literary and cultural figures, including biographies of Henry David Thoreau and Ralph Waldo Emerson."

SIDELIGHTS: James R. Mellow's *Charmed Circle: Gertrude Stein and Company* "is a busy, ambitious book packed with tangy anecdotes and self-dramatization recalled both by and about [American expatriate writer Gertrude] Stein and her famous coterie," describes Susan Heath in the *Saturday Review.* In preparing his account of Stein's circle of writer and artist friends that included Ernest Hemingway, F. Scott Fitzgerald, Sherwood Anderson, Henri Matisse, and Pablo Picasso, Mellow "appears to have talked to everybody and read everything that might conceivably be relevant," observes *New York Times* critic Anatole Broyard. The result is a detailed narrative which, according to *New York Review of Books* contributor Donald Sutherland, "is wonderful [in] how the proliferation of topics and anecdotes on the side does not destroy the main shape of the story but enriches it." Adds the critic: "In many ways the work is a triumph."

Despite this praise, Sutherland also observes that because the book moves steadily "and with the blandness of an old-fashioned novel," the author "cannot very well re-create the ferocity of the literary and artistic quarrels in the story, or the great excitement of radically new works when they first appeared." *Charmed Circle* "consolidates rather than extends our understanding of an extraordinary time and its heroic actors," remarks Herbert Leibowitz in the *New York Times Book Review,* adding that the book "lacks the intellectual excitement of discovery." But Martha Duffy believes that the author's methodical approach is appropriate to the subject of Stein's circle; writing in *Time,* Duffy notes that "their lives had some of the character and texture of an old-fashioned, well-upholstered novel. It is James Mellow's achievement that he has told the story carefully and unpretentiously in clear, uncluttered prose."

While he may fault the author for not conveying enough excitement, Sutherland also comments that "Mr. Mellow's prose is anything but stilted. It is easy and ordinary, except that often, especially when he is on his dearest subject, painting, it can rise to a beautiful eloquence." The critic believes that Mellow's visual orientation to the biography "is appropriate enough to Gertrude Stein's own sense of things." Heath makes a similar assertion, stating that "Mellow revives Stein brilliantly, illuminating the connections between her daily life . . . and the themes and characters of her fiction. And he suffuses it all with the hothouse atmosphere of the Stein milieu." "[Mellow's] portrait of [Stein] is as good, in its way, as Picasso's," comments Broyard. Concludes the critic: "Not the least of the charms of 'Charmed Circle' is its evocation of a time when Paris favorably compared with the Florence of the Renaissance."

Mellow uses a similar method in *Nathaniel Hawthorne in His Times,* which, "as the title suggests, places the novelist clearly in the midst of [the] events and the distinguished personages with whom he lived, showing Hawthorne as a man shaped by—in agreement or in conflict with—the dominant ideas of his age," states Michael True in *Commonweal.* As he did for Stein's biography, Mellow "has nicely recreated Hawthorne's milieu and nicely sketched his acquaintances," says Charles Nicol in the *Saturday Review,* "drawing on them for the apt citations that keep Hawthorne's character continually before us." But while *New York Times Book Review* contributor Alfred Kazin also calls the work "a charming and very full period piece," he also believes that it "adds little to our understanding of Hawthorne the writer. Despite the title, it adds little to what we know of Hawthorne's politics," and fails to address several other important issues. But *Newsweek*'s Walter Clemons does perceive a new aspect of the author in Mellow's depiction of "the steely determination that underlay Hawthorne's reclusive exterior. Mellow also brings to life in witty detail the mid-nineteenth-century New England society in which Hawthorne moved." In addition, the critic comments that in his investigation of the friendship between Hawthorne and fellow author Herman Melville, Mellow conducts "the most searching and pertinent discussion I've yet seen of the puzzling phenomenon of nineteenth-century friendships in which homoerotic ardor was hotly avowed but totally, innocently unrecognized." And further dispelling the criticism that the work presents nothing new, True claims that the vivid scenes and "pertinent biographical details" of *Nathaniel Hawthorne in His Times* "send the reader back to the novels with a new understanding of how and why Hawthorne dealt with various aspects of human life."

Because of the great number of biographies previously written about his subjects, "James R. Mellow has accomplished an extraordinary feat in *Invented Lives: F. Scott and Zelda Fitzgerald,*" comments Wendy Smith in the *Wall Street Journal.* "He's taken the oft-told tale of the Jazz Age's most famous couple, used essentially the same material as scores of biographers before him, and written a book with a completely fresh perspective." Mellow approaches the story of the two novelists by theorizing that the Fitzgeralds "invented" roles for themselves and acted them out in their experiences and in their fiction. Despite this new angle, Morris Dickstein comments in the *New York Times Book Review* that while *Invented Lives* "is readable, polished and professional . . . Mr. Mellow has little new to add." But Elizabeth Janeway asserts in the *Los Angeles Times Book Review* that Mellow is "interpreting the effect on American lives of commanding and pervasive myths." The critic elaborates that while the story is well-told, "the force of the book, in the end, is not really any new revelation, but [instead] an added strand in the weaving of the myth."

Although this interpretation of the Fitzgeralds' behavior brings a semi-psychological approach to Mellow's account of the Fitzgeralds, Kenneth S. Lynn believes the author does not carry it far enough; writing in the *Washington Post Book World,* Lynn comments that "unfortunately and unaccountably, Mellow hurries both his subjects into adulthood without adding anything of significance to the psychological insights into their childhoods." Similarly, Michiko Kakutani notes in the *New York Times* that by avoiding the standard romanticization of F. Scott's behavior, Mellow dwells "solely on the spoiled part of his character [and] fails to achieve the sympathy necessary for illuminating his subject's heart and mind." But Dickstein believes that "Mellow is most effective when he resists the charm and glamour of their self-created legend," for then he can cut through the legend to make "refreshingly cold-eyed observation[s]." Because he avoids over-analysis, "Mellow's rare virtue as a biographer is to leave the mysteries of human behavior unsolved, untidy, and organically complex," states Geoffrey Wolff in *Vogue.* Adds the critic: "Mellow's impulse is not to debunk (though that is often the effect) but to bore through the carapace of 'type' to get at two individuals, Scott and Zelda."

"*Invented Lives,* whatever its shortcomings, is a consistently readable and well-constructed biography," maintains Leon Edel in the *New Republic.* Part of this construction lies in the author's ability to reconstruct the era of his subject. Calling Mellow "perhaps the most evocative prose stylist now working in American literary biography," Lynn comments that the author "has an especially strong visual sense, and in his latest biography the portraits of the principal places . . . are wonderfully vivid." While

Dickstein also remarks that "Mellow's forte is the group biography that aims to bring a writer's whole circle and cultural context alive around him," the critic feels that *Invented Lives* "is not inventive enough to breathe life into its secondary characters." But Kakutani differs, noting that "Mellow has a sure storytelling gift, and as he did in his previous biographies of Nathaniel Hawthorne and Gertrude Stein, he conjures up the glittering worlds the Fitzgeralds inhabited with almost painterly precision." As he has demonstrated in his other portraits, "Mellow believes in giving a shape and form to the lives he writes," notes Edel; "he has an artistic goal."

Mellow told *CA:* "Context is of vital importance to the series of nineteenth-century biographical studies that I regard as my principal long-term project. My theory, based on [Thomas] Carlyle's dictum that 'History is the essence of innumerable biographies,' is that a biography, even one dealing with a supposedly reclusive figure like Hawthorne, if it covers the subject's major and minor personal relationships, inevitably engages most of the social, cultural and political issues of an age. In the 'Lost Generation' trilogy which I am currently working on, Hemingway, who had a wide range of acquaintanceship with the world-at-large as an ambulance-driver and then a war correspondent in World Wars I and II, and as a political journalist, literary man, sportsman and international celebrity, is meant to be the culminating figure of the period covered.

"The sequence of three books (as I hope the quartet on nineteenth-century American writers will also do) is intended to form a detailed study of a major episode in American cultural history. It will not only cover the lives of the principals—Stein, the Fitzgeralds and Hemingway—but will explore an expanded network of literary and social relationships, incorporating different phases in the careers of such figures as Ezra Pound, John Dos Passos, Edmund Wilson, Max Perkins, the American expatriates abroad and others. Through them, it will explore the shifting political allegiances and changing cultural values of the times. I don't entirely agree with Emerson's dictum: 'There is no history: only biography,' but I do feel that biography is the most immediate and engaging form of history."

AVOCATIONAL INTERESTS: Art, architecture, design, food, travel, gardening.

BIOGRAPHICAL/CRITICAL SOURCES:

PERIODICALS

Commonweal, October 9, 1981.
Detroit News, December 9, 1984.
Los Angeles Times Book Review, November 25, 1984.
New Republic, December 3, 1984.
Newsweek, February 11, 1974, October 6, 1980.
New Yorker, February 25, 1974.
New York Review of Books, May 30, 1974.
New York Times, January 30, 1974, September 20, 1980, October 23, 1984.
New York Times Book Review, February 3, 1974, September 21, 1980, November 4, 1984.
Saturday Review, March 9, 1974, September, 1980.
Time, March 4, 1974.
Times (London), February 14, 1985.
Times Literary Supplement, November 8, 1974, August 2, 1985.
Vogue, November, 1984.
Wall Street Journal, November 5, 1984.
Washington Post Book World, October 5, 1980, December 23, 1984.

—Sketch by Diane Telgen

MELOAN, Taylor Wells 1919-

PERSONAL: Born July 31, 1919, in St. Louis, Mo.; son of Taylor Wells (an industrialist) and Edith (Graham) Meloan; married Anna Geraldine Leukering, December 17, 1944 (divorced, 1974); married Jane Innes Bierlich, January 30, 1975; children: (first marriage) Michael David, Steven Lee. *Education:* St. Louis University, B.S. (cum laude), 1949; Washington University, St. Louis, Mo.; M.B.A., 1950; Indiana University, D.B.A., 1953. *Religion:* Protestant.

ADDRESSES: Office—Department of Business Administration, University of Southern California, University Park, Los Angeles, Calif. 90007.

CAREER: Herz and Co., St. Louis, Mo., advertising manager, 1941-42; Ligget and Myers Tobacco Co., St. Louis, sales promotion supervisor, 1942-43; University of Oklahoma, Norman, assistant professor of marketing, 1953; Indiana University, Bloomington, assistant professor, 1953-55, associate professor of marketing, 1955-59; University of Southern California, Los Angeles, professor of marketing, 1959—, Robert E. Brooker Professor of Marketing Management, 1970—, chairman of marketing department, 1959-69, interim dean of school of business administration, 1969-71, associate vice president for academic administration and research, 1971-81. Visiting professor, University of Karachi, 1962, and Instituto Post Universitario Per Lo Studio Dell Organizzazione Aziendale, 1964; distinguished visiting professor, University of Witwatersrand, 1978. Consultant to industry and government, 1953—. Member of executive review board, Green Power Foundation, 1971—; member of board of directors, Council of Better Business Bureaus, Inc., 1978-84. *Military service:* U.S. Maritime Service. U.S. Naval Reserve, 1943-46; became lieutenant junior grade.

MEMBER: American Marketing Association (president of Los Angeles chapter, 1964-64; national publications chairman, 1965-67), American Economic Association, Newcomen Society in North America, Rotary Club International, Order of Artus, Beta Gamma Sigma, Delta Pi Epsilon.

WRITINGS:

Mobile Homes: The Growth and Business Practices of the Industry, Irwin, 1957.

(With others) *Trading Stamp Practice and Pricing Policy,* Bureau of Business Research, Indiana University, 1958.

(With John M. Rathmell) *Selling: Its Broader Dimensions,* Macmillan, 1960.

(Editor with Charles M. Whitlo) *Competition in Marketing,* University of Southern California, 1964.

(Contributor) Victor B. Buell, editor, *Handbook of Modern Marketing,* McGraw, 1970.

(Editor with Samuel V. Smith and John J. Wheatley; also contributor) *Managerial Marketing: Policies and Decision,* Houghton, 1970.

Also author of *Internalizing the Business Curriculum,* 1968, *New Career Opportunities,* 1978, and *Innovation Strategy and Management,* 1979. Editorial advisor in business administration, Houghton Mifflin Co., 1959-73; member, board of editors, *Journal of Marketing,* 1965-72.

WORK IN PROGRESS: Study of franchise marketing, and of antitrust policy and impact.*

MENDEL, Arthur 1905-1979

PERSONAL: Born June 6, 1905, in Boston, Mass.; died October 14, 1979, in Newark, N.J.; son of Philip (a businessman) and Gertrude (Newman) Mendel; married Elsa M. Wissell, August 23, 1934. *Education:* Harvard University, B.A., 1925; studied with Nadia Boulanger, Paris, France, 1925-27. *Politics:* Independent. *Religion:* None.

CAREER: Worked for Columbia Broadcasting System and for *Musical America,* New York City, 1927-30; G. Schirmer, Inc. (music publishers), New York City, literary editor, 1930-38; free-lance editor, teacher, conductor, and scholar in New York City, 1938-52, including posts as teacher at Diller-Quaile School of Music, and as teacher and president at Dalcroze School of Music; lecturer in music history at Columbia University, New York City, and University of California, Berkeley, 1950-51; Princeton University, Princeton, N.J., professor of music, 1952-69, Henry Putnam University Professor of Music, 1969-73, professor emeritus, 1973-79, chairman of department, 1952-57. Music critic, *Nation,* New York City, 1930-33; conductor of Cantata Singers, 1936-53; editor, Associated Music Publishers, Inc., 1941-46. Authority on the works of Johann Sebastian Bach, and scholar in the field of sixteenth- through eighteenth-century music.

MEMBER: International Musicology Society, German Musicology Society, Italian Society of Musicology, American Musicological Society (editor, 1941-44; vice-president, 1962-63; honorary member, 1975-79).

AWARDS, HONORS: J. K. Paine Traveling Fellow in Paris, 1925-27; Guggenheim fellow, 1949-50; American Council of Learned Societies fellow, 1962-63; National Endowment for the Humanities senior fellow, 1967-68; American Academy of Arts and Sciences fellow, 1973; Mus.Doc., Rutgers University, 1973; D.H.L., Brandeis University, 1976.

WRITINGS:

(Translator) Paul Bekker, *The Changing Opera,* Norton, 1935.
(Contributor) John Tasker Howard, *Our Contemporary Composers: American Music in the Twentieth Century,* Crowell, 1941, reprinted, Books for Libraries Press, 1975.
(Translator) Paul Hindemith, *The Craft of Musical Composition,* Volume 1: *Theoretical Part,* Associated Music Publishers, 1942, reprinted, Schott, 1970.
(Translator with Nathan Broder) Alfred Einstein, *Mozart: His Character, His Work,* Oxford University Press, 1945, 6th edition, Cassell, 1966.
(Editor with Hans T. David) *The Bach Reader,* Norton, 1945, revised edition, with supplements, 1966.
(Editor) Heinrich Schuetz, *The Christmas Story,* G. Schirmer, 1949.
(Editor) J. S. Bach, *The St. John Passion* (vocal score), G. Schirmer, 1951.
(Editor) Mozart, *Missa Brevis,* G. Schirmer, 1954.
(Editor) Schuetz, *A German Requiem,* G. Schirmer, 1955.
(With Curt Sachs and Carroll C. Pratt) *Some Aspects of Musicology: Three Essays by Arthur Mendel, Curt Sachs and Carroll C. Pratt,* Bobbs-Merrill, 1957.
(With A. J. Ellis) *Studies in the History of Musical Pitch,* Frits Knuf, 1968.
(Editor) J. S. Bach, *Passion nach dem Evangelisten Johannes,* Neue Bach-Ausgabe, 1973-74.
Pitch in Western Music since 1500: A Re-examination, Baerenreiter (Kassel, West Germany), 1979.

Contributor to musicological journals. Member of international editorial board for *Neue Bach Ausgabe,* a new critical edition of the collected works of Bach, beginning 1950.

WORK IN PROGRESS: Research on the masses and motets of Joaquin Des Prez (c. 1440-1521), including a search for objective criteria of their style, chronology, and authenticity; further research on Bach.*

* * *

MENNINGER, Edwin A(rnold) 1896-

PERSONAL: Born March 18, 1896, in Topeka, Kan.; son of Charles Frederick (a physician) and Flora Vesta (a teacher; maiden name, Knisely) Menninger; married Patsy Underhill, May 19, 1928; children: Jane Menninger McCrocklin, John U., Edwin, Jr., Barbara. *Education:* Washburn University, A.B., 1916; Columbia University, graduate study, 1916-18. *Religion:* Christian Scientist.

ADDRESSES: Home—P.O. Box 107, 129 Martin Ave., Stuart, Fla. 33495. *Agent*—Carol Woodward, Painter Hill Rd., Roxbury, Conn. 06783.

CAREER: New York Tribune, New York, N.Y., telegraph editor, 1917-22; *Palm Beach Post,* Palm Beach, Fla., city editor, 1922; owner and publisher of newspapers in Stuart, Fla., including the *South Florida Developer,* 1922-27, *Stuart Daily News,* 1928-31, and *Stuart News,* 1931-58; secretary and general manager of Southeastern Printing Co., ending 1980; currently owner and operator of Horticultural Books, Inc.

MEMBER: American Horticultural Society (life member), Royal Horticultural Society (fellow), Botanical Society of South Africa, Florida Press Association (president, 1945), Rotary Club (former president, Stuart chapter).

AWARDS, HONORS: Distinguished service award, Washburn University Alumni Association, 1956; American Horticultural Council citation, 1957; Rio de Janeiro Sesquicentennial Medal, 1958; Thomas Barbour Medal, Fairchild Tropical Gardens (Miami), 1958; D.Sc., Florida State University, 1964; Gold Medal for individual achievement in horticulture, Florida Federation of Garden Clubs, 1980; D.Sc. Washburn University, 1981.

WRITINGS:

(With David Sturrock) *Shade and Ornamental Trees for South Florida and Cuba,* privately printed, 1946.
Descriptive Catalog of Flowering Tropical Trees, privately printed, 1947.
Flowering Tropical Trees, Doubleday, 1956.
What Flowering Tree Is That?: A Handbook for the Tropics, privately printed, 1956, 2nd edition, 1958.
The Cultivated Eugenias in American Gardens, privately printed, 1959.
Flowering Trees of the World for Tropics and Warm Climates, Hearthside, 1962.
Seaside Plants of the World: A Guide to Planning, Planting, and Maintaining Salt-Resistant Gardens, Hearthside, 1964.
Fantastic Trees, Viking, 1967.
(With others), *Flowering Vines of the World: An Encyclopedia of Climbing Plants,* Hearthside, 1970.
Edible Nuts of the World, Horticultural Books, 1977.

Also author of *Catalog of New Tropical Flowering Trees,* 1953, and *Color in the Sky,* 1975. Contributor of articles on tropical trees to horticultural magazines.*

MENNINGER, Karl (Augustus) 1893-

PERSONAL: Born July, 1893, in Topeka, Kan.; son of Charles Frederick (a physician) and Flora Vesta (a teacher; maiden name, Knisely) Menninger; married Grace Gaines, September 9, 1916 (divorced, 1941); married Jeanetta Lyle (editor of *Bulletin of the Menninger Clinic*), September 8, 1941; children: (first marriage) Julia (Mrs. A. H. Gottesman), Martha (Mrs. William Nichols), Robert Gaines; (second marriage) Rosemary Jeanetta Karla. *Education:* Attended Washburn College (now Washburn University of Topeka), 1910-12, and Indiana University, summer, 1910; University of Wisconsin, Madison, A.B., 1914, B.S., 1915; Harvard Medical School, M.D. (cum laude), 1917. *Religion:* Presbyterian.

ADDRESSES: Home—1819 Westwood Circle, Topeka, Kan. 66604. *Office*—Menninger Foundation, Box 829, Topeka, Kan. 66601; Topeka Veterans Administration Hospital, Topeka, Kan.; and Washburn University, Topeka, Kan.

CAREER: The Menninger Foundation (formerly the Menninger Clinic), Topeka, Kan., partner with father, Charles Frederick Menninger, 1919-25, chief of staff, 1925-46, director of education, 1946-70, chairman of board of trustees, 1954-70, member of education committee, 1967-70. Kansas City General Hospital, Kansas City, Mo., intern, 1917-18; Harvard Medical School, Cambridge, Mass., instructor in neuropathology, 1918-20; Boston Psychopathic Hospital, Boston, Mass., assistant physician, 1918-20; Tufts Medical School, Medford, Mass., assistant in neurology, 1919-20; Christ's Hospital and St. Francis Hospital, Topeka, staff member, 1919—; Winter Veterans Administration Hospital, Topeka, manager, 1945-48, chairman of dean's committee and senior consultant, 1948-55; Menninger School of Psychiatry, Topeka, founder, 1946, dean, 1946-70; University of Kansas City (now University of Missouri—Kansas City) Medical School, clinical professor of psychiatry, 1946-62; Topeka Institute of Psychoanalysis, Topeka, director, 1960—; University of Kansas, Lawrence, professor of medicine, 1970-76, professor at large, 1976—. Visiting professor, University of Cincinnati Medical School. Trustee, Albert Deutsch Memorial Foundation, 1961, and Aspen Institute for Humanistic Studies, 1961-64. Advisor to the Surgeon General, U.S. Army, 1945; consultant, Veteran Administration Hospital, Topeka, 1948—; consultant in psychiatry to State of Illinois Department of Welfare, and Governor of Illinois, 1953-54; consultant, Office of Vocational Rehabilitation, Department of Health, Education, and Welfare, 1953-55; consultant, Bureau of Prisons, Department of Justice, 1956—; consultant, Forbes Air Force Base Hospital and Stone-Brandel Center, 1958—; member of advisory committee, International Survey of Correctional Research and Practice, California, 1960—; consultant to various other institutes and associations.

MEMBER: International Association for Suicide Prevention, World Society of Ekistics, Masons, Central Neuropsychiatric Association (co-founder; secretary, 1922-32; president, 1932-33), Central Psychiatric Hospital Association, American Orthopsychiatric Association (secretary, 1926-27; president, 1927-28), American Psychiatric Association (life fellow; counselor, 1928-29, 1941-43), American Psychological Association, American Psychoanalytic Association (life member; president, 1941-43), American Academy of Psychiatry and Law, American Society of Criminology, American Justice Institute (member of advisory committee), American Civil Liberties Union (vice-chairman of national committee), American Medical Association (fellow), American College of Physicians (life fellow), American College of Psychiatrists, American Medical Writers Association (life member; 2nd vice-president, 1957-58; 1st vice-president, 1958-59), American Association for the Advancement of Science, American Association for Child Psychoanalysis, National Commission for the Prevention of Child Abuse (co-chairman of honorary board), American Association of Suicidology (honorary member), Medical Association for the Research of Nervous and Mental Diseases, Royal College of Psychiatrists (honorary fellow), Association of Clinical Pastoral Education, Association for Psychiatry Treatment Offenders, Sigmund Freud Archives, American Humanities Foundation, NAACP, National Congress of the American Indian, American Association of Botanical Gardens and Arboreta, American Horticultural Council, Friends of the Earth, Sierra Club, Save the Tallgrass Prairie Inc. (chairman of national honorary board), Kansas Medical Society, Illinois Academy of Criminology, Illinois Committee on Family Law, Aspen Institute for Humanistic Studies (former trustee; currently honorary trustee), Chicago Psychoanalytic Association, American Indian Center (Chicago grand council), Chicago Orchestral Association (governor), Sigmund Freud Society (Vienna), University Presbyterian Club (Chicago), Country Lodge Presbyterian Club (Topeka, Kan.).

AWARDS, HONORS: D.Sc., Washburn University, 1949, University of Wisconsin, 1965, Oklahoma City University, 1966; L.H.D., Park College, 1955, St. Benedict College, 1963, Loyola University, 1972, DePaul University, 1974; LL.D., Jefferson Medical College of Philadelphia, 1956, Parsons College, 1960, Kansas State University, 1962, Baker University, 1965, Pepperdine University, 1974, John Jay College of Criminal Justice, 1978; Isaac Ray Award, 1962, First Distinguished Service Award, 1965, and First Founders Award, 1977, all from American Psychiatric Association; T. W. Salmon award, New York Academy of Medicine, 1967; Good Samaritan award, Eagles Lodge, 1968, 1969; Annual Service award, John Howard Association, 1969; Good Shepherd award, The Lambs (Chicago), 1969; American Academy of Psychiatry and Law award, 1974; Roscoe Pound award, National Council of Crime and Delinquency, 1975; Kansas Department of Corrections special award, 1976; Sheen award, American Medical Association, 1978; Presidential Medal of Freedom, 1981; numerous other awards.

WRITINGS:

The Human Mind, Knopf, 1930, 2nd edition, 1945.

Man against Himself, Harcourt, 1938, reprinted, 1985.

(With wife, Jeanetta Menninger) *Love against Hate,* Harcourt, 1942.

(With G. Devereux) *A Guide to Psychiatric Books,* Grune & Stratton, 1950, 3rd revised edition, 1972.

A Manual for Psychiatric Case Study, Grune & Stratton, 1952, revised edition, 1962.

Theory of Psychoanalytic Technique, Basic Books, 1958, revised edition with Philip Holzman, 1973.

A Psychiatrists World (selected papers), Viking, 1959.

The Vital Balance: The Life Process in Mental Health and Illness, Viking, 1963, reprinted, Peter Smith, 1983.

The Crime of Punishment, Viking, 1968.

Sparks, edited by Lucy Freeman, Crowell, 1973.

A Celebration Issue Honoring Karl Menninger on His 80th Birthday: A Selection of His Previously Published Papers, Menninger Foundation, 1973.

Whatever Became of Sin?, Hawthorn, 1973, reprinted, Bantam, 1988.

The Human Mind Revisited, International University Press, 1978.

(With Sarah R. Haavik) *Sexuality, Law, and the Developmentally Disabled Person: Legal and Clinical Aspects of Marriage, Parenthood, and Sterilization,* Paul Brookes, 1981.

Also author with others of *Why Men Fail,* 1918, *The Healthy-Minded Child,* 1930, and *America Now,* 1938. Editor in chief, *Bulletin of the Menninger Clinic,* 1936—; member of editorial board, *Archives of Criminal Psychodynamics, Psychoanalytic Quarterly, Excerpta Criminologica,* and *Academic Achievement.*

WORK IN PROGRESS: The Suicidal Intention of Nuclear Armament Manufacture and Storage.

SIDELIGHTS: With his father Charles and brother William, Karl Menninger founded the famous Menninger Clinic in 1919, which later became the Menninger Foundation. The importance of the clinic was noted in the citation of the Albert Lasker Group Award for 1955: "The Menninger Foundation and Clinic, headed by Drs. Karl and William Menninger, has provided a sustained and highly productive attack against mental disease for many years. Inspired by their father, Dr. Charles Frederick Menninger, these brothers have developed an outstanding institution which has served as an example for other mental disease hospitals. . . . The influence of the Menninger Foundation and Clinic in increasing professional and public interest in the care of the mentally ill cannot be measured, but it is indelibly recorded as a great service to mankind."

BIOGRAPHICAL/CRITICAL SOURCES:

BOOKS

Chandler, Caroline A., *Famous Modern Men of Medicine,* Dodd, 1965.

Davis, Elizabeth L., *Fathers of America,* Revell, 1958.

PERIODICALS

Chicago Tribune, June 16, 1979.
Look, September 30, 1958.
Los Angeles Times, September 18, 1983.
New York Times, November 6, 1955.
New York Times Book Review, December 29, 1964.
Saturday Evening Post, April 7, 1962.
Saturday Review, January 25, 1964.

* * *

MERRIAM, Eve 1916-

PERSONAL: Born July 19, 1916, in Philadelphia, Pa.; children: Guy Michel, Dee Michel (sons). *Education:* Attended Cornell University; University of Pennsylvania, A.B., 1937; graduate study at University of Wisconsin and Columbia University.

ADDRESSES: Office—101 West 12th St., New York, N.Y. 10011. *Agent*—Marian Reiner, 71 Disbrow Lane, New Rochelle, N.Y. 10804.

CAREER: Poet, playwright, fiction and nonfiction writer. Copywriter, 1939-42; radio writer, mainly of documentaries and scripts in verse, for Columbia Broadcasting System, Inc. (CBS-Radio), and other networks, and conductor of weekly program on modern poetry for radio station WQXR, New York City, 1942-46; *PM,* New York City, author of daily verse column, 1945; *Deb,* New York City, fashion editor, 1946; *Glamour,* New York City, fashion copy editor, 1947-48; free-lance magazine and book writer, 1949—. Teacher of creative writing at City College of the City University of New York, 1965-69. Member of field project staff, Bank Street College of Education, 1958-60. Public lecturer, 1956—.

MEMBER: Dramatists Guild Council, Authors League Council.

AWARDS, HONORS: Yale Younger Poets Prize for first volume of verse by a promising American poet, 1946, for *Family Circle;* Star Fiction Award from *Collier's,* 1949, for "Make Something Happen"; William Newman Poetry Award, 1957; drama-writing grant from Columbia Broadcasting System, Inc., 1959; Obie Award from *Village Voice,* 1976, for play "The Club"; National Council of Teachers of English Award for excellence in poetry for children, 1981.

WRITINGS:

JUVENILE POETRY

There Is No Rhyme for Silver (first book in trilogy; Junior Literary Guild selection), illustrated by Joseph Schindelman, Atheneum, 1962.

It Doesn't Always Have to Rhyme (second book in trilogy), illustrated by Malcolm Spooner, Atheneum, 1964.

Catch a Little Rhyme (third book in trilogy), illustrated by Imero Gobbato, Atheneum, 1966.

Independent Voices (biographical sketches in verse form), illustrated by Arvis Stewart, Atheneum, 1968.

Finding a Poem (Junior Literary Guild selection), illustrated by Seymour Chwast, Atheneum, 1970.

I Am a Man: Ode to Martin Luther King, Jr., illustrated by Suzanne Verrier, Doubleday, 1971.

Out Loud, illustrated by Harriet Sherman, Atheneum, 1973.

Rainbow Writing, Atheneum, 1976.

The Birthday Cow, illustrated by son Guy Michel, Knopf, 1978.

A Word or Two with You: New Rhymes for Young Readers, illustrated by John Nez, Atheneum, 1981.

If Only I Could Tell You: Poems for Young Lovers and Dreamers, illustrated by Donna Diamond, Knopf, 1983.

Jamboree: Rhymes for All Times, illustrated by Walter Gaffney-Kessell, Dell, 1984.

Blackberry Ink: Poems, pictures by Hans Wilhelm, Morrow, 1985.

Fresh Paint: New Poems, woodcuts by David Frampton, Macmillan, 1986.

A Sky Full of Poems, illustrated by Gaffney-Kessell, Dell, 1986.

Halloween ABC, illustrated by Lane Smith, Macmillan, 1987.

You Be Good and I'll Be Night: Jump on the Bed Poems, Morrow, 1988.

OTHER JUVENILE BOOKS

The Real Book about Franklin D. Roosevelt, illustrated by Bette J. Davis, Garden City, 1952.

The Real Book about Amazing Birds, Garden City, 1954.

(Contributor) *Believe and Make-Believe* (anthology), Dutton, 1957.

The Voice of Liberty: The Story of Emma Lazarus, illustrated by Charles W. Walker, Farrar, Straus, 1959.

A Gaggle of Geese, illustrated by Paul Galdone, Knopf, 1960.

(Contributor) *Let's Read More Stories,* Garden City, 1960.

Mommies at Work, illustrated by Beni Montressor, Knopf, 1961.

Funny Town, illustrated by Evaline Ness, Macmillan, 1963.

What's in the Middle of a Riddle?, illustrated by Murray Tinkelman, Collier, 1963.

What Can You Do with a Pocket?, illustrated by Sherman, Knopf, 1964.

Small Fry, illustrated by Garry MacKenzie, Knopf, 1965.

Don't Think about a White Bear, illustrated by Tinkelman, Putnam, 1965.

The Story of Benjamin Franklin, illustrated by Brinton Turkle, Four Winds, 1965.

Do You Want to See Something?, illustrated by Abner Graboff, Scholastic Books, 1965.

Miss Tibbett's Typewriter, illustrated by Rick Schreiter, Knopf, 1966.

Andy All Year 'Round: A Picture Book of Four Seasons and Five Senses, illustrated by Margo Huff, Funk & Wagnalls, 1967.

(Reteller) *Epaminondas,* illustrated by Trina Schart Hyman, Follett, 1968, republished as *That Noodle-Head Epaminondas,* Scholastic Books, 1972.

Project 1-2-3 (counting book), illustrated by Sherman, McGraw, 1971.

(Translator) Hana Doskocilova, *Animal Tales,* illustrated by Mirko Hanak, Doubleday, 1971.

Bam! Zam! Boom!: A Building Book, illustrated by William Lightfoot, Walker & Co., 1972.

Boys and Girls, Girls and Boys, illustrated by Sherman, Holt, 1972.

Ab to Zogg: A Lexicon for Science-Fiction and Fantasy Readers, illustrated by Albert Lorenz, Atheneum, 1977.

Unhurry Harry, illustrated by Gail Owens, Four Winds, 1978.

Good Night to Annie (alphabet book), illustrated by John Wallner, Four Winds, 1980.

A Book of Wishes for You, Gibson, 1985.

The Christmas Box (picture book), illustrated by David Small, Morrow, 1985.

The Birthday Door, illustrated by Peter Thornton, Morrow, 1986.

ADULT POETRY

Family Circle, edited, and with a foreword, by Archibald MacLeish, Yale University Press, 1946.

Tomorrow Morning, Twayne, 1953.

Montgomery, Alabama, Money, Mississippi, and Other Places (pamphlet), Cameron, 1957.

The Double Bed from the Feminine Side, Cameron, 1958, reprinted, M. Evans, 1972.

The Trouble with Love, Macmillan, 1960.

The Inner City Mother Goose, photographs by Lawrence Ratzkin, Simon & Schuster, 1969.

The Nixon Poems, illustrated by John Gerbino, Atheneum, 1970.

A Husband's Notes about Her, Collier, 1976.

ADULT PLAYS

Out of Our Fathers' House (based on Merriam's book *Growing up Female in America: Ten Lives;* also see below; first produced in New York City at Theatre of the Riverside Church, November, 1977), Samuel French, 1975.

The Club (first produced Off-Broadway at Circle in the Square Theatre, 1976), Samuel French, 1976.

"Viva Reviva," first produced in Lenox, Mass., at Lenox Arts Center, 1977.

At Her Age (first produced in New York City at Theatre for Older People, 1979), Samuel French, 1979.

"The Good Life: Lady Macbeth of Westport," first produced in Ithaca, New York, at Ithaca College, 1979.

Dialogue for Lovers: Sonnets of Shakespeare Arranged for Dramatic Presentation (first produced in New York City at Symphony Space, 1980), Samuel French, 1981.

And I Ain't Finished Yet, Samuel French, 1982.

"Plagues for Our Time," first produced Off-Broadway at La Mama Experimental Theatre Club, April, 1983.

OTHER ADULT BOOKS

Emma Lazarus: Woman with a Torch (biography), Citadel, 1956.

Figleaf: The Business of Being in Fashion (nonfiction), illustrated by Burmah Burris, Lippincott, 1960.

Basics: An I-Can-Read-Book for Grownups, illustrated by Robert Osborn, Macmillan, 1962.

After Nora Slammed the Door: American Women in the 1960s—The Unfinished Revolution, World Publishing, 1964.

Man and Woman: The Human Condition, Research Center on Women, 1968.

Equality, Identity, and Complementarity, Research Center on Women, 1968.

(Editor and author of introduction) *Growing up Female in America: Ten Lives,* Doubleday, 1971, reprinted, Beacon Press, 1987.

(Editor with Nancy Larrick) *Male and Female under Eighteen: Frank Comments from Young People about Their Sex Roles Today,* Avon, 1973.

OTHER

Also contributor to journals, including *Nation, New Republic, Saturday Evening Post, Saturday Review, Village Voice, Newsweek, Washington Post,* and *Ms.*

Merriam's manuscripts are part of the Kerlan Collection at the University of Minnesota in Minneapolis; the de Grummond Collection at the University of Southern Mississippi in Hattiesburg; and the Schlesinger Library at Radcliffe College in Cambridge, Mass.

SIDELIGHTS: According to Eve Merriam, the choice to be a poet was not her own. From her earliest years, the rhythmic, rhyming nature of poetry impassioned her so much that being a poet was something of a necessity for her. "I find it difficult to sit still when I hear poetry or read it out loud. I feel a tingling feeling all over, particularly in the tips of my fingers and in my toes, and it just seems to go right from my mouth all the way through my body. It's like a shot of adrenalin or oxygen when I hear rhymes and word play," remarked Merriam to *Language Arts* interviewer Glenna Sloan. Merriam has worked for over two decades to create these same feelings in young readers. Indeed, she is one of America's most respected contemporary poets for children, having authored numerous poetry volumes for youths and having garnered the National Council of Teachers of English Award for excellence in children's poetry in 1981. In her *Learning 85* article "Some Pearls from Eve Merriam on Sharing Poetry with Children," Merriam urges: "Whatever you do, find ways to read poetry. Eat it, drink it, enjoy it, and share it."

When Merriam was a child, she read poetry out loud from the verse column of the *Philadelphia Bulletin* and she was moved by the poetic quality of the many Gilbert and Sullivan musicals she and her brother were taken to see. She began writing her own poems when she was seven or eight years old and later contributed poems to her high school magazine and weekly newspaper. After graduating with an A.B. degree from the University of Pennsylvania in 1937, Merriam moved to New York to pursue graduate studies at Columbia University. However, one afternoon she abruptly quit her studies and began working, first as a copywriter and later as a radio writer for Columbia Broadcasting System, Inc., and for other networks. Eventually Merriam became fashion copy editor for *Glamour* magazine. In the meantime, her first collection of adult poetry, entitled *Family Circle,* won the 1946 Yale Younger Poets Prize. A few years after this welcome recognition, Merriam devoted her full energies to free-lance magazine and book writing. Her literary endeavors for both the adult and children's literary scene have been prolific, but Merriam is recognized foremost as a children's poet; in fact, Laura M. Zaidman remarks in the *Dictionary of Literary Biography* that Merriam's "contributions to numerous poetry anthologies and many respected magazines have made her a most influential voice in educating teachers of children's literature."

According to Sloan, one of Merriam's chief aims as a writer of children's poetry is to instill in youth the same fascination with language that she experiences: "*Out Loud* is not only the title of a book of poems by Eve Merriam, it is also her teaching philosophy in two words. She maintains that no one learns to love poetry without hearing it read out loud . . . [and Merriam concludes that] 'if we can get teachers to read poetry, lots of it, out loud to children, we'll develop a generation of poetry readers; we may even have some poetry writers, but the main thing, we'll have language appreciators.' " Again with the intention of drawing children to the side of poetry, Merriam includes a section "Writing a Poem" in her book *Finding a Poem.* "Writing a Poem" contains a step-by-step illustration of how Merriam developed her poem "Landscape," an undertaking which involved twelve revisions.

As one who practices what she preaches, Merriam's poetry is particularly conducive to being read out loud. Her poems exemplify her fascination with language, as evidenced by her puns and word puzzles, her concentration on the eccentricities and idiosyncracies of the English language, and her broad use of poetic devices, like onomatopoeia, inner rhyme, alliteration, assonance, metaphor, and so forth, in addition to traditional rhyming. "How to Eat a Poem," originally from Merriam's second children's poetry collection, *It Doesn't Always Have to Rhyme,* illustrates Merriam's use of metaphor, but it is also "a poem of the invitational mode," notes Zaidman. Accordingly, "How to Eat a Poem" exclaims: "Don't be polite./ Bite in./ Pick it up with your fingers and lick the juice that may run down your chin./ It is ready and ripe now, whenever you are." Overall, Zaidman believes *It Doesn't Always Have to Rhyme* could serve "as an excellent minicourse in the elements of poetry" because it contains the distinctive poems "Metaphor," "Simile: Willow and Ginkgo," "Couplet Countdown," "Quatrain," "Learning on a Limerick," "Beware of Doggerel," "Onomatopoeia," and "A Cliche." Merriam also works with the positioning of the words on the page, thus bringing the visual sense into her verse more fully.

Besides being oriented to sensory appeal, Merriam's poetry is noted for its instructive, social strain. According to Sloan, Merriam was astonished when an anthologist once categorized her as the only children's poet who addressed social issues. Merriam is of the opinion that war, pollution, sexism, racism, television addiction, and the like, are issues that touch children's lives as well as adults's lives, notes Sloan. *Finding a Poem,* in particular, contains poems of political and social satire. Diane Farrell describes this volume in *Horn Book* as "an irresistible collection of poems that satirize our empty, 'plastic' society, the verses reflect some of the slick sheen of contemporary life and should have 'instant' appeal for those seeking instant satisfactions." Additionally, Barbara H. Baskin and Karen H. Harris remark in *Books for the Gifted Child* that "such poems as 'The Wholly Family,' 'Umbilical,' and 'Alarm Clock' . . . [focus on how] humanity's need for the latitude to pursue individual, unfettered, and natural interests conflicts with the demands of a highly structured, technologically obsessed, and plasticized world. People caught in various traps—sometimes of their own devising, but more commonly as a spinoff from the rat race they were scarcely aware they had entered—is a recurring theme in [*Finding a Poem*]." According to Zaidman, "Merriam did not always feel free to express her concerns about social issues, but like other poets in the late 1960s and 1970s, she began to focus on more relevant topics. Poems about nature, animals, family, and the everyday experiences children encounter never disappeared from her children's books, yet she stretched beyond these traditional sensibilities of childhood and shifted her concerns to reflect the inner emotional conflicts and stark realities of the world facing children: anxieties, alienation, racial and social injustice, war, inhumane technology, and the struggles of urban life."

In general, critics are impressed with Merriam's poetry for young readers. They applaud her serious attempt to get children involved in poetry by providing poems that are pleasurable, approachable, and stimulating to both the intellect and the senses. In the *Children's Literature Association Quarterly,* Rebecca Lukens writes: "Reading Merriam through, end to end, awakens all our senses to sharpness, but touches our intellects, too. The unexpected juxtapositions, the keen contrasts, the onomatopoeic series, even the cliches freshened to surprise—all are parts of Merriam's own pleasure, and now of ours." Complaints that do arise often relate to unevenness of quality, especially in regard to Merriam's more recent collections. For instance, whereas *School Library Journal* critic Peter Neumeyer believes "Merriam's touch remains authoritative" in her 1981 volume *A Word or Two with You: New Rhymes for Young Readers,* Nancy C. Hammond for *Horn Book* is of the opinion that "unevenness haunts both the poems and the volume. With only seventeen poems . . . weak ones are glaring."

Merriam's approach to educating children goes beyond verse. *Independent Voices,* for example, contains biographical sketches, albeit in verse form, of seven prominent Americans, including Benjamin Franklin, Henry David Thoreau, and Elizabeth Blackwell. *The Voice of Liberty: The Story of Emma Lazarus* is Merriam's fictionalized biography of Lazarus, a poet and prose writer who championed the cause of Jewish refugees in America at the turn of the century. Also included in Merriam's body of work for children are counting books, alphabet books, and books presenting the equality of the sexes, like *Boys and Girls, Girls and Boys,* which "energetically tries to stamp out separate roles for males and females and show that boys and girls are really alike," notes Marilyn R. Singer in *School Library Journal.* Merriam's playfulness and inventiveness is apparent in these works as in her poetry.

Merriam is also an established author of adult works. Included among these are poetry volumes, such as *Family Circle, Tomorrow Morning,* and *The Trouble with Love;* feminist writings, like *The Double Bed from the Feminine Side, After Nora Slammed the Door: American Women in the 1960s—The Unfinished Revolution,* and *Growing up Female in America: Ten Lives;* and political satires, including *The Inner City Mother Goose* and *The Nixon Poems,* both of which are poetry collections. Most recently, Merriam's attention has been drawn to writing for the theatre. Her indictment of the ghetto experience in her poetry volume *The Inner City Mother Goose* was adapted for the theatre as "Inner City: A Street Cantata" and appeared on Broadway in the early 1970s. Since then, Merriam has written a number of adult plays, including "Out of Our Fathers' House," "At Her Age," and her OBIE Award-winning "The Club." As with some of her poetry, Merriam's plays could be characterized as social or political satire. In the *New York Times,* Stephen Holden writes of "Plagues for Our Time": "[It] amusingly implies that the unpleasant banalities of everyday—everything from meaningless work to presweetened food and spray cans—are plagues that we have brought upon ourselves. . . . Merriam's accumulation of everyday indignities is not just an amusing indictment of kitsch culture, but a pointed critique of a society that offers its pets hundreds of varieties of food, yet won't adequately feed all its elderly."

Merriam is an author with a broad literary range, from adult feminist tracts to pictorial counting books for the very young. However, for decades her main thrust has been inspiring in others her passion for poetic language. As Zaidman explains, "Merriam's excellence in poetry has given her readers a better appreciation for a wide range of topics expressing the varieties of a child's experiences, and her insights into the way in which children should approach poetry have greatly influenced the ability of parents and teachers to help them enjoy it. By inviting two generations of readers into her world of words, Eve Merriam has greatly enriched children's poetry."

MEDIA ADAPTATIONS: The musical play "Inner City: A Street Cantata," based on *The Inner City Mother Goose,* was first produced on Broadway at the Ethel Barrymore Theatre, December, 1971, with music by Helen Miller and lyrics by Merriam; John Braswell's production "Sweet Dreams," also based on *The Inner City Mother Goose,* was first produced Off-Broadway at La Mama Experimental Theatre Company, February, 1984.

AVOCATIONAL INTERESTS: Travel, swimming, walking, folk dancing, group singing, the city in the winter, the ocean in the summer, the theatre, frequenting public libraries and second-hand bookstores.

BIOGRAPHICAL/CRITICAL SOURCES:

BOOKS

Baskin, Barbara H. and Karen H. Harris, *Books for the Gifted Child,* Bradford Publishing, 1980.

Children's Literature Review, Volume 14, Gale, 1988.

Dictionary of Literary Biography, Volume 61: *American Writers for Children since 1960—Poets, Illustrators, and Nonfiction Authors,* Gale, 1987.

Haviland and Smith, *Children and Poetry,* Library of Congress, 1969.

Larrick, Nancy, editor, *Somebody Turned on a Tap in These Kids,* Delacorte, 1971.

PERIODICALS

Children's Literature Association Quarterly, winter, 1981.

Christian Science Monitor, January 8, 1970, March 15, 1970.

Dramatists Guild Quarterly, autumn, 1982.

Horn Book, October, 1970, April, 1982.

Language Arts, November-December, 1981.

Learning 85, September, 1985.

Library Journal, September, 1970, May 15, 1971.

Nation, January 31, 1959, March 21, 1959, June 23, 1962, December 14, 1964, June 7, 1965, October 7, 1968, February 7, 1972.

New Republic, November 16, 1959, October 9, 1976.

Newsweek, July 2, 1962, August 2, 1976.

New York Times, December 22, 1963, July 23, 1976, May 30, 1980, April 17, 1983, December 9, 1987.

New York Times Book Review, August 16, 1964, March 2, 1969, November 1, 1970, June 25, 1972, March 13, 1977.

New York Times Magazine, May 2, 1971.

School Library Journal, February, 1973, January, 1982.

—Sketch by Cheryl Gottler

MERY, Fernand 1897-1984

PERSONAL: Born February 11, 1897, in Clermont l'Herault, France; died February, 1984; son of Fernand (an industrialist) and Berthe (Berquet) Mery; married Wilhelmine Massonneau, July 2, 1934. *Education:* Attended Faculte des Lettres de Montpelier, Ecole Veterinaire de Lyon, and Ecole Veterinaire d'Alfort. *Politics:* "Apolitical." *Religion:* Roman Catholic.

ADDRESSES: *Home—*22 bis avenue de Suffren, 75015 Paris, France. *Office—*c/o *Point-de-Vue-Images du Monde,* 116 bis Champs Elysee, 75008 Paris, France.

CAREER: Veterinarian and free-lance writer. President of Academie Veterinaire de France, 1962, and Conseil National de la Protection Animale. Free-lance lecturer and radio broadcaster. *Military service:* French Cavalry, 1914-18; French Army, 1940, director of army canine service and creator of the training code for army dogs; became captain.

MEMBER: International Society for the Protection of Animals (former president), World Wildlife Federation, International PEN, Association des Ecrivains Combattants, Medecins Ecrivains, Societe des Gens de Lettres, Societe des Auteurs, Association des Amis des Betes (founder and president), Academie Grammont.

AWARDS, HONORS: Grand Prix of the Societe des Gens de Lettres, 1966; Prix litteraire of the Academie Francaise; honorary president, Assistance aux Animaux; Officier des Palmes Academiques; officer of French Legion of Honor.

WRITINGS:

Betes et gens devant l'amour, Flammarion, 1933.

Les chiens de chasse, photographs by Dim, Payot, 1951.

Ames de betes, Denoel, 1952.

Avoir un chien, illustrated by O'Klein, Denoel, 1953.

Ici: Les betes, Denoel, 1954.

Les coulisses du monde animal, Prisma, 1956, Hachette, 1973.

Sa majeste le chat, Denoel, 1956, translation by Elizabeth King and John Rosenberg published as *Her Majesty the Cat,* Criterion, 1957 (published in England as *Just Cats,* Quartet Books, 1973).

Notre ami le chien, illustrated by Colyann, Denoel, 1957.

(Editor with P. C. Blin and others) *Le chien,* illustrated by Lucy Dawson and Roger Reboussin, Librairie Larousse, 1959.

Encyclopedies du chat et du chien, Larousse, 1959.

Medicin des betes, Laffont, 1961.

Les animaux celebres, illustrated by Daniel Colin, Denoel, 1964.

Entre chiens, illustrated by Albert Debout, Editions du Livre (Monte Carlo), 1964.

Le chat: Sa vie, son histoire, sa magie, Pont Royal, 1966, translation by Emma Street published as *The Life, History, and Magic of the Cat,* Hamlyn, 1967, Madison Square Press, 1968.

Chiens d'utilite et de compagnie, Marguerat, 1966.

Le chien: Son mystere, Pont Royal, 1968, translation published as *The Life, History, and Magic of the Dog,* Grosset & Dunlap, 1970 (published in England as *The Dog,* Cassell, 1970).

Le chow-chow, Crepin-Leblond, 1970.

Les betes aussi ont leurs languages, Editions France-Empire, 1971, translation by Michael Ross published as *Animal Languages,* Saxon House, 1975.

(Editor with R. P. Audras and others) *Le chat,* Larousse, 1973.

Les mysteres du monde animal, Hachette, 1975.

Le chat et son enigme, Robert Laffont, 1981.

Le chat, Denoel, 1982.

Also author of *Les joies du chien*, Realites; *Entre chats*, illustrated by Dubout, Editions Solar; *Moumour le panthere; L'homme et l'animal; Les enfants et les betes;* and *Les chiens de compagnie: Bichons, chihuahuas, chow-chows.* Contributor of articles to *Point-de-Vue-Images du Monde, France-Soir, Le Parisien Libere,* and other magazines.

SIDELIGHTS: As a veterinarian and animal behaviorist, Fernand Mery devoted his life to the study of animals and was recognized as an authority on animal habits. Although active in the study and protection of wild species, Mery was particularly interested in man's domesticated animal companions. Many of his books, generously illustrated, reveal his delight in dogs and cats. The authors other books reflect his fascination for and wide knowledge of the animal world.

One of Mery's books, *Animal Languages*, discusses communication among birds, insects, amphibians, fish, and mammals and between man and these animals. The book met with mixed reception. While some critics considered it to be well-documented, others found the book's sources unreliable or outdated. Margery C. Coombs of the University of Massachusetts department of zoology speculated that "students and more sophisticated readers are more likely to profit" from *Animal Languages* than the general reader. On the other hand, Maurice Burton noted in *Books and Bookmen* that some readers will "enjoy [Mery's] racy style."

BIOGRAPHICAL/CRITICAL SOURCES:

PERIODICALS

Books and Bookmen, May, 1975.
Library Journal, August, 1975.

[Sketch reviewed by wife, Wilhelmine Massonneau]

* * *

MICHAELS, Ski
See PELLOWSKI, Michael (Joseph)

* * *

MIDDLETON, Christopher 1926-

PERSONAL: Born June 10, 1926, in Truro, Cornwall, England; son of Hubert Stanley (a professor of music) and Dorothy (Miller) Middleton; married Mary Freer, April 11, 1953 (divorced, 1970); children: Sarah, Miranda, Benjamin. *Education:* Merton College, Oxford, B. A., 1951, D.Phil., 1954.

ADDRESSES: *Home*—Austin, Tex. *Office*—Department of German, University of Texas, Austin, Tex. 78712.

CAREER: Zurich University, Zurich, Switzerland, lecturer in English, 1952-55; University of Texas, Austin, visiting professor, 1961-62, 1966, professor of German literature, 1966—; King's College, University of London, London, England, senior lecturer, 1965-66. *Military service:* Royal Air Force, 1944-48; became sergeant.

AWARDS, HONORS: Sir Geoffrey Faber Memorial Prize, 1964, for *Torse 3: Poems, 1949-1961;* Guggenheim fellow, 1974-75; National Endowment for the Arts fellow, 1980.

WRITINGS:

The Metropolitans (libretto), Alkor, 1964.
Der Taschenelefant, Verlag Neue Rabenpresse, 1969.
Wie wir Grossmutter zum Markt bringen, Eremiten-presse, 1970.
Bolshevism in Art, and Other Expository Writings, Carcanet Press, 1978, Humanities Press, 1980.
The Pursuit of the Kingfisher (essays), Carcanet Press, 1983.

POETRY

Poems, Fortune Press, 1944.
Nocturne in Eden, Fortune Press, 1945.
Torse 3: Poems, 1949-1961, Harcourt, 1962.
(With David Holbrook and David Wevill) *Penguin Modern Poets 4*, Penguin, 1963.
Nonsequences: Selfpoems, Longmans, Green, 1965, Norton, 1966.
Our Flowers and Nice Bones, Horizon Press, 1969.
The Fossil Fish: 15 Micropoems, Burning Deck, 1970.
Briefcase History: 9 Poems, Burning Deck, 1972.
Fractions from Another Telemachus, Sceptre Press, 1974.
Wildhorse, Sceptre Press, 1975.
The Lonely Suppers of W. V. Balloon, David Godine, 1975.
Razzmatazz, W. Thomas Taylor, 1976.
Eight Elementary Inventions, Sceptre Press, 1977.
Pataxanadu and Other Prose, Carcanet Press, 1977.
Carminalenia, Carcanet Press, 1980.
Woden Dog, Burning Deck, 1982.
111 Poems, Carcanet Press, 1983.
Serpentine, Oasis Books, 1985.
Two Horse Wagon Going By, Carcanet Press, 1987.

Also author of *Anasphere*, Burning Deck.

EDITOR

(With others) *Ohne Hass und Fahne*, Rowolt Verlag, 1959.
(And translator with Michael Hamburger) *Modern German Poetry, 1910-1960: An Anthology with Verse Translations*, Grove, 1962.
(And translator with William Burford) *The Poet's Vocation: Selections from the Letters of Hoelderlin, Rimbaud and Hart Crane*, University of Texas Press, 1962.
German Writing Today, Penguin, 1967.
Selected Poems by Georg Trakl, J. Cape, 1968.
(And translator with others) *Goethe: Selected Poems*, Suhrkamp Insel, 1983.

TRANSLATOR

Robert Walser, *The Walk and Other Stories*, Calder, 1957.
(With others) Gottfried Benn, *Primal Vision*, New Directions, 1960.
(With others) Hugo von Hofmannsthal, *Poems and Verse Plays*, Pantheon, 1961.
(With Hamburger) Guenter Grass, *Selected Poems*, Harcourt, 1966.
Walser, *Jakob von Gunten*, University of Texas Press, 1969.
Friedrich Nietzsche, *Selected Letters*, University of Chicago Press, 1969.
(With Hamburger) Grass, *Poems*, Penguin, 1969, published as *Selected Poems*, 1980.
Christa Wolf, *The Quest for Christa T.*, Farrar, Straus, 1970.
(With Hamburger) Paul Celan, *Selected Poems*, Penguin, 1972.
Friedrich Hoelderlin and Eduard Moerike, *Selected Poems*, University of Chicago Press, 1972.
Grass, *Inmarypraise*, Harcourt, 1974.
Elias Canetti, *Kafka's Other Trial: The Letters to Felice*, Schocken, 1974.
(With Hamburger) Grass, *In the Egg, and Other Poems*, Harcourt, 1977.
Walser, *Selected Stories*, Farrar, Straus, 1982.
Gerd Hofmann, *The Spectacle at the Tower*, Fromm, 1985.

SIDELIGHTS: Christopher Middleton is "one of the most scrupulous of British poets involved in following the innovations of modernism," according to Douglas Dunn of *Encounter.* Writing in the *Times Literary Supplement,* George Steiner praises Middleton's "characteristic tautness, his sinewy elegance and reach of invocation". Middleton has earned a considerable reputation for his translations as well. As Alfred Corn remarks in the *New York Times Book Review,* Middleton "is a distinguished translator of Goethe, Rilke and Trakl, among others." Steiner believes that Middleton "is at his best when he writes as a translator, when he places his own gifts at the exigent service of a master."

"Although its roots are in surrealism . . . and German Expressionism," Brian Swann comments in the *Library Journal,* "Middleton's poetry is unlike any other. He specializes in lively juxtapositions, incongruities of collage, the play of forms. . . . Vistas recede in a number of poems into the prehistoric so we are aware of mysterious correlations." One of Middleton's continuing concerns has been the shaping of each individual poem to suit its particular subject. "His concern to produce an individual structure of perception for every place, thought and experience he writes about," notes Alan Brownjohn in the *New Statesman,* "results in a ceaseless and challenging originality." Alan Young of the *Dictionary of Literary Biography* describes Middleton as a writer who sees "the art and craft of writing as a hazardous, disruptive, and visionary enterprise, one in which the poet as maker undertakes to shape a language into original ways of saying and, therefore, of knowing for a shaken and uncertain world."

Because of his beliefs about what poetry should be, Middleton is often at odds with the British poetry mainstream. In his collection of essays entitled *The Pursuit of the Kingfisher,* Middleton calls for an "exigent poetry, hard-bitten poetry, which goes to the limits of the conceivable and thus relocates the centre." He also decries the "suave poetry" which he sees as dominating the British literary scene. Steiner argues that Middleton's "linguistic range, the severe seriousness of his conception of the role of the poet and of the poet's reader in these 'terrible times', his unembarrassed celebration of the visionary, 'transcendent' potentialities in art and the imagination, are correctives to the retrenched provincialism of the current English manner."

Middleton's approach has not always been popular with the critics, who sometimes misunderstand his intentions or do not appreciate his innovations. Even some critics who understand his intentions believe that Middleton does not always succeed in fulfilling them in his poems. Corn, for one, states that Middleton's "effort is to escape the artifice of received literacy, and he has at least succeeded in doing that; his poems don't sound like anyone in particular, not even his models. The gain brings with it definite losses." Reviewing *Pataxanadu and Other Prose* for the *Times Literary Supplement,* Alan Young claims that Middleton "likes to make up new rules and does not really seem to care which way he is playing. . . . *Pataxanadu and Other Prose* . . . exhibits more than ever before those cultivated eccentricities of Middleton's art which by turns fascinate, mystify and exasperate his readers."

Among Middleton's most successful poetry collections is *The Lonely Suppers of W. V. Balloon,* a book that "ranges through many countries, times, and moods, but [exhibits] throughout a consistently high level of performance," according to Young in his *Dictionary of Literary Biography* article. Writing in the *Chicago Review,* Jay Parini finds *The Lonely Suppers of W. V. Balloon* to be "a daring and, largely, successful book." The collection moved Brownjohn to call Middleton "easily the most intelligent and serious of our innovators, a poet with a disconcerting knack of making it new in a different way in almost every poem." Dunn, in his review of the book, called Middleton "a poet of considerable importance—an avant-garde poet we can actually *read.*"

The collection *111 Poems,* a selection from several of Middleton's books, has also been well received by the critics. Writing in the *London Review of Books,* Denis Donoghue states that "metrically inventive and various, these poems are remarkably alive to 'the unknown thing beside us'; they listen for 'the due sound', and, as if watching birds, register 'the timed flight of words.' " Although acknowledging Middleton's reputation as "a poet of re-markable oddity," John Mole of *Encounter* finds in his review of the book that "Middleton can write fine poems." And Mole explains that Middleton's work is often concerned with "definitions of poetry — its possibilities and limits." In similar terms, Robert Nye remarks in the London *Times* that Middleton "has a reputation for being eccentric to the point of obscurity. The present volume shows that reputation to be more apparent than real." Nye compares Middleton to Wordsworth: "Middleton demonstrates that the essence of his talent is for a kind of passionate description not all that far away from Wordsworth. . . . I very much like both the tone and the substance."

Although Middleton has lived in Texas for over twenty years—and is, as Steiner explains, "at odds with what he takes to be the English literary, spiritual climate"—he is still a vital part of the contemporary English poetry scene. As Young notes in the *Dictionary of Literary Biography,* "Middleton has been an increasingly important influence on writing in English since the mid-1950s. His poems, stories, translations, and essays have demonstrated consistent refusal to disregard the more unsettling discoveries of both romanticism and high modernism."

BIOGRAPHICAL/CRITICAL SOURCES:

BOOKS

Contemporary Literary Criticism, Volume 13, Gale, 1980.
Dictionary of Literary Biography, Volume 40: *Poets of Great Britain and Ireland since 1960,* Gale, 1985.
Middleton, Christopher, *The Pursuit of the Kingfisher,* Carcanet Press, 1983.
Young, Alan, *Dada and After: Extremist Modernism and English Literature,* Humanities Press, 1981.

PERIODICALS

Chicago Review, Volume 29, number 1, 1977.
Encounter, September, 1975, October, 1979, December, 1983.
Hudson Review, autumn, 1962.
Library Journal, November 15, 1975.
London Magazine, February, 1966.
London Review of Books, October 4, 1984.
New Statesman, December 24, 1965, September 5, 1975, June 3, 1983.
New York Times Book Review, October 24, 1982, May 20, 1984, November 15, 1987.
Ninth Decade, Number 2, 1983.
Observer, January 2, 1966.
PN Review, Number 18, 1980.
Stand, spring, 1981.
Times (London), June 9, 1983.
Times Literary Supplement, February 17, 1966, January 13, 1978, May, 16, 1980, March 9, 1984.
Voice Literary Supplement, March, 1982.
Yale Review, autumn, 1963.

—Sketch by Thomas Wiloch

MILGRAM, Stanley 1933-1984

PERSONAL: Born August 15, 1933, in New York, N.Y.; died December 20, 1984, in New York City; son of Samuel (a cake baker and shop owner) and Adele (Israel) Milgram; married Alexandra Menkin (a psychiatric social worker), December 10, 1961; children: Michele Sara, Marc Daniel. *Education:* Queens College (now Queens College of the City University of New York), A.B., 1954; Harvard University, Ph.D., 1960.

CAREER: Yale University, New Haven, Conn., assistant professor of psychology, 1960-63; Harvard University, Cambridge, Mass., assistant professor of social psychology, 1963-67; City University of New York, New York City, professor of psychology, 1967-79, Distinguished Professor of Psychology, beginning 1980. Consultant, Polaroid Corp., Cambridge, 1977.

MEMBER: American Association for the Advancement of Science (fellow, 1971), American Psychological Association, Association of Independent Film and Television Producers, American Academy of Arts and Sciences.

AWARDS, HONORS: Ford Foundation fellowship, 1954-55; Harvard University fellowship, 1955-57; Social Science Research Council fellowship, 1957-59; American Association for the Advancement of Science socio-psychological prize, 1964, for experiments examining obedience to authority; grant from CBS, Inc., 1969-72, to study effects of television violence; Guggenheim fellowship, 1972-73, to study psychological maps of Paris; New York International Film and Television Festival silver medal, 1974, for "The City and the Self"; National Book Award nomination, 1975, for *Obedience to Authority: An Experimental View.*

WRITINGS:

(With R. Lance Shotland) *Television and Anti-Social Behavior,* Academy Press, 1973.
Obedience to Authority: An Experimental View, Harper, 1974.
(Editor) *Psychology in Today's World,* Little, Brown, 1975.
The Individual in a Social World: Essays and Experiments, Addison-Wesley, 1977.

OTHER

Also writer and producer for the films "Obedience," 1968, "The City and the Self," 1974, "Conformity and Independence," 1974, "Invitation to Social Psychology," 1974, "Human Aggression," 1976, and "Nonverbal Communication," 1976.

SIDELIGHTS: Stanley Milgram, who died at age fifty-one, was recognized as one of America's foremost social psychologists for his experiments on human conformity and aggression. He was perhaps best known for his experiments on obedience, the results of which he published as *Obedience to Authority: An Experimental View.* In the first chapter of the book, Milgram noted: "Obedience is as basic an element in the structure of social life as one can point to. Some system of authority is a requirement of all communal living, and it is only the man dwelling in isolation who is not forced to respond, through defiance or submission, to the commands of others."

Using Adolph Hitler and the Nazi Party to exemplify submission to authority, Milgram pointed out that the mass slaughter of millions of people was the idea of just one man, Hitler, and that the killings would not have happened if people had not obeyed Hitler's orders. Concluded Milgram: "Facts of recent history and observation in daily life suggest that for many people obedience may be a deeply ingrained behavior tendency, indeed a prepotent impulse overriding training in ethics, sympathy, and moral conduct."

In Milgram's famous test to determine if obedience supersedes moral and ethical consciousness, a laboratory technician instructed a subject to give a verbal test to a learner and to punish incorrect answers by administering electric shocks of increasing voltage to the learner. The learner, actually an actor, received no real shocks at all, but simulated responses to the punishments supposedly administered by the test subject. The learner responded to low-voltage shocks with a groan and begged for release as the shocks worsened. If the subject hesitated to continue, the technician ordered him or her to proceed, assuring the subject that the technician himself would assume full responsibility for any harm done. Despite the screams of the learner and the hesitancy of the subjects, two-thirds of those tested obeyed the technician's command to continue, all the while believing the learner was being harmed. Some of the subjects nearly broke down from the strain of the test, but even they persisted.

Milgram postulated that the "most fundamental lesson" of his study is that "ordinary people, simply doing their jobs, and without any particular hostility on their part, can become agents in a terrible destructive process. Moreover, even when the destructive effects of their work become patently clear, and they are asked to carry out actions incompatible with fundamental standards of morality, relatively few people have the resources needed to resist authority."

The psychologist was both praised and criticized for this study of human behavior. The American Association for the Advancement of Science applauded Milgram's efforts, but some critics claimed his experiment was immoral and unethical because it placed people under extreme stress that could be psychologically harmful. Nevertheless, few denied the test's impact. Peter S. Prescott of *Newsweek* commented: "We can argue that the experiments were cruel and should not have been undertaken. We can question whether much truth can be abstracted from [deception]. . . . But the results of the experiment remain: they are real, they have been repeated, their implications are appalling, and they must not be dismissed." In the view of a *Times Literary Supplement* writer, "If it is immoral to find out about ourselves in a way we do not like, these experiments are certainly immoral. But then, as the experiments show, morality—at least in its public form—may have quite a lot to answer for."

MEDIA ADAPTATIONS: A television drama, "The Tenth Level," was based on Milgram's experiments on obedience.

BIOGRAPHICAL/CRITICAL SOURCES:

BOOKS

Milgram, Stanley, *Obedience to Authority: An Experimental View,* Harper, 1974.

PERIODICALS

Newsweek, January 28, 1974.
New York Times Book Review, January 13, 1974.
Psychology Today, March, 1985.
Spectator, July 20, 1974.
Times Literary Supplement, June 7, 1974.
Virginia Quarterly Review, summer, 1974.
Washington Post Book World, February 3, 1974.

OBITUARIES:

PERIODICALS

Los Angeles Times, December 26, 1984.
New York Times, December 22, 1984.

MILLER, Anita 1926-

PERSONAL: Born August 31, 1926, in Chicago, Ill.; daughter of Louis and Clara (Ruttenberg) Wolfberg; married Jordan Miller (a publisher), December 19, 1948; children: Mark Crispin, Bruce Joshua, Eric Lincoln. *Education:* Roosevelt University, B.A., 1948; Northwestern University, M.A., Ph.D., 1972.

ADDRESSES: *Home*—334 Hawthorn, Glencoe, Ill. 60022. *Office*—Academy Chicago, 213 West Institute Pl., Chicago, Ill. 60610.

CAREER: University of Wisconsin—Parkside, Kenosha, lecturer in English, 1969-70; Northwestern University, Evanston, Ill., lecturer in English, 1970-77; Academy Chicago (publisher), Chicago, Ill., editorial director, 1976—.

WRITINGS:

Arnold Bennett: An Annotated Bibliography, 1887-1932, Garland Publishing, 1972.
(With Jean M. Weiman) *The Fair Women,* Academy Chicago, 1981.
(Editor) *Beyond the Front Page,* Academy Chicago, 1983.
(Editor) *Feminismo!,* Academy Chicago, 1988.
(Editor) *The Trial of Levi Weeks,* Academy Chicago, 1989.
(Translator) Hella Haarse, *In a Dark Wood Wandering* (novel), Academy Chicago, 1989.

Editor, *Arnold Bennett Newsletter;* contributing editor, *English Literature in Translation.*

WORK IN PROGRESS: A book of light nonfiction.

SIDELIGHTS: Anita Miller told *CA:* "My major concern is reviving interest in worthwhile but now neglected writers. As a writer myself, I am also involved in producing primarily well-written, informative nonfiction and amusing light fiction."

* * *

MINCHINTON, W(alter) E(dward) 1921-

PERSONAL: Born April 29, 1921, in Dulwich, London, England; son of Walter Edward (a clerk) and Anne (Clark) Minchinton; married Marjorie Sargood (a medical social worker), August 18, 1945; children: Paul Richard, Anne Border, Susan Clare, David Walter. *Education:* London School of Economics and Political Science, B.Sc., 1947.

ADDRESSES: *Home*—53 Homefield Rd., Exeter EX1 2QX, England.

CAREER: University of Wales, University College of Swansea, assistant lecturer, 1948-50, lecturer, 1950-59, senior lecturer in history, 1959-64; University of Exeter, Exeter, England, professor of economic history, 1964-86, head of department, 1974-83. Visiting professor, Fourah Bay College, University of Sierra Leone, 1965, and LaTrobe University, 1981-82. *Military service:* British Army; served in Royal Signal Corps, 1942-45; became lieutenant.

MEMBER: Economic History Society, British Agricultural History Society, Royal Historical Society (fellow).

AWARDS, HONORS: Alexander Prize, Royal Historical Society, 1953, for article "Bristol: The Metropolis of the South West in the Eighteenth Century"; Rockefeller Foundation research fellow, 1959-60.

WRITINGS:

The British Tinplate Industry: A History, Oxford University Press, 1957.
The Port of Bristol in the Eighteenth Century, Bristol Branch of the Historical Association, 1962.
Industrial Archaeology in Devon, Devon County Council, 1968, 4th edition, 1984.
(With John Perkins) *Tidemills of Devon and Cornwall,* Exeter Industrial Archaeology Group, 1971.
Devon at Work, David & Charles, 1974.
Windmills of Devon, Exeter Industrial Archaeology Group, 1977.
A Guide to Industrial Archaeology Sites in Britain, Paladin Books, 1984.
(With Celia King and Peter Waite) *Virginia Slave-Trade Statistics, 1698-1775,* Virginia State Library, 1984.
Devon's Industrial Past: A Guide, Dortington Amenity Research Trust, 1986.
Life to the City: An Illustrated History of Exeter's Water Supply, Devon Books, 1987.

EDITOR

The Trade of Bristol in the Eighteenth Century, Bristol Record Society, 1957.
Politics and the Port of Bristol in the Eighteenth Century, Bristol Record Society, 1963.
Essays in Agrarian History, two-volume reprints edition, Augustus M. Kelley, 1968.
Industrial South Wales, 1750-1914: Essays in Welsh Economic History, Augustus M. Kelley, 1968.
Mercantilism: System or Expediency?, Heath, 1969.
(And author of introduction) *The Growth of English Overseas Trade in the Seventeenth and Eighteenth Centuries,* Methuen, 1969, Barnes & Noble, 1970.
Wage Regulation in Pre-Industrial England, David & Charles, 1971.
Farming and Transport in the South West, University of Exeter, 1972.
(With H. E. S. Fisher) *Transport and Shipowning in the West Country,* University of Exeter, 1973.
Population and Marketing: Two Studies in the History of the South-West, University of Exeter, 1976.
Capital Formation in South-West England, University of Exeter, 1978.
Reactions to Social and Economic Changes, 1750-1939, University of Exeter, 1979.
Agricultural Improvement: Medieval and Modern, University of Exeter, 1981.
(With Peter Harper) *American Manuscripts in the House of Lords Record Office,* Microform, 1983.
A Limekiln Miscellany: The South-West and South Wales, Exeter Industrial Archaeology Group, 1984.
The Baltic Grain Trade: Five Essays, Association for the History of the Northern Seas, 1985.
Britain and the Northern Seas: Some Essays, Lofthouse Publications, 1988.

* * *

MITCHELL, Juliet (Constance Wyatt) 1940-

PERSONAL: Born October 4, 1940, in Christchurch, New Zealand; married; one daughter. *Education:* St. Anne's College, Oxford, B.A. (honors), 1961. *Politics:* Socialist. *Religion:* Agnostic.

ADDRESSES: *Agent*—Deborah Rogers, 20 Powis Mews, London W11 1JN, England.

CAREER: University of Leeds, Leeds, England, assistant lecturer in English, 1962-63; University of Reading, Reading, England, lecturer in English, 1965-71; free-lance writer, broadcaster, and lecturer, 1971—; auxiliary nurse, University College Hospital psychiatric unit, 1974-75; psychotherapist, at Paddington Centre for Psychotherapy, 1975-76, and in private practice, 1976-77; psychoanalyst in private practice, 1978—. Lecturer at universities and institutes in the United States, Canada, Europe, Australia, and New Zealand, including service as Henry Luce Scholar, Yale University, 1983-84.

MEMBER: Institute of Psychoanalysis (associate member).

WRITINGS:

Women: The Longest Revolution (essay), New Left Review, 1966.

Women's Estate, Penguin, 1971, Pantheon, 1972.

Psychoanalysis and Feminism, Pantheon, 1974.

(Editor and author of introduction with Ann Oakley) *The Rights and Wrongs of Women,* Penguin, 1976.

(Editor and author of introduction) Daniel Defoe, *The Fortunes and Misfortunes of the Famous Moll Flanders,* Penguin, 1978.

(Editor with Jacqueline Rose) *Feminine Sexuality: Jacques Lacan and the Ecole Freudienne,* Macmillan (London), 1982, Norton, 1983.

Women: The Longest Revolution (anthology), Pantheon, 1984.

(Editor with Oakley) *What Is Feminism?: A Re-Examination by Nancy Cott, Linda Gordon, Judith Stacey, Juliet Mitchell, Ann Oakley, and Six Other Major Feminist Thinkers,* Pantheon, 1986.

(Editor) Melanie Klein, *The Selected Melanie Klein: The Essential Writings,* Penguin, 1986, Free Press, 1987.

Contributor to *New Left Review, Nation, New York Times,* and other journals and newspapers. Member of editorial boards, *New Left Review, Social Praxis,* and *Dialectic: A Journal of Feminist Thought.*

SIDELIGHTS: Juliet Mitchell "is a provocative English theorist, a Marxist and feminist, whose interests have often anticipated those of the women's movement or run beside them as a gloss," notes Ann Snitow in the *Nation.* Mitchell published the essay *Women: The Longest Revolution* in 1966, and even "if she had written nothing else," comments Snitow, "[she] would still hold an honored place in the history of feminism for this extraordinary essay—a detailed, fully developed feminist analysis of the complex, coordinated layers of female oppression." Mitchell, however, has continued developing her feminist theories in several books which are distinguished by their broad scope of ideas, flexibility of discussion, and absence of rigid rhetoric.

Women's Estate, for example, is "a small book whose clear thinking and lucid argument are a grateful contrast to the heat without light generated by a good deal of the literature of the women's movement," remarks a *Times Literary Supplement* reviewer. Taking a Marxist approach to analyzing the female experience, *Women's Estate* explores the ordinary situations of women, both at home and in the workplace. *Book World* contributor Elizabeth Janeway believes this work is an important contribution to feminist literature: "Mitchell reveals herself in this book as a humane, wide-ranging, and toughminded critic and guide. Her Marxist background has not turned her into a stereotypical thinker. She questions the Revolutionary Fathers and their contemporary descendents on their attitudes toward women." While Jill Tweedie finds *Woman's Estate* too "jargon-ridden," she admits in the *New Statesman* that "every revolutionary movement needs theoretical underpinning and Miss Mitchell's discussion [and comparisons] . . . are all useful and thought-provoking." And Janeway concludes that "there is much meat in this valuable book, for which I wish a wide readership."

Mitchell continues challenging conventional assumptions in *Psychoanalysis and Feminism,* "a book of provocative imagination which sets out to transform our view of [Sigmund] Freud and history," states Elsa First in the *New York Times Book Review.* While traditional feminists have often rejected Freud's theories of sexual attitudes and gender development as too outmoded to be applicable to current society, Mitchell claims that "Freud tells us far more about [the basis of] women's degradation than the enemies of Freud can ever begin to tell us," describes *New York Review of Books* contributor Christopher Lasch. The critic observes that Mitchell's "book not only challenges orthodox feminism, . . . it defies the conventions of social thought in the English-speaking countries. . . . *Psychoanalysis and Feminism,*" asserts Lasch, "is a brave and important book, and its influence will not be confined to feminists. Anyone who thinks Freud's work has been conclusively revised, updated, or overthrown will have to contend for a long time to come with this withering rejoinder." "*Psychoanalysis and Feminism* is an important and provocative book," remarks Ellen Willis in *Ms.* "I sympathize with its purpose and admire its boldness." While Willis faults Mitchell for being overly theoretical and impractical, she concedes that the treatise "begins a long overdue exploration. I hope other feminists will carry it on."

Published in 1984, *Women: The Longest Revolution* is a retrospective of Mitchell's writings; the collection, according to *New Statesman* contributor Jean Radford, "reads like a narrative of these [last fifteen] years as well as the story of one woman's intellectual development. The title essay was written in 1966, before the women's liberation movement started in [Great Britain]." The critic notes that Mitchell's early tract "became what *New Left Review* would call a 'seminal' text for socialist-feminists, so it's excellent to have it available in book form." Snitow also believes that *Women: The Longest Revolution* presents "a retrospective of [the author's] evolution." Although the critic finds the essays less compelling than they were upon their original publication, she observes that Mitchell's accompanying commentary is helpful: "She assumes, I think rightly, that such a narrative of her own development will echo larger themes in the history of recent political thought."

"Of all the feminist thinkers of our time, Juliet Mitchell is the one who genuinely understands how to cross subject boundaries," writes Judith Hughes in *Encounter.* Snitow similarly praises the author's ability "to take on the big men—Marx, Engels, Mill, Meredith, Dickens, James, Defoe, Freud, Lacan—something feminists have understandably but regrettably been leery of doing. She offers us much thereby," continues the critic, adding that "it's a pleasure to see her at ease with such difficult mentors, granting them their greatness without being overawed by their authority." "In a year which has seen the publication of several books by feminists looking back . . . , it's doubly good to read one which so tenaciously pursues the question of sexual difference," says Radford. *Women: The Longest Revolution* "tells *one* version of the story so far," concludes the critic. "Since the longest revolution still has a long way to go, this is both necessary and valuable."

BIOGRAPHICAL/CRITICAL SOURCES:

PERIODICALS

Book World, January 30, 1972.
Encounter, November, 1984.
London Review of Books, April 4, 1985, November 6, 1986.
Ms., August, 1974.
Nation, October 13, 1984, February 7, 1987.
New Statesman, December 3, 1971, May 3, 1974, June 8, 1984.
New York Review of Books, April 20, 1972, October 3, 1974.
New York Times Book Review, May 19, 1974, March 15, 1987.
Times Literary Supplement, December 17, 1971, May 3, 1974, September 28, 1984, December 4, 1987.

* * *

MOAT, John 1936-

PERSONAL: Born September 11, 1936, in India; married Antoinette Galletti; children: Elsbeth Merlin, Ben John. *Education:* Oxford University, M.A., 1960.

ADDRESSES: Agent—A.D. Peters & Co., 10 Buckingham St., London WC2N 6BU, England.

CAREER: Writer.

WRITINGS:

6d. per annum (poems), Phoenix Press, 1966.
(Self-illustrated) *Heorot* (novel), Cresset, 1968.
A Standard of Verse, Phoenix Press, 1969.
Thunder of Grass (poems), Cresset, 1970.
The Tugen and the Toot (novel), Barrie & Jenkins, 1973.
The Ballad of the Leaf (verse), Arc Publications, 1974.
Bartonwood (novel), Chatto & Windus, 1978.
Fiesta (verse), Enitharmon Press, 1980.
Skeleton Key (verse), Phoenix Press, 1982.
Mai's Wedding (novel), Collins, 1983.
(Self-illustrated) *The Missing Moon* (novel), Green Books, 1988.
The Miraculous Mandarin (verse), Enitharmon, 1989.

* * *

MOHAN, Brij 1939-

PERSONAL: Born August 9, 1939, in Mursan, India; came to the United States in 1975, naturalized citizen, 1983; son of Ram Pershad Sharma and Ram Shreedevi Sharma; married Prem Sharma; children: Anupama Sharma, Apoorva Sharma. *Education:* Agra University, B.A., 1958, M.S.W., 1960; University of Lucknow, Ph.D., 1964.

ADDRESSES: Home—1573 Leycester Dr., Baton Rouge, La. 70808. *Office*—School of Social Work, Louisiana State University, Baton Rouge, La. 70803.

CAREER: University of Lucknow, Lucknow, India, research supervisor and research scholar, 1960-64, lecturer in social work, 1964-75; University of Wisconsin—Oshkosh, academic specialist, 1975-76; Louisiana State University, Baton Rouge, associate professor, 1976-81, professor of social work, 1981—, dean of School of Social Work, 1981-86.

MEMBER: International Sociological Association, International Association of Schools of Social Work, International Consortium on Social Development, National Association of Social Workers, Council on Social Work Education.

AWARDS, HONORS: Government of India University Grants Commission research scholar, 1960-63; fellow of UNESCO, 1968.

WRITINGS:

India's Social Problems, Indian International Publications, 1972.
Social Psychiatry in India, Minerva Associates, 1973.
New Horizons of Social Welfare and Policy, Schenkman, 1985.
(Editor) *Toward Comparative Social Welfare,* Schenkman, 1985.
Denial of Existence: Essays on the Human Condition, C. C Thomas, 1987.
The Logic of Social Welfare, St. Martin's, 1988.
Glimpses of International and Comparative Social Welfare, ISFED, Inc., 1988.

Contributor of about one hundred articles and reviews to journals in the social sciences. Founder and editor-in-chief of *Journal of International and Comparative Social Welfare;* member of editorial board of *Psychology: A Journal of Human Behavior.*

WORK IN PROGRESS: Rediscovery of India; Beyond Nonviolence.

SIDELIGHTS: Brij Mohan told *CA:* "To me, writing has always been a 'painkiller'; it relieves me of 'existential anxieties.' Commitment to human conditions has been the main drive prompting me to analyze social realities that impact human experience and quality of life. *India's Social Problems* was an unorthodox approach to understanding the dehumanization of one-seventh of the total of humanity. In *Social Psychiatry in India,* I uncovered the anguish of mental patients. *New Horizons of Social Welfare and Policy* and *Toward Comparative Social Welfare* seek to explore international dimensions in policy analysis. A comparative-analytic paradigm is proffered as a tool for cross-cultural analyses and understanding." He continues: "My recent books, *Denial of Existence* and *The Logic of Social Welfare,* proffer detailed exposes of the human condition and societal arrangements. My forthcoming book, *Rediscovery of India,* is an exploration of the phenomenon 'new ethnicity.' In *Beyond Nonviolence,* I seek to present a framework for a nonviolent 'bioglobal' strategy of peaceful co-existence.

"It is hard to be an author; it is a kind of self-execution. Especially when you find that your work is not duly rewarded while mediocrity and pathology of power continue to flourish, one gets depressed. But writing helps when everyone else betrays; it gives you a sense of purpose, a satisfaction that is a reward in itself. A writer alone *exists!*"

* * *

MOORE, Lander
See FENSCH, Thomas

* * *

MORAN, Tom 1943-

PERSONAL: Born December 5, 1943, in Philadelphia, Pa.; son of George F. and Alice Moran; married Marilyn Groch (an artist), June, 1978; children: Rachel L., Michael T. *Education:* California State Polytechnic College (now University), San Luis Obispo, B.S., 1965; California State College (now University), Long Beach, M.S., 1968.

ADDRESSES: Home—Venice, Calif. *Office*—218 Howland Canal, Venice, Calif. 90291.

CAREER: California Institute of Technology, Pasadena, research engineer at Jet Propulsion Laboratory, 1966-69; freelance journalist, 1969-74; aide to Los Angeles city council member Pat Russell, 1974-78; *Ocean Front Weekly,* Venice, Calif., editor, 1979; free-lance journalist, 1979-82; Loral Electro Optical Systems, Pasadena, aerospace technical writer, 1982-1983; Rockwell, Inc.-North American Aircraft, El Segundo, Calif., supervisor of technical publications, 1983—. Member of board of directors of Project Heavy West, 1976-78, and Venice U.S.A., 1980-82; member of Los Angeles Regional Criminal Justice Planning Board, 1976.

WRITINGS:

(Author of text) *The Photo Essay: Paul Fusco and Will McBride,* photographs by Fusco and McBride, Crowell, 1974.
(With Tom Sewell) *Fantasy by the Sea,* Peace Press, 1980.
Roller Skating Is for Me (juvenile; with own photographs), Lerner, 1982.
Frisbee Disc Flying Is for Me (juvenile; with own photographs), Lerner, 1982.
(With Andrew David) *River Thrill Sports* (juvenile), Lerner, 1983.
Kite Flying Is for Me (juvenile; with own photographs), Lerner, 1984.
Canoeing Is for Me (juvenile), Lerner, 1984.
Bicycle Motocross Racing (juvenile), Lerner, 1986.
A Family in Ireland (juvenile; with own photographs), Lerner, 1986.
A Family in Mexico (juvenile; with own photographs), Lerner, 1987.

Contributor to magazines, including *California Living, Chic, Los Angeles, Swank, Canoe,* and *Beyond Baroque.*

WORK IN PROGRESS: A book on California art and poetry during the 1950s, completion expected in 1990; a book on the U.S. Army for Lerner.

SIDELIGHTS: Tom Moran told *CA:* "*Fantasy by the Sea* is a history of the eccentric southern California community of Venice, my home for many years and a constant source of friendship and inspiration."

* * *

MORGAN, (Walter) Jefferson 1940-

PERSONAL: Born March 30, 1940, in Salt Lake City, Utah; son of Thomas Ralph (an executive) and Althea (a pharmacist and nurse; maiden name, Ball) Morgan; married Patricia Williams, 1960 (divorced, 1965); married Jinx Adams (a writer), March 26, 1971; children: Stacy, Derick, Coulter. *Education:* University of California, teaching credential, 1967; also attended Diablo Valley College, Oakland City College, University of Chicago, University of California, Berkeley, Stanford University, and Harvard University.

ADDRESSES: Home and office—The Sugar Mill, P.O. Box 425, Road Town, Torfola, British Virgin Islands. *Agent*—Carl Brandt, Brandt & Brandt, 1501 Broadway, New York, N.Y. 10036.

CAREER: Oakland Tribune, Oakland, Calif., copyboy, 1957-58, police reporter, 1958-59, assistant state editor, 1959-60, courthouse bureau chief, 1960-63, city desk rewrite man, 1963-69, special writer, 1969-76, author of column "Dining with Wine," 1976; free-lance writer, 1976—. Western U.S. correspondent for Manchester *Guardian,* 1967—. Instructor at Peralta Colleges, 1967-69. Member of Society of Nieman Fellows.

MEMBER: Royal Commonwealth Society, Confrerie de la Marmite, San Francisco Press Club, Harvard Club.

AWARDS, HONORS: Newswriting prizes from Associated Press, 1966, 1969, 1971, 1973; William F. Knowland Award, 1966, 1969, 1970; first prize from San Francisco Press Club, 1970, 1973; Nieman fellow at Harvard University, 1971-72; McQuade Award from Association of Catholic Newsmen, 1974; award from California Taxpayers Association, 1974.

WRITINGS:

Guide to California Wines, Dutton, 1968, 3rd edition, 1975.
Adventures in the Wine Country, Chronicle Books, 1971, revised edition, 1976.
Why Have They Taken Our Children?, Delacorte, 1978.
(With Donald T. Lunde) *The Die Song: A Journey into the Mind of a Mass Murderer,* Norton, 1980.
(With wife, Jinx Morgan) *Two Cooks in One Kitchen,* Doubleday, 1983.
(With J. Morgan) *The Sugar Mill Cookbook,* TMC Ltd., 1987.

Contributor to popular magazines, including *Reader's Digest, National Wildlife, Bon Appetit, Parade,* and *Travel and Leisure.*

WORK IN PROGRESS: Completing a mystery novel set in the Caribbean; magazine writing.

SIDELIGHTS: Jefferson Morgan's book *The Die Song: A Journey into the Mind of a Mass Murderer* is a study of Herbert Mullin, a paranoid schizophrenic, and is based on psychiatrist Donald T. Lunde's examination of this convicted killer. Describing the writing as "excellent," *Los Angeles Times Book Review* critic Robert Kirsch adds that in *The Die Song* the reader clearly sees "the skewed nature of the person in the grip of his disorder, the swing between normal behavior and the grip of a delusional system that seems to the killer logical and determined."

Morgan told *CA* that "cooking helps keep *me* sane."

BIOGRAPHICAL/CRITICAL SOURCES:

PERIODICALS

Los Angeles Times Book Review, April 13, 1980.
New York Times Book Review, March 30, 1980.

* * *

MORGAN, Robin 1941-

PERSONAL: Born January 29, 1941, in Lake Worth, Fla.; daughter of Faith Berkeley Morgan; married Kenneth Pitchford (a poet, novelist and playwright), September 19, 1962; children: Blake Ariel Morgan-Pitchford. *Education:* Attended Columbia University. *Politics:* "Radical Feminist." *Religion:* "Wiccean Atheist."

ADDRESSES: Home—New York, N.Y. *Office*—c/o *Ms.,* 119 West 40th St., New York, N.Y. 10018. *Agent*—Georges Borchardt, Inc., 145 East 52nd St., New York, N.Y. 10022.

CAREER: Curtis Brown, Ltd., New York, N.Y., associate literary agent, 1960-62; free-lance editor, 1964-70; writer, 1970—; contributing editor, *Ms.* magazine, 1977—. International lecturer on feminism, 1970-76; guest professor at New College, Sarasota, Fla., 1972; has given poetry readings all over the United States. Member of board of directors, Women's Law Center, Feminist Self-Help Clinics, Battered Women's Refuge, Women's Institute Freedom Press, and National Alliance of Rape Crisis Centers.

MEMBER: Women's International Terrorist Conspiracy from Hell (founding member), Authors Guild, Authors League of America, Women's Anti-Defamation League, Susan B. Anthony

National Memorial Association, Poetry Society of America, National Women's Political Caucus, Women Against Pornography (founding member), Feminist Writers Guild (founding member), New York Radical Women (founding member).

WRITINGS:

(Editor with Charlotte Bunch-Weeks and Joanne Cooke) *The New Women: A Motive Anthology on Women's Liberation,* Bobbs-Merrill, 1970.

(Editor) *Sisterhood Is Powerful: An Anthology of Writings from the Women's Liberation Movement,* Random House, 1970.

Monster: Poems, Random House, 1972.

Lady of the Beasts: Poems, Random House, 1976.

Going Too Far: The Personal Chronicle of a Feminist, Random House, 1977.

Depth Perception: New Poems and a Masque, Anchor/ Doubleday, 1982.

The Anatomy of Freedom: Feminism, Physics, and Global Politics, Anchor/Doubleday, 1982.

(Contributor) Karen Payne, editor, *Between Ourselves: Letters between Mothers and Daughters,* Houghton, 1984.

(Contributing editor) *Sisterhood Is Global: The International Women's Movement Anthology,* Anchor, 1985.

Dry Your Smile (novel), Doubleday, 1987.

The Demon Lover: On the Sexuality of Terrorism, Norton, 1989.

OTHER

"Our Creations Are in the First Place Ourselves" (in two cassettes), Iowa State University of Science and Technology, 1974.

Also author of "Their Own Country," a play, 1961. Works represented in many anthologies, including *No More Masks!,* edited by Howe and Bass, for Doubleday; *The Young American Writers,* edited by Kostelanetz, for Funk; and *Campfires of the Resistance,* edited by Gitlin, for Bobbs-Merrill. Contributor of articles and poems to about a hundred literary and political journals, including *Atlantic, New York Times, Hudson Review,* and *Feminist Art Journal.*

WORK IN PROGRESS: Tales of the Witches, historical fiction; a book of poems; a cycle of verse plays.

SIDELIGHTS: "One discovery of this decade has been a hitherto unplumbed, forbidden, inexpressible depth of female rage. Robin Morgan—one of the most honestly angry women since Antigone—has rightly become a feminist heroine for her expression of it," notes Alicia Ostriker in the *Partisan Review.* Indeed, for more than twenty years, Morgan has been known as both an active leader in the international feminist movement and an accomplished poet. "I am an artist and a political being as well," Morgan once told *CA.* "My aim has been to forge these two concerns into an integrity which affirms language, art, craft, form, beauty, tragedy, and audacity with the needs and visions of women, as part of an emerging new culture which could enrich us all."

Morgan is best known for having edited "one of the first of the good anthologies of the women's movement, *Sisterhood Is Powerful* [*: An Anthology of Writings from the Women's Liberation Movement*]," notes Kathleen Wiegner in the *American Poetry Review.* Published soon after Kate Millett's *Sexual Politics,* Morgan's feminist reader has "profoundly affected the way that many of us think about women and the relations between the sexes," Paul Robinson says in a *Psychology Today* article. Reviewers concur with Jean Gardner of the *New York Times Book Review* that the collection maintains a distinctly anti-male tone; in fact, a *New Leader* contributor expressed a fear that its strident cast might eclipse "some basic truths: that women have indeed been discriminated against, their talents wasted or misused, by many institutions and many men for a very long time, and that an end to this inequality is still not in sight." Particularly hazardous are the book's dogmatic features, such as "The Drop Dead List of Books to Watch Out For," Gardner suggests. *Commonweal* contributor Kathy Mulherin sees these hazards as well, but recommends *Sisterhood Is Powerful* nonetheless because it relates "to the real conditions of women and is worth looking into."

She argues, "The worst aspects of the book can't really be helped; they are also the worst aspects of the women's liberation movement," which at that time was just beginning to address the concerns of women outside white middle-class status. Writing in the *Nation,* Muriel Haynes also defends the essays: "This is good personal journalism, some of it flecked with wit, though it is rarely amusing."

Morgan's next anthology, *Sisterhood Is Global: The International Women's Movement Anthology,* "clearly demonstrates that there is a vital international women's movement," observes *Choice* contributor S. E. Jacobs, who deems it, therefore, "one of the most important books to appear in the past decade." Reviewers such as Andrew Hacker question the validity and accuracy of certain statistics in the book; at the same time, Hacker, writing in the *New York Times Book Review,* admires the book's range: "By temperament, the editor and almost all the contributors veer toward the left. Yet, as Simone de Beauvoir points out in her article on France, if that side of the spectrum has been 'the chosen friend' of militant women, it has also been their 'worst enemy.'. . . Virtually every left-leaning regime has put women's issues on the back burner or ignored them altogether." The collection's other successes include "the reports from feminists perhaps many of us did not know existed—Senegalese, Tahitian, Nepalese—who describe working, sexual, marital, political and economic life in their respective countries," remarks Vivienne Walt in the *Nation.*

Contributors to the anthology met with Morgan in New York City in 1984 to define a strategy for the Sisterhood Is Global Institute. Members of the institute plan to "address the problems of women everywhere, including illiteracy; the care of the elderly; refugee populations and war victims; the crisis of world population; [and] the welfare, health, rights, and education of children," one participant told Marilyn Hoffman for a *Los Angeles Times* article. It also aims to translate books by women's rights activists; to investigate and impede the practice of sex tourism; and to expose religious groups they have identified "as being particularly adverse to women," Hoffman reports. Morgan, together with leaders from Greece, Portugal, New Zealand and Palestine, is one of the institute's founders.

"Morgan is a feminist, to be sure; she is also an accomplished and original poet," Jay Parini observes in a *Poetry* review. Because Morgan's political concerns are foremost, she sometimes deliberately relaxes her attention to poetic technique. As a result, says May Swenson in the *New York Times Book Review,* Morgan's first book of poems, *Monster,* offers some poems that are "strongly wrought" among others that are "polemical" and "formless." David Lehman, writing in *Poetry,* echoes this assessment, praising the poems that "attain an anger purer than prejudice, stereotype, or slogan." Particularly effective is the title poem, which records Morgan's reflections on the demands of political activism and in which she accepts the darker aspects of that role. "At her best," says Annette Niemtzow in the *Los Ange-*

les Times, Morgan possesses "a voice of passion, a gift of rhetoric and commitment, a verbal gesture which moves toward prophecy." Adrienne Rich, writing in the *Washington Post Book World,* values Morgan's "acute, devouring sense of her own potential, of the energy she and all women in patriarchal society expend in simply countering opposition—and of what that energy might achieve if it could be released from combat (and self-punishment) into creation."

Reviewing Morgan's second volume of poems, Wiegner comments, "*Monster* . . . dealt with female consciousness as an emerging political issue. Now, in *Lady of the Beasts* . . . she melds this consciousness with the Jungian theory of archetypes to present women in their mythic roles as mother, consort, sister, and finally, divine. . . . Her work appears to give power to women by showing the reader how, in some historic or mythic past, women held power through roles which have, in recent times, fallen into disrepute." *Lady of the Beasts* surpasses *Monster* while it contains more "engage poetry, the most difficult of . . . modes," Parini notes. In all of the poems, he goes on, "Morgan commands a wealth of technical resources," but her skill, he feels, is most evident in the poems "Voices from Six Tapestries" and "The Network of the Imaginary Mother."

Both poems are ambitious, reviewers explain. " 'Voices . . .' interprets the fifteenth-century *Lady with the Unicorn* tapestries, which hang in the Musee de Cluny in Paris, as the expression of a woman-centered pre-Christian religious system. It is also a moving, sustained love poem," Ostriker states. "The Network of the Imaginary Mother," notes Parini, is an "intricate long poem" that looks at Morgan's relationships with her mother, husband, woman lover, son, and self. Ostriker observes that this "descent into self has brought her to the sea floor where autobiography meets mythology." For example, its five sections "are laced together with horrifying lists of murdered prototypes of the women's liberation movement"—female veterinarians, herbalists, mystics, and others accused of witchcraft, Parini reports. These lists, he says, draw "taut the stitches between the concrete particulars of one life and their mythic potential." Though reviewers disagree about how well these poems serve the poet's intent, even those who see room for improvement find the poems successful on the emotional level. Ostriker, for example, comments, "I do not quarrel with Morgan's seriousness, her sense of the issues, or her conviction that poetry can make things happen. I have been touched and changed by her work, and presume that other contemporary women, and men, will be so also."

Morgan's later books place her continuing commitment to women's rights into context against a wider field of vision. *Depth Perception: New Poems and a Masque,* her third book of poems, takes her farther from "the unassimilated feminism of her first collection, *Monster,* and has gradually absorbed its ideas and concerns into an eloquent and forceful lyricism," says Parini in the *New York Times Book Review.* Essays in *Anatomy of Freedom: Feminism, Physics and Global Politics* claim a basis for human freedom in quantum physics, where particles in motion sometimes behave erratically. *Dry Your Smile,* a first novel, treats some of the same concerns in a fictional account of one woman writer's feelings as she writes her first novel. *Going Too Far: The Personal Chronicle of a Feminist* contains autobiographical nonfiction giving insight into the range of her opinions from 1962 to 1977. Critics comment on the unevenness in this selection, even though Morgan had explained in a *Ms.* "Forum" article that she meant to honestly represent her development by including some weaker pieces: "Ten years ago my poems quietly began muttering something about my personal pain as a woman—unconnected, of course, to anyone else, since I saw this merely as my own inadequacy, my own battle. I think a lot these days about the intervening decade and the startling changes it brought about, especially since the current book I'm working on [*Going Too Far*] is an assemblage of my own essays on feminism, dating back to the early 1960s: a graph of slow growth, defensiveness, struggle, painful new consciousness, and gradual affirmation. My decision to leave each piece 'as it was'—warts and all—has necessitated an editorial process redolent with a nostalgia punctuated by fits of embarrassed nausea."

Like other women writers who share her political concerns, Morgan has received "slings and arrows from all sides," she said in a later interview for the *Women's Review of Books.* She concluded, "Somehow there has to be more support for these women. In a country where the written word is not particularly esteemed, and where the message of feminism is complex and vast and not monolithic—and threatening—part of the problems that we're all of us having, well, they just come with the territory. And we have to keep fighting. There are no simple solutions. We chose this."

BIOGRAPHICAL/CRITICAL SOURCES:

BOOKS

Contemporary Literary Criticism, Volume 2, Gale, 1974.
Morgan, Robin, *Going Too Far: The Personal Chronicle of a Feminist,* Random House, 1977.
Payne, Karen, editor, *Between Ourselves: Letters between Mothers and Daughters, 1750-1982,* Houghton, 1984.

PERIODICALS

America, February 17, 1973.
American Book Review, March, 1983.
American Poetry Review, January, 1977.
Black World, August, 1971.
Choice, May, 1985.
Christian Century, March 31, 1971.
Christian Science Monitor, May 29, 1971, January 15, 1973.
Commonweal, April 2, 1971, January 15, 1973.
Library Journal, December 1, 1970.
Los Angeles Times, December 21, 1982, November 23, 1984.
Motive, March 4, 1969.
Ms., September, 1975, March, 1977.
Nation, December 14, 1970, March 2, 1985.
New Leader, December 14, 1970.
New Pages, spring, 1987.
New York Times, October 29, 1970.
New York Times Book Review, November 22, 1970, February 21, 1971, November 19, 1972, January 27, 1985, September 27, 1987.
Partisan Review, January 10, 1980.
Poetry, December, 1973, August, 1975, August, 1977.
Progressive, January, 1977, August, 1977.
Psychology Today, January, 1983.
San Francisco Review of Books, January, 1983.
Times Educational Supplement, January 10, 1987.
Times Literary Supplement, November 12, 1982.
Virginia Quarterly Review, spring, 1971.
Washington Post Book World, November 19, 1972, December 31, 1972, June 12, 1977.
Women's Review of Books, July 8, 1987.*

—Sketch by Marilyn K. Basel

MORGENSTERN, S.
See GOLDMAN, William W.

* * *

MORRIS, Henry M(adison, Jr.) 1918-

PERSONAL: Born October 6, 1918, in Dallas Tex.; son of Henry M. (a realtor) and Emily Ida (Hunter) Morris; married Mary Louise Beach (a librarian), January 24, 1940; children: Henry M. III, Kathleen (Mrs. Leslie Bruce), John, Andrew, Mary Rebecca. *Education:* Rice University, B.S.C.E. (with distinction), 1939; University of Minnesota, M.S., 1948, Ph.D., 1950. *Politics:* Republican. *Religion:* Independent Baptist.

ADDRESSES: Home—6733 El Banquero Pl., San Diego, Calif. 92119. *Office*—Institute for Creation Research, P.O. Box 2167, El Cajon, Calif. 92021.

CAREER: Member of Texas State Highway Department, Houston, Tex., 1938-39; International Boundary and Water Commission, El Paso, Tex., junior engineer, 1939-41, assistant hydraulic engineer, 1941-42; Rice University, Houston, instructor in civil engineering, 1942-46; University of Minnesota, St. Anthony Falls Hydraulic Laboratory, Minneapolis, instructor, 1946-50, assistant professor of civil engineering, 1950-51, research project leader, 1947-51; University of Southwestern Louisiana, Lafayette, professor of civil engineering, 1951-56, head of department, 1951-56, acting dean of engineering, fall, 1956; Southern Illinois University at Carbondale, professor of applied science, 1957; Virginia Polytechnic Institute and State University, Blacksburg, professor of hydraulic engineering and chairman of department of civil engineering, 1957-70; Christian Heritage College, San Diego, Calif., vice-president for academic affairs, 1970-78, president for academic affairs, 1978-80, Institute for Creation Research, director, 1970-80, president, 1980—.

MEMBER: Trans-National Association of Christian Schools (president, 1982—), American Association for the Advancement of Science (fellow), American Society of Civil Engineers (fellow), American Geophysical Union, American Geological Institute, Geological Society of America, American Society for Engineering Education, Engineers Council for Professional Development, Creation Research Society (president, 1967-73), Evolution Protest Movement (member of council, 1968—), Phi Beta Kappa, Sigma Xi, Tau Beta Pi, Chi Epsilon.

AWARDS, HONORS: LL.D., Bob Jones University, 1966.

WRITINGS:

(With R. S. Stephens) *Report on the Rio Grande Water Conservation Investigation,* El Paso International Boundary and Water Commission, 1942.
That You Might Believe, Good Books, 1946, end edition, 1978.
(With C. L. Larson) *Hydraulics of Flow in Culverts,* University of Minnesota Press, 1948.
A New Concept of Flow in Rough Conduits, University of Minnesota Press, 1950.
The Bible and Modern Science, Moody, 1951, revised edition, 1968.
(With John C. Whitcomb) *The Genesis Flood,* Presbyterian & Reformed, 1961.
The Twilight of Evolution, Baker Book, 1963.
Applied Hydraulics in Engineering, Ronald, 1963, revised edition (with J. M. Wiggert), Wiley, 1972.
Science, Scripture, and Salvation, Baptist Publications, 1965, revised edition, 1971.
Studies in the Bible and Science, Presbyterian & Reformed, 1966.
Evolution and the Modern Christian, Baker Book, 1968.
Hydraulics of Energy Dissipation, Virginia Polytechnic Institute and State University, 1968.
Biblical Cosmology and Modern Science, Craig, 1970.
The Bible Has the Answer, Craig, 1971, 2nd edition, 1976.
A Biblical Manual on Science and Creation, Institute for Creation Research, 1972.
The Remarkable Birth of Planet Earth, Institute for Creation Research, 1972.
(Editor) *Scientific Creationism,* Creation-Life, 1974, revised edition, 1985.
Many Infallible Proofs, Creation-Life, 1974.
The Troubled Waters of Evolution, Creation-Life, 1975.
(Editor) *The Battle for Creation,* Creation-Life, 1976.
The Genesis Record, Baker Book, 1976.
Education for the Real World, Creation-Life, 1977, revised edition, 1982.
The Scientific Case for Creation, Creation-Life, 1977.
Sampling the Psalms, Creation-Life, 1978.
The Beginning of the World, Accent, 1979.
King of Creation, Creation-Life, 1980.
Men of Science, Men of God, Master Books, 1981, revised edition, 1988.
(With G. E. Parker) *What Is Creation Science?,* Master Books, 1981, revised edition, 1987.
Evolution in Turmoil, Master Books, 1982.
The Revelation Record, Tyndale, 1983.
History of Modern Creationism, Master Books, 1984.
The Biblical Basis of Modern Science, Baker Book, 1984.
Creation and the Modern Christian, Master Books, 1985.
Days of Praise, Master Books, 1986.
Science and the Bible, Moody, 1986.
The God Who Is Real, Baker Book, 1988.
The Remarkable Record of Job, Baker Book, 1988.

Contributor of about two hundred articles on hydraulics and on the Bible to technical journals, magazines, and newspapers.

* * *

MOTT, Michael (Charles Alston) 1930-

PERSONAL: Born December 8, 1930, in London, England; son of Eric Alston (a solicitor) and Margaret (Berger) Mott; married Margaret Ann Watt (a weaver), May 6, 1961; children: Sophia Jane and Amanda Margaret (twins). *Education:* Oriel College, Oxford, 1950-51; Courtauld and Warburg Institutes, London, B.A. (honors), 1971; Central School of Arts, London, diploma; Law Society School, London, intermediate diploma.

ADDRESSES: Home—128 North Maple St., Bowling Green, Ohio 43402. *Office*—Creative Writing Program, Department of English, Bowling Green State University, Bowling Green, Ohio 43403. *Agent*—A. D. Peters, 10 Buckingham St., London WC2, England.

CAREER: Writer. Writer-in-residence, Kenyon College, Gambier, Ohio, 1966-70, Emory University, Atlanta, Ga., 1970-77, and College of William and Mary, Williamsburg, Va., 1978-79, and 1985-86; professor of English, Bowling Green State University, 1980—. Visiting professor, Kenyon College, 1966-70, State University of New York at Buffalo, 1968, and Concordia University, 1970 and 1974. Editor of fine arts books, Thames & Hudson, London, 1961-64. *Military service:* British Army; became captain.

MEMBER: Royal Geographical Society (fellow), Authors Guild, Amnesty International, Geographical Club, Arts Club.

AWARDS, HONORS: Georgia Governor's Award in the Fine Arts, 1974; Guggenheim fellowship, 1979-80; H.D.L., St. Mary's College, 1983; Christopher Award, 1984, and Pulitzer Prize nomination, Ohioana Award, and OCEA Nancy Dasher Award, all 1985, all for *The Seven Mountains of Thomas Merton;* Olscamp Research Award, 1985.

WRITINGS:

POETRY

The Cost of Living, Adam Poets, 1957.
Tales of Idiots, Adam International Review, 1961.
New Exile, Adam International Review, 1961.
A Book of Pictures, Outposts Publications, 1962.
Absence of Unicorns, Presence of Lions, Little, Brown, 1976.
Counting the Grasses, Anhinga, 1980.
Corday, Beacham Publishing, 1986.

NOVELS

The Notebooks of Susan Berry, Deutsch, 1962, Macmillan, 1963.
Helmets and Wasps, Deutsch, 1964, Houghton, 1966.
Master Entrick: An Adventure, 1754-1756 (juvenile), Deutsch, 1965, Delacorte, 1966, reprinted, 1986.
The Blind Cross: A Novel of the Children's Crusade (juvenile), Delacorte, 1968.

OTHER

The Seven Mountains of Thomas Merton (Book-of-the-Month Club alternate selection), Houghton, 1984.

Work appears in anthologies. Contributor of more than two hundred poems to *Poetry, Encounter, Iowa Review, Southern Review, Georgia Review,* and other publications. Editor, *Air Freight* (trade journal; London), beginning 1956; assistant editor, *Adam International Review,* 1956-66; assistant editor, *Geographical Magazine* (London), 1964-66; poetry editor, *Kenyon Review,* 1967-70.

SIDELIGHTS: Before the appearance of his best-selling biography of American monk and writer Thomas Merton, *The Seven Mountains of Thomas Merton,* Michael Mott was primarily known as a poet and novelist. Although he had written ten books prior to beginning work on the story of Merton's life, he soon discovered that writing biography—particularly this biography—would be like nothing he had ever done before in his life. For nearly five years Mott found work and research on the book consumed all of the time left over from a full teaching schedule, intruded on his family life—one room of his house became filled with information about Thomas Merton—and ate up his life savings.

But, whatever the cost to Mott personally, the end result appeared to be worth the effort: the book's publication was a major literary event of 1984. Lead reviews of the biography appeared in the *New York Times Book Review,* the *Boston Globe,* the *Washington Post,* and nearly every other important newspaper across the country, it maintained a berth on the *New York Times* non-fiction bestseller list for nine weeks, and gained Mott a Pulitzer Prize nomination. The critical and popular success of the biography far outshone Mott's previous work and ensured his reputation as an important biographer for years to come. Critic Kieran Quilan wrote in his *Georgia Review* essay on the book, "In both the sensitivity of its judgments and the depth of its exploration, this may well be the best biography that has been written about any twentieth-century author."

The tale of Mott's connection with the work begins in the spring of 1978 when he was first approached by Houghton Mifflin about the possibility of doing the biography. Although the Thomas Merton Trust had nearly ten years earlier named writer and photographer John Howard Griffin Merton's official biographer, Griffin soon thereafter became too ill to continue the work and Mott was asked to take over the project. As "official biographer," Mott had access to more than ten years of Merton's detailed journals denied to other scholars until twenty-five years after his death (in 1968) as specified in Merton's will. Mott also consulted Merton's writings, published and unpublished, and thousands of letters. Although Mott had no previous experience as a biographer, he shared certain similarities of background with Merton that would aid him in his task: the men were both poets, novelists and teachers, were both born to English/American parents, and were both raised in England.

The title Mott chose for his story of Merton's life borrows from that of Merton's best-selling autobiography, *The Seven Storey Mountain,* which itself refers to Dante's seven-storied Mount Purgatory from *The Inferno.* The mountains in Mott's title allude to seven mountains prominent in Merton's life, starting with Mount Canigou in southern France near his birthplace to Mount Kanchenjunga in Asia near the place where he died. *America* contributor James E. Milord and *Chicago Tribune Book World* contributor Eugene Kennedy praise Mott's seven-part organization of the biography. Milord notes that Mott "casts his images of Merton into seven settings, a felicitous choice for the monk who was always so deeply moved and galvanized by the sense of place." Kennedy similarly states: "Mott structures his work on the seven mountains of challenge and struggle that he sees in his subject's life experience. This happy choice provides a framework for this very satisfying book."

Besides the task of organizing the vast amount of material available on Merton, another major concern for Mott while writing the biography was sketching a cohesive portrait of a man who, because of his vast array of interests, had always defied classification. Critics find Mott successful in this regard, as well. William H. Shannon seems to summarize critical opinion on this point when he writes in *Commonweal:* "Mott has managed to put together a remarkable, coherent, and eminently readable portrait of the different Mertons that emerge from the published writings, the journals, the life events, and the many friendships of Gethsemani's [the abbey where Merton lived] most famous monk. Surely no small feat. One does not have to agree with everything that Mott has said, but nonetheless from now on anyone who writes about Merton must reckon with this biography."

BIOGRAPHICAL/CRITICAL SOURCES:

BOOKS

Contemporary Literary Criticism, Gale, Volume 15, 1980, Volume 34, 1985.
Contemporary Authors Autobiographical Series, Volume 7, Gale, 1988.

PERIODICALS

America, November 24, 1984.
Boston Globe, December 23, 1984.
Chicago Tribune Book World, January 27, 1985.
Christian Science Monitor, May 22, 1985.
Commonweal, October 19, 1984.
Georgia Review, fall, 1977, summer, 1985.
Irish Times, July 19, 1986.
Los Angeles Times Book Review, December 30, 1984.
Newsweek, December 10, 1984.
New York Times, December 20, 1984.

New York Times Book Review, February 20, 1966, December 23, 1984.
Parnassus: Poetry in Review, spring-summer, 1977.
Saturday Review, July 2, 1966.
Spectator, February 8, 1986.
Sunday Telegraph (London), February 2, 1985.
Times Literary Supplement, December 9, 1965, June 26, 1969, May 23, 1986.
Washington Post Book World, December 16, 1984.

* * *

MOYES, Patricia
See HASZARD, Patricia Moyes

* * *

MROZEK, Slawomir 1930-

PERSONAL: Born June 26, 1930, in Borzecin, Poland; son of Antoni (a post office clerk) and Zofia (Kedzior) Mrozek; married Maria Obremba, 1959. *Education:* Studied architecture, oriental culture, and painting, in Krakow, Poland.

ADDRESSES: *Home*—5, Avenue Franco-Russe, 75007 Paris, France. *Agent*—Tessa Sayle, 11 Jubilee Place, London SW3 3TE, England.

CAREER: Worked as a caricaturist for various newspapers and magazines, and as a journalist, in Krakow, Poland. Director, editor, and producer of films, S. D. R., Stuttgart, West Germany, 1977 and 1979. Full-time writer.

AWARDS, HONORS: Prix de l'Humeur Noir, 1964.

WRITINGS:

FICTION

Opowiadania z Trzmielowej Gory (short stories; title means "Stories from Buble Bee Hill"), [Warsaw, Poland], 1953.
Polpancerze praktyczne (short stories; title means "Practical Half-Armours"), [Krakow, Poland], 1953.
Malenkie lato (satirical novel; title means "The Small Summer"; originally published in *Dziennik Polski,* 1955-56), Wydawnictwo Literackie (Krakow), 1956.
Slon (short stories; title means "The Elephant"), illustrations by Daniel Mroz, Wydawnictwo Literackie, 1957, translation from the Polish by Konrad Syrop published as *The Elephant,* Grove Press, 1963.
Wesele w Atomicach (short stories; title means "A Wedding at Atomville"), Wydawnictwo Literackie, 1959.
Deszcz (satire; title means "Rain"), Wydawnictwo Literackie, 1962.
Opowiadania (short stories), Wydawnictwo Literackie, 1964.
The Urgupu Bird (short stories), translation from the Polish by Syrop, Macdonald & Co., 1968.
Dwa listy i inne opowiadania (short stories; title means "Two Letters and Other Stories"; also see below), Instytut Literacki (Paris), 1970.
Dwa listy (short story), Wydawnictwo Literackie, 1974.
Opowiadania (short stories), Wydawnictwo Literackie, 1974.
Moniza Clavier (short story; originally published in *Tworczosc,* number 6, 1967), Wydawnictwo Literackie, 1983.

PLAYS

Meczenstwo Piotra Oheya (three-act; title means "The Ordeal of Peter Ohey"; first produced in Krakow, at the Groteska Theatre, 1959; also see below), *Dialog,* number 6, 1959.
Indyk (two-act; title means "The Turkey"; first produced in Krakow at Stary Theatre, 1960), *Dialog,* number 10, 1960.
Karol (first produced in Zakopane, Poland, at the Modrzejewska Theatre, 1961; also see below), *Dialog,* number 3, 1961.
The Policemen (originally published as *Policja* in *Dialog,* number 6, 1958; first produced in Warsaw at Dramatyczny Theatre, 1958; translation from the Polish by Edmund Ordon produced Off-Broadway at Phoenix Theatre, November, 1961; also see below), Hart Stenographic Bureau, 1961.
Na pelnym morzu (title means "On the Open Sea"; first produced in Zakopane at the Modrzejewska Theatre, 1961; translation from the Polish by Mai Rodman produced as "At Sea" Off-Broadway at Mermaid Theatre, January, 1962; also see below), *Dialog,* number 2, 1961.
Striptease (first produced in Zakopane at the Modrzejewska Theatre, 1961; also see below), *Dialog,* number 6, 1961.
Kynolog w rozterce (title means "A Dog Fancier in a Quandary"; first produced in Krakow at the Muzyczny Theatre, 1967), *Dialog,* number 11, 1962.
Zabawa (title means "Having a Ball"; first produced in Wroclaw, Poland, at Dramatyczny Theatre, 1963; also see below), *Dialog,* number 10, 1962.
Czarowna noc (title means "An Enchanting Evening"; first produced in Krakow at Groteska Theatre, 1963; also see below), *Dialog,* number 3, 1963.
Smierc porucznika (one-act with prologue and epilogue; title means "Death of the Lieutenant"; first produced in Warsaw at Dramatyczny Theatre, 1963), *Dialog,* number 5, 1963.
Utwory sceniczne (collection; title means "Stage Plays"), Wydawnictwo Literackie, 1963.
Dom na granicy (title means "The House on the Frontier"; first produced in Krakow at Groteska Lalka i Maski Theatre, 1968), *Dialog,* number 5, 1967.
Poczworka (title means "The Quarternion"; first produced in Gdansk, Poland, at the Wybrzeze Theatre, 1967), *Dialog,* number 1, 1967.
Testarium, published in *Dialog,* number 11, 1967.
Six Plays (contains *The Police, The Martyrdom of Peter Ohey, Out at Sea, Charlie, The Party,* and *An Enchanted Night*), translation from the Polish by Nicholas Bethell, Grove Press, 1967.
Drugie danie (title means "Main Course"; first produced in Lodz, Poland, at Nowy Theatre, 1979), *Dialog,* number 5, 1968.
Tango: A Play in Three Acts (originally published in *Dialog,* number 11, 1964; first produced in Warsaw at the Wspolczesny Theatre, 1964; produced on the West End at Aldwych Theatre, 1966; produced Off-Broadway at Pocket Theater, January, 1969; also see below), translation from the Polish by Ralph Manheim and Teresa Dzieduscycka, Grove Press, 1968, reprinted, Polska Macierz Skolna, [London], 1983.
Vatzlav: A Play in 77 Scenes (first produced in Stratford, Ontario, Canada, at the Festival Theatre, August, 1970; produced in New York City at the Quaigh, February, 1982; also see below), translation from the Polish by Manheim, Grove Press, 1970, reprinted, Applause Theatre Book Publications, 1986.
Striptease, Repeat Performance, and The Prophets: Three Plays, translations from the Polish by Dzieduscycka, Lola Gruenthal, and Manheim, Grove Press, 1972.
Utwory sceniczne (collection), Wydawnictwo Literackie, 1973.
Szczesliwe wydarzenie (title means "A Happy Event"; first produced in Warsaw at Wspolczesny Theatre, 1973), *Dialog,* number 4, 1973.

Rzeznia (radio play; title means "The Abattoir"; first produced in Warsaw at Dramatyczny Theatre, 1975), *Dialog,* number 9, 1973.

Utwory sceniczne nowe (collection; title means "New Stage Plays"), Wydawnictwo Literackie, 1975.

Garbus (title means "The Hunchback"; first produced in Krakow at Stary Theatre, 1975; also see below), *Dialog,* number 9, 1975.

Wyspa roz (teleplay; title means "Island of Roses"), *Dialog,* number 5, 1975.

Serenada (title means "Serenade"; first produced in Zabrze, Poland, at the Nowy Theatre, 1977; also see below), *Dialog,* number 2, 1977.

Lis filozof (title means "The Philosopher Fox"; first produced in Zabrze at the Nowy Theatre, 1977; also see below), *Dialog,* number 3, 1977.

Polowanie na lisa (title means "The Fox Hunt"; first produced in Zabrze at Nowy Theatre, 1977; also see below), *Dialog,* number 5, 1977.

Krawiec (title means "The Tailor"; first produced in Szczecin, Poland, at Wspolczesny Theatre, 1978; also see below), *Dialog,* number 11, 1977.

Lis aspirant (title means "Fox the Aspirant"; also see below), *Dialog,* number 7, 1978.

Amor (teleplay; originally published in *Dialog,* number 3, 1978; contains *Amor, The Tailor, The Hunchback, The Fox Hunt, Serenade, The Philosopher Fox,* and *Fox the Aspirant*), Wydawnictwo Literackie, 1979.

Striptease, Tango, Vatzlav: Three Plays, translations from the Polish by Gruenthal and others, Grove Press, 1981.

Pieszo, Czytelnik (Warsaw), 1983.

The Emigrants (originally published as *Emigranci* in *Dialog,* number 8, 1974; first produced in Warsaw at Wspolczesny Theatre, 1975; translation from the Polish by Maciej Wrona, Teresa Wrona, and Robert Holman produced Off-Broadway at the Brooklyn Academy of Music, 1979), translation from the Polish by Henry Beissel, S. French, 1984.

Also author of "Jelen" (title means "The Stag"), 1963, and the "Ambassador," 1981. Author and director of teleplay "Return."

CONTRIBUTOR TO ANTHOLOGIES

John Lahr, editor, *Grove Press Modern Drama,* Grove Press, 1975.

Wybor dramatow i opowiadan, Wydawnictwo Literackie, 1975.

OTHER

Polska w obrazach (satirical drawings; title means "Poland in Pictures"), [Krakow], 1957.

Postepowiec: Organ Slawomira Mrozka (satirical drawings; title means "The Progressive: Organ of Slawomir Mrozek"), Iskry, 1960.

Ucieczka na poludnie (comic book; title means "Flight to the South"), Iskry (Warsaw), 1961.

Przez okulary Slawomira Mrozka (humorous drawings; title means "Through Slawomir Mrozek's Eyeglasses"), Iskry, 1968.

Male listy (feuilletons), Wydawnictwo Literackie, 1982.

Rysunki, Iskry, 1982.

Donosy, Puls (London), 1983.

Alfa, Instytut Literacki, 1984.

Also contributor to *Dziennik Polski* (Krakow), 1955, and of cartoons to the weekly periodical *Przekroj.*

WORK IN PROGRESS: Short stories and plays.

SIDELIGHTS: Polish playwright and satirist Slawomir Mrozek has lived in exile since the Polish government withdrew his passport for having criticized its role in the Soviet occupation of Czechoslovakia. He began his career as a journalist, and then drew satirical cartoons before becoming a playwright and author of numerous short stories. Recognized primarily for his plays, several of which have been staged worldwide, Mrozek is fluent in English, French, and Italian, and his work has been published in several countries outside Poland and the United States, including Czechoslovakia, Denmark, West Germany, Finland, France, Great Britain, Greece, Holland, Hungary, Italy, Japan, Portugal, Rumania, Spain, Switzerland, the Soviet Union, and Yugoslavia. And although Mrozek is not well known in the United States, a few of his plays have been produced Off-Broadway.

Of his many plays, Mrozek is perhaps best known for "Tango," which according to Clive Barnes in the *New York Times,* "is a fascinating piece" and "created a sensation" when it was first performed and later banned in Poland. Walter Kerr describes the plot in the *New York Times:* "A family that discovered every kind of personal freedom for itself—freedom in art, freedom from religion—along about 1914 is now living contentedly in a house gone thoroughly to seed. . . . But, in however slovenly a way, these people are quite happy. Except for the son of the house . . . [who] would very much like to restore the conventions that were abandoned when his parents so courageously took to doing the tango. . . . Unfortunately, as he tries to bring the new/old order into being he discovers that it is empty. A convention cannot be restored simply because it is a convention; it must have an impulse, an idea, inside it, if it is going to work." In another *New York Times* piece, Barnes considered "Tango" to be "one of the most rewarding plays to come out of Eastern Europe in many years."

Remarking on the complexity of "Tango," Martin Esslin writes in his *The Theatre of the Absurd:* "It has been described as a parody or paraphrase of *Hamlet* in that it shows a young man horrified by the behaviour of his parents, deeply ashamed by his mother's promiscuity and his father's complacency. It is also, clearly, a bitter attack by a young man on the previous generation which has plunged his country into war, occupation and devastation." As such, Esslin suggests that the play has relevance for the West as well; Barnes concurs: "Like Chekhov's 'The Cherry Orchard,' Mr. Mrozek's play is based on a family household that is intended to serve as a microcosm to the outside world. Indeed Mr. Mrozek is intentionally allegorical, and his play is intended to describe the decline of the West, postulating that our present laissez faire, hedonistically materialist society will . . . give way first to intellectual authoritarianism, and finally to the chaos of rule by brute force."

Praising Mrozek's "sharp, almost unerring ability to show things in a new perspective," Marketa Goetz Stankiewicz comments in *Contemporary Literature* that the reason Mrozek's play speaks especially to the Western world "lies in his ability to fuse three currents of contemporary drama . . . into a single medium of expression: first, the artist's acute sense of disaster evoked by the historical events of this century; second, the sensitivity to the false values and stultifying effects of a variety of social systems and man's subsequent change . . . to a vegetating weed without conscience or consciousness; third, the desire to recreate forms of the pre-literary theater expressing inexplicable and indefinable fears and hopes." Suggesting that Mrozek is writing within the tradition of the theatre of the absurd, Mardi Valgemae notes in *Contemporary Drama* that "Tango" exemplifies "a particular type of East European theatre of the absurd that differs somewhat from the French school of Beckett and his colleagues. For most French absurdists tend to concentrate on basic metaphysical issues, whereas many East European playwrights simply use absurd images in order to create social and political allegories."

In *Mrozek,* however, Jan Klossowicz disagrees with the tendency to categorize Mrozek within the absurdist tradition, offering instead the assessment that his plays must be "viewed within the framework of the tradition from which they sprang and of the experience by which they were determined." Klossowicz maintains that although Mrozek's plays employ devices of the absurdist theatre of the fifties, such as "emotional ambivalence, the grotesque technique, a mixture of the tragic and the comic, disregard for conventional plot and psychological motivation, ahistorical action, creation of a stage metareality, a new approach to the time of action and the duration of the play on stage," he is rather responding to the tradition of Polish Romanticism which, as Klossowicz explains, "stands for the tendency to proclaim political and social ideas in art (the struggle for freedom and criticism of the existing social structure), it stands for patriotism, exaltation, coupled with fantasy, sentimentalism and the professed superiority of 'emotion to mind.'" And according to Klossowicz, "Mrozek's works are a virtually ideal example of the anti-Romantic stance."

"Parody and imitation of the Romantic style is dominant in his writing," adds Klossowicz, who contends that "Mrozek's works as a whole may best be described by the term parabolic. His plays and most of his short stories are allegories. The characters are symbolic representation while situations illustrate theses." Klossowicz indicates that "instead of transcribing political or philosophical discourses into dialogue, Mrozek writes parables that illustrate the theses of these discourses, instead of devoting himself to the reconstruction of historical events, he writes fables where he narrates these events in the form of a metaphor." Klossowicz believes that Mrozek's work springs not from "the conviction of the absurdity of life and of the world, but a conviction of the absurdity of certain phenomena." As a satirist, Mrozek "scoffed at the surrounding world in the name of a laudable goal, and he remained faithful to this concept of literature later in life as well," observes Klossowicz, indicating that "the singular charm and originality" in his work rests in its "reflection of a specific social and historical situation."

BIOGRAPHICAL/CRITICAL SOURCES:

BOOKS

Contemporary Literary Criticism, Gale, Volume 3, 1975, Volume 13, 1980.

Esslin, Martin, *The Theatre of the Absurd,* revised edition, Doubleday, 1969.

Klossowicz, Jan, *Mrozek,* translation from the Polish by Christina Cenkalski, Authors Agency and Czytelnik (Warsaw), 1980.

PERIODICALS

Comparative Drama, spring, 1971.

Contemporary Literature, spring, 1971.

Nation, August 2, 1975.

New Statesman, July 9, 1976.

New York Times, November, 22, 1961, April 24, 1962, January 1, 1968, January 20, 1969, February 9, 1969, August 23, 1970, October 29, 1979, February 7, 1982.

Times Literary Supplement, April 20, 1967, March 21, 1968.

Virginia Quarterly Review, summer, 1973.

Washington Post, February 3, 1982.*

—*Sketch by Sharon Malinowski*

* * *

MUIR, Frank (Herbert) 1920-

PERSONAL: Surname is pronounced *Mew*-er; born February 20, 1920, in Ramsgate, England; son of Charles James and Margaret (Harding) Muir; married Polly McIrvine, July 16, 1949; children: Jamie, Sally. *Education:* Attended high school in Leyton County, England. *Politics:* "Not committed to a party." *Religion:* Church of England.

ADDRESSES: Home—Anners, Thorpe, Egham, Surrey TW20 8UE, England. *Agent*—Hilary Rubenstein, A. P. Watt Ltd., 26 Bedford Row, London WC1R 4HL, England.

CAREER: Free-lance writer for radio and television. Worked as consultant, with Denis Norden, on light entertainment for television for British Broadcasting Corp. (BBC), 1960-64, assistant head of Television Light Entertainment Group, 1964-67; London Weekend Television Ltd., London, England, head of entertainment, 1968-69; currently "self-unemployed." University of St. Andrews, St. Andrews, Scotland, rector, 1977-79. Panelist, with Norden, on game shows "My Word!," 1956—, and "My Music," 1967—. *Military service:* Royal Air Force, 1940-46.

MEMBER: Johnson Society (president, 1975-76), Savile Club.

AWARDS, HONORS: Screenwriters Guild Award for best contribution to light entertainment, 1961, and Variety Club of Great Britain Award for best radio personality of the year, 1977, both with Denis Norden; Writers' Guild award for best radio feature script, 1973, with Simon Brett; LL.D., University of St. Andrews, 1978; Commander, Order of the British Empire, 1980; D.Litt, University of Kent, 1982.

WRITINGS:

(With Patrick Campbell) *Call My Bluff: Frank Muir Versus Patrick Campbell,* Eyre Methuen, 1972.

Christmas Customs and Traditions, Sphere Books, 1975, Taplinger, 1977.

An Irreverent and Thoroughly Incomplete Social History of Almost Everything, Stein & Day, 1976, published in England as *The Frank Muir Book: An Irreverent Companion to Social History,* Heinemann, 1976.

(With Simon Brett) *Frank Muir Goes Into . . .,* Robson Books, 1978.

(With Denis Norden) *The Glums: Based on the Original Radio Scripts,* Robson Books, 1979.

(With Brett) *The Second Frank Muir Goes Into . . .,* Robson Books, 1979.

(Contributor) Steve Race, *My Music!,* Robson Books, 1979.

(With Brett) *Frank Muir on Children,* Heinemann, 1980.

(With Brett) *The Third Frank Muir Goes Into . . .,* Robson Books, 1980.

(With wife, Polly Muir) *Frank and Polly Muir's Big Dipper,* Heinemann, 1981.

(With son, Jamie Muir) *A Treasury at Christmas,* Robson Books, 1981.

(With Brett) *The Fourth Frank Muir Goes Into . . .,* Robson Books, 1981.

A Book at Bathtime, Heinemann, 1982, published as *An Irreverent and Almost Complete Social History of the Bathroom,* Stein & Day, 1983.

(Editor with Brett) *Frank Muir Presents the Book of Comedy Sketches,* Elm Tree, 1982.

WITH DENIS NORDEN; "MY WORD!" STORIES

You Can't Have Your Kayak and Heat It: Stories from "My Word!" (also see below), introduction by Jack Longland, Eyre Methuen, 1973.
Upon My Word!: More Stories from "My Word!" (also see below), Eyre Methuen, 1974.
The "My Word!" Stories (contains *You Can't Have Your Kayak and Heat It* and *Upon My Word!*), Eyre Methuen, 1976, Stein & Day, 1977.
Take My Word for It: Still More Stories from "My Word," Eyre Methuen, 1978.
Oh, My Word!: A Fourth Collection of Stories from "My Word," a Panel Game Devised by Edward J. Mason and Tony Shryane, Eyre Methuen, 1980.
The Complete and Utter "My Word!" Collection: Stories from the Panel Game Devised by Edward J. Mason and Tony Shryane, Eyre Methuen, 1983.
You Have "My Word!": Stories from the Panel Game, Eyre Methuen, 1989.

"WHAT-A-MESS" SERIES; JUVENILES

What-a-Mess (also see below), Doubleday, 1977.
What-a-Mess the Good (also see below), Doubleday, 1978.
What-a-Mess [and] *What-a-Mess the Good,* Ernest Benn, 1979.
Prince What-a-Mess, Ernest Benn, 1979.
Super What-a-Mess, Ernest Benn, 1980.
What-a-Mess and the Cat-Next-Door, Ernest Benn, 1981.
What-a-Mess in Spring, Ernest Benn, 1982.
What-a-Mess in Summer, Ernest Benn, 1982.
What-a-Mess in Autumn, Ernest Benn, 1982.
What-a-Mess in Winter, Ernest Benn, 1982.
What-a-Mess at the Seaside, Ernest Benn, 1983.
What-a-Mess Goes to School, Ernest Benn, 1984.
What-a-Mess Has Breakfast, Black, 1986.
What-a-Mess Has Lunch, Black, 1986.
What-a-Mess Has Supper, Black, 1986.
What-a-Mess Has Tea, Black, 1986.
What-a-Mess Goes on Television, Wather Books, 1989.

OTHER

Also collaborator with Denis Norden, 1947-64, on scripts for television and radio shows, including "Take It from Here," 1947-58, "Bedtime with Braden," 1950-54, "And so to Bently," 1956, and "Whack-O!," 1958-60.

WORK IN PROGRESS: The Oxford Book of Humorous Prose, for Oxford University Press.

SIDELIGHTS: Frank Muir writes: "After twenty-five years of writing for radio and television comedy, I am now deeply—and happily—embedded in books. I enjoy talking in public about books. I have made speeches at conventions in Chicago and Atlanta on the perils of authorship and authors' promotional tours.

"I only write humour. Sometimes I write humorous fiction, as in my children's books and the 'My Word!' stories, and sometimes I write non-fiction, as in my examination of the ludicrous and laughable elements in our social history. I think this is because I have a very low threshold of boredom. I bore easily and am therefore desperately anxious not to bore others."

AVOCATIONAL INTERESTS: Book collecting, staring silently into space.

BIOGRAPHICAL/CRITICAL SOURCES:

PERIODICALS

Los Angeles Times Book Review, May 10, 1981.
Observer, September 19, 1976.
Times Literary Supplement, December 24, 1982.
Washington Post Book World, October 14, 1984.

* * *

MUN
See LEAF, (Wilbur) Munro

* * *

MURPHY, Shirley Rousseau 1928-

PERSONAL: Born May 20, 1928, in Oakland, Calif.; daughter of Otto Francis (a horse trainer) and Helen (an artist; maiden name, Hoffman) Rousseau; married Patrick J. Murphy (a U.S. probation officer), August 5, 1951. *Education:* California School of Fine Arts (now San Francisco Art Institute), A.A., 1951.

ADDRESSES: Home—Route 1, Box 59-J, Grandview Lake, Jasper, Ga. 30143.

CAREER: Sam Kweller, Designer, Los Angeles, Calif., packaging designer, 1952-53; Bullock's (department store), Los Angeles, interior decorator, 1953-55; San Bernardino Valley College, San Bernardino, Calif., teacher of mosaics, 1957-59; Canal Zone Library-Museum, Canal Zone, Panama, documents assistant, 1964-67; writer, painter, and sculptor. Had a dual show with mother, Helen Rousseau, at Instituto Panameno de Arte, 1964, and eight one-woman shows in California, 1957-63; paintings, drawings, and sculpture also exhibited at group and juried shows in California, Arizona, and Nevada, and traveling exhibits.

MEMBER: American Library Association, Society of Children's Book Writers, California Water Color Society, San Francisco Art Institute, San Francisco Women Artists, Marin Society of Artists.

AWARDS, HONORS: Received eight awards for sculpture and four for paintings at San Francisco Museum and other exhibitions, 1956-62.

WRITINGS:

White Ghost Summer, Viking, 1967.
The Sand Ponies, Viking, 1967.
Elmo Doolan and the Search for the Golden Mouse, Viking, 1970.
(With husband, Patrick J. Murphy) *Carlos Charles,* Viking, 1971.
Poor Jenny, Bright as a Penny, Viking, 1974.
The Grass Tower, Atheneum, 1976.
(Contributor) Sylvia Engdahl, editor, *Anywhere, Anywhen,* Atheneum, 1976.
Silver Woven in My Hair, Atheneum, 1977.
The Ring of Five, Atheneum, 1977.
The Flight of the Fox (Junior Literary Guild selection), Atheneum, 1978.
The Pig Who Could Conjure the Wind, Atheneum, 1978.
Soonie and the Dragon, Atheneum, 1979.
The Wolf Bell, Atheneum, 1979.
The Castle of Hape, Atheneum, 1980.
Caves of Fire and Ice, Atheneum, 1980.
(With P. J. Murphy) *Mrs. Tortino's Return to the Sun,* Lothrop, 1980.
The Joining of the Stone, Atheneum, 1981.

Tattie's River Journey, Dial, 1983.
Valentine for a Dragon, Atheneum, 1984.
Nightpool, Harper, 1986.
The Ivory Lyre, Harper, 1987.
The Dragonbards, Harper, 1988.
(With Welch Suggs) *Medallion of the Black Hound,* Harper, 1989.
Wind Child, Harper, 1990.
The Silver Parfait Ripple Mouse, Harper, 1990.
The City of Jewels, Harper, 1990.

Contributor to *The Advocate.*

SIDELIGHTS: Shirley Rousseau Murphy told *CA:* "By writing for young readers, I can write for my young self, who is still quite alive somewhere, who is still, like younger readers, trying to figure things out. I take the notion that people who consider themselves adult and have everything figured out, can be dangerous.

"When I was young, I thought that getting old was all a state of mind. Now in a different sense I can see that that is quite true. As a child reader I was trying to find my way through to a particular place of enchantment where the state of mind never petrifies. Now as I write, I am still trying to get there. If I write the book I strive to write, the perfect one, the next one over the hill, that fantasy world will open and I will step through.

"But you can't write fantasy without real things. Real threats, real fears, real problems and weaknesses and strengths. They are the solid core of all worlds. Fantasy is about the super real, the primal powers and fears that dwell inside us all. You must be brave to read fantasy, as a child reader is brave."

BIOGRAPHICAL/CRITICAL SOURCES:

BOOKS

Rasmusen, H., and A. Grant, *Sculpture from Junk,* Reinhold, 1967.
Twentieth-Century Children's Writers, 3rd edition, St. James Press, 1989.

* * *

MUTO, Susan Annette 1942-

PERSONAL: Born December 11, 1942, in Pittsburgh, Pa.; daughter of Frank and Helen (Scardamalia) Muto. *Education:* Duquesne University, B.A., 1964; University of Pittsburgh, M.A., 1967, Ph.D., 1970. *Politics:* Democrat. *Religion:* Roman Catholic.

ADDRESSES: Home—2223 Wenzell Ave., Pittsburgh, Pa. 15216. *Office*—Epiphany Association, 1145 Beechwood Blvd., Pittsburgh, Pa. 15206.

CAREER: United Jewish Federation, Pittsburgh, Pa., assistant director of public relations, 1964-65; *Jewish Chronicle,* Pittsburgh, society editor, 1965-66; Duquesne University, Pittsburgh, professor, 1965—, assistant director of Institute of Man, 1966-80, member of institute workshop and conference team, 1971—, director of Institute of Formative Spirituality, 1980-88, Graduate School of Arts and Sciences, adjunct professor of literature and spirituality, 1988—; Epiphany Association (ecumenical lay center), Pittsburgh, executive director, 1988—. Guest lecturer at numerous colleges, universities, workshops, and seminars throughout the U.S. and Canada. Member of Pittsburgh Advisory Council, Project for Moral and Spiritual Development in the Workplace, 1987—.

MEMBER: Society for Scientific Study of Religion, Edith Stein Guild (lifetime member), Phi Kappa Phi.

WRITINGS:

Celebrating the Single Life: A Spirituality for Single Persons in Today's World, Doubleday, 1982.
Blessings That Make Us Be: Living the Beatitudes, Crossroad/Continuum, 1982.
(Editor with Adrian van Kaam) *Creative Formation of Life and World,* University Press of America, 1982.
Pathways of Spiritual Living, Doubleday, 1984.
Meditation in Motion, Doubleday, 1986.
(With van Kaam) *Commitment: Key to Christian Maturity,* Paulist Press, 1989.

PUBLISHED BY DIMENSION

(With van Kaam) *The Emergent Self,* 1968.
(With van Kaam) *The Participant Self,* 1969.
Approaching the Sacred: An Introduction to Spiritual Reading, 1973.
Steps along the Way: The Path of Spiritual Reading, 1975.
A Practical Guide to Spiritual Reading, 1976.
The Journey Homeward: On the Road of Spiritual Reading, 1977.
(With van Kaam) *Tell Me Who I Am,* 1977.
(With van Kaam) *Am I Living a Spiritual Life?,* 1978.
Renewed at Each Awakening: The Formative Power of Sacred Words, 1979.
(With van Kaam) *Practicing the Prayer of Presence,* 1980.

OTHER

Contributor of approximately sixty articles to religious magazines and theology journals, including *Spiritual Life, Cross and Crown,* and *Contemplative Review.* Managing editor of *Envoy* and *Humanitas,* both 1966-79, and of *Studies in Formative Spirituality,* 1979—.

WORK IN PROGRESS: Women and the Church, for Crossword.

SIDELIGHTS: Susan Muto told *CA:* "After a brief career in journalism and public relations, I became assistant director of the Institute of Man, a position that changed the direction of my life and led me into my present dedication to teaching, speaking, writing, and research in the field of foundational formation. As a single laywoman living my vocation in the world and supported by over twenty-one years of experience at the Institute, I am qualified to address the formation concerns of laity, clergy, and religious. My time is spent doing what I love most—reading and writing within the framework of the Christian formation tradition, especially as it is recorded in the writings of both pre- and post-Reformation spiritual masters. This work continues in a marvelous way in my new position as executive director of the ecumenical lay center with which I am affiliated in Pittsburgh, the Epiphany Association.

"The aim of one of my best-known books, *Celebrating the Single Life,* is to suggest—on the basis of lived experience—concrete dynamic ways and means in which men and women are formed in this vocation to the single life as fully human, fully Christian people. Most of its contents are applicable to anyone who wants to live a seriously committed, spiritually-grounded single life. Their formation as single persons enables them to participate in a special way in the transformation of self and world.

"The single state is the foundation of all human formation. We are born single (that is, unique), and we die single. In this world, before one chooses any other state of life, he or she is single. Only to the degree that persons accept this blessing of uniqueness can they enjoy the togetherness offered by marriage or community membership. Married couples, who really love one another, know how much the preservation of their relationship depends on respect for their spouse's uniqueness. Vowed religious agree that their solidarity as a community finds its greatest resource in each one's solitude before God. He calls them all to give witness temporarily or for a lifetime to the originating uniqueness that is his gift to every human being."

N

NAIMAN, Arthur 1941-

PERSONAL: Born May 12, 1941, in Chicago, Ill.; son of Albert (a salesman) and Juliette (a clerk and secretary; maiden name, Gibian) Naiman. *Education:* Brandeis University, B.A., 1962; Bank Street College, M.S., 1976. *Politics:* "Left." *Religion:* "Atheist (Jewish by birth)."

ADDRESSES: Home and office—Box 7635, Berkeley, CA 94707.

CAREER: Teacher at junior and senior high schools in New York City, 1965-67; Ogilvy & Mather, New York City, copywriter, 1967-68; Scali, McCabe, Sloves, New York City, copywriter, 1968-70; Young & Rubicam, New York City, copywriter, 1970-72; teacher at alternative high school in East Harlem, N.Y., 1972-73; teacher at grammar schools in South Bronx, N.Y., 1975-76, and in Berkeley, Calif., 1977-78; author, 1980—. Founder, Hotcake Press, 1978; president, Goldstein & Blair (publisher), 1984—. Free-lance advertising copywriter in New York City, 1967-76, and San Francisco, Calif., 1977-82. Creative director of Public Media Center, San Francisco, 1977. Instructor at Open Education Exchange, Oakland, Calif., 1977, New School for Democratic Management, San Francisco, 1978, University of California, Extension, San Francisco, 1979-81, and Media Alliance, San Francisco, 1980-81. Painter and photographer.

WRITINGS:

Every Goy's Guide to Common Jewish Expressions, Houghton, 1981.
Introduction to WordStar, Sybex, 1982, 2nd edition, 1983.
Word Processing Buyer's Guide, McGraw, 1982.
The IBM Personal Computer Made Easy, Houghton, 1983.
The First Book to Read about the IBM Personal Computer, Houghton, 1983.
(Editor) *Computer Dictionary for Beginners,* Ballantine, 1983.
Introduction to the Lisa, Addison-Wesley, 1984.
What Every Kid (and Adult) Should Know about Computers, Hayden, 1985.
MacBook: The Indispensable Guide to Macintosh Software and Hardware, Hayden, 1985.
Mastering WordStar on the IBM PC, Sybex, 1986.
(With Dale Coleman) *The Macintosh Bible,* Goldstein & Blair, 1987, 2nd edition, 1988.
(And editor with Kelly Horan) *Supercharging WordStar* (sequel to *Introduction to WordStar*), Goldstein & Blair, 1987.
(Editor) *The Macintosh Bible Book-Disk Combination,* Goldstein & Blair, 1988.

Also author of articles, booklets and speeches. Author of column, "The Sleaze Patrol," in *User's Guide* magazine, and "Making Books," in *Desktop Publishing* magazine.

WORK IN PROGRESS: "An introductory guide to Central American politics that covers the history of all seven countries up to the present day and includes a glossary and five other reference chapters; an attempt at a unified field theory of psychology, politics, anthropology and history; an unusual kind of almanac; a sort of autobiographical pastiche or collage; a collection of essays and humorous writing on computer subjects; an introductory book on the Macintosh computer."

SIDELIGHTS: Arthur Naiman's "how-to" books on computer systems and word processing have been well received by critics. Art Kleiner writes about *Word Processing Buyer's Guide* in *Co-Evolution Quarterly:* "The writing's clear, concise, gossipy and full of thorough details. . . . Though I'm usually bored by computer books after the first two pages, I read this all the way through in one sitting." According to *Personal Computing* contributor David Galel, the guide is "a standout. . . . Whether you're a novice or a hacker, you'll find this book informative and fun. Naiman's style is conversational, yet clear and succinct. The book covers the word-processor field better than most works of this type which is praise enough."

In order to get his books into the market before the software became obsolete, Naiman founded his own publishing company. *The Macintosh Bible,* a general guide, was his first book published by Goldstein & Blair. Charles Rubin observes in the *San Jose Mercury News,* that "computer books often have a short shelf life because information changes quickly but the Mac Bible solves this problem by including two free, 40-page updates with the purchase price." Rubin continues, "Another plus is the book's punchy, down-to-earth style, which makes it a pleasure to read. Although it's designed as a reference work, I found myself reading whole sections of tips at a time. . . . This book presents a lot of useful information in a very accessible way. Anyone who owns a Macintosh will get more out of it with the Macintosh Bible." And *New York Times* reviewer Peter H. Lewis says the book is "like having a Macintosh expert at your side whenever you need one."

Naiman wrote *CA:* "Having made a success of writing (and now publishing) computer books—something I fell into almost by accident—I want to transfer my skill at making complicated subjects accessible (and even enjoyable) to the area of politics. If the left's main stock in trade is the truth—and if it isn't, what hope is there?—then the left's main job is education. Yet most leftists talk to the already converted, in language (and with a design sense), that only the already converted will put up with. I think there's a much wider audience for political truths, and I'm going to try to address it."

BIOGRAPHICAL/CRITICAL SOURCES:

PERIODICALS

Co-Evolution Quarterly, summer, 1983.
New York Times, February 10, 1987.
Personal Computing, June, 1983.
San Jose Mercury News, March 29, 1987.

* * *

NEVILLE, Robert C(ummings) 1939-

PERSONAL: Born May 1, 1939, in St. Louis, Mo.; son of Richard Perry (a chemist) and Rose (Cummings) Neville; married Elizabeth Egan (an artist and teacher), June 8, 1963; children: Gwendolyn (deceased), Naomi, Leonora. *Education:* Yale University, B.A., 1960, M.A., 1962, Ph.D., 1963.

ADDRESSES: Home—49 Harbor Circle, Centerport, N.Y. 11721. *Office*—Department of Religion, Boston University, 745 Commonwealth Ave., Boston, Mass. 02215.

CAREER: Ordained minister of United Methodist Church. Yale University, New Haven, Conn., instructor in philosophy, 1963-65; Wesleyan University, Middletown, Conn., visiting instructor, 1964-65, assistant professor of philosophy, 1966-67; Fordham University, Bronx, N.Y., assistant professor, 1965-68, associate professor of philosophy, 1968-71; State University of New York College at Purchase, associate professor, 1971-74, professor of philosophy, 1974-77; State University of New York at Stony Brook, professor of philosophy and religious studies, 1977-87, dean of humanities and fine arts, 1982-85; Boston University, Boston, Mass., professor of religion, philosophy, and theology, 1987—, chairman of department of religion, 1987—. Director of Stony Brook Center for Religious Studies, 1978-82.

MEMBER: American Philosophical Association, American Theological Society, American Academy of Religion, Metaphysical Society of America (president, 1988), Society for the Study of Process Philosophy, Institute of Society, Ethics and the Life Sciences (fellow).

WRITINGS:

God the Creator: On the Transcendence and Presence of God, University of Chicago Press, 1968.
The Cosmology of Freedom, Yale University, 1974.
(Editor with Willard Gaylin and Joel Meister) *Operating on the Mind,* Basic Books, 1975.
(Co-editor) *Encyclopedia of Bioethics,* Free Press, 1977.
Soldier, Sage, Saint, Fordham University Press, 1978.
Creativity and God, Seabury, 1980.
Reconstruction of Thinking, State University of New York Press, 1981.
The Tao and the Daimon, State University of New York Press, 1982.
The Puritan Smile, State University of New York Press, 1987.
(Editor) *New Essays in Metaphysics,* State University of New York Press, 1987.

Contributor of articles and reviews to periodicals, including *Journal of the American Medical Association, Man and World,* and *Review of Metaphysics.*

WORK IN PROGRESS: Recovery of the Measure; System and Systems.

BIOGRAPHICAL/CRITICAL SOURCES:

PERIODICALS

Christian Century, June 5, 1968.
Southern Journal of Philosophy, Volume X, number 1, 1972.
Theological Studies, Volume XXX, number 1, 1969.

* * *

NEWMAN, Peter C(harles) 1929-

PERSONAL: Born May 10, 1929, in Vienna, Austria; moved to Canada, 1940; naturalized Canadian citizen, 1945; son of Oskar and Wanda (Newman) Newman; married Camilla Jane Turner, August 5, 1978; children: (previous marriage) Ashley (daughter). *Education:* University of Toronto, B.A., 1950, M.Com., 1953.

ADDRESSES: Home—4855 Major Rd., Cordova Bay, Victoria, British Columbia, Canada, V8Y 2L8. *Office*—Maclean Hunter Bldg., 777 Bay St., Toronto, Ontario, Canada M5W 1A7.

CAREER: Financial Post, Toronto, Ontario, assistant editor, 1953-57; *Maclean's* (magazine), Toronto, assistant editor, 1957-59, Ottawa editor, 1959-63, national affairs editor, 1963-64; *Toronto Daily Star,* Toronto, Ottawa editor, 1964-69, editor-in-chief, 1969-71; *Maclean's,* editor, 1971-82, currently senior contributing editor. Visiting associate professor of political science, McMaster University, 1970, and York University, 1980. Professor of creative writing, University of Victoria, 1985. *Military service:* Royal Canadian Navy Reserve; became captain.

MEMBER: International Press Institute (deputy chairman for Canada, 1970-72), Royal Canadian Yacht Club (Toronto), Rideau Club (Ottawa).

AWARDS, HONORS: National Newspaper Award for feature writing, 1964; Wilderness Award, Canadian Broadcasting Association, 1967; Doctor of Laws, Brock University, 1974; Doctor of Letters, York University, 1975; Officer in Order of Canada, 1978; Knighthood in Order of St. Lazarus, 1980; Knight of Lippe, 1980.

WRITINGS:

Flame of Power: Intimate Profiles of Canada's Greatest Businessmen, Longmans, Green, 1960.
Renegade in Power: The Diefenbacker Years, McClelland & Stewart, 1963, Bobbs-Merrill, 1964, reprinted, McClelland, 1977.
The Distemper of Our Times: Canadian Politics in Transition, 1963-1968, McClelland & Stewart, 1968, 2nd edition, Carleton University Press, 1978, published as *A Nation Divided: Canada and the Coming of Pierre Trudeau,* Knopf, 1969.
Home Country, McClelland & Stewart, 1973.
The Canadian Establishment, Volume 1, McClelland & Stewart, 1975, Volume 2: *The Acquisitors,* Seal Books, 1981.
King of the Castle, Atheneum, 1979.

Bronfman Dynasty: The Rothschilds of the New World, Seal Books, 1979.

The Establishment Man: A Portrait of Power, McClelland & Stewart, 1982.

(Editor with Sir Iain Moncreiffe) *Debrett's Illustrated Guide to the Canadian Establishment,* Methuen, 1983.

True North, Not Strong and Free: A Study of Canada's Defence Dilemma, McClelland & Stewart, 1983, published as *True North, Not Strong and Free: Defending the Peaceable Kingdom in the Nuclear Age,* Penguin, 1984.

Company of Adventurers: The Story of the Hudson's Bay Company, Penguin, Volume 1, 1985, Volume 2: *Caesars of the Wilderness,* 1987.

Sometimes a Great Nation: Will Canada Belong to the Twenty-First Century?, McClelland & Stewart, 1988.

Contributor of more than 500 articles on various aspects of Canadian politics and economics to magazines, newspapers, and journals.

SIDELIGHTS: Canadian journalist Peter C. Newman's presentation of the celebrities of Canadian politics and business in *Debrett's Illustrated Guide to the Canadian Establishment* "is pure entertainment," reports Wallace Clement in Toronto's *Globe and Mail.* Previous books focusing on the upper strata of Canadian society were more serious, but no doubt suggested the satirical approach taken in the *Illustrated Guide,* believes Clement: "I do not think Newman consciously started out with parody in mind. Rather he was pulled along by the momentum created by The Canadian Establishment, into [its second volume] The Acquisitors and The Establishment Man, catalyzed by his own wry sense of humor." Characteristic of this "social tour," relates Clement, is Newman's early statement that "much of the Canadian business community moved from primitive to decadent without ever becoming particularly civilized."

Newman collects support for this broad generalization in his three-volume history of the Hudson's Bay Company, *Company of Adventurers.* "Newman writes with force and elegance," Bruce Brown remarks in the *Washington Post Book World.* "His intimate knowledge of the company's history . . . fills *Company of Adventurers* with wonderful details about the evolving nature of venture capitalism." Under scrutiny in the first two volumes is the era between the opening of the company in 1670 and 1869, when it yielded its control over western Canada to the national government. "The period abounds with colorful characters and drama, and is thus eminently suited to Newman's high-octane style of writing," offers *Globe and Mail* contributor William French. In the opinion of *Times Literary Supplement* reviewer Richard Davenport-Hines, "Newman excels when writing of the company's lowest servants or of its pervasive influence on Canadian historical consciousness, but is less convincing when dealing with high politics or European merchant princes. Few books . . . have as well conveyed the oppressive stillness of Canada's cold northern reaches. Newman is at his best when exploring the psychological isolation of the trappers and company men, the price of whose freedom he sees as cultural disinheritance and social malignity." Setting Newman's book apart from typical nonfiction "is his fascination with his own research, and his utter inability to leave out a good yarn merely because it has little or nothing to do with the story of the Hudson's Bay Company and its entrepreneurial rivals," claims *Los Angeles Times* contributor Jonathan Kirsch, who says the result is "not purely a work of history, but rather an armchair adventure with novelistic touches." Several reviewers mention that, at times, Newman takes liberties with his materials and descriptive language. However, French concedes, "perhaps some literary hyperbole is needed to change the minds of those who insist our history is dull. That's a four-letter word that doesn't exist in Newman's vocabulary."

BIOGRAPHICAL/CRITICAL SOURCES:

BOOKS

Newman, Peter C., editor, *Debrett's Illustrated Guide to the Canadian Establishment,* Methuen, 1983.

PERIODICALS

Book World, September 28, 1969.
Canadian Forum, December, 1968.
Chicago Tribune Book World, March 25, 1979.
Globe and Mail (Toronto), December 3, 1983, October 24, 1987.
Los Angeles Times, March 3, 1988.
National Review, March 10, 1970.
New York Times, March 20, 1979.
New York Times Book Review, November 23, 1969, March 11, 1979, December 15, 1985, December 20, 1987.
Saturday Night, November, 1968.
Times Literary Supplement, May 23, 1986.
Tribune Books (Chicago), December 20, 1987.
Washington Post Book World, December 29, 1985.

* * *

NEWPORT, John P(aul) 1917-

PERSONAL: Born June 16, 1917, in Buffalo, Mo.; son of Marvin Jackson and Mildred (Morrow) Newport; married Eddie Belle Leavell; children: Martha Ellen, Frank Marvin, John Paul, Jr. *Education:* William Jewell College, B.A., 1938; Southern Baptist Theological Seminary, Louisville, Ky., Th.M., 1941, Th.D., 1946; University of Edinburgh, Ph.D., 1953; Texas Christian University, M.A., 1963; also attended Tulsa University, 1948-49, Tulane University, 1951-52, Harvard University, 1958-59, Union Theological Seminary, 1965, University of Basel, and University of Zurich.

ADDRESSES: Office—Southern Baptist Theological Seminary, Fort Worth, Tex. 76122.

CAREER: Baylor University, Waco, Tex., associate professor of religion and director of graduate studies of religion, 1949-51; New Orleans Baptist Theological Seminary, New Orleans, La., associate professor of philosophy of religion and New Testament, 1952-53; Southwestern Baptist Theological Seminary, Fort Worth, Tex., professor of philosophy of religion and chairman of the department, 1953-76; Rice University, Houston, Tex., Chavanne Professor of Religious Studies, 1976-79; Southwestern Baptist Theological Seminary, vice-president for academic affairs and provost, 1979—. Field work director, Boston University School of Theology, 1958-59; visiting professor, Golden Gate Baptist Theological Seminary, 1970, Rice University, 1974-75, and Princeton Theological Seminary, 1982. Rockwell Visiting Distinguished Theologian, University of Houston, 1984. Lecturer and speaker at colleges and universities in United States and Asia.

MEMBER: American Academy of Religion (president of Southwestern division, 1967-68), Society of Biblical Literature and Exegesis, Southwestern Philosophical Association, North American Paul Tillich Society.

AWARDS, HONORS: Rockefeller Foundation grant, Harvard University, 1958-59; D.Lett., William Jewell College, 1967.

WRITINGS:

(Contributor) Norman Wade Cox, editor, *Encyclopedia of Southern Baptists,* Broadman, 1958.
Theology and Contemporary Art Forms, Word Books, 1971.
(Contributor) Clifton D. Allen, editor, *Broadman Commentary,* Volume 1, Broadman, 1971.
Demons, Demons, Demons: A Christian Guide through the Murky Maze of the Occult, Broadman, 1972.
Why Christians Fight over the Bible, Thomas Nelson, 1974.
(Contributor) John W. Montgomery, editor, *Demon Possession,* Bethany Fellowship, 1976.
Christ and the New Consciousness, Broadman, 1978.
Christianity and Contemporary Art Forms, Word Books, 1979.
(Editor) *Nineteenth-Century Devotional Thought,* Broadman, 1981.
Makers of the Modern Theological Mind: Paul Tillich, Word Books, 1984.
What Is Christian Doctrine?, Broadman, 1984.
The Lion and the Lamb: The Book of Revelation for Today, Broadman, 1986.
Life's Ultimate Questions, Word Books, 1989.

Also author of *Questions People Ask about a Christian Philosophy of Religion* (two volumes), *Biblical Philosophy and the Modern Mind, A Guide to Religious Authority and Biblical Interpretation to the Thought of John Calvin,* and *Religious Authority, Biblical Interpretation and the Modern Mind,* all privately printed. Contributor to *Review and Expositor, Southwestern Journal of Theology, Baptist Student,* and other publications.

* * *

NORDEN, Denis 1922-

PERSONAL: Born February 6, 1922, in London, England; son of George and Jenny (Lubell) Norden; married Avril Rosen, 1943; children: one son, one daughter. *Education:* Attended schools in London, England.

CAREER: Broadcaster and scriptwriter. Theatre manager, 1939-42; Variety Agency, staff writer, 1945-47; writer and broadcaster, 1947—. Chairman of "Looks Familiar," a program on Thames Television, 1973—, and "It'll Be Alright on the Night," on London Weekend Television, 1977-85. Worked as consultant, with Frank Muir, on light entertainment for television for British Broadcasting Corp. (BBC), 1960-64. Panelist, with Muir, on game shows "My Word!," 1956—, and "My Music," 1967—. *Military service:* Royal Air Force, 1942-45.

MEMBER: Saturday Morning Odeon Club, Queen's Club.

AWARDS, HONORS: Screenwriters Guild Award for best contribution to light entertainment, 1961, and Variety Club of Great Britain Award for best radio personality of the year, 1977, both with Frank Muir; Commander, Order of the British Empire, 1980; Male TV Personality of the Year, 1980.

WRITINGS:

WITH FRANK MUIR

You Can't Have Your Kayak and Heat It: Stories from "My Word!" (also see below), introduction by Jack Longland, Eyre Methuen, 1973.
Upon My Word!: More Stories from "My Word!" (also see below), Eyre Methuen, 1974.
The "My Word!" Stories (contains *You Can't Have Your Kayak and Heat It* and *Upon My Word!*), Eyre Methuen, 1976, Stein & Day, 1977.
Take My Word for It: Still More Stories from "My Word," Eyre Methuen, 1978.
The Glums: Based on the Original Radio Scripts, Robson Books, 1979.
Oh, My Word!: A Fourth Collection of Stories from "My Word," a Panel Game Devised by Edward J. Mason and Tony Shryane, Eyre Methuen, 1980.
The Complete and Utter "My Word!" Collection: Stories from the Panel Game Devised by Edward J. Mason and Tony Shryane, Eyre Methuen, 1983.
You Have "My Word!": Stories from the Panel Game, Eyre Methuen, 1989.

FILMSCRIPTS

(With Alec Coppel) "The Bliss of Mrs. Blossom," Paramount, 1968.
(With Melvin Frank and Sheldon Keller) "Buona Sera, Mrs. Campbell," United Artists, 1969.
"The Best House in London," Metro-Goldwyn-Meyer, 1969.
"The Statue," Cinerama, 1971.

OTHER

(Contributor) Steve Race, *My Music!,* Robson Books, 1979.
(With Sybil Harper and Norma Gilbert) *Coming to You Live!: Behind-the-Screen Memories of Forties and Fifties Television,* Eyre Methuen, 1985.

Also author of television commercials and revues. Scriptwriter of "Every Home Should Have One" and "Twelve Plus One." Also collaborator with Frank Muir, 1947-64, on scripts for television and radio shows, including "Take It from Here," 1947-58, "Bedtime with Braden," 1950-54, "And so to Bently," 1956, and "Whack-O!," 1958-60.

AVOCATIONAL INTERESTS: Reading, loitering.

BIOGRAPHICAL/CRITICAL SOURCES:

PERIODICALS

Los Angeles Times Book Review, May 10, 1981.
Times Educational Supplement, November 29, 1985, December 26, 1986.

* * *

NORRIS, Christopher (Charles) 1947-

PERSONAL: Born November 6, 1947, in London, England; son of Charles F. (an accountant) and Edith E. (Ward) Norris; married Alison Newton (a teacher), 1971; children: Clare, Jennifer. *Education:* University of London, B.A. (first class honors), 1970; Ph.D., 1975. *Politics:* Socialist (Labour). *Religion:* None.

ADDRESSES: Home—14 Belle Vue Terrace, Penarth, South Glamorgan CF6 1DB, Wales. *Office*—Department of English, University of Wales Institute of Science and Technology, Colum Dr., Cardiff CF1 3EU, Wales.

CAREER: University lecturer in English in Duisburg, West Germany, 1974-76; *Books and Bookmen,* London, England, assistant editor, 1976-78; University of Wales Institute of Science and Technology, Cardiff, Wales, lecturer in English, 1978—, appointed to personal chair, 1987. Visiting fellow at Northwestern University, 1983, and visiting professor at University of California, Berkley, 1986, and City University of New York, 1988.

WRITINGS:

William Empson and the Philosophy of Literary Criticism, Athlone Press, 1978.

Deconstruction: Theory and Practice, Methuen, 1982.

(Editor) *Shostakovich: The Man and His Music,* Lawrence & Wishart, 1982.

The Deconstructive Turn: Essays in the Rhetoric of Philosophy, Methuen, 1983.

(Editor) *Inside the Myth: George Orwell—Views from the Left,* Lawrence & Wishart, 1984.

Jacques Derrida, Fontana, 1987.

(Editor with Richard Machin) *Post-Structuralist Readings of English Poetry,* Cambridge University Press, 1987.

Also author of *The Contest of Faculties: Philosophy and Theory after Deconstruction,* 1985, *Paul de Man: Deconstruction and the Critique of Aesthetic Ideology,* 1988, *Deconstruction and the Interests of Theory,* 1988, and co-author of *What Is Deconstruction?,* 1989. Contributor of articles and review to journals and periodicals, including *Times Literary Supplement, London Review of Books, Essays in Criticism, Mind, Philosophy and Literature,* and *Critical Quarterly.* General editor of "Critics of the Twentieth Century" series, Routledge.

WORK IN PROGRESS: A book on Spinoza and the influence of his thought on present-day critical theory; editing a volume of essays on the work of William Empson and another on music, politics, and cultural form.

SIDELIGHTS: Christopher Norris told *CA:* "My main motivation is to help shake British criticism out of its dogmatic slumber. I also want to build bridges between philosophy and literary theory. My interest in these matters was first awakened by (among others) William Empson, Frank Kermode, Jacques Derrida, and Paul de Man. My main activities and the pleasures aside from all this are teaching, listening to music, and doing what I can to help turn back the tide of Thatcherite ignorance, hypocrisy and greed."

BIOGRAPHICAL/CRITICAL SOURCES:

PERIODICALS

London Review of Books, October 21, 1982.

Times Literary Supplement, June 4, 1982, July 2, 1982.

* * *

NORTHCOTT, Kenneth J(ames) 1922-

PERSONAL: Born November 25, 1922, in London, England; son of Frank (a gardener) and Emily Ida (Russell) Northcott; divorced; children: Victoria, Julian, Michael, Felicity. *Education:* Attended Christ's Hospital, Horsham, 1934-39; King's College, London, B.A., 1950, M.A., 1952. *Politics:* Liberal. *Religion:* Church of England.

ADDRESSES: *Office*—Department of Germanic Languages, Wb 204, University of Chicago, 5801 Ellis Ave., Chicago, Ill. 60637.

CAREER: University of Glasgow, Glasgow, Scotland, assistant, 1952-53; University of Sheffield, Sheffield, England, lecturer in medieval German literature, 1953-61; University of Chicago, Chicago, Ill., associate professor, 1961-64, professor of medieval German literature, 1964-73, professor of comparative literature, 1973—, chairman of department of Germanic languages and literature, 1969-78, acting chairman of department of comparative studies and literature, 1977-78, dean of students division of humanities, 1966-68. Institute of European Studies, chairman of board of governors, 1966-70, deputy chairman, 1970—. *Military service:* British Army, Intelligence, 1942-46; became sergeant major.

MEMBER: Modern Language Association of America, Mediaeval Academy of America, American Association of Teachers of German, Midwest Modern Language Association (president, 1971-73), British Association of University Teachers.

WRITINGS:

(Author of text and commentary) *Peter Schlemihl,* Thomas Nelson, 1955.

(Translator) Hans Kuehner, *Encyclopedia of the Papacy,* Philosophical Library, 1958.

(Translator) Emerich Schaffran, *Dictionary of European Art,* Philosophical Library, 1958.

(Editor with Werner Betz and Evelyn Coleman, and contributor) *Taylor Starck: Festschrift,* Mouton, 1964.

(Translator and author of introduction) Gotthold E. Lessing, *Minna von Barnhelm,* University of Chicago Press, 1972.

(Editor) Friedrich von Schiller, *Wilhelm Tell,* translation by William F. Mainland, University of Chicago Press, 1972.

(Editor) J. M. Lenz, *Tutor and the Soldiers,* translation by William E. Yuill, University of Chicago Press, 1973.

(Translator) *Watther von der Vogehreide,* Scribner, 1982.

(Translator) Arnold Hauser, *The Sociology of Art,* University of Chicago Press, 1982.

(Translator with Elizabeth Lutzeier) Hans J. Nissen, *The Early History of the Ancient Near East, 9000-2000 B.C.,* University of Chicago Press, 1988.

(Translator) Wolfgang Braunfels, *Urban Design in Western Europe: Regime and Architecture, 900-1000,* University of Chicago Press, 1988.

Also general editor of *A Literary History of Germany* (eight volumes), Barnes & Noble, and *German Literary Classics in Translation,* University of Chicago Press.

AVOCATIONAL INTERESTS: Theater.*

* * *

NORWICH, John Julius (Cooper) 1929-

PERSONAL: Born September 15, 1929, in London, England; son of Alfred Duff (an historian and statesman; first Viscount Norwich) and Lady Diana (Manners) Cooper; married Anne Francis May Clifford (a painter), August 5, 1952 (marriage dissolved, 1983); children: Artemis Cooper, Jason Cooper. *Education:* Attended University of Strasbourg, and New College, Oxford.

ADDRESSES: *Home*—24 Blomfield Rd., London W. 9, England. *Agent*—Felicity Bryan, 2A North Parade, Oxford, England (literary); and Curtis Brown Ltd., 162-168 Regent St., London W1R 5TA, England (television and radio).

CAREER: Her Majesty's Foreign Service, 1952-64, served as third secretary at British Embassy in Belgrade, Yugoslavia, 1955-57, as second secretary at British Embassy in Beirut, Lebanon, 1957-60, and as first secretary in Foreign Office, London, England, 1961-64, member of British delegation to Disarmament Conference, Geneva, Switzerland, 1962-63; Serenissima Travel, London, chairman, 1972-87. Lecturer on conservation, travel, history, and the fine arts; chairman of British Theatre Museum, 1966-71; member of Executive Committee, National Trust, 1969—; chairman of Venice in Peril Fund. Host of some 30 television documentaries; host of radio programme, "My Word!" for British Broadcasting Corp. Radio. *Military service:* Royal Navy, writer, 1947-49.

MEMBER: Royal Society of Literature (fellow), Royal Geographical Society (fellow), Beefsteak Club.

WRITINGS:

(With Reresby Sitwell) *Mount Athos,* illustrated with photographs by the authors and A. Costa, Harper, 1966.

The Other Conquest, Harper, 1967 (published in England as *The Normans in the South, 1016-1130,* Longmans, Green, 1967).

Sahara, illustrated with photographs by the author and by A. Costa, Weybright & Talley, 1968.

The Kingdom in the Sun, 1130-1194 (sequel to *The Other Conquest*), Harper, 1970.

(Editor) *Great Architecture of the World,* foreword by N. Pevsner, Random House, 1975.

Venice: The Rise to Empire (also see below), Allen Lane, 1977.

(Compiler) *Christmas Crackers: Ten Commonplace Selections, 1970-1979,* Allen Lane, 1980.

Venice: The Greatness and the Fall (also see below), Allen Lane, 1981.

A History of Venice, Volume 1: *The Rise to Empire,* Volume 2: *The Greatness and the Fall,* Knopf, 1982.

(Editor) *The Italian World: History, Art, and the Genius of a People,* Abrams, 1983.

(Editor) *Britain's Heritage,* Granada, 1983.

(Author of introduction) Suomi La Valle, *Hashish,* Quartet Books, 1984.

(Author of introduction) *The World Atlas of Architecture,* G. K. Hall, 1984.

(Author of introduction) Laura Ralson, compiler, *Tuscany: An Anthology,* Facts on File, 1984.

The Architecture of Southern England, photographs by Jorge Lewinski and Mayotte Magnus, Macmillan, 1985.

Fifty Years of Glyndebourne: An Illustrated History, J. Cape, 1985.

(Editor and compiler) *A Taste for Travel: An Anthology,* Macmillan (London), 1985, Knopf, 1987.

Byzantium: The Early Centuries, Knopf, 1989.

Also author of historical documentary films for British Broadcasting Corp. television. General editor, *Great Architecture of the World,* Mitchell Beazley, 1975, and *Shell Guides to Britain,* 1987—. Contributor to *Sunday Times, Spectator, History Today,* and other publications.

SIDELIGHTS: John Julius Norwich, says J. G. Links in the *Spectator,* "has been everywhere, read everything, and has been anthologising for years." A veteran of the British diplomatic service with a strong interest in the unusual, Norwich has produced books ranging from descriptions of exotic places and architecture, anthologies of traveler's tales and other oddities, and histories of the Normans in Italy and the Venetian Republic. In short, states Fiona MacCarthy in the London *Times,* "Lord Norwich is a huge, and an infectious, enthusiast."

Representative of Norwich's travel literature is the anthology *A Taste for Travel.* J. Y. Smith of the *Washington Post Book World* reports, "This is an anthology of pieces about traveling when getting there was half the fun of it and there was more to having an adventure along the way than losing your luggage or missing a connection." "Norwich's purpose is to share with us the excitement and drama the simple act of going abroad can still arouse, 'the endless fascination of the unknown,' as he puts it," remarks *Los Angeles Times Book Review* contributor William Murray. Norwich's own journeys have taken him to locations over the world, including Mount Athos in Greece and the Sahara Desert.

Another series of excursions led Norwich to write *The Architecture of Southern England.* This book, says MacCarthy, "purports to set before us the best buildings of the country, south (roughly) of the line from the Severn to the Wash." However, many reviewers have found *The Architecture of Southern England* limited in the range of buildings Norwich chooses to include: "No one," MacCarthy continues, "could fail to find its range and energy remarkable. But it is also startling in the things it leaves out." In Norwich's introduction, states *Times Literary Supplement* reviewer J. M. Richards, the author "declares that the buildings he describes are simply his personal choice, and he defines his reactions to architecture as 'almost depressingly orthodox,' which means that with few exceptions he limits himself to the pre-Victorian." Gavin Stamp, writing in the *Spectator,* points out that Norwich neglects Victorian and twentieth-century architecture almost entirely. Nonetheless, concludes Richards, *The Architecture of Southern England* "is an enjoyable reference book."

Norwich displays his fascination with the unique and outlandish in his anthology of miscellany called *Christmas Crackers: Ten Commonplace Selections, 1970-1979.* When he was in the Foreign Service, explains Mary Blume in the *Los Angeles Times,* Norwich began keeping a log of "phrases that caught his fancy, and from these culled the first Christmas Cracker." These included, she adds, quotations and a couple of dictionary definitions: the Italian word *buffona,* meaning "woman with a not unpleasing mustache," and *carphology,* "delirious fumbling with the bed-clothes, etc." Other Norwich favorites in the collection include all sorts of palindromes (lines which read the same backward or forward), evocative lines of poetry, mnemonics, and various entreating notes his late mother left on her windshield to avoid being ticketed for illegal parking. "His range knows no bounds," comments William Haley in the *Times Literary Supplement;* " 'a chance remark, a letter from a friend, an opera programme, an advertisement, the instruction book for the new washing machine . . . can reveal the unexpected nugget of pure gold.' "

More famous than Norwich's anthologies, however, are his popular histories. *The Other Conquest* and *The Kingdom in the Sun, 1130-1194,* two of his early books, trace the events which led to the establishment of the Norman kingdom of Sicily. While lacking in original scholarship, says *Saturday Review* contributor Gabriel Gersh, Norwich's work is valuable for its "triumph[al] . . . evoking [of] this fascinating island. His descriptions are well wrought and give his work an added dimension. The total result is an excellent assessment." "Lord Norwich does not always display the professional scholarship one finds, for example, in Steven Runciman's books on the Crusades—but he has enough for his purpose," declares Thomas Caldecot Chubb in the *New York Times Book Review.* His work, the reviewer continues, "is an orderly—and, on the whole, accurate—account of things that really happened."

Norwich continues to examine Mediterranean history in his two-volume *A History of Venice.* This work traces the long story of the Venetian Republic from its foundation as a refuge from barbarian invaders in the fifth century, through its period of empire and dominion over much of northern Italy, Greece, Cyprus, and the Levant, to its collapse and conquest by Napoleon in 1805. Reviewers praise Norwich's depiction of the Republic, commenting especially on his writing style and historical acumen. For example, Edward Condren states in the *Los Angeles Times Book Review,* "John Julius Norwich has written a handsome history of Venice that precisely captures the essence of that endlessly fascinating republic." "Viscount Norwich is a good writer," says Felix Gilbert in the *New Republic,* "and, from the beginning to the end, the book is pleasant to read . . ." *Washington Post Book World* contributor Lauro Martines declares that "there is much here to appeal to the [general reader]. The book has zest, vigor, and an unflinching narrative line. Travelers, laymen, local librarians, and all who enjoy the exploits and panache of old regimes are certain to find satisfaction in it."

Although many reviewers praise Norwich's history, others maintain that it does not significantly advance historical scholarship. Norwich himself admits this: "I'm not a scholar, I'm a popularizer," he told Blume. "I only use printed sources, I don't go burrowing down into dusty libraries." Gilbert asserts that "the principal defect of this story of Venice lies not in what is told or in how it is told, but in what the book fails to tell us." Martines declares that the book "offers no analysis of problems and does not rely on the fullness of modern scholarship, with the result that it is wrong about the 14th-century population, wrong about guilds, about the even-handed administration of justice, about the equitable distribution of taxes, about entry into the special class of 'citizens,' and about other matters of little interest to the general reader."

On the other hand, Martines points out that Norwich's history has value as a document that exudes the author's deep feeling for the city. "He takes sides, he emphasizes, he castigates, he shakes his head, he sighs, and he draws lessons," the reviewer comments. Such judgments, Martines declares, reinterpret Venetian history; instead of presenting the city as "repressive and wickedly oligarchical," Norwich shows "Venice as humane and fair." Martines concludes by hoping that readers "find the light [*A History of Venice*] throws on the ways in which our present determines our understanding of that past, for in this regard Norwich's book—a bit of live history itself—is a resonant human document."

AVOCATIONAL INTERESTS: Travel (has traveled in Sicily and the Sahara), theatre, music (especially opera).

BIOGRAPHICAL/CRITICAL SOURCES:

PERIODICALS

Best Sellers, December 1, 1970.
Christian Science Monitor, September 7, 1967.
Economist, April 29, 1967.
Los Angeles Times, December 3, 1986.
Los Angeles Times Book Review, August 29, 1982, August 21, 1983, November 6, 1983.
New Republic, December 9, 1967, November 8, 1982.
New Statesman, June 19, 1970.
New Yorker, May 10, 1982.
New York Review of Books, May 27, 1982.
New York Times, May 4, 1982, May 30, 1982.
New York Times Book Review, December 4, 1966, September 10, 1967, December 1, 1968.
Saturday Review, December 3, 1966, March 6, 1971.
Spectator, March 31, 1967, March 14, 1969, June 20, 1970, December 24, 1977, September 19, 1981, November 28, 1981, December 17, 1983, November 2, 1985, September 6, 1986.
Time, August 25, 1967.
Times (London), October 27, 1966, November 3, 1977, September 17, 1981, March 23, 1984, July 11, 1985, March 20, 1987.
Times Books for Christmas, December 21, 1980.
Times Literary Supplement, June 15, 1967, February 26, 1971, December 19, 1975, December 19, 1980, June 11, 1982, September 20, 1985, December 27, 1985.
Washington Post Book World, January 31, 1971, May 30, 1982, December 4, 1983, March 22, 1987.
Yale Review, December, 1970.

—*Sketch by Kenneth R. Shepherd*

NOYCE, Gaylord B. 1926-

PERSONAL: Born July 8, 1926, in Burlington, Iowa; son of Ralph Brewster (a clergyman) and Harriet (Norton) Noyce; married Dorothy Caldwell (a school psychologist), May 25, 1949; children: Elizabeth Ann, Karen Virginia, Timothy Brewster. *Education:* Miami University, Oxford, Ohio, B.A., 1947; Yale University, M.Div., 1952.

ADDRESSES: Home—56 Morse St., Hamden, Conn. 06517. *Office*—Divinity School, Yale University, 409 Prospect St., New Haven, Conn. 06510.

CAREER: Clergyman of United Church of Christ; Robert College, Istanbul, Turkey, instructor in mathematics, 1947-49; assistant minister of congregational church in Lexington, Mass., 1952-54; pastor of United Community Church in Raleigh, N.C., 1954-60; Yale University, Divinity School, New Haven, Conn., assistant professor, 1960-65, associate professor, 1965-80, professor of pastoral theology, 1980—. *Military service:* U.S. Navy, 1944-46.

WRITINGS:

The Church Is Not Expendable, Westminster, 1969.
The Responsible Suburban Church, Westminster, 1970.
Survival and Mission for the City Church, Westminster, 1975.
New Perspectives on Parish Ministry: A View from the Third World, Judson, 1981.
The Art of Pastoral Conversation, John Knox, 1981.
(With Parker Rossman) *Helping People Care on the Job,* Judson, 1985.
Pastoral Ethics: Professional Responsibilities of the Clergy, Abingdon, 1988.
The Minister: A Moral Counselor, Abingdon, 1989.

SIDELIGHTS: Gaylord B. Noyce wrote *CA,* "Most of my work is an attempt to enhance the religious vision and competence of congregations, their pastors, and the individuals in the pews."

* * *

NYE, Robert 1939-

PERSONAL: Born March 15, 1939, in London, England; son of Oswald William and Frances Dorothy (Weller) Nye; married first wife Judith Preyed, 1959 (divorced, 1967); married second wife, Aileen Campbell (an artist, poet, and psychologist), 1968; children: (first marriage) Jack, Taliesin, Malory; (second marriage) Owen, Sharon, Rebecca. *Education:* Attended schools in England.

ADDRESSES: Home—Cork, Ireland. *Agent*—Anthony Sheil Associates, Ltd., 2/3 Morwell St., London WC1B 3AR, England; and Wallace, Aitken & Sheil, Inc., 118 East 61st St., New York, N.Y. 10021.

CAREER: Writer. Worked as a newspaper reporter, milkman, market garden laborer, and sanatorium orderly; *Times,* London, England, poetry critic, 1971—. Poetry editor, *Scotsman,* 1967—; fiction reviewer, *Guardian,* London. Writer in residence, University of Edinburgh, 1976-77.

MEMBER: Royal Society of Literature (fellow).

AWARDS, HONORS: Eric Gregory Award, 1963, for *Juvenilia 2;* Scottish Arts Council bursary, 1970, 1973, and publication award, 1970, 1976; James Kennaway Memorial Award, 1970, for *Tales I Told My Mother; Guardian* fiction prize, 1976, and Hawthornden Prize, 1977, both for *Falstaff.*

WRITINGS:

FOR CHILDREN

Taliesin (novel; also see below), Faber, 1966, Hill & Wang, 1967.

March Has Horse's Ears (short stories), Faber, 1966, Hill & Wang, 1967.

Beowulf: A New Telling (novel; also see below), illustrated by wife Aileen Campbell Nye, Hill & Wang, 1968 (published in England as *Bee Hunter: Adventures of Beowulf,* Faber, 1968, reprinted as *Beowulf, the Bee Hunter,* Faber, 1972).

Wishing Gold (novel; also see below), illustrated by Helen Craig, Macmillan (London), 1970, Hill & Wang, 1971.

Poor Pumpkin (short stories), Macmillan (London), 1971, published as *The Mathematical Princess and Other Stories,* Hill & Wang, 1972.

Cricket: Three Stories, pictures by Shelly Freshman, Bobbs-Merrill, 1975 (published in England as *Once upon Three Times,* Benn, 1978).

Out of the World and Back Again, illustrated by Joanna Troughton, Collins, 1977, published as *Out of This World and Back Again,* Bobbs-Merrill, 1978.

The Bird of the Golden Land, illustrated by Krystyna Turska, Hamish Hamilton, 1980.

Harry Pay the Pirate (novel), Hamish Hamilton, 1981.

Three Tales: Beowulf, Taliesin, Wishing Gold, Hamish Hamilton, 1983.

FOR ADULTS

Doubtfire (novel), Calder & Boyars, 1967, Hill & Wang, 1968.

Tales I Told My Mother (short stories), Hill & Wang, 1969.

(Contributor) *Penguin Modern Stories 6,* Penguin, 1970.

Lines Review 38 (includes four stories, poems, and a filmscript), [Edinburgh], 1971.

Falstaff: Being the "Acta Domini Johannis Fastolfe"; or, "Life and Valiant Deeds of Sir John Faustoff"; or, "The Hundred Days War," as told by Sir John Fastolf, K. G., to His Secretaries William Worcester, Stephen Scrope, Fr. Brackley, Christopher Hanson, Luke Nanton, John Bussard, and Peter Bassett—Now First Transcribed, Arranged, and Edited in Modern Spelling by Robert Nye (novel), Little, Brown, 1976.

Merlin (novel), Hamish Hamilton, 1978, Putnam, 1979.

Faust: Being the Historia von D. Johann Fausten dem Wietbeschreyten Zauberer und Schwartzkuenstler; or, History of Dr. John Faust the Notorious Magician and Necromancer, as Written by His Familiar Servant and Disciple Christopher Wagner, Now for the First Time Englished from the Low German (novel), Putnam, 1980.

The Voyage of the Destiny (novel), Putnam, 1982.

The Facts of Life and Other Fictions (short stories), Hamish Hamilton, 1983.

POEMS

Juvenilia 1, Scorpion Press, 1961.

Juvenilia 2, Scorpion Press, 1963.

Darker Ends, Hill & Wang, 1969.

Divisions on a Ground, Carcanet Press, 1976.

PLAYS

(With William Watson) *Sawney Bean* (also see below; first produced in Edinburgh, Scotland, 1969, produced in New York, 1982), Calder & Boyars, 1970.

"Sisters" (also see below), first produced as a radio play by British Broadcasting Corp. (BBC Radio), 1969, first stage production in Edinburgh, Scotland, 1973.

"A Bloody Stupit Hole," BBC Radio, 1970.

"Reynolds, Reynolds," BBC Radio, 1971.

"Penthesilea" (adaptation of a play by Heinrich von Kleist; also see below), BBC Radio, 1971, first stage production in London, 1983.

The Seven Deadly Sins: A Mask (first produced in Stirling, Scotland, at the Stirling Festival, 1973), Omphalos Press, 1974.

"Mr. Poe: A Public Lecture with Private Illustrations," first produced in Edinburgh, Scotland, and London, 1974.

Three Plays: Penthesilia, Fugue, and Sisters, Marion Boyars, 1975.

(With Humphrey Searle) "The Devil's Jig" (play adaptation of a work by Thomas Mann), BBC Radio, 1980.

EDITOR

(And author of introduction) *A Choice of Sir Walter Raleigh's Verse,* Faber, 1972.

William Barnes of Dorset: A Selection of His Poems, Carcanet Press, 1973.

(And author of introduction) *A Choice of Swinburne's Verse,* Faber, 1973.

The Book of Sonnets, Oxford University Press (New York), 1976 (published in England as *The Faber Book of Sonnets,* Faber, 1976).

The English Sermon 1750-1850: An Anthology, Carcanet Press, 1976.

P.E.N. New Poetry I, Quartet Books, 1986.

WORK IN PROGRESS: A volume of collected poems.

SIDELIGHTS: Robert Nye is a writer of poetry, short stories, and novels for children and adults. He has also tried his hand at plays and scriptwriting, and has become a noted critic and editor, contributing reviews to the London *Times* and *Guardian.* Although his poetry and short stories have won the Eric Gregory Award and the James Kennaway Award respectively, Nye is best known for his novels *Merlin, Faust,* and *Falstaff;* the lattermost won the Hawthornden Prize in 1977 and was adapted for the stage. These books are examples of the author's tendency to borrow old story lines from myths and legends (usually of English, Welsh, and Celtic origin) and use literary and historical figures, reworking these two elements into tales with frequently humorous and ribald plots. Michael Wood in the *New York Review of Books,* along with other critics, compares Nye's style to that of French satirist Francois Rabelais, and London *Times* reviewer David Williams detects an influence of James Joyce in the author's work. Despite an early dissatisfaction with poetry, in 1988 the author told *CA:* "I . . . regard myself primarily as a poet." He further added that he writes prose "as a relief from the truth-telling which poetry requires of his adherents."

In a *Dictionary of Literary Biography* entry written by Elizabeth Allen, the author says his penchant for writing was first inspired by his mother, who, he relates, "was possessed of an innate peasant storytelling ability." By his early teens, Nye knew that he wanted to pursue a writing career. He decided against any further formal education after high school, concentrating instead on his poetry while working odd jobs to support himself and, later, his family. Though *Juvenilia 2* and *Darker Ends* were both well received by critics, these early poetry collections did not draw much income. His first collection of poetry, *Juvenilia 1,* was dismissed by critics, as one *Times Literary Supplement* article notes, for its "immaturity of attitude and elusiveness of meaning." This is not surprising, however, since Nye wrote many of the poems in *Juvenilia 1* while still a teenager.

According to the same article, by the time *Juvenilia 2* was written Nye's style had matured to the point where he could be called a "true poet." But after he published *Darker Ends* in 1969, the poet abandoned the genre for several years. In a 1967 *Books and Bookmen* interview, Nye explains his disenchantment with poetry: "Poetry on every side is announcing to all who still have an ear for its voice that it is a factitious and unsatisfactory means of expression." Instead, he says that he has turned to the novel because it "has in the last 50 years been surreptitiously taking over from poetry the field it once claimed as its own exclusive right." The field to which he refers is "the true history of the race: a permanent record of man's deepest moments of feeling, seeing, being."

Doubtfire, Nye's first novel, is faithful to his idea that novels should depict life poetically. It is "an exercise in word-imagery with allegorical overtones," describes Anthony Horner in *Books and Bookmen. New Statesman* contributor Gillian Freeman summarizes the book as being "a ranging exploration of the mind of an adolescent boy who, developing towards sexual maturity, is unable to sort out reality from fantasy." By telling the story from within the mind of a confused adolescent, Nye explores the nature of reality. "The Reality of Nye's intricately clever 'nowhere somewhere else' is not real because he teaches us that no reality is real," writes *Northwest Review* critic P. H. Porosky. "Madness, grotesque bizarreness replace so-called lucidity because, as Nye's characters learn, lucidity is really a fiction, a process of imagination, the minor image, or finally, . . . the poem." Porosky expresses frustration with Nye's obtuse, poetic approach in *Doubtfire,* remarking that "at times one wonders if there is any coherence at all." But in a London *Times* article Michael Wood brings to the reader's attention that not storyline, but "language is the hero" in *Doubtfire.* It is, says Wood, a "brilliantly sustained [book], . . . a poem-novel with careful syntax, proliferating pictures and a strong sense of the concrete."

Similarly, Nye's short stories are a departure from the norm, due to the author's unique use of language, characters, and plot. David Williams remarks that, as with *Doubtfire,* it is difficult to say what the stories in Nye's *Tales I Told My Mother* are about. He suggests that one will "probably get farther if he proceeds by way of similes rather than epitomes." To compose his stories, the writer uses a liberal mixture of characters and objects without much regard to the limitations of time, place, or reality. "Among other people and things," writes David Montrose in the *Times Literary Supplement,* Nye incorporates into his stories "various members of the Pre-Raphaelite Brotherhood, a Chinese giant, a reinterpretation of Chatterton's suicide, the Wandering Jew, and a lost novel by Emily Bronte." The reviewer concludes that *Tales I Told My Mother* displays "plenty of ingenuity." One original aspect of the book involves the way the author intertwines these elements to form an interconnected whole. In the *British Book News,* Neil Philip calls this approach to the short story "an immature 'experimental' attempt which nevertheless repays attention. Nye's prose is dazzling even at its most opaque, and his sheer delight in language is a delight for the reader, too."

His more recent collection of short stories, *The Facts of Life and Other Fictions,* also "confirms Nye's wonderful gift for language," asserts Montrose; but, the reviewer adds, the inventiveness of the author's earlier collection is lacking. Again, the author mixes various famous characters such as James Joyce and Anne Hathaway into the same storyline, but the plots in this case are unconnected and do not include "the dark imaginings" of *Tales I Told My Mother,* says Montrose. However, he claims the story "Adam Kadmon" in *The Facts of Life* contains a previously undisclosed key to Nye's writing which "could almost be applied to the entire collection. The story, we learn, is 'a pack of lies'. . . . It has no other function or meaning."

This insight, when applied to Nye's *Falstaff,* explains this novel's content. With much extrapolation by the author, Shakespeare's comical character from *Henry IV* and *The Merry Wives of Windsor* dictates his own version of his life to several secretaries. Nye asks the reader to accept that, although Shakespeare tells us that Falstaff dies in *Henry IV: Part II,* his "death" was actually a ruse to avoid his creditors. Falstaff can then go on to describe what really happened at the Battle of Shrewsbury, the robbery at Gadshill, and other events from Shakespeare's plays, while adding many ribald adventures and explicit monologues about human bodily functions and parts of the corpulent storyteller's anatomy. In these memoirs Falstaff's character becomes heroic, logical, and noble. For example, he explains that he actually allowed Prince Hal to steal the booty from him at Gadshill because, as *Time* reviewer John Sklow puts it, any other course of action "would have destroyed the confidence of the next King of England." At the conclusion of the book, however, Falstaff confesses to a priest that his memoirs are really "lies about my whole life." The riddle comes when he adds: "But try & explain: some *true* lies?" Peter Conrad comments on this in the *Spectator:* "Falstaff's dying admission that his memoirs are a tissue of prurient lies only confirms his creative genius: he turns life into art, whereas Shakespeare can only make feeble art from the transcription of that life."

To *Village Voice* contributor Katherine Bouton, though, Falstaff's tales are "sometimes apt, but more often it is simply Shakespeare paraphrased." Bouton also finds the details of Falstaff's sexual exploits, which contain many suggestive puns, "tiresomely repetitive." She complains that there is "no plot or character development." West similarly believes that the rotund prevaricator "wears his welcome out." To a certain extent, Michael Wood supports this viewpoint; but he adds that the bawdiness in the novel "generally . . . takes on a rather attractive pathos, for we are rarely allowed to forget that Falstaff is not bragging, but *lying,* and that his 'cunterbury tales,' as he calls them, are a requiem for a life he never lived."

The two books which follow *Falstaff, Merlin* and *Faust,* are also largely based upon ribald adventures and incredible tales. Again, these novels borrow old, familiar stories and tell them from new perspectives. *Merlin* relates the events of the Arthurian legend from the viewpoint of the wizard, whom Nye describes as the offspring of a virgin and Satan. He is a kind of "failed Antichrist," who, when imprisoned in the crystal cave, "becomes the ultimate voyeur and cosmospectator," says *Times Literary Supplement* contributor T. A. Shippey. Mary Hope describes the book in the *Spectator* as "a gallimaufrey and hotch potch, linked by one splendid shaggy dog story." Like *Falstaff, Merlin* does not fall easily into the category of the novel because of its de-emphasis of character and plot development. It is more of an exercise with "language, images, and psychological implications," asserts *Atlantic* contributor Phoebe-Lou Adams. As in the author's other books, *New Statesman* reviewer Helen McNeil says that the "giggling, scratching, farting, cursing, pissing, birching (lots of that), frigging, . . . only lead one away from any suspicion that these [characters] have ever lived or that they resemble us."

But even though "the novel fizzes along on a charge of multilevelled, inconsequential anecdote," comments Shippey, *Merlin* is "not as inconsequential as it looks." Through Merlin's eyes, the reader gains certain "sensational" insights which lead Shippey to believe that the moral of the story "is that the world is a book and the devil writes it . . . —an idea which all great Arthurians of the past would, I'm sure, find repugnant." Nevertheless, Nye does succeed in presenting this familiar story in a new way. Unhindered by any need to honor the Arthurian myth, the author is free to present a new perspective of the legend.

The author also brings originality to the legend of Faust through his customary shift in viewpoint, which in this case comes from Faust's protege Christopher (Kit) Wagner. Kit relates the last days of Faust before his contract with Satan expires and he is condemned to damnation in Hell. Contrary to Goethe's and Marlowe's versions, Nye's Faust is portrayed by Kit as a "chronic old lecher and drunken fool," according to *British Book News* reviewer Christopher Norris. The story relates the events of Faust's and Kit's travels as they journey to Rome "in a final bid to secure reprieve" from the Pope, writes *Spectator* critic Paul Ableman, but the trip deteriorates into a spree of debauchery which *Times Literary Supplement* reviewer J. B. Steane finds "tiresome, [especially] when 'come' cannot pass without a pun."

"The whole book," summarizes Norris, "is really a compendium of jokes, some of them told straight off on the flimsiest of narrative pretexts, others having a more subtle relation to the legend and tradition of Faust." He concludes that *Faust* is not a book "for the squeamish or custodians of moral sweetness and light." In Nye's version, however, the plot has "an original twist which gives the whole tale something of the nature of a metaphysical thriller with a surprise ending," says Ableman. It is, Norris adds, "a spirited piece of novelistic daring. A thoroughly enjoyable book."

In a combined review of *Falstaff* and *Faust,* Alan Franks concludes in the London *Times:* "These most ambitious novels could so easily have become inchoate . . ., but it is always the sheer vigour of Nye's language which pulls them back from the brink." Franks continues, "His is a highly individual diction, forever lancing its own pretensions with the use of tough, strangely timeless vernacular. The mixture of erudition and sheer belly mirth is potent indeed." Because his primary interest is poetry, Nye's continuing experimentations with language have tended to place plot and characterization in subordinate positions within his novels. This has sometimes made his work difficult for critics to interpret. In the *Dictionary of Literary Biography,* Allen summarizes Nye's writing as being "both traditional and highly individual: traditional in that he works with archetypal themes and myths available to all writers of story and legend both oral and literary, and individual in the forms in which he recreates them." It is this originality of form in perspective and language which has made Nye a noted contributor to English literature.

MEDIA ADAPTATIONS: Falstaff was produced as a radio play in 1981.

BIOGRAPHICAL/CRITICAL SOURCES:

BOOKS

Dictionary of Literary Biography, Volume 14: *British Novelists since 1960,* Gale, 1983.

PERIODICALS

Atlantic, June, 1979.
Books and Bookmen, May, 1967, March, 1968.
British Book News, December, 1980, June, 1982.
Listener, February 29, 1968.
New Statesman, February 9, 1968, September 15, 1978.
New York Review of Books, January 20, 1977.
New York Times Book Review, November 7, 1976.
Northwest Review, summer, 1968.
Spectator, September 4, 1976, October 18, 1980, September 23, 1987.
Time, November 8, 1976.
Times (London), January 27, 1968, December 20, 1969, June 30, 1983, January 4, 1986.
Times Literary Supplement, July 26, 1963, September 15, 1978, October 17, 1980, June 17, 1983.
Village Voice, December 27, 1976.

—*Sketch by Kevin S. Hile*

O

OAKES, Philip (Barlow) 1928-

PERSONAL: Born January 31, 1928, in Burslem, Staffordshire, England; son of Sam (a traveler) and Constance (a teacher; maiden name, Barlow) Oakes; married Stella Fleming (a librarian), September 9, 1950; children: Susan Jill, Toby Alan, Josy. *Education:* Attended school in Darwen, Lancashire, England. *Politics:* Radical. *Religion:* None.

ADDRESSES: Agent—Elaine Green Ltd., 31 Newington Green, London N16 9PU, England.

CAREER: Eric R. Sly's Court Reporting Service Ltd., London, England, reporter, 1945-46, 1949-55; *Daily Express,* London, reporter and author of column, "The World I Watch," 1955-56; *Evening Standard,* London, film critic, 1956-58; Granada Television Film Unit, London, scriptwriter, 1959-61; *Sunday Telegraph,* London, film critic, 1963-65; *Sunday Times Magazine,* London, assistant editor, 1965-67; *Sunday Times,* London, arts columnist, 1965-80. *Military service:* British Army, newspaper writer, 1946-49; served in Cairo and Athens.

WRITINGS:

Unlucky Jonah (poems), University of Reading Press, 1955.

Exactly What We Want (novel), M. Joseph, 1962.

(Editor) *The Film Addict's Archive: Poetry and Prose of the Cinema,* Beekman, 1966.

In the Affirmative (poems), Deutsch, 1968.

Miracles: Genuine Cases Contact Box 340 (novel), John Day, 1969 (published in England as *The Godbotherers,* Deutsch, 1969).

Notes by the Provincial Governor (poems), Poem-of-the-Month Club, 1972.

Experiment at Proto (novel), Coward, 1973, published as *The Proto Papers,* Quartet Books, 1974.

Married/Singular (poems), Deutsch, 1973.

Tony Hancock (biography), Woburn, 1975.

(Editor) *The Entertainers,* Woburn, 1975.

A Cast of Thousands (novel), Gollancz, 1976.

From Middle England: A Memory of the 1930s, Deutsch, 1980, St. Martin's, 1983.

Dwellers All in Time and Space: A Memory of the 1940s, Deutsch, 1981, St. Martin's, 1984.

Selected Poems, Deutsch, 1982.

At the Jazz Band Ball: A Memory of the 1950s, Deutsch, 1983.

Author, with Tony Hancock, of screenplay "The Punch and Judy Man," 1962; author, with Desmond Morris, of more than one hundred fifty filmscripts on animal behavior; author of documentary programs and plays for television. Work anthologized in numerous collections. Columnist and literary editor, *Truth,* 1955-56.

WORK IN PROGRESS: A novel.

SIDELIGHTS: While many childhood memoirs are frequently over-dramatized or sentimental, novelist and poet Philip Oakes's *From Middle England: A Memory of the 1930s* "has adroitly steered around these pitfalls," writes Vernon Scannell of the *Times Literary Supplement.* Oakes was sent to boarding school at the age of eight; his father had died when the child was four, and his mother was bedstricken, a weakening invalid following a brain operation. Although these circumstances appear miserable, *London Review of Books* contributor Penelope Lively notes that Oakes's book "is a good-humoured and unsentimental account. . . . The descriptions of place and mood are precise and accurate, owing their detachment, one feels, to the shrewd eye of the child as much as to the distancing of adult experience: the view is the one seen at the time, not another recovered with the alterations of hindsight." In addition, Scannell claims that because Oakes is a poet, "*From Middle England* contains the best kind of poetic prose"; as the critic elaborates, Oakes's writing contains "a precision and sharp-eyed focusing on itself, a knack of conveying the emotion through the exact presentation of a particular object, event or spoken phrase." Scannell concludes: "[*From Middle England*] is continuously enjoyable, sharply observed, funny, tender and, in its closing pages dealing with the outbreak of war, tactfully and quite unsentimentally moving."

In his next volume, *Dwellers All in Time and Space: A Memory of the 1940s,* Oakes continues his story with his expulsion from school and subsequent enrollment in a Methodist children's home. Seemingly oblivious to the effects of war around him, the young Philip begins a period of sexual exploration, including the impregnation of a house mother fifteen years his senior. More than its predecessor, "*Dwellers All in Time and Space* is autobiography which employs many of the procedures of fiction," notes Scannell; "conversations which took place forty years ago are recorded *verbatim.*" Several critics are uncomfortable with the amount of dialogue Oakes uses in this volume, however; *Listener* contributor Patricia Beer comments that "the book does not sound like an autobiography at all. . . . The technique throughout *Dwellers* is that of highly competent fiction." Despite this fictional bent, Lively believes that "Oakes has to be congratulated on his reconstruction of what it was like to be 14 and despatched unconsulted to an institution which, while not exactly grim or uncharitable, was tough and uncompromising." As Sarah Newell states in the *New York Times Book Review:* "[Oakes's] characters are all the more intriguing for being real, and one is left wondering what will happen to them. . . . We're left hankering for more, looking forward to the 1950's installment of this readable life."

"In the same way that a novelist may write about his own life, disguising it as a tale about imaginary people, autobiography may be a sly form of fiction," remarks Nina Bawden in the *London Review of Books.* "And it follows that the success of an autobiography depends on whether or not he makes a good story of it. Philip Oakes has succeeded superbly." Detailing the author's late adolescence and young adulthood working as a reporter and writer, *At the Jazz Band Ball: A Memory of the 1950s* "is a very funny, lively and often enthralling record," says Bawden, adding that the book is "convincing in its detail, and set down with verve and style." Comparable to his two previous volumes, Oakes "shows a quite unusual gift for pitilessly accurate self-portraiture," maintains Scannell. "It is the kind of honesty that is unusual in any author . . . but in a middle-aged writer it is particularly rare." *New Statesman* contributor Nigella Lawson also sees a similarity of technique throughout Oakes's memoirs: "As in his earlier volumes, it is the quiet, understated perceptiveness which marks Philip Oakes's prose." *At the Jazz Band Ball* concludes with the death of Oakes's aging and deteriorating mother, "a scene written with perfect tact and precision," as Scannell describes it. "I found this [scene] very moving and the whole trilogy deserves a place among those few autobiographies of the twentieth century that demand to be preserved."

Oakes told *CA:* "I write mostly about the world in which I've worked—the world of media. I'm interested in how people communicate and the difficulties they have in doing so. I've been described as mordant and pessimistic. Not so; I believe I am painfully realistic."

AVOCATIONAL INTERESTS: Cats, fishing.

BIOGRAPHICAL/CRITICAL SOURCES:

BOOKS

Oakes, Philip, *From Middle England: A Memory of the 1930s,* Deutsch, 1980, St. Martin's, 1983.

Oakes, Philip, *Dwellers All in Time and Space: A Memory of the 1940s,* Deutsch, 1981, St. Martin's, 1984.

Oakes, Philip, *At the Jazz Band Ball: A Memory of the 1950s,* Deutsch, 1983.

PERIODICALS

Listener, June 19, 1980, April 8, 1982, December 8, 1983.

London Review of Books, April 1, 1982, February 2, 1984.

New Statesman, June 13, 1980, January 13, 1984.

New York Times Book Review, July 22, 1984.

Observer, November 20, 1983.

Times (London), May 29, 1980, April 15, 1982.

Times Literary Supplement, June 27, 1980, May 7, 1982, May 27, 1983, December 30, 1983.

* * *

O'DAY, Cathy
See CRANE, Barbara (Joyce)

ODIER, Daniel 1945-
(Delacorta)

PERSONAL: Born May 17, 1945, in Geneva, Switzerland; son of J. P. (a businessman) and Doris (Kenny) Odier; married Nell Gotkovsky (a violinist). *Education:* Ecole Superieure de Journalisme, Paris, diploma, 1966; Ecole des Hautes Etudes Internationales, Paris, diploma, 1967; Ecole des Hautes Etudes Sociales, Paris, diploma, 1967. *Religion:* Buddhist.

ADDRESSES: Home—9 Grande Rue, 78610 Auffargis, France; and 4748 South Harvard #79, Tulsa, Okla. 74135.

CAREER: Journal de Geneve, London, England, art critic, 1967-68; free-lance writer for *Tribune De Geneve* and *Gazette De Lausanne,* Geneva, Switzerland, and for *Le Magazine Litteraire* and *La Quinzaine Litteraire,* Paris, France, 1968—; currently senior fellow and instructor in comparative literature at University of Tulsa, Tulsa, Okla. Lecturer on literary subjects.

WRITINGS:

Transparence (poems), Perret-Gentil, 1964.

Le soleil dans la poche (poems), Perret-Gentil, 1965.

Rouge, Editions 317, 1967.

(With William S. Burroughs) *Entretiens,* P. Belfond, 1969, translation by Odier published as *The Job,* Grove, 1970.

Sculptures tantriques du Nepal, Editions du Rocher, 1971.

Le Voyage de John O'Flaherty (novel), Seuil, 1972.

Les Mystique orientales, Denoel, 1972.

Nuit contre nuit (poems), Oswald, 1972.

La Voie sauvage (novel), Seuil, 1974.

Nepal, Seuil, 1975.

Nirvana-Tao: The Secret Meditation Techniques of the Taoist and Buddhist Masters, R. Laffont, 1976, Inner Traditions, 1986.

Ming (novel), R. Laffont, 1976.

Splendor Solis (novel), Stock, 1976.

L'annee du lievre (novel), R. Laffont, 1978.

Le milieu du monde (novel), R. Laffont, 1979.

Petit dejeuner sur un tapis rouge (novel), Fayard, 1982.

Gioconda (novel), Fayard, 1984.

(With Marc de Smedt) *Essais sur les mystiques orientales,* A. Michel, 1984.

Le Baiser cannibale, Mazarine, 1987.

UNDER PSEUDONYM DELACORTA

Nana: A Novel, translation by Victoria Reiter, Seghers, 1979, Summit Books, 1983.

Diva: A Novel, translation by Lowell Bair, Seghers, 1979, Summit Books, 1984.

Luna: A Novel, translation by Reiter, Seghers, 1979, Summit Books, 1984.

Rock, Fayard, 1981, translation by Reiter published as *Lola: A Novel,* Summit Books, 1984.

Vida: A Novel, translation by Reiter, Summit Books, 1985.

WORK IN PROGRESS: Alba; a novel about America.

SIDELIGHTS: Although he has written several novels under his own name, Swiss author Daniel Odier is best known for the new-wave thrillers he writes under the pseudonym Delacorta. The novels all involve a middle-aged Parisian con artist named Serge Gorodish and his 13-year-old companion, Alba. Together, they solve crimes involving gangsters, millionaire psychopaths, teenage rock stars, and other colorful characters. All of these novels have become popular with readers, and two of them have been made into movies. In a quote from Jon D. Markman's *Los Angeles Times* article, Odier advises other aspiring thriller authors to write "fast and without self-consciousness. . . . Most writers think too much when they slum, and it doesn't come out right."

MEDIA ADAPTATIONS: *La Voie sauvage* was produced as "Light Years Away" for New Yorker Films in 1983. *Diva* was made into a movie in France in 1982, and *Lola* was also made into a film.

BIOGRAPHICAL/CRITICAL SOURCES:

PERIODICALS

Globe and Mail (Toronto), January 18, 1986.
Los Angeles Times, June 29, 1983, December 4, 1983.
Los Angeles Times Book Review, July 28, 1985, November 3, 1985.
New York Times Book Review, April 21, 1985, October 13, 1985.
Times (London), January 16, 1986, July 31, 1986.
Washington Post Book World, October 20, 1985.*

* * *

OGILVIE, Mardel 1910-

PERSONAL: Born February 2, 1910, in Middletown, N.Y.; daughter of John Alex and Mary Helen (Milne) Ogilvie. *Education:* Cornell University, B.A., 1931, M.A., 1932; Columbia University, Ph.D., 1941.

ADDRESSES: *Home*—196-15A 65 Crescent, Flushing, N.Y. 11365. *Office*—Department of Speech and Theater, Herbert H. Lehman College of the City University of New York, Bedford Park Blvd. W., Bronx, N.Y. 10468.

CAREER: High school teacher in South Fallsburg, N.Y., 1933-35; Mexico Academy, Mexico, N.Y., teacher of English and speech, 1935-37; State Teacher's College (now State University of New York College at Fredonia), Fredonia, 1937-49, began as assistant professor, became professor of speech; Queen's College of the City University of New York, Flushing, professor of speech, 1949-67; Herbert H. Lehman College of the City University of New York, Bronx, N.Y., professor of speech, 1967-80, professor emeritus, 1980—.

MEMBER: Speech Association of America, National Education Association, American Association of University Professors, National Council of Teachers of English, Speech Association of Eastern States, New York State Speech Association (president, 1939-41), Pi Lambda Theta, Phi Kappa Delta.

WRITINGS:

Terminology and Definitions of Speech Defects, Teachers College, Columbia University, 1942, reprinted, AMS Press, 1972.
Speech in the Elementary School, McGraw, 1954.
(With Jon Eisenson) *Speech Correction in the Schools,* Macmillan, 1957, 5th edition published as *Communicative Disorders in Children,* 1983.
Teaching Speech in the High School: Principles and Practices, Appleton-Century-Crofts, 1961.
(With Norma S. Rees) *Communication Skills: Voice and Pronunciation,* McGraw, 1969.

Contributor to education journals. *Speech Teacher,* advisory editor, 1952-54, consulting editor, 1955-60.

* * *

OINAS, Felix J(ohannes) 1911-

PERSONAL: Born March 6, 1911, in Tartu, Estonia (now Estonian Soviet Socialist Republic); came to the United States in 1949, naturalized in 1955; son of Ernst (a businessman) and Marie (Saarik) Oinas; married Lisbet Kove (a librarian), July 10, 1937; children: Helina (Mrs. Charles Anthony Piano), Valdar. *Education:* Attended Budapest University, 1935-36; Tartu State University, M.A., 1938; additional study at University of Heidelberg, 1946-48; Indiana University, Ph.D., 1952. *Religion:* Evangelical Lutheran.

ADDRESSES: *Home*—2513 East Eighth St., Bloomington, Ind. 47401. *Office*—Department of Slavic Languages and Literatures, Ballantine Hall 502, Indiana University, Bloomington, Ind. 47405.

CAREER: Budapest University, Budapest, Hungary, lecturer in Finno-Ugric languages, 1938-40; Baltic University, Hamburg, Germany, lecturer in Estonian language, 1946-48; Indiana University at Bloomington, lecturer, 1951-52, instructor, 1952-55, assistant professor, 1955-61, associate professor, 1961-65, professor of Slavic and Finno-Ugric languages and fellow of the Folklore Institute, 1965-71, professor emeritus, 1971—.

MEMBER: American Association of Teachers of Slavic and East European Languages, Linguistic Society of America, American Folklore Society, Finno-Ugrian Society (fellow), Finnish Academy of Sciences, Finnish Literary Society (fellow), Baltisches Forschungsinstitut (fellow), Finnish Folklore Society (fellow).

AWARDS, HONORS: Fulbright grant, 1961-62; Guggenheim grants, 1961-62 and 1966-67; Ford International Studies grants, 1962 and 1967; Fulbright-Hays grant, 1964-65; American Philosophical Society grant, 1965; American Council of Learned Societies travel grant, 1973; National Endowment for the Humanities research grant, 1974; Arthur Puksow Foundation first prize award, 1980.

WRITINGS:

Petoefi, Estonian Literary Society, 1939.
The Karelians, Human Relations Area Files Press, 1955.
The Development of Postpositional Cases in Balto-Finnic Languages, Finno-Ugric Society, 1961.
Estonian General Reader, Indiana University Publications, 1963, 2nd edition, 1972.
Basic Course in Estonian, Indiana University Publications, 1966, 4th edition, 1975.
Studies in Finnic-Slavic Folklore Relations, Finnish Academy, 1969.
Kalevipoeg kuetkeis ja muid esseid, Mana, 1979.
Vargamae tode ja oigus, Valis-Eesti, 1984.
Studies in Finnic Folklore, Finnish Literature Society, 1985.
Essays in Russian Folklore and Mythology, Slavica Publishers, 1985.

EDITOR

(With Karl Inno) *Eesti,* Eesti Rahvusfond, 1949.
Language Teaching Today, Research Center, Indiana University, 1960.
The Study of Russian Folklore, Mouton, 1975.
(Co-editor) *Tractata Altaica: Denis Sinor sexagenario optime de rebus altaicis merito dedicata,* Otto Harrassowitz, 1976.
(Co-editor) *Folklore Today: Festschrift in Honor of Richard M. Dorson,* Research Center, Indiana University, 1976.
The Heroic Epic and Saga, Indiana University Press, 1978.
Folklore, Nationalism and Politics, Slavica Publishers, 1978.
European Folklore, Trickster Press, 1981.

OTHER

Contributor of about 150 articles to *Word, Journal of American Folklore, Slavic Review, General Linguistics, Studia Fennica,* and other publications. Review editor, *Slavic and East European Journal,* 1957-64.

WORK IN PROGRESS: Working on problems of mythology and ancient history.

SIDELIGHTS: Felix J. Oinas told *CA:* "My field of research is rather broad, and includes Slavic, Finno-Ugric, and Siberian folklore, mythology, literature, and languages. This variety of interests provides me with an abundance of fascinating research problems, frequently cross-cultural, which can then be viewed from a unifying vantage point. I am currently applying myself to intensive research in an effort to make up for the ten years lost during World War II."

* * *

OLSEN, Jack
See OLSEN, John Edward

* * *

OLSEN, John Edward 1925-
(Jack Olsen; Jonathan Rhoades, a pseudonym)

PERSONAL: Born June 7, 1925, in Indianapolis, Ind.; son of Rudolph O. (a salesman) and Florence (Drecksage) Olsen; married Su Peterson, 1966; children: John Robert, Susan Joyce, Jonathan Rhoades, Julia Crispin, Evan Pierce, Barrie Elizabeth, Emily Sara Peterson, Harper Alexander Peterson. *Education:* Attended University of Pennsylvania, 1945-46.

ADDRESSES: Office—7954 Northeast Baker Hill Rd., Bainbridge Island, Wash. 98110. *Agent*—Scott Meredith Literary Agency, 845 Third Ave., New York, N.Y. 10022.

CAREER: San Diego Union Tribune, San Diego, Calif., reporter, 1947-48; *San Diego Journal,* San Diego, reporter, 1949-50; *Washington Daily News,* Washington, D.C., reporter, 1950-51; WMAL-TV, Washington, D.C., television news editor and broadcaster, 1950-51; *New Orleans Item,* New Orleans, La., reporter, 1952-53; *Chicago Sun-Times,* Chicago, Ill., reporter, 1954-55; *Time* magazine, correspondent, 1956-58, chief of Midwest bureau, 1959; *Sports Illustrated,* New York, N.Y., senior editor, 1960-74; writer. *Military service:* U.S. Army, Office of Strategic Services, 1943-44.

MEMBER: Authors Guild, Authors League of America, Defenders of Wildlife.

AWARDS, HONORS: National Headliner Award, Press Club of Atlantic City; Page One Award, Chicago Newspaper Guild; Washington Governor's Award; Special Edgar Award, Mystery Writers of America; citations from Indiana University and Columbia University; recipient of five Pulitzer Prize nominations.

WRITINGS:

(Under pseudonym Jonathan Rhoades) *Over the Fence Is Out,* Holt, 1961.

UNDER NAME JACK OLSEN

The Mad World of Bridge, Holt, 1960.
The Climb up to Hell, Harper, 1962.
(With Charles Goren) *Bridge Is My Game,* Doubleday, 1965.
Black Is Best: The Riddle of Cassius Clay, Putnam, 1967.
Silence on Monte Sole, Putnam, 1968.
The Black Athlete: A Shameful Story, Time-Life, 1968.
Night of the Grizzlies, Putnam, 1969.
(With Fran Tarkenton) *Better Scramble than Lose,* Four Winds Press, 1969.
The Bridge at Chappaquiddick, Little, Brown, 1970.
Aphrodite: Desperate Mission, Putnam, 1970.
Slaughter the Animals, Poison the Earth, Simon & Schuster, 1971.
The Girls in the Office, Simon & Schuster, 1972.
The Girls on the Campus, Pocket Books, 1974.
Sweet Street, Ballantine, 1974.
The Man with the Candy: The Story of the Houston Mass Murders, Simon & Schuster, 1974.
Alphabet Jackson, Playboy Press, 1974.
Massy's Game, Playboy Press, 1975.
The Secret of Fire Five, Random House, 1977.
Night Watch, Times Books, 1979.
Missing Persons, Atheneum, 1981.
Have You Seen My Son?, Atheneum, 1982.
"Son," A Psychopath and His Victims, Atheneum, 1983.
Give a Boy a Gun: The True Story of Law and Disorder in the American West, Delacorte, 1985.
Cold Kill: The True Story of a Murderous Love, Atheneum, 1987.
"Doc": The Rape of the Town of Lovell, Atheneum, 1989.

Contributor to *Sports Illustrated, Life, Reader's Digest, Fortune, This Week, Time, Nouvelle Candide, Daily Sketch,* and other periodicals. Contributor to anthologies.

SIDELIGHTS: A long-time reporter and author of numerous nonfiction works and novels, Jack Olsen is probably best known for his contributions to the "fact crime" genre with such works as *The Man with the Candy: The Story of the Houston Mass Murders* and *Give a Boy a Gun: A True Story of Law and Disorder in the American West.* While many probes of real-life crimes tend to exploit the lurid aspects of violent actions, Olsen's books avoid focusing on the more prurient elements of criminal cases and instead provide detailed portraits of both the perpetrators and their victims. In *The Man with the Candy,* for example, which investigates the abuse and murders of almost thirty young boys, Olsen "has dissected the sociology of the neighborhood in some depth," notes Dorothy Rabinowitz in the *Saturday Review/World.* "More to the point, his brief sketches of the families from which the murder victims came do much to dispel the unreality that surrounds these boys and their fate."

Reviewers have also commented on Olsen's method of presenting a complete and thorough story while leaving his readers to make judgments for themselves. In *Give a Boy a Gun,* the account of Claude Dallas, a self-proclaimed "mountain man" who executed two Idaho game wardens and avoided capture for over a year, Olsen "does a very commendable job of refraining from indulging in social commentary and delivering the facts of the case," states Theodore J. Johnson in *Best Sellers.* The author creates such portraits with a variety of information; *Newsweek* writer Gene Lyons remarks that *Give a Boy a Gun* contains many "virtues," including "a crisp, unambiguous style, a gift for interviewing people in their own terms . . . and an ear for the apposite quote." And in *Cold Kill: The Story of a Murderous Love,* "Olsen has another winner," states a *Publishers Weekly* reviewer. This study of a woman who convinces her lover to murder her parents "is a somewhat unusual true-crime study," asserts the critic, not because of its topic but for "its searching psychological depiction of the killers."

The study of a young real estate agent who is exposed as a brutal serial rapist, *"Son," A Psychopath and His Victims* is Olsen's best known work. It is certainly one that intrigued its author, for Olsen spent seventeen months and fifty thousand dollars of his own researching the episodes. "This case had all the wonderful elements for a crime book," Olsen told *Publishers Weekly*'s Lisa See, "a detective story filled with mystery, human tragedy on the scale of *Hamlet,* revenge, avarice, hatred, terror and irony. Most people have a hobby like collecting stamps or wood-working. [Convicted rapist Fred] Coe's hobbies were looking, peeping, making obscene phone calls and attacking women. In two years, 42 rapes in Spokane had the same MO." The case was further complicated when after Coe's conviction, his mother attempted to hire a hit man to kill the presiding judge and prosecutor of the trial. "Such are the makings of this true story," describes Lowell Cauffiel in the *Detroit News.* "It is bizarre on its own merits, but in the practiced hands of veteran journalist Jack Olsen . . . it becomes a riveting look at the monster lurking beneath a criminal psychopath's polished exterior."

Time contributor J. D. Reed observes that while most true crime narratives are "almost pernicious as the criminals" in their focus on psychological rationalizations of the criminal's behavior, "Jack Olsen will have none of this. In *'Son'* he is out to study the evildoer and to finger those who made him go wrong." Other critics, such as *Times Literary Supplement* contributor Clancy Sigal, feel that Olsen focuses too much on the details of the crime and does not do enough to "make interesting links between the multiple rapist's respectable origins and his crimes." Cauffiel, however, believes that these "detailed vignettes shun psychobabble, allowing the reader to speculate for himself." In addition, "Olsen manages to keep the horror of the crimes and subsequent court case before us," states Carolyn Banks in the *Washington Post.* "He gives us you-are-there accounts by several of the victims, erasing any urge to laugh [at the Coe family's bizarre behavior]." Marty Lieberman concurs, writing in the *Los Angeles Times Book Review* that "Olsen succeeds on all levels," including his "compassionate treatment of rape victims." "The story of the Coe family is a good one on its own," concludes Banks; "because of Jack Olsen's selectivity and skill, it's even better."

Olsen told *CA:* "I have spent forty years trying to tell it like it is. It hasn't been easy."

BIOGRAPHICAL/CRITICAL SOURCES:

PERIODICALS

Best Sellers, November 15, 1974, March, 1986.
Detroit News, March 11, 1984.
Los Angeles Times Book Review, February 12, 1984.
Newsweek, December 9, 1985.
New York Times, July 21, 1972.
New York Times Book Review, July 2, 1972, September 27, 1981, February 5, 1984, January 12, 1986.
Publishers Weekly, November 19, 1983, October 2, 1987.
Saturday Review/World, November 2, 1974.
Time, July 31, 1972, March 19, 1984.
Times Literary Supplement, August 17, 1984.
Washington Post, February 13, 1984.

* * *

OPLER, Morris E(dward) 1907-

PERSONAL: Born May 16, 1907, in Buffalo, N.Y.; son of Arthur (a businessman) and Fanny (Haas) Opler; married Catherine Hawkins, September 15, 1930 (died, 1956); married Lucille Ritter, July 29, 1957. *Education:* University of Buffalo, B.A. (summa cum laude), 1929, M.A., 1930; University of Chicago, Ph.D., 1933.

ADDRESSES: Home—926 McCall Dr., Norman, Okla. 73069. *Office*—Department of Anthropology, 506 Dale Hall, University of Oklahoma, Norman, Okla. 73069.

CAREER: University of Chicago, Chicago, Ill., research assistant, 1933-34, research associate in anthropology, 1934-35; Bureau of Indian Affairs, Washington, D.C., assistant anthropologist, 1936-37; Reed College, Portland, Ore., visiting lecturer in sociology, 1937-38; Claremont Colleges, Claremont, Calif., assistant professor of anthropology, 1938-42; War Relocation Authority, Manzanar, Calif., social science analyst, 1943-44; Office of War Information (later part of U.S. Department of State), Washington, D.C., social science analyst, 1944-45, deputy chief of Foreign Morale Analysis Division, 1945, chief, 1946; Harvard University, Cambridge, Mass., assistant professor of education and anthropology, 1946-48; Cornell University, Ithaca, N.Y., professor of anthropology and Asian studies, 1948-69, professor emeritus, 1969—; University of Oklahoma, Norman, professor of anthropology, 1969—. Fellow of Laboratory of Anthropology of Santa Fe, summer, 1931; fellow of center for Advanced Study in the Behavioral Sciences, 1956-57. Lecturer at University of Wisconsin, summer, 1941; visiting professor at Howard University, fall, 1945, and Lucknow University, 1953-54. Member of board of trustees of American Institute of Indian Studies, 1963-66.

MEMBER: International Union of Anthropological and Ethnological Sciences (member of national advisory committee), American Anthropological Association (fellow; member of executive board, 1949-52; president-elect, 1961-62; president, 1962-63), Society for Applied Anthropology (fellow), Association for Asian Studies, American Ethnological Society, American Folklore Society (fellow; first vice president, 1946-47; member of executive committee, 1950; member of council, 1957-60), Sigma Xi, Phi Beta Kappa, Alpha Kappa Delta, Phi Delta Kappa.

AWARDS, HONORS: Social Science Research Council fellowships, 1932-33, 1946-47; Guggenheim fellowship, 1942-43; National Endowment for the Humanities senior fellowship, 1968-69.

WRITINGS:

(With Edward F. Castetter) *The Ethnobiology of the Chiracahua and Mescalero Apache,* University of New Mexico Press, 1936.

(Contributor) Fred Eggan, editor, *Social Anthropology of North American Tribes,* University of Chicago Press, 1937, 2nd edition, 1955.

Dirty Boy: A Jicarilla Tale of Raid and War, American Anthropological Association, 1938.

(With Harry Hoijer) *Chiracahua and Mescalero Apache Texts,* University of Chicago Press, 1938, reprinted, AMS Press, 1977.

Myths and Tales of the Jicarilla Apache Indians, G. E. Stechert, 1938, Kraus Reprints, 1977.

Myths and Tales of the Lipan Apache Indians, J. J. Augustin, 1940, Kraus Reprints, 1977.

An Apache Life-Way: The Economic, Social and Religious Institutions of the Chiracahua Indians, University of Chicago Press, 1941, reprinted, Cooper Square, 1965.

Myths and Tales of the Chiracahua Apache Indians, G. Banta, 1942, Kraus Reprints, 1977.

The Character and Derivation of the Jicarilla Holiness Rite, University of New Mexico Press, 1943, Kraus Reprints, 1977.
Childhood and Youth in Jicarilla Apache Society, Southwest Museum, 1946, reprinted, AMS Press, 1980.
(Editor and contributor) *Cultural Patterns,* Delphian Society, 1950.
India (pamphlet), Fund for Adult Education, 1952.
Social Aspects of Technical Assistance in Operation, Drukkerji, 1954.
(With Henry F. Dobyns and others) *Recommendations for Future Research on the Process of Cultural Change,* Comparative Studies of Cultural Change, Department of Anthropology, Cornell University, 1966.
(With Dobyns and others) *Some Principals of Cultural Change,* Comparative Studies of Cultural Change, Department of Anthropology, Cornell University, 1967.
Chris; Apache Odyssey: A Journey between Two Worlds, Holt, 1969, reprinted, Irving Publishers, 1983.
(Editor with Keith H. Basso, and contributor) *Apachean Culture History and Ethnology,* University of Arizona Press, 1971.
(Contributor) Mario D. Zamora and Zeus A. Salazar, editors, *Anthropology, Range and Relevance: A Reader for Non-Anthropologists,* Kayumangii, 1972.
(Contributor) J. Michael Majar, editor, *The Untouchables in Contemporary India,* University of Arizona Press, 1972.
(Editor) *Grenville Goodwin among the Western Apache: Letters from the Field,* University of Arizona Press, 1973.
Lipan and Mescalero Apache in Texas, Clearwater Publishers, 1973 (bound with Verne F. Ray, *Ethnohistorical Analysis of Documents Relating to the Apache Indians of Texas,* Garland, 1974).

Contributor to more than a dozen books on social science, anthropology, and cultural change. Contributor to proceedings and to social science journals, including *American Anthropologist, Southwestern Journal of Anthropology, Ethnology, Human Organization, Current Anthropology,* and *American Journal of Sociology.* Member of editorial advisory board of *Journal of Asian Studies,* 1955-58; associate editor of *Journal of American Folklore,* 1959-64, and *Journal of Asian and African Studies,* 1964—.

WORK IN PROGRESS: Research on the cultures of various Apache tribes.

BIOGRAPHICAL/CRITICAL SOURCES:

BOOKS

Zamora, Mario D. and others, editors, *Themes in Culture: Essays in Honor of Morris E. Opler,* Kayumangii, 1971.*

* * *

ORGILL, Douglas 1922-1984
(J. D. Gilman, a joint pseudonym)

PERSONAL: Born August 10, 1922, in Walsall, England; died February, 1984; son of William Henry (an industrialist) and Madeline (Platt) Orgill; married Margaret Chance Walker (a journalist); children: Richard, Andrew. *Education:* Attended Royal Military College, Sandhurst, 1943; Keble College, Oxford, M.A., 1948.

ADDRESSES: Office—Daily Express, 121 Fleet St., London EC4P 4JT, England. *Agent*—Ursula Winnant, Winnant Towers, 14 Cliffords Inn, London EC4, England.

CAREER: Journalist, military historian, and novelist. *Newcastle Journal,* Newcastle-upon-Tyne, England, reporter, 1949-50, subeditor, 1950-52, leader writer, 1952-53; *Daily Mail,* London, England, subeditor, 1953-59, deputy chief subeditor, 1957-59; *Daily Express,* London, chief subeditor, 1966-73, special writer, beginning 1973. *Military service:* British Army, 1944-46; served in Italy and Austria and with Arab Legion.

MEMBER: Royal United Services Institute for Defence Studies, Royal Geographic Society (fellow), Savage Club.

WRITINGS:

NOVELS

The Death Bringers, P. Davies, 1962, published as *Journey into Violence,* Morrow, 1963.
Ride a Tiger, P. Davies, 1963, published as *The Cautious Assassin,* Morrow, 1964.
The Days of Darkness, P. Davies, 1965.
Man in the Dark, Morrow, 1965, reprinted, State Mutual Book, 1987.
The Astrid Factor, Walker & Co., 1968.
The Jasius Pursuit, St. Martin's, 1973.
(Under joint pseudonym J. D. Gilman with Jack Fishman, and with John Clive) *KG 200: A Novel,* Simon & Schuster, 1977 (published in England as *KG 200: The Force with No Face,* Souvenir Press, 1977).
(With John Gribbin) *The Sixth Winter,* Simon & Schuster, 1979.
(With Gribbin) *Brother Esau,* Harper, 1982.

NONFICTION

The Gothic Line: The Autumn Campaign in Italy, 1944, Norton, 1967.
The Tank: Studies in the Development and Use of a Weapon, Heinemann, 1970.
T-34: Russian Armor, Ballantine, 1971.
Armoured Onslaught: August, 1918, Ballantine, 1972.
Lawrence (biography of T. E. Lawrence), Ballantine, 1973.
German Armour, Ballantine, 1974.

OTHER

Contributor to *Purnell's History of the Second World War.* Contributor to British newspapers and to professional journals.

SIDELIGHTS: Douglas Orgill once commented to *CA:* "I work in two fields: as a novelist and as a historian. I believe that *as a novelist* my task is, in essence, to tell a story: to place a number of characters into situations which they cannot wholly control, and then to observe the degree of success or failure with which they struggle to overcome them. For me, two things matter: the characters must engage the reader's sympathy, and the situations, while sometimes bizarre, must never become unbelievable.

"I believe that *as a historian* my first and absolute duty is accuracy: any interpretation of historical events based on inaccuracy is a house built on sand. My next duty is an attempt, sometimes intuitively, to try to understand why men did what they did, to what extent they had any choice at all, and what material and other factors influenced them in their decisions."

AVOCATIONAL INTERESTS: Entomology, military history, travel.

BIOGRAPHICAL/CRITICAL SOURCES:

PERIODICALS

Los Angeles Times Book Review, March 6, 1983.
New York Times Book Review, October 23, 1977, January 27, 1980.*

OSBORNE, Mary Pope 1949-

PERSONAL: Born May 20, 1949, in Fort Sill, Okla.; daughter of William P. (a U.S. Army colonel) and Barnette (Dickens) Pope; married Will Osborne (an actor and writer), May 16, 1976. *Education:* University of North Carolina at Chapel Hill, B.A., 1971.

ADDRESSES: Home and office—325 Bleecker St., New York, N.Y. 10014.

CAREER: Writer; has worked as a medical assistant in Monterey, Calif., and as a travel agent in Washington, D.C., and New York City; *Scholastic News Trials,* New York City, assistant editor, 1973-79.

WRITINGS:

JUVENILES

Run, Run as Fast as You Can (novel), Dial, 1982.
Love Always, Blue (novel), Dial, 1984.
Best Wishes, Joe Brady (novel), Dial Books for Young Readers, 1984.
Last One Home (novel), Dial Books for Young Readers, 1986.
Mo to the Rescue (easy to read), Dial Books for Young Readers, 1986.
Beauty and the Beast, Scholastic, Inc., 1987.
Christopher Columbus, Admiral of the Ocean Sea, Yearling Books, 1987.
Pandora's Box, Scholastic, Inc., 1987.
(With husband, Will Osborne) *Jason and the Argonauts,* Scholastic, Inc., 1987.
(With W. Osborne) *The Deadly Power of Medusa,* Scholastic, Inc., 1988.
Mo and His Friends (easy to read), Dial Books for Young Readers, 1989.
Favorite Greek Myths (Book-of-the-Month Club selection), Scholastic, Inc., 1989.
A Visit to Sleep's House (picture book), Knopf, 1989.
Moon-Horse (picture book), Knopf, 1990.
The Biography of George Washington, Dial Books for Young Readers, 1990.
The Biography of Benjamin Franklin, Dial Books for Young Readers, 1990.
(Adaptor) *American Tall Tales* (collection), Knopf, 1990.

SIDELIGHTS: Mary Pope Osborne's novels for young adults focus on the problems, conflicts, and difficult situations encountered by many adolescents. *Run, Run as Fast as You Can,* for example, relates the story of Hallie, who wants to join a group of popular girls at school; facing the clique's rejection as well as her younger brother's fatal illness, however, forces Hallie to reexamine her values. It is Osborne's treatment of this self-analysis that transforms the novel into what London *Times* contributor Jennie Ingham calls "a compulsively gripping story." Osborne presents similarly well-developed characters in her most recent novel, *Last One Home,* the story of Bailey, a young girl torn between her alcoholic mother and her father, who has just remarried; a *Publishers Weekly* writer notes that "all the characters, including the heedless mother whose abuses Bailey forgets in her wistful dreams, are skillfully humanized," while Phyllis Graves comments in *School Library Journal* that the author's "finely crafted characterization enhances this affecting story about the difficulties of coping."

Osborne told *CA:* "My childhood was spent on different Army posts with my parents, two brothers, and sister. We lived mostly in the southern United States with a three-year stay in Salzburg, Austria. When I was fifteen my father retired and my family settled permanently in North Carolina." After a series of jobs and travels, the author married actor Will Osborne, and "the day after our wedding we took off on a theatre tour. While on the road with Will, I began writing," Osborne relates. "In 1979, I wrote a young adult novel, *Run, Run as Fast as You Can,* about a girl whose family retires from the military and settles in the South. Dial Press bought the manuscript and my editor, Amy Ehrlich, helped me develop it. Amy has also been a big influence on my other [novels], *Love Always, Blue,* about a southern teenager who travels to Greenwich Village to visit her playwright father, and *Best Wishes, Joe Brady,* about a North Carolina girl who falls in love with an actor performing in a local dinner theatre—and *Last One Home,* a novel inspired by a scene I witnessed on the Florida Coast: a young girl leading a dishevelled mother down a fishing pier. The girl became Bailey, and the book revolved around her coming to terms with the loneliness of having an alcoholic mother.

"For the last few years my work has taken several new directions, as I've been concentrating on mythology and fairy tale retellings, picture books and biographies," the author continued, noting that "I've been very lucky in that I've been able to channel so many different interests into books for children and young people. I imagine I'll probably focus next on the natural world. After having lived exclusively in New York City for the last fourteen years, my husband and I now spend part of each week in a cabin in Pennsylvania, and as a result of this, I feel a new passion developing for animals and nature. The wonderful thing about a career as a children's book writer is that there are so many different forms in which to fill different sorts of content. Choosing the vehicle that will carry a new story or passion out into the world is half the fun."

BIOGRAPHICAL/CRITICAL SOURCES:

PERIODICALS

Baltimore Sun, May 16, 1982.
Publishers Weekly, March 21, 1986.
School Library Journal, May, 1986.
Times (London), August 23, 1983.
Times Literary Supplement, September 30, 1983.

* * *

OUGHTON, Frederick 1923-

PERSONAL: Born February 22, 1923, in Coventry, England; son of Ernest Frederick and Amy Cheetham (Willocks) Oughton; married to Eve Mary Aggiss. *Education:* Attended private schools.

ADDRESSES: 2 Holly Rd., Retford, Nottinghamshire DN22 6BE, England.

CAREER: Author and publisher. British Picture Corp. Ltd., Elstree, England, scriptwriter, 1950-55; held positions with various newspapers, including feature writer and editor for *Northern News,* Ndola, Northern Rhodesia; managing director of Frederick Oughton Publishers Ltd., 1965-68; Her Majesty's Stationery Office, London, England, marketing director, 1968-75; Mansard Press Ltd., London, director, 1984—. Broadcaster for British Broadcasting Corp.; also has worked as radio producer. Tutor, TV Writers' School, London; executive director, Capital School of Specialist Writing, London. *Military service:* Royal Air Force, 1939-45; Merchant Navy.

MEMBER: Fellow, Royal Arts Society; Freeman, City of London, for *Grinling Gibbons and the English Woodcarving Tradition.*

WRITINGS:

Brother Lunatic, Spearman, 1957.
Pitfall, Spearman, 1958.
Breakout, Spearman, 1959.
The Siege of Sidney Street (based on the screenplay by Jimmy Sangster), Pan Books, 1960.
The Aces, Putnam, 1960.
Ten Guineas a Day: A Portrait of a Private Detective, John Long, 1961.
The Two Lives of Robert Ledru: An Interpretative Biography of a Man Possessed, Muller, 1963.
(With Vernon Smyth) *Ace with One Eye: The Life and Combats of Major Edward Mannock, V.C., DSO (2 Bars), MC (1 Bar), Royal Flying Corps and Royal Air Force,* Muller, 1963.
The Big Steal: The Realities of Robbery, Spearman, 1963.
Combat World War I (anthology), Delacorte, 1964.
Tape Recording and Hi-Fi, Collins, 1964.
(Author of introduction and notes) *The Personal Diary of Major Edward "Mick" Mannock,* Spearman, 1966.
The History and Practice of Woodcarving, Allman, 1969, Woodcraft Supply Corp. (Woburn, Mass.), 1976.
Value Analysis and Value Engineering, Pitman, 1969.
The Finishing and Re-finishing of Wood, Constable, 1969.
Research and Development in Industry, Times Management Library, 1971.
Fraud and White Collar Crime, Elek, 1971.
Murder Investigation, Elek, 1971.
Total Industrial Automation, Longman, 1971.
Lapidary Practice: A Manual, Batsford, 1971.
Woodworking Tools, Constable, 1973.
Wood Technology, Macdonald Educational, 1975.
(Revisor) Thomas Osbert Howard, *Joinery,* 2nd edition, Teach Yourself Books, 1975.
Creative Crafts, Teach Yourself Books, 1976.
Grinling Gibbons and the English Woodcarving Tradition, Stobart, 1979.
The Complete Manual of Wood Finishing, Stobart, 1982, Stein & Day, 1983.

Murder Investigation has been translated into Spanish. Former editor, *Voice of Welsh Industry, Welsh Nation, World Naturalist* and *Community Broadsheet.*

AVOCATIONAL INTERESTS: Science, natural history, medieval history, modern American prose, acoustics, sound engineering, book collecting, microscopy, criminology, psychiatry, psychotherapy, wood-carving, industrial technology.

BIOGRAPHICAL/CRITICAL SOURCES:

PERIODICALS

New York Times Book Review, December 4, 1960.
Times Literary Supplement, November 5, 1971, March 21, 1980.

* * *

OWEN, Clifford
See HAMILTON, Charles (Harold St. John)

* * *

OWEN, Tobias Chant 1936-

PERSONAL: Born March 20, 1936, in Oshkosh, Wis.; son of George C. (a physician) and Mona (Volkert) Owen; married Linda Lewis (a psychotherapist), September 2, 1960; children: Jonathan Dylan, David Trevor. *Education:* University of Chicago, B.A., 1955, B.S., 1959, M.S., 1960; attended University of Frankfurt, 1956-57; University of Arizona, Ph.D., 1965.

ADDRESSES: Home—6 Ivy Lane, Setauket, N.Y. 11733. *Office*—Department of Earth and Space Sciences, State University of New York at Stony Brook, Stony Brook, N.Y. 11794.

CAREER: Illinois Institute of Technology Astro Sciences Center, Chicago, Ill., associate physicist, 1964-65, scientific adviser, 1969-70; California Institute of Technology, Pasadena, visiting associate professor of planetary science, 1970; State University of New York at Stony Brook, associate professor, 1970-72, professor of astronomy, 1972—. Vernadasky Lecturer at U.S.S.R. Academy of Sciences, 1982.

National Aeronautics and Space Administration (NASA), principal investigator on Apollo 15 and 16 Lunar Orbit Experiments Team, 1969-72, member of astronomy working group for International Ultraviolet Explorer, 1973-76, member of molecular analysis team for Viking 1975 Mars Landing, member of imaging science team for Voyager 1977 flybys of Jupiter, Saturn, Uranus, and Neptune, 1972—, interdisciplinary scientist and member of probe mass spectrometer team for Galileo 1995 Jupiter Orbiter Probe, 1978—. Member of NASA working groups on imaging and IR spectroscopy for outer planets grand tour, 1971-72, comets and asteroids, 1972-74, outer planet probes, 1974-75, strategy for outer planet exploration, 1974-75, Comet Halley science working group, 1977-81, and exobiology workshops, 1977-81, chairman of working group on comet missions, 1975; chairman of science workshop on the origin of life, 1979-81; member of solar system exploration committee, 1981-82; chairman of U.S. delegation, joint science study team for ESA-NASA Cassini project, 1984—. National Academy of Sciences, member of exchange team in U.S.S.R., 1967, chairman of working group on planetary astronomy, 1970-71, member of space astronomy panel, 1970-71, and planetary panel, 1979-81.

MEMBER: International Association of Geochemistry and Cosmochemistry, International Astronomical Union (president of Commission for the Physical Study of Planets and Satellites, 1976-79), International Society for the Study of the Origin of Life, American Association for the Advancement of Science (fellow; chairman of astronomy section, 1980), American Astronomical Society, American Geophysical Union, Royal Astronomical Society, Astronomical Society of the Pacific, Associated Universities for Research in Astronomy (member of board of directors, 1973-76).

AWARDS, HONORS: NASA group achievement award, 1971, for lunar orbit experiments team, and 1981, for Voyager imaging science investigation; NASA medal for exceptional scientific achievement, 1977; medal from Aero Club of Cairo, 1977; Newcomb Cleveland Prize, American Association for the Advancement of Science, 1977, for articles on NASA's Viking Mission; alumni professional achievement award, University of Chicago, 1983.

WRITINGS:

(Editor with Carl Sagan and H. J. Smith, and contributor) *Planetary Atmospheres,* D. Reidel, 1971.
(With Donald Goldsmith) *The Search for Life in the Universe,* Benjamin-Cummings, 1980.
(With David Morrison) *The Planetary System,* Addison-Wesley, 1988.

CONTRIBUTOR

L. H. Ahrens, editor, *Proceedings of the Symposium on the Origin and Distribution of the Elements,* Pergamon, 1968.

J. S. Hall, editor, *Planetary Astronomy: An Appraisal of Ground Based Opportunities,* National Academy of Sciences, 1968.

S. I. Rasool, editor, *Physics of the Solar System,* National Aeronautics and Space Administration, 1972.

G. P. Kuiper and Elizabeth Roemer, editors, *Comets: Scientific Data and Missions,* University of Arizona Press, 1972.

Daniel Gautier, editor, *Physics of Planets,* Observatoire de Meudon, 1973.

E. Whalley, S. J. Jones, and L. W. Gold, editors, *Physics and Chemistry of Ice,* Royal Society of Canada, 1973.

Andrzej Woszczyk and Cecylia Iwaniszewska, editors, *Exploration of the Planetary System,* D. Reidel, 1974.

D. M. Hunten, editor, *Proceedings of Uranus Atmosphere Workshop,* Ames Research Center, National Aeronautics and Space Administration, 1975.

A. P. Vinogradov, editor, *Kosmochimiya Luni i Planet* (title means "On Cosmochemistry of the Moon and Planets"), Nauka, 1975.

A. Vallance Jones, editor, *Proceedings of a Symposium on Planetary Atmospheres,* Royal Society of Canada, 1978.

E. C. Alexander, Jr., and M. Ozima, editors, *Terrestrial Rare Gases,* Center for Academic Publications (Japan), 1978.

Tom Gehrels, editor, *The Moon and the Planets,* D. Reidel, 1978.

Joan Oro, J. C. Verges, and J. A. Plana Castellvi, editors, *Els Planetes Comparats* (title means "Comparisons of the Planets"), Sirocco, 1980.

G. Hunt, editor, *Uranus and the Outer Planets,* Cambridge University Press, 1982.

Andre Brahic, editor, *Formation of Planetary Systems,* Centre National d'Etudes Spatiales, 1982.

(With D. Gautier) D. Black and M. Matthews, editors, *Protostars and Planets II,* University of Arizona Press, 1985.

(With D. Morrison and L. Soderblom) J. A. Burns and M. S. Matthews, editors, *Satellites,* University of Arizona Press, 1986.

J. Kerridge and M. S. Matthews, editors, *Meteorites,* University of Arizona Press, 1987.

Contributor to *Encyclopaedia Britannica* and *Encyclopaedia of Science and Technology.*

OTHER

Contributor of more than two hundred articles and reviews to scientific journals and popular magazines, including *Newsday, Future Life,* and *Scientific American.* Associate editor of *Fundamentals of Cosmic Physics,* 1970-76, and *Icarus,* 1970—; member of editorial committee of *Annual Reviews of Astronomy and Astrophysics,* 1976-80.

WORK IN PROGRESS: Research on planetary and satellite atmospheres with ground-based and orbiting telescopes, the Voyager spacecraft, and the Galileo Project; research on physics and chemistry of the solar system, spectroscopy of planets, satellites, and comets, laboratory gas-phase spectoscopy, and investigations of planetary environments from spacecraft.

SIDELIGHTS: Tobias Chant Owen once told *CA:* "My interest in the solar system received a strong stimulus during a summer spent as a research associate at the Yerkes Observatory in 1956. Mars was at a favorable opposition, and it was possible from time to time to use the observatory's large refractor to study it. Trying to see detail on that distant world while speculating about what conditions could be like there was a fascinating experience. Twenty years later with the successful Viking landings, I suddenly knew what Mars was really like. In the intervening years, I had the privilege of doing my doctoral research with the late Gerard Kuiper, who in those days was the only astronomer who was totally devoted to studying planets and satellites. One of the projects we worked on together was a determination of the composition and surface pressure of the Martian atmosphere.

"I also began studying the outer planets during that time, including a determination of the temperature on Jupiter as part of my doctoral dissertation. The outer solar system is now the main focus of my work, both with the Voyager spacecraft and with a variety of telescopes: ground-based and in Earth orbit. A recent highlight of this work has been the growing awareness that Titan, Saturn's largest satellite, represents a world effectively frozen in time at a very early stage of its development. This means that chemical evolution is occurring on Titan now that has strong parallels to processes postulated for the primitive Earth. On our planet, these processes ultimately led to the origin of life. Titan is too cold for life to originate, but it offers us a giant natural laboratory where we can test our ideas about pathways to life's origin.

"It is these larger problems that make the study of the solar system so interesting. Are we alone in the universe or are there other intelligent civilizations inhabiting planets around other stars? We can't answer this question yet, but the information we have gained about our own family of planets indicates that solar systems should be relatively common, that planets like the Earth are not desperately rare, and that the first steps toward the chemical complexity necessary for life are easy. These considerations suggest that other civilizations indeed exist, but there is much more to be done before this suggestion can be changed to certainty. In our own solar system, we need to go back to Mars to hunt for fossils of primitive organisms and we need to study the products of chemical syntheses on Titan and in the comets. We are also just acquiring the capabilities needed to search for planets around other stars.

"All of these intermediate steps can be bypassed by the direct detection of signals from another advanced civilization elsewhere in the galaxy. Here too, great progress is being made in improving the sensitivity and frequency range of radio receivers. An undergraduate doing a summer research job today might well expect to know the answer to this question within the next twenty-five years, if only our own civilization can restrain its self-destructive tendencies."

P

PALLONE, Nathaniel John 1935-

PERSONAL: Born October 30, 1935, in Chicago, Ill.; son of Louis Thomas (an engineer) and Adeline T. (Tenkach) Pallone; married Nicolina Tiranno, June 30, 1956 (divorced, 1980); married Jacqueline B. Lewis, July 1, 1981 (died, 1982); married Letitia M. Clarke, 1983; children: (first marriage) Andrea Marie, Angela Therese. *Education:* Catholic University of America, A.B., 1957, A.M., 1960; Columbia University, graduate study, 1960-61; New York University, Ph.D., 1963. *Politics:* Social Democrat. *Religion:* Apostate Catholic.

ADDRESSES: *Home*—1234 Woodland Ave., Plainfield, N.J. 07060. *Office*—Rutgers University, Lucy Stone Hall, New Brunswick, N.J. 09803.

CAREER: Bullis School, Silver Spring, Md., teacher and counselor, 1957-60; St. Francis College, Brooklyn, N.Y., psychologist, 1960-63; University of Notre Dame, Notre Dame, Ind., assistant professor, 1963-66; New York University, New York, N.Y., associate professor, 1966-68, professor of counseling psychology and chairman of department, 1968-72; University of Hartford, West Hartford, Conn., professor and associate dean, 1972-73; Rutgers University, New Brunswick, N.J., professor and dean of University College, 1973-78, academic vice-president, 1978-87, University Distinguished Professor of Clinical Psychology and Criminal Justice, 1981—. Private practice in counseling and psychotherapy, 1963—.

Hill Foundation distinguished visiting professor in the behavioral sciences, University of Minnesota, 1979; visiting professor, School of Public Health, Harvard University, 1987-88; lecturer at numerous universities throughout the world. Licensed psychologist, New Jersey, 1968; registered psychotherapist, New Jersey Rehabilitation Commission, 1970; diplomate, American Board of Professional Psychology, 1980. Chairman, Classification Review Board for Sex Offenders, New Jersey Department of Corrections, 1976-82. Consultant in group psychotherapy, New York State Narcotics Control Commission, 1967-72; research consultant, Connecticut Department of Corrections, 1971-74. *Military service:* U.S. Army Reserve, 1952-54; U.S. Air Force ROTC, 1953-56; U.S. Air Force Reserve, 1954-60.

MEMBER: American Psychological Association (fellow), American College of Forensic Psychology (fellow), Phi Beta Kappa.

WRITINGS:

(With James M. Lee) *Guidance and Counseling in Schools: Foundations and Processes,* McGraw, 1966.

(Editor with Lee) *Readings in Guidance and Counseling,* Sheed, 1966.

(Editor) *Readings for Catholic Counselors,* National Catholic Guidance Conference, 1966.

(With George H. Moreau) *Guidelines for Guidance,* National Catholic Education Association, 1968.

(With Donald Wehmyer, Peter Grande, and Richard Tirman) *Instructional Group Size and Learning Outcomes,* Ford Foundation, 1969.

(With William H. Liu) *Catholic/USA: Perspectives on Social Change,* Wiley, 1970.

(With Robert B. Hurley and Fred S. Rickard) *Race, Sex, and Social Mobility: An Exploration of Occupational Aspirations and Expectations among Black and White Youth in Four New York State Cities,* New York University Center for Field Research, 1970.

(Editor) *Learning for Living,* Association for Continuing Higher Education, 1976.

On the Social Utility of Psychopathology: A Deviant Majority and Its Keepers?, Transaction Books, 1988.

Also author of chapters in books and of eight research monographs. Consulting editor for a series in psychology and social policy, Transaction Books, 1987—. Contributor of more than 125 articles to professional journals. Editor, *National Catholic Guidance Conference Journal,* 1963-68, and *New York State Personnel and Guidance Journal,* 1969-72; member of editorial board, *Offender Rehabilitation,* 1978—, *Criminal Justice and Behavior,* 1981—, and *Current Psychological Research,* 1985—.

WORK IN PROGRESS: Toward a Process Psychology of Criminal Behavior; New Perspectives on the Outpatient Treatment of the Criminal Offender; The Over-Education of Ordinary Minds: Higher Education and American Social Policy, 1935-85.

SIDELIGHTS: Nathaniel John Pallone told *CA* that his principle interests are in "psychotherapy and psychopathology, with a particular focus on the dynamics and treatment of criminal offenders, with a strong interest in effects of sociocultural forces on the definition and treatment of psychological and criminal deviance." He adds that he "has become a visible practitioner of the application of psychological research to the definition of social policy—though at the expense of court decisions," citing two instances in which his research was used in consumer advocacy cases and in testing the legality of state treatment laws.

* * *

PAVLOWITCH, Stevan K. 1933-

PERSONAL: Born September 7, 1933, in Belgrade, Yugoslavia; son of Kosta (a diplomat) and Mara (Dyoukitch) Pavlowitch; married France Raffray; children: Kosta (a son). *Education:* University of Paris and University of Lille, licence es lettres, 1956; King's College, London, B.A., 1956, M.A., 1959.

ADDRESSES: Office—Department of History, University of Southampton, Highfield, Southampton S09 5NH, England.

CAREER: Employed in field of public relations as a journalist in Brussels, Stockholm, Milan, and London, 1958-65; University of Southampton, Highfield, Southampton, England, 1965—, began as lecturer, currently reader in Balkan history, department of history and Centre for International Policy Studies.

WRITINGS:

Anglo-Russian Rivalry in Serbia, 1837-1839: The Mission of Colonel Hodges, Mouton, 1961.
Yugoslavia, Praeger, 1971.
Bijou d'Art: Histoires de la vie, de l'ouvre et du milieu de Bojidar Karageorgevitch, artiste parisien et prince balkanique, L'Age d'Homme, 1978.
(Contributor) R. Clogg, editor, *Balkan Society in the Age of Greek Independence,* Macmillan, 1981.
The Albanian Problem in Yugoslavia: Two Views, Institute for Study of Conflict, 1982.
Unconventional Perceptions of Yugoslavia, 1940-45, Columbia University Press, 1985.
(Contributor) L. Kaplan and others, editors, *NATO and the Mediterranean,* Scholarly Resources, 1985.
The Improbable Survivor: Yugoslavia and Its Problems, 1918-88, Hurst and Ohio State University Press, 1988.
(Contributor) P. Ramet, editor, *Eastern Christianity and Politics in the Twentieth Century,* Duke University Press, 1988.

Contributor to numerous periodicals, including *Journal of Contemporary History, War and Society, European History Review, European Journal of International Affairs, L'Autre Europe, Commentaire,* and *Vingtieme Siecle.*

WORK IN PROGRESS: A biography of J. B. Tito.

SIDELIGHTS: Stevan K. Pavlowitch told *CA:* "I try to understand and thereby to explain, the history of Yugoslavia. In doing so, I enjoy studying the reverse of medals and the people who have not won wars and come out on top."

* * *

PEALE, Norman Vincent 1898-

PERSONAL: Born May 31, 1898, in Bowersville, Ohio; son of Charles Clifford (a physician and minister) and Anna (DeLaney) Peale; married Loretta Ruth Stafford, June 20, 1930; children: Margaret Ann (Mrs. Paul F. Everett), John Stafford (an ordained minister and philosophy professor), Elizabeth Ruth (Mrs. John M. Allen). *Education:* Ohio Wesleyan University, B.A., 1920; Boston University, M.A., 1924, S.T.B., 1924. *Politics:* Republican.

ADDRESSES: Home—1030 Fifth Ave., New York, N.Y. 10028; and "Quaker Hill," Pawling, N.Y. 12564. *Office*—1025 Fifth Ave., New York, N.Y. 10028.

CAREER: Ordained into Methodist Episcopal Church, 1922; *Morning Republican,* Findlay, Ohio, 1920, reporter; *Detroit Journal,* Detroit, Mich., 1920, reporter; pastor in Berkeley, R.I., 1922-24, Brooklyn, N.Y., 1924-27, Syracuse, N.Y., 1927-32; Marble Collegiate Reform Church, New York, N.Y., pastor, 1932-84; writer, 1937—. Chaplain, American Legion, Kings County, N.Y., 1925-27. Co-founder and member, Institutes of Religion and Health; co-founder, Foundation for Christian Living, 1940. Host of a weekly radio program on NBC, "The Art of Living," 1935—, a program on station WOR, 1954-84, "American Character," 1975—, "Positive Thinking Network, with Norman Vincent Peale," 1981—, and "The Angelus Hour," and television programs, "What's Your Trouble," and "Guideposts Presents Norman Vincent Peale." Lecturer on public affairs and personal effectiveness. President of Protestant Council of New York, 1965-69, and the Reformed Church of America, 1969-70. Acting chairman, committee for Constitutional Government; member of executive committee of Presbyterian Ministers Fund for Life Insurance, and trustee, Ohio Wesleyan University and Central College. Technical advisor for film, "One Foot in Heaven,". Warner Brothers, 1963.

MEMBER: National Temperance Society (president), American Authors Guild, Lotos Club, Episcopal Actors Guild, Sons of the American Revolution, Ohio Society of New York (president, 1952-55), Rotary Club, Masons, Metropolitan Club, Union League, Alpha Delta, Phi Gamma Delta.

AWARDS, HONORS: Honorary degrees from many institutions, including Duke University, 1938, and Brigham Young University, 1967; numerous awards, including Freedoms Foundation award, 1952, 1955, 1959, 1973, 1974; Horatio Alger Award, 1952; American Education award, 1955; Government Service Award for Ohio, 1956; National Salvation Army Award, 1956, 1957; Distinguished Salesman's Award from New York Sales Executives, 1957; International Human Relations Award from the Dale Carnegie Club International, 1958; Clergyman of the Year Award, Religious Foundation of America, 1964; Paul Harris Fellow Award from Rotary International, 1972; Distinguished Patriot Award from Sons of the American Revolution, 1973; Order of Aaron and Hur, Chaplains Corps, U.S. Army, 1975; All-Time Great Ohioan Award, 1976; joint recipient with wife of medallion, Society for Family of Man, 1981; Treasure Award, 1984; Medal of Freedom National Award, 1983; Religion in Media Gold Angel, 1984; Caleb B. Smith Medal of Honor, Grand Lodge of Indiana, 1984; Bowery Savings Bank 150th Anniversary Distinguished New Yorker Award, 1984; International Rotary Award, 1984. Co-recipient with wife of special citation, Laymen's National Committee.

WRITINGS:

SELF-HELP BOOKS

The Art of Living (essays), Abingdon, 1937, new edition published as *The New Art of Living,* Worlds Work, 1975.
You Can Win (essays), Abingdon, 1939.
(With Smiley Blanton) *Faith Is the Answer: A Psychiatrist and a Pastor Discuss Your Problems,* Abingdon-Cokesbury, 1940, enlarged and revised edition, Guideposts Associates, 1955.
A Guide to Confident Living, Prentice-Hall, 1948, reprinted, Fawcett, 1975.
(With Blanton) *The Art of Real Happiness,* Prentice-Hall, 1950, revised edition, Fawcett, 1976.
(Author of introduction) *Guideposts* editors, *What Prayer Can Do,* Doubleday, 1953.

The Power of Positive Thinking, Prentice-Hall, 1952, reprinted, Fawcett, 1976, abridged edition published as *The Power of Positive Thinking for Young People,* Prentice-Hall, 1954.
Inspiring Messages for Daily Living, Prentice-Hall, 1955.
Stay Alive All Your Life, Prentice-Hall, 1957.
The Amazing Results of Positive Thinking, Prentice-Hall, 1959.
(Author of foreword) Blanton, *The Healing Power of Poetry,* Crowell, 1960.
The Tough-Minded Optimist, Prentice-Hall, 1961, revised edition published as *Positive Thinking for a Time Like This,* 1975.
Sin, Sex and Self-Control, Doubleday, 1965.
The Healing of Sorrow, Doubleday, 1966.
Enthusiasm Makes the Difference, Prentice-Hall, 1967.
You Can if You Think You Can, Prentice-Hall, 1974.
The Positive Principle Today: How to Renew and Sustain the Power of Positive Thinking, Prentice-Hall, 1976.
Positive Imaging, Revell, 1981.
Have a Great Day, Revell, 1984.

BOOKS ON THE LIFE OF CHRIST

The Coming of the King (juvenile), Prentice-Hall, 1956.
He Was a Child (juvenile), Prentice-Hall, 1957.
Jesus of Nazareth: A Dramatic Interpretation of His Life from Bethlehem to Calvary, Prentice-Hall, 1966.
The Story of Jesus (juvenile), Gibson, 1976.
The Positive Power of Jesus Christ, Tyndale, 1980.

EDITOR

Guideposts: Personal Messages of Inspiration and Faith, Prentice-Hall, 1948.
The Guideposts Anthology, Guideposts Associates, 1953.
Faith Made Them Champions, Guideposts Associates, 1954.
Sermon on the Mount, engravings by John de Pol, World, 1955.
Unlock Your Faith-Power, Guideposts Associates, 1957.
Guideposts to a Stronger Faith, Guideposts Associates, 1959.

OTHER

Adventures in the Holy Land, Prentice-Hall, 1963.
Norman Vincent Peale's Treasury of Courage and Confidence (anthology), Doubleday, 1970.
Bible Stories (juvenile), F. Watts, 1973.
Norman Vincent Peale's Treasury of Joy and Enthusiasm, Revell, 1981.
The True Joy of Positive Living (autobiography), Morrow, 1984.

Also editor of several volumes of testimonials from *Guideposts* magazine. Also author of newspaper columns, "Confident Living" and "Positive Thinking." Co-author with wife, Ruth Stafford Peale, of syndicated column, "There's an Answer." Contributor to periodicals, including *Christian Herald, Reader's Digest, Look.* Publisher and editor-in-chief, *Guideposts* magazine, New York City, 1945—; publisher with wife of *PLUS: The Magazine for Positive Thinking.*

SIDELIGHTS: Norman Vincent Peale is "one of the most noted preachers of the century . . . [and] one of the most influential Americans of our age," writes a *Parade* contributor. One of the first religious leaders to recognize the potential of mass media, Peale has used books, television, and radio, along with the pulpit, to communicate to Americans his message of self-help through positive thinking and prayer. Peale is a dynamic speaker, and his sermons have helped increase membership in every church in which he has served. As minister for three years in a struggling Brooklyn congregation, Peale collected enough funds to build a new church, while raising membership from forty to nearly nine hundred. In 1932, he became pastor of the historic but decaying New York City Marble Collegiate Church, where he initially preached to five hundred people. But by the end of his fifty–year pastorate, closed circuit television had been installed to accommodate the more than four thousand people attending the church.

Peale's primary success came with *The Power of Positive Thinking,* the most famous of his many books stressing the cultivation of a positive attitude as the key to happiness. As have many self-help writers, Peale happened upon his principles through working on his own problems. "I was a very shy, self-doubting boy," he told Miriam Berkley for *Publishers Weekly,* "and I put myself down all the time. It's a miserable way to live. I went out and I prayed and I told the Lord if he could turn a drunk into a sober person and a thief into an honest man, he could certainly help me get over this terrible thing. I struggled with it a long time, then got the answer. So I wrote a book. Since the answer was faith, I wanted faith in the title and called it *The Power of Faith.*" Peale disliked the book after finishing it, however, and threw it in the waste basket. But, as Peale told Berkley, his wife, Ruth, retrieved the manuscript and took it to Myron Boardman of Prentice-Hall, who "came to me and said, 'Who do you want this book to be read by, church people?' I said 'No, everybody.' 'Well,' he said, '*The Power of Faith* won't do it.' " Boardman decided that 'positive thinking' was a recurrent theme in the book, and chose it for the title.

The Power of Positive Thinking soared to the top of the *New York Times* best seller list, where it remained for three years, breaking the previous all-time record set by Lloyd Douglas' novel, *The Robe.* As Georgia Dullea puts it in the *New York Times, The Power of Positive Thinking* "became a model for self-help books." Although "over the years, the concept of positive thinking has been variously dismissed by religious and secular critics as simplistic and selfish, as using religion to gain fame or wealth," observes Dullea, sales of the book have now topped fifteen million copies worldwide. Douglas T. Miller in the *Journal of Popular Culture,* explains the minister's approach to problems: "The underlying assumption of Peale's teaching was that nearly all basic problems were personal, the result of inner conflicts and especially 'negative thinking.' We 'manufacture our own unhappiness,' he told readers. 'By our thoughts and attitudes we distill out of the ingredients of life either happiness or unhappiness for ourselves.' 'Unhappiness' could be avoided by following one of his simple formulas. As he wrote in the introduction to *The Power of Positive Thinking,* 'you do not need to be defeated by anything . . . you can have peace of mind, improved health, and a never-ceasing flow of energy. . . . By using the techniques outlined here you can modify or change the circumstances in which you now live, assuming control over them. . . . You will become a more popular, esteemed, and well-liked individual." Peale, while not overstating his book's literary merit, believes strongly in its message. "I don't think this is the greatest work of art or literature that ever came down the road," he told the *Parade* interviewer. "But it has sensible principles. If a person were to live by it, he wouldn't be free of trouble, but he'd know how to handle trouble. He'd have a good life."

Peale also broke new ground, and irritated some religious leaders, by using psychology in counseling parishioners. In the 1930s, Peale began working with psychiatrist Dr. Smiley Blanton to initiate a religio-psychiatric outpatient clinic, which eventually became the nonprofit Institutes of Religion and Health. Staffed by clergymen of all denominations, psychiatrists and social workers, the organization treats approximately six hundred patients a week at its New York City headquarters, and has established branches in Harlem, Chicago, and Green Bay, Wisconsin.

In a *Los Angeles Times* interview with Beth Ann Krier, J. Harold Ellens, the founder and editor of the *Journal of Psychology and Christianity* observes, "It is a very significant fact that Dr. Peale was three-quarters of a century ahead of the times with his emphasis on the relationship between psychology and religious experience. He saw psychology and Christian experience as very compatible . . . he had the courage to stand pat on this position in spite of the opposition of the entire Christian church for nearly half a century. His genius was that he . . . translated psychotheology into the language of the people."

Peale's message also appears monthly in *Guideposts* magazine. According to a *New Yorker* contributor, "Each month, *Guideposts* features inspiring stories of people who have walked up to adversity and kicked it." Founded by the Peales in conjunction with Lowell Thomas, Thomas E. Dewey, Raymond Thornburg, and Captain Eddie Rickenbacker in 1945, the magazine started as a four-page spiritual newsletter for businessmen. It now runs forty-eight pages, with a circulation of about four and a half million and an estimated readership of fourteen and a half million. In 1940, the Peales founded the Foundation for Christian Living, which distributes Peale's numerous books and those of other writers, as well as publishing an inspirational magazine, *PLUS: The Magazine of Positive Thinking.*

Peale's autobiography, *The True Joy of Positive Living* sums up a lifetime of work spent in attempting to improve people's lives. While it is filled with anecdotes about the minister's acquaintances, both famous and unknown, "one emerges from it with little private knowledge of the public man," writes Berkley. But John Fraunces in *Best Sellers* finds *The True Joy of Positive Living* "an unconscious telling of how [Peale's] personality developed, and how this very unusual man came to be an integral part of the American scene. . . . In this book he makes it sound as if Christ himself were speaking rather than a practiced, polished preacher."

Oddly enough, Peale does not see himself as the outgoing, constantly cheerful figure that he portrays. "Oh, I live in misery," he told Dullea. "But I overcome it by affirmations, by 'imaging,' by positive thinking. I suppose the day I'm lying in my casket the minister could say, 'Here's a shy boy.' "

MEDIA ADAPTATIONS: Excerpts of *The Power of Positive Thinking* were recorded for RCA Victor in 1953.

BIOGRAPHICAL/CRITICAL SOURCES:

BOOKS

Authors in the News, Volume 1, Gale, 1976.
Davis, Elisabeth L., *Fathers of America,* Revell, 1958.
Gordon, Arthur, *Norman Vincent Peale: Minister to Millions,* Prentice-Hall, 1958.
Peale, Norman Vincent, *The Power of Positive Thinking,* Prentice-Hall, 1952.
Westphal, Clarence, *Norman Vincent Peale: Christian Crusader,* Denison, 1964.

PERIODICALS

American, June, 1949.
Best Sellers, November, 1984, August, 1986.
Booklist, February 1, 1982, August, 1984.
Cleveland Press, March 9, 1974.
Good Housekeeping, January, 1956.
Journal of Popular Culture, summer, 1975.
Los Angeles Times, June 5, 1988.
Los Angeles Times Book Review, December 9, 1984.
Newsweek, December 28, 1953.
New Yorker, February 25, 1985.
New York Times, May 26, 1988.
Parade, May 17, 1987.
Publishers Weekly, January 14, 1974, July 12, 1976, September 28, 1984.
Quarterly Journal of Speech, December, 1954.
Reader's Digest, February, 1954.
Time, November 1, 1954.
Washington Post Book World, October 17, 1982.
West Coast Review of Books, February, 1982.

—*Sketch by Jani Prescott*

* * *

PEALE, Ruth Stafford 1906-

PERSONAL: Born September 10, 1906, in Fonda, Iowa; daughter of Frank Burton (a minister) and Anna Loretta (Crosby) Stafford; married Norman Vincent Peale (a minister), June 20, 1930; children: Margaret Ann (Mrs. Paul F. Everett), John Stafford, Elizabeth Ruth (Mrs. John M. Allen). *Education:* Syracuse University, A.B., 1928. *Religion:* Dutch (member of Reformed Church in America).

ADDRESSES: Home—1030 Fifth Ave., New York, N.Y. 10028; and "Quaker Hill," Pawling, N.Y. 12564. *Office*—1025 Fifth Ave., New York, N.Y. 10028.

CAREER: Central High School, Syracuse, N.Y., mathematics teacher, 1928-31; Reformed Church in America, national president of Women's Board of Domestic Missions, 1936-46, member of Board of Domestic Missions, 1955-56, and North American Missions board, 1963-69, president, 1967-69, commission member, 1966-69, general program council member, 1968—; secretary, Protestant Film Commission, 1946-51; Foundation for Christian Living, Pawling, N.Y., co-founder, 1940, president, general secretary and editor-in-chief, 1945—; *Guideposts* magazine, New York, N.Y., co-editor and publisher, 1957—. Appeared on national television program "What's Your Trouble," 1952-68; appeared on national radio program, 1968—. Member of board of governors, Norman Vincent Peale Telephone Center, 1977. Member of national women's board, Northwood Institute, 1981. Member of board of executive commissioners, Institutes of Religion and Health. Chairman, American Mother's Commission, 1948-49. Home Missions Council of North America, national president, 1942-44, national chairman, 1948-51; National Council of Churches, general board member, 1951-66, vice-chairman of broadcasting and film commission, 1951-55, vice-president, 1952-54, program chairman of general assembly, 1966; vice-president, Council of Churches of the City of New York, 1964-65; vice-president, Protestant Council of New York City, 1964-66; member of American Foundation of Religion and Psychiatry and Planners of Equal Opportunity. Trustee, Hope College, Champlain College, Stratford College, Lenox School, and Syracuse University. Member of board of directors, Cook Christian Training School and Lord's Day Alliance.

MEMBER: United Bible Societies of the World (vice-president), American Bible Society (member of board and executive committee, 1953—, currently director), New York Federation of Women's Clubs (chairman of religion, 1951-53, 1957-58), Sorosis (president, 1953-56), Lotos, Alpha Phi.

AWARDS, HONORS: LL.D., Syracuse University, 1953; Litt.D., Hope College, 1962; New York state Mother of the

Year, 1963; Cum Laude award, Syracuse University Alumni Association of New York, 1965, for outstanding service to the university, church, and community; Honor Iowans' award, Buena Vista College, 1966; Churchwoman of the Year award, Religious Heritage of America, 1969; American Mother's Commission award, 1970; Honorary Chancellor of Webber College, 1972; Champlain College Distinguished Citizen Award; Distinguished Service Award, Council of Churches of the City of New York, 1973; Honorary Life President, Alpha Phi, 1975; Distinguished Citizen Award, Champlain College, 1976; Francis W. Willard Award of Achievement, Alpha Phi 1976; Distinguished Service to Community and Nation award, General Federation of Women's Clubs, 1977; Horatio Alger Award, 1977; joint recipient with husband of medallion, Society for Family of Man, 1981; Distinguished Woman of the Year award, National Art Association; co-recipient with husband of special citation, Laymen's National Committee; honorary life member, National League of American Pen Women.

WRITINGS:

I Married a Minister, Abingdon-Cokesbury, 1942.

(With Arthur Gordon) *The Adventure of Being a Wife,* Prentice-Hall, 1971.

Secrets of Staying in Love, Thomas Nelson, 1984.

Co-author with husband, Norman Vincent Peale, of syndicated column, "There's an Answer." Contributor to *Reader's Digest, Woman's Day, Saturday Evening Post,* and other periodicals. Co-editor and publisher, *Guideposts* magazine, 1947—; publisher with husband of *PLUS: The Magazine of Positive Thinking.*

SIDELIGHTS: Ruth Stafford Peale has been an instrumental part of her husband, Norman Vincent Peale's, work in the area of "positive thinking." Together, they started the Foundation for Christian Living, which publishes and distributes inspirational literature. In 1964 Ruth Peale was portrayed in "One Man's Way," a motion picture based on her husband's life and work.

For more information, see Norman Vincent Peale's sketch in this volume.

* * *

PELLETIER, Kenneth R. 1946-

PERSONAL: Born April 27, 1946, in New Hampshire; son of Roger N. (a designer) and Lucy B. Pelletier. *Education:* University of California, Berkeley, B.A., 1969, Ph.D., 1974; graduate study at University of Pennsylvania, 1969, and C.G. Jung Institute of Analytical Psychology, Zurich, Switzerland, 1970-71.

ADDRESSES: Home—Shaughnessy Farms, 5 Country Oak Lane, Danville, Calif. 94526. *Office*—University of California, School of Medicine, 400 Parnassus Ave., A 405, San Francisco, Calif. 94143. *Agent*—Robert Briggs Associates, P.O. Box 9, Mill Valley, Calif. 94941.

CAREER: University of California Extension Division, Berkeley, San Francisco, Santa Cruz, Davis, Santa Barbara, Los Angeles, Irvine, and San Diego, Calif., instructor of psychology, psychiatry, and postgraduate medicine, and program coordinator, 1971—; Everett A. Gladman Memorial Hospital, Oakland, Calif., clinical psychologist, 1974—; Behavioral Medicine Clinic, Berkeley, director, 1976-81. University of California, San Francisco, School of Medicine, Department of Psychiatry, and Langley Porter Neuropsychiatric Institute, intern, 1973-74, clinical instructor, 1974-78, assistant clinical professor, 1978-85, associate clinical professor, 1986—; University of California, San Francisco, School of Medicine, Department of Medicine—Division of Internal Medicine, assistant clinical professor, 1982-86, associate clinical professor and member of attending staff, 1986—.

Licensed clinical psychologist in State of California, 1976—; registrant of Council for the National Register of Health Service Providers in Psychology, 1976—; certified biofeedback practitioner in the State of California, 1977—; registered provider for California State Psychological Health Plan, 1979—. Member of advisory boards or committees of numerous organizations, including Biofeedback Society of California, 1974-76, Golden Gate National Recreation Area, U.S. Department of the Interior, 1976-79, Health Steps program of Blue Cross of California and Blue Cross of America, 1983—, Preventive Medicine Research Institute, 1987—, National Survey of Worsite Health Promotion, 1987—, and SyberVision, Inc., 1988—. Member of editorial board, Hume Companies, 1987—. Senior consultant, Johnson & Johnson Health Management, Inc., 1985—. Research and clinical practice have been the subject of numerous national television programs, including the "Today" show, "Good Morning, America," several segments of "ABC World News," and the award-winning British Broadcasting Corporation series "The Long Search."

MEMBER: American Psychological Association, American Association for the Advancement of Science, Academy of Psychosomatic Medicine, Society for Psychophysiological Research, Biofeedback Society of America, Association for Fitness in Business, Society of Behavioral Medicine, American Holistic Medical Association, Phi Beta Kappa.

AWARDS, HONORS: Research grants, John E. Fetzer Foundation, 1974-75, Taylor Foundation, 1979-80, Dextra, Baldwin & McGonagle Foundation, 1980-82, Minneapolis Foundation and Minnesota Mott Foundation, 1980-83, Mary A. Crocker Foundation, 1981-84, San Francisco Foundation, 1982-84, and 1987—, Levi Strauss Foundation, Koret Foundation, and Burden Foundation, 1983-85, Ichinose Family Foundation, 1983-86, Institute of Noetic Sciences, 1986-87, Institute of Human Development, 1986—, Pacific Telesis Foundation, 1987—, Laurance S. Rockefeller, Transamerica-Pasteur Institute Foundation, and New Cycle Foundation, 1988—. First place mental health media award in national network programming, National Mental Health Association, 1987, for "Unwinding the Spring."

WRITINGS:

(With C. Garfield) *Consciousness: East and West,* Harper, 1976.

Mind as Healer, Mind as Slayer: A Holistic Approach to Preventing Stress Disorders, Delacorte, 1977.

Toward a Science of Consciousness, Delacorte, 1978.

Holistic Medicine: From Stress to Optimum Health, Delacorte, 1979.

Longevity: Fulfilling Our Biological Potential, Delacorte, 1981.

Healthy People in Unhealthy Places: Stress and Fitness at Work, Delacorte, 1983.

(With R. Lutz and N. L. Klehr) *That's Life!: Learning to Manage Life's Stress* (workbook and audiotape), California Department of Mental Health, 1988.

CONTRIBUTOR

Demetri Kanellakos and Jerome Lukas, editors, *The Psychobiology of Transcendental Meditation,* W. A. Benjamin, 1974.

P. G. Zimbardo and F. L. Ruch, editors, *Psychology and Life,* Scott, Foresman, 1975.

L. Domash, J. Farrow, and David Orme-Johnson, editors, *Scientific Research on Transcendental Meditation: Collected Papers,* Maharishi International University Press, 1976.

(With A. E. Gladman and T. H. Mikuriya) *Handbook of Physiological Feedback,* Autogenic Systems, 1976.

Gay Hendricks and James Fadiman, editors, *Transpersonal Education,* Prentice-Hall, 1976.

Kenneth Blum, editor, *Social Psychology,* Basic Books, 1977.

Dolores Krieger, editor, *The Persistent Reality,* Quest Books, 1977.

Zimbardo and C. Maslach, editors, *Psychology for Our Times: Readings,* 2nd edition, Scott, Foresman, 1977.

Orme-Johnson, editor, *Scientific Research on the Transcendental Meditation Program,* Volume 1, MIU Press, 1977.

C. Garfield, editor, *Stress and Survival: The Emotional Realities of Life-Threatening Illness,* Mosby, 1979.

(Author of introduction) D. Saltoon, *The Common Book of Consciousness,* Chronicle Books, 1979.

(With E. Peper and B. Tandy) Peper, S. Ancoli, and M. Quinn, editors, *Mind/Body Integrations: Essential Readings in Biofeedback,* Plenum, 1979.

C. F. Wilson and D. L. Hall, editors, *Stress Management for Educators,* U.S. Department of Education, 1980.

A. Hastings, Fadiman, and J. S. Gordon, editors, *Holistic Medicine: An Annotated Bibliography,* National Institute of Mental Health, 1980, published as *Health for the Whole Person,* Westview, 1980.

K. Blum, J. Cull, and G. G. Meyer, editors, *Folk Healing and Herbal Medicine,* C. C Thomas, 1981.

Bresler, J. Gordon, and D. Jaffe, editors, *Body, Mind, and Health: Toward an Integral Medicine,* National Institute of Mental Health, 1981.

(Author of introduction) Wilson and D. Hall, *Preventing Burnout in Education,* Wright Publishing Group, 1981.

J. Manuso, editor, *Occupational Clinical Psychology,* Praeger, 1982.

D. H. Shapiro, Jr., and R. N. Walsh, editors, *The Art and Science of Meditation: A Reader,* Aldine, 1982.

K. Wilber, editor, *The Holographic Paradigm and Other Paradoxes,* Shambala Publishers, 1982.

J. S. J. Manuso, editor, *Occupational Clinical Psychology,* Praeger, 1983.

H. Selye, editor, *Selye's Guide to Stress Research,* Volume 3, Van Nostrand, 1983.

D. E. Bresler, D. A. Jaffe, and J. S. Gordon, editors, *Mind, Body, and Health,* Human Sciences Press, 1983.

C. Van Dyke, L. Temoshok, and L. S. Zegans, editors, *Emotions in Health and Illness: Clinical Applications,* Grune & Stratton, 1984.

Wellness Perspectives, University of Nebraska, 1984.

Shapiro, Jr., and Walsh, editors, *Meditation: Classic and Contemporary Perspectives,* Aldine, 1984.

J. P. Opatz, editor, *Wellness Promotion Strategies,* University of Wisconsin and the Stevens Point Foundation with Kendall/Hunt Publishing, 1984.

L. Erlicht and A. R. Schneider, editors, *The Human Mind—The Brain and Beyond,* American Broadcasting Companies, 1984.

K. Dychtwald, editor, *Wellness and Health Promotion for the Elderly,* Aspen Publishing Systems, 1986.

(Author of foreword) E. Miller, *Feeling Good—How to Stay Healthy,* Ten Speed Press, 1986.

M. F. Cataldo and T. C. Coates, editors, *Health and Industry—A Behavioral Medicine Perspective,* Wiley, 1986.

R. J. Carlson and B. A. Newman, editors, *For Your Health,* C. V. Mosby, 1986.

J. Bland, editor, *Review of Molecular Medicine,* JSB and Associates, 1986.

R. Bellingham and B. Cohen, editors, *The Wellness Sourcebook,* Human Resource Development Press, 1987.

J. S. Gordon, D. T. Jaffe, and D. E. Bresler, editors, *Mind, Body, and Health: Toward an Integral Medicine,* Human Sciences Press, 1987.

A. A. Sheikh and K. S. Sheikh, editors, *Eastern and Western Approach to Healing,* Wiley, 1988.

(Author of preface) J. Travis, *The Wellness Workbook,* 2nd edition, Hershey Publications, 1988.

DOCUMENTARY FILMS, AUDIOTAPES, VIDEOTAPES

"The Nature of Things," Canadian Broadcasting Company (CBC-TV), 1975.

"The New Medicine," National Broadcasting Corp. (NBC-TV), 1976.

"The Search for Something Special," NBC-TV, 1976.

"I Move," American Broadcasting Company (ABC-TV), 1976.

"Mental Stress and Physical Illness" (*Psychology Today* audio cassette), Ziff-Davis Publishing, 1977.

"Two Techniques for Treating Stress Disorders" (*Psychology Today* audio cassette), Ziff-Davis Publishing, 1977.

"The New Medicine," RAI-TV National Television of Italy, 1977.

"Frontiers of Holistic Medicine," Hartley Productions, 1977.

"New Boundaries for Health," Boston Family Institute, 1977.

"The Energy Workshop," NBC-TV, 1978.

"The Long Search" (twelfth program in a thirteen-part series), British Broadcasting Corp. (BBC-TV), 1978.

"A Neurophysiological Stress Profile" (professional training videotape), Autogenic Systems, Inc., 1978.

"Stress: Are We Killing Ourselves?" (five-part series), ABC-TV, 1979.

"Nutrition for Optimum Physical and Mental Health" (*Psychology Today* audio cassette), Ziff-Davis, 1979.

"Exercise for Optimum Physical and Mental Health" (*Psychology Today* audio cassette), Ziff-Davis, 1979.

"Stress: The Silent Killer," Westinghouse Broadcasting Co., 1980.

"Here's to Your Health," Public Broadcasting Service (PBS-TV), 1981.

"A Whole New Medicine," Pacificon Productions and State of California Department of Mental Health, 1981.

"Stress Management: A Positive Strategy," Time-Life Video Corp., 1982.

"Magic or Miracle" (special pilot), NBC-TV, 1983.

"Health in the Workplace," CBS-TV, 1983.

"Frontiers of Medicine" (documentary), University of New Mexico School of Medicine, Department of Family Medicine, 1983.

"Longevity: Fulfilling Our Biological Potential" (audio cassettes), Institute for the Study of Human Knowledge, 1984.

"Healthy Executives: The AT&T Experience" (videotape), Southwestern Bell Corp., 1985.

"Healthy Super Executives: What Sets Them Apart?" (*Psychology Today* audio cassette), American Psychological Association, 1986.

"Visualization: Accessing the Higher Self" (*Psychology Today* audio cassette), American Psychological Association, 1986.

"Unwinding the Spring" (five half-hour stress management programs), Hospital Satellite Network (Los Angeles), 1987.

"The Neuropsychology of Executive Health" (audio and video cassettes), SyberVision, 1987.
"The Neuropsychology of Staying Young" (audio and video cassettes), SyberVision, 1987.
"Corporate Health Promotion Programs" (videotape), Southwestern Bell Corp., 1987.
"The Mind-Body Connection," CBS-TV, 1988.
"The Neuropsychology of Quitting Smoking for Life" (audio and video cassettes), SyberVision, 1988.
"The Neuropsychology of Mastering Stress" (audio and video cassettes), SyberVision, 1988.
"The Neuropsychology of Healthy Hearts" (audio and video cassettes), SyberVision, 1988.

OTHER

Contributor to *Collier's Encyclopedia,* Macmillan, 1977; contributor to University of California School of Medicine, *Extension Division Catalog,* 1976; contributor to proceedings of biofeedback societies, including Biofeedback Research Society, 1974, 1975, and 1976, and Biofeedback Society of America, 1977. Contributor of more than one hundred articles on behavioral medicine, clinical biofeedback, and neurophysiology to professional journals, including *Journal of Biofeedback, Journal of Altered States of Consciousness, Journal of Contemporary Psychotherapy, Journal of Holistic Health, Journal of Humanistic Psychology, Western Journal of Medicine,* and *American Journal of Clinical Biofeedback.*

Editor, database section of *American Journal of Health Promotion,* 1986—, *Health Companies: Innovation and Evaluation,* 1987—. Contributing editor, *Newsletter of the American Institute of Stress* and *Medical Self Care,* 1981—, and *Healthline,* 1982-84; consulting editor, *International Journal of Psychosomatics,* 1984—. Member of editorial board, *Clinical Biofeedback* and *Journal of Mind and Behavior,* 1978—, *Journal of Holistic Medicine,* 1981-87, *Advances: Journal of the Institute for the Advancement of Health,* 1982—, and the Time-Life series, *Fitness, Health, and Nutrition: Managing Stress—From Morning to Night,* 1987—. Member of editorial advisory board, *Journal of Individual, Family and Community Wellness,* 1982—, *American Health: Fitness of Body and Mind,* 1984—, and *Holistic Medicine: Journal of the British Holistic Medicine Association,* 1985—.

AVOCATIONAL INTERESTS: Sailing, tennis, horseback riding, foreign travel (Europe, North Africa, Mexico, and Canada).

BIOGRAPHICAL/CRITICAL SOURCES:

PERIODICALS

Washington Post Book World, October 4, 1981.

* * *

PELLOWSKI, Michael (Joseph) 1949-
(Ski Michaels)

PERSONAL: Born January 24, 1949, in New Brunswick, N.J.; son of Michael (a construction worker) and Charlotte (Novack) Pellowski; married Judith Audrey Snyder (a banker), August 6, 1971; children: Morgan Jason, Matthew Joshua, Melanie Judith, Martin Jude. *Education:* Rutgers University, B.A., 1971.

ADDRESSES: Home—Hillsborough, N.J. *Office*—P.O. Box 726, Bound Brook, N.J. 08805.

CAREER: Professional football player affiliated with the New England Patriots, 1971-73; Gibbons School, New Brunswick, N.J., teacher of philosophy and art, and director of health and physical education, 1973-75; free-lance writer, 1975—. Creator, writer, host, and producer of children's series "Fun Stop," and stand-up comedian, under name Ski Michaels.

MEMBER: Elks.

AWARDS, HONORS: Nomination for Ace Award, Academy for Cable Excellence, 1982, for "Fun Stop."

WRITINGS:

FOR CHILDREN

The Great Sports Question and Answer Book, Waldman Publishing, 1979.
A Child's Book of the Bible, Playmore, 1980.
Jokes: Hours of Laughs, Playmore, 1980.
Clara Joins the Circus, Parents Magazine Press, 1981.
Great Baseball Quiz Book, Moby Books, 1982.
Great Football Quiz Book, Moby Books, 1982.
Amazing but True Sports Stories, Moby Books, 1982.
Double Trouble, Willowisp, 1986.
Ghost Toasties, Willowisp, 1986.
Where's Teddy?, Willowisp, 1986.
Maxwell Finds a Friend, Troll Associates, 1986.
Benny's Bad Day, Troll Associates, 1986.
Who Can't Follow an Ant?, Troll Associates, 1986.
Magic Broom, Troll Associates, 1986.
The Messy Monster, Troll Associates, 1986.
Moosey Saves Money, Troll Associates, 1986.
Teddy on Time, Troll Associates, 1986.
Copycat Dog, Troll Associates, 1986.
No Fleas, Please!, Troll Associates, 1986.
The Duck Who Loved Puddles, Troll Associates, 1986.
(Under pseudonym Ski Michaels) *The Baseball Bat,* Troll Associates, 1986.
(Under pseudonym Ski Michaels) *The Big Surprise,* Troll Associates, 1986.
(Under pseudonym Ski Michaels) *Felix, the Funny Fox,* Troll Associates, 1986.
(Under pseudonym Ski Michaels) *Fun in the Sun,* Troll Associates, 1986.
(Under pseudonym Ski Michaels) *Mystery of the Missing Fuzzy,* Troll Associates, 1986.
(Under pseudonym Ski Michaels) *Mystery of the Windy Meadow,* Troll Associates, 1986.
(Under pseudonym Ski Michaels) *Something New to Do,* Troll Associates, 1986.
(Under pseudonym Ski Michaels) *Wake Up, Sam!,* Troll Associates, 1986.
Photon-Attack of the Tunnel-Dwellers, Putnam, 1987.
Birthday Bear and the Runaway Skateboard, Willowisp, 1987.
Ghost Bumps, Willowisp, 1987.
The Puppy Who Wanted a Playmate, Willowisp, 1987.
Fire Fighter, Troll Associates, 1988.
Forest Ranger, Troll Associates, 1988.
Ghost in the Library, Troll Associates, 1988.
Mixed-up Magic, Troll Associates, 1988.
Professor Possum's Great Adventure, Troll Associates, 1988.

Also author of *Silly Sidney.*

JUVENILES; ADAPTOR

Howard the Duck: The Movie Storybook, Putnam, 1986.
Silverhawks: The Menace of Moon Star, Putnam, 1987.
Silverhawks: The Planet-Eater, Putnam, 1987.
Silverhawks: The Sun Bandits, Putnam, 1987.
Silverhawks: The Terror of the Time-Stopper, Putnam, 1987.

OTHER

Also author of *My Sister the Mess-up*, and *Triple Trouble, Trouble Twins* (part of "Trouble Twins" series), both published by Willowisp, and *That's So Funny I Fell Off My Dinosaur Laughing.* Author of syndicated comic strip, *Archie*, for King Features. Author of comedy scripts for stand-up comedians.

SIDELIGHTS: Michael Pellowski once wrote *CA:* "I'm interested in three major topics, to which I devote myself as a person and in my work—humor, children, and sports. I strive for pieces that do not force adulthood on youngsters too quickly. I close my weekly television show with the words, 'Don't grow up too fast, because it's great to be a kid.' That sums up my cause in life."

* * *

PENNOCK, J(ames) Roland 1906-

PERSONAL: Born February 4, 1906, in Chatham, Pa.; son of James Levis and Alice Rakestraw (Carter) Pennock; married Helen B. Sharpless, January 24, 1931; children: Joan (Mrs. V. John Barnard), Judith Carter (Mrs. Albert F. Lilley). *Education:* Attended London School of Economics and Political Science, 1925-26; Swarthmore College, B.A., 1927; Harvard University, M.A., 1928, Ph.D., 1932. *Politics:* Democrat. *Religion:* Quaker.

ADDRESSES: Home—The Quadrangle, 3300 Darby Rd., Haverford, Pa. 19041-1095. *Office*—Department of Political Science, Swarthmore College, Swarthmore, Pa. 19081.

CAREER: Swarthmore College, Swarthmore, Pa., instructor, 1929-32, assistant professor, 1932-41, associate professor, 1941-45, professor of political science, 1945-62, Richter Professor Emeritus, 1976—, chairman of department, 1941-70. Administrative specialist, U.S. Social Security Board, 1936-37; principal divisional assistant, Office of Foreign Relief, U.S. Department of State, 1943; panel chairman, Regional War Labor Board, 1943-45. Social Science Research Council, chairman of Committee on Political Theory and Legal Philosophy Fellowships, 1954-60, member of board of directors, 1960-66. Visiting professor at Columbia University, 1950, and University of California, San Diego, 1978; Hill Distinguished Visiting Professor at University of Minnesota, 1979; visiting lecturer, Harvard University, 1953, and University of Pennsylvania, 1976.

MEMBER: American Political Science Association (member of council, 1953-55; vice president, 1963-64), American Society of Political and Legal Philosophy (editor, 1965-86; president, 1968-70), Phi Beta Kappa.

AWARDS, HONORS: Guggenheim fellow, 1954-55.

WRITINGS:

Administration and the Rule of Law, Farrar & Rinehart, 1941.

Liberal Democracy: Its Merits and Prospects, Rinehart, 1950.

(With others) *Democracy in the Mid-Twentieth Century: Problems and Prospects,* Department of Political Science, Washington University, 1960.

(With David G. Smith) *Political Science: An Introduction,* Macmillan, 1964.

(Contributor) Oliver Garceau, editor, *Political Research and Political Theory,* Oxford University Press, 1968.

Democratic Political Theory, Princeton University Press, 1979.

(Contributor) Geoffrey Brennan and Loren E. Lomasky, editors, *The Justification of Democracy,* Cambridge University Press, in press.

EDITOR

Self-Government in Modernizing Nations, Prentice-Hall, 1965.

(And contributor with John W. Chapman) *Nomos* (yearbook of American Society for Political and Legal Philosophy), Atherton, Volume 4: *Equality,* 1967, Volume 5: *Representation,* 1968, Volume 6: *Voluntary Associations,* 1969, Volume 7: *Political and Legal Obligation,* 1970, Volume 8: *Privacy,* 1971, Volume 14: *Coercion,* 1972, Volume 15: *The Limits of Law,* 1974, Volume 16: *Participation in Politics,* 1974, Volume 17: *Human Nature in Politics,* 1977, Volume 18: *Due Process,* 1977, Volume 19: *Anarchism,* 1978, Volume 20: *Constitutionalism,* 1979, Volume 21: *Compromise in Ethics, Law, and Politics,* 1979, Volume 22: *Property,* 1980, Volume 23: *Human Rights,* 1981, Volume 24: *Ethics, Economics, and the Law,* 1982, Volume 25: *Liberal Democracy,* 1983, Volume 26: *Marxism,* 1983, Volume 27: *Criminal Justice,* 1985, Volume 28: *Justification,* 1986, Volume 29: *Authority Revisited,* 1987, Volume 30: *Religion, Morality, and the Law,* 1988, Volume 31: *Markets and Justice,* 1989.

OTHER

Contributor to *A Dictionary of the Social Sciences, International Encyclopedia of the Social Sciences, Encyclopaedia Britannica,* and to other dictionaries and encyclopedias; contributor of articles to numerous professional journals, including *University of Pennsylvania Law Review, Georgetown Law Review, Annals of the American Academy, Western Political Quarterly, Journal of Politics, Behavioral Science, World Politics,* and *Ethics.* Member of board of editors and contributor, *American Political Science Review,* 1968-69, 1973-76.

WORK IN PROGRESS: Articles on democratic theory.

SIDELIGHTS: J. Roland Pennock told *CA:* "Perhaps more scholar than 'writer' in happy retirement (although I greatly enjoyed teaching), I continue to read, write, and edit in my chosen field, political theory. If my work is in any way distinctive, it is probably because I have always attempted to bridge the gap between normative and empirical theory, a gap that too frequently divides our discipline into warring camps. The 'happy medium' sometimes is attacked from both sides. So be it. As to style, I strive, not always successfully, for precision and economy of words."

AVOCATIONAL INTERESTS: Tennis, travel, and using his computer.

* * *

PETERS, Robert L(ouis) 1924-

PERSONAL: Born October 20, 1924, in Eagle River, Wis.; son of Samuel (a welder and farmer) and Dorothy (Keck) Peters; married Jean Louise Powell, October 22, 1950 (divorced, 1972); children: Robert II, Meredith Jean, Richard Nathaniel (deceased), Jefferson Marlowe. *Education:* University of Wisconsin, B.A., 1948, M.S., 1949, Ph.D., 1952.

ADDRESSES: Home—9431 Krepp Dr., Huntington Beach, Calif. 92646. *Office*—Department of English, University of California, Irvine, Calif. 92717.

CAREER: University of Idaho, Moscow, instructor in English, 1951-52; Boston University, Boston, Mass., assistant professor of humanities, 1952-54; Ohio Wesleyan University, Delaware, assistant professor of English, 1954-57; Wayne State University, Detroit, Mich., associate professor of English, 1957-63; University of California, Riverside, associate professor, 1963-66, professor of Victorian literature, 1966-68; University of California, Irvine, professor of English and comparative literature, 1968—. Visiting professor, University of California, Los Angeles, 1965, University of Utah, 1967. Has given readings of his poetry across the United States and Europe. Member of board, Wayne State University Press, 1960-62. *Military service:* U.S. Army, 1943-46; became technical sergeant.

MEMBER: PEN, Modern Language Association of America, Authors Guild, Authors League of America, Poetry Society of America, American Society for Aesthetics (trustee and member of board, 1965-68).

AWARDS, HONORS: Grant-in-aid, American Council of Learned Societies, 1963; Hilberry Publication Prize, Wayne State University Press, 1965, for *The Crowns of Apollo: Swinburne's Principles of Literature and Art, a Study in Victorian Criticism and Aesthetics;* Guggenheim fellowship, 1966-67; poems selected for Borestone Mountain Awards, 1967; fellowship to Yaddo, The MacDowell Colony, and Ossabaw Island Project, 1973-74; National Endowment for the Arts fellowship, 1974; Alice Faye de Castagnola Prize, 1984; Larry P. Fine Award for Criticism, 1985.

WRITINGS:

(Editor) *A Splendid Will: From the Writings of Rev. Walter B. Pedersen,* privately printed, 1958.

(Editor) *Victorians on Literature and Art,* Appleton, 1961.

The Crowns of Apollo: Swinburne's Principles of Literature and Art, a Study in Victorian Criticism and Aesthetics, Wayne State University Press, 1965.

(Editor with David Halliburton) *Edmund Gosse's Journal of his Visit to America,* Purdue University Press, 1966.

(With George Hitchcock) *Pioneers of Modern Poetry,* Kayak, 1967.

(Editor with Herbert Schueller) *The Letters of John Addington Symonds,* three volumes, Wayne State University Press, 1967-69.

Songs for a Son (poems), Norton, 1967.

Fourteen Poems, privately printed, 1967.

The Sows Head and Other Poems, Wayne State University Press, 1968.

Eighteen Poems, privately printed, 1973.

Byron Exhumed: A Verse Suite, Windless Orchard Press, 1973.

(Editor with Timothy d'Arch Smith) *Gabriel: A Poem by John Addington Symonds,* Hartington Publishers, 1974.

Connections: In the English Lake District (poems), Anvil Press, 1974.

Cool Zebras of Light (poems), Christopher's Books, 1974.

Red Midnight Moon (poems), Empty Elevator Shaft Press, 1974.

Holy Cow: Parable Poems, Red Hill, 1974.

Bronchial Tangle, Heart System (poems), Granite Books, 1975.

The Gift to be Simple: A Garland for Mother Ann Lee, Liveright, 1975.

(Editor) John Steinbeck, *The Collected Poems of Amnesia Glasscock,* Manroot Books, 1976.

Gaugin's Chair: Selected Poems, 1967-74, Crossing Press, 1977.

Hawthorne: Poems Adapted from Journals, Red Hill, 1977.

The Drowned Man to the Fish (poems), New Rivers Press, 1978.

The Poet as Ice-Skater (poems), Manroot Books, 1978.

Ikagnak: The North Wind, with Dr. Kane in the Arctic (poems), Kenmore Press, 1978.

The Lost Ghazals of the First Century Persian Poet Harun abu-Hatim al-Farskin, Raccoon Press, 1979.

The Great American Poetry Bake-Off: First Series, Scarecrow, 1979, . . . *Second Series,* 1982, . . . *Third Series,* 1987.

What Dillinger Meant to Me (poems), Sea Horse, 1981.

Celebrities: In Memory of Margaret Dumond, Dowager of the Marx Brothers Movies (poems), Somber Reptiles Press, 1981.

Love Poems for Robert Mitchum, privately printed, 1981.

The Picnic in the Snow: Ludwig of Bavaria, New Rivers Press, 1981.

The Peters Black and Blue Guide to Current Literary Journals, Cherry Valley, 1983, 2nd edition published as *The Second Peters Black and Blue Guide to Current Literary Journals,* 1985, 3rd edition published as *Peters Third Black and Blue Guide to Literary Journals,* Dustbooks, 1987.

Hawker (poems), Unicorn Press, 1984.

Kane (poems), Unicorn Press, 1985.

Ludwig of Bavaria: A Verse Biography and a Play for Single Performer, Cherry Hill, 1986.

The Blood Countess: Erzebet of Hungary (poems and a play), Cherry Valley, 1987.

Shaker Light (poems), Unicorn Press, 1987.

(Editor) *Letters to a Tutor: The Tennyson Family Letters to Henry Graham Dakyns (1861-1911), with the Audrey Tennyson Death-Bed Diary,* Scarecrow, 1988.

Crunching Gravel: Growing Up in the Thirties, Mercury House, 1988.

Hunting the Snark (criticism), Paragon, 1989.

Haydon (poems), Unicorn Press, 1989.

Author of a play produced at the Cubiculo Theatre, 1971. Poems anthologized in *Best Poems of 1967: Borestone Mountain Poetry Awards,* edited by Lionel Stevenson and others, Pacific Books, 1968. Contributor to *Victorian Studies, Prairie Schooner, Western Humanities Review, American Book Review, Fiddlehead, Kayak, The Little Square Review,* and other magazines and professional journals; contributor of reviews to the *Los Angeles Times, Library Journal, American Book Review, Paintbrush,* and *Gargoyle. English Literature in Transition,* bibliographer, 1958-68, member of editorial board, 1962-68; associate editor, *Criticism: A Quarterly of Literature and the Arts,* 1961-63; assistant editor and bibliographer, *Journal of Aesthetics and Art Criticism,* 1963-65; American poetry editor, *Ikon;* consulting editor to *American Book Review,* 1976—, *Contact II,* 1977—, *Bachy,* 1979, and *Paintbrush,* 1987—; editor, *American Poets' Series,* Scarecrow, 1981—.

WORK IN PROGRESS: Brueghel's Pig, for Illuminati.

SIDELIGHTS: In an interview with Eric Baizer and Richard Peabody in *Gargoyle,* Robert L. Peters addresses the issue of modern poetry and criticism. "We need better poems and fewer theories," he tells Baizer and Peabody. "Theories abound, particularly fashionable ones. . . . I teach in a University full of theories about literature. Not much contemporary poetry is read by these theory-profs. They seem to stop with [Wallace] Stevens and [William Carlos] Williams. When my *Great American Poetry Bake-Off* appeared and I was reviewed by my colleagues for a pay-boost, I received [few] Brownie points for the book, since, as one beguiling colleague said to me: 'We didn't know what to do with it; why do you write about people we've never heard of?' " When asked by his interviewers about his own poetry, Peters remarks: "I used to fantasize that I could be just as good a nature poet as [Theodore] Roethke. That's hubris, of course, since Roethke is God. There are times when I feel like Adam first discovering the physical universe. And there is a mystique—the more objects you can love and value and incorporate in your work, the more your own mortality, symbolically, becomes a lie."

BIOGRAPHICAL/CRITICAL SOURCES:

BOOKS

Contemporary Authors Autobiography Series, Volume 8, Gale, 1989.
Contemporary Literary Criticism, Volume 7, Gale, 1976.

PERIODICALS

American Book Review, January-February, 1981.
Gargoyle, January, 1981.
Los Angeles Times Book Review, August 25, 1985.
New York Times Book Review, December 28, 1975, May 8, 1988.
Village Voice, October 20, 1975.

* * *

PETERSHAM, Maud (Sylvia Fuller) 1890-1971 (Maud Fuller)

PERSONAL: Born August 5, 1890, in Kingston, N.Y.; died on November 29, 1971, in Ravenna, Ohio; daughter of a Baptist minister; married Miska Petersham (author and illustrator of books for children), 1917 (died May 15, 1960); children: Miki (a son). *Education:* Graduated from Vassar College, 1912; studied art at the New York School of Fine and Applied Art.

ADDRESSES: Home—Woodstock, N.Y.

CAREER: Author and illustrator of books for children. Worked in art department of International Art Service (advertising agency), New York, N.Y.

AWARDS, HONORS: Runner-up, with husband, Miska Petersham, for Caldecott Medal, 1942, for *An American ABC;* Caldecott Medal, with husband, Miska Petersham, 1946, for *The Rooster Crows: A Book of American Rhymes and Jingles.*

WRITINGS:

CO-AUTHOR AND ILLUSTRATOR WITH HUSBAND, MISKA PETERSHAM; JUVENILES

Miki, Doubleday, Doran, 1929, reprinted, Cadmus, 1946.
The Ark of Father Noah and Mother Noah, Doubleday, Doran, 1930.
The Christ Child, as Told by Matthew and Luke, Doubleday, Doran, 1931.
Auntie and Celia Jane and Miki, Doubleday, Doran, 1932.
The Story Book of Things We Use, Winston, 1933.
The Story Book of Houses, Winston, 1933.
The Story Book of Transportation, Winston, 1933.
The Story Book of Food, Winston, 1933.
The Story Book of Clothes, Winston, 1933.
Get-a-Way and Hary Janos, Viking, 1933.
Miki and Mary: Their Search for Treasures, Viking, 1934.
The Story Book of Wheels (also see below), Winston, 1935.
The Story Book of Ships (also see below), Winston, 1935.
The Story Book of Trains (also see below), Winston, 1935.
The Story Book of Aircraft (also see below), Winston, 1935.
The Story Book of Wheels, Ships, Trains, Aircraft (contains *The Story Book of Wheels, The Story Book of Ships, The Story Book of Trains,* and *The Story Book of Aircraft*), Winston, 1935.
The Story Book of Gold (also see below), Winston, 1935.
The Story Book of Coal (also see below), Winston, 1935.
The Story Book of Oil (also see below), Winston, 1935.
The Story Book of Iron and Steel (also see below), Winston, 1935.
The Story Book of the Earth's Treasures: Gold, Coal, Oil, Iron and Steel (contains *The Story Book of Gold, The Story Book of Coal, The Story Book of Oil,* and *The Story Book of Iron and Steel*), Winston, 1935.
The Story Book of Wheat (also see below), Winston, 1936.
The Story Book of Corn (also see below), Winston, 1936.
The Story Book of Rice (also see below), Winston, 1936.
The Story Book of Sugar (also see below), Winston, 1936, published as *Let's Learn about Sugar,* with illustrations by James E. Barry, Harvey House, 1969.
The Story Book of Foods from the Field: Wheat, Corn, Rice, Sugar (contains *The Story Book of Wheat, The Story Book of Corn, The Story Book of Rice,* and *The Story Book of Sugar*), Winston, 1936.
Joseph and His Brothers: From the Story Told in the Book of Genesis (also see below), Winston, 1938.
Moses: From the Story Told in the Old Testament (also see below), Winston, 1938, reprinted, Macmillan, 1958.
Ruth: From the Story Told in the Book of Ruth (also see below), Winston, 1938.
David: From the Story Told in the First Book of Samuel and the First Book of Kings (also see below), Winston, 1938.
Stories from the Old Testament: Joseph, Moses, Ruth, David (contains *Joseph and His Brothers, Moses, Ruth,* and *David*), Winston, 1938.
The Story Book of Cotton (also see below), Winston, 1939.
The Story Book of Wool (also see below), Winston, 1939.
The Story Book of Rayon (also see below), Winston, 1939.
The Story Book of Silk (also see below), Winston, 1939, published as *Let's Learn about Silk,* Harvey House, 1939.
The Story Book of Things We Wear (contains *The Story Book of Cotton, The Story Book of Wool, The Story Book of Rayon,* and *The Story Book of Silk*), Winston, 1939.
An American ABC, Macmillan, 1941, reprinted, 1966.
America's Postage Stamps: The Story of One Hundred Years of U.S. Postage Stamps, Macmillan, 1947, reprinted, 1967.
My Very First Book, Macmillan, 1948.
The Box with Red Wheels, Macmillan, 1949, reprinted, 1973.
The Circus Baby, Macmillan, 1950, reprinted, 1972.
The Story of the Presidents of the United States of America, Macmillan, 1953.
Off to Bed: Seven Stories for Wide-Awakes, Macmillan, 1954.
The Boy Who Had No Heart, Macmillan, 1955.
A Silver Mace: A Story of Williamsburg, Macmillan, 1956.
The Peppernuts, Macmillan, 1958.

ILLUSTRATOR WITH HUSBAND, MISKA PETERSHAM; JUVENILES

Franklin T. Baker and Ashley H. Thorndike, *Everyday Classics: Primer—Second Reader,* Macmillan, 1917.
Ada Maria Skinner and Frances Gillespy Wickes, compilers, *A Child's Own BOok of Verse,* three volumes, Macmillan, 1917.
John Stuart Thomson, *Fil and Filippa: Story of Child Life in the Philippines,* Macmillan, 1917.
Mary Lydia Bolles Branch, *Guld the Cavern King,* Bookshop for Boys and Girls and Women's Educational and Industrial Union, 1918.
John Walter Wayland, *History Stories for Primary Grades,* Macmillan, 1919.
William Bowen, *Enchanted Forest,* Macmillan, 1920.
Elsie S. Eells, *Tales of Enchantment from Spain,* Harcourt, 1920.
Louise Lamprey, *Children of Ancient Britain,* Little, Brown, 1921, published as *Long Ago People: How They Lived in Britain before History Began,* Little, Brown, 1921.
Anna Cogswell Tyles, compiler, *Twenty-four Unusual Stories for Boys and Girls,* Harcourt, 1921.

Ethel May Gate, *The Broom Fairies,* Silver, Burdett, 1922.

Carl Sandburg, *Rootabaga Stories,* Harcourt, 1922, reprinted, 1974.

Charles Lamb and Mary Lamb, *Tales from Shakespeare,* Macmillan, 1923.

Mabel Guinnip La Rue, *Under the Story Tree,* Macmillan, 1923.

Sandburg, *Rootabaga Pigeons,* Harcourt, 1923.

Sisters of Mercy (St. Xavier College, Chicago), *Marquette Readers,* Macmillan, 1924.

La Rue, *The F-U-N Book,* Macmillan, 1924.

La Rue, *In Animal Land,* Macmillan, 1924, revised edition, 1929.

Margery Clark, *Poppy Seed Cakes,* Doubleday, 1924.

Inez M. Howard, Alice Hawthorne, and Mae Howard, *Language Garden: A Primary Language Book,* Macmillan, 1924.

Harriott Fansler and Isidoro Panlasigui, *Philippine National Literature,* Macmillan, 1925.

Bessie Blackstone Coleman, Willis L. Uhl, and James Fleming Hosic, *Pathway to Reading: Primer,* Silver, Burdette, 1925.

Florence C. Coolidge, *Little Ugly Face, and Other Indian Tales,* Macmillan, 1925.

Olive Beaupre Miller, translator, *Nursery Friends from France,* Book House for Children, 1925.

Miller, editor, *Tales Told in Holland,* Book House for Children, 1926.

Jean Young Ayer, *The Easy Book: First Lessons in Reading,* Macmillan, 1926.

Howard, Hawthorne, and Howard, *Number Friends: A Primary Arithmetic,* Macmillan, 1927.

Elizabeth C. Miller, *Children of the Mountain Eagle,* Doubleday, 1927.

La Rue, *The Billy Bang Book,* Macmillan, 1927.

Everyday Canadian Primer, Macmillan, 1928.

Marguerite Clement, *Where Was Bobby?,* Doubleday, Doran, 1928.

Wilhelmina Harper and Aymer Jay Hamilton, compilers, *Pleasant Pathways,* Macmillan, 1928.

Ayer, Baker, and Thorndike, *Everyday Stories,* Macmillan, 1929.

Harper and Hamilton, compilers, *Winding Roads,* Macmillan, 1929.

Harper and Hamilton, compilers, *Heights and Highways,* Macmillan, 1929.

Harper and Hamilton, compilers, *Far Away Hills,* Macmillan, 1929.

E. Miller, *Pran of Albania,* Doubleday, Doran, 1929.

Marie, Queen of Roumania, *The Magic Doll of Roumania: A Wonder Story in which East and West Do Meet,* Stokes, 1929.

La Rue, *Little Indians,* Macmillan, 1930, revised edition, 1934.

Sydney Vanferson Rowland, William Dodge Lewis, and Elizabeth J. Marshall, compilers, *New Trails: Book IV,* Winston, 1930.

Rowland, Lewis, and Marshall, compilers, *Treasure Trove: Book V,* Winston, 1930.

Rowland, Lewis, and Marshall, compilers, *Rich Cargoes: Book VI,* Winston, 1931.

Rowland, Lewis, and Marshall, compilers, *Beckoning Road: Book VII,* Winston, 1931.

Rowland, Lewis, and Marshall, compilers, *Wings of Adventure: Book VIII,* Winston, 1931.

E. Miller, *Young Trajan,* Doubleday, Doran, 1931.

Marie Barringer, *Martin, the Goose Boy,* Doubleday, Doran, 1932.

La Rue, *Zip, the Toy Mule and Other Stories,* Macmillan, 1932.

Carlo Collodi, *Adventures of Pinocchio,* Garden City Publishing, 1932.

Johanna Spyri, *Heidi,* Garden City Publishing, 1932.

Ayer, *Picnic Book,* Macmillan, 1934.

Post Wheeler, *Albanian Wonder Tales,* Doubleday, Doran, 1936.

Barringer, *The Four and Lena,* Doubleday, Doran, 1938.

Miriam Evangeline Mason, *Susannah, the Pioneer Cow,* Macmillan, 1941.

Emilie Louise Dickey Johnson, *A Little Book of Prayers,* Viking, 1941.

Story of Jesus: A Little New Testament, Macmillan, 1942, reprinted, 1967.

Ethan Allen Cross and Elizabeth Lehr, editors, *Literature: A Series of Anthologies,* seven volumes, Macmillan, 1943-46.

The Rooster Crows: A Book of American Rhymes and Jingles, Macmillan, 1945, reprinted, Aladdin Books, 1987.

Told under the Christmas Tree, Macmillan, 1948.

Washington Irving, *Rip Van Winkle* [and] *The Legend of Sleepy Hollow,* Macmillan, 1951.

Benjamin Franklin, *Bird in the Hand: Sayings from "Poor Richard's Almanack" by the Wise American Benjamin Franklin,* Macmillan, 1951.

Eric P. Kelly, *In Clean Hay,* Macmillan, 1953.

Mason, *Miss Posy Longlegs,* Macmillan, 1955.

ILLUSTRATOR

(Under name Maud Fuller) *The Cambridge Book of Poetry for Children,* Putnam's, 1916.

The Shepherd Psalm, Macmillan, 1962.

OTHER

Contributor of illustrations to children's magazines, including *St. Nicholas, Child Life, Story Parade,* and *Jack and Jill.*

SIDELIGHTS: Maud Petersham claimed she learned more from working with her husband, Miska, than in all the years she had taken formal art training. The two met at an advertising agency in New York City, where both worked in the art department. After their marriage in 1917 they began work as free-lance illustrators of books for children. Two of the most popular books they illustrated were Olive Beaupre Miller's *Nursery Friends from France* and *Tales Told in Holland.* These volumes were part of a set published by Book House for Children that sold nearly ten thousand copies a year in the late 1920s and early 1930s.

The Petershams got their start as writers of books for children when they outlined the text and pictures for a book of their own and sent it to their editor at Doubleday. Although they thought that the book they had roughly put together would be turned over to an experienced author for rewriting, they soon learned—much to their surprise—that the book would be published just as they had planned it. *Miki,* their story of a boy who goes to Hungary, became the first book they both illustrated and wrote together. It was just one of the many books they wrote and illustrated and the even larger number of books they illustrated for other authors which, according to *Dictionary of Literary Biography* contributor Sharyl G. Smith, "established the Petershams as important, skilled craftsmen of the bookmaking art."

In an interview with Lee Bennett Hopkins appearing in *Books Are By People,* Maud Petersham recalled some of the hard work that went into the production of her and her husband's books as well as some of the lighter moments. "Miska and I had fun working on books for children," she reminisced, "for it often meant travel with sketchbook in hand. We wandered about in Palestine for three months before we made the illustrations for our book *The Christ Child.* . . . A visit to Sarasota, where the Ringling

Brothers Circus made its winter quarters, gave us the idea for *Circus Baby* . . . , and the hunting lodge where we ourselves spent one summer inspired *The Peppernuts*. . . . Our life and work [were] so closely related that anyone who knows our books knows us."

AVOCATIONAL INTERESTS: Gardening, modeling clay, embroidering pictures in yarn.

BIOGRAPHICAL/CRITICAL SOURCES:

BOOKS

Dictionary of Literary Biography, Volume 22: *American Writers for Children, 1900-1960,* Gale, 1983.
Hopkins, Lee Bennett, *Books Are By People,* Citation, 1969.
Montgomery, Elizabeth Rider, *Story behind Modern Books,* Dodd, 1949.

PERIODICALS

Horn Book, July-August, 1946.
Library Journal, July, 1946.
New York Herald Tribune Book Review, May 17, 1953.
New York Times, October 1, 1950.
Pubishers Weekly, October 20, 1934, June 22, 1946.

OBITUARIES:

PERIODICALS

New York Times, November 30, 1971.
Publishers Weekly, December 13, 1971.
Washington Post, December 3, 1971.*

* * *

PETERSHAM, Miska 1888-1960

PERSONAL: Given name, Petrezselyem Mihaly; born September 20, 1888, in Toeroekszemtmiklos, near Budapest, Hungary; died May 15, 1960; immigrated to United States, 1912, became naturalized citizen; married Maud Sylvia Fuller (author and illustrator of books for children), 1917 (died November 29, 1971); children: Miki (a son). *Education:* Attended Royal Academy of Art, Budapest, Hungary; additional study at art schools in Italy and England.

ADDRESSES: Home—Woodstock, N.Y.

CAREER: Author and illustrator of books for children. Worked in art department of International Art Service (advertising agency), New York, N.Y.

AWARDS, HONORS: Runner-up, with wife, Maud Petersham, for Caldecott Medal, 1942, for *An American ABC;* Caldecott Medal, with wife, Maud Petersham, 1946, for *The Rooster Crows: A Book of American Rhymes and Jingles.*

WRITINGS:

CO-AUTHOR AND ILLUSTRATOR WITH WIFE, MAUD PETERSHAM; JUVENILES

Miki, Doubleday, Doran, 1929, reprinted, Cadmus, 1946.
The Ark of Father Noah and Mother Noah, Doubleday, Doran, 1930.
The Christ Child, as Told by Matthew and Luke, Doubleday, Doran, 1931.
Auntie and Celia Jane and Miki, Doubleday, Doran, 1932.
The Story Book of Things We Use, Winston, 1933.
The Story Book of Houses, Winston, 1933.
The Story Book of Transportation, Winston, 1933.
The Story Book of Food, Winston, 1933.
The Story Book of Clothes, Winston, 1933.
Get-a-Way and Hary Janos, Viking, 1933.
Miki and Mary: Their Search for Treasures, Viking, 1934.
The Story Book of Wheels (also see below), Winston, 1935.
The Story Book of Ships (also see below), Winston, 1935.
The Story Book of Trains (also see below), Winston, 1935.
The Story Book of Aircraft (also see below), Winston, 1935.
The Story Book of Wheels, Ships, Trains, Aircraft (contains *The Story Book of Wheels, The Story Book of Ships, The Story Book of Trains,* and *The Story Book of Aircraft*), Winston, 1935.
The Story Book of Gold (also see below), Winston, 1935.
The Story Book of Coal (also see below), Winston, 1935.
The Story Book of Oil (also see below), Winston, 1935.
The Story Book of Iron and Steel (also see below), Winston, 1935.
The Story Book of the Earth's Treasures: Gold, Coal, Oil, Iron and Steel (contains *The Story Book of Gold, The Story Book of Coal, The Story Book of Oil,* and *The Story Book of Iron and Steel*), Winston, 1935.
The Story Book of Wheat (also see below), Winston, 1936.
The Story Book of Corn (also see below), Winston, 1936.
The Story Book of Rice (also see below), Winston, 1936.
The Story Book of Sugar (also see below), Winston, 1936, published as *Let's Learn about Sugar,* with illustrations by James E. Barry, Harvey House, 1969.
The Story Book of Foods from the Field: Wheat, Corn, Rice, Sugar (contains *The Story Book of Wheat, The Story Book of Corn, The Story Book of Rice,* and *The Story Book of Sugar*), Winston, 1936.
Joseph and His Brothers: From the Story Told in the Book of Genesis (also see below), Winston, 1938.
Moses: From the Story Told in the Old Testament (also see below), Winston, 1938, reprinted, Macmillan, 1958.
Ruth: From the Story Told in the Book of Ruth (also see below), Winston, 1938.
David: From the Story Told in the First Book of Samuel and the First Book of Kings (also see below), Winston, 1938.
Stories from the Old Testament: Joseph, Moses, Ruth, David (contains *Joseph and His Brothers, Moses, Ruth,* and *David*), Winston, 1938.
The Story Book of Cotton (also see below), Winston, 1939.
The Story Book of Wool (also see below), Winston, 1939.
The Story Book of Rayon (also see below), Winston, 1939.
The Story Book of Silk (also see below), Winston, 1939, published as *Let's Learn about Silk,* with illustrations by Barry, Harvey House, 1939.
The Story Book of Things We Wear (contains *The Story Book of Cotton, The Story Book of Wool, The Story Book of Rayon,* and *The Story Book of Silk*) Winston, 1939.
An American ABC, Macmillan, 1941, reprinted, 1966.
America's Postage Stamps: The Story of One Hundred Years of U.S. Postage Stamps, Macmillan, 1947, reprinted, 1967.
My Very First Book, Macmillan, 1948.
The Box with Red Wheels, Macmillan, 1949, reprinted, 1973.
The Circus Baby, Macmillan, 1950, reprinted, 1972.
The Story of the Presidents of the United States of America, Macmillan, 1953.
Off to Bed: Seven Stories for Wide-Awakes, Macmillan, 1954.
The Boy Who Had No Heart, Macmillan, 1955.
The Silver Mace: A Story of Williamsburg, Macmillan, 1956.
The Peppernuts, Macmillan, 1958.

ILLUSTRATOR WITH WIFE, MAUD PETERSHAM; JUVENILES

Franklin T. Baker and Ashley H. Thorndike, *Everyday Classics: Primer—Second Reader,* Macmillan, 1917.

Ada Maria Skinner and Frances Gillespy Wickes, compilers, *A Child's Own Book of Verse,* three volumes, Macmillan, 1917.

John Stuart Thomson, *Fil and Filippa: Story of Child Life in the Philippines,* Macmillan, 1917.

Mary Lydia Bolles Branch, *Guld the Cavern King,* Bookshop for Boys and Girls and Women's Educational and Industrial Union, 1918.

John Walter Wayland, *History Stories for Primary Grades,* Macmillan, 1919.

William Bowen, *Enchanted Forest,* Macmillan, 1920.

Elsie S. Eells, *Tales of Enchantment from Spain,* Harcourt, 1920.

Louise Lamprey, *Children of Ancient Britain,* Little, Brown, 1921, published as *Long Ago People: How They Lived in Britain before History Began,* Little, Brown, 1921.

Anna Cogswell Tyles, compiler, *Twenty-four Unusual Stories for Boys and Girls,* Harcourt, 1921.

Ethel May Gate, *The Broom Fairies,* Silver, Burdett, 1922.

Carl Sandburg, *Rootabaga Stories,* Harcourt, 1922, reprinted, 1974.

Charles Lamb and Mary Lamb, *Tales from Shakespeare,* Macmillan, 1923.

Mabel Guinnip La Rue, *Under the Story Tree,* Macmillan, 1923.

Sandburg, *Rootabaga Pigeons,* Harcourt, 1923.

Sisters of Mercy (St. Xavier College, Chicago), *Marquette Readers,* Macmillan, 1924.

La Rue, *The F-U-N Book,* Macmillan, 1924.

La Rue, *In Animal Land,* Macmillan, 1924, revised edition, 1929.

Margery Clark, *Poppy Seed Cakes,* Doubleday, 1924.

Inez M. Howard, Alice Hawthorne, and Mae Howard, *Language Garden: A Primary Language Book,* Macmillan, 1924.

Harriott Fansler and Isidoro Panlasigui, *Philippine National Literature,* Macmillan, 1925.

Bessie Blackstone Coleman, Willis L. Uhl, and James Fleming Hosic, *Pathway to Reading: Primer,* Silver, Burdette, 1925.

Florence C. Coolidge, *Little Ugly Face, and Other Indian Tales,* Macmillan, 1925.

Olive Beaupre Miller, translator, *Nursery Friends from France,* Book House for Children, 1925.

Miller, editor, *Tales Told in Holland,* Book House for Children, 1926.

Jean Young Ayer, *The Easy Book: First Lessons in Reading,* Macmillan, 1926.

Howard, Hawthorne, and Howard, *Number Friends: A Primary Arithmetic,* Macmillan, 1927.

Elizabeth C. Miller, *Children of the Mountain Eagle,* Doubleday, 1927.

La Rue, *The Billy Bang Book,* Macmillan, 1927.

Everyday Canadian Primer, Macmillan, 1928.

Marguerite Clement, *Where Was Bobby?,* Doubleday, Doran, 1928.

Wilhelmina Harper and Aymer Jay Hamilton, compilers, *Pleasant Pathways,* Macmillan, 1928.

Ayer, Baker, and Thorndike, *Everyday Stories,* Macmillan, 1929.

Harper and Hamilton, compilers, *Winding Roads,* Macmillan, 1929.

Harper and Hamilton, compilers, *Heights and Highways,* Macmillan, 1929.

Harper and Hamilton, compilers, *Far Away Hills,* Macmillan, 1929.

E. Miller, *Pran of Albania,* Doubleday, Doran, 1929.

Marie, Queen of Roumania, *The Magic Doll of Roumania: A Wonder Story in which East and West Do Meet,* Stokes, 1929.

La Rue, *Little Indians,* Macmillan, 1930, revised edition, 1934.

Sydney Vanferson Rowland, William Dodge Lewis, and Elizabeth J. Marshall, compilers, *New Trails: Book IV,* Winston, 1930.

Rowland, Lewis, and Marshall, compilers, *Treasure Trove: Book V,* Winston, 1930.

Rowland, Lewis, and Marshall, compilers, *Rich Cargoes: Book VI,* Winston, 1931.

Rowland, Lewis, and Marshall, compilers, *Beckoning Road: Book VII,* Winston, 1931.

Rowland, Lewis, and Marshall, compilers, *Wings of Adventure: Book VIII,* Winston, 1931.

E. Miller, *Young Trajan,* Doubleday, Doran, 1931.

Marie Barringer, *Martin, the Goose Boy,* Doubleday, Doran, 1932.

La Rue, *Zip, the Toy Mule and Other Stories,* Macmillan, 1932.

Carlo Collodi, *Adventures of Pinocchio,* Garden City Publishing, 1932.

Johanna Spyri, *Heidi,* Garden City Publishing, 1932.

Ayer, *Picnic Book,* Macmillan, 1934.

Post Wheeler, *Albanian Wonder Tales,* Doubleday, Doran, 1936.

Barringer, *The Four and Lena,* Doubleday, Doran, 1938.

Miriam Evangeline Mason, *Susannah, the Pioneer Cow,* Macmillan, 1941.

Emilie Louise Dickey Johnson, *A Little Book of Prayers,* Viking, 1941.

Story of Jesus: A Little New Testament, Macmillan, 1942, reprinted, 1967.

Ethan Allen Cross and Elizabeth Lehr, editors, *Literature: A Series of Anthologies,* seven volumes, Macmillan, 1943-46.

The Rooster Crows: A Book of American Rhymes and Jingles, Macmillan, 1945, reprinted, Aladdin Books, 1987.

Told under the Christmas Tree, Macmillan, 1948.

Washington Irving, *Rip Van Winkle* [and] *The Legend of Sleepy Hollow,* Macmillan, 1951.

Benjamin Franklin, *Bird in the Hand: Sayings from "Poor Richard's Almanack" by the Wise American Benjamin Franklin,* Macmillan, 1951.

Eric P. Kelly, *In Clean Hay,* Macmillan, 1953.

Mason, *Miss Posy Longlegs,* Macmillan, 1955.

OTHER

Contributor of illustrations to children's magazines, including *St. Nicholas, Child Life, Story Parade,* and *Jack and Jill.*

SIDELIGHTS: Dictionary of Literary Biography contributor Sharyl G. Smith presented the following summary of Maud and Miska Petersham's contributions to juvenile literature: "The Petershams were innovators. In the 1920s and 1930s, their most significant period of work, they were among the first illustrators to try new printing processes, even working with their printer in one instance to develop a new technique for making originals for photo-offset lithography, a printing process just then coming into its own commercially. Through their illustrations and book design, they helped to introduce the graphic art of Munich and Vienna, particularly that of Vienna Secession [into the United States]. With *Miki* they created what was possibly one of the first American children's picture books set in a foreign country."

BIOGRAPHICAL/CRITICAL SOURCES:

BOOKS

Dictionary of Literary Biography, Volume 22: *American Writers for Children, 1900-1960,* Gale, 1983.
Hopkins, Lee Bennett, *Books Are By People,* Citation, 1969.
Montgomery, Elizabeth Rider, *Story behind Modern Books,* Dodd, 1949.

PERIODICALS

Horn Book, July-August, 1946.
Library Journal, July, 1946.
New York Herald Tribune Book Review, May 17, 1953.
New York Times, October 1, 1950.
Pubishers Weekly, October 20, 1934, June 22, 1946.

OBITUARIES:

PERIODICALS

New York Times, May 16, 1960.
Publishers Weekly, May 23, 1960.*

* * *

PHILLIPS, Gerald M. 1928-

PERSONAL: Born December 1, 1928, in Cleveland, Ohio; son of Oskar (a laborer) and Henrietta (Sawimer) Philkofsky; married Nancy Faye Koslen, June 19, 1949; children: Dean Richard, Judith Miriam, Ellen Rose, Abigail Beth. *Education:* Case Western Reserve University, B.A., 1949, M.A., 1950, Ph.D., 1956. *Politics:* "Opposed." *Religion:* Secular Humanist.

ADDRESSES: Home—1212 South Pugh St., State College, Pa. 16802. *Office*—225 Sparks Building, Pennsylvania State University, University Park, Pa. 16802.

CAREER: Pennsylvania State University, University Park, 1964—, currently professor of speech communication; president, Communication Training and Consulting, 1966—. Consulting editor, Harper & Row Publishers, Inc.

MEMBER: Speech Communication Association, Eastern Communication Association, Pennsylvania Speech Association.

WRITINGS:

(With S. Crandell and J. Wigley) *Speech: A Course in Fundamentals,* Scott, Foresman, 1963.
Communication and the Small Group, Bobbs-Merrill, 1966, 2nd edition, 1973.
(With D. Butt, R. Dunham, and R. Brubaker) *Development of Oral Communication in the Classroom,* Bobbs-Merrill, 1969.
(With E. Murray and D. Truby) *Speech: Science-Art,* Bobbs-Merrill, 1970.
(With E. Erickson) *Interpersonal Dynamics in the Small Group,* Random House, 1971.
(With Butt and N. Metzger) *Communication and Education,* Holt, 1975.
(With Metzger) *Intimate Communication,* Allyn & Bacon, 1976.
(With J. Zolten) *Structuring Speech,* Bobbs-Merrill, 1976.
(With D. Pedersen and J. Wood) *Group Discussion: A Practical Guide for Participants and Leaders,* Houghton, 1981.
Help for Shy People, Prentice-Hall, 1981.
Communicating in Organizations, Macmillan, 1982.
(With Wood) *Communication and Human Relationships: The Study of Interpersonal Communication,* Macmillan, 1982.
(With H. Goodall) *Loving and Living,* Prentice-Hall, 1983.
Support Your Cause and Win, University of South Carolina Press, 1984.
(With Wood) *Emergent Issues in Decision Making,* Southern Illinois University Press, 1984.
(With K. Kougl and L. Kelly) *Communicating in Public and Private,* Bobbs-Merrill, 1984.
(With Zolten) *Speaking in Front of People,* Bobbs-Merrill, 1984.
(With Goodall) *Making It in the Organization,* Prentice-Hall, 1984.
(With Wood and Pedersen) *Group Discussion,* Harper, 1984.
(With J. A. Jones) *Communicating with Your Doctor,* Southern Illinois University Press, 1988.
(With N. J. Wyatt) *Studying Organizational Communications: A Case Study of the Farmers Home Administration,* Ablex, 1988.
(With Kelly and L. Lederman) *Communicating in the Workplace,* Harper, 1989.

Contributor of more than one hundred articles to speech and communication journals.

WORK IN PROGRESS: Books on credit for poor farmers, on overcoming mid-life crisis, and on sources of myths about male-female relationships.

SIDELIGHTS: Speech communications expert Gerald M. Phillips states in his book *Help for Shy People* that shyness is "not a 'defect' but a lack of skills." In a *Washington Post Book World* review of the book, Curt Suplee finds the author "wonderfully, ruthlessly practical" in his advice. " 'The only way you can see how you look to others is to examine how others respond to you,' " Suplee quotes Phillips. The author demonstrates, Suplee continues, "with breathtaking cynicism, how to get those responses—always insisting on very specific, concrete goals."

BIOGRAPHICAL/CRITICAL SOURCES:

BOOKS

Phillips, Gerald M., *Help for Shy People,* Prentice-Hall, 1981.

PERIODICALS

Washington Post Book World, October 17, 1982.

* * *

PICKERING, James H(enry) 1937-

PERSONAL: Born July 11, 1937, in New York, N.Y.; son of James Henry and Anita (Felber) Pickering; married Patricia Paterson, August 18, 1962; children: David Scott, Susan Elizabeth. *Education:* Williams College, B.A., 1959; Northwestern University, M.A., 1960, Ph.D., 1964. *Religion:* Protestant.

ADDRESSES: Home—13602 Queensbury Lane, Houston, Tex. 77079. *Office*—College of the Humanities and Fine Arts, University of Houston—University Park, Houston, Tex. 77004.

CAREER: Michigan State University, East Lansing, assistant professor, 1965-68, associate professor, 1968-72, professor of English, 1972-81, associate chairman of department and director of graduate study, 1968-75, director of Honors College, 1975-81; University of Houston, Houston, Tex., dean of College of Humanities and Fine Arts, and professor of English, 1981—.

MEMBER: College English Association (director, 1976-79; president, 1980-81), National Collegiate Honors Council (member of executive committee, 1980-83), Phi Beta Kappa, Omicron Delta Kappa, Phi Kappa Phi, Golden Key.

WRITINGS:

(Editor) Herman Melville, *Five Tales,* Dodd, 1967.
(Editor with E. Fred Carlisle) *The Harper Reader,* Harper, 1971.
(Editor) James Fenimore Cooper, *The Spy,* College & University Press, 1971.
(Compiler) *Fiction 100: An Anthology of Short Stories,* Macmillan, 1974, 5th edition, 1988.
(Editor) *The World Turned Upside Down: Poetry and Prose of the American Revolution,* Kennikat, 1975.
(Author of introduction) H. L. Barnum, *The Spy Unmasked,* Harbor Hill, 1975.
(Editor) *The City in American Literature,* Harper, 1977.
(With Jeffrey D. Hoeper) *Concise Companion to Literature,* Macmillan, 1981.
(With Hoeper) *Literature: An Anthology,* Macmillan, 1982, 2nd edition, 1986.
Mountaineering in Colorado, University of Nebraska Press, 1987.
(Editor) Joe Mills, *A Mountain Boyhood,* University of Nebraska Press, 1988.
(Editor) Enos Abijah Mills, *Wild Life on the Rockies,* University of Nebraska Press, 1988.
Spell of the Rockies, University of Nebraska Press, 1989.
(With Hoeper) *Purpose and Process,* Macmillan, 1989.

Contributor to history and literature journals.

WORK IN PROGRESS: Research on colonial, revolutionary, and early nineteenth-century American literature, Western American history and literature, the writing process, and the teaching of writing.

* * *

PINERO, Miguel (Antonio Gomez) 1946-1988

PERSONAL: Born December 19, 1946, in Gurabo, Puerto Rico; died of cirrhosis of the liver, June 16 (some sources say June 17), 1988, in New York, N.Y.; son of Miguel Angel Gomez Ramos and Adelina Pinero; married Juanita Lovette Rameize, 1977 (divorced, 1979); children: Ismael Castro (adopted). *Education:* Attended public schools in New York City; received high school equivalency diploma.

ADDRESSES: *Agent*—Niel I. Gantcher, Cohn, Glickstein, Lurie, 1370 Avenue of the Americas, New York, N.Y. 10019.

CAREER: Writer and actor. Founder of NuYorican Poets' Theatre, New York, N.Y., 1974.

AWARDS, HONORS: New York Drama Critics Circle Award, Obie Award, and Drama Desk Award, all 1974, all for *Short Eyes: The Killing of a Sex Offender by the Inmates of the House of Detention Awaiting Trial.*

WRITINGS:

PLAYS

"All Junkies," first produced in New York City, 1973.
"The Gun Tower," first produced in New York City, 1976.
"The Sun Always Shines for the Cool" (also see below), produced in New York City at 78th Street Theater Lab, 1977.
"Eulogy for a Small-Time Thief" (also see below), first produced Off-Off Broadway at Ensemble Studio Theatre, 1977.
(With Neil Harris) "Straight from the Ghetto," first produced New York City, 1977.
"Paper Toilet," first produced in Los Angeles, c. 1979.
"Cold Beer," first produced in New York City, 1979.
"NuYorican Nights at the Stanton Street Social Club," first produced in New York City at NuYorican Poets' Cafe, 1980.
"Playland Blues," first produced in New York City at Henry Street Settlement Theatre, 1980.
"A Midnight Moon at the Greasy Spoon" (two acts; also see below) first produced in New York City at Theater for the New City, 1981.

PUBLISHED PLAYS

Short Eyes: The Killing of a Sex Offender by the Inmates of the House of Detention Awaiting Trial (first produced in New York City at Theater of Riverside Church, January, 1974; produced Off-Broadway at New York Shakespeare Festival Public Theater, March, 1974; produced on Broadway at Vivian Beaumont Theatre, May, 1974; also see below), Hill & Wang, 1975.
The Sun Always Shines for the Cool, A Midnight Moon at the Greasy Spoon, Eulogy for a Small-Time Thief, Arte Publico (Houston), 1984.
Outrageous: One-Act Plays, Arte Publico, 1986.

OTHER

(Editor with Miguel Algarin) *Nuyorican Poets: An Anthology of Puerto Rican Words and Feelings,* Morrow, 1975.
"Short Eyes" (screenplay adapted from his play "Short Eyes: The Killing of a Sex Offender by the Inmates of the House of Detention Awaiting Trial"), Film League, Inc., 1977.
La Bodega Sold Dreams (poetry), Arte Publico Press, 1980.

Also author of scripts for television series, "Baretta," and unproduced and unpublished play, "The Cinderella Ballroom."

WORK IN PROGRESS: "Every Form of Refuge Has Its Price," a play set in the intensive-care unit of a hospital, to be produced at the New York Shakespeare Public Theater.

SIDELIGHTS: Joseph Papp, head of the New York Shakespeare Festival Public Theater hailed Miguel Pinero in the *New York Times* as "the first Puerto Rican playwright to really break through and be accepted as a major writer for the stage" and as "an extraordinarily original talent." During Pinero's short life, however, the playwright probably heard more condemnation than praise. Born in Puerto Rico, he and his family moved to New York City when he was four years old. A few years later, his father abandoned the family of four children who were forced to live on the streets of Manhattan for several months until their mother (who was pregnant) could find a source of income. Pinero began a life punctuated by brushes with the law, spending time in juvenile detention centers and, eventually, serving two prison terms for robbery and drug possession convictions. In 1971, he was incarcerated in the New York State prison at Ossining, known as Sing Sing, for armed robbery. His life seemed to turn around during this last term in prison, when he happened upon a playwright's workshop and wrote the first draft of what was to be his best-known play, "Short Eyes: The Killing of a Sex Offender by the Inmates of the House of Detention Awaiting Trial." "I really got hooked on theatre," Pinero told the *New York Times*'s Mel Gussow. "It was like a shot of dope."

The play, which deals with the murder of a "short eyes" (prison slang for a child molester) at the hands of his fellow inmates, was produced after Pinero was paroled from prison. It received such favorable reviews that the production was soon moved to Broadway from the small church theater where it had opened. Critics hailed Pinero as a bright new face on the theatrical scene and saw the play as brutally realistic. In *Newsweek* Jack Kroll, for example, wrote: " 'Short Eyes' needs absolutely no apology—it isn't occupational therapy and it isn't a freak show; it's an authentic, powerful theatrical piece that tells you more about the anti-universe of prison life than any play outside the work of Jean Genet." *People* contributor Leroy Aarons noted: "It was a smash. Pinero's unsentimental drama in which black, Puerto Rican and white prisoners systematically destroy a fellow inmate accused of molesting a child . . . sizzled like a dynamite fuse to an explosive conclusion." In a *Contemporary Dramatists* essay, Gaynor F. Bradish calls the play "the most ruthlessly exciting drama with a prison setting so far produced by the American theater. Harrowing, brutal, yet suffused with a transforming, unsettling sensuality, it succeeds in imparting a special kind of understated, deliberately minimal poetic beauty and compassion to the rather terrifying events it dramatizes."

Pinero was surprised by his rapid success. "Here I was with $60 one day and all of a sudden somebody was giving me $15,000," he told Aarons. "I was being asked to lecture at Princeton, at Rutgers, at Pratt Institute. Here I have no education whatsoever and I am working as a mentor to the top students at Pratt Institute. What the hell am I doin' here?" Further commercial success alluded the playwright, however, and when the film version of "Short Eyes" opened in 1976 Pinero was fighting conviction for an arrest for armed robbery, and possession of drugs and a dangerous weapon.

BIOGRAPHICAL/CRITICAL SOURCES:

BOOKS

Contemporary Dramatists, 4th edition, St. James Press, 1988.
Contemporary Literary Criticism, Volume 4, Gale, 1974.

PERIODICALS

New Republic, April 20, 1974.
Newsweek, April 8, 1974.
New York Times, March 27, 1974, May 5, 1974, January 23, 1977, September 28, 1977, September 28, 1979, April 27, 1981.
People, November 14, 1977.
Times (London), June 27, 1987.
Village Voice, March 28, 1974.

OBITUARIES:

PERIODICALS

Chicago Tribune, June 19, 1988.
Los Angeles Times, June 18, 1988.
New York Times, June 18, 1988.
Times (London), June 17, 1988.
Washington Post, June 16, 1988.*

* * *

PLAIN, Belva 1919-

PERSONAL: Born October 9, 1919, in New York, N.Y.; daughter of Oscar and Eleanor Offenberg; married Irving Plain (a physician), June 14, 1941 (died December, 1982); children: three. *Education:* Graduated from Barnard College.

ADDRESSES: *Home*—New Jersey. *Agent*—Dorothy Olding, Harold Ober Associates, Inc., 40 East 49th St., New York, N.Y. 10017.

CAREER: Writer.

WRITINGS:

NOVELS

Evergreen (Literary Guild selection), Delacorte, 1978.
Random Winds, Delacorte, 1980.
Eden Burning, Delacorte, 1982.
Crescent City, Delacorte, 1984.
The Golden Cup, Delacorte, 1987.
Tapestry, Delacorte, 1988.
Blessings, Delacorte, 1989.

OTHER

Contributor of several dozen short stories to periodicals, including *McCall's, Good Housekeeping, Redbook,* and *Cosmopolitan.*

WORK IN PROGRESS: A novel, "the completion of the story begun in *Evergreen.*"

SIDELIGHTS: Best-selling author Belva Plain began her successful writing career by writing formula fiction for women's magazines in the 1940s. *Cosmopolitan* and *Good Housekeeping* printed her stories of women in love who toyed with the idea of having extramarital affairs, but chose to honor their vow in the end. Her enthusiasm for writing this kind of story waned in comparison with the activities of family life, so for about twelve years, she wrote almost nothing for publication. However, she remained an avid reader. Jewish characters in novels she read during that time were slight variations on stereotypes that she found repugnant and inaccurate, and by the 1950s, she was moved to provide an alternative view of Jewish American life in her first book-length work. *Evergreen*—the story of a young immigrant maid who falls in love with her boss's son—became the first of many best sellers for Plain, of which there are more than eleven million copies in a dozen languages.

Unlike the dominating, hysterical Jewish mothers of contemporary myth, Plain's female characters are good mothers, discrete lovers, and emotionally strong. As capable in business as in domestic affairs, they make the best of unchangeable circumstances, finding fulfillment despite repeated disappointment. They often have to overcome the problems of immigration and other challenges related to their heritage, yet they elicit the interest of many readers outside the ethnic circle. "Forbidden love is all over the more than 2,000 collective pages of Plain's books," explains Laura Kavesh in the *Chicago Tribune.* Time and again, notes Kavesh, "Plain characters march through life courageously and usually with great success—but bearing private, searing aches over love just out of reach, the kind that sneaks along behind its slaves forever, jumping out in front of them now and again to shake things up."

Plain's novels also take readers to other places and times. *Eden Burning* takes place on a Caribbean island, and *Crescent City* goes back to the Civil War era. "It's all here," writes Gay Courter in the *Washington Post,* "moss and mansions, languid afternoons and clandestine evenings, repressed old maids and irresistable quadroons, the glamour and gore of war, chance encounters and missed opportunities." Furthermore, the novel uncovers little-known details about Jewish life during that period of American history. For example, Jews stood on both sides of the conflict over slavery, but only those on the Confederate side were allowed to have chaplains until Lincoln learned of this inequity among the Northern troops. The surprise ending, remarks Courter, lends a seldom-seen view of "American Jewry and southern history" that incites readers to research further on historical figures of the Civil War era.

Following the same sense of fair play that inspired *Evergreen,* Plain takes a second look at Anna's life in *The Golden Cup,* this time to fully explore her story from Paul's point of view. *Tapestry,* the third book in the Werner family saga, looks at the lives of Anna's grandchildren. The chronicle is informed by the author's own family experiences, she told *CA:* "I had always been curious about my own grandmother, who came here from Europe at the age of sixteen. Such courage! I think of her still saying a final goodbye and sailing toward an unknown world so long ago. She never saw her people again. Of course, all that is a common American adventure: the loneliness, the struggles and failures—and sometimes, the rise to shining affluence. *Evergreen* is everybody's story whether he be of Irish, Italian, Polish, or any other stock." Kavesh reports that readers admire the portraits of Jewish womanhood and family values in Plain's books. When asked to explain their popularity, Plain told Kavesh, "I think I show real people and a real understanding of human nature, how people function and react to their environment. And there's a good story line."

MEDIA ADAPTATIONS: Evergreen was produced as a miniseries by the National Broadcasting Co. in 1985.

CA INTERVIEW

CA interviewed Belva Plain by telephone on March 1, 1989, at her home in Short Hills, New Jersey.

CA: There was a long period between your short stories, written and published during the forties and fifties, and the novels, which began with the publication of Evergreen *in 1978. Did you give up the writing altogether during that time?*

PLAIN: Oh, no. I did a lot of writing, but I didn't publish anything. I never finished anything; I had lots of family obligations and some problems with a child, and I just didn't feel that I had the energy to commit myself to anything big at that time.

CA: It seems quite a leap from the long period of inactivity as a writer to such a big novel as Evergreen, *and a first novel at that. How did it happen?*

PLAIN: The magazine stories became fewer and farther between because they were not really what I wanted to do. I don't say this to denigrate them, but I wanted to write something deeper and more significant.

CA: Had you grown up wanting to write?

PLAIN: Yes, I had. I had always written for school magazines, and I was editor of the school paper. In fact, I did start to publish very soon. Right after college I married and sold my first story; I think I was twenty- five.

CA: According to Laura Kavesh in the Chicago Tribune, *you also started writing novels with some firm ideas about what you didn't want to do, what you'd seen too much of in other books. Would you comment on that?*

PLAIN: I wanted to avoid stereotypes. I think so many novelists stereotype their characters: the Jewish mother is a demanding woman who has a heart attack every time her children want to do something that she doesn't like; the Irish family always has a perennial drunk; the Italians are always burdened with somebody who's in the Mafia. These things get to be sickening after a while. Even the people we call WASPs, white Anglo-Saxon Protestants—a term I don't like—are stereotyped. The term is stupid, to begin with; if you're Anglo-Saxon, you're white. Also it's a pejorative term, because Anglo-Saxons are usually portrayed as very uptight people who never show any emotion. That's the sort of thing I resented in fiction.

CA: I'm interested in the research you must do for your books. Not only do you set the larger scene, the place and time, but you provide so many details from everyday life, down to food and clothing and furniture. How do you go about gathering all this information?

PLAIN: That's really the fun part of the writing. I enjoy this much more than I enjoyed doing research in school and college, when I had to. What I like about studying history is not just learning of great events, but learning what living was like, how people went about getting along from one day to the next. I learn by reading, reading, and reading. I have lots of books. I keep things forever; I have books that were given to me when I was in my teens—books on costumes, for instance. When I did *Crescent City,* the book set in New Orleans before and during the Civil War, I used my costume books, so that I could see exactly what the ladies wore at a wedding, for instance. I could glean little things such as the fact that engagement rings at that time always contained a ruby—not a diamond, but a ruby. Second-hand books can be great. Going back to *Crescent City,* I got a lot of information when I was in New Orleans by going to second-hand book stores and finding books written shortly after the Civil War, so contemporary that you got the feeling of the time and all the details. I did the same for *Eden Burning,* the book that was written about a Caribbean island. I read the local newspapers—not newspapers brought onto the island, but the local weekly sheets that tell what's going on. That's the fun part of it for me. There are so many sources—museums too, as well as books.

CA: The clothes are especially fun to read about. Your skill in dressing your characters tells the reader so much about them. I think for example, of Mimi in a dress with an Elizabethan-type collar.

PLAIN: Yes. I try to convey a lot with the clothes—not only from a historical point of view, but from that of the character. You know from your acquaintances that clothes say so much about people. Paul's wife was a very austere and proper lady. One of his paramours, Leah, liked flash. She was in the clothing business; she was up to date and looked it.

CA: Leah is a great character, by the way. She's able to get over the bumps and keep going, to make the very best of even the toughest things.

PLAIN: All the characters are composites, of course. But we have all known women who just have a flair for clothes, who know how to put things together even when they don't have much money—how to wear a scarf, how to make do. Then when they do get some money, they really produce an effect! Leah was like that.

CA: You've created some vivid characters, among them Anna Friedman, who began in Evergreen; *Hennie Roth, one of the stars of* The Golden Cup; *Miriam, from* Crescent City; *Kate Tarbox in* Eden Burning. *Do they go through a long process of development in your mind before you first put them down on paper?*

PLAIN: They do. I think this is what happens: there is a kernel, something that strikes me when I know a person very well, or—paradoxically, I can just see a person I don't really know and something flashes toward me. After I get that start, that impetus, then I start to put my mind to work and think about how that person would react in different situations. How would a certain person react to the death of a child, for example? You've seen the person, or known the person, and you can say, this one would be stoic and not let anyone see her cry; or, this one would have a total collapse. That's true also of less drastic events, of things that happen every day. But I have to get the start, to see somebody or know somebody who gives me that beginning.

CA: It strikes me that most of your star characters are very much outsiders in one sense or another, having to come to terms with their differences from the society around them in order to live in it comfortably. Is that a theme you're conscious of in creating them?

PLAIN: It's very interesting to hear you say that, because I truly am not aware of planning to create such characters. Maybe it says something about me that I don't know about myself!

CA: Enough of your characters care deeply for animals to make me suspect that's taken from life. Are you a great animal lover?

PLAIN: Yes, yes, and yes. Right now I'm most interested in People for the Ethical Treatment of Animals. They've done a lot of things that need to be done. And of course I care about all the humane societies and all the local homes for stray animals. I'll tell you something that made a great impression on me. I was reading Milan Kundera's book *The Unbearable Lightness of Being,* a very different book, and there was a sentence at the end of it that brought me up short. It said that the ultimate test of the morality of any human being is the way he treats animals. There's no reward in treating an animal well. With people you can get love in return; you can get many other things from people, as we all know—money, admiration, power, influence, everyday pleasure from their company. When you're nice to people, you're making an investment, in a sense. But an animal can't do anything for you, and he's totally dependent on you. It says such dreadful things about us, but I read that on the Galapagos Islands, where animals are not accustomed to seeing people, they're not afraid. In other places of the world, animals must have told each other, "Watch out for the two-legged ones." You're right, there are animals in all my stories, usually a dog.

CA: Has your work on settings taken you to all the places that have figured in your stories?

PLAIN: I've been to all the European settings. Yes, I've never really written about any place that I haven't seen, because I think that's artificial; it's phony. Readers are intelligent. They can sense when you've made something up. Even for the one book that took place far back in history, a time I couldn't have known firsthand, the Civil War, still I went through Louisiana plantations that have been restored and opened to the public. You can see from them exactly how people lived—the wash basins in the bedrooms, the chamber pots, everything as it was. I always do write about what I have actually seen.

CA: For the reader, your stories unwind and interconnect—sometimes from book to book—in a way that seems quite natural, but I suspect this results from a lot of careful planning on your part. How much do you know about your characters or your story before you start writing?

PLAIN: Everything. After I did *Evergreen,* I did some books that were not about that family. I wrote *Random Winds,* for example, which was about a doctor in a farming community in upstate New York, where I had also lived for a while. But I was so involved with the characters in *Evergreen,* I finally thought, I will tell about Paul's side of the story. *Evergreen* only tells about Anna; Paul is a two-dimensional figure who comes into her life, but you don't know anything about him from that first book. So I decided to do *The Golden Cup* and tell something about Paul and his family. And then I continued with *Tapestry,* telling about the next generation. Then I left them and did something entirely different. The title of that is *Blessings,* and it will be out in August of 1989. It has nothing to do with the characters who began in *Evergreen.* I'm working now on another story, a conclusion for that family.

Yes, I do know all about my characters and my plot is clear in my mind before I write the first word. Actually, I could write the end before I start the opening chapter.

CA: It must be fun for you as their creator to live with those characters as they go on from book to book.

PLAIN: It really is. That's probably a reflection of my reading; I've always liked books, especially the Victorians, that start with a person almost at birth and show you his growth, like a vine that spreads and puts out tendrils. You see people grow up, marry—or not marry!—and go through a whole series of events, reach out to other areas and other people; yet you always have the background of childhood in your mind, so you know the character quite thoroughly and know how he's going to react to whatever happens. I enjoy reading books like that, and I enjoy writing them.

CA: Do you happen to have a favorite among your characters?

PLAIN: That truly is a hard question to answer, but if you press me I'll say perhaps Paul, from *Evergreen, The Golden Cup* and *Tapestry.* He really is a man to fall in love with, I think any woman would agree.

CA: In your article "A Valentine to Love," in the February 16, 1988, issue of Woman's Day, *you lamented the coldness and lack of commitment in many of today's relationships between men and women. Do you believe, as many people do, that there's a backlash forming, a return to marriage and family?*

PLAIN: I've read about it, but I think it's too early to tell yet. I don't think the divorce rate has dropped at all, has it? But maybe that will be a self-fulfilling prophecy; I hope so. Children are always the victims of divorce. I've been reading a new book, a study of children of divorce ten and twenty years after the fact. It shows that children may look as if they have recovered nicely, but that years later all the pain comes back. For instance, a young woman falling in love is afraid that love won't last, because of what happened to her parents. Five divorces out of ten marriages—it's really shocking. I don't mean that some marriages shouldn't be dissolved—of course they should. Some should never have taken place, and the sooner you get out of them, the better. But not half of them; I don't believe it! I have a friend who's a psychiatrist and he told me that very often women come into his office—maybe men would do the same if they went as frequently—and they say, "Looking back, I think I would have done better to stay in my marriage. It really wasn't all that bad, and there's a very cold, uncaring world out there." It's too easy to leave a marriage now; there's no stigma attached. When divorce was unthinkable, I think people tried to work things out; they got over the hump. They might have been terribly angry, but since there was nothing they could do but stay, they bore with their anger and they got over it. Now they don't give things a chance. They just walk away.

CA: For all our liberation as women and our success in the workplace, many women who choose to have families and careers are obviously having a hard time meeting the demands of both. What are your feelings about this problem?

PLAIN: I think it's insoluble because of biology. It's just plain hard for women, and there's no sense saying it's easy. You either have to say to yourself, I'm going to do both and I'm going to be exhausted, or else you have to make a choice and say, I'm going to have children and delay my ambitions, or I'm going to forge ahead—as a lawyer, let's say—and become senior partner, but I'm not going to have children. In some few cases there's enough so that a woman can go ahead and become senior partner and hire wonderful people to take her place in the home. Of course that's not the same as having Mommy at home, but it can be very good. You have to have a great deal of money to live that way and it's not something that can apply to more than a fraction of a percent of women. For most people it's tough, getting up extra early in the morning to rush the child off to nursery or day care; and if the child is sick, you have to stay home and the job is affected. Just tough, but worth it to many women and a necessity for many, too.

CA: Do you have a lot of contact with your readers?

PLAIN: I get many, many fine letters. I'm very fortunate: I can count on my fingers over all the years those letters that haven't been friendly. Some of them were very moving too—especially with regard to this last little article you mentioned, the one in *Woman's Day.* I got a letter that was so sad, from a woman who said that she was about to give up because her husband had had a complete psychiatric breakdown. She said that she was thinking of committing suicide; she could no longer bear the strain, the pity for him and for herself. While I find it hard to believe, she said that when she read my article, it gave her some hope. That letter was written last year. Recently I heard from her again; she told me that things were much, much better, and she thought I would like to know that. It's very moving, the power of the word.

CA: Can you say more about Blessings?

PLAIN: Yes, I can. I think it will be a timely story. The idea for it came because I'd been reading about adoptees, how so many of them are now trying to break through the fence of laws that up to now has prevented them from finding out who they are. There are three sides to the problem, as I see it: there's the adoptee, the parent or parents who brought him into the world, and then the people who gave the child a home and became his parents. I've written a novel about that. It's not a tract; it's just a story, my imagination working on certain situations, and how people are affected.

CA: What hopes do you have for your books when they go out to readers? What would you like people to get from them?

PLAIN: Of course I'd love to help readers as the woman whom I mentioned earlier was helped. But that was most unusual. In the main I would say: some thought and some pleasure. Entertainment, too, because a novelist is primarily an entertainer. Even the most distinguished authors—the Tolstoys, the all-time world-wide greats—are really entertainers. They're storytellers. Of course, they are also more than that. In my very modest way, making no comparison with the great ones, I would still like to help readers to do some thinking about relationships, how people can work out their problems. Perhaps some of my characters can relate to the reader's problems. I have, I'm glad to say, had some letters from people who've said that certain things in my books have affected their relationships. Maybe they'd had a quarrel, and something I had written had made them look more deeply into their own motivations. Things like that. So I would say that I'd like my readers to get some pleasure from my books and to do some thinking about life, as well.

BIOGRAPHICAL/CRITICAL SOURCES:

PERIODICALS

Best Sellers, August, 1978, August, 1980, September, 1982, November, 1984, December, 1986.
Books, February, 1988.
Chicago Tribune, October 12, 1984.
New York Times Book Review, July 30, 1978, August 22, 1982, October 7, 1984.
Publishers Weekly, May 21, 1979, March 28, 1980, March 18, 1988.
Washington Post, September 28, 1984.
Woman's Day, February 16, 1988.

—Interview by Jean W. Ross

* * *

POLA
See WATSON, Pauline

* * *

POTEET, G(eorge) Howard 1935-

PERSONAL: Born March 31, 1935, in Baltimore, Md.; son of G. Howard (a computer operator) and Catherine (Aro) Poteet; married Hilda Klock, January 21, 1956 (divorced, 1961); married Frances Rosenthal (a teacher), October 3, 1961 (divorced, 1983); married Anna Cheng, October 21, 1983; children: Cynthia, Christopher, Jennifer. *Education:* Shippensburg State College, B.S., 1961; Columbia University, M.A., 1964, Prof.Dip., 1965, Ed.D., 1971.

ADDRESSES: Home—21 Princeton St., Nutley, N.J. 07110. *Office*—Department of English, Essex County College, 303 University Ave., Newark, N.J. 07102.

CAREER: English teacher in public schools in Pennsylvania and New Jersey, 1957-68; Essex County College, Newark, N.J., associate professor, 1968-74, professor of English, 1974—, head of department, 1968-75. President, G. Howard Poteet, Inc. (publishing firm). Film and linguistics consultant to schools and businesses; educational consultant to various home study and correspondence schools.

MEMBER: National Council of Teachers of English (chairman of committee on film study), Modern Language Association of America, National Education Association.

AWARDS, HONORS: Award of Excellence, Sixteenth Annual Exhibition of *Communications Arts* (magazine), 1975, for *Tom Swift and His Electric English Teacher.*

WRITINGS:

Film Criticism in Popular American Periodicals: 1933-1967, Revisionist Press, 1971.
Sentence Strategies: Writing for College, Harcourt, 1971.
The Compleat Guide to Film Study, National Council of Teachers of English, 1972.
Tom Swift and His Electric English Teacher, Pflaum-Standard, 1974.
Radio!, Pflaum-Standard, 1975.
Death and Dying: A Bibliography, Whitston Publishing, 1976, supplement, 1978.

How to Live in Your Van and Love It!, Trail-R-Club of America, 1976.
Published Radio, TV, and Film Scripts: A Bibliography, Whitston Publishing, 1976.
Workbench Guide to Tape Recorder Servicing, Parker Publishing, 1976.
The Complete Guide to Making Money, G. Howard Poteet, Inc., 1976.
Treasure Hunting in the City, Ram Publishing, 1977.
Your Career in Chiropractic, Richard Rosen, 1977, revised edition, 1985.
Suicide, Whitston Publishing, 1978.
Complete Guide to the Use and Maintenance of Hand and Power Tools, Parker Publishing, 1978.
There's a School in Your Mailbox, National Home Study Council, 1979, revised edition, 1980.
Complete Illustrated Guide to Basic Carpentry, Parker Publishing, 1980.
Professional Photography, SCI, 1986.
We Succeeded through Home Study, National Home Study Council, 1986.
Powerboating, PC, 1987.

Author of tape-and-text series "The English Program," Williamsville Publishing, 1976; also author of numerous other lessons, tapes, and texts for home study schools in photography, locksmithing, and building trades. Contributor of poetry, short stories, and articles to numerous magazines and newspapers, including *English Journal, Media and Methods, Reading Instruction Journal, Mechanix Illustrated,* and *New York Times.* Member of editorial board, *New Jersey Audio-Visual News;* contributing editor, *Film Journal Newsletter;* editor, *College English Notes* and *Printing Trade Secrets* newsletter; editor in chief, *How to Make Extra Money Newsletter.*

WORK IN PROGRESS: The Complete Guide to Writing Well with a Computer Using Videocameras.

SIDELIGHTS: G. Howard Poteet told *CA:* "I have always wanted to write. When I was a young child, I took delight in writing stories. In the seventh grade I wrote a short story a week. My first published article, a description of winter in the country, was published during the summer between when I was in the eighth and ninth grades. I wrote for my high school papers in various schools that I attended and wrote for the newspaper and literary magazine while attending Shippensburg State College.

"However, I have always wanted to write for money and even today, I think that that is what proves a writer's worth. Even Shakespeare wrote for money, didn't he? Fame and all the trappings are less important than being paid cash for words. I know that most of my colleagues who are scholars will disagree (for after all, I have spent my life as a scholar—of sorts and I have the degree or union card, made it to become a full professor—tenured, of course, and have been active in scholarly organizations). However, I fail to see why writers shouldn't be proud of the fact that someone is willing to pay to read what they've written."

AVOCATIONAL INTERESTS: Photography, bicycling, antiques, electronics.

* * *

POZZETTA, George Enrico 1942-

PERSONAL: Born October 29, 1942, in Great Barrington, Mass.; son of Attilio L. (an electrician) and Mary (Ciolina) Pozzetta; married Sandra Magdalenski (a teacher), September 17, 1966; children: James, Adrienne. *Education:* Providence College, B.A., 1964, M.A., 1965; University of North Carolina, Ph.D., 1971. *Religion:* Roman Catholic.

ADDRESSES: Home—2624 Northwest 34th Terrace, Gainesville, Fla. 32605. *Office*—Department of History, University of Florida, Gainesville, Fla. 32611.

CAREER: Providence College, Providence, R.I., instructor in history, 1965-66; University of Maryland, Far East Division, Can Rahn Bay, South Vietnam, instructor in history, 1968; University of Florida, Gainesville, assistant professor, 1971-76, associate professor, beginning 1976, currently professor. *Military service:* U.S. Army, 1966-68; served in Vietnam; became first lieutenant; received Bronze Star.

MEMBER: American Historical Association (chair, Marraro Prize committee), Organization of American Historians, American Italian Historical Association (member of executive board, 1976—; president, 1978-80), Immigration History Society (member of executive board, 1982-84; chair, nominating committee, 1983-84), Southern Historical Association (member of membership committee, 1982-84).

AWARDS, HONORS: Florida Endowment for the Humanities grant, 1974 and 1981; American Philosophical Society grant, 1978; teacher of the year, University College, University of Florida, 1978; Cavaliere nell'Ordine al Merito della Republica Italiana, 1984; Theodore Saloutos Award, 1987, for best book in immigration history.

WRITINGS:

(Editor with David R. Colburn) *America and the New Ethnicity,* Kennikat, 1978.
(Contributor) Robert F. Harney, editor, *Italian Immigrant Women in North America,* Multicultural History Society, 1978.
(Contributor) J. H. Shofner and L. V. Ellsworth, editors, *Ethnic Minorities in Gulf Coast Society,* Gulf Coast History and Humanities Conference, 1979.
Pane e Lavoro: The Italian American Working Class, Multicultural History Society, 1980.
(Contributor) Harney, editor, *Little Italies in North America,* Multicultural History Society, 1981.
Reform and Reformers in the Progressive Era, Greenwood Press, 1983.
(With G. R. Mormino) *The Immigrant World of Ybor City: Italians and Their Latin Neighbors in Tampa, Florida, 1885-1985,* University of Illinois Press, 1987.
(With Randall Miller) *Shades of the Sunbelt: Essays on Race, Ethnicity, and the Urban South,* Greenwood Press, 1988.

Chairman of editorial board of "Social Science Monograph Series," University of Florida, 1981—; senior consultant for *Encyclopedia of Southern Culture.* Contributor to history and ethnic studies journals.

WORK IN PROGRESS: A study of the impact of World War II on America's major European ethnic groups.

SIDELIGHTS: George Enrico Pozzetta told *CA:* "Ethnicity is one of America's most important, but least understood, social forces. This 'nation of immigrants' has often assumed that the experience of immigration would ultimately not matter, that assimilation would do its work quickly and efficiently. And yet, millions of Americans still find relevance in their ethnic background and draw from the reservoir of self-understanding and self-confidence that resides there. Both my professional and personal lives have been shaped by these facts. The realization that both diversity and uniformity can exist together first crystallized in the late 1960s, during the resurgence of interest in ethnicity taking place at that time (the so-called 'New Ethnicity'). To the extent that American society can recognize its long-standing abilities to harmonize the particular with the universal, then to that extent will ours be a healthier and more secure nation. Such realizations are all the more important today, when newcomers continue to seek our shores in ever greater numbers."

* * *

PRAWER, S(iegbert) S(alomon) 1925-

PERSONAL: Surname is pronounced Prah-ver; born February 15, 1925, in Cologne, Germany (now West Germany); came to England, 1939; naturalized British citizen, 1945; son of Marcus (owner of a clothing business) and Eleonora (Cohn) Prawer; married Helga Alice Schaefer, December 25, 1949; children: David Marcus (died, 1968), Daniela Sylvia, Deborah Joy, Jonathan Roy. *Education:* Attended Jesus College, Cambridge; Christ's College, Cambridge, B.A., 1947, M.A., 1950; University of Birmingham, Ph.D., 1953; Cambridge University, Litt.D., 1962; Oxford University, M.A. and D.Litt., 1969.

ADDRESSES: Home—9 Hawkswell Gardens, Oxford OX2 7EX, England.

CAREER: University of Birmingham, Birmingham, England, assistant lecturer, 1948-51, lecturer, 1951-58, senior lecturer in German, 1958-63; University of London, Westfield College, London, England, professor of German, 1964-69, Taylor Professor of German Language and Literature, 1969-86, professor emeritus, 1986—; free-lance graphic artist, 1986—. Visiting professor at numerous colleges and universities, including Harvard University, 1968, Hamburg University, 1969, and Australian National University, 1980. Queen's College, Oxford, fellow, 1969—, Dean of Degrees, 1978—; resident fellow of Knox College, Dunedin, New Zealand, 1976; honorary fellow, London University Institute of Germanic Studies, 1987. Honorary director of University of London Institute of Germanic Studies, 1966-68; member of board, Leo Baeck Institute.

MEMBER: British Comparative Literature Association (president, 1984-87), English Goethe Society (member of council, 1964-84), Conference of University Teachers of German in Great Britain and Northern Island, Modern Language Association of America (honorary member).

AWARDS, HONORS: Goethe Medal, 1973; Isaac Deutscher Memorial Prize, 1977, for *Karl Marx and World Literature;* D.Phil., Cologne University, 1985; Friedrich Gundolf Prize, the German Academy, 1986; D.Litt., University of Birmingham, 1988.

WRITINGS:

German Lyric Poetry, Routledge & Kegan Paul, 1952.
Moerike und seine Leser (title means "Moerike and His Readership"), E. Klett (Stuttgart), 1960.
Heine's "Buch der Lieder": A Critical Study, Edward Arnold, 1960.
Heine: The Tragic Satirist, Cambridge University Press, 1961.
(Editor and translator) *The Penguin Book of Lieder,* Penguin, 1964.
(Editor with V. J. Riley) *Theses in Germanic Studies: 1962-67,* Institute of Germanic Studies, University of London, 1969.
(Editor with R. H. Thomas and Leonard W. Forster) *Essays in German Language, Culture, and Society,* Institute of Germanic Studies, University of London, 1969.
(Editor) *The Romantic Period in Germany,* Schocken, 1970.
(Editor) *Seventeen Modern German Poets,* Oxford University Press, 1971.
Comparative Literary Studies: An Introduction, Duckworth, 1973, Barnes & Noble, 1974.
Karl Marx and World Literature, Oxford University Press, 1976.
Caligari's Children: The Film as Tale of Terror, Oxford University Press, 1978.
Heine's Jewish Comedy: A Study of His Portraits of Jews and Judaism, Oxford University Press, 1983.
Frankenstein's Island: England and the English in the Writings of Heinrich Heine, Cambridge University Press, 1986.

Contributor of numerous articles on German, English, and comparative literature to scholarly journals, including *Cambridge Journal, German Review, Modern Language Review,* and *Modern Philology.* Co-editor, *Oxford German Studies,* 1971-75, and *Anglica Germanica,* 1973-79.

WORK IN PROGRESS: Graphic artwork.

SIDELIGHTS: German-born S. S. Prawer "is the doyen of [Heinrich] Heine scholars in England," as *Times Literary Supplement* contributor Theodore Ziolkowski describes him, and has written several illuminating works on the nineteenth-century German poet and journalist. Prawer's most renowned inquiry is *Heine's Jewish Comedy: A Study of His Portraits of Jews and Judaism,* in which he investigates the role that Heine's Jewish background played in his writing. Prawer "has written a masterful study of the ambiguities attendant on the formation of [Heine's Jewish] identity," notes Sander L. Gilman in his *Times Literary Supplement* review. While other analyses "tend to isolate the question of [Heine's] Jewish identity from the totality of his literary production," continues Gilman, "Prawer manages to integrate it into an analysis of Heine's work as a whole." The scholar uses numerous sources on Heine as the basis of his examination; as Gabriele Annan details in the *New York Review of Books,* Prawer examines Heine's famous journalistic pieces on France and Germany, "the original as well as the final version of each; he also pays attention to all Heine's rejected or unpublished output in verse and prose. These labors," asserts the critic, "enable him to chart every change in Heine's perpetually vacillating attitude to Jewishness, and to come to some very interesting conclusions."

Gilman similarly praises the professor's "extraordinarily productive" method, remarking that "by limiting the field of his investigation to Heine's explicit statements about Jews and Judaism, [Prawer] avoids the pitfall of seeing all of Heine's works as unmediated response to his Jewishness. In this way a pattern emerges which sheds much light on Heine's political and ethical stance in contexts seemingly remote from the question of Jewishness." *Observer* contributor John Gross, who calls Prawer "a critic of rare penetration, equally at home . . . in English and German and traditional Jewish culture," concurs with this assessment: "[Prawer] also has an admirable sense of proportion: however deeply he pursues his chosen theme, he never forgets that it was only one strand in the pattern of Heine's work, and that to concentrate on it is inevitably to give it more prominence than it had in the original design." "Prawer's study may serve as the paradigm for future studies of the role which literary production plays in the formation of ethnic identity," states Gilman, adding that "Prawer's book is a milestone in the study of how aesthetic responses interact with a writer's sense of his ethnic identity." *Heine's Jewish Comedy,* he continues, "is also the best introduction we have to Heine's work as a reflection of the poet's life and world, an 'inner biography' written with intelligence and great subtlety." Gross likewise concludes that Prawer's analysis "is an important book, which does full justice to its theme—and that means both that it is a work of solid learning, and that it is written with an unprofessorial freshness and sparkle."

AVOCATIONAL INTERESTS: Portrait drawing.

BIOGRAPHICAL/CRITICAL SOURCES:

PERIODICALS

New York Review of Books, February 16, 1984.
Observer, August 14, 1983.
Times Literary Supplement, February 1, 1974, February 4, 1977, December 2, 1983, August 21, 1987.

* * *

PREVERT, Jacques (Henri Marie) 1900-1977

PERSONAL: Born February 4, 1900, in Neuilly-sur-Seine, France; died April 11, 1977, in Omonville-La-Petite, France; son of Andre (a clerk) and Suzanne (Catusse) Prevert; married Simone Dienne, April 30, 1925 (marriage ended); married Janine Tricotet, March 4, 1947. *Education:* Educated in Paris, France.

ADDRESSES: Home—Cite Veron, 82 Blvd. de Clichy, 75018 Paris, France.

CAREER: Poet, screenwriter, and dramatist. Exhibitions of his collages held in Paris, 1957 and 1982, and in Antibes, 1963. Appeared as an actor in several of his films.

AWARDS, HONORS: Grand Prix from Societe des Auteurs et Compositeurs Dramatiques, 1973; Grand Prix National from *Cinema,* 1975.

WRITINGS:

IN ENGLISH TRANSLATION

Paroles (poetry), Editions du Point du Jour, 1945, revised and augmented edition, Gallimard, 1966, translation by Lawrence Ferlinghetti published as *Selections from 'Paroles,'* City Lights, 1958.
(With Albert Lamorisse) *Bim, le petit ane* (juvenile), Guilde du Livre, 1951, translation by Bette Swados and Harvey Swados published as *Bim, the Little Donkey,* Doubleday, 1973.
(Author of introduction) *Couleur de Paris,* illustrated with photographs by Peter Cornelius, La Bibliotheque des Arts, 1961, translation by Jonathan Griffin and Margaret Shenfield published as *Paris in Colour,* Thames & Hudson, 1962, Bramhall House, 1963.
(Author of preface) *Les Halles: L'Album du coer de Paris,* illustrations by Romain Urhausen, Editions des Deux-Mondes, 1963, translation published as *Les Halles: The Stomach of Paris,* Atlantis Books, 1964, published as *Les Halles de Paris* (French, German, and English text), Moos, 1980.
Prevert II (anthology), translation by Teo Savory, Unicorn Press, 1967.
Les Enfants du paradis (screenplay), Lorrimer Publishing, 1968, translation by Dinah Brooke published as *Children of Paradise,* Simon & Schuster, 1968.
Le Jour se leve (screenplay), translation by Brooke and Nicola Hayden, Simon & Schuster, 1970.
To Paint the Portrait of a Bird—Pour faire le portrait d'un oiseau (juvenile; bilingual French/English text), translation by Ferlinghetti, Doubleday, 1971.
Words for All Seasons: Selected Poems, translation by Teo Savory, Unicorn Press, 1979.
Blood and Feathers: Selected Poems of Jacques Prevert, translation by Harriet Zinnes, Schoken, 1987.

POETRY

(With Andre Verdet) *Histoires* (title means "Stories"), Editions du Pre Aux Clercs, 1946, reprinted, Gallimard, 1974.
Grand Bal du printemps (title means "Grand Ball of Spring"; also see below), illustrated with photographs by Izis Bidermanas, Guilde du Livre, 1951.
Charmes de Londres (title means "The Charms of London"; also see below), illustrated with photographs by Bidermanas, Guilde du Livre, 1952.
Lumieres d'homme (title means "Lights of Man"), Guy Levis Mano, 1955.
La Pluie et le beau temps (title means "Rain and Fine Weather"; also see below), Gallimard, 1955.
(With Joseph L. Artigas) *Miro,* Maeght, 1956.
(Contributor) Henry Decanaud, *La Pierre dans le souffle* (title means "The Stone in the Wind"), Seghers, 1959.
Poemes, edited by J. H. Douglas and D. J. Girard, Harrap, 1961.
Histoires et d'autres histoires (title means "Stories and Other Stories"), Gallimard, 1963.
Varengeville, illustrations by Georges Braque, Maeght, 1968.
Poesies (includes *Spectacle* [also see below] and *La Pluie et le beau temps*), Newton Compton, 1971.
Choses et autres (title means "Things and Others"), Gallimard, 1972.
Grand Bal du printemps suivi de Charmes de Londres, Gallimard, 1976.
Anthologie Prevert (anthology with French text), edited and with English introduction and notes by Christiane Mortelier, Methuen Educational, 1981.

SCREENPLAYS

(With Paul Grimault) *La Bergere et le remoneur* (title means "The Shepherdess and the Chimneysweep"), Les Gemeaux, 1947.
Les Amants de Verone, Nouvelle Edition, 1949.
Guy Jacob, Andre Heinrich, and Bernard Chardere, editors, *Jacques Prevert* (anthology), Imprimerie du Bugey, 1960.
"Les Visiteurs du soir," published in *Deux films francais: Les Visiteurs du soir* [and] *Le Feu follet,* edited by Robert M. Hammond and Marguerite Hammond, Harcourt, 1965.
Drole le drame (also see below), Balland, 1974.
Jenny; Le quai des brumes: Scenarios, preface by Marcel Carne, Gallimard, 1988.
La fleur de l'age; Drole de drame: scenarios, Gallimard, 1988.

Also author of other screenplays, including "L'Affaire est dans le sac," 1932, "Ciboulettte," 1933, "L'Hotel du Libre-Echange," 1934, "Un Oiseau rare," 1935, "Le Crime de Monsieur Lange," 1936, "Ernest le Revelle," 1938, "Le Soleil a toujours raison," 1941, "Les Visiteurs du soir," 1942, "Lumiere d'ete," 1943, "Sortileges," 1945, "Les Portes de la nuit," 1946, "Notre Dame de Paris," 1953, and "Les Amours celebres," 1961.

OTHER

Contes pour les enfants pas sages (title means "Stories for Naughty Children"; juvenile), Editions du Pre aux Clercs, 1947, reprinted, Gallimard, 1984.
(With Camilla Koffler) *Le Petit Lion* (title means "The Little Lion"), illustrated with photographs by Ylla, Arts et Metiers Graphiques, 1947.
(Contributor) Joseph Kosman, *Le Rendezvous: Ballet en trois tableaux* (piano scores), Enoch, 1948.
(With Verdet) *C'est a Saint Paul de Vence,* Nouvelle Edition, 1949.

Spectacle (poems, plays, and prose), Gallimard, 1949, reprinted, 1972.

Des Betes (title means "The Animals"), illustrated with photographs by Ylla, Gallimard, 1950.

Guignol (title means "Puppet Show"), illustrations by Elsa Henriquez, Guilde du Livre, 1952.

Lettres des Iles Baladar (title means "Letter from the Baladar Islands"), Gallimard, 1952.

L'Opera de la lune (title means "Moon Opera"), lyrics by Christiane Verger, Guilde du Livre, 1953, reprinted, Editions G.P., 1974.

(With Georges Ribemont-Dessaignes) *Joan Miro,* Maeght, 1956.

(With Ribemont-Dessaignes) *Arbres* (title means "Trees"), Gallimard, 1956, 2nd edition, 1976.

Images (title means "Pictures"), Maeght, 1957.

Dix-sept Chansons de Jacques Prevert (title means "Seventeen Songs by Jacques Prevert"), music by Joseph Kosma, Folkuniversitetets Foerlag, 1958.

Portraits de Picasso (title means "Portraits of Picasso"), illustrated with photography by Andre Villers, Muggiani, 1959, reprinted, Ramsay, 1981.

(Contributor) Ylipe, *Magloire de Paris,* Losfeld, 1961.

(With Max Ernst) *Les Chiens ont soif* (title means "The Dogs Are Thirsty"), Pont des Arts, 1964.

Jacques Prevert presente "Le Circle d'Izis" (title means "Jacques Prevert Presents 'The Circle of Izis'")), illustrated with photographs by Bidermanas, A. Sauret, 1965.

(With Helmut Grieshaber) *Carl Orff: Carmina Burana,* Manus Presse, 1965.

Georges, illustrations by Ribemont-Dessaignes, Cagnes, 1965.

(Contributor) Alexander Calder, *Calder,* Maeght, 1966.

Fatras, illustrations by the author, Livre de Poche, 1966.

Prevert vous parle (title means "Prevert Speaks to You"), Prentice-Hall, 1968.

(Contributor) Cesare Vivaldi, *Mayo,* Instituto Editoriale Italiano, 1968.

Imaginaires (title means "Make-Believe"), A. Skira, 1970.

(With Andre Pozner) *Hebdomadaires* (title means "Weeklies"; interview), G. Authier, 1972.

(With Rene Bartele) *Images de Jacques Prevert* (title means "Pictures by Jacques Prevert"), Filipacchi, 1974.

Le Jour des temps, illustrations by Max Papart, Galerie Bosquet and Jacques Goutal Darly, 1975.

A travers Prevert (title means "Through Prevert"), Gallimard, 1975.

Soleil de nuit, Gallimard, 1980.

Pages d'ecriture (juvenile), Gallimard, 1980.

Couleurs de Braque, Calder, Miro, Maeght, 1981.

(Illustrator) Andre Pozner, *Jacques Prevert: Collages,* Gallimard, 1982.

La cinquieme saison, Gallimard, 1984.

Chanson des cireurs de souliers, illustrations by Marie Gard, Gallimard, 1985.

Chanson pour chanter a tue-tete et a cloche-pied, illustrations by Gard, Gallimard, 1985.

Also author of *Le Cheval de Troie,* 1946, *L'Ange gardechiourme,* 1946, and *Vignette pour les vignerons,* 1951. Also author of farces, pantomimes, ballets, and skits, including "Baptiste" (mime play) and "La Famille tuyau de poele" (title means "Top-hat Family"), 1935, and of lyrics for numerous popular songs, including "Les Feuilles mortes" (title means "Autumn Leaves"), set to music by Joseph Kosma. Work represented in numerous anthologies, including *Let's Get a Divorce,* edited by E. R. Bentley, Hill & Wang, 1958, and *Selections from French Poetry,* edited by K. F. Canfield, Harvey House, 1965. Contributor to *Coronet, Kenyon Review, Poetry,* and other periodicals.

SIDELIGHTS: On Jacques Prevert's death, Marcel Carne, the producer with whom Prevert collaborated on several major films, told the *New York Times:* "Jacques Prevert [was] the one and only poet of the French cinema. He created a style, original and personal, reflecting the soul of the people. His humor and poetry succeeded in raising the banal to the summit of art." Between 1937 and 1950 Prevert collaborated with Carne on eight major films and became one of France's most important screenwriters.

Prevert was a poet as well as a screenwriter, so the comparison Carne made between Prevert's cinematic work and poetry was not surprising. Prevert's general appeal as a poet was such that *New Republic* contributor Eve Merriman called the Frenchman "France's most popular poet of the 20th century." He began writing poetry in the early thirties but did not see his first volume of poetry, *Paroles,* published until 1946. The book was a best-seller, selling hundreds of thousands of copies. In *Jacques Prevert* William E. Baker noted that the titles of several of Prevert's early books of poetry—including *Paroles*—"in a very general way" described the poet's stylistic tendencies: "*Paroles* because the poet has a genius for making all sorts of ordinary idiom highly expressive, *Spectacle* because his verbal tricks often correspond to the antics of a clown or a magician, and *La Pluie et le beau temps* because the emotional tones of his symbols can have the classic simplicity of the summer-and-winter, sunshine-and-rain cycle of life and love."

BIOGRAPHICAL/CRITICAL SOURCES:

BOOKS

Baker, William E., *Jacques Prevert,* Twayne, 1967.
Contemporary Literary Criticism, Volume 15, 1980.

PERIODICALS

Modern Language Journal, October, 1949.
Times Literary Supplement, January 19, 1973.
Wisconsin Studies in Contemporary Literature, summer, 1966.

OBITUARIES:

PERIODICALS

AB Bookman's Weekly, June 20, 1977.
New Republic, July 9 & 16, 1977.
New York Times, April 12, 1977.*

* * *

PRICKETT, (Alexander Thomas) Stephen 1939-

PERSONAL: Born June 4, 1939, in Freetown, Sierra Leone; son of William Ewart and Barbara (Lyne) Prickett; married Diana Mabbutt, 1966; children: Ruth. *Education:* Trinity Hall, Cambridge, B.A. (first class honors), 1961, M.A., 1965, Ph.D., 1968; University College, Oxford, Dipl.Ed., 1962.

ADDRESSES: Home—40 Quiros St., Red, Hill, Canberra, ACT 2603, Australia. *Office*—Department of English, Australian National University, P.O. Box 4, Canberra, ACT 2600, Australia.

CAREER: Methodist College, Uzuakoli, East Nigeria, English teacher, 1962-64; University of Sussex, School of English and American Studies, Brighton, Sussex, England, assistant lecturer, then lecturer, 1967-78, reader in English, 1978-82, sub-dean of School of English and American Studies, 1972-75, chairman of English department, 1980-82; Australian National University,

Canberra, Australia, professor of English, 1983—, head of department, 1985-88. Regius Professor of English Language and Literature, University of Glasgow, 1988. Lecturer at numerous universities in the United States, Europe, the Middle East, Australia, Asia, and China. Founder, Australian Globe Theatre Trust and Australian Shakespeare Centre, 1988.

MEMBER: Australasian Victorian Studies Association (member of executive committee, 1983—), Australian Academy of the Humanities (fellow), United Kingdom National Conference on Literature and Religion (vice-president, 1983—), University Teachers Group (chairman, 1971-82).

AWARDS, HONORS: Edward George Harwood Prize, 1961; Member's Prize, Cambridge University, 1964; Fulbright scholarship, 1979; Conference on Christianity and Literature Book Award, Modern Language Association, 1987, for *Words and the Word: Language, Poetics, and Biblical Interpretation.*

WRITINGS:

Do It Yourself Doom (fiction), Gollancz, 1962.
Coleridge and Wordsworth: The Poetry of Growth, Cambridge University Press, 1970.
(Editor with Philip Booth and Nicholas Taylor) *Cambridge New Architecture,* 3rd edition, International Textbook, 1970.
Wordsworth and Coleridge: The Lyrical Ballads, Edward Arnold, 1975.
Romanticism and Religion: The Tradition of Coleridge and Wordsworth in the Victorian Church, Cambridge University Press, 1976.
Victorian Fantasy, Indiana University Press, 1979.
(Editor and contributor) *The Romantics,* Holmes & Meier, 1981.
(Editor with Pat Dobrez, and contributor) *Proceedings of the Australasian Victorian Studies Association,* Australian National University, 1984.
Words and the Word: Language, Poetics, and Biblical Interpretation, Cambridge University Press, 1986.
England and the French Revolution, Macmillan, 1988.

Also author of numerous cassette tapes on the works of Wordsworth and Coleridge, for Everett/Edwards. Contributor to numerous anthologies on literature and Biblical studies; contributor to magazines and journals, including *Times Literary Supplement, Journal of European Studies, Wordsworth Circle,* and *Theology.* Advisor to 5th edition of *Norton Anthology of English Literature;* member of editorial advisory boards, *Seven: An Anglo-American Literary Review,* 1980—, and *Literature and Theology,* 1986—.

WORK IN PROGRESS: Editing a collection of essays on biblical interpretation and literary criticism for Basil Blackwell, tentative title *Reading the Text: Biblical Interpretation and Literary Theory;* a volume on the Bible, with Robert Barnes, for the "Landmarks of World Literature" series of Cambridge University Press; a book on radicalism during the French Revolution, provisionally titled *Radical Satire: Preachers, Pigs, and Pornographers in the French Revolution Debate.*

SIDELIGHTS: Stephen Prickett's *Victorian Fantasy* "is required reading for anyone who has ever derived pleasure and puzzlement from [Edmund] Lear and [Lewis] Carroll" among other writers, notes Benny Green in the *Spectator.* Tracing the development of early fantasy literature, Prickett infuses his scholarly study with a "fresh" approach that "is complex, lively and convincing," writes an *Economist* contributor. "Indeed he holds each author he discusses up to the light in an original, sympathetic and analytical fashion." Green concurs, commenting that while "the convolutions of [Prickett's] thought [are] occasionally self-defeating, . . . there is no question that once he is launched into the lives and works of the writers who interest him, he conducts his explorations in a style which reflects much of the fascination of the models from which he is working."

Prickett brings a similarly engaging style to *Words and the Word: Language, Poetics, and Biblical Interpretation,* a study which "first addresses problems that have arisen with the plethora of new Bible translations, then provides a magisterial survey of the Bible's role in modern literary history," describes the *Christian Science Monitor*'s Thomas D'Evelyn. "Prickett takes the reader on an exhilarating tour through Western consciousness," observes a *Christianity and Literature* reviewer, "from the ancient Hebrews through the Romantic poets to modern critical theory. Along the way are stimulating close readings of poetry . . . as well as mind-opening discussions of the thought [of Biblical scholars]." "It all turns out to be far from academic," states D'Evelyn; "a brief summary does scant justice to the sustained energy and pithy eloquence of these pages. It's refreshing to read." J. H. Sims likewise remarks in *Choice* that "Prickett's brilliant insights and his closely woven and cogently argued style" make *Words and the Word* "a delight (finally) to the mind." While these critics find Prickett's study entertaining as well as enlightening, *Times Literary Supplement* contributor C. H. Sisson asserts that *Words and the Word* also serves as a scholarly work: "It is an immensely well-informed survey, the usefulness of which is by no means confined to the elucidation of the 'structure and mode of expression' of the Bible which is the main purpose of the book." As the *Christianity and Literature* critic concludes, Prickett's book "exemplifies what it claims, that literary and Biblical scholarship can support each other, and that all of our fragmented fields and specialties can come together in terms of the Word."

BIOGRAPHICAL/CRITICAL SOURCES:

PERIODICALS

Choice, September, 1987.
Christianity and Literature, winter, 1988.
Christian Science Monitor, May 13, 1987.
Economist, August 25, 1979.
Spectator, September 29, 1979.
Times Literary Supplement, October 2, 1970, January 30, 1987.

* * *

PURTILL, Richard L. 1931-

PERSONAL: Born March 12, 1931, in Chicago, Ill.; son of Joseph T. (a businessman) and Bertha (Walker) Purtill; married Elizabeth Banks (a statistician), June 20, 1959; children: Mark, Timothy, Steven. *Education:* University of Chicago, B.A., 1958, M.A., 1960, Ph. D., 1965; University of California, Los Angeles, postgraduate study, 1960-62. *Politics:* Independent. *Religion:* Roman Catholic.

ADDRESSES: Home—1708 Douglas Ave., Bellingham, Wash. 98225. *Office*—Department of Philosophy, Western Washington University, Bellingham, Wash. 98225.

CAREER: Western Washington University, Bellingham, instructor, 1962-65, assistant professor, 1965-68, associate professor, 1968-72, professor of philosophy, 1972—, acting chairman of department, 1970-71. Visiting lecturer, San Francisco State College (now University), 1968-69. Textbook consultant to Prentice-Hall, and other publishers. *Military service:* U.S. Army, 1949-52; became sergeant.

MEMBER: American Philosophical Association, American Association of University Professors, Authors Guild, Authors League of America, Science Fiction Writers of America, Sierra Club.

AWARDS, HONORS: National Endowment for the Humanities summer grant, 1970.

WRITINGS:

Logic for Philosophers, Harper, 1971.
Logical Thinking, Harper, 1972.
Lord of the Elves and the Eldils: Philosophy and Fantasy in C. S. Lewis and J. R. R. Tolkien, Zondervan, 1974.
Reason to Believe, Eerdmans, 1974.
(Contributor) Thomas Beauchamp, editor, *Ethics and Public Policy,* Prentice-Hall, 1975.
Philosophically Speaking, Prentice-Hall, 1975.
Thinking about Ethics, Prentice-Hall, 1976.
(Contributor) Peter J. Schackel, editor, *The Longing for a Form: Essays on the Fiction of C. S. Lewis,* Kent State University Press, 1977.
Thinking about Religion, Prentice-Hall, 1978.
Logic: Argument, Refutation and Proof, Harper, 1979.
The Golden Gryphon Feather, DAW Books, 1979.
The Stolen Goddess, DAW Books, 1980.
C. S. Lewis's Case for the Christian Faith, Harper, 1981.
Murdercon, Doubleday, 1982.
The Mirror of Helen, DAW Books, 1983.
The Parallel Man, DAW Books, 1984.
J. R. R. Tolkien: Myth, Morality and Religion, Harper, 1984.
Enchantment at Delphi (young adult), Harcourt, 1986.
A Logical Introduction to Philosophy, Prentice-Hall, 1989.

Contributor of more than thirty articles to philosophy journals. Contributor of short stories to *Magazine of Fantasy and Science Fiction, Isaac Asimov's Science Fiction Magazine,* and *Alfred Hitchcock's Mystery Magazine.*

WORK IN PROGRESS: Making Moral Decisions, an ethics textbook; *On the Soul,* a philosophical monograph.

SIDELIGHTS: Richard L. Purtill told *CA:* "I have gradually moved from [writing] textbooks to trade non-fiction and fiction, though I have some textbook editing projects in process. Fiction is more enjoyable to write, but I sometimes become fascinated with a subject area about which I want to write nonfiction, such as my recent Tolkien book or my current project on the soul. As a result of my various interests I move in a number of different circles: Christian philosophers, C. S. Lewis and J. R. R. Tolkien enthusiasts, science fiction fans, mystery writers and readers. I find diversity interesting and I often find one area of interest impinging on another, as when I set a mystery novel at a science fiction convention (*Murdercon*). I have also lead tours to Greece and have become fascinated with ancient and modern Greek culture, an interest which comes out in much of my writing. To quote R. L. Stevenson: 'The world is so full of a number of things I'm sure we should all be as happy as kings.' "

AVOCATIONAL INTERESTS: Reading, food, wine.

BIOGRAPHICAL/CRITICAL SOURCES:

PERIODICALS

New York Times Book Review, September 12, 1982.

Q

QUANDT, Richard E(meric) 1930-

PERSONAL: Born June 1, 1930, in Budapest, Hungary; came to United States, 1949, naturalized citizen, 1954; son of Richard F. and Elizabeth (Toth) Quandt; married Jean H. Briggs, August 6, 1955; children: Stephen. *Education:* Princeton University, B.A., 1952; Harvard University, M.A., 1955, Ph.D., 1957.

ADDRESSES: Home—Princeton, N.J. *Office*—Department of Economics, Princeton University, Princeton, N.J. 08544-1017.

CAREER: Princeton University, Princeton, N.J., lecturer, 1956-57, assistant professor, 1957-59, associate professor, 1959-64, professor of economics, 1964—, Ford Foundation research professor, 1967-68, chairman of department of economics, 1968-71, 1985-88. Consultant to various firms, including Mathematica, Inc., 1961-67.

MEMBER: American Economic Association, American Statistical Association (fellow), Econometric Society (fellow), Regional Science Association.

AWARDS, HONORS: Guggenheim fellow, 1958-59; McCosh fellow, 1964; National Science Foundation senior postdoctoral fellow, 1971-72.

WRITINGS:

(With J. M. Henderson) *Microeconomic Theory: A Mathematical Approach,* McGraw, 1958, 3rd edition, 1980.
(With W. L. Thorp) *The New Inflation,* McGraw, 1959.
(With Burton G. Malkiel) *Strategies and Rational Decision in the Securities Options Market,* MIT Press, 1969.
(Editor) *The Demand for Travel: Theory and Estimation,* Heath, 1970.
(With S. M. Goldfeld) *Nonlinear Methods in Econometrics,* North-Holland Publishing, 1972.
(With Goldfeld) *Studies in Nonlinear Estimation,* Ballinger, 1976.
Statistical Analyses of Aircraft Hijackings and Political Assassinations, Econometric Research Program, Princeton University, 1976.
Classical and Bayesian Hypothesis Testing, Princeton University, 1981.
On the Optimal Level of Complexity in Regulation, Department of Economics, Princeton University, 1981.
(With Peter Asch and Malkiel)) *Racetrack Betting and Efficient Markets,* Department of Economics, Princeton University, 1981.
(With Asch) *Racetrack Betting: The Professors' Guide to Strategies,* Auburn House, 1986.
(With M. H. Peston) *Prices, Competition and Equilibrium,* B & N Imports, 1986.

Contributor of numerous articles to various periodicals, including *Journal of Political Economy,* and *Economic Journal.* Associate editor of *Bell Journal of Economics, Econometrica, Journal of the American Statistical Association,* and *Review of Economics and Statistics.*

* * *

QUELCH, John A(nthony) 1951-

PERSONAL: Born August 8, 1951, in London, England; came to the United States in 1972; son of Norman (an accountant) and Laura S. (a nurse; maiden name, Jones) Quelch; married Joyce Ann Huntley. *Education:* Oxford University, B.A., 1972, M.A., 1976; University of Pennsylvania, M.B.A., 1974; Harvard University, D.B.A., 1977, M.S., 1978.

ADDRESSES: Home—57 Baker Bridge Rd., Lincoln, Mass. 01773. *Office*—Harvard Business School, Harvard University, Soldiers Field, Boston, Mass. 02163.

CAREER: University of Western Ontario, London, assistant professor of business, 1977-79; Harvard University, Harvard Business School, Boston, Mass., assistant professor, 1979-84, associate professor, 1984-88, professor of business, 1988—. President of Marque Associates, Inc.; director of Reebock International Ltd., and WWP Group PLC.

WRITINGS:

Advertising and Promotion Management, Chilton, 1983.
Cases in Advertising and Promotion Management, Business Publications, 1983.
Consumer Behavior for Marketing Managers, Allyn & Bacon, 1984.
Marketing Management, three volumes, Irwin, 1985.
Cases in Consumer Behavior, Prentice-Hall, 1986.
Multinational Marketing Management, Addison-Wesley, 1988.
Sales Promotion Management, Prentice-Hall, 1989.
How to Market to Consumers, Wiley, 1989.

The Marketing Challenge of 1992, Addison-Wesley, in press.

Contributor to business journals.

BIOGRAPHICAL/CRITICAL SOURCES:

PERIODICALS

Harvard Business School Bulletin, December, 1983.

R

RACINA, Thom
See RAUCINA, Thomas Frank

* * *

RAE, Hugh C(rauford) 1935-
(James Albany, Robert Crawford, R. B. Houston, Jessica Stirling; Stuart Stern, joint pseudonym)

PERSONAL: Born November 22, 1935, in Glasgow, Scotland; son of Robert Tennant (a printer) and Isobel (a clerk; maiden name, McNair) Rae; married Elizabeth McMillan Dunn, September 12, 1960; children: Gillian Faulkner (daughter). *Education:* Attended school in Glasgow, Scotland. *Politics:* Conservative. *Religion:* Presbyterian.

ADDRESSES: Home—Drumore Farm Cottage, Gartness Rd., Balfron Station, Stirlingshire, Scotland. *Agent*—Fraser & Dunlop Ltd., 91 Regent St., London W1R 8RU, England.

CAREER: John Smith & Son Ltd. (antiquarian booksellers), Glasgow, Scotland, assistant, 1952-65; full-time writer, 1965—. Lecturer in creative writing, University of Glasgow. *Military service:* Royal Air Force, National Service, 1954-56.

MEMBER: Society of Authors, Scottish Association of Writers (president, 1970-77), Scottish Arts Council (member of literature committee, 1973-80), Romantic Novelists' Association: Scotland (president, 1986—).

WRITINGS:

UNDER PSEUDONYM JAMES ALBANY

Warrior Caste, Pan Books, 1982.
Mailed Fist, Pan Books, 1982.
Deacon's Dagger, Pan Books, 1982.
Close Combat, Pan Books, 1983.
Marching Fire, Pan Books, 1983.
Last Bastion, Pan Books, 1984.
Borneo Story, Pan Books, 1984.

UNDER PSEUDONYM ROBERT CRAWFORD

Cockleburr, Constable, 1969, Putnam, 1970.
The Shroud Society, Putnam, 1969.
Kiss the Boss Goodbye, Constable, 1970, Putnam, 1971.
The Badger's Daughter, Constable, 1971.
Whip Hand, Constable, 1972.

UNDER PSEUDONYM JESSICA STIRLING

(With Peggy Coghlan) *The Spoiled Earth: A Novel,* Hodder & Stoughton, 1974, published as *Strathmore,* Delacorte, 1975.
(With Coghlan) *The Dresden Finch: A Novel,* Delacorte, 1976.
(With Coghlan) *The Hiring Fair: A Novel,* Hodder, 1975.
(With Coghlan) *Call Home the Heart: A Novel,* St. Martin's, 1977.
(With Coghlan) *The Dark Pasture,* Hodder, 1977, St. Martin's, 1978.
(With Coghlan) *The Deep Well at Noon,* Hodder, 1979.
(With Coghlan) *The Drums of Time,* St. Martin's, 1980.
(With Coghlan) *The Blue Evening Gone,* Hodder, 1981, St. Martin's, 1982.
(With Coghlan) *The Gates of Midnight,* St. Martin's, 1983.
(With Coghlan) *Treasures on Earth,* St. Martin's, 1985.
Creature Comforts, St. Martin's, 1986.
Hearts of Gold, St. Martin's, 1987.
The Good Provider, St. Martin's, 1988.
The Asking Price, St. Martin's, 1989.

OTHER

Skinner, Viking, 1965.
Night Pillow, Viking 1967.
A Few Small Bones, Coward, 1969.
The House at Balnesmoor, Coward, 1969.
The Interview: A Novel, Coward, 1969.
The Saturday Epic, Coward, 1970.
The Marksman, Coward, 1971.
"The Freezer" (radio play), British Broadcasting Corp., 1972.
(Under pseudonym R. B. Houston) *Two for the Grave,* Robert Hale, 1972.
The Shooting Gallery, Coward, 1972.
The Rock Harvest, St. Martin's, 1973.
The Rookery: A Novel of the Victorian Underworld, Constable, 1974, St. Martin's, 1975.
Harkfast: The Making of the King, St. Martin's, 1976.
(Under joint pseudonym Stuart Stern, with S. Ungar) *The Minotaur Factor,* Playboy Press, 1977.
(Under joint pseudonym Stuart Stern, with Ungar) *The Poison Tree,* Playboy Press, 1978.
Sullivan, Playboy Press, 1978.
(Editor) *Scottish Short Stories,* Collins, 1978.
The Travelling Soul, Avon, 1978.
The Haunting at Waverly Falls, Constable, 1980.

Privileged Strangers, Hodder & Staughton, 1982.

Also author of plays, television scripts, short stories, poems, radio plays, and literary articles.

WORK IN PROGRESS: As Jessica Stirling, *The Wise Child.*

SIDELIGHTS: Hugh C. Rae described himself to *CA* as a "compulsive writer. . . . No strong desire to travel. No foreign languages. No strong commitment to any specific cause through development of an 'innocent bystander' attitude. Boringly single-minded."

AVOCATIONAL INTERESTS: The cinema and theater, television, reading, sports (tennis and golf).

* * *

RAINE, Craig 1944-

PERSONAL: Born December 3, 1944, in Bishop Auckland, England; son of Norman Edward and Olive Marie Raine; married Ann Pasternak Slater (a professor), August 12, 1974; children: Nina, Isaac, Moses, Vaska. *Education:* Received B. Phil. from Exeter College, Oxford.

ADDRESSES: Office—Faber & Faber, 3 Queen Sq., London W.C. 1, England.

CAREER: Faber & Faber, London, England, poetry editor, 1981—. Broadcaster for British Broadcasting Corp..

AWARDS, HONORS: First prize, Cheltenham Festival Poetry Competition, 1977, for poem, "Flying to Belfast, 1977," and, 1978, for poem, "Mother Dressmaking"; second prize, National Poetry Competition, 1978, for poem, "In the Mortuary"; *New Statesman*'s Prudence Farmer Award, 1979, for poem, "A Martian Sends a Postcard Home," and, 1980, for poem, "Laying a Lawn"; Cholmondeley Award, Society of Authors (Great Britain), 1983.

WRITINGS:

POETRY

The Onion, Memory, Oxford University Press, 1978.
A Journey to Greece, Sycamore Broadsheets, 1979.
A Martian Sends a Postcard Home, Oxford University Press, 1979.
A Free Translation, Salamander Press, 1981.
Rich, Faber, 1984.

OTHER

(Contributor) *Poetry Introduction 4,* Faber, 1978.
(Contributor) Blake Morrison and Andrew Motion, editors, *The Penguin Book of Contemporary British Poetry,* Penguin, 1982.
The Electrification of the Soviet Union (libretto; based on Boris Pasternak's novella, *The Last Summer*), Faber, 1986.
(Editor) *A Choice of Kipling's Prose,* Faber, 1987.

Book editor, *New Review,* 1977-78; poetry editor, *New Statesman,* 1981.

SIDELIGHTS: Craig Raine is considered by many to be among the foremost contemporary British poets. *A Martian Sends a Postcard Home,* possibly his best-known work, has spawned a group of young British poets called the Martian poets or the Metaphor Men. Their poetry pays homage to the "long-awaited return to exuberant playfulness" which *New Statesman* contributor Andrew Motion finds defines the book's poetic style. While *A Martian Sends a Postcard Home* is written from the point of view of an alien visitor who describes our world in humorous terms to his fellow inhabitants of Mars, not all of Raine's work is so far removed from everyday life. In Michael Hulse's *Dictionary of Literary Biography* essay, the critic specifically warns against applying "the Martian tag" to Raine's work since *A Martian Send a Postcard Home.* On the contrary, Hulse finds the remainder of Raine's poetry to be "very much of this world, indeed his passion is all for the domestic and ordinary, however he transforms it."

BIOGRAPHICAL/CRITICAL SOURCES:

BOOKS

Dictionary of Literary Biography, Volume 40: *Poets of Great Britain and Ireland since 1960,* Gale, 1985.

PERIODICALS

New Statesman, June 23, 1978, October 20, 1978, December 4, 1979.

* * *

RAUCHER, Herman 1928-

PERSONAL: Surname is pronounced *Row*-sher; born April 13, 1928, in New York, N.Y.; son of Benjamin Brooks and Sophie (Weinshank) Raucher; married Mary Kathryn Martinet, April 20, 1960; children: Jacqueline Leigh, Jennifer Brooke. *Education:* New York University, B.S., 1949. *Religion:* Hebrew.

ADDRESSES: Home—Cos Cob, Conn.

CAREER: Writer. Advertising writer in Hollywood, Calif., for Twentieth Century-Fox, 1950-54, and Walt Disney, 1954-55; worked at Calkins & Holden (advertising), New York City, 1956-57; Reach, McClinton (advertising), New York City, vice president, creative director, 1963-64; Gardner (advertising), New York City, vice president, creative director, 1964-65; Benton & Bowles (advertising), New York City, consultant, 1965-67. *Military service:* U.S. Army, 1950-52; became second lieutenant.

MEMBER: Writers Guild of America, Dramatists Guild, Authors League of America.

WRITINGS:

"Sweet November" (screenplay), Warner Bros., 1968.
"Can Heironymus Merkin Ever Forget Mercy Humppe and Find True Happiness?" (screenplay), Regional Film Distributors, 1969.
"Watermelon Man" (screenplay), Columbia, 1970 (novelization published as *Watermelon Man,* Ace Books, 1970).
"Summer of '42" (screenplay), Warner Bros., 1971 (novelization published as *Summer of '42,* Putnam, 1971, reprinted, 1986).
A Glimpse of Tiger (novelization), Putnam, 1971.
"Class of '44" (screenplay; sequel to "Summer of '42"), Warner Bros., 1972.
"Ode to Billy Joe" (screenplay), Warner Bros., 1976 (novelization published as *Ode to Billy Joe,* Dell, 1976).
"The Other Side of Midnight" (screenplay based on novel of same title by Sidney Sheldon), Twentieth Century-Fox, 1977.
There Should Have Been Castles, Delacorte Press, 1978.
Maynard's House, Putnam, 1980.

Also author of original television dramas for "Studio One," "Alcoa Hour," and "Goodyear Playhouse," 1956-58.

AVOCATIONAL INTERESTS: "Amorphic and everchanging."

BIOGRAPHICAL/CRITICAL SOURCES:

PERIODICALS

Atlantic, July, 1971.
Commonweal, May 21, 1971.
Los Angeles Times Book Review, October 5, 1980.
New York Times Book Review, September 28, 1980.
Punch, July 29, 1970.
Times Literary Supplement, May 1, 1981.
Washington Post, March 15, 1971, October 4, 1980.

* * *

RAUCINA, Thomas Frank 1946-
(Thom Racina; pseudonyms: Tom Anicar, Grant Tracy Saxon, Lisa Wells)

PERSONAL: Born June 4, 1946, in Kenosha, Wis.; son of Frank (a dry cleaner) and Esther (Benko) Raucina. *Education:* Attended University of New Mexico, 1964-66; Art Institute of Chicago, B.F.A., 1969, M.F.A., 1971. *Politics:* Democrat.

ADDRESSES: Home—3449 Waverly Dr., Los Angeles, Calif. 90027. *Agent*—George Diskant & Associates, 1033 Gayley Ave., Los Angeles, Calif. 90024.

CAREER: Goodman Theatre, Chicago, Ill., assistant director, 1966-69, playwright in residence, 1969-71; writer, 1971—; children's television writer in Hollywood, Calif., for Hanna-Barbera, 1973-74, and MTM Enterprises, Inc., 1974-76; associate head writer for "General Hospital," American Broadcasting Companies, Inc., 1981-84; co-head writer for "Days of Our Lives" daytime series, 1984-86, "Another World" daytime series, 1986-88, and "Generations" daytime series, 1988—, all for National Broadcasting Co. Has worked as a church organist, a price-check boy on roller skates in a discount store, a night club pianist, and a piano teacher.

WRITINGS:

Lifeguard (novel), Warner Paperback, 1976.
(Under pseudonym Tom Anicar) *Secret Sex* (novel), New American Library, 1976.
(Under pseudonym Grant Tracy Saxon) *The Happy Hustler* (nonfiction), Warner Books, 1976.
(Ghostwriter) Marilyn Chambers, *Marilyn Chambers: My Story* (nonfiction), Warner Books, 1976.
(Under pseudonym Grant Tracy Saxon) *Making Love* (nonfiction), Warner Books, 1977.
(Ghostwriter) Xaviera Hollander and Marilyn Chambers, *Xaviera Meets Marilyn Chambers,* Warner Books, 1977.
The Great Los Angeles Blizzard (novel), Putnam, 1977.
Quincy, M.E. (novel), Berkley Publishing, 1977.
Kojak in San Francisco (novel), Berkley Publishing, 1977.
Palm Springs (novel), Seaview, 1978.
FM (novel), Jove, 1978.
Sweet Revenge (novel), Berkley Publishing, 1978.
The Gannon Girls (novel), Jove, 1979.
Nine to Five (novel), Bantam, 1980.
Tomcat (novel), Ace Books, 1981.
(Under pseudonym Lisa Wells) *Magda* (novel), Ace Books, 1982.

PLAYS

(Adaptor) William Shakespeare, "A Midsummer Night's Dream" (musical for children), first produced in Chicago, Ill., at Goodman Theatre, 1968.
"Allison," first produced in Chicago, at Goodman Theatre, January 30, 1970.
Allison Wonderland (musical for children), Samuel French, 1970.
The Marvelous Misadventure of Sherlock Holmes (musical for children), Samuel French, 1971.
"Sherlock," first produced in Chicago at Goodman Theatre, July 6, 1971.

WORK IN PROGRESS: Three, a novel.

SIDELIGHTS: Thomas Frank Raucina, who sometimes writes under the names Thom Racina, Tom Anicar, Grant Tracy Saxon, and Lisa Wells, once told *CA:* "I have no desire to write literature, only the kinds of books I like to read, novels which are real escapist entertainment. The motivation to do much and do it well and be happy at the same time comes from a long history of battling the disease pancreatitis. Having been faced with death several times, it is always a joy to have one more pain-free day to be able to write a few more pages."

AVOCATIONAL INTERESTS: Travel (including the Soviet Union), gourmet cooking, swimming, driving his BMW, playing the piano, and "sharing an eleven room house with two cats, Saxon and Sherman, and a dog named Herschel."

BIOGRAPHICAL/CRITICAL SOURCES:

PERIODICALS

New York Times Book Review, November 13, 1977.

* * *

RAVENSCROFT, Arthur 1924-

PERSONAL: Born June 24, 1924, in Oudtshoorn, South Africa; son of James (a storekeeper) and Inez Mary (King) Ravenscroft; married Nesta Alice Tudhope, April 4, 1953; children: William, Anne, Jill. *Education:* University of Cape Town, B.A., 1944, M.A., 1945, Cambridge University, B.A., 1952, M.A., 1961. *Religion:* Anglican.

ADDRESSES: Home—Leeds, England. *Office*—School of English, University of Leeds, Leeds LS2 9JT, England.

CAREER: University of Cape Town, Cape Town, South Africa, junior lecturer in English, 1946; University of Stellenbosch, Stellenbosch, South Africa, lecturer, 1947-57, senior lecturer in English, 1957; University College of Rhodesia and Nyasaland, Salisbury, Rhodesia (now Zimbabwe), lecturer in English, 1958-63; University of Leeds, Leeds, England, lecturer, 1963-66, senior lecturer in English literature, 1966-84, honorary lecturer, 1984—. *Military service:* South African Defence Force, 1942-44.

MEMBER: African Studies Association of the United Kingdom, Association for Commonwealth Literature and Language Studies, English Association (Zimbabwe; chairman, 1960-63), Association of University Teachers (Zimbabwe; vice-chairman, 1962-63), Stellenbosch Film Society, University College Film Society (Zimbabwe, chairman, 1958-61).

AWARDS, HONORS: British Council Scholarship, 1950-52; African Universities Program fellowship for Chicago, Ill., 1958.

WRITINGS:

(Translator with C.K. Johnman) *Van Riebeeck's Journal, 1659-1662,* Balkema, 1958.
Chinua Achebe, Longmans, Green, 1969, 2nd edition, Longman, 1977.
Nigerian Writers and the African Past, Karnatak University, 1978.

(With Harry Blamires and Peter Quartermaine) *A Guide to Twentieth-Century English, Irish, and Commonwealth Literature,* Methuen, 1983.

"Teaching Words" in African Literature: The McAlpin Lecture 1984, Dhvanyaloka, Mysore, 1986.

CONTRIBUTOR

Kenneth Parker, editor, *The South African Novel in English,* Macmillan, 1978.

Douglas Jefferson and Graham Martin, editors, *The Uses of Fiction,* Open University Press, 1982.

Shirley Chew, editor, *Re-visions of Canadian Literature,* University of Leeds, 1985.

Robert Welch and Suheil B. Bushrui, editors, *Literature and the Art of Creation,* Barnes & Noble, 1988.

Ian Ousby, editor, *New Cambridge Guide to Literature in English,* Cambridge University Press, 1988.

OTHER

Contributor to literature journals. Co-editor of *Film Review,* 1949-55; editor of *Journal of Commonwealth Literature,* 1965-79.

WORK IN PROGRESS: Research on politics and literature in the Third World; collaborating with three friends on a book about Commonwealth literatures since 1970.

SIDELIGHTS: Arthur Ravenscroft told *CA* that his most urgent concern is "trying to understand the savagery at the center of European (indeed, North Atlantic) civilization when it has unleashed itself on the Third World, trying to understand why any human beings can imagine themselves dignified by their humiliation of their fellows." He adds, "Such wondering about a civilization that has produced both Beethoven and Buchenwald has arisen out of my South African origins, the intimate relationship between apartheid and Auschwitz, and, in the last twenty years, my reading of Third World literature."

AVOCATIONAL INTERESTS: Literature, film, the theatre, television, walking, "mild gardening."

* * *

RAY, Man 1890-1976

PERSONAL: Born Emmanuel Radensky (some sources show surname as Rudnitsky), August 27, 1890, in Philadelphia, Pa.; died in his sleep, November 18, 1976, in Paris, France; married Donna Lacroix Loupov (a poet), 1914 (divorced); married Juliet Browner (a dancer), 1946. *Education:* Attended National Academy of Design, 1908.

ADDRESSES: Home—Paris, France.

CAREER: Painter, filmmaker, photographer, art constructor. Held first one-man exhibition in New York, N.Y., 1915.

WRITINGS:

Self Portrait (autobiography), Little, Brown, 1963, reprinted, New York Graphic Society, 1988.

Opera Grafica, L. Anselmino, 1973.

Man Ray: The Photographic Image, translated by Murtha Baca, Barron's, 1977.

Photographs by Man Ray: 1920-1934, Dover, 1980.

Man Ray: Photographs, Thames & Hudson, 1982.

Objects of My Affection, Thames & Hudson, 1987.

Also author of screenplays, including "Retour a la raison," 1923, "Emak Bakia," 1927, (with Robert Desnos) "L'Etiole de Mer," 1927, and "Les Mysteres du Chateau de De," 1929. Artwork represented in various published collections, and in numerous U.S. and foreign catalogs. Co-designer and editor of *New York Dada,* April, 1921.

SIDELIGHTS: Although little is known about the early years of Emmanuel Radensky, whose parents wanted him to become an engineer or an architect and disapproved of the five-year-old's interest in painting, he became famous worldwide as the artist and photographer Man Ray. Skilled in mechanical and free-hand drawing, he rejected a scholarship to study architecture in college for a job in New York City, where he was eventually introduced to photography by Alfred Stieglitz and stimulated by the artistic innovations of Paul Cezanne and Pablo Picasso. Introduced by Marcel Duchamp to Dadaism, which sought to supplant all other forms of art, Man Ray became synonymous with that revolutionary artistic movement and founded a New York branch. At the age of thirty, he moved to Paris, where his experimental photographs—called "Rayographs" and achieved by setting dark models against light-sensitive paper—gained the artist a wide clientele and an international reputation. Even years after his death, Man Ray's work continues to be anthologized and critiqued as a major influence in modern art, and is collected at prestigious museums worldwide. "In his lifelong engagement in several arts—painting, photography, object-making and movies—he craved, and often won, renown," according to Dore Ashton in a *Washington Post Book World* article. "The drive to succeed was cloaked by a carefully cultivated quiet manner, but it was there, burning, in this son of Russian-Jewish immigrants who fought his way out of Brooklyn into the great world with an enterprising intelligence and an uncanny gift for being in the right place at the right time."

BIOGRAPHICAL/CRITICAL SOURCES:

BOOKS

Baldwin, Neil, *Man Ray: American Artist,* Clarkson Potter, 1988.

Foresta, Merry, and others, *Perpetual Motif: The Art of Man Ray,* Abbeville Press, 1988.

Penrose, Roland, *Man Ray,* New York Graphic Society, 1975.

Ray, Man, *Self Portrait,* Little, Brown, 1963, reprinted, New York Graphic Society, 1988.

Schwarz, Arturo, *Man Ray: The Rigour of Imagination,* Rizzoli, 1977.

PERIODICALS

Newsweek, November 28, 1988.

New York Times Book Review, July 1, 1979.

Times Literary Supplement, November 14, 1980.

Washington Post Book World, December 18, 1988.*

* * *

RAYNER, Mary 1933-

PERSONAL: Born December 30, 1933, in Mandalay, Burma; daughter of A. H. and Yoma Grigson; married E. H. Rayner, 1960 (divorced, 1982); married Adrian Hawksley, 1985; children: Sarah, William, Benjamin. *Education:* University of St. Andrews, M.A. (second class honors), 1954.

ADDRESSES: Home—Wiltshire, England. *Office*—c/o Macmillan London Ltd., 4 Little Essex St., London W.C.2, England.

CAREER: Former production assistant at Hammond, Hammond Ltd. (publisher), London, England; Longmans, Green &

Co. Ltd. (publisher), London, copywriter, 1959-62; free-lance writer and book illustrator, 1974—.

MEMBER: Society of Authors.

AWARDS, HONORS: Horn Book Honor List citation, 1977, for *Mr. and Mrs. Pig's Evening Out,* 1978, for *Garth Pig and the Ice Cream Lady,* and 1986, for *Babe: The Gallant Pig;* Parents Choice Award, 1987, for *Mrs. Pig Gets Cross.*

WRITINGS:

SELF-ILLUSTRATED JUVENILES

The Witch-Finder, Morrow, 1976.
Mr. and Mrs. Pig's Evening Out, Atheneum, 1976.
Garth Pig and the Ice Cream Lady, Atheneum, 1977.
The Rain Cloud, Atheneum, 1980.
Mrs. Pig's Bulk Buy, Atheneum, 1981.
Crocodarling, Collins, 1985, Bradbury, 1986.
Mrs. Pig Gets Cross, Collins, 1986, Dutton, 1987.
Reilly, Gollancz, 1987.
Oh Paul!, Heinemann, 1988.
Marathon and Steve, Dutton, 1989.
Rug, Collins, 1989.

OTHER

Contributor to anthologies, including *All Sorts of Poems, Young Winters' Tales Seven, Allsorts Six, Allsorts Seven,* and *Hidden Turnings.* Contributor of stories to *Cricket.* Also illustrator of numerous juvenile books, including *Lost and Found, Thank You for the Tadpole,* and *Babe: The Gallant Pig.*

SIDELIGHTS: Juvenile author and illustrator Mary Rayner frequently writes about a family of two pigs and ten mischievous piglets. The youngsters usually find themselves facing both the results of their own youthful mischief and the more malign actions of nearby wolves. *Mr. and Mrs. Pig's Evening Out* is considered by *Times Literary Supplement* reviewer Elaine Moss to have "style, wit, excitement, high drama, and pathos." "If humour and terror (resolved) are the ingredients of treasured nursery stories," Moss believes, *Mr. and Mrs. Pig's Evening Out* "will be loved till its sturdy binding falls off." In the *Garth Pig and the Ice Cream Lady,* a wolf masquerades as a friendly ice cream peddler in order to lure the piglets to her home. G. A. Woods comments in the *New York Times Book Review:* "Of course, the story is another variant of the classic wolf vs. pig theme," but concludes that "color, detail and story make this one a prime selection." In describing the collection of stories *Mrs. Pig Gets Cross, New York Times Book Review* contributor Merri Rosenberg relates: "Once again Mrs. Rayner amusingly, and honestly, deals with the ordinary experiences of family life in a manner that is entertaining to the small fry—and blessedly comforting to the parent." Rosenberg continues: "[*Mrs. Pig Gets Cross*] is one of those rare finds that are as much fun for a parent to read as they are for a child to hear."

BIOGRAPHICAL/CRITICAL SOURCES:

PERIODICALS

New York Times Book Review, October 23, 1977, October 12, 1980, June 7, 1981, November 1, 1981, May 17, 1987.
Times Literary Supplement, July 16, 1976, December 2, 1977, July 24, 1981.

* * *

REDWAY, Ralph
See HAMILTON, Charles (Harold St. John)

REDWAY, Ridley
See HAMILTON, Charles (Harold St. John)

* * *

REES, Joan 1927-
(Joan Alice Gladys Rees; pseudonyms: June Avery, Ann Bedford, Susan Strong)

PERSONAL: Born May 8, 1927, in London, England; daughter of George William Robert (a company director) and Alice (Bedford) Rees; married Frank Louis Cyprien (a visual aids adviser), April 20, 1965. *Education:* University of London, Diploma in Literature. *Politics:* "Internationally-minded liberal." *Religion:* Unaffiliated.

ADDRESSES: Home—Flat 20, Harraby Green, Broadstone, Dorsetshire BH18 8NG, England. *Agent*—Mary Irvine, 11 Upland Park Rd., Oxford OX2 7RU, England.

CAREER: Journal of British Kinematograph Society, London, England, editorial assistant, 1953-55; United Nations Food and Agriculture Organization, Rome, Italy, editorial assistant, 1957-64; writer.

MEMBER: Society of Authors, Romantic Novelists Association, Jane Austen Society, Keats-Shelley Memorial Association, Bronte Society.

WRITINGS:

First Adventure, John Gresham, 1962.
Lesson of Love, John Gresham, 1962.
Voyage to Happiness, John Gresham, 1963.
Ticket to Romance, John Gresham, 1963.
Crossroads of Love, John Gresham, 1964.
Bright Star: The Story of John Keats and Fanny Brawne, Harrap, 1968.
The Queen of Hearts, R. Hale, 1974.
Jane Austen: Woman and Writer, St. Martin's, 1976.
The Bride in Blue, R. Hale, 1978.
The Lass from the Sea, R. Hale, 1979.
The Winter Queen, R. Hale, 1983.
Shelley's Jane Williams, Kirk, 1985.
Profligate Son: Branwell Bronte and His Sisters, R. Hale, 1986.

UNDER NAME JOAN ALICE GLADYS REES; PUBLISHED BY JOHN GRESHAM

First Love, 1965.
Between Strangers, 1967.
The Decoy, 1967.

UNDER PSEUDONYM JUNE AVERY

Voyage of Dreams, John Gresham, 1967.

UNDER PSEUDONYM ANN BEDFORD

Adventure in Rome, John Gresham, 1965.

UNDER PSEUDONYM SUSAN STRONG; PUBLISHED BY R. HALE

This Thing Called Love, 1969.
My Own True Love, 1971.
Error of Judgement, 1977.
Love Remembered, 1979.
Will to Love, 1982.
Drama of Love, 1982.
By Love Cast Out, 1982.
Far East Assignment, 1983.

Jo's Awaking, 1984.
North to the Sun, 1985.
Swedish Rhapsody, 1987.
Romantic Assignment, 1988.

OTHER

Also author, under name Joan Rees, of *The Summer of 1560,* 1977, and of short stories.

WORK IN PROGRESS: A study of Charlotte Bronte's friendship with Mrs. Gaskell.

SIDELIGHTS: Joan Rees has spent a number of months in India and visited many other countries, including Thailand, North Africa, and Australia.

AVOCATIONAL INTERESTS: Music, the theater.

BIOGRAPHICAL/CRITICAL SOURCES:

PERIODICALS

Good Housekeeping (British edition), January, 1964.
Times (London), August 5, 1968.

* * *

REES, Joan Alice Gladys
See REES, Joan

* * *

REMY, Richard C. 1942-

PERSONAL: Born December 9, 1942, in Chicago, Ill.; son of Paul (an accountant) and Helen (a secretary; maiden name, Stevens) Remy; married August 22, 1966; children: Steven, Sharon. *Education:* Loyola University, Chicago, Ill., B.S., 1964; Northwestern University, M.A., 1968, Ph.D., 1971.

ADDRESSES: Home—7083 Cooper Rd., Westerville, Ohio 43081. *Office*—199 West 10th Ave., Columbus, Ohio 43201.

CAREER: Associated with Continental Insurance Co., 1964-65; Jenner Elementary School, Chicago, Ill., teacher, 1965-67; Ohio State University, Columbus, director of citizenship development program at Mershon Center, 1972—, associate professor of political science and humanities education, 1976—. Member of board of directors of ERIC Clearinghouse for Social Science/Social Studies Education.

WRITINGS:

Citizenship Decision-Making: Skill Activities, Addison-Wesley, 1978.
Civics for Americans, Scott, Foresman, 1980.
Lessons on the U.S. Constitution, American Historical Association/American Political Science Association, 1984.
Approaches to World Studies, Allyn & Bacon, 1989.
Teaching About National Security, Addison-Wesley, 1989.
Government in the United States, Macmillan, 1989.

Member of editorial board of *International Journal of Political Education,* 1980-82, and *Journal of Research and Development in Education.*

* * *

RENO, Clint
See BALLARD, (Willis) Todhunter

RESNIK, Hank
See RESNIK, Harry S.

* * *

RESNIK, Henry S. 1940-
(Hank Resnik)

PERSONAL: Born April 3, 1940, in New Haven, Conn.; son of Howard B. (a lawyer and financier) and Muriel (Spitzer) Resnik. *Education:* Yale University, B.A., 1962, M.A.T., 1963.

CAREER: High school teacher of English in Great Neck, N.Y., 1963-65; writer.

AWARDS, HONORS: Grants from Rockefeller Foundation and Thomas Skelton Harrison Foundation, 1968, to write *Turning on the System: War in the Philadelphia Public Schools.*

WRITINGS:

UNDER NAME HANK RESNIK

Turning on the System: War in the Philadelphia Public Schools, Pantheon, 1970, reprinted, 1985.
(With Joan Pizza) *The School Team Approach: Preventing Alcohol and Drug Abuse by Creating Positive Environments for Learning and Growth,* illustrations by Linda Wartell and Jon Sagen, U.S. Department of Education, Alcohol and Drug Abuse Education Program, 1980.
(With William Thomas Adams) *Channel One: A Government-Private Sector Partnership for Drug Abuse Prevention,* U.S. Department of Health and Human Services, Public Health Service, Alcohol, Drug Abuse and Mental Health Administration, 1981.
(With Adams) *Teens in Action: Creating a Drug-free Future for America's Youth,* U.S. Department of Health and Human Services, Public Health Service, Alcohol, Drug Abuse and Mental Health Administration, National Institute on Drug Abuse, Division of Prevention and Communications, 1985.
(Editor) Gary R. Collins and others, *Changes: Becoming the Best You Can Be,* Quest National Center (Columbus, Ohio), 1985.

Contributor of articles and reviews to *Saturday Review, Vogue,* and other magazines.

WORK IN PROGRESS: Magazine articles.

AVOCATIONAL INTERESTS: "Magic, mysticism, communes, tripping, travel, yoga, sailing, skiing, jogging, bicycling, women, women's liberation, revolution, counter culture, music, guitar, movies, media, children, money, survival, death, dropping out, organic food—not in order of importance; this varies from day to day."*

* * *

REYNOLDS, Barbara 1914-

PERSONAL: Born June 13, 1914, in Bristol, Gloucestershire, England; daughter of Alfred Charles (a composer) and Barbara (a singer; maiden name, Florac), Reynolds; married Lewis Thorpe (a professor of French at the University of Nottingham), September 5, 1939; children: Adrian Charles, Kerstin. *Education:* Attended schools in Detroit, Mich., 1922-26, Chicago, Ill., 1926-27, and St. Paul's Girls School, London, England, 1927-32; University College, University of London, B.A. (honors in French), 1935, B.A. (honors in Italian), 1936, Ph.D., 1948; Cambridge University, M.A., 1940. *Religion:* Church of England.

ADDRESSES: Home—220 Milton Rd., Cambridge CB4 1LQ, England.

CAREER: London School of Economics, University of London, London, England, assistant lecturer in Italian, 1937-40; Cambridge University, Cambridge, England, lecturer in Italian, 1940-62; University of Nottingham, Nottingham, England, lecturer in Italian and warden of a hall of residence, 1963-69, reader in Italian studies, 1969-78. Member of council of senate, Cambridge University, 1960-62.

MEMBER: Society for Italian Studies (honorary secretary, 1948-52; member of executive committee, 1946-62), University Women's Club (chairman, 1988—), Dorothy L. Sayers Society (chairman).

AWARDS, HONORS: Silver Cultural medal, 1964, for services to Italian culture; Edmund Gardner prize, 1964, for original Italian scholarship; Monselice International Prize, 1976, for translation of Ariosto's *Orlando Furioso;* Cavaliere Ufficiale al Merito della Repubblica Italiana, 1978.

WRITINGS:

(Editor and author of introduction and notes, with K. T. Butler) *Tredici novelle moderne,* Macmillan (New York), 1947, 2nd edition, Cambridge University Press, 1959.

The Linguistic Writings of Alessandro Manzoni: A Textual and Chronological Reconstruction, Heffer, 1950.

(Editor) M. A. Orr, *Dante and the Early Astronomers,* 2nd edition, Wingate, 1956.

(General editor and chief contributor) *The Cambridge Italian Dictionary,* Cambridge University Press, Volume 1, 1962, Volume 2, 1980.

(Translator with Dorothy L. Sayers) Dante Alighieri, *The Comedy of Dante Alighieri, the Florentine: Paradise,* Penguin, 1962.

(With husband, Lewis Thorpe) *Guido Farina,* Valdonega (Verona), 1967.

(Translator) Dante, *La vita nuova: Poems of Youth,* Penguin, 1969.

Concise Cambridge Italian Dictionary, Cambridge University Press, 1975.

(Translator) Lodovico Ariosto, *Orlando Furioso: The Frenzy of Orlando, a Romantic Epic,* Penguin, Volume 1, 1975, Volume 2, 1977.

(Editor) *Cambridge-Signorelli Italian-English English-Italian Dictionary,* Cambridge University Press, 1986.

(Editor with William Radice) *The Translator's Art: Essays in Honor of Betty Radice,* Penguin, 1987.

The Passionate Intellect: Dorothy L. Sayers' Encounter with Dante, Kent State University Press, 1989.

Contributor of stories and poetry to the *Detroit News.* Managing editor and co-founder of *Seven: An Anglo-American Literary Review.*

BIOGRAPHICAL/CRITICAL SOURCES:

PERIODICALS

Times (London), September 19, 1987.

Times Literary Supplement, May 9, 1986.

* * *

RHOADES, Jonathan
See OLSEN, John Edward

RICHARDS, Frank
See HAMILTON, Charles (Harold St. John)

* * *

RICHARDS, Hilda
See HAMILTON, Charles (Harold St. John)

* * *

RICHARDSON, Robert D(ale), Jr. 1934-

PERSONAL: Born June 14, 1934, in Milwaukee, Wis.; son of Robert Dale (a clergyman) and Lucy (Marsh) Richardson; married Elizabeth Hall, November 7, 1959; married second wife, Annie Dillard (a writer), December 10, 1988; children: (first marriage) Elizabeth, Anne. *Education:* Harvard University, B.A., 1956, Ph.D., 1961.

ADDRESSES: Home—158 Mt. Vernon St., Middletown, Conn. 06457.

CAREER: Harvard University, Cambridge, Mass., instructor in English, 1961-63; University of Denver, Denver, Colo., assistant professor, 1963-68, associate professor, 1968-72, professor of English, beginning 1972, Phipps Professor of Humanities, 1979-82, head of department of English, 1968-73. Visiting professor at universities, including Harvard University, summer, 1976, Sichuan University, 1983, and University of Colorado, 1987. Member of board of directors, David R. Godine Publishers; trustee, Meadville-Lombard Theological School and University of Chicago.

MEMBER: Modern Language Association of America, American Studies Association, American Association of University Professors, American Civil Liberties Union, Phi Beta Kappa.

AWARDS, HONORS: Huntington Libraries fellow, 1973-74; Melcher Book Award, 1986.

WRITINGS:

Literature and Film, Indiana University Press, 1969.

(With Burton Feldman) *The Rise of Modern Mythology,* Indiana University Press, 1972.

Myth and Literature in the American Renaissance, Indiana University Press, 1978.

Henry Thoreau: A Life of the Mind, University of California Press, 1986.

Also author of *Myth and Romanticism,* a reprint series of fifty-two volumes of major myth sources used by the English Romantics. Contributor of articles and reviews to professional journals. *Denver Quarterly,* associate editor, 1967-76, book review editor, 1976—; member of editorial board, *Western Review.*

WORK IN PROGRESS: An intellectual biography of Ralph Waldo Emerson.

SIDELIGHTS: Critics praise Robert D. Richardson, Jr.'s skill as a biographer displayed in his *Henry Thoreau: A Life of the Mind. Los Angeles Times Book Review* contributor Ronald Gottesman, for example, calls the book a "major contribution to Thoreau studies" and recommends it "to research specialists and general readers alike. That this biography may be recommended enthusiastically to any serious reader is a tribute to the power of Richardson's prose, which is vivid, supple and clear." In his *Virginia Quarterly Review* essay on the book, David Robinson comments, "Richardson has mastered all that Thoreau himself had mastered, but done so with the understanding that the fundamental biography of Thoreau was not what he read, but why he read it, and what he thought of it. . . . The success of Richardson's reconstruction of Thoreau's intellectual development will make it *the* book on him for a very long time."

BIOGRAPHICAL/CRITICAL SOURCES:

PERIODICALS

Los Angeles Times Book Review, November 30, 1986.
Virginia Quarterly Review, autumn, 1987.

*　　*　　*

RICKS, Chip
See RICKS, Nadine

*　　*　　*

RICKS, Nadine 1925-
(Chip Ricks)

PERSONAL: Born February 20, 1925, in Texas; daughter of Sidney Leeman (a rancher) and Mabel (Bollinger) Wilson; married Albert Conwell Ricks (a stockbroker), May 5, 1944; children: Cynthia Ann (Mrs. E. H. Littlejohn), Connie Jean (Mrs R. Engel), Richard Alan. *Education:* University of Texas, B.A., 1954; University of Nebraska, M.A., 1964. *Religion:* Nazarene.

ADDRESSES: Home—505 St. Andrews Way, Lompoc, Calif. 93436. *Office*—Trinity Nazarene Church, 500 East North Ave., Lompoc, Calif. 93436.

CAREER: Aroostook State Teachers College (now University of Maine at Presque Isle), Presque Isle, Me., instructor in English, 1960; University of Nebraska, Lincoln, instructor in English, 1964-67; Allan Hancock College, Santa Maria, Calif., instructor in English, 1967-84; Trinity Nazarene Church, Lompoc, Calif., director of adult education, 1984-87.

WRITINGS:

(With Marilyn Marsh) *Patterns in English,* Scribner, 1969.
(With Marsh) *How to Write Your First Research Paper,* Wadsworth, 1971, revised edition, Kendall/Hunt, 1982.

UNDER PSEUDONYM CHIP RICKS

Beyond the Clouds, Tyndale, 1979.
Carol's Story, Tyndale, 1980.
John and 1st John, Tyndale, 1982.
How to Write for Christian Periodicals, Broadman, 1985.
Understanding the Bible, Virgil Hensley, Inc., Volume 1: *The Five Books of Moses,* Volume 2: *The Twelve History Books,* Volume 3, and Volume 4, 1989, Volumes 5-7, 1990-91.

SIDELIGHTS: Nadine Ricks, also known to readers as Chip Ricks, told *CA:* "My latest books in a series titled *Understanding the Bible* are by far the most exciting writing assignment I have ever had. Actually there are sixty-six books in the Bible and the themes in these ancient books were here even centuries before they became the basis for our English and American literature. Themes of life and death, light and darkness, good and evil, sacrifice and redemption—these and more run like threads through these sixty-six books. My task is to help the reader understand how these themes come together in the relationship of God and man—the two major characters."

ROBBINS, Raleigh
See HAMILTON, Charles (Harold St. John)

*　　*　　*

ROBBINS, Thomas Eugene 1936-
(Tom Robbins)

PERSONAL: Born in 1936, in Blowing Rock, N.C.; son of Katherine (Robinson) Robbins; married second wife, Terrie (divorced); children: (second marriage) Fleetwood Star (son). *Education:* Attended Washington and Lee University, 1950-52, Richmond Professional Institute (now Virginia Commonwealth University), and University of Washington.

ADDRESSES: Home—LaConner, Wash. *Agent*—Pheobe Larmore, 228 Main St., Venice, Calif. 90291.

CAREER: Writer. *Richmond Times-Dispatch,* Richmond, Va., copy editor, 1960-62; *Seattle Times* and *Seattle Post-Intelligence,* Seattle, Wash., copy editor, 1962-63; *Seattle Magazine,* Seattle, reviewer and art critic, 1964-68. Conducted research in New York City's East Village for an unwritten book on Jackson Pollock. *Military service:* U.S. Air Force; served in Korea.

WRITINGS:

UNDER NAME TOM ROBBINS

Guy Anderson (biography), Gear Works Press, 1965.
Another Roadside Attraction (novel), Doubleday, 1971.
Even Cowgirls Get the Blues (novel), Houghton, 1976.
Still Life with Woodpecker (novel), Bantam, 1980.
Jitterbug Perfume (novel), Bantam, 1984.

SIDELIGHTS: Tom Robbins was a critically admired but low-selling novelist until the mid-1970s, when his first two works of fiction, *Another Roadside Attraction* and *Even Cowgirls Get the Blues,* went into paperback editions. Only then did the books become accessible to students, and they took to the novels with an enthusiasm that made the author "the biggest thing to hit the 'youth market' in years," according to *New York Times Magazine* reporter Mitchell S. Ross. Much of Robbins's popularity among young readers, most critics agree, can be attributed to the fact that his novels encompass the countercultural "California" or "West Coast" school of writing, whose practitioners also include the likes of Ken Kesey and Richard Braughtigan. In the words of R. H. Miller, writing in a *Dictionary of Literary Biography Yearbook* piece, the West Coast school emphasizes "the themes of personal freedom, the pursuit of higher states of being through Eastern mysticism, the escape from the confining life of urban California to the openness of the pastoral Pacific Northwest. Like the writings of his mentors, Robbins's own novels exhibit an elaborate style, a delight in words for their own sake, and an open, at times anarchical, attitude toward strict narrative form."

All of these qualities are evident in the author's first novel, *Another Roadside Attraction.* In this story, a collection of eccentrics with names like Plucky Purcell and Marx Marvelous gets involved with the mummified body of Jesus Christ, which somehow ends up at the Capt. Kendrick Memorial Hot Dog Wildlife Preserve, formerly Mom's Little Dixie Diner. As Ross sees it, the novel's plot "is secondary to the characters and tertiary to the style. [These characters] are nothing like your next-door neighbors, even if you lived in Haight-Ashbury in the middle '60s." Jerome Klinkowitz, digging deeper into the novel's meaning, declares in his book *The Practice of Fiction in America: Writers from Hawthorne to the Present* that in *Another Roadside Attrac-*

tion Robbins "feels that the excessive rationalization of Western culture since [17th-century philosopher Rene] Descartes has severed man from his roots in nature. Organized religion has in like manner become more of a tool of logic and control than of spirit. Robbins' heroine, Amanda, would reconnect mankind with the benign chaos of the natural world, substituting magic for logic, style for substance, and poetry for the analytical measure of authority." Klinkowitz also finds the author is "a master of plain American speech . . . and his greatest trick is to use its flat style to defuse the most sacred objects."

Robbins followed *Another Roadside Attraction* with what would become his best-known novel to date. In *Even Cowgirls Get the Blues,* the author "shows the same zest of his earlier book, but the plot is focused and disciplined, mostly because Robbins had learned by this time to use the structure of the journey as a major organizing principle in the narrative," according to Miller. This tale concerns one Sissy Hankshaw, an extraordinary hitchhiker due mainly to the fact that she was born with oversized thumbs. One of her rides takes her to the Rubber Rose Ranch, run by Bonanza Jellybean and her cowgirls, "whom Sissy joins in an attempt to find freedom from herself, as she participates in their communal search for that same freedom," as Miller relates. "They yearn for an open, sexual, unchauvinistic world, much like that of the Chink, a wizened hermit who lives near the ranch and who has absorbed his philosophy of living from the Clock people, a tribe of Indians, and from Eastern philosophy."

Again, plot takes a backseat to the intellectual forces that drive the characters on. To *Nation* critic Ann Cameron, *Even Cowgirls Get the Blues* shows "a brilliant affirmation of private visions and private wishes and the power to transform life and death. A tall tale and a parable of essential humanness, it is a work of extraordinary playfulness, style and wit." In his study *Tom Robbins,* author Mark Siegel sees two "major paradoxes in [the author's ideas]. One is the emphasis he places on individual fulfillment while he simultaneously castigates egotism. The second is his apparent devotion to Eastern philosophies in *Another Roadside Attraction,* although he warns against adopting Eastern religions in *Cowgirls.* Actually the two issues are closely related, both stemming from Robbins's notion that any truly fulfilling way of life must evolve from the individual's recognition of his true, personal relationship to the world. Thus, although Americans can learn from Oriental philosophies much about liberation from the ego, Western man must nevertheless find a way of liberation that is natural to him in his own world."

"Robbins has an old trunk of a mind," says Thomas LeClair in a *New York Times Book Review* piece on *Cowgirls.* "[He] knows the atmosphere on Venus, cow diseases, hitchhiking manuals, herbs, the brain's circuitry, whooping cranes, circles, parades, Nisei internment," and that these visions "add up to a primitivism just pragmatic enough to be attractive and fanciful enough to measure the straight society." In Ross's opinion, the author's style "generates its own head of steam and dances past the plot, characters and clockwork philosophy. . . . Oddly, it is a style without a single voice. At times, Robbins booms out like a bard; the next instant he forces us to mourn the loss of the next Bob Hope to beautiful letters." Ross notes too that "a piling on of wisecracks is made to substitute for description."

Robbins's penchant for cracking wise represents a sore point in his next novel, *Still Life with Woodpecker,* according to Julie B. Peters in the *Saturday Review.* Peters states that in this tale of a princess's romance with an outlaw, the prose "is marbled with limping puns heavily splattered with recurrent motifs and a boyish zeal for the scatalogical." Taking a similar tack, *Commonweal* critic Frank McConnell points out that "a large part of the problem in reading Robbins [is that] he's so *cute:* his books are full of cute lines populated by unrelentingly cute people, even teeming with cute animals—frogs, chipmunks and chihuahuas in *Still Life with Woodpecker.* No one ever gets hurt very badly . . . , and although the world is threatened by the same dark, soulless business cartels that threaten the worlds of [Thomas] Pynchon, [Norman] Mailer, and our century, in Robbins it doesn't seem, finally, to matter. Love or something like it really does conquer all in his parables, with a mixture of stoned gaiety, positive thinking, and Sunday Supplement Taoism."

In telling the story of the unusual relationship between Princess Leigh-Cheri, heiress of the Pacific island of Mu, and good-hearted terrorist Bernard Micky Wrangle, alias Woodpecker, the author also frames the tale by a monologue "having to do with his [Robbins's] efforts to type out his narrative on a Remington SL-3 typewriter, which at the end fails him, and he has to complete the novel in longhand," says Miller, who also finds that the moral of *Still Life with Woodpecker* "is not as strong as that of the earlier two [novels], and while the plot seems more intricately interlaced, it has the complexity and exoticism of grand opera but little of its brilliance."

The generally disappointed reaction of critics to *Still Life with Woodpecker* left some writers wondering whether Robbins, with his free-form style, was addressing the needs of fiction readers in the upwardly mobile 1980s. The author answered his critics with *Jitterbug Perfume,* published in 1984. In this novel, Seattle waitress Priscilla devotes her life to inventing the ultimate perfume. The challenge is taken up in locales as varied as New Orleans and Paris, while back in Seattle, Wiggs Dannyboy, described by *Washington Post Book World* reviewer Rudy Rucker as "a Timothy Leary work-alike who's given up acid for immortality research" enters the scene to provide insights on the 1960s.

Comparing *Jitterbug Perfume* to the author's other works, Rucker notes that the first two novels were '60s creations—"filled with mushrooms and visions, radicals and police. *Still Life with Woodpecker* is about the '70s viewed as the aftermath of the '60s." And in *Jitterbug Perfume,* "Robbins is still very much his old Pan-worshipping self, yet his new book is lovingly plotted, with every conceivable loose end nailed down tight. Although the ideas are the same as ever, the form is contemporary, new-realistic craftsmanship. Robbins toys with the 1980s' peculiar love/hate for the 60s through his invention of the character Wiggs Dannyboy." To John House, the work "is not so much a novel as an inspirational fable, full of Hallmark sweetness, good examples and hope springing eternal." House, in a *New York Times Book Review* article, goes on to say that he finds Robbins's style "unmistakable—oblique, florid, willing to sacrifice everything for an old joke or corny pun." While *Jitterbug Perfume* "is still less exuberant than 'Cowgirls,' " according to Don Strachan in the *Los Angeles Times Book Review,* the former is still "less diminished than honed. The author may still occasionally stick his foot in the door of his mouth, as he would say in one of those metaphors he loves to mix with wordplay salads, but then he'll unfurl a phrase that will bring your critical mind to its knees."

"Robbins's contribution to the West Coast novel lies in his athletic style and iconoclastic attitude toward form," concludes Miller. "He refuses to be disciplined by the critics. His message is like the dying call of the whooping cranes in *Even Cowgirls Get the Blues,* a plea for freedom, naturalness, and peace, but it is a rather lonely voice echoing the concerns of an earlier decade, even an earlier generation." The author himself summed up his appeal in a *Detroit News* interview conducted by Randy Sue Coburn. "I'm an ordinary, sweet, witty guy who happens to possess a luminous cosmic vision and a passionate appreciation of fine sentences," Robbins says. "There. Now let's talk about books. Let's talk about life, death and goofiness. Best of all, let's talk about lunch."

BIOGRAPHICAL/CRITICAL SOURCES:

BOOKS

Contemporary Literary Criticism, Gale, Volume 9, 1978, Volume 32, 1985.

Dictionary of Literary Biography Yearbook: 1980, Gale, 1981.

Klinkowitz, Jerome, *The Practice of Fiction in America: Writers from Hawthorne to the Present,* Iowa State University Press, 1980.

Nadeau, Robert, *Readings from the New Book on Nature: Physics and Metaphysics in the Modern Novel,* University of Massachusetts Press, 1981.

Siegel, Mark, *Tom Robbins,* Boise State University Press, 1980.

PERIODICALS

Chicago Review, autumn, 1980.

Commonweal, March 13, 1981.

Detroit News, October 5, 1980, Janaury 6, 1985.

Los Angeles Times Book Review, December 16, 1984.

Nation, August 28, 1976, October 25, 1980.

New Boston Review, December, 1977.

New Republic, June 26, 1971.

New Statesman, August 12, 1977.

Newsweek, September 29, 1980.

New York Times Book Review, May 23, 1976, September 28, 1980, December 9, 1984.

New York Times Magazine, February 12, 1978.

Saturday Review, September, 1980.

Times Literary Supplement, October 31, 1980.

Washington Post Book World, October 25, 1980.

—*Sketch by Susan Salter*

* * *

ROBBINS, Tom
See ROBBINS, Thomas Eugene

* * *

ROEBUCK, Derek 1935-

PERSONAL: Born January 22, 1935, in Stalybridge, England; son of John (a postal worker) and Jessie (a bookbinder) Roebuck; married Susanna Hoe (a writer), August 18, 1981; children: two sons, one daughter. *Education:* Hertford College, Oxford, M.A., 1960; University of New Zealand, M.Conn.

ADDRESSES: Home—Flat 5B/1 Cavendish Heights, Jardihe's Lookout, Hong Kong. *Office*—Law Department, City Polytechnic of Hong Kong, Kowloon, Hong Kong.

CAREER: Solicitor in England, 1957-62; Victoria University of Wellington, Wellington, New Zealand, lecturer in law, 1962-67; University of Tasmania, Hobart, Australia, senior lecturer, 1967-69, professor of law, 1969-78; Amnesty International, London, England, head of research at International Secretariat, 1979-82; University of Papua New Guinea, Port Moresby, professor of law, 1982-87; City Polytechnic of Hong Kong, Kowloon, professor and head of department of law, 1987—.

MEMBER: International Association of Democratic Lawyers, International Commission of Jurists, Law Society, Selden Society.

WRITINGS:

Law in the Study of Business, Pergamon, 1967.

(With Peter C. Duncan and Alexander Szakats) *Law of Commerce,* Wellington, Sweet & Maxwell, 1968.

(Editor with David E. Allan and Mary E. Hiscock) *Asian Contract Law: A Survey of Current Problems,* Melbourne University Press, 1969.

(With Allan, Hiscock, and others) *Credit and Security: The Legal Problems of Development Financing,* ten volumes, Queensland University Press, 1974.

Law of Contract: Text and Materials, Law Book Co., 1974.

(With Wilfred Burchett) *The Whores of War,* Penguin, 1977.

Custom and Usage: Australian and New Zealand Commentary on the Laws of England, Butterworth, 1979.

(With D. K. Srivastava and J. Nonggorr) *Context of Contract,* University of Papua New Guinea Press, 1984.

(With Srivastava and Nonggorr) *Pacific Contract Law,* University of Papua New Guinea Press, 1987.

The Background of the Common Law, Oxford University Press, 1988.

Cheques, Hong Kong University Press, 1989.

AVOCATIONAL INTERESTS: Football, cricket.

* * *

ROGERS, Robert
See HAMILTON, Charles (Harold St. John)

* * *

ROOT, Waverley (Lewis) 1903-1982

PERSONAL: Born April 15, 1903, in Providence, R.I.; died of pulmonary edema, October 31, (one source says October 30), 1982, in Paris, France; son of Francis Solomon and Florence Mae (Lewis) Root; married first wife, Jeanne Rose Albinelli, July, 1937; married Colette Debenais, April 8, 1959; children: (former marriage) Diane Lane. *Education:* Tufts University, student, 1920-23, B.A. (as of class of 1924), 1941. *Politics:* No political affiliation. *Religion:* No church affiliation.

ADDRESSES: Home—124 rue de Cherche-Midi, Paris 6E, France.

CAREER: Chicago Tribune, Chicago, Ill., correspondent in Paris and London, 1927-1930, editor of Paris edition, 1930-34; *Politiken,* Copenhagen, Denmark, Paris correspondent, 1932-40; United Press, New York City, Paris correspondent, 1934-38; *Time,* New York City, Paris correspondent, 1938; Mutual Broadcasting System, New York City, Paris radio correspondent, 1938-40; WINS-Radio, New York City, commentator, 1940-45; *New York Daily Mirror,* New York City, editor of "World behind Headlines," 1941-42; Press Alliance, New York City, syndicated columnist, 1941-53; Opera Mundi, Paris, ghostwriter, 1950-52; "Fodor's Modern Guides," editor in The Hague, Netherlands, 1952-55; *Washington Post,* Washington, D.C., Paris correspondent, 1958-67; Paris editor, *Holiday* (magazine), 1968-71.

MEMBER: Overseas Press Club (New York City; vice-president, 1943-45), Anglo-American Press Association of Paris (president, 1967).

AWARDS, HONORS: Officer of the Legion of Honor (France).

WRITINGS:

(With Philip Dutton Hurn) *The Truth about Wagner,* Stokes Publishing, 1929.
The Secret History of the War, three volumes, Scribner, 1945-46.
The Food of France, Knopf, 1958, 2nd edition, 1970.
(With Richard de Rochement) *Contemporary French Cooking,* Random House, 1962.
The Cooking of Italy, Time-Life, 1968.
Paris Dining Guide, Atheneum, 1969.
The Food of Italy, Atheneum, 1971.
(Editor) Luigi Veronelli, *The Best of Italian Cooking,* Grosset & Dunlap, 1974.
(With de Rochement) *Eating in America: A History,* Morrow, 1976.
Food: An Authoritative and Visual History and Dictionary of the Foods of the World, Simon & Schuster, 1980.
(Editor with others) *Herbs and Spices: The Pursuit of Flavor,* McGraw, 1980, revised edition published as *Herbs and Spices: A Guide to Culinary Seasoning,* Van der Marck, 1985.
The Paris Edition: The Autobiography of Waverley Root, 1927-1934, North Point Press, 1987.

Contributor to a number of American periodicals, including *Chicago Times, Holiday, American Scholar, Gourmet, Esquire,* and *New York Times Magazine.*

WORK IN PROGRESS: The Food of Ancient Greece and Rome, for Dodd.

SIDELIGHTS: The late Waverley Root was an American journalist and expert on international cuisine who spent most of his life in Paris. Prior to World War II, Root served as a Paris correspondent to the *Chicago Tribune.* He also edited the Paris edition of the same newspaper and served as a literary critic and columnist with strong feelings on experimental literature. Root was the first Paris correspondent for the *Washington Post,* holding that position from 1958 until 1967. Simultaneously he began to write and edit books on the cuisine of France and Italy, and these created his reputation as a connoisseur of fine food. More than mere compilations of recipes, Root's books such as *The Food of France, The Food of Italy,* and *Eating in America: A History* "brought a historical dimension to cooking, describing how various foods were used down through the ages," to quote a *Los Angeles Times* reporter. Indeed, Root's most popular book, *The Food of France,* has never been out of print since its publication in 1958, even though it is simply a region-by-region assessment of French cooking techniques.

Root was born in Providence, Rhode Island, but he grew up in Fall River, Massachusetts. In 1920 he entered Tufts University, where he served as campus correspondent for a Boston newspaper and the Associated Press. He left Tufts without a degree in 1923 and sought journalism work in New York city (the university awarded him a B.A. *ex ordinem* in 1941). While in New York, Root worked for a variety of trade publications and wrote capsule reviews for the *World,* hoping to land a staff job on a newspaper. Acting on a whim in the spring of 1927, he took a transatlantic steamer to France, ostensibly just for a short visit. As Anne Chamberlain puts it in the *Washington Post Book World,* "Normandy was adrift in apple blossoms when he got there; Paris aglow with enchantment. Days passed before his feet even touched the ground, and for more than 50 years the magic never wore off." Root stayed in Paris from 1927 until the war threatened his safety in 1940; his numerous jobs included book reviewer, editor, and feature writer for the Paris *Tribune* (an English language daily), correspondent for the *Chicago Tribune,* and radio correspondent for the Mutual Broadcasting System. After the war he returned to Europe, living and working there until his death in 1982.

Root became an authority on regional foods after he began to compile dining guides for Americans visiting France and Italy. While most of his books contain recipes, they are first and foremost accounts of the histories and eccentricities of regional cuisine. Paramount in this genre is *Eating in America,* a work that explores the multinational influences on diet and food preparation in the United States. *Saturday Review* contributor Evan Jones describes *Eating in America* as "the kind of book that will stimulate talk—perhaps most of it irritated, defensive, combative—and, yes, nostalgic discussion. Above all, it should give rise to further considerations of what the American cuisine really is."

Root died of pulmonary edema on October 31, 1982, at his home in Paris. His posthumously published *The Paris Edition: The Autobiography of Waverley Root, 1927-1934* recounts his early years as a working journalist in France.

AVOCATIONAL INTERESTS: Scientific developments, especially in biology and psychology; chess, bridge, tennis, classical music.

BIOGRAPHICAL/CRITICAL SOURCES:

BOOKS

Dictionary of Literary Biography, Volume 4: *American Writers in Paris, 1920-1939,* Gale, 1980.
Root, Waverley, *The Paris Edition: The Autobiography of Waverley Root, 1927-1934,* North Point Press, 1987.

PERIODICALS

American Scholar, summer, 1977.
Los Angeles Times, July 1, 1987.
Newsweek, December 6, 1971.
New York Times, August 15, 1981.
New York Times Book Review, March 19, 1967, December 1, 1968, November 21, 1976, August 16, 1987.
Saturday Review, October 16, 1976.
Time, November 29, 1976, November 24, 1980.
Washington Post Book World, December 7, 1980, May 31, 1987.

OBITUARIES:

PERIODICALS

Chicago Tribune, November 2, 1982.
Los Angeles Times, November 1, 1982.
New York Times, November 2, 1982.
Washington Post, November 1, 1982.*

* * *

ROSITZKE, Harry A(ugust) 1911-

PERSONAL: Born February 25, 1911, in Brooklyn, N.Y.; son of Emil H. and Anna (Brockman) Rositzke; married Barbara Bourgeois, May 11, 1942; children: John Brockman, Anne Elizabeth. *Education:* Union College, Schenectady, N.Y., A.B., 1931; Harvard University, Ph.D., 1935. *Politics:* Democrat.

ADDRESSES: Home—Fox Den, Middleburg, Va. 22117.

CAREER: Harvard University, Cambridge, Mass., tutor in English, 1936-37; University of Omaha, Omaha, Neb., instructor in English, 1937-38; University of Rochester, Rochester, N.Y., instructor in English, 1938-42; U.S. Central Intelligence Agency (CIA), Washington, D.C., foreign intelligence officer in Munich,

West Germany, and New Delhi, India, 1947-70; free-lance writer, 1970—. *Military service:* U.S. Army, 1942-46; became major.

WRITINGS:

The C-Text of the Old English Chronicles, Poeppinghaus, 1940.
The Peterbrough Chronicle, Columbia University Press, 1951.
The U.S.S.R. Today, John Day, 1973.
Left On! (novel), Quadrangle, 1973.
The CIA's Secret Operations: Espionage, Counterespionage, and Covert Action, Reader's Digest Press, 1977.
The KGB: The Eyes of Russia, Doubleday, 1980.
Managing Moscow: Guns or Goods?, Morrow, 1984.

WORK IN PROGRESS: A Short History of the Human Soul; The Making of a Christian Atheist.

SIDELIGHTS: Harry A. Rositzke spent twenty-five years as the Central Intelligence Agency's agent assigned to monitoring the Soviet Union's intelligence operations, beginning his career by organizing the first unit to focus on Soviet activities. Rositzke lends this expertise to two books on the workings of espionage: *The CIA's Secret Operations: Espionage, Counterespionage, and Covert Action,* and *The KGB: The Eyes of Russia.* The latter study, while not presenting much new information, is "a serviceable primer on the KGB," comments David Wise in the *Washington Post Book World,* "useful for anyone who is interested in the operations of the Soviet spy service, but whose interest does not extend to plowing through a lot of individual books on the subject." Paul G. Levine similarly notes in the *Los Angeles Times Book Review* that "Rositzke is most effective in his broad overview of Soviet capabilities . . . [and in] unravel[ing] the workings of the Soviet intelligence bureaucracy." Containing first-hand accounts of CIA procedures, *The CIA's Secret Operations* "is—like Rositzke's own long and dedicated professional career—a felicitous blend of intelligence philosophy and intelligence operations," writes *National Review* contributor Howard Hunt, "and the author has not refrained from describing CIA failures as well as some mitigating successes." The result, concludes the critic, "is by far the best written and most authentic book on the CIA I have ever read."

AVOCATIONAL INTERESTS: Raising Angus cattle, playing tennis, visiting New York, "ruminat[ing] about nature, death, the Russians, and our dehumanized society."

BIOGRAPHICAL/CRITICAL SOURCES:

PERIODICALS

Los Angeles Times Book Review, August 23, 1981.
National Review, July 8, 1977, September 18, 1981.
Spectator, February 13, 1982.
Washington Post Book World, July 26, 1981.

* * *

ROSOWSKI, Susan J(ean) 1942-

PERSONAL: Born January 2, 1942, in Topeka, Kan.; daughter of William H. and Alice E. (Winegar) Campbell; married James R. Rosowski (a professor of botany), June 22, 1963; children: Scott Merritt, David William. *Education:* Whittier College, B.A., 1964; University of Arizona, M.A., 1967, Ph.D., 1974.

ADDRESSES: Home—3405 South 28th St., Lincoln, Neb. 68502. *Office*—Department of English, University of Nebraska, Lincoln, Neb. 68588-0333.

CAREER: University of Nebraska at Omaha, instructor, 1971-76, assistant professor, 1976-78, associate professor of English, 1978-82; University of Nebraska—Lincoln, associate professor, 1983-86, professor of English, 1986—. Co-director of National Seminar on Willa Cather, 1983; executive council member, Center for Great Plains Studies, University of Nebraska, 1984-87; member of board of governors of Willa Cather Pioneer Memorial and Educational Foundation.

MEMBER: Modern Language Association of America, Midwest Modern Language Association, Western Literature Association (member of executive committee, 1980-83; president, 1986-87), Golden Key Society (University of Nebraska—Lincoln chapter; honorary member).

AWARDS, HONORS: Danforth associate, 1980—; Great Teacher Award, University of Nebraska at Omaha, 1981; Annis Chaikin Sorensen Award for distinguished teaching in the humanities, University of Nebraska—Lincoln, 1986.

WRITINGS:

(With Billie Jo Inman and Ruth Gardner) *Reading and Exercises for English I* (textbook and manual), University of Arizona, 1967, 2nd edition, 1968.
(Editor with Helen Stauffer) *Women and Western American Literature,* Whitston Publishing, 1982.
The Voyage Perilous: Willa Cather's Romanticism, University of Nebraska Press, 1986.
(Editor and contributor) *Approaches to Teaching Cather's "My Antonia,"* Modern Language Association of America, 1989.

CONTRIBUTOR

Arthur R. Husboe and William Geyer, editors, *Where the West Begins,* Center for Western Studies, Augustana College (Sioux Falls, S.D.), 1978.
Elizabeth Abel, Marianne Hirsch, and Elizabeth Langland, editors, *The Voyage In: Fictions of Female Development,* University of New England Press, 1983.
Paul Simpson-Housley and William Mallory, editors, *Geography and Literature,* Syracuse University Press, 1987.
Hollister Sturgis, editor, *Jules Breton and the French Rural Tradition,* Joslyn Art Museum, 1987.
Bernard Koloski, editor, *Approaches to Teaching Chopin's "The Awakening,"* Modern Language Association of America, 1988.
Kathryn N. Benzel and Lauren De La Vars, editors, *Women's Artistry: Re-envisioning the Female Self,* Edwin Mellen, in press.

OTHER

Contributor of articles on Willa Cather and other writers to journals, including *Studies in the Novel, Novel, Western American Literature, Journal of Narrative Technique, Great Plains Quarterly, Women's Studies, English Journal, Prairie Schooner,* and *Literature and Belief.* Editor-in-chief, *Cather Studies.*

WORK IN PROGRESS: A book on gender and the significance of the frontier in American literature; editing, with James Woodress, a scholarly edition of Willa Cather's works.

SIDELIGHTS: Susan J. Rosowski once told *CA:* "Work on Willa Cather has enabled me to combine my personal and professional interests in an extremely satisfying way. Cather contributed heroic women to a western American literature dominated by a masculine ethos, and she provided revelations of spiritual value in a modern tradition dominated by themes of alienation and loneliness. Cather once wrote, 'Miracles . . . rest not so much upon faces or voices or healing power coming suddenly near to us from afar off, but upon our perceptions being made finer, so that for a moment our eyes can see and our ears can hear what is there about us always.' Her writing offers the 'miracle' of such moments."

* * *

ROSS, Leonard M(ichael) 1945-1985

PERSONAL: Born July 7, 1945, in Los Angeles, Calif.; died of apparent drowning, May 1, 1985, in Santa Clara, Calif.; son of William and Pauline (Lieberman) Ross. *Education:* Attended Reed College, 1959-62; University of California, Los Angeles, B.A., 1963; Yale University, LL.B., 1967, Ph.D. candidate in economics, beginning 1967.

ADDRESSES: Office—Department of Business Management, California State Polytechnic University, 380 West Temple Ave., Ponoma, Calif. 91768.

CAREER: Harvard University, Law School, Cambridge, Mass., Thayer teaching fellow, 1970-71; Columbia University, Law School, New York, N.Y., assistant professor of law, beginning 1971; became affiliated with department of business management, California State Polytechnic University, Ponoma, Calif. Executive director of Council for President's Task Force on Communications Policy, President's Commission on Campus Unrest, Rand Corp., Arthur D. Little, Inc., New England Economic Research Foundation, and Sloan Commission on Cable Television.

WRITINGS:

(With David Kendall) *The Lottery and the Draft: Where Do I Stand,* Harper, 1970.
(With Peter Passell) *Communications Satellite Tariffs for Television* (monograph), International Broadcast Institute, c. 1972.
(With Passell) *The Retreat from Riches: Affluence and Its Enemies,* Viking, 1973.
(With Passell) *The Best,* Farrar, Straus, 1974.
Economic and Legal Foundations of Cable Television, Sage Publications, 1974.
(With Passell) *State Policies and Federal Programs: Priorities and Constraints,* Praeger, 1978.

Contributor of articles and reviews to several publications. Editor-in-chief, *Yale Law Journal,* 1966-67.

SIDELIGHTS: The apparent suicide of former child prodigy Leonard M. Ross stunned his colleagues and left a raft of unanswered questions. But on one point his friends and loved ones seemed to agree: that Ross' publicity as a genius took a toll on the youngster's emotional life. From his earliest years, Ross was in the spotlight. "He had attracted national attention by passing a Federal examination for a ham radio operator's license when he was 7 and, three years later, as the 'whiz kid' who won $164,000 on two television quiz shows for his precocious answers about the stock market," according to Maureen Dowd in a *New York Times* article.

Entering Yale Law school at age eighteen brought more attention to the young man. By the time Ross had graduated, "his friends had great expectations" for him, Dowd continued. A number of political assignments made up the bulk of Ross' career, with a half-dozen books and monographs completing the picture. But even as Ross' reputation preceded him everywhere, the author's personality worried many. Toward the end of his life, Ross was "already losing his confidence in his ability to do sustained work," as writing partner Peter Passell told Dowd. "He thought he would embarrass himself." Passell further characterized Ross as an eccentric who "had bad table manners and . . . dressed sloppily. At some level he was proclaiming that he was a child who needed to be taken care of." A previous suicide attempt, over a failed romance, alerted Ross' friends to the author's deep-seated problems; but on May 1, 1985, he was discovered floating in a motel swimming pool in Santa Clara, California.

OBITUARIES:

PERIODICALS

Chicago Tribune, May 5, 1985.
Los Angeles Times, May 4, 1985.
New York Times, May 6, 1985, May 25, 1985.*

* * *

ROTHMAN, Barbara Katz 1948-

PERSONAL: Born June 21, 1948, in Brooklyn, N.Y.; daughter of Daniel H. (a refrigeration mechanic) and Marcia (a social worker; maiden name, Charnow) Katz; married Herschel M. Rothman (a programmer), August 24, 1969; children: Daniel Colb, Leah Colb. *Education:* Brooklyn College of the City University of New York, B.A., 1969, M.A., 1972; New York University, Ph.D., 1979. *Politics:* "Feminist."

ADDRESSES: Office—Department of Sociology, Baruch College of the City University of New York, 17 Lexington Ave., New York, N.Y. 10010. *Agent*—Carol Mann Literary Agency, 168 Pacific St., Brooklyn, N.Y. 11201.

CAREER: Associated with branches of the city and state Universities of New York, 1970-78; Bernard M. Baruch College of the City University of New York, New York City, professor of sociology, 1979—. Member of the faculty of Graduate School and University of the City University of New York, 1982—.

MEMBER: American Sociological Association, Sociologists for Women in Society, Society for the Study of Social Problems, Eastern Sociological Society.

AWARDS, HONORS: Pericles Foundation Award, Society for the Study of Social Problems, 1979; National Endowment for the Humanities summer stipend, 1981; Cheryl Miller lecturer, 1988.

WRITINGS:

(Contributor) Jo Freeman, editor, *Women: A Feminist Perspective,* Mayfield, 1979.
(Contributor) Shelley Romalis, editor, *Childbirth,* University of Texas Press, 1981.
In Labor: Women and Power in the Birthplace, Norton, 1982, published as *Giving Birth,* Penguin, 1982.
(Contributor) Henry Etzkowitz, editor, *Alternative Sociological Theories,* West Publishing, 1984.
The Tentative Pregnancy: Prenatal Diagnosis and the Future of Motherhood, Viking/Penguin, 1986, Pandora Press, 1988.
Recreating Motherhood: Ideology and Technology in a Patriarchal Society, Norton, 1989.

Contributor of articles to *Ms., Social Problems, Symbolic Interaction, Mothering,* and *Journal of Nurse Midwifery.*

SIDELIGHTS: Barbara Katz Rothman's first book, a sociological study entitled *In Labor: Women and Power in the Birthplace,* compares midwife-assisted home births with doctor-assisted births in hospitals. Childbirth is a normal, natural process for nine out of ten women, Rothman argues. Yet, in America, most babies are born in hospitals where, despite highly trained doctors and sophisticated equipment, the infant and maternal mortality rates are higher than in Holland, for example, where home births are the norm. Rothman supports her argument with data from books, articles, and interviews with professionals concerned with her subject, and provides personal insights into the positive aspects of home delivery based upon her own experience with two home births.

Writing in the *Washington Post Book World,* Beryl Lieff Benderly calls *In Labor* a "perceptive, robust, and original analysis of American birthing practices," and recommends that it "should be read by women, by men, and especially by doctors." Rothman told *CA* that *The Tentative Pregnancy: Prenatal Diagnosis and the Future of Motherhood* is "a study of women's experiences with amniocentesis and other prenatal testing and selective abortion." Her third book, *Recreating Motherhood: Ideology and Technology in a Patriarchal Society,* she said, "offers a woman-centered, class-sensitive way of understanding motherhood in a changing world." Speaking more generally of her works, she wrote, "The basic question in my work has been how do we know what we know, and who controls that knowledge? I am a feminist and a sociologist, a sociologist and a feminist; my work and my life reflect the interplay of those two perspectives. My two more recent books develop these same theses while examining new procreative technology."

BIOGRAPHICAL/CRITICAL SOURCES:

PERIODICALS

New York Times Book Review, April 16, 1989.
Washington Post Book World, August 1, 1982.

* * *

ROWAN, Ford 1943-

PERSONAL: Born May 31, 1943, in Houston, Tex. *Education:* Tulane University, B.A., 1968; American University, M.A., 1972; Georgetown University, J.D., 1976.

ADDRESSES: Office—Independent Network News, 220 East 42nd St., New York, N.Y. 10017.

CAREER: Broadcast journalist. WDSU-TV, New Orleans, La., reporter and anchorman, 1964-69; WTOP-TV, Washington, D.C., White House correspondent, 1969-72; WRC-TV, Washington, D.C., urban affairs reporter, 1972-75; Television News, Inc., Washington, D.C., reporter, 1973-74; Washington correspondent, "NBC News," National Broadcasting Corp. (NBC-TV), 1974-80; Independent Network News, New York City, reporter, beginning 1980.

AWARDS, HONORS: Journalism fellow, University of Chicago Center for Policy Studies, 1972.

WRITINGS:

Technospies: The Secret Network That Spies on You—and You, Putnam, 1978.
Broadcast Fairness: Doctrine, Practice, Prospects, Longman, 1984.

SIDELIGHTS: Among Ford Rowan's most notable assignments as a Washington television news correspondent have been the Nixon administration, the Watergate investigation, and investigations into the CIA and FBI.*

RUDELIUS, William 1931-

PERSONAL: Born September 2, 1931, in Rockford, Ill.; son of Carl William (an accountant) and Clarissa Euclid (Davis) Rudelius; married Jacqueline Urch Dunham, July 3, 1954; children: Robert, Jeanne, Katherine, Kristi. *Education:* University of Wisconsin, B.S., 1953; University of Pennsylvania, M.B.A., 1959, Ph.D., 1964.

ADDRESSES: Home—1425 Alpine Pass, Minneapolis, Minn. 55416. *Office*—Carlson School of Management, University of Minnesota, 271 19th Ave. S., Minneapolis, Minn. 55455.

CAREER: General Electric Co., Philadelphia, Pa., engineer, 1956-57, 1959-61; University of Minnesota, Minneapolis, lecturer, 1961-64, assistant professor of marketing, 1964; North Star Research and Development Institute, Minneapolis, senior economist and director of research, 1964-66, consultant, 1966—; University of Minnesota, Carlson School of Management, associate professor, 1966-72, professor of marketing, 1972—. *Military service:* U.S. Air Force, 1954-55; became first lieutenant.

MEMBER: American Marketing Association.

WRITINGS:

(With W. Bruce Erickson) *An Introduction to Contemporary Business,* Harcourt, 1973, 4th edition, 1985.
(With Eric N. Berkowitz and Roger A. Kerin) *Marketing,* Irwin, 1986, 2nd edition, 1989.

Contributor to professional journals.

SIDELIGHTS: William Rudelius told *CA:* "I write textbooks because I find it a challenge to try to organize and present material to students in a way that is both interesting *and* educational. I believe we have had some success in this in *Marketing* and *An Introduction to Contemporary Business.* . . . Writing books is a lonely occupation. The hope that a book explains complex ideas in a simple, understandable way is what prompts me to do it."

* * *

RUTTER, Michael (Llewellyn) 1933-

PERSONAL: Born August 15, 1933, in Brummana, Lebanon; son of Llewellyn Charles (a medical practitioner) and Winifred (Barber) Rutter; married Majorie Heys (a nurse practitioner and psychosexual counselor), December 27, 1958; children: Sheila Carol Rutter Mellish, Stephen Michael, Christine Ann. *Education:* University of Birmingham, M.B., Ch.B. (with distinction), 1955, M.D. (with honors), 1963; University of London, D.P.M. (with distinction), 1961.

ADDRESSES: Home—London, England. *Office*—Department of Child and Adolescent Psychiatry, Institute of Psychiatry, University of London, De Crespigny Park, London SE5 8AF, England.

CAREER: Held various training positions in pediatrics, neurology, and internal medicine, 1955-58; Maudsley Hospital, London, England, registrar, 1958-61, senior registrar, 1961, member of scientific staff of Medical Research Council Social Psychiatry Research Unit, 1962-65, honorary consultant child psychiatrist, 1966—; University of London, Institute of Psychiatry, London, senior lecturer, 1965-68, reader, 1968-73, professor, 1973—, honorary director of Medical Research Council Psychiatry Unit, 1984—. Fellow of Center for Advanced Study in the Behavioral Sciences, Palo Alto, Calif., 1979-80.

MEMBER: Association for Child Psychology and Psychiatry (chairman, 1973-74), British Paediatric Association, Royal College of Physicians (fellow), Royal College of Psychiatrists (fellow), Royal Society of Medicine (fellow), British Psychological Society (honorary fellow), American Academy of Pediatrics (honorary fellow), American Academy of Child Psychiatry (honorary member).

AWARDS, HONORS: Nuffield medical traveling fellow, Yeshiva University, 1961-62; Belding traveling scholar in United States, 1963; Goulstonian Lecturer, Royal College of Physicians, 1973; research award, American Association on Mental Deficiency, 1975; Rock Carling fellow, Nuffield Provincial Hospitals Trust, 1979; C. Anderson Aldrich Award, American Academy of Pediatrics, 1981; Commander of the Order of the British Empire, 1985; Fellow of the Royal Society, 1987.

WRITINGS:

Children of Sick Parents: An Environmental and Psychiatric Study, Oxford University Press, 1966.
(With Philip Graham and William Yule) *A Neuropsychiatric Study in Childhood,* Heinemann, 1970.
(Editor with Jack Tizard and Kingsley Whitmore) *Education, Health, and Behaviour,* Longmans, Green, 1970, Robert E. Krieger, 1981.
(Editor) *Infantile Autism: Concepts, Characteristics, and Treatment,* Churchill Livingstone, 1970.
Maternal Deprivation Reassessed, Penguin, 1972, 2nd edition, 1981, published as *The Qualities of Mothering: Maternal Deprivation Reassessed,* Jason Aronson, 1974.
(Editor with J. A. M. Martin) *The Child with Delayed Speech,* Heinemann, 1972.
(With David Shaffer and Michael Shepherd) *A Multi-Axial Classification of Child Psychiatric Disorders,* World Health Organization, 1975.
Helping Troubled Children, Penguin, 1975, Plenum, 1976.
(With Nicola Madge) *Cycles of Disadvantage,* Heinemann Educational, 1976.
(Editor with Lionel Abraham Hersov) *Child Psychiatry: Modern Approaches,* Blackwell Scientific Publications, 1977, 2nd edition published as *Child and Adolescent Psychiatry: Modern Approaches,* 1985.
(Editor with Eric Schopler) *Autism: A Reappraisal of Concepts and Treatment,* Plenum, 1978.
(With Barbara Maughan, Peter Mortimer, and others) *Fifteen Thousand Hours: Secondary Schools and Their Effects on Children,* Harvard University Press, 1979.
Changing Youth in a Changing Society: Patterns of Adolescent Development and Disorder, Nuffield Provincial Hospital Trust, 1979, Harvard University Press, 1980.
(Editor) *Scientific Foundation of Developmental Psychiatry,* Heinemann Medical Books, 1980.
(With Henri Giller) *Juvenile Delinquency: Trends and Perspectives,* Penguin, 1983.
(Editor with Norman Garmezy) *Stress, Coping, and Development in Children,* McGraw, 1983.
(Editor) *Developmental Neuropsychiatry,* Guilford, 1983.
(Editor with R. Russell Jones) *Lead versus Health: Sources and Effects of Low Level Lead Exposure,* Wiley, 1983.
(Contributor) E. M. Hetherington, editor, *Carmichael's Manual of Child Psychology,* Volume 4: *Social and Personality Development,* Wiley, 1983.
A Measure of Our Values: Goals and Dilemmas in the Upbringing of Children, Quaker Home Service Committee, 1983.
(Editor with Carroll Izard and Peter Read) *Depression in Young People: Developmental and Clinical Perspectives,* Guilford, 1986.
(With Patricia Howlin) *Treatment of Autistic Children,* Wiley, 1987.
(With Yule) *Language Development and Disorders,* MacKeith, 1987.
(Editor with A. Hussain Tuma and Irma S. Lann) *Assessment and Diagnosis in Child Psychopathology,* Guilford, 1988.
(With David Quinton) *Parenting Breakdown: The Making and Breaking of Inter-generational Links,* Avebury (Brookefield, Vt.), 1988.
(Editor) *Studies of Psychosocial Risk: The Power of Longitudinal Data,* Cambridge University Press, 1989.

European editor of *Journal of Autism and Developmental Disorders,* 1974—; member of editorial boards of *Journal of Child Psychology and Psychiatry, Psychological Medicine, Journal of Special Education, Child Psychiatry and Human Development, Journal of Abnormal Child Psychology, Applied Psycholinguistics,* and *Applied Research in Mental Retardation.*

WORK IN PROGRESS: Conducting a study of "normal and abnormal child development, with particular focus on the links between experiences in childhood and functioning in adult life, factors in the child and in his environment leading to resilience in the face of adversity, the characteristics that make for effective schooling, the skills involved in interviewing, the characteristics of good parenting and the factors that facilitate it, and the study of autistic, depressed, and hyperkinetic children."

BIOGRAPHICAL/CRITICAL SOURCES:

PERIODICALS

APA Monitor, June, 1980.
New Society, Volume 62, number 1049/50, 1982.

* * *

RYBCZYNSKI, Witold (Marian) 1943-

PERSONAL: Born March 1, 1943, in Edinburgh, Scotland; son of Witold K. (an engineer) and Ann (a lawyer; maiden name, Hoffman) Rybczynski; married Shirley Hallam, 1974. *Education:* McGill University, B. Arch., 1966, M.Arch., 1972.

ADDRESSES: Home—206 Covey Hill Rd., Hemmingford, Quebec, Canada J0L 1H0. *Office*—School of Architecture, McGill University, 815 Sherbrooke St. W., Montreal, Quebec, Canada. *Agent*—Carl D. Brandt, Brandt & Brandt Literary Agents, Inc., 1501 Broadway, New York, N.Y. 10036.

CAREER: Worked as architect and planner for Moshe Safdie on Habitat 67 and as planner of housing and new towns in northern Canada, 1966-71; in practice as registered architect, 1970-82; McGill University, Montreal, research associate, 1972-74, assistant professor, 1975-78, associate professor, beginning 1978, currently professor of architecture. Consultant to World Bank, United Nations, International Research Center, and Banco de Mexico in Nigeria, India, the Philippines, and Mexico, 1976—.

WRITINGS:

Paper Heroes: A Review of Appropriate Technology, Doubleday, 1980.
Taming the Tiger: The Struggle to Control Technology, Viking, 1983.
Home: A Short History of an Idea, Viking, 1986.
The Most Beautiful House in the World, Viking, 1989.

SIDELIGHTS: In general, reviewers of *Home: A Short History of an Idea* conclude that architect Witold Rybczynski had two basic aims in mind: the first, to provide a survey of the gradual establishment of ease and comfort in the home over the centuries, and the second, to fault modernism with ignoring these past achievements and turning to aesthetics instead. With regard to Rybczynski's first aim, Jonathan Yardley notes in his *Washington Post Book World* article that "the idea of 'home' . . . may seem as old as the hills, but as . . . Rybczynski demonstrates in this exceptionally interesting and provocative book, it is a relatively modern notion that did not really begin until after the Middle Ages." As history would have it, living conditions in medieval times were sober, indeed; for one, family members, as well as servants and visitors, had all of their activities confined to one room. As Rybczynski maintains, "in the Middle Ages, people didn't so much live in their houses as camp in them." According to Rybczynski, with the advent of both the separation of the workplace from the home in the seventeenth century and technological advances that were to flourish from that time on, a house started to take on the richness of a home. Privacy, intimacy, and comfort became increasingly possible and meaningful. Rybczynski moves through the centuries recording the domestic changes that characterize this progression from public house to private home, and includes such highlights as the popularization of the extremely comfortable furniture of the Rococo movement in France in the eighteenth century and the Georgian tradition of the same time in England which consisted of a decor that was practical yet refined. In the opinion of Brina Caplan in the *Nation,* "as a historical survey, *Home* traces the technological and psychological changes that produced our modern sense of domestic ease. But while Rybczynski is explaining how we achieved comfort, he is also arguing that we are well on the way to losing it. He has a case to make against the 'fundamental poverty of modern architectural ideas.' "

According to Wendy Smith in the *Village Voice,* Rybczynski feels the "fundamental poverty" of modern architecture is due to the failure of architects to learn from history; "unlike [Tom Wolfe's] *From Bauhaus to Our House,* however, *Home* is no hysterical polemic against modernism. Rybczynski's concern isn't with shouting condemnation from the rooftops a la Tom Wolfe, but with understanding how contemporary architects came to ignore 300 years of experience in arranging comfortable, convenient homes. . . . It's not the appearance of older buildings he misses . . . it's the attitude they reflected: an attention to human needs in the creation of spaces that were practical as well as pleasing to the eye. His closing chapter calls for a return to the idea of comfort in the home, an acknowledgement that houses are places for people to live, not forums for architects' aesthetic manifestos." Rybczynski, for example, criticizes the domestic decor of French architect and theorist Le Corbusier, describing it as cubelike, austere, and conducive to mass production, notes Christopher Lehmann-Haupt in the *New York Times.* Lehmann-Haupt further maintains that "Rybczynski knows the way out of the dilemma that he believes Modernism has led us into. It is, simply enough, to rediscover what is *comfortable,* and to do so not just by recapturing bourgeois styles of the past, but instead by re-examining bourgeois traditions."

When *Home* was published in 1986, Rybczynski "became an overnight authority on the subject of comfort," writes *Globe & Mail* contributor Adele Freedman. As is the case with other critics, William H. Gass for the *New York Times Book Review* feels Rybczynski "tells the story of the development of the private dwelling from house to home . . . in a sensitive and balanced way." Additionally, remarks Gass, "Rybczynski's call for a re-examination of the bourgeois tradition is one that should be heeded, and when he remarks, for example, that the 17th-century Dutch interior can teach us a good deal about living in small spaces he is surely right." When it comes to Rybczynski's criticism of modern architecture, however, some critics disagree with Rybczynski's stance. As Gass sees it, "what remains a problem is [Rybczynski's] basic opposition of art and comfort and the question whether an artist can really come to any kind of decent terms with the values of the middle class—because if living well remains a good revenge, living beautifully is yet better, indeed, best." Freedman likewise responds that "it was in the cards, but nonetheless wearisome, that a champion of intimacy, privacy, coziness, convenience and pragmatism would blame 'modernity' for banishing comfort in the name of esthetics." Such complaints aside, Yardley views *Home* as "highly persuasive," and Lehmann-Haupt considers it a "delightful, intelligent book." Moreover, *New Yorker* contributor John Lukacs deems it "exquisitely readable . . . a triumph of intelligence."

BIOGRAPHICAL/CRITICAL SOURCES:

BOOKS

Rybczynski, Witold, *Home: A Short History of an Idea,* Viking, 1986.

PERIODICALS

Chicago Tribune, July 28, 1986, June 2, 1989.
Globe & Mail (Toronto), November 7, 1987.
Los Angeles Times Book Review, July 13, 1986.
Nation, December 20, 1986.
Newsweek, August 18, 1986.
New Yorker, September 1, 1986.
New York Review of Books, December 4, 1986.
New York Times, July 14, 1986, June 8, 1989.
New York Times Book Review, November 6, 1983, August 3, 1986, May 21, 1989.
Time, August 4, 1986.
Times Literary Supplement, May 6, 1988.
Village Voice, August 12, 1986.
Washington Post, June 17, 1980.
Washington Post Book World, September 25, 1983, July 6, 1986, May 7, 1989.

S

SABLE, Martin Howard 1924-

PERSONAL: Born September 24, 1924, in Haverhill, Mass.; son of Benjamin (a distributor) and Ida (Saberlinsky) Sable; married Minna Gibbs, February 5, 1950; children: James S., Charles D. *Education:* Boston University, A.B., 1946, M.A., 1951; Universidad Nacional Autonoma de Mexico, Doctorate, 1952; Simmons College, M.S., 1959.

ADDRESSES: Home—4518 North Larkin St., Milwaukee, Wis. 53211.

CAREER: Northeastern University, Boston, Mass., staff librarian and bibliographer, 1959-63; California State College at Los Angeles (now California State University, Los Angeles), language librarian, 1963-64; Los Angeles County Library, Hawthorne, Calif., reference librarian, 1964-65; University of California, Los Angeles, assistant research professor at Latin American Center, 1965-68; University of Wisconsin—Milwaukee, School of Library and Information Science, associate professor, 1968-72, professor, 1972—. Visiting professor at Hebrew University of Jerusalem, 1972-73. Bibliographer, Office of Latin American Studies, Harvard University, 1962-63.

MEMBER: Institute of International Education, International Federation for Documentation, Society for Latin American Studies—United Kingdom (U.S. Correspondent), Library Association of Colombia (honorary member), American Library Association, Conference on Latin American History, Association of Library Science Educators, Latin American Studies Association, American Association of University Professors, Midwest Association for Latin American Studies, North Central Council of Latin Americanists.

WRITINGS:

A Selective Bibliography in Science and Engineering, G. K. Hall, 1964.

Master Directory for Latin America, University of California, Latin American Center, 1965.

Periodicals for Latin American Economic Development, Trade and Finance: An Annotated Bibliography, University of California, Latin American Center, 1965.

A Guide to Latin American Studies, two volumes, University of California, Latin American Center, 1967.

UFO Guide: 1947-1967, Rainbow Press, 1967.

Unamuno: Creator and Creation, edited by Jose Rubia Barcia and M. A. Zeitlin, University of California Press, 1967.

Communism in Latin America, an International Bibliography: 1900-1945, University of California, Latin American Center, 1968.

A Bio-Bibliography of the Kennedy Family, Scarecrow, 1969.

Urbanization Research, with Special Reference to Latin America: An Inventory, University of Wisconsin—Milwaukee, Center for Latin America, 1970.

Latin American Agriculture: A Bibliography, University of Wisconsin—Milwaukee, Center for Latin America, 1970.

Latin American Studies in the Non-Western World and Eastern Europe: A Bibliography on Latin America in the Languages of Africa, Asia, the Middle East, and Eastern Europe, Scarecrow, 1970.

Latin American Urbanization: A Guide to the Literature, Organizations and Personnel, Scarecrow, 1971.

International and Area Studies Librarianship: Case Studies, Scarecrow, 1973.

The Guerilla Movement in Latin America since 1950: A Bibliography, University of Wisconsin—Milwaukee, Center for Latin America, 1977.

Exobiology: A Research Guide, Green Oak, 1978.

A Guide to Nonprint Materials for Latin American Studies, Blaine Ethridge, 1979.

The Latin American Studies Directory, Blaine Ethridge, 1981.

A Bibliography of the Future for Arts-Recreation-Culture, Communication, Economy-Employment, Education, Health and Wellbeing, Housing, Land Use, Public Safety, and Transportation, Goals for Greater Milwaukee 2000, 1981.

Protection of the Library and Archive: An International Bibliography, Haworth Press, 1984.

Industrial Espionage and Trade Secrets: An International Bibliography, Haworth Press, 1985.

(Editor) *Research Guides to the Humanities, Social Sciences, Sciences and Technology: An Annotated Bibliography of "True Guides" to Library Resources and Usage, Arranged by Subject and Discipline,* Pierian, 1986.

Jewish Holocaust Studies: A Dictionary and Bibliography of Bibliographies, Penkevill, 1987.

Mexican and Mexican-American Agricultural Labor in the United States: An International Bibliography (supplement to *Behavioral and Social Sciences Librarian, Vol. 4*), Haworth Press, 1987.

(Series initiator and compiler) *Materials on Latin America for Elementary and Secondary Schools,* 5th edition, Center for Latin America, University of Wisconsin—Milwaukee, 1987.

Also author of *Latin American Jewry: A Research Guide,* 1978, *Latin American Research Resources,* 1985, *An International Bibliography of the Shuadit Language and Culture of the Provence,* 1988, *A Guide to the Writings of Pioneer Latinamericanists of the United States,* 1989, and *Las Maquiladoras: Assembly and Manufacturing Plants on the United States-Mexico Border: An International Bibliography,* 1989. Contributor to *Encyclopedia of Library and Information Science,* to "Scripta Hierosolymitana" series, and to periodicals, including *Current History, Reference Librarian, International Library Review,* and *New England Modern Language Association Bulletin.* Advisory editor for Latin America, *Encyclopedia Americana,* 1967—; member of editorial board, *International Library Review* (London), 1983—, and *Reference Librarian,* 1987—.

WORK IN PROGRESS: The Latin American Foreign Debt: An International Bibliography; "Outline for a Course in Peace and World Order Studies."

SIDELIGHTS: "Learning is the greatest adventure of all," Martin Howard Sable once told *CA.* "Contributions to knowledge and progress distinguish mankind from the rest of the animal kingdom. I am grateful for the great teachers I've been privileged to learn from, many of whom I attempt to emulate in my teaching methods. I hope to have been instrumental in my students' success in their respective careers."

BIOGRAPHICAL/CRITICAL SOURCES:

PERIODICALS

International Library Review, number 20, 1988.

* * *

SANDS, Leo G(eorge) 1912-1984
(Lee Craig, Jack Helmi)

PERSONAL: Born March 20, 1912, in Spokane, Wash.; died October 27, 1984, of Parkinson's disease, in San Diego, Calif.; son of Jacob Herman and Helmi (Laasanen) Sands; married Rhea Meuron, May 6, 1944; children: Lee Meuron, Craig Jacob. *Education:* Attended University of California, Berkeley, 1933-34, and Golden Gate College, 1935.

ADDRESSES: Home and office—10222 Challenge Blvd., La Mesa, Calif. 92041.

CAREER: Free-lance writer. Electronic engineer, U.S. War Department, Sacramento, Calif., 1942-44, and Curtiss-Wright Corp., Bloomfield, N.J., 1944-45; Bendix Corp., product sales manager, regional sales manager, and director of public relations and advertising in Baltimore, Kansas City, and Chicago, 1945-51; Bogue Electric Manufacturing Co., Paterson, N.J., marketing director, 1951-53; RCA Corp., Camden, N.J., administrator, 1953-54; Sands Technology Corp., New York, N.Y., president, 1954-74, chairman, 1974-84. Santa Barbara (Calif.) Safety Council, vice president and director, 1954-56.

MEMBER: Institute of Electrical and Electronics Engineers (life senior member), Radio Club of America (fellow member).

WRITINGS:

Industrial Sound Systems, Howard W. Sams, 1958.
Guide to Mobile Radio, Gernsback Library, 1958, revised edition, Chilton, 1967.
Marine Electronics Handbook, Howard W. Sams, 1959, 3rd revised edition, TAB Books, 1973.
(Under pseudonym Jack Helmi) *Two-Way Mobile Radio Handbook,* Ziff-Davis Publishing, 1960, 2nd revised edition, 1964.
Class D Citizens Radio, Ziff-Davis Publishing, 1960.
ABCs of Radiotelephony, Howard W. Sams, 1962.
Commercial Sound Installer's Handbook, Bobbs-Merrill, 1962, 3rd edition published as *Sound Systems Installers Handbook,* Howard W. Sams, 1973.
(With Joseph A. Risse) *Introduction to Electronics,* International Correspondence Schools, 1962.
Fundamentals of Radio Control, Howard W. Sams, 1962.
CB Radio Servicing Guide, Howard W. Sams, 1963, 3rd edition, 1974.
UHF Business Radio Handbook, Howard W. Sams, 1963.
Audel's Handbook of Commercial Sound Installations, Audel, 1965.
Mobile and Marine Station License Manual, Howard W. Sams, 1965.
101 Questions and Answers about Transistors, Howard W. Sams, 1966.
Having Fun in Electronics, Howard W. Sams, 1966.
Traffic Signal Control Systems, Hayden Book Co., 1967.
Microwave Equipment Guide, Howard W. Sams, 1967.
Power Supplies for Electronic Equipment, John F. Rider, 1967.
(With Kenneth L. Dumas) *Microwave Systems Planning,* Hayden Book Co., 1967.
Rapid Radio Repair, TAB Books, 1967.
(With G. Geoffrey Tellet) *VHF-FM Marine Radio,* Chilton, 1967.
Walkie-Talkie Handbook, Howard W. Sams, 1967.
101 Questions and Answers about CB Operations, Howard W. Sams, 1967, 2nd edition published as *Questions and Answers about CB Operations,* 1972.
(With Dumas) *Microwave Systems Planning,* Hayden Book Co., 1967.
Easy Way to Service Radio Receivers, TAB Books, 1968.
Electronics Handbook for the Electrician, Chilton, 1968.
101 Questions and Answers about Auto Tape Units, Howard W. Sams, 1968, 2nd edition published as *Questions and Answers about Auto Tape Units,* 1973.
101 Questions and Answers about Color TV, Howard W. Sams, 1968, 2nd edition published as *Questions and Answers about Color TV,* 1972.
101 Questions and Answers about Fixed Radiocommunications, Howard W. Sams, 1968.
(With Tellet) *VHF-FM Marine Radio,* Chilton, 1968.
CBers' How-To Book, Hayden Book Co., 1969.
(With Fred Shunaman) *101 Questions and Answers about Hi-Fi and Stereo,* Howard W. Sams, 1969.
(With Kenneth Bourne) *101 Questions and Answers about Amateur Radio,* Howard W. Sams, 1969.
(With Lionel Rodgers) *Automobile Traffic Signal Control Systems,* Chilton, 1969.
CB Radio, A. S. Barnes, 1970, revised edition, 1976.
Mobile-Radio Systems Planning, Howard W. Sams, 1970.
101 Questions and Answers about Transistor Circuits, Howard W. Sams, 1970.
101 Questions and Answers about Electricity, Howard W. Sams, 1971.
(With Robert Burns) *Citizen's Band Radio Service Manual,* TAB Books, 1971.
101 Questions and Answers about AM, FM, and SSB, Howard W. Sams, 1972.

Realistic Guide to Hi-Fi and Stereo, Radio Shack, 1972.
Electronic Security Systems, Audel, 1973.
Mobile Radio Handbook, TAB Books, 1973.
Installing TV and FM Antennas, TAB Books, 1974.
CB Radio Accessories, Howard W. Sams, 1974, published as *Leo Sands' Complete Guide to CB Radio,* 1978.
Auto Test Circuits You Can Build, TAB Books, 1974.
Electronic Test Equipment You Can Build, TAB Books, 1974.
Small Appliance Repair Guide, two volumes, TAB Books, 1974.
Mobile Radio Servicing Made Easy, Howard W. Sams, 1975.
(With George deLucenay Leon) *Dial 911: Modern Emergency Communications Networks,* Hayden Book Co., 1975.
(With Donald R. Mackenroth) *Encyclopedia of Electronic Circuits,* Parker Publishing Co., 1975.
Questions and Answers about CB Interference, Howard W. Sams, 1976.
Questions and Answers about CB Radio Repair, Howard W. Sams, 1977.

Author of numerous texts for International Correspondence Schools, McGraw, RCA Institutes, CB Radio Repair Course, Inc., and technical instruction books and sales manuals for U.S. Air Force, U.S. Navy, Hughes Aircraft Co., Bell Telephone Co., and other firms; has also ghostwritten books for industry, and edited trade journals. Contributor, sometimes under pseudonyms of Lee Craig and Jack Helmi, of some three thousand articles for more than sixty popular and technical magazines, including *True, House Beautiful, Plant Engineering, Popular Electronics, Mechanix Illustrated, Motor Boating, Missiles & Space,* and *Communications.* Editor, *CB Magazine,* 1964.

WORK IN PROGRESS: Several books under contract, on electronics, management, and communications.

OBITUARIES:

PERIODICALS

San Diego Union, October 31, 1984.*

* * *

SAVAGE, Blake
See GOODWIN, Harold L(eland)

* * *

SAXON, Grant Tracy
See RAUCINA, Thomas Frank

* * *

SCHLEE, Ann 1934-

PERSONAL: Born May 26, 1934, in Greenwich, Conn.; daughter of Duncan and Nancy (Houghton) Cumming; married D. Nicholas Schlee (in advertising), July 27, 1957; children: Emily, Catherine, Duncan, Hannah. *Education:* Attended Downe House, 1947-51; Somerville College, Oxford, B.A., 1955.

ADDRESSES: *Home*—London, England. *Agent*—Deborah Rogers, Ltd., 20 Powis Mews, London W11 1JN, England.

CAREER: Tutor and writer.

AWARDS, HONORS: Guardian Award commendation, 1977, and "Best Book" citation, *School Library Journal,* 1982, both for *Ask Me No Questions;* Guardian Award, 1980, Carnegie Medal commendation, 1980, Notable Children's Trade Book in the field of Social Studies, National Council for Social Studies and the Children's Book Council, 1982, all for *The Vandal;* Booker McConnell Prize for Fiction finalist, 1981, for *Rhine Journey.*

WRITINGS:

JUVENILE NOVELS

The Strangers, Macmillan, 1971, Atheneum, 1972.
The Consul's Daughter, Atheneum, 1972.
The Guns of Darkness, Macmillan, 1973, Atheneum, 1974.
Ask Me No Questions, Macmillan, 1976.
Desert Drum, Heinemann, 1977.
The Vandal, Macmillan, 1979.

ADULT NOVELS

Rhine Journey, Holt, 1981.
The Proprietor, Holt, 1983.
Laing, Macmillan, 1987.

SIDELIGHTS: After ten years of writing historical books for juveniles, in 1981 Ann Schlee published her first novel for adults, *Rhine Journey.* Victorian in setting and style, the narrative follows a middle class family on their tour of the Rhine river by paddle steamer, focusing in particular on the spinster aunt who is tempted to escape from her repressive lifestyle. Although authors frequently use nineteenth century mores and people as subjects, *Encounter* contributor Penelope Lively believes Schlee is superior to most: "Ann Schlee has none of those vices of the historical novelist that can put one off the form for life—the fatal urge to instruct, the confusion of fiction with history, the need to have all that arduous research show in the text—and has written a brief and powerful novel about the emotional crisis of a fortyish spinster, Charlotte Morrison." Holly Eley makes a similar comparison in the *Times Literary Supplement,* commenting that while on the surface *Rhine Journey* appears a typical, light example of the genre, "a not immediately discernible seriousness of purpose underpins the entertainment." In addition, "*Rhine Journey* skirts some well-established prejudices about Victorians [typical of the genre] . . . with a chaste diction, a ceremonious and circumlocutory sureness of tone with the social voice of the age, which marks its intensity of engagement with the kind of experience it imagines," states Philip Horne in the *London Review of Books.*

Although Schlee reproduces the Victorian style and manner in *Rhine Journey,* some critics fault the relative weakness of the novel's plot; *Saturday Review* contributor Susan Ochshorn finds the historical parallels to Charlotte's situation "somewhat labored, as is the contrived similarity between her own adolescent love affair and her niece's infatuation with a Prussian soldier." Nevertheless, the critic observes that "Schlee's taut, elegant prose is ample compensation for the plot's lack of subtlety." "What matters [in the end]," comments Anthony Thwaite in the *Observer,* "is that Ann Schlee has created a haunting, fastidiously delicate and yet plainly tough story which escapes any accusation of being a pastiche Victorian piece, though its sense of time, place and tone is perfect." And a *New Yorker* reviewer echoes this evaluation: "[*Rhine Journey*] is a first novel only in name. In its empathetic evocation of period, in its understanding of people enchained by piety and caste, in the bite and luminosity of its style, it is entirely mature, and a finished work of art."

"Ann Schlee's strength, exhibited first in *Rhine Journey* and now again in *The Proprietor,* is that she neither adopts a position of modern superiority towards those repressions and hypocrisies by which we have come to characterize an age," remarks Laura Marcus in the *Times Literary Supplement,* "nor renders her characters wholly blind to their own psychologies." Explains the critic: "If [the characters] cannot put their insights to use, they are at least aware of the limits to their freedom." Like its predecessor, *The Proprietor* is set in the mid-nineteenth century, but it covers two decades in the lives of the inhabitants of two neighboring islands. The title character is Augustus Warner, the owner of the islands who wishes to create a self-sufficient, "ideal" community; in his attempts to achieve this goal, however, Augustus alienates the islanders and ultimately fails in his purpose. "Plot, however, is not the strong point of *The Proprietor,*" asserts John Mellows in *London Magazine,* for "place and time give the book its power." The critic elaborates: "Ann Schlee has mastered exactly the right style for a story set in [the 1830s to 1850s], a decorous and discreetly elegant style, unhurried, precise and sharp in its descriptions yet leaving reflections and echoes in the mind's eye and ear. While not directly imitative, the style strikes one as utterly appropriate." Although Schlee recreates the age authentically, she "does not allow herself the easy means of creating a period 'feel' through descriptions of costumes or quaint turns of phrase," states Marcus. Isabel Colegate also sees a calculated effort in Schlee's style; she writes in the *Washington Post Book World* that "the book is full of such echoes, reflections and re-enactments, partly because of a skillful technique, used with great restraint, of going over the same incident more than once, so that time, place and incident ebb and flow with an effect which is almost musical." Concludes the critic: "Ann Schlee has a faultless sense of period and place, and an ability to convey very delicate sense impressions."

While *The Proprietor* "is a fine, and solidly written period piece," remarks Elaine Feinstein in the London *Times,* ". . . it is also a slow and bitter book; generating emotion chiefly from an oppressive claustrophobia." The critic adds that the distance of the setting means that "we care much less" for the protagonists. "Schlee keeps her readers outside the intimacy of the circle," observes *Spectator* contributor Harriet Waugh. "They are treated as acquaintances and like acquaintances can only see the outward behaviour of the people they observe—but when intimacy does come," continues Waugh, "it gives great satisfaction." And a *New Yorker* reviewer finds the distance and unfamiliarity of the characters entirely appropriate: "It is a measure of Mrs. Schlee's vigorous comprehension of the period that even when her characters behave most exasperatingly (by our notions) we accept and respect their reasons." "Such a sense of motion and motive testifies to a rare imaginative grasp," notes Horne. "Ann Schlee's enabling faith in an essential continuity of experience . . . is disciplined and substantiated by her submission to the special historical conditions which dictate so much in her characters' lives." Concludes the critic: "This grounding in constraint yields valuable rewards: mysterious and frightening moments when people stand outside the restriction of their lives and are lost to themselves."

Schlee's third novel, *Laing,* is similarly "historical in the best sense: not a panorama peppered with well-known characters and references to events . . . but an intimate view of a group of people whose story is rooted in a particular time and place," asserts Isabel Raphael in the London *Times.* "Ann Schlee possesses a remarkable gift for enabling the reader to enter a past world, enlightened but unshackled by modern concepts and prejudices." Based on actual correspondences between explorer Alexander Laing and the British Consul to Tripoli, Schlee's novel follows Laing's journey through Africa and his search for Timbuctoo. Complicating and complementing Laing's exchange with the consul Colonel Warrington is his relationship with the Colonel's daughter, Emma Warrington, whom he marries on the eve of his departure. Told mainly through the letters of these three characters, "*Laing*'s effects arise, in fact, from the steady accumulation of detail," comments Christopher Burns in the *London Review of Books.* While "the pace is deceptively slow," adds Burns, "imperceptibly, a hypnotic power takes hold." But *Times Literary Supplement* contributor Christopher Hawtree finds this pace tedious, calling the novel "muddled and lifeless" and "swamped by rumination, sentence after freighted sentence of it."

Christina Koning differs with this assessment, however, remarking in *New Statesman* that "Schlee depends for her effects on the slow accretion of detail. Laing's ennui and frustration are felt, rather than explicitly stated." Raphael similarly notes that "the emotional claustrophobia captured so subtly in Rhine Journey and The Proprietor is caught again here. . . . The wholly admirable result is a strong sense of rightness, almost of the destiny Laing himself believes in, which justifies the apparent excesses of this strange tale." Other critics maintain that the slow pace of Schlee's narrative is suited to these restrained times; for example, Liz Heron observes in the *Listener* that "strongly imagined, its period and its settings evoked with an uncanny weight of atmosphere, *Laing* is also splendidly equivocal in its offer of access to the past." "The observation is keen, the depiction sure," states Burns. "The lyricism is kept in check by a succession of short, at times almost truncated sentences. After a while a sense of apparently paradoxical restriction sets in, so that the tone becomes remarkably similar to passages in [American writer] Paul Bowles." The critic adds that "Ann Schlee is very much her own writer, however, and her talent is considerable."

BIOGRAPHICAL/CRITICAL SOURCES:

BOOKS

Contemporary Literary Criticism, Volume 35, Gale, 1985.

PERIODICALS

Encounter, August, 1981.
Listener, December 31, 1987.
London Magazine, October, 1983.
London Review of Books, September 1, 1983, March 31, 1988.
Los Angeles Times, November 7, 1983.
New Statesman, September 16, 1983, January 15, 1988.
New Yorker, January 26, 1981, January 16, 1984.
New York Times Book Review, August 29, 1982, January 22, 1984.
Observer, March 22, 1981.
Saturday Review, January, 1981.
Spectator, January 14, 1984.
Times (London), September 1, 1983, November 5, 1987.
Times Literary Supplement, March 20, 1981, September 16, 1983, December 11, 1987.
Washington Post Book World, December 11, 1983.

—Sketch by Diane Telgen

* * *

SCHLISSEL, Lillian 1930-

PERSONAL: Born February 22, 1930, in New York, N.Y.; daughter of Abraham and Mae (Isaacson) Fischer; children: Rebecca Claire, Daniel. *Education:* Brooklyn College (now Brooklyn College of the City University of New York), B.A., 1951; Yale University, Ph.D., 1957.

ADDRESSES: Office—Department of English, Brooklyn College of the City University of New York, Brooklyn, N.Y. 11210.

CAREER: Brooklyn College of the City University of New York, Brooklyn, N.Y., instructor, 1957-65, assistant professor, 1965-69, associate professor, 1969-71, professor of English, 1971—, director of American studies program, 1971—.

MEMBER: American Studies Association, Organization of American Historians.

WRITINGS:

(Editor) *The World of Randolph Bourne,* Dutton, 1965.
(Editor) *Conscience in America: A Documentary History of Conscientious Objection in the United States, 1757-1967,* Dutton, 1968.
(Contributor) Mary Kelley, editor, *Women, Identity and Vocation in American History,* G. K. Hall, 1979.
(With Walter Reigart) *The Journals of Washington Irving,* Twayne, 1981.
(Contributor) Sam Girgus, editor, *The American Self,* University of New Mexico Press, 1981.
Women's Diaries of the Westward Journey, preface by Carl N. Degler, Schocken, 1982.
(Editor with V. Ruiz and J. Monk) *Western Women: Their Land, Their Lives,* University of New Mexico Press, 1988.
(With Byrd Gibbens and E. Hampsten) *Far from Home: Families of the Westward Journey,* preface by Robert Coles, Schocken, 1989.
Bawdy Women: A History of Women on the Stage, Pantheon, 1990.

Contributor to *Frontiers* and *American Studies.*

SIDELIGHTS: "The most astonishing revelation of Lillian Schlissel's marvelous book about the women of the Westward migration is that they didn't want to go," *Ms.* contributor Susan Dworkin explains in discussing *Women's Diaries of the Westward Journey.* The book is a collection of letters and diaries written by women travelling to California and Oregon between 1840 and 1870 via the Overland Trail. In the *New York Times,* Emid Nemy notes that while the "story of the covered wagons wending their way West has been told before . . . , it is doubtful if anything available in the past has been more accurate or revealing than this compilation from actual diaries. The excerpts . . . provide a stark day-by-day account." *Christian Science Monitor* contributor S. R. Williams applauds Schlissel's approach, which focuses on men's and women's contrasting roles and emotions on the journey, and claims that the author "has moved scholarship ahead by two giant steps." And while Nemy remarks that the book "is not light summer reading," she continues that "it is important for anyone who wants a clearer understanding of the people, and particularly the women, who shaped a good part of the nation."

BIOGRAPHICAL/CRITICAL SOURCES:

PERIODICALS

Christian Science Monitor, April 14, 1982.
Ms., April, 1982.
New York Times, July 21, 1982.

* * *

SCHMALENBACH, Werner 1920-

PERSONAL: Born September 13, 1920, in Goettingen, Germany (now West Germany); son of Herman and Sala (Muentz) Schmalenbach; married Esther Grey, December 15, 1950; children: Peggy, Corinne. *Education:* Basel University, Prof.Dir., 1945.

ADDRESSES: Home—Poststrasse 17, 4005 Meerbusch 1, West Germany. *Office*—Kunstsammlung Nordrhein-Westfalen, Jacobistrasse, 2 4000 Duesseldorf, West Germany.

CAREER: Gewerbemuseum Basel, Basel, Switzerland, curator, 1945-55; Kestner-Gesellschaft Hannover, Hannover, West Germany, director, 1955-62; Kunstsammlung Nordrhein-Westfalen, Duesseldorf, West Germany, director, 1962—.

MEMBER: Association Internationale des Critiques d'Art, PEN.

WRITINGS:

(With Peter Baechlin and Georg Schmidt) *Der Film: Wirtschaftlich, Gesellschaftlich, Kuenstlerisch,* Holbein-Verlag, 1947, translation by Hugo Weber and Roger Manvell published as *The Film: Its Economic, Social and Artistic Problems,* Falcon Press, 1948.
Die Kunst Afrikas, Holbein-Verlag, 1953, translation by Glyn T. Hughes published as *African Art,* Macmillan, 1954.
Adel des Pferdes: Kleiner Galopp durch die Kunstgeschichte, Walter-Verlag, 1959, translation by Daphne M. Goodall published as *The Noble Horse: A Journey through the History of Art,* J. A. Allen, 1962.
Julius Bissier: Farbige Miniaturen, Piper, 1960.
Bissier, Abrams, 1963.
Kurt Schwitters, Verlag DuMont Schauberg, 1967, English translation published under same title, Abrams, 1970.
Die Kunstsammlung Nordrhein-Westfallen in Duesseldorf, Verlag DuMont Schauberg, 1970, translation by Sarah Twohig published as *Picasso to Lichtenstein: Masterpieces of Twentieth-Century Art from the Nordrhein-Westfallen Collection in Duesseldorf,* Tate Gallery Publications, 1974.
Antoni Tapies: Zeichen und Strukturen, Propylaeen-Verlag, 1974.
Fernand Leger, Abrams, 1976.
Eduardo Chillida: Zeichnungen, Propylaeen-Verlag, 1977.
Julius Bissier: Tuschen und Aquarelle (text in German, French, and English), Propylaeen-Verlag, 1978.
Marc Chagall, Draeger-Vilo, 1979.
Emil Schumacher (text in German and English), Verlag DuMont Schauberg, 1981.
Joan Miro: Zeichnungen aus den spaeten Jahren, Propylaeen-Verlag, 1982.
Bilder des zwanzigsten Jahrhunderts, Prestel Verlag, 1986.
Paul Klee, Prestel Verlag, 1986.
Afrikanische Kunst, Prestel Verlag, 1988.

BIOGRAPHICAL/CRITICAL SOURCES:

PERIODICALS

Observer, April 11, 1969.

* * *

SCHOOR, Gene 1921-

PERSONAL: Surname is pronounced Shore; born July 26, 1921, in Passaic, N.J.; son of Bernard and Marie (Winstone) Schoor; married Frances Stampler (a nursery school consultant), September, 1942. *Education:* Miami University, Coral Gables, Fla., B.P.E., 1938.

CAREER: Athletic instructor at New York University, New York City, 1938-39, University of Minnesota, Minneapolis, 1939-41, and City College (now of the City University of New York), New York City, 1941-42; professional writer. Owner of Gene Schoor Steak House, New York. *Military service:* U.S. Navy, public relations, 1942-45.

AWARDS, HONORS: Awards from Boys' Clubs of America for *The Jim Thorpe Story: America's Greatest Athlete, Joe DiMaggio:*

The Yankee Clipper, Young John Kennedy, The Army-Navy Game: A Treasury of Football Classics, and *Young Robert Kennedy.*

WRITINGS:

(Editor) Samuel Nisenson, *Giant Book of Sports,* Garden City Publishing, 1948.
Picture Story of Franklin Delano Roosevelt, Fell, 1950.
The Thrilling Story of Joe DiMaggio, Fell, 1950.
General Douglas MacArthur: A Pictorial Biography, Rudolph Field, 1951.
Sugar Ray Robinson, Greenburg, 1951.
(With Henry Gilfond) *The Jim Thorpe Story: America's Greatest Athlete,* Messner, 1951.
(With Gilfond) *Red Grange: Football's Greatest Halfback,* Messner, 1952.
(Wtih Gilfond) *The Story of Ty Cobb: Baseball's Greatest Player,* Messner, 1952.
(With Gilfond) *Casey Stengel: Baseball's Greatest Manager,* Messner, 1953.
(With Gilfond) *Christy Mathewson: Baseball's Greatest Pitcher,* Messner, 1953.
(With Gilfond) *The Ted Williams Story,* Messner, 1954.
The Leo Durocher Story, Messner, 1955.
Joe DiMaggio: The Yankee Clipper, Messner, 1956.
The Pee Wee Reese Story, Messner, 1956.
(With Gilfond) *The Jack Dempsey Story,* Nicholas Kaye, 1956.
Jackie Robinson: Baseball Hero, Putnam, 1958.
Bob Turley: Fireball Pitcher, Putnam, 1959.
Mickey Mantle of the Yankees, Putnam, 1959.
Roy Campanella: Man of Courage, Putnam, 1959.
Lew Burdette of the Braves, Putnam, 1960.
Willy Mays: Modest Champion, Putnam, 1960.
The Red Schoendienst Story, Putnam, 1961.
Bob Feller: Hall of Fame Strikeout Star, Doubleday, 1962.
(Editor) *A Treasury of Notre Dame Football,* Funk, 1962.
Young John Kennedy, Harcourt, 1963.
(Editor) *The Army-Navy Game: A Treasury of Football Classics,* Dodd, 1967.
Courage Makes the Champion, Van Nostrand, 1967.
Young Robert Kennedy, McGraw, 1969.
Football's Greatest Coach: Vince Lombardi, Doubleday, 1974.
(With Robert J. Antonacci) *Track and Field for Young Champions,* McGraw, 1974.
(With wife, Fran Schoor) *Luechow's German Festival Cookbook,* Doubleday, 1976.
The Story of Yogi Berra, Doubleday, 1976.
Bart Starr: A Biography, Doubleday, 1977.
Babe Didrikson, the World's Greatest Woman Athlete, Doubleday, 1978.
Joe DiMaggio: A Biography, Doubleday, 1980.
Billy Martin, Doubleday, 1980.
The Scooter: The Phil Rizzuto Story, Scribner, 1982.
Dave Winfield, the 23 Million Dollar Man, Stein & Day, 1982.
The Complete Dodgers Record Book, Facts on File, 1984.
A Pictorial History of the Dodgers: Brooklyn to Los Angeles, Scribner, 1984.
Yogi: A Fascinating Biography of One of Baseball's Most Illustrious Hall-of-Famers, Morrow, 1985.
Seaver: A Biography, Contemporary Books, 1986.
One Hundred Years of Notre Dame Football, Morrow, 1987.

SIDELIGHTS: Gene Schoor attended Miami University on an athletic scholarship and was on the university boxing team for three years; as an amateur boxer he won eighteen city, state, and national championships and reached the boxing finals in the 1936 Olympics.

BIOGRAPHICAL/CRITICAL SOURCES:

PERIODICALS

New York Times Book Review, November 9, 1969.
Washington Post Book World, July 20, 1980.*

* * *

SCHWARTZ, Amy 1954-

PERSONAL: Born April 2, 1954, in San Diego, Calif.; daughter of I. Henry (a writer and newspaper columnist) and Eva (a professor of chemistry; maiden name, Herzberg) Schwartz. *Education:* Attended Antioch College; California College of Arts and Crafts, B.F.A., 1976.

ADDRESSES: Agent—Jane Feder, 305 East 24th St., New York, N.Y. 10010.

CAREER: Author and illustrator of books for children.

AWARDS, HONORS: Has received many awards for books and illustrations from organizations, libraries, and periodicals, including Parents' Choice Award from Parents' Choice Foundation for *The Crack of Dawn Walkers,* Award for Best Picture Book from Association of Jewish Libraries for *Mrs. Moskowitz and the Sabbath Candlesticks, Parents* Certificate of Excellence from *Parents* Magazine for *Annabelle Swift, Kindergartner,* and Christopher Award for *The Purple Coat.*

WRITINGS:

SELF-ILLUSTRATED

Bea and Mr. Jones, Bradbury, 1982.
Begin at the Beginning, Harper, 1983.
Mrs. Moskowitz and the Sabbath Candlesticks, Jewish Publication Society, 1983.
Her Majesty, Aunt Essie, Bradbury, 1984.
Yossel Zissel and the Wisdom of Chelm, Jewish Publication Society, 1986.
Oma and Bobo, Bradbury, 1987.
Annabelle Swift, Kindergartner, Orchard Books, 1988.

ILLUSTRATOR

Amy Hest, *The Crack-of-Dawn Walkers,* Macmillan, 1984.
Eve Bunting, *Jane Martin, Dog Detective,* Harcourt, 1984.
Joanne Ryder, *The Night Flight,* Four Winds, 1985.
Donna Guthrie, *The Witch Who Lives Down the Hall* (Junior Literary Guild selection), Harcourt, 1985.
Hest, *The Purple Coat,* Four Winds, 1986.
Elizabeth Lee O'Donnell, *Maggie Doesn't Want to Move,* Four Winds, 1987.
Mary Stolz, *The Scarecrows and Their Child,* Harper, 1987.
Larry King, *Because of Lozo Brown,* Viking, 1988.
I. Henry Schwartz, *How I Captured a Dinosaur,* Orchard, 1989.
Lucretia Hale, *The Lady Who Put Salt In Her Coffee,* Harcourt, 1989.
Hest, *Fancy Aunt Jess,* Morrow, 1990.
Nancy White Carlstrom, *Blow Me A Kiss, Miss Lillie,* Morrow, 1990.

WORK IN PROGRESS: Illustrating *Mother Goose's Little Misfortunes.*

SIDELIGHTS: Amy Schwartz has been recognized by many reviewers as a talented writer and gifted illustrator of children's books. Her stories have been praised for their realistic, yet sensitive portrayal of childhood experiences. Maureen J. O'Brien in a *Publishers Weekly* interview with Schwartz notes that "virtually all of Schwartz's books include one overriding theme: that anything is achievable if you just put your mind to it." And Schwartz relates to O'Brien during the interview: "When I'm trying to come up with a story, I think I am more inclined to write about internal victories." As she explains further to *CA:* "I often pick these rather stubborn and determined types as main characters—both in little girls and grandmotherly figures. I think it's a part of me, a part of the people in my family."

Schwartz goes on to describe her early love of books to *CA* in this manner: "Looking back on my childhood, I can easily see a progression of interests that led to my writing and illustrating children's books. Some of my strongest memories from my childhood involve books. I always had the most number of stars in the class for 'Books Read' on the elementary school book awards. I remember looking forward each year to the annual ritual of receiving a book from my grandmother on my birthday.

"I wrote stories and plays in elementary school, and adapted my favorite picture books for school theater productions. I was shy and awkward in real life, but I had an active fantasy life. I was also a real ham on stage. I also loved to draw and paint when I was young, as I still do. I would draw after school, either with friends or on my own. I was usually enrolled in an art class on Saturday mornings. This interest in drawing and painting has been continuous throughout my life."

CA INTERVIEW

CA interviewed Amy Schwartz by telephone on July 13, 1988, while she was staying in San Francisco, California.

CA: Since you're in what would seem the enviable position of being both writer and illustrator of your books for children, you must approach a new one as both storyteller and artist. Does the story always come first in the hatching process?

SCHWARTZ: Yes, it does. A book always starts with a story idea.

CA: Is the story usually pretty well refined before you start on the drawings?

SCHWARTZ: Yes, it is. When I first started making picture books, sometimes I would get impatient to start on the artwork during the lengthy writing and revising process, and I'd work on an illustration while I was still writing. But usually I wait until my story is really finished to begin drawing. It seems to me that it has to work that way. It would be very frustrating to have to redo an illustration because it no longer fit a revised story, or if my editor and I had decided on a different trim size for the book. My characters become very real to me as I write; they exist for me without a visual representation.

CA: Your young characters are very stalwart little creatures, all with distinct personalities. Are they ever hard to capture in pictures?

SCHWARTZ: I've usually gotten my children pretty readily. Sometimes my adult characters take me a bit longer, and I'm not sure why that is.

CA: Good children's books have a simplicity that I suspect may be deceptive. Do you find them hard to write?

SCHWARTZ: Yes, I do, and the process hasn't gotten any easier.

CA: What do you find hardest about the writing?

SCHWARTZ: My stories usually involve the heroine solving a problem she has, usually a combination of an internal and external problem. It is difficult to have my characters come to their realizations and solutions in ways that make sense, are real and understandable, happen neither too quickly nor too slowly, and are not overstated, moralistic or cliched.

CA: Do you have to get yourself into a childlike state of mind on some level to write your books, or are the child's imagination and emotions always there, readily available?

SCHWARTZ: I think that part comes fairly naturally to me. I assume that my heroine's emotions are the same as my own, only the situations which provoke these emotions might be different for a child than for myself. Sometimes, as in *Begin at the Beginning,* in which Sara struggles with producing a piece of art, even the situation is familiar to me.

CA: How do you usually go about working out the illustrations for a story, from ideas to final version?

SCHWARTZ: First I make a dummy, a paged mock-up, of the story. If I'm the author of the story, I've often already done this while writing. Then I make a dummy with sketches of the illustrations and do a first sample illustration. The dummy, which might look primitive, is actually the most important part for me of illustrating a book. Here is where all of my planning takes place. Not only the content and composition of each illustration, but also how each page relates to the preceding and following pages, is decided here. My first finished illustration also takes some time because I'm figuring out not only what my characters will look like, but also which style and medium I want to use. So the beginning is the hard part. By the time I'm working on the finished art, I usually have everything pretty well planned out.

CA: What medium do you most often work in?

SCHWARTZ: Lately I've been working in watercolor and pen and ink. I use a simple set of watercolors in a tin, a crowquill pen and Rives BFK paper. My first books were done in pencil. I like using simple and easily accessible materials.

CA: Besides not having to write the text, obviously, how does the illustration process differ when you're doing it for someone else's book?

SCHWARTZ: One difference is that the text comes to me as a foreign object, rather than something I've been living with for some time. It takes me a while to feel like the story is mine. Sometimes I first visualize the story with someone else's illustrations, a project I am still looking at from the outside. I might not realize at first what a large part I will have in creating the mood of the book, that that is why I was hired. Sometimes I think I've been hired as a counterpoint to a story, to add a light touch. A nice thing about illustrating a text by another author is that I'm given an opportunity to illustrate a kind of story, or a setting, or theme, that I would never have come up with on my own.

CA: And you normally get the text after it's completed rather than working with the writer?

SCHWARTZ: Yes. There have been several exceptions where an author and I have submitted a project together. But it's more common for an editor to do the matching up. Sometimes I've talked a little with the author about settings and such, but more usually I am on my own, with my editor or art director as my guide.

CA: Are there illustrators who have similarly served as models or inspirations for your art work?

SCHWARTZ: That's a difficult question to answer, there are so many illustrators whom I admire. And at different times different artists' works have felt personally encouraging to me for so many different reasons. I've always admired Garth Williams's work. I remember studying his illustrations for Laura Ingalls Wilder's books, when I was a child.

CA: Were you an avid reader as a child?

SCHWARTZ: Yes, I was. I used to try to get the most stars in the class on my Book Award for Most Books Read. I loved to tell myself stories and lose myself in daydreams. I could lose myself in a book in a way that is just not possible for me as an adult.

CA: Mrs. Moskowitz and the Sabbath Candlesticks *is different from your other books, partly because its central character is a grown-up. How did it come about?*

SCHWARTZ: The children's book editor at the Jewish Publication Society, David Adler, suggested to me that I write a book about the Sabbath, and I told him I was interested. I'm Jewish, but I didn't grow up in a family that observed the Sabbath. After talking to David, I went home and made a list of my different associations with Sabbath. I thought of some friends I had made when I first moved to New York from California who had looked after me and made me feel at home when I was new in the city. They were observant Jews, and sometimes invited me over on Sabbath. So I associated the feeling of being in a new place and creating a home with the comforting feelings that arise from observing a ritual like the Sabbath. That was the beginning of the book. My grandmother lived with us when I was growing up, and she was probably the inspiration for the Mrs. Moskowitz character.

CA: And your grandmother is Oma in Oma and Bobo, *which you said in an interview a while back was your favorite book.*

SCHWARTZ: Yes, I am fond of *Oma and Bobo.* The book is based on my grandmother and her relationship with our family dog, and her relationship with my family. So the book means a great deal to me personally. I felt very close to my grandmother. I suppose the book is an affectionate memorial to her, and also sort of a fulfillment of a childhood fantasy, to make one's family "famous."

I'm also fond of *Bea and Mr. Jones* because it was my first book, and because it makes people laugh. And I think a great deal of a text by my father which I've just finished illustrating, *How I Captured a Dinosaur.*

CA: Is there a single one of your books that's been most popular among readers?

SCHWARTZ: I couldn't really say. *Bea and Mr. Jones* seems to be popular, and my latest book, *Annabelle Swift, Kindergartner,* has been well received.

CA: How do you generally get your feedback from readers? I imagine some of them are too young really to write letters to you, and some may have the books read to them.

SCHWARTZ: I do go and speak at schools, and get a little feedback that way. A lot of the feedback I do get is rather formalized; often the questions I get asked have been rehearsed beforehand. I do like speaking to a prepared class, but what's the most special is getting spontaneous reactions if I read something new. It's a lot of fun to see kids get caught up in a story. I also get letters from children, which I enjoy.

CA: What would you like your books to do for their readers? Is there something you hope for beyond entertainment?

SCHWARTZ: I like to make people laugh. And to touch them in some way.

CA: How well do you think children's books are treated by reviewers?

SCHWARTZ: I've been treated pretty generously. And people I know who review children's books seem to take their work very seriously. I do think there should be much more reviewing of children's books in newspapers and magazines. They should get much more attention than they do.

CA: Your book Bea and Mr. Jones *has appeared on PBS-TV's "Reading Rainbow." Is there more television in the offing?*

SCHWARTZ: The Purple Coat, by Amy Hest, which I illustrated, is also going to be on "Reading Rainbow" in 1989.

CA: Do you think of yourself more as a writer than an artist?

SCHWARTZ: I actually think of myself as an illustrator first, I suppose because I do more illustrating than writing. And I've drawn and painted since I was a child, whereas the writing still feels fairly new to me.

CA: You came to writing as a means of working as an illustrator, and only after a long and discouraging struggle to find good work in your field. Is there any advice you'd give aspiring artists from your own experience?

SCHWARTZ: With me it mainly took sticking with it, being persistent. I'm very glad that I did stick with it, that I didn't give up early and drop the whole thing. Also, before I started doing this, I had the idea—especially with writing—that it was something you did all on your own. With practically all my writing I've gotten help from somebody: a teacher, a friend, my agent, an editor. I think that's also good to know, that it's not something you have to do from start to finish all on your own without getting advice from someone else, an outside reader.

CA: If you could pick any art assignment imaginable, what would strike you as ideal?

SCHWARTZ: Just doing a story that touches me, that I really like. And I do also like stories that have a special personal meaning to me; that's why I liked working on *Oma and Bobo,* and that's why I liked working on the story that my father wrote. It's nice when there's some personal history behind a story.

CA: What's ahead in your work that you'd like to mention?

SCHWARTZ: The story I'm doing with my father, *How I Captured a Dinosaur,* will be out in the spring of 1989. It takes place in Southern California and Baja California. It's very witty; it has a kind of sophisticated but silly humor that I like, where there are jokes behind jokes, very deadpan. And I'm just completing the illustrations for *The Lady Who Put Salt in Her Coffee,* a story from a collection of Victorian children's stories by Lucretia Hale, called *The Peterkin Papers.* They're about a quite foolish family, the Peterkins. I liked these stories when I read them as a child. They're silly and cleverly told. I have a fantasy of myself as a child watching myself as an adult working with this story."

MEDIA ADAPTATIONS: Bea and Mr. Jones was adapted for television and broadcast on "Reading Rainbow," Public Broadcasting System, 1983; *The Purple Coat* was adapted for television and broadcast on "Reading Rainbow," Public Broadcasting System, 1989.

BIOGRAPHICAL/CRITICAL SOURCES:

PERIODICALS

New York Times Book Review, May 17, 1987.
Publishers Weekly, February 26, 1988.

—Interview by Jean W. Ross

* * *

SCHWARZ, Boris 1906-1983

PERSONAL: Born March 13, 1906 (some sources say March 26), in St. Petersburg, Russia (now Leningrad, U.S.S.R.); died December 31, 1983, in New York, N.Y.; son of Joseph (a pianist) and Rose (Kaplan) Schwarz; married Patricia Yodido, June 15, 1941; children: Joseph J., K. Robert. *Education:* Attended Sorbonne, University of Paris, 1925-26; University of Berlin, cand.phil., 1935; Columbia University, Ph.D., 1950.

ADDRESSES: Home—50-16 Robinson St., Flushing, N.Y. 11355. *Agent*—Beorger Borchardt, Inc., 136 East 57th St., New York, N.Y. 10022.

CAREER: Violinist, conductor, and musicologist. Arthur Jordan Conservatory, Indianapolis, Ind., artist-teacher, 1937-38; Settlement Music School, Philadelphia, Pa., member of faculty, 1938-41; Queens College of the City University of New York, Flushing, N.Y., instructor, 1941-47, assistant professor, 1947-57, associate professor, 1957-58, professor of music, 1958-76, professor emeritus, 1976-83, founder-conductor, Queens College Orchestral Society, 1946-76, chairman of music department, 1949-52, 1953-56. Concertmaster, Indianapolis Symphony, 1937-38; first violinist, NBC-Toscanini Symphony, 1938-39; member of New Friends Music Quartet, 1950-51; consultant to Columbia Masterworks, 1974-83.

MEMBER: International Musicological Society, American Musicological Society, Gesellshaft fuer Musikforschung.

AWARDS, HONORS: Ford Foundation award, 1952; Guggenheim fellow, 1959-60; American Council of Learned Societies cultural exchange fellow, Academy of Science, Moscow, 1962; award from American Society of Composers, Authors, Publishers for *Music and Musical Life in Soviet Russia, 1917-1970.*

WRITINGS:

(Contributor) Paul H. Lang, editor, *Igor Stravinsky: A New Appraisal,* Norton, 1963.
(Contributor) Lang, editor, *Contemporary Music in Europe,* Norton, 1965.
(Contributor) Paul L. Horecki, editor, *Russia and the Soviet Union* (bibliographical guide), University of Chicago Press, 1965.
(Editor and translator) Carl Flesch, *Violin Fingering,* Barrie & Rockliff, 1966.
Music and Musical Life in Soviet Russia: 1917-1970, Norton, 1972, enlarged edition published as *Music and Musical Life in Soviet Russia: Enlarged Edition, 1917-1981,* Indiana University Press, 1983.
French Instrumental Music between the Revolutions (1789-1830), DaCapo, 1978.
Great Masters of the Violin: From Corelli and Vivaldi to Stern, Zuckerman and Perlman, Simon & Schuster, 1983.
Russian and Soviet Music: Essays for Boris Schwarz, edited by Malcolm Hamrick Brown, UMI Research Press, 1984.

Contributor to *The New Grove Dictionary of Music and Musicians* and *Die Musik in Geschichte und Gegenwart;* contributor to *Saturday Review* and to music journals.

WORK IN PROGRESS: Two Hundred Years of Russian Music, for Prentice-Hall.

BIOGRAPHICAL/CRITICAL SOURCES:

PERIODICALS

Los Angeles Times Book Review, January 29, 1984.
New York Times Book Review, April 16, 1972, June 4, 1972, December 3, 1972, October 27, 1985.
Times Literary Supplement, March 24, 1972.
Washington Post, January 17, 1984.
Washington Post Book World, July 3, 1983.

OBITUARIES:

PERIODICALS

New York Times, January 2, 1984.*

* * *

SCOTT, Anthony Dalton 1923-

PERSONAL: Born August 2, 1923, in Vancouver, British Columbia, Canada; son of Sydney Dunn and Edith Evelyn Scott; married Barbara Wilson, December 13, 1952; children: Nicholas, Margot. *Education:* University of British Columbia, B.Comm., 1946, B.A., 1947; Harvard University, M.A., 1949; London School of Economics and Political Science, Ph.D., 1953.

ADDRESSES: Office—Department of Economics, University of British Columbia, Vancouver, British Columbia, Canada V6T 1W5.

CAREER: University of British Columbia, Vancouver, lecturer in economics, summer, 1949; Cambridge University, Cambridge, England, junior research worker in applied economics, 1949-50; University of London, London School of Economics and Political Science, London, England, assistant lecturer in economics, 1950-53; University of British Columbia, lecturer, 1953-54, instructor, 1954, assistant professor, 1954-57, associate professor, 1957-61, professor of economics, 1961—; University of Chicago, Chicago, Ill., Lilly fellow, 1964-65; Harvard University, Cambridge, Mass., MacKenzie King Professor of Canadian Studies, 1983-84. Visiting professor, University of York, 1987. Executive, British Columbia Natural Resources Conference, 1963-68; member of National Advisor Council on Water Resources, 1966-71; commissioner, International Joint Commission, 1968-73; consultant to the environmental directorate, Organization for Economic Cooperation and Development, 1971-75; professional fellow, Reserve Bank of Australia, 1977-78. *Military service:* Canadian Army, 1943-45.

MEMBER: Social Science Research Council of Canada, Canadian Political Science Association (member of executive committee, 1956-57; president, 1966-67), Royal Society of Canada (president, 1966-67; fellow, 1969—), Canadian Economics Association, Law of the Sea Institute (member of executive board, 1978-79), American Economic Association (member of executive board, 1966-70), American Association for Environmental Economics (member of board of officers, 1975-78; vice-president, 1978-80).

AWARDS, HONORS: Canada Council senior research fellow, 1959-60, 1971-72, Killam fellow, 1972, Killam senior research fellow, 1973-74, 1986-87; LL.D., University of Guelph, 1980; Officer of the Order of Canada, 1982; grants from Energy, Mines, and Resources Development and Environmental and Provincial Institute for Policy Analysis, Development and Environmental Fisheries, Canada Council, and Donner Foundation.

WRITINGS:

(With William C. Hood) *Output: Labour and Capital in the Canadian Economy,* [Ottawa], 1958.

(With T. N. Brewis, H. E. English, and Pauline Jewett) *Canadian Economic Policy,* Macmillan, 1961, revised edition, 1965.

(With W. R. D. Sewell, John Davis, and D. W. Ross) *Guide to Benefit-Cost Analysis,* Queen's Printer, 1962.

(With F. T. Christy, Jr.) *The Common Wealth in Ocean Fisheries,* Johns Hopkins Press, 1966, 2nd edition, 1973.

(Editor) Paul A. Samuelson, *Economics* (Canadian edition), McGraw, 1966, 5th edition, 1980.

(Editor with J. D. Rae) Stefan Stykolt, *Efficiency in the Open Economy: Collected Writings on Canadian Economic Problems and Policies,* Oxford University Press, 1969.

(Editor and contributor) *Economics of Fisheries Management: A Symposium,* Institute of Animal Resource Ecology, University of British Columbia, 1970.

Government Policy and Self Sufficiency, University of Calgary Press, 1976.

(Editor and contributor) *Natural Resource Revenues: A Test of Federalism,* University of British Columbia Press, 1976.

(With H. G. Grubel) *The Brain Drain: Determinants, Measurement and Welfare Effects,* Sir Wilfred Laurier University Press, 1977.

(With Albert Breton) *The Economic Constitution of Federal States,* University of Toronto Press, 1978.

(With Breton) *The Design of Federations,* Institute for Research on Public Policy, 1980.

(With P. A. Neher) *The Public Regulation of Commercial Fisheries in Canada,* Supply and Services, 1981.

Progress in Natural Resource Economics, Oxford University Press, 1985.

Water Exports, Inquiry on Federal Water Policy (Ottawa), 1985.

CONTRIBUTOR

Natural Resources: The Economics of Conservation, University of Toronto Press, 1955, revised edition, McClelland & Stewart, 1973.

Ralph Turvey and Jack Wiseman, editors, *The Economics of Fisheries,* PAO (Rome), 1958.

R. Goldsmith and C. Saunders, editors, *Income and Wealth,* Bowes & Bowes, 1959.

Wesley Ballaine, editor, *Taxation and Conservation of Privately Owned Timber,* Bureau of Business Research, University of Oregon, 1960.

R. M. Clark, editor, *Canadian Issues: Essays in Honour of Henry F. Angus,* University of Toronto Press, 1961.

R. Hamlisch, editor, *Economic and Biologic Aspects of Fishery Regulation,* United Nations Food and Agriculture Organization, 1962.

Marion Clawson, editor, *Natural Resources and International Development,* Johns Hopkins Press, 1964.

D. B. Turner, editor, *Inventory of the Natural Resources of British Columbia,* Queen's Printer, 1964.

Mason Gaffney, editor, *Extractive Resources and Taxation,* University of Wisconsin Press, 1967.

M. Blaug, editor, *Economics of Education,* Penguin, 1969.

William J. McNeil, editor, *Marine Aquiculture,* Oregon State University Press, 1970.

W. Lee Hansen, editor, *Education, Income, and Human Capital: Studies in Income and Wealth,* Columbia University Press, 1970.

Charles Kindleberger and Andrew Shonfield, editors, *North American and Western European Economic Policies,* Macmillan, 1971.

Problems of Environmental Economics, Organization for Economic Cooperation and Development (Paris), 1972.

D. A. Auld, editor, *Economic Thinking and Pollution Problems,* University of Toronto Press, 1972.

P. J. Crabbe and I. M. Spry, editors, *Natural Resource Development in Canada: A Multi-Disciplinary Seminar,* University of Ottawa Press, 1973.

Problems in Transfrontier Pollution, Organization for Economic Cooperation and Development, 1973.

P. H. Pearse, editor, *The Mackenzie Pipeline,* McClelland & Stewart, 1974.

Ingo Walter, editor, *Studies in International Environmental Economics,* Wiley, 1976.

Annette B. Fox, A. O. Hero, and J. S. Nye, editors, *Canada and the United States: Transnational and Transgovernmental Relations,* Columbia University Press, 1976.

Emilio Gerelli and others, editors, *Economics of Transfrontier Pollution,* Organization for Economic Cooperation and Development, 1976.

Neil Swainson, editor, *Managing the Water Environment,* University of British Columbia Press, 1976.

Walter, editor, *Studies in International Environmental Economics,* New York University Press, 1976.

Michael Crommelin, editor, *Minerals Leasing,* Institute for Economic Policy, University of British Columbia, 1976.

William McKillup and Walter Mead, editors, *Timber Policy Issues in British Columbia,* University of British Columbia Press, 1976.

D. Hartle and Geoffrey Young, editors, *Intergovernmental Relations,* Ontario Economic Council, 1977.

(With Breton) M. S. Feldsein and R. P. Inman, editors, *The Economics of Public Services,* Macmillan, 1977.

S. D. Berkowitz, editor, *Canada's Third Option,* Macmillan, 1978.

Horst Siebert, Klaus Zimmerman, and Walter, editors, *Regional Environmental Policy: The Economic Issues,* New York University Press, 1979.

Todd Sandler, editor, *Theories and Structures of International Political Economy,* Westview, 1980.

(With David LeMarquand) O. Dwivedi, editor, *Resources and the Environment,* McClelland & Stewart, 1980.

(With Harry F. Campbell) P. Nemetz, editor, *Resource Policy: International Implications,* Institute for Research on Public Policy, 1980.

(With G. Rosebluth) D. M. Nowland and R. Bellaire, editors, *Financing Canadian Universities,* Institute for Public Policy, University of Toronto, 1981.

OTHER

Contributor and advisor to *Encyclopedia Americana, International Encyclopedia of the Social Sciences, Pelgrave's Dictionary of Economics,* and *Canadian Encyclopedia;* contributor to proceedings; contributor of articles and reviews to numerous professional journals. Member of board of editors of *Western Economic Journal,* 1968-71, *Land Economics,* 1969-75, and *Journal of Environmental Economics and Management,* 1973—; special editor of *British Columbia Studies,* 1972; *Canadian Public Policy,* member of board of editors, 1980-82, editor, 1982—.

WORK IN PROGRESS: Articles on the origin or development of several kinds of property rights in land or natural resources; a book.

* * *

SEIBEL, Hans Dieter 1941-

PERSONAL: Born February 1, 1941, in Muelheim, Germany; son of Peter (an administrative director) and Anna (Gross) Seibel; children: Saskia Tatjana, Tjark Errit, Greta, Lena. *Education:* University of Freiburg, Dr.phil., 1966; University of Muenster, Dr.phil.habil., 1972; attended University of London and University of Ibadan.

ADDRESSES: Office—University of Cologne, Gronewaldstrasse 2, 5000 Koeln 41, Germany.

CAREER: Arnold-Bergstraesser Institute, Freiburg, Germany, chairman of Africa department, 1966-67; University of Liberia, Monrovia, associate professor of sociology and chairman of department of sociology and anthropology, 1967-69; Princeton University, Princeton, N.J., visiting lecturer, 1969-72; Manhattanville College, Purchase, N.Y., associate professor of sociology and chairman of department, 1972-75; Paedagogische Hochschule Ruhr, Dortmund, Germany, professor of sociology, 1975-80; University of Cologne, Cologne, Germany, professor of sociology, 1980—. Visiting professor, University of Muenster, 1971-72.

MEMBER: American Sociological Association, Nigerian Economic Society, Deutsche Gesellschaft fuer Soziologie.

AWARDS, HONORS: German Academic Exchange Service fellowship, 1967-69; Tubman Center of African Culture grant, 1967-68; German Research Council grant, 1968-69, 1969-71; Thussen Foundation grant, 1968-69; Princeton University and Kraus-Thomson Organization grant, 1973; Volkswagen Foundation grant, 1974-75, 1983-85; Minister fuer Wissenschaft und Forschung NW grant, 1978-80; German Research Council grant, 1983-85; various Ministry for Economic Co-operation grants, 1984-88.

WRITINGS:

(Contributor) Dieter Oberndoerfer, editor, *Africana Cellecta,* Bertelsmann Universitaetsverlag, Volume 1: *Beitraege zum Studium von Politik, Gesellschaft und Wirtschaft afrikanischer Laender,* 1968, Volume 2: *Beitraege zu Geschichte, Gesellschaft, Politik und Wirtschaft afrikanischer Laender,* 1971.

(With Michael Koll) *Einheimische Genossenschaften in Afrika: Formen wirtschaftlicher Zusammenarbeit bei westafrikanischen Staemmen* (title means "Indigenous Cooperatives in Africa: Types of Economic Cooperation among West African Tribes"), Bertelsmann Universitaetsverlag, 1968.

Industriearbeit und Kulturwandel in Nigeria (title means "Industrial Labor and Cultural Change in Nigeria"), Westdeutscher Verlag, 1968.

(Contributor) Robert A. Scott and Jack D. Douglas, editors, *Theoretical Perspectives on Deviance,* Basic Books, 1972.

Gesellschaft im Leistungskonflikt (title means "The Dilemma of the Achieving Society"), Bertelsmann Universitaetsverlag, 1973.

(Editor and contributor with Ukandi G. Damachi) *Social Change and Economic Development in Nigeria,* Praeger, 1973.

The Dynamics of Achievement: A Radical Perspective, Bobbs-Merrill, 1974.

(With Andreas Massing) *Traditional Organizations and Economic Development: Studies of Indigenous Cooperatives in Liberia,* Praeger, 1974.

(With Guenter Schroeder) *Ethnographic Survey of Southeastern Liberia: The Liberian Kran and the Sapo,* Liberian Studies Association in America (Newark, Del.), 1974.

(Editor with Lester Trachtman and contributor with Damachi) *Industrial Relations in Africa,* Macmillan, 1979.

Struktur und Entwicklung der Gesellschaft (title means "Structure and Development of Society"), Kohlhammer Verlag, 1980.

(With Damachi) *Self-Management in Yugoslavia and the Developing World,* Macmillan, 1982.

(With Damachi) *Self-Help Organizations: Guidelines and Case Studies for Development Planners and Field Workers—A Participative Approach,* Friedrich-Ebert-Stiftung Bonn, 1982.

(With Horst Luehring) *Arbeit und psychische Gesundheit* (title means "Work and Mental Health"), Verlag fuer psychologie Dr. C. J. Hogrefe, 1984.

Ansatzmoeglichkeiten fuer die Mobilisierung von Sparkapital zur Entwicklungsfinanzierung: Genossenschaften und autochthone Spar- und Kreditvereine in Nigeria (title means "Mobilizing Savings for Development Finance: Cooperatives and Indigenous Savings and Credit Associations in Nigeria"), Koeln, Weltforum Verlag, 1984.

(With Damachi) *Management Problems in Africa,* Macmillan, 1986.

Laendliche Entwicklung als Austauschprozess: Einheimische Sozialsysteme, staatliche Entwicklungsstrukturen und informelle Finanzinstitutionen in der Republik Elfenbeinkueste (with English summary; title means "Rural Development as an Exchange Process: Indigenous Social Systems Governmental Development Organizations and Informal Financial Institutions in Ivory Coast"), Verlag Breitenbach, 1987.

(With Michael T. Marx) *Dual Financial Markets in Africa: Case Studies of Linkages between Informal and Formal Financial Institutions,* Verlag Breitenbach, 1987.

(With Helmut Anheier) *Small-Scale Industries and Economic Development in Ghana: Business Behavior and Strategies in Informal Sector Economies,* Verlag Breitenbach, 1987.

Einheimische Selbsthilfeorganisationen in der Volksrepublik Kongo (title means "Indigenous Self-Help Organizations in the People's Republic of Congo"), Verlag Breitenbach, 1987.

(With Damachi and Detlev Holloh) *Industrial Labour in Africa: Continuity and Change among Nigerian Factory Workers,* Verlag Breitenbach, 1988.

(With Holloh) *Handwerk in Nigeria: Unternehmensorganisation, Verbandsstruktur und Foerderungsansaetze* (title means "Craft Industries in Nigeria"), Verlag Breitenbach, 1988.

(With Marx and Volker Moenikes) *Soziokulturelle Faktoren der Entwicklung in afrikanischen Gesellschaften: Entwicklung von oben oder Entwicklung von unten?* (title means "Sociocultural Factors of Development in African Societies: Development from Above or from Below?"), Verlag Breitenbach, 1988.

Contributor of articles and book reviews to journals, including *American Journal of Sociology, Nigerian Journal of Social and Economic Research, Soziale Welt, Internationales Afrikaforum, Koelner Zeitschrift fuer Soziologie und Sozialpsychologie,* and *Zeitschrift fuer Soziologie.*

WORK IN PROGRESS: Work and Mental Health.

AVOCATIONAL INTERESTS: International travel, windsurfing, tennis, and skiing.

* * *

SELZ, Peter (Howard) 1919-

PERSONAL: Born March 27, 1919, in Munich, Germany (now West Germany); came to the United States, 1936; became naturalized citizen, 1942; son of Eugene and Edith (Drey) Selz; married Thalia Cheronis, 1948 (divorced, 1965); married Carole Schemmerling, December 14, 1983; children: (first marriage) Tanya Nicole Eugenia, Gabrielle Hamlin. *Education:* University of Chicago, M.A., 1949, Ph.D., 1954; attended University of Paris, 1949-50, and Columbia University.

ADDRESSES: Office—Department of Art History, University of California, Berkeley, Calif. 94720.

CAREER: University of Chicago, Chicago, Ill., instructor, 1949-53; Institute of Design, Chicago, assistant professor of art history and head of art education department, 1949-55; Pomona College, Claremont, Calif., chairman of art department and director of art gallery, 1955-58; Museum of Modern Art, New York, N.Y., curator of department of painting and sculpture exhibitions, 1958-65; University of California, Berkeley, founding director of university art museum, 1965-72, professor of art history, 1965—. Fulbright scholar, University of Paris and Ecole de Louvre, 1949-50, and Musees Royaux d'Art et d'Histoire, 1953. Guest professor, University of Jerusalem, 1976, and City University of New York, 1987; lecturer at universities and museums in the United States and Europe. Has had his art works selected for U.S. representation at I Biennale de Paris; director of numerous art exhibitions touring museums in United States and Europe. Member of president's council on art and architecture, Yale University, 1971-76; trustee, American Craft Council, 1980-86. *Military service:* U.S. Army, Office of Strategic Services, 1941-46.

MEMBER: International Art Critics Association, College Art Association of America (director, 1958-64, 1966-71), American Federation of Arts, American Association of University Professors, Society for Ethical Culture.

AWARDS, HONORS: Fulbright grant for Paris, 1949-50; Belgian-American Educational Foundation fellowship, 1953; Medal for American Scholars, New York Public Library, 1961; Order of Merit, Federal Republic of Germany, 1967; D.F.A., California College of Arts and Crafts, 1967; National Endowment for the Humanities senior fellowship, 1972-73.

WRITINGS:

German Expressionist Painting, University of California Press, 1957.

New Images of Man, Doubleday for the Museum of Modern Art, 1959.

(Editor with Mildred Constantine) *Art Nouveau: Art and Design at the Turn of the Century,* Doubleday for the Museum of Modern Art, 1960, reprinted, Ayer Co., 1976.

Mark Rothko, Doubleday for the Museum of Modern Art, 1961.

Fifteen Polish Painters, Doubleday for the Museum of Modern Art, 1961.

The Work of Jean Dubuffet, Doubleday for the Museum of Modern Art, 1962, reprinted, Arno Press, 1980.

Emil Nolde, Doubleday for the Museum of Modern Art, 1963, reprinted, Arno Press, 1980.

(Editor with others) *Max Beckmann,* Doubleday for the Museum of Modern Art, 1964, reprinted, Arno Press, 1980.

(Editor) *Alberto Giacometti,* Doubleday for the Museum of Modern Art, 1965.

Directions in Kinetic Sculpture, University of California, 1966.

Seven Decades of Modern Art, 1895-1965: Crosscurrents in Modern Art, [New York, N.Y.], 1966.

Funk, University of California, 1967.

(Contributor) Herschel Browning Chipp, *Theories of Modern Art: A Source Book by Artists and Critics,* University of California, 1968.

Ferdinand Hodler, University of California, 1972.

Harold Paris: The California Years, University of California, 1972.

Sam Francis, Abrams, 1975, revised edition, 1982.

(With Thomas C. Blaisdell) *The American Presidency in Political Cartoons, 1776-1976,* Peregrine Smith, 1976.

Zwei Jahrzehnte amerikanische Malerei, 1920-1940, Kunsthalle (Duesseldorf), 1979.

Art in Our Times: A Pictorial History, 1890-1980, Harcourt, 1981.

Art in a Turbulent Era, edited by Donald Kuspit, UMI Research Press, 1985.

Chillida, Abrams, 1986.

(With Friedrich Duerrenmatt) *Varlin, 1900-1977: Paintings,* translated by Felice Ross and Mimi Levitt, C. Bernard Gallery, 1986.

Dramas of Human Encounter: The Work of Bedri Baykam, Screen Productions, 1986.

BIOGRAPHICAL/CRITICAL SOURCES:

PERIODICALS

New York Times Book Review, May 24, 1981.

* * *

SENIOR, Donald 1940-

PERSONAL: Born January 1, 1940, in Philadelphia, Pa.; son of Vincent E. (a business executive) and Margaret (Tiernan) Senior. *Education:* Passionist Seminary College, Chicago, Ill., B.A., 1963; University of Louvain, lic. theology, 1970, S.T.D., 1972; postdoctoral study at Harvard University and Hebrew Union College, Cincinnati, Ohio.

ADDRESSES: Home—5401 South Cornell Ave., Chicago, Ill. 60615. *Office*—Catholic Theological Union, 5401 South Cornell Ave., Chicago, Ill. 60615.

CAREER: Entered Passionist Religious Congregation, 1960, ordained Roman Catholic priest, 1967; Catholic Theological Union, Chicago, Ill., assistant professor, 1972-77, associate professor, 1977-82, professor of New Testament studies and director of Israel Study Program, 1982-88, president, 1988—. Lecturer and conductor of retreats in the United States, Canada, Israel, Asia, and Africa. Member of Roman Catholic/Southern Baptist Scholars Dialogue, 1977-80. Has appeared on Chicago's Catholic television network (CTN/C).

MEMBER: Pax Christi International, Society of Biblical Literature, Catholic Biblical Association of America, Catholic Theological Society of America, Chicago Society of Biblical Research, Studiorum Novi Testamenti Societas.

WRITINGS:

Matthew: A Gospel for the Church, Franciscan Herald, 1973.
Matthew: Read and Pray, Franciscan Herald, 1974.
Jesus: A Gospel Portrait, Pflaum, 1975.
The Passion Narrative according to Matthew, University of Louvain Press, 1975.
Invitation to Matthew, Doubleday, 1977.
(Editor) Wilfrid Harrington, *Mark,* Michael Glazier, 1980.
Loving and Dying, NCR Publications, 1979.
I and II Peter, Michael Glazier, 1980.
God the Son, Argus, 1981.
What Are They Saying about Matthew?, Paulist Press, 1983.
(With Carroll Stuhlmueller) *The Biblical Foundations for Mission,* Orbis, 1983.
(Editor) *Biblical and Theological Reflections on the Challenge to Peace,* Michael Glazier, 1984.
The Passion of Jesus in the Gospel of Mark, Michael Glazier, 1984.
The Gospel of Matthew, Michael Glazier, 1985
The Passion of the Gospel of Luke, Michael Glazier, 1989.

EDITOR WITH W. HARRINGTON

Adela Y. Collins, *Apocalypse,* Michael Glazier, 1979.
Daniel J. Harrington, *Interpreting the New Testament: A Practical Guide,* Michael Glazier, 1979.
Robert J. Karris, *Pastoral Epistles,* Michael Glazier, 1979.
James McPolin, *John,* Michael Glazier, 1979.
Jerome Crowe, *The Acts,* Michael Glazier, 1980.
Eugene H. Maly, *Romans,* Michael Glazier, 1980.
Pheme Perkins, *Johannine Epistles,* Michael Glazier, 1980.

OTHER

General editor with W. Harrington of "New Testament Message" series, twenty-two volumes. Creator of tape cassette series "The Gospel of Mark" and "The Gospel of Matthew." Contributor of articles and reviews to periodicals, including *American Benedictine Review, Bible Today, Biblical Research, Biblical Theology Bulletin, Catholic Biblical Quarterly, Catechist, Commonweal, Cross and Crown, Emmanuel, Interpretation, New Theology Review, Worship, U.S. Catholic, Review and Expositor, Horizons, St. Anthony's Messenger, Sign,* and *Spirituality Today.* Associate editor of *Bible Today.*

WORK IN PROGRESS: Research on the Gospels, particularly on their presentation of the death of Jesus, and on the biblical attitudes to body and health.

SIDELIGHTS: Donald Senior writes *CA:* "My career has been shaped by two main influences: my professional training in critical biblical scholarship and my vocation as a Catholic priest. I have tried to keep faith with both by serious scholarship and by a heavy schedule of lectures and writings to disseminate the results of biblical scholarship for the sake of Christians interested in contemporary interpretation of the Bible. I have had the opportunity to travel and lecture throughout the United States and Canada, have spent five years in Europe, and in 1977, spent five months in Korea, Japan, and the Philippines lecturing to and learning from people there. All of this helps me understand more about the art of interpreting a treasured tradition in a new world."

* * *

SEYMOUR, A(rthur) J(ames) 1914-

PERSONAL: Born January 12, 1914, in Georgetown, British Guiana (now Guyana); son of James Tudor (a land surveyor) and Philippine (Dey) Seymour; married Elma E. Bryce, July 31, 1937; children: Ann Seymour Boys, Joan, Margaret Seymour Outridge, James T., Guy, Philip. *Education:* Attended high school in Georgetown, British Guiana. *Religion:* Methodist.

ADDRESSES: Home—23 North Rd., Bourda, Georgetown, Guyana.

CAREER: Bureau of Public Information, British Guiana, assistant public information officer, 1943-54; Government Information Services, Georgetown, British Guiana, chief information officer, 1954-62; Caribbean Organization, San Juan, Puerto Rico, development officer for information and cultural collaboration, 1962-64; Demerara Bauxite Co., Ltd., Mackenzie, Guyana, community relations officer, 1965-70; Guyana Bauxite Co., Ltd., Georgetown, public relations officer, 1970-73; Ministry of Information, Culture, and Youth, Georgetown, cultural relations adviser, 1973—. Director of creative writing for Guyana's Institute of Creative Arts, 1974-79. Lecturer at University of Puerto Rico, 1963, and at University of Brasilia, Federal University of Bahia, and Catholic University of Fluminense, all 1973; visiting professor of journalism, University of Western Ontario, 1979; lecturer in Brazil, the U.S. Virgin Islands, Cuba, and England. Secretary of British Guiana Union of Cultural Clubs, 1943-50; literary coordinator of Caribbean Festival of the Creative Arts, 1972—; chairman of National Commission for Research Materials on Guyana, and deputy chairman of National History and Arts Council and National Trust, all 1973—. Participant in international conferences of United Nations Educational, Scientific, and Cultural Organization. Broadcasted weekly literary programs in the 1950s; conducts writers' workshops.

AWARDS, HONORS: Golden Arrow of Achievement from president of Guyana, 1970; D.Litt., University of the West Indies, 1983.

WRITINGS:

POETRY

Verse, Daily Chronicle (Georgetown, British Guiana), 1937.
More Poems, Daily Chronicle (Georgetown), 1940.
Over Guiana, Clouds, Demerera Standard, 1945.
Sun's in My Blood, Demerera Standard, 1945.
The Guiana Book, Argosy, 1948.
Leaves from the Tree, Kyk-over-al, 1951.
Water and Blood: A Quincunx, Kyk-over-al, 1952.
Selected Poems, privately printed, 1965, reprinted, Labour Advocate Job Print, 1983.
Monologue, privately printed, 1968.
Patterns, privately printed, 1970.
I, Anancy, privately printed, 1971.
Black Song, privately printed, 1972.
Passport, privately printed, 1973.
Song to Man, privately printed, 1973.
Italic, privately printed, 1974.
Love Song, privately printed, 1975.
Images of Majority: Collected Poems, 1968-78, Labour Advocate Printery, 1978.
AJS at 70, edited by Ian McDonald, [Guyana], 1984.

Also author of *Six Songs,* 1946, *Shape of the Crystal,* 1977, *Religious Poems,* 1980, *Lord of My Life,* 1981, *Poems for Export Only,* 1982.

NONFICTION

A Survey of West Indian Literature, Kyk-over-al, 1950.
Edgar Mittelholzer: The Man and His Work, National History and Arts Council (Georgetown, Guyana), 1968.
An Introduction to Guyanese Writing, National History and Arts Council (Georgetown), 1971.
Looking at Poetry, privately printed, 1974.
I Live in Georgetown, privately printed, 1974.
Growing Up in Guyana (first volume of autobiography), Labour Advocate Printery, 1976.
Cultural Policy in Guyana, United Nations Educational, Scientific, and Cultural Organization, 1977.

Also author of *Caribbean Literature* (radio talks), 1951, *Window on the Caribbean,* 1952, *Nine Caribbean Essays,* 1977, *Family Impromptu,* 1977, *Pilgrim Memories* (second volume of autobiography), 1978, *The Making of Guyanese Literature,* 1979, *Studies in West Indian Poetry,* 1981, *Thirty Years a Civil Servant* (third volume of autobiography), 1982, *The Poetry of Frank A. Collymore,* 1982, *The Poetry of Phyllis Shand Allfrey,* 1982, *Studies of Ten Guyanese Poems,* 1982, *The Years in Puerto Rico and Mackenzie* (fourth volume of autobiography), 1983.

EDITOR

The Miniature Poets, Kyk-over-al, Series A, 1951, Series B, 1952.
An Anthology of West Indian Poetry, Kyk-over-al, 1952, revised edition published as *The Kyk-over-al Anthology of West Indian Poetry,* 1952.
An Anthology of Guianese Poetry, Kyk-over-al, 1954.
Themes of Song, privately printed, 1959.
(With wife, Elma Seymour) *My Lovely Native Land,* Longman, 1971.
New Writing in the Caribbean, Carifesta, 1972.
Independence Ten: Guyanese Writing, 1966-76, [Georgetown], 1977.
(With E. Seymour) *Dictionary of Guyanese Biography,* [Guyana], 1984.

Also editor of *A Treasury of Guyanese Poetry,* 1980.

OTHER

Author of introduction to *Dictionary of Guyanese Folklore,* 1975. Contributor to anthologies, including *Schwarz Orpheus,* [Munich, Germany], and *You'd Better Believe It,* Penguin. Editor of "Miniature Poet Series," Kyk-over-al, 1945-61; editor of *Kyk-over-al* (literary magazine), 1945-61, editor with Ian McDonald, 1984—; poetry editor of *Kaie,* 1965.

WORK IN PROGRESS: Study of the cultural development of Guyana.*

* * *

SHEPHERD, J(ohn) Barrie 1935-

PERSONAL: Born February 25, 1935, in Halifax, Yorkshire, England; came to the United States in 1960; son of John Jenkinson (a baker) and Florence (Woodhead) Shepherd; married Mhairi Catherine Macfarlane Primrose (a teacher of modern languages), July 26, 1962; children: Alison Catherine, Kirstin Fiona, Nicola Mairi, Ailsa Catriona. *Education:* University of Edinburgh, M.A., 1960; Yale University, M.Div. (cum laude), 1964, M.A., 1965; Hartford Seminary Foundation, M.A., 1972.

ADDRESSES: Home—107 Yale Ave., Swarthmore, Pa. 19081. *Office*—Swarthmore Presbyterian Church, 727 Harvard Ave., Swarthmore, Pa. 19081.

CAREER: Ordained Presbyterian minister, 1965; J. J. & F. Shepherd (confectioners), Bathgate, Scotland, in sales, 1950-53, manager, 1955-58; Chicago City Missionary Society (now Community Renewal Society), Chicago, Ill., intern, 1962-63; University of Connecticut, Storrs, director of Campus Christian Foundation, 1965-67; Connecticut College for Women (now Connecticut College), New London, chaplain and assistant professor of religion, 1967-72; senior minister of Presbyterian church in Wooster, Ohio, 1972-76; Swarthmore Presbyterian Church, Swarthmore, Pa., senior minister, 1976—. Guest preacher in London, England, and Edinburgh, Scotland; guest lecturer and preacher at Cornell University, Harvard University, Yale University, Dartmouth College, Dickinson College, Kenyon College, Wittenberg University, Hartford Seminary Foundation, Philadelphia Lutheran Seminary, Gettysburg Lutheran Seminary, and Princeton Theological Seminary; guest on Philadelphia television programs. Member and chairperson of Committee on Worship of Advisory Council on Discipleship and Worship of the Presbyterian General Assembly, 1981-86; moderator of Presbytery of Muskingum Valley, 1976; member of Presbytery Permanent Judicial Commission; conducted field work at New Haven Young Men's Christian Association, Presbyterian churches in Stamford, Conn., and Yale Hope Mission. *Military service:* Royal Air Force, 1953-55; became senior aircraftsman. Royal Air Force Reserve, 1955-59.

AWARDS, HONORS: D. Litt., Muskingum College, 1986.

WRITINGS:

Diary of Daily Prayer, Augsburg, 1975.
A Diary of Prayer: Daily Meditations on the Parables of Jesus, Westminster, 1981.
Encounters: Poetic Meditations on the Old Testament, Pilgrim Press (New York, N.Y.), 1983.
Prayers from the Mount, Westminster, 1986.
Praying the Psalms, Westminster, 1987.
A Child Is Born, Westminster, 1988.
A Pilgrim's Way, Westminster, 1989.

Contributor of nearly five hundred articles, poems, and prayers to magazines and newspapers, including *Christian Century, New Republic, Living Church, Cresset, Christianity Today,* and *Youth.*

SIDELIGHTS: J. Barrie Shepherd commented: "Most of my writing tends to be a by-product of—and at times a release from—my work as a minister of a very large and active congregation. The daily variety and challenges of a pastor's life—from management to marriage counseling, from sermon preparation to sickbed visitation—provide a rich source of experiences."

Shepherd's languages include Hebrew, Greek, Latin, French, Aramaic, and some German.

* * *

SHEPHERD, John
See BALLARD, (Willis) Todhunter

* * *

SHILLING, Dana 1953-

PERSONAL: Born January 22, 1953, in Brooklyn, N.Y.; daughter of Norman Hyman (an attorney) and Janet (a novelist;

maiden name, Silverstein) Shilling. *Education:* Goucher College, A.B. (magna cum laude), 1972; Harvard University, J.D., 1975.

ADDRESSES: Home and office—Plaintext, 41 Mercer St., Jersey City, N.J. 07302. *Agent*—Peter Ginsburg, Curtis Brown Ltd., 575 Madison Ave., New York, N.Y. 10021.

CAREER: Malcolm A. Hoffmann (antitrust law firm), New York City, associate, 1975; Corporation Counsel of the City of New York, New York City, attorney-trainee, 1976-77; Institute for Business Planning, Port Washington, N.Y., writer and editor of *Pay Planning Ideas* and *Life Insurance Ideas,* 1978-79; New York City Department of Housing Preservation and Development, New York City, attorney, 1979; Plaintext, Jersey City, N.J., president, 1980—. Administrative law judge for New York City Environmental Control Board, 1980. Staff writer for Siegel & Gale, New York City, 1979.

MEMBER: New York County Lawyers' Association, Phi Beta Kappa.

WRITINGS:

(With Howard Hillman) *Howard Hillman's Encyclopedia of World Cuisines,* Penguin, 1979.
(With Hillman) *The Cook's Book,* Avon, 1981.
Fighting Back: A Consumer's Guide for Getting Satisfaction, Morrow, 1982.
Be Your Own Boss, Morrow, 1983.
Making Wise Decisions, Morrow, 1983.
(Editor) William Averill, *Estate Valuation Handbook,* Wiley, 1983.
Redress for Success: Using the Law to Enforce Your Rights as a Woman, Viking/Penguin Books, 1985.
(Co-author) *William E. Donaghue's Lifetime Funeral Planner,* Harper, 1987.
(With John Hancock Financial Services Staff) *Real Life, Real Answers,* Arbor House, 1988.
Law and Aging, CCH, 1989.
(With David Horowitz) *The Business of Business,* Harper, 1989.

Author of "Rights and Responsibilities," a column in *Current Consumer,* 1981-84, and "Women and the Law," a column in *Vogue,* 1983. Contributing editor of *Business Planning,* 1982-84.

WORK IN PROGRESS: Winning Defenses in Drunk Driving Cases, for Prentice-Hall.

SIDELIGHTS: Dana Shilling's book *Fighting Back: A Consumer's Guide for Getting Satisfaction,* tells consumers how to go about seeking restitution when they are dissatisfied with a product or service. Shilling "offers consumer advice of a very practical kind," explains Ben Reuven in the *Los Angeles Times Book Review.* In her "relaxed but snappy tone," Shilling gives the reader "the feeling that a problem with a product, a company, the media or government is neither insoluble nor reason for a holy crusade. It's simply something that must be resolved, step by clear-headed step," writes Stevenson O. Swanson in the *Chicago Tribune.* To aid the consumer in his quest for satisfaction, Shilling provides a series of sample letters that, according to Swanson, "cover just about every situation a consumer is likely to find himself in when he is seeking restitution. One can find blank requests for information under the Freedom of Information Act, letters to elected officials, and even complaints to bar associations, in addition to the more predictable letters to manufacturers." With her "lawyer's mind for precision and order and a consumer advocate's fervor for the little guy," Shilling has provided disgruntled consumers with an exceptionally complete and helpful guide to "fighting back." "Best of all," Swanson concludes, "she writes well."

Be Your Own Boss is intended for the optimistic but serious individual desiring to start a small business. According to *Washington Post Book World* contributor Mary E. Ames: "Especially instructive in *Be Your Own Boss* are lists, intended to reveal unmistakably what lies ahead: what the IRS and other government agencies will require, how to incorporate or create a partnership, what to consider when choosing a location, what sources of financing to tap, what ratios to examine to know how the business is going. These are essential details and Shilling, apparently . . . , does a great job of elucidating them."

Redress for Success: Using the Law to Enforce Your Rights as a Woman advises women on taking their suits to court. "Shilling has a clear, penetrating analysis of the inadequacies of our legal system, and presents in every instance strong, convincing representative cases that elucidate the law for any layperson," commends Laura J. Lederer in the *Los Angeles Times Book Review.* Lederer does take issue with Shilling's frequent use of puns and jokes, but concludes, "this book is helpful, and there may be those who would argue that the informal, joke-a-minute style is necessary when dealing with the complexities of our legal system."

Shilling once told *CA:* "I hate obfuscation, and it makes me angry when people are deprived of information and therefore deprived of free exercise of legal and moral rights. Therefore, I spend a fair amount of time designing forms, putting things into plain English, and otherwise explaining things. I suppose I'm a sort of class traitor; I should be making it *harder* for people to understand, which would increase the volume and duration of litigation and enhance the images of lawyers as demiurges rather than tradesmen."

AVOCATIONAL INTERESTS: Reading, ballet dancing, racquetball.

BIOGRAPHICAL/CRITICAL SOURCES:

PERIODICALS

Chicago Tribune, February 20, 1983.
Los Angeles Times Book Review, September 5, 1982, November 17, 1985.
Washington Post Book World, March 6, 1983.

* * *

SHUMWAY, Floyd M(allory, Jr.) 1917-

PERSONAL: Born September 8, 1917, in New York, N.Y.; son of Floyd Mallory, Sr. (a business executive) and Mary Elvira (Spencer) Shumway; married Margaret Frances Rabling, June 27, 1942 (divorced, 1960); married Emma Jean Clifton, July 1, 1960; children: (first marriage) Spencer Thomas, Jean Todd, Peter Mallory. *Education:* Yale University, B.A., 1939; Columbia University, M.A., 1965, Ph.D., 1968. *Religion:* Unitarian.

ADDRESSES: Home—37 Temple Ct., New Haven, Conn. 06511.

CAREER: Prentice-Hall, Inc., New York City, editorial assistant, 1940-41; John David, Inc. (men's clothing stores), New York City, floorman, 1941-42; Liberty Mutual Insurance Co., New York City, employee in claims department, 1942-43; General Electric Co., Bridgeport, Conn., and Chicago, Ill., began as clerk, became sales executive, 1943-52; Shumway-Fresen Co. (manufacturer's agency), Chicago, partner, 1952-58; R. H. Wilson Co. (management consultants), Mountain Lakes, N.J., associate, 1955-60; Remsen-Whitney Publishing Corp., Manhassett, N.Y., vice-president and editor, 1961-62; Rutgers University, Douglass College, New Brunswick, N.J., history instructor, 1968; Columbia University, New York City, instructor, 1968, assistant professor, 1969-70, adjunct associate professor of history, 1976-78, assistant dean of School of General Studies, 1970-73; New Haven Colony Historical Society, New Haven, Conn., executive director, 1978-85. Adjunct assistant professor, New York University, 1980-81; visiting lecturer, Yale University, 1983, 1986, 1987.

MEMBER: American Historical Association; member of numerous genealogical societies, including Sons of the American Revolution.

WRITINGS:

David and Nathaniel Shipman: The Two Leatherstockings, privately published, 1963.
(With John E. Pomfret) *Founding the American Colonies, 1583-1660,* Harper, 1970.
Seaport City: New York in 1776, South Street Seaport Museum, 1975.
(Editor with Richard B. Morris) *John Jay: The Making of a Revolutionary, 1745-1780,* Harper, 1975.
(Editor with Richard Hegel) *New Haven: An Illustrated History,* Windsor Publications, 1981, 2nd edition, 1987.

Also author of numerous privately published genealogies. Contributor to encyclopedias and historical journals. Editor of *NATO Journal,* 1961-62; associate editor, "John Jay Papers," Columbia University, 1973-76.

* * *

SIEGEL, Mark Richard 1949-

PERSONAL: Born March 14, 1949, in Buffalo, N.Y.; son of Marvin L. (a retailer) and Joyce (a teacher; maiden name, Sapowitch) Siegel; married Carole Elaine Drew (a community health nursing specialist), 1972; children: Amanda Drew, Max Drew. *Education:* Williams College, B.A., 1971; State University of New York at Buffalo, M.A.H., 1972; University of Arizona, Ph.D., 1976.

ADDRESSES: Home—4258 East Edgewood, Mesa, Ariz. 85206.

CAREER: Arizona State University, Tempe, assistant professor of English, 1976-77; University of Wyoming, Laramie, assistant professor, 1977-83, associate professor of English, 1983-85, acting department head, 1985; Blue Sky Press, Inc., Mesa, Ariz., publisher, 1987—. Free-lance consultant, 1975-87. Visiting professor at Osaka University, 1983-84.

WRITINGS:

Pynchon: Creative Paranoia in "Gravity's Rainbow," Kennikat, 1978.
Tom Robbins, Boise State University, 1980.
(Contributor) Carl Yoke and Donald Hassler, editors, *Death and the Serpent,* Greenwood Press, 1983.
A Reader's Guide to James Tiptree, Jr., Starmount House, 1984.
Savage Society: American Culture through the American Western Movie, Eiosha Press, 1984.
(Contributor) Brian Rose, editor, *TV Genres,* Greenwood Press, 1984.
(With Vicki Patraka) *Sam Shepard,* Boise State University, 1985.
The World According to Evan Mecham, Blue Sky Press, 1987.
Hugo Gernsback: Father of American Science Fiction, Borgo, 1988.
(With Barry Wolfson) *Tax-Cheating: Hide and Seek with the IRS,* Blue Sky Press, 1988.
The Arizona Conspiracy, Blue Sky Press, 1988.

Also contributor to *The Survey of Fantasy Literature,* edited by Keith Neilson, 1983, *The Literary History of the American West,* edited by Tom Lyons and others, 1984, and *Popular Culture in Japan,* edited by Richard Gid Powers, 1987. Contributor of approximately sixty articles to periodicals, including *Extrapolation, Critique,* and *Science-Fiction Studies.*

WORK IN PROGRESS: "Primarily fiction."

SIDELIGHTS: Mark Richard Siegel told *CA:* "I've always been in danger of being overwhelmed by my own interests, which I don't really see as diverse, but as necessarily connected pipes in the plumbing of our culture. Pynchon, Shepard, Tiptree, Robbins, and Gernsback are all completely different 'kinds' of writers, but all are responding and contributing to American culture—by which I mean the total pattern of our social behavior.

"Teaching and writing about popular culture was an attempt to unify my interests somewhat. I finally felt that I needed some distance from all this, and since my wife and I had always had an interest in the Orient, we decided to take advantage of an invitation from Osaka University to come to Japan for a couple of years. That distance merely [served] to increase my desire to explore and experience.

"I quit my tenured position and left academia in 1985 for a number of personal reasons, at least one of which was personal growth. I wanted to learn new things in a different way. While working with businessmen, lawyers, and politicians for a living, I've managed to succeed in writing a number of commercially successful nonfiction books designed for the local market in Arizona and to gather experiences that I hope will make me more successful as a writer of fiction."

* * *

SILBER, William L. 1942-

PERSONAL: Born November 26, 1942, in New York, N.Y.; son of Joseph F. (a businessman) and Pauline (Rothstein) Silber; married Lillian Frank, January 26, 1964; children: Jonathan, Daniel, Tammy. *Education:* Yeshiva University, B.S., 1963; Princeton University, M.A., 1965, Ph.D., 1966.

ADDRESSES: Office—Department of Economics/Finance, New York University, Washington Sq., New York, N.Y. 10003.

CAREER: New York University, New York, N.Y., assistant professor, 1966-71, associate professor, 1971-74, professor of economics and finance, 1974—, director of doctoral program, Graduate School of Business Administration. Visiting senior lecturer, Hebrew University of Jerusalem, 1970. Consultant to various government agencies, including service as senior staff economist, Council of Economic Advisors, Executive Office of the President, 1970-71.

MEMBER: American Economic Association, American Finance Association.

AWARDS, HONORS: Social Science Research Council faculty research grant, 1970.

WRITINGS:

(With Lawrence S. Ritter) *Money,* Basic Books, 1970, 5th revised edition, 1984.

Portfolio Behavior of Financial Institutions, Holt, 1970.

(With Ritter) *Principles of Money, Banking, and Financial Markets,* Basic Books, 1974, 6th revised edition, 1988.

(Editor) *Financial Innovation,* Heath, 1975.

Municipal Revenue Bond Costs and Bank Underwriting: A Survey of the Evidence, Salomon Brothers Center for the Study of Financial Institutions, 1980.

(Contributor) Richard Michael Cyert, *The American Economy, 1960-2000: A Retrospective and Prospective Look,* Collier, 1983.

Contributor of articles to professional journals. Associate editor, *Review of Economics and Statistics,* and *Journal of Finance.**

* * *

SIMON, John Y. 1933-

PERSONAL: Born June 25, 1933, in Highland Park, Ill.; son of Jay (a banker) and Jane (Younker) Simon; married Harriet Furst, July 22, 1956; children: Philip, Ellen. *Education:* Swarthmore College, B.A., 1955; Harvard University, M.A., 1956, Ph.D., 1961.

ADDRESSES: *Home*—805 Glenview Dr., Carbondale, Ill. 62901. *Office*—Ulysses S. Grant Association, Morris Library, Southern Illinois University, Carbondale, Ill. 62901.

CAREER: Ohio State University, Columbus, instructor in history, 1960-62, on leave, 1962-64; Southern Illinois University at Carbondale, executive director and managing editor, Ulysses S. Grant Association, 1962—, associate professor, 1964-71, professor of history, 1971—. Faculty member, Institute for the Editing of Historical Documents, 1975, 1979. Member of historians' advisory committee, Illinois Sesquicentennial Commission, 1965-68; chairman of Founders Award committee, Museum of the Confederacy, 1973-75. Member, Illinois State Historical Records Advisory Board, 1976-79, and Governor of Illinois Advisory Task Force on Historic Preservation, 1985. Panel member and consultant, National Endowment for the Humanities, 1979. Historical consultant to "Ohio Has Saved the Union," WOSU-TV, 1965; consultant to Illinois Humanities Council, 1975-76, and to Chicago Historical Society, 1987.

MEMBER: American Historical Association, Organization of American Historians, Association for Documentary Editing (chairman of steering committee, 1978; president, 1978-83; chairman of constitution and bylaws committee, 1983-85; chairman of documentary heritage trust steering committee, 1986-88; placement officer, 1987—), Illinois Association for the Advancement of History (member of steering committee, 1981-83; president, 1983-84; director, 1984-87; member of nominating committee, 1986—), Illinois State Historical Society (vice-president, 1966-67; director, 1967-70), Abraham Lincoln Association (director, 1984—, member of executive committee, 1986—), Lincoln Group of Boston (associate member), Lincoln Fellowship of Wisconsin (honorary member).

AWARDS, HONORS: Illinois State Historical Society award of merit, 1970; Harry S Truman Award, Kansas City Civil War Round Table, 1972; Fletcher Pratt Award, Civil War Round Table of New York, 1973; Delta Award, Friends of Morris Library, 1976; Moncado Prize Award, American Military Institute, 1982; Founders Award, Confederate Memorial Literary Society, 1983; Distinguished Service Award, Association for Documentary Editing, 1983; D.H.L., Lincoln College, 1983; Nevins-Freeman Award, Chicago Civil War Round Table, 1985.

WRITINGS:

Ulysses S. Grant Chronology, Ohio Historical Society for Ulysses S. Grant Association and Ohio Civil War Centennial Commission, 1963.

(Editor) *General Grant by Matthew Arnold with a Rejoinder by Mark Twain,* Southern Illinois University Press, 1966.

(Editor) *The Papers of Ulysses S. Grant,* Southern Illinois University Press, Volume 1: *1837-1861,* 1967, Volume 2: *April-September, 1861,* 1969, Volume 3: *October 1, 1861-January 7, 1862,* 1970, Volume 4: *January 8-March 31, 1862,* 1972, Volume 5: *April 1-August 31, 1862,* 1973, Volume 6: *September 1-December 8, 1862,* 1977, Volume 7: *December 9, 1862-March 31, 1863,* 1979, Volume 8: *April 1-July 6, 1863,* 1979, Volume 9: *July 7-December 31, 1863,* 1982, Volume 10: *January 1-May 31, 1864,* 1982, Volume 11: *June 1-August 15, 1864,* 1984, Volume 12: *August 16-November 15, 1864,* 1984, Volume 13: *November 16, 1864-February 20, 1865,* 1985, Volume 14: *February 21-April 30, 1865,* 1985, Volume 15: *May 1-December 31, 1865,* 1988, Volume 16: *1866,* 1988.

(Editor) *The Personal Memoirs of Julia Dent Grant,* Putnam, 1975.

(Contributor) *Encyclopedia of Southern History,* Louisiana State University Press, 1979.

(Editor and contributor, with David L. Wilson) *Ulysses S. Grant: Essays and Documents,* Southern Illinois University Press, 1981.

(Contributor) Roger D. Bridges and Rodney O. Davis, editors, *Illinois: Its History and Legacy,* River City Publishers (St. Louis, Mo.), 1984.

(Contributor with editor Gunnar Boalt) *Competing Belief Systems,* Almqvist & Wiksell International (Stockholm), 1984.

(Contributor) Henry F. Groff, editor, *The Presidents: A Reference History,* Scribner, 1984.

(Contributor) *U. S. Grant: The Man and the Image* (National Portrait Gallery exhibition catalogue), Southern Illinois University Press, 1985.

House Divided: Lincoln and His Father, Louis A. Warren Lincoln Library and Museum (Fort Wayne, Ind.), 1987.

OTHER

(Author of introduction) Rachel Sherman Thorndike, editor, *The Sherman Letters: Correspondence between General and Senator Sherman from 1837 to 1891,* Da Capo Press, 1969.

(Author of foreword) Thomas M. Pitkin, *The Captain Departs: Ulysses S. Grant's Last Campaign,* Southern Illinois University Press, 1973.

(Author of foreword) William M. Anderson, *They Died to Make Men Free: A History of the 19th Michigan Infantry in the Civil War,* Hardscrabble Books, 1980.

(Author of foreword) Charles G. Ellington, *The Trial of U. S. Grant: The Pacific Coast Years 1852-1854,* Arthur H. Clark, 1987.

(Author of introduction) Arthur Charles Cole, *The Era of the Civil War 1848-1870,* University of Illinois Press, 1987.

Contributor of articles on Ulysses S. Grant to *Encyclopaedia Britannica,* 1970, and *World Book Encyclopedia,* 1971. Contributor of articles and reviews to numerous journals, including *Journal of the Illinois State Historical Society, Civil War History, Journal of American History, Military Affairs,* and *Ohio History.* Civil War editor, *Manuscripts,* 1967-72; editor of Ulysses S. Grant Association's *Newsletter,* 1963-73. Member of advisory committee, *Papers of Daniel Chester French,* 1975—; member of editorial board, *The Papers of Jefferson Davis,* Louisiana State University

Press, 1980—, *Documentary History of the First Federal Elections,* University of Wisconsin Press, 1980—, and *Charles Sumner Correspondence,* 1986—.

SIDELIGHTS: Considered one of America's foremost experts on Ulysses S. Grant, John Y. Simon has devoted more than twenty years to editing the multi-volume *The Papers of Ulysses S. Grant,* in which he presents the life of the military leader and eighteenth president of the United States through an estimated thirty thousand documents. Praised by the *New York Time's* Herbert Mitgang for his "immaculate editorship," Simon includes such documents as Grant's personal correspondence with his family and friends as well as his official and military correspondence with members of his staff and commanders.

"This collection, when complete, will be definitive," writes R. J. Haylik in *Library Journal,* "and will help to assure General Grant his proper place in history as an extraordinary man who had his share of human failings, but had an inner strength." *The Papers of Ulysses S. Grant* "is an enterprise of archival importance, of course, but . . . it will have a more lively interest," according to a *New Yorker* reviewer who adds that more than one hundred of the letters are those to Grant's longtime fiancee Julia Dent Grant: "Through them we perceive a rather different person from the taciturn and colorless figure of many histories, for here, speaking for himself, is a man of quick feelings and perceptions." As a *Choice* contributor comments, "The personal letters to wife, father, and father-in-law are the most interesting because they reveal the intimate Grant."

BIOGRAPHICAL/CRITICAL SOURCES:

PERIODICALS

Annals of the American Academy of Political and Social Science, March, 1970.
Choice, February, 1970.
Library Journal, September 15, 1967.
New Yorker, August 26, 1967.
New York Times, December 1, 1982, July 13, 1985.
Times Literary Supplement, September 28, 1967.

* * *

SIMON, Seymour 1931-

PERSONAL: Born August 9, 1931, in New York, N.Y.; son of David and Clara (Liftin) Simon; married Joyce Shanock (a travel agent), December 25, 1953; children: Robert Paul, Michael Alan. *Education:* City College (now City College of the City University of New York), B.A., 1953, graduate study, 1955-60.

ADDRESSES: *Home*—4 Sheffield Rd., Great Neck, N.Y. 11021.

CAREER: Writer. New York City public schools, science teacher, 1955-79. *Military service:* U.S. Army, 1953-55.

MEMBER: Authors Guild, Authors League of America.

AWARDS, HONORS: Children's Book Showcase Award from Children's Book Council, 1972, for *The Paper Airplane Book;* awards from National Science Teachers Association and Children's Book Council, 1972-88, for outstanding science books for children; Best Children's Science Book of the Year Award from New York Academy of Sciences, 1988, for *Icebergs and Glaciers;* Eva L. Gordon Award from American Nature Society, for contributions to children's science literature.

WRITINGS:

JUVENILES

Animals in Field and Laboratory: Projects in Animal Behavior, McGraw, 1968.
The Look-It-Up Book of the Earth, Random House, 1968.
Motion, Coward, 1968.
Soap Bubbles, Hawthorn, 1969.
Weather and Climate, Random House, 1969.
Exploring with a Microscope, Random House, 1969.
Handful of Soil, Hawthorn, 1970.
Science in a Vacant Lot, Viking, 1970.
Science at Work: Easy Models You Can Make, F. Watts, 1971.
Chemistry in the Kitchen, Viking, 1971.
The Paper Airplane Book, Viking, 1971.
Science at Work: Projects in Space Science, F. Watts, 1971.
Science Projects in Ecology, Holiday House, 1972.
Science Projects in Pollution, Holiday House, 1972.
Science at Work: Projects in Oceanography, F. Watts, 1972.
From Shore to Ocean Floor: How Life Survives in the Sea, F. Watts, 1973.
The Rock Hound's Book, Viking, 1973.
A Tree on Your Street, Holiday House, 1973.
A Building on Your Street, Holiday House, 1973.
Projects with Plants, F. Watts, 1973.
Birds on Your Street, Holiday House, 1974.
Life in the Dark: How Animals Survive at Night, F. Watts, 1974.
Projects with Air, F. Watts, 1975.
Pets in a Jar: Collecting and Caring for Small Wild Animals, Viking, 1975.
Everything Moves, Walker & Co., 1976.
The Optical Illusion Book, Four Winds, 1976.
Life on Ice, F. Watts, 1976.
Ghosts, Lippincott, 1976.
Life and Death in Nature, McGraw, 1976.
Animals in Your Neighborhood, Walker & Co., 1976.
The Saltwater Tropical Aquarium Book: How to Set Them up and Keep Them Going, Viking, 1976.
What Do You Want to Know about Guppies?, Four Winds, 1977.
Beneath Your Feet, Walker & Co., 1977.
Space Monsters, Lippincott, 1977.
Look to the Night Sky, Viking, 1977.
Exploring Fields and Lots, Garrard, 1978.
Killer Whales, Lippincott, 1978.
About Your Lungs, McGraw, 1978.
Animal Fact/Animal Fable, Crown, 1979.
Danger from Below, Four Winds, 1979.
The Secret Clocks, Viking, 1979.
Meet the Giant Snakes, Walker & Co., 1979.
Creatures from Lost Worlds, Lippincott, 1979.
The Long View into Space, Crown, 1979.
Deadly Ants, Four Winds, 1979.
About the Foods You Eat, McGraw, 1979.
Meet Baby Animals, Random House, 1980.
Animals Nobody Loves, Random House, 1980.
Strange Mysteries, Four Winds, 1980.
Goony Birds, Bush Babies, and Devil Rays, Random House, 1980.
Mirror Magic, Lothrop, 1980.
Silly Animal Jokes and Riddles, McGraw, 1980.
Poisonous Snakes, Four Winds, 1981.
Mad Scientists, Weird Doctors, and Time Travelers, Lippincott, 1981.
About Your Brain, McGraw, 1981.
Strange Creatures, Four Winds, 1981.

Body Sense, Body Nonsense, Lippincott, 1981.
The Smallest Dinosaurs, Crown, 1982.
How to Be a Space Scientist in Your Own Home, Lippincott, 1982.
The Long Journey from Space, Crown, 1982.
Little Giants, Morrow, 1983.
Hidden Worlds: Pictures of the Invisible, Morrow, 1983.
Earth: Our Planet in Space, Four Winds, 1984.
Moon, Four Winds, 1984.
Dinosaur Is the Biggest Animal That Ever Lived, Harper, 1984.
Computer Sense, Computer Nonsense, Harper, 1984.
Chip Rogers I, Computer Whiz, Morrow, 1984.
Shadow Magic, Lothrop, 1985.
Soap Bubble Magic, Lothrop, 1985.
Meet the Computer, Harper, 1985.
How to Talk to Your Computer, Harper, 1985.
Your First Home Computer, Crown, 1985.
101 Questions and Answers about Dangerous Animals, Macmillan, 1985.
Bit and Bytes: A Computer Dictionary for Beginners, Harper, 1985.
The Basic Book, Harper, 1985.
Turtle Talk: A Beginner's Book of Logo, Harper, 1986.
The Largest Dinosaurs, Macmillan, 1986.
How to Be an Ocean Scientist in Your Own Home, Harper, 1988.
Whales, Harper, 1989.

"DISCOVERING" SERIES

Discovering What Earthworms Do, McGraw, 1969.
. . . *What Frogs Do,* McGraw, 1969.
. . . *What Goldfish Do,* McGraw, 1970.
. . . *What Gerbils Do,* McGraw, 1971.
. . . *What Crickets Do,* McGraw, 1973.
. . . *What Garter Snakes Do,* McGraw, 1975.
. . . *What Puppies Do,* McGraw, 1977.

"LET'S TRY IT OUT" SERIES

Let's Try It Out: Wet and Dry, McGraw, 1969.
. . . *Light and Dark,* McGraw, 1970.
. . . *Finding out with Your Senses,* McGraw, 1971.
. . . *Hot and Cold,* McGraw, 1972.
. . . *About Your Heart,* McGraw, 1974.

"EINSTEIN ANDERSON" SERIES

Einstein Anderson, Science Sleuth, Viking, 1980.
. . . *Shocks His Friends,* Viking, 1980.
. . . *Makes up for Lost Time,* Viking, 1981.
. . . *Tells a Comet's Tale,* Viking, 1981.
. . . *Goes to Bat,* Viking, 1982.
. . . *Lights up the Sky,* Viking, 1982.
. . . *Sees through the Invisible Man,* Viking, 1983.

"SPACE PHOTOS" SERIES

Jupiter, Morrow, 1985.
Saturn, Morrow, 1985.
The Sun, Morrow, 1986.
The Stars, Morrow, 1986.
Icebergs and Glaciers, Morrow, 1987.
Mars, Morrow, 1987.
Uranus, Morrow, 1987.
Galaxies, Morrow, 1988.
Volcanoes, Morrow, 1988.

WORK IN PROGRESS: Science dictionary for children, for Harper; an introductory series of books on earth science; photo essay series on animals.

SIDELIGHTS: Seymour Simon taught science, creative writing, and other subjects to middle-grade students for more than twenty years. He had his first book published in 1968 and has since become a full-time writer. His more than a hundred books for children cover a wide range of topics in the pure and applied sciences. Simon's earliest books were nonfiction pieces which sought to bring children closer to science by providing them with projects and questions which motivated the children into learning by doing. His "Discovery" series, for example, introduced youth to the study and care of those animals—frogs, goldfish, puppies, and so forth—which frequently become classroom pets. In the 1980s, Simon moved to include the fiction genre in his writing. Simon addresses science and computers most often in these works, as illustrated by his "Einstein Anderson" series in which the main character is a science whiz kid who solves local mysteries. The series has been compared to the *Encyclopedia Brown* books by Donald Sobol. In the *Lion and the Unicorn,* Simon told Geraldine De Luca and Roni Natov that he feels it is "very important to get kids to read science books from a very young age. If they're not reading books about science by the time they're twelve, you've probably lost them. When they grow up, they will view science with a great deal of fear and misinformation. Thus, if we want a literate citizenry, we have to start children on science books when they're young. They have no fear at a young age, and they will stay familiar with science all of their lives."

Simon wrote to *CA:* "To me, science is a way of finding out about the world. It's easy enough to read what an authority says about a particular subject, but it's so much more satisfying and rewarding to find out the answer to a question by working at it yourself. Many of the books I write are really in the nature of guidebooks to unknown territories. Each territory has to be discovered again by a child venturing into it for the first time."

AVOCATIONAL INTERESTS: Reading, collecting books and art, playing chess and tennis, listening to music, traveling, computers.

BIOGRAPHICAL/CRITICAL SOURCES:

BOOKS

Children's Literature Review, Volume 9, Gale, 1985.

PERIODICALS

Lion and the Unicorn, Volume 6, 1982.

* * *

SISSON, Rosemary Anne 1923-

PERSONAL: Surname rhymes with "listen"; born October 13, 1923, in London, England; daughter of Charles Jasper (a professor) and Vera (Ginn) Sisson. *Education:* University College, London, B.A. (with honors), 1946; Cambridge University, M.Lit., 1948. *Politics:* Conservative. *Religion:* Church of England.

ADDRESSES: Agent—Andrew Mann Ltd., 1 Old Compton St., London W.1, England.

CAREER: Writer. University of Wisconsin—Madison, instructor in English, 1949-50; University of London, University College, London, England, assistant lecturer in American literature, 1950-54; University of Birmingham, Birmingham, England, assistant lecturer in English, 1954-55; *Stratford-upon-Avon Herald,* Stratford-upon-Avon, England, drama critic, 1955-57. Member of Coventry Cathedral Drama Council. *Military service:* Royal Observer Corps, 1943-45.

MEMBER: Writers Guild of Great Britain, Writers Guild of America.

AWARDS, HONORS: Repertory Players Award, 1964, for "The Royal Captivity."

WRITINGS:

The Adventures of Ambrose, Harrap, 1951, Dutton, 1952.
The Impractical Chimney-Sweep, St. Martin's Press, 1956.
The Queen and the Welshman: A Play in Three Acts (acting edition; also see below), Samuel French, 1958, reprinted, Arrow Books, 1980.
Fear Came to Supper: A Play, Samuel French, 1959.
The Isle of Dogs, St. Martin's Press, 1959.
The Young Shakespeare, Roy Publishers, 1959.
The Young Jane Austen, Parrish, 1962.
The Young Shaftesbury, Parrish, 1964.
Bitter Sanctuary: A Play, Samuel French, 1964.
The Acrobats: A Play in One Act, Samuel French, 1965.
(Contributor) *The Six Wives of Henry VIII* (television screenplays; also see below), edited by J. C. Trewin, Ungar, 1972.
The Exciseman, R. Hale, 1973.
The Killer of Horseman's Flats, Doubleday, 1973.
Catherine of Aragon (stage version of original television screenplay; also see below), adapted by Herbert E. Martin, Dramatic Publishing, 1973.
(Contributor) *The Six Wives of Henry VIII* (includes stage version of *Catherine of Aragon*), adapted by Martin, Dramatic Publishing, 1973.
(With Robert Morley) *A Ghost on Tiptoe: A Comedy* (play), Samuel French, 1975.
"Ride a Wild Pony" (screenplay; adaptation of James Aldridge's *A Sporting Proposition*), Walt Disney Productions, 1975.
The Stratford Story, W. H. Allen, 1975, published as *Will in Love,* Morrow, 1976.
"The Littlest Horse Thieves" (screenplay; also see below), Walt Disney Productions, 1976.
(With Burt Kennedy) *The Littlest Horse Thieves* (screenplay novelization), Pocket Books, 1976 (published in England as *Escape from the Dark,* W. H. Allen, 1976).
(With David Swift) "Candleshoe" (screenplay), Walt Disney Productions, 1978.
The Queen and the Welshman (novelization), W. H. Allen, 1979.
The Dark Horse: A Play, Samuel French, 1979.
The Manions of America (based on a story by Agnes Nixon; also see below), Dell, 1981.
(With Brian Cleens and Harry Soalding) "The Watcher in the Woods" (screenplay), Walt Disney Productions, 1981.
Bury Love Deep, Love Stories, 1985.
Beneath the Visiting Moon, Love Stories, 1986.
The Bretts (also see below), Viking/Penguin Books, 1987.

Also author of produced plays "The Splendid Outcasts," "Home and the Heart," "The Royal Captivity," "Bitter Sanctuary," and, with Robert Morley, "A Ghost on Tiptoe." Author of screenplays, including "Anstice," and "The Talking Parcel" and "The Wind in the Willows," both animated versions, both for Cosgrove Hall Productions; author of television plays, including "The Vagrant Heart," "The Man from Brooklyn," "The Ordeal of Richard Feveral" (adapted from the novel by George Meredith), "The Mill on the Floss" (adapted from the novel by George Eliot), "The Marriage Game" (in the "Elizabeth R." series), "Beyond Our Means," "Let's Marry Liz," "The Irish R.M.," "Mistral's Daughter" (adapted from the novel by Judith Krantz), and "The Bretts." Scriptwriter for British Broadcasting Corp. television series, including "Compact," "Upstairs, Downstairs," "Within These Walls," and "The Duchess of Duke Street." Author of scripts for miniseries "The Manions of America" for E.M.I. and American Broadcasting Companies (ABC-TV). Contributor of poetry and short stories to magazines, and articles to *Sunday Times* and *Daily Telegraph.*

SIDELIGHTS: Rosemary Anne Sisson told *CA:* "From my earliest childhood, my sole ambition was to be an actress, and my dearest love was the theatre. This ambition was frustrated by the outbreak of the Second World War while I was still at school, and when I began writing novels, it was as a sort of desperate second-best. It was not until I wrote my first play that I realized that my ambition could be fulfilled by writing plays for others to act, instead of acting them myself.

"I wrote seven more plays before that first one was produced, and rewrote the first one seven times before its production in 1957 turned me into a professional writer. Its adaptation for television led me into writing my first original play for television, and, many years later, television led to my writing my first film. But it has only been since I returned to writing novels as well that I have realized that all my writing is essentially theatrical—to act a story out in the minds and hearts of an audience. The different media demand different crafts, but in them all, my ambition is essentially that first ambition of all, and I feel profoundly grateful to have been allowed to fulfill it."

AVOCATIONAL INTERESTS: Riding, gardening, cooking, housework.

* * *

SLADE, Jack
See BALLARD, (Willis) Todhunter

* * *

SLIDE, Anthony 1944-

PERSONAL: Born November 7, 1944, in Birmingham, England; son of Clifford Frederick and Mary (Eaton) Slide. *Education:* Attended grammar school in Birmingham, England. *Politics:* None. *Religion:* None.

ADDRESSES: Office—4118 Rhodes Ave., Studio City, Calif. 91604.

CAREER: Silent Picture (quarterly devoted to the art and history of silent film), London, England, founder and editor, 1968-74; American Film Institute, Washington, D.C., associate archivist, 1972-75; Academy of Motion Picture Arts and Sciences, Beverly Hills, Calif., resident film historian, 1975-80; freelance writer and researcher, 1980—. Co-owner, Producers Library Service, 1986—. Organizer of first silent film festival ever held in Europe, 1970. Research associate, American Film Institute, 1971-72. Lecturer, Museum of Modern Art, Pacific Film Archive, Columbia University, and Library of Congress. Consultant on silent film programming, National Film Theatre, London.

WRITINGS:

Sir Michael Balcon (monograph), British Film Institute, 1969.
Lillian Gish (monograph), British Film Institute, 1969.
(With Paul O'Dell) *Griffith and the Rise of Hollywood,* A. S. Barnes, 1970.
(With O'Dell) *Early American Cinema,* A. S. Barnes, 1971.
The Griffith Actresses, A. S. Barnes, 1973.

(With Edward Wagenknecht) *The Films of D. W. Griffith*, Crown, 1975.
The Idols of Silence, A. S. Barnes, 1976.
The Big V: A History of the Vitagraph Company, Scarecrow, 1976, revised edition, 1988.
Early Women Directors, A. S. Barnes, 1977, revised edition, Da Capo Press, 1984.
Aspects of American Film History Prior to 1920, Scarecrow, 1978.
Films on Film History, Scarecrow, 1979.
The Films of Will Rogers (monograph), Academy of Motion Picture Arts and Sciences, 1979.
The Kindergarten of the Movies: A History of the Fine Arts Studio, Scarecrow, 1980.
(With Wagenknecht) *Fifty Great American Silent Films: 1912-1920*, Dover, 1980.
The Vaudevillians, Arlington House, 1981.
Great Radio Personalities in Historic Photographs, Dover, 1982, revised edition, Vestal, 1988.
A Collector's Guide to Movie Memorabilia, Wallace-Homestead, 1983.
(Editor) *International Film, Radio and Television Journals*, Greenwood Press, 1984.
Fifty Classic British Films: 1932-1982, Dover, 1985.
A Collector's Guide to TV Memorabilia, Wallace-Homestead, 1985.
The American Film Industry: A Historical Dictionary, Greenwood Press, 1986.
The Great Pretenders, Wallace-Homestead, 1986.
(Editor) *Filmfront*, Scarecrow, 1986.
(With Judith Katten) *Movie Posters: The Paintings of Batiste Madalena*, Abrams, 1986.
Fifty Classic French Films: 1912-1982, Dover, 1987.
(Editor) *Selected Radio and Television Criticism*, Scarecrow, 1987.
The Cinema and Ireland, McFarland & Co., 1988.
(Editor) *Selected Vaudeville Criticism*, Scarecrow, 1988.
(Editor) *Picture Dancing on a Screen*, Vestal, 1988.
One Hundred Rare Books from the Margaret Herrick Library (monograph), Academy of Motion Picture Arts and Sciences, 1988.
(With Patricia King Hanson and Stephen L. Hanson) *Sourcebook for the Performing Arts*, Greenwood Press, 1988.

EDITOR OF "SELECTED FILM CRITICISM" SERIES

Selected Film Criticism: 1896-1911, Scarecrow, 1982.
. . . *1912-1920*, Scarecrow, 1982.
. . . *1921-1930*, Scarecrow, 1982.
. . . *1931-1940*, Scarecrow, 1982.
. . . *1941-1950*, Scarecrow, 1983.
. . . *Foreign Films, 1930-1950*, Scarecrow, 1984.
. . . *1951-1960*, Scarecrow, 1985.

EDITOR OF "SELECTED THEATRE CRITICISM" SERIES

Selected Theatre Criticism: 1900-1919, Scarecrow, 1985.
. . . *1920-1930*, Scarecrow, 1985.
. . . *1931-1950*, Scarecrow, 1986.

OTHER

Also editor of "Filmmakers" series for Scarecrow. Contributor to several books on cinema, including *The International Dictionary of Films and Filmmakers*, *Film Review Annual*, and *Magill's Survey of Cinema*. Contributor of articles on the history of film to numerous periodicals. Member of editorial board, *Film History*.

WORK IN PROGRESS: The International Film Industry: A Historical Dictionary, for Greenwood Press; revised edition of *Early American Cinema*, for Vestal.

* * *

SMALL, Bertrice 1937-

PERSONAL: Born December 9, 1937, in New York, N.Y.; daughter of David R. (a broadcaster) and Doris S. (a broadcaster) Williams; married George S. Small (a photographer and designer), October 5, 1963; children: Thomas David. *Education:* Attended Western College for Women, 1955-58, and Katharine Gibbs Secretarial School, 1958-59. *Politics:* "I vote for candidates, not parties." *Religion:* Anglican.

ADDRESSES: Home—P.O. Box 765, Southold, N.Y. 11971. *Agent*—Edward J. Acton, Inc., 928 Broadway, Suite 301, New York, N.Y. 10010.

CAREER: Secretary in New York City, 1959-61; Edward Petry & Co., New York City, sales assistant, 1961-63; free-lance writer, 1969—.

MEMBER: Authors Guild, Authors League of America, Southold Association of Merchants (member of board of directors, 1977-78).

AWARDS, HONORS: Honorable mention, Porgie Awards from *West Coast Review of Books*, 1979; Historical Romance Novelist of the Year Award, 1983, and Best Historical Series Author Award, 1986, both from *Romantic Times;* Silver Pen Award, 1988.

WRITINGS:

HISTORICAL ROMANCES

The Kadin, Avon, 1978.
Love Wild and Fair, Avon, 1978.
Adora, Ballantine, 1980.
Skye O'Malley, Ballantine, 1980.
Unconquered, Ballantine, 1982.
Beloved, Ballantine, 1983.
All the Sweet Tomorrows, Ballantine, 1984.
This Heart of Mine, New American Library, 1985.
A Love for All Time, New American Library, 1986.
Enchantress Mine, New American Library, 1987.
Blaze Wyndham, New American Library, 1988.
Lost Love Found, Ballantine, 1989.

WORK IN PROGRESS: Several historical books.

SIDELIGHTS: Bertrice Small writes *CA:* "I consider myself one of the most fortunate people alive to be able to earn my living doing something that I love doing—writing historical fiction. My career has put me in contact with other authors, which is a great blesssing for me, since novelists, like whooping cranes, are a very endangered species and enjoy congregating together occasionally with their own kind. It's nice to be with people who don't think you're strange because you earn your living doing something everyone always told you you couldn't possibly do and be successful.

"The greatest blessing of this rather odd lifestyle of mine, however, is that I have come in contact with the readers. I am amazed by the variety of people who read historical romance: men and women of all ages, educational backgrounds, and socioeconomic groupings. I have gained a great respect for the readers, and I only wish the publishers knew them as well as I do. My mail comes in from all over the world, including South Africa, where, I understand, I am banned! My books are translated into French, Dutch, Italian, German, Norweigan, Swedish, Danish, and Japanese. My ex-secretary, now a nurse, says I am, in my correspondence, a para-professional shrink, operating on the same level as bartenders and hairdressers. It's comforting to know that I've done something worthwhile with my otherwise wastral existence!"

* * *

SMITH, Harry 1936-

PERSONAL: Born October 15, 1936, in New York, N.Y.; son of Harry Joseph (a banker) and May A. (Dinkelmeyer) Smith; married Marion Camilla Petschek (a psychologist), February 21, 1959; children: Tristram, Lisa, Rebecca. *Education:* Brown University, A.B., 1957, graduate study, 1957-58. *Politics:* "Harmless anarchist."

ADDRESSES: Home—Brooklyn, N.Y. *Office*—Generalist Association, 5 Beekman St., New York, N.Y. 10038.

CAREER: Southbridge Evening News, Southbridge, Mass., reporter, photographer, and sports editor, 1958; *Worcester Telegram,* Worcester, Mass., reporter-photographer, 1959; *Modern Server* (alcoholic beverage industry trade publication), New York City, managing editor, 1959-61; *Recess* (legal newspaper), New York City, editor-in-chief, 1962-63; *Smith,* New York City, publisher, 1964—.

MEMBER: International PEN, Committee of Small Magazine Editors and Publishers (member of board of directors, 1968-74; chairman, 1971-73), Coordinating Council of Literary Magazines, Generalist Association (president, 1972—).

AWARDS, HONORS: Lucile Medwick Memorial Award from International PEN, 1976.

WRITINGS:

Rainscent (lyric poetry), Stephen Dwoskin, 1962.
Trinity (epic poem), Horizon Press, 1975.
The Early Poems, Ghost Dance Press, 1977.
Summer Woman (love poems), Allegra Press, 1978.
(Translator) Menke Katz, *Water-Rose* (poems), Allegra Press, 1978.
Me, the People (selected poems), State of the Culture Press, 1979.
(With Katz) *Two Friends* (verse dialogues and dialects), State of the Culture Press, 1981.
(With Dick Higgins, Richard Morris, and Donald Phelps) *The Word and Beyond: Cosmologists of the Word* (essays), The Smith, 1982.
(With Marshall Brooks) *Snow Poems,* Arts End Books, 1985.
Ballads for the Possessed, Birch Brook Press, 1987.
(With Katz) *Two Friends II,* Birch Brook Press, 1988.

Editor-in-chief of *Newsletter on the State of Culture,* 1968-80.

WORK IN PROGRESS: Gawaine Greene, an epic.

SIDELIGHTS: Harry Smith wrote *CA:* "The poet is the primal revolutionary. The poet is everyman."

* * *

SOMERVILLE, John (P. M.) 1905-

PERSONAL: Born March 13, 1905, in New York, N.Y.; married in 1929; children: two. *Education:* Columbia University, A.B. (with honors), 1926, M.A., 1929, Ph.D., 1938.

ADDRESSES: Home—1426 Merritt Dr., El Cajon, Calif. 92020.

CAREER: College of the City of New York (now City College of the City University of New York), New York City, instructor in philosophy, 1928-35; Columbia University, New York City, lecturer in philosophy, 1937-39; Hunter College of the City University of New York, New York City, instructor, 1939-60, assistant professor, 1961-63, associate professor to professor of philosophy, 1964-67, professor emeritus, 1967—; United States International University, San Diego, Calif., professor of philosophy, 1962-72. Visiting lecturer at universities, including Stanford University, University of Southern California, Cornell University, University of Michigan, and others; has also lectured in Russian at Charles University (Prague), University of Bucharest, and Institute of Philosophy (Moscow and Armenia); lectured in French at University of Bucharest. Has conducted field research in the Soviet Union and Nazi Germany. Participant in UNESCO international research projects, 1948-54; speaker at international conferences. President of Colloquium on Peace at World Congress of Philosophy, 1973; co-founder and president of American chapter, Union of American and Japanese Professionals Against Omnicide, 1978—; founding president, International Philosophers for the Prevention of Nuclear Omnicide, 1983—.

MEMBER: International Committee on Scientific Humanism (member of executive committee, 1949-54), American Philosophical Association, American Sociological Association, American Society for the Philosophical Study of Dialectical Materialism (vice-president, 1962-63; president, 1963—), Society for Religious Culture, American Association for Political and Legal Philosophy, Society for the Psychological Study of Social Issues, Society for the Study of Social Problems, American Association for the Advancement of Science.

AWARDS, HONORS: Cutting Traveling fellowship, Columbia University, 1935-36, 1936-37; Rockefeller Foundation grant, Hoover Institution on War, Revolution and Peace, 1948-49; D.H.L., Denison University, 1980; Peace Messenger Award, United Nations, 1987; Gandhi Peace Award, Promoting Enduring Peace, Inc., 1987; Bertrand Russell Peace Award, 1987.

WRITINGS:

Methodology in Social Science: A Critique of Marx and Engels, Lewin, 1938.
(With Jacques Maritain, Bertrand Russell, John Dewey, and others) *Twentieth Century Philosophy,* Philosophical Library, 1943.
Soviet Philosophy: A Study of Theory and Practice, Philosophical Library, 1946.
The Philosophy of Peace, Gaer, 1949, revised edition, with introductory letters by Albert Einstein and Thomas Mann, Liberty Press, 1954.
(With Maritain, Mahatma Gandhi, Richard McKeon, F. S. C. Northrop, and others) *Human Rights: A Symposium Prepared by UNESCO,* [London], 1949.
(With McKeon, Edgar S. Brightman, S. K. Chatterji, and others) *Interrelations of Cultures: Their Contributions to International Understanding,* UNESCO, 1953.
The Way of Science: Its Growth and Method, Schuman, 1953.
The Enjoyment of Study, Schuman, 1954.
(With McKeon, Marvin Farber, Charles Hartshorne, Jacques Rueff, H. K. Pos, and others) *Inquiry into Freedom: A Symposium Jointly Sponsored by UNESCO and the International Federation of Societies of Philosophy,* Hermann, 1954.
The Communist Trials and the American Tradition, Cameron, 1956.

(With Karl Barth, Simone de Beauvoir, Lewis Mumford, Sarvepalli Radhakrishnan, and others) *Contemporary Thought* (in Japanese), Iwanami Shoten (Tokyo), 1957.

(With Carl Friedrich, Margaret Spahr, and others) *On Freedom: Yearbook of the American Society for Political and Legal Philosophy,* Atherton, 1962.

(With Dewey, Max Black, Ernest Nagel, and others) *Introductory Readings in Philosophy,* Scribner, 1962.

(Editor with Ronald E. Santoni) *Social and Political Philosophy: Readings from Plato to Gandhi,* Doubleday, 1963.

The Philosophy of Marxism: An Exposition, Random House, 1967.

Philosophy and Politics Today (in Japanese), Iwanami Shoten, 1968.

(Contributor) Paul Kurtz, editor, *Moral Problems in Contemporary Society: Essays in Humanistic Ethics,* Prentice-Hall, 1969.

(Contributor) Robert Ginsberg, editor, *The Critique of War: Contemporary Philosophical Explorations,* Regnery, 1969.

(Contributor) George McLean, editor, *Current Issues in Modern Philosophy,* Catholic University of America Press, 1969.

Durchbruch zum Frieden: Eine amerikanische Gesellschaftskritik, Darmstaedter Blaetter, 1973, published as *The Peace Revolution: Ethos and Social Process,* Greenwood Press, 1975.

(Editor with Howard L. Parsons) *Dialogues on the Philosophy of Marxism: Proceedings of the Society for the Philosophical Study of Dialectical Materialism,* Greenwood Press, 1974.

The Crisis: The True Story about How the World Almost Ended, a Play in Four Acts (first produced in Japan, 1976), privately printed, 1976.

(Editor with Parsons) *Marxism, Revolution, and Peace: From the Proceedings of the Society for the Philosophical Study of Dialectical Materialism,* Gruener (Amsterdam), 1977.

(Editor and author of introduction) *Soviet Marxism and Nuclear War: An International Debate, from the Proceedings of the Special Colloquium of the Fifteenth World Congress of Philosophy,* Greenwood Press, 1981.

Contributor to *Dictionary of Philosophy* and *Encyclopedia Americana.* Contributor to philosophy journals, including *Journal of Philosophy, Philosophical Review, Philosophy and Phenomenological Research, Philosophy of Science, Ethics* and *Humanist.* Member of editorial board of *Philosophic Abstracts,* 1940-50; editor-in-chief, *Soviet Studies in Philosophy* (translation journal), 1962-87. Somerville's books have been published in Danish, German, Japanese, Swedish, and Russian.

* * *

SOMMERS, Joseph 1924-1979

PERSONAL: Born June 21, 1924, in New York, N.Y.; died March 9, 1979; son of Samuel (a textile merchant) and Leah (Ray) Sommers; married Letitia Innes, April 30, 1949 (divorced, 1971); children: William. *Education:* Attended University of Havana, 1942; Cornell University, B.A., 1943; University of Wisconsin, M.A., 1960, Ph.D., 1962.

ADDRESSES: Office—Department of Literature, University of California, San Diego, La Jolla, Calif. 92093.

CAREER: University of Washington, Seattle, assistant professor, 1963-65, associate professor, 1965-68, professor of Spanish literature, 1969-74; University of California at San Diego, La Jolla, professor of Spanish literature, 1974-79. Occasional researcher and teacher in Mexico, 1961-79. *Military service:* U.S. Army, 1943-45; became sergeant; received Purple Heart.

MEMBER: Instituto Internacional de Literatura Iberoamericana, Asociacion Internacional de Hispanistas, Modern Language Association of America, American Association of Teachers of Spanish and Portuguese (national executive council, 1966-68), American Association of University Professors, Phi Beta Kappa.

AWARDS, HONORS: Ford Foundation grant, 1962-63, Joint Committee on Latin American Studies fellow, 1976-77; Woodrow Wilson fellow.

WRITINGS:

Francisco Rojas Gonzalez: Exponente literario del nacionalismo mexicano, University of Veracruz, 1966.

After the Storm: Landmarks of the Modern Mexican Novel, University of New Mexico Press, 1968.

(Contributor) Angel Flores and Raul Silva Caceres, editors, *La novela hispanoamericana,* Las Americas, 1971.

(Editor with Antonia Castaneda Shular) *Literatura chicana: Texto y contexto,* Prentice-Hall, 1972.

(Contributor) Andrew Deicki and Enrique Tupo Walter, editors, *Studies Dedicated to Jose Juan Arrom,* University of North Carolina Press, 1974.

(Editor) *La narrativa de Juan Rulfo: Interpretaciones criticas,* Sep-Setentas, 1974.

(Editor with Tomas Ybarra-Frausto) *Modern Chicano Writers: A Collection of Critical Essays,* Prentice-Hall, 1979.

Contributor to *Nation, Books Abroad, Revista Iberoamericana, Cuadernos Americanos,* and to professional journals in both English and Spanish.

WORK IN PROGRESS: Research for a book of essays on the subject of ideology and Latin American literature.

BIOGRAPHICAL/CRITICAL SOURCES:

PERIODICALS

Books Abroad, spring, 1969.*

* * *

SOUSTER, (Holmes) Raymond 1921- (John Holmes, Raymond Holmes)

PERSONAL: Born January 15, 1921, in Toronto, Ontario, Canada; son of Austin Holmes and Norma (Baker) Souster; married Rosalia Lena Geralde (a bank clerk), June 24, 1947. *Education:* Attended Humberside Collegiate Institute, 1938-39. *Politics:* New Democratic Party. *Religion:* United Church of Canada.

ADDRESSES: Home—39 Baby Point Rd., Toronto, Ontario, Canada M6S 2G2.

CAREER: Poet and editor. Canadian Imperial Bank of Commerce, Toronto, Ontario, accountant, 1939-84. *Military service:* Royal Canadian Air Force, 1941-45; leading aircraftsman.

MEMBER: League of Canadian Poets.

AWARDS, HONORS: Canada's Governor-General Award, 1964, for *The Colour of the Times;* President's Medal, University of Western Ontario, 1967; Centennial Medal, 1967; Canadian Silver Jubilee Medal, 1977; City of Toronto Book Award, 1979.

WRITINGS:

(Contributor) Ronald Hambleton, editor, *Unit of Five,* Ryerson, 1944.

When We Are Young (poetry), First Statement Press, 1946.
Go to Sleep, World (poetry), Ryerson, 1947.
City Hall Street (poetry), Ryerson, 1951.
(Compiler) *Poets 56: Ten Younger English-Canadians,* Contact Press, 1956.
Selected Poems, Contact Press, 1956.
Crepe-hanger's Carnival: Selected Poems, 1955-58, Contact Press, 1958.
Place of Meeting: Poems, 1958-60, Gallery Editions, 1962.
A Local Pride: Poems, Contact Press, 1962.
The Colour of the Times: The Collected Poems, Ryerson, 1964.
12 New Poems, Goosetree Press, 1964.
Ten Elephants on Yonge Street (poetry), Ryerson, 1965.
As Is (poetry), Oxford University Press, 1967.
(Editor with John Robert Colombo) *Shapes and Sounds: Poems of W. W. E. Ross,* Longmans, Green, 1968.
Lost & Found: Uncollected Poems by Raymond Souster, Clarke, Irwin, 1968.
So Far So Good: Poems 1938/1968, Oberon, 1969.
(Editor) *Made in Canada,* Oberon, 1970.
(Editor) *New Wave Canada,* Oberon, 1970.
(Editor with Richard Woollatt) *Generation Now* (poetry anthology), Longmans, Green, 1970.
The Years (poetry), Oberon, 1971.
Selected Poems, Oberon, 1972.
(Under pseudonym John Holmes) *On Target* (novel), Village Book Store Press, 1973.
(Editor with Woollatt) *Sight and Sounds* (poetry anthology), Macmillan (Toronto), 1973.
Change-Up (poetry), Oberon, 1974.
(Editor with Douglas Lochhead) *100 Poems of Nineteenth Century Canada* (poetry anthology), Macmillan (Toronto), 1974.
(Editor with Woollatt) *These Loved, These Hated Lands* (poetry anthology), Doubleday (Toronto), 1975.
Double-Header (poetry), Oberon, 1975.
Rain-Check (poetry), Oberon, 1975.
Extra Innings (poetry), Oberon, 1977.
(Compiler and author of introduction) *Vapour and Blue: Souster Selects Campbell* (selected poetry of William Wilfred Campbell), Paget Press, 1978.
(With Douglas Alcorn) *From Hell to Breakfast* (war memoirs), Intruder Press, 1978.
(Editor) *Comfort of the Fields* (selected poetry of Archibald Lampman), Paget Press, 1979.
Hanging In (poetry), Oberon, 1979.
(Editor with Woollatt) *Poems of a Snow-Eyed Country* (poetry anthology), Academic Press of Canada, 1980.
Collected Poems of Raymond Souster, Oberon, Volume 1: *1940-1955,* 1980, Volume 2: *1955-1962,* 1981, Volume 3: *1962-1974,* 1982, Volume 4: *1974-1977,* 1983, Volume 5: *1977-1983,* 1984, Volume 6: *1984-1986,* 1988.
Going the Distance (poetry), Oberon, 1983.
Jubilee of Death: The Raid on Dieppe, Oberon Press, 1984.
Queen City (poetry), Oberon, 1984.
The Flight of the Roller Coaster (juvenile), Oberon, 1985.
It Takes All Kinds (poetry), Oberon, 1985.
The Eyes of Love (poetry), Oberon, 1987.
Asking for More (poetry), Oberon, 1988.
Running Out the Clock (poetry), Oberon, 1990.

Also author, under pseudonym Raymond Holmes, of novel *The Winter of Time,* 1949.

SIDELIGHTS: Raymond Souster "is the most Torontocentric of Canadian poets," writes Robert Fulford in *Saturday Night.* What Souster has "been doing, all these years," Fulford declares, "is writing hymns of praise to the Toronto he loves and the professionals he admires." According to *Canadian Forum* reviewer David Jackel, "Souster's greatest strength is his ability to go on finding, in his own life and in the ordinary life around him, materials for poetry." *Canadian Literature* critic Mike Doyle comments that "singing small seems to be Raymond Souster's way of being a poet in the world," taking for his subject matter "the face of the ragged postcard seller on Yonge Street, the movement of cats . . . [and] of small birds, the shapes and colours of old buildings, the small immediate actions of people." "Souster's Toronto is not so much vivid as it is simply, palpably there," points out *Tamarack Review* critic Hayden Carruth, "the great northern city, bare, cold, ugly, windswept, yet full of life, indispensible to that life. And this is the freshness that Souster brings to so much of his writing."

BIOGRAPHICAL/CRITICAL SOURCES:

BOOKS

Contemporary Literary Criticism, Gale, Volume 5, 1976, Volume 14, 1980.
Whitman, Bruce, *Collected Poems of Raymond Souster: A Descriptive Bibliography,* Oberon, 1984.

PERIODICALS

Canadian Forum, December, 1968, February, 1969, June, 1975, August, 1977.
Canadian Literature, fall, 1964, autumn, 1972, winter, 1974.
Globe and Mail (Toronto), October 13, 1984.
Saturday Night, December, 1971, July, 1977.
Tamarack Review, winter, 1965.

* * *

SPATE, O(skar) H(ermann) K(hristian) 1911-

PERSONAL: Born March 30, 1911, in London, England; son of Karl (a hotel-keeper) and Olive (Tester) Spate; married Daphne Jessica Huband, August 27, 1937 (divorced); married Browning Hervey Daneke, July 2, 1960; children: (first marriage) Virginia, Andrew, Alastair. *Education:* St. Catharine's College, Cambridge, B.A. (with first class honors), 1933, Ph.D., 1937. *Politics:* "No affiliations, rather left of center." *Religion:* None.

ADDRESSES: Home—3 Spencer St., Turner, ACT 2601, Australia.

CAREER: University of Rangoon, Rangoon, Burma, lecturer in geography, 1937-41; London School of Economics and Political Science, London, England, 1946-51, began as lecturer, became reader in geography; Australian National University, Canberra, New South Wales, professor of geography, 1951-67, director of Research School of Pacific Studies, 1967-72. Convenor of working party on economic development of New Guinea for Minister of Territories, Canberra, 1953; conducted inquiry into Fijian economic problems for Fiji government and Ministry of Overseas Development, 1957-58. Member of Commission on Higher Education in Papua New Guinea, 1963-64, Council of University of Papua New Guinea, Port Moresby, 1965-71, and Council of University of the South Pacific, Suva, Fiji, 1967-70. Convenor, National Committee for Geography, 1956-62; president, Institute of Australian Geographers, 1959; fellow, Australian Academy of the Humanities. Consultant to Ahmadiyya Muslims, Punjab Partition Enquiry, 1947. *Military service:* British Army, 1941-45; served with antiaircraft regiment in Burma, as military press censor in Bombay, India, and as officer in charge of Burma section, Inter-Services Topographical Department, Southeast Asia Command; became temporary major.

MEMBER: Geographical Association (United Kingdom; council member, 1950-51), Royal Geographical Society, Australian and New Zealand Association for Advancement of Science (president of geographical section, 1954; council member, 1954-57).

AWARDS, HONORS: Charles Garnier Medal, Societe de Geographie (Paris); Nehru Medal, National Geographical Society of India; Charles P. Daly Gold Medal, American Geographical Society; Victoria Medal, Royal Geographical Society; Comendador, Order of Isabel la Catolica (Spain); LL.D., University of Papua New Guineas; D.Litt., Australian National University; honorary fellow, Australian Academy of Social Sciences.

WRITINGS:

Burma Setting, Orient Longmans, 1943.
(Editor with W. G. East and contributor) *The Changing Map of Asia,* Methuen, 1950, 5th edition, 1971.
India and Pakistan: A General and Regional Geography, Dutton, 1954, 3rd edition (with A. T. A. Learmonth), 1967.
Australia, New Zealand and the Pacific, Oxford University Press, 1956, 2nd edition, 1965.
The Fijian People: Economic Problems and Prospects, Fiji Legislative Council, 1958.
(Co-author) *Report of the Commission on Higher Education in Papua and New Guinea,* Department of Territories (Canberra), 1964.
Let Me Enjoy: Essays, Partly Geographical, Methuen, 1965.
Australia, Praeger, 1968.
The Pacific since Magellan, University of Minnesota Press, Volume 1: *The Spanish Lake,* 1979, Volume 2: *Monopolists and Freebooters,* 1982.
Paradise Found and Lost, ANU/Pergamon, 1988.

Contributor to geography journals and to *Meanjin* (Melbourne), *Historical Studies* (Melbourne), and *Journal of Pacific History* (Canberra). Editor, *Australian Geographer* (Sydney), 1952-61. *India and Pakistan: A General and Regional Geography* has been translated into Russian; *The Pacific since Magellan* has been translated into Italian.

SIDELIGHTS: O. H. K. Spate's two-volume history, *The Pacific since Magellan,* relates the account of Pacific exploration from the early 1600s to the 1760s. In the *Times Literary Supplement,* Raymond Carr explains the author's intent: "O. H. K. Spate, a distinguished Australian geographer, seeks . . . to give to the Pacific a historical personality." *New York Review of Books* contributor J. H. Elliott appreciates Spate's viewpoint. He states: "Even if it is not always perfectly realized, it is precisely [*The Pacific since Magellan*'s] imaginative attempt to approach the past with fresh perspectives that makes a work like Professor Spate's so valuable historically. What he has sought to do, and with a fair measure of success, is to shift the center of historical gravity for a traditionally Western-minded readership. . . . Most of all, he is concerned to depict *one* world, or, more accurately, one world in the making, as the activities of a handful of sailors and soldiers, merchants and missionaries, begin to bind its different parts together."

Geofrey Parker in *History Today* calls *The Spanish Lake* "an outstanding work of scholarship," and relates that the book "received unqualified critical acclaim. It was a bold and ambitious venture, yet the author manifested total mastery of his sources . . . and told his tale with wit and insight." In *Monopolists and Freebooters,* Parker continues, "the same clear, engaging style is evident; so is the mastery of French, English, Spanish and Portuguese sources." While *The Spanish Lake* received wide praise, *Monopolists and Freebooters* gained mixed reviews. Donald C. Cutter sums up the second volume in *American Historical Review:* "By design, this many-sided book attempts to treat the Pacific as a whole. Yet that immense area's diversity and the varied intentions of the actors on that watery stage make it more convenient to concentrate on particular regions and focus on particular national groups. The result is kaleidoscopic, but seldom dull. The writing is good, at times even lyrical, but not always easy to follow. Political geography and economic history are supported by many well-chosen illustrations that enhance the text, but there is little effort at primary research, as the author customarily uses published contemporary accounts rather than manuscript sources. Notwithstanding this preference, much of his interpretation is fresh." Elliott concludes: "The facility of the writing should not be allowed to conceal the magnitude and difficulty of the enterprise. . . . The overwhelming need at this moment is for someone to sift through and organize the vast quantity of material in print . . . and to produce a readable narrative within a coherent frame. This is what Professor Spate set out to do, and what he has triumphantly achieved."

Spate wrote *CA:* "Having finished *The Pacific since Magellan,* which nearly finished me, I can look back on a life in which I think I have lived up to the motto I have prescribed to generations of students: 'You don't have to be solemn to be serious.' It has been a life with its share of suffering, even anguish, private and public, but on the whole very enjoyable, and although my dearest and unattained wish was to have been able to write real poetry, much of the enjoyment has come from translating hard and often drudging work into honest prose which others besides myself have felt to have some sparkle, colour and force."

BIOGRAPHICAL/CRITICAL SOURCES:

PERIODICALS

American Historical Review, June, 1984.
History Today, February, 1985.
New York Review of Books, October 13, 1983.
Times Literary Supplement, September 9, 1983.

* * *

SPRINGER, Haskell S(aul) 1939-

PERSONAL: Born November 18, 1939, in New York, N.Y.; son of Harry A. (an accountant) and Edith (Guttman) Springer; married Marlene Ann Jones (a professor of English); children: Ann, Rebecca. *Education:* Queens College of the City University of New York, B.A., 1961; Indiana University, M.A., 1965, Ph.D., 1968.

ADDRESSES: Home—1611 Kentucky St., Lawrence, Kan. 66044. *Office*—Department of English, University of Kansas, Lawrence, Kan. 66045.

CAREER: University of Virginia, Charlottesville, instructor in English, 1966-68; University of Kansas, Lawrence, assistant professor, 1968-72, associate professor, 1972-78, professor of English, 1978—, courtesy professor of American studies, 1980—, director of freshman-sophomore English, 1984-89. Fulbright professor at Federal University of Rio de Janeiro and Pontifical Catholic University of Rio de Janeiro, 1975-76; visiting professor, University of Paris, 1985-86.

MEMBER: Modern Language Association of America, American Culture Association, American Association of University Professors, Melville Society.

AWARDS, HONORS: Grant from National Endowment for the Humanities, 1971.

WRITINGS:

Studies in Billy Budd, C. E. Merrill, 1970.

(Contributor) Andrew B. Myers, editor, *Washington Irving: A Tribute,* Sleepy Hollow Restorations, 1972.

(Contributor) Guy Owen, editor, *Modern American Poetry: Essays in Criticism,* Everett/Edwards, 1972.

(Editor and author of introduction) Washington Irving, *Rip Van Winkle and the Legend of Sleepy Hollow,* Sleepy Hollow Restorations, 1975.

Washington Irving: A Reference Guide, G. K. Hall, 1976.

(Editor) Irving, *The Sketch Book of Geoffrey Crayon, Gent.,* Twayne, 1978.

(Contributor) Patricia A. Carlson, editor, *Literature and Lore of the Sea,* RODOPI (Amsterdam), 1986.

(Editor with wife, Marlene Springer) *Plains Woman: The Diary of Martha Farnsworth, 1888-1922,* Indiana University Press, 1986.

(Contributor) Emory Elliott, editor, *Columbia Literary History of the United States,* Columbia University Press, 1988.

Contributor of articles and reviews to literature and American studies journals.

WORK IN PROGRESS: America and the Sea: A Literary History; research on American literature and the sea.

* * *

STABLEFORD, Brian (Michael) 1948-
(Brian Craig)

PERSONAL: Born July 25, 1948, in Shipley, Yorkshire, England; son of William Ernest (an aircraft designer) and Joyce (a teacher; maiden name, Wilkinson) Stableford; married Vivien Owen, September 3, 1973 (divorced, 1985); married Roberta Jane Rennie, May 16, 1987; children: (first marriage) one son, one daughter. *Education:* University of York, B.A., 1969, D.Phil., 1979.

ADDRESSES: Home—113 St. Peter's Rd., Reading, Berkshire, RG6 1PG, England.

CAREER: Writer of speculative fiction; University of Reading, Reading, Berkshire, England, lecturer in sociology, 1976, 1977-88.

MEMBER: Science Fiction Writers of America.

AWARDS, HONORS: Distinguished Scholarship Award, International Association for the Fantastic in the Arts, 1987.

WRITINGS:

SCIENCE FICTION NOVELS

Cradle of the Sun, Sidgwick & Jackson, 1969, published with *The Wizards of Senchuria* by K. Bulmer, Ace Books, 1969.

The Blind Worm, Sidgwick & Jackson, 1970, published with *Seed of the Dreamers* by E. Petaja, Ace Books, 1970.

The Days of Glory ("Dies Irae" series), Ace Books, 1971.

In the Kingdom of the Beasts ("Dies Irae" series), Ace Books, 1971.

Day of Wrath ("Dies Irae" series), Ace Books, 1971.

To Challenge Chaos, DAW Books, 1972.

Halcyon Drift ("Hooded Swan" series), DAW Books, 1972.

Rhapsody in Black ("Hooded Swan" series), DAW Books, 1973.

Promised Land ("Hooded Swan" series), DAW Books, 1974.

The Paradise Game ("Hooded Swan" series), DAW Books, 1974.

The Fenris Device ("Hooded Swan" series), DAW Books, 1974.

Man in a Cage, John Day, 1975.

Swan Song ("Hooded Swan" series), DAW Books, 1975.

Realms of Tartarus, Volume I: *The Face of Heaven,* Quartet, 1975, published in omnibus edition with Volume II: *A Vision of Hell,* and Volume III: *A Glimpse of Infinity,* DAW Books, 1977.

The Mind-Riders, DAW Books, 1976.

The Florians ("Daedalus" series), DAW Books, 1976.

Critical Threshold ("Daedalus" series), DAW Books, 1977.

Wildeblood's Empire ("Daedalus" series), DAW Books, 1977.

The City of the Sun ("Daedalus" series), DAW Books, 1978.

The Last Days of the Edge of the World (juvenile), Hutchinson, 1978, Berkley Publishing, 1985.

Balance of Power ("Daedalus" series), DAW Books, 1979.

The Paradox of Sets ("Daedalus" series), DAW Books, 1979.

The Walking Shadow, Fontana, 1979.

Optiman, DAW Books, 1980 (published in England as *War Games,* Pan, 1981).

The Castaways of Tanagar, DAW Books, 1981.

Journey to the Center ("Asgard" trilogy), DAW Books, 1982.

The Gates of Eden, DAW Books, 1983.

The Empire of Fear, Simon & Schuster, 1988.

(Under pseudonym Brian Craig) *The Doom of Zaragoz,* G. W. Books, 1989.

Invaders from the Center ("Asgard" trilogy), New English Library, 1990.

The Center Cannot Hold ("Asgard" trilogy), New English Library, 1990.

OTHER

Scientific Imagination in Literature (literary history), Futura, 1975.

The Mysteries of Modern Science, Routledge & Kegan Paul, 1978, Littlefield Adams, 1980.

A Clash of Symbols: The Triumph of James Blish, Borgo Press, 1979.

Masters of Science Fiction: Essays on Six Science Fiction Authors, Borgo Press, 1982.

(With Peter Nicholls and David Langford) *The Science in Science Fiction,* Joseph, 1982, Knopf, 1983.

Future Man: Brave New World or Genetic Nightmare?, Crown, 1984.

(With Langford) *The Third Millenium: A History of the World A.D. 2000-3000,* Knopf, 1985.

Scientific Romance in Britain, 1890-1950, St. Martin's, 1985.

The Cosmic Perspective (bound with *Custer's Last Stand*), Drumm Books, 1985.

The Sociology of Science Fiction, Borgo Press, 1987.

The Way to Write Science Fiction, Elm Tree Books, 1989.

Contributor to numerous reference books on science fiction and fantasy; contributor of science fiction stories, occasionally under pseudonym Brian Craig, and articles on science fiction to numerous anthologies and magazines.

WORK IN PROGRESS: A trilogy for Simon & Schuster, *The Werewolves of London,* expected 1991, *The Angel of Pain,* expected 1992, and *The Carnival of Destruction,* expected 1993; more books in the series begun with *The Doom of Zaragoz,* under pseudonym Brian Craig, for G. W. Books.

SIDELIGHTS: Although he is a prolific writer of science fiction novels, sociologist Brian Stableford is perhaps better known for his literary criticism and surveys of the genre. *The Science in Sci-*

ence Fiction, for example, written with Peter Nicholls and David Langford, "is, as billed, a vivid and careful evaluation of the science in science fiction," describes *Discover* contributor Mayo Mohs. In researching early works and traditional theories of science fiction, Stableford and his co-authors "go well beyond judging the quality of the science [in the fiction]; they explain it. With instructive diagrams and in lucid prose," continues Mohs, "they address a wide range of often difficult concepts." K. V. Bailey similarly praises the author's ability to integrate his knowledge of theory and fiction in *Scientific Romance in Britain 1890-1950;* the critic notes in the *New Statesman* that "Stableford brings to this book the skills of a sociologist and the insights of a successful science fiction novelist." While *Times Literary Supplement* contributor Brian Aldiss faults this study of a precursor of modern science fiction for being somewhat lifeless, he comments that it illumines "the traffic of its time," and adds that "Stableford is to be applauded, not only for his dedication, but for refusing to lament too strenuously the passing of the genre he anatomizes." In contrast, Bailey not only finds the study "documented by lively precis and adroitly chosen quotation," but also remarks that "taken as a whole [this] contribution to the critical literature of this field is scholarly, comprehensive—and a pleasure to read."

BIOGRAPHICAL/CRITICAL SOURCES:

PERIODICALS

Discover, March, 1983.
Foundation, January, 1979.
Interzone, January-February, 1989.
Los Angeles Times Book Review, November 24, 1985.
New Statesman, October 4, 1985.
Times Literary Supplement, February 14, 1986.

* * *

STANHOPE, Eric
See HAMILTON, Charles (Harold St. John)

* * *

STANLEY, Robert
See HAMILTON, Charles (Harold St. John)

* * *

STEADMAN, Ralph (Idris) 1936-

PERSONAL: Born May 15, 1936, in Wallasey, Cheshire, England; son of Lionel Raphael (a commercial traveler) and Gwendoline (Welsh) Steadman; married Sheila Thwaite, September 5, 1959 (divorced, 1972); married Anna Deverson (a teacher), December 8, 1972; children: (first marriage) Suzannah, Genevieve, Theo, Henry; (second marriage) Sadie. *Education:* Attended East Ham Technical College, 1959-66, and London College of Printing and Graphic Arts, 1961-65. *Politics:* "Apolitical." *Religion:* Church of England.

ADDRESSES: Agent—Abner Stein, 10 Roland Gardens, London SW7 3PH, England; and Nat Sobel Associates, Inc., 146 East 19th St., New York, N.Y. 10003.

CAREER: Free-lance cartoonist and illustrator. Early in career worked at odd jobs, including trainee manager with F. W. Woolworth Co., Colwyn Bay, North Wales, and as pool attendant in Rhyl, North Wales; de Havilland Aircraft Co., Broughton, Chester, Cheshire, England, apprentice aircraft engineer, 1952; Kemsley (Thomson) Newspapers, London, England, cartoonist, 1956-59; did free-lance work for *Punch, Private Eye,* and *Telegraph* during the 1960s. Work exhibited at the National Theatre, 1977. *Military service:* Royal Air Force, 1954-56.

MEMBER: Chelsea Arts Club.

AWARDS, HONORS: Francis Williams Book Illustration Award, 1972, for *Lewis Carroll's Alice in Wonderland;* gold award, Designers and Art Directors Association, 1977, for outstanding contributions to illustration; silver award, Designers and Art Directors Association, 1977, for outstanding editorial illustration; recipient of merit award and voted illustrator of the year, American Institute of Graphic Arts, 1979; Silver Pencil Award (Holland) for children's book illustrations, 1982, for *Inspector Mouse;* W. H. Smith Illustration Award for Best Illustrated Book, 1987, for *I, Leonardo;* BBC Design Award, 1987, for Halley's Comet postage stamps; Critici in Erba Prize, Bologna Children's Book Fair, 1987, for *That's My Dad.*

WRITINGS:

SELF ILLUSTRATED

Jelly Book (juvenile), Dobson, 1967, Scroll Press, 1970.
(With Fiona Saint) *The Yellow Flowers,* Dobson, 1968, Southwest Book Service, 1974.
The Little Red Computer (juvenile), McGraw, 1969.
Still Life with Raspberry; or, the Bumper Book of Steadman, Rapp & Whiting, 1969.
(With Richard Ingrams) *The Tale of Driver Grope,* Dobson, 1969.
Dogs Bodies, Abelard-Schuman, 1970, Paddington Press, 1977.
Bumper Book of Boobs, Deutsch, 1973.
Ralph Steadman's Bumper to Bumper Book for Children, Pan Books, 1973.
The Bridge (juvenile), Collins (London), 1974, Collins & World (Cleveland), 1975.
America, Straight Arrow Books, 1974.
Flowers for the Moon, Nord Sud Verlag, 1974.
Zwei Esel und eine Brueke, Nord Sud Verlag, 1974, published as *Two Donkeys and a Bridge,* Andersen Press, 1983.
Cherrywood Cannon (juvenile; based on a story told by Dimitri Sidjanski), Paddington Press, 1978.
Sigmund Freud, Paddington, 1979.
A Leg in the Wind and Other Canine Curses, Putnam, 1982.
I, Leonardo, Summit Books, 1983.
No Good Dogs, Perigee, 1983.
Between the Eyes, J. Cape, 1984, Summit Books, 1986.
Paranoids, Harrap, 1986.
That's My Dad, Andersen Press, 1986, David & Charles, 1987.
Scar Strangled Banger, Salem House, 1988.
The Big I Am, Summit Books, 1988.
No Room to Swing a Cat, Andersen, 1989.

ILLUSTRATOR

Frank Dickens, *Fly Away Peter* (juvenile), Dobson, 1963, Scroll Press, 1970.
Mischa Damjan, *Das Eichhorn und das Nashornchen,* Nord Sud Verlag, 1964, published as *The Big Squirrel and the Little Rhinoceros,* Norton, 1965.
Daisy Ashford and Angela Ashford, *Love and Marriage,* Hart-Davis, 1965, reprinted, Oxford University Press, 1982.
D. Ashford, *Where Love Lies Deepest,* Hart-Davis, 1966.
Damjan, *Die Falschen Flamingos* (juvenile), Nord Sud Verlag, 1967, published as *The False Flamingoes,* Dobson, 1968, Scroll Press, 1970.

Charles L. Dodgson, *Lewis Carroll's Alice in Wonderland* (also see below), Dobson, 1967, C. N. Potter, 1973.

Harold Wilson, *The Thoughts of Chairman Harold,* compiled by Tariq Ali, Gnome Press, 1967.

Damjan, *The Little Prince and the Tiger Cat,* McGraw-Hill, 1968.

Randolph Stow, *Midnite: The Story of a Wild Colonial Boy,* Penguin, 1969, reprinted, Bodley Head, 1984.

Tony Palmer, *Born under a Bad Sign,* Kimber, 1970.

Damjan, *Two Cats in America,* Longman Young Books, 1970.

Patricia Mann, *150 Careers in Advertising: With Equal Opportunity for Men and Women,* Longman, 1971.

Brian Patten, *And Sometimes It Happens,* Steam Press, 1972.

John Fuller, *Boys in a Pie,* Bernard Stone, 1972.

Contemporary Poets Set to Music, Turret Books, 1972.

Kurt Baumann, *Der Schlafhund und der Wachlund,* Nord Sud Verlag, 1972, published as *Dozy and Hawkeye,* Hutchinson, 1974.

Hunter S. Thompson, *Fear and Loathing in Las Vegas: A Savage Journey to the Heart of the American Dream,* Paladin Press, 1972.

Ted Hughes, *In the Little Girl's Angel Gaze,* Steam Press, 1972.

Dodgson, *Lewis Carroll's Through the Looking Glass, and What Alice Found There* (also see below), MacGibbon & Kee, 1972, C. N. Potter, 1973.

Edward Lucie-Smith, *Two Poems of Night,* Turret Books, 1972.

John Letts, compiler, *A Little Treasury of Limericks Fair and Foul,* Deutsch, 1973.

Jane Deverson, *Night Edge,* Bettiscombe Press, 1973.

Flann O'Brien, *The Poor Mouth: A Bad Story about the Hard Life,* Hart-Davis/MacGibbon, 1973, Viking, 1974.

Thompson, *Fear and Loathing: On the Campaign Trail,* Allison & Busby, 1974.

Steam Press Portfolio, Steam Press, Number 2, 1974, Number 3, 1977.

Dodgson, *The Hunting of the Snark: An Agony in Eight Fits* (also see below), Studio Vista, 1975, C. N. Potter, 1976.

Bernard Stone, *Emergency Mouse: A Story* (juvenile), Prentice-Hall, 1978.

Hughes, *The Threshold,* Steam Press, 1979.

Stone, *Inspector Mouse* (juvenile), Andersen Press, 1980, Holt, 1981.

Thompson, *The Great Shark Hunt,* Paladin, 1980.

Adrian Mitchell, *For Beauty Douglas: Adrian Mitchell's Collected Poems, 1953-79,* Allison & Busby, 1982.

Alan Sillitoe, *Israel Sketchbook,* Steam Press, 1983.

Thompson, *The Curse of Lono,* Bantam, 1983.

Stone, *Quasimodo Mouse,* Andersen Press, 1984.

Robert Louis Stevenson, *Treasure Island,* Harrap, 1985.

Dodgson, *The Complete Alice and Hunting of the Snark* (contains *Lewis Carroll's Alice in Wonderland, Lewis Carroll's Through the Looking Glass, and What Alice Found There,* and *The Hunting of the Snark: An Agony in Eight Fits*), Salem House, 1986.

SIDELIGHTS: "Extended exposure to the art of Ralph Steadman is rather like inserting your eyeballs into an electric outlet," comments *New York Times Book Review* contributor Draper Hill. Steadman began his career as an illustrator and cartoonist for the British magazines *Punch* and *Private Eye,* honing his talents as a caricaturist and satirist. In 1969, "Gonzo" journalist Hunter S. Thompson was searching for an artist to prepare illustrations for his "Fear and Loathing" series; Steadman accompanied the writer on his coverage of the Kentucky Derby, and the resultant cartoons presented the ugly side of the "beautiful" people found there. The artist continued to find subjects in the United States, working regularly for the magazine *Rolling Stone.* Many of these early drawings are collected in *America,* a volume in which "Steadman, because of [his] 'demented' view of society . . . [draws] powerful personal statements that are as disturbing today as they were in their time," asserts *Washington Post Book World* contributor K. Francis Tanabe. As Steve Appleford describes in the *Washington Post,* "to Steadman, the United States was the most vulgar embodiment of all that he found evil and wrong-headed with Western society. Its culture, leaders and people fascinated and repelled him. . . . It was inspirational."

In this "impressively consistent high-energy fury, Steadman has developed an unevenly spluttering calligraphy which would probably suggest to an orthodox graphologist that the penman was mad," comments Patrick Skene Catling in a *Spectator* review of *Between the Eyes,* a twenty-five year retrospective of the artist's work. "Steadman is not really mad; he is certainly no madder than any other extremely ardent believer. He is indignant, as anybody is bound to be who reads the newspapers, listens to the radio and watches television." Because the artist is often "wildly subjective" in his portraits, *Los Angeles Times Book Review* writer Alex Raksin believes that it may be "easy to dismiss Steadman's sparse text . . . as threadbare." The critic admits, however, that whatever the subject "it's difficult to remain unaffected by [Steadman's] art."

Although Steadman has gained his fame through his cartoons, "more recently his 'biography' 'Sigmund Freud' and his 'autobiography' 'I, Leonardo' provided evidence that his abilities as a writer are a natural complement to his remarkable gifts as a draftsman," notes Hill. A tribute to the father of psychoanalysis, *Sigmund Freud* "comes across as a remarkable book: wild, inventive, disturbing and explosively funny," writes Hill in his review. Grounded in Freud's own writings about humor, Steadman's "principal drawings are potent fusions of intuitive force, linear grace and comic outrage," continues the critic, "evocations of the twilight zone of borderline psychosis enveloping teacher, patient and disciple." *Newsweek* writer Peter Prescott similarly calls *Sigmund Freud* "a surprisingly complex work" with drawings "as vigorous and witty as anything being done in the genre today." "With this book," maintains David Finkle in the *Village Voice,* "Steadman subtly establishes himself as a far-sighted disciple passing around a magnifying glass for closer perusal and understanding of who Freud was and why he thought as he did." In *I, Leonardo,* Steadman creates an invented "autobiography" of famed artist and inventor Leonardo da Vinci. With "characteristically uninhibited ink-and-stipple illustrations" and recreations of Leonardo's own work, "Steadman captures the human feelings behind the genius," states a *Macleans* reviewer. The author spent three years researching and preparing the text, and attempts to get inside the artist's personality. The result, remarks Joyce Wadler in the *Washington Post,* "is Leonardo filtered through Steadman, written so you're never quite sure where one begins and the other leaves off. He did this on purpose," adds the critic, "and purposely included inaccuracies—just to twit the academics, whom he loathes."

When asked where the rage that motivates much of his work originates, Steadman replied to Wadler: "How the —— should I know finally where it comes from? Except that it continually burns me and I really can't draw unless I'm angry and that's unfortunately why one gets drunk, you try and crank it up. . . ." As the artist once told *CA:* "I started my drawing career more as a cause than a business. I thought I could change the world, but I now realize that is a hopeless dream. However, I still try. Fundamentally, man is an idiot with aspirations."

MEDIA ADAPTATIONS: "The Bridge" was made into a filmstrip with cassette by Listening Library, 1976.

AVOCATIONAL INTERESTS: Gardening, collecting, writing, fishing, sculpture. astronomy.

BIOGRAPHICAL/CRITICAL SOURCES:

PERIODICALS

Los Angeles Times Book Review, March 13, 1988.
Macleans, December 12, 1983.
Newsweek, December 10, 1979.
New York Times Book Review, December 14, 1980, January 11, 1987.
New York Times Magazine, October 9, 1983.
Spectator, October 13, 1984, December 12, 1987.
Times Literary Supplement, January 20, 1984.
Village Voice, January 7, 1980.
Washington Post, December 31, 1983, April 28, 1988.
Washington Post Book World, April 3, 1977.

* * *

STEFANSSON, Thorsteinn 1912-

PERSONAL: Born December 1, 1912, in Lodmundarfiord, Iceland; son of Stefan (a farmer) and Herborg (Bjoernsdottir) Thorsteinsson. *Politics:* "Individualism and social justice." *Religion:* "Faith in After-Life."

ADDRESSES: Home—Teglgardsvej 531, DK 3050, Humlebaek, Denmark.

CAREER: Writer. Worked as cowman, fisherman, dockworker, hodman, debt collector, language teacher, and translator.

MEMBER: Dansk Forfatterforening.

AWARDS, HONORS: Hans Christian Andersen Medal from Danish literary committee of judges, 1958, for *The Golden Future.*

WRITINGS:

Fra oedrum hnetti (novel; title means "From Another Planet"), [Reykjavik], 1935.
Dalen (novel; title means "The Valley"), Nyt Nordisk Forlag, 1942.
Als het hart in woorden zingt (novel; title means "When the Heart Sings"), Zuid-Hollandsche, 1950.
Den gyldne Fremtid (novel), Nyt Nordisk Forlag, 1958, translation by the author published as *The Golden Future,* Oxford University Press, 1974.
(Contributor) *Datskaya Novella XIX-XX,* Leningrad, 1967.
(Translator) Kristmann Gudmundsson, *Sommer i Selavik* (novel; title means "Summer in Selavik"), Birgitte Hoevrings Biblioteksforlag, 1974.
(Translator) Gudmundsson, *Ild og Aske* (novel; title means "Fire and Ashes"), Birgitte Hoevrings Biblioteksforlag, 1975.
Wo sich die Wege Kreuzen (novel; title means "At Crossroads"), Herder Verlag, 1976.
Dybgroenne tun (novel; title means "Deep Green Tuns"), Birgitte Hoevrings Biblioteksforlag, 1976.
Soelvglitrende hav (novel; title means "Silvery Ocean"), Birgitte Hoevrings Biblioteksforlag, 1976.
Paa lovens grund (short stories; title means "With the Sanction of the Law"), Birgitte Hoevrings Biblioteksforlag, 1977.
Forlovelsesringen (novel; title means "The Engagement Ring"), Birgitte Hoevrings Biblioteksforlag, 1977.
(Translator) Olafur Johann Sigurdsson, *The Nest* (novel), Birgitte Hoevrings Biblioteksforlag, 1978.
Du, som kom (poetry collection; title means "You Who Came"), Birgitte Hoevrings Biblioteksforlag, Volume I, 1979, Volume II, 1980, Volume III, 1981.
(Contributor) *Anthology of Icelandic Short Stories in Russian,* Mockba, 1980.
Vinden blaeser (novel; title means "The Wind Blows"), Birgitte Hoevrings Biblioteksforlag, 1983.
Men det koster (novel; title means "But, You Will Have to Pay for It"), Birgitte Hoevrings Biblioteksforlag, 1985.

OTHER

Also author of radio drama, "Lagsystir manns" (title means "Comradeship with a Man"), 1975. Contributor of short stories to literature periodicals, including *Norseman, American-Scandinavian Review, Vaerldens, Beraettare, Ord och Bild,* and *Eimreidin.*

WORK IN PROGRESS: Translating *The Wedding Gown* by Kristmann Gudmundsson.

SIDELIGHTS: Thorsteinn Stefansson told *CA,* "All fiction must represent the greatest drama: life itself." *The Valley* has also been published in French.

AVOCATIONAL INTERESTS: Outdoor life, swimming, psychic research, protecting animals and environments.

* * *

STEINER, Joerg 1930-

PERSONAL: Born October 26, 1930, in Biel, Switzerland; son of Paul (an engineer) and Margrit (Flueckiger) Steiner; married Silvia Schluep (a tour guide), February 7, 1955; children: Rachel, Sarah. *Education:* Attended Munstalden (seminary), Bern, Switzerland, 1950-52.

ADDRESSES: Home and office—Seevorstadt 57, CH-2502 Biel, Switzerland.

CAREER: Writer, 1956—.

MEMBER: PEN International, Gruppe Olten.

AWARDS, HONORS: Charles Veillon Prize, 1966, for *Ein Messer fuer den ehrlichen Finder;* Mildred L. Batchelder Award, American Library Association Children's Service Division, 1979, for *Rabbit Island.*

WRITINGS:

JUVENILES; IN ENGLISH TRANSLATION

(Adapter) *Der Baer der ein Baer bleiben wollte* (illustrated by Joerg Mueller), Sauerlaender, 1976, translation by Anthea Bell published as *The Bear Who Wanted to Be a Bear,* Atheneum, 1977.
Die Kanincheninsel (illustrated by Mueller), Sauerlaender, 1977, translation by Ann Conrad Lammers published as *Rabbit Island,* Harcourt, 1978.
Die Menschen im Meer (illustrated by Mueller), Sauerlaender, 1981, translation published as *The Sea People,* Gollancz, 1982.

IN GERMAN

Episoden aus Rabenland (poems; title means "Episodes in Crowland"), Tschudi, 1957.

Abendanzug zu verkaufen (fiction; title means "Evening Suit for Sale"), Benteli, 1961.

Strafarbeit (novel; title means "Punishment Work"), Walter, 1962.

Polnische Kastanien (fiction; title means "Polish Chestnuts"), Brechbuehl, 1963.

Der schwarze Kasten: Spielregeln (juvenile; title means "The Black Box: A Play"), Walter, 1965.

Ein Messer fuer den ehrlichen Finder (novel; title means "A Knife for the True Finder"), Walter, 1966.

"Das Bett" (play; title means "The Bed"), broadcast by Studio Radio Basel, 1967.

Auf dem Berge Sinai sitzt der Schneider Kikrikri: Ein Geschichtenbuch (storybook; title means "The Tailor Kikrikri on Mount Sinai: A Storybook"), Luchterhand, 1969.

"Peles Bruder" (television play; title means "Brother Peles"), broadcast by SRG (Zurich), 1972.

Pele sein Bruder (picture book; illustrated by Werner Maurer; title means "Pele's Brother"), Middelhauve, 1972.

Schnee bis in die Niederungen (fiction; title means "Snow in the Valley"), Luchterhand, 1973.

Als es noch Grenzen gab (poems; title means "When There Were Borders"), Suhrkamp, 1976.

Das Netz zerreissen (novel; title means "The Tearing of the Net"), Suhrkamp, 1982.

Olduvai (stories), Suhrkamp, 1985.

Der Eisblumenwald (novel for children), Sauerlaender, 1985.

Der Mann vom Baerengraben (picture book; illustrated by Mueller), Sauerlaender, 1987.

SIDELIGHTS: Joerg Steiner told *CA:* "In Swiss literature there is no children's literature to speak of. This is one big reason why I like to write for children. I write for them as much as for my adult readers. Children understand more of life than many adults believe. I am happy that the children do not reject me because I also write for adults."

* * *

STERN, Stuart
See RAE, Hugh C(rauford)

* * *

STEVENSON, Janet 1913-

PERSONAL: Born February 4, 1913, in Chicago, Ill.; daughter of John C. (an investment banker) and Atlantis (McClendon) Marshall; married second husband, Benson Rotstein (an educator), 1964; children: (previous marriage) Joseph Stevenson, Edward Stevenson. *Education:* Bryn Mawr College, B.A. (magna cum laude), 1933; Yale University, M.F.A., 1937. *Religion:* Unitarian Universalist.

ADDRESSES: Home—Route 5, Astoria, Ore. 97103.

CAREER: University of Southern California, Los Angeles, lecturer in drama, 1951-53; Grambling College, Grambling, La., assistant professor of English, 1966-67; Portland State University, Portland, Ore., lecturer, 1968.

MEMBER: Authors League of America, PEN.

AWARDS, HONORS: International Bicentennial Playwriting Prize, 1976, for "The Third President"; Friends of American Writers awards for *Weep No More* and *The Ardent Years;* National Arts of the Theatre Award, for "Weep No More" (dramatic version of book); John Golden fellowship in playwriting.

WRITINGS:

Weep No More: A Novel, Viking, 1957.

The Ardent Years: A Novel, Viking, 1960.

Painting America's Wildlife: John James Audubon (juvenile biography), Kingston House, 1961.

Marian Anderson: Singing to the World (juvenile biography), Encyclopaedia Britannica Press, 1963.

Sisters and Brothers: A Novel, Crown, 1966.

Pioneers in Freedom: Adventures in Courage (juvenile history), Reilly & Lee, 1969.

Spokesman for Freedom: The Life of Archibald Grimke (juvenile biography), Crowell-Collier, 1969.

Woman Aboard (travel), Crown, 1969, new edition, Chandler & Sharp, 1981.

Soldiers in the Civil Rights War: Adventures in Courage (juvenile history), Reilly & Lee, 1971.

The Montgomery Bus Boycott, December, 1955: American Blacks Demand an End to Segregation (juvenile history), F. Watts, 1971.

Women's Rights (juvenile history), F. Watts, 1972.

The School Segregation Cases (Brown v. Board of Education of Topeka and Others): The United States Supreme Court Rules on Racially Separate Public Education (juvenile history), F. Watts, 1973.

"The Third President" (drama), first produced at Laboratory Theatre, Southern Illinois University at Carbondale, 1976.

The Undiminished Man: A Political Biography of Robert Walker Kenny, Chandler & Sharp, 1980.

(Contributor) *A Sense of History: The Best Writing from the Pages of American Heritage,* American Heritage Press/Houghton, 1985.

Departure, Harcourt, 1985.

Also author of plays "Declaration" and "Counter-Attack," in collaboration with Philip Stevenson, and "Weep No More." Author of motion picture scripts, short stories, and reading texts.

WORK IN PROGRESS: A novel with an 1850 maritime background concerning a woman navigator; "Days without Names," a screenplay.

SIDELIGHTS: Janet Stevenson told *CA:* "Like many other women, I carried, during what are usually considered the 'best years of your life,' responsibilities that competed for the time and energy that might have gone into writing. I raised two sons (who seem to me worth every erg of the energy they absorbed) and I helped two quite different husbands achieve at least part of their life goals. I also spent a lot of those years fighting as a citizen to avert the disaster that seemed to me to hang over not only our country, but our human race.

"I learned a lot in that process of living, but I used up those best writing years with not nearly enough to show for them. Now I am trying to use the not-best years—with plenty of time, but not as much energy—to put what I learned into literary or dramatic form. And I find I am still trying to avert the same omen, convinced at last that writing a book (or a play) that helps people to feel themselves inside other people is the way I should be doing it."*

* * *

STIRLING, Jessica
See RAE, Hugh C(rauford)

STRASBERG, Lee 1901-1982

PERSONAL: Born November 17, 1901, in Budanov, Austria-Hungary (now in U.S.S.R.); brought to United States, 1909; became U.S. citizen, 1936; died February 17, 1982, in New York, N.Y.; son of Baruch Meyer and Ida (Diner) Strasberg; married Paula Miller, March 16, 1934 (deceased); married Anna Mizrahi, January 7, 1968; children: (second marriage) Susan (an actress), John; (third marriage) Adam Lee, David Lee. *Education:* Studied at American Laboratory Theatre under Richard Boleslavski and Maria Ouspenskaya.

ADDRESSES: Home—135 Central Park West, New York, N.Y. 10023.

CAREER: Began acting in productions at a New York settlement house; started Broadway career with the Theatre Guild, 1924, as assistant stage manager for the Lynn Fontanne and Alfred Lunt play, "The Guardsman," and appeared in "Red Rust" and several other Guild presentations, 1925-31; joined actors and directors interested in the "Method" theory of Constantin Stanislavski (Moscow Art Theatre) in founding the Group Theatre, 1931, and was co-director of the Group's first Broadway hit, "The House of Connelly," 1931, and director of the Pulitzer Prize-winning "Men in White," 1933, and "Johnny Johnson," 1936; resigned from Group Theatre, 1937, staging plays independently before going to Hollywood in 1942; returned to Broadway in 1948 as director of "Skipper Next to God" and, later, "The Big Knife"; artistic director of Actors Studio, Inc., 1962-66; director for "Three Sisters," 1964; artistic director for "The Silent Partner, Felix". Established Lee Strasberg Institute of Theatre in New York City and Los Angeles, 1969. Lecturer at Harvard University, Brown University, Yale University, Brandeis University, and Northwestern University. Made film debut in "The Godfather—Part II," also appeared in films "And Justice for All" and "Going in Style."

MEMBER: American Federation of Television and Radio Artists, Screen Actors Guild.

AWARDS, HONORS: Kelcey Allen award, New York City, 1961; Centennial Gold Medal for excellence in dramatic arts, Boston College, 1963; Academy Award nomination for best supporting actor, 1974, for "The Godfather—Part II"; elected to Theatrical Hall of Fame, 1982; building named in his honor at Hebrew University; honorary degree, University of Florida.

WRITINGS:

(Editor) *Famous American Plays of the 1950's,* Dell, 1963.
Strasberg at the Actors Studio, edited by Robert H. Hethmon, Viking, 1965.
Lee Strasberg on Acting, Harper, 1973.
A Dream of Passion: The Development of the Method, Little, Brown, 1987.

Also author of articles on acting; contributed to *Encyclopaedia Britannica,* 15th edition.

SIDELIGHTS: Until this century, actors were trained primarily for the classics, mastering the Greek chorus style or Shakespeare's iambic pentameter. But the advent of modern drama, characterized in the United States by the plays of Clifford Odets, Eugene O'Neill, and Tennessee Williams, demanded a new breed of actor, one who could project the strong inner turmoil of these contemporary characters. Enter Lee Strasberg, actor, teacher, and proponent of "the Method," the introspective, highly expressive acting mode developed by Russia's Constantin Stanislavski. Strasberg devoted his life to his theatrical pursuits, though mostly behind the scenes. In fact, he "retired" from stage acting in 1929, and didn't make his film debut until 1974, when Strasberg earned an Academy Award nomination for playing an elderly mobster in "The Godfather—Part II."

Always a controversial figure, Strasberg as acting coach and director oversaw a generation of talent whose number includes Robert DeNiro, Paul Newman, and Joanne Woodward. But while many of his students went on to gain success, Strasberg's detractors remained vocal. "Lee Strasberg?" stated fellow teacher Stella Adler in a 1979 *New York Times Magazine* article. "I think what he does is sick. Too many of his students have come to me ready for an institution."

What Strasberg did was to use the Method as an emotional tool, an exercise by which "an actor draws upon events, sometimes traumatic, in his own life in order to help understand the life of a character," in the words of *New York Times* critic Mel Gussow. In the same article, actress Ellen Burstyn, another Stasberg protege, elaborated: "For Stanislavski, behavior defined character. That's true in any style of theatre—if you're doing Brecht, Shakespeare or Clifford Odets. I would be hard pressed to find a really good actor who was not a Method actor. About the charge that you can only use the Method to play yourself, the answer to that objection is Dustin Hoffman, who is a great character actor and a Method actor."

The Actors Studio, run by Strasberg as a Method workshop, gained a reputation as an elite organization where neophytes and stars alike gathered to refine their technique. There Strasberg was known as tough teacher to please, innovative yet headstrong. "Most acting teachers employ a method similar to Strasberg's," noted Steven Hager in *Horizon,* "but [his] classes differ from many in their use of affective memory. Affective memory has caused more confusion and disagreement among actors than any other aspect of the Method. It is used to create intense emotions on stage and involves a past event in the actor's life. Suppose, for example, a character in a play is jilted by his girlfriend," Hager continued. "The actor playing the role would be asked to recall a similar experience of his own and list every detail he could remember: the exact time of day he found out, what the girl was wearing at the time, the look on her face, etc. Rather than concentrate on an emotion, the actor looks for a physical detail that is psychologically linked to the emotion. Once he finds the detail, he needs only to recall it the moment he needs it in the play."

Many of the actors who disparage the Method, Gussow pointed out, came from a more traditional background. He cited Laurence Olivier as one Method critic who once advised young actors to "work on a building site rather than go to a [Method] studio." On a more agreeable note, actress Estelle Parsons told Gussow that she had never been entirely comfortable with the technique, although it does "enable you to use your emotional apparatus." But, she added, "it's not much use without professional discipline." Other performers believe strongly in the Method. Among them is Academy Award winner Shelley Winters, who revealed to Gussow that "for 30 years I called 'affective memory' effective memory because it is so effective." And to Cloris Leachman, speaking at a Strasberg tribute covered by Nancy Platze for *People,* the instructor brought her "a sense of discovering experience and experiencing discovery."

Strasberg had not performed publicly for some 40 years when he made his film debut in 1974. The immediate acclaim for his role in "The Godfather—Part II" led to a string of other roles. In an interview with Gene Siskel in 1979, Strasberg told the *Chicago Tribune Book World* critic that if he were a film reviewer, he would "try to give a sense of what the actor was trying to do, because otherwise I would always write what I thought he should be doing, then I would think he was bad. But, no, he may be very good doing what he thinks he should be doing."

On the weekend before his death, Strasberg had appeared on stage in an uncharacteristic role—a member of an all-male kickline performing at a benefit. The news of his passing brought a flood of tributes, and, as *Washington Post* writer Joyce Wadler reported, his funeral "was packed, Standing Room Only." At a memorial service, student Marlo Thomas recalled seeing Strasberg at a posh state dinner. "From the receiving line, Strasberg saw a line of young, good-looking waiters," described Wadler, now quoting Thomas: " 'Actors?' he asked, and when they said yes, he left the receiving line to visit. He won so many awards and he once said, 'I don't want any tributes, the work is the tribute.' "

BIOGRAPHICAL/CRITICAL SOURCES:

BOOKS

Adams, C.H., *Lee Strasberg: The Imperfect Genius of the Actors Studio,* Doubleday, 1980.
Hethmon, Robert H., editor, *Strasberg at the Actors Studio,* Viking, 1965.
Strasberg, Lee, *Lee Strasberg on Acting,* Harper, 1973.
Strasberg, Lee, *A Dream of Passion: The Development of the Method,* Little, Brown, 1987.
Strasberg, Susan, *Bittersweet,* Putnam, 1980.

PERIODICALS

Chicago Tribune Book World, December 16, 1979.
Esquire, October, 1961.
Horizon, January, 1980.
New Republic, December 1, 1962.
New York Times, July 20, 1958, April 14, 1987.
New York Times Book Review, June 10, 1984, November 29, 1987.
New York Times Magazine, October 7, 1979.
People, November 24, 1980.
Time, October 6, 1967, December 16, 1974.
U.S. News and World Report, June 16, 1980.
Washington Post, February 19, 1982, February 21, 1982.

OBITUARIES:

PERIODICALS

Chicago Tribune, February 18, 1982.
New York Times, February 18, 1982.
Time, March 1, 1982.
Times (London), February 18, 1982.
Washington Post, February 18, 1982.*

—Sketch by Susan Salter

* * *

STRONG, Susan
See REES, Joan

* * *

STROTHER, Pat Wallace 1929-
(Pat Wallace Latner, Patricia Strother, Pat Wallace; pseudonyms: Patricia Cloud, Vivian Lord, Pat West)

PERSONAL: Born March 11, 1929, in Birmingham, Ala.; daughter of Claude Hunter (in insurance) and Gladys Eleanor (English) Wallace; married Lee Levitt (a public relations executive), June, 1951 (divorced, 1957); married David G. Latner, August, 1958 (divorced, 1969); married Robert A. Strother (a building contractor), July, 1980; stepchildren: (third marriage) Robert, Andrea, Douglas. *Education:* Attended University of Tennessee, 1947-51, and Columbia University, 1962. *Politics:* Liberal Democrat. *Religion:* None.

ADDRESSES: Home—117 West 13th St., Apt. 20, New York, N.Y. 10011. *Agent*—Jane Rotrosen Agency, 318 East 51st St., New York, N.Y. 10022.

CAREER: WGNS-Radio, Murfreesboro, Tenn.; women's program director, 1951-52; WMAK-Radio, Nashville, Tenn., copy chief and announcer, 1952-54; *Civil Service Leader,* New York City, assistant to editor, 1955-57; International Brotherhood of Teamsters, Local Union 237, New York City, secretary to the president, 1957-76; full-time writer, 1975—.

MEMBER: Authors Guild, Authors League of America.

WRITINGS:

UNDER NAME PAT WALLACE

House of Scorpio, Avon, 1975.
The Wand and the Star, Pocket Books, 1978.
Silver Fire, Silhouette Romances, 1982.
My Loving Enemy, Silhouette Romances, 1983.
Sweetheart Contract, Silhouette Romances, 1983.
Shining Hour, Silhouette Romances, 1984.
Objections Overruled, Silhouette Romances, 1984.
Love Scene, Silhouette Romances, 1985.
Star Rise, Silhouette Romances, 1985.

UNDER NAME PATRICIA STROTHER

The Constant Star, New American Library, 1986.
Grand Design, New American Library, 1988.
Silvermore, New American Library, 1989.

UNDER PSEUDONYM VIVIAN LORD

Traitor in My Arms, Fawcett, 1979.
The Voyagers, Fawcett, 1980.
Once More the Sun, Fawcett, 1982.
Summer Kingdom, Fawcett, 1983.
Unyielding Fire, Fawcett, 1985.

OTHER

(Under pseudonym Patricia Cloud) *This Willing Passion,* Putnam, 1978.
(Under pseudonym Pat West) *Under the Sign of Scorpio,* Dell, 1986.
(Under pseudonym Pat West) *A Wife for Ransom,* Dell, 1986.

Contributor of short stories, under name Pat Wallace Latner, and poems to periodicals.

WORK IN PROGRESS: A fourth novel for New American Library under name Patricia Strother; a sequel to *House of Scorpio* under name Pat Wallace Strother.

SIDELIGHTS: "I started writing poetry at eleven," Pat Wallace Strother once told *CA,* "and this was my major interest until 1971, when I began writing novels and invented the astrological novel genre. My interest in astrology goes back to 1963 when Ree Dragonette . . . introduced me to the subject. Though I am not a professional astrologer, my studies and observations have been intense."

BIOGRAPHICAL/CRITICAL SOURCES:

PERIODICALS

Washington Post Book World, March 4, 1979.

* * *

STROTHER, Patricia
See STROTHER, Pat Wallace

* * *

SUCHLICKI, Jaime 1939-

PERSONAL: Born December 8, 1939, in Havana, Cuba; U.S. citizen; son of Salomon (a businessman) and Ana (Greinstein) Suchlicki; married Carol Meyer, January 26, 1964; children: Michael Ian, Kevin Donald, Joy Michelle. *Education:* Attended University of Havana, 1959-60; University of Miami, A.B. (cum laude) 1964, M.A., 1965; Texas Christian University, Ph.D., 1967.

ADDRESSES: Office—Institute of Interamerican Studies, University of Miami, 1531 Brescia Ave., Miami, Fla. 33124.

CAREER: University of Miami, Coral Gables, Fla., assistant professor, 1967-71, associate professor, 1971-75, professor of history, 1975—, Center for Advanced International Studies, research associate, 1967-70, associate director, 1979-80, Institute of Interamerican Studies, associate director, 1970-71, director, 1971-73, 1982—.

MEMBER: Conference on Latin American History, Latin American Studies Association, B'nai B'rith, Phi Alpha Theta.

WRITINGS:

(Contributor) Robert E. McNicoll, editor, *Latin American Panorama,* Putnam, 1968.

(Contributor) Donald K. Emmerson, editor, *Students and Politics in Developing Nations,* Praeger, 1968.

The Cuban Revolution: A Documentary Bibliography, 1952-1968, Center for Advanced International Studies, University of Miami, 1968.

University Students and Revolution in Cuba, 1920-1968, University of Miami Press, 1969.

(Editor and author of introduction) *Cuba, Castro and Revolution,* University of Miami Press, 1972.

(With Irving B. Reed and Dodd L. Harvey) *The Latin American Scene of the Seventies: A Basic Fact Book,* Center for Advanced International Studies, University of Miami, 1972.

Cuba: From Columbus to Castro, Scribner, 1974, 2nd edition, Pergamon, 1986.

(With staff of Cuban Studies Conference) *Cuba: Continuity and Change,* Institute of Interamerican Studies, University of Miami, 1985.

Historical Dictionary of Cuba, Scarecrow, 1988.

Contributor to encyclopedias. Contributor to professional journals.

* * *

SUNY, Ronald Grigor 1940-

PERSONAL: Born September 25, 1940, in Philadelphia, Pa.; son of George and Arax Suny; married Armena Pearl Marderosian, August 14, 1971; children: Grikor Martiros (deceased), Sevan Siranoush Suni, Anoush Tamar Suni. *Education:* Swarthmore College, B.A. (with high honors), 1962; Columbia University, M.A. and Certificate in Russian, both 1965, Ph.D., 1968.

ADDRESSES: Home—1723 Wells, Ann Arbor, Mich. 48104. *Office*—Department of History, University of Michigan, Ann Arbor, Mich. 48109.

CAREER: Columbia University, New York, N.Y., lecturer in Russian history, 1967-68; Oberlin College, Oberlin, Ohio, assistant professor, 1968-72, associate professor of history, 1972-81; University of Michigan, Ann Arbor, Alex Manoogian Professor of Modern Armenian History, 1981—. Senior fellow at Columbia University's Russian Institute, 1976; fellow at Harvard University's Russian Research Center, 1980-81. Visiting professor at University of Michigan, 1977-78; John and Haigouhie Takakjian Lecturer at Columbia University, 1981; distinguished visiting professor at University of California, Irvine, 1987. Public speaker in the United States and the U.S.S.R. Coordinator and chairman of Conference on Nationalism and Social Change in Transcaucasia at Kennan Institute for Advanced Russian Studies, 1980.

MEMBER: American Association for the Advancement of Slavic Studies, American Historical Association, Society for Armenian Studies (member of administrative council, 1978-79, 1980-81; chairman, 1981), British Study Group on the Russian Revolution, Phi Beta Kappa.

AWARDS, HONORS: H. H. Powers grants from Oberlin College, 1970, 1975, 1979; grants from International Research and Exchanges Board for the U.S.S.R., 1971-72, 1975-76; Fulbright grant, 1975-76; fellow of National Endowment for the Humanities, 1980-81; Guggenheim fellow, 1983-84.

WRITINGS:

The Baku Commune, 1917-1918: Class and Nationality in the Russian Revolution, Princeton University Press, 1972.

(Contributor) Stephen F. Cohen, Alexander Rabinowitch, and Robert Sharlet, editors, *The Soviet Union since Stalin,* Indiana University Press, 1980.

(Contributor) Richard G. Hovannisian, editor, *The Armenian Image in History and Literature,* Undena, 1981.

Armenia in the Twentieth Century, Scholars Press, 1983.

(Editor) *Transcaucasia, Nationalism, and Social Change,* Michigan Slavic Publications, 1983.

The Making of the Georgian Nation, Indiana University Press, 1988.

(Author of foreword) Maurice Hindus, *Red Beard,* Indiana University Press, 1988.

Contributor to *Modern Encyclopedia of Russian and Soviet History.* Contributor of about forty articles and reviews to history journals and Armenian newspapers. Member of editorial board of *Journal of the Society for Armenian Studies;* member of editorial committee of *Soviet Studies in History.*

WORK IN PROGRESS: A biography of the young Stalin from 1879-1924, *Stalin and the Revolutionary Movement in Russia.*

SIDELIGHTS: Ronald Grigor Suny told *CA:* "My interest in the history of Armenia, Georgia, and Russia stems from my father's stories of his youth in Tiflis. Raised as an Armenian in America, I have been engaged in a lifelong attempt to understand the past of this small people so desperate to preserve their unique ethnic personality. But to my mind, the history of the Armenians, especially in Transcaucasia, cannot be understood without a deep study of the history of their neighbors, particularly the Russians and Georgians."

BIOGRAPHICAL/CRITICAL SOURCES:

PERIODICALS

American Historical Review, April, 1974.
Times Literary Supplement, April 21, 1989.

* * *

SYLVIA
See ASHTON-WARNER, Sylvia (Constance)

T

TALBOT, Toby 1928-
(Rebecca Josephs)

PERSONAL: Born November 29, 1928, in New York, N.Y.; daughter of Joseph and Bella (Nager) Tolpen; married Daniel Talbot (a film producer and founder of New Yorker Theatre and New York Films), January 6, 1951; children: Nina, Emily, Sarah. *Education:* Queens College (now Queens College of the City University of New York), B.A., 1949; Brooklyn College (now Brooklyn College of the City University of New York), M.A., 1952; Columbia University, graduate student, 1953-55.

ADDRESSES: Home—180 Riverside Dr., New York, N.Y. 10024. *Office*—New York University, 19 University Place, New York, N.Y. 10003. *Agent*—Watkins, Loomis Agency, 150 East 35th St., Suite 530, New York, N.Y. 10016.

CAREER: Syracuse University, Syracuse, N.Y., instructor in Spanish, 1949-50; Long Island University, Brooklyn, N.Y., instructor in Spanish, 1950-53; Columbia University, Columbia College, New York City, lecturer in Spanish, 1958-65; Long Island University, lecturer in Spanish, 1967-68; John Jay College of Criminal Justice of the City University of New York, New York City, assistant professor of Spanish, 1974-79; New York University, New York City, adjunct professor of Spanish, 1980—. Lecturer in Latin American film and film documentary, New School for Social Research, New York City, 1974-75.

WRITINGS:

JUVENILE

I Am Maria, Cowles, 1969.
My House Is Your House, Cowles, 1970.
Count Lucanor's Tales, Dial, 1970.
Once Upon a Truffle, Cowles, 1971.
Coplas: Spanish Folk Poems (bilingual), Four Winds, 1972.
The Night of the Radishes, Putnam, 1972.
The Rescue, Putnam, 1973.
Away Is So Far, Four Winds, 1974.
Two by Two, Follett, 1974.
A Bucketful of Moon, Lothrop, 1975.
Dear Greta Garbo, Putnam, 1977.

TRANSLATOR

Benito Perez Galdos, *Compassion,* Ungar, 1962.
Jose Ortega y Gasset, *On Love: Aspects of a Single Theme,* Meridian Books, 1966.
Ortega y Gasset, *The Origin of Philosophy,* Norton, 1968.
Felix Marti Ibanez, *Ariel,* MD Publications, 1969.
Roberto Conde, *The First Stages of Modernization in Latin America,* Harper, 1973.
Jacobo Timerman, *Prisoner without a Name, Cell without a Number,* Random House, 1982.
Humberto Constantini, *The Gods, the Little Guys and the Police,* Harper, 1984.

OTHER

(Editor) *The World of the Child: Clinical and Cultural Studies from Birth to Adolescence,* Doubleday, 1962.
A Book about My Mother, Farrar, Straus, 1980.
(Under pseudonym Rebecca Josephs) *Early Disorder,* Farrar, Straus, 1980.

Also author of a documentary film, "Berimbau," 1972. Education editor, *El Diario de Nueva York,* 1951-53.

BIOGRAPHICAL/CRITICAL SOURCES:

PERIODICALS

Washington Post Book World, May 25, 1980.

*   *   *

TATE, James (Vincent) 1943-

PERSONAL: Born December 8, 1943, in Kansas City, Mo.; son of Samuel Vincent Appleby (a pilot) and Betty Jean Whitsitt. *Education:* Attended University of Missouri, 1963-64; Kansas State College, B.A., 1965; University of Iowa, M.F.A., 1967.

ADDRESSES: Home—16 Jones Rd., Pelham, Mass. 01002. *Office*—Department of English, University of Massachusetts, Amherst, Mass. 01003.

CAREER: University of Iowa, Iowa City, instructor in creative writing, 1966-67; University of California, Berkeley, visiting lecturer, 1967-68; Columbia University, New York, N. Y., assistant professor of English, 1969-71; University of Massachusetts at Amherst, beginning 1971, began as associate professor, currently professor of English. Poet in residence, Emerson College, 1970-71. Consultant to the Coordinating Council of Literary Magazines, 1971-74, and to the Kentucky Arts Commission,

1979. Member of Bollingen Prize Committee, 1974-75; judge for several poetry contests, including the Lucille Medwick Prize, 1978, the Elliston Book Award, 1978, and the Charles and Cecilia Wagner Award, 1980.

MEMBER: PEN.

AWARDS, HONORS: Yale Younger Poets Award, 1966, for *The Lost Pilot;* named Poet of the Year, Phi Beta Kappa, 1972; National Institute of Arts and Letters award for poetry, 1974; Massachusetts Arts and Humanities fellow, 1975; Guggenheim fellow, 1976; National Endowment for the Arts fellow, 1980.

WRITINGS:

POETRY

Cages, Shepherd's Press, 1966.
The Destination, Pym-Randall Press, 1967.
The Lost Pilot, Yale University Press, 1967, reprinted, Ecco Press, 1982.
Notes of Woe: Poems, Stone Wall Press, 1968.
Camping in the Valley, Madison Park Press, 1968.
The Torches, Unicorn Press, 1968, revised edition, 1971.
Row with Your Hair, Kayak, 1969.
Is There Anything?, Sumac Press, 1969.
Shepherds of the Mist, Black Sparrow Press, 1969.
Amnesia People, Little Balkans Press, 1970.
(With Bill Knott) *Are You Ready Mary Baker Eddy,* Cloud Marauder Press, 1970.
Deaf Girl Playing, Pym-Randall Press, 1970.
The Oblivion Ha-Ha, Little, Brown, 1970.
Wrong Songs, Halty Ferguson Press, 1970.
Hints to Pilgrims, Halty Ferguson Press, 1971, 2nd edition, University of Massachusetts Press, 1982.
Absences, Little, Brown, 1972.
Apology for Eating Geoffrey Movius' Hyacinth, Unicorn Press, 1972.
Hottentot Ossuary, Temple Bar Bookshop, 1974.
Viper Jazz, Wesleyan University Press, 1976.
Riven Doggeries, Ecco Press, 1979.
Land of Little Sticks, Metacom Press, 1981.
Constant Defender, Ecco Press, 1983.
Reckoner, Wesleyan University Press, 1986.

BROADSIDES

Mystics in Chicago, Unicorn Press, 1968.
Nobody Goes to Visit the Insane Anymore, Unicorn Press, 1971.
A Dime Found in the Snow, Little Balkans Press, 1973.
Marfa, University of Connecticut Library, 1974.
Suffering Bastards, Hearsay Broadsheets, 1975.
Who Gets the Bitterroot?, Rook Press, 1976.
The Rustling of Foliage, the Memory of Caresses, Massachusetts Review, 1979.
If It Would All Please Hurry, Shanachie Press, 1980.

OTHER

(With Knott) *Lucky Darryl: A Novel,* Release Press, 1977.

Contributor to *Paris Review, Transatlantic Review, New Yorker, Nation, Atlantic, Poetry, Quarterly Review of Literature, Shenandoah,* and other publications. Poetry editor, *Dickinson Review,* 1967-76; trustee and associate editor, Pym-Randall Press, 1968-80; associate editor, Barn Dream Press.

CONTRIBUTOR

Lucien Stryk, editor, *Heartland: Poets of the Midwest,* Northern Illinois University Press, 1967.
Hazard Adams, editor, *Poetry: An Introductory Anthology,* Little, Brown, 1968.
Paul Carroll, editor, *The Young American Poets,* Follett, 1968.
Nancy Larrick, editor, *On City Streets: An Anthology of Poetry,* M. Evans, 1968.
George Plimpton and Peter Ardery, editors, *The American Literary Anthology/2: The Second Annual Collection of the Best from the Literary Magazines,* Random House, 1969.
The New Yorker Book of Poems, Viking, 1969.
Charles Newman and William A. Henkin, Jr., editors, *Under 30: Poetry, Fiction and Criticism of the New American Writers,* Indiana University Press, 1969.
Mark Strand, editor, *The Contemporary American Poets: American Poetry since 1940,* World Publishing, 1969.
Louis Untermeyer, compiler, *Modern American Poetry,* Harcourt, 1969.
Plimpton and Ardery, editors, *The American Literary Anthology/3: The Third Annual Collection of the Best from the Literary Magazines,* Viking, 1970.
Voices, Rand McNally, 1970.
John Malcolm Brinnin and Bill Reed, editors, *The Modern Poets: An American-British Anthology,* 2nd edition, McGraw, 1970.
X. J. Kennedy, editor, *An Introduction to Poetry,* 2nd edition, Little, Brown, 1971.
George Hitchcock, editor, *Losers, Weepers,* Kayak, 1971.
Dennis Saleh and James McMichael, editors, *Just What the Country Needs, Another Poetry Anthology,* Wadsworth Publishing, 1971.
Al Lee, editor, *The Major Younger Poets,* World Publishing, 1971.
Robert Killoren and Joseph Clark, editors, *The Missouri Poets: Sesquicentennial Edition,* Eads Bridge Press, 1971.
Wang Hui-Ming, editor, *The Land on the Tip of a Hair,* Barre Publishers, 1972.
Robert Baylor and Brenda Stokes, editors, *Fine Frenzy: Enduring Themes in Poetry,* McGraw, 1972.
Richard Kostelanetz, editor, *In Youth,* Ballantine, 1972.
Milton Klonsky, editor, *Shake the Kaleidoscope: A New Anthology of Modern Poetry,* Pocket Books, 1973.
Kennedy, editor, *Messages: A Thematic Anthology of Poetry,* Little, Brown, 1973.
Richard Ellman and Robert O'Clair, editors, *The Norton Anthology of Modern Poetry,* W. W. Norton, 1973.
Oscar Williams and Hyman J. Sobiloff, editors, *The Pocket Book of Modern Verse,* Pocket Books, 1973.
John Frederick Nims, editor, *Western Wind: An Introduction to Poetry,* Random House, 1974.
Klonsky, editor, *The Best of Modern Poetry,* Pocket Books, 1975.
Robin Skelton, editor, *The Poet's Calling,* Heinemann, 1975.
Daniel Halpern, editor, *The American Poetry Anthology,* Avon, 1975.
Michael Benedikt, editor, *The Prose Poem: An International Anthology,* Dell, 1976.
Alberta T. Turner, editor, *50 Contemporary Poets: The Creative Process,* David McKay, 1977.
Edward B. Germain, editor, *English and American Surrealist Poetry,* Penguin, 1978.
Edward Field, editor, *A Geography of Poets: An Anthology of the New Poetry,* Bantam, 1979.
George E. Murphy, Jr., editor, *The Poet's Choice,* Tendril, 1980.

SIDELIGHTS: Described by John Ash in the *New York Times Book Review* as "an elegant and anarchic clown, a lord of poetic misrule with a serious, subversive purpose," James Tate writes poetry concerned with the playful and creative aspects of language, as well as the limits of what language can express. Some critics fault him for slighting his poetic subjects in favor of the language in which the poems are written, but for Tate, the language of the poem is the poem's ultimate subject. As Philip Dacey remarks in the *American Book Review,* Tate's "subject matter is the folly of subject matter."

A typical Tate poem begins with an unlikely or whimsical situation. Writing in the *Dictionary of Literary Biography,* Stephen Gardner maintains that Tate's poems "are rooted in landscapes that are often—if not generally—bizarre and surreal." His language is charged with metaphor and linguistic inventiveness, similar to that of the surrealist or absurdist writers, and is meant to illustrate the inability of language to express human emotion. Because of his willingness to take extreme chances, Tate tends to "err on the side of adventure rather than caution," according to Harold Jaffe in the *Christian Science Monitor.* "Tate," Dacey comments, "writes as if he were translating from a foreign language he did not understand, relying solely on word-association for method. . . . He has his fun at the expense of language rather than vice versa, acting less to employ it than to expose it."

According to a critic for the *Virginia Quarterly Review,* the strengths and weaknesses of Tate's work "are characteristic of the poet's generation. Freshness, attractive eccentricity, winning irreverence, and a laudable independence give these poems a flavor quite their own; but most of them lack something vital: a purpose, a sense of direction, a goal." Pointlessness is a charge raised by some other critics as well. William Logan of *Poetry* characterizes Tate's poems as "invention without control, ingenuity without purpose, they careen like driverless automobiles, ending at times in a crash of irrelevant simile." In like terms, Dick Allen of the *Hudson Review* has "the feeling that these are mainly smarty-pants nonsense poems, going for the easy chuckle and the virtuoso dance of language."

But many commentators value Tate's work for its ingenuity, exhilarating language, and sheer energy. Norman Rosten in *Saturday Review,* for example, calls Tate "a poet of verbal excitement, sometimes opaque, sometimes of dazzling clarity. His is a unique vision of a man tuned in to a private cosmos with its little mysteries." "Tate's power," claims Marianne Boruch in the *American Poetry Review,* "has always been his verbal energy, his expert and dead serious play which resists conventional design and the sentimental reduction it risks." Though Ash admits that sometimes "Tate's jazzy, oddball version of Surrealism threatens to become automatic," he argues that "these reservations are insignificant when set against the poet's consistent originality and inventiveness." Harper Barnes, writing in the *Washington Post Book World,* believes that Tate "must be included in any discussion of major American poets."

In 1966 Tate won the prestigious Yale Younger Poets Award, the youngest poet, at the age of 23, to ever do so in the award's seventy-three year history. The manuscript that earned him the prize was *The Lost Pilot,* which was published by Yale University Press in 1967. The book's title refers to Tate's father, a pilot who was reported missing over Germany during the Second World War. Critical response to the collection was enthusiastic. Gardner notes that "most reviewers" reacted with "simultaneous praise and amazement—praise for the accomplishment and amazement that one so young had done so much so well." Several reviewers believed that Tate had already developed his own poetic voice: Tate's "low-keyed, off-hand style is his own," as Jaffe remarks. Julian Symons, writing in *New Statesman,* found Tate to be "an ironical, original, self-absorbed poet who glances with amusement at love, humanity, himself."

In subsequent collections Tate has established himself as one of the leading poets of his generation. According to Barnes, "Tate is that rare American phenomenon, the prodigy fulfilled." Among his most critically praised books is *Absences,* a collection that Julian Moynahan in the *New York Times Book Review* describes as "meditative, introverted, self-reliant, funny, alarming, strange, difficult, intelligent and beautifully crafted." Brian Swann, in his review of the book for *Library Journal,* calls Tate "a real poet: vigorous, effervescent, adventurous." Speaking of the collection in the *American Poetry Review,* Mark Rudman claims that "*Absences* still moves me more than anything else [Tate has] written. In it he retains elements of despair, anger, rage; it is surrealism with a razor-edge and transcends the boundaries of any *ism.*"

Constant Defender has also been praised by many reviewers. In his analysis of the book, Logan believes that Tate "tests himself too little and congratulates himself too much." Yet he describes Tate as "a clever and resourceful poet. He can take a bizarre premise and with it mock the grave anthropologists. . . . He can turn a meditation on an old photograph of himself into an Icelandic saga." Mark Irwin, writing in *World Literature Today,* explains that "Tate has succeeded perhaps more than anyone else in defining 'the disinheritedness' of American culture. His new volume confirms in a wry yet terrifying manner the shallow and confusing nature of our orphaned past."

In an article for the *American Poetry Review,* Donald Revell sees *Constant Defender* as a long meditation on the relationship between our treatment of death and our use of language to describe and deal with death. He explains that the poem "If It Would All Please Hurry," included in the collection and also published separately as a broadside, "engages every one of Tate's major themes—love, death, and the career of words among the loving and the dying—in a single, urgent occasion." In this poem, according to Revell, Tate attacks the language typically found in eulogies. "He reserves his most forceful, moving language for the assault on those rituals surrounding death," Revell writes. "Tate distills that language to an awful clarity. . . . The prescribed ritual speech of the man presiding over the funeral is dead because it is irrelevant. It cannot comfort; it cannot speak to the situation of grief at all."

Rudman's overview of Tate's work supports Revell's argument concerning the poems found in *Constant Defender.* Rudman sees Tate as struggling "to make language counteract the banality of everyday life and the threat of 'oblivion.' Tate's aesthetic position is such that even if we could make sense out of our experience we couldn't express it in words since expressive language and poetic diction consist of two components, both negative—cliches and hyperboles—and he uses them so unusually that he highlights their absurdity."

According to Gardner, "Tate's importance in contemporary poetry needs no defense. . . . [His] poetry provides a lively and jolting characterization of the universe. His language is fresh and highly suggestive. And unlike many surrealists—including those who are his followers—he is clearly able to control the situations he creates." Rosten calls Tate "a risk-taker, likely to get out on that real or metaphysical limb and keep cutting, not caring much whether the saw is between him and the tree or not. This is the heady spirit that encourages the adventure of poetry."

BIOGRAPHICAL/CRITICAL SOURCES:

BOOKS

Contemporary Literary Criticism, Gale, Volume 2, 1974, Volume 6, 1976, Volume 25, 1983.

Dictionary of Literary Biography, Volume 5: *American Poets since World War II,* Gale, 1980.
The Making of Poetry, Yale University Press, 1967.
Shaw, Robert B., editor, *American Poetry since 1960: Some Critical Perspectives,* Dufour Editions, 1974.

PERIODICALS

AB Bookman's Weekly, July 11-18, 1977.
American Book Review, November-December, 1987.
American Poetry Review, November-December, 1976, July-August, 1981, January-February, 1987, January-February, 1988.
Carleton Miscellany, fall, 1967.
Christian Science Monitor, July 11, 1967, October 28, 1976.
Commonweal, September 11, 1987.
Encounter, December, 1967.
Hudson Review, summer, 1967, winter, 1972-73, spring, 1980, autumn, 1987.
Library Journal, June 15, 1972, January, 1987.
Nation, April 24, 1967.
New Statesman, June 16, 1967.
New York Times Book Review, November 12, 1972, March 1, 1987.
Poetry, February, 1968, March, 1971, October, 1971, July, 1977, August, 1980, November, 1984.
Saturday Review, June 3, 1967, August 12, 1972.
Sewanee Review, summer, 1980.
Southern Review, winter, 1972.
Times Literary Supplement, May 18, 1967.
Virginia Quarterly Review, summer, 1967, spring, 1969, autumn, 1970, winter, 1980.
Washington Post Book World, December 31, 1972.
World Literature Today, spring, 1984.
Yale Review, summer, 1967.

—*Sketch by Thomas Wiloch*

* * *

TATUM, Charles M(ichael) 1943-

PERSONAL: Born August 10, 1943, in El Paso, Tex.; son of Robert E. (an accountant) and Eloisa (a teacher; maiden name, Pomeroy-Ainsa) Tatum; married Sandra L. Stephens, June 17, 1963 (divorced December 31, 1981); married Anne Hutchins (a journalist), May 22, 1982; children: Regina Gabriela, Maura Raquel, Michael Christopher. *Education:* University of Notre Dame, B.A., 1965; Stanford University, M.A., 1968; University of New Mexico, Ph.D., 1971.

ADDRESSES: Office—Department of Spanish and Portuguese, University of Arizona, Tucson, Ariz. 85721.

CAREER: University of Minnesota at Minneapolis, St. Paul, assistant professor of Spanish, 1971-74; College of the Holy Cross, Worcester, Mass., assistant professor of Spanish, 1974-76; New Mexico State University, Las Cruces, associate professor, 1976-83, professor of Latin American literature and department head, 1983-87; University of Arizona, Tucson, professor of Latin American literature and head of department of Spanish and Portuguese, 1987—.

MEMBER: Modern Language Association of America, American Association of Teachers of Spanish and Portuguese, Popular Culture Association, Latin American Studies Association.

AWARDS, HONORS: Fulbright fellow at University of Madrid, 1965-66; fellow of National Endowment for the Humanities, 1980-81.

WRITINGS:

(Compiler) *A Selected and Annotated Bibliography of Chicano Studies,* Society of Spanish and Spanish American Studies, 1976.
Chicano Literature: A Critical History, Twayne, 1982.
(Editor with Harold E. Hinds, Jr.) *Handbook of Latin American Culture,* Greenwood Press, 1985.
Literatura Chicana, Secretaria de Educacion Publica, 1985.

Contributor of articles and reviews to literature and Latin American studies journals. Co-editor of *Studies in Latin American Popular Culture.*

WORK IN PROGRESS: The Mexican Comic Book, with Hinds.

SIDELIGHTS: Charles M. Tatum commented to *CA:* "I believe that a mark of the vital professional in any field is to remain open to new interests and fields of research. In this light, my training in Latin American literature has served as a springboard for my current research on Chicano literature and popular culture. While all three are not always directly related, they have served to keep me fresh and stimulated over the years."

* * *

TAYLOR, Paul S(chuster) 1895-1984

PERSONAL: Born June 9, 1895, in Sioux City, Iowa; died March 13, 1984; son of Henry James (an attorney) and Rose Eugenia (Schuster) Taylor; married Katharine Page Whiteside, May 15, 1920 (divorced, 1935); married Dorothea Lange, December 6, 1935 (died, 1965); children: (first marriage) Ross Whiteside (deceased), Katharine Page Taylor Loesch, Margot Agnes Taylor Fanger. *Education:* University of Wisconsin, Madison, A.B., 1917; University of California, Berkeley, M.A., 1920, Ph.D., 1922. *Politics:* Democrat.

ADDRESSES: Home—1163 Euclid Ave., Berkeley, Calif. 94708. *Office*—Department of Economics, University of California, 275 Barrows Hall, Berkeley, Calif. 94720.

CAREER: University of California, Berkeley, instructor, 1922-24, assistant professor, 1924-29, associate professor, 1929-39, professor of economics, 1939-62, professor emeritus, beginning 1962, head of department, 1952-56, chairman, Institute of International Studies, 1956-62. Visiting professor at University of Alexandria, 1962-63. Chief Investigator of Mexican Labor in U.S., Social Science Research Council, 1927-29; regional labor adviser, Resettlement Administration, 1935-36; field director, Rural Rehabilitation Division of California Emergency Relief Administration, 1935-36; president, California Rural Rehabilitation Corp., 1936-43; research director, California Labor Federation, 1970. Member of advisory council of California Department of Employment, 1935-42; member, Governor's Commission on Reemployment, 1939, California Board of Agriculture, 1940-44. Consultant to U.S. Department of the Interior, United Nations, Ford Foundation, and other governmental and private organizations. *Military service:* U.S. Marine Corps, American Expeditionary Forces, 1917-19; served in France; became captain; received Purple Heart.

MEMBER: American Economic Association, Academia Nacional de Ciencias (Mexico; honorary corresponding member), Phi Beta Kappa, Chi Phi, Phi Alpha Delta, Delta Sigma Pi, Delta Sigma Rho, Cosmos Club, Faculty Club (University of California, Berkeley).

AWARDS, HONORS: Guggenheim Latin-American Fellow, 1931; LL.D., University of California, Berkeley, 1965; Henry

Wagner Award, California Historical Society, 1977, for work in California history; Conservation Service Award, U.S. Department of the Interior, 1980.

WRITINGS:

The Sailors' Union of the Pacific, Ronald, 1923, reprinted, Ayer Co., 1971.

Mexican Labor in the United States, three volumes, University of California Press, 1928-34, reprinted in two volumes, Johnson Reprint, 1966.

A Spanish-Mexican Peasant Community: Arandas in Jalisco, Mexico, University of California Press, 1933.

An American-Mexican Frontier: Nueces County, Texas, University of North Carolina Press, 1934, reprinted, Russell & Russell, 1971.

(With wife, Dorothy Lange) *An American Exodus: A Record of Human Erosion,* Reynal, 1939, revised edition, Yale University Press, 1969.

Adrift on the Land, Public Affairs Committee, 1940.

Principles and Practices of Community Development, Institute of International Studies, University of California, Berkeley, 1960.

Georgia Plan, 1732-1752, Institute of Business and Economic Research, University of California, Berkeley, 1971.

(Contributor) Arthur F. Corwin, editor, *Immigrants—and Immigrants: Perspectives on Mexican Migration to the United States,* Greenwood Press, 1978.

Stuart Bruchey, editor, *Essays on Land, Water, and the Law in California: An Original Anthology,* introduction by Taylor, foreword by Paul W. Gates, Ayer Co., 1979.

(With Lange) *Dorothea Lange: Farm Security Administration Photographs, 1935-1939: From the Library of Congress,* Text-Fiche, 1980.

Labor on the Land: Collected Writings, 1936-70, Ayer Co., 1981.

On the Ground in the Thirties, G. M. Smith, 1983.

Also author of *Slave to Freedman,* 1970, and *Communist Strategy and Tactics of Employing Peasant Dissatisfaction over Conditions of Land Tenure for Revolutionary Ends in Vietnam,* 1970.

WORK IN PROGRESS: Research on excess land and residency requirements of U.S. reclamation law.

SIDELIGHTS: Paul S. Taylor once told *CA:* "My interest in land tenure was stimulated by fifteen months service with the American Expeditionary Forces. The Bolshevik revolution of 1917 released German troops on the Eastern Front to attack the Allies on the Western Front. We stopped them at Chateau-Thierry-Bouresches-Belleau Wood, where I was gassed. When I researched the Mexican migration of 1927-32, I saw the effects of the Mexican revolution in both the United States and Mexico. The Russian slogan was 'Peace, Bread, and the Land'; the Mexican slogan was 'Land and Liberty.' In 1958 I spent two weeks evaluating General Douglas MacArthur's land reform in Japan. I researched the land reform program in Vietnam in 1958 and 1967. Incidentally, one of the important reasons for our failure in Vietnam was our failure to press for land reform in that country. The Viet Cong thus had two main charges against us: we were foreigners splitting their country, and we were backing a landlord-based government."

Taylor also commented about his research methods: "I have always sought to do my research at ground level, whether literally in the fields for contemporary research in the United States, Asia, Latin America, or elsewhere. In historical research I sought ground level sources in the sense of original documents of the time and subject. In other words, I wanted primary rather than secondary sources."

BIOGRAPHICAL/CRITICAL SOURCES:

BOOKS

Riess, Suzanne B., *Paul Schuster Taylor, California Social Scientist: An Interview,* three volumes, Bancroft Library, University of California, Berkeley, 1973.

OBITUARIES:

PERIODICALS

Los Angeles Times, March 17, 1984.*

* * *

TEBBEL, John (William) 1912-

PERSONAL: Born November 16, 1912, in Boyne City, Mich.; son of William Farr and Edna Mae Tebbel; married Kathryn Carl (a copy editor), April 29, 1939; children: Judith Elaine Tebbel Smith. *Education:* Central Michigan University, A.B., 1935; Columbia University, M.S., 1937. *Politics:* Independent.

ADDRESSES: *Home*—876-A Heritage Village, Southbury, Conn. 06488.

CAREER: *Times-News,* Mt. Pleasant, Mich., city editor, 1935-36; affiliated with *Newsweek,* 1937; *Detroit Free Press,* Detroit, Mich., reporter, 1937-39; *Providence Journal,* Providence, R.I., feature writer and Sunday music editor, 1939-41; *American Mercury,* New York City, managing editor, 1941-43; *New York Times,* New York City, Sunday staff writer, 1943; E. P. Dutton & Co., Inc., New York City, associate editor, 1943-46; New York University, New York City, assistant professor, 1949-52, associate professor, 1952-54, professor of journalism, 1954-76, head of department, 1954-65, director of Graduate Institute of Book Publishing, 1958-62. Part-time instructor at Columbia University, 1941-46. Free-lance writer, 1943—. Member of board of directors of Public Interest Public Relations, 1975-78; consultant to Ford Foundation.

MEMBER: Society of Professional Journalists, Authors Guild, Authors League of America, Players Club, New York University Club.

AWARDS, HONORS: Litt.D., Central Michigan University, 1948; alumni award, Journalism Alumni Association of Columbia Univeristy, 1975; Annual Printing History Award, 1981; member of Publishing Hall of Fame.

WRITINGS:

An American Dynasty: The Story of the McCormicks, Medills, and Pattersons, Doubleday, 1947, reprinted, Greenwood Press, 1968.

The Marshall Fields, Dutton, 1947.

George Horace Lorimer and the Saturday Evening Post, Doubleday, 1948, reprinted, Easton Press, 1988.

(Editor) Francis Parkman, *The Battle for North America,* Doubleday, 1948.

(With Kenneth N. Stewart) *Makers of Modern Journalism,* Prentice-Hall, 1950.

Your Body: How to Keep It Healthy, Harper, 1951.

The Conqueror (novel), Dutton, 1951.

Touched with Fire (historical novel), Dutton, 1952.

The Life and Good Times of William Randolph Hearst, Dutton, 1952.

George Washington's America, Dutton, 1954.

A Voice in the Streets (novel), Dutton, 1954.

The Magic of Balanced Living: A Man's Key to Health, Well-Being, and Peace of Mind, Harper, 1956.
(With Keith Jennison) *The American Indian Wars,* Harper, 1960.
The Inheritors: A Study of America's Great Fortunes and What Happened to Them, Putnam, 1962.
(Editor with Anne Seranne) *The Epicure's Companion,* McKay, 1962.
The Human Touch in Business: The Story of Charles R. Hook, Who Rose from Office Boy to Internationally-Known Business Leader, Otterbein Press, 1963.
David Sarnoff: Putting Electrons to Work (juvenile), Encyclopaedia Britannica, 1963.
Paperback Books: A Pocket History, Pocket Books, 1963.
The Compact History of the American Newspaper, Hawthorn, 1963, revised edition, 1969.
From Rags to Riches: Horatio Alger, Jr. and the American Dream, Macmillan, 1964.
Red Runs the River: The Rebellion of Chief Pontiac (juvenile), Hawthorn, 1966.
The Compact History of the Indian Wars, Hawthorn, 1966.
Open Letter to Newspaper Readers, James Heineman, 1968.
The Compact History of American Magazines, Hawthorn, 1969.
(With Ramon Eduardo Ruiz) *South by Southwest: The Mexican-American and His Heritage* (juvenile), Doubleday, 1969.
The Battle of Fallen Timbers, August 20, 1974: President Washington Secures the Ohio Valley (juvenile), F. Watts, 1972.
A History of Book Publishing in the United States, Bowker, Volume 1: *The Creation of an Industry, 1630-1865,* 1972, Volume 2: *The Expansion of an Industry, 1865-1919,* 1975, Volume 3: *The Golden Age: Between Two Wars, 1920-1940,* 1978, Volume 4: *The Great Change: 1940-1980,* 1980.
The Media in America: A Social and Political History, Crowell, 1974.
Opportunities in Publishing Careers, National Textbook Company, 1975.
Opportunities in Journalism, National Textbook Company, 1977.
Opportunities in Magazine Publishing, National Textbook Company, 1980.
(With Sarah Miles Watts) *The Press and the Presidency: Washington to Reagan,* Oxford University Press, 1985.
Opportunities in Book Publishing, National Textbook Company, 1986.
Bewteen Covers: The Rise and Transformation of American Book Publishing, Oxford University Press, 1987.
A Certain Club: 100 Years of The Players, Weiser, 1989.
The Magazine in America, 1741-1991, Oxford University Press, 1990.

Also author of about forty ghost-written books. Contributor of more than five hundred articles to popular magazines, including *Saturday Review.*

SIDELIGHTS: John Tebbel told *CA:* "I agree with Samuel Johnson that no man but a blockhead ever wrote for anything but money. Yet Johnson knew, as every writer knows, that he also writes because there is no alternative. At ten, living on a farm in the middle of Michigan, with Manhattan as remote from me as the moon, I told inquiring relatives that when I grew up I intended to go to New York and be a writer. A dozen or so years later, I was doing just that. I could not then, nor could I now, conceive of any other kind of life—except for music, a life I sampled briefly with my violin, but fortunately had sense enough to realize was not my real talent. The experience, however, gave me a lifetime of listening enjoyment, as well as an opportunity to write about music on occasion.

"Newspapers were the springboard I used to attain the literary life, as so many others have done, from Dickens onward, and I still regard it as an ideal preparation. The news is life itself, the same materials the writer uses for nonfiction or, enhanced, as fiction. Reporting as I did, from the small town to the big city, gives a writer basic perspectives and perceptions about life that stay with him always.

"A year spent at the Graduate School of Journalism, Columbia University, was the turning point in my life. It translated me from a Michigan small town life to metropolitan dailies, besides subjecting my writing for the first time to the critical eye of top-flight professionals, and demonstrating to me that although I had been writing for money since I was fourteen, I had a great deal to learn about the craft. I am still learning.

"Another turning point came in 1949. I had topped off a career on newspapers and magazines with four years as a publisher's editor, a job I had enjoyed more than anything I'd ever done. After ghostwriting a few books for the publisher, E. P. Dutton, I had quit with a two-book contract from Doubleday and freelanced for three years—enough time to convince me I could never cope with the constant anxiety of the freelancer's life. Then my Columbia classmate, Vance Packard, who has been my good friend for more than fifty years, helped me get a job in the journalism department of New York University. As so many other writers have discovered, I found that teaching and writing made an ideal combination as a way of life, particularly since teaching gave me nearly as much satisfaction.

"My books have had reasonably good sales, for the most part, and one (*The Inheritors*) was on the *New York Times* best-seller list for a week. Some have been translated and distributed in the U.K., Spain, West Germany, Sweden, Italy, Brazil, and Australia. Of them all, the greatest satisfaction has come from the four-volume *A History of Book Publishing in the United States.* For me, it was not only a rewarding absorption for the past twenty years, but extremely satisfying in the sense that I created something unique that will outlast me and be useful to future generations. No writer could ask for more.

"As for advice to aspiring writers, Epictetus said it all in his *Discourses,* and I repeated it for twenty years in my fiction workshop at N.Y.U.: 'If you would be a writer, write.' "

* * *

TENNYSON, Charles (Bruce Locker) 1879-1977

PERSONAL: Born November 8, 1879, in London, England; died June 22, 1977, in England; son of Lionel and Eleanor Bertha Mary (Locker) Tennyson; married Ivy Gladys Pretious, 1909 (died, 1958); children: Hallam, two other sons (killed in action, 1941 and 1945). *Education:* King's College, Cambridge, M.A.

CAREER: Called to the Bar of Gray's Inn, 1906; British Office of Works, junior equity counsel, 1909-11; British Colonial Office, assistant legal adviser, 1911-19; Federation of British Industries, deputy director, beginning 1919; Dunlop Rubber Co., secretary, 1928-48. British delegate at New Hebrides Conference, 1914. Chairman, Board of Trade Utility Furniture Committee, 1943, Furniture Production Committee, 1944. President, Union of Educational Institutions, 1948; chairman of council, Bedford College, London, 1946-53.

MEMBER: Royal College of Art (honorary fellow), Royal Society of Literature (fellow).

AWARDS, HONORS: Honorary fellow, King's College, Cambridge; Companion of the Order of St. Michael and St. George, 1915; LL.D., Cambridge University, D.Litt., University of Leicester; Order of the British Empire, 1945.

WRITINGS:

Cambridge from Within, illustrations by Harry Morley, G. W. Jacobs, 1913.

Concordance to the Devil and the Lady, [England], 1931, Macmillan, 1949.

(Editor) Alfred Tennyson, *Unpublished Early Poems* (also see below), Macmillan, 1932, reprinted, Folcroft Library Editions, 1974.

Alfred Tennyson (biography), Macmillan, 1949, amended edition published as *Alfred Tennyson, by His Grandson,* 1968, Archon Books, 1969.

Life's All a Fragment (memoirs of Charles D. Fisher, John C. Snaith, Roy F. Truscott, Penrose Tennyson, and Julian Tennyson), Cassell, 1953, reprinted, Century Bookbindery, 1983.

Six Tennyson Essays, Cassell, 1954, reprinted, S. R. Publishers, 1972.

(Editor and author of introductions) Alfred Tennyson, *The Idylls of the King* [and] *The Princess,* Collins, 1956.

Stars and Markets (autobiography), Chatto & Windus, 1957.

The Somersby Tennysons, Victorian Studies (Bloomington, Ind.), 1963.

(Editor) Alfred Tennyson, *The Devil and the Lady* [and] *Unpublished Early Poems,* Indiana University Press, 1964.

(Editor with F. T. Baker) Arthur Henry Hallam, *Some Unpublished Poems,* West Virginia University Library, 1965.

(With Christine Fall) *Alfred Tennyson: An Annotated Bibliography,* University of Georgia Press, 1967.

(Editor with Hope Dyson) *Dear and Honored Lady: The Correspondence between Queen Victoria and Alfred Tennyson,* Macmillan (London), 1969, Farleigh Dickinson University Press, 1971.

(Compiler and editor, with son, Hallam Tennyson) *Victorian Poetry, 1830-1890,* Ginn, 1971.

(With Dyson) *The Tennysons: Background to Genius,* Macmillan, 1974.

Studies in Tennyson, edited by H. Tennyson, Macmillan (London), 1981.

OTHER

(Editor and author of foreword and annotations) Usher Gallery, *Tennyson Collection,* Lincoln Libraries, Museum and Art Gallery Committee, 1963.

Reminiscences of the Poet by His Grandson (sound recording), Tennyson Society (London), 1973.

Also author of many papers for Tennyson Society, and contributor to periodicals.

SIDELIGHTS: "Sir Charles Tennyson, a grandson of the poet, has rendered good service to literature in this new biography of the English Virgil," wrote Alfred Noyes in the *Saturday Review of Literature* about Tennyson's best known work, *Alfred Tennyson.* "Moreover," declared a *Christian Century* contributor, "his own qualifications—cultural, literary and professional—fit him for the task of interpreting sensitively and presenting effectively the life and character of the poet against the background of English literary society through the greater part of the Victorian era." And although Ernest Jones maintained in a *Nation* review that "for all the unostentatious dusting off of family skeletons, the prevailing tone is one of scissors and paste and filial piety," most critics shared Naomi Lewis's *New Statesman and Nation* assessment of the biography as "an excellent book." Some critics, however, faulted it for a lack of critical commentary, and believed as W. C. DeVane did in the *Yale Review,* "For the biography we must be grateful; for a definitive study of the poetry we shall have to wait for a different writer and a longer time."

In editing *Dear and Honored Lady: The Correspondence between Queen Victoria and Alfred Tennyson,* Tennyson and Hope Dyson provided an account of the friendship that grew between Queen Victoria and the then poet laureate of England. A *Times Literary Supplement* contributor wrote: "Illuminated by the narrative, the letters and other documents are always interesting and sometimes moving." However, while Keith Cushman found it "charming to observe two fascinating human beings gradually emerging from behind their public facades," he added in *Library Journal* that the correspondence itself yielded "few surprises."

Tennyson and Dyson worked together again on *The Tennysons: Background to Genius,* a study of Alfred Tennyson's family—many of whom also wrote poetry—and especially of the dark influence of the poet's father upon his family. In a *New Statesman,* Alethea Hayter remarked that "this delightful book about them, though it does not gloss over their melancholy and indolence, dwells much more on their extremely amusing oddities and enjoyments, and their remarkable talents." However, Hayter added that "to treat this book simply as a anthology of amusing oddities, though it certainly is that," would be unfair and would "ignore the tragic figure [of] . . . the Reverend George Tennyson, the poet's father. . . . This darker undercurrent flows on beneath the bright bubbles of anecdotes about George Tennyson's children." Hayter concluded that "why this one brother should have had that extra, totally different element which is genius remains, as always, inexplicable."

BIOGRAPHICAL/CRITICAL SOURCES:

BOOKS

Tennyson, Charles, *Stars and Markets,* Chatto & Windus, 1957.

PERIODICALS

Christian Century, September 7, 1949.
Library Journal, December 15, 1971.
Nation, August 27, 1949.
New Statesman, December 6, 1974.
New Statesman and Nation, October 15, 1949.
Observer, February 1, 1970.
Saturday Review of Literature, July 23, 1949.
Times Literary Supplement, January 8, 1970, March 14, 1975.
Yale Review, autumn, 1949.

OBITUARIES:

PERIODICALS

AB Bookman's Weekly, September 12, 1977.*

*   *   *

THOMAS, F(ranklin) Richard 1940-

PERSONAL: Born August 1, 1940, in Evansville, Ind.; son of Franklin Albert (a refrigeration engineer) and Lydia (a nurse; maiden name, Klausmeier) Thomas; married Sharon Kay Myers (a teacher), June 2, 1962; children: Severn Rhyl (son), Caerllion (daughter). *Education:* Purdue University, A.B., 1963, M.A., 1964; further graduate study at University of Minnesota, 1965; Indiana University, Ph.D., 1970.

ADDRESSES: Home—145 Kenberry Dr., East Lansing, Mich. 48823. *Office*—Department of American Thought and Language, Michigan State University, East Lansing, Mich. 48824.

CAREER: Purdue University, Calumet Campus, Calumet, Ind., instructor, 1969-70, assistant professor of English, 1970-71; Michigan State University, East Lansing, assistant professor, 1971-76, associate professor, 1976-81, professor of American thought and language, 1981—. Research associate in American Studies, Indiana University, 1978-79. Has given poetry readings in the United States and Denmark, and on radio and television programs. Member of American-Scandinavian Foundation.

MEMBER: American Studies Association, Poets and Writers, Committee of Small Magazine Editors and Publishers, Coordinating Council of Literary Magazines, Society for the Study of Midwestern Literature, Associated Writing Programs, Fulbright Alumni Association, Michigan Poetry Resource Center, Scandinavian Society of Greater Lansing.

AWARDS, HONORS: Fulbright teaching grant for Copenhagen, Denmark, 1974-75; National Endowment for the Arts grant for *Centering*, 1978; MacDowell Colony fellowship, 1979; Fulbright lecture award for Odense, Denmark, 1985-86.

WRITINGS:

Fat Grass (poetry chapbook), Nosferatu Press, 1970.
(Editor with Charles B. Tinkham, and contributor) *The Day after Yesterday* (anthology of Midwestern poets), Catalyst Press, 1971.
(Editor with Roger Pfingston and Richard Pflum, and contributor) *Stoney Lonesome: Forty Poets*, Nosferatu Press, 1971.
Alive with You This Day (poems), Raintree, 1980.
Frog Praises Night (poems), Southern Illinois University Press, 1980.
The Landlocked Heart (Indiana place-poems), Indiana Writers Press/Indiana University, 1980.
Literary Admirers of Alfred Stieglitz, Southern Illinois University Press, 1983.
Heart Climbing Stairs (poems), Odense University, 1986.
Corolla, Stamen, and Style (poems), Odense University, 1986.
(Editor) *Americans in Denmark* (essays by expatiate artists, writers, and teachers), Southern Illinois University Press, 1988.
The Whole Mystery of the Bregn (poems), Canoe Press, 1988.

Work represented in anthologies, including *A Globe of Fruit*, 1963, *Other Men's Flowers: A Continuing Anthology of the Best Poems from Today's Poetry Magazines and Literary Journals*, *Michigan State Anthology*, edited by David Anderson, 1983, *Writing Poetry*, 1983, and *Light Year*, 1985 and 1988-89. Contributor of more than a hundred poems, articles, and a story to magazines, including *Poet Lore*, *Beloit Poetry Journal*, *Images*, *Sparrow*, and *Midwest*. Editor of *Centering: A Magazine of Poetry*, 1973—; editor/publisher of Years Press (publishes *Centering* and chapbooks of poetry and photography); former assistant editor of *Purdue English Notes*, *Quartet: A Magazine of the Arts*, *Abstracts of Folklore Studies*, and *Trial Flight;* former associate editor of *Bard*.

WORK IN PROGRESS: Poems and Prism, a novel.

SIDELIGHTS: F. Richard Thomas told *CA:* "My writing career began when I met three eye-opening friends and fellow students during my freshman year in college: a musician, a writer, and a painter. Their influence caused me to turn away from my goal to become a chemical engineer. My downfall was complete when I dropped out of school for better than half a year between my sophomore and junior year to travel Europe, live a romantic and semi-bohemian life-style, read provocative (and sometimes banned in the U.S.A.) books, and keep a daily journal. The *romance* of being a writer, a doubter, and a searcher has kept me going. Even when I have questioned the value of my finished written *products*, the *process* of writing has continued to excite me in a way similar to being in Paris and looking for the local bakery with the best *baguette*.

"I have not forgotten my early training to become a scientist. I count popular science books and magazines among my favorite reading, and chemists and physicists among my favorite friends. And my book on Stieglitz deals with the influence of technology on literature.

"I consider my poetry, especially, to be domestic. I generally deal with subjects close to home: family and friends."

AVOCATIONAL INTERESTS: Family, friends, southern Indiana, Scandinavia, travel, soccer.

* * *

THOMPSON, Kenneth W(infred) 1921-

PERSONAL: Born August 29, 1921, in Des Moines, Iowa; son of Thor Carlyle and Agnes (Rorbeck) Thompson; married Lucille Elizabeth Bergquist, February 4, 1948; married Beverly Cornelia Bourret; children: (first marriage) Kenneth Carlyle, Paul Andrew, James David; (second marriage) Carolyn Annette. *Education:* Augustana College, Sioux Falls, S.D., A.B., 1943; University of Chicago, M.A., 1948, Ph.D., 1950.

ADDRESSES: Home—Route 3, Box 369, Charlottesville, Va. 22901. *Office*—Miller Center of Public Affairs, University of Virginia, P.O. Box 5106, Charlottesville, Va. 22905.

CAREER: University of Chicago, Chicago, Ill., lecturer in social sciences, 1948, assistant professor of political science, 1951-53; Northwestern University, Evanston, Ill., assistant professor of political science and chairman of international relations committee, 1951-55; Rockefeller Foundation, New York, N.Y., consultant in international relations, 1953-55, assistant director, 1955-57, associate director, 1957-60, director for social sciences, 1960-61, vice-president, 1961-74; University of Virginia, Charlottesville, Commonwealth Professor of Government and Foreign Affairs, 1975-78, White Burkett Miller Professor of Government and Foreign Affairs, 1979-86, J. Wilson Newman Professor of Government and Foreign Affairs, 1986—, director of Miller Center of Public Affairs, 1978—. Seminar associate, Columbia University, 1957—. Featured lecturer at numerous colleges and universities; trustee, member of board of directors, or director of numerous institutes, educational organizations, and colleges. *Military service:* U.S. Army, Infantry and Intelligence, 1943-45, Counter-Intelligence, 1944-46; became first lieutenant.

MEMBER: International Studies Association, American Political Science Association, Council of Foreign Relations, United Nations Association of the United States of America, American Committee on East West Accord (committee member), American Universities Field Staff (member of governing board), Society for Religion in Higher Education (fellow), American Academy of Arts and Sciences (fellow), Council on Religion and International Affairs (director of ethics and foreign policy project), Phi Beta Kappa, Sigma Nu, Raven Society, Century Club.

AWARDS, HONORS: LL.D., University of Notre Dame, 1964, Bowdoin College, 1972, St. Michael's College, 1973, and St. Olaf College, 1974; L.H.D., West Virginia Wesleyan University, 1970, Nebraska Wesleyan College, 1971, University of Denver,

1984, and Augustana College, 1986; Annual Medal, University of Chicago, 1974.

WRITINGS:

(With Karl de Schweinitz) *Man and Modern Society: Conflict and Choice in the Industrial Era,* Holt, 1953.

Ethics and National Purpose (pamphlet), Church Peace Union, 1957.

Christian Ethics and the Dilemmas of Foreign Policy, Duke University Press, 1959.

Political Realism and the Crisis of World Politics: An American Approach to Foreign Policy, Princeton University Press, 1960, reprinted, University Press of America, 1982.

(With Ivo D. Duchacek) *Conflict and Cooperation among Nations,* Holt, 1960.

American Diplomacy and Emergent Patterns, New York University Press, 1962.

The Moral Issue in Statecraft: Twentieth-Century Approaches and Problems, Louisiana State University Press, 1966.

(With Hans J. Morgenthau and Jerald C. Brauer) *U.S. Policy in the Far East: Ideology, Religion, and Superstition,* Council on Religion and International Affairs, 1968.

Foreign Assistance: A View from the Private Sector, University of Notre Dame Press, 1972.

Higher Education for National Development, Interbook, 1972.

Reconstituting the Human Community, Hazen Foundation, 1972.

Understanding World Politics, University of Notre Dame Press, 1975.

(With James Rosenau and Gavin Boyd) *World Politics,* Free Press, 1976.

Interpreters and Critics of the Cold War, University Press of America, 1978.

Ethics, Functionalism and Power in International Politics: Crisis in Values, Louisiana State University Press, 1979.

Masters of International Thought, Louisiana State University Press, 1980.

The Moral Imperatives of Human Rights: A World Survey, University Press of America, 1980.

Morality and Foreign Policy, Louisiana State University Press, 1980.

Cold War Theories, Volume 1: *World Polarization, 1943-53,* Louisiana State University Press, 1981.

The President and the Public Philosophy, Louisiana State University Press, 1981.

American Diplomacy and Emergent Patterns, University Press of America, 1983.

Winston Churchill's World-View, Louisiana State University Press, 1983.

(With Morgenthau) *Politics among Nations,* 6th revised edition, Knopf, 1984.

Toynbee's Philosophy of History and Politics, Louisiana State University Press, 1985.

Moralism and Morality in Politics and Diplomacy, University Press of America, 1985.

Theory and Practice in International Relations, University Press of America, 1987.

EDITOR

(With Morgenthau) *Principles and Problems of International Politics: Selected Readings,* Knopf, 1950.

(And contributor and author of introduction with Joseph E. Black) *Foreign Policies in a World of Change,* Harper, 1963.

(With Barbara R. Fogel) *Higher Education and Social Change: Promising Experiments in Developing Countries,* Volumes 1-2, Praeger, 1976.

(With Robert J. Myers) *Truth and Tragedy: A Tribute to Hans J. Morgenthau,* New Republic Press, 1977.

(With Louis J. Halle) *Foreign Policy and the Democratic Process: The Geneva Papers,* University Press of America, 1978.

(With Herbert Butterfield) *The Ethics of History and Politics,* University Press of America, 1979.

(With Graeme Salaman) *Control and Ideology in Organizations,* MIT Press, 1980.

(With Morgenthau) *Principles and Problems of International Politics: Selected Reading,* University Press of America, 1982.

Papers on Presidential Disability and the Twenty-Fifth Amendment by Six Medical, Legal and Political Authorities, University Press of America, 1988.

SERIES EDITOR

The Virginia Papers on the Presidency: The White Burkett Miller Center Forums, Volumes 1-25, University Press of America, 1979-86.

American Values Projected Abroad, Volumes 1-20, University Press of America, 1980-83.

The American Presidency: Principles and Problems, Volumes 1-3, University Press of America, 1982-84.

The Credibility of Institutions, Policies and Leadership, Volumes 1-20, University Press of America, 1983-86.

The Presidential Nominating Process, Volumes 1-4, University Press of America, 1983-86.

The Presidency and the Press, Volumes 1-6, University Press of America, 1983-86.

Portraits of American Presidents, Volumes 1-8, University Press of America, 1983-88.

Ethics and Foreign Policy, Volumes 1-2, Transaction Books, 1984-85.

The American Presidency: Perspectives from Abroad, Volumes 1-2, University Press of America, 1986.

Presidential Transitions and Foreign Policy, Volumes 1-6, University Press of America, 1986-87.

The Presidency and Science Advising, Volumes 1-7, University Press of America, 1986-88.

Rhetoric and Political Discourse, Volumes 1-20, University Press of America, 1987-88.

Arms Control, Volumes 1-13, University Press of America, 1987-88.

OTHER

Also author of monograph series on international affairs, 1974—. Contributor to numerous anthologies on politics, foreign policy, cultural affairs, theology, education, and history; contributor of articles to periodicals, including *Reporter, World Politics, Interpretation, Worldview,* and *International Organization.* Contributing editor, *Christianity and Crisis,* 1956-62, and *Worldview,* 1969—; member of editorial board, *International Organization,* 1956-76, *Virginia Quarterly Review, Society,* and *Atlantic Quarterly;* associate editor, *Review of Politics,* 1974—.

WORK IN PROGRESS: History of the Cold War.

AVOCATIONAL INTERESTS: Travel, gardening, hiking, watching football and basketball.

BIOGRAPHICAL/CRITICAL SOURCES:

PERIODICALS

Christian Century, December 13, 1967.

Political Science Quarterly, December, 1963.
Times Literary Supplement, March 5, 1982.
Virginia Quarterly Review, summer, 1967.

* * *

THORAT, Sudhakar S. 1935-

PERSONAL: Born March 4, 1935, in Karmala, District Sholapur, Maharashtra, India; son of Shankar Laxman (inspector of schools and teacher) and Mathura B. (Deshmane) Thorat; married Indu S. Surkar, May 24, 1964; children: Anand Sudhakar, Arun Sudhakar (sons), Deepali (daughter). *Education:* College of Agriculture, Pune, B.S. (with honors), 1956; Kansas State University, M.S., 1960; Michigan State University, Ph.D., 1966.

ADDRESSES: Home—c/o Shri S. G. Thorat, Advocate, Shaikh Mohalla, Indapur, District Pune, Maharashtra, India. *Office*—Department of Agricultural Extension, Mahatma Phule Agricultural University, Rahuri 413 722, District Ahmednagar, Maharashtra, India.

CAREER: College of Agriculture (constituent college of Mahatma Phule Agricultural University), Pune, India, instructor, 1957-59, assistant professor, 1964-65, professor of agricultural extension education, 1969-75, rector of agricultural college hostels, 1969-75; Ford Foundation research assistant in sociology, New Delhi, India, 1963; National Institute of Rural Development, Hyderabad, India, deputy director of Diffusion of Innovations Project, 1966-68; Mahatma Phule Agricultural University, Ahmednagar, India, head of department of agricultural extension, 1975—.

MEMBER: Indian Society of Extension Education.

WRITINGS:

(With George H. Axinn) *Modernizing World Agriculture: A Comparative Study of Agricultural Extension Education Systems,* Praeger, 1972.
(Editor) *Report of a Seminar on Agricultural Production and Productivity in Maharashtra State, Mahatma Phule Agricultural University, July 1975,* Mahatma Phule Agricultural University, 1976.

Contributor to behavioral science journals; contributor of articles on agriculture and of personal essays to *Sakal* (Marathi language newspaper, Pune). Editor, *MPKV News Letter;* member of editorial board, *Indian Journal of Extension Service.*

WORK IN PROGRESS: Teaching and guiding graduate students in research on agricultural extension education, on rural sociology, and on communication.

* * *

THORNE, Christopher 1934-

PERSONAL: Born May 17, 1934, in Surrey, England; married; children: two daughters. *Education:* Attended St. Edmund Hall, Oxford, 1955-58.

ADDRESSES: Office—University of Sussex, Sussex, England.

CAREER: Charterhouse, Godalming, Surrey, England, senior history master, 1951-56; British Broadcasting Corp. Radio, London, England, head of further education, 1966-68; University of Sussex, Sussex, England, 1968—, began as lecturer, currently professor of international relations. *Military service:* Royal Navy, 1953-55; became lieutenant.

AWARDS, HONORS: Elected fellow of the British Academy; Bancroft Prize, 1979, for *Allies of a Kind;* D.Litt., Oxford University.

WRITINGS:

Ideology and Power, Macmillan, 1965.
Chartism, Macmillan, 1966.
The Approach of War, 1938-39, St. Martins, 1967.
The Limits of Foreign Policy, Hamish Hamilton, 1972, Putnam, 1973.
Allies of a Kind: The United States, Britain, and the War against Japan, 1941-1945, British Academy, 1982.
The Issue of War: States, Societies, and the Far Eastern Conflict of 1941-1945, Oxford University Press, 1985.
The Far Eastern War, Allen & Unwin (London), 1987, (Boston), 1988.
American Political Culture and the Asian Frontier, 1943-1973, British Academy, 1988.
Border Crossings: Studies in International History, Oxford University Press, 1988.

Reviewer for various periodicals, including *Times Literary Supplement.*

WORK IN PROGRESS: An inquiry into the notion of 'consensus' within the United States regarding foreign policy in the post-war years.

SIDELIGHTS: In his award-winning book *Allies of a Kind: The United States, Britain, and the War against Japan, 1941-1945,* historian Christopher Thorne explores the relationship between the United States and Great Britain in their struggle against Japan. "His main aim and his main achievement is to illuminate the character of Anglo-American relations," observes Paul Addison in the *New Statesman.* Despite their united purpose in Europe, "east of the Suez the two nations were competitors as well as allies. The Americans made no secret of the fact that they intended to inherit not only the white man's burden but his trade and investments." And Britain, aware that her status as a world power was dwindling, wanted to maneuver the United States in such a way that England's continued participation in world commerce was assured. Thorne sums up their positions this way: "On the American side [there were] suspicions of the British and an assumption of conflicting interests; on the part of the British, a belief in mutual long-term Anglo-American interests and hopes for close collaboration." According to Thorne, both nations were guilty of imperialism and white supremacy.

Unlike historians who draw their account solely from records of formal transactions between nations, Thorne focuses much of his study on the men who shaped such policies—in this case, Franklin Delano Roosevelt and Winston Churchill. "Great care is taken to be scrupulously fair to both parties," reports Richard Storry in the *Times Literary Supplement,* "although Thorne in no way conceals his own dislike of Churchill's political opinions. He refers more than once to Churchill's 'racism,' describing this as 'ignorant, ugly and at times vicious.' He clearly regards Churchill as hopelessly reactionary. Yet he concedes that Churchill had 'the strength of genuineness,' that he was temperamentally unsuited to intrigue. . . . By contrast, Roosevelt, his style 'a combination of halo-polishing and hard politics,' emerges as much the smaller man."

In summary of Thorne's treatment, Addison observes that the author "combines the cold qualities of control and the warm qualities of passion and imagination which flow together in the making of a first-class history. As a writer he is cool, patient and judicious, never reaching a verdict without a meticulous reckoning of the pros and cons. Yet the overall effect is far-reaching: the most searching, the most imaginative, and the most radical analysis we have yet had of the relations between John Bull and Uncle Sam in the 20th century."

Responses to *The Issue of War: States, Societies, and the Far Eastern Conflict of 1941-1945* have also been generally favorable. "This book has all the qualities one has come to associate with Christopher Thorne—scholarship, imagination, breadth of knowledge, and the ability to present an elaborate argument with great lucidity," writes C. J. Bartlett in a *History* review. *Times Literary Supplement* contributor Paul Kennedy reacts with "a mixture of disbelief and admiration" because "Thorne's approach is so wide-ranging—asking questions about political change, to be sure, but also about culture and race, about Western and Eastern concepts of 'civilization,' about the role of women," and other concerns, amounting to "a veritable Cook's Tour of much of the history of the globe during the 1930s and 1940s." Though the general reader—and even the well-informed—may find this global range daunting, Kennedy credits Thorne with "bridging the 'gap' between East and West in ways Kipling never dreamt of, and forcing us to look at the Far-Eastern war from a new, wider and altogether more satisfying perspective."

Thorne's discussion of the goals and victories of Japan and the United States are the subject of Ian Buruma's article on *The Issue of War* in the *New York Review of Books*. According to a London *Times* reviewer, Thorne's book supports the argument that changes in Europe brought about by the second World War will perhaps come to be viewed as less significant than Japan's bid for power. Though Japan suffered military defeat, it led the general "Asian quest for independence" in which "500 years of European domination were overturned," notes the *Times* reviewer. The victorious United States also emerged as a loser in the sense that its provincial attitudes left it unprepared to deal effectively with conflicts in Asian countries during the 1970s, adds Buruma, who concludes: "Thorne's book, which should be obligatory reading for all admirers of violent liberation movements, is an eloquent warning of what happens when nations resist it by turning to atavistic fantasies [i.e., inherited but outdated political attitudes]. Nuclear bombs are nothing but tools; it is the fantasies that could burn us all."

AVOCATIONAL INTERESTS: Music, sports (played cricket for England Schools team and for British Navy), and Crete.

BIOGRAPHICAL/CRITICAL SOURCES:

BOOKS

Thorne, Christopher, *Allies of a Kind: The United States, Britain, and the War against Japan, 1941-1945,* Oxford University Press, 1978.

Thorne, Christopher, *Border Crossings: Studies in International History,* Oxford University Press, 1988.

PERIODICALS

American History Review, June, 1986.
Economist, June 15, 1985.
History, February, 1986.
Listener, June 8, 1978.
London Review of Books, January 23, 1986.
New Statesman, March 24, 1978.
New York Review of Books, May 17, 1973, March 13, 1986.
Times (London), October 17, 1985.
Times Literary Supplement, February 2, 1973, June 2, 1978, August 9, 1985.

THUBRON, Colin (Gerald Dryden) 1939-

PERSONAL: Surname is pronounced *Thoo*-bron; born June 14, 1939, in London, England; son of Gerald Ernest (a brigadier in the British Army) and Evelyn (Dryden) Thubron. *Education:* Attended Eton College.

ADDRESSES: *Home*—Garden Cottage, 27 St. Ann's Villas, London W11 4RT, England.

CAREER: Hutchinson & Co. Ltd., London, England, member of editorial staff, 1959-62; British Broadcasting Corp. Television, London, free-lance filmmaker, 1963-64; Macmillan Co., New York, N.Y., member of editorial staff, 1964; writer.

MEMBER: Royal Society of Literature.

AWARDS, HONORS: PEN Silver Pen Award, 1985, for *A Cruel Madness;* Thomas Cook Travel Award, and Hawthornden Prize, both 1988, both for *Behind the Wall: A Journey through China.*

WRITINGS:

Mirror to Damascus, Heinemann, 1967, Little, Brown, 1968, reprinted, Century Hutchinson, 1986.
The Hills of Adonis: A Quest in Lebanon, Little, Brown, 1968, reprinted, Penguin, 1987.
Jerusalem, Little, Brown, 1969, reprinted, Century Hutchinson, 1986.
Journey into Cyprus, Heinemann, 1975.
The God in the Mountain (novel), Heinemann, 1977, Norton, 1978.
Emperor (novel), Heinemann, 1978.
(With the editors of Time-Life Books) *The Venetians,* Time-Life, 1980.
(With the editors of Time-Life Books) *The Ancient Mariners,* Time-Life, 1981.
The Royal Opera House, Covent Garden, Hamish Hamilton, 1982.
Among the Russians, Heinemann, 1983, published as *Where Nights Are Longest: Travels by Car through Western Russia,* Random House, 1984.
A Cruel Madness (novel), Heinemann, 1984, Atlantic Monthly Press, 1985.
Behind the Wall: A Journey through China, Heinemann, 1987, Atlantic Monthly Press, 1988.
Falling, Heinemann, 1989.

Has also scripted and filmed three documentary motion pictures on Turkey, Morocco, and Japan for television in the United States and Britain.

SIDELIGHTS: A veteran world traveler, Colin Thubron has written of his voyages in a series of books that several critics consider superior to the average travelogue. The typical Thubron book is a blend of history, description, and personal observation; the author approaches each of his subjects with a perspective which, according to a *Choice* reviewer, goes "beyond the facade of the monuments and events" to evoke a "beautifully poetic but not romantic" portrait of the people and places he has come to know. In a *Times Literary Supplement* review of *Journey into Cyprus,* for example, David Hunt observes that "the book is mainly about people," adding that it "is full of the most fascinating conversations." Even though *Journey into Cyprus* focuses on "personalities and on village life," Hunt concludes that "it will also serve very well as a guide-book. The principal antiquities are poetically but accurately described, and history is so subtly interwoven into the narrative that by the end the reader has learnt painlessly all he needs to know of it." A *Times Literary Supple-*

ment reviewer presents a similar assessment of *Mirror to Damascus:* "[Thubron's] narrative [exhibits] one great quality often missing from modern books of travel: its continual reference to the reality of another society and its actual people. His hosts and their relatives emerge as individuals, not as stereotypes." The critic concludes that "all this provides a pungent counterpoint of personal involvement and adventure to a solid account of the city's present flavour and past development, and the way Mr. Thubron has woven these elements together is a lesson for anyone who tries to combine entertainment with instruction."

"Colin Thubron's latest book, *Among the Russians* [published in the United States as *Where Nights Are Longest: Travels by Car through Western Russia*], can only serve to enhance his reputation," comments Fitzroy Maclean in the *Spectator.* "I enjoyed every page of it. It is well observed, well written and, unlike many books about Russia, gives proof of an unusual and penetrating insight into the character of the country and people." The book "is compiled from the notebooks of [Thubron's] extraordinary 10,000 mile journey across the Soviet Union in an old Morris Marina," describes *New Statesman* contributor Olga Semenova, "from Leningrad and the Baltic, to Moscow and central Russia, the Ukraine and Kiev, the Caucasus and Armenia. The result is a beautiful and poetic work, which captures much of the spirit of Russia." The critic notes that while "Thubron conveys the feel of places and their past with wonderful intensity," he also portrays "the ugliness and emptiness of modern Russian life, with its tawdry tower blocks, interminable queues and tension, radiating outwards from the Kremlin."

Although the Soviet Union is a subject that has been studied and analyzed many times before, Nigel Ryan believes that "new" information is not the author's purpose. Writing in the *Times Literary Supplement,* Ryan suggests that "with [Thubron], one experiences the bewildering and disorientating contrasts of vast loneliness, of cruelty and indifference to human life on a horrifying scale, and of sudden extravagant gusts of personal warmth, generosity and desire to confide; of a deep national melancholia at odds with a fierce patriotism. If we have heard most of it before," states the critic, "we have seldom heard it so elegantly or powerfully put." Another difference, maintains Gail Pool of the *Christian Science Monitor,* is that "to a large degree, Thubron's journey through Russia is an exploration of attitudes, the Soviets' and his own. . . . If he is looking *at* everything, he is also looking *for* something, always moving beyond description to penetrate the texture of Russian life and compare it with his own world."

While some critics praise this personal angle in Thubron's work, *Washington Post Book World* contributor Joel Conarroe faults the author for bringing a biased attitude to his work: "Thubron is mesmerized by rampant alcoholism, by bribery, and by 'universal political hypocrisy.' About these and other matters he tends invariably to confuse first impressions with wisdom. . . . The author is himself quite willing to draw conclusions from skimpy evidence." The *Los Angeles Times*'s Richard Eder similarly believes that Thubron has not brought enough diverse elements to his account; he specifically cites as a "disabling defect . . . that Thubron rarely is good at describing and conveying the particular quality of the people he meets. They blur into each other, and their conversations, whether official, dissident or simply private, have a uniformity rarely lightened by wit or individuality."

Other critics, however, praise the author for an honest, self-cognizant approach; Douglas Hill of the Toronto *Globe and Mail,* for example, claims that "what wins a reader over is Thubron's palpable honesty. . . . He gives the impression of complete candor, especially about himself, his enthusiasms, surprises and frustrations." The critic also observes that the author "makes quick but profound friendships; the connections he forges with the most unlikely people are explored sensitively, and they are often quite moving." *New York Times Book Review* contributor S. Frederick Starr echoes this opinion, writing that "the appeal of Mr. Thubron's account is deepened by his keen self-awareness, which pervades his narrative like an inner dialogue." The critic elaborates: "[Thubron] reports with surprise how he gradually ceased to be disappointed by the shortcomings he perceived in Soviet life and began to feel comforted by them. Then he stopped himself, realizing he had become like the Soviet visitor to the West who is at first disgusted and then smugly relieved by the flaws he observes around him." Starr also notes that Thubron, whom he calls "a subtle and humane writer," is able to "capture the fleeting words and gestures that define a culture." "Thubron is a limpid writer who has all the sharpness of eye . . . and can also present his version of Russia with a particular sweet-sour flavor," remarks Rosemary Dinnage in the *New York Review of Books,* adding that Thubron "has a novelistic gift for dialogue and settings." Citing Thubron's "fine writing," Ryan concludes that "the extraordinary dimensions [of the Soviet people] come through in *Among the Russians.* It is one of the best—and best written—travel books of recent years."

Thubron embarked on a similar voyage to prepare for *Behind the Wall: A Journey through China,* an account which *Times Literary Supplement* contributor Jonathan Mirsky claims that "many China specialists who disdain 'I saw China' books will wish they had written . . . [for it] contains remarkable insights into the country." After learning enough Mandarin Chinese to be able to travel without a guide, Thubron toured the country by fourth-class train, staying off the beaten tourist track and meeting many Chinese. "The result," writes Robin Hanbury-Tenison in *Spectator,* "is a rare first-hand account of a country seen through the eyes of one who has experienced what he describes and who is in a position to understand what he sees." The critic also comments that all the discomforts Thubron endured have produced "rich encounters, the special stuff of this author's writing. The world seems to be full of extraordinary people with amazing tales to tell, if a writer but puts himself in a position, however uncomfortable, to hear them." Because he was a lone British visitor, Thubron found himself approached by many Chinese, who found him a curiosity, as Patrick Taylor-Martin details in the *Listener:* "As an outsider, [Thubron] receives confidences from the Chinese, and throws much light on the mystery which still surrounds this nation of a billion uncomprehended people. Talking to him, people confess their sorrow at having no children, their longing to go to America to study medieval European art, [and] their hatred of communism," among other topics.

It is this personal aspect of *Behind the Wall* that impresses many critics. While Hanbury-Tenison observes that "the countryside through which [the author] travels for lonely months, the satanic industrial cities, the deserted but reviving temples he visits are vividly described," he maintains that "they come alive through the characters [Thubron] contrives to meet." "The distinction of his book is in the way, with conviction and elegance and humour, he describes through chance conversations, bits of history and visions of understanding the country's total *being,* its Chinaness," claims Nicholas Wollaston in the *Observer.* "A travel book, to quote his own essay again, is one civilisation reporting on another: which is what this one does marvellously." And as with his other travelogues, Thubron brings a novelist's eye to his writing: "Thubron, as readers of his earlier books, especially the excellent *Among the Russians,* already know, is a wonderfully perceptive writer," notes Mirsky. Taylor-Martin similarly states that the author's "style is impeccable. The book is full of beautifully composed scenes, orchestrated as if for a novel, and exquisite passages of description. . . . It should be read for the intelligence and poetic insight which went into its making," concludes the critic. Calling *Behind the Wall* "an even better book than *Among the Russians,*" London *Times* contributor Victoria Glendinning notes that Thubron's "characteristic lyricism is in this book a controlled calligraphy of ideas and images, its richness cut by splashes of monosyllables. . . . At the end I turned to look—again, as I thought—at the pictures. There are none, except in the mind," adds the critic. "Writing as vivid as this needs no illustrations."

Having been praised for the intricate, lyrical descriptions in his travel books, it is not surprising that Thubron has turned his hand to fiction as well. Although his first two novels were not widely noticed, *A Cruel Madness,* his third, "sees Thubron in full possession of considerable talents as a novelist," claims *Times Literary Supplement* contributor Jayne Pilling, adding that "the book is a quietly extraordinary *tour de force.*" The novel begins as Daniel, a prep school teacher who volunteers weekends at a local mental hospital, believes he sees on the grounds of the asylum a woman with whom he once had a brief but disastrous affair. As he painfully realizes she is a patient there, Daniel recalls his original passion for her, including passages from her point of view. As the novel progresses, however, the reader becomes aware that Daniel is untrustworthy as a narrator, that he is actually a patient at the asylum and that his visions and recollections may be delusions.

Although many books have been written about the illusory nature of human perception, *Los Angeles Times Book Review* contributor Sharon Dirlam believes that Thubron's book "isn't just another novel about madness and despair." Calling *A Cruel Madness* "spellbinding," the critic describes the novel as "a gripping tale of passion, however misspent, and the failure of an entire set of characters to come to grips with life seems not as distant from 'normal' as one might think, but simply a look deeper into the mind than most of us dare to probe." Pilling concurs, writing that "what is so impressive about *A Cruel Madness* is the way it transcends the conventional 'novelized' case history." The critic elaborates: "Thubron's descriptions of the hospital and its inmates are vividly convincing—fearfully so in their sad banality. The defences of a character traumatized by loss and separation—the madman's traditional cunning in weaving compulsive fictions—are appropriated by the novelist to impressive effect."

While *Washington Post Book World* contributor Stephen Koch also finds *A Cruel Madness* "an intriguing and sometimes rather moving novel about insanity and love, illusion and reality," he faults the author for the structure of the novel. In particular the critic dislikes what he terms "the absurdly simple device of omitting major pieces of information from an otherwise perfectly ordinary story. . . . This is what happens in *A Cruel Madness,* and I for one find it a cheap trick, an effort to make a story more portentous, merely because it is more perplexing." Other critics, however, find Thubron's use of Daniel's ambiguous narration very effective and well written; John Wheatcroft, for example, states in the *New York Times Book Review* that "to experience this montage through Daniel's eyes and to hear through his ears echoes that are not perfectly congruent with what they supposedly repeat compels us to try to discover what actually has happened and what really is happening. As we do so," continues the critic, "all the apparently solid ground on which the narrative has built begins to shift, to reveal gaps and inconsistencies." "In such of his non-fiction as *Among the Russians,*" observes Francis King in the *Spectator,* "Mr. Thubron gives the impression of being the most rational and well-balanced of people. It is therefore all the more remarkable that he should have been able to enter so convincingly into a mind so disturbed. With a terrifying vividness, Mr. Thubron creates a phantasmagoric world in which . . . the demarcation between reality and delusion becomes harder to perceive." In its persuasive use of narrative, *A Cruel Madness* "brings to mind other novels set in the microcosmic world of a hospital," asserts Wheatcroft, including "Thomas Mann's 'Magic Mountain,' Aleksandr Solzhenitsyn's 'Cancer Ward,' Ken Kesey's 'One Flew over the Cuckoo's Nest'. . . . Among such distinguished company, Mr. Thubron's novel holds its own," concludes the critic. And a *New Yorker* reviewer claims that Thubron's novel is "a study in madness so compelling that it is hard to believe we are not experiencing it at first hand," adding that *A Cruel Madness* is "a remarkable achievement."

BIOGRAPHICAL/CRITICAL SOURCES:

PERIODICALS

Choice, December, 1968.
Christian Science Monitor, September 8, 1987.
Globe and Mail (Toronto), September 7, 1985.
Listener, September 22, 1977, September 24, 1987.
Los Angeles Times, April 4, 1984.
Los Angeles Times Book Review, October 6, 1985.
New Statesman, October 21, 1983.
New Yorker, October 7, 1985.
New York Review of Books, June 13, 1985.
New York Times Book Review, May 18, 1969, December 7, 1969, July 15, 1984, November 10, 1985, November 27, 1988.
Observer, September 27, 1987.
Spectator, July 7, 1984, September 1, 1984, September 19, 1987.
Times (London), December 15, 1983, July 25, 1985, September 17, 1987.
Times Literary Supplement, December 21, 1967, October 31, 1968, June 6, 1975, December 30, 1977, June 22, 1984, September 7, 1984, September 11, 1987.
Washington Post Book World, June 17, 1984, November 17, 1985, September 11, 1988.

—Sketch by Diane Telgen

* * *

TIDYMAN, Ernest 1928-1984

PERSONAL: Born January 1, 1928, in Cleveland, Ohio; died July 14, 1984 (one source says July 15), of a perforated ulcer and other complications in London, England; son of Benjamin (a journalist) and Catherine (Kascsak) Tidyman; married second wife, Susan Katherine Gould (a writer), December 25, 1970 (divorced); married fourth wife, Chris Clark; children: (first marriage) Benjamin, Nathaniel; (second marriage) Adam, Nicholas. *Education:* Educated in Cleveland, Ohio.

ADDRESSES: Office—Ernest Tidyman International, Ltd., Rossiter Rd., Washington, Conn. 06793.

CAREER: Cleveland News, Cleveland, Ohio, newsman, 1954-57; *New York Post,* New York City, newsman, 1957-60; *New York Times,* New York City, editor, 1960-66; *Signature,* New York City, managing editor and writer, 1966-69; free-lance screenwriter, author, and film, producer, 1969-84. Founder of and producer for Ernest Tidyman International, Ltd. Lecturer. *Military service:* U.S. Army, 1945-46.

MEMBER: Academy of Motion Picture Arts and Sciences, American Film Institute, British Film Institute, Writers Guild of America-West, Mystery Writers of America.

AWARDS, HONORS: Academy Award, Writers Guild of America Award, and Edgar Allan Poe Award of Mystery Writers of America, all 1971, all for screenplay "The French Connection"; National Association for the Advancement of Colored People (NAACP) Image Award, 1971, for *Shaft;* Peabody Award and Gavel Award from American Bar Association, both 1980, both for teleplay "Dummy."

WRITINGS:

Flower Power, Paperback Library, 1968.
Absolute Zero, Dial, 1971.
High Plains Drifter, Bantam, 1973.
Dummy, Little, Brown, 1974.
Line of Duty, Little, Brown, 1974.
Starstruck, W. H. Allen, 1975.
Table Stakes: A Novel, Little, Brown, 1978.
Big Bucks: The True Story of the Plymouth Mail Robbery and How They Got Away with It, Norton, 1982.

"SHAFT" SERIES

Shaft, Macmillan, 1970.
Shaft among the Jews, Dial, 1972.
Shaft's Big Score, Bantam, 1972.
Shaft Has a Ball, Bantam, 1973.
Goodbye, Mr. Shaft, Dial, 1973.
Shaft's Carnival of Killers, Bantam, 1974.
The Last Shaft, Weidenfeld & Nicolson, 1975.

OTHER

Also author of *The Billion Dollar Snatch.* Author of screenplays, including "The French Connection" (based on the novel by Robin Moore), 1971, "Shaft," 1971, "Shaft's Big Score," 1972, "High Plains Drifter," 1973, "Report to the Commissioner" (with Abby Mann), 1975, "The Street People," 1976, "A Force of One," 1979, "Forfeit" (based on the novel by Dick Francis), and "Please Be Careful, Barney Noble." Also author of the teleplays "To Kill a Cop," 1978, and "Power: An American Saga," 1980; author and co-producer of teleplays "Dummy," 1979, "Guyana Tragedy: The Story of Jim Jones," 1980, and "Alcatraz: The Whole Shocking Story," 1980.

SIDELIGHTS: Although Ernest Tidyman spent twenty-five years as a magazine and newspaper journalist for such publications as the *Cleveland News, New York Post,* and *New York Times,* he was known in Hollywood primarily as an author and screenwriter. For one, Tidyman penned the seven "Shaft" novels about a tough, black detective named John Shaft. In a 1970 *Library Journal* interview, Tidyman explained the character of Shaft: "Shaft is a black man, you will discover in going down the list of delineators to his existence, but he is also very much a man first and a complex human being beneath the surface of pigmentation." The original *Shaft* novel won Tidyman an Image Award from the National Association for the Advancement of Colored People (NAACP). Tidyman also received much respect, including an Academy Award, for his screenplay adaptation of Robin Moore's novel *The French Connection.* Other acknowledged works by Tidyman include his novel and screenplay "High Plains Drifter," which starred Clint Eastwood, and the screenplay "Report to the Commissioner," which he co-authored. If anything, it was Tidyman's hope that his stories would "reach out and grab the reader by the scruff of his emotional response and give him a thorough shaking," quotes the *Library Journal* reviewer. Tidyman's awards and recognition attest to his success in this respect.

OBITUARIES:

PERIODICALS

Chicago Tribune, July 17, 1984.
New York Times, July 16, 1984.*

* * *

TIMMERMAN, John H(ager) 1945-

PERSONAL: Born January 19, 1945, in Grand Rapids, Mich.; son of John Johnson (a professor of English) and Carolyn Jane (Hager) Timmerman; married Patricia Lynn (a nurse), August, 1966; children: Jeffrey, Betsy, Tamara, Joel. *Education:* Calvin College, A.B., 1968; Ohio University, M.A., 1971, Ph.D., 1973.

ADDRESSES: Office—Department of English, Calvin College, Grand Rapids, Mich. 49506.

CAREER: Grove City College, Grove City, Pa., assistant professor of philosophy, 1973-77; Calvin College, Grand Rapids, Mich., associate professor, 1977-81, professor of English, 1981—. *Military service:* U.S. Army, 1968-70; served in Vietnam; received Bronze Star.

WRITINGS:

Frederick Manfred: A Bibliography and Publishing History, Center for Western Studies, Sioux Falls, S.D., 1981.
(Editor) John Johnson Timmerman, *Markings on a Long Journey,* Baker Book, 1982.
Shaper (fiction), Chosen Books, 1983.
Other Worlds: The Fantasy Genre, Bowling Green University, 1983.
At the Name of Jesus, Tyndale House, 1984.
John Steinbeck's Fiction: The Aesthetics of the Road Taken, University of Oklahoma Press, 1986.
The Way of Christian Living, Eerdmans, 1987.
A Season of Suffering, Multnomah, 1987.
John Steinbeck's Short Stories, University of Oklahoma, 1989.

Contributor to *Studies in the Twentieth Century, Christian Scholar's Review, Southwest Review, Wisconsin Review,* and other journals.

SIDELIGHTS: John H. Timmerman commented: "I divide my time, both in books and for journals, pretty evenly between academic, scholarly writing necessary to survive in an academic career and my private loves—fiction and poetry. *Shaper* is a religious fantasy analogous to the temptation of Jesus in the wilderness. Fantasy in theory and fiction remains a favorite subject, and I continue to lecture widely at colleges on the subject."

* * *

TODD, Peter
See HAMILTON, Charles (Harold St. John)

* * *

TOMALIN, Ruth

PERSONAL: Born in County Kilkenny, Ireland; daughter of Thomas Edward (a professional gardener and writer) and Elspeth Rutherford (Mitchell) Tomalin; divorced; married William N. Ross (a journalist), 1971; children: (first marriage) Nicholas

Leaver. *Education:* King's College, London, diploma in journalism.

ADDRESSES: Home and office—c/o Barclay's Bank, 15 Langham Pl., London W.1, England.

CAREER: Journalist and writer. Began newspaper work in 1942 with *Portsmouth Evening News,* Portsmouth, Hampshire, England, and has since been a staff reporter, at various times, for other newspapers in England, and a press agency reporter in London law courts. *Military service:* Women's Land Army, 1941-42.

MEMBER: Society of Authors.

WRITINGS:

Threnody for Dormice (poems), Fortune Press, 1947.
The Day of the Rose (essays and portraits), Fortune Press, 1947.
Deer's Cry (poem), Fortune Press, 1952.
All Souls (novel), Faber, 1952.
W. H. Hudson (biography), Philosophical Library (Witherby), 1954.
The Daffodil Bird (juvenile novel), Faber, 1959, A. S. Barnes, 1960.
The Sea Mice (juvenile novel), Faber, 1962.
The Garden House (novel), Faber, 1968.
The Spring House (novel), Faber, 1968.
(Editor) *Best Country Stories,* Faber, 1969.
Away to the West (novel), Faber, 1972.
A Green Wishbone (juvenile novel), Faber, 1975.
A Stranger Thing (juvenile novel), Faber, 1975.
The Snake Crook (juvenile novel), Faber, 1976.
Gone Away (juvenile novel), Faber, 1979.
(Contributor) Brocard Sewell, editor, *Henry Williamson, the Man, the Writings: A Symposium,* Tabb House, 1980.
W. H. Hudson: A Biography, Faber, 1982.
Little Nasty (juvenile novel), Faber, 1985.
A Summer Ghost (juvenile novel), Faber, 1986.
Another Day (juvenile novel), Faber, 1988.
Long Since (novel), Faber, 1989.

WORK IN PROGRESS: The Orchard House, fourth novel in the "A Day in the Country" series about country homes in England and Ireland; a juvenile textbook on ecology, for Faber; Sussex ecology records, 1930—.

AVOCATIONAL INTERESTS: Country life and wildlife preservation.

BIOGRAPHICAL/CRITICAL SOURCES:

PERIODICALS

New Statesman & Nation, March 1, 1952.
New York Times Book Review, March 13, 1983.
Times (London), March 22, 1964, January 13, 1982.
Times Literary Supplement, November 3, 1972, December 5, 1975, November 26, 1982.

* * *

TORRANCE, Thomas F(orsythe) 1913-

PERSONAL: Born August 30, 1913, in Chengdu, Sichuan, China; son of Thomas (a missionary) and Annie Elizabeth (Sharp) Torrance; married Margaret Edith Spear, October, 1946; children: Thomas Spear, Iain Richard, Alison Meta Elizabeth. *Education:* University of Edinburgh, M.A., 1934, B.D., 1937, D.Litt., 1970; University of Basel, graduate study, 1937-38, D.Theol., 1946; Oriel College, Oxford, graduate study, 1939-40.

ADDRESSES: Home—37 Braid Farm Rd., Edinburgh EH10 6LE, Scotland.

CAREER: Clergyman of Church of Scotland. Auburn Theological Seminary, Auburn, N.Y., professor of theology, 1938-39; Alyth Barony Parish, Perthshire, Scotland, minister, 1940-47; Beechgrove Church, Aberdeen, Scotland, minister, 1947-50; University of Edinburgh, Edinburgh, Scotland, professor of church history, 1950-52, professor of Christian dogmatics, 1952-79. Hewett Lecturer, Newton Center and Cambridge, Mass., and New York, N.Y., 1959; moderator of Church of Scotland, 1976-77; has worked for ten years for Faith and Order Commission, World Council of Churches. *Military service:* Chaplain, 1943-45.

MEMBER: Academie Internationale des Sciences Religieuses (president, 1972-81), Academie Internationale de Philosophie des Sciences, Societe Internationale pour l'Etude de la Philosophie Medievale, Society for the Study of Theology (founding member; honorary president, 1966-68), Scottish Church Theology Society (former president), Church Service Society of Church of Scotland (honorary president, 1970-71), Societe de l'Histoire du Protestantisme Francais (foreign member).

AWARDS, HONORS: Member, Order of the British Empire, 1945; D.D., Presbyterian College, Montreal, 1950, St. Andrews University, 1960; D.Theol., University of Paris, 1959, University of Geneva, 1959, University of Oslo, 1961, Theological Academy of the Reformed Church, Debrecen, Hungary, 1988; Cross of St. Mark (first class), 1970; Collins Biennial Religious Book Award, 1970, for *Theological Science;* Templeton Foundation Prize, 1978; Fellow of the Royal Society of Edinburgh, 1979; Fellow of the British Academy, 1982; D.Sc., Heriot-Watt University, Edinburgh, 1983.

WRITINGS:

The Modern Theological Debate, Inter-Varsity Fellowship of Evangelical Unions, 1941.
The Doctrine of Grace in the Apostolic Fathers, Oliver & Boyd, 1948, Eerdmans, 1959.
Calvin's Doctrine of Man, Lutterworth, 1949, 2nd edition, Eerdmans, 1957, reprinted, Greenwood Press, 1977.
Royal Priesthood, Oliver & Boyd, 1955.
Kingdom and Church: A Study in the Theology of the Reformation, Essential Books, 1956.
When Christ Comes and Comes Again, Eerdmans, 1957.
(Author of historical notes and introduction) John Calvin, *Tracts and Treatises on the Reformation of the Church,* three volumes, Oliver & Boyd, 1958, Eerdmans, c. 1959.
The Apocalypse Today, Eerdmans, 1959.
Conflict and Agreement in the Church, Lutterworth, Volume 1, 1959, Volume 2, 1960.
Karl Barth: An Introduction to His Early Theology, 1910-1931, S.C.M. Press, 1962.
(Author of introduction) Karl Barth, *Theology and Church: Shorter Writings, 1920-1928,* Westminster, 1962.
Theology in Reconstruction, S.C.M. Press, 1965, Eerdmans, 1966.
Space, Time and Incarnation, Oxford University Press, 1969.
(With Piet Frans Fransen) *Intelligent Theology,* Franciscan Herald Press, 1969.
Theological Science, Oxford University Press, 1969.
God and Rationality, Oxford University Press, 1971.

Newton, Einstein, and Scientific Theology (Keese Lecture for 1971), University of Tennessee at Chatanooga, 1971.

Theology in Reconciliation: Essays towards Evangelical and Catholic Unity in East and West, Eerdmans, 1975.

Space, Time and Resurrection, Eerdmans, 1976.

The Ground and Grammar of Theology, University of Virginia Press, 1980.

Christian Theology and Scientific Culture, Christian Journals (Belfast), 1980, Oxford University Press, 1981.

Divine and Contingent Order, Oxford University Press, 1981.

Reality and Evangelical Theology, Westminster, 1982.

Juridical Law and Physical Law, Scottish Academic Press, 1982.

The Mediation of Christ, Paternoster Press, 1983, Eerdmans, 1984.

Transformation and Convergence in the Frame of Knowledge: Exploration in the Interrelations of Scientific and Theological Enterprise, Eerdmans, 1984.

The Christian Frame of Mind, Handsel Press, 1985, enlarged edition, Helmers & Howard, 1989.

Reality and Scientific Theology, Scottish Academic Press, 1985.

Theological Dialogue between Orthodox and Reformed Churches, Scottish Academic Press, 1985.

The Trinitarian Faith, T. & T. Clark, 1988.

The Hermeneutics of John Calvin, Scottish Academic Press, 1988.

EDITOR

(With G. W. Bromiley, and others) Karl Barth, *Church Dogmatics,* translation from the German by Bromiley, Volume 1, part 1: *The Doctrine of the Word of God: Prolegomena to Church Dogmatics,* T. & T. Clark, 1975, Volume 1, part 2: *The Doctrine of the Word of God: The Revelation of God, Holy Scripture, the Proclamation of the Church,* T. & T. Clark, 1956, Volume 2, part 1: *The Doctrine of God: The Knowledge of God,* T. & T. Clark, 1957, Volume 2, part 2: *The Doctrine of God: The Election of God, the Command of God,* T. & T. Clark, 1957, Volume 3, part 1: *The Doctrine of Creation: The Work of Creation,* T. & T. Clark, 1958, Volume 3, part 2: *The Doctrine of Creation: The Creature,* T. & T. Clark, 1960, Volume 3, part 3: *The Doctrine of Creation: The Creator and His Creature,* T. & T. Clark, 1961, Volume 3, part 4: *The Doctrine of Creation: The Command of God the Creator,* T. & T. Clark, 1961, Volume 4, part 1: *The Doctrine of Reconciliation: The Subject Matter and Problems of the Doctrine of Reconciliation,* T. & T. Clark, 1956, Volume 4, part 2: *The Doctrine of Reconciliation: Jesus Christ, the Servant as Lord,* T. & T. Clark, 1958, Volume 4, part 3: *The Doctrine of Reconciliation: Jesus Christ, the True Witness,* two volumes, T. & T. Clark, 1961, Volume 4, part 4, *The Doctrine of Reconciliation: The Christian Life (fragment)—Baptism as Foundation of the Christian Life,* T. & T. Clark, 1969, Volume 5: *Index, with Aids for the Preacher,* T. & T. Clark, 1977.

(And translator) Robert Bruce, *The Mystery of the Lord's Supper* (sermons), James Clarke, 1958.

(And translator, and author of introduction) *The School of Faith: The Catechisms of the Reformed Church,* Harper, 1959.

(With R. S. Wright) Henry J. Wotherspoon and J. M. Kirkpatrick, *A Manual of Church Doctrine According to the Church of Scotland,* 2nd edition, revised and enlarged, Oxford University Press, 1960.

William Manson, *Jesus and the Christian,* Eerdmans, 1967.

Belief in Science and in Christian Life: The Relevance of Michael Polanyi's Thought for Christian Faith and Life, Handsel Press, 1980.

Theology and Scientific Culture, five volumes, Christian Journals (Belfast), 1980-83.

The Incarnation: Ecumenical Studies in the Nicene-Constantinopolitan Creed, A.D. 381, Handsel Press, 1981.

(And author of introduction) James Clerk Maxwell, *A Dynamical Theory of the Electromagnetic Field,* Scottish Academic Press, 1982.

Theology and Science at the Frontiers of Knowledge, several volumes, Scottish Academic Press, 1985—.

EDITOR WITH DAVID W. TORRANCE; JOHN CALVIN'S NEW TESTAMENT COMMENTARIES

The Gospel According to St. John: Chapters 1-10, translation by T. H. L. Parker, Eerdmans, 1959.

Commentary on Corinthians I, translation by J. W. Fraser, Eerdmans, 1960.

The Gospel According to St. John: Chapters 11-21, translation by Parker, Eerdmans, 1961.

Commentary of Romans and Thessalonians, translation by R. Mackenzie, Eerdmans, 1961.

Epistle of Paul the Apostle to the Hebrews and the First and Second Epistles of St. Peter, translation by W. B. Johnston, Eerdmans, 1963.

Second Epistle of Paul the Apostle to the Corinthians and the Epistles to Timothy, Titus and Philemon, translation by T. A. Smail, Eerdmans, 1964.

Acts of the Apostles, Volume 1, translation by Fraser and W. J. G. McDonald, Oliver & Boyd, 1965, Volume 2, translation by Fraser, Eerdmans, 1966.

Harmony of the Gospels, Volume 1, translation by A. W. Morrison, St. Andrew Press, 1972, Volume 2, translation by Parker, St. Andrew Press, 1972, Volume 3, translation by Morrison, Eerdmans, 1972.

OTHER

Founder-editor with J. K. S. Reid, *Scottish Journal of Theology,* 1948-82.

WORK IN PROGRESS: The Doctrine of God the Father; The Doctrine of God the Son; The Doctrine of God the Holy Spirit; Karl Barth, Evangelical Theologian; Exploration in the History of Hermeneutics.

AVOCATIONAL INTERESTS: Golf, fishing, travel in China.

* * *

TOURNIER, Paul 1898-1986

PERSONAL: Born May 12, 1898, in Geneva, Switzerland; died October 6, 1986, in Geneva; son of Louis (a clergyman) and Elisabeth (Ormond) Tournier; married Nelly Bouvier, October 4, 1924 (died, 1974); married second wife, Corinne, 1984; children: (first marriage) Jean-Louis, Gabriel. *Education:* University of Geneva, M.D., 1923. *Religion:* "Reformed."

ADDRESSES: Home and office—Chemin Ormand 50, 1256 Troinex, Geneva, Switzerland.

CAREER: Physician in private practice; writer. *Military service:* Physician in Swiss Army, 1939-45.

WRITINGS:

(With Philippe Mottu and Charles F. Ducommun) *Pierres d'angles de la reconstruction nationale,* Delachaux & Niestle, 1941.

Medecine de la personne, Delachaux & Niestle, 1945, translation by Edwin Hudson published as *The Healing of Persons,*

Harper, 1965, reprinted, 1983, published as *Tournier's Medicine of the Whole Person,* Word Books, 1973.
(With Jacques Ellul and Rene Gillouin) *L'Homme mesure de toute chose,* Centre Protestant d'Etudes, 1947.
Desharmonie de la vie moderne, Delachaux & Niestle, 1947.
Les Forts et les faibles, Delachaux & Niestle, 1948, translation by Hudson published as *The Strong and the Weak,* Westminster Press, 1963.
Le Personnage et la personne, Delachaux & Niestle, translation by Hudson published as *The Meaning of Persons,* Harper, 1957, reprinted, 1982.
Bible et medecine, Delachaux & Niestle, translation by Hudson published as *A Doctor's Casebook in the Light of the Bible,* Harper, 1960, reprinted, 1976.
Vrai ou fausse culpabilite, Delachaux & Niestle, 1958, translation by Arthur W. Heathcote and others published as *Guilt and Grace: A Psychological Study* (also see below), Harper, 1962, reprinted, 1983.
De la solitude a la communnaute, Delachaux & Niestle, translation by John S. Gilmour published as *Escape from Loneliness,* Westminister Press, 1962.
Des Cadeaux pourquoi?, Labor et Fides, 1961, translation by Gilmour published as *The Meaning of Gifts,* John Knox Press, 1963.
Les Saisons de la vie (also see below), Labor et Fides, 1961, translation by Gilmour published as *The Seasons of Life,* John Knox Press, 1963.
Tenir tete ou ceder (also see below), Labor et Fides, 1962, translation by Gilmour published as *To Resist or to Surrender,* John Knox Press, 1964, reprinted, 1980.
Difficultes conjugales: Pour les surmonter, il faut chercher a se comprendre, Labor et Fides, 1962, translation by Gilmour published as *To Understand Each Other* (also see below), John Knox Press, 1967.
Le Secret, Labor et Fides, 1963, translation by Joe Embry published as *Secrets,* John Knox Press, 1965.
Solitude de l'homme moderne, Westminster Press, 1964.
L'Aventure de la vie, Delachaux & Niestle, translation by Hudson published as *The Adventure of Living,* Harper, 1965.
Desharmonie de la vie moderne, Delachaux & Niestle, translation by John Doberstein and Helen Doberstein published as *The Whole Person in a Broken World: A Biblical Remedy for Today's World,* Collins & World, 1965, reprinted, Harper, 1981.
Technique et foi, Delachaux & Niestle, translation by Hudson published as *The Person Reborn* (also see below), Harper, 1966.
L'Homme et son lieu: Psychologie et foi, Delachaux & Niestle, 1966, translation by Hudson published as *A Place for You: Psychology and Religion,* Harper, 1968.
Dynamique de la guerison, Delachaux & Niestle, 1968.
Problemes de vie (includes *Les Saisons de la vie, Des Cadeaux, pourquoi?,* and *Tenir tete de ceder*), Labor et Fides, 1970.
Apprendre a vieiller, Delachaux & Niestle, 1971, translation by Hudson published as *Learning to Grow Old,* Harper, 1972, published as *Learn to Grow Old,* 1983.
Quel nom lui donnerez-vous?, Labor et Fides, 1974, translation by Hudson published as *The Naming of Persons,* Harper, 1975 (published in England as *What's in a Name?,* SCM Press, 1975).
Reflections on Life's Most Crucial Questions (extracts from author's works), Harper, 1976 (published in England as *A Tournier Companion,* SCM Press), published as *Reflections: A Personal Guide for Life's Most Crucial Questions,* Westminster Press, 1982.
The Best of Paul Tournier (includes *Guilt and Grace, The Meanings of Persons, The Person Reborn,* and *To Understand Each Other*), Iverson-Norman, 1977.
Violence te puissance, Delachaux & Niestle, 1977, translation published as *The Violence Within,* Harper, 1978 (published in England as *The Violence Inside*), 2nd edition, 1982.
La Mission de la femme, Delachaux & Niestle, 1979, translation by Hudson published as *The Gift of Feeling,* John Knox Press, 1981.
Face a la souffrance, Labor et Fides, 1981, translation published as *Creative Suffering,* Harper, 1983.
Vivre a l'ecoute, translation published as *A Listening Ear: Reflections on Christian Caring,* Augsburg Publishing, 1984.

Also editor of *Surmenage et repos,* 1963, translation by James H. Farley published as *Fatigue in Modern Society.*

SIDELIGHTS: Throughout his long career as a psychiatrist and author, Paul Tournier sought to explain what he perceived to be the links between physical illness and the mind, and the correspondingly close alignment between priest and physician. Although his theories, outlined in *La Medicine de la personne (The Healing of Persons),* were initially received "with criticism and ridicule from both theologians and doctors," states the London *Times,* his ideas have "nevertheless, become increasingly popular" in the more scientific study of psychosomatic medicine. In addition to English, Tournier's books have been translated into numerous other languages, including Finnish, Dutch, Norwegian, Greek, Chinese, and Spanish.

BIOGRAPHICAL/CRITICAL SOURCES:

PERIODICALS

Christian Century, August 29, 1973, August 17, 1977.
Christianity Today, May 11, 1973.
Times (London), October 29, 1986.
Times Literary Supplement, November 11, 1965.

OBITUARIES:

PERIODICALS

Times (London), October 29, 1986.*

* * *

TOWNLEY, Rod
See TOWNLEY, Roderick

* * *

TOWNLEY, Roderick 1942-
(Rod Townley)

PERSONAL: Born June 7, 1942, in Orange, N.J.; son of William Richard (a businessman) and Elise (Fredman) Townley; married Libby Blackman, April 4, 1970 (divorced, 1980); married Wyatt Baker (a writer and performer), February 15, 1986; children: (first marriage) Jesse Blackman; (second marriage) Grace Whitman. *Education:* Attended Hamilton College, 1960-61, and University of Chicago, 1961-62; Bard College, A.B., 1965; Rutgers University, M.A., 1970, Ph.D., 1972.

ADDRESSES: Home—492 Henry St., Brooklyn, N.Y. 11231. *Office*—*TV Guide,* 1290 Avenue of the Americas, New York, N.Y. 10104. *Agent*—Lois de la Haba, 142 Bank St., New York, N.Y. 10014.

CAREER: Passaic County Community College, Paterson, N.J., associate professor of world literature, 1972-73; free-lance writer in Philadelphia, Pa., 1973-80; *TV Guide,* New York, N.Y., editorial writer, 1980—. Fulbright professor of English at University of Concepcion, Chile, 1978-79.

WRITINGS:

UNDER NAME ROD TOWNLEY

Blue Angels Black Angels (poetry), privately printed, 1972.
(Contributor) Daniel Hoffman, editor, *University and College Poetry Prizes: 1967-1972,* Academy of American Poets, 1974.
(Contributor) Ray Boxer, editor, *Eleven Young Poets: The Smith Seventeen* (anthology), The Smith, 1975.
The Early Poetry of William Carlos Williams (criticism), Cornell University Press, 1975.
Summer Street (chapbook), The Smith, 1975.
Minor Gods (novel), St. Martin's, 1976.
Three Musicians (poetry), The Smith, 1978.
(Contributor) Carroll F. Terrell, editor, *William Carlos Williams: Man and Poet,* National Poetry Foundation, 1983.
The Year in Soaps: 1983, Crown, 1984.

OTHER

Safe and Sound: A Parent's Guide to Child Protection, Simon & Schuster, 1985.
Final Approach (poetry), Countryman Press, 1986.
(Translator) Rene Escudie, *Paul and Sebastian* (children's book), Kane/Miller Books, 1988.
(Ghostwriter) Gerald Jackson, *The Inner Executive,* Pocket Books, 1989.

Contributor to *Studies in Short Fiction, Philadelphia, New York Times, Washington Post, Village Voice, Detroit Free Press,* and other publications.

WORK IN PROGRESS: A novel; a volume of poetry.

SIDELIGHTS: Roderick Townley told *CA:* "I've found that earning a living by writing entails compromise, but that compromise has a positive side. It pulls down one's vanity, and it leads one in unexpected directions. My books are in five genres, and I hope to explore others."

* * *

TRANI, Eugene P(aul) 1939-

PERSONAL: Born November 2, 1939, in Brooklyn, N.Y.; son of Frank Joseph (a civil engineer) and Rose (Kelly) Trani; married Lois Elizabeth Quigley (a nurse anesthetist), June 2, 1962; children: Anne N., Frank J. *Education:* University of Notre Dame, B.A. (cum laude), 1961; Indiana University, M.A., 1963, Ph.D., 1966.

ADDRESSES: *Office*—Academic Affairs, University of Missouri, 5100 Rockhill Rd., Kansas City, Mo. 64110-2499.

CAREER: Ohio State University, Columbus, instructor in history, 1965-67; Southern Illinois University, Carbondale, assistant professor, 1967-71, associate professor, 1971-75, professor of history, 1975-76; University of Nebraska, Lincoln, assistant vice president for academic affairs and professor of history, 1976-80; University of Missouri—Kansas City, vice chancellor for academic affairs and professor of history, 1980—. Visiting research fellow, Princeton University, 1969-70; senior Fulbright lecturer, Moscow State University, 1981.

MEMBER: Council on Foreign Relations, American Historical Association, American Association for the Advancement of Slavic Studies, Society for Historians of American Foreign Relations, Organization of American Historians.

AWARDS, HONORS: Research and project grants from Southern Illinois University, 1967-69, 1970-72; grants from American Philosophical Society, summers, 1968 and 1972; fellow, National Historical Publications Commission, 1969-70; Younger Humanist Award, National Endowment for the Humanities, 1972-73; fellow, Woodrow Wilson International Center for Scholars; grant from Lilly Endowment, 1975-76; grant from Sloan Commission on Government in Higher Education, 1978.

WRITINGS:

(Author of notes) Charles Sawyer, *Concerns of a Conservative Democrat,* foreword by John Wesley Snyder and Dean Acheson, Southern Illinois University Press, 1968.
The Treaty of Portsmouth: An Adventure in American Diplomacy, University of Kentucky Press, 1969.
The Secretaries of the Department of the Interior: 1849-1969, National Anthropological Archives, Smithsonian Institution, 1975.
(With David L. Wilson) *The Presidency of Warren G. Harding,* University Press of Kansas, 1977.

Contributor of numerous articles to scholarly journals.

WORK IN PROGRESS: *Woodrow Wilson and Russia, 1913-1921.*

* * *

TRIGGER, Bruce G(raham) 1937-

PERSONAL: Born June 18, 1937, in Preston (now Cambridge), Ontario, Canada; son of John Wesley and Gertrude E. (Graham) Trigger; married Barbara Marian Welch, December, 1968; children: Isabel Marian, Rosalyn Theodora. *Education:* University of Toronto, B.A., 1959; Yale University, Ph.D., 1964. *Politics:* Liberal. *Religion:* None.

ADDRESSES: *Home*—3495 rue de la Montagne, Apt. 603, Montreal, Quebec H3G 2A5, Canada. *Office*—Department of Anthropology, McGill University, 855 Sherbrooke St., Montreal, Quebec H3A 2T7, Canada.

CAREER: Chief archaeologist with Pennsylvania-Yale expedition to Egypt, 1962, and Oriental Institute expedition to Sudan, 1964; Northwestern University, Evanston, Ill., assistant professor of anthropology, 1963-64; McGill University, Montreal, Quebec, 1964—, began as assistant professor, currently professor of anthropology, chairman of department, 1970-75. Leave fellow, Social Sciences and Humanities Research Council of Canada, 1983. Member of council of the Institute for American History and Culture, 1980-83, and of board of directors, McCord Museum, 1980-85.

MEMBER: American Anthropological Association (foreign fellow), Royal Anthropological Institute (fellow), Canadian Society for Archaeology Abroad, Royal Society of Canada (fellow), Sigma Xi.

AWARDS, HONORS: Canada Council fellowships, 1968, 1977; Killam research fellowships, 1971, 1990; Queen's Silver Jubilee Medal, 1977; Cornplanter Medal, 1979, for Iroquois research; Innis-Gerin Medal, Royal Society of Canada, 1985; D.Sc. (honoris causa), University of New Brunswick, 1987; John Porter Prize, Canadian Sociology and Anthropology Association, 1987.

WRITINGS:

History and Settlement in Lower Nubia, Yale University Publications in Anthropology, 1965.
The Late Nubian Settlement at Arminna West, Publications of the Pennsylvania-Yale Expedition to Egypt, Number 2, 1967.
Beyond History: The Methods of Prehistory, Holt, 1968.
The Huron: Farmers of the North, Holt, 1969.
The Meroitic Funerary Inscriptions from Arminna West, Publications of the Pennsylvania-Yale Expedition to Egypt, Number 4, 1970.
(With James F. Pendergast) *Cartier's Hochelaga and the Dawson Site,* McGill-Queen's University Press, 1972.
The Children of Aataentsic: A History of the Huron People to 1660, two volumes, McGill-Queen's University Press, 1976, 2nd edition, 1987.
Nubia under the Pharaohs, Thames & Hudson, 1976.
Time and Traditions: Essays in Archaeological Interpretation, Columbia University Press, 1978.
(Editor) *Handbook of North American Indians,* Smithsonian Institution, 1978.
Gordon Childe, Columbia University Press, 1980.
(With B. Kemp, D. O'Connor and A. Lloyd) *Ancient Egypt: A Social History,* Cambridge University Press, 1983.
Natives and Newcomers: Canada's "Heroic Age" Reconsidered, McGill-Queen's University Press, 1985.
A History of Archaeological Thought, Cambridge University Press, 1989.

WORK IN PROGRESS: Co-editing North American volume of *Cambridge History of the Native Peoples of the Americas;* beginning a major comparative study of the social organization of early civilizations.

SIDELIGHTS: Bruce G. Trigger, states M. T. Kelly in the Toronto *Globe and Mail,* "may be the best-kept secret in Canadian scholarship." Although largely unknown to the public, Trigger's *The Children of Aataentsic: A History of the Huron People to 1660,* "was a seminal work that changed forever how many people viewed the Jesuits and Hurons." "In *The Children of Aataentsic,*" writes Boyce Richardson in *Saturday Night,* "[Trigger] wrote an undoubted masterpiece, a work of such historical imagination and literary quality that Trigger deserves to rank with Harold Innis, Northrope Frye, and Marshall McLuhan—Canadian academics known abroad for their critical imaginations and honoured at home for their contributions to Canadian self-knowledge."

BIOGRAPHICAL/CRITICAL SOURCES:

PERIODICALS

American Anthropologist, April, 1969, April, 1971, August, 1973, December, 1978, September, 1979.
Globe and Mail (Toronto), December 14, 1985.
Saturday Night, July, 1986.
Times Literary Supplement, November 28, 1980, January 27, 1984.

* * *

TRUMAN, (Mary) Margaret 1924-

PERSONAL: Born February 17, 1924, in Independence, Mo.; daughter of Harry S. (the U.S. president) and Elizabeth Virginia (Wallace) Truman; married E. Clifton Daniel, Jr. (a newspaper editor), April 21, 1956; children: Clifton, William, Harrison, Thomas. *Education:* George Washington University, A.B., 1946. *Politics:* Democrat. *Religion:* Episcopalian.

ADDRESSES: Home—New York, N.Y. *Agent*—Scott Meredith, Scott Meredith Literary Agency, Inc., 845 Third Ave., New York, N.Y. 10022.

CAREER: Writer. Opera coloratura, touring nationwide and appearing on radio and television, 1947-54; host of radio program "Authors in the News," 1954-61; co-host, with Mike Wallace, of radio program "Weekday," 1955-56; host of television program "CBS International Hour," 1965; summer stock actress. Director of Riggs National Bank, Washington, D.C.; trustee of Harry S. Truman Institute at Georgetown University; secretary of Harry S. Truman Scholarship Fund.

AWARDS, HONORS: L.H.D., Wake Forest University, 1972; Litt.D., George Washington University, 1975; H.H.D., Rockhurst College, 1976.

WRITINGS:

(With Margaret Cousins) *Souvenir: Margaret Truman's Own Story,* McGraw, 1956.
White House Pets, McKay, 1969.
Harry S. Truman (Book-of-the-Month Club selection), Morrow, 1972.
Women of Courage, Morrow, 1976.
(Editor) *Letters from Father: The Truman Family's Personal Correspondence,* Arbor House, 1981.
Bess W. Truman, Macmillan, 1986.

MYSTERY NOVELS

Murder in the White House, (Book-of-the-Month Club alternate selection), Arbor House, 1980.
Murder on Capitol Hill, Arbor House, 1981.
Murder in the Supreme Court (Book-of-the-Month Club alternate selection), Arbor House, 1982.
Murder in the Smithsonian, Arbor House, 1983.
Murder on Embassy Row, Arbor House, 1984.
Murder at the FBI, Arbor House, 1985.
Murder in Georgetown, Arbor House, 1986.
Murder in the CIA, Random House, 1987.

SIDELIGHTS: When Margaret Truman published her first mystery novel in 1980, *Murder in the White House,* some observers scoffed at her. As the daughter of U.S. President Harry S. Truman, she had long been a familiar figure to the nation's news media, and had garnered a reputation as a concert singer, radio and television personality, and nonfiction writer. But her move to fiction writing was unexpected, even by her. Although she had long been a reader of mystery novels, trying her hand at writing one was accidental. Speaking to Carol Lawson of the *New York Times Book Review,* Truman explains: "I had been working on a nonfiction book—a history of White House children—but lost interest in it. I was with my agent one day . . ., and I told him I had an idea for a mystery: 'Murder in the White House.' I don't know where those words came from." Because she had unique credentials to write a mystery set in the White House, having lived there for seven years during her father's administration, her agent encouraged her to do the book. "It's a combination of the setting and my name . . . ," Lawson quotes Truman as saying about the book's appeal. "Seeing my name with this setting startles people, don't you think?"

Murder in the White House centers on the murder of Lansard Blaine, the corrupt Secretary of State, who is found strangled to death in the family quarters of the White House. Because Blaine had been a shady businessman, a powerful politican, and a womanizer, there are numerous suspects in the case. "Blaine may have been put out of business by one of these females," Chris Chase of the *Chicago Tribune* explains, "or he may have been killed by the agent of a foreign power . . ., or he may have been killed by 'someone fairly highly placed in the White House.' " The ensuing investigation of the murder exposes personal and political scandals among the First Family and their staff.

Critics were divided as to the merits of *Murder in the White House,* pointing out that Truman handled some elements of the novel better than others. William French of the Toronto *Globe and Mail* notes that "Miss Truman seems to have studied Agatha Christie on how to introduce false leads, point to the wrong suspect and generally confuse the issue. She does this with a certain amount of technical dexterity, but it's too mechanical and juiceless." Edwin J. Miller of *Best Sellers* maintains that the idea for the novel "could have made a first-rate book," but that Truman's story was only an "excellent outline." Peter Andrews of the *New York Times Book Review* claims that "a bit more thought and some rudimentary editing might have turned the book into a really interesting story. . . . All the evidence indicates that Margaret Truman is capable of doing much more interesting work than this." Reactions from the reading public were far more positive. *Murder in the White House* made the bestseller lists, was optioned for a television movie, and earned Truman over $200,000 for the paperback rights alone.

After her initial success as a mystery writer Truman settled into a one-novel-a-year writing schedule, and these subsequent mysteries have proven to be popular with readers and critics alike. In each one, she draws on her intimate knowledge of Washington and its environs, setting her mysteries in such famous locations as the CIA headquarters, the Supreme Court, the Smithsonian Institution, the U.S. Congress, and the offices of the FBI. "From reading Margaret Truman," writes Dan McCoubrey in the *Washington Post,* "one would gather that the cleaning people in Washington spend much of their time washing blood from the floors of our most noted public buildings."

Charles Champlin notes in the *Los Angeles Times Book Review* that Truman also "draws on her close knowledge of government as seen from the White House" to write her novels. And, Champlin admits, "she is very good." Her characters are bureaucrats, diplomats, and the other influential men and women who are found in Washington society, and she views them with a cynical eye. Her plots are complicated and fast-moving, while the Washington milieu is painted with precision. Jean M. White of the *Washington Post Book World* reports that Truman "writes a lively Washington scene with the sure hand of one who knows her way around the streets, institutions, restaurants, watering holes, people and politics." McCoubrey concludes: "I suspect Truman's novels of Washington will continue to entertain both mystery and Washington buffs. Even now, Give-'em-Hell Harry's daughter likely is zooming in on her next historical site."

Despite the success of her mystery novels, Truman has admitted on several occasions that she does not find writing to be a pleasant activity. "Writing," she told *CA,* "is the hardest and most exacting career I've ever had." And Truman has had several careers. For many years before she began to write, Truman was a concert singer. She debuted in 1947 on a national radio program with the Detroit Symphony Orchestra and was soon touring the nation, performing a program of operatic arias and light classics. Live concerts soon led to regular appearances on radio and television, and in 1949 she signed a recording contract with RCA-Victor Records. In 1956, while a host of the radio program "Weekday" with Mike Wallace, Truman married Clifton Daniel, an editor at the *New York Times.* Except for acting in summer stock, Truman quit her performing work at this time.

She was prompted to write her first book, *Souvenir: Margaret Truman's Own Story,* only because an unauthorized biography was in the planning stages and she wanted to head it off. *Souvenir* recounts incidents from her girlhood in Missouri, her years living in the White House as the president's only child, and her successful career as a concert singer. N. L. Browning of the *Chicago Sunday Tribune* calls the book "a fascinating chronicle. . . . It projects the simple dignity, warmth, and genuine modesty of a plain, unaffected midwest girl." Ishbel Ross of the *New York Herald Tribune Book Review* finds *Souvenir* to be "a gracefully written tale of an average American girl drawn by chance into the White House."

After the success of *Souvenir* in 1956, Truman did not write another book until 1969, when her *White House Pets,* a far less ambitious work, enjoyed some popularity with readers. But in 1972 Truman completed a project she had long wanted to do, a biography of her father. Her biography, published as *Harry S. Truman,* provides a behind-the-scenes look at Harry Truman as president and family man, revealing his personal side in a way no other biography could do. In her review for the *Christian Science Monitor,* Pamela Marsh explains that in this book, the former president is "shown through the eyes of a deeply loving, loyal daughter" who "can give what no one else can, a closeup of an undramatic man dramatically thrust into awesome power—and coping with it." Vera Glaser of the *Akron Beacon Journal* calls the book "a warm memoir based on her father's personal papers and [Margaret Truman's] own recollections." While disagreeing with some of the book's partisan judgments about Truman and his administration, Wilson C. McWilliams of the *New York Times Book Review* sees value in the portrait it gives of Truman. He finds that "it is the personal, familial side of [Truman's] biography that makes it valuable. . . . Every anecdote adds human dimension to the Trumans as a family and to Harry as a man." The book has sold well over one million copies and was a selection of a major book club.

In 1986 Truman followed up her success by publishing a biography of her mother, entitled *Bess W. Truman,* a book considered by several critics to be of special interest for its intimate portrait of the president's wife. Because her mother preferred to burn her correspondence rather than let historians read it, little is known of Bess Truman's private thoughts and emotions. Her daughter's biography is one of the few personal accounts available. It is, according to Helen Thomas of the *New York Times Book Review,* "a refreshing, real and touching biography." Similarly, the critic for *Time* terms the book "a gentle, warmhearted biography." A. L. Yarnell of *Choice* calls *Bess W. Truman* "the most revealing view of the personal side of the Truman relationship now available."

Although White maintains that Truman "has proved herself to be a competent professional writer of mysteries" and both her mystery novels and biographies have been bestsellers, Truman is nonetheless still uneasy about the writing life. "I am always glad," she told *CA,* "when a book or a magazine article is finished. I promise myself never to write another one, but I shall probably do one."

MEDIA ADAPTATIONS: Film rights to *Murder in the White House* have been sold to Dick Clark Cinema Productions.

BIOGRAPHICAL/CRITICAL SOURCES:

BOOKS

Truman, Margaret, *Souvenir: Margaret Truman's Own Story,* McGraw, 1956.

PERIODICALS

Akron Beacon Journal, March 3, 1974.
Armchair Detective, spring, 1986.
Best Sellers, July, 1980.
Biography News, April, 1974.
Chicago Sunday Tribune, May 27, 1956.
Chicago Tribune, July 6, 1980.
Chicago Tribune Book World, June 21, 1981.
Choice, September, 1986.
Christian Science Monitor, January 3, 1973.
Globe and Mail (Toronto), June 26, 1980.
Los Angeles Times Book Review, November 1, 1987.
New York Herald Tribune Book Review, May 20, 1956.
New York Times, April 24, 1980, June 24, 1983.
New York Times Book Review, December 24, 1972, July 20, 1980, August 17, 1980, April 13, 1986.
People, June 16, 1980.
Time, May 19, 1986.
Washington Post, June 27, 1983.
Washington Post Book World, July 19, 1981, August 18, 1985, November 15, 1987.

—Sketch by Thomas Wiloch

* * *

TURNER, Clay
See BALLARD, (Willis) Todhunter

* * *

TUTOROW, Norman E. 1934-

PERSONAL: Born July 23, 1934, in Mishawaka, Ind.; son of Virgil Walter (a mechanic) and Violet Evelyn (Chadwick) Tutorow; married Sue Carol Fanning (a secretary), November 25, 1954 (marriage ended); children: James Andrew. *Education:* San Diego State College (now University), A.B. (with high honors), 1958; Stanford University, M.A., 1960, Ph.D., 1967, M.A., 1983; San Jose State College (now University), M.A., 1965.

ADDRESSES: Home—50 Adair Lane, Portola Valley, Calif. 94025.

CAREER: Instructor in philosophy, West Valley Junior College, Campbell, Calif., and Foothill Junior College, Los Altos Hill, Calif., 1964-67; San Jose State College (now University), San Jose, Calif., instructor in history, 1964-67; University of Santa Clara, Santa Clara, Calif., assistant professor of history, 1967-69; Los Angeles Federal Records Center, Bell, Calif., chief of the archives branch, 1969-70; Tutorow Estate Agents (formerly Golden State Realty), Los Altos, Calif., founder, owner and real estate broker, beginning 1970; Anthony School, Menlo Park, Calif., instructor in real estate, 1973-78; Foothill Junior College, instructor in real estate economics, 1973-78. Consultant, San Francisco Federal Records Center, 1970-71. *Military service:* U.S. Marine Corps, 1952-55; became sergeant.

MEMBER: American Historical Association, Organization of American Historians, Society of American Archivists, National Association of Real Estate Brokers, California Historical Society, Southern California Historical Society, California Association of Real Estate Teachers.

WRITINGS:

(With Don E. Fehrenbacher) *California: An Illustrated History,* Van Nostrand, 1968.
The Early Years of Leland Stanford, New Yorker Who Built the Central Pacific Railroad (pamphlet), Dewitt Historical Society of Tomkins County (New York), 1969.
Leland Stanford: Man of Many Careers, Pacific Coast Publishers, 1970.
Texas Annexation and the Mexican War: A Political Study of the Old Northwest, Chadwick House, 1978.
The Mexican-American War: An Annotated Bibliography, Greenwood Press, 1981.
War Crimes, War Criminals, and War Crimes Trials: An Annotated Bibliography, Greenwood Press, 1985.

Contributor to periodicals, including *Picturescope, Wisconsin Then and Now,* and *Quarterly Review.**

U

UBLE, T(homas) R(alph) O(bermeyer) 1931-

PERSONAL: Surname rhymes with "bubble"; born January 1, 1931, in White Plains, N.Y.; son of William Obermeyer Edward and Beatrice (Hasty) Uble; married Iris Nancyann Rush, October, 1955; children: Mortimer R. *Education:* Attended Academy of Data Processing, 1951-52; Seyburn Institute of Technology, B.S., 1953.

ADDRESSES: Home and office—9568 Columbia, Redford, Mich. 48239.

CAREER: Radical Techniques, Inc., Revere, Mich., head of key punch department, 1954-55; Soft Wear Unlimited, Upsala, Mich., head programmer, 1955-63; New Day Co., Sylvanopolis, Mich., manager of computer composition department, 1963-64, vice-president, 1964-67, president, 1967-82; Uble Systems, Redford, Mich., president, 1982—. Publisher, Uble Books, 1987—. McGill County Community College, Upsala, instructor, 1962-73, head of graphics department, 1974-86.

WRITINGS:

Symbolic Ambience in the Automation Approach, Fairweather, 1959.

Facilitating the Understanding of Human Behavior in Relation to Computer Dynamics, New Day, 1963.

How to Be Responsive to Change in Methods, Goals, Points of View, New Day, 1964.

Applying Computer Techniques to Publishing, New Day, 1966.

Eliminating the Human Factor, New Day, 1967.

The Struggle to Oblivion, Pap Press, 1970.

Grow with Your Computer, New Day, 1972.

About Face!: Interfacing with Students, New Day, 1973.

Everything but the Tool Crib, McGill County Community College Press, 1973, revised edition, New Day, 1984.

Running on Overdrive (collection of newspaper columns), New Day, 1981.

Computers Are Our Friends (elementary textbook), New Day, 1986.

All My Friends Have Computers (humorous sketches), Uble Press, 1989.

Columnist, *Sylvanopolis Herald,* 1974-83. Contributor to *High Tech Directions.*

WORK IN PROGRESS: Computer Foods.

SIDELIGHTS: T. R. O. Uble wrote *CA:* "I am currently researching ways that computers can be used to create formulas and recipes for new (and nutritious) foods."

* * *

UHNAK, Dorothy 1933-

PERSONAL: Born in 1933, in Bronx, N.Y.; married Tony Uhnak (an electrical engineer), 1950; children: Tracy. *Education:* Attended City College (now of the City University of New York); John Jay College of Criminal Justice of the City University of New York, B.S., 1968.

ADDRESSES: Home—37 Nostrand Parkway, Shelter Island, N.Y. 11964. *Office*—c/o Simon & Schuster, 1230 Avenue of the Americas, New York, N.Y. 10020.

CAREER: New York City Transit Police, New York, N.Y., policewoman, 1953-55, detective second grade, 1955-67; full-time writer, 1967—. Former counselor-group leader for Rivington Street settlement house, Family Welfare Shelter, and an East Bronx settlement house.

AWARDS, HONORS: Outstanding Police Duty Medal, New York City Transit Police, 1955, for heroism above and beyond the call of duty; Edgar Award for best first mystery, Mystery Writers of America, 1968, for *The Bait;* Leonard Reisman Award for Achievement, John Jay College of Justice of the City University of New York, 1968; La grande Prix de la litterature policiere, 1970, for *The Ledger.*

WRITINGS:

Policewoman: A Young Woman's Initiation into the Realities of Justice (semi-autobiographical), Simon & Schuster, 1964.

The Bait (novel), Simon & Schuster, 1968.

The Witness (novel), Simon & Schuster, 1969.

The Ledger (novel), Simon & Schuster, 1970.

Law and Order (novel; Literary Guild selection), Simon & Schuster, 1973.

The Investigation (novel; Literary Guild selection), Simon & Schuster, 1977.

False Witness (novel; Literary Guild selection), Simon & Schuster, 1981.

Victims (novel; Literary Guild selection), Simon & Schuster, 1985.

WORK IN PROGRESS: Secrets and Mysteries, a generational novel.

SIDELIGHTS: "The one quality of [crime novelist Dorothy] Uhnak's writing that has consistently caught the attention of critics and reviewers is her faithful portrayal of the reality of the police world, based upon her own experiences as a policewoman," notes Jane S. Bakerman in *And Then There Were Nine . . .: More Women of Mystery.* "Almost invariably, any review of her [work] . . . will remark on her fourteen years of experience in the New York Police Department," the critic adds, during which time she was awarded two citations for bravery. Uhnak began publishing with a nonfiction account of her years as a policewoman, and shortly after quit her job due to sex discrimination—a circumstance which is reflected in the experiences of *Victims* protagonist Miranda Torres. Uhnak then wrote *The Bait,* which earned her an Edgar Award for best first novel. Introducing Detective Second-Grade Christie Opara, *The Bait* is "the first true American policewoman-procedural novel, and a highly enjoyable one," claims a *New York Times Book Review* contributor. Uhnak followed with two more novels featuring the complex detective, but instead of continuing with the character and perpetuating a formula, she changed course with *Law and Order,* which became a best seller. An intergenerational saga of New York City policemen, *Law and Order* "skillfully evokes the passage of cultural history, as generational attitudes change and clash," comments *New York Times* writer Christopher Lehmann-Haupt.

Uhnak stirred controversy with her next best-selling novel, *The Investigation,* whose basic situation closely mirrors that of the 1965 Alice Crimmins case, where a young mother was accused of murdering her two children. The similarities between the novel and reality have led some critics to accuse the author of appropriating material; Uhnak, however, has told *CA* that she "did not research anything about Alice Crimmins; there is absolutely no single person in *The Investigation* based on any real person." The author explains: "I took the voice of a male investigator, Joe Peters, and as a writer (and as an experienced police investigator) I took the case, step by step, through my fictional story, in a logical direction. I was later told by people 'in the know' that many of my created characters and situations had counterparts in reality. This didn't surprise me, since I proceeded logically as a writer and certain areas would almost have to parallel reality." And critics, while noting these parallels, stress that *The Investigation* works well as a story in itself; *New York Times Book Review* contributor Barbara Gelb, for example, instructs the reader to "ignore the story's derivation and suppress curiosity about what is real and what is invented, and [there] is a well-plotted whodunit, adequately mystifying, that at times achieves the fashionably tough, cynical flavor of Hammett or Chandler for which it seems to strive." The *New York Times*'s John Leonard similarly observes that Uhnak's characters are "credible," as is the investigation itself, "in grubby detail, with all the politicking in the Police Department and the District Attorney's office."

Law and Order and *The Investigation* have both been popular successes, and *False Witness,* "virtually perfect in plot and pace and tone, should complete the hat-trick," states Eliot Fremont-Smith in the *Village Voice.* "The book opens with a crisply written scene of pure horror," describes the *Washington Post*'s Joseph McLellan, "just after the attempted murder" of Sanderalee Dawson, a famous black television star who has been brutally raped and mutilated. "If you can get past that [opening] paragraph," asserts McLellan, "it's hard to stop reading the rest of the book, up to the point where it ends with a simple, logical and finely prepared last twist of the plot that completely changes its perspective. It is all managed not only with finesse but with a kind of technical integrity too rare in popular fiction today," the critic adds. While this opening scene is graphic—it features the victim's severed hand—Uhnak "has a very sound reason for that added gory detail," claims Lehmann-Haupt. "In fact, there's a sound reason for every detail in the novel. . . . Especially the novel's title, because throughout your reading of the book you keep asking yourself who the 'false witness' can possibly be, as the list of candidates keeps growing and shifting."

In addition, Fremont-Smith observes that Uhnak "has become a master of momentum . . . and here she deftly interweaves the necessaries with ongoing investigation and foreshadowing of what's to come, which produces a ripple effect." While Lehmann-Haupt comments that *False Witness* "is primarily an entertainment—in this case a whodunit thriller that works so well that it's even surprising to learn who the suspect is," Uhnak's novel also "achieves greater intensity than she has ever done before." The critic explains that this is primarily due to the author's "clever plotting" in addition to "the ethnic mix of her characters and the extremes of conflict among them." Because the victim is a black woman with ties to the PLO, and the suspects include a prominent Jewish surgeon, "*False Witness* isn't simply a police procedural, but a political procedural as well," states Fremont-Smith. Walter Clemons similarly maintains in *Newsweek* that while the novel has too many "gimmicks, . . . the best thing in her book is the intrusion of political issues into the usually hermetic world of the murder novel." "In fact, it's tempting to call 'False Witness' a lesson in nonstereotype thinking," Lehmann-Haupt states, except that "the novel's main concern is not to teach any lessons, but instead to keep you absorbed and entertained until its very last paragraph and sentence. This," the critic concludes, *False Witness* "does most successfully."

"Everything that takes place in a Uhnak novel results from pictures of believable characters who become real people as they wrestle with troubles and dilemmas," claims Philip I. Mitterling in the *Journal of Popular Culture,* "articulating their attitudes and beliefs in thoughts and words, behaving in certain ways and interrelating in a mosaic of dramatic, fast-moving, crisply-described, often vivid scenes. Her books are not the product of narrative abundance," the critic continues, "but rather collections of scenes." Bakerman concurs, stating that "undoubtedly, one reason for [Uhnak's] varied approach is that her interest is not primarily detection or mystery, but people, who must be considered as human beings apart from the crimes they commit or those committed against them." In addition, Mitterling asserts, "the popularity of [Uhnak's] books rests on her characterizations of the perplexities of police work and her depiction of justice and morality. . . . [She presents] convincing pictures of a social environment stained by corruption and of police officers who know life cannot be lived within the boundaries of justice. . . . In this way," the critic concludes, "Dorothy Uhnak has become an authentic writer in the minds of her readers."

MEDIA ADAPTATIONS: Uhnak's novels about policewoman Christie Opara were the basis for the ABC television series, "Get Christy Love," broadcast during the 1974-1975 season; *Law and Order* was made into a movie and broadcast on NBC in 1975; *The Investigation* was broadcast by CBS in 1987 as "Kojak: The Price of Justice"; *False Witness* is being produced for NBC by New World Television Productions.

AVOCATIONAL INTERESTS: Animal rescue/welfare, study of political systems, study of complexity of drug traffic.

BIOGRAPHICAL/CRITICAL SOURCES:

BOOKS

Authors in the News, Volume 1, Gale, 1976.

Bakerman, Jane S., *And Then There Were Nine . . .: More Women of Mystery,* Bowling Green State University Popular Press, 1985.

Budd, Elaine, *Thirteen Mistresses of Murder,* Ungar, 1986.

PERIODICALS

Akron Beacon Journal, April 29, 1973.

Globe and Mail (Toronto), August 16, 1986.

Journal of Popular Culture, summer, 1982.

Newsweek, August 22, 1977, August 10, 1981.

New York Times, May 4, 1973, August 1, 1977.

New York Times Book Review, April 28, 1968, May 27, 1973, August 21, 1977, October 25, 1981, February 23, 1986.

Village Voice, July 22, 1981.

Washington Post, August 14, 1981, May 6, 1986.

—*Sketch by Diane Telgen*

* * *

UNGAR, Sanford J. 1945-

PERSONAL: Born June 10, 1945, in Wilkes-Barre, Pa.; son of Max H. (a businessman) and Tillie (Landau) Ungar; married Beth L. Pollock (a physician), November 1, 1969; children: Lida, Philip Samuel. *Education:* Harvard University, A.B., (magna cum laude), 1966; London School of Economics and Political Science, University of London, M.Sc., 1967.

ADDRESSES: Home—3753 Jenifer St. N.W., Washington, D.C. 20015. *Office*—309 Mary Graydon Center, American University, 4400 Massachusetts Ave. N.W., Washington, D.C. 20016. *Agent*—Robert Lescher, 67 Irving Pl., New York, N.Y. 10003.

CAREER: Boston Globe, Cambridge, Mass., stringer, 1964-66; *Time,* London, England, stringer, 1966-67; United Press International, Paris, France, correspondent, 1967-69; *Newsweek,* Nairobi, Kenya, correspondent, 1969; *Washington Post,* Washington, D.C., staff writer, 1969-73; Adlai Stevenson Institute of International Affairs, Chicago, Ill., resident fellow, 1973-74; *Atlantic,* Washington, D.C., Washington editor, 1975-77; *Foreign Policy,* Washington, D.C., managing editor, 1977-80; National Public Radio, Washington, D.C., host of "Communique," 1979-82, "All Things Considered," 1980-82, and "NPR Dateline," 1983; Carnegie Endowment for International Peace, Washington, D.C., 1983-85, began as resident associate, became senior associate; American University, Washington, D.C., dean of School of Communications, 1986—. Has appeared on television, including program "What This Country Needs," WTTW-TV (Chicago), 1982, and in public affairs programming on public television WETA-TV (Washington, D.C.); has also appeared in foreign radio and television productions. Visiting reporter, *Argus* newspapers of South Africa, 1967; feature and editorial writer, *Daily Nation,* Kenya, 1969. Member of board of trustees, National Humanities Faculty, Concord, Mass. Consultant, "Closeup" segment on J. Edgar Hoover and the FBI, American Broadcasting Corp. News, 1982.

MEMBER: International Institute of Strategic Studies, International Human Rights Law Group (member of board), National Humanities Faculty, National Press Club, Society of Professional Journalists, French-American Foundation, Council on Foreign Relations, Overseas Development Council (member of national council), South-North News Service (board member), African Studies Association, American Friends of the London School of Economics, Authors Guild, Authors League of America, Washington Independent Writers, Washington Press Club, Harvard Club of Washington (member of schools and scholarship committee).

AWARDS, HONORS: Certificate of merit, American Bar Association, 1972, for *Washington Post* coverage of May Day activities; George Polk Memorial Award, 1973, for *The Papers and the Papers;* American Association of University Women award, 1982, for work on "All Things Considered"; Emmy award, 1983, for work on television documentary "What This Country Needs."

WRITINGS:

(With Allan Priaulx) *The Almost Revolution: France, 1968,* Dell, 1969.

The Papers and the Papers: An Account of the Legal and Political Battle over the Pentagon Papers, Dutton, 1972, revised edition, Columbia University Press, 1989.

FBI: An Uncensored Look behind the Walls, Little, Brown, 1976.

(Editor and author of introduction) *Estrangement: America and the World,* Oxford University Press, 1985.

Africa: The People and Politics of an Emerging Continent, Simon & Schuster, 1985, 3rd revised edition, 1989.

CONTRIBUTOR

(With Robert L. Heilbroner, Morton Mintz, and others) *In the Name of Profit: Profiles in Corporate Irresponsibility,* Doubleday, 1972.

Richard Pollak, editor, *Stop the Presses, I Want to Get Off!,* Random House, 1975.

Great Decisions 1980, Foreign Policy Association, 1980.

Great Decisions 1981, Foreign Policy Association, 1981.

John Barratt and Alfred O. Hero, Jr., editors, *The American People and South Africa,* Lexington Books, 1981.

Great Decisions 1982, Foreign Policy Association, 1982.

Wayne S. Smith and Esteban Morales Dominguez, editors, *Subject to Solution: Problems in Cuban-U.S. Relations,* Lynne Rienner Publishers, 1988.

OTHER

Contributor of articles to magazines and newspapers, including *New Republic, Newsweek, Saturday Review, U.S. News and World Report, Harvard Review, Washington Post,* and *Boston Globe.* Special correspondent, *Economist,* 1973-86; contributing editor, *Atlantic,* 1977—.

WORK IN PROGRESS: A book on immigration for Simon & Schuster.

SIDELIGHTS: Sanford J. Ungar's *Africa: The People and Politics of an Emerging Continent,* states Xan Smiley in the *New York Times Book Review,* is a "thoughtful safari through sub-Saharan Africa [and] is a valuable contribution to the library of contemporary writing on the most misunderstood of continents. It is dead accurate and sympathetic to the plight of Africa without being too prim or pious." Ungar "approaches a difficult subject—the political, social and economic problems of a generally non-understood continent—," says *Washington Post Book World* reviewer Jerry Funk, "in ways that are entertaining as well as thoughtful." Ungar's book, Funk concludes, "should be required reading for all would-be Africanists and will be a stimulating review for 'old Africa hands.' "

BIOGRAPHICAL/CRITICAL SOURCES:

PERIODICALS

Los Angeles Times Book Review, September 29, 1985.
New York Times Book Review, September 1, 1985, December 22, 1985.
Times Literary Supplement, November 14, 1986.
Washington Post Book World, September 8, 1985, January 12, 1986.

* * *

UPTON, Robert

PERSONAL: Born in Chicago, Ill.; married wife, Patricia; children: Kathleen, Jeffrey. *Education:* Attended Florida State University, Northwestern University, Yale University, and University of San Francisco.

ADDRESSES: Home—419 West 22nd St., New York, N.Y. 10011.

CAREER: Novelist and author of screenplays and musicals. *Military service:* U.S. Army.

AWARDS, HONORS: LL.B., Stetson University, 1962.

WRITINGS:

Who'd Want to Kill Old George?, Putnam, 1977.
A Golden Fleecing, St. Martin's, 1979.
Fade Out, Viking, 1984.
Dead on the Stick, Viking, 1985.
The Faberge Egg, Dutton, 1988.
The Flaming Man, Dutton, 1990.

Also author of plays, screenplays, and musicals, including "Ambassador," a musical based on *The Ambassadors* by Henry James.

SIDELIGHTS: Robert Upton's tough, hard-drinking private eye Amos McGuffin makes his third appearance in the mystery novel *Dead on the Stick,* which takes place in the vicinity of an exclusive club in the Bahamas. Newgate Callendar notes in the *New York Times Book Review* that "Mr. Upton has a good time sticking pins with malicious intent into the hides of the cynical, manipulative upper crust of American society." He concludes that *Dead on the Stick* "is a well-worked-out, snappily written and often irreverent mystery novel."

BIOGRAPHICAL/CRITICAL SOURCES:

PERIODICALS

New York Times Book Review, August 10, 1986.

* * *

URBAN, Michael E(dward) 1947-

PERSONAL: Born May 28, 1947, in Los Angeles, Calif.; son of Edward Leonard (a truck driver) and Rose Kiska Urban; married Veronica Joan McGill, April 28, 1971; children: Emily, George, Michael. *Education:* Seattle University, B.A., 1969; University of Alberta, M.A., 1972; University of Kansas, Ph.D., 1976.

ADDRESSES: Home—369 Payne St., Auburn, Ala. 36830. *Office*—Department of Political Science, Auburn University, Auburn, Ala. 36849.

CAREER: University of Montana, Missoula, assistant professor of political science and public administration, 1976-78; State University of New York College at Oswego, assistant professor of political science, Soviet politics, and public administration, 1978-82; Auburn University, Auburn, Ala., assistant professor, 1982-84, associate professor, 1984-89, professor of political science and Soviet and East European politics, 1989—. Vice-president of United University Professions, 1980-82.

MEMBER: American Political Science Association, American Association for the Advancement of Slavic Studies, Southern Political Science Association.

AWARDS, HONORS: Fellow of International Research and Exchanges Board in Moscow, U.S.S.R., 1979-80, and 1988; National Science Foundation research grant, 1987-88.

WRITINGS:

The Ideology of Administration: American and Soviet Cases, State University of New York Press, 1982.
An Algebra of Soviet Power, Cambridge University Press, 1989.
More Power to the Soviets, Edward Elgar Publishing, 1990.

Contributor to political science journals.

SIDELIGHTS: Michael E. Urban commented to *CA:* "I am researching political reform and democratization in the U.S.S.R. from the point of view of a transition from weak to strong structures in the Soviet order. Politically, this process seems to involve the transfer of power from the apparatus of the Communist Party to the organs of representative government, the Soviets—at all levels in the system—and the development of democratic processes, such as competitive nominations and elections, and freedom of speech, press, and assembly, in order to infuse these institutions with a popular content and real authority. As the architects of the reform understand the matter, these changes are essential to the project of transforming a system in which power is used by small groups of administrators in irresponsible ways, with the result that enormous waste and social harm are regularly incurred, to one in which decision making becomes publicly accountable and power is contained within effective legal forms. Having studied the first major phase of this transition . . . I am convinced that Soviet society has indeed embarked upon the long and arduous road of the radical reform known as *perestroika.*"

V

VANDERSEE, Charles (Andrew) 1938-

PERSONAL: Born March 25, 1938, in Gary, Ind.; son of Harvey F. and Louise (Bauer) Vandersee. *Education:* Valparaiso University, B.A., 1960; University of California, Los Angeles, M.A., 1961, Ph.D., 1964. *Religion:* Lutheran.

ADDRESSES: Office—205 Garrett Hall, University of Virginia, Charlottesville, Va. 22903.

CAREER: University of Virginia, Charlottesville, assistant professor, 1964-70, associate professor of English, 1970—, assistant dean of College of Arts and Sciences, 1970—, director of Echols Scholars Program, 1973—.

MEMBER: Modern Language Association of America, Society for Values in Higher Education, Raven Society, Omicron Delta Kappa.

AWARDS, HONORS: Danforth fellowship, 1960; Woodrow Wilson fellowship, 1960; Bruern fellow in American literature, University of Leeds, 1968-69; American Council of Learned Societies fellowship, 1972-73; National Endowment for the Humanities editorial project grant, 1977-86; Bayly Museum poetry prize, 1988; Coolidge research colloquium, 1988; James Bass Award, Southern Humanities Council, 1989.

WRITINGS:

(Editor) John Hay, *The Bread-Winners,* College & University Press, 1973.

(Author of introduction) *The Henry Adams Papers* (microedition), Massachusetts Historical Society, 1979.

(Editor with J. C. Levenson, Ernest Samuels, and Viola Hopkins Winner) *The Letters of Henry Adams,* Harvard University Press, Volumes 1-3: *1858-1892,* 1982, Volumes 4-6: *1892-1918,* 1988.

Columnist for *Cresset,* 1969-72, 1982—. Contributor of articles, notes, and reviews to numerous periodicals, including *Resources for American Literary Study, South Atlantic Review, American Speech, American Literary Realism, South Atlantic Quarterly, American Quarterly, Shakespeare Survey, Journal of American Studies, Papers on Language and Literature,* and *Studies in Bibliography;* contributor of poetry to *Georgia Review, Southern Poetry Review, Sewanee Review, Poetry, Ironwood, American Poetry Review, Iris, Poetry East, Boundary 2, Poetry Northwest, Writer's Eye,* and other publications.

VanGUNDY, Arthur B(oice), Jr. 1946-

PERSONAL: Born May 24, 1946, in Lancaster, Ohio; son of Arthur B. (a physician) and Sarajane (Miesse) VanGundy; married Denilyn Wilson, June 20, 1971; children: Sarah E., Laura S. *Education:* Ohio Wesleyan University, B.A., 1968; Miami University, M.S., 1970; Ohio State University, Ph.D., 1975.

ADDRESSES: Home—2328 Houston Ave., Norman, Okla. 73071. *Office*—Communication Department, University of Oklahoma, Norman, Okla. 73019.

CAREER: Capital University, Columbus, Ohio, director of housing, 1970-72; civilian organization development consultant to U.S. Air Force, 1975; University of Oklahoma, Norman, assistant professor, 1976-82, associate professor of human relations, 1982-86, chairperson of department, 1982-87, professor of communication, 1987—.

MEMBER: Product Development and Management Association, American Society for Training and Development.

WRITINGS:

Techniques of Structured Problem Solving, Van Nostrand, 1981, 2nd edition, 1988.

Training Your Creative Mind, Prentice-Hall, 1982.

One Hundred Eight Ways to Get a Bright Idea, Prentice-Hall, 1983.

Managing Group Creativity, American Management Association, 1984.

Creative Problem Solving: A Guide for Trainers and Management, Quorum Books, 1987.

Stalking the Wild Solution: A Problem Finding Approach to Creative Problem Solving, Bearly, 1988.

WORK IN PROGRESS: Designing and Facilitating Problem Solving Groups.

SIDELIGHTS: Arthur B. VanGundy, Jr., told *CA:* "I write for the challenge of producing something that begins as an ill-defined concept. Writing also helps me educate myself. It is possible to learn much more from writing than from reading alone.

"My focus on creativity and problem-solving stems from my concern that too many people suppress their native creative and problem-solving abilities. Society has conditioned many of us to believe that we either are creative or we are not. In fact, we all are creative to the degree that we have been able to develop our creative potential. However, most societal rewards stem from logical thinking. As a result, we may both consciously and unconsciously believe that we were handed a given unit of creativity that cannot be improved upon. Our educational system, for example, stresses the scientific method and rewards those who can think logically and scientifically. The tragedy is that science also requires creative thinking, but it is not always allowed to bloom.

"Our society requires both logical *and* creative thinking. This also is true of the sexes, although the creativity of women is not suppressed as much as that of men, since we perpetuate the myth that it is acceptable for women to be creative. From a historical perspective, women have always been given greater cultural rein in expressing their creativity. Although things have begun to change, we still have a long way to go. Creativity is neither feminine nor masculine; it is a basic human trait.

"To awaken our innate creative potentials we need to start with our educational systems—from preschool on up to higher education. Problem-solving as a genetic skill needs to be incorporated into the curriculum. And, the 'gifted' programs we now offer should be expanded to include all students. Each individual also bears some responsibility for the development of his or her own creativity. By reading, workshops, and practice, we can all do a lot to increase our creative potentials. All it takes is the motivation to try."

AVOCATIONAL INTERESTS: Travel (Europe and the Pacific), jogging, bicycling, swimming.

* * *

VERNANT, Jean-Pierre 1914-

PERSONAL: Born January 4, 1914, in Provins, France; son of Jean (a journalist) and Anna (Heilbron) Vernant; married Lida Nahimovitch (a professor), November 30, 1939; children: Claude. *Education:* Sorbonne, University of Paris, agrege de philosophie, 1937.

ADDRESSES: Home—112 Grand-Rue, 92310 Sevres, France. *Office*—Department of Ancient Religions, College de France, 11 Place Marcelin, Berthelot, 75005 Paris, France.

CAREER: In charge of research at Centre National de la Recherche Scientifique, 1948-57; director of studies at Ecole Pratique des Hautes-Etudes, 1957-75; College de France, Paris, professor of the comparative study of ancient religions, 1975-84, honorary professor, 1984—. *Military service:* French Army, 1937-45, served in infantry; became lieutenant colonel; received Croix de Guerre and Croix de la Liberation, was made officer of French Legion of Honor.

MEMBER: Academie Royale de Belgique (associe).

AWARDS, HONORS: Honorary doctorates from University of Chicago, 1979, and University of Bristol, 1987.

WRITINGS:

Les Origines de la pensee greque, Presses Universitaires de France, 1962, 6th edition, 1988, translation published as *The Origins of Greek Thought,* Cornell University Press, 1982.

Mythe et pensee chez les grecs: Etudes de psychologie historique, Maspero (Paris), 1965, 10th edition, 1985, translation by Janet Lloyd published as *Myth and Thought among the Greeks,* Routledge & Kegan Paul.

(Editor) *Problemes de la guerre en Grece ancienne* (title means "Problems of War in Ancient Greece"), La Haye, Mouton & Co., 1968, 2nd edition, 1985.

(Author of introduction) Marcel Detienne, *Les Jardins d'Adonis* (title means "The Gardens of Adonis"), Gallimard, 1972.

(With Pierre Vidal-Naquet) *Mythe et tragedie en Grece ancienne,* Maspero, 1972, 6th edition, 1986, translation by Lloyd published as *Tragedy and Myth in Ancient Greece,* Harvester Press, 1981.

Mythe et societe en Grece ancienne, Maspero, 1974, 3rd edition, 1981, translation by Lloyd published as *Myth and Society in Ancient Greece,* Harvester Press, 1980, Methuen, 1982.

(With Detienne) *Les Ruses de l'intelligence: La Metis des grecs,* Flammarion, 1974, 2nd edition, 1978, translation by Lloyd published as *Cunning Intelligence in Greek Culture and Society,* Humanities, 1978.

(Contributor) *Divination et rationalite* (title means "Divination and Rationality"), Seuil, 1974.

La Cuisine du sacrifice en pays grec, Gallimard, 1979, 2nd edition, 1983.

Religions, histoires, raisons (title means "Religion, History, Reason"), Maspero, 1979.

(With Gherardo Gnoli) *La Mort, les morts dans les societes anciennes,* Cambridge University Press, 1982.

La Mort dans les yeux, Hachette, 1985, 2nd edition, 1986.

(With Vidal-Naquet) *Mythe et tragedie deux,* Decouverte, 1986.

(With Charles Malamoud) *Corps des dieux,* Gallimard, 1986.

(With Vidal-Naquet) *Oedipe et ses mythes,* Complexe, 1988.

(With Vidal-Naquet) *Travail et esclavage en Grece ancienne,* Complexe, 1988.

L'Individo, la mort, l'amour, Gallimard, 1989.

SIDELIGHTS: Jean-Pierre Vernant told *CA:* "My work tries to be a contribution to the foundation of a historical anthropology of ancient Greece." About the body of Vernant's work, Charles Segal notes in *Arethusa* that "one is struck by the coherence and the logical progression of his thought, his feeling for the integral relation between literature and society, language and social institutions." Segal admires the writer's depth of study and concludes that "Vernant's work is of seminal importance."

Myth and Society in Ancient Greece, a collection of Vernant's essays, illustrates the relationship between myth and societal institutions in ancient Greek culture. According to John Gould in a *Times Literary Supplement* review, the essays analyze myths comparatively, "refer[ring] the logic of the myth to a network of related concepts which makes up the 'deep structure' of ancient Greek thinking about the social nature of man." Gould judges Vernant's book to be "an important work, of rare intelligence, stimulating and discerning."

BIOGRAPHICAL/CRITICAL SOURCES:

PERIODICALS

Arethusa, spring, 1982, fall, 1982.

Times Literary Supplement, August 22, 1980, October 29, 1982, November 12, 1982, September 26, 1986.

* * *

VIGNA, Judith 1936-

PERSONAL: Surname is pronounced *Veen*-ya; born April 27, 1936, in Gedney, England; came to the United States in 1958; naturalized citizen, 1968; daughter of Audrey Brackenridge; married Arnaldo Vigna, December, 1960 (divorced). *Education:* Attended St. Martin's School of Art, 1956, School of Visual Arts, 1960, and Queens College of the City University of New York.

ADDRESSES: Home—Whitestone, N.Y. *Agent*—Curtis Brown Ltd., 10 Astor Place, New York, N.Y. 10003.

CAREER: Lincolnshire Standard, Boston, England, journalist and artist, 1953-55; Dorville House, London, England, public relations assistant, 1955-57; Henry Morgan Co., Montreal, Quebec, advertising copywriter, 1957-58; Young & Rubicam, Inc., New York, N.Y., copywriter, 1958-65; free-lance writer and illustrator, 1965—.

MEMBER: Authors Guild, PEN.

AWARDS, HONORS: 1987 Jane Addams Children's Book Award for *Nobody Wants a Nuclear War.*

WRITINGS:

JUVENILES; SELF-ILLUSTRATED

Gregory's Stitches, Albert Whitman, 1974.
The Little Boy Who Loved Dirt and Almost Became a Superslob, Albert Whitman, 1975.
Couldn't We Have a Turtle Instead?, Albert Whitman, 1975.
Everyone Goes as a Pumpkin, Albert Whitman, 1977.
Anyhow, I'm Glad I Tried, Albert Whitman, 1978.
The Hiding House, Albert Whitman, 1979.
She's Not My Real Mother, Albert Whitman, 1980.
Daddy's New Baby, Albert Whitman, 1982.
Grandma Without Me, Albert Whitman, 1984.
Nobody Wants a Nuclear War, Albert Whitman, 1986.
Mommy and Me by Ourselves Again, Albert Whitman, 1987.
I Wish Daddy Didn't Drink So Much, Albert Whitman, 1988.
Boot Weather, Albert Whitman, 1989.

WORK IN PROGRESS: Picture books and novels for children.

SIDELIGHTS: Judith Vigna told *CA:* "An addiction to books as a child in England—particularly those of Beatrix Potter and Kenneth Grahame—motivated me early on to write and illustrate children's books, but I did not realize that ambition until my mid-thirties. My goal in putting together a picture book is to approach common childhood problems such as a new baby or loss of a precious possession, with a humorous touch that can help a child over a painful experience. Most of the situations in my books are dug up from my own childhood—remembering uncomfortable feelings, minor calamities (that seemed major at the time!)—or overwhelming joy. In trying to keep in touch with a child's feelings, I find it helpful to remember that many emotions we experience as adults are enormously intensified in children. Always acknowledging the marvelous sense of humor children have, I try to combine these emotions with a bit of fun and whimsy."

AVOCATIONAL INTERESTS: Conducting workshops for children, portrait painting, music, skiing, books, travel.

BIOGRAPHICAL/CRITICAL SOURCES:

PERIODICALS

Chicago Tribune Book World, February 1, 1981.
Los Angeles Times Book Review, August 31, 1986.

* * *

VO-DINH, Mai 1933-

PERSONAL: Born November 14, 1933, in Hue, Vietnam; came to United States, 1960, naturalized citizen, 1976; son of Thang (a civil servant) and Do-Thi (Hanh) Vo-Dinh; married Helen Coutant Webb (a teacher), August 17, 1964 (divorced June, 1986); children: Katherine, Hannah. *Education:* Attended Faculte des Lettres, Sorbonne, Paris, 1956, Academie de la Grande Chaumiere, Paris, 1957, and Ecole Nationale Superieure des Beaux Arts, Paris, 1959.

ADDRESSES: Home and office—c/o Mai Studio, P.O. Box 425, Burkittsville, Md. 21718.

CAREER: Aritist, writer, and translator. Painting instructor, Hood College, Frederick, Md., summers, 1985 and 1986. Artist-in-residence, Synechia Arts Center, 1974, Middletown Middle School, 1985 and 1986, Brunswick Middle School, 1986. Work exhibited at Mars Hill College, 1981, Arsenal Gallery, 1982, Touchstone Gallery, 1983, Master Eagle Gallery, 1983, and George Mason University, 1987.

AWARDS, HONORS: Christopher Foundation Award, 1975; National Endowment for the Arts fellowship, 1983-84.

WRITINGS:

SELF-ILLUSTRATED

The Toad Is the Emperor's Uncle, Doubleday, 1970.
The Jade Song, Chelsea House, 1970.
Xu Sam Set, LaBoi Press (Paris), 1980.
Xu Sam Set, II, Van Nghe House, 1987.

ILLUSTRATOR

Wind Play: The Kite, UNICEF, 1964.
Birds, Frogs, and Moonlight, translation by Sylvia Dassedy and Kunihiro Suetake, Doubleday, 1967.
Nhat Hanh, *The Cry of Vietnam,* Unicorn Press, 1968.
All Year Long, Unicorn Press, 1969.
(And translator) Doan-Quoc-Sy, *The Stranded Fish,* Sang-Tao Press (Saigon), 1971.
(And translator) Hanh, *The Path of Return Continues the Journey,* Hoa-Binh Press, 1972.
James Kirkup, *The Magic Drum,* Knopf, 1973.
Helen Coutant, *First Snow,* Knopf, 1974.
Daniel Berrigan and Hanh, *The Raft Is Not the Shore,* Beacon Press, 1976.
(And translator) Hanh, *Zen Poems of Nhat Hnah,* Unicorn Press, 1976.
Hanh, *The Miracle of Mindfulness,* Beacon Press, 1976.
Ron Roy, *One Thousand Pails of Water,* Knopf, 1978.
The Way of Everyday Life, Center Publications, 1978.
(And translator) *Fragrance of Zen,* Buddhist Cultural Center, 1981.
(And translator) *Tuyet Dau Mua,* LaBoi Press, 1981.
The Land I Lost, Harper, 1982.
The Brocaded Slipper, Harper, 1982.
The Happy Funeral, Harper, 1982.
A Flash of Lightning, International Zen Institute of America, 1983.
Angel Child, Dragon Child, Carnival Press, 1983.
The Gift, Knopf, 1983.
(And translator) *The Pine Gate,* White Pine Press, 1988.
(And translator) *The Moon Bamboo,* Parallax Press, 1989.

PORTFOLIOS

The Crimson Silk Portfolio, VDM Editions, 1968.
Unicorn Broadsheet #4, Unicorn Press, 1969.
Let's Stand Beside Each Other, Fellowship Publications, 1969.
Recent Works by Vo-Dinh, Suzuki Graphics, 1972.
The Woodcuts of Vo-Dinh, Hoa-Binh Press, 1974.

OTHER

Views of a Vietnam Artist (lecture), Southern Illinois University Press, 1972.

(Translator) *A Flower for You,* Nam-Tuyen Temple (Virginia), 1983.
(Translator) *A Day to Dispose Of,* Rowan Tree, 1985.

Contributor to English language publications, including *Vietnam Forum, Webster Review, Unicorn Journal,* and *Vietnam Culture Journal,* and to Vietnamese language publications, including *Van Hoc, Diendan Tudo, Ngay Nay, Doc Lap,* and *Dat Moi.*

WORK IN PROGRESS: Writing a collection of short stories in English.

SIDELIGHTS: Mai Vo-Dinh told *CA:* "Naturally, the war in Vietnam affected me, an artist, profoundly as it did, in other ways, all Vietnamese. An entire generation grew up, lived, and died with it. Yet, my work cannot, except for occasional flarings of outrage and sorrow, be called violent or pessimistic. If anything, the war between Vietnamese and between Vietnamese and Americans has reinforced my faith in the miracle of life. It is a faith beyond hope or despair.

"Surprisingly enough, the paintings that I, born and bred in Vietnam, am most fond of are by two Britishers, Francis Bacon and Graham Sutherland. I also like Georgia O'Keefe, a great American lady, very much. I also greatly admire Isaac Bashevis Singer.

"My opinion of modern art? I hope it counts! Modern art is but a reflection of modern life. Do you know the story from that Buddhist text?; 'A man gallops by on his horse. Someone shouts at him: "Where are you going?" The man hollers back: "Don't know! Ask the horse!"' "

* * *

VOIGHT, Ellen Bryant 1943-

PERSONAL: Born May 9, 1943, in Danville, Va.; daughter of Lloyd (a farmer) and Zue (an elementary school teacher; maiden name, Yeatts) Bryant; married Francis George Wilhelm Voight (a college dean), September 5, 1965; children: Jula Dudley, William Bryant. *Education:* Converse College, B.A., 1964; University of Iowa, M.F.A., 1966.

ADDRESSES: Home—P.O. Box 16, Marshfield, Vt. 05658.

CAREER: Iowa Wesleyan College, Mount Pleasant, instructor in English, 1966-69; Goddard College, Plainfield, Vt., teacher of literature and writing, 197-78, director of writing program, 1975-78; Massachusetts Institute of Technology, Cambridge, associate professor of creative writing, 1979-82; Warren Wilson College, M.F.A. program for writers, Swannanoa, N.C., visiting faculty member, 1981—. Professional pianist. Member of board of directors of Associated Writing Programs; has given poetry readings at schools and colleges, and served as judge of poetry contests.

AWARDS, HONORS: Grants from Vermont Council on the Arts, 1974-75, National Endowment for the Arts, 1976-77, and the Guggenheim Foundation, 1978-79; Pushcart Prize, 1983; Emily Clark Balch award, *Virginia Quarterly Review,* 1987.

WRITINGS:

Claiming Kin (poems), Wesleyan University Press, 1976.
(Contributor) *Poetry in Public Places* (anthology), American International Sculptors Symposium, 1977.
(Contributor) David Rigsby, editor, *Ardis Anthology of New American Poetry,* Ardis, 1977.
(Contributor) *The Norton Anthology of Poetry,* 3rd edition, Norton, 1983.
(Contributor) *The Breadloaf Anthology of Contemporary Poetry,* University Press of New England, 1983.
The Forces of Plenty (poems), Norton, 1983.
(Contributor) *The Morrow Anthology of Younger American Poets,* Morrow, 1985.
(Contributor) *The Ploughshares Reader,* Ploughshares Books, 1987.
(Contributor) *The Antaeus Anthology,* Bantam, 1987.
The Lotus Flowers (poems), Norton, 1987.

Works represented in numerous anthologies. Contributor to *Nation, New Yorker, Atlantic,* and *New Republic,* and to literary journals, including *Shenandoah, Sewanee Review, American Poetry Review, Southern Review,* and *Poetry.* Advisory editor, *Arion's Dolphin,* 1971-75.

WORK IN PROGRESS: Poetry.

SIDELIGHTS: In her first book of poems, *Claiming Kin,* Ellen Bryant Voight reveals "a Southerner's devotion to family and a naturalist's devotion to the physical world," Edward Hirsch observes in his *Nation* review. The title poem of the collection reflects both impulses, for in addressing her early life in her mother's house, Voight compares herself to a barren plant: "Mother, this poem is from your middle / child who, like your private second self / rising at night to wander the dark / house / grew in the shady places: / a green plant in a brass pot, / rootbound, without blossoms."

What Peter Schjeldahl finds interesting about Voight's poems, he writes in the *New York Times Book Review,* "is evidence of a pretty ferocious sensibility: powerful sexual yearnings and repulsions, fascinations with physical rot and murderous impulses." And Hirsch alludes to "a sort of Plathean intensity, a bleak energy of mourning" permeating her work. "As a book," Hirsch concludes, "*Claiming Kin* is restless, sometimes violent, always physical. Its poems stand on both sides of a barren winter. But in the end, through the magical, saving grace of language, Ellen Bryant Voight's poems resist and transcend their seasons of hard weather. *Claiming Kin* is a stunning first collection."

The Lotus Flowers, Voight's third book of poems, shows the poet's maturity as craftsman and storyteller, reviewers note. "At various times she has written in tight forms and free verse; with adjectives and without; personally and objectively," remarks *Poetry* reviewer Peter Stitt. "In [*The Lotus Flowers*] she seems to bring all of this together and it makes for both a pleasing variety and an inherent toughness." Michael Collier, writing in the *Partisan Review,* recommends the book to readers "who believe that a poem should be clear and accessible and concern itself with the rescue and transformation of a life."

BIOGRAPHICAL/CRITICAL SOURCES:

PERIODICALS

American Poetry Review, July, 1977, January, 1988.
Chicago Tribune Book World, June 10, 1984.
Hudson Review, spring, 1988.
Nation, August 6, 1977.
New York Times Book Review, May 1, 1977, July 17, 1983, August 23, 1987, May 22, 1988.
Partisan Review, summer, 1988.
Poetry, February, 1984, June, 1988.

WALLACE, Nigel
See HAMILTON, Charles (Harold St. John)

* * *

WALLACE, Pat
See STROTHER, Pat Wallace

* * *

WALZER, Norman 1943-

PERSONAL: Born March 17, 1943, in Mendota, Ill.; son of Elmer and Anna (Johnson) Walzer; married Dona Lee Maurer, August 21, 1970; children: Steve, Mark. *Education:* Illinois State University, B.S., 1966; University of Illinois, M.A., 1969, Ph.D., 1970.

ADDRESSES: Home—727 Auburn Dr., Macomb, Ill. 61455. *Office*—Department of Economics, 442 Stipes Hall, Western Illinois University, Macomb, Ill. 61455.

CAREER: Western Illinois University, Macomb, assistant professor, 1970-74, associate professor, 1974-78, professor of economics, 1978—, director of Public Policy Research Institute, 1974—, chairman of department, 1980—. Visiting professor at University of Illinois, 1977-78, 1979-80; research director of Illinois General Assembly's Illinois Cities and Villages Municipal Problems Commission, 1974-1983.

MEMBER: American Economic Association, Regional Science Association, Midwest Economic Association, Illinois Economic Association (president, 1979-80), Knights of Columbus (grand knight, 1983-84).

AWARDS, HONORS: Grants from Illinois Municipal League, 1971—, Southwestern Illinois Law Enforcement Commission, 1972, Western Illinois Crime Commission, 1972, Illinois Division of Vocational and Technical Education, 1972, 1973, 1974, U.S. Army Corps of Engineers, 1974, Municipal Problems Commission, 1974, 1975, U.S. Department of Labor, 1979, State of Illinois, 1980, 1981, and Community Information and Education Service, 1983.

WRITINGS:

(Contributor) A. S. Bunker and T. S. Hutchinson, editors, *Roads of Rural America,* U.S. Department of Agriculture, 1979.

(Editor with David L. Chicoine) *Financing State and Local Governments in the 1980s,* Oelgeschlager, Gunn & Hain, 1981.

(With Glenn W. Fisher) *Cities, Suburbs, and Property Taxes,* Oelgeschlager, Gunn & Hain, 1981.

(Contributor) T. N. Clark, editor, *Fiscal Austerity and Urban Innovation,* Jai Press, 1983.

(Editor) *Financing Local Infrastructure in Nonmetropolitan Areas,* Praeger, 1986.

(Editor) *Financing Economic Development,* Praeger, 1986.

(Editor) *Financing Rural Health Care,* Praeger, 1988.

Contributor of several dozen articles and reviews to professional journals. Editor of *Papers and Proceedings of the Illinois Economic Association,* 1981-83. Also author, with David L. Chicoine, of *Governmental Structure and Local Public Finance,* 1984.

SIDELIGHTS: Norman Walzer told *CA:* "The study of urban economics is particularly interesting to an economist because of the opportunities to see prices and markets work. Many of the urban related problems arise because there is no explicit price to operate as a rationing agent. There is renewed interest among academics and professional writers to identify new methods of incorporating price information into service delivery systems in American cities.

"The fiscal retrenchment which has faced American cities in recent years has been a mixed blessing. In many instances, local officials have experienced considerable difficulty balancing budgets during rapidly rising prices for inputs at the same time that residents were resisting property tax increases. In response, local officials have turned to new methods of finance that reflect innovations which, in the absence of fiscal austerity, might not have been considered. There is a general view that many local governments came out of the recent recession in a much more efficient stance. Of course, there are other cities whose economy has been severely damaged and major efforts are needed to reconstruct the tax base."

* * *

WARD, Eric
See EBON, Martin

WARNER, Sylvia (Constance) Ashton
See ASHTON-WARNER, Sylvia (Constance)

* * *

WATSON, Pauline 1925-
(POLA)

PERSONAL: Born July 24, 1925, in New Iberia, La.; daughter of Luke and Rosalie (Catalano) Bennett; married Jimmy T. Watson, October 19, 1947; children: Cindy (Mrs. Scott Walling), Jim, Duke, Vicki, Mike. *Education:* Palmer Institute of Authorship, graduate, 1951.

ADDRESSES: Home—24420 Stuebner Airline, Tomball, Tex. 77375.

CAREER: Accountant and office manager for an automobile dealership in New Iberia, La., 1942-47; writer, 1950—. Guest speaker at, participant in, and conductor of workshops.

MEMBER: International Toastmistress Club (secretary and publicity chairman of Houston's Noonday branch, 1968—), Houston Writer's Workshop (president, 1970—), Associated Authors of Children's Literature, (Houston; president, 1975—), Federated Woman's Club (Beaumont, Tex.).

WRITINGS:

JUVENILES

A Surprise for Mother, Prentice-Hall, 1976.
Curley Cat Baby-Sits, Harcourt, 1977.
Days with Daddy, Prentice-Hall, 1977.
(With the editors of *Cricket* magazine) *Cricket's Cookery,* Random House, 1977.
Wriggles: The Little Wishing Pig, Seabury, 1978.
What Would You Do?, Prentice-Hall, 1979.
The Walking Coat, Walker & Co., 1980.
Christmas Legends Wrapped in Song, Pola Press, 1982.
Casey's Shapes to Share (with tape), Playskool, 1984.

OTHER

Also author of *My Turn, Your Turn,* Prentice-Hall. Work anthologized in *Cricket's Choice,* edited by Clifton Fadiman and Marianne Carus, Open Court, 1975. Author of weekly column, "Post Oak Patter," in *Bellaire Texan,* 1969, and of monthly columns, "Kitchen Klatter," 1972-79, and, under pseudonym POLA, "Washboard Wisdom," 1974-79, both syndicated by Features Unlimited. Contributor of stories, articles, and poems to periodicals, including *My Weekly Reader, Woman's Day, Southern Living, Reader's Digest, Highlights for Children, Tempo,* and *Parents' Magazine.*

WORK IN PROGRESS: "There is always a story or an article or a poem in my typewriter."

SIDELIGHTS: Pauline Watson sold her first story in 1950 while taking a home-study course in creative writing. She told *CA* that she tries "to learn something new everyday and to have a long-range plan of study toward goals that I have privately set for myself." Though her articles, stories, and poems have appeared in numerous publications for both adults and children, she considers writing for children more rewarding because it keeps her feeling young. "An added joy in writing for children," she confides, "is the fun of getting to speak to hundreds of them about writing and books, and how poems can be found hiding inside each of us. [One] summer I discovered Polly Popcorn inside of me when I became the story lady at our local library. I enjoyed being this character so much [that] I will surely use her again, somewhere, in my writing."

She adds: "I was a guest speaker at the first *Highlights* Writers Workshop at Chautauqua, July 13-20, 1985. That experience inspired me to develop workshops for adults, using 'off the wall' exercises to awaken creativity. I conduct these frequently, now.

"During Young Authors' Day celebrations, I use my art creations made from dried fruit and vegetable peelings to stretch the imagination of the students. The girls and boys agree that if it is possible to turn a banana peel into an octopus, [then] it is possible to turn an idea into a story. My greatest delight is making up a story with a class of enthusiastic, handwaving young students."

BIOGRAPHICAL/CRITICAL SOURCES:

PERIODICALS

Woodlands Sun, July 20, 1977.

* * *

WEART, Spencer R(ichard) 1942-

PERSONAL: Surname rhymes with "Burt"; born March 8, 1942, in Detroit, Mich.; son of Spencer A. and Janet (Streng) Weart; married Carole Ege, 1971; children: Lara Kimi, Spencer Gen. *Education:* Cornell University, B.A., 1963; University of Colorado, Ph.D., 1968; University of California, Berkeley, postdoctoral study, 1971-73. *Politics:* Independent.

ADDRESSES: Home—12 Buena Vista Dr., Hastings, N.Y. 10706. *Office*—American Institute of Physics, 335 East 45th St., New York, N.Y. 10017.

CAREER: Mount Wilson and Palomar Observatories, Pasadena, Calif., research fellow, 1968-70; University of California, Berkeley, research assistant in history department, 1971-74; American Institute of Physics, New York, N.Y., director of Center for History of Physics, 1974—.

MEMBER: American Astronomical Society, History of Science Society, Society for Social Studies of Science.

WRITINGS:

Light: A Key to the Universe (juvenile), illustrated by Mark Binn, Coward, 1968.
(Self-illustrated) *How to Build a Sun* (juvenile), Coward, 1970.
(Contributor) Russell McCormmach, editor, *Historical Studies in the Physical Sciences,* Volume 5: *Physics circa 1900: Personnel, Funding, and Productivity of the Academic Establishment,* Princeton University Press, 1975.
(Editor) *Selected Papers of Great American Physicists: The Bicentennial Commemorative Volume of the American Physical Society, 1976,* American Institute of Physics, 1976.
(Editor with Gertrud Weiss Szilard) *Leo Szilard: His Version of the Facts—Selected Recollections and Correspondence,* MIT Press, 1978.
Scientists in Power, Harvard University Press, 1979.
(Editor with Melba Phillips) *History of Physics: Readings from "Physics Today,"* American Institute of Physics, 1985.
Nuclear Fear: A History of Images, Harvard University Press, 1988.

SIDELIGHTS: In *Nuclear Fear: A History of Images,* Spencer R. Weart argues that humanity's fear of nuclear energy originated years before the first atomic explosion at Hiroshima. According to Alfred Kazin in the *New York Times Book Review,*

"Weart . . . has gone beyond anyone else in collecting what I have called 'evidences' and he calls 'images.' 'Nuclear Fear: A History of Images' is a prodigious demonstration, item after item, of how Americans have responded to the new world of nuclear energy and its militarization. The new consciousness is revealed to be, under pressure, a very old, primitive, long-buried world of archaic images. Mr. Weart has been tireless in searching out even old movies, comic strips, forgotten best sellers, equally perishable military and official governmental pronouncements." In terms of archaic images, Weart points to the commonly held visions of total earthly destruction by mad scientists, the appearance of mutant monsters due to radiation exposure, and Garden of Eden-type utopias. Although fears and misconceptions concerning atomic energy are prevalent among nonscientists, Weart indicates that many of these images were actually fostered by scientists themselves. British chemist Frederick Soddy, for instance, predicted in a 1908 book that if man had the ability to transmute matter "such a race could transform a desert continent, thaw the frozen poles and make the whole world one smiling Garden of Eden," Weart records. Overall, Weart's purpose is to reveal the flaws in some of these recurring but misleading images. "Doomsday thinking is so common," writes Kazin, ". . . that a valuable feature of this book is Mr. Weart's effort to correct 'images' that do not correspond to the facts."

Critical response to Weart's study varies. Reviewer Peter Gorner for the *Chicago Tribune* expresses that "a few works have 'important' written all over them, and this is one. . . . [Weart] has spent 15 years indefatigably compiling countless 'images,' or symbolic associations, that have led to the thinking of our times. . . . If Weart has an axe to grind, it is that all of us, pro- and antinuclear proponents alike, have been conned by image-makers." In turn, *Los Angeles Times Book Review* contributor Alex Raksin believes Weart's main argument—that much of humanity's fear of atomic energy is based on false images—will surely "provoke the ire" of anti-nuclear activists. Additionally, Raksin finds Weart's emphasis on the safety of nuclear power plants unrealistic: "Weart . . . is too quick to discount disasters such as Chernobyl. . . . Power plants are not always designed and operated perfectly. . . . To dismiss this book for its underestimation of nuclear dangers, however, would be to miss its extraordinary value as a detailed, probing study of American hopes, dreams and insecurities in the 20th Century."

One additional complaint expressed by both Kazin and John Gross in the *New York Times* is that Weart's history of atomic fear emphasizes psychological factors at the expense of sociopolitical factors. As Gross maintains, there is a "limit . . . to what you can usefully say if you push politics and policies so firmly into the background. . . . While Mr. Weart doesn't altogether ignore hard political considerations, the reasons he advances are mainly psychological: habituation, strategies of denial and so forth. . . . 'Nuclear Fear' certainly deserves to be read: it is never less than intelligent and absorbing. But it still leaves you feeling that although imagery is an important aspect of history, it is only an aspect." In a like manner, Kazin finds "insufficient and occasionally misleading the emphasis [Weart] puts on individual psychology rather than on social and economic factors. He suggests that . . . deprivation of early maternal support links such very different 'apocalyptic' thinkers as Mary Shelley, Frederick Soddy, Jack London, Philip Wylie, J. B. Priestley, Bertrand Russell, [and] Dr. Helen Caldicott. . . . Suggestive as it is to relate the 'interior holocaust,' as Mr. Weart sensationally puts it, to the turbulence of the atomic age, there is all too little here about the defense contractors . . . actively promoting the fantasy of Star Wars." Nevertheless, Kazin concludes that Weart's study is "a true history of our age—a cutting, indispensable, deeply troubling book. I trust it will trouble you."

AVOCATIONAL INTERESTS: Hiking, skiing.

BIOGRAPHICAL/CRITICAL SOURCES:

BOOKS

Weart, Spencer R., *Nuclear Fear: A History of Images,* Harvard University Press, 1988.

PERIODICALS

Bulletin of the Atomic Scientists, August, 1985.
Chicago Tribune, May 4, 1988.
Los Angeles Times Book Review, May 15, 1988.
New York Times, April 29, 1988.
New York Times Book Review, May 1, 1988.

* * *

WEBSTER, James 1925-1981

PERSONAL: Born March 8, 1925, in New Barhet, Hertfordshire, England; died in a glider crash, June 16, 1981, in Stratford-upon-Avon, England; son of James Joscelyn (a bank manager) and May (an organist; maiden name, Spearman) Webster; married Mary Barbara Windeatt (an artist); children: Adrian William, Martin Guy. *Education:* Attended St. Luke's College, Exeter, 1947-49, and Central School of Speech, London, 1949-50; University of London, F.L.C.M., 1955, L.R.A.M., 1956. *Politics:* "Very liberal views." *Religion:* "Very liberal views."

ADDRESSES: Home—"Westward Ho!," St. Ouen, Jersey C.1, United Kingdom.

CAREER: Newton Park College of Education, Bath, England, lecturer in education, 1959-61; Redland College of Education, Bristol, England, senior lecturer in education, 1961-63; University of Bristol, Bristol, visiting lecturer, 1963-77. Founder of clinic for dyslexic children, 1964. *Military service:* Royal Air Force, navigator, 1943-47.

AWARDS, HONORS: Guiness trophy for gliding, 1964, 1965, 1966; Evening World trophy in gliding, 1968, 1977, 1978, for height gain.

WRITINGS:

Practical Reading: Some New Remedial Techniques, Evans Brothers, 1964.
The Four Aces, Jonathan Cape, 1965.
The Red Robber of Larado, Pitman, 1966.
The Ladybird Book of Tricks and Games and Others, Wiggs & Hepborough, 1966.
Reading Failure, with Particular Reference to Rescue Reading, Ginn, 1967, revised edition published as *Reading Failure,* 1971.
Rescue Stories, Ginn, 1967.
More Rescue Stories, Ginn, 1967.
Rescue Adventures, Ginn, 1967.
First Helpings, Thomas Nelson, 1970.
Help Stories, Thomas Nelson, 1970.
Help Yourself Stories, Thomas Nelson, 1970.
The Webster Test for Dyslexics, Ginn, 1972.
Ghosts!, Thomas Nelson, 1974.
The Spy!, Thomas Nelson, 1974.
The Red Sweater, Thomas Nelson, 1974.
Lads and Ladders, Thomas Nelson, 1974.
Dream Holiday, Thomas Nelson, 1974.
When the Glass Went Down, Thomas Nelson, 1974.

The Day I Was Buried Alive, Thomas Nelson, 1974.
The Day We Saved the Flats, Thomas Nelson, 1974.
The Day We Found Fang Island, Thomas Nelson, 1974.
Water, Wills & Hepborough, 1974.
Man in the Air, Wills & Hepborough, 1974.
The Night I Had a Pain, Thomas Nelson, 1974.
The Night I Heard a Noise, Thomas Nelson, 1974.
The Night I Felt a Ghost, Thomas Nelson, 1974.
Ghost Train, Thomas Nelson, 1975.
Razor Rock, Thomas Nelson, 1975.
The Man in the Black Jacket, Thomas Nelson, 1975.
Witches' Wood, Thomas Nelson, 1975.
The Kite Bike, Thomas Nelson, 1975.
Tall Boy, Thomas Nelson, 1975.
Help for Reluctant Readers, Thomas Nelson, 1975.
Ladybird Readers, Wiggs & Hepborough, 1975.
Man and His Car, Wills & Hepborough, 1975.
Man on the Sea, Wills & Hepborough, 1976.
Rewards, Arnold, 1976.
Roads, Wills & Hepborough, 1976.
Homes, Wills & Hepborough, 1976.
Fire, Wills & Hepborough, 1976.
Webster's English Work Books, Thomas Nelson, 1976.
Under the Ground, Wills & Hepborough, 1977.
The Secret Wish, Hart-Davis Educational, 1978.
Bomber Pilot, Macmillan, 1979.
Spitfire Pilot, Macmillan, 1979.
Airline Pilot, Macmillan, 1979.
Air Taxi Pilot, Macmillan, 1979.
Glider Pilot, Macmillan, 1980.
Spy Pilot, Macmillan Educational, 1980.
Chopper Pilot, Macmillan, 1980.
Reading Matters: A Practical Philosophy, McGraw, 1982.

Also author of more than two hundred books on literacy. Author of *Space Pilot.* Author of material for British Broadcasting Corp. (BBC) and Instructional Television (ITV).

"RESCUE ADVENTURES" SERIES

Adventure in Jersey, Ginn, 1967.
Adventure in Scotland, Ginn, 1967.
Adventure on the Road, Ginn, 1967.
City Adventure, Ginn, 1967.
Adventure Underground, Ginn, 1967.
Adventure in Space, Ginn, 1970.

"RESCUE READING" SERIES

Shorty and the Bank Robbers, Ginn, 1967.
Sally the Seagull, Ginn, 1967.
Martin the Mouse, Ginn, 1967.
Shorty and Tom Rabbit, Ginn, 1967.
Shorty the Hero, Ginn, 1967.
Snowball, Ginn, 1967.
Trouble the Fox, Ginn, 1967.
Patrick the Parrot, Ginn, 1967.
Firewater, Ginn, 1967.
Shorty Again, Ginn, 1967.
Hoppy the Second, Ginn, 1967.
Brown Beauty, Ginn, 1968.
Young Shorty Books (twelve volumes), Ginn, 1978.
More Young Shorty Books (twelve volumes), Ginn, 1980.
Young Shorty Again (twelve volumes), Ginn, 1981.

Also author of "Shorty" activity books. Author of reading packs, discussion packs, and workbooks.

"BEAUTIES" SERIES

Book 1: The Secret Wish, Hart-Davis, 1978.
Book 2: Missing!, Hart-Davis, 1978.
Book 3: A Real Beauty!, Hart-Davis, 1978.
Book 4: The Letter, Hart-Davis, 1978.
Book 5: Beauty and the Bus, Hart-Davis, 1978.
Book 6: Beauty, Bess and Bottle, Hart-Davis, 1978.
Book 7: The Man in the Mist, Hart-Davis, 1978.
Book 8: Poached Eggs, Hart-Davis, 1979.
Book 9: Pups!, Hart-Davis, 1979.
Book 10: Copper, Hart-Davis, 1979.

"ROUNDABOUTS" SERIES

The Secret Room, Arnold, 1978.
Buried Treasure at the Secret Room, E. J. Arnold, 1978.
A Lucky Day at the Secret Room, Arnold, 1978.
Trouble at the Secret Room, Arnold, 1978.

"REWARDS" SERIES

Book 1: Steve Meets Chunky, E. J. Arnold, 1976.
Book 2: A Chunky Jacket, E. J. Arnold, 1976.
Book 3: Chunky at School, E. J. Arnold, 1976.
Book 4: Smoky, E. J. Arnold, 1976.
Book 5: Chunky Tries Flying, E. J. Arnold, 1976.
Book 6: Chunky at the Circus, E. J. Arnold, 1976.
Book 7: The Big Man, E. J. Arnold, 1976.
Book 8: The Big Man Again, E. J. Arnold, 1976.

"ECHOES" SERIES

Story 1: What Happened to Sam, Macmillan, 1979.
Story 2: What Happened in the Park, Macmillan, 1979.
Story 3: What Happened in the Hills, Macmillan, 1979.
Story 4: What Happened on Hallowe'en, Macmillan, 1979.
Story 5: What Happened at Nine O'Clock, Macmillan, 1979.
Story 6: What Happened in School, Macmillan, 1979.
Story 7: What Happened at Breakfast, Macmillan, 1979.
Story 8: What Happened on the Number Twelve Bus, Macmillan, 1979.
Story 9: What Happened to Sam's Grandad, Macmillan, 1979.
Story 10: What Happened to Pam's Song, Macmillan, 1979.
Story 11: What Happened at the Match, Macmillan, 1979.
Story 12: What Happened in Space, Macmillan, 1979.

Also author of twelve "Echoes" workbooks.

SIDELIGHTS: James Webster, founder of England's first clinic for dyslexic children, once wrote *CA:* "My writing stems not so much from creative urge, although I am never free from the disease, as from an obsessive desire to slay the dragon of illiteracy. Much of my work arose from the resident reading clinics for dyslexics and is based on I.C.G. (Informational Contextual Guessing)."

AVOCATIONAL INTERESTS: Gliding, sportscars.

OBITUARIES:

PERIODICALS

Chicago Tribune, June 17, 1981.

[Sketch updated by wife, Barbara Webster]

* * *

WEINBERG, Herman G(ershon) 1908-1983

PERSONAL: Born August 6, 1908, in New York, N.Y.; died November 7, 1983, of a heart attack in New York, N.Y.; son of

Julius (a merchant) and Mary (Levine) Weinberg; married Etta Polano, October 1, 1942 (died, 1948); children: Gretchen Berg (professional name). *Education:* Attended high school in Astoria, N.Y., and Institute of Musical Art, New York, N.Y.

ADDRESSES: Home—Coliseum House, 228 West 71st St., New York, N.Y. 10023.

CAREER: Fifth Avenue Playhouse, New York City, musical consultant, 1926-27; Fifty-Fifth Street Playhouse, New York City, publicist, 1928; Little Carnegie Playhouse, New York City, publicist, 1928-29; Little Theatre, Baltimore, Md., managing director, 1929-36; free-lance translator of foreign film dialogue into subtitles, 1929-70; City College of the City University of New York, New York City, lecturer in film, 1960-76; Division of Graduate Studies of the City University of New York, New York City, lecturer in film, 1973. Prepared exhibit, "Homage to Erich von Stroheim," Montreal Film Festival, 1964.

AWARDS, HONORS: Jury Awards from Venice Film Festival, 1953, San Francisco Film Festival, 1960, and Vancouver Film Festival, 1961.

WRITINGS:

(Editor) *Fifty Years of Italian Cinema,* Carlo Bestetti (Rome), 1954.
(Editor) *Fifty Years of Ballet in Italy,* Carlo Bestetti, 1956.
Josef von Sternberg (French text), Seghers (Paris), 1966, revised edition (English text), Dutton, 1967.
The Lubitsch Touch, Dutton, 1968, revised and expanded edition, Dover, 1977.
Saint Cinema: Writings on Film, 1929-1970, Drama Book Specialists, 1970, revised edition, Dover, 1973, 2nd revised edition, with a new foreword by Weinberg, Ungar, 1980.
The Complete "Greed," Arno, 1972, published as *Greed: A Reconstruction of the Complete Erich Von Stroheim Film from Stills,* Ayer, 1972.
Stroheim: A Pictorial Record of His Nine Films, Dover, 1973.
The Complete "Wedding March," Little, Brown, 1974.
Fritz Lang, Gordon Press, 1979.
Robert Flaherty and Hans Richter, Gordon Press, 1979.
An Index to the Creative Work of Erich von Stroheim, Gordon Press, 1980.
A Manhattan Odyssey: A Memoir (autobiography), Anthology Film Archives, 1983.
Coffee, Brandy and Cigars: A Kaleidoscope of the Arts and That Strange Thing Called Life (collection of syndicated columns), Anthology Film Archives, 1983.

Also author of *The Complete "Merry Widow" of Erich von Stroheim,* 1983. Editor of series, "Indexes on Directors," for British Film Institute. Contributor to anthologies, including *Twenty Years of Cinema in Venice, Introduction to the Art of the Movies, The Cinema between Two World Wars,* and *International Dictionary of Films and Filmmakers,* Volume 2: *Directors,* 1984. Author of syndicated column, "Coffee, Brandy and Cigars," which appeared in *Variety, Films in Review, Film Culture,* and other film periodicals. Film critic for *Film Culture, Film Quarterly,* and *Playboy,* 1960-76. Film editor for *Liberty Magazine.*

OBITUARIES:

PERIODICALS

New York Times, November 8, 1983.
Times (London), December 5, 1983.*

WEINMAN, Paul 1940-

PERSONAL: Born April 11, 1940, in Albany, N.Y.; son of Philip Pius (a house builder) and Jessie (Thomas) Weinman; children: Erika, Heidi, Stefan, Meadow. *Education:* Harpur College, B.A., 1962.

ADDRESSES: Home—79 Cottage Ave., Albany, N.Y. 12203.

CAREER: New York State Museum, Albany, museum education supervisor, 1963—.

MEMBER: New York State Archaeological Association (fellow).

AWARDS, HONORS: CAPS award for poetry, Center Press, 1982; award for innovative fiction, 1983; achievement award from New York State Archaeological Association.

WRITINGS:

My Sister's Underwear, Zeitgeist, 1969.
For We He Bleeds, Vega Books, 1982.
Frog Eyes and Forgiveness, Modern Images, 1983.
Gathering Fish, Center Press, 1983.
The Bestiary about Me, MAF Press, 1986.
Hardball Ain't All Bucolic, Samisdat Press, 1986.
(Editor with Peter H. Gordon and Sydney Waller) *Diamonds Are Forever,* Chronicle Books, 1987.
Three Fingers, MAF, 1988.
Adam's at Bat, Samisdat Press, 1988.
Central American Poems, Vergin, 1988.
White Boy's a Punk, Mutated Viruses, 1989.
Pack Your Pocket, Minatour, 1989.

* * *

WELLS, Lisa
See RAUCINA, Thomas Frank

* * *

WELLS, Stanley W(illiam) 1930-

PERSONAL: Born May 21, 1930, in Hull, England; son of Stanley Cecil and Doris (Atkinson) Wells; married Susan Hill (a novelist and playwright), April 23, 1975; children: Jessica, Clemency. *Education:* University College, London, B.A., 1951; University of Birmingham, Ph.D., 1961. *Politics:* None.

ADDRESSES: Home—Midsummer Cottage, Church Lane, Beckley, Oxford, England. *Office*—The Shakespeare Institute, Church St., Stratford-upon-Avon, Warwickshire CV37 6HP, England.

CAREER: Shakespeare Institute, University of Birmingham, Stratford-upon-Avon, England, fellow, 1961-77, reader in English, 1972-77, honorary fellow, 1979—, director, 1988—; Oxford University Press, Oxford, England, head of Shakespeare department and general editor of *The Oxford Shakespeare,* 1978-88; Oxford University, Balliol College, Oxford, senior research fellow, 1980-88; University of Birmingham, Birmingham, England, professor of Shakespeare studies, 1988—. Royal Shakespeare Theatre, director of summer school, 1971—, member of executive council and governor, 1974—; trustee, Shakespeare Birthplace Trust, 1975-81, 1984—.

MEMBER: Malone Society (member of council), Society for Theatre Research.

AWARDS, HONORS: D.Litt., Furman University, 1978.

WRITINGS:

Shakespeare: A Reading Guide, Oxford University Press, 1969.
Literature and Drama with Special Reference to Shakespeare and His Contemporaries, Routledge & Kegan Paul, 1970.
Royal Shakespeare: Studies of Four Major Productions at the Royal Shakespeare Theatre, Stratford-upon-Avon, Furman University, 1976 (published in England as *Royal Shakespeare: Four Major Productions at Stratford-upon-Avon,* Manchester University Press, 1977).
Shakespeare: The Writer and His Work, Scribner, 1978 (published in England as *Shakespeare,* Longman, 1978).
Shakespeare: An Illustrated Dictionary, Oxford University Press, 1978, revised edition, 1985.
Modernizing Shakespeare's Spelling (bound with *Three Studies in the Text of Henry V,* by Gary Taylor), Oxford University Press, 1980.
Re-editing Shakespeare for the Modern Reader, Oxford University Press, 1984.
(With Taylor and others) *William Shakespeare: A Textual Companion,* Oxford University Press, 1987.

EDITOR

Thomas Nash, *Selected Writings: "Pierce Penniless, His Supplication to the Devil," and Selected Writings,* Edward Arnold, 1964, published as *Selected Writings: "Pierce Penniless, His Supplication to the Devil," "Summer's Last Will and Testament," "The Terrors of the Night," "The Unfortunate Traveller," and Other Writings,* Harvard University Press, 1965.
William Shakespeare, *A Midsummer Night's Dream,* Penguin, 1967.
A Book of Masques in Honour of Allardyce Nicoll, Cambridge University Press, 1967.
Shakespeare, *King Richard the Second,* Penguin, 1967.
Shakespeare, *The Comedy of Errors,* Penguin, 1972.
Charles Jasper Sisson, *Boar's Head Theatre: An Inn-yard Theatre of the Elizabethan Age,* Routledge & Kegan Paul, 1972.
Shakespeare: Select Bibliographical Guides, Oxford University Press, 1973.
English Drama, Excluding Shakespeare: Select Bibliographical Guides, Oxford University Press, 1975.
Nineteenth-Century Shakespeare Burlesques, Diploma Press, Volume 1: *John Poole and His Imitators,* 1977, Volume 2: *Maurice Dowling, 1834, to Charles Beckington, 1847,* 1978, Volume 3: *The High Period: Francis Talfourd, 1849, to Andrew Halliday, 1859,* 1978, Volume 4: *The Fourth Phase: F. C. Burnand, W. S. Gilbert, and Others, 1860-1882,* 1978, Volume 5: *American Shakespeare Travesties, 1852-1888,* 1978.
(With Kenneth Muir) *Aspects of Hamlet: Articles Reprinted from "Shakespeare Survey,"* Cambridge University Press, 1979.
(With R. L. Smallwood) Thomas Decker, *The Shoemaker's Holiday,* Johns Hopkins University Press, 1979.
(With Muir) *Aspects of Shakespeare's Problem Plays: Articles Reprinted from "Shakespeare Survey,"* Cambridge University Press, 1982.
(With Muir) *Aspects of King Lear,* Cambridge University Press, 1982.
Shakespeare's Sonnets, Oxford University Press, 1985.
Twelfth Night: Critical Essays, Garland Publishing, 1986.
(With Taylor and others) *William Shakespeare: The Complete Works,* Oxford University Press, 1986.
(With Taylor and others) *William Shakespeare: The Complete Works* (original spelling edition), Oxford University Press, 1986.
The Cambridge Companion to Shakespeare Studies, Cambridge University Press, 1986.
An Oxford Anthology of Shakespeare, Oxford University Press, 1987.

OTHER

Reviewer for British Broadcasting Corp. program "Kaleidoscope." Contributor of articles and reviews to the *Times Literary Supplement* and to Shakespeare and English study journals. Editor, *Shakespeare Survey: An Annual Survey of Shakespearian Study and Production,* Cambridge University Press, 1980—.

WORK IN PROGRESS: The Oxford Companion to Shakespeare.

BIOGRAPHICAL/CRITICAL SOURCES:

PERIODICALS

Times Literary Supplement, April 8, 1983, April 10, 1987.

* * *

WEST, E(dwin) G(eorge) 1922-
(Edwin G. West)

PERSONAL: Born February 27, 1922, in Goldthorpe, England; son of Sydney Millard and Tessie (Fey) West; married Ann Revett, March 31, 1959; children: John, Sarah, Caroline. *Education:* University of Exeter, B.Sc. and B.A., 1949; University of London, M.Sc., 1959, Ph.D., 1964.

ADDRESSES: Office—Department of Economics, Carleton University, Ottawa, Ontario, Canada, K1A 5B6.

CAREER: University of Newcastle upon Tyne, Newcastle upon Tyne, England, lecturer in economics, 1962-65; University of Chicago, Chicago, Ill., fellow of Law and Economics Center, 1965-66; University of Kent at Canterbury, Canterbury, England, reader in economics, 1966-70; Carleton University, Ottawa, Ontario, professor of economics, 1970—. Visiting research scholar, University of California, Berkeley, 1974; visiting professor, Virginia Polytechnic Institute and State University, 1975-77. Chief examiner of economics, University of London, 1967-69. Consultant, British Restrictive Trade Practices Committee, 1968-70.

MEMBER: American Economics Association.

WRITINGS:

Education and the State, Institute of Economic Affairs, 1965, 2nd edition, Transatlantic Arts, 1970.
(Co-author) *Education: A Framework for Choice,* Institute of Economic Affairs, 1967.
Economics, Education, and the Politician, Institute of Economic Affiars, 1968.
(Contributor) *Rural Poverty and Regional Progress in Urban Society,* U.S. Chamber of Commerce, 1969.
Adam Smith: The Man and His Works, Arlington House, 1969.
(Author of introduction) Adam Smith, *The Theory of Moral Sentiments,* Arlington House, 1969.
(With Graham Hallett and Peter Randall) *Regional Policy Forever: Essays on the History, Theory and Political Economy of Forty Years of Regionalism,* London Institute of Economic Affairs, 1973.
Education and the Industrial Revolution, Barnes & Noble, 1975.
Student Loans: A Reappraisal; with Special Reference to Ontario's and Canada's Changing Needs in Educational Finance, Ontario Economic Council, 1976.
(Editor) *Nonpublic School Aid: The Law, Economics, and Politics of American Education,* Lexington Books, 1976.

(Under name Edwin G. West; with Roger LeRoy Miller) *Canadian Economics Today,* Harper, Volume 1: *The Macro View,* 1978, Volume 2: *The Micro View,* 1978.
(Under name Edwin G. West; with Michael McKee) *Minimum Wages: The New Issues in Theory, Evidence, Policy, and Politics,* Economic Council of Canada, 1980.
The Economics of Education Tax Credits, Heritage Foundation, 1981.

Contributor to economics, philosophy, and history journals.

BIOGRAPHICAL/CRITICAL SOURCES:

PERIODICALS

National Review, June 16, 1970.
Times Literary Supplement, November 7, 1975.*

* * *

WEST, Edwin G.
See WEST, E(dwin) G(eorge)

* * *

WEST, Pat
See STROTHER, Pat Wallace

* * *

WESTWOOD, Jennifer 1940-
(Jennifer Chandler)

PERSONAL: Born May 1, 1940, in England; daughter of Wilfrid James (a builder) and Beatrice Fulcher (a teacher); married Trevor Frank Westwood in 1958 (divorced, 1966); married Brian Herbert Chandler (a director of management training), 1968; children: (first marriage) Jonathan James. *Education:* St. Anne's College, Oxford, B.A., 1963, M.A., 1970; New Hall, Cambridge, B.A., 1965, M.A., 1972. *Religion:* Church of England.

ADDRESSES: Home—133 Shepherdess Walk, London, N.1, England; and The Cottage, The Street, Norton Subcourse, Norfolk, England.

CAREER: Cambridge University, Cambridge, England, conductor of university classes and tutorials in Old Norse and Anglo-Saxon, 1965-68; free-lance editor and publishing adviser, 1969—. Presenter and reviewer, "The Children's Illustrated Book Review" on British cable television Arts Channel, 1985—. Guide and lecturer for "Magical Britain" tours, Gothic Image Ltd., Glastonbury, England.

AWARDS, HONORS: M.Litt., Cambridge University, 1973.

MEMBER: Viking Society for Northern Research, Folklore Society (committee member), British Hedgehog Preservation Society.

WRITINGS:

(Adaptor and translator) *Medieval Tales,* illustrations by Pauline Baynes, Hart-Davis, 1967, Coward, 1968.
Gilgamesh and Other Babylonian Tales, illustrations by Michael Charlton, Bodley Head, 1968, Coward, 1970.
(Compiler) *The Isle of Gramarye,* Hart-Davis, 1970.
Tales and Legends, illustrations by Baynes, Coward, 1971.
Stories of Charlemagne (young adult), Bodley Head, 1972, S. G. Phillips, 1976.
Alfred the Great (juvenile), Wayland, 1978.
(Adaptor) Oscar Wilde, *The Star Child: A Fairy Tale* (picture-book), illustrations by Fiona French, Four Winds, 1979.
(Contributor under name Jennifer Chandler) *The Book of London,* St. Michael/Automobile Association, 1979.
Fat Cat, illustrations by French, Abelard, 1984.
Going to Squintum's: A Foxy Folktale (juvenile), illustrations by French, Dial, 1985.
Albion: A Guide to Legendary Britain, Granada, 1985.
(Adaptor) Cecile Donner and Jean-Luc Caradeau, *Dictionary of Superstitions,* Granada, 1985.
(Contributor) *Secret Britain,* Automobile Association, 1986.
(Editor and contributor) *The Atlas of Mysterious Places: The World's Unexplained Sacred Sites, Symbolic Landscapes, Ancient Cities and Lost Lands,* Weidenfeld & Nicolson, 1987.
(Contributor) *Gardens and Garden Centres in Britain,* Automobile Association, 1987.

Also author of *Gothic Guides: Hertfordshire* and *Gothic Guides: Norfolk,* for Shire; author of *A Dictionary of Legends,* for Grafton. Also contributor to anthologies, including *Northern Lights: Legends, Sagas and Folk-tales,* Faber, 1987. *Times Literary Supplement* reviewer of children's books, as Jennifer Chandler, 1975-78, and of Folklore/Fairytale, as Jennifer Westwood, 1986—. Contributor to *British Heritage.*

SIDELIGHTS: "I began writing whilst still at university, for the amusement of my son Jonathan," Jennifer Westwood once wrote *CA.* "What he liked most in the world was stories, and it so happened that—after reading Old and Middle English language and literature at Oxford, and the Anglo-Saxon Tripos at Cambridge—stories was what I knew. I realized that I had access to a fund of stories in dead languages that were either unavailable to children or available only in Victorian retellings long since out of print. I set about trying to retell some of these in intelligible modern English whilst keeping the flavor and style of the originals—particularly in *Gilgamesh,* where a semi-liturgical style was aimed at.

"One thing has led to another: I now write also on Dark Age history and archaeology for children (*Alfred the Great* and contributions on the Anglo-Saxons and Vikings to *British Heritage*), and on legends and folktales for adults. . . . A most exciting development in my career has been to work with the British illustrator Fiona French, with whom I have long been close friends. Our abridged picture-book version of Oscar Wilde's fairytale *The Star Child* is now published in several languages, including Japanese. . . . *Fat Cat,* a classic Danish folktale, [is] virtually the first piece of Danish I ever managed to read. I stayed in Denmark for a time as a child, living in a Danish family, and again as a student, and the book is a token of the gratitude I feel for those good times.

"As a student I've also lived in Sweden and Iceland, and with my family have lived for a year each in Iran (1976-77) and the United States (1978-79). My interest in ancient monuments has led to extensive travels in Europe and the Middle East, and of course my own country. I speak French, and much less Danish and Icelandic than I used to do; on the other hand, I have learned to read and write in Farsi (Persian). Of the dead languages, I can get by in Latin, Anglo-Saxon (Old English), Old Norse and Old French."

BIOGRAPHICAL/CRITICAL SOURCES:

PERIODICALS

Times (London), August 15, 1985.

WHITE, Barbara A(nne) 1942-

PERSONAL: Born October 25, 1942, in Norwich, N.Y.; daughter of Frank (an electrician) and Mary (an office nurse; maiden name, Busacker) White; married Harvey Epstein (an engineer); children: Elizabeth. *Education:* Cornell University, A.B., 1964; University of Wisconsin—Madison, M.A., 1965, Ph.D., 1974; Simmons College, M.S., 1976.

ADDRESSES: Home—34 Mast Rd., Lee, Durham, N.H. 03824. *Office*—Women's Studies Program, University of New Hampshire Library, Durham, N.H. 03824.

CAREER: Northwestern University, Evanston, Ill., instructor in English, 1970-72; research assistant, University of Wisconsin, 1972-74; University of Louisville, Louisville, Ky., assistant professor of English, 1974-75; University of New Hampshire, Durham, associate professor and curator of rare books and manuscripts, 1976-87, co-coordinator of women's studies program, 1980-81, associate professor of women's studies, 1987—. Project humanist and filmscript writer for New Hampshire Council of the Humanities project, "New Hampshire Writers View the Small Town," 1980-81. Member, Committee for a New England Bibliography, 1978-81, and New Hampshire Governor's Historical Records Advisory Board, 1980—. Reader for University of Oklahoma Press, University of Pennsylvania Press, *Signs,* and *Tulsa Studies in Women's Literature.* Consultant to Frederick Ungar Publishing Co., 1978-84.

MEMBER: National Women's Studies Association, Modern Language Association of America, MELUS, Phi Beta Kappa, Phi Kappa Phi, Beta Phi Mu.

AWARDS, HONORS: Koppelman Award for "Best Multi-Authored or Edited Book of 1985," Popular Culture Association and American Culture Association, for *Hidden Hands: American Women Writers, 1790-1870, an Anthology.*

WRITINGS:

(Contributor) *Female Studies IV: Teaching about Women,* Know, Inc., 1971.

American Women Writers: An Annotated Bibliography of Criticism, Garland Publishing, 1977.

(Contributor) Lina Mainiero, editor, *American Women Writers,* Ungar, Volume I, 1979, Volume II, 1980, Volume III, 1981, Volume IV, 1982.

(Contributor) Annis Pratt, editor, *Archetypal Patterns in Women's Fiction,* Indiana University Press, 1981.

(Author of foreword) Jane E. Vallier, *Poet on Demand: The Life, Letters, and Works of Celia Thaxter,* Down East, 1982.

(Contributor) Susan Koppelman, editor, *Short Stories Written by Women in the United States,* Feminist Press, 1983.

Growing up Female: Adolescent Girlhood in American Fiction, Greenwood Press, 1985.

(With Lucy M. Freibert) *Hidden Hands: American Women Writers, 1790-1870, an Anthology,* Rutgers University Press, 1985.

(Contributor) *The New Hampshire Image: As We and Others See Us,* Friends of the Humanities in New Hampshire, 1985.

Also contributor to Paul Lauter, editor, *Reconstructing American Literature,* Heath, and William Grant, editor, *American Short Story Writers to World War II,* Gale; also co-compiler of *A Bibliography of Books about Women in the Dimond Library.* Contributor to numerous literature journals.

WORK IN PROGRESS: A bibliography of criticism on American women writers of fiction, 1790-1870, for Garland Publishing; a book on short stories of Edith Wharton, for G.K. Hall.

SIDELIGHTS: Barbara A. White told *CA:* "I have studied writings by women since 1970 when I taught one of the earliest women's studies courses. A novel we discussed in that course—Carson McCullers's *The Member of the Wedding*—led me to question why girls in coming-of-age novels differ so markedly from the boys we are more familiar with, for example, Huck Finn, Stephen Dedalus, Holden Caulfield. I have since found, even in contemporary novels, that adolescent heroines are portrayed as ambivalent about growing up to womanhood, a state they view as powerless and inferior.

"I am also interested in earlier fiction by women, especially the so-called 'sentimental' or 'domestic' fiction written in America before the Civil War. I think some of these much-maligned novels were important contributions to the growth of realism and the development of the novel. Feminist critics have thus far been building a critical theory, discovering 'lost' women writers, and reinterpreting works of individual women; now we must begin to write women's literary history."

* * *

WHITE, William 1910-

PERSONAL: Born September 4, 1910, in Paterson, N.J.; son of Noel D. (a chemist) and Beccia (Firkser) White; married Gertrude Mason (a professor of English), June 20, 1951; children: Geoffrey M., Roger W. *Education:* University of Tennessee at Chattanooga, B.A., 1933; graduate study at University of California, Los Angeles, 1935-40; University of Southern California, M.A., 1937; further study at University of Dijon, 1951; University of London, Ph.D., 1953. *Politics:* Democrat. *Religion:* Methodist.

ADDRESSES: Home—555 South Woodward Ave., Apt. 903, Birmingham, Mich. 48009.

CAREER: Whitman College, Walla Walla, Wash., instructor in English, 1941-42; Mary Hardin-Baylor College (now University of Mary Hardin-Baylor), Belton, Tex., assistant professor of journalism, 1946-47; Ohio Wesleyan University, Delaware, assistant professor of journalism, 1947; Wayne State University, Detroit, Mich., assistant then associate professor, 1947-60, professor of journalism, 1960-74, adjunct professor of American studies, 1974-80, adjunct professor of journalism, 1978-80, acting chairman of journalism department, 1956-57, 1965-66, chairman of American studies program, 1967-74; Oakland University, Rochester, Mich., professor of speech communications and director of journalism program, 1974-81, coordinator of American studies program, 1980-81. Visiting professor at numerous colleges and universities in the United States, Israel, and South Korea. Reporter, columnist, and editor for fourteen local daily and weekly newspapers, 1924—. *Military service:* U.S. Army, intelligence service, 1942-45; also associated with several serviceman's newspapers.

MEMBER: American Association of University Professors, Modern Language Association of America, Bibliographical Society of America, American Association for the History of Medicine, Association for Education in Journalism, American Studies Association, Modern Humanities Research Association, Thoreau Society, Whitman Birthplace Association, Private Libraries Association, Michigan Academy of Science, Arts and Letters, Book Club of Detroit, Friends of Detroit Public Library, Cranbrook Writers Guild (trustee, 1980—), Sigma Delta Chi, Blue Key, Theta Chi.

AWARDS, HONORS: Foundation for Economic Education fellowship, 1956; Wayne State University research grants, 1957,

1963, 1966; Fulbright fellowship, 1963-64; American Philosophical Society fellowship, 1965; National Endowment for the Humanities grants, 1967-70, 1972; Distinguished Service Award, Baylor School Alumni Association, 1971; Oakland University research grants, 1978, 1980; Distinguished Alumnus Award, University of Tennessee at Chattanooga, 1984.

WRITINGS:

A Henry David Thoreau Bibliography, 1908-1937, Faxon, 1939.
(Editor) A. E. Housman, *Three Comic Poems,* Jake Zeitlin, 1941.
John Donne since 1900: A Periodical Bibliography, Faxon, 1942.
D. H. Lawrence: A Checklist, 1931-50, Wayne State University Press, 1950.
(Editor) *This Is Detroit, 1701-1951: 250 Years in Pictures,* Wayne State University Press, 1951.
Sir William Osler: Historian and Literary Essayist, Wayne State University Press, 1951.
John Ciardi: A Bibliography, Wayne State University Press, 1959.
(Editor with H. W. Blodgett) *Walt Whitman: An 1855-56 Notebook,* Southern Illinois University Press, 1959.
(Editor) *A. E. Housman: A Centennial Memento,* Oriole Press, 1959.
(Editor) *A. E. Housman to Joseph Ishill: Five Unpublished Letters,* Oriole Press, 1959.
W. D. Snodgrass: A Bibliography, Wayne State University Press, 1960.
Karl Shapiro: A Bibliography, Wayne State University Press, 1960.
(Editor) Walt Whitman, *The People and John Quincy Adams,* Oriole Press, 1961, revised edition, 1962.
Ernest Hemingway: Guide to a Memorial Exhibition, University of Detroit Library, 1961.
(With Zoltan G. Zeke) *George Orwell: A Selected Bibliography,* Boston Linotype Print, 1962.
(Consulting editor) Housman, *A Shropshire Lad,* Avon, 1966.
Wilfred Owen, 1893-1918: A Bibliography, Kent State University Press, 1967.
(Editor) *By-Line: Ernest Hemingway* (Literary Guild selection), Scribner, 1967.
(Contributor) *American Literary Scholarship,* Duke University Press, 1967-71.
Walt Whitman's Journalism: A Bibliography, Wayne State University Press, 1968.
Studies in "The Sun Also Rises," C. E. Merrill, 1969.
Guide to Ernest Hemingway, C. E. Merrill, 1969.
Checklist of Ernest Hemingway, C. E. Merrill, 1970.
(Editor) *Walt Whitman in Our Time: Four Essays,* Wayne State University Press, 1970.
Edwin Arlington Robinson: A Supplemental Bibliography, 1936-1970, Kent State University Press, 1971.
(Editor with Roger Asselineau) *Walt Whitman in Europe Today,* Wayne State University Press, 1972.
(Editor) Ernest Bramah, *Kai Lung: Six Uncollected Stories from Punch,* Non-Profit Press, 1974.
Nathanael West: A Comprehensive Bibliography, Kent State University Press, 1975.
(Editor) *The Bicentennial Walt Whitman,* Wayne State University Press, 1976.
(Editor) *Walt Whitman: Daybooks and Notebooks,* New York University Press, 1978.
(Editor with others) *Walt Whitman: Leaves of Grass, A Textual Variation of the Printed Poems,* New York University Press, 1980.
(Editor) *1980: Leaves of Grass at 125,* Wayne State University Press, 1980.
(Editor with Gertrude Traubel) Horace Traubel, *With Walt Whitman in Camden,* Volume 6, Southern Illinois University Press, 1982.
A. E. Housman: A Bibliography, St. Paul's Bibliographies, 1982.
(Editor) Ernest Hemingway, *Dateline—Toronto: Hemingway's Complete "Toronto Star" Dispatches, 1920-1924,* Scribner, 1985.

General editor, the "Serif Series in Bibliography," Kent State University Press, 1966-75. Contributor to *The New Cambridge Bibliography of English Literature,* Volumes 3 and 4; contributor of over 2400 articles and reviews to professional journals, including *Bulletin of Bibliography, Choice,* and *Reprint Bulletin: Book Reviews. Annual Bibliography of English Language and Literature,* editor, 1947-63, contributing editor, 1963—. Editor, *Walt Whitman Review,* 1956—, *Wayne Journalism Newsletter,* 1956-74, *SDX Times,* 1977, *Odyssey: A Journal of the Humanities,* 1977-81, and *Journal of the Book Club of Detroit,* 1978; associate editor, *American Books Collector,* 1965-77; editorial advisor, *Dickinson Studies (Emily Dickinson Bulletin),* 1971—, *Hemingway Notes,* 1972-74, 1979-81, *Hemingway Review,* 1981—, and *University of Mississippi Studies in English,* 1980—.

WORK IN PROGRESS: Editing, with eight others, *The Collected Writings of Walt Whitman,* for New York University Press; *Ernest Bramah,* for Twayne; *John P. Marquand: A Bibliography,* for Yale University Library; editing Volumes 7-10 of Horace Traubel's *With Walt Whitman in Camden,* for Southern Illinois University Press; updated bibliographies of W. D. Snodgrass and Nathanael West; *Walt Whitman: Critical Reception,* for Burt Franklin.

BIOGRAPHICAL/CRITICAL SOURCES:

PERIODICALS

Chicago Tribune Book World, May 4, 1986.
Globe and Mail (Toronto), January 16, 1986.
New York Times Book Review, May 28, 1967.
Time, May 19, 1967.
Times Literary Supplement, December 10, 1982.
Washington Post Book World, November 3, 1985.

* * *

WHITMAN, Alden 1913-

PERSONAL: Born October 27, 1913, in New Albany, Nova Scotia, Canada; son of Frank S. (a teacher) and Mabel (Bloxsom) Whitman; married Joan McCracken (an editor), November 13, 1960; children: Pamela, Peter, Harriet, Daniel. *Education:* Harvard University, A.B., 1934.

ADDRESSES: *Home*—Major's Path, Southampton, N.Y. 11968.

CAREER: *New York Herald Tribune,* New York City, copy editor, 1943-51; *New York Times,* New York City, copy editor, 1951-64, chief obituary writer, 1964-76; freelance book critic, 1976—. Adviser, *Dictionary of Literary Biography,* Bruccoli-Clark, Inc.; editor, *Great American Reformers,* 1979.

MEMBER: Century Club.

WRITINGS:

Early American Labor Parties, International Publishers, 1944.
Portrait: Adlai E. Stevenson, Harper, 1965.
The Obituary Book, Stein & Day, 1971.
(Co-author) *The End of a Presidency,* Bantam Books, 1974.

Come to Judgment, Viking Books, 1980.

Contributor of book reviews to *Times Literary Supplement, New York Times, Los Angeles Times,* and other publications.

SIDELIGHTS: *Come to Judgment,* a collection of obituaries Alden Whitman wrote for the *New York Times,* sold well despite publishers' apprehensions to the contrary. Favorably reviewed in several major newspapers, the book "turns out to be an unusual 20th century history, carefully constructed on the flesh and bones of the individuals who made it. Film stars, personalities, politicians, publishers, scientists, humanitarians, emperors and artists: Whitman gently paints them all as human beings, complete with flaws and handicaps, and without adulation or scorn," reports Ben Burns in the *Detroit News.* "Essentially, what Alden Whitman has done," offers Kendall Mitchell in the *Chicago Tribune Book World,* "is piece together and sort out the often complicated lives of these personages. He has dealt with physics, movies, politics in France, music, economics, philosophy, architectural and literary movements, gossip, war, cosmetics, poetry, the shifting tides of public opinion, and the currents of world history. He has done it all with skill, perspective, and balance." Burns adds, "For the journalistic community, 'Come to Judgment' is a primer on the proper construction of an obituary."

BIOGRAPHICAL/CRITICAL SOURCES:

PERIODICALS

Chicago Tribune Book World, July 20, 1980, July 26, 1981.
Detroit News, June 29, 1980.
New York Times Book Review, July 26, 1981.
Publishers Weekly (interview), July 4, 1980.

* * *

WHITTEN, Leslie H(unter) 1928-

PERSONAL: Born February 21, 1928, in Jacksonville, Fla.; son of Leslie Hunter (an electrical engineer) and Linnora (Harvey) Whitten; married Phyllis Webber, November 11, 1951; children: Leslie Hunter III, Andrew Cassisus, Daniel Lee, Deborah Wilson Gordon. *Education:* Lehigh University, B.A. (magna cum laude), 1950.

ADDRESSES: *Home*—114 Eastmoor Dr., Silver Spring, Md. 20901. *Office*—1531 P St. N.W., Washington, D.C. 20005. *Agent*—Curtis Brown, Ltd., 575 Madison Ave., New York, N.Y. 10022.

CAREER: Radio Free Europe, news editor in Munich, Germany, 1952-55, news chief in New York, N.Y., 1955-57; International News Service, desk editor, Washington, D.C., 1957-58; United Press International, Columbia, S.C., newsman, 1958; *Washington Post,* Washington, D.C., reporter, 1958-62; Hearst Newspapers, Washington, D.C., reporter, 1963-66, assistant bureau chief, 1966-69, columnist with Jack Anderson, 1969—. Visiting associate professor, Lehigh University, 1968-70; adjunct professor, Southern Illinois University, 1984. *Military service:* U.S. Army, 1946-48; became staff sergeant.

MEMBER: American Civil Liberties Union.

AWARDS, HONORS: Honorable mention, Washington Newspaper Guild Public Service Award, 1963; California Hospital Association News Award, 1965; Edgerton Award from American Civil Liberties Union, 1974; in 1983, Lehigh University instituted a scholarship program in Whitten's name.

WRITINGS:

Progeny of the Adder (mystery novel), Doubleday, 1965.
Moon of the Wolf (mystery novel), Doubleday, 1967.
Pinion, the Golden Eagle (juvenile), Van Nostrand, 1968.
(Translator) Charles Baudelaire, *The Abyss,* The Smith, 1970.
F. Lee Bailey (biography), Avon, 1971.
The Alchemist (novel), Charterhouse Books, 1973.
Conflict of Interest (novel), Doubleday, 1976.
Sometimes a Hero (novel), Doubleday, 1979.
Washington Cycle (poems), Horizon/The Smith, 1980.
A Killing Pace (novel), Atheneum, 1983.
A Day without Sunshine (mystery novel), Atheneum, 1985.
The Lost Disciple (historical novel), Atheneum, 1989.

WORK IN PROGRESS: A novel; more poems; more translations from Baudelaire.

SIDELIGHTS: Les Whitten has traveled in the United States, Latin America, Europe, Asia, the Middle East, and elsewhere as a newsman.

BIOGRAPHICAL/CRITICAL SOURCES:

BOOKS

Downie, Leonard, *The New Muckrakers,* New Republic Book Co., 1976.
Dygent, James, *One Investigative Journalist,* Prentice-Hall, 1976.
Hume, Brit, *Inside Story,* Doubleday, 1974.

PERIODICALS

Chicago Tribune Book World, June 26, 1983.
New York Times, July 16, 1986.
Washington Post Book World, June 24, 1979, June 3, 1983, August 18, 1985.

* * *

WILBUR, Richard (Purdy) 1921-

PERSONAL: Born March 1, 1921, in New York, N.Y.; son of Lawrence Lazear (a portrait artist) and Helen Ruth (Purdy) Wilbur; married Mary Charlotte Hayes Ward, June 20, 1942; children: Ellen Dickinson, Christopher Hayes, Nathan Lord, Aaron Hammond. *Education:* Amherst College, A.B., 1942; Harvard University, A.M., 1947. *Politics:* Independent. *Religion:* Episcopal.

ADDRESSES: *Home*—Dodwells Rd., Cummington, Mass. 01026. *Office*—Department of English, Smith College, Northampton, Mass. 01063. *Agent*—(Theatrical) Gilbert Parker, William Morris Agency, 1350 Avenue of the Americas, New York, N.Y. 10019.

CAREER: Harvard University, Cambridge, Mass., Society of Fellows, junior fellow, 1947-50, assistant professor of English, 1950-54; Wellesley College, Wellesley, Mass., associate professor of English, 1955-57; Wesleyan University, Middletown, Conn., professor of English, 1957-77; Smith College, Northampton, Mass., writer in residence, 1977-86; Library of Congress, Washington, D.C., Poet Laureate of the United States, 1987-88. Lecturer at colleges, universities, and Library of Congress. U.S. State Department cultural exchange representative to the U.S.S.R., 1961. *Military service:* U.S. Army, Infantry, 1943-45; became staff sergeant.

MEMBER: American Academy and Institute of Arts and Letters (president, 1974-76; chancellor, 1976-78), American Academy of Arts and Sciences, PEN, Academy of American Poets (chancellor), Dramatists' Guild, Authors League of America, Century Club, Chi Psi.

AWARDS, HONORS: Harriet Monroe Memorial Prize, *Poetry* magazine, 1948, 1978; Oscar Blumenthal Prize, *Poetry* magazine, 1950; M.A., Amherst College, 1952; Guggenheim fellowships, 1952-53, 1963; Prix de Roma fellowship, American Academy of Arts and Letters, 1954; Edna St. Vincent Millay Memorial Award, 1957; Pulitzer Prize for poetry and National Book Award for poetry, both 1957, for *Things of This World;* Boston Festival Award, 1959; Ford Foundation fellowship for drama, 1960; Melville Cane Award, 1962; co-recipient, Bollingen Prize for translation, Yale University Library, 1963, for *Tartuffe,* and for poetry, 1971, for *Walking to Sleep;* Sarah Josepha Hale Award, 1968; Creative Arts Award, Brandeis University, 1971; Prix Henri Desfeuilles, 1971; Shelley Memorial Award, 1973; *Book World*'s Children's Spring Book Festival award, 1973, for *Opposites: Poems and Drawings;* PEN translation Prize, 1983, for *Moliere: Four Comedies;* St. Botolph's Club Foundation Award, 1983; Drama Desk Award, 1983; Chevalier, Ordre des Palmes Academiques, 1983; named Poet Laureate of the United States, Library of Congress, 1987-88; *Los Angeles Times* Book Prize, 1988, Pulitzer Prize, 1989, for *New and Collected Poems;* Taylor Poetry Award, *Sewanee Review* and University of the South, 1988. L.H.D., Lawrence College (now Lawrence University of Wisconsin), 1960, Washington University, 1964, Williams College, 1975, University of Rochester, 1976, and Carnegie-Mellon University, 1980; Litt.D., Amherst College, 1967, Clark University, 1970, American International College, 1974, Marquette University, 1977, Wesleyan University, 1977, and Lake Forest College, 1982.

WRITINGS:

The Beautiful Changes and Other Poems, Reynal, 1947.

Ceremony and Other Poems, Harcourt, 1950.

Things of This World: Poems (also see below), Harcourt, 1956.

Poems, 1943-1956, Faber, 1957.

(With Robert Hillyer and Cleanth Brooks) *Anniversary Lectures,* U.S. Government Printing Office, 1959.

(With Louise Bogan and Archibald MacLeish) *Emily Dickinson: Three Views* (criticism), Amherst College Press, 1960.

Advice to a Prophet, and Other Poems, Harcourt, 1961.

Loudmouse (juvenile), illustrated by Don Almquist, Collier, 1963, Harcourt, 1982.

The Poems of Richard Wilbur, Harcourt, 1963.

(Translator) Philippe de Thaun, *The Pelican from a Bestiary of 1120* (poem), privately printed, 1963.

Prince Souvanna Phouma: An Exchange between Richard Wilbur and William Jay Smith (poem), limited edition, Phoenix Book Shop, 1968.

Walking to Sleep: New Poems and Translations, Harcourt, 1969.

Digging to China: Poem (Child Study Association book list; first published in *Things of This World*), Doubleday, 1970.

(Self-illustrated) *Opposites: Poems and Drawings* (children's poems), Harcourt, 1973.

Seed Leaves: Homage to R. F. (poem), limited edition, David R. Godine, 1974.

Responses: Prose Pieces, 1953-1976, Harcourt, 1976.

The Mind-Reader: New Poems, Harcourt, 1976.

Seven Poems, Abbatoir Editions, 1981.

(Translator) *The Whale and Other Uncollected Translations,* Boa Editions, 1982.

Richard Wilbur's Creation, University of Michigan Press, 1983.

New and Collected Poems, Harcourt, 1988.

PLAYS

(Translator) Jean Baptiste Poquelin Moliere, *The Misanthrope: Comedy in Five Acts, 1666* (also see below; first produced in Cambridge, Mass., by the Poet's Theatre, October 25, 1955; produced Off-Broadway at Theatre East, November 12, 1956), Harcourt, 1955.

(Lyricist with John Latouche, Dorothy Parker, Lillian Hellman, and Leonard Bernstein) Voltaire, *Candide: A Comic Operetta Based on Voltaire's Satire* (musical; based on adaptation by Lillian Hellman; music by Leonard Bernstein; first produced on Broadway at Martin Beck Theatre, December 1, 1956; produced on the West End at Saville Theatre, April 30, 1959), Random House, 1957.

(Translator) Moliere, *Tartuffe: Comedy in Five Acts, 1669* (also see below; first produced in Milwaukee, Wis., at Fred Miller Theatre, January, 1964; produced on Broadway at ANTA Theatre, January 14, 1965), Harcourt, 1963.

(Translator) Moliere, *The Misanthrope* [and] *Tartuffe,* Harcourt, 1965.

(Translator) Moliere, *The School for Wives: Comedy in Five Acts, 1662* (first produced on Broadway at Lyceum Theatre, February 16, 1971), Harcourt, 1971.

(Translator) Moliere, *The Learned Ladies: Comedy in Five Acts, 1672* (first produced in Williamstown, Mass., at the Williamstown Festival Theatre, 1977), Harcourt, 1978.

(Translator) Jean Racine, *Andromanche: Tragedy in Five Acts, 1667,* Harcourt, 1982.

(Translator) *Moliere: Four Comedies,* Harcourt, 1982.

(Translator) Racine, *Phaedra,* Harcourt, 1986.

EDITOR

(With Louis Untermeyer and Karl Shapiro) *Modern American and Modern British Poetry,* revised abridged edition, Harcourt, 1955.

A Bestiary (anthology), Pantheon, 1955.

(And author of introduction and notes) Edgar Allan Poe, *Poe: Complete Poems,* Dell, 1959.

(Editor of section on Poe) *Major Writers of America,* Harcourt, 1962.

(With Alfred Harbage, and author of introduction) William Shakespeare, *Poems,* Penguin, 1966, revised edition published as *Shakespeare, the Narrative Poems and Poems of Doubtful Authenticity,* 1974.

(And author of introduction) Poe, *The Narrative of Arthur Gordon Pym,* David R. Godine, 1974.

(And author of introduction) Witter Bynner, *Selected Poems,* Farrar, Straus, 1978.

OTHER

(Contributor) Gygory Kepes, editor, *The New Landscape in Art and Science,* Paul Theobald, 1955.

"Poems" (recording), Spoken Arts, 1959.

(Contributor) Don C. Allen, editor, *The Moment of Poetry,* Johns Hopkins Press, 1962.

(Lyricist) "On Freedom's Ground" (cantata; music by William Schuman), first produced in New York City at the Lincoln Center for the Statue of Liberty Centennial, October, 1986.

Also recorded "Richard Wilbur Reading His Own Poems," for Caedmon. Translator of *The Funeral of Bobo,* by Joseph Brodsky, for Ardis. Work represented in anthologies. Contributor of critical reviews to periodicals. General editor, "Laurel Poets" series, for Dell; former member of poetry board, Wesleyan University Press.

SIDELIGHTS: Richard Wilbur "is a poet for all of us, whose elegant words brim with wit and paradox," announced Librarian of Congress Daniel J. Boorstin when the poet succeeded Robert Penn Warren to become the second Poet Laureate of the United

States. Elizabeth Kastor further quotes Boorstin in her *Washington Post* article: "He is also a poet's poet, at home in the long tradition of the traveled ways of the great poets of our language. . . . His poems are among the best our country has to offer." The new poet laureate has won the Pulitzer Prize and National Book Award for his collection *Things of This World: Poems,* among other numerous awards for his poetry. His translations of French verse, especially Voltaire's *Candide,* and the plays of Jean-Baptiste Moliere and Jean Racine, are also highly regarded by critics; his translation of Moliere's *Tartuffe* won the 1971 Bollingen Prize. But because of Wilbur's dedication to the traditional forms of rhyme and meter, and unwillingness to compose experimental poetry, his work has in the past stirred controversy among critics.

The son of a commercial artist, Wilbur was interested in painting as a youth; but he eventually opted to pursue writing as his avocation, a decision he attributes to the influence of his mother's father and grandfather, both of whom were editors. As a student, Wilbur wrote stories, editorials, and poems for his college newspaper and magazine, but, as the poet comments in *Twentieth Century Authors: A Biographical Dictionary of Modern Literature:* "It was not until World War II took me to Cassino, Anzio, and the Siegfried Line that I began to versify in earnest. One does not use poetry for its major purposes, as a means to organize oneself and the world, until one's world somehow gets out of hand." Witnessing war firsthand has had a major effect on Wilbur's poetry. "Many of his first poems had a common motive," writes Richard L. Calhoun in the *Dictionary of Literary Biography,* "the desire to stress the importance of finding order in a world where war had served as a reminder of disorder and destruction."

Because of this motivation, Wilbur's first collection, *The Beautiful Changes and Other Poems,* contains "more poetic exercises on how to face the problems of disorder and destruction than laments over the losses occasioned by the war," notes Calhoun. The poems in this book, according to Donald L. Hill in his *Richard Wilbur,* also demonstrate "a pervasive good humor, a sweetness of spirit, unusual among the major poets of the century." This generally light-hearted approach that Wilbur uses in his poetry has caused some critics of his early work to charge the poet with avoiding tragic themes by covering them with purely aesthetic verse. James Dickey, for example, writes in his book, *Babel to Byzantium,* that one has "the feeling that the cleverness of phrase and the delicious aptness of Wilbur's poems sometimes mask an unwillingness or inability to think or feel deeply; that the poems tend to lapse toward highly sophisticated play." John Reibetanz speculates in *Modern Poetry Studies* that this is because "for Richard Wilbur, the sights offered by World War II contradict and threaten his most basic beliefs, as we can infer them from his writings: that love is more powerful than hatred; that nature is a source of values and of reassurance; and that there is a strong creative urge in both man and nature which constantly seeks and finds expression in images of graceful plenitude." "But in the 1940's," Reibetanz concludes, "the utter disparity between what he saw and what he wished to see made him run for cover."

The explanation for his choice of subjects and preference for a light-hearted tone in his poetry is, in Wilbur's view, not so much a matter of running from reality as it is a matter of affirming a philosophical conviction. "I feel that the universe is full of glorious energy," he explains in an interview with Peter Stitt in the *Paris Review,* "that the energy tends to take pattern and shape, and that the ultimate character of things is comely and good. I am perfectly aware that I say this in the teeth of all sorts of contrary evidence, and that I must be basing it partly on temperament and partly on faith, but that's my attitude." Still, the poet does not completely refuse to address serious issues. Robert B. Shaw comments in *Parnassus: Poetry in Review* that while "it is true that some of Wilbur's earlier poems veer with disconcerting abruptness from the naturalistic to the esthetic. . . . He has never, in fact, avoided negative subject matter as completely as some critics have charged." The critic later asserts that several poems in his third collection, *Things of This World,* deal directly with humane and political issues.

Certain reviewers have persisted in their arguments that it is necessary for a poet to occasionally use a tragic tone of voice in order to capture all the aspects of life in his poetry. Hill maintains: "A bitter or anguished poet, if he is equally skillful and equally just in his response to his experience, may strike even more deeply into our feelings." Echoing this sentiment, *Sewanee Review* contributor Paul Ramsey feels that Wilbur's tone tends to mar his work. The critic declares in an article on *The Mind-Reader: New Poems* that "the calm precision of touch, the middle-distanced eye, the self-awareness of technique, which make for a comfortably joyful light verse, tend to undercut more serious occasions." But even though Wilbur's is not the tragic mind that many readers sometimes expect to see in poets, Dickey retorts that the poems "are as true and heartening a picture as we are ever likely to have of the best that the twentieth-century American can say of himself or have said about him." Commenting on his 1988 book, *New and Collected Poems,* Robert Richman also reminds critics in his *New York Times Book Review* article: "If it were not for writers like [Wilbur], future students might wonder if there were no poets in the late 20th century who championed beauty . . . or who were capable of rising above all the despair and doubt."

But changes in attitudes toward poetry in the 1960s alienated the future laureate from his fellow poets, as David H. Van Biema's *People* article explains: "American poetry appeared to be moving away from the style at which [Wilbur] excelled. Younger poets such as Allen Ginsberg, Gregory Corso and Robert Creeley were tossing away the traces of metric form completely or engaging in an uncooked, violently confessional poetry that Wilbur would not emulate." The new approaches did not appeal to Wilbur, who comments on the subject in an interview collected in William Packard's *The Craft of Poetry: Interviews from the New York Quarterly:* "I don't like, I can't adjust to, simplistic political poetry, the crowd-pleasing sort of anti-Vietnam poem. I can't adjust to the kind of Black poetry that simply cusses and hollers artlessly. And most of all I can't adjust to the sort of poem, which is mechanically, prosaically 'irrational,' which is often self-pitying, which starts all its sentences with 'I,' and which writes constantly out of a limply subjective world."

While Wilbur obdurately composed reflective, optimistic poetry, using traditional patterns of rhyme and meter, the changing poetic movements that flowed by him caused his image to change over the years. "His poetry was judged too impersonal for the early 1960s," testifies Calhoun; "it was not politically involved enough during the literary protests against the war in Vietnam in the later 1960s, and, in the 1970s, not sufficiently postmodernist." Calhoun does note that Wilbur's poems of the 1960s show some experimentation, "but in comparison with what other poets, Robert Lowell and John Berryman for example, were doing by 1961, the experimentation is comparatively minor." His skill at using rhyme and meter, however, is generally acknowledged among critics like *London Magazine* reviewer Roy Fuller, who believes that "Wilbur is excellent at inventing stanza forms, and his stanzas rhyming in pairs are particularly effective." "His intricately patterned poems reflect the discovery of patterns of natural beauty," adds Shaw.

"I think that critics of Wilbur's urbane formalism have often failed to appreciate the deep emotional needs met by it, and so have overlooked the seriousness of his commitment to it," opines Reibetanz. Indeed, according to Wilbur in a *Paris Review* interview with Ellesa Clay High and Helen McCloy Ellison, his poetic style and need for order in the world are related. The poet remarks: "One of the jobs of poetry is to make the unbearable bearable, not by falsehood but by clear, precise confrontation." Because his formal technique is a matter of personal preference, Wilbur emphasizes that he is not against others using free verse. "I'm thought to have a quarrel with free-verse poets," he tells David Dillon in the *Southwest Review.* "I really don't at all. I just choose to write free verse that happens to rhyme or to fall into a stanza pattern." "We must recognize that meter in itself is not rigid—," he remarks to Stitt, "it depends on how you use it."

Wilbur's insistence on formalism, critics soon found, was naturally suited to his work in translating French poetry and plays. Speaking of his "tactful, metrical and speakable translation of verse drama," *Hudson Review* critic Alan Shaw comments: "Wilbur's [translations] are almost the solitary example of this kind in English. And it is precisely, I think, because he has stood somewhat apart from the tradition on English-language poetry in this century . . . that he has been able to achieve this." He concludes that "Richard Wilbur's translations of classic French drama are among the undiscovered treasure of our recent literature." The expertise and importance of the poet's translations of plays by Moliere, Voltaire, and Racine has been little questioned by reviewers. "The rendition [of Moliere's *The Misanthrope*], delightful and literate, made Moliere accessible for the first time to a wide American audience and was the start of a lucrative sideline for the poet," writes Van Biema. Compared to other translators, *Saturday Review* contributor John Ciardi believes that "instead of cognate-snapping, as the academic dullards invariably do, [in his translation of *The Misanthrope*] Wilbur has found English equivalents for the turn and nuance of the French, and the fact that he has managed to do so in rhymed couplets that not only respect themselves as English poetry but allow the play to be staged . . . with great success is testament enough."

Contrary to the view that Wilbur's poems have not evolved over the years, several critics feel that the translations have had a noticeable effect on his verse. X. J. Kennedy avers in the *Los Angeles Times Book Review* that "his recent poems are more easily speakable—a result, I suspect, of his translating so much Moliere. More often now, the poems tell stories." And Wilbur admits in a *Time* article by Patricia Blake: "The experience of translating Moliere has enlarged the voice of my own poems. . . . Sometimes I have the illusion that I speak for him." In an article he wrote, which appears in *Shenandoah,* Wilbur says that his "writing is now plainer and more straightforward than it used to be." "Another change in my work has been a partial shift from the ironic meditative lyric toward the dramatic poem," he adds.

Analyzing the laureate's book *New and Collected Poems, Los Angeles Times Book Review* contributor Joshua Odell believes these newer poems "clearly show a continued evolution in style from an ornate elegance found particularly in Wilbur's first collection, 'The Beautiful Changes,' toward a simple, direct and crisp verse." Still, poems like those in *The Mind Reader* manage "to stand up against every kind of poetic chic," according to Bruce Michelson in *Southern Review.* And as some critics have noted, the changes in Wilbur's poetry have not affected the basic philosophy his verses have always shown. "He seems to be seeking even firmer and more affirmative statements of the need for order and responsibility; and his tone in the later poems is more confident, more self-assured," asserts Calhoun. This is a need that Wilbur feels all poets should attempt to meet in their work. In his book, *Responses: Prose Pieces, 1953-1976,* the laureate declares: "Every poet is impelled to utter the whole of the world that is real to him, to respond to that world in some spirit, and to draw all its parts toward some *coherence.*"

Through his efforts to illustrate an optimistic viewpoint, while using traditional techniques on meter and rhyme, Wilbur is able to show considerable depth in his poems, according to William Heyen in *Southern Review.* "There is for me in the poetry of Richard Wilbur something just past the threshold of realization," writes Heyen, "something elusive, something toward which his formal structures edge and with which they bump shoulders, something that criticism can only hope to graze. This something, I think, is feeling, passion." *P.N. Review* contributor J. D. McClatchy also sees that there is more to Wilbur's poetry than is readily apparent. "Scrupulous questioning and elegant rhetoric, in such skilful hands," he maintains, "can better contour the chaos than the wildest poem; can make us feel the tension between the light touch and the darkness it holds back. One has to watch carefully, beneath the performance that would convince us otherwise, for the harsher realities on which these poems are founded."

AVOCATIONAL INTERESTS: Tennis, herb gardening, walking.

CA INTERVIEW

CA interviewed Richard Wilbur by telephone on June 15, 1988, at his home in Cummington, Massachusetts.

CA: In the New York Times Book Review, *Robert Richman called the publication of your* New and Collected Poems *"an occasion to celebrate." This fall will also mark the end of your year as Poet Laureate of the United States. Have these rather public events occasioned a time of quiet introspection as well as celebration?*

WILBUR: I've enjoyed these events very much, being the Laureate for a year in Washington and also finally getting all my books between two covers. But I shouldn't say quiet introspection, no. I think that however one chooses to handle the Laureate appointment in Washington, it's going to be much more public than life usually is for poets. I suppose there are some practical, efficient poets around, but I'm not one of them. I find that when I'm put into the position of having a desk with telephones on it and having a calendar with dates on it—in fact with hours on it—I cannot think of very much else. I certainly can't be deeply introspective. So I'm looking forward to a year of doing very little of a public nature and getting in touch with myself again, learning once again how to write a poem.

CA: Do you think the still new position of Poet Laureate signifies a greater appreciation of poets and their work?

WILBUR: I think it does. I don't really know how all of the members of Congress feel about poetry, but I do know that Senator Matsunaga, who for many years in the House of Representatives and in the Senate has been pushing for the Laureate appointment, recently managed to get his bill put through. That should signify a change of heart to some extent. However the appointment may be meant by the Congress and by the government, it certainly has the effect of bringing much more attention to poetry, of honoring American poetry in a way that I think is the most important aspect of the new position. That is to say, I don't think the importance of it is that a particular person holds it at a particular time; I think the importance of it is that the job exists at all.

CA: One of the delights of your poetry is its wide and rich vocabulary, the joy it seems to demonstrate in right words. Were you enchanted with words early on?

WILBUR: Yes. I've always been crazy about words, and I suppose that one really wouldn't consider trying to be a poet if that weren't a continual delight and obsession. I can't think offhand of any poet whose work I like in whom I don't find a keen pleasure in the words of our common language, and also in the historical roots of those words, the etymologies of those words, and in the uses which they've had in other and earlier hands.

CA: Your father was a painter, and paintings have inspired many of your poems. Did you ever consider art as a possible choice for a career?

WILBUR: Yes, I did, in a way. In the house where I grew up, all sorts of arts were practiced in a sort of easygoing and, in most cases, nonprofessional way. But we enjoyed everything we tried our hand at. Of course I tried to paint, and I did one or two things my father was kind about. But I don't think I showed any particular color genius. I also think that my father was a much handier man than I, much better with his hands in all respects. You have to be that in order to be a painter. A painter really does work in a physical way with this art, from the stretching of the canvasses to the framing. I tried it, but it didn't seem to me that I was going to be outstanding. I did do a lot of drawing and cartooning when I was a young man. When I was at college, I did cartoons for the undergraduate magazine at Amherst. And as late as the late 1940s I was thinking of myself as somebody who *could,* if he struck out on all other matters, become a political cartoonist or even a comic-strip artist.

CA: That's interesting. It certainly is obvious from your writing that art plays a big part in it.

WILBUR: Yes, it does. Especially in my early poems I tended to write about objects of art and about paintings. But of course poetry itself is a very visual art; that's the major sense which the poet employs. There's a considerable affinity between poetry and painting—always has been.

CA: While it may be impossible to write for an audience—and I tend to believe it is—do you think consciously of what readers might "get" from your poems, or see in them? Do you have some hope for them when they go out to readers?

WILBUR: When they go out, yes; not while I'm writing them. I think that the only times I've ever thought keenly about an audience while writing in verse was when I was writing lyrics for Broadway shows. If you're writing for a show like *Candide,* for which I wrote most of the lyrics back in 1956, you really do have to think about what people understand, what words they're familiar with, and what things will amuse them. I don't think one does that in writing poems. I agree with you that that's an unlikely thing. I. A. Richards once, however, put the answer to this question in a very satisfying way, I think he said that the poet, though he may not address a particular audience consciously, is always addressing some "condition of the language." That is, if you're the kind of poet who uses a word like *eleemosynary* in his poem, you're not directly thinking, perhaps, of a public which will understand that work or be willing to look it up, but you're creating an object which implies that kind of a public. You think of some state of the language rather than of an audience. But an audience, I suppose, is always implicit.

CA: You've said that you sometimes spend years writing a poem. Do you always have a sure sense of when a poem is right, complete?

WILBUR: I generally do. Sometimes I have a sudden firm sense that, for all the time I've given it, the poem I've just finished is wrong, and that I'd better not send it out. But mostly, working as slowly and self-critically as I do, I won't have moved ahead with a poem without feeling that what's behind me is OK. So, if I manage to find a satisfactory close for the poem, I usually feel that I've done the best I could with the material that had occurred to me.

CA: In one of the Paris Review *interviews you said in response to a question about formalism's liberating rather than confirming the imagination, "I think you have to be using your brains all the time, yes, but your brains have to be attentive to the stupid part of you." Will you talk about the "stupid part," what that term meant to you and how it figures in the process of making poems?*

WILBUR: Of course that word *stupid* was a sassy way of saying it. I could find some resonant and Jungian word, I suppose, for the part of the self I was speaking of when I said "stupid." I do think that when you're writing on all eight, you write with reaches of your own nature and depths of your own experience which aren't readily available to you at ordinary times. And one way to commune with the deeper and stranger parts of one's self, I think, is by taking advantage of the irrational suggestions that adherence to certain formal demands can make. In that interview I said that the need to rhyme often brings to mind all sorts of unexpected words, some of which may turn out to tell you what it was you semiconsciously or unconsciously meant to say.

CA: How satisfying it must be when things click in just that way.

WILBUR: It is. It's like having a good throw at dice, and you feel scarcely more responsible for it.

CA: Has the process of writing become easier or harder for you, or otherwise changed over the years?

WILBUR: I think it's probably become a little harder. Robert Frost has often been quoted as answering, when asked why he wrote poems, that he wrote poems to see if he could make them all different. Of course that's an evasive answer, and yet there's some truth in it. You don't want doggedly and consciously to repeat yourself. I think that everybody who's at all serious as a poet will find himself returning to certain concerns and working them over again, perhaps finding out something a little new about them. But you don't want to write the same poem twice. And since everybody has a finite imagination, I suppose it happens when you're a young poet that you cover a lot of your potential territory with first poems, and then it becomes a little harder to return, however obliquely, however unsuspectingly, to the same territory and find something new in it. So, for that reason, it gets harder to write as you go along. You don't want to repeat yourself; you do want to continue to interest yourself, and to be changing.

CA: You have homes in Cummington, Massachusetts, and Key West. Is one place more conducive to writing than the other?

WILBUR: I write about as well in one place as in the other. The odd difference for me between the two places is that the world of New England is the one which seems like the familiar and serious world to me. In it I find all sorts of things ready to hand to write about—or to mention, at any rate. I still haven't managed to incorporate jasmine and orchid trees and mangroves and many of the charming things about Key West into my poems. I'll do it in time, I know. But I've been going to Key West since 1964, so I've been making a sort of slow imaginative adjustment to the place, which will probably bear fruit next year or the next.

CA: How do you feel your work as a translator of Moliere and Racine has benefitted your original poetry?

WILBUR: It benefits you in various ways. Of course there are drawbacks too, but one thing that any kind of translation does is to broaden you. I don't think poetry is much good unless you hear a speaking human voice in it—not necessarily an actor's voice, but something approaching it. I think all good poetry has to have some quality of the dramatic. If you do a translation effectively and truly, it involves a kind of justifiable act of impersonation. That extends your range. It extends the range of what you have been able to put down on paper in the way of ideas and feelings. There's some transference from that to your own original work. And no doubt there are other benefits. I think that if you translate as many plays as I have done—I've now done six classical French plays—the writing of dramatic speeches inclines you, simply out of momentum, to be in some sense more dramatic in your own work.

CA: It must be tremendously exciting to see that work you've translated being performed on the stage. I wonder if it isn't very much the same feeling that the original playwright has.

WILBUR: I think so. Although I try to be very, very faithful to the originals, I put a great deal of myself into them. I write as slowly when I'm translating as I do when I'm writing my own work, and I confess that by the time I'm finished doing a play by Moliere, I very much feel that it's mine. It's full of my choices. So I'm very anxious for Moliere or Racine in my translation to be properly acted. I continually stand up for those dead fellows and try to get them their rights.

CA: Do you read fiction?

WILBUR: I'm not very good anymore at reading the old three-decker, the very thick novel. But I do read quite a lot of fiction, maybe twenty novels in a year, and I read quite a bit of light fiction. I have some detective writers and some humor writers whom I favor very much.

CA: In your essay "Explaining the Obvious" you noted that "it is one mark of the good critic that he abstain from busywork." What do you feel are the proper functions of criticism, and how well do you think poetry criticism is being done now?

WILBUR: This is going to sound simple-minded, but I'll defend myself: I think the main thing to do in criticism is to tell somebody else who might be about to read what you've just read what you see in it and what he just possibly might miss if he read with a little less care or experience than you have read with. It's mostly a matter of appreciative mediation, I think. Of course there's a higher level of criticism at which the critic dares to say whether something should have been written at all, dares to think that he knows what the intent of the author was and that he can judge whether the author has succeeded or failed. Those are considerable altitudes. What most interests me is simply to give people my reactions, which I hope are sympathetic and painstaking.

CA: As a long-time teacher, what part of writing do you think can be taught, and how can aspiring poets best be helped in a classroom or workshop setting?

WILBUR: There are various things you can do. People are always asking those who have taught writing classes whether they can actually teach writing and the answer is: No, of course you can't; there are certain horses you just can't lead to water. But it seems to me that you can give people a sympathetic and at the same time sharp and demanding hearing. You can try to be the best possible kind of an audience for young writers or for struggling writers. You can sometimes discover what someone's strong point is and help him to know that a little sooner than he might otherwise. You can ask people, it they're willing, to do little light-hearted exercises which can in one way or another shake up the imagination, broaden the approach to writing. I used to ask my students to write riddles, for example. That's not a very coercive thing to ask, and it turned out to be fun for almost everybody. But if people are willing to take your suggestion and try their hands at riddles, then they find themselves writing wit poetry, a thing they might not have essayed otherwise. All sorts of suggestions of that kind can limber people up a little and perhaps help them discover their possibilities.

CA: Would you like to see more magazines or special journals that publish poetry?

WILBUR: No. It seems to me that there are quantities of magazines publishing poetry in America right now, maybe more than we need. That probably sounds unpleasant, but I do think there are many magazines which are not very demanding and which are not awfully readable. Maybe it would be better if we had a smaller number of very choosy magazines to which writers could aspire. But in any case, I think that back in the teens and twenties of this century there was a fairly justified feeling on the part of many experimental writers that the commercial publishers weren't venturesome enough, that the popular magazines were stodgy, that they had to create their own so-called little magazines and hope for new presses which would dare to publish their innovative work. That's just not the situation now. I think that anybody who writes at all well has a pretty good chance of being published in America today.

CA: How badly do you think American poetry has been hurt by the confessional mood and work that became so acceptable in the sixties?

WILBUR: There were some really fine, indeed brilliant, practitioners of the confessional style. The trouble with it is, if you're going to talk about your own life and mind, you'd better have an interesting life and mind. And not all of the people who in the last couple of decades have been writing a very personal, chatty, unambitious, and prosaic sort of verse seem to me to be interesting in either way. So I'm glad that the period of prevalence of the confessional seems to be passing. I think it's important, at any rate, that our most talented people be challenged to be broader than that—broader than that is likely to be in some hands, anyway. Altogether too much of it sounds like the ramblings of the man on the next bar stool.

CA: Do you see or anticipate—or hope for—new trends in poetry?

WILBUR: I haven't really any particular notions about that. I hear people saying what I think is true: that there is a revival of interest in the fundamental techniques of poetry, in meters and rhymes and stanzas and all that. I'm glad of that, because it will be a change and it will extend some of our poets and give them new leases on life. It'll probably have an effect on our sense of content in poetry as well. I don't think that one would do a lot of bar-stool rambling in stanzaic form. And I think the fact that there is a certain reviving interest in traditional means will probably have a salutary effect on the tonal range of poetry.

CA: You said in the beginning of this talk that you're looking forward to getting beck to quiet and to writing. Are there specific things you want to write that you can talk about?

WILBUR: At the moment I'm tinkering a little with a lecture I gave at the Library of Congress in May, called "The Persistence of Riddles." I'm trying to polish that up so that it can be published in a magazine and also published in pamphlet form by the Library. After that, I've taken care not to be involved in any musical shows or translations or anything else for the time being. I'm just going to wait and see if some poems don't hit me.

BIOGRAPHICAL/CRITICAL SOURCES:

BOOKS

Contemporary Literary Criticism, Gale, Volume 3, 1975, Volume 6, 1976, Volume 9, 1978, Volume 14, 1980, Volume 53, 1989.

Cummins, Paul F., *Richard Wilbur,* Eerdmans, 1971.

Dickey, James, *Babel to Byzantium,* Farrar, Straus, 1968.

Dictionary of Literary Biography, Volume 5: *American Poets since World War II,* Gale, 1980.

Field, John, *Richard Wilbur: A Biographical Checklist,* Kent State University Press, 1971.

French, Warren, editor, *The Fifties: Fiction, Poetry, Drama,* Everett/ Edwards, 1970.

Hill, Donald L., *Richard Wilbur,* Twayne, 1967.

Hungerford, Edward, editor, *Poets in Progress,* Northwestern University Press, 1962, new edition, 1967.

Jarrell, Randall, *Poetry and the Age,* Knopf, 1953.

Jarrell, Randall, *The Third Book of Criticism,* Farrar, Straus, 1969.

Kunitz, Stanley, and Vineta Colby, *Twentieth Century Authors: A Biographical Dictionary of Modern Literature,* H. W. Wilson, 1955.

Packard, William, editor, *The Craft of Poetry: Interviews from the New York Quarterly,* Doubleday, 1974.

Nemerov, Howard, editor, *Poets on Poetry,* Basic Books, 1966.

Rosenthal, M. L., *The Modern Poets,* Oxford University Press, 1965.

Stepanchev, Stephen, *American Poetry since 1945,* Harper, 1965.

Wilbur, Richard, *Responses: Prose Pieces, 1953-1976,* Harcourt, 1976.

PERIODICALS

Bulletin of Bibliography, January-March, 1980.

Christian Century, March 19, 1958.

Hollins Critic, April, 1977.

Hudson Review, summer, 1969, summer, 1987.

London Magazine, July, 1957.

Los Angeles Times, March 17, 1983, April 18, 1987, October 13, 1987.

Los Angeles Times Book Review, July 31, 1988, October 9, 1988.

Modern Poetry Studies, Volume 2, numbers 1 and 2, 1982.

Nation, November 3, 1956.

National Review, September 2, 1988.

New Republic, June 5, 1976.

New York Times, January 28, 1983.

New York Times Book Review, December 14, 1969, December 26, 1982, April 18, 1987, May 29, 1988.

Paris Review, winter, 1977.

Parnassus: Poetry in Review, spring/summer, 1977.

People, October 5, 1987.

P.N. Review, Volume 13, number 5, 1987.

Saturday Review, August 18, 1956.

Sewanee Review, spring, 1978.

Shenandoah, fall, 1965.

Southern Review, summer, 1973, July, 1979.

Southwest Review, summer, 1973.

Time, November 19, 1984.

Times Literary Supplement, May 20, 1977.

Tribune Books (Chicago), July 24, 1988.

Washington Post, July 25, 1976, October 6, 1987.

—Sketch by Kevin S. Hile

—Interview by Jean W. Ross

* * *

WILEY, David Sherman 1935-

PERSONAL: Born November 9, 1935, in Eldorado, Ill.; son of Kenneth L. (an auto dealer) and Martha Louise (Summers) Wiley; married Christine A. Root, August 25, 1985; children: Stephen B., Thomas M. C., Mark A. Root-Wiley. *Education:* Wabash College, B.A., 1957; Yale University, M.Div., 1961; Princeton University and Theological Seminary, Ph.D., 1971. *Religion:* Protestant.

ADDRESSES: Home—729 Sunset Ln., East Lansing, Mich. 48823. *Office*—African Studies Center, Michigan State University, East Lansing, Mich. 48824-1035.

CAREER: University of Zambia, instructor, 1966-67; University of Wisconsin—Madison, assistant professor of sociology, 1968-76, chairman of African studies program, 1972-76; Michigan State University, East Lansing, assistant professor and director of African Studies Center, beginning 1977-84; associate professor of sociology, 1984—. Co-chairperson, Task Force on Elementary, Secondary, and Undergraduate Education, National Council on Foreign Language and International Studies, 1980-85; vice-chairperson, U.S. National Commission for United Nations Educational, Scientific, and Cultural Organization, 1983-87; chairperson, National Science Foundation International Advisory Committee, 1987—.

MEMBER: American Sociological Association (chairperson of various committees), American Association for the Advancement of Science (chairperson of various committees), Society for Scientific Study of Religion, African Studies Association.

WRITINGS:

African Language Instruction in the United States: Directions and Priorities for the 1980s, African Studies Center, Michigan State University, 1980.

(With Marylee C. Crofts) *The Third World: Africa,* Pendulum Press, 1972, 2nd edition, 1981.

(And co-editor) *Southern Africa: Society, Economy, and Liberation,* African Studies Center, Michigan State University, 1982.

Africa on Film and Videotape, 1960-1981, African Studies Center, Michigan State University, 1983.

(With Frank H. Rosegren) *Internationalizing Your School,* National Council on Foreign Language and International Studies, 1983.
Education for South Africans and Namibians, African Studies Center, Michigan State University, 1989.
Group Portrait: International Education in the Academic Disciplines, National Council on Foreign Language and International Studies, 1989.

Guest editor and editorial advisor, *Issue,* 1973-74.

WORK IN PROGRESS: A study of housing, health, education, and the labor force in Zambia; a book on urban society in Zambia.

SIDELIGHTS: David Sherman Wiley once told *CA* that he is "deeply concerned with United States policy concerning Southern Africa and Africa in general; [he is] involved in extension of information and interest concerning Africa into schools and universities; [and is] working actively in policy-related research for the development of independent African nations."

* * *

WILLIAMS, Benjamin H(arrison) 1889-1974

PERSONAL: Born March 23, 1889, in Eugene, Ore.; died September 11, 1974; son of John Monroe (an attorney) and Jennie Mary (Gwin) Williams; married Helene Frances Ogsbury, June 17, 1917 (died, 1948); married Evelyn Ernestine Allemong, August 25, 1951; children: (first marriage) Patricia Gwynne (Mrs. Robert Case McMann), Stanton Monroe. *Education:* University of Oregon, A.B., 1910, A.M., 1912; attended Harvard Law School, 1912-13; University of California, Berkeley, Ph.D., 1921; studied in Europe. *Politics:* Independent Democrat. *Religion:* Unitarian-Universalist.

ADDRESSES: Home—3 Forestdale Dr., Asheville, N.C. 28803.

CAREER: State Industrial Accident Commission, Salem, Ore., statistician, 1914-16, Extension Division, secretary of social welfare, 1916-17; University of Pennsylvania, Philadelphia, instructor in political science, 1921-23; University of Pittsburgh, Pittsburgh, Pa., assistant professor, 1923-27, associate professor, 1927-30, professor of political science, 1930-43; U.S. Department of War, analyst in Military Intelligence Division, 1943; U.S. Department of State, division assistant, 1943-44; Industrial College of the Armed Forces, member of staff in political economy, 1944-59, specialist in education, 1950-59; researcher and writer, beginning 1959. Visiting summer professor, University of Oregon, 1921, 1923, 1925, 1927; lecturer, Bryn Mawr College, 1923. Consultant to U.S. Information Agency, 1960. *Military service:* U.S. Army, 1917-19; became first lieutenant.

MEMBER: American Association for the Advancement of Science (chairman of section K, 1956; vice president; fellow), National Academy of Economics and Political Science (chairman, 1948-59), University of Oregon Alumni Association (chairman, 1914), Pisgah Council Girl Scouts (treasurer, 1963-66), Civitan (scholarship chairman, 1964-70).

AWARDS, HONORS: Decoration for exceptional civilian service, U.S. Department of the Army, 1959.

WRITINGS:

Economic Foreign Policy of the United States, McGraw, 1929, reprinted, Fertig, 1967.
A Series of Twelve Radio Talks on the London Naval Conference: Its Background and Results, University of Pittsburgh, 1930.
The United States and Disarmament, McGraw, 1931, reprinted, Kennikat, 1973.
American Diplomacy: Policies and Practice, McGraw, 1936, reprinted, Century Bookbindery, 1980.
Foreign Loan Policy of the United States since 1933, Council on Foreign Relations, 1939.
Mutual Security, Industrial College of the Armed Forces, 1959.
Retrospect and Prospect, [Washington, D.C.], 1963.
(With Harold J. Clem) *United States Foreign Economic Policy,* Industrial College of the Armed Forces, 1965.
The United States in the Nuclear Age, Sadna Prakashan, 1970.
Humbug, Brainwash, and Other Verse, Carlton, 1972.

Also author of *The London Naval Conference,* 1930. Editor, *The Search for National Security,* 1951. General editor, "Economics of National Security," twenty-two volumes, Industrial College of the Armed Forces, 1952-58. Contributor to journals. Associate editor, *Scholastic,* 1927-28, and *Social Science,* 1955.

WORK IN PROGRESS: Research on U.S. foreign policy.*

* * *

WILLIAMS, Herbert Lee 1918-

PERSONAL: Born June 1, 1918, in Birmingham, Ala.; son of William Percy and Lucy McMillan (Cowan) Williams; married Mary Elizabeth Roberts, July 9, 1948; children: Herbert Lee II, John Kirby, William Creighton. *Education:* Murray State College (now University), B.A., 1940; University of Mississippi, M.A., 1941; University of Missouri, Ph.D., 1950. *Religion:* Baptist.

ADDRESSES: Home—4145 Grandview St., Memphis, Tenn. 38117. *Office*—Department of Journalism, Memphis State University, Memphis, Tenn. 38152.

CAREER: Boston University, Boston, Mass., assistant professor of journalism, 1949-51; University of Missouri—Columbia, assistant professor of journalism, 1951-54; Michigan State University, East Lansing, associate professor of journalism, 1954-56; Memphis State University, Memphis, Tenn., professor of journalism, beginning 1956, founding chairman of department, beginning 1956. *Military service:* U.S. Naval Reserve, 1941-46; became lieutenant junior grade; awarded three theater citations.

MEMBER: Association for Education in Journalism, American Society of Journalism School Administrators, National Conference of Editorial Writers, Kappa Tau Alpha, Sigma Delta Chi, Pi Delta Epsilon.

WRITINGS:

(With F. W. Rucker) *Newspaper Organization and Management,* Iowa State College Press, 1955, 5th edition, Iowa State University Press, 1978.
Modern Journalism, Pitman, 1962.
No Room for Doubt, Broadman, 1976.
The Newspaperman's President: Harry S. Truman, Nelson-Hall, 1984.

Also ghost writer for Harry S. Truman's *Memoirs,* 1954. Copy editor, *Memphis Commercial Appeal,* beginning 1956.

AVOCATIONAL INTERESTS: Music, gardening.

* * *

WINTERS, Janet Lewis
See LEWIS, Janet

WINTON, Harry N(athaniel) M(cQuillian) 1907-1977(?)

PERSONAL: Born December 10, 1907, in San Francisco, Calif.; deceased; son of Ulysses Nathaniel and Alice Bartley (McQuillian) Winton. *Education:* Stanford University, A.B., 1932, A.M., 1934. *Politics:* Democrat. *Religion:* Presbyterian.

CAREER: Stanford University, Stanford, Calif., instructor in history, 1937-40; University of Washington, Seattle, editorial associate of *Pacific Northwest Quarterly,* 1940-42; United Nations, New York City, chief of Documents Index Unit, 1945-50, librarian, United Nations Collection, 1950-61, chief of Documents Reference Section, Dag Hammarskjold Library, 1962-67; UNIPUB, Inc., New York City, bibliographer and editor, 1971-72; R. R. Bowker Co., New York City, managing editor of *International Bibliography, Information, Documentation (IBID),* 1973-74, consulting editor, beginning 1975. Consultant on League of Nations and United Nations documentation. *Military service:* U.S. Army, Signal Corps, 1942-46.

MEMBER: Association of International Libraries, American Society of Indexers.

AWARDS, HONORS: Special fellow, United Nations Institute for Training and Research (UNITAR), 1975-78.

WRITINGS:

(Editor) *Sea-bed 1968,* six volumes, Arno, 1970.
(Editor) *Sea-bed 1969,* eight volumes, Arno, 1971.
(Editor) *Man and the Environment: A Bibliography of Selected Publications of the United Nations System,* Bowker, 1972.
Publications of the United Nations System: A Reference Guide, Bowker, 1972.
(Compiler with Alfred George Moss) Alfred George Moss, *A New International Economic Order: Selected Documents, 1945-75,* UNITAR, c. 1976.
International Organizations and the Oceans, UNIPUB, 1977.

Contributor to *Pacific Northwest Quarterly* and *College and Research Libraries.**

* * *

WITHERSPOON, Naomi Long
See MADGETT, Naomi Long

* * *

WOLF, William J(ohn) 1918-

PERSONAL: Born January 17, 1918, in Hartford, Conn.; son of William Henry (a printer) and Mabel Bodine (Griggs) Wolf; married Eleanor Hale Dun, August 10, 1946; children: Edwin Mershon, John De Nervaud (deceased), Stephen Hale (deceased). *Education:* Trinity College, Hartford, Conn., B.A., 1940; Episcopal Theological School, B.D. (with honors), 1943; Union Theological Seminary, New York, N.Y., S.T.M., 1944, Ph.D., 1945.

ADDRESSES: Home—2A St. John's Rd., Cambridge, Mass. 02138 (winters); P. O. Box 131, Heath, Mass. 01346 (summers). *Office*—Episcopal Divinity School, 99 Brattle St., Cambridge, Mass. 02138.

CAREER: Ordained Episcopal minister, 1943; Grace Episcopal Church, New York, N.Y., assistant minister, 1943-45; Episcopal Divinity School, Cambridge, Mass., instructor, 1945-48, assistant professor, 1948-51, professor, 1951-54, Howard Chandler Robbins Professor of Theology, 1954-83, emeritus professor, 1983—, theologian in residence, 1983—, Kellogg Lecturer, 1976, 1987. Founder and minister of Episcopal church in Sudbury, Mass., 1948-51. Dudleian Lecturer at Harvard University, 1970; visiting professor at St. John's Seminary; member of board of trustees of Boston Theological Institute. Acting director of World Council of Churches Laity Institute in Celigny, Switzerland, 1952; Anglican observer at Second Vatican Council; chairman of Massachusetts Council of Churches committee for study of Christian unity; past chairman of Greater Boston Ecumenical Seminar; member of Interorthodox and Pan-Anglican Joint Doctrinal Commission; member of Anglican-Roman Catholic Commission, Anglican Theological Commission for Joint Doctrinal Discussions With Eastern Orthodox Churches, and Joint Commission of Ecumenical Relations of the Episcopal Church. Member of town planning board of Health, Mass.

MEMBER: American Theological Society, Thoreau Society, Society for Theological Discussion, Heath Historical Society (acting president).

AWARDS, HONORS: D.S.T. from Kenyon College, 1959, Trinity College, Hartford, Conn., 1960, and General Theological Seminary, 1973.

WRITINGS:

Man's Knowledge of God, Doubleday, 1955.
No Cross, No Crown: A Study of the Atonement (Pulpit Book Club selection), Doubleday, 1957.
The Almost Chosen People: A Study of the Religion of Abraham Lincoln (Religious Book Club selection), Doubleday, 1959, reprinted as *The Religion of Abraham Lincoln,* Seabury, 1963, reprinted as *Lincoln's Religion,* Pilgrim Press (Philadelphia, Pa.), 1970.
Thoreau: Mystic, Prophet, Ecologist, United Church Press, 1973.
Freedom's Holy Light: American Identity and the Future of Theology, Parameter Press, 1977.
Benedict Arnold (novel), Paideia Press, 1989.

EDITOR

(With John Francis Porter) *Toward the Recovery of Unity: The Thought of Frederick Denison Maurice,* Seabury, 1963.
Protestant Churches and Reform Today, Seabury, 1964.
The Spirit of Anglicanism: Hooker, Maurice, Temple, Morehouse, 1979.
Thomas Traherne's Centuries of Meditations, Forward Movement Publications, 1980.
Anglican Spirituality, Morehouse, 1982.
Maurice, *An Abridgment of Maurice's Kingdom of Christ,* University Press of America, 1983.

OTHER

Also author of *Plan of Church Union: Catholic, Evangelical, and Reformed,* and of *Bicentennial Addresses to Towns of Rowe and Heath,* 1989.

Contributor of essays and chapters to numerous books. Also contributor to *Encyclopaedia Britannica, New Schaff-Herzog Encyclopedia of Religious Knowledge,* and *Encyclopedia of Religion.*

WORK IN PROGRESS: Lincoln's Politics of Morality (tentative title).

SIDELIGHTS: William J. Wolf told *CA:* "In ecumenics my conviction is that the churches are impelled by the gospel to seek liberation of oppressed peoples and union by steps and stages, with many differences in organization, faith, and liturgy, including the right of conscientious objection to religious traditions. I feel that the power of bureaucrats holds back the widespread grassroots desire for greater oneness in First World countries. Here courageous action by laity and clergy in the local community is needed to shake and move establishments forward. In Third World countries many effective unions have already been achieved. My *Plan of Church Union: Catholic, Evangelical, and Reformed* tried to apply some of the wisdom of Third World unions to the American scene. The *Plan* has been influential in the drafting of the Proposed Plan of Union for the Consultation on Church Union (ten member churches) and for similar developments abroad. The ordination of women is a necessity for church renewal and liberation.

"In writing, my chief interest is in American intellectual history. The impact of the Bible, often without denominational wrapping, explains many of the values inherited by our writers and expressed in the American advocacy of democracy. We really are 'the nation with the soul of a church.' The negative side is that Lincoln's theme of 'the almost chosen people' has been debased abroad by a mindless imperialism with an increasing pluralistic and secular culture. Lincoln, whose 'Second Inaugural' is the finest theological interpretation of the American experience, was a master of the politics of morality. Jefferson, much more than the Deist he is widely thought to be, spent many an evening in the White House abridging privately the gospels to produce 'the morals of Jesus.' Thoreau, hostile to the denominations of his day, combined nature mysticism with an almost Hebrew prophetic view of God in human communities in the spirit and often in the words of the Bible.

"My writing on such pillars of integrity as Jefferson, Thoreau, and Lincoln has stimulated me to risk a novel on Benedict Arnold, usually considered our most notorious 'traitor.' What was the tragic flaw in this man who was probably the most effective fighting general of our revolution? Does his change of sides tell us anything about our current American fear of revolution? Does the panic reaction to his treason by his contemporaries partly explain an endemic paranoia in American life?"

* * *

WOLFF, Geoffrey (Ansell) 1937-

PERSONAL: Born November 5, 1937, in Los Angeles, Calif.; son of Arthur Saunders (an engineer) and Rosemary (Loftus) Wolff; married Priscilla Porter, August 21, 1965; children: Nicholas Hinckley, Justin Porter. *Education:* Princeton University, A.B. (summa cum laude), 1961; attended Churchill College, Cambridge, 1963-64. *Politics:* Independent. *Religion:* None.

ADDRESSES: Home—302 Angell St., Providence, R.I. 02906. *Agent*—Robert Lescher, 155 East 71st St., New York, N.Y. 10021.

CAREER: Robert College, Istanbul, Turkey, lecturer in comparative literature, 1961-63; Istanbul University, Istanbul, lecturer and chairman of department of American civilization, 1962-63; *Washington Post,* Washington, D.C., book editor, 1964-69; Maryland Institute, College of Art, Baltimore, lecturer in aesthetics, 1965-69; Corcoran School of Art, Washington, D.C., lecturer, 1968-69; *Newsweek,* New York City, book editor, 1969-71; Princeton University, Princeton, N.J., visiting lecturer in creative arts, 1970-71, 1972-74; *New Times,* New York City, book editor, 1974-79; *Esquire,* New York City, contributing editor, 1979—; Brandeis University, Waltham, Mass., writer in residence, 1982—. Visiting lecturer in English literature at Middlebury College, 1976; Ferris Professor, Princeton University, 1980; lecturer, Brown University, 1981.

AWARDS, HONORS: Woodrow Wilson fellow, 1961-62, 1963-64; Fulbright scholar, 1963-64; Guggenheim fellow in creative writing, 1971-72; National Endowment for the Humanities senior fellow, 1974-75; National Endowment for the Arts fellow, 1987.

WRITINGS:

Bad Debts (novel), Simon & Schuster, 1969.
The Sightseer (novel), Random House, 1974.
Black Sun: The Brief Transit and Violent Eclipse of Harry Crosby (biography), Random House, 1976.
(Editor and author of introduction) *The Edward Hoagland Reader,* Random House, 1976.
Inklings (novel), Random House, 1977.
The Duke of Deception: Memories of My Father (biography), Random House, 1979.
Providence (novel), Viking, 1986.
Herman Melville: Biography, Viking, 1987.

Contributor of essays and reviews to *American Scholar, New Leader, New Republic, Atlantic, Saturday Review,* and other periodicals.

SIDELIGHTS: A book critic and author of several nonfiction works and novels, Geoffrey Wolff creates narratives distinguished by realistic characterizations, a highly comic and satiric approach to their subjects, and a sensitivity to dialogue. *New York Times* reviewer John Leonard comments that *Bad Debts,* Wolff's first novel, "deals wittily with a collection of people . . . whose possibilities appear to have been poisoned at the source, as though birth itself were a fatal wound. Looking at them through Mr. Wolff's savage eye is like being trapped at a disastrous dinner party, or being one among a dozen conscripts in a malfunctioning elevator." *Bad Debts* follows the misadventures of Benjamin Freeman, a spendthrift who lies and cheats to cover up his misbehavior, and those of his wife and son, who are equally degenerate. The scenes of confrontation between these characters "are in the same league with the best bitterly comic writing of recent years," remarks Richard P. Brickner in the *New York Times Book Review.* The critic comments that "even though it ends up failing for lack of emotional thrust, *Bad Debts* is a novel with honest-to-God touchstones in it, a novel to be recommended for virtues rare enough that one is grateful for even their qualified appearance."

Similarly, Sara Blackburn observes in *Book World* that "it's obvious from the first page of this funny, sad book that its author is a real writer, and it's just as evident by the last that he is better than his material." The critic adds that Wolff "is a writer of such imagination and skill that one feels he is being confined by his material instead of using it and taking risks at broader and (shudder) more important work." Calling *Bad Debts* "technically very accomplished [although] not original," John Wain writes in the *New York Review of Books* that the novel "is a work of a writer who has an excellent ear for the way people talk, an understanding eye for the way comedy intertwines with pathos, and a penetrating curiosity about human beings." "*Bad Debts* is a rigorously moral novel without a clear moral focus," concludes Paul Edward Gray in the *Yale Review.* "It is also, improbable as this may sound, extremely funny, and its appearance provides promising evidence of a new comic talent."

Penned between other, less successful novels, Wolff's biography *Black Sun: The Brief Transit and Violent Eclipse of Harry Crosby,* "is a timely document," notes James Atlas in the *Village Voice,* "unsentimental about the '20s and determined not to elevate the importance of his subject." The critic adds that Wolff's book "tells a dramatic, vivid story without claiming to be social history." Harry Crosby, the rich and privileged nephew of J. P. Morgan, Jr., shocked his family and Boston society by eloping with a married woman, devoting himself to poetry, and finally committing double suicide with one of his many lovers. *New Republic* contributor J. M. Edelstein describes the biography as "a good story, with all the elements of a spellbinder: the passionate rich, Paris in the '20s, sex, sometimes kinky, scandal in high society and the foreordained ending of tragedy. Geoffrey Wolff makes the most of these exciting elements, writing in a cool and skillful way."

Nevertheless, Edelstein faults *Black Sun* as "a story which has lost its point in the telling, and for that reason it is troubling." The critic explains that "Wolff doesn't claim anything for Harry Crosby; he knows that Harry was not a poet and that his life was neither Art nor artful. As a result, this long and dramatically written book has about as much meaning as most of Harry Crosby's own writing." But D. Keith Mano, writing in the *National Review,* believes that *Black Sun* "is engrossing, chiefly because of those notables who intersect, or were paid to intersect, with Harry Crosby's stupid and selfish brief transit." The *New York Times*'s Christopher Lehmann-Haupt concurs: "One has read Mr. Wolff's dramatic narrative from beginning to end; one has relished his many literary anecdotes, the best of which are very good indeed; respected his intelligent social commentaries on Paris in the 1920's and the effects of World War I on its literary generation; and savored detached and ironic prose." The critic concludes that "whatever else he may have been, Harry Crosby was symptomatic of something about his times. They were interesting times, and Mr. Wolff has caught them."

Wolff returned to biography with *The Duke of Deception: Memories of My Father,* an intimate portrait of the man who drifted through various jobs, debts, and scams, leaving his son with ambivalent memories. "To write about one's father—anyone's father—is apt to be an oedipal act," comments Harold Beaver in the *Times Literary Supplement,* "a bid at working him out of the system. Geoffrey Wolff's first shot was a novel, *Bad Debts.*" The critic continues, asserting that "ten years later, [Wolff has] come to terms with his [father's] ghost. His second try is triumphant." In telling the story of the man who produced such conflicting emotions in him, "Wolff writes with care and craft, and also with a certain exhilaration, as if this were a story he had wanted to tell for a good long while," observes an *Atlantic* reviewer. As the author told Stella Dong in a *Publishers Weekly* interview, "I wrote the book primarily for my sons. I wanted to show them that even though in the eyes of the world their grandfather might be considered a 'bad' man, that he was not a bad father to me. I had no identity of my own to hang onto when I was growing up, and I wanted to give them as clear a record as possible." Wolff added that "in a way, I realized that I was the connector between my father and my sons." "As a portrait of Arthur [Saunders] Wolff," describes Lehmann-Haupt, *The Duke of Deception* "is simply superb. Mr. Wolff manages, without pulling any punches, to convey the full horror of the man, whose appearance did not exactly match his reality."

Although stories of "confidence men" are common in biography and literature, *Time* contributor Paul Gray finds that "Wolff's account of this misspent life is absorbing throughout. It is not just the story of 'a wreck of a desperado,' as he calls the Duke at one point; it is an engrossing, often moving search for the troubled bond between sons and fathers that is known as love." This bond is illustrated throughout the author's narrative, for as John Irving explains in the *New York Times Book Review, The Duke of Deception* "is a book abundant with the complexities and contradictions of family sympathy. Keenly perceptive of family ties and family shame, Geoffrey Wolff has succeeded in being true to his emotionally complicated subject while also being divinely easy to read." The critic continues by noting that "in the delicate telling of his father's story, the son manages to bring all versions of 'Duke' Wolff to light." Lehmann-Haupt echoes this assessment, claiming that "without apologizing for any of his father's shortcomings, Wolff also makes us understand the enormous appeal of the man—his erratic genius for self-creation." "Each of us has experienced the feeling of having been deceived by a father or mother or older brother," states Tim O'Brien in the *Saturday Review.* "And this is what gives Geoffrey Wolff's story, with its extreme litany of deception followed by eroding fatherly images, such power and universal truth." Concludes the reviewer: "*The Duke of Deception* awakens us to our own emotions, enlivens our own memories, and compels us to examine our own familial histories."

Several reviewers have also remarked on Wolff's ability to avoid the pitfalls traditionally present in portraits of difficult family relationships. For example, Donald Hall claims in the *National Review* that "the problem in writing this book was a problem of tone," explaining that "if we see the old man through the mature Geoffrey, we see him through the mature Geoffrey watching the young Geoffrey, necessarily a distorting lens." Despite this hazard, Hall believes that Wolff "handles this problem with delicacy, restraint, and intelligence, so that we are able to feel compassion for the old man while the young man rages, at the same time as we feel compassion for the young man saddled with this impossible father." L. J. Davis similarly claims that in a tale of difficult adolescence, "only a rare [book] can survive cheap empathy, and only a remarkable one deploy its usual occasions and use them to a good purpose. *The Duke of Deception* is one such remarkable book." *Los Angeles Times Book Review* contributor Herbert Gold praises in particular Wolff's ability to portray his father "with neither vengefulness and hatred nor false unction. That must have been a task difficult far beyond the normal one of setting down a bizarre account." "This book, in its honesty and lucidity, affirms the son's faithfulness to the father," asserts O'Brien. "It does not condescend, nor judge harshly, nor forgive gratuitously; it does not ignore the father's failings but neither does it wallow in them. Indeed, in many instances, Geoffrey Wolff celebrates his father's gutty audacity, his flair, his enormous capacity for the outlandish and outlawish." Concludes a *New Yorker* critic: "In this extraordinary memoir—both biography and autobiography—Mr. Wolff recalls, examines, depicts, reaches toward understanding, and brings to the full complexity of life a most exceptional man. . . . It is an achievement of a high order."

When Wolff wrote *The Duke of Deception,* "I wasn't just writing because I was a writer anymore," he told David Remnick of the *Washington Post.* "I wrote it out of need." The author told Remnick that a comparable need inspired *Providence,* a novel that grew out of Wolff's experience with a burglary at his home. *Providence* relates the troubles of Adam Dwyer, a criminal lawyer whose house is robbed shortly after he learns he is dying of leukemia; also appearing are Baby and Skippy, the two hoods who rob Adam, Skippy's girlfriend Lisa, and a cop who becomes involved with both Lisa and the local mob. "In this, his fourth novel, [Wolff] has taken the sense of drama and irony that made [his previous] works so stunningly effective and fused it onto a well-plotted sociological/psychological/moral tale," writes M. George Stevenson in the *Village Voice.* "It is difficult to describe exactly *how* artfully everything is interconnected. . . . Which might lead you to believe that *Providence* is a humorless, arcane and stultifying 'high art' novel," continues the critic, adding that "it ain't." As James Carroll explains in the *New York Times Book Review*, *Providence* "is a novel to be read for pleasure, for pure enjoyment, because it brings a supremely light touch to its heavy subject. With unfailing irony and profound affection for all his characters, Mr. Wolff presents their awful story as if he thinks it is funny." In heightening this comic aspect, "there is a sense of pure reality to these passages," comments Bruce Cook in the *Chicago Tribune Book World*. "Wolff creates the feeling that this is truly the way a man like Adam Dwyer would react."

Critics observe that Wolff's successful recreation of Providence and its inhabitants is based in part on his effective use of language. Carroll, for example, maintains that "there is nothing mere about the words in this novel. They are exactly right. Mr. Wolff has an ear for the way the nuances of English tease one another," he continues. "His paragraphs sparkle because he is a writer at play. Thus each of the five wildly different characters has a distinct voice that is in its way hilarious." In telling the story of the corruption of these characters, "Wolff has deliberately employed a wacky, loose and often wonderful style that breaks most of the rules of grammar known to man," states Ross Thomas in the *Washington Post Book World*. "Yet the style serves the story well, for Wolff is writing largely about civic rot and decay and the various maggots that dwell therein." And a *Time* reviewer remarks that "the atmosphere is entertainingly breezy and sleazy, with a wise-cracking, side-of-the-mouth narrator and some of the tightest, meanest dialogue this side of Elmore Leonard."

Because of the success Wolff enjoys in recreating the different vernaculars of Providence, Lehmann-Haupt believes that the language "is sometimes too dazzling—to the point that it overshadows the people and behavior it purports to be describing. . . . Paradoxically, what purports to be the way people talk sometimes becomes mere literary conceit." Cook similarly finds it distracting that Wolff "programmatically interrupts his narrative with lectures on the social history of Providence and on the structure of organized crime there." "Fortunately, Mr. Wolff's vision of corruption is too powerful and amusing to be undermined by his infatuation with language," concludes Lehmann-Haupt, adding that "a reader is too entranced to be put off by affectations of style." One aspect of this vision of corruption, according to Celia McGee, is "a reckoning with old-fashioned providence—divine foreknowledge and unavoidable destiny," the critic writes in the *New Republic*. "But Wolff goes one, modern, step further. He positions himself as the all-seeing, all-knowing force behind the story, wielding the power of foresight and informed distance that only storytellers have. This novel," continues McGee, "shows him relishing the role, playing games with genre . . . , creating and destroying lives, speaking in Providence's many different voices." "*Providence* is distinguished both in conception and execution," claims Stevenson. "As a narrative, an essay in novelistic effect, a meditation on degeneration, or a stylistic tour de force, there is little in recent fiction that can equal it." "If the mark of a good novel is that it leaves you with a lingering aftertaste, good or bad," concludes Thomas, "than Geoffrey Wolff has written a very good and witty novel indeed."

MEDIA ADAPTATIONS: The Duke of Deception has been optioned for a movie; Tri-Star Pictures has purchased the rights to *Providence*.

BIOGRAPHICAL/CRITICAL SOURCES:

BOOKS

Contemporary Literary Criticism, Volume 41, Gale, 1987.

PERIODICALS

Atlantic, May, 1974, September, 1979, February, 1986.
Book World, November 23, 1969.
Chicago Tribune Book World, August 26, 1979, March 2, 1986.
Detroit News, August 19, 1979.
Los Angeles Times Book Review, July 8, 1979.
Nation, November 3, 1979.
National Review, November 12, 1976, October 26, 1979.
New Republic, April 27, 1974, November 6, 1976, March 11, 1978, August 18, 1979, June 16, 1986.
Newsweek, November 17, 1969, February 18, 1974, September 6, 1976, August 27, 1979.
New Yorker, October 8, 1979, May 5, 1986.
New York Review of Books, February 26, 1970, February 17, 1977.
New York Times, November 12, 1969, February 11, 1974, September 6, 1976, September 24, 1976, January 2, 1978, August 13, 1979, February 10, 1986.
New York Times Book Review, February 1, 1970, March 3, 1974, August 22, 1976, January 8, 1978, August 12, 1979, February 16, 1986, March 1, 1987.
Publishers Weekly, September 3, 1979.
Saturday Review, January 21, 1978, September 29, 1979.
Time, January 5, 1970, September 6, 1976, August 13, 1979, July 7, 1986.
Times (London), June 26, 1980.
Times Literary Supplement, June 11, 1970, August 31, 1974, January 14, 1977, July 4, 1980, November 28, 1986.
Village Voice, November 12, 1976, September 17, 1979, March 18, 1986.
Washington Post, January 29, 1978, March 22, 1986.
Washington Post Book World, February 10, 1974, August 8, 1976, August 12, 1979, December 2, 1979, February 23, 1986.
Yale Review, March, 1970.*

—Sketch by Diane Telgen

* * *

WORONOFF, Jon 1938-

PERSONAL: Born January 19, 1938, in New York, N.Y.; son of Jules and Sophie (Tabor) Woronoff. *Education:* New York University, B.A., 1959; University of Geneva, Diploma of Interpreters School, 1962, License in Political Science of Graduate Institute of International Studies, 1966.

ADDRESSES: Home—340 East 64th St., New York, N.Y. 10021.

CAREER: Free-lance interpreter and translator for United Nations and other organizations, working in Europe, Africa, Asia, and the United States, 1962-73; managing director, Interlingua Language Services Ltd., 1973-78; free-lance journalist based in Tokyo, Japan.

WRITINGS:

Organizing African Unity, Scarecrow, 1970.
West African Wager, Scarecrow, 1972.
Japan: The Coming Economic Crisis, Lotus Press, 1979.
Hong Kong: Capitalist Paradise, Heinemann, 1980.
Japan: The Coming Social Crisis, Lotus Press, 1980.
Inside Japan, Inc., Lotus Press, 1982.
Japan's Wasted Workers, Rowman & Allenheld, 1983.
World Trade War, Praeger, 1983.
Korea's Economy, Man-Made Miracle, Si-sa-yong-o-sa Publishers, 1983.

Japan's Commercial Empire, Lotus Press, 1984.
The Japan Syndrome, Transaction Books, 1985.
Asia's "Miracle" Economies, M. E. Sharpe, 1986.
Politics: The Japanese Way, Macmillan and St. Martin's, 1988.

Regular contributor to periodicals, including *Asian Business, Modern Asia, Oriental Economist, Japan Economic Journal, South China Morning Post,* and *Mainichi Daily News.*

WORK IN PROGRESS: Studies of the newly-industrialized countries of East Asia; studies of the Confucian ethic; comparisons between Asian and American economies and business practices.

* * *

WYNYARD, Talbot
See HAMILTON, Charles (Harold St. John)

Y

YAO, Esther Lee 1944-

PERSONAL: Born July 21, 1944, in Szechuan, China; came to the United States in 1967, naturalized citizen, 1976; daughter of Wei-Chin and Phoebe Lee; married Stanton Yao; children: Pin-Ping (daughter), Irene. *Education:* National Taiwan Normal University, B.S., 1967; Northern Illinois University, M.S., 1969; Purdue University, Ph.D., 1971.

ADDRESSES: *Home*—15714 Sylvan Lake, Houston, Tex. 77062. *Office*—School of Education, University of Houston at Clear Lake, 2700 Bay Area Blvd., Houston, Tex. 77058.

CAREER: High school teacher of music in Taiwan, 1964-67; University of Houston at Clear Lake, Houston, Tex., associate professor of multicultural education and developmental psychology, 1975—. Commissioner of the U.S. Congressional Commission for the Study of International Migration and Cooperative Economic Development, 1987-90.

MEMBER: Organization of Chinese Americans (member of national board of directors, 1980-81), Organization of Chinese-American Women (national vice president).

AWARDS, HONORS: First place in national piano competition in Taiwan, 1965; Outstanding Young Women of America award, 1978; grants from U.S. Department of Health, Education, and Welfare, 1978-79, and 1987-90, Pacific Cultural Foundation, 1979, and Melrose-Thompson Fund, 1982-83; Presidential Achievement Award, 1982; Tribute Award from Minority Women's Convention, 1982; Fulbright fellowship to India, 1987; president's distinguished service award, University of Houston, 1988.

WRITINGS:

Teacher's Handbook for Teaching and Working with Oriental Students and Their Parents, Educational Resources Information Center, 1979.

Together in Three Generations, Baptist Press, 1982.

Chinese Women: Past and Present, Ide House, 1983.

Contemporary Chinese, Crown, 1987.

Viewing Contemporary Chinese from Global Perspective, Crown, 1987.

Author of "Christians and Family," a column in *Houston Chinese Church Newsletter,* 1973-77, "Family Life," a column in *Overseas,* 1974-75, and "Overseas Chinese," a weekly column in *World Journal,* 1979-88. Contributor of more than one hundred articles to magazines and journals, including *Urban Education, Reading Improvement, Contemporary Education, Journal of Psychology, Journal of Education, Cornell Journal of Social Relations, International Journal of Sociology of the Family, Business Marketing,* and to newspapers.

WORK IN PROGRESS: Research on the cognitive style and family characteristics of Asian-American learners.

SIDELIGHTS: Esther Lee Yao told *CA:* "My writing interests are very broad, not just the topics but also the style. Writings which can be visualized and preserved give me a sense of accomplishment and also at times serve as an emotional outlet. Regardless of the language (Chinese or English), contents (business, education, family, and even politics), or format (essay, story, research report, commentary) of my writings, I am inclined to try to bridge the cultural gaps and promote mutual understanding among various ethnic and racial groups.

"After all the years of writing, it has been my experience that the pen is mightier than the sword. Writing is a very powerful tool for communication which has profound influence on people's attitude and thinking. Unfortunately, today, many of our youngsters are not aware of the impact writing has and show little interest in it. I am concerned about the future. Will our country still be a democratic society if the government policy is directed and controlled by so few people who are good writers? I would like to challenge parents, teachers and concerned citizens to reverse the trend by encouraging youngsters to become involved in writing as early as possible in their life."

AVOCATIONAL INTERESTS: Playing the piano.

* * *

YOLEN, Jane (Hyatt) 1939-

PERSONAL: Born February 11, 1939, in New York, N.Y.; daughter of Will Hyatt (a public relations man and journalist) and Isabelle (a social worker; maiden name, Berlin) Yolen; married David W. Stemple (a college professor and computer expert), September 2, 1962; children: Heidi Elisabet, Adam Douglas, Jason Frederic. *Education:* Smith College, B.A., 1960; University of Massachusetts, M.Ed., 1976. *Politics:* Liberal Democrat. *Religion:* Jewish/Quaker.

ADDRESSES: Home—Phoenix Farm, Box 27, 31 School St., Hatfield, Mass. 01038. *Agent*—Marilyn Marlow, Curtis Brown Ltd., 10 Astor Pl., New York, N.Y. 10003.

CAREER: Saturday Review (magazine), New York City, production assistant, 1960-61; Gold Medal Books (publishers), New York City, assistant editor, 1961-62; Rutledge Books (publishers), New York City, associate editor, 1962-63; Alfred A. Knopf, Inc. (publishers), New York City, assistant juvenile editor, 1963-65; full-time professional writer, 1965—. Lecturer, Smith College; chairman of board of library trustees, Hatfield, Mass., 1976-83; member of arts council, Hatfield, Mass.; editor of imprint, Jane Yolen Books, Harcourt Brace Jovanovich, 1988—.

MEMBER: Society of Children's Book Writers (board of directors, 1974—), Children's Literature Association (board of directors, 1977-79), Science Fiction Writers of America (president, 1986-88), Science Fiction Poetry Association, National Association for the Preservation and Perpetuation of Storytelling (NAPPS), Bay State Writers Guild, Western New England Storytelling Guild (founder, 1984), Western Massachusetts Illustrators Guild (founder, 1980).

AWARDS, HONORS: Boys Clubs of America Junior Book Award, 1968, for *The Minstrel and the Mountain;* American Library Association Notable Book citation, *New York Times* Best Book of the Year citation, Lewis Carroll Shelf Award, and Caldecott Honor Book citation, all 1968, all for *The Emperor and the Kite;* Lewis Carroll Shelf Award, and Children's Book Showcase selection, both 1973, both for *The Girl Who Loved the Wind;* Gold Kite Award, Society of Children's Book Writers, 1974, and National Book Award nomination, 1975, both for *The Girl Who Cried Flowers and Other Tales;* Gold Kite Honor Book citation, 1975, for *The Transfigured Hart,* and 1976, for *Moon Ribbon and Other Tales;* Children's Book Showcase selection, 1976, for *The Little Spotted Fish;* Christopher Medal, 1978, for *The Seeing Stick;* LL.D., College of Our Lady of the Elms, 1981; *School Library Journal* Best Books for Young Adults citation, 1982, for *The Gift of Sarah Barker;* Garden State Children's Book Award, 1983, for *Commander Toad in Space;* Mythopoeic Society award, 1986, for *Cards of Grief;* Daedelus Award, 1987, for body of short fantasy fiction; Kerlan Award, 1988, for body of work; World Fantasy Award, 1988, for *Favorite Folktales from Around the World,* 1988; Caldecott Medal, 1988, for *Owl Moon;* Jewish Book Council Award, Association of Jewish Libraries Sydney J. Taylor Award, Judy Lopez Honor Book, and Nebula Award finalist, all 1989, all for *The Devil's Arithmetic.*

WRITINGS:

FICTION

The Witch Who Wasn't, Macmillan, 1964.
Gwinellen, the Princess Who Could Not Sleep, Macmillan, 1965.
(With Anne Huston) *Trust a City Kid,* Lothrop, 1966.
Isabel's Noel, Funk, 1967.
The Emperor and the Kite, World Publishing, 1967, reprinted, Philomel, 1987.
The Minstrel and the Mountain: A Tale of Peace, World Publishing, 1968.
Greyling: A Picture Story from the Islands of Shetland, World Publishing, 1968, reprinted with new illustrations, Philomel, 1989.
The Longest Name on the Block, Funk, 1968.
The Wizard of Washington Square, World Publishing, 1969.
The Inway Investigators; or, The Mystery at McCracken's Place, Seabury Press, 1969.
The Seventh Mandarin, Seabury Press, 1969.
Hobo Toad and the Motorcycle Gang, World Publishing, 1970.
The Bird of Time (also see below), Crowell, 1971.
The Girl Who Loved the Wind, Crowell, 1972, reprinted, Harper, 1987.
The Girl Who Cried Flowers and Other Tales (short stories), Crowell, 1974.
Rainbow Rider, Crowell, 1974.
The Adventures of Eeka Mouse, Xerox, 1974.
The Boy Who Had Wings, Crowell, 1974.
The Magic Three of Solatia, Crowell, 1974.
The Little Spotted Fish, Seabury Press, 1975.
The Transfigured Hart, Crowell, 1975.
The Moon Ribbon and Other Tales (short stories), Crowell, 1976.
Milkweed Days, Crowell, 1976.
The Sultan's Perfect Tree, Parents' Magazine Press, 1977.
The Seeing Stick, Crowell, 1977.
The Lady and the Merman, Pennyroyal Press, 1977.
The Hundredth Dove and Other Tales, Crowell, 1977.
The Giants' Farm, Seabury Press, 1977.
Hannah Dreaming, Springfield Museum of Fine Arts, 1977.
The Mermaid's Three Wisdoms, Collins World, 1978.
No Bath Tonight, Crowell, 1978.
The Simple Prince, Parents' Magazine Press, 1978.
Spider Jane, Coward McCann, 1978.
Dream Weaver, Collins, 1979, new edition, 1989.
The Giants Go Camping, Seabury Press, 1979.
Spider Jane on the Move, Coward McCann, 1980.
Mice on Ice, Dutton, 1980.
Commander Toad in Space, Coward McCann, 1980.
The Robot and Rebecca: The Mystery of the Code-Carrying Kids, Random House, 1980.
Shirlick Holmes and the Case of the Wandering Wardrobe, Coward McCann, 1981.
Uncle Lemon's Spring, Dutton, 1981.
The Boy Who Spoke Chimp, Knopf, 1981.
Brothers of the Wind, Philomel, 1981.
The Gift of Sarah Barker (young adult), Viking, 1981.
The Acorn Quest, Crowell, 1981.
The Robot and Rebecca and the Missing Owser, Knopf, 1981.
Sleeping Ugly, Coward McCann, 1981.
Dragon's Blood: A Fantasy (young adult; first volume in trilogy), Delacorte, 1982.
Commander Toad and the Planet of the Grapes, Coward McCann, 1982.
Neptune Rising: Songs and Tales of the Undersea Folk, Philomel, 1982.
Commander Toad and the Big Black Hole, Coward, 1983.
Tales of Wonder (adult; short stories), Schocken Books, 1983.
Children of the Wolf (historical novel), Viking, 1984.
Heart's Blood (young adult; second volume in trilogy), Delacorte, 1984.
The Stone Silenus (young adult), Philomel, 1984.
Cards of Grief (adult science fiction), Ace Books, 1984.
Commander Toad and the Dis-Asteroid, Coward, 1985.
Dragonfield and Other Stories (adult short stories), Ace Books, 1985.
Merlin's Booke (adult short stories), Ace Books, 1986.
Commander Toad and the Intergalactic Spy, Coward, 1986.
The Sleeping Beauty, Knopf, 1986.
Commander Toad and the Space Pirates, Coward, 1987.
Piggins, Harcourt, 1987.
A Sending of Dragons (young adult; third volume in trilogy), Delacorte, 1987.
Owl Moon, Philomel, 1987.
The Devil's Arithmetic (young adult), Viking, 1988.

Picnic with Piggins, Harcourt, 1988.
Sister Light, Sister Dark (adult fantasy), Tor Books, 1988.
Piggins and the Royal Wedding, Harcourt, 1989.
Dove Isabeau, Harcourt, 1989.
White Jenna (adult fantasy; sequel to *Sister Light, Sister Dark*), Tor Books, 1989.
The Faerie Flag and Other Stories, Orchard Books, 1989.
Baby Bear's Bedtime Book, Harcourt, 1990.
Tam Lin, Harcourt, 1990.
Elfabet, Little, Brown, 1990.
The Dragon's Boy, Harper, 1990.
Sky Dogs, Harcourt, 1990.

NONFICTION

Pirates in Petticoats (juvenile), McKay, 1963.
World on a String: The Story of Kites (juvenile), World Publishing, 1968.
Writing Books for Children, Writer, Inc., 1973, revised edition, 1982.
Friend: The Story of George Fox and the Quakers (juvenile), Seabury Press, 1972.
The Wizard Islands (juvenile), Crowell, 1973.
Ring Out! A Book of Bells (juvenile), Seabury Press, 1975.
Simple Gifts: The Story of the Shakers (juvenile), Viking, 1976.
Touch Magic: Fantasy, Faerie, and Folktale in the Literature of Childhood, Philomel, 1981.
Guide to Writing for Children, Writer, Inc., 1989.

EDITOR

The Fireside Song Book of Birds and Beasts, music by Barbara Green, Simon & Schuster, 1972.
Zoo 2000: Twelve Stories of Science Fiction and Fantasy Beasts, Seabury Press, 1973.
Rounds about Rounds, music by Barbara Green, F. Watts, 1977.
Shape Shifters: Fantasy and Science Fiction Tales about Humans Who Can Change Their Shapes, Seabury Press, 1978.
The Lullaby Songbook, music by Adam Stemple, Harcourt, 1986.
(With Martin H. Greenberg and Charles G. Waugh) *Dragons and Dreams,* Harper, 1986.
Favorite Folktales from Around the World, Pantheon, 1986.
(With Greenberg and Waugh) *Spaceships and Spells: A Collection of New Fantasy and Science Fiction Stories,* Harper, 1987.
(With Greenberg) *Werewolves: A Collection of Original Stories,* Harper, 1988.
The Laptime Song and Play Book, music by Adam Stemple, Harcourt, 1989.
(With Greenberg) *Things That Go Bump in the Night,* Harper, 1989.
2040 A.D., Delacorte, 1990.

CONTRIBUTOR

Orson Scott Card, editor, *Dragons of Light,* Ace Books, 1981.
Terri Windling and Mark Alan Arnold, editors, *Elsewhere, Volume I,* Ace Books, 1981.
Windling and Arnold, editors, *Elsewhere, Volume II,* Ace Books, 1982.
Susan Schwartz, editor, *Hecate's Cauldron,* DAW Books, 1982.
Jessica Amanda Salmonson, editor, *Heroic Visions,* Ace Books, 1983.
Windling, editor, *Faery!,* Ace Books, 1983.
Will Shetterly and Emma Bull, editors, *Liavek,* Ace Books, 1985.
Schwartz, editor, *Moonsinger's Friends,* Bluejay, 1985.
Robin McKinley, editor, *Imaginary Lands,* Greenwillow, 1985.
Shetterly and Bull, editors, *Liavek: The Players of Luck,* Ace Books, 1986.
Donald R. Gallo, editor, *Visions,* Delacorte, 1987.
Shetterly and Bull, editors, *Liavek: Wizard's Row,* Ace Books, 1987.
Schwartz, editor, *Arabesques: More Tales of the Arabian Nights,* Avon, 1988.
Shetterly and Bull, editors, *Liavek: Spells of Binding,* Ace Books, 1988.
Parke Godwin, editor, *Invitation to Camelot,* Ace Books, 1988.
Bruce Coville, editor, *The Unicorn Treasury,* Doubleday, 1988.

OTHER

See This Little Line? (verse), McKay, 1963.
"Robin Hood" (play; music by Barbara Green), produced in Boston, 1967.
It All Depends (verse), Funk, 1969.
An Invitation to the Butterfly Ball: A Counting Rhyme (verse), Parents' Magazine Press, 1976.
All in the Woodland Early: An ABC Book, music by the author, Collins, 1979.
How Beastly! A Menagerie of Nonsense Poems, Collins, 1980.
Dragon Night and Other Lullabies (verse), Methuen, 1980.
"The Bird of Time" (play; based on novel of same title; music by Karen Simon), first produced in Northampton, Mass., 1982.
Ring of Earth: A Child's Book of Seasons, Harcourt, 1986.
The Three Bears Rhyme Book, Harcourt, 1987.
Best Witches (verse), Putnam, 1989.
Bird Watch (poetry), Philomel, 1990.
Dinosaur Dances (verse), Putnam, 1990.

Author of column, "Children's Bookfare," *Daily Hampshire Gazette.* Contributor of articles, reviews, poems, and short stories to *Writer, Parabola, New York Times, Horn Book, Magazine of Fantasy and Science Fiction, Isaac Asimov's Science Fiction Magazine, Language Arts, NAPPS Journal,* and other periodicals. Member of editorial board, *New Advocate* and *NAPPS Journal.* Many of Jane Yolen's manuscripts are in the Kerlan Collection of the University of Minnesota, Minneapolis.

WORK IN PROGRESS: Novels *Wizard's Hall* and *Many Mansions;* picture books *All Those Secrets of the World, Letting Swift River Go, Grandpa Bill's Song, Wings, The Seaman, Mouse's Birthday, Merlin and the Two Dragons,* and *Encounter; Moon Songs,* a book of verse; the screenplay for *The Devil's Arithmetic.*

SIDELIGHTS: Jane Yolen's interests and activities almost outnumber her books. Although best known as a children's author, she is also a folksinger, playwright, poet, editor, and outspoken exponent of fantastic literature. She has held influential posts in important writing organizations, including the Science Fiction Writers of America, the Society of Children's Book Writers, and the Children's Literature Association, and has spoken to children and children's literature groups all over the United States. "Her special talents, however," declares *Dictionary of Literary Biography* contributor William E. Kreuger, "lie in the writing of literary folktales, noted for their beauty of language and imagery and their abstract, philosophic mode."

Yolen's effective use of language is characteristic of her work. Her books, declares *New York Times Book Review* contributor Jane Langton, "are told with sober strength and native wit. They are simple and perfect, with not a word too much." Raised in a family with a strong storytelling heritage—her father's grandfather was a teller of tales in his native Finno-Russian village, her father was a journalist, and her mother wrote short stories—

Yolen developed a style that owes much to the oral tradition of storytelling. She told *CA:* "I write a sentence and then read it out loud before going on to the next. Then the paragraph is read aloud. Finally, the entire book is read and reread to the walls, to the bathtub, to the blank television, to my long-suffering husband."

Unlike many other writers, Yolen works primarily with characters who are more symbols than individuals. One of the major concerns of her books is the disappearance from Western culture of the folklore, fables and myths that use these symbolic characters. "In our need to update the educational standards," she writes in *Touch Magic: Fantasy, Faerie, and Folktale in the Literature of Childhood,* "we have done away with the old gods. And now we have names without faces, mnemonics without meaning." Four "functions of myth and legend and folklore," Yolen continues in *Touch Magic,* "make the listening to and learning of the old stories one of the most basic elements of our education: a landscape of allusion, the understanding of other cultures that leads to an understanding of our own, an adaptable tool of therapy, and the ability to express a symbolic or metaphoric statement of existence. I draw on all those aspects of mythology and folklore when I write, for I write fantasy and fairy tales."

Much of Yolen's work employs symbols and allusion; in *The Moon Ribbon and Other Tales, Dream Weaver, The Girl Who Cried Flowers and Other Tales,* and *The Magic Three of Solatia,* for instance, she uses elements from the Greek myth of Daphne and Apollo, and the fairy tale of Cinderella to create new and vivid stories that take place not in a real world of blood and bruise, but in a world of the mind. "Some critics," states Krueger, "have commented that her characters . . . are 'remote,' that they lack sharpness. Actually the characters are no more remote than those in other quest tales, particularly the Grail stories. The remoteness undoubtedly is due to the ethereal quality of the settings and themes."

Even in Yolen's books that are not folktales—such as her fantasy novel *Dragon's Blood,* its sequel *Heart's Blood,* and the trilogy's conclusion *A Sending of Dragons*—the author employs symbols and metaphor to enrich her stories. The dragon itself serves as both symbol and character; in *Dragon's Blood,* it is by means of his dragon that the slave boy Jakkin gains his freedom, while in *Heart's Blood,* it serves as a shelter from the cold after it is slain. "When Jakkin and Akki [his friend] climb inside the dragon's body to keep from freezing, they are transformed," explains Krueger; "when they emerge the next day, they . . . have new insights and are stronger than they have ever been. Thus the dragon becomes a symbol of human potential, of inner strength necessary to overcome any adversary."

"But the wonderful thing about stories," declares Yolen in her *Something about the Author Autobiography Series* entry, "is that other folk can turn them around and make private what is public; that is, they take into themselves the story they read or hear and make it their own. Stories do not exist on the page or in the mouth, they exist *between.* Between writer and reader, between teller and listener. I wrote *The Girl Who Loved the Wind* for myself, out of my own history. But recently I received a letter from a nurse who told me that she had read the story to a dying child, and the story had eased the little girl through her final pain. The *story* did that—not me. But if I can continue to write with as much honesty and love as I can muster, I will truly have touched magic—and passed it on."

MEDIA ADAPTATIONS: "The Seventh Mandarin" (movie), Xerox Films, 1973; "The Emperor and the Kite" (filmstrip with cassette), Listening Library, 1976; "The Girl Who Cried Flowers and Other Tales" (cassette), Weston Words, 1983; "Dragon's Blood" (animated television film), CBS Storybreak, 1985; "Dragonfield" (cassette); "Touch Magic" (cassette with a variety of stories and poems), Weston Words; "Owl Moon" (cassette), Weston Words; "Piggins" and "Picnic with Piggins" (cassette package), Caedmon.

CA INTERVIEW

CA interviewed Jane Yolen by telephone on February 6, 1989, at her home in Hatfield, Massachusetts.

CA: Storytelling goes way back in your family, according to everything I've read about you. When did you begin to join in the telling yourself?

YOLEN: If you mean oral telling, not until about the last seven or eight years. If you mean writing it down, I did that from a very young age. I was a writer from the time I learned how to write. In first grade I wrote the class musical, and I was a performer in it too. It was all about vegetables. I played a carrot, and we all ended up doing the big finale in a salad together.

CA: Do you feel that working as an editor early in your career helped you later on as a writer?

YOLEN: Yes. I think one thing that happens when you work in the publishing world is that you see so many examples of bad writing that would never make it to the stage of being published that you are given a sense that you can surely do better. You see so many mistakes you know you don't want to replicate. You also have an idea of what it takes physically to put a book together, so you might not be as adventurous, perhaps, as someone else because you know what the limitations are. You know how difficult writers can make things for editors, so you have a tendency to hold back, to be "good." I don't think I do that now, but at the beginning I certainly worked within very comfortable forms and formats.

CA: That may be a good thing for a writer to do at the beginning.

YOLEN: Well, yes and no. If you are a genius, you can violate rules and make it work. But for most of us, who are not geniuses, yes, it's probably better at least to know the form of a sonnet before you attempt to destroy it.

CA: Your own children have figured in some of your books for young people. When they were small, did you often try out your story ideas on them for a first response?

YOLEN: I didn't, for several reasons. Children will let you know if they like or dislike something by wiggling, wriggling, trying to get off your lap, falling asleep, yawning, asking for a chocolate-chip cookie. But normally they can't articulate what it is that's wrong. They can't tell you there's a hole in the plot, they can't tell you the characters aren't deep enough, they can't tell you that your language is flat where it should be singing. They don't have that critical ability, which is a learned response. So it's useless trying to find out that kind of information from them. And, in fact, I've always felt that the audience I'm writing for is myself—the child that I was and the child who is still inside me. Therefore, I have to please *that* child. So that's the child that I would read my things to, not to my own children.

CA: You've written not only for children but for young adults and for adults. I wonder how you feel about those divisions. Do you see them as different kinds of writing that require different basic approaches?

YOLEN: Mainly I simply tell a story or write a poem and think afterwards about the audience. Obviously with some things—if I'm writing a Commander Toad book, for example—it's clear that I'm not writing primarily for an adult audience, though there are a lot of adults who love those books. I don't normally say, "All right, now I am going to write a children's book," or, "I am going to write a young adult book." I tend first to figure out what the story is I want to tell, and the story itself tells me eventually who the audience is. Still, I don't write to that audience. I write to tell a story. That may be why a lot of my things seem to cross boundaries.

CA: Yes. It's nice that that happens despite the categorization of books in libraries and stores—which of course has its uses, but may restrict the readership for certain books.

YOLEN: I'm involved in the Science Fiction Writers of America, and I'm always the person who shouts, "Go into the children's room. You'll find some of the best fantasy novels and science fiction novels around there." But we do have these arbitrary divisions: this one is a children's book; this one is not. What can you say about *The Little Prince?* What can you say about *The Bat Poet?* What can you say about Robin McKinley's *Beauty?* What can you say about *Lord of the Rings?* Are those adult books or are those children's books? They're books that are enjoyed. When my children were younger, I read them *The Secret Garden* out loud. My children were then four, six, and eight, and I was in my late thirties, and all four of us loved the book. I had read it as a child. I loved it again, reading it to them. It was a children's book, but it wasn't. There were many things that it was saying to me as an adult. C. S. Lewis once said, "I hold it as canon that a children's book that cannot be enjoyed by adults is a bad children's book." It's true, absolutely, that these books cross lines, if they're wise books—*Alice in Wonderland, The Wizard of Earthsea, Charlotte's Web.*

Librarians sometimes come up to me angrily and say, "We don't know where to shelve you. You write so many different things. We don't know how to categorize you." And I say—that's not my problem. If I were going to write the same book over and over again, I might as well take a factory job. But I love to read a whole variety of things, I'm interested in a lot of things, so I write a lot of things. What they should do—I tell them—is pretend there's a different author for each of my books!

CA: You're a folksinger as well as a writer. What sort of part does music play in the composition of your prose?

YOLEN: My prose is very musical to begin with, and I can't listen to any music while I am writing because it forces a different rhythm. Some of my prose can practically be sung—*Greyling,* for example, one of my picture books. All of my stuff is read out loud, because it's very important for me to please the ear as well as the eye. A lot of my themes, also, and magical figures come out of folk songs. And I have written music to go along with a number of my things. For example, *All in the Woodland Early* has a song at the end that I wrote. I have an adult fantasy novel, *Sister Light, Sister Dark,* and its sequel, *White Jenna,* which is about to come out. *Sister Light, Sister Dark* has seven or eight songs with piano accompaniment at the end of the book, poems that have appeared earlier in the book, but set to music at the end. And then there are ten in the second book. Music is very important to me.

CA: In an article in the Writer, *you told how serendipity has been such a big help in your work, and about the need to be ready for it to happen. Aside from being in the car, the shower, the bed, or other places where you get inspired, are there conscious ways you have of cultivating that readiness for things to happen?*

YOLEN: At this point in my writing career I don't, because I seem to be in that constant state of readiness. In fact, about twenty years ago when doing alpha waves was the big thing, my husband and I had a friend who had a machine that—supposedly—could chart your alpha waves. The friend hooked his machine up to my husband's head and David tried to meditate, but he couldn't get any alpha waves. Then I was hooked up to the machine and it began chattering away immediately. Supposedly alpha waves have something to do with creativity. I don't know; it may have been all gimmick. But at this point I really seem to be totally receptive all of the time. In fact, I have to force myself *not* to think of ideas. At one time I had different gimmicks: I would write lists of titles; I would read things and say to myself, "What then? What if . . ." and the ideas would begin to come to me. But I've reached a point now where it's a little bit like a spigot that I turn on and ideas come flowing out. Sometimes, in fact, the idea tap just drips, drips, drips all the time and I can't turn it off completely.

CA: Some of your books are so beautifully illustrated, among others The Seventh Mandarin, The Owl Moon, The Girl Who Cried Flowers.

YOLEN: Normally the author doesn't get to choose the artist; it's up to the publisher. But because I have so many books out now and I have been an editor, I have a relationship with certain publishers, certain editors, that allows me either to suggest the artist or actually bring in the artist. That's rare; I've been extraordinarily lucky. But I've also been told by various illustrators that they have done their best work on my books, because my books called forth their best work, which always makes me feel terrific. If I had my druthers, I'd be an artist, but I can't draw.

CA: How much contact do you have with your readers of all ages?

YOLEN: I get lots of fan mail. For twenty-some years I went around talking at schools and libraries, seminars and conferences. This year I've taken a sabbatical from it. My husband, who is a professor, had an actual sabbatical and we were in Scotland for the fall semester. I'm taking all of 1989 basically off just to recharge.

CA: Scotland must be very inspiring for a writer like you, in touch with fantasy.

YOLEN: Yes. I have a book coming out in the fall called *The Faery Flag and Other Stories,* and the title story comes out of a legend that I found out about when we visited Dunvegan Castle on the Isle of Skye. There were about three lines on a plaque on the wall of the castle that said, "This is the Faery Flag and this is how it happened . . ." and I made up the rest of the story, it was so inspiring.

CA: What do you think accounts for the tremendous revival of interest now in storytelling, the gatherings large and small?

YOLEN: Part of it is a real feeling that we've gotten so far away from family, from the center of life, in this big, sprawling, modern country of ours, that there's a great need to go back to the hearth fire. And what do you do when you sit around the hearth fire? You tell stories. It's also been helped by the work done by NAPPS, the National Association for the Preservation and Perpetuation of Storytelling, an organization that's only about ten or twelve years old. I think that there's been a lot of interest in our *story* as in *history,* and that has called people back. We were afraid of losing it; those people who know the stories of the past are dying off, and we are trying desperately to retain that heritage.

CA: You've taught children's literature at Smith College and lectured at many other places. What do you feel is most important to convey to students of children's literature?

YOLEN: That the history of children's literature is very long and very wide, very varied; that some of the best books that have been written in literature, especially in the English language, have been in the children's section. We tend to forget that. And that the books that we read in childhood affect us more than anything else we read until the end of our days. Children's books are important. We can all recite nursery rhymes we heard as children, songs we heard as children, stories we heard as children, and yet we can't remember the adult novel we read yesterday.

CA: Would you tell me something about your work with the Society of Children's Book Writers?

YOLEN: The organization was started sixteen or seventeen years ago by two young writers who wanted to join an organization of children's book writers to find out more about the field that they wanted to enter. They were looking around to decide which one of the many organizations they could join, and they discovered there weren't any. The original two were Lin Oliver and Stephen Mooser. They ran into Sue Alexander, who helped them organize the whole thing, and I was really the first member who signed up, because I had met Sue at a conference where I was teaching and she was a student. And it's just grown; there are now 4,600 members around the country. It's an organization that combines both novices and people like Judy Blume and Sid Fleischman and Tomie de Paola and Patricia MacLachlan—all the top children's book writers and illustrators. It's an organization that expands the knowledge of the people who want to write and illustrate for children as well as being an effective lobby for those issues that directly affect children's literature and books.

CA: How did you go about gathering and selecting the tales for the 1986 book Favorite Folktales from around the World?

YOLEN: I went through hundreds and hundreds of books! For someone who loves folklore, it was wonderful to be able to buy so many books, many of them second-hand, and to be able to spend a year and a half reading stories and calling it research. It was a lot of fun. I would hear a story told by a storyteller and track that story down to see if I liked the written version as well as I liked the spoken version, because it was going to be a written book. In my first culling I had 500 stories I wanted to print, and the publisher said, "No, no, cut it in half." So then I had 250, and they said, "No, no, cut it in half again," and we argued about that and finally ended up with about 170 stories.

CA: I imagine it could have been an encyclopedia.

YOLEN: Oh yeah, it's endless, the folklore of the world. After a while, reading so many stories, I would say, "Oh, I heard that story before, but I heard it in a different way." So I would go back and find the cards where I had annotated everything. At one point, while I was in the middle of the project and working on the notes for the back of the book, my storytelling group, the Western New England Storytelling Guild, had a weekend storytelling retreat. Each time someone would tell a story, they would try to stump me. "Has Jane found it?" they'd ask. And I'd say, "Oh, that's a version of . . ." or, "That's a variant of . . ." or, "That's tale type number whatever." I can't do it any more because I don't remember the numbers now, but I could identify them by tale type numbers. We spent two and a half days at the retreat, and they couldn't find a story to stump me. It was really funny.

CA: You've said you wrote the 1988 book The Devil's Arithmetic *for your children, because they needed "to learn, and to remember" the tragedy of the Holocaust. What response to the book have you had from readers?*

YOLEN: I've had people sobbing. My daughter called me up the other day—she's in college now—and she was crying on the phone. I said, "Honey, what's wrong?" and she said, "I just read *The Devil's Arithmetic* and it is the most wonderful book in the world. This book has to be read next to *The Diary of Anne Frank* in every classroom in the country and I'm going to tell them." I said, "How are you going to tell them, honey?" and she said, "I don't know, but I'm going to. Thank you, I love you," and she hung up. I just got a letter today from Penina Schram, who is probably the most important Jewish storyteller in America, telling me, "Your new novel reached me in more ways than one. . . . What a storyteller you are. . . . and what is true about the book are ways to extend the story into our very lives and to lead us into retelling and remembering." For me, the real exciting thing is that there's going to be a German-language edition published in Vienna. So I've been having conversations with the translator, very interesting.

The book didn't win any of the big children's book awards, but it was the most discussed book, evidently, at the Newberry-Caldecott meetings. People were arguing and screaming. It either makes people really, really moved or it makes them really, really angry. I'm not really quite sure why, except that there are people who own the Holocaust. Either they were there or they had family there, or they have become Holocaust fanatics. And there are many people also who feel that we should not tell our children about it, because it was such a horrible period. This is the only book for children that I know of which actually takes place in the camps.

CA: You've recently been given your own imprint at Harcourt Brace Jovanovich. Tell me about your work there.

YOLEN: What I want to publish are books that other people might not publish, because they are different or they are all-ages books or they are the books that I wanted to read when I was a child and had to seek out. I'm publishing picture books as well as novels, but I'm concentrating on fantasy and science fiction and books of the imagination.

CA: What's in the works that you'd like to talk about besides The Faery Flag and Other Stories?

YOLEN: I have eight or nine books coming out this year. There are several things in the works that are really exciting. This fall I have a book called *Dove Isabeau,* a fairy tale that's incredibly illustrated by Dennis Nolan. One might even call it a feminist fairy tale, though I wouldn't! It's a full fairy tale with a dragon and a witch-stepmother and a transformation and a girl who rescues the young man and the young man who comes to rescue her and has to do it in what's really a very feminist way. He can't fight with a sword; he has to give her three kisses and sacrifice himself. I also have *White Jenna,* the sequel I mentioned earlier to *Sister Light, Sister Dark.*

I have a number of picture books coming out in the next few years, including an alphabet book called *Elfabet,* with little elves doing the letters—for example, "A—Apple Elf Always Acrobatic" and "B—Bottle Elf Boldly Balancing"—with incredible pictures by Lauren Mills, who is married to Dennis Nolan. I have a sequel to *Three Bears Rhyme Book* called *Baby Bear's Bedtime Book* that Jane Dyer is doing the illustrations for; knowing her work, I'm sure it's going to be fantastic. I have a novel called *The Dragon's Boy,* based on one of my Merlin short stories, that is going to be published as a children's novel in the fall of 1990. I have three picture books coming out that I'm especially fond of. One is called *Sky Dogs,* which is going to have pictures by Barry Moser and is about the coming of the horse to the Blackfeet Indians. And one is called *All Those Secrets of the World,* with pictures by Leslie Baker, which is a childhood memory of mine about the time my father went off to World War II and we were living in Virginia with my grandparents. My cousin Michael and I waded in the Chesapeake Bay, which we weren't supposed to do because it was fouled with fuel oil from the great destroyers and tankers that were sailing off from Norfolk. And then one called *Letting Swift River Go,* for which Barbara Cooney is going to do the pictures. It's the story of what happened right here in our area of Massachusetts in the 1930s when they drowned a bunch of little towns to make the big reservoir for Boston. And I have a big collection of poems called *Bird Watch* with pictures by Ted Lewin and a collection of Halloween poems called *Best Witches* with hysterically funny illustrations by Elise Primavera and . . . and . . . I have about fourteen books ahead. I love to write!

BIOGRAPHICAL/CRITICAL SOURCES:

BOOKS

Children's Literature Review, Volume 4, Gale, 1982.

Dictionary of Literary Biography, Volume 52: *American Writers for Children since 1960: Fiction,* Gale, 1986.

Something about the Author Autobiography Series, Volume 1, Gale, 1986.

Yolen, Jane, *Touch Magic: Fantasy, Faerie, and Folktale in the Literature of Childhood,* Philomel, 1981.

PERIODICALS

Fantasy Newsletter, September, 1983.

New York Times Book Review, May 5, 1974, September 19, 1976, November 20, 1977, January 1, 1978, February 18, 1979, October 28, 1979, May 23, 1982, January 25, 1987, January 3, 1988.

Writer, May, 1986.

—*Interview by Jean W. Ross*

* * *

YOLEN, Will(iam Hyatt) 1908-1985 (Phillips H. Lord)

PERSONAL: Born February 25, 1908; came to U.S., 1912; naturalized U.S. citizen, 1939; died of complications related to Parkinson's disease, November 19, 1985, in Holyoke, Mass.; son of Sampson (a soldier and merchant) and Mina (Hyatt) Yolen; married Isabelle (a social worker; maiden name, Berlin), February 23, 1934 (died May 30, 1970); children: Jane (Mrs. David Stemple), Steven. *Education:* Attended University of Alabama, 1929, and Yale University, 1976. *Politics:* Democrat.

ADDRESSES: *Home*—Box 27, 31 School St., Hatfield, Mass. 01038.

CAREER: Newspaper and radio news editor and reporter, 1928-34; Radio News Service, Los Angeles, Calif., editor, 1931; columnist for United Features, New York City; feature writer for *New Haven Register* (Conn.) and *Madison Eagle* (N.J.), 1934-35; free-lance writer in Europe; publicity director of New York World's Fair Amusement Area, 1939-40; promotion director for Warner Brothers, 1940-44; American Broadcasting System in Europe (secret radio station working with Underground), London, England, managing editor, 1944-45; public relations executive for station WNEW, 1946-47; president of Yolen, Ross & Associates (publicists), 1947-49; free-lance writer, 1950-51; Hill & Knowlton, Inc. (public relations counsel), New York City, vice-president and editor of books and magazines, 1952-70. Consultant to U.S. Department of Commerce, 1970-74, and Hill & Knowlton, Inc., 1970-85. *Military service:* National Guard, infantry officer.

MEMBER: International Kite Fliers Association (president, 1950-85), Overseas Press Club (board of governors, 1956-57; secretary, 1958-61; first vice-president, 1961-62; president, 1963; chairman of book publishing committee; life governor), National Association of Science Writers, Mystery Writers of America, Authors League of America, Society of Children's Book Writers, American Kite Fliers Association, Dramatists Guild, Twelfth Regiment Veteran Officers Association, Sigma Delta Xi, Explorers Club, Dutch Treat Club, Silurians (New York), Players Club, Adventurers Club.

WRITINGS:

The Young Sportsman's Guide to Kite Flying, Nelson, 1963.

(Editor) *I Can Tell It Now,* Dutton, 1964.

(Editor) *How I Got That Story,* Dutton, 1967.

(Editor with Malcolm Malone Johnson) *Current Thoughts on Public Relations,* M. W. Lads, 1968.

(Editor with Kenneth Giniger) *Hero for Our Times,* Stackpole, 1968.

(Editor-in-chief) *Newsbreak,* Stackpole, 1975.

The Complete Book of Kites and Kite Flying, Simon & Schuster, 1976.

Also author of plays, "Fit to Print," 1940, and with Will Oursler, "Family Story," 1969. Author of radio scripts for National Broadcasting Company, including serial "Hiss the Villain," 1934; author, under pseudonym Phillips H. Lord, of "Gangbusters" filmscripts for King Features. Contributor to *Book of Knowledge* encyclopedia, and to periodicals, including *Life, This Week, Parade, American Weekly, Today's Health, Reader's Digest, Catholic Digest,* and *Mature Living.*

SIDELIGHTS: "Most of my life I have been a journalist," wrote Will Yolen, "even when I worked as a public relations man to eke out a living. Most of my PR jobs—many of long duration—were taken with the understanding that I would return to journalism." Yolen was cup holder and world championship winner at an international kite flying event in India in 1959, and for many years was world champion. He once kept 178 kites in the air at one time and was cited in the *Guinness Book of World Records* for keeping a kite aloft for 179 hours with a team made up of Sunrise Hotel staffers in Fort Lauderdale, Florida. In 1976, he trained a summer-session kite team at Yale University.

BIOGRAPHICAL/CRITICAL SOURCES:

PERIODICALS

Newsweek, August 23, 1976.
New York Sun, August 18, 1944.
New York Times, August 9, 1976.
Springfield Union (Mass.), February 9, 1968.
Wall Street Journal, May 26, 1978.

OBITUARIES:

PERIODICALS

New York Times, November 22, 1985.

[Sketch reviewed by daughter, Jane Yolen]

* * *

YOUNG, Alison 1922-

PERSONAL: Born June 18, 1922, in Hove, England; daughter of Andrew John (a clergyman and poet) and Janet (Green) Young; married Edward Lowbury (a physician and poet), June 12, 1954; children: Ruth, Pauline, Miriam. *Education:* University of Edinburgh, Mus.Bac., 1943; Royal College of Music, London, G.R.S.M., A.R.C.M., 1944. *Politics:* Moderate Labour. *Religion:* Agnostic.

ADDRESSES: Home—79 Vernon Rd., Birmingham B16 9SQ, England.

CAREER: Music teacher, pianist, free-lance musician, author.

WRITINGS:

(With husband, Edward Lowbury, and Timothy Salter) *Thomas Campion: Poet, Composer, Physician,* Barnes & Noble, 1970.
(Editor with Lowbury) Andrew Young, *The Poetical Works of Andrew Young,* Secker & Warburg, 1986.

WORK IN PROGRESS: With Edward Lowbury, *To Shirk No Idleness: A Critical Biography of Andrew Young.*

* * *

YOUNG, Andrew (John) 1885-1971

PERSONAL: Born April 29, 1885, in Elgin, Scotland; died of heart failure, November 25, 1971, in Bognor Regis, England; married Janet Green, September 8, 1912; children: Anthony, Alison. *Education:* New College, University of Edinburgh, M.A., 1907, postgraduate study in theology, 1908-12.

CAREER: Ordained minister, United Free Church, 1912; Wallace Green Presbyterian Church, Berwick on Tweed, assistant minister, 1914; minister at Temple, Midlothian, Scotland, 1914-20; minister at Hore Presbyterian Church, 1920-38; inducted into the Church of England, 1939; vicar of Stonegate, Sussex, England, 1941-59; canon of Chichester Cathedral, 1948-71. *Military service:* Superintendent at Army rest camp near Bologne, 1916-17.

AWARDS, HONORS: A. C. Benson Silver Medal, Royal Society of Literature, 1940, for poetry; Heinemann Award, 1946; LL.D., University of Edinburgh, 1951; Queen's Gold Medal for Poetry, 1952; Duff Cooper Memorial Prize, 1960, for *The Collected Poems.*

WRITINGS:

Songs of Night, A. Moring, 1910.
Boaz and Ruth, and Other Poems, J. G. Wilson, 1920.
(Contributor) *Cecil Barclay Simpson: A Memorial by Two Friends,* [Edinburgh], 1918.
The Death of Eli and Other Poems, J. G. Wilson, 1921.
The Adversary (verse play), J. G. Wilson, 1923.
The Bird Cage (poems), J. & E. Bumpus, 1926.
The Cuckoo Clock (poems), J. & E. Bumpus, 1928.
The New Shepherd (poems), J. & E. Bumpus, 1931.
Winter Harvest (poems), Nonesuch Press, 1933.
The White Blackbird (poems), J. Cape, 1935.
Collected Poems, J. Cape, 1936.
Nicodemus: A Mystery, J. Cape, 1937.
Speak to the Earth (poems), J. Cape, 1939.
A Prospect of Flowers: A Book about Wild Flowers, J. Cape, 1945.
The Green Man (poems), J. Cape, 1947.
A Retrospect of Flowers, J. Cape, 1950.
Collected Poems of Andrew Young, J. Cape, 1950.
Into Hades (long poem; also see below), Hart-Davis, 1952.
A Prospect of Britain, Harper, 1956.
Out of the World and Back: "Into Hades" and "A Traveller in Time" (two poems), Hart-Davis, 1958.
Quiet as Moss: Thirty-six Poems, Hart-Davis, 1959, Dufour, 1963.
The Collected Poems, arranged by Leonard Clark, Hart-Davis, 1960.
The Poet and the Landscape (criticism), Hart-Davis, 1962, Dufour, 1963.
The New Poly-Olbion: Topographical Excursions, Hart-Davis, 1967.
Burning as Light (poems), arranged by Clark, Hart-Davis, 1967.
The Poetic Jesus, Harper, 1972.
Complete Poems, arranged and introduced by Clark, Secker & Warburg, 1974.
The Poetical Works of Andrew Young (centenary edition), edited by Edward Lowbury and Alison Young, Secker & Warburg, 1985.

SIDELIGHTS: A cleric, poet, and botanist, Andrew Young "neither influenced nor—remarkably—was influenced by any of the passing trends in English poetry," writes Ted Walker in the *New Statesman. Times Literary Supplement* contributor Grevel Lindop explains that Young's early work, which the poet repudiated in later life, "can conveniently be summed up as 'Decadent.' " "Gradually, however," Lindop continues, "in the poems written between 1910 and 1931, out of the welter of wine, wounds and pagan deities there began to emerge touches of vivid landscape-description, black humour and terse verbal facility," and it is these later works for which the poet is remembered. Young's best poems, declares Robert Nye in the London *Times,* are "neither old nor new, but something seemingly remembered even the first time we read it."

According to a *Times Literary Supplement* reviewer, critics who are confronted with the poetic peculiarities of Andrew Young—"whose structures and substance . . . are not of the most intricate, and do not fit usefully into their scheme of relationships and their critical formulae"—often choose to ignore him or to reduce him "to a simplistic property, to a 'nature poet.' " Several reviewers, however, including those cited above, regard such a dismissal or reduction as unjust, claiming that either action misconstrues what Young's poetry is about.

Leslie Norris, writing in *London Magazine,* considers the designation "nature poet" accurate enough "as far as it goes, since [Young] writes with grace and economy of the countryside and the plants and animals living there." But Norris maintains that Young "uses nature for a more important purpose than merely to observe it even with his clear eye and the knowledge of a fine naturalist. He was a metaphysical poet, exploring the layers of meaning that exist within a single word, now playfully, now transforming a small lyric into an important and profound statement by a single stroke of the imagination."

Walker, too, characterizes Young as the author of "a metaphysical poetry full of wit and intellectual conceits; a poetry very far removed from the nature-notes of his Georgian contemporaries. Natural objects are used, with love, sometimes for their own sake; but usually they are no more than the starting-points from which the poet presents a world, a life, a way of seeing, which we might never have perceived for ourselves." Commenting in *Andrew Young: Prospect of a Poet* on both the oddity and brilliance of Young's metaphysical poetry, Leonard Clark writes: "It was as if the childlike, elfin hand of [William] Blake had guided [Young] on his explorations."

BIOGRAPHICAL/CRITICAL SOURCES:

BOOKS

Clark, Leonard, editor, *Andrew Young: Prospect of a Poet,* Hart-Davis, 1957, Dufour, 1964.
Contemporary Literary Criticism, Volume 5, Gale, 1976.
Sall, Roger D., *Transposing Ghost: A Critical Study of Andrew Young,* Acte Academiae Aboensis [Finland], 1978.

PERIODICALS

Encounter, September, 1974.
Listener, March 7, 1974.
London Magazine, June-July, 1974.
New Statesman, February 22, 1974.
Stand, Volume 15, number 4, 1974.
Times (London), March 28, 1985.
Times Literary Supplement, June 8, 1967, April 12, 1974, June 13, 1986.

[Sketch reviewed by daughter Alison Young and son-in-law Edward Lowbury]

* * *

YOUNG, Axel
See McDOWELL, Michael

Z

ZIMAN, John M(ichael) 1925-

PERSONAL: Surname is pronounced *Zy*-man; born May 16, 1925, in Cambridge, England; son of Solomon Netheim (a civil servant) and Nellie Frances (Gaster) Ziman; married Rosemary Dixon, September 15, 1951; children (adopted): Clare, Matthew, Gregory, Katharine. *Education:* Victoria University of Wellington, B.Sc., 1945, M.Sc., 1946; Balliol College, Oxford, B.A., 1949, M.A. and D.Phil., 1952.

ADDRESSES: *Office*—Policy Support Group, Imperial College of Science and Technology, Exhibition Rd., London SW7 2PG, England.

CAREER: Oxford University, Oxford, England, junior lecturer in mathematics, 1951-53, research fellow at Clarendon Laboratory, 1953-54; Cambridge University, Cambridge, England, lecturer in physics at Cavendish Laboratory, 1954-64, fellow at King's College, 1957-64, tutor for advanced students at King's College, 1959-63; University of Bristol, Bristol, England, professor of theoretical physics, 1964-69, Melville Wills Professor of Physics, 1969-76, Henry Overton Will Professor of Physics, 1976-82, director of H. H. Wills Physics Lab, 1976-81; Imperial College of Science and Technology, London, England, visiting professor in School of Management, 1982—, chairman, Science Policy Support Group, 1986—. Visiting professor, University of California, Berkeley, 1964; director of courses on condensed matter, International Centre for Theoretical Physics, Trieste, 1967, 1970, 1972; Rutherford Memorial Lecturer of Royal Society in India and Pakistan, 1968.

MEMBER: European Association for Study of Science and Technology (chairman), Royal Society (fellow), Institute of Physics (fellow), Institute of Mathematics and Its Applications (fellow), American Physical Society, Council for Science and Society (member of executive committee; chairman), Council for National Academic Awards, Society of Authors.

AWARDS, HONORS: Hopkins Prize, Cambridge Philosophical Society, 1964; D.Sc., Victoria University of Wellington, 1985.

WRITINGS:

Electrons and Phonons: Theory of Transport Phenomena in Solids, Oxford University Press, 1960.

Electrons in Metals, Taylor & Francis, 1963, reprinted, 1980.

(With Jasper Rose) *Camford Observed,* Gollancz, 1964.

Principles of the Theory of Solids, Cambridge University Press, 1964, 2nd revised edition, 1979.

Public Knowledge: An Essay Concerning the Social Dimension of Science, University Press, 1968, new edition, 1975.

Elements of Advanced Quantum Theory, Cambridge University Press, 1969.

(Editor with R. G. Chambers and J. L. Olsen) *Electron Mean Free Paths in Metals* (conference proceedings), Springer-Verlag, 1969.

(Editor) *The Physics of Metals,* Volume I: *Electrons,* Cambridge University Press, 1969-75.

(Editor) *Reports on Progress in Physics,* Institute of Physics, Volume XXXVII, Parts 1-4, 1974-75, Volume XXXVIII, Part 1, 1975.

The Force of Knowledge: The Scientific Dimension of Society, Cambridge University Press, 1976.

Reliable Knowledge: An Exploration of the Grounds for Belief in Science, Cambridge University Press, 1978.

Deciding about Energy Policy, Council for Science and Society, 1979.

Models of Disorder: The Theoretical Physics of Homogeneously Disordered Systems, Cambridge University Press, 1979.

Teaching and Learning about Science and Society, Cambridge University Press, 1980.

Puzzles, Problems, and Enigmas: Occasional Pieces on the Human Aspects of Science, Cambridge University Press, 1981.

An Introduction to Science Studies: The Philosophical and Social Aspects of Science and Technology, Cambridge University Press, 1984.

(With Paul Sieghart and John Humphrey) *The World of Science and the Rule of Law: A Study of the Observance and Violations of the Human Rights of Scientists in the Participating States of the Helsinki Accords,* Oxford University Press, 1986.

Knowing Everything about Nothing: Specialization and Change in Research Centres, Cambridge University Press, 1987.

Contributor of scientific papers to professional journals; occasional contributor of articles and reviews to *Listener, New Statesman,* and *Minerva.* General editor, "Cambridge Monographs on Physics." Editor, *Cambridge Review,* 1958-59, and *Science Progress,* 1964—.

WORK IN PROGRESS: Scientific work in theoretical physics; cogitation on various aspects of the sociology of science.

SIDELIGHTS: "An eminent scientist and commentator on science," as *Times Literary Supplement* contributor Joseph Agassi describes him, John M. Ziman has written several discussions of the social and political aspects of science. *Puzzles, Problems, and Enigmas: Occasional Pieces on the Human Aspects of Science,* for example, is written in a "witty, very agreeable style" with a "masterly exposition of opinions and prejudices current among leading scientists," comments Agassi. Similarly, in *An Introduction to Science Studies: The Philosophical and Social Aspects of Science and Technology,* "Ziman undertakes the task eschewed by [others]" in this broad survey, observes Paul T. Durbin in *Science.* "His is a masterly summary of the whole range of the science studies literature, from philosophy of science to sociology of science to science and technology policy studies. At the same time," adds the critic, "it is a personal summary, depending explicitly on Ziman's earlier formulations." Calling *An Introduction to Science Studies* "a *tour de force,*" Durbin concludes that previous anthologists of science studies had "lamented the fact that the perspective of a spokesperson for science would not fit into the scheme of the volume. Now there is such a voice."

AVOCATIONAL INTERESTS: Gardening, cabinet making.

BIOGRAPHICAL/CRITICAL SOURCES:

PERIODICALS

New Statesman, May 28, 1976, April 16, 1982.
Science, August 2, 1985.
Times Literary Supplement, June 25, 1982.*

* * *

ZIRING, Lawrence 1928-

PERSONAL: Born December 11, 1928, in Brooklyn, N.Y.; son of Israel and Anna (Berg) Ziring; married Raye Marlene Ralph, August 10, 1962; children: Leona, Sarah. *Education:* Columbia University, B.S., 1955, M.I.A., 1957, Ph.D., 1962.

ADDRESSES: Home—5139 Greenhill, Portage, Mich. 49081. *Office*—Department of Political Science, Western Michigan University, Kalamazoo, Mich. 49008.

CAREER: University of Dacca, Dacca, East Pakistan (now Bangladesh), lecturer in political science, 1959-60; Columbia University, New York, N.Y., lecturer in political science, 1960-61; Lafayette College, Easton, Pa., assistant professor of political science, 1961-64; Syracuse University, Syracuse, N.Y., assistant professor of political science, 1964-67; Western Michigan University, Kalamazoo, associate professor, 1967-73, professor of political science, 1973—, director of Institute of Government and Politics, 1979—. U.S. Information Agency lecturer in Pakistan, 1959-60, 1974-75, 1976, 1981, 1983, 1985, India, 1981, and Nepal, 1983; lecturer at Defense Intelligence School, 1964, Foreign Service Institute, 1967, 1983-84, 1986, and Canadian Defense College, 1968. Adviser to Pakistan Administrative Staff College, 1964-66; external examiner, Karachi University, 1973—, University of Toronto, 1974, and Quaid-i-Azam University, 1988-89; member of board of trustees, American Institute of Pakistan Studies, 1973—. Consultant to U.S. Department of State. *Military service:* U.S. Army, 1951-53.

MEMBER: Association for Asian Studies (chairman of Pakistan Studies Development Committee, 1972-77).

AWARDS, HONORS: Jones Superior Teaching Award, Lafayette College, 1963-64; Institute of Oriental Studies fellow, Soviet Union Academy of Sciences, 1974, 1981, and 1983; American Council of Learned Societies fellow, 1974-75; Distinguished Scholar award, Western Michigan University, 1982; American University research affiliate, 1983-84; Oxford University fellow, 1984, 1989.

WRITINGS:

The Ayub Khan Era: Politics in Pakistan, 1958-1969, Syracuse University Press, 1971.
(Editor with Ralph Braibanti and Howard Wriggins, and contributor) *Pakistan: The Long View,* Duke University Press, 1977.
(With C. I. Eugene Kim) *An Introduction to Asian Politics,* Prentice-Hall, 1977.
(Editor and contributor) *The Subcontinent in World Politics: India, Its Neighbors, and the Great Powers,* Praeger, 1978, 2nd edition, 1982.
Pakistan: The Enigma of Political Development, Dawson, 1980.
Iran, Turkey, and Afghanistan: A Political Chronology, Praeger, 1981.
The Middle East Political Dictionary, American Bibliographical Center-Clio Press, 1983.
(With Kim) *The Asian Political Dictionary,* American Bibliographical Center-Clio Press, 1985.
(Editor with Kim, and contributor) *Changing Asia,* Asian Studies Program, Western Michigan University, 1987.
(Editor and contributor) *Asian Security Issues: National Systems and International Relations,* Institute of Government and Politics, Western Michigan University, 1988.

CONTRIBUTOR

G. S. Birkhead, editor, *Administrative Problems in Pakistan,* Syracuse University Press, 1966.
Anwar Dil, editor, *Toward Developing Pakistan,* Abbottabad Bookservice, 1970.
J. Henry Korson, editor, *Contemporary Problems of Pakistan,* E. J. Brill, 1974.
Wriggins, editor, *Pakistan in Transition,* Islamabad University Press, 1975.
Eric Gustafson, editor, *Pakistan and Bangladesh: Bibliographic Essays in the Social Sciences,* Southern Asian Institute, Columbia University, 1976.
R. G. C. Thomas, editor, *The Great Power Triangle and Asian Security,* Lexington Books, 1983.
Surendra Chopra, editor, *Studies in India's Foreign Policy,* Gurunanek Dev University Press, 1983.
Chopra, editor, *Perspectives on Pakistan's Foreign Policy,* Gurunanek Dev University Press, 1983.
Leo Rose and Noor A. Husein, editors, *U.S.-Pakistan Relations,* Institute of East Asian Relations, 1985.
S. H. Hashmi, editor, *The Governing Process in Pakistan,* Aziz Publishers, 1987.
Hafeez Malik, editor, *Soviet-American Relations with Pakistan, Iran, and Afghanistan,* St. Martin's, 1987.

OTHER

Also co-author of *Pakistan: A Country Study,* edited by Richard Nyrop, 1984. Contributor to *Funk and Wagnalls Encyclopedia Yearbook,* 1984, and *Collier's Encyclopedia,* 1984. Contributor of more than one hundred articles and reviews to periodicals.

WORK IN PROGRESS: Bangladesh: A Political Analysis; continuing research in political forecasting.

SIDELIGHTS: Lawrence Ziring told *CA* that his "several volumes and numerous articles on Pakistan represent a comprehensive analysis of that country's political history. Students and researchers interested in identifying the character and patterns of political life in Pakistan will find useful information and insight. I have devoted more than thirty years to this study and I believe my findings and projections will stand the test of time.

"As for my other work, I continue to be involved in the examination of South Asian and Middle East politics and am attempting to assemble data useful in forecasting national political behavior and how it impacts on foreign policy decision-making."